**Fodor's** 2012

# FLORIDA

Fodor's Travel Publications   New York, Toronto, London, Sydney, Auckland
www.fodors.com

# Eugene Fodor:
## The Spy Who Loved Travel

As Fodor's celebrates our 75th anniversary, we are honoring the colorful and adventurous life of Eugene Fodor, who revolutionized guidebook publishing in 1936 with his first book, *On the Continent, The Entertaining Travel Annual.*

Eugene Fodor's life seemed to leap off the pages of a great spy novel. Born in Hungary, he spoke six languages and graduated from the Sorbonne and the London School of Economics. During World War II he joined the Office of Strategic Services, the budding spy agency for the United States. He commanded the team that went behind enemy lines to liberate Prague, and recommended to Generals Eisenhower, Bradley, and Patton that Allied troops move to the capital city. After the war, Fodor worked as a spy in Austria, posing as a U.S. diplomat.

In 1949 Eugene Fodor—with the help of the CIA—established Fodor's Modern Guides. He was passionate about travel and wanted to bring his insider's knowledge of Europe to a new generation of sophisticated Americans who wanted to explore and seek out experiences beyond their borders. Among his innovations were annual updates, consulting local experts, and including cultural and historical perspectives and an emphasis on people—not just sites. As Fodor described it, "The main interest and enjoyment of foreign travel lies not only in 'the sites,' . . . but in contact with people whose customs, habits, and general outlook are different from your own."

Eugene Fodor died in 1991, but his legacy, Fodor's Travel, continues. It is now one of the world's largest and most trusted brands in travel information, covering more than 600 destinations worldwide in guidebooks, on Fodors.com, and in ebooks and iPhone apps. Technology and the accessibility of travel may be changing, but Eugene Fodor's unique storytelling skills and reporting style are behind every word of today's Fodor's guides.

Our editors and writers continue to embrace Eugene Fodor's vision of building personal relationships through travel. We invite you to join the Fodor's community at fodors.com/community and share your experiences with like-minded travelers. Tell us when we're right. Tell us when we're wrong. And share fantastic travel secrets that aren't yet in Fodor's. Together, we will continue to deepen our understanding of our world.

Happy 75th Anniversary, Fodor's! Here's to many more.

Tim Jarrell, Publisher

## FODOR'S FLORIDA 2012

**Editors:** Laura M. Kidder (*northern and central Florida, including Orlando and its theme parks*) and Stephanie E. Butler (*southern Florida*)

**Editorial Contributors:** Carolyn Galgano (Orlando hotel and restaurant editor), Heidi Leigh Johansen
**Writers:** Elise Allen, Kate Bradshaw, Rona Gindin, Jennifer Greenhill-Taylor, Lynne Helm, Jennie Hess, Dorothea Hunter Sönne, Chelle Koster Walton, Steve Master, Gary McKechnie, Megan Peck, Paul Rubio, Connie Sharpe, Mary Thurwachter, Sharon Weightman Hoffmann, Jaimie Wilson, Ashley Wright

**Production Editor:** Jennifer DePrima
**Maps & Illustrations:** David Lindroth; Mark Stroud, *cartographers;* Bob Blake, Rebecca Baer, *map editors;* William Wu, *information graphics*
**Design:** Fabrizio La Rocca, *creative director;* Guido Caroti, *art director;* Tina Malaney, Nora Rosansky, Chie Ushio, Jessica Walsh, *designers;* Melanie Marin, *associate director of photography*
**Cover Photo:** (pink flamingos, Everglades) aceshot1/Shutterstock
**Production Manager:** Angela L. McLean

## COPYRIGHT

ISBN 978-0-679-00969-6

ISSN 0193-9556

## SPECIAL SALES

This book is available at special discounts for bulk purchases for sales promotions or premiums. Special editions, including personalized covers, excerpts of existing books, and corporate imprints, can be created in large quantities for special needs. For more information, write to Special Markets/Premium Sales, 1745 Broadway, MD 3-2, New York, NY 10019, or e-mail specialmarkets@randomhouse.com.

## AN IMPORTANT TIP & AN INVITATION

Although all prices, opening times, and other details in this book are based on information supplied to us at press time, changes occur all the time in the travel world, and Fodor's cannot accept responsibility for facts that become outdated or for inadvertent errors or omissions. So **always confirm information when it matters,** especially if you're making a detour to visit a specific place. Your experiences—positive and negative—matter to us. If we have missed or misstated something, **please write to us.** Share your opinion instantly through our online feedback center at fodors.com/contact-us.

PRINTED IN COLOMBIA

10 9 8 7 6 5 4 3 2 1

# CONTENTS

## Fodor's Features

## MAPS

# ABOUT
# THIS BOOK

## Our Ratings
At Fodor's, we spend considerable time choosing the best places in a destination so you don't have to. By default, anything we recommend in this book is worth visiting. But some sights, properties, and experiences are so great that we've recognized them with additional accolades. Orange **Fodor's Choice** stars indicate our top recommendations; black stars highlight places we deem **Highly Recommended**; and **Best Bets** call attention to top properties in various categories. Disagree with any of our choices? Care to nominate a new place? Visit our feedback center at www.fodors.com/feedback.

## Hotels
Hotels have private bath, phone, and TV, and do not offer meals unless we specify that in the review. We always list facilities but not whether you'll be charged an extra fee to use them.

> For expanded hotel reviews, visit **Fodors.com**

## Restaurants
Unless we state otherwise, restaurants are open for lunch and dinner daily. We mention dress only when there's a specific requirement and reservations only when they're essential or not accepted—it's always best to book ahead.

## Credit Cards
We assume that restaurants and hotels accept credit cards. If not, we'll note it in the review.

## Budget Well
Hotel and restaurant price categories from ¢ to $$$$ are defined in the opening pages of the respective chapters. For attractions, we always give standard adult admission fees; reductions are usually available for children, students, and senior citizens.

### Listings
- ★ Fodor's Choice
- ★ Highly recommended
- ⊠ Physical address
- ✛ Directions or Map coordinates
- 🕮 Mailing address
- ☎ Telephone
- 🖷 Fax
- ⊕ On the Web
- ✍ E-mail
- 🎫 Admission fee
- ⊙ Open/closed times
- Ⓜ Metro stations
- ⊟ No credit cards

### Hotels & Restaurants
- 🏨 Hotel
- 🛏 Number of rooms
- ⚲ Facilities
- ⦿ Meal plans
- ✕ Restaurant
- ⚱ Reservations
- 🏛 Dress code
- ⤢ Smoking

### Outdoors
- 🏌 Golf
- ⛺ Camping

### Other
- ☾ Family-friendly
- ⇨ See also
- ⊠ Branch address
- ☞ Take note

# Experience
# Florida

# WHAT'S NEW

Each year more than 80 million visitors, representing all age groups and interests, flock to Florida. Its sun, sand, and sea are obvious draws, yet these account for only part of the narrow state's broad appeal. Theme-park enthusiasts come for first-class rides and attractions, while nature lovers find the outdoor options (ranging from snorkeling and fishing to boating and bird-watching) irresistible. Moreover, spring breakers, seniors, and sophisticated sybarites alike are lured by a diverse arts-and-entertainment scene. With such activities in play, the entire state exudes a vacationland vibe that keeps people coming back. For those returning, there's always something new under the sun.

## Worlds of Magic

Just in time for 2012 Legoland will open its doors in Orlando on the 150-acre plot that was the home of Florida's first theme park, Cypress Gardens. Expect more than 50 family-focused attractions, including rides, playgrounds, shows, and, of course, make-you-go-oooh Lego displays. The Wizarding World of Harry Potter at Universal's Islands of Adventure, bewitches Muggles with its near-perfect re-creation of Hogwarts and Hogsmeade, where visitors down glasses of butterbeer and have a wands selected at Ollivander's. At this writing, Disney's Magic Kingdom's Toontown will be closed until 2013. Favorite characters have taken up temporary home on Main Street USA, and when they return, they'll have full-size replicas of their homes and castles, a Little Mermaid ride, an expanded Dumbo attraction, and a Tinkerbell fairy playground.

## Call of the Wild

Going from zero to 60 mph in seconds is short work for cheetahs, the world's fastest cats. Now at Busch Gardens in Tampa you can see them in action at their 13-acre Cheetah Run habitat and *feel* their speed on board Cheetah Hunt, the park's newest (and longest!) coaster. Interactive learning displays and zoo trainers educate visitors on the show-stopping sprinters. For those with a need for speed, zip-line courses have been popping up across the state, combining thrills with the beauty of the great outdoors. Three alone landed in the Orlando area in recent years—Florida EcoSafaris at the Forever Florida wildlife conservation area, the arboreal obstacle course ZOOm Air Adventure Park at the Central Florida Zoo & Botanical Gardens, and Gatorland's soar-over-alligators experience. Get up close and personal with the animals at Zoo Miami; a rhino encounter area, where you can stroke or scratch their backs, joined the enormously popular giraffe feeding station. At the zoo's Wacky Barn pet miniature horses and other exotic farm animals.

## Making a Splash

Tourists may still cast a skeptical eye toward Florida's beaches in light of the Deepwater Horizon disaster on April 20, 2010, but all is well in the Sunshine state's waters. Cleaning crews quickly swept up an oil slick off the coast and tarballs that washed up on the Western Panhandle's shore, and all health advisories for swimming and recreational fishing were lifted by the end of summer 2010. Along the gulf and elsewhere, the Florida Fish and Wildlife Conservation Commission has continued to build up artificial reefs, with roughly a hundred structures added each year. Those, along with intentional wrecks like the 2009 USS *Vandenberg* sinking and the maintenance of underwater archaeological preserves (⊕ *museumsinthesea. org*), have transformed the entire coastline into a divers' paradise. For a controlled

environment, SeaWorld's Discovery Cove just unveiled the Grand Reef, a nearly million-gallon snorkeling zone with rare spotted eagle rays, zebra sharks, and venomous lionfish (the latter two separated from snorkelers by glass). And for armchair adventurers, plenty of high seas booty—including one of only two known Jolly Roger skull-and-bones flags —is in store at the Pirate and Treasure Museum in St. Augustine.

## Must-See Museums

At a fitting time of 11:11 am on 1/1/11, the new Dalí Museum burst onto St. Petersburg's art scene, celebrating the surrealist with 2,971 of his pieces in its permanent collection. The building itself is a work of art with more than 1,000 different-size triangular glass pieces wrapping around the structure in an homage to the painter's melting clocks. Nearby, the Tampa Museum of Art, the Glazer Children's Museum, and the Curtis Hixon Waterfront Park all opened on Tampa's Riverwalk. Farther south, the children's museum C'mon is making its debut in Naples with 13 galleries of interactive play exhibits. The Charles Hosmer Morse Museum of American Art in central Florida, featuring the world's largest collection of works by Louis Comfort Tiffany, doubled in size. Farther north, Pensacola's National Naval Aviation Museum, where thousands flock to see the famous Blue Angels stunt team in flight, will open the doors to the National Flight Academy in 2012. Miami is transforming Bicentennial Park into a museum campus with glittering LEED-certified facilities for the Museum of Science and Industry and the Miami Art Museum.

## Let the Games Begin

The Orlando Magic's shiny new 875,000-square-foot arena will host the NBA's All-Star Weekend in February 2012. If you can't make it for that talent showcase, catch the Heat in action at their Downtown Miami arena, and judge the skills of Chris Bosch, Dwayne Wade, and LeBron James for yourself. The highly anticipated opening of the Marlins Ballpark in Miami's Little Havana will happen in time for the 2012 baseball season. The retractable roof and air-conditioning will solve two problems: the hot summer weather and frequent thunderstorms.

## The Suite Life

You gotta give Florida's hoteliers credit for opening new properties—like Jimmy Buffett's 162-room Margaritaville Beach Hotel on the Gulf and Jacksonville's Aloft in Tapestry Park, a luxurious Starwood hotel—amid one of the worst recessions the country has ever seen. Many properties have also undergone massive renovations and expansions, including luxury destinations like Orlando's Peabody, which added a 35-story tower and English garden among other improvements.

## Airport Facelifts

A whopping $100,000 million has been spent per year over the last several, expanding and adding to Florida's airports. But the biggest news is Miami International's soup-to-nuts overhaul. Every single inch of MIA has been renovated over a six-year period, and the huge Miami Intermodal Center (MIC), a public transportation hub, will hold all rental cars companies and Tri-Rail (a commuter train connecting southeast Florida counties), Metrorail (to downtown Miami), and Amtrak stops.

# WHAT'S WHERE

*The following numbers refer to chapters.*

**2 The Panhandle.** Southern gentility and redneck rambunctiousness make the Panhandle a colorful place—but it's the green gulf waters and sugar-white sand that keep devotees coming back.

**3 Northeast Florida.** Though time rewinds in historic St. Augustine, it's on fast-forward in Daytona Beach and the Space Coast, where horse-drawn carriages are replaced by race cars and rocket ships.

**4 Orlando and Environs.** It's theme parks that draw most visitors to the area, yet downtown Orlando, Kissimmee, and Winter Park have enough sites, shops, and restaurants to make them destinations in their own right.

**5 Walt Disney World.** The granddaddy of attractions, Disney is four theme parks in one—Magic Kingdom, Animal Kingdom, Epcot, and Hollywood Studios. Plus it has a pair of water parks and Downtown Disney (an entertainment zone featuring Cirque du Soleil).

**6 Universal Orlando.** The movies are brought to life at Universal Studios while Islands of Adventure delivers gravity-defying rides and special-effects surprises—and the Wizarding World of Harry Potter. Nearby Wet 'n Wild is full of watery adventures.

**7 SeaWorld Orlando.** Marine mammals perform in SeaWorld's meticulously choreographed shows, and thrill seekers find their adrenaline rush on coasters. Sister park Discovery Cove offers a day-long, swim-with-the-dolphins escape. At Aquatica water park, one slide even dips into a dolphin habitat.

**8 The Tampa Bay Area.** Tampa's Busch Gardens and Ybor City are only part of the area's appeal. Culture vultures flock to St. Petersburg and Sarasota for concerts and museums; while eco-adventurers veer north to the Nature Coast.

**9 The Lower Gulf Coast.** Blessed with beaches, this was the last bit of coast to be settled. But as Naples's manicured golf greens and Fort Myers's mansions-cum-museums prove, it is far from uncivilized.

**10 Palm Beach and the Treasure Coast.** This area scores points for diversity. Palm Beach and environs are famous for their golden sand and glitzy residents, whereas the Treasure Coast has unspoiled natural delights.

**11 Fort Lauderdale and Broward County.** The town *Where the Boys Are* has

grown up. The beaches that first attracted college kids are now complemented by luxe lodgings and upscale entertainment options.

**12 Miami and Miami Beach.** Greater Miami is hot—and we're not just talking about the weather. Art deco buildings and balmy beaches set the scene. Vacations here are as much about lifestyle as locale, so prepare for power shopping, club hopping, and decadent dining.

**13 The Everglades.** Covering more than 1.5 million acres, the fabled "River of Grass" is the state's greatest natural treasure. Biscayne National Park (95% of which is underwater) runs a close second. It's the largest marine park in the United States.

**14 The Florida Keys.** This slender necklace of landfalls, strung together by a 113-mi highway, marks the southern edge of the continental United States. It's nirvana for anglers, divers, literature lovers, and Jimmy Buffett wannabes.

GEORGIA

ATLANTIC OCEAN

Chattahoochee
Quincy
TALLAHASSEE
65
319
98
Eastpoint
Apalachicola

75
19
10
Perry
98
19

Osceola National Forest

St. Mary's R.

Amelia Island

95
Jacksonville

3
St. Augustine

75
Lake City
Gainesville
301
41
Ocala
27

Santa Fe R.

Ocala National Forest

1
40
Daytona Beach

Cedar Keys

St. Johns R.

5  6  7
Orlando
4
Titusville
50
Kennedy Space Center
Cape Canaveral
528
Cocoa Beach
Merritt Island
Melbourne
Sebastian Inlet Recreation Area

Walt Disney World
Kissimmee

Tarpon Springs
Clearwater
75
Tampa
Winter Haven
4
8
St. Petersburg
Tampa Bay
Bradenton
Sarasota
Venice
75

Florida's Turnpike

95
Vero Beach
Fort Pierce
Hutchinson Island

Kissimmee R.

Lake Okeechobee
70
27
Singer Island
10
West Palm Beach
Palm Beach
80
27
Boca Raton
11
Fort Lauderdale
Miami Beach
12
Miami

9
Caloosahatchee R.
Cape Coral
Fort Myers
Captiva Island
Sanibel Island
Big Cypress National Preserve
75
Naples
Everglades City

41
Florida City
Biscayne Bay
Homestead

Everglades National Park
13  9336
Cape Sable
Key Largo
Florida Bay

Gulf of Mexico

Key West
FLORIDA
1
KEYS
14

0        50 miles
0        75 kilometers

# FLORIDA
# TOP ATTRACTIONS

### Walt Disney World

**(A)** Like one of Snow White's dwarfs, Orlando was sleepy until Uncle Walt arrived more than 40 years ago. Today the city is booming—and so is Walt Disney World, which has grown into a 39-square-mi complex with four separate parks, scores of hotels, and satellite attractions like Blizzard Beach and Downtown Disney. Thanks to innovative rides and dazzling animatronics, these parks feature prominently in every child's holiday fantasy. Adults, however, don't have to channel their inner eight-year-old to have fun, because Walt Disney World also has grown-up amenities including championship golf courses, sublime hotels and spas, and fine restaurants that rank among North America's best.

### South Beach

**(B)** You can't miss the distinctive forms, vibrant colors, and extravagant flourishes of SoBe's architectural gems. The world's largest concentration of art deco edifices is right here; and the Art Deco District, with more than 800 buildings, has earned a spot on the National Register of Historic Places. (⇨ *See "A Stroll Down Deco Lane" In-Focus feature in Chapter 12.*) The 'hood also has enough beautiful people to qualify for the Register of Hippest Places. The glitterati, along with assorted vacationing hedonists, are drawn by über-trendy shops and a surfeit of celeb-studded clubs. Divine eateries are the icing—umm, better make that the ganache—on South Beach's proverbial cake.

### The Florida Keys

**(C)** These 800-plus islands are at once a unique landmass and a mass of contradictions. Long years of geographic isolation not only allowed tropical flora and fauna to flourish here, they enabled locals to nurture a quirky one-of-a-kind culture. Unfortunately, increased traffic on the Overseas Highway linking the Upper,

Middle, and Lower Keys to the mainland has threatened both. So the Keys now have a split personality. On one hand, they are a reef-rimmed paradise occupied by free spirits; on the other, a relatively mainstream realm composed of shopping malls and trailer parks. Avoiding the latter can be tricky. But the charm of the former is ample reward.

## Kennedy Space Center

**(D)** Though there are enough wide-open expanses to justify the area's moniker, it was NASA that put the "space" in Space Coast—and this is its star attraction. Space memorabilia and aeronautic antiques, ranging from Redstone rockets to the *Apollo XIV* command module, turn an outing here into a trip back in time for anyone who lived through the space race. Yet for contemporary kids its interactive bells and whistles open up a brave new world. (⇨ *See "Soaring High" In-Focus feature in Chapter 3.*) More down-to-earth types can

also visit the Merritt Island National Wildlife Refuge (originally created as a buffer for the space program) and Canaveral National Seashore.

## Tampa

**(E)** As a vibrant city with exceptional beaches, Tampa is perfect for indecisive folks who want to enjoy surf and sand without sacrificing urban experiences. Families will love Busch Gardens, a major zoo and theme park. Football and hockey fans will relish the chance to see the Buccaneers and Lightning play. Baseball is big, too: the Rays are based here, and the Yankees descend annually for spring training. (*See "Spring Training, Florida-Style" In-Focus feature in Chapter 8.*) When you need a break from the city, St. Pete Beach (famous for surreally beautiful strands) and St. Petersburg (home to the new Dalí Museum, with the largest collection of the surrealist's artwork outside of his native Spain) are a short drive away.

## Go Fish

**(F)** Each October, Destin proves it is the "World's Luckiest Fishing Village" by inviting anglers young and old to compete in the monthlong Destin Fishing Rodeo. However, if you'd prefer to throw fish rather than catch them, head to Pensacola in late April for the Interstate Mullet Toss. (Participants line up to throw dead fish across the Florida–Alabama state line.) Epicures will be relieved to hear that Pensacola also stages a September Seafood Festival. As if fish fried, broiled, battered, or grilled weren't appealing enough, gourmet options are added to the menu.

## Hang 10

**(G)** Cocoa Beach, on the northeast coast, is Surf City for Floridians. Baby boomers may remember it as the place where Major Nelson dreamed of Jeannie. The community is better known today as the hometown of surfing's biggest celeb, Kelly Slater. He has won a record-breaking 10 world championships, and totally tubular types can learn to emulate him at the Ron Jon Surf School. It offers group classes as well as semiprivate and one-on-one lessons for any level of expertise. Loaner equipment is included, but you can also purchase your own nearby at the massive Ron Jon Surf Shop.

## Act Goofy

**(H)** If you have time for only one megapark, choose the original, Walt Disney World's Magic Kingdom. Approached with an open mind (and a couple of well-behaved kids), it really can feel like the "happiest place on Earth." Start by waving to Mickey on Main Street USA, then fly with Dumbo and catch the nighttime fireworks display over Cinderella's Castle. As an FYI, flume lovers can also have a blast on Splash Mountain. Just be forewarned—ride it more than once and

you'll spend the rest of your trip humming Brer Rabbit's theme song.

### Enjoy the High Life

**(I)** If money could talk, you'd hardly be able to hear above the din in Palm Beach. The upper crust started calling it home, during winter at least, in the early 1900s. And today it remains a ritzy, glitzy enclave for both old money and the nouveau riche (a coterie led by the Donald himself, who owns the landmark Mar-a-Lago Club). Simply put, Palm Beach is the sort of place where shopping is a full-time pursuit and residents don't just wear Polo—they play it. Ooh and aah to your heart's content; then, for more conspicuous consumption, continue south on the aptly named Gold Coast.

### Float Your Boat

**(J)** Mariners should set their compass for Fort Lauderdale (aka the Venice of America), where vessels from around the world moor along some two dozen finger isles between the beach and the mainland. Sailors can cruise Broward County's 300 mi of inland waterways by water taxi and tour boat, or bob around the Atlantic in a chartered yacht. If you're in a buying mood, come in late October for the annual Fort Lauderdale International Boat Show. Billed as the world's largest, it has $3 billion worth of boats in every conceivable size, shape, and price range.

### Live La Vida Local

**(K)** On the streets of Miami's Little Havana, just west of downtown, salsa tunes blare and the smell of spicy chorizo fills the air. (You can get a good whiff of tobacco, too, thanks to the cigar makers who still hand-roll their products here.) For nearly 50 years, the neighborhood's undisputed heart has been Calle Ocho, the commercial thoroughfare that hosts

Carnaval Miami (⊕ *www.carnavalmiami. com*). The roaring 10-day block party each March culminates with the world's longest conga line. Ambience- and amenity-wise, it is as close as you'll get to Cuba without running afoul of the federal government. (⇨ *See "Caribbean Infusion" In-Focus feature in Chapter 12.*)

### Join the Papa-Papa-razzi

(L) Who's Your Papa? Ask that question around Key West and the answer will invariably be "Ernest Hemingway." The author lived and worked here for 11 years, during which time he penned *For Whom the Bell Tolls* and *A Farewell to Arms*. Today, touring his former digs (Ernest Hemingway Home and Museum) and toasting his memory at Sloppy Joe's Bar on Duval Street is almost mandatory. To fully understand the importance of being Ernest, though, come in late July for Hemingway Days. Events include a

fishing tournament and look-alike contest featuring Papa impersonators.

### Feel Swamped

(M) No trip to southern Florida is complete without seeing the Everglades. At its heart is a river—50 mi wide but merely 6 inches deep—flowing from Lake Okeechobee into Florida Bay. For an up-close look, speed demons can board an airboat that careens through the marshy waters. Purists, alternately, may placidly canoe or kayak within the boundaries of Everglades National Park. Just remember to keep your hands in the boat. The critters that call this unique ecosystem home (alligators, Florida panthers, and cottonmouth snakes for starters) can add real bite to your visit!

### Be Beachy-Keen

(N) Ready to do something slightly more vigorous than applying SPF 45 and rolling over? Trade beach-bumming for

beachcombing in Sanibel, the "Shell Capital of the World." Conchs, cockles, clams, coquinas—they're all here (the bounty is due to this barrier island's unusual east–west orientation). Of course, if you'd rather construct sand castles than do the Sanibel Stoop, you need only cross the 3-mi causeway to Fort Myers Beach. It has the finest building material and, every November, professional and amateur aficionados prove it during the American SandSculpting Championship. (⇨ *See "Shell-Bent on Sanibel Island" In-Focus feature in Chapter 9.*)

Clown Around

(O) Sarasota, once winter headquarters for Ringling Bros. and Barnum & Bailey, is proud of its circus heritage. Several troupes are still based here, including Royal Hanneford, Walker Brothers, and Circus Sarasota. Visitors who can't get enough of sawdust and sequins can see an impressive collection of vintage costumes, props, and parade wagons at the Ringling Circus Museum. The adjacent Tibbals Learning Center houses a mind-boggling ¾-inch-scale miniature circus with almost a million pieces. Sarasota even has a Circus Ring of Fame with bronze plaques honoring big-top bigwigs.

# QUINTESSENTIAL FLORIDA

## H2O

Spanish explorer Ponce de León didn't find the Fountain of Youth when he swung through Florida in 1513. But if he'd lingered longer, he could have located 7,700 lakes, 1,700 rivers and creeks, and an estimated 700 springs. Over the centuries these have attracted American Indians, immigrants, opportunists, and, of course, countless outdoor adventurers. Boaters come for inland waterways and a 1,200-mi coast, and anglers are lured by more than 700 species of fish. Snorkelers and divers curious to see what lies beneath can get face time with the marine life that thrives on the world's third-largest coral reef or bone up on maritime history in underwater archaeological preserves (⊕ *www. museumsinthesea.com*). Back on dry land, all those beaches are pretty impressive, too.

## Theme Parks

Children tend to think of Florida as a playland that's liberally sprinkled with pixie dust. And who can blame them? Orlando's theme parks are among the most popular (and most publicized) attractions on earth. Walt Disney World opened the first of its four Floridian parks in 1971. Competitors like SeaWorld and Universal followed suit, transforming a swampy cattle-and-citrus town into Fun Central. Today, dozens of smaller Orlando venues—including kitschy parks like Dinosaur World and Gatorland—vie for visitors' dollars; and Busch Gardens in Tampa (85 mi southwest) scrambles for a piece of the pie with its own roundup of rides. Some locals love them. Others lament the dawn of the Disney Era. All, however, recognize that theme parks are now a fact of life.

Florida is synonymous with sunshine, and visitors routinely come to revel in it. However, the people who actually live here—a diverse group that includes Mouseketeers, millionaires, surfers, and rocket scientists—know that the state's appeal rests on more than those reliable rays.

## Superlative Sports

Florida is teeming with teams—and residents take the games they play *very* seriously. Baseball fans regularly work themselves into a fever pitch: after all, the state has a pair of Major League franchises and hosts another 13 in spring when the Grapefruit League goes to bat (*see "Spring Training, Florida-Style" In-Focus feature in Chapter 8*). Those with a preference for pigskin might cheer for NFL teams in Jacksonville, Miami, and Tampa. But the state is also home to top-rated college teams, and two (the Gators and 'Noles) have especially fervent followings. Basketball lovers, meanwhile, feel the "Heat" in Miami or the "Magic" in Orlando, and hockey addicts stick around to watch the Florida Panthers and Tampa Bay Lightning. The Professional Golfers Association (PGA) is headquartered here.

## Fabulous Food

Geography and gastronomy go hand in hand in Florida. Seafood, for instance, is a staple almost everywhere. Yet locals will point out that the way it is prepared changes considerably as you maneuver around the state. Northern restaurants show their regional roots with Cajun classics and Dixieland dishes. (It seems that virtually any fish can be crusted with pecans and served with greens!) In Southern Florida, menus typically highlight Floribbean cuisine, which marries Floridian, Caribbean, and Latin flavors. (Think mahimahi with mango salsa.) Inland, expect catfish, gator tails, and frogs' legs, all of which are best enjoyed at a Cracker-style fish camp with a side order of hush puppies. In keeping with the regional emphasis, assorted seafood—along with peanuts, sweet corn, watermelons, and citrus fruits—all merit their own down-home festivals.

# WHEN TO GO

Although Florida is a year-round vacation venue, it divides the calendar into regional tourism seasons. Holidays and school breaks are major factors. However, the clincher is weather, with the best months being designated as peak periods.

High season in southern Florida starts with the run-up to Christmas and continues through Easter. Snowbirds migrate down then to escape frosty weather back home, and festivalgoers flock in because major events are held this time of year to avoid summer's searing heat and high humidity. Winter is also *the* time to visit the Everglades as temperatures, mosquito activity, and water levels are all lower (making wildlife easier to spot).

Northern Florida, conversely, receives the greatest influx of visitors from Memorial Day to Labor Day. Costs are highest then, but so are temperatures. (In winter, when the mercury dips into the 40s, you'd get a chilly reception on Panhandle beaches.) Specific areas, like Panama City Beach or Daytona Beach, attract throngs—and thongs—during spring break, too. In the latter location, expect revved-up revelers during Speedweeks (late January and February) and Bike Week (early March).

Thanks to its theme parks, Central Florida is a magnet for children, meaning the largest crowds gather, logically enough, whenever class lets out. Line-ups at attractions do shrink after they return to school, though this area's hopping all year, with large numbers of international families and kid-free adults coming in the off-season. Spring and fall shoulder seasons are the optimal time to visit, both weatherwise and pricewise.

## Climate

Florida is rightly called the Sunshine State—areas like Tampa Bay report 361 days of sunshine a year! But it could also be dubbed the Humid State. From June through September, 90% humidity levels aren't uncommon, nor are accompanying thunderstorms. In fact, more than half of the state's rain falls during these months. Florida's two-sided coastline also makes it a target for tropical storms. Hurricane season officially begins June 1 and ends November 30.

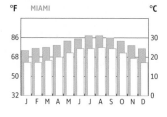

# FAQS

**I'm not crazy about spending seven nights in hotels. Any affordable alternatives?** If you want to pretend you're lucky enough to live here, try a vacation rental. Aside from providing privacy, rentals let you set your own schedule and do your own cooking. The caveat is you may have to rent in weekly—not nightly—increments. Several companies specialize in the Orlando area, Magical Memories (☎ 866/535–7851 ⊕ *www.magicalmemories.com*) being one reliable bet. But in terms of coverage, geographically and pricewise, HomeAway (☎ 877/228–3145 ⊕ *www. homeaway.com*) wins, listing more than 20,000 Floridian condos, cottages, beach houses, and villas. ⇨ *See Apartment and House Rentals under Accommodations in Travel Smart Florida.*

**Will I need a car?** Public transportation is limited here. So unless you'll be spending your whole vacation on-site at Walt Disney World (where complimentary shuttles are available to resort guests) or in Miami Beach (where dense traffic and limited parking is the norm), having a vehicle is recommended. Renting one on arrival is wise, unless you drive your own. To make car time less tedious, consider occasionally taking the road less traveled. The National Scenic Byways Program Web site (⊕ *www.byways.org*) spotlights memorable routes within the state, including the Overseas Highway, which has been designated as an "All-American Road" and is one of only 31 roads countrywide to be so honored.

**How do I pick between Orlando's parks and Tampa's Busch Gardens?** That's a tough call, especially if you haven't yet seen newer attractions like Manta at SeaWorld or Jungala at Busch Gardens. The good news is you don't have to choose, because the Busch Gardens Shuttle Express (☎ 407/423–5566 ⊕ *www. mearstransportation.com*) offers same-day round-trip service between designated locations in Orlando and the Tampa venue for only $10. The trip is free when you buy a six-park Orlando Flex Ticket Plus (good for 14 days unlimited entry to Universal, Islands of Adventure, SeaWorld, Aquatica, Wet 'n Wild, and Busch Gardens) or any Busch Gardens combination ticket.

**Is Miami OK for families?** Absolutely. Despite all the attention paid to G-strings, it retains areas with genuine G-rated appeal. Beyond the beaches, attractions like the interactive Children's Museum and MiaSci (a museum of science) draw kids in droves. Want to go wild? Bypass the nightclubs and head instead to Zoo Miami or the Seaquarium. If you dream of being named "best parent ever," sign your offspring up for a sleepover at the former or a dolphin swim at the latter.

**Will the Deepwater Horizon oil spill affect my vacation?** Deepwater Horizon, an offshore oil-drilling platform owned by Transocean Ltd and under contract to BP, exploded on April 20, 2010. The rig leaked approximately 210,000 gallons per day into the Gulf of Mexico near Louisiana before it was capped three months later. Although a heavy blanket of oil didn't coat Florida's shoreline, more than 100 mi of its northwest coast felt the effects of the crisis. By October 2010, only 2 mi experienced "moderate impacts," like tar balls and beach erosion. For up-to-date information about the oil spill's impact, see ⊕ *www. restorethegulf.gov.*

# IF YOU LIKE

## Animal Encounters

Florida is home to one supersized mouse and makes an ideal habitat for party animals. Yet there are other types of wildlife here, too. In terms of biodiversity, the state ranks third in the country with approximately 1,200 different kinds of critters.

■ **Alligators.** Florida has more than 1.3 million resident alligators. You can witness them doing tricks at places like Gatorland, but gator spotting in swamps or roadside waterways is itself a favorite pastime. Eating the official state reptile in deep-fried-nugget form is popular, too. Mmm . . . tastes like chicken.

■ **Birds.** Poised on two major migratory routes, Florida draws about 500 species of birds—and the 2,000-mi Great Florida Birding Trail helps you track them down. Through detailed guides and highway signs, it identifies sites where you may spy anything from bald eagles and burrowing owls to pink flamingos.

■ **Manatees.** They're nicknamed sea cows and resemble walruses. But Florida's official marine mammals are most closely related to elephants, which may account for their slow pace and hefty frames. In winter, scan the water for a telltale glassy patch (called a "footprint"), indicating that a manatee swims below.

■ **Sea Turtles.** Ready for a late-night rendezvous with the massive leatherbacks and loggerheads that lumber onto Floridian beaches to lay their eggs between March and October? Archie Carr National Wildlife Refuge, the Western Hemisphere's largest loggerhead nesting site, organizes free turtle watches in June and July.

## Life in the Fast Lane

The Sunshine State has been satisfying visitors' need for speed ever since Henry Ford and his snowbird buddies started using Ormond Beach as a test track. Today roller coasters, stock cars, supersonic jets, and spaceships add momentum to your vacation.

■ **Tampa.** If you think the pursuit of happiness is a high-speed activity, head for Busch Gardens, Florida's premier roller-coaster location. SheiKra is one of the world's tallest dive coasters, Kumba features one of the world's largest vertical loops, and Montu (a gut-churning inverted coaster) delivers a G-force of 3.85.

■ **Daytona Beach.** Daytona 500, NASCAR's most prestigious event, pulls in legions of devotees each February. But any time of year you can slip into a driving suit, then into the driver's seat of a Winston Cup–style stock car courtesy of the Richard Petty Driving Experience at Daytona International Speedway.

■ **Pensacola.** The National Museum of Naval Aviation displays 150-plus military aircraft and has motion-based simulators that let you "fly" an F/A-18. Better yet, the U.S. Navy Precision Flight Team (familiar to most of us as the Blue Angels) is based here, so you may get to observe them in action at 700 mph.

■ **Kennedy Space Center.** Whether you admire Buzz Aldrin or Buzz Lightyear, this spot has the right stuff. See a rocket launch or take your own giant leap with the Astronaut Training Experience. The half-day program consists of realistic training exercises culminating in a simulated mission.

## Something Old, Something New

You don't have to look far for "New Florida." It's evident in skyscrapers and sprawling suburbs, in malls, multiplexes, and the ubiquitous condo complexes that obscure parts of the coast. Yet it is easy enough to find reminders of the state's rich past.

■ **St. Augustine.** Fortify yourself at Castillo de San Marcos. Built by the Spanish to defend *La Florida*, this formidable 17th-century structure is America's oldest masonry fort. Even kids whose interest in architecture stops at Cinderella's Castle will be impressed by its turrets, moat, and double drawbridge.

■ **Apalachicola.** A booming cotton-and-lumber industry turned this Panhandle town into a bustling port in the 19th century. Now it's part of the Forgotten Coast. Hundreds of preserved buildings, ranging from antebellum warehouses to gracious Victorian-style homes, give it a time-warped appeal.

■ **Coral Gables.** You can soak up 1920s architecture in Miami Beach. But in nearby Coral Gables you can soak *in* it at the Venetian Pool, a vintage municipal lagoon fashioned from a quarry. Back in the day, it attracted Johnny Weissmuller, Esther Williams, and other legendary swimmers.

■ **Cross Creek.** The backwoods scrub immortalized by Marjorie Kinnan Rawlings in the *Dirty Thirties* hasn't changed much. Nor has the Cracker-style house where the Pulitzer prizewinner wrote *The Yearling.* You can tour it from October through July and visit the surrounding farm and grove year-round.

## Hitting the Greens

With more courses than any other state and weather that allows for year-round play, Florida is a dream destination for golfers. Ready to go fore it? The tourism board's new, dedicated golf site (⊕ *www.golf.visitflorida.com*) will point you in the right direction.

■ **The Breakers.** Floridian's fascination with golf began in 1897 when the state's first course opened at this Palm Beach resort. (Rockefellers, Vanderbilts, and Astors are all listed in the guest book.) Today, the original 70-par Ocean Course offers spectacular Atlantic views and challenging shots on 140 acres.

■ **PGA Village.** Owned and operated by the PGA, this Port St. Lucie venue boasts three championship courses designed by Tom Fazio and Pete Dye, plus a 35-acre Golf Learning and Performance Center that can turn weekend duffers into scratch players. A free museum of golf memorabilia is also on-site.

■ **Doral Golf Resort & Spa.** The Blue Monster understandably grabs the spotlight here: the par-72 course has been a stop on the PGA tour for more than 45 years. But the Miami resort has four other championship courses (including the new Jim McLean Signature Course) as well as McLean's own golf school.

■ **Reunion Resort.** This spot near Orlando just keeps upping its game. Not content with having courses laid out by Tom Watson, Arnold Palmer, and Jack Nicklaus, it recently added the Annika Academy, a golf school named for LPGA phenom Annika Sörenstam and overseen by her coach, Henri Reis.

# GREAT ITINERARIES

Florida is a long, lean peninsula anchored to the mainland by a "panhandle," so the distances between destinations may surprise you. Panama City, for example, is closer to New Orleans than to Orlando; and Tallahassee, though only 8 mi from the Georgia border, is a whopping 465 mi from Miami Beach. Key West, similarly, is 494 mi from Jacksonville, yet only 90 mi from Cuba. When plotting your dream trip, study a map to determine how easy it will be to connect the dots—or simply follow one of these tried-and-true itineraries. If you have two or more weeks to drive through the state, you can do them all.

## 3 to 4 Days: Orlando

Anyone can easily spend a week doing the attractions. (Remember, Walt Disney World alone is roughly the size of San Francisco!) But unless you're a die-hard ride hound, a few days will let you sample them and still enjoy some of Orlando's other amenities. The hard part is deciding where to start. The Magic Kingdom has the greatest concentration of classic sites, and Epcot proves this really is a small world. Film buffs can get reel at Disney's Hollywood Studios or Universal Studios, and thrill seekers can get their hearts pumping at Islands of Adventure. As for wildlife encounters, you can do like Dolittle at Disney's Animal Kingdom or SeaWorld. On top of all that, there's a sufficient number of water parks—including both old favorites such as Wet 'n Wild and newer entries like Aquatica—to make you forget you're inland. In the city itself, art connoisseurs can survey the collection of modern paintings at the Orlando Museum of Art; and flower fans can check out Orlando blooms in the 50-acre Harry P. Leu Gardens. Boaters can take advantage of the area's numerous lakes, and golfers can link up on courses designed by the sport's biggest stars.

## 2 to 3 Days: Panhandle

Let's be honest: people come to Florida's Panhandle primarily for those white-sand beaches. Some of the best in the country are along this coastline, affectionately known as the Redneck Riviera. But it's possible to work on a tan and still work in some sightseeing. At Gulf Islands National Seashore, for instance, you can soak up the sun, cast a fishing net, take a hike, tour centuries-old forts, and have time left for a trip into historic Pensacola. After beach time around Apalachicola Bay, head north through the canopied roads around Apalachicola National Forest. Then get a true taste of the Old South in moss-draped Tallahassee. Yet another day could be devoted to glorious Grayton Beach, where diving and kayaking can be followed up with a relaxing drive along Route 30A to cute, nostalgia-inducing communities like WaterColor and Seaside. When planning your trip, bear in mind that the Panhandle not only has its own time zone but its own tourism season—summer, and that's prime time for beach going.

## 2 to 3 Days: Space Coast

If you need proof that Florida was the first part of the United States to be settled, look no further than St. Augustine. It was founded by the Spanish in 1565, and visiting Castillo de San Marcos (its colonial-era fortress) or strolling the streets of the Old City that grew up around it allows you to experience life in the past lane. Taking in the stellar sites at the 150,000-acre Kennedy Space Center has just the opposite effect. Although it may seem centuries removed, the nation's oldest continuously inhabited city is less than two hours by car from our launch pad to the moon. Between them, you can hear the call of the wild at Merritt Island

National Wildlife Refuge, catch a wave like local surfing legend Kelly Slater, or blissfully hit the beach at Canaveral National Seashore (the 24-mi preserve remains undeveloped. So you lounge in the shelter of dunes, not the shadow of high-rises). Racier options also await—just reset your GPS for Daytona Beach. Its International Speedway, which has hosted NASCAR's Daytona 500 every February since 1959, is a must-see for stock-car enthusiasts, and there's plenty to do here year-round even if it's not a race day.

## 2 to 3 Days: Gold Coast and Treasure Coast

The opulent mansions of Palm Beach's Ocean Boulevard give you a glimpse of how the richer half lives. For exclusive boutique shopping, art gallery browsing, and glittery sightseeing, sybarites should wander down "The Avenue" (that's Worth Avenue to non–Palm Beachers). The sporty set will find dozens of places to tee up (hardly surprising given that the PGA is based here), along with tennis courts, polo clubs, even a croquet center. Those who'd like to see more of the Gold Coast can continue traveling south through Boca Raton to Fort Lauderdale (justifiably known as the

"Yachting Capital of the World"). But to balance the highbrow with the low-key, turn northward for a tour of the Treasure Coast. Notable for its outdoor opportunities and Old Florida ambience, this region was named for the booty spilled by a fleet of Spanish galleons shipwrecked here in 1715, and for centuries treasure kept washing ashore south of Sebastian Inlet. These days you're more likely to discover manatees and golden surfing opportunities. You can also look for the sea turtles that lay their own little treasures in the sands from March through October.

## 2 to 3 Days: Miami Area

Greater Miami lays claim to the country's most celebrated strand—South Beach—and lingering on it tops most tourist itineraries. (The Ocean Drive section, lined with edgy clubs, boutiques and eateries, is where the see-and-be-seen crowd gathers.) Once you've checked out the candy-color art deco architecture, park yourself to ogle the parade of stylish people. Or join them in browsing Lincoln Road Mall, and be sure to check out its latest addition, the glittering Frank Gehry–designed New World Symphony. Later, merengue over to Calle Ocho, the epicenter of Miami's Cuban community. Elsewhere in the area,

Coconut Grove, Coral Gables, and the Miami Design District (an 18-block area crammed with showrooms and galleries) warrant a visit as well. Since Miami is the sole U.S. city with two national parks and a national preserve in its backyard, it is also a convenient base for eco-texcursions. You can take a day trip to the Everglades; get a spectacular view of the reefs from a glass-bottom boat in Biscayne National Park; then spot some rare wood storks in Big Cypress Swamp, which is best explored via Alligator Alley (Interstate 75).

## 2 to 3 Days: Florida Keys

Some dream of "sailing away to Key Largo," others of "wasting away again in Margaritaville." In any case, almost everybody equates the Florida Keys with relaxation. And they live up to their reputation, thanks to offbeat attractions and that fabled come-as-you-are, do-as-you-please vibe. Key West, alternately known as the Conch Republic, is a good place to get initiated. The Old Town has a funky, laid-back feel. So take a leisurely walk; pay your respects to Ernest Hemingway; then (if you haven't imbibed too much at one of the renowned watering holes) rent a moped to tour the rest of the island. Clear waters and abundant marine life make underwater activities another must. After scoping out the parrotfish, you can head back into town and join local Parrotheads in a Jimmy Buffett sing-along. When retracing your route to the mainland, plan a last pit stop at Bahia Honda State Park (it has ranger-led activities plus the Keys' best beach) or John Pennekamp Coral Reef State Park, which offers unparalleled snorkeling and scuba-diving.

### TIPS

Now that one-way airfares are commonplace, vacationers visiting multiple destinations can fly into and out of different airports. Rent a car in between, picking it up at your point of arrival and leaving it at your point of departure. If you do this itinerary as an entire vacation, your best bet is to fly into and out of Orlando and rent a car from there.

Inquire about scheduled activities when visiting national and state parks or preserves. Many of them run free or low-cost ranger-led programs that run the gamut from walks and talks to campfires and canoe trips.

## 2 to 3 Days: Tampa Bay Area

Whether you bypassed Orlando's theme parks or simply want to add another one to your list, Busch Gardens is a logical starting point. With hair-raising rides and more than 2,000 animals, it appeals to adrenaline junkies and 'fraidy cats alike. Later you can catch a pro-sporting event (Tampa has Major League Baseball, football, and hockey teams) or catch an act in the Spanish-inflected Ybor City entertainment district. If you're more interested in catching some rays, try Caladesi Island State Park to the west of the city or Fort De Soto Park at the mouth of Tampa Bay. After exploring the Riverwalk's new museums, culture vultures can take day trips to the galleries in St. Petersburg and to Sarasota's thriving arts scene. Nature lovers proceed north to Crystal River, where you can snorkel with the manatees that congregate in the warm water November through March.

# SOAKING IN THE SUN: FLORIDA'S BEST BEACHES

by Mary Thurwachter

Long before the world's most famous mouse took up residence here, Florida reeled in hordes of visitors who wanted to bask in the sun and splash in the surf. The 447-mi peninsula lays claim to 1,100 mi of flip-flop–friendly beaches, each with its own distinct character. Some shores are blessed with snow-white sand, some with an abundance of shells. Others have golden sand perfect for sandcastle-building or sea-turtle nesting. Ready to join the sun-and-sand set? Here's a roundup of Florida's best beaches in seven categories.

# BEACH PLANNING

## CHOOSING YOUR BEACH

When planning a beach trip to Florida, the first thing to decide is whether you want to be on the ocean or on the gulf.

**Florida's ocean-side beaches** are blessed with golden sands—some even packed hard enough to drive on—and clear turquoise-blue waters. Come here if you want to surf, dive, or watch the sunrise. On the downside, ocean-side beaches have to contend at times with the twin menaces of jellyfish and sea lice, which can sting and cause a rash.

**Florida's gulf-coast beaches** have white sandy shores; the best can be found in the Panhandle, where the water is emerald green. Come here if you want to collect seashells or watch a sunset. On the downside, gulf-side beaches seasonally endure red-tide algae that can make it difficult to breathe and cause itchy eyes. Jellyfish also are here, particularly in the late summer and fall.

The next thing to consider is when you're going, as beaches are not warm year-round. If you're going in the winter, choose a South Florida destination.

## SAFETY TIPS

If you plan to swim, note the water's condition. Rip currents, caused when the tide rushes out through a narrow break in the water, can overpower even the strongest swimmer. If you do get caught in one, resist the urge to swim straight to shore—you'll tire before you make it. Instead, swim parallel to the shoreline until you are outside the current's pull, then head to the shore.

■TIP➔ See our chapter beach spotlights for more regional information.

Seeing the stars at Lummus Park.

## CELEBRITY SIGHTINGS

Chosen for their close proximity to top-notch hotels—the places that fluff pillows for stars—these beaches are palm-tree-adorned slices of paradise. The sand is soft enough to comfortably walk barefoot, and the water is warm and inviting. Tanning butlers, private cabanas, and trendy nightclubs are never far away—nor are paparazzi!

❶ **Lummus Park (South Beach),** Ocean Drive between 5th and 15th streets, Miami Beach. It's no accident that the park opens at 5 AM, when bars close and revelers totter over to watch the sun rise. Later in the day stars such as Lindsay Lohan, Jennifer Lopez, and Will Smith come out to freshen tans, frolic in the surf, play volleyball, or rollerblade on the boardwalk. Topless sunbathers are not uncommon.

❷ **Ponte Vedra Beach,** near Ponte Vedra Inn & Club, Northeast Florida

❸ **Lantana Beach,** near the Ritz-Carlton Palm Beach (in Manalapan), Palm Beach and the Treasure Coast

❹ **St. Pete Beach,** near the Don CeSar, Tampa Bay area

❺ **Islamorada Beach,** near The Moorings and Cheeca Lodge, the Florida Keys

❻ **Vanderbilt Beach,** near the Ritz-Carlton, Naples, the Lower Gulf Coast

❼ **Seagrove Beach,** near Seaside, in the Panhandle

Kids play at Clearwater Beach.

Fido gets his paws wet at a Florida beach.

## FAMILIES

To be considered for this category, beaches had to have picnic areas, showers, lifeguards, and sand suitable for building great sandcastles. Also, beachgoers to these slices of sand wear bathing (not birthday) suits. Having a playground area and being a site for annual festivals or events were not required but were worth bonus points.

❶ **Clearwater Beach,** Tampa Bay area. This gem for families features gorgeous white sand, attentive lifeguards, shallow waters that are clear and warm, a pier, and plenty of showers and restrooms. Bring some cash for renting certain amenities, like a beach umbrella or cabana, or for taking a whirl in the waves aboard a watercraft. Kids will want a pail and shovel, especially if you're coming during the Clearwater Fun 'n Sun Festival in April and May, where sandcastle-building contests are part of the festivities.

❷ **Delray Beach,** Palm Beach and the Treasure Coast

❸ **Hollywood Beach,** Hollywood, Fort Lauderdale and Broward County

❹ **Siesta Beach,** near Sarasota, Tampa Bay area

❺ **Harry Harris Park,** Tavenier (mile marker 92.5), the Florida Keys

❻ **Anastasia State Park,** St. Augustine, Northeast Florida

❼ **Fort Myers Beach,** the Lower Gulf Coast

## ANIMALS

Most beaches do not allow dogs. These Fido-friendly spots do, giving a pup a chance to dig up a seashell, chase a sand crab, fetch a Frisbee, and maybe even bodysurf. Most provide fresh water so our four-legged pals can quench their thirst and have sand soft enough for an easy-on-the-paws hike along the shore.

❶ **Jupiter Beach,** Jupiter, Palm Beach County. At this well-maintained 2.5-mi patch from Juno Beach north to Carlin Park boarded crosswalks framed by sea grapes lead you to the shoreline, and doggie bags are provided at each entrance. Dogs need to be leashed unless they respond well to your commands, in which case they can take a mad dash into the surf for a refreshing untethered swim.

❷ **St. Joe Beach,** Port St. Joe, north of Apalachicola, the Panhandle

❸ **Dog Beach,** Key West, adjacent to Louie's Backyard Restaurant near the southernmost point, the Florida Keys

❹ **Smyrna Dunes Park,** New Smyrna Beach, Northeast Florida

❺ **Rickenbacker Causeway and Beach,** Key Biscayne, Miami & Miami Beach

❻ **Abercrombie Park,** on Park Street at 38th Ave. N., St. Petersburg, the Tampa Bay Area

❼ **Flagler Beach,** north and south of 10th Street (but not at the 10th Street pier), Flagler Beach, Northeast Florida

Gathering in a handful of shells on the beach.

Enjoying a sunset at Caladesi Island State Park.

## SEASHELLS

These pretty beaches were picked for their abundance of seashells and how easy it was to find them. In other words, these are places you won't have to dig deep to find a gift from the sea—from whelks to olives to conchs.

❶ **Bowman's Beach,** on Sanibel Island, the Lower Gulf Coast. While most beaches in Sanibel and Captiva are worthy hunting grounds for shell devotees, Bowman's, the most remote, tops them all. Guests reach this wide sandy beach by traipsing from the parking area through beach grass, pines, wetland, and a picnic area cooled by the shade of pine trees and sea grapes. The likelihood of leaving with a bag full of gorgeous shells is high. You might even score one of the island's most coveted shells, the junonia. Time spent here is worth enduring "the Sanibel Stoop," the nickname islanders have given the hunched-over position shell seekers assume.

❷ **Holmes Beach,** Anna Maria Island, the Lower Gulf Coast

❸ **St. Joe State Park,** on Cape San Blas, the Panhandle

❹ **Sombrero Beach,** Marathon, the Florida Keys

❺ **Vero Beach,** Palm Beach & the Treasure Coast

❻ **Turtle Beach,** Siesta Key, Tampa Bay area

❼ **Jacksonville Beach,** Northeast Florida

## SOLITUDE & ROMANCE

We looked for shorelines that were uncrowded but beautiful, places you could walk a few hundred steps and find a strech of sand all to yourself or with your main squeeze. These selections are not public beaches where the masses come to drink in the sun; here the water laps gently against a silent shore.

❶ **Caladesi Island State Park,** a mile west of Dunedin, Tampa Bay Area. For a getting-away-from-it-all beach, this island retreat more than fits the bill: you can't even get to it by car but must take a boat. With crystal-clear waters and tiny waves, it's a good spot for swimming and fishing. You can paddle a kayak through the mangroves, hike on the nature trail, search for seashells, or just unwind with a romantic picnic on the white-sand shore.

❷ **Lovers Key State Park,** on County Rd. 865 between Fort Myers Beach and Bonita Beach in Lee County, the Lower Gulf Coast

❸ **Bahia Honda State Park,** Bahia Honda Key (mile marker 37), the Florida Keys

❹ **John U. Lloyd Beach Recreation Area,** Dania Beach, Fort Lauderdale and Broward County

❺ **St. George Island State Park,** St. George Island, the Panhandle

❻ **Blowing Rocks Preserve,** Jupiter, Palm Beach and the Treasure Coast

❼ **Canaveral National Seashore,** Titusville, Northeast Florida

Diving at John Pennekamp Coral Reef State Park.

Playing volleyball at Panama City Beach.

## DIVING IN

Water clarity and warmth were key factors here, but we also looked for beaches that offer interesting things to eyeball underwater. Strap on a mask and snorkel and you'll definitely see something eye-catching, from colorful coral reefs and schools of fish, to the remains of shipwrecks in their watery graves.

❶ John Pennekamp Coral Reef State Park, mile marker 102.5, Key Largo, the Florida Keys. With shallow water reefs, submerged sculptures, and 55 kinds of coral, Pennekamp has been hailed as the Diving Capital of the World. The country's first underwater park showcases an eight-and-a-half-foot bronze sculpture "Christ of the Deep." Those who don't want to dive in can see the coral reefs—and some of the nearly 600 varieties of fish who live there—on a glass-bottom boat tour. A visitor center sports a 30,000-gallon aquarium and nature theater.

❷ Bahia Honda State Park, Bahia Honda Key (mile marker 37), the Florida Keys

❸ Fort Lauderdale Beach, Fort Lauderdale and Broward County

❹ Fort Walton Beach, the Panhandle

❺ St. Andrew's State Recreational Area, Panama City, the Panhandle

❻ Egmont Key, Tampa Bay, southwest of Fort DeSoto Beach, the Tampa Bay Area

❼ Vero Beach, Palm Beach and the Treasure Coast

## PARTYING

Girls just wanna have fun, and that urge often takes them where the boys are. The ones they find at these beaches are tolerant of rowdiness and are never too far from bars, bands, and food. These beaches attract spring-breakers more than families with young children.

❶ Panama City Beach, the Panhandle. Seventeen miles of snowy-white sand and sparkling emerald-green water are enough to attract any beach lover, but at the Spring Break Capital of the World collegiate party animals find a special lure. MTV's televised concerts during spring break add fuel to the already hot word-of-mouth fire. When they're not drinking and dancing, free spirits looking for a legal high can tether themselves to a parachute and a speed boat for a bit of parasailing, and party girls can get a pedicure or scour the shops at Pier Park.

❷ Cocoa Beach, Northeast Florida

❸ Lummus Beach (South Beach), Miami Beach

❹ Smathers Beach in Key West, the Florida Keys

❺ Lynn Hall Memorial Park, Fort Myers Beach, the Lower Gulf Coast

❻ Riviera Beach Municipal Beach, on Singer Island, Palm Beach and the Treasure Coast

❼ Fort Lauderdale Beach, Fort Lauderdale and Broward County

# The Panhandle

**WORD OF MOUTH**

"I have been vacationing in Destin, Florida, for the past eight years, and nothing beats it! It's a great family vacation for rest, relaxation, and tons of things to do in a beautiful part of the world!"

—DestinDearestDestiny

# WELCOME TO THE PANHANDLE

## TOP REASONS TO GO

★ **Snowy White Beaches:** Most of the Panhandle's Gulf Coast shoreline is relatively unobstructed by high-rise condos and hotels, and the white-powder sand is alluring.

★ **Lots of History:** Spanish, American Indian, and, later, French and English influences shaped the direction of this region and are well represented in architecture, historic sites, and museums.

★ **Slower Pace:** The Panhandle is sometimes referred to as "LA," or Lower Alabama. Southern through and through, the pace here is as slow as molasses—a fact Tallahassee plays up by claiming to be "Florida with a Southern accent."

★ **Capital Sites:** As the state capital (chosen because it was midway between the two earlier Spanish headquarters of St. Augustine and Pensacola), Tallahassee remains intriguing thanks to its history, historical museums, universities, and quiet country charm.

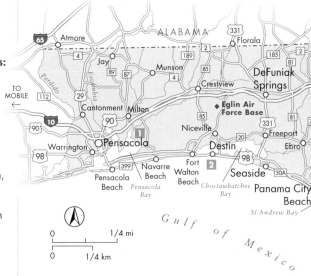

**1 Around Pensacola Bay.** By preserving architecture from early Spanish settlements, the city earns points for retaining the influence of these early explorers. The downtown district is compact and unique, plus there's the city's Naval Air Museum and its nearby beaches.

**2 The Emerald Coast.** A nature reserve spans thousands of square miles of Gulf Coast land, and miles of shoreline between Pensacola and Destin is nearly void of development. The area is known for its blue-green waters and sugarlike sand beaches made of Appalachian quartz crystals. Panama City offers unique attractions.

2

## GETTING ORIENTED

The Panhandle is a large area, and there are a number of regional airports to access the largest cities. Two major east–west routes will introduce you to some breathtaking waterfront drives. From Tallahassee, U.S. 90 is an early byway that roughly parallels its modern cousin, Interstate 10, but goes through small Old Florida towns like Marianna and DeFuniak Springs on its way to Pensacola. From Pensacola, U.S. 98 generally skirts along the Gulf of Mexico through seaside towns and communities like Fort Walton Beach, Destin, Panama City Beach, and Apalachicola.

**3** Inland Towns. The shoreline gets most tourist business, so the areas north are lightly trafficked, giving this region great appeal and access to Old Florida's small towns, vibrant history, rolling hills, and deep forests.

**4** Tallahassee. In the state capital you can see the old and new capitols, visit the state's historical museum, attend an FSU football game, and go for a country ride down canopied roads.

# PANHANDLE BEACHES

Not every stretch of Florida coastline features great beaches; some have rough sands, and others may find you contending with rocks, mud, and stingrays when you wade in. What's appealing about the Panhandle—especially the Emerald Coast—are beaches that are marked by soft, powdery sands and clear clean water.

Pensacola Beach has soft sand perfect for playing in.

### WHEN TO GO

The Panhandle beaches are best visited in the summer months. In late summer and fall, jellyfish can be a problem. Northwest Florida's beaches also offer some of Florida's best vacation packages come fall and winter, when the crowds thin out and the weather is comfortably cooler.

About 20 quiet beach communities are clustered along Route 30A, which breaks off U.S. 98 east of Sandestin and runs along the water for more than 17 mi before rejoining with U.S. 98. Here, sugar-white, quartz-crystal sands and emerald-green waters make for some of the finest stretches of sand and sea in the country. Known as the Beaches of South Walton, many are little more than a wide spot in the road, and all are among the least known and least developed in the Gulf Coast, even though Grayton Beach, near Route 283, is regularly ranked among the country's top 20 beaches.

## THE PANHANDLE'S BEST BEACHES

### PENSACOLA BEACH

Here you get miles of pristine beach and a convenient location, fringed by a commercial district and just over the bridge from Pensacola itself. Santa Rosa Island, home of Pensacola Beach, is a barrier island and part of the Gulf Island National Seashore. There's plenty of room to roam from Fort Pickens to the west to Opal Beach to the east, especially with the reopening of CR 399, which is pleasantly absent of development. Just east of Pensacola Beach, it's a lovely stretch of nothing but sand and some convenient pull-outs. All in all, the beaches here provide a nice balance that blends privacy and accessibility, as well as passive lounging and active beach recreation. The sand is white and soft, and water adventures include scuba diving (explore the sunken USS *Oriskany*), fishing (the Pensacola Fishing Pier is 1,471 feet long!), kayaking, sailing, surfing, and swimming. The water temperatures are in the 80s in the summer and in the 60s in the winter. For shopping, there's the Quietwater Beach Boardwalk, which also offers delicious dining options.

### GRAYTON BEACH

This area will take you back to Old Florida, where there were no condos, no strip malls, and no beach concessions.

Instead, there's a state park that has preserved the area and its sea oats and miles of walking trails for a laid-back time in the outdoors. The park has even added cabins (sans telephones and televisions), so you can experience Florida's Gulf Coast in its natural state. There are big dunes, camping, ample bird-watching and wildlife viewing, and on-the-water activities like canoeing, fishing, sailing, and swimming. It may be too slow-paced for kids, but just right for adults who want to ditch the schedule and get into the rhythm of nature.

### PANAMA CITY BEACH

If your visit to the Panhandle is based purely on beach access and activities, then this is where you want to be. Granted, Front Beach Road can get crowded, but parallel roads can move you up and down the coast fairly swiftly. Then again, once you check into your condo or hotel you may never need to hit the road. Instead, plant yourself by the pool, which is usually no more than a few feet away from the Gulf waters. A popular family retreat most times, families tend to steer clear during spring break, when it gets a bit crazy, but arrive in droves in the summer seeking attractions from pirate ships to go-karts. For a peaceful excursion, arrive in the winter. You won't be able to swim, but the views are still splendid.

By Ashley
Wright

The sugar-white sands of the Panhandle's beaches stretch 227 mi from Pensacola east to Apalachicola. Sprinkle in clear emerald waters, towering dunes, and laid-back small towns where the fish are always biting and the folks are friendly, and you have a region with local color that's beloved by Floridians and visitors alike.

There are sights in the Panhandle, but sightseeing isn't the principal activity. The region is better known for its rich history, ample fishing and diving, and its opportunities for relaxation. Here it's about Southern drawls, a gentle pace, fresh seafood, and more grits and old-fashioned hospitality than anywhere else in the state. Sleepy beach towns offer world-class golf, deep-sea fishing, relaxing spa treatments, and unbeatable shopping.

There's glamour here, too. Look for it in winning resorts throughout the region and in the abundance of nightlife, arts, and culture—from local symphonies to boutique art galleries—particularly in the more metropolitan areas. And then there's the food: from fresh catches of the day to some of the nation's finest oysters to mom-and-pop favorites offering fried seafood goodness.

Jump in a car, rent a bike, or buy a spot on a charter boat—you're never too far from outdoor adventure with more miles of preserved coastline than anywhere else in the state. Destin is, after all, dubbed "The World's Luckiest Fishing Village" and the sport of Yolo Boarding (this region's term for the popular paddleboarding craze) has invaded the area in full force, offering a unique point of view to all the region's unspoiled, natural beauty.

Don't forget to veer off the beach roads and venture into some of the area's picturesque historic districts. Pensacola is known as America's first settlement, and the rest of the region follows suit with rich history dating from the first settlers. The state's capital, Tallahassee, has its own unique history woven of politics, varying cultures, and innovation. Between the local charm, natural splendor, outdoor adventures, and miles of coastline, it's no wonder that the Panhandle is so beloved.

# THE PANHANDLE PLANNER

## WHEN TO GO

Peak season is Memorial Day to Labor Day, with another spike during spring break. Inland, especially in Tallahassee, high season is during the fall (football) and March to April. Vendors, attractions, and other activities will be in full swing in the summer. There's a "secret season" that falls around October and November: things quiet down as students go back to school, but restaurants and attractions keep normal hours and the weather is moderate.

## GETTING HERE

In May 2010, the first American international airport to open since 1995 arrived on the east shore of Panama City's West Bay. The Northwest Florida Beaches International Airport (ECP) debuted with flights to six U.S. cities through Southwest Airlines and Delta. In addition, there are passenger airports in Pensacola, Tallahassee, and a public airport—Northwest Florida Regional Airport—in Fort Walton Beach on the Eglin Air Force Base. Many major carriers will stop by at least one of these airports.

Transportation Contacts **Northwest Florida Beaches International Airport** (☎ 850/763-7651 ⊕ www.newpcairport.com). **Northwest Florida Regional Airport** (☎ 850/651-7160 ⊕ www.flyvps.com). **Pensacola Gulf Coast Regional Airport** (☎ 850/436-5005 ⊕ www.flypensacola.com). **Tallahassee Regional Airport** (☎ 850/891-7800 ⊕ www.talgov.com/airport).

## GETTING AROUND

The main east–west arteries across the top of the state are Interstate 10 and U.S. 90. Interstate 10 can be monotonous, but U.S. 90 piques your interest by routing you along the main streets of several county seats. U.S. 98 snakes eastward along the coast, splitting into 98 and 98A at Inlet Beach before rejoining at Panama City and continuing on to Port St. Joe and Apalachicola. The view of the gulf from U.S. 98 can be breathtaking, especially at sunset.

If you need to get from one end of the Panhandle to the other in a timely manner, drive inland to Interstate 10, where the speed limit runs as high as 70 mph in places. Major north–south highways that weave through the Panhandle are (from east to west) U.S. 231, U.S. 331, Route 85, and U.S. 29. From U.S. 331, which runs over a causeway at the east end of Choctawhatchee Bay between Route 20 and U.S. 98, the panorama of barge traffic and cabin cruisers on the twinkling waters of the Intracoastal Waterway will get your attention.

## ABOUT THE RESTAURANTS

An abundance of seafood is served at coastal restaurants: oysters, crab, shrimp, scallops, and a variety of fish. Of course, that's not all there is on the menu. This part of Florida still impresses diners with old-fashioned comfort foods such as meat loaf, fried chicken, beans and cornbread, okra, and fried green tomatoes. You'll also find small-town seafood shacks where you can dine on local favorites such as deep-fried mullet, cheese grits, coleslaw, and hush puppies. Restaurants, like resorts, vary their operating tactics off-season, so call first if visiting during winter months.

## ABOUT THE HOTELS

Many of the lodging selections here revolve around extended-stay options: resorts, condos, and time-shares that allow for a week or more in simple efficiencies, as well as fully furnished homes. There are also cabins, such as the ones that rest between the dunes at Grayton Beach. In any case, these are great for families and get-togethers, allowing you to do your own housekeeping and cooking and explore the area without tour guides.

Local visitors' bureaus often act as clearinghouses for these types of properties, and you can also search online for vacation rentals. On the coast, but especially inland, the choices seem geared more toward mom-and-pop motels in addition to the usual line of chain hotels. ■TIP➔During the summer and over holiday weekends, always reserve ahead for top properties.

| WHAT IT COSTS | | | | | |
|---|---|---|---|---|---|
| | ¢ | $ | $$ | $$$ | $$$$ |
| Restaurants | under $10 | $10–$15 | $15–$20 | $20–$30 | over $30 |
| Hotels | under $80 | $80–$100 | $100–$140 | $140–$220 | over $220 |

Restaurant prices are per person for a main course at dinner. Hotel prices are for a standard double room, excluding 6% sales tax (more in some counties) and 1%–4% tourist tax.

# PENSACOLA BAY

In the years since its founding, Pensacola has come under the control of five nations, earning this old Southern city its nickname, the City of Five Flags. Spanish conquistadors, under the command of Don Tristan de Luna, landed on the shores of Pensacola Bay in 1559, but, discouraged by a succession of destructive tropical storms and dissension in the ranks, de Luna abandoned the settlement two years after its founding.

In 1698 the Spanish again established a fort at the site, and during the early 18th century control jockeyed between the Spanish, the French, and the British. Finally, in 1821, Pensacola passed into U.S. hands, although during the Civil War it was governed by the Confederate States of America and flew yet another flag. Across the bay lies Pensacola Beach on Santa Rosa Island.

## PENSACOLA

*59 mi east of Mobile, Alabama via I-10.*

Pensacola consists of three distinct districts—Seville, Palafox, and North Hill—though they are easy to explore as a unit. Stroll down streets mapped out by the British and renamed by the Spanish, such as Cervantes, Palafox, Intendencia, and Tarragona. An influx of restaurants and bars has brought new nightlife to the historic districts, especially Palafox Street, which is now home to a thriving entertainment district.

At the southern terminus of Palafox Street is Plaza DeLuna, a 2-acre park with open grounds, interactive water fountains, and an amphitheater. It's a quiet place to sit and watch the bay, fish, or enjoy the city's Thursday-evening sunset celebration.

### GETTING HERE AND AROUND

Pensacola Regional Airport has dozens of daily flights and is served by AirTran, American Airlines (American Eagle), Continental, Delta, United, and US Airways. From the Pensacola Regional Airport via Yellow Cab it costs about $14 to go downtown or about $32 to Pensacola Beach.

In Pensacola and Pensacola Beach, Escambia County Area Transit provides regular citywide bus service ($1.75), downtown trolley routes, tours through the historic districts, and free summer trolley service to the beach from mid-May to Labor Day on Friday, Saturday, and Sunday evenings as well as Saturday afternoons.

### ESSENTIALS

Transportation Contacts **Escambia County Area Transit** (*ECAT* ☎ *850/595–3228* ⊕ *www.goecat.com*). **Pensacola Regional Airport** (☎ *850/436–5000* ⊕ *www.flypensacola.com*). **Yellow Cab** (☎ *850/433–3333*).

Visitor Information **Pensacola Visitor Information Center** (✉ *1401 E. Gregory St.* ☎ *850/434–1234 or 800/874–1234* ⊕ *www.visitpensacola.com*).

### EXPLORING

#### TOP ATTRACTIONS

Fodor's Choice
★
**Pensacola Naval Air Station.** Locals almost unanimously suggest this as *the* must-see attraction of Pensacola. As you drive near it, don't be alarmed if you're suddenly struck with the shakes—they're probably caused by the U.S. Navy's Blue Angels' aerobatic squadron buzzing overhead. This is their home base, and they practice maneuvers here on Tuesday and Wednesday mornings at 8:30 from March to November.

The Naval Air Station's bleachers hold about 1,000 people and they fill up fast, so get here early. Then stay late—the pilots stick around after the show to shake hands and sign autographs. During the show, cover your ears as the six F/A 18s blast off in unison for 45 minutes of thrills and skill. Watching the Blue Angels practice their aerobatics is one of the best "free" shows in all of Florida (your tax dollars are already paying for these jets). ✉ *1750 Radford Blvd.* ☎ *850/452–3604 or 850/452–3606* ⊕ *www.navalaviationmuseum.org* ⛶ *Free, IMAX film $8, 2 films for $13* ⊙ *Daily 9–5.*

**National Museum of Naval Aviation.** Within the Pensacola Naval Air Station, the 300,000-square-foot National Museum of Naval Aviation has more than 140 historic aircraft. Among them are the NC-4, which in 1919 became the first plane to cross the Atlantic; the famous World War II fighter the F-6 *Hellcat*; and the Skylab Command Module.

**TOP GUN**

The National Museum of Naval Aviation is one of only two locations nationwide that feature "Top Gun," four real F-14 military flight-training simulators with all the actual controls. Experience mock air-to-air combat, practice carrier landings, or simply cruise over Las Vegas, Iraq, Miramar, California, and other simulated sites during a 20-minute joyride. The $25 experience includes "cockpit orientation training."

Other attractions include an atomic bomb (it's defused, we promise), and the restored Cubi Bar Café—a very cool former airmen's club transplanted here from the Philippines. Relive the morning's maneuvers in the 14-seat motion-based simulator as well as an IMAX theater playing *Fighter Pilot, The Magic of Flight,* and other educational films. Pensacola, also known as the "Cradle of Naval Aviation," celebrated the 100th Anniversary of Naval Aviation in 2011. ☎ *850/452–3604*

**Seville Square Historic District.** Established in 1559, this is the site of Pensacola's first permanent Spanish settlement (it beat St. Augustine's by six years). Its center is Seville Square, a live oak–shaded park bounded by Alcaniz, Adams, Zaragoza, and Government streets. Roam these brick streets past honeymoon cottages and homes set in a parklike setting. Many buildings have been converted into restaurants, offices, and shops that overlook broad Pensacola Bay and coastal road U.S. 98, which you'll use to access the Gulf Coast and beaches.

**Historic Pensacola Village.** Within the Seville Square Historic District is this complex of several museums and historic homes whose indoor and outdoor exhibits trace the area's history back 450 years. The Museum of Industry (✉ *200 E. Zaragoza St.*), in a late-19th-century warehouse, is home to permanent exhibits dedicated to the lumber, maritime, and shipping industries—once mainstays of Pensacola's economy. A reproduction of a 19th-century streetscape is displayed in the Museum of Commerce (✉ *201 E. Zaragoza St.*). Also in the village are the Julee Cottage (✉ *210 E. Zaragoza St.*), the "first home owned by a free woman of color," 1871 Dorr House (✉ *311 S. Adams St.*), and French-Creole Lavalle House (✉ *205 E. Church St.*).

Strolling through the area gives you a good (and free) look at many architectural styles, but to enter some of the buildings you must purchase an all-inclusive ticket at the Village gift shop in the Tivoli High House—which was once in the city's red-light district but now is merely a calm reflection of a restored home. Opt for the guided tour (11 am, 1 pm, and 2:30 pm), and you'll experience the history of Pensacola as you visit the 1805 Lavalle House, the 1871 Dorr House, Old Christ Church, and the 1890s Lear-Rocheblave House. Tours last one hour to 90 minutes. For information on home and museum tours within the district, contact Historic Pensacola Village. ⊠ *Tivoli High House, 205 E. Zaragoza St.* ☎ *850/595–5985* ⊕ *www.historicpensacola.org* 🖻 *$6* ⊙ *Tues.–Sat. 10–4.*

**T.T. Wentworth, Jr. Florida State Museum.** Even if you don't like museums, this one is worth a look. Housed in the elaborate, Renaissance revival– style former city hall, it has an interesting mix of exhibits illustrating life in the Florida Panhandle over the centuries. One presentation you'll want to see is the City of Five Flags, which provides a good introduction to Pensacola's history. Mr. Wentworth was quite a collector (as well as a politician and salesman), and his eccentric collection includes a mummified cat (creepy) and the size 37 left shoe of Robert Wadlow, the world's tallest man (not creepy, but a really big shoe). A wide range of both permanent and traveling exhibits include a rare collection of dollhouses, Black Ink (a look at African-Americans' role in printing), Hoops to Hips (a review of the fashion history), Civil War exhibits, and a kid-size interactive area with a ship and fort where kids can play and pretend to be colonial Pensacolans. ⊠ *330 S. Jefferson St.* ☎ *850/595– 5990* ⊕ *www.historicpensacola.org* 🖻 *Free* ⊙ *Tues.–Sat. 10–4.*

**WORTH NOTING**

**North Hill Preservation District.** Pensacola's affluent families, many made rich in the turn-of-the-20th-century timber boom, built their homes in this area where British and Spanish fortresses once stood. Residents still occasionally unearth cannonballs in their gardens. North Hill occupies 50 blocks, with more than 600 homes in Queen Anne, neoclassical, Tudor revival, and Mediterranean styles. Take a drive through this community, but remember these are private residences. Places of general interest include the 1902 Spanish mission–style Christ Episcopal Church; Lee Square, where a 50-foot obelisk stands as a tribute to the Confederacy; and Fort George, an undeveloped parcel at the site of the largest of three forts built by the British in 1778.

**Palafox Historic District.** Palafox Street is the main stem of historic downtown Pensacola and the center of the Palafox Historic District. The commercial and government hub of Old Pensacola is now an active cultural and entertainment district. Note the opulent, renovated Spanish Renaissance–style Saenger Theater, Pensacola's 1925 movie palace, which hosts performances by the local symphony and opera, as well as national acts, and the Bear Block, a former wholesale grocery with wrought-iron balconies that are a legacy from Pensacola's creole past.

On Palafox between Government and Zaragoza streets is a statue of Andrew Jackson that commemorates the formal transfer of Florida from Spain to the United States in 1821. While in the area, stop by Veterans Memorial Park, just off Bayfront Parkway near 9th Avenue. The ¾-scale replica of the Vietnam Memorial in Washington, D.C., honors the more than 58,000 Americans who lost their lives in the Vietnam War.

## SPORTS AND THE OUTDOORS

### CANOEING AND KAYAKING

**Adventures Unlimited.** This outfitter on Coldwater Creek rents light watercraft as well as campsites and cabins along the Coldwater and Blackwater rivers in the Blackwater State Forest. Canoe season lasts roughly from March through mid-November, but Adventures Unlimited rents year-round. ⊠ *Rte. 87* ☎ *850/623–6197 or 800/239–6864* ⊕ *www.adventuresunlimited.com.*

**Blackwater Canoe Rental.** Canoe and kayak rentals for exploring the Blackwater River—the purest sand-bottom river in the nation—are available from this outfitter, northeast of Pensacola off Interstate 10 Exit 31. ⊠ *6974 Deaton Bridge Rd., Milton* ☎ *850/623–0235 or 800/967–6789* ⊕ *www.blackwatercanoe.com.*

### DIVING

**USS *Oriskany.*** It's called the "Mighty O," but it was formerly known as the USS *Oriskany.* The retired aircraft carrier was sunk 24 mi off the Pensacola Pass in 2006, and now the superstructure is the world's largest artificial reef. The "island" is accessible just 67 feet down, and the flight deck can be reached at 137 feet. ☎ *850/455–7702* ⊕ *www.mbtdivers.com.*

### DOLPHIN TOURS

**Chase-N-Fins.** To catch a glimpse of a friendly porpoise, try climbing aboard this 50-foot navy utility launch that cruises Pensacola Bay along Ft. Pickens, Pensacola Pass, and the Lighthouse at Pensacola Naval Air Station in search of dolphins. ⊠ *655 Pensacola Beach Blvd.,* Pensacola Beach ☎ *850/492–6337 or 800/967–6789* ⊕ *www.chase-n-fins.com.*

### FISHING

**Beach Marina.** For a full- or half-day deep-sea charter, try the Beach Marina, which represents several charter outfits. Bottom-fishing is best for amberjack and grouper, offshore trolling trips are searching for tuna, wahoo, and sailfish, and inshore charters are out to hook redfish, cobia, and pompano. For a complete list of local fishing charters, visit ⊕ *www.visitpensacola.com.* ⊠ *655 Pensacola Beach Blvd.* ☎ *877/650–3474 or 850/932–0304* ⊕ *www.pensacolabeachmarina.net.*

### GOLF

**Club at Hidden Creek.** This 18-hole course is in Santa Rosa County, 20 mi from Pensacola. Greens fees are $20–$53 (with cart). ⊠ *3070 PGA Blvd., Navarre* ☎ *850/939–1939* ⊕ *www.hiddengolf.com.*

---

### DEEPWATER SPILL

The beaches of Northwest Florida were threatened by the Deepwater Horizon Oil Spill that unraveled in the early months of 2010. And although some beaches did report pollution in local waterways, with the capping of the well, many of the area's beaches have cleaned up and reported very limited disturbances. Isolated impacts may still occur, mainly in the form of scattered tar balls; state and local emergency management officials have ensured they're removed quickly and efficiently. The beaches largely remain as pure-white as ever and the waters as emerald as they ever were.

**Lost Key Golf Club.** A public, par-71, 18-hole Arnold Palmer Signature Design Course, this was the first golf course in the world to be certified as an Audubon International Silver Signature Sanctuary. Greens fees are $40–$84 (with cart). ✉ *625 Lost Key Dr., Perdido Key Beach* ☎ *850/549–2160 or 888/256–7853* ⊕ *www.lostkey.com.*

**Perdido Bay Golf Club.** The 18-hole course here is well-kept. Greens fees are $29–$45 (with cart). ✉ *1 Doug Ford Dr., Pensacola* ☎ *850/492–1223* ⊕ *www.perdidobaygolf.com.*

## SHOPPING

Pensacola's Palafox and Seville historic districts are enjoyable areas for browsing.

**Cordova Mall.** Ten miles north of the Historic District, this mall is anchored by large stores such as Dillards, Best Buy, and World Market. There are also more than 125 specialty shops and a food court. ✉ *5100 N. 9th Ave.* ☎ *850/477–5355.*

**Quayside Art Gallery.** The largest co-op art gallery in the Southeast has items by local artists in a variety of mediums. Other shops here display glass, wood, metal, paintings, and jewelry. ✉ *17 E. Zaragoza St.* ☎ *850/438–2363* ⊕ *www.quaysidegallery.com.*

## NIGHTLIFE

**Hopjacks Pizza Kitchen and Taproom.** It's a restaurant with a full bar and one of the Panhandle's most extensive and unique specialty beer selections. There are more than 150 beers, including 36 on tap. *10 S. Palafox St.* ☎ *850/497–6073* ⊕ *www.hopjacks.com.*

**Hub Stacey's.** On the corner by Seville Square, this friendly neighborhood local pub has bottled beer, numerous drink specials, sidewalk tables, and a good vibe. ✉ *312 E. Government St.* ☎ *850/469–1001* ⊕ *www. hubstaceys.com.*

**McGuire's Irish Pub.** Those of Irish descent and anyone else who enjoys cold home-brewed ales, beers, or lagers will feel at home in this restaurant and microbrewery. Its 8,500-bottle wine cellar includes vintages ranging from $14–$20,000. If you want a quiet drink, steer clear on Friday and Saturday nights—when crowds abound and live entertainment enlivens the masses. ✉ *600 E. Gregory St.* ☎ *850/433–6789* ⊕ *www. mcguiresirishpub.com.*

**New York Nick's.** This place is a little of everything: a sports bar, a rock-and-roll club, a shrine to Bruce Springsteen, and a popular downtown bar and grill. It's an "A+" spot for all the best "Bs" in life—beer, billiards, burgers, and the Boss. ✉ *9–11 S. Palafox St.* ☎ *850/469–1984* ⊕ *www.newyorknicks.net.*

**Seville Quarter.** In the heart of the Historic District is Pensacola's equivalent of New Orleans's French Quarter. In fact, you may think you've traveled to Louisiana when you enter any of its seven bars and two courtyards offering an eclectic mix of live music. College students pack the place on Thursday, tourists come on the weekend, and military men and women from six nearby bases are stationed here nearly all the time. This is a classic Pensacola nightspot. ✉ *130 E. Government St.* ☎ *850/434–6211* ⊕ *www.sevillequarter.com.*

Like an Old West town with a Victorian twist, historic Pensacola is eye candy for architecture buffs.

## THE ARTS

**Saenger Theatre.** The restored 1925 Sanger presents touring Broadway shows and concerts by **Pensacola's Symphony Orchestra** (☎ 850/435–2533 ⊕ *www.pensacolasymphony.com*) and **Pensacola Opera** (☎ 850/433–6737 ⊕ *www.pensacolaopera.com*). ⊠ *118 S. Palafox St.* ☎ *850/595–3880* ⊕ *www.pensacolasaenger.com.*

## WHERE TO EAT

**$$$**
SEAFOOD
✕ **Fish House.** Come one, come all, come hungry, and come at 11 am to witness the calm before the lunch storm. By noon the Fish House is packed with professionals, power players, and poseurs. The wide-ranging menu of fish dishes is the bait, and each can be served in a variety of ways: ginger-crusted, grilled, blackened, pecan-crusted, or Pacific-grilled, which puts any dish over the top. The attentive service, bay-front setting, and signature "Grits a Ya-Ya" (fresh gulf shrimp on a bed of smoked Gouda-cheese grits smothered with a portobello mushroom sauce) keeps diners in the net. Steaks, delicious homemade desserts, a sushi bar, more than 300 varieties of wine, and a full-service bar don't hurt the popularity of this restaurant either. ⊠ *600 S. Barracks St.* ☎ *850/470–0003* ⊕ *www.fishhousepensacola.com.*

**$$**
ECLECTIC
✕ **Global Grill.** Come hungry to this trendy downtown Pensacola restaurant, and fill your eyes, plate, and belly from the selection of more than 40 different tapas, 11 entrées, and eight salads. Among the tapas are the high-demand lamb lollipops, Israeli couscous, sundried tomato au jus, spicy seared tuna with five-pepper jelly, or the andouille-Manchego empanadas with cucumber cream. To jazz things up, entrées have been added as well, with filet mignon, gulf shrimp, duck breast, fresh

2

fish, and New York strip competing with the light appetizers. ✉ *27 S. Palafox* ☎ *850/469–9966* ⊕ *www.dineglobalgrill.com* ⊗ *Closed Sun. and Mon.*

**$$$**
IRISH
✕ **McGuire's Irish Pub**. Since 1977 this authentic Irish pub has promised its patrons "feasting, imbibery, and debauchery" seven nights a week. A sense of humor pervades the place, evidenced by the range of prices on hamburgers—$10–$100 depending on whether you want it topped with cheddar or served with caviar and champagne. Beer is brewed on the premises, and the wine cellar has more than 8,500 bottles. Menu items include corned beef and cabbage, great steaks, and a hickory-smoked prime rib. In an old firehouse, the pub is replete with antiques, moose heads, Tiffany-style lamps, and Erin-go-bragh memorabilia. As for the "richness" of the decor—on the walls and ceiling are nearly $250,000 in bills signed and dated by "Irishmen of all nationalities." ✉ *600 E. Gregory St.* ☎ *850/433–6789* ⊕ *www.mcguiresirishpub.com.*

**WHERE TO STAY**
*For expanded hotel reviews, visit Fodors.com.*

**$$$**
HOTEL
⌂ **Crowne Plaza–Pensacola Grand Hotel**. On the site of the restored historic Louisville & Nashville (L&N) railroad passenger depot, the Crowne Plaza has a 15-story glass tower, attached to the train depot by a glass atrium, and incredible views of historic Pensacola. **Pros:** great location near downtown; amenities perfect for business travelers. **Cons:** it's a box; there are more intimate choices closer to downtown. ✉ *200 E. Gregory St.* ☎ *850/433–3336 or 800/348–3336* ⊕ *www. pensacolagrandhotel.com* ⟿ *200 rooms, 10 suites* ⚶ *In-room: Wi-Fi. In-hotel: restaurant, bar, pool, gym.*

**$$–$$$**
B&B/INN
★
⌂ **New World Inn**. If you like your inns small, warm, and cozy, with the bay on one side and a short two-block walk to the downtown historic area on the other, then this is the inn for you. **Pros:** perfect location downtown; unique boutique hotel. **Cons:** could use a spring-cleaning. ✉ *600 S. Palafox St.* ☎ *850/432–4111* ⊕ *www.newworldlanding.com* ⟿ *14 rooms, 1 suite* ⚶ *In-room: Wi-Fi. In-hotel: bar* ⑂ *BP.*

**$$–$$$**
HOTEL
⌂ **Residence Inn by Marriott**. In the downtown bay-front area, this immaculately kept all-suites hotel is perfect for extended stays, whether for business or pleasure. **Pros:** self-serve meal and dining options make a family retreat easier. **Cons:** ordinary hotel style. ✉ *601 E. Chase St.* ☎ *850/432–0202* ⊕ *www.marriott.com* ⟿ *78 suites* ⚶ *In-room: kitchen. In-hotel: tennis court, pool, gym, some pets allowed* ⑂ *BP.*

# PENSACOLA BEACH

*5 mi south of Pensacola via U.S. 98 to Rte. 399 (Bob Sikes) Bridge.*

One of the longest barrier islands in the world, Pensacola Beach offers a low-key, family-friendly feel with many local hangouts, fishing galore, and historic Fort Pickens. Connected to Pensacola by two long bridges, the island offers both a gulf-front and "sound" side for those seeking a calmer seaside experience. Public beaches abound in the area, including Casino Beach at the tip of Pensacola Beach Road, which offers live entertainment at its pavilion in the summer, as well as showers and bathrooms. Quietwater Beach Boardwalk, across the street from Casino Beach, also offers boutique shopping, eateries, nightlife, and shopping.

Long home to chain hotels as well as locally owned motels, the beach has opened a number of condominiums and resorts in recent years, with even more development slated for the near future. And don't forget to rent a bike or take a drive to explore both Fort Pickens Road and J. Earle Bowden Way (which connects Pensacola Beach to the Navarre Beach area), which have reopened after many years of being closed to vehicular traffic and offer breathtaking, unobstructed views of the gulf.

### EXPLORING

**Fort Pickens.** Constructed of more than 21 million locally made bricks, this fort, dating back to 1834, once served as a prison for Apache chief Geronimo. A National Park Service plaque describes the complex as a "confusing jumble of fortifications," but the real attractions here are the beach, nature exhibits, a large campground, an excellent gift shop, and breathtaking views of Pensacola Bay and the lighthouse across the inlet. It's the perfect place for a picnic lunch and a bit of history, too. ⊠ *At western tip of island, Ft. Pickens Rd.* ☎ *850/934–2635* ⊠ *$8 per car* ☉ *Daily 7 am–10 pm.*

### BEACH

**Casino Beach.** It was named for the Casino Resort, which was the first tourist spot on the island when it opened in 1931, the same day the first Pensacola Beach Bridge opened. The area offers everything from live entertainment during peak season to public restroom facilities and showers. ⊠ *735 Pensacola Beach Blvd.*

### SPORTS AND THE OUTDOORS

**Pensacola Beach Gulf Pier.** The 1,471-foot-long pier touts itself as the "the most friendly pier around." This peerless pier hosts serious anglers who find everything they'll need here—from pole rentals to bait—to land that big one, but those looking to catch only a beautiful sunset are welcome, too. Check the pier's website for the latest reports on what's biting. ⊠ *41 Ft. Pickens Rd.* ☎ *850/934–7200* ⊕ *www.fishpensacolabeachpier.com* ⊠ *Observers $1.25, fishing $7.50.*

### WHERE TO EAT AND STAY

*For expanded hotel reviews, visit Fodors.com.*

$$
SEAFOOD
✕ **Flounder's Chowder and Ale House.** The wide and peaceful gulf spreads out before you at this casual restaurant where, armed with a fruity libation, you're all set for a night of "floundering" at its best. Funkiness comes courtesy of an eclectic collection of objets d'art; tastiness is served in specialties such as seafood nachos and the shrimp-boat platter. Most signature dishes are charbroiled over a hardwood fire, and to cater to those who love the sea but not seafood, the extensive menu reveals more choices. Live entertainment is presented every night in season, with performances limited to weekends off-season. ⊠ *800 Quietwater Beach Blvd.* ☎ *850/932–2003* ⊕ *www.flounderschowderhouse.com.*

$$$-$$$$
HOTEL
🏨 **Margaritaville Beach Hotel.** This tropical getaway, inspired by the lyrics of Jimmy Buffett, gives you the relaxed, fun, Margaritaville experience with the amenities of a top-notch hotel that oozes barefoot elegance. **Pros:** clean, inviting atmosphere; lots of dining options; local spa

services available. **Cons:** somewhat off the beaten path to other local dining and nightlife. options. ✉ *165 Fort Pickens Rd.* ☎ *850/916–9755* ⊕ *www.margaritavillehotel.com* ⤴ *162 rooms* ⚇ *In-hotel: restaurants, bar, pool.*

# THE EMERALD COAST

On U.S. 98, several towns, each with its own personality, are strung along the shoreline from Pensacola southeast to St. George Island. The side-by-side cities of Destin and Fort Walton Beach seemingly merge into one sprawling destination and continue to spread as more condominiums, resort developments, shopping centers, and restaurants crowd the skyline each year. The view changes drastically—and for the better—farther along the coast as you veer off 98 and enter Route 30A, the main coastal road that leads to a quiet stretch known as the Beaches of South Walton. Here building restrictions prohibit high-rise developments, and the majority of dwellings are privately owned homes, most of which are available to vacationers.

Continuing southeast on U.S. 98, you'll find Panama City Beach, whose "Miracle Strip," once crammed with carnival-like amusement parks, junk-food vendors, T-shirt shops, and go-kart tracks, has been nearly replaced by up-to-date shopping and entertainment complexes and new condos that have given the area a much-needed face-lift. Farther east, past the up-and-coming sleeper cities of Port St. Joe and Mexico Beach, you'll come to the quiet blue-collar town of Apalachicola, Florida's main oyster fishery. Watch oystermen ply their trade, using long-handled tongs to bring in their catch. Cross the Apalachicola Bay via the Bryant Patton Bridge to St. George Island. This unspoiled 28-mi-long barrier island offers some of America's most scenic beaches, including St. George Island State Park, which has the longest beachfront of any state park in Florida.

### GETTING HERE AND AROUND

Northwest Florida Regional Airport in North Eglin on Highway 85 is served by American Airlines (American Eagle), Delta (Delta Connection), Continental (Continental Express), US Airways, and Vision Airlines. From here you can take a number of car and cab services, including Checker Cab, to destinations such as Fort Walton Beach ($18) or Destin ($24).

### ESSENTIALS

Transportation Contacts **Northwest Florida Regional Airport** (☎ *850/651–7160* ⊕ *www.flyvps.com*). **Checker Cab** (☎ *850/650–8294*).

Visitor Information **Emerald Coast Convention and Visitors Bureau** (☎ *850/651–7131 or 800/322–3319* ⊕ *www.emeraldcoastfl.com*).

## FORT WALTON BEACH

*46 mi east of Pensacola via U.S. 98.*

This coastal town dates from the Civil War but had to wait more than 75 years to come into its own. Patriots loyal to the Confederate cause

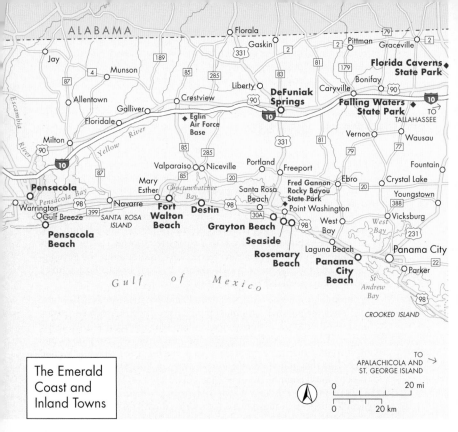

Florala
Gaskin
Pittman Graceville
Jay
Munson
Florida Caverns
State Park
Liberty
Caryville
Bonifay
Allentown
Crestview
DeFuniak
Springs
Falling Waters
State Park
Galliver
TO
TALLAHASSEE
Floridale
Eglin
Air Force
Base
Milton
Vernon
Wausau
Valparaiso Niceville
Portland
Freeport
Fountain
Mary
Esther
Choctawhatchee
Bay
Santa Rosa
Beach
Fred Gannon
Rocky Bayou
State Park
Ebro
Crystal Lake
Pensacola
Navarre
Fort
Walton
Beach
Destin
Point Washington
Youngstown
Warrington
Pensacola Bay
Gulf Breeze
SANTA ROSA
ISLAND
Grayton Beach
West
Bay
West
Bay
Vicksburg
Pensacola
Beach
Seaside
Laguna Beach
Panama City
Rosemary
Beach
Panama
City
Beach
Parker
St.
Andrew
Bay
Gulf of Mexico
CROOKED ISLAND

The Emerald
Coast and
Inland Towns

TO
APALACHICOLA AND
ST. GEORGE ISLAND

0        20 mi
0        20 km

organized Walton's Guard (named in honor of Colonel George Walton, onetime acting territorial governor of West Florida) and camped at a site on Santa Rosa Sound, later known as Camp Walton. In 1940 fewer than 90 people lived in Fort Walton Beach, but within a decade the city became a boomtown, thanks to New Deal money for roads and bridges and the development of Eglin Field during World War II.

The military is now Fort Walton Beach's main source of income (the area's Eglin Air Force Base, which is off-limits to civilians) encompasses 724 square mi of land, with 10 auxiliary fields and a total of 21 runways), but tourism runs a close second. Despite the inland sprawl of the town, independent merchants have created a cute little shopping district along U.S. 98.

### EXPLORING

★ **Air Force Armament Museum.** The collection at this museum just outside the Eglin Air Force Base's main gate contains more than 5,000 armaments (aka missiles, bombs, and aircraft) from World Wars I and II and the Korean and Vietnam wars. Included are uniforms, engines, weapons, aircraft, and flight simulators. You can't miss the museum—there's a squadron of aircraft including a B-17 Flying Fortress, an SR-71 Blackbird, a B-52, a B-25, and helicopters parked on the grounds in front. A continuously playing 32-minute movie, *Arming the Future*, features current weapons and Eglin's history and its role in their development. ✉ *100 Museum Dr. (Rte. 85), Eglin Air Force Base* ☎ *850/651–1808* ⊕ *www.afarmamentmuseum.com* 🎟 *Free* ☾ *Mon.–Sat. 9:30–4:30.*

**Gulfarium.** Opened in 1955, this is the oldest continuously operating marine park in Florida. In the style of several modest oceanographic attractions, it tosses in an assortment of sea life–themed shows and exhibits. Its main attraction is the Living Sea, a 60,000-gallon tank that simulates conditions on the ocean floor, and there are campy performances by trained porpoises, plus sea-lion shows and marine-life exhibits. Among other species here are otters, penguins, alligators, harbor seals, and sharks. The old-fashioned Dolphin Reef gift shop sells anything from conch shells to beach toys. There's also the Dolphin Meet and Greet program, in which you sit on a ledge in a pool as spotted dolphins swim up to your lap. That experience lasts about 15–20 minutes and allows you to pet and feed the dolphins. Visit the park's website for details. ✉ *U.S. 98 E* ☎ *850/243–9046 or 800/247–8575* ⊕ *www. gulfarium.com* 🎟 *$19.25, Dolphin Meet and Greet $50* ☾ *Daily 9–4; Jan., Feb., and part of Mar. closed Mon. and Tues.*

### BEACH

**John C. Beasley Wayside Park.** Resting tranquilly atop the dunes is Fort Walton Beach's seaside playground on Okaloosa Island. Across the dunes, a boardwalk leads to the beach, where there are a dozen covered picnic tables, pavilions, changing rooms, and freshwater showers. Lifeguards are on duty in summer. ✉ *Okaloosa Island* ☎ *No phone.*

### SPORTS AND THE OUTDOORS

**Eglin Air Force Base Reservation.** With 810 mi of creeks and plenty of challenging, twisting wooded trails, this 1,045-square-mi base appeals to outdoors enthusiasts, who can hunt, fish, canoe, and swim here. For $10 you can buy a day pass to camp or hike or mountain bike on the Timberlake Trail, which is open from 7 am to 4:30 pm, Monday through Thursday. Hours may change on Friday and Saturday, so call ahead. Obtain permits from the Jackson Guard. ✉ *107 Rte. 85 N, Niceville* ☎ *850/882–4164* ⊕ *www.eglin.af.mil.*

#### FISHING

**Okaloosa Island Pier.** Don't miss a chance to go out to the end of this ¼-mi-long pier. It costs two bucks to walk the plank, $7.50 if you'd like to fish. (You can buy bait and tackle, and rent poles.) ☎ *850/244–1023* ⊕ *www.okaloosaislandpier.com.*

#### GOLF

**Fort Walton Beach Golf Club.** It's a 36-hole municipal course whose links (Oaks and Pines) lie about 400 yards from each other. The two courses are considered by many to be among Florida's best public layouts; greens fee $32–$43 (with a shared cart). ✉ *Rte. 189* ☎ *850/833–9528.*

**Shalimar Pointe Country Club.** There's a pleasing mix of water and bunkers at this 18-hole course. Greens fees are $28–$45 (with cart); if you book online you can save a little money. ✉ *302 Country Club Dr., Shalimar* ☎ *850/651–1416* ⊕ *www.shalimarpointe.com.*

## NIGHTLIFE

**The Boardwalk.** This massive dining-and-entertainment complex at the entrance to the Okaloosa Island Pier includes several restaurants (Crab Trap Seafood, Oyster House, Floyd's Shrimp House, and Angler's) as well as an assortment of nightclubs. ⊠ *1450 Miracle Strip Pkwy.*

**Howl at the Moon.** Dueling pianos and furious singalongs make this Boardwalk spot extremely popular. The show starts at 8 pm and rocks until 2. ☎ *850/301–0111.*

## WHERE TO EAT

**$$**
AMERICAN

✕ **Angler's.** Unless you sit in the water, you can't dine any closer to the gulf than at this casual beachside bar and grill next to the Gulfarium. Located at the entrance to Okaloosa Island Pier (and within a complex of other nightclubs and restaurants), Angler's houses the requisite sports bar with televisions (including in the elevators and bathrooms) broadcasting sports events. Outside, a volleyball net tempts diners onto the sands. Snack on nachos and quesadillas or sample the fresh-catch dishes such as king crab and prawns or try the Smoked Tuna Dip, a lightly smoked yellowfin tuna dip served with warm crisp tortilla strips. A perfect waterfront setting captures your image of a picturesque Gulf Coast eatery. ⊠ *1030 Miracle Strip Pkwy. SE* ☎ *850/796–0260* ⊕ *www.anglersbeachside.com.*

**$$$**
STEAK
★

✕ **Pandora's Steakhouse and Lounge.** On the Emerald Coast, the name Pandora's is synonymous with prime rib. Steaks are cooked over a wood-burning grill, and you can order your prime rib regular or extra-thick cut; fish aficionados should try the char-grilled yellowfin tuna or one of the daily specials. Cozy up in an alcove to enjoy your meal in peace or head to the lounge, where the mood turns a bit more gregarious with live entertainment Wednesday through Saturday. ⊠ *1226 Santa Rosa Blvd.* ☎ *850/244–8669* ⊕ *www.pandorassteakhouse.com* ⊗ *Closed Mon.*

**$$$**
AMERICAN

✕ **Staff's.** Reputed to be Florida's oldest family-owned restaurant, this garage-turned-eatery, which serves up steaks and seafood dishes like Florida lobster and char-grilled amberjack, has been attracting folks since 1913. Also on the chock-full menu are items including seafood gumbo with okra, grouper, soft-shell crabs, scallops, and oysters. The grand finale is a trip to the delectable dessert bar; try a generous wedge of cherry cheesecake. Sip a Tropical Depression or a rum-laced Squall Line while you peruse a menu tucked into the centerfold of a tabloid-size newspaper filled with snippets of local history and family memorabilia, including bathing-beauty pix of the family's 1920 all-girl swim team. An even grander finale may be stopping in the quite authentic "Margaritaville-style" neighborhood lounge that features a pool table and a true Old Florida vibe. Don't miss it. ⊠ *24 Miracle Strip Pkwy. SE* ☎ *850/243–3482* ⊕ *www.staffrestaurant.com.*

## WHERE TO STAY

*For expanded hotel reviews, visit Fodors.com.*

**$$**
B&B/INN

🛏 **Aunt Martha's Bed and Breakfast.** Although it has been pampering and charming its guests since 2001, Aunt Martha's can transport you back half a century to when Florida was still a sleepy little state. **Pros:**

quiet sanctuary on the waterfront but with access to dining, shopping, and sites. **Cons:** not suited for kids and families; primarily for romance and privacy. ⊠ *315 Shell Ave. SE* ☎ *850/243–6702* ⊕ *www. auntmarthasbedandbreakfast.com* ↰ *5 rooms.*

**$–$$** **Ramada Plaza Beach Resort.** If your family loves the water, splash
RESORT down at this beachside extravaganza, where activity revolves around a 194,000-gallon pool (allegedly the area's largest) with a spectacular swim-through waterfall that tumbles down from an island oasis; there's also a separate kiddie pool, a beachwear and beach-toy shop, as well as an 800-foot private beach. **Pros:** extravagant offerings for a family-friendly vacation—the pool may please the kids more than the gulf. **Cons:** may be too busy for romance travelers or seniors seeking peace and quiet. ⊠ *1500 Miracle Strip Pkwy. SE* ☎ *850/243–9161 or 800/874–8962* ⊕ *www.ramadafwb.com* ↰ *335 rooms, 18 suites* ⌂ *In-hotel: restaurant, bars, pools, gym, beach.*

## DESTIN

*8 mi east of Fort Walton Beach via U.S. 98.*

Fort Walton Beach's "neighbor" lies on the other side of the strait that connects Choctawhatchee Bay with the Gulf of Mexico. Destin takes its name from its founder, Leonard A. Destin, a Connecticut sea captain who settled his family here sometime in the 1830s. For the next 100 years, Destin remained a sleepy little fishing village until the strait, or East Pass, was bridged in 1935. Then recreational anglers discovered its white sands, blue-green waters, and abundance of some of the most sought-after sport fish in the world. More billfish are hauled in around Destin each year than from all other gulf-fishing ports combined, giving credence to its nickname, the World's Luckiest Fishing Village.

But you don't have to be the rod-and-reel type to love Destin. There's plenty to entertain the sand-pail set as well as senior citizens, and there are many nice restaurants, which you'll have an easier time finding if you remember that the main drag through town is referred to as both U.S. 98 and Emerald Coast Parkway. The name makes sense, but part of what makes the gulf look so emerald in these parts is the contrasting whiteness of the sand on the beach. Actually, it's not sand—it's pure, powder-soft Appalachian quartz that was dropped off by a glacier a few thousand years back. Since quartz doesn't compress (and crews clean and rake the beach each evening), your tootsies get the sole-satisfying benefit of soft, sugary "sand." Sand so pure it squeaks.

### ESSENTIALS

**Visitor Information Destin Chamber of Commerce** (☎ *850/837–6241* ⊕ *www. destinchamber.com*).

### EXPLORING

**Big Kahuna's Lost Paradise.** The seasonal water park is the big draw here, with the Honolulu Half-pipe (a perpetual surfing wave), flume rides, steep and slippery slides, and assorted other methods of expending hydro-energy appealing to travelers who prefer freshwater thrills over the gulf (which is just across the street). This complex also has

Billfish, like the large blue marlin, are easy to find off Destin's coast and a favorite catch of sportfishers.

year-round family-friendly attractions: 54-hole miniature golf course, two go-kart tracks, an arcade, thrill rides for kids of all ages, and an amphitheater. ⊠ *1007 U.S. 98 E* ☎ *850/837–8319* ⊕ *www.bigkahunas. com* ⊠ *Grounds free, water park $36.99, miniature golf $6.99, go-karts $6.99, combination ticket (water park, golf, and 2 go-kart tickets) $54.99* ⊗ *Water park: early May–Memorial Day, open 10–5. Check website or call for hrs.*

## SPORTS AND THE OUTDOORS

### FISHING

Destin has the largest charter-boat fishing fleet in the state. You can also pier-fish from the 3,000-foot-long Destin Catwalk and along the East Pass Bridge.

**Adventure Charters.** This company represents more than 90 charter services that offer deep-sea, bay-bottom, and light-tackle fishing excursions. ⊠ *East Pass Marina, 288 U.S. 98 E* ☎ *850/654–4070* ⊕ *www. destinfishingservice.com.*

**Destin Dockside.** It's a great place to pick up bait, tackle, and most anything else you'd need for a day of fishing. ⊠ *East Pass Marina, 288 U.S. 98 E* ☎ *850/837–2622* ⊕ *www.boatrentalsindestin.com.*

**Harbor Walk Marina.** At this rustic-looking waterfront complex you can get bait, gas, tackle, and food. Party-fishing-boat excursions cost as little as $55, a cheaper alternative to chartering or renting your own boat. ⊠ *66 Harbor Blvd., U.S. 98 E* ☎ *850/337–8250* ⊕ *www.harborwalk-destin.com.*

## GOLF

**Indian Bayou Golf Club.** Greens fees are $30–$59 (with cart) at this 27-hole course. ✉ *1 Country Club Dr. E, off Airport Rd., off U.S. 98* ☎ *850/837–6191* ⊕ *www.indianbayougolf.com.*

**Kelly Plantation Golf Club.** Designed by Fred Couples and Gene Bates, this semiprivate 18-hole course runs along Choctawhatchee Bay; greens fee $59/$139 (with cart). ✉ *307 Kelly Plantation Dr.* ☎ *850/650–7600* ⊕ *www.kellyplantationgolf.com.*

**Regatta Bay Golf and Country Club.** Here you'll find an 18-hole, semiprivate course. Greens fees are $59–$129. ✉ *465 Regatta Bay Blvd.* ☎ *850/337–8080* ⊕ *www.regattabay.com.*

**Sandestin Golf and Beach Resort.** For sheer number of holes, Sandestin tops the list, with 72. There are four courses, and peak fees are as follows (although prices can change seasonally): Baytowne Golf Club at Sandestin, greens fee: $54–$89; Burnt Pines Course, greens fee: $109–$155; Links Course, greens fee: $49–$75; and the Raven Golf Club, greens fee: $79–$129. Note that this is also a top tennis resort, whose 15 courts have grass, hard, or Rubico surfaces. ✉ *9300 U.S. 98 W* ☎ *850/267–8211* ⊕ *www.sandestin.com.*

## SCUBA DIVING

Although visibility here isn't on par with the reefs of the Atlantic Coast, local divers can explore artificial reefs, wrecks, and a limestone shelf. The views are about 50 feet and diving depths up to 90 feet.

**Emerald Coast Scuba.** You can take diving lessons, arrange excursions, and rent all the necessary equipment through this operation. ✉ *503 Harbor Blvd.* ☎ *850/837–0955 or 800/222–0955* ⊕ *www.divedestin. com.*

**The Scuba Shop.** The specialty here is wreck diving. ✉ *348 S.W. Miracle Strip Pkwy. No. 19* ☎ *850/243–1600.*

## SHOPPING

**Destin Commons.** Don't call it a mall. Call it an "open-air lifestyle center." More than 70 high-end specialty shops are here, as well as a 14-screen theater, Hard Rock Cafe, a miniature train and a nautical theme park for kids. ✉ *4300 Legendary Dr.* ☎ *850/337–8700* ⊕ *www. destincommons.com.*

**Market at Sandestin.** The two dozen or so upscale shops in this elegant Sandestin complex peddle everything from expensive chocolates to designer clothes. ✉ *9300 Emerald Coast Pkwy. W, Sandestin* ☎ *850/267–8092.*

**Silver Sands Factory Stores.** It's one of the Southeast's largest retail designer outlets. More than 100 shops sell top-name merchandise. ✉ *10562 Emerald Coast Pkwy. W* ☎ *850/654–9771* ⊕ *www.silversandsoutlet. com.*

## NIGHTLIFE

**AJ's Seafood & Oyster Bar.** Folks come by boat and car to this supercasual bar and restaurant overlooking the marina. Nightly live music means young lively crowds pack the dance floor. ✉ *116 U.S. 98 E* ☎ *850/837–1913* ⊕ *www.ajs-destin.com.*

**Harbor Docks.** Affiliated with Pensacola's Dharma Blue, this favorite with the local seafaring set has been around since 1979. The incredibly casual feel is marked by picnic tables and hibachi grills. There's live music Thursday through Saturday. There's also a sushi bar. ⊠ *538 U.S. 98 E* ☎ *850/837–2506* ⊕ *www.harbordocks.com.*

**Hog's Breath Saloon.** The festive atmosphere is enhanced by a solo performer during the week and more musicians showing up on the weekend to present good live music. The food—steaks, burgers, salads—isn't bad, either. ⊠ *541 U.S. 98 E* ☎ *850/837–5991.*

**Nightown.** This nightclub has an expansive dance floor, VIP access with bottle service, seven bars, live music, pool tables, and plenty of drink specials and themed evenings. It's open Wednesday through Saturday until 4 am. ⊠ *140 Palmetto St.* ☎ *850/837–7625* ⊕ *www.nightown. com.*

**Sandestin Village of Baytowne Wharf.** You can find funky blues, great sushi, and a set of dueling pianos here any night of the week. Music guests have included Graffiti & the Funky Blues Shack and John Wehner's Village Door Nightclub. ⊠ *9300 Emerald Coast Pkwy. W* ☎ *800/622–1038.*

### WHERE TO EAT

¢ ╳**Another Broken Egg Café.** With six locations in Northwest Florida,
SEAFOOD you can still find the café by following the line to this local-favorite breakfast-and-lunch retreat, especially in Destin. This is the kind of restaurant you crave when you're on the road, where each morning starts with platters of pancakes, waffles, and French toast with special twists like blackberry grits and more than a dozen styles of omelet, including the "Hey Ricky," a Spanish omelet with avocado slices, green chilies, and onions. It's crowded—and for a reason. ⊠ *979 Hwy. 98 (Harbor Blvd.)* ☎ *850/650–0499* ⊙ *No dinner. Closed Mon.*

$$$ ╳**Marina Café.** A harbor view, impeccable service, and sophisticated
SEAFOOD fare create one of the finest dining experiences on the Emerald Coast.
★ The ocean motif is expressed in shades of aqua, green, and sand accented with marine tapestries and sea sculptures. The chef calls his creations contemporary Continental, offering diners a choice of thick USDA steaks, classic creole, Mediterranean, or Pan Asian dishes. One regional specialty is the popular pan-seared yellow-edge grouper with a blue-crab-meat crust. A special sushi menu is available, the wine list is extensive, and happy hour runs from 5 to 7. ⊠ *404 U.S. 98 E* ☎ *850/837–7960* ⊙ *No lunch.*

### WHERE TO STAY

*For expanded hotel reviews, visit Fodors.com.*

$$$$ ⛱**Emerald Grande Harbor Walk Village.** Even locals seek out the views
RESORT at this harborfront oasis that is a destination within a destination with luxurious hotel accommodations and a full menu of amenities, including a full-service spa, marina, health club, indoor/outdoor pools, and more. **Pros:** great for larger families and groups; many top-rated amenities are part of the complex. **Cons:** very family-oriented, so it's not ideal for a romantic couples getaway; must water-taxi to the beach. ⊠ *10 Harbor Blvd.* ☎ *800/676–0091* ⊕ *www.emeraldgrande.com* ⤴ *269*

*Continued on page 66*

# GONE FISHIN'

by Gary McKechnie

My favorite uncle has a passion for fishing.

It was one I didn't really understand—I'm more of a motorcycle guy, not a fishing pole–toting one. But one day he piqued my curiosity by telling me that fishing has many of the same enticements as motorcycling. Come again? He beautifully described the peaceful process of it all—how the serenity and solitude of the sport wash away concerns about work and tune him into the wonder of nature, just like being on a bike (minus the helmet and curvy highways).

I took the bait, and early one morning a few weeks later, my Uncle Bud and I headed out in a boat to a secluded cove on the St. Johns River near DeLand. We'd brought our rods, line, bait, and tackle—plus hot chocolate and a few things to eat. We didn't need much else. We dropped in our lines and sat silently, watching the fog hover over the water.

There was a peaceful stillness as we waited (and waited) for the fish to bite. There were turtles sunning themselves on logs and herons perched in the trees. We waited for hours for just a little nibble. I can't even recall now if we caught anything, but it didn't matter. My uncle was right: it was a relaxing way to spend a Florida morning.

# REEL TIME

Florida is recognized as the "Fishing Capital of the World" as well as the "Bass Capital of the World." It's also home to some of the nation's most popular crappie tournaments.

Florida and fishing have a bond that goes back to thousands of years before Christ, when Paleo-Indians living along Florida's rivers and coasts were harvesting the waters just as readily as they were harvesting the land. Jump ahead to the 20th century and along came amateur anglers like Babe Ruth, Clark Gable, and Gary Cooper vacationing at central Florida fishing camps in pursuit of bream, bluegill, and largemouth bass, while Ernest Hemingway was scouring the waters off Key West in hopes of snagging marlin, tarpon, and snapper. Florida was, and is, an angler's paradise.

When he wasn't writing, Ernest Hemingway loved to fish in the Florida Keys. He's shown here in Key West in 1928.

A variety of fish and plentiful waterways—7,800 lakes and 1,700 rivers and creeks, not to mention the gulf and the ocean—are just two reasons why Florida is the nation's favorite fishing spot. And let's not forget the frost-free attributes: unlike their northern counterparts, Florida anglers have yet to drill through several feet of ice just to go fishing in the wintertime. Plus, a well-established infrastructure for fishing—numerous bait and tackle shops, boat rentals, sporting goods stores, public piers, and charters—makes it easy for experts and first-time fishermen to get started. For Floridians and the visitors hooked on the sport here, fishing in the Sunshine State is a sport of sheer ease and simplicity.

An afternoon on the waters of Charlotte County in southwest Florida.

## CASTING WIDE

The same way Florida is home to rocket scientists and beach bums, it's home to a diverse variety of fishing methods. What kind will work for you depends on where you want to go and what you want to catch.

From the Panhandle south to the Everglades, fishing is as easy as finding a quiet spot on the bank or heading out on freshwater lakes, tranquil ponds, spring-fed rivers, and placid inlets and lagoons.

Perhaps the biggest catches are found offshore—in the Atlantic Ocean, Florida Straits, or the Gulf of Mexico. For saltwater fishing, you can join a charter, be it a private one for small groups or a large party one; head out along the long jetties or public piers that jut into the ocean; or toss your line from the shore into the surf (known as surf casting). Some attempt a tricky yet effective form of fishing called net casting: tossing a circular net weighted around its perimeter; the flattened net hits the surface and drives fish into the center of the circle.

Surf casting on Juno Beach, about 20 mi north of Palm Beach.

## FRESHWATER FISHING VS. SALTWATER FISHING

### FRESH WATER

With nearly 8,000 lakes to choose from, it's hard to pick the leading contenders, but a handful rise to the top: Lake George, Lake Tarpon, Lake Weohyakapka, Lake Istokpoga, Lake Okeechobee, Crescent Lake, Lake Kissimmee, Lake George, and Lake Talquin. Florida's most popular freshwater game fish is the largemouth bass. Freshwater fishermen are also checking rivers and streams for other popular catches, such as spotted bass, white bass, Suwannee bass, striped bass, black crappie, bluegill, redear sunfish, and channel catfish.

### SALT WATER

The seas are filled with some of the most challenging (and tasty) gamefish in America. From piers, jetties, private boats, and charter excursions, fishermen search for bonefish, tarpon, snook, redfish, grouper, permit, spotted sea trout, sailfish, cobia, bluefish, snapper, sea bass, dolphinfish (the short, squat fish, not Flipper), and sheepshead.

Tarpon

**DID YOU KNOW?**

The Florida Keys is the Sportfishing Capital of the World. Among the bounty brought in are all kinds of tuna—blackfin, skipjack, blue, or yellowfin.

| | | |
|---|---|---|
| Florida Largemouth Bass | Striped Bass | Black Crappie |
| Channel Catfish | Bluegill | Redear Sunfish |
| Bonefish | Dolphinfish (Mahi-Mahi) | Red Snapper |
| Sheepshead | Snook | Sailfish |

(top six) freshwater, (bottom six) saltwater

## HERE'S THE CATCH

The type of fish you're after will depend on whether you fish in Florida's lake, streams, and rivers, or head out to sea. The Panhandle has an abundance of red snapper, while Lake Okeechobee is the place for bass fishing—although the largemouth bass is found throughout the state (they're easiest to catch in early spring, when they're in shallower waters). If you're looking for a good charter, Destin has a very large charter-boat fishing fleet. In the Florida Keys, you can fish by walking out in the very shallow water for hundreds of yards with the water only up to your knees; the fish you might reel in this way include bonefish, tarpon, and permit.

## CHARTING THE WATERS

| TYPE OF TRIP | COST | PROS | CONS |
| --- | --- | --- | --- |
| LARGE PARTY BOAT | Approx. $40/person for 4 hrs. | The captain's fishing license covers all passengers; you keep whatever you catch. | Not much privacy, assistance, or solitude: boats can hold as many as 35 passengers. |
| PRIVATE CHARTER | Roughly $1,200 for up to six people for 9 hrs. | More personal attention and more time on the water. | Higher cost ($200 per person instead of $40); tradition says you split the catch with the captain. |
| GUIDED TRIP FOR INLAND WATERS | Around $300–$400 for one or two people for 6 hrs. | Helpful if your time is limited and you want to make sure you go where the fish are biting. | Can be expensive and may not be as exciting as deep-sea fishing. |
| GOING SOLO | Cost for gear (rod, line, bait, and tackle) and license ($30–$100 depending on where you fish and if you need gear). | Privacy, flexibility, your time and destination are up to you; you can get fishing tips from your fellow anglers. | If you require a boat, you need to pay for and operate it yourself, plus pay for gear and a fishing license and find a fishing spot! |

With a little hunting (by calling marinas, visiting bait and tackle stores, asking at town visitor centers), you can find a fishing guide who will lead you to some of the best spots on Florida's lakes and rivers. The guide provides the boat and gear, and his or her license should cover all passengers. A guide is not generally necessary for freshwater fishing, but if you're new to the sport, it might be a worthwhile investment.

On the other hand, if you're looking for fishing guides who can get you into the deep water for tarpon, redfish, snook, snapper, and dolphinfish, your best bet is to hang out at the marinas along the Florida coast and decide whether price or privacy is more important. If it's price, choose one of the larger party boats. If you'd prefer some privacy and the privilege of creating an exclusive passenger list, then sign up for a private charter. The average charter runs about nine hours, but some companies offer overnight and extended trips, too. Gear is provided in both charter-boat methods, and charters also offer the service of cleaning your catch. All guided trips encourage tipping the crew.

Most people new to the sport choose to do saltwater fishing via a charter party boat. The main reasons are expert guidance, convenience, and cost. Plus, fishing with others can be fun. Charter trips depart from marinas throughout Florida.

### CREATING A FLOAT PLAN

If you're fishing in a boat on your own, let someone know where you're headed by providing a float plan, which should include where you're leaving from, a description of the boat you're on, how many are in the boat with you, what survival gear and radio equipment you have onboard, your cell phone number, and when you expect to return. If you don't return as expected, your friend can call the Coast Guard to search for you. Also be sure to have enough life jackets for everyone on board.

## RULES AND REGULATIONS

To fish anywhere in (or off the coast of) Florida, you need a license, and there are separate licenses for freshwater fishing and saltwater fishing.

For non-residents, either type of fishing license cost $47 for the annual license, $30 for the 7-day one, or $17 for a 3-day license. Permits/tags are needed for catching snook ($2), crawfish/lobster ($2), and tarpon ($51.50). License and permit costs help generate funds for the Florida Fish and Wildlife Conservation Commission, which reinvests the fees into ensuring healthy habitats to sustain fish and wildlife populations, to improve access to fishing spots, and to help ensure public safety.

You can purchase your license and permits at county tax collectors' offices as well as wherever you buy your bait and tackle, such as Florida marinas, specialty stores, and sporting goods shops. You can also buy it online at ⊕ www.myfwc. com/license and have it mailed to you; a surcharge is added to online orders.

If you're on a charter, you don't need to get a license. The captain's fishing license covers all passengers. Also, some piers have their own saltwater fishing licenses that cover you when you're fishing off them for recreational purposes—if you're pier fishing, ask the personnel at the tackle shop if the pier is covered.

### RESOURCES

For the latest regulations on gear, daily limits, minimum sizes and seasons for certain fish, and other fishing requirements, consult the extraordinary **Florida Fish and Wildlife Conservation Commission** (☎ 888/347–4356 ⊕ www.myfwc.com).

**WEB RESOURCES**
Download the excellent, and free, Florida Fishing PDF at www.visitflorida.com/guides. Other good sites:
www.floridafishinglakes.net
www.visitflorida.com/fishing
www.floridasportsman.com

rooms ⟡ *In-room: kitchen, Wi-Fi. In-hotel: restaurant, bar, pool, gym, spa, parking.*

**$–$$$**
**RESORT**
**Fodor's Choice**
**★**

▦ **Sandestin Golf and Beach Resort.** It's almost a city in itself and certainly its own little world with shopping, charter fishing, spas, salons, tennis, water sports, golf, and special events—so it's no wonder newlyweds, conventioneers, and families all find their fit in this 2,400-acre resort with accommodations spread across five areas: beachfront, beachside, village, bay side, and dockside. **Pros:** has everything you'd ever need in a resort—and more. **Cons:** lacks the personal touches of a modest retreat. ✉ *9300 Emerald Coast Pkwy. W* ☎ *850/267–8000 or 800/277–0800* ⊕ *www.sandestin.com* ⤳ *1,400 condos, villas, town homes and variety of guest rooms* ⟡ *In-room: kitchen (some), Wi-Fi. In-hotel: restaurants, bars, golf courses, tennis courts, pools, gym, spa, beach.*

# BEACHES OF SOUTH WALTON

The 26-mi stretch of coastline between Destin and Panama City Beach is referred to as the Beaches of South Walton. From the middle of this mostly residential stretch of the Panhandle you can see the monolithic condos of Destin and Panama City Beach in either direction, like massive bookends in the distance, flanking the area's low-slung, less imposing structures. A decidedly laid-back, refined mood prevails in these parts, where vacation homes go for millions and selecting a dinner spot is usually the day's most challenging decision.

Accommodations consist primarily of private-home rentals, the majority of which are managed by local real estate firms. Also scattered along Route 30A are a growing number of boutiques selling everything from fine art and unique hand-painted furniture to jewelry, gifts, and clothes.

### ESSENTIALS

**Visitor Information Beaches of South Walton Visitor Information Center** (☎ *850/267–1216 or 800/822–6877* ⊕ *www.beachesofsouthwalton.com*).

## GRAYTON BEACH

*18 mi east of Destin via U.S. 98 on Rte. 30A (Exit 85).*

Inland, pine forests and hardwoods surround the area's 14 dune lakes, giving anglers ample spots to drop a line and kayakers a peaceful refuge. Grayton Beach, the oldest community in this area, was founded in 1890. You can still see some of the old weathered-cypress homes scattered along narrow, crushed-gravel streets. The secluded off-the-beaten-path town has been noticed with the addition of adjacent WaterColor, a high-end development of vacation homes with a stylish boutique hotel as its centerpiece. The architecture is tasteful, development is carefully regulated—no buildings taller than four stories are allowed—and bicycles and kayaks are the preferred methods of transportation. Stringent building restrictions, designed to protect the pristine beaches and dunes, ensure that Grayton maintains its small-town feel and look.

### EXPLORING

**Eden Gardens State Park.** Scarlett O'Hara could be at home here on the lawn of an antebellum mansion amid an arcade of moss-draped live oaks in nearby Point Washington. Tours of the mansion are given every hour on the hour, and furnishings inside the spacious rooms date as far back as the 17th century. The surrounding grounds—the perfect setting for a picnic lunch—are beautiful year-round, but they're nothing short of spectacular in mid-March, when the azaleas and

dogwoods are in full bloom. ⊠ *Rte. 395, Point Washington* ☎ *850/267–8320* 🖘 *Gardens $4, mansion tours $4* ⊙ *Daily 8–sunset, mansion tours hourly Thurs.–Mon. 10–3.*

Fodor's Choice ★ **Grayton Beach State Park.** This is the place to see what Florida looked like when only American Indians lived here. One of the most scenic spots along the Gulf Coast, this 2,220-acre park is composed primarily of untouched Florida woodlands within the Coastal Lowlands region. It also has salt marshes, rolling dunes covered with sea oats, crystal-white sand, and contrasting blue-green waters. The park has facilities for swimming, fishing, snorkeling, and camping, and there's an elevated boardwalk that winds over the dunes to the beach, as well as walking trails around the marsh and into the piney woods. Notice that the "bushes" you see are actually the tops of full-size slash pines and Southern magnolias, an effect created by the frequent shifting of the dunes. Even if you are just passing by, the beach here is worth the stop. Thirty fully equipped cabins are available for rent, and a campground loop with 24 new sites (with sewer, electric, and water) gives even more visitors a chance to see Old Florida. ⊠ *357 Main Park Rd., off Rte. 30A* ☎ *850/267–8300* ⊕ *www.floridastateparks.org/graytonbeach* 🖘 *$5 per vehicle, up to 8 people* ⊙ *Daily 8–sunset.*

### SHOPPING

**Magnolia House.** At this shop under the shade trees of Grayton Beach, you can browse for gifts, bath products, and home accessories, while the owner entertains you on her grand piano. ⊠ *2 Magnolia St.* ☎ *850/231–5859* ⊕ *www.magnoliahouse.com.*

**Shops of Grayton.** In the eight cottages of this colorful complex you can buy gifts, artwork, and antiques. ⊠ *Rte. 283 Grayton Rd., 2 mi south of U.S. 98* ☎ *No phone.*

### NIGHTLIFE

**Red Bar.** The local watering hole presents red-hot blues or jazz acts every night. On Friday and Saturday nights it's elbow-to-elbow at the truly funky and colorful bar that would be right at home on Miami's South Beach or in New York City's Greenwich Village. ⊠ *70 Hotz Ave.* ☎ *850/231–1008.*

### WHERE TO EAT

$$$$ 
ECLECTIC 
Fodor's Choice ★ ✕ **Fish Out of Water.** Time your appetite to arrive at sunset and you'll witness the best of both worlds: sea oats lumbering on gold-dusted dunes outside and a stylish interior that sets new standards of sophistication for the entire Panhandle. Colorful, handblown-glass accent lighting that "grows" out of the hardwood floors, plush taupe banquettes, oversize handmade lamp shades, and a sleek bar area create an atmosphere

If you saw *The Truman Show*, you may recognize several places in Seaside, where the movie was filmed.

worthy of the inventive cuisine. Menus are seasonal, but often range in influences from Southern (Low Country shrimp and scallops with creamy grits) to classic Continental, but all are convincingly wrought and carefully presented. The extensive wine list keeps pace with the menu offerings. ⊠ *34 Goldenrod Circle, 2nd fl. of WaterColor Inn 5979* ☎ *850/534–5050* ⊕ *www.watercolorresort.com* ⊗ *No lunch.*

**$$**
**SEAFOOD**
★
✕ **Picolo Restaurant and Red Bar**. You could spend weeks here just taking in all the funky-junky, eclectic toy-chest memorabilia—from Marilyn Monroe posters to flags to dolls—dangling from the ceiling and tacked to every available square inch of wall. The contemporary menu is small, although it includes what you'd expect to find in the Panhandle: crab cakes, shrimp, and crawfish, to name a few. It also serves breakfast. In season, it can feed hundreds of people a day, so expect a wait. Blues and jazz musicians play nightly in the Red Bar. You can't make up a place like this. ⊠ *70 Hotz Ave.* ☎ *850/231–1008* ⊕ *www.theredbar. com* ⊟ *No credit cards.*

**WHERE TO STAY**

**$$**
★
⌂ **Cabins at Grayton Beach State Park**. Back-to-nature enthusiasts and families love to visit these stylish accommodations set among the sand pines and scrub oaks of this pristine state park. **Pros:** rare and welcome preservation of Old Florida; pure peace and quiet; what a gulf vacation is meant to be. **Cons:** if you're accustomed to abundant amenities, you won't find them here. ⊠ *357 Main Park Rd.* ☎ *800/326–3521 for reservations* ⊕ *www.reserveamerica.com* ⤳ *30 cabins* ⌂ *In-room: kitchen, no TV.*

**$$$$**
Fodor'sChoice
★
⌂ **WaterColor Inn and Resort**. Nature meets seaside chic at this boutique property, the crown jewel of the area's latest—and largest—planned communities. **Pros:** perhaps the ultimate vacation experience on the

gulf; upscale and fancy. **Cons:** you may feel like it caters exclusively to Ivy Leaguers and CEOs, which might make it hard to relax. ✉ *34 Goldenrod Circle* ☎ *850/534–5000* ⊕ *www.watercolorresort.com* ↷ *60 rooms* ♿ *In-room: safe, Wi-Fi. In-hotel: restaurant, pool, beach, business center* ❦ *BP.*

## SEASIDE AND ROSEMARY BEACH
*2 mi east of Grayton Beach on Rte. 30A.*

**Seaside.** Seaside is a thriving planned community with old-fashioned Victorian architecture, brick streets, restaurants, retail stores—and a surfeit of art galleries. The brainchild of Robert Davis, Seaside was designed to promote a neighborly, old-fashioned lifestyle, and there's much to be said for an attractive, billboard-free village where you can park your car and walk everywhere you need to go. Pastel-color homes with white-picket fences, front-porch rockers, and captain's walks are set along redbrick streets, and all are within walking distance of the town center and its unusual cafés and shops. The community is so reminiscent of a storybook town that producers chose it for the set of the 1998 film *The Truman Show,* starring Jim Carrey.

The community has come into its own in the last few years, achieving a comfortable, lived-in look and feel that had escaped it since its founding in the late 1970s: some of the once-shiny tin roofs are starting to rust around the edges, and the foliage has matured, creating pockets of privacy and shade. There are also more signs of a real neighborhood with bars, record shops, and bookstores added to the mix. Still, while Seaside's popularity continues to soar, it retains a suspicious sense of *Twilight Zone* perfection that can weird out some visitors.

**Rosemary Beach.** About a dozen miles east down Route 30A is Rosemary Beach, a fledgling development that is a variation on the theme pioneered by Seaside's founders. Incidentally, between Seaside and Rosemary Beach a few other "New Urbanism"–style planned neighborhoods are trying to carve out a niche as they deal with the new reality of an enduring recession. Of these artificially realistic towns, though, Rosemary Beach seems to have a head start with a few restaurants and shops. Despite the attempts at jump-starting growth, the focus here is still on preserving the local environment (the landscape is made up completely of indigenous plants) and maintaining its small-town appeal. You can already see a nascent sense of community sprouting at the Town Green, a perfect patch of manicured lawn fronting the beach, where locals gather with their wineglasses to toast the sunset.

## SPORTS AND THE OUTDOORS
**Butterfly Bike & Kayak.** A few miles from Seaside in Seagrove Beach, this outfitter rents bikes, kayaks, scooters, and golf carts and has free delivery and pickup. ✉ *3657 E. Rte. 30A* ☎ *850/231–2826* ⊕ *www. butterflybikerentals.com.*

**Yolo Board.** The biggest craze in the region is Yolo Boarding, or stand-up paddling, on what looks like a surfboard. It can be found at many resorts in the region and privately through Yolo Board. ✉ *820 N. County Hwy. 393* ☎ *850/622–5760* ⊕ *www.yoloboard.com.*

## SHOPPING

Seaside's central square and open-air market, along Route 30A, offer a number of unusual and whimsical boutiques carrying clothing, jewelry, and arts and crafts. In the heart of Seaside, there's a collection of small shops and artists' galleries in an area called Ruskin Place that has everything from toys and pottery to fine works of art.

**Perspicacity.** This shop sells simply designed women's clothing and accessories perfect for easy, carefree, beach-town casualness. ⊠ *178 Market St.* ☎ *850/231–5829.*

## NIGHTLIFE

**Courtyard Wine & Cheese.** Rosemary Beach's sophisticated wine bar (with free Wi-Fi) opens onto a Tuscan-style courtyard and stocks 150 wines, fine cheeses, and artwork, too. It's closed Monday. ⊠ *66 Main St., Rosemary Beach* ☎ *850/231–1219* ⊕ *www.courtyardwineandcheese.com.*

## WHERE TO EAT

**$$$$** ✕ **Bud & Alley's.** This down-to-earth beachside bistro (named for a pet
CONTINENTAL cat and dog) has been a local favorite since 1986. Tucked in the dunes by the gulf, the rooftop Tarpon Club bar makes a great perch for a sunset toast (guess the exact moment the sun will disappear and win a drink). Daily salad specials are tangy introductions to such entrées as grilled black grouper, seared diver scallops with creamy grits, a marinated pork chop with sweet-potato hash browns, and a taco bar. ⊠ *2236 E. Rte. 30A, Seaside* ☎ *850/231–5900* ⊕ *www.budandalleys. com* ☉ *No lunch.*

**$$$$** ✕ **Café Thirty-A.** About a mile and half east of Seaside in a beautiful
CONTINENTAL Florida-style home with high ceilings and a wide veranda, this res-
★ taurant has an elegant look—bolstered by white linen tablecloths— and impeccable service. The menu changes nightly and includes such entrées as wood-oven-roasted wild king salmon, sesame-crusted rare yellowfin tuna, and grilled Hawaiian butterfish. Even if you're not a Southerner, you should try the appetizer of grilled Georgia quail with creamy grits and sage fritters. With nearly 20 creative varieties, the martini menu alone is worth the trip. ⊠ *3899 E. Rte. 30A, Seagrove Beach* ☎ *850/231–2166* ⊕ *www.cafethirtya.com* ☉ *No lunch.*

**$$$** ✕ **The Great Southern Cafe.** Jim Shirley, founder of Pensacola's very
SEAFOOD popular Fish House, brought Grits a Ya Ya here as well, putting this restaurant right on the town square in Seaside. Breakfast is served from 8 to 11, before the menu segues to regional fare, including gulf shrimp, Apalachicola oysters, and fresh sides such as collards, okra, black-eyed peas, fried green tomatoes, and sweet potatoes. Oysters and po'boys stuffed with shrimp bring a little of N'awlins to the beach. Beer and wine and a full liquor bar are here to boot. ⊠ *83 Central Sq.* ☎ *850/231–7327* ⊕ *www.thegreatsoutherncafe.com.*

## WHERE TO STAY

*For expanded hotel reviews, visit Fodors.com.*

**$$$$** ⌂ **Seaside Cottage Rental Agency.** When residents aren't using their
RENTAL homes, they rent out their pricey one- to six-bedroom, porticoed,
★ faux-Victorian cottages. **Pros:** gulf breezes blowing off the water; unspoiled sugar-white beaches are a short stroll away. **Cons:** not much

here for those who just want the basic comforts of a full-service hotel. ✉ *Rte. 30A, Box 4730* ☎ *850/231–2222 or 866/966–2565* ⊕ *www. cottagerentalagency.com* ⤳ *275 units* ☺ *In-room: a/c, kitchen, Wi-Fi (some). In-hotel: tennis courts, pools.*

## PANAMA CITY BEACH

*21 mi southeast of Seaside off U.S. 98.*

In the early 2000s, a dizzying number of high-rises built along the Miracle Strip—about two dozen in total—led to the formation of a new moniker for this stretch of the Panhandle: the "Construction Coast." But most of the new buildings have been condominiums, not hotels, many (but certainly not all) of the older mom-and-pop motels that once gave this town its beach-resort flavor have fallen victim to the wrecking ball, and the recession has eased the threat of overdevelopment.

Still, the spate of invasive growth did turn the main thoroughfare, Front Beach Road, into a dense mass of traffic that peaks in spring and between June and August when college students descend en masse from neighboring states. The bright side of the changing landscape is that many of the attractions that gave parts of this area a seedy reputation (i.e., strip joints and dive bars) were driven out and replaced by new retailers and the occasional franchise "family" restaurant or chain store.

The one constant in this sea of change, however, is the area's natural beauty that, in some areas at least, manages to excuse its gross over-commercialization. The shoreline in town is 17 mi long, so even when a mile is packed with partying students, there are 16 more where you can toss a beach blanket and find the old motels that managed to survive. What's more, the beaches along the Miracle Strip, with their powder-soft sand and translucent emerald waters, are some of the finest in the state; in one sense, anyway, it's easy to understand why so many condos are being built here.

Cabanas, umbrellas, sailboats, WaveRunners, and floats are available from any of dozens of vendors along the beach. For an aerial view, for about $30 you can strap yourself beneath a parachute and go parasailing as you're towed aloft behind a speedboat a few hundred yards offshore. And St. Andrews State Park, on the southeast end of the beaches, is treasured by locals and visitors alike. The area's incredible white sands, navigable waterways, and plentiful marine life that attracted Spanish conquistadors today draw invaders of the vacationing kind—namely families, the vast majority of whom hail from nearby Georgia and Alabama. ■TIP➔ When coming here, be sure to set your sights for Panama City Beach. Panama City is its beachless inland cousin.

### GETTING HERE AND AROUND

The Northwest Beaches International Airport opened in May 2010 on the east shore of Panama City's West Bay, with routes operated by Delta and Southwest. From the airport to the beach area, depending on the location of your hotel, it's about $15–$27 by taxi. Try Yellow Cab or Checker Cab.

When navigating Panama City Beach by car, don't limit yourself to Front Beach Road—the stop-and-go traffic will drive you nuts. You can avoid the congestion by following parallel roads like Back Beach Road and U.S. 98. Also, anywhere along this long stretch of beachfront, look for "sunrise" signs that indicate an access point to the beach—they're a treasure to find, especially when you happen across one in the midst of a quiet residential neighborhood and know that a private, quiet beach experience is just a few feet away. The Baytown Trolley serves Bay County, including downtown Panama City and the beaches ($1.50, $3 for an all-day pass).

### ESSENTIALS

**Transportation Contacts Baytown Trolley** (☎ 850/769–0557 ⊕ www. baytowntrolley.org). **Checker Cab** (☎ 850/784–1115). **Northwest Florida Beaches International Airport** (☎ 850/763–6751 ⊕ www.iflybeaches.com). **Yellow Cab** (☎ 850/763–4691).

**Visitor Information Panama City Beach Convention and Visitors Bureau** (☎ 850/233–5070 or 800/722–3224 ⊕ www.visitpanamacitybeach.com).

### EXPLORING

**Gulf World Marine Park.** It's certainly no SeaWorld, but with a tropical garden, tropical-bird theater, plus alligator and otter exhibits, the park is still a winner with the kids. The stingray petting pool and the shark-feeding and scuba demonstrations are big crowd pleasers, and the old favorites—performing sea lions, otters, and bottle-nosed dolphins—still hold their own.

If you're really nautically minded, consider some of the specialty programs, including the Trainer for a Day program, which allows you to go behind the scenes to assist in food preparation and training sessions and make an on-stage appearance in the Dolphin Show. The $199, six-hour program includes a souvenir photo, lunch, and a trainer T-shirt. In the Swim with a Dolphin program, you'll spend some time being pulled around the dolphin habitat, receive a dolphin kiss, and get a dolphin "handshake." Priced at $150, the session lasts between 60 and 90 minutes. Park admission is included with both programs. ⊠ *15412 Front Beach Rd.* ☎ *850/234–5271* ⊕ *www.gulfworldmarinepark.com* ⊠ *$27* ⊗ *Late May–early Sept., daily 9–7; call for hrs at other times of year.*

**Shipwreck Island Waterpark.** Once part of the now-defunct Miracle Strip Amusement Park operation, this 6-acre water park has everything from speedy slides and tubes to the slow-moving Lazy River. Oddly enough, admission is based on height: 50 inches, $33; between 35 and 50 inches, $28; under 35 inches, free. Wear flats. ⊠ *12201 Middle Beach Dr.* ☎ *850/234–0368* ⊕ *www.shipwreckisland.com* ⊠ *$33* ⊗ *Mid-Apr.– May, weekends and some weekdays 10:30–4:30; June and July, daily 10:30–5; Aug. and Sept. 10:30–4:30.*

**St. Andrews State Park.** At the southeastern tip of Panama City Beach, all at once the hotels and condos and traffic stops and there suddenly appears a pristine 1,260-acre park that includes beaches, pinewoods, and marshes. Complete camping facilities are here and a snack bar, too, as well as places to swim, pier-fish, and hike on clearly marked

Fodor's Choice
★

Get up close and personal with intriguing seashells on undeveloped Shell Island.

nature trails. Board a ferry to Shell Island—a 700-acre barrier island in the Gulf of Mexico with some of the best shelling between here and southwest Florida's Sanibel Island. A rock jetty creates a calm, shallow play area that is perfect for young children. Come to this spectacular park for a peek at what the entire beach area looked like before developers sank their claws into it. ✉ *4607 State Park La.* ☎ *850/233–5140* ⊕ *www.floridastateparks.org* ✉ *$8 per vehicle, up to 8 people* ⊙ *Daily 8 until sundown.*

## SPORTS AND THE OUTDOORS

### CANOEING

**Econofina Creek Canoe Livery.** Rentals for a trip down Econofina Creek—known as Florida's most beautiful canoe trail—are supplied by this outfitter. Single kayaks are $35, double kayaks and canoes rent for $45. No checks or credit cards. ✉ *Strickland Rd., north of Rte. 20, Youngstown* ☎ *850/722–9032* ⊕ *www.canoeeconfinacreek.net.*

### DIVING

Snorkeling and scuba diving are extremely popular in the clear waters here. If you have the proper certification, you can dive among dozens of ships sunk by the city to create artificial reefs.

**Panama City Dive Center.** Here you can arrange for instruction, gear rental, and charters. ✉ *4823 Thomas Dr., Panama City Beach* ☎ *850/235–3390* ⊕ *www.pcdivecenter.com.*

### GOLF

**Bay Point Golf Resort & Spa.** There are two courses open to the public at this country club: the **Nicklaus Course** and the **Meadows Course.** Greens fees are $29–$59. This resort also has five lighted clay tennis courts.

✉ *4200 Marriott Dr.* ☎ *850/235–6950 or 877/235–6950* ⊕ *www. baypointgolf.com.*

**Hombre Golf Club.** This 27-hole course occasionally hosts professional tours. Greens fees are $25–$39 (with cart). ✉ *120 Coyote Pass* ☎ *850/ 234–3673* ⊕ *www.hombregolfclub.com.*

### SHOPPING

**Pier Park.** Occupying a huge swath of land that was one an amusement park is this diverse 900,000-square-foot entertainment/shopping/dining complex that creates the downtown that Panama City Beach lacked. Anchor stores including Dillard's, JCPenney, and Target keep things active during the day, and clubs like Jimmy Buffett's Margaritaville and the 16-screen Grand Theatre keep things hopping after dark. Other stores like Ron Jon Surf Shop and a Fresh Market offer even more reason to see this vibrant and enjoyable complex. ✉ *16230 Front Beach Rd.* ☎ *850/236–9974* ⊕ *www.discoverpierpark.com.*

### NIGHTLIFE

**Boatyard.** This multilevel, indoor-outdoor waterfront nightclub and restaurant presents a regular lineup of bands, ranging from blues to steel drums to classic rock and beyond (DJs round out the entertainment roster). ✉ *5325 North Lagoon Dr.* ☎ *850/249–9273* ⊕ *www. boatyardclub.com.*

**Club La Vela.** Among the offerings that guarantee a full-tilt party here are a slate of concerts (acts have included Aerosmith, Creed, and Ludacris); international DJs; 48 bar stations; swimming pools; a tropical waterfall; and dance halls with names like Thunderdome, Underground, Night Gallery, Rock Arena, and the Pussykat Lounge. At spring-break time this club is transformed into a whirlpool of libido. ✉ *8813 Thomas Dr.* ☎ *850/234–1061 or 850/234–3866* ⊕ *www.clublavela.com.*

**Pineapple Willy's.** This eatery and bar is geared to families and tourists— as well as sports fans. The signature rum drink, the Pineapple Willy, was the inspiration for its full slate of tropical drinks and the hangout's tiki attitude. ✉ *9875 S. Thomas Dr.* ☎ *850/235–0928* ⊕ *www.pwillys.com.*

### WHERE TO EAT

$$$
AMERICAN

✗**Boars Head.** An exterior that looks like an oversize thatch-roof cottage sets the mood for dining in this ersatz-rustic restaurant and tavern. Inside you'll find the dark woods and dim lighting of steak restaurants of the 1970s, which is understandable considering that Boar's Head opened in 1978. From opening day, prime rib has been the number-one people pleaser—with blackened seafood and broiled shrimp with crabmeat stuffing always a close second. Its motto: "Good food, simply prepared." ✉ *17290 Front Beach Rd.* ☎ *850/234–6628* ⊕ *www. boarsheadrestaurant.com* ⊙ *No lunch.*

$$$
SEAFOOD

✗**Boatyard.** The same folks who operate Schooners on the beach side opened this larger, more stylish establishment overlooking a marina on the Grand Lagoon. For dinner, choose from the five-spice seared tuna, spicy bowtie pasta with shrimp, or the aptly named Fried Shrimp You Can't Live Without. The coconut-and-plantain-crusted grouper is a knockout, as is the pan-roasted catch with bacon, mushrooms, and grits (this is definitely the South). There are a kids' menu, an extensive wine list, a full bar, and flat-screen televisions, and the upstairs deck area is a great place to get away from the beach for a long, lazy lunch or romantic sunset dinner. Be aware that Boatyard kicks into high gear at sundown, transforming into one of the hottest nightspots in town. ✉ *5325 N. Lagoon Dr.* ☎ *850/249–9273* ⊕ *www.boatyardclub.com.*

**$$$**
**SEAFOOD**
✕ **Capt. Anderson's.** Come early to watch the boats unload the catch of the day on the docks, and to beat the long line that forms each afternoon in this noted restaurant that projects a real family feel. Here since 1953, it doesn't seem to have changed much and that's a good thing. A nautical theme is reinforced by tables made of hatch covers in the attached bar, which attracts longtime locals. The Greek specialties aren't limited to feta cheese and shriveled olives; charcoal-broiled grouper, amberjack, and yellowfin tuna, crab-stuffed jumbo shrimp, stuffed fillet of grouper, whole oven-broiled stuffed Florida lobster, and steaks have a prominent place on the menu as well. If you're visiting in the off-season, call to make sure it's adhering to the posted hours before venturing out. ✉ *5551 N. Lagoon Dr.* ☎ *850/234–2225* ⊕ *www.captainandersons.com* ⟡ *Reservations not accepted* ⊙ *Closed Sun. and Nov.–Jan. No lunch.*

**$$**
**SEAFOOD**
✕ **Schooners.** Thanks to a clientele that's mostly local, this beachfront spot—which is really tucked away down a small avenue—bills itself as the "last local beach club," and more boldly, "the best place on Earth." It's actually a perfect spot for a casual family lunch or early dinner: kids can have burgers and play on the beach while Mom and Dad enjoy grown-up drinks and more substantial fare such as homemade gumbo, steak, or simply prepared seafood like crab-stuffed shrimp, gulf-fresh grouper, and grilled tuna steaks. One sign of Schooner's casual atmosphere is the ceremonial firing of the cannon when the sun disappears into the gulf, a crowd favorite that fires up an all-around good vibe. Late-night folks pile in for live music and dancing. ✉ *5121 Gulf Dr.* ☎ *850/235–3555* ⊕ *www.schooners.com.*

## WHERE TO STAY

*For expanded hotel reviews, visit Fodors.com.*

**$$–$$$**
**RESORT**
**Fodor's Choice**
★
🛏 **Bay Point Golf Resort & Spa.** Across the Grand Lagoon from St. Andrews State Park, this expansive property exudes sheer elegance. **Pros:** quiet and away from the madness of Panama City Beach; complete range of services and activities. **Cons:** may be too expansive and generic for those seeking a small, intimate resort. ✉ *4200 Marriott Dr.* ☎ *850/236–6000 or 800/874–4025* ⊕ *www.marriottbaypoint.com* 🛏 *316 rooms, 60 1- and 2-bedroom golf villas* ⟡ *In-room: Wi-Fi. In-hotel: restaurants, bars, golf courses, pools, gym, spa.*

**$$–$$$**
**RESORT**
★
🛏 **Edgewater Beach Resort.** You can sleep at least four and as many as eight in the luxurious one-, two-, and three-bedroom apartments in beachside towers and golf course villas. **Pros:** variety of lodging options; 110 acres of beautiful beachfront property. **Cons:** overwhelming for those looking for a quiet getaway. ✉ *11212 Front Beach Rd.* ☎ *850/235–4044 or 800/874–8686* ⊕ *www.edgewaterbeachresort.com* 🛏 *520 apartments* ⟡ *In-room: kitchen. In-hotel: restaurants, bars, golf course, tennis courts, spa, beach, business center.*

$$–$$$   ⌧ **Legacy by the Sea.** Nearly every room at this 14-story, pastel-peach
HOTEL   hotel has a private balcony with commanding gulf views. **Pros:** shopping, dining, and attractions are within walking distance; all the amenities a family (or college kids) need. **Cons:** in the heart of a crowded
and congested district; can be difficult to access in peak seasons.
☒ *15325 Front Beach Rd.* ☎ *850/249–8601 or 888/886–8917* ⊕ *www.
legacybythesea.com* ⇨ *139 rooms and suites* ⟁ *In-room: kitchen. In-
hotel: pool* ⍩ *CP.*

## APALACHICOLA

*65 mi southeast of Panama City Beach off U.S. 98.*

It feels like a long haul between Panama City Beach and here. Add an
odd name and a town's below-the-radar reputation to that long drive
and you may be tempted to skip Apalachicola. But you shouldn't. It's a
weirdly fascinating town that, for some reason, has a growing cosmopolitan veneer. And that makes it worth a visit.

Meaning "land of the friendly people" in the language of its original
American Indian inhabitants, Apalachicola—known in these parts as
simply Apalach—lies on the Panhandle's southernmost bulge. European settlers began arriving in 1821, and by 1847 the southern terminus of the Apalachicola River steamboat route was a bustling port
town. Although the town is now known as the Oyster Capital of
the World, oystering became king only after the local cotton industry flagged—the city's extra-wide streets, built to accommodate bales
of cotton awaiting transport, are a remnant of that trade—and the
sponge industry moved down the coast after depleting local sponge
colonies.

But the newest industry here is tourism, and visitors have begun dis-
covering the Forgotten Coast, as the area is known, flocking to its
intimate hotels and B&Bs, dining at excellent restaurants, and browsing in unique shops selling anything from handmade furniture to brass
fixtures recovered from nearby shipwrecks. If you like oysters or want
to go back in time to the Old South of Gothic churches and spooky
graveyards, Apalachicola is a good place to start.

### ESSENTIALS

**Visitor Information Apalachicola Bay Chamber of Commerce** (☎ *850/653-
9419* ⊕ *www.apalachicolabay.org*).

### SHOPPING

The best way to shop in Apalachicola is just to stroll around the tiny
downtown area. There are always new stores joining old favorites
and somewhere along the way you'll find something that'll pique your
interest.

**Grady Market.** On the first floor of the Consulate Inn is a collection of
more than a dozen boutiques, including several antiques dealers and the
gallery of Richard Bickel, known for his stunning black-and-white photographs of local residents. ☒ *76 Water St.* ☎ *850/653–4099* ⊕ *www.
gradymarket.com.*

2

**Tin Shed.** This shop has an impressive collection of antiques and knick-knacks, from brass luggage tags to 1940s nautical charts to sponge-diver wet suits to hand-glazed tiles and architectural elements salvaged from demolished buildings. It's closed Sunday. ⊠ *170 Water St.* ☎ *850/ 653–3635.*

## WHERE TO EAT

$$  CONTINENTAL
✕**Apalachicola Seafood Grill.** Where will you find the world's largest fish sandwich? Right here in downtown Apalachicola. Here since 1908, it's where the locals go for lunch and dinner, noshing on blue-crab cakes, seafood gumbo, fresh grouper, shrimp, and hamburgers. The decor is iconic diner, with a giant flamingo on the ceiling for that added Florida charm. ⊠ *100 Market St.* ☎ 850/653–9510 ⊘ *No dinner Sun.*

$$  SEAFOOD
✕**Boss Oyster.** "Shut up and shuck." That's the advice from this rustic Old Florida restaurant—and it should know, since many consider this the top oyster restaurant in Florida's oyster capital. Located at the Apalachicola River Inn, this is where you can eat your oysters fried, Rockefeller-style, on the half shell, or Greek, Mexican, English, with garlic, with shrimp, with crab, with hot peppers, with—oh, just eat 'em with gusto at this laid-back eatery overlooking the Apalachicola River. In addition to oysters, it lays down jumbo gulf shrimp, blue crabs, bay scallops, and fresh gulf grouper. Eat alfresco at picnic tables or inside in the busy, rustic dining room, but don't let the modest surroundings fool you—oysters aren't cheap here or anywhere in Apalach. The menu also includes such staples as steak and pizza. ⊠ *123 Water St.* ☎ *850/653–9364* ⊕ *www.apalachicolariverinn.com/ boss.html.*

$$  CONTINENTAL  ★
✕**Magnolia Grill.** Chef-owner Eddie Cass has earned local and regional acclaim from major food critics who have discovered the culinary pearl in this oyster town. In addition to meat dishes such as char-grilled pork tenderloin served with raspberry-bordelaise sauce, Eddie pays tribute to local seafood with a broiled seafood feast that includes three of the freshest market fish served with locally harvested shrimp, scallops, and Apalachicola Bay oysters. Dinners here tend to be leisurely events (this is the South, after all), and the stellar desserts—anything chocolate will wow you—deserve an hour of their own. The restaurant is small, so reservations are recommended. ⊠ *99 11th St.* ☎ 850/653–8000 ⊘ *Closed Sun. No lunch.*

$$  AMERICAN
✕**Owl Café.** Located in a behemoth clapboard building on a prime corner in downtown Apalachicola, this old-fashioned, charming lunch-and-dinner spot pleases modern palates, both in the white-linen elegance of the dining room and in the colorful garden terrace. The food is an artful blend of old and new as well: the chicken wrap seems as much at home on the lunch menu as the crab quesadillas. Dinner seafood specials are carefully prepared and include lump-crab cakes, Atlantic salmon, and authentic jambalaya. Fine wines for adults and special menu selections for children along with a cluttered gift shop make this a family-friendly place. At night, the mood shifts to a casual lounge setting with a full liquor bar—and if the liquor bar lacks enough choices there's a 3,000-bottle wine cellar featuring 250 selections from around

the world. ⊠ *15 Ave. D* ☎ *850/653–9888* ⊕ *www.owlcafeflorida.com* ⊗ *No dinner Sun.*

**$$$**
LATIN AMERICAN
★
×**Tamara's Café.** Mixing Florida flavors with South American flair, Tamara, a native Venezuelan, opened this colorful bistro more than a decade ago. Now owned by her daughter and son-in-law, the restaurant resides in a 1920s-era building, complete with stamped-tin ceiling and original brick walls. For starters, try the creamy black-bean soup or the pleasantly spicy oyster stew; for dinner choose from seafood paella, prosciutto-wrapped salmon with mango-cilantro sauce, or margarita chicken and scallops with a tequila-lime glaze. All entrées come with black beans and rice, fresh vegetables, and focaccia bread, but if you still have room for dessert, try the fried-banana split or the *tres leches* (cake soaked in three types of milk), a South American favorite. The chef, who keeps watch over the dining room from an open kitchen, is happy to accommodate most any whim. ⊠ *71 Market St.* ☎ *850/653–4111* ⊕ *www.tamarascafe.com.*

## WHERE TO STAY

*For expanded hotel reviews, visit Fodors.com.*

**$$$–$$$$**
HOTEL
**The Consulate.** These four elegant suites, on the second story of the former offices of the French consul, range in size from 650 to 1,650 square feet and combine a 19th-century feel with 21st-century luxury. **Pros:** large rooms; more character than you'd find in a chain hotel. **Cons:** a bit pricey, especially for Apalachicola. ⊠ *76 Water St.* ☎ *850/927–2282 or 800/341–2021* ⊕ *www.consulatesuites.com* ⇝ *4 suites* △ *In-room: kitchen. In-hotel: laundry facilities.*

**$$–$$$**
B&B/INN
**Coombs Inn.** A combination of neighboring homes and a carriage house, this is an entire complex created with a Victorian flair. **Pros:** clean and comfortable; on-site, friendly owner who's happy to assist with travel tips and suggestions. **Cons:** be prepared to meet and greet other guests at the inn; if you favor complete privacy, a hotel may suit you better. ⊠ *80 6th St.* ☎ *850/653–9199* ⊕ *www.coombshouseinn.com* ⇝ *23 rooms* △ *In-room: Wi-Fi* ❍ *BP.*

**$$–$$$**
B&B/INN
**Gibson Inn.** One of a few inns on the National Register of Historic Places still operating as a full-service facility, this turn-of-the-20th-century hostelry in the heart of downtown is easily identified by its wraparound porches, intricate fretwork, and captain's watch. **Pros:** smack dab in the center of town; peaceful veranda. **Cons:** may get a little busy when weddings are taking place in the main lobby. ⊠ *51 Ave. C* ☎ *850/653–2191* ⊕ *www.gibsoninn.com* ⇝ *28 rooms, 2 suites* △ *In-room: Wi-Fi. In-hotel: restaurant, bar, some pets allowed.*

# ST. GEORGE ISLAND

*8 mi southeast of Apalachicola via Bryant Patton Bridge off U.S. 98.*

Cross the long, long bridge leading east out of Apalachicola and then look to your right for another lengthy span that will take you south to pristine St. George Island. Sitting 5 mi out into the Gulf of Mexico, the island is bordered by both Apalachicola Bay and the gulf, offering the best of both to create a nostalgic seaside retreat.

The rich bay is an angler's dream, whereas the snowy-white beaches and clear gulf waters satisfy even the most finicky beachgoer. Indulge in bicycling, hiking, canoeing, and snorkeling, or find a secluded spot for reading, gathering shells, or bird-watching. Accommodations mostly take the form of privately owned, fully furnished condos and single-family homes.

### EXPLORING

**Fodor's**Choice ★  **St. George Island State Park.** This is Old Florida at its undisturbed best. On the east end of the island are 9 mi of undeveloped beaches and dunes—the longest beachfront of any state park in Florida. Sandy coves, salt marshes, oak forests, and pines provide shelter for many birds, including bald eagles and ospreys. Spotless restrooms and plentiful parking make a day at this park a joy. ⊠ *1900 E. Gulf Beach Dr.* ☎ *850/927–2111* ⊕ *www.floridastateparks.org/stgeorgeisland* ⊠ *$6 per vehicle, up to 8 people* ⊙ *Daily 8–sunset.*

### WHERE TO EAT

¢  ✕ **BJs.** In any other locale you might think twice before dining at a res-
PIZZA  taurant that advertises "kegs-to-go" on the menu, but this is an island, so establishments tend to wear several hats (some even sell live bait). Fear not. This simple beach shack serves solid, if predictable, sandwiches (grilled chicken, turkey club, BLT), salads (Caesar, tuna, fried chicken), and appetizers (buffalo wings, cheese sticks, onion rings), but the pizza is definitely worth stopping for. Pies range from white pizza with chicken and bacon to shrimp-and-mozzarella to build-your-own personal pie (choose from 15 toppings). Beer and wine are available, and there are pool tables to pass the time while you wait for your order. ⊠ *105 W. Gulf Beach Dr.* ☎ *850/927–2805* ⚑ *Reservations not accepted.*

$$$  ✕ **Blue Parrot.** You'll feel like you're sneaking in the back door as you
SEAFOOD  climb the side stairs leading to an outdoor deck overlooking the gulf (this is Apalach's only restaurant on the beach). Or if you can, grab a table indoors. During special-event weekends, the place is packed, and service may be a little slow. The food is hard to beat if you're not looking for anything fancy. Baskets of shrimp, oysters, and crab cakes—fried or char-grilled and served with fries—are more than one person can handle. Daily specials are listed on the blackboard. ⊠ *68 W. Gorrie Dr.* ☎ *850/927–2987* ⊕ *www.blueparrotcafe.net.*

# INLAND TOWNS

Inland, where the northern reaches of the Panhandle butt up against the back porches of Alabama and Georgia, you'll find a part of Florida that goes a long way toward explaining why the state song is "Swannee River" (and why its parenthetical title is "Old Folks at Home"). Stephen Foster's musical genius notwithstanding, the inland Panhandle area is definitely more Dixie than Sunshine State, with few lodging options other than the chain motels that flank the Interstate 10 exits and a decidedly slower pace of life than you'll find on the tourist-heavy Gulf Coast.

But the area's natural attractions—hills and farmland, untouched small towns, pristine state parks—make for great day trips from the coast should the sky turn gray or the skin red. Explore underground caverns where eons-old rock formations create bizarre scenes, visit one of Florida's up-and-coming wineries, or poke around small-town America in DeFuniak Springs. Altogether, the inland area of the Panhandle is one of the state's most satisfyingly soothing regions.

## DEFUNIAK SPRINGS

*28 mi east of Crestview on U.S. 90 off I–10.*

This scenic spot has a rather unusual claim to fame: at its center lies a nearly perfectly symmetrical spring-fed lake, one of only two such naturally circular bodies of water in the world (the other is in Switzerland). A sidewalk encircles the lake, which is dotted by pine and shade trees, creating a very pleasing atmosphere for a long-distance mosey. In 1848 the Knox Hill Academy was founded here, and for more than half a century it was the only institution of higher learning in northwestern Florida.

In 1885 the town was chosen as the location for the New York Chautauqua educational society's winter assembly. The Chautauqua programs were discontinued in 1922, but DeFuniak Springs attempts to revive them, in spirit at least, by sponsoring a countywide Chautauqua Festival in April. Christmas is a particularly festive time, when the sprawling Victorian houses surrounding the lake are decorated to the nines.

There's not a tremendous amount to see here, but if you have the good sense to travel U.S. 90 to discover Old Florida, at least take the time to travel Circle Drive to see its beautiful Victorian homes. Also take a little time to walk around the small downtown area and drop in its bookstores, cafés, and small shops.

### EXPLORING

**Chautauqua Winery.** Open since 1989, this winery and its vintages have slowly won respect from oenophiles wary of what was once considered to be an oxymoron at best: "Florida wine." The winery has won honors in national and international competitions, with wines that vary from dry, barrel-fermented wines to Southern favorites like sweet muscadine and blueberry wines. Fourteen vats ranging in size from 1,500 to 6,000 gallons generate a total of 70,000 gallons of wine. Take a free tour to see how ancient art blends with modern technology; then retreat to the tastefully decorated tasting room and gift shop. ✉ *I–10 and U.S. 331* ☎ *850/892–5887* ⊕ *www.chautauquawinery.com.*

2

**TAKE A TOUR**

Circle Drive. Some of the finest examples of Victorian architecture in the state can be seen while you are walking or motoring around Circle Drive, the road that wraps around Circle Lake. The circumference is marked with beautiful Victorian specimens like the Walton-DeFuniak Public Library, the Dream Cottage, and the Pansy Cottage. Most of the other notable structures are private residences, but you can still admire them from the street.

### WHERE TO STAY
*For expanded hotel reviews, visit Fodors.com.*

¢–$

B&B/INN

⊞ **Hotel DeFuniak.** You can't miss this sweet, Depression-era two-story redbrick structure on a quiet corner a few blocks from peaceful Lake DeFuniak—just look for the two-tone 1937 Buick permanently moored out front. **Pros:** applause for the owners who created a sweet little retreat in the heart of downtown. **Cons:** DeFuniak can be eerily empty and quiet at night. ⊠ *400 E. Nelson Ave.* ☎ *850/892–4383 or 877/333–8642* ⊕ *www.hoteldefuniak.com* ⇝ *8 rooms, 3 suites* ⚿ *In-hotel: restaurant* ⏹ *BP.*

## FALLING WATERS STATE PARK

*35 mi east of DeFuniak Springs via U.S. 90 and Rte. 77.*

**Falling Waters State Park.** This site of a Civil War–era whiskey distillery and, later, an exotic plant nursery (some species still thrive in the wild) is best known for also being the site of the Falling Waters Sink. The 100-foot-deep cylindrical pit provides the background for a waterfall, and there's an observation deck for viewing this natural phenomenon. The water freefalls 67 feet to the bottom of the sink, but where it goes after that is a mystery. ⊠ *Rte. 77A, Chipley* ☎ *850/638–6130* ⊕ *www.floridastateparks.org/fallingwaters* ⊠ *$5 per vehicle, up to 8 people* ☉ *Daily 8–sunset.*

## FLORIDA CAVERNS STATE PARK

*13 mi northeast of Falling Waters off U.S. 90 on Rte. 166.*

**Florida Caverns State Park.** Marianna is a cute and pristine community, and a short drive from the center of town you can see what's behind, or—more accurately—what's beneath it all. Take a ranger-led cave tour to see stalactites, stalagmites, soda straws, columns, rim stones, flowstones, and "waterfalls" of solid rock at these underground caverns where the temperature hovers at an oh-so-pleasant 68°F year-round. Some of the caverns are off-limits to the public or open for scientific study only with a permit, but you'll still see enough to fill a half-day or more—and you'll be amazed that caverns of this magnitude exist anywhere in the Sunshine State. Don't forsake the quiet, preserved, and peaceful woodlands, which encompass 10 distinct communities including upland glade, hardwood forests, and floodplains, forests, and swamps. There are also hiking trails, campsites, and areas for swimming, horseback riding, and canoeing on the Chipola River. ⊠ *3345 Caverns Rd. (off U.S. 90 on Rte. 166), Marianna* ☎ *850/482–9598, 800/326–3521 for camping reservations* ⊕ *www.floridastateparks.*

*org/floridacaverns* 🏞 *Park $5 per vehicle, up to 8 people; caverns $8* ☉ *Daily 8–sunset; cavern tours Thurs.–Mon. 9–4.*

# TALLAHASSEE

*61 mi southeast of Florida Caverns on I–10.*

Tallahassee is Florida with a Southern accent. It maintains a tranquillity quite different from the sun-and-surf coastal towns. The only Southern capital spared in the Civil War, Tallahassee has preserved its past. Vestiges of the city's colorful past are found throughout. For example, in the capitol complex, the turn-of-the-20th-century Old Capitol building is strikingly paired with the New Capitol skyscraper.

The canopies of ancient oaks and spring bowers of azaleas line many streets; among the best "canopy roads" are St. Augustine, Miccosukee, Meridian, Old Bainbridge, and Centerville, all dotted with country stores and antebellum plantation houses. If you visit between March and April, you'll find flowers in bloom, the legislature in session, and the Springtime Tallahassee festival in full swing.

### GETTING HERE AND AROUND

Just 14 mi south of the Georgia border, Tallahassee is midway between Jacksonville and Pensacola and is nearer to Atlanta than Miami. Tallahassee Regional Airport is served by American Airlines, Continental, Delta, Northwest, and US Airways (US Airways Express). From the airport to downtown is around $20 via City Taxi or Yellow Cab.

### ESSENTIALS

Transportation Contacts **City Taxi** (☎ *850/562–4222*). **Tallahassee Regional Airport** (☎ *850/891–7800* ⊕ *www.talgov.com/airport*). **Yellow Cab** (☎ *850/575–1022*).

Visitor Information **Tallahassee Area Convention and Visitors Bureau** (☎ *850/606–2305 or 800/628–2866* ⊕ *www.visittallahassee.com*).

## EXPLORING

### DOWNTOWN

**Downtown Tallahassee Historic Trail.** A route originally mapped and documented by an eager Eagle Scout as part of a merit-badge project, this trail has become a Tallahassee sightseeing staple. The starting point is the New Capitol, where you can pick up maps and descriptive brochures at the visitor center. You'll walk through the Park Avenue and Calhoun Street historic districts, which will take you back to territorial days and the era of postwar reconstruction. The trail is dotted with landmark churches and cemeteries, along with outstanding examples of Greek revival, Italianate, and prairie-style architecture. Some houses are open to the public.

The **Brokaw-McDougall House** (✉ *329 N. Meridian St.* 🎫 *Free* ☉ *Weekdays 9–3*) is a superb example of the Greek revival and Italianate styles. The **Meginnis-Monroe House** (✉ *125 N. Gadsden St.*

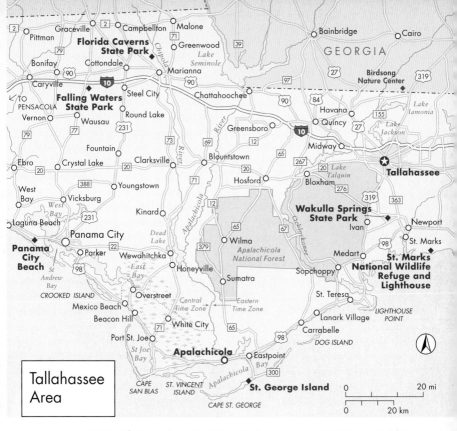

Tallahassee Area

*Free ⏱ Tues.–Sat. 10–5, Sun. 2–5)* served as a field hospital during the Civil War and is now an art gallery.

**Museum of Florida History.** If you thought Florida was founded by Walt Disney, stop here. The displays explain the state's past by highlighting the unique geological and historical events that have shaped the state. Exhibits include a mammoth armadillo grazing in a savanna, the remains of a giant mastodon found in nearby Wakulla Springs, and a dugout canoe that once carried American Indians into Florida's backwaters. Florida's history also includes settlements by the Spanish, British, French, and Confederates who fought for possession of the state.

Gold bars, weapons, flags, maps, furniture, steamboats, and other artifacts underscore the fact that although most Americans date the nation to 1776, Florida's residents were building settlements hundreds of years earlier. If this intrigues you, one floor up is the Florida State Archives and Library, where there's a treasure trove of government records, manuscripts, photographs, genealogical records, and other materials. ■TIP→ It was in these archives that researchers found footage of a young Jim Morrison appearing in a promotional film for Florida's universities. ✉ *500 S. Bronough St.* ☎ *850/245–6400, 850/245–6600 library, 850/245–6700 archives* ⊕ *www.museumoffloridahistory.com* *Free ⏱ Weekdays 9–4:30, Sat. 10–4:30, Sun. noon–4:30.*

## DID YOU KNOW?

There are many types of speleothems (cave formations). The two you hear spelunkers say the most are probably stalactites and stalagmites. Formed from dripping water, stalactites (shown here at Florida Caverns State Park) are conical formations that hang down from a cave ceiling. Formations that go the other direction—from the ground up, due to mineral deposits—are called stalagmites.

Guided tours are given daily at Florida's Old Capitol in Tallahassee. It sits in front of the 22-story New Capitol.

★ **New Capitol.** In the 1960s, when there was talk of relocating the capital to a more central location like Orlando, Panhandle legislators got to work and approved the construction of a 22-story skyscraper that would anchor the capital right where it was. It's perfectly placed at the crest of a hill, sitting prominently behind the low-rise Old Capitol. The governor's office is on the first floor, along with the Florida Artists Hall of Fame, a series of plaques that pay tribute to Floridians such as Ray Charles, Burt Reynolds, Tennessee Williams, Ernest Hemingway, and Marjorie Kinnan Rawlings.

The House and Senate chambers on the fifth floor provide viewer galleries for when the legislative sessions take place (March to May). Catch a panoramic view of Tallahassee and the surrounding countryside all the way into Georgia from the fabulous 22nd-floor observation deck. Although budget cuts have stopped scheduled guided tours, a free brochure can get you around; if you're traveling in a group you can call ahead to have a guide usher you around. To pick up information about the area, stop at the Florida Visitors Center on the plaza level, and check out the plaque on the north wall facing the elevators. It's dedicated to Senator Lee Wissenborn " . . . whose valiant effort to move the Capitol to Orlando was the prime motivation for the construction of this building." ✉ *400 S. Monroe St.* ☎ *850/488–6167* ⊕ *www.myfloridacapitol. com* ✉ *Free* ☉ *Visitor center weekdays 8–5.*

★ **Old Capitol.** The centerpiece of the capitol complex, this 1842 structure has been added to and subtracted from several times. Having been restored, the jaunty red-and-white-striped awnings and combination gas-electric lights make it look much as it did in 1902. Inside, it houses a must-see museum of Florida's political history as well as the old Supreme Court chambers and Senate Gallery—a very interesting peek into the past. ⊠ *S. Monroe St. at Apalachee Pkwy.* ☎ *850/487–1902* ✈ *Free* ☉ *Self-guided tours weekdays 9–4:30, Sat. 10–4:30, Sun. noon–4:30; call ahead for guided tours.*

## AWAY FROM DOWNTOWN

**Alfred B. Maclay Gardens State Park.** Starting in December, the grounds at this 1,200-acre estate are afire with azaleas, dogwood, Oriental magnolias, spring bulbs of tulips and irises, banana shrubs, honeysuckle, silverbell trees, pansies, and camellias. Allow half a day to wander past the reflecting pool into the tiny walled garden and around the lakes and woodlands. The Maclay residence (open January through April only) is furnished as it was in the 1920s; picnic areas, gardens, and swimming and boating facilities are open to the public. ⊠ *3540 Thomasville Rd.* ☎ *850/487–4556* ⊕ *www.floridastateparks.org/ maclaygardens* ✈ *$6 per vehicle, up to 8 people; extra $6 per person for garden admission Jan.–Apr. (blooming season); free rest of year* ☉ *Daily 8–sunset.*

**Fodor's Choice** ★  **Edward Ball Wakulla Springs State Park.** Known for having one of the deepest springs in the world, this very picturesque and highly recommended park remains relatively untouched, retaining the wild and exotic look it had in the 1930s, when the films *Tarzan* and *Creature from the Black Lagoon* were shot here. Even if they weren't, you'd want to come here and see what Florida really looks like. Beyond the lodge is the spring where glass-bottom boats set off deep into the lush, jungle-lined waterways to catch glimpses of alligators, snakes, nesting limpkins, and other waterfowl. It costs $50 to rent a pontoon boat and go it alone—it may be worth it since an underground river flows into a pool so clear you can see the bottom more than 100 feet below. The park is 15 mi south of Tallahassee on Route 61. If you can't pull yourself away from this idyllic spot, spend the night in the 1930s Spanish Mediterranean–style lodge. ⊠ *550 Wakulla Park Dr., Wakulla Springs* ☎ *850/926–0700* ⊕ *www.floridastateparks.org/ wakullasprings* ✈ *$6 per vehicle, up to 8 people; boat tour $8* ☉ *Daily 8–sunset; boat tours offered 9:30–4:30.*

**San Luis Archaeological and Historic Site.** Long before New England's residents began gaining a foothold in America, the native Apalachee Indians as well as Spanish missionaries settled here. On the site of a 17th-century Spanish mission and Apalachee Indian town sites, this museum focuses on the archaeology of the late 1600s, when the Apalachee village here had a population of at least 1,400. By 1704, however, threatened by Creek Indians and British forces, the locals burned the village and fled. About once a year, researchers will conduct digs and then spend the rest of the year analyzing their findings. If you're here when they are, you can watch them dig, although chances are you'll have to be content with roaming around the re-creation of a 17th-century Spanish village and speaking with the living-history guides who will offer tours if you call in advance. Even without the sight of researchers digging for clues, this is still a cool experience and a great way to learn about Florida's impressive history. A 24,000-square-foot, state-of-the-art visitor center

## WHERE TO STAY

*For expanded hotel reviews, visit Fodors.com.*

**$$$-$$$$**
**B&B/INN**
★

**Governors Inn.** Only a block from the capitol, this plushly restored historic warehouse is abuzz during the week with politicians, press, and lobbyists. **Pros:** a few steps from museums, restaurants, and the capitol; the rooms and lobby are warm and inviting. **Cons:** during session and football season, the district can get crowded and busy, and accessing the area may be a challenge. ⊠ *209 S. Adams St.* ☎ *850/681–6855 or 800/342–7717* ⊕ *www.thegovinn.com* ⇆ *29 rooms, 12 suites* ⛉ *In-room: Wi-Fi. In-hotel: parking* ⏐○⏐ *CP.*

**¢**
**HOTEL**

**Super 8.** The quiet courtyard with its own pool and the darkly welcoming cantina (where a complimentary Continental breakfast is served) convey the look of old Spain. **Pros:** close to the capitol; great rates. **Cons:** it's a Super 8, so it lacks the character of higher-priced lodging. ⊠ *2801 N. Monroe St.* ☎ *850/386–8286* ⊕ *www.super8.com* ⇆ *108 rooms, 23 suites* ⛉ *In-room: Wi-Fi. In-hotel: pool* ⏐○⏐ *CP.*

# Northeast Florida

## WORD OF MOUTH

"The beaches are beautiful. There are lots of casual restaurants. There are lots of families in the area, both young and old. . . . There's lots to do both near the beaches and in Jacksonville . . . shopping, movies, museums, and you're only minutes from St. Augustine. I think you'll enjoy!"

—khern

# WELCOME TO NORTHEAST FLORIDA

## TOP REASONS TO GO

★ **Get Out and Play:**
Beautiful beaches and a wealth of state and national parks mean swimming, sunbathing, kayaking, fishing, hiking, bird-watching, and camping opportunities are all nearby.

★ **Golfer's Paradise:**
"Above par" describes the golf scene, from award-winning courses to THE PLAYERS Championship to the World Golf Hall of Fame.

★ **Start Your Engines:**
Few things will get racing fans as revved up as tours of Daytona International Speedway, home of the Daytona 500, Coke Zero 400, and Rolex 24 at Daytona.

★ **Be in the Now:**
Whether you want a yoga retreat or the ultimate in sybaritic pampering, the oceanfront spas at Amelia Island and Ponte Vedra Beach make this region the place to be.

★ **The Rest Is History:**
The nation's oldest city, St. Augustine, is a must-see for anyone interested in history.

**1 Jacksonville.** With a metro-area population of 1.3 million, Jacksonville has the social and cultural appeal of a big city (think pro sports teams, fine dining, museums, nightlife, and shopping) but the down-to-earth charm of a small town. At Amelia Island/Fernandina Beach, just to the north, you'll find a historic downtown, beautiful beaches, and two superlative resorts: The Omni Amelia Island Plantation Resort and the Ritz-Carlton.

**2 St. Augustine.** You don't have to be a history buff to enjoy one of America's oldest cities, founded in 1565. Foodies, golfers, art lovers, and beach bums generally find plenty to do here, too.

**3 Daytona Beach and Inland Towns.** The Daytona 500, Bike Week, and spring break put it on the map, but places like the Ocala National Forest and Ocala are popular with vacationing families, too. Gainesville is home to the University of Florida and its Gators.

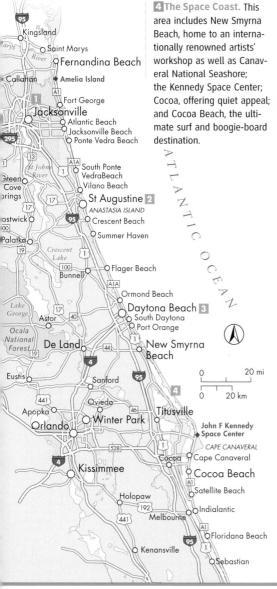

**4** **The Space Coast.** This area includes New Smyrna Beach, home to an internationally renowned artists' workshop as well as Canaveral National Seashore; the Kennedy Space Center; Cocoa, offering quiet appeal; and Cocoa Beach, the ultimate surf and boogie-board destination.

## GETTING ORIENTED

3

Northeast Florida has historic port cities like Amelia Island/Fernandina Beach and St. Augustine and inland towns like Micanopy and Gainesville, as well as the urban hub of Jacksonville. About two hours south of the city, on Interstate 95, Titusville, the entry point for the Kennedy Space Center, marks the northern perimeter of the Space Coast, which includes Cocoa and Melbourne. If you take U.S. 1, it lengthens the trip, but the scenery makes up for the inconvenience. Route A1A/Atlantic Avenue is the main road on all the barrier islands. In many places on A1A, you can see the area's beautiful beaches from your car window.

# NORTHEAST FLORIDA'S BEACHES

Northeastern Florida's primary draw is its beaches. Hugging the coast are long, slender barrier islands whose entire eastern sides make up a broad band of spectacular sand. Development has been modest in many places, and beaches are edged with funky, appealing little towns.

Just below the Georgia border are Fernandina Beach with its well-preserved Victorian buildings, and Amelia Island, an idyllic playland with its acclaimed resorts in lush, natural surroundings.

Separated from the mainland by the Intracoastal Waterway, Jacksonville's main beaches include those in the laid-back towns of Atlantic Beach, Neptune Beach, Jacksonville Beach, and Ponte Vedra Beach. To the south are Vilano Beach; historic St. Augustine, with its beach on Anastasia Island; Daytona Beach; and the surfer's paradise of Cocoa Beach.

## QUIETER BEACHES

Small and scenic, **Paradise Beach** is a 1,600-foot stretch of sand that's part of a 10-acre park north of Indialantic, about 20 mi south of Cocoa Beach on Route A1A. It has showers, restrooms, picnic tables, a refreshment stand, and lifeguards in summer. Meanwhile, **Satellite Beach**, about 15 mi south of Cocoa Beach on Route A1A, is popular for family vacations because of its lack of crowds.

## NORTHEAST FLORIDA'S BEST BEACHES

### AMELIA ISLAND/FERNANDINA BEACH

Far from the madness of some of the popular spring break beaches, the shores of Amelia Island put you close to nature. Here, you can swim or body surf; pound the beach on horseback; or fish for tarpon, kingfish, and amberjack. Public parking beach access is available at the north end of Fletcher Avenue.

### COCOA BEACH

The Surfing Capital of the East Coast is home to Ron Jon Surf Shop, the world's largest surf shop; the Cocoa Beach Surf Company, the world's largest surf complex, complete with the East Coast Surfing Hall of Fame and Museum; and the birthplace of 10-time world surfing champion Kelly Slater. Grommets looking to follow in his aqua shoes should head to the beach at Third Street North (aka Slater Way), where he learned the basics. Stretching 800 feet over the Atlantic, the Cocoa Beach Pier is an everyday hangout and a grandstand for launches from nearby Kennedy Space Center. There's a bait shop, souvenir shops, bars, and restaurants. It costs $3 to park, and $1 to access the fishing part of the pier.

### DAYTONA BEACH

The World's Most Famous Beach is fronted by tall condos and apartments, hotels, low-rise motels, and flashy

nightclubs. Throughout the year, events such as Bike Week, spring break, and auto racing ensure that the beach is busy. Traffic can get backed up, as driving on the sand is allowed (be careful, because cars can, and do, get stuck). No-car zones are less frenetic and more family-friendly.

### JACKSONVILLE BEACHES

The northernmost of Jacksonville's beaches, Atlantic Beach is one of the more subdued, thanks to expensive housing that keeps most young people from settling here. Adjacent Neptune Beach and Jacksonville Beach draw the current crop of tanned bodies in bikinis and board shorts, particularly in the vicinity of 1st Street, where cars often yield to bicyclists and in-line skaters.

It's fun to drive south along A1A to Ponte Vedra Beach and have a look at its multimillion-dollar homes. Unless you stay at an area resort, though, it's fiendishly difficult to reach the sand. Yes, there are designated public-access points between houses, but parking and right-of-way restrictions make true access difficult and keep most stretches practically private. Head farther south still; there's public parking at Mickler's Landing and Guana River State Park.

Note that on the more populated area beaches, lifeguards are on duty 10–6 in summer.

3

Updated by
Sharon Hoff-
mann, Steve
Master, Gary
McKechnie,
and Jaimie
Wilson

For many travelers, Florida is about fantasy, thanks, in no small part, to central Florida's make-believe kingdoms. But the northeastern part of the state—you could call it "authentic Florida—has its own allure, with unspoiled beaches and rivers and historic small towns, and urban arts and culture.

Northeastern Florida's beaches have wide, shell-strewn expanses of soft sand and breakers just the right height for kids to jump. Thanks to waters warmed by the Gulf Stream and to the temperate climate, these beaches are a year-round playground—when it's too cold to swim, you can still enjoy surf-fishing or just strolling the shoreline looking for shells and shark's teeth.

Sun and surf aren't the only reasons to explore northeastern Florida, though. There's historic St. Augustine and its horse-drawn carriages, Daytona and its classic spring break flavor, and Space Coast and its sense of discovery. Along the way is an array of little towns—from Fernandina and its shrimp fleets to Micanopy and its antiques stores—that invite quiet exploration.

There's city life in the northeast, too. In the last decade or so, Jacksonville has revitalized its institutions and infrastructure. And with the revitalization has come an arts renaissance—from virtuoso productions in the theaters of the Times-Union Center for the Performing Arts to world-class exhibits in the Museum of Contemporary Art.

So, even if the ultimate reason for your Florida sojourn is Mickey and his friends, there's no reason to miss the northeast. Indeed, you'll find some authentic benefits—among them, a dearth of crowds and lines and an abundance of Southern hospitality and good value for money.

# NORTHEAST FLORIDA PLANNER

## WHEN TO GO

It's not 90°F and sunny here every day. In winter, the weather is fair, averaging in the low 50s in Jacksonville and low 60s in Cocoa Beach, but the temperature sometimes dips below freezing for a day or two. Summer temperatures hover around 90, but the humidity makes it seem hotter, and late afternoon thunderstorms are frequent. April and May are good months to visit, since the ocean is beginning to warm up, and the beaches aren't yet packed. Fall is usually pleasant, too.

## TOURS

**TourTime, Inc.** This company offers custom group and individual motor-coach tours of Jacksonville, Amelia Island, Jeckyll Island, and St. Augustine, as well as river cruises and overnight trips to Silver Springs, Kennedy Space Center, Orlando, Okefenokee Swamp, and New Orleans. Prior arrangements are required. ☎ *904/282–8500 or 800/822–4278 ⊕ www.tourtimeinc.com.*

## GETTING HERE

Jacksonville International Airport (JAX) is the region's air hub. A welcome center with information on local attractions, including St. Augustine and Amelia Island, is on the ground floor of Jacksonville International Airport at the foot of the escalator near baggage claim. It is open daily 9 am–10 pm.

Daytona Beach International (DAB) and Gainesville Regional (GNV) are smaller operations with fewer flights; that said, they may be more convenient in certain travel situations.

Although Orlando isn't part of the area, visitors to northeastern Florida often choose to arrive at Orlando International Airport (MCO) since cheaper flights are often available. Driving east from Orlando on toll-road 528 (aka, the Beachline Expressway) brings you to Cocoa Beach in about an hour; to reach Daytona from Orlando, take the Beachline Expressway to Interstate 95 and drive north for an hour or so.

# GETTING AROUND

East–west traffic travels the northern part of the state on Interstate 10, a cross-country highway stretching from Jacksonville, FL, to Santa Monica, CA. Farther south, Interstate 4 connects Florida's west and east coasts. Signs on Interstate 4 designate it an east–west route, but actually the road rambles northeast from Tampa to Orlando, then heads north–northeast to Daytona. Two interstates head north–south on Florida's peninsula: Interstate 95 on the east coast and Interstate 75 on the west.

If you want to drive as close to the Atlantic as possible, choose Route A1A, but accept the fact it will add considerably to your drive time. It runs along the barrier islands, changing its name several times along the way.

The Buccaneer Trail, which overlaps part of Route A1A, goes from St. Augustine north to Mayport, through marshlands and beaches, and then finally into Fort Clinch State Park. The extremely scenic Route 13, also known as the William Bartram Trail, runs from Jacksonville to East Palatka along the east side of the St. Johns River through tiny hamlets. U.S. 17 travels the west side of the river, passing through Green Cove Springs and Palatka. Route 40 runs east–west through the Ocala National Forest, giving a nonstop view of stately pines and bold wildlife.

## ABOUT THE RESTAURANTS

The ocean, St. Johns River, and numerous lakes and smaller rivers are teeming with fish, and so, naturally, seafood dominates local menus. Northeast Florida also has fine-dining restaurants, and its ethnic eateries include some excellent Middle Eastern places. And then there are the barbecue joints—more of them than you can shake a hickory chip at.

## ABOUT THE HOTELS

For the busy seasons—during summer in and around Jacksonville and during summer and holiday weekends all over Florida—reserve well ahead for top properties. Jacksonville's beach hotels fill up quickly for PGA's THE PLAYERS Championship in mid-May. Daytona Beach presents similar problems during the Daytona 500 (mid-February), Bike Week (late February–early March), spring break (March), and the Coke Zero 400 (early July).

St. Augustine stays busy all year. In fall rates are low and availability is high, but it is also hurricane season. Although the area hasn't been hit directly since 1964, it's possible for threatening storms to disrupt plans.

| WHAT IT COSTS | | | | |
|---|---|---|---|---|
| ¢ | $ | $$ | $$$ | $$$$ |
| Restaurants | under $10 | $10–$15 | $15–$20 | $20–$30 | over $30 |
| Hotels | under $80 | $80–$100 | $100–$140 | $140–$220 | over $220 |

Restaurant prices are per person for a main course at dinner. Hotel prices are for a standard double room, excluding 6% sales tax (more in some counties) and 1%–4% tourist tax.

# JACKSONVILLE

*399 mi north of Miami, on I–95.*

Jacksonville is an underrated vacation spot. It offers appealing downtown riverside areas, handsome residential neighborhoods, a thriving arts scene, and, for football fans, the NFL's Jaguars and the NCAA Gator Bowl.

Although the city has become the largest in area of the continental United States (841 square mi), its Old South flavor remains, especially in the Riverside/Avondale historic district. Here moss-draped oak trees frame prairie-style bungalows and Tudor-revival mansions and palm trees, Spanish bayonet, and azaleas populate the landscape.

## EXPLORING JACKSONVILLE

### GETTING HERE AND AROUND

The main airport for the region is Jacksonville International Airport. Free shuttles run from the terminal to all parking lots (except the garage) around the clock, and transportation service into the city is available from numerous companies in vehicles that range from taxis to vans to elegant limousines. Check beforehand on prices, which vary widely, and on which credit cards are accepted. The average cost per person from airport to downtown is $35 to $45; it's $45 to $55 for trips to the beaches. The larger companies usually operate 24/7, but the smaller (and often less expensive ones) may be by appointment only.

Connecting the north and south banks of the St. Johns River, S.S. *Marine* water taxi runs between several locations, including the Crowne Plaza Jacksonville Riverfront and the Jacksonville Landing. The one-way trip takes about five minutes. During football season the water taxi also makes trips to EverBank Field on game days and for special events like the Florida/Georgia game. The water taxi runs Sunday through Thursday 11–9; Friday and Saturday 11–11 (except during rain or other bad weather), with special hours on game days and for special events. One-way fare is $3, special-event fare is $5.

Jacksonville Transportation Authority buses and shuttles serve the city and its beaches. The city also operates a small monorail system that links the convention center and a few downtown areas to several other stations across the river on the Southbank and San Marco. It costs only 35 cents and runs weekdays from 6 am to 11 pm.

### ESSENTIALS

Transportation Contacts **Carey Jacksonville** (☎ *904/221–5466*). **Gator City Shuttle** (☎ *904/741–8294*). **Gator City Taxi** (☎ *904/741–0008*). **Jacksonville International Airport** (*JAX* ☎ *904/741–4902* ⊕ *www.jia.aero*). **Jacksonville Transportation Authority** (*JTA* ☎ *904/630–3100* ⊕ *www.jtafla.com*). **S.S. Marine Taxi** (☎ *904/733–7782* ⊕ *www.jaxwatertaxi.com*). **Yellow Cab–Jacksonville** (☎ *904/355–8294*).

Visitor Information **Visit Jacksonville** (✉ *208 N Laura St., Suite 102, Jacksonville* ☎ *904/798–9104 or 800/733–2668* ⊕ *www.visitjacksonville.com*).

## EXPLORING

Jacksonville was settled along both sides of the twisting St. Johns River, and a number of attractions are on or near its banks. Both sides of the river, which is spanned by myriad bridges, have downtown areas and waterfront complexes of shops, restaurants, parks, and museums.

Rainbox Lorikeet might pop by and say hello while you're touring the Jacksonville Zoo.

You can reach some attractions by water taxi or Skyway Express monorail system—scenic alternatives to driving back and forth across the bridges. That said, a car is generally necessary.

In addition to the visitor information center at the airport, there's one at the Jacksonville Landing marketplace and another in Jacksonville Beach at the Beaches Historical Museum (380 Pablo Avenue), open Tuesday through Saturday 10–4:30.

## TOP ATTRACTIONS

**Cummer Museum of Art & Gardens.** The Wark Collection of early-18th-century Meissen porcelain is just one reason to visit this former riverfront estate, which includes 13 permanent galleries with more than 5,500 items spanning more than 8,000 years, and 3 acres of riverfront gardens reflecting northeast Florida's blooming seasons and indigenous varieties. Art Connections allows kids to experience art through hands-on, interactive exhibits. One of the museum's newest additions, the Thomas H. Jacobsen Gallery of American Art, focuses on works by American artists, including Max Weber, N.C. Wyeth, and Paul Manship. ⊠ 829 Riverside Ave. ☎ 904/356-6857 ⊕ www.cummer.org 🖃 $10, free Tues. 4–9 ☉ Tues. 10–9, Wed.–Sat. 10–5, Sun. noon–5.

**Jacksonville Landing.** During the week, this riverfront market caters to locals and tourists alike, with specialty shops, full-service restaurants—including a sushi bar, Italian bistro, and a steak house—and an internationally flavored food court. The Landing hosts more than 250 weekend events each year, ranging from the good clean fun of the Lighted Boat Parade and Christmas Tree Lighting to the just plain obnoxious Florida/Georgia game after-party, as well as live music (usually of the local

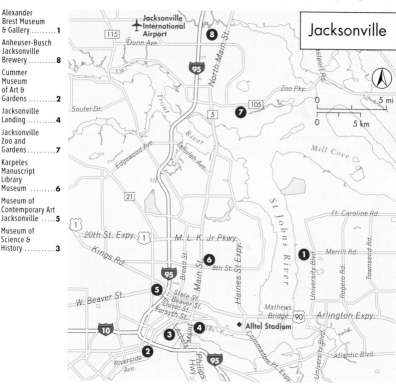

cover-band variety) in the courtyard. ⊠ *2 W. Independent Dr.* ☎ *904/353–1188* ⊕ *www.jacksonvillelanding.com* ✉ *Free* ⊙ *Mon.–Thurs. 10–8, Fri. and Sat. 10–9, Sun. noon–5:30; restaurant hrs vary.*

**Jacksonville Zoo and Gardens.** What's new at the zoo? Plenty. Not only has it seen the births of a rare Amur leopard and a greater kudu calf, it has opened Tuxedo Park, a controlled environment for a group of Magellanic penguins. Among the other highlights are the rare waterfowl and the Serona Overlook, which showcases some of the world's most venomous snakes. The Florida Wetlands is a 2½-acre area with black bears, bald eagles, white-tailed deer, and other animals native to Florida. The African Veldt has alligators, elephants, and white rhinos, among other species of African birds and mammals; and the Range of the Jaguar, winner of the Association of Zoos and Aquarium's Exhibit of the Year, includes 4 acres of exotic big cats as well as 20 other species of animals. New additions include Play Park, complete with a splash park, forest play area, maze, and discovery building; and Stingray Bay, a 17,000-gallon pool where visitors can pet and feed the mysterious creatures. Parking is free. ⊠ *370 Zoo Pkwy., off Heckscher Dr. E* ☎ *904/757–4463* ⊕ *www.jaxzoo.org* ✉ *$13.95* ⊙ *Daily 9–5; extended hrs offered during summer weekends and holidays.*

Fodor'sChoice **Museum of Contemporary Art Jacksonville.** In this loftlike downtown build-
★ ing, the former headquarters of the Western Union Telegraph Company,
a permanent collection of 20th-century art shares space with traveling
exhibitions. The museum encompasses five galleries and ArtExplorium, a
highly interactive educational exhibit for kids, as well as a funky gift shop
and Café Nola, open for lunch on weekdays and for dinner on Thursday
and Friday. MOCA Jacksonville also hosts film series, and workshops
throughout the year, and packs a big art-wallop into a relatively small
14,000 square feet. The Art Matters lecture series is free; Sunday is free
for families; a once-a-month Art Walk is free to all. ⊠ *Hemming Plaza,
333 N. Laura St.* ☎ *904/366–6911* ⊕ *www.mocajacksonville.org* 🎫 *$8*
⊙ *Tues., Wed., Fri., and Sat. 10–4, Thurs. 10–8, Sun. noon–4; Art Walk
5–9 1st Wed. of month, hrs subject to change.*

## WORTH NOTING

ℭ **Alexander Brest Museum & Gallery.** Boehm and Royal Copenhagen porcelain and Steuben glass are among the collections at this Jacksonville University museum. Also on display are cloisonné pieces, pre-Columbian
artifacts, and one of the finest collections of ivory anywhere from the
early 17th to the late 19th century. ⊠ *Jacksonville University, Phillips
Fine Arts Bldg., 2800 University Blvd. N* ☎ *904/256–7371* ⊕ *arts.ju.edu*
🎫 *Free* ⊙ *Weekdays 9–4.*

**Anheuser-Busch Jacksonville Brewery Tour.** Guided tours give a behind-the-
scenes look at how barley, malt, rice, hops, and water form the "King
of Beers." Or you can hightail it through the self-guided tour and head
straight to the free beer tastings (if you're 21 years or older, that is).
⊠ *111 Busch Dr.* ☎ *904/696–8373* ⊕ *www.budweisertours.com* 🎫 *Free*
⊙ *Mon.–Sat. 10–4; guided tours based on availability; call for hrs.*

**Karpeles Manuscript Library Museum.** File this one under "hidden treasure," given that even many residents have never visited Karpeles. That's
too bad, because this 1921 neoclassical building on the outskirts of
downtown has displayed some priceless documents: the original draft
of the Bill of Rights, the Emancipation Proclamation signed by Abraham Lincoln, handwritten manuscripts of Edgar Allan Poe and Charles
Dickens, and musical scores by Beethoven and Mozart. Manuscript
exhibits change every three months or so and coincide with monthly
art exhibits. Also on the premises is an antique-book library, with volumes dating from the late 1800s, and a children's museum. ⊠ *101 W.
1st St.* ☎ *904/356–2992* ⊕ *www.rain.org/~karpeles/jax.html* 🎫 *Free*
⊙ *Mon.–Sat. 10–3.*

ℭ **Museum of Science & History.** MOSH, once known in Jacksonville as
"the children's museum," is for all ages these days, especially with the
installation of the Konica Minolta Super MediaGlobe II. Translation?
It's the next generation of planetarium, one that can project shows of
all kinds on the dome—from blockbuster movies to live NASA feeds to
the 3-D laser shows that accompany the ever-popular, weekend Cosmic
Concerts. The resolution here is four times sharper than that of the most
hi-def TV currently on the market, so whether you're a kid "flying" on
a snowflake or an adult falling into darkness during *Black Holes: The
Other Side of Infinity,* the experience is awesome.

MOSH also has a wide variety of interactive exhibits like the JEA Science Theatre, where you can participate in live experiments related to electricity and electrical safety; the Florida Naturalist's Center, where you can explore northeast Florida wildlife; and the Universe of Science, where you'll learn about properties of physical science through hands-on demonstrations. ⊠ *1025 Museum Circle* ☎ *904/396–6674* ⊕ *www.themosh.org* ⊇ *$10 adult for museum; $15 for museum and planetarium; except Fri. $5 all admissions, Cosmic Concerts $7–$9; Fri. $5* ☉ *Mon.–Thurs. 10–5, Fri. 10–8, Sat. 10–6, Sun. 1–6.*

## SPORTS AND THE OUTDOORS

### BASEBALL

**Jacksonville Suns.** The AA minor-league affiliate of the Florida Marlins plays at the $34 million Baseball Grounds of Jacksonville. The Suns were Southern League champions in 2009 and 2010. ⊠ *301 A. Philip Randolph Blvd.* ☎ *904/358–2846.*

### BOAT TOURS

**River Cruises.** Relaxing lunch and dinner-dancing cruises and private sightseeing charters are aboard this operation's *Annabelle Lee* and *Lady St. Johns* paddleboats; schedules and prices vary. ☎ *904/306–2200* ⊕ *www.jaxrivercruises.com.*

### FOOTBALL

**EverBank Field.** The home of NFL's Jacksonville Jaguars also kicks off each year with a New Year's Day bowl game, the Konica Minolta Gator Bowl, which usually features NCAA top-10 teams from the ACC, Big East, or Big 12 conferences, or Notre Dame. Billed as the "World's Largest Outdoor Cocktail Party," the Florida versus Georgia Football Classic, or the Florida/Georgia Game, as it's better known, celebrates one of college football's most heated rivalries—between the Florida Gators and Georgia Bulldogs—every fall at Everbank Field. ⊠ *1 EverBank Field* ☎ *904/633–6100* ⊕ *www.jaxevents.com.*

### GOLF

Northeast Florida's most famous golf courses are not technically within Jacksonville, but rather just south of the city in Ponte Vedra Beach. The Tournament Players Club at Sawgrass offers two courses: the Dye's Valley course and the Stadium Course (with its world-renowned Island Green), which hosts THE PLAYERS Championship each year. There are, in addition, many excellent public courses in Jacksonville and in the neighboring towns of Orange Park and Green Cove Springs in Clay County.

**Champions Club at Julington Creek.** The course here is well maintained and reasonably priced; greens fees are $39 or $52, depending on whether you're a resident. ⊠ *1111 Durbin Creek Blvd., Jacksonville* ☎ *904/287–4653.*

**Cimarrone Golf Club.** The 6,891-yard course has a water or marsh feature on every hole. Greens fees are $35 or $40 (discounts available online). ⊠ *2800 Cimarrone Blvd., Jacksonville* ☎ *904/287–2000* ⊕ *www.cimarronegolf.com.*

## JACKSONVILLE'S BASEBALL HISTORY

Jacksonville became Major League Baseball's first spring training location when the city hosted the Washington Statesmen in 1888. Many of baseball's greatest African-American players, both white and black, have wowed fans at Jacksonville's J.P. Small Park, including Hank Aaron, Satchel Paige, Roy Campanella, and James "Cool Papa" Bell.

A truly historic moment—Jackie Robinson breaking the color barrier—could have happened here in 1942, but he wasn't allowed to take the field with his teammates on the minor league Royals team. Rather than let him play, the stadium was padlocked.

Spring training has moved south, but the baseball tradition here continued. Some of the sport's best players—Nolan Ryan, Tom Seaver, Randy Johnson, and Alex Rodriguez—did stints on Jacksonville's farm-league teams.

**Eagle Harbor Golf Club.** The 18-hole, par-72 course is designed by Clyde Johnston and has a driving range, club rentals, and discount packages. Greens fees are $49 or $59. ✉ *2217 Eagle Harbor Pkwy., Orange Park* ☎ *904/269–9300.*

**Magnolia Point Golf and Country Club.** The "player-friendly" course has beautiful scenery and wildlife. Greens fees are $29–$33. ✉ *3670 Clubhouse Dr., Green Cove Springs* ☎ *904/284–3559.*

**Windsor Parke Golf Club.** The course's 18 holes (par 72) are on tree-lined fairways and amid natural marshlands. Greens fees are $39 or $55. ✉ *13823 Sutton Park Rd., Jacksonville* ☎ *904/223–4653* ⊕ *www.windsorparke.com.*

## SHOPPING

### DISTRICT

**Five Points.** This small but funky shopping district less than a mile southwest of downtown has new and vintage-clothing boutiques, shoe stores, and antiques shops. It also has a handful of eateries and bars, not to mention some of the city's most colorful characters. ✉ *Intersection of Park, Margaret, and Lomax Sts., Riverside.*

### MALLS

**San Marco Square.** The dozens of interesting apparel, home, and jewelry stores and restaurants are in 1920s Mediterranean-revival–style buildings. ✉ *San Marco and Atlantic Blvds.*

**The Shoppes of Avondale.** The highlights here include upscale clothing and accessories boutiques, art galleries, home-furnishings shops, a chocolatier, and trendy restaurants. ✉ *St. Johns Ave., between Talbot Ave. and Dancy St.*

**St. Johns Town Center.** Some of the shops at this huge outdoor "lifestyle center" aren't found anywhere else in northeast Florida, including Anthropologie, Apple, Lucky Brand Jeans, and Sephora, as well as the

Cheesecake Factory, P.F. Chang's China Bistro, and Maggiano's Little Italy. ✉ *4663 River City Dr., Southside* ☎ *904/998–7156.*

## MARKET

**Riverside Arts Market.** The unique location—under the Fuller-Warren Bridge, a block from the Cummer Museum of Art & Gardens—might be as much of a draw as the merchandise. Regardless, since its first Saturday in April 2009, RAM has attracted larger and larger crowds of singles, couples, families, and their dogs. They all come to shop for locally created art and crafts, sample food from vendors that include some excellent area restaurants, and check out street performers or the live music shows on the riverfront stage.

Quality is high in every aspect—artists and vendors all go through a fairly rigorous application/audition process—and what there is to see or hear or eat varies from week to week. Sometimes there's also a farmers' market, with licensed farmers and growers selling everything from just-laid eggs and local honey to salad greens that were still in the earth the day before. Inside the Children's Activity Center tent, several organizations offer free educational arts activities to kids.

Because it's sheltered by the bridge, RAM goes on rain or shine. Free parking is available at Fidelity National Financial and other adjacent businesses, and a "bike valet" service encourages people to travel on two wheels. At this writing, there's buzz that the market might open on more than just Saturday; check the website for updates. ✉ *Riverside Ave. at I–95, Riverside* ☎ *904/554–6865* ⊕ *www.riversideartsmarket. com* ☑ *Free* ☉ *Sat. 10–4; hrs may change in 2012; call to check.*

# NIGHTLIFE AND THE ARTS

## THE ARTS

### MAJOR VENUES

**Jacksonville Veterans Memorial Arena.** The 16,000-seat arena hosts major concerts and sporting events. ✉ *300 A. Philip Randolph Blvd.* ☎ *904/630–3900.*

**Times-Union Center for the Performing Arts.** The biggest rock concerts are held in Jacksonville Veterans Memorial Arena, and the next biggest shows—as well as touring Broadway productions—are held here. ✉ *300 W. Water St.* ☎ *904/633–6110.*

Jacksonville Symphony Orchestra. The Times-Union Center's Jacoby Music Hall is home to the city's symphony orchestra, which also gives outdoor concerts at downtown's Metro Park. ☎ *904/354–5547.*

FCCJ Artist Series. Northeast Florida's major presenter of professional national and international touring attractions is responsible for bringing Broadway shows—among other things—to the Times-Union Center's Moran Theater. ✉ *501 W. State St.* ☎ *904/632–3373.*

### THEATERS

**Florida Theatre.** This 1920s theater presents concerts, dance productions, and special events, as well as a classic-movie series. ✉ *128 E. Forsyth St.* ☎ *904/355–2787.*

## DID YOU KNOW?

The Jacksonville Jazz Festival takes place within a five-block area centered around Laura Street in the heart of downtown. Festival highlights include performances by renowned jazz musicians and jazz piano and youth jazz talent competitions.

**Ritz Theatre.** Dubbed "the Harlem of the South" in the 1920s, historic La Villa is the site of the Ritz, which hosts musical and theatrical events of particular interest to the African-American community. ⊠ *829 N. Davis St.* ☎ *904/632–5555.*

**Theatre Jacksonville.** One of the oldest continuously operating community theaters in the United States, Theatre Jacksonville presents outstanding productions ranging from Shakespeare to programs for children. ⊠ *2032 San Marco Blvd.* ☎ *904/396–4425.*

## NIGHTLIFE

**Comedy Zone.** The area's premier comedy club is inside the Ramada Inn Mandarin. ⊠ *3130 Hartley Rd.* ☎ *904/292–4242* ⊕ *www.comedyzone. com.*

**Eclipse.** This dance club serves up a mix of moods and music styles for the twentysomething set. ⊠ *4219 St. Johns Ave.* ☎ *904/387–3582.*

**The Grotto.** Wine snobs, rejoice! Here you can enjoy more than 70 wines by the glass. ⊠ *2012 San Marco Blvd.* ☎ *904/398–0726* ⊕ *www. grottowine.com.*

**Harmonious Monks.** This place claims to have "the world's most talented waitstaff." They certainly might be the most energetic, performing throughout the night and encouraging customers to dance on the bar. ⊠ *10550 Old St. Augustine Rd.* ☎ *904/880–3040.*

**Jack Rabbits.** It's the place to catch the latest and greatest indie bands and budding rock stars. ⊠ *1528 Hendricks Ave.* ☎ *904/398–7496* ⊕ *www. jackrabbitsonline.com.*

**Latitude 30.** Latitude 30 could be called a pleasure-complex, offering "luxury bowling," game arcade, billiards, casual restaurants, sports bars, "cinegrille" movie screening rooms and more, all at one 45,000 square foot facility. ⊠ *10370 Phillips Hwy., Southside* ☎ *904/365–5555* ⊕ *www.latthirty.com* ✉ *No admission at door; bowling $4–$5 game; others vary* ☉ *Thurs.–Sat. 11 am–2 am, Sun. 11 am–midnight.*

**Mark's.** This self-proclaimed "neighborhood lounge with a dash of dance club style" attracts beautiful people for theme nights like Indie Lounge Tuesdays. ⊠ *315 E. Bay St.* ☎ *904/355–5099* ⊕ *www.marksjax.com.*

**Metro.** It's more than just a gay bar: it's like seven gay bars rolled into one, including a piano bar, dance club, lounge, and drag-show cabaret. ⊠ *2929 Plum St.* ☎ *904/388–8719* ⊕ *www.metrojax.com.*

**Plush.** At 12,000 square feet, Plush is certainly Jacksonville's largest nightclub. It's also the loudest. ⊠ *845 University Blvd. N* ☎ *904/743– 1845* ⊕ *plushjax.com.*

**Square One.** The upscale singles' scene here is complemented by live music on weekends. ⊠ *1974 San Marco Blvd.* ☎ *904/306–9004.*

**TSI.** Billing itself as the city's premier underground venue, TSI hosts local and national indie bands like Bonde do Role, VHS or Beta, the Death Set, and Black Kids. ⊠ *333 E. Bay St.* ☎ *904/424–3531* ⊕ *www. clubtsi.com.*

**Twisted Martini.** This glitzy meat market is complete with designer martinis, chichi bar food, and a VIP area with bottle service. It also has live music, hosting stars like Colbie Caillat. ⊠ *Jacksonville Landing, 2 Independent Dr.* ☎ *904/353–8464* ⊕ *www.thetwistedmartini.com.*

## WHERE TO EAT

**$**

AMERICAN

★

✕ **bb's.** Sleek yet cozy, this hip bistro is as popular with corporate muckety-mucks looking to close a deal as it is with young lovebirds seemingly on the verge of popping the question (though shouting the question might be more appropriate, considering how loud the dining room can get on weekends). The concrete floors and a stainless-steel wine bar provide an interesting backdrop for comfort-food-inspired entrées and daily specials that might include char-grilled beef tenderloin, prosciutto-wrapped pork chops, or mushroom *triangoli* (triangle) ravioli. On the lighter side, grilled pizzas, sandwiches, and salads, especially warm goat-cheese salad, are favorites. Although a wait is practically guaranteed, you can pass the time sizing up the display of diet-destroying desserts. ⊠ *1019 Hendricks Ave., Southbank* ☎ *904/306–0100* ⊕ *www. bbsrestaurant.com* ⊘ *Closed Sun.*

**¢**

AMERICAN

✕ **Biscottis.** The local artwork on the redbrick walls is a mild distraction from the jovial yuppies, soccer moms, and metrosexuals—all of whom are among the crowd jockeying for tables in this midsize restaurant. Elbows almost touch, but no one seems to mind. The menu offers the unexpected: wild mushroom ravioli with a broth of corn, leek, and dried apricot; or curry-grilled swordfish with cucumber-fig bordelaise sauce. Be sure to sample from Biscottis's decadent dessert case (we hear the peanut butter ganache is illegal in three states). Brunch, a local favorite, is served until 3 on weekends. ⊠ *3556 St. Johns Ave., Avondale* ☎ *904/387–2060* ⊕ *www.biscottis.net* ⌂ *Reservations not accepted.*

**$$$**

ECLECTIC

✕ **Bistro Aix.** When a Jacksonville restaurant can make Angelinos feel like they haven't left home, that's saying a lot. With its slick black-leather booths, 1940s brickwork, velvet drapes, and intricate marbled globes, Bistro Aix (pronounced "X") is just that place. Regulars can't get enough of the creamy onion soup, crispy calamari, and house-made potato chips with warm blue-cheese appetizers or entrées like oak-fired fish Aixoise, grilled salmon, and filet mignon. Adventurous diners can sample diverse dishes on a prix-fixe menu for $29. Aix's resident pastry chef ensures no sweet tooth leaves unsatisfied. For the most part, wait-staff are knowledgeable and pleasant, though some patrons find their demeanor snooty, except, of course, the ones from L.A. Call for preferred seating. ⊠ *1440 San Marco Blvd., San Marco* ☎ *904/398–1949* ⊕ *www.bistrox.com* ⊘ *No lunch weekends.*

**$–$$**

SEAFOOD

✕ **Clark's Fish Camp.** It's out of the way and hard to find, but every mile and missed turn will be forgotten once you step inside this former bait shop overlooking Julington Creek. Clark's has more than 160 appetizers and entrées, including the usual—shrimp, catfish, and oysters—and the unusual—ostrich, rattlesnake, and kangaroo. In keeping with the more bizarre entrées is the decor, best described as early American taxidermy: hundreds of stuffed critters gaze upon you in the main dining room, and preserved lions, gazelles, baboons, even a rhino, keep a watchful eye in the bar. One person's kitschy may be another's creepy. Be careful not to park illegally—tickets are expensive. ⊠ *12903 Hood*

*Landing Rd., Mandarin* ☎ *904/268–3474* ⊕ *www.clarksfishcamp.com* ⊙ *No lunch weekdays.*

¢ ✕ **European Street Café.** Wicker baskets and lofty shelves brimming with
AMERICAN European confections and groceries like Toblerone and Nutella fill
★ practically every inch of space not occupied by café tables. The menu
is similarly overloaded, with nearly 100 deli sandwiches and salads.
Notable are raspberry-almond chicken salad and the "Blue Max," with
pastrami, corned beef, Swiss cheese, sauerkraut, hot mustard, and blue-
cheese dressing. This quirky spot is favored by area professionals looking for a quick lunch, as well as the under-forty set doing 23-ounce curls
with one of the restaurant's 20-plus beers on tap (plus more than 100 in
bottles). The San Marco and Beach Boulevard locations offer live music
Thursday and Saturday nights, respectively. ✉ *2753 Park St., Riverside*
☎ *904/384–9999* ✉ *1704 San Marco Blvd., Marco* ☎ *904/398–9500*
✉ *5500 Beach Blvd., Southside* ☎ *904/398–1717* ≈ *Reservations not
accepted.*

$$$ ✕ **Matthew's.** Local foodies sing chef Matthew Medure's praises not
ECLECTIC only for his culinary creativity but also his dazzling presentation, which
Fodor's Choice stands out quite strikingly against the very spare interior of stainless
★ steel, polished bronze, and terrazzo flooring. The menu changes nightly,
but might include lemon-roasted Amish chicken with honey-truffle spa-
ghetti squash, or herb-roasted rack of lamb with mustard-pistachio
crust. Complement your meal with one of 450 wines (topping out at
more than $1,000 per bottle), then dive into one of the warm souf-
flés for dessert. ✉ *2107 Hendricks Ave., San Marco* ☎ *904/396–9922*
⊙ *Closed Sun. No lunch.*

$ ✕ **Sticky Fingers.** In the South, barbecue joints are a dime a dozen, yet
SOUTHERN this chain smokehouse manages to stand out year after year. Perhaps it's
the atypical environment—meals are served on real dishes rather than
paper plates, soft lighting replaces harsh fluorescents, and B.B. King
plays in the background instead of Tim McGraw. Maybe it's because
the staff go out of their way to make sure you're satisfied. Probably, it's
the classic, Memphis-style smoked ribs, slow-cooked over aged hickory
and available in five versions, including Memphis-style dry, Tennessee
whiskey, and Carolina sweet. A full bar sweetens the deal. ✉ *8129 Point
Meadows Way, Southside* ☎ *904/493–7427* ⊕ *www.stickyfingers.com*
✉ *13150 City Station Dr., Northside* ☎ *904/309–7427.*

## WHERE TO STAY

*For expanded hotel reviews, visit Fodors.com.*

$ ⊡ **Hotel Indigo.** Despite the name, don't expect this Southside hotel to
HOTEL be moody and blue: it's bright, bold, and visually different from any
other Jacksonville property. **Pros:** reasonable rates; free Wi-Fi through-
out; 24-hour business center; loaner PC; rental car desk. **Cons:** wood
floors can be noisy; convenient to business parks but not downtown
and its sights; rush hour in this area is the worst. ✉ *9840 Tapestry
Park Circle, Southside* ☎ *904/996–7199 or 877/270–1392* ⊕ *www.
hotelindigo.com* ⇥ *96 rooms, 4 suites* ⌂ *In-room: a/c, Wi-Fi. In-hotel:*

*restaurant, bar, pool, gym, laundry facilities, business center, parking, some pets allowed.*

**$$**
**B&B/INN**
☒ **House on Cherry Street.** Guests of this early-20th-century Avondale inn rave about its gracious and fascinating hostess, owner Victoria Freeman, who bends over backward to make every stay memorable. **Pros:** riverfront location; warm hospitality; afternoon tea; evening cocktails. **Cons:** only four rooms, all on 2nd floor; no in-room phones; closed April through September. ☒ *1844 Cherry St.* ☎ *904/384–1999* ⊕ *www. houseoncherry.com* ⤴ *4 rooms* ♿ *In-room: Wi-Fi. In-hotel: parking, some age restrictions* ⑂ *Breakfast.*

**$$**
**HOTEL**
☒ **Hyatt Regency Jacksonville Riverfront.** It doesn't get much more convenient than this 19-story, downtown, waterfront hotel within walking distance of Jacksonville Landing, Florida Theatre, Times-Union Center, corporate office towers, and the county courthouse. **Pros:** riverfront location; rooftop pool and gym; free Wi-Fi in public areas; 24-hour business center; hypoallergenic rooms available. **Cons:** not all rooms are riverfront; slow valet service; no minibars; no in-room Wi-Fi or high-speed Internet. ☒ *225 Coastline Dr.* ☎ *904/588–1234* ⊕ *www. jacksonville.hyatt.com* ⤴ *963 rooms, 21 suites* ♿ *In-room: Internet. In-hotel: restaurants, bar, pool, gym, laundry facilities, parking, some pets allowed.*

**$$$**
**B&B/INN**
★
☒ **The Inn at Oak Street.** This romantic bed-and-breakfast may have been constructed in 1902, but it's up-to-date when it needs to be: free Wi-Fi, whirlpool tubs, and a laptop station just in case you left your i-Book at home. **Pros:** spa room with dry sauna; personal chef available; meticulously clean; walking distance to restaurants; wine and refreshments each evening. **Cons:** hardwood floors can be noisy; not for families with small children; no pool. ☒ *2114 Oak St.* ☎ *904/379–5525* ⊕ *www. innatoakstreet.com* ⤴ *6 rooms, 1 suite* ♿ *In-room: Internet. In-hotel: gym, parking, some age restrictions* ⑂ *Breakfast.*

**$$**
**HOTEL**
★
☒ **Omni Jacksonville Hotel.** Spacious guest rooms in Jacksonville's most luxurious and glamorous hotel are decorated in a chic urban style (think neutral grays and creams, dark wood, stainless steel) and have flatscreen TVs. **Pros:** four-diamond on-site restaurant; downtown location; large rooms; rooftop pool; great kids offerings. **Cons:** congested valet area; restaurant pricey; can be chaotic when there's a show at the Times-Union Center across the street. ☒ *245 Water St.* ☎ *904/355–6664 or 800/843–6664* ⊕ *www.omnijacksonville.com* ⤴ *354 rooms, 4 2-bedroom suites* ♿ *In-room: kitchen (some), Wi-Fi. In-hotel: restaurant, bar, pool, gym, parking, some pets allowed.*

**$$$**
**B&B/INN**
☒ **Riverdale Inn.** In the early 1900s, Jacksonville's wealthiest residents built mansions along Riverside Avenue—dubbed the Row—and the three-story Riverdale Inn is only one of two such homes remaining. **Pros:** on-site restaurant and pub; close to area restaurants and shops; private baths. **Cons:** small rooms; restaurant and pub can be noisy; limited parking. ☒ *1521 Riverside Ave.* ☎ *904/354–5080* ⊕ *www.riverdaleinn. com* ⤴ *7 rooms, 3 suites* ♿ *In-room: Wi-Fi. In-hotel: restaurant, bar, parking, some pets allowed, some age restrictions* ⑂ *Breakfast.*

**$**
**B&B/INN**
☒ **The St. Johns House.** You can enjoy the grace and elegance of the past and all the modern amenities at this surprisingly inexpensive

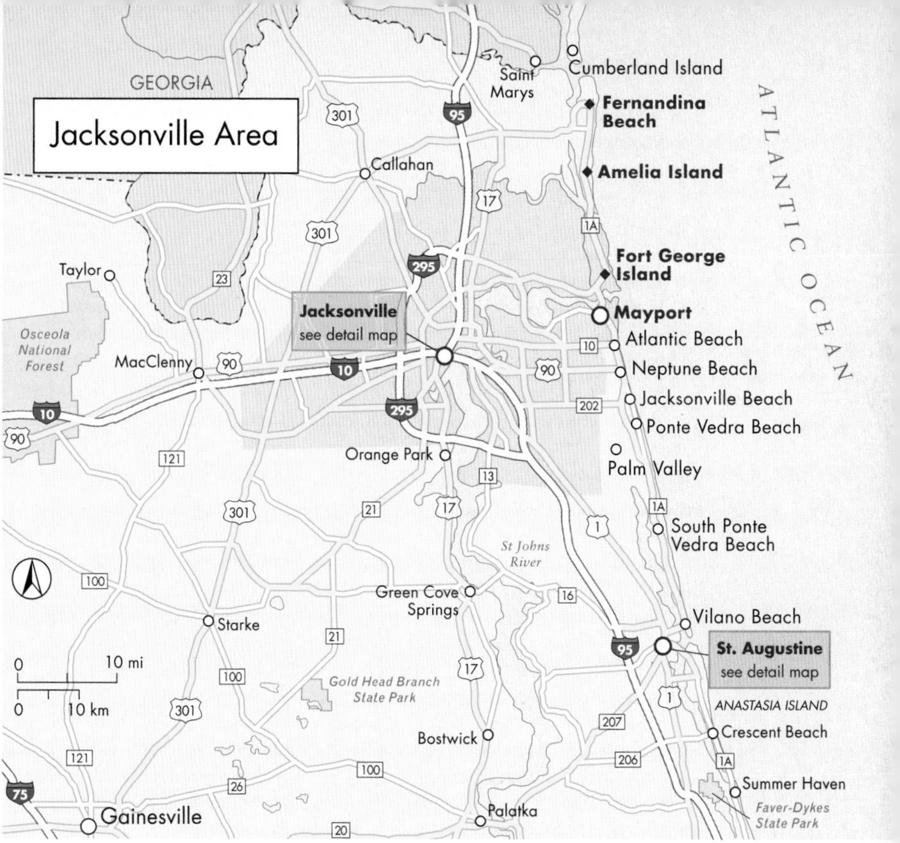


B&B. **Pros:** historic home; beautiful Riverside location near parks, restaurants and river; elegant antique furnishings. **Cons:** only open six months a year. ✉ *1718 Osceola St., Riverside* ☎ *904/384–2724* 🌐 *www.stjohnshousebb.com* *3 rooms* *In-room: a/c, Wi-Fi. In-hotel: parking* ⏲ *Closed Apr.–Oct.* 🍽 *Breakfast.*

## JACKSONVILLE AREA

### JACKSONVILLE BEACHES

*20 mi east of Jacksonville, on U.S. 90 (Beach Blvd.).*

Perhaps because the Intracoastal Waterway isn't all that wide where it separates the mainland from the beaches, people here aren't likely to think of themselves as "islanders." But they are, indeed, living on a barrier island, functioning with its own rhythms and led by its own elected officials. And, while there's only one island, there are four beaches/beach communities each with its own mayor and city officials, tax base, and local legislation. They are, from north to south: Atlantic Beach, Neptune Beach, Jacksonville Beach, and Ponte Vedra Beach. Technically, Ponte Vedra is just across the border between Duval County and St. Johns County, but the four communities are all considered "Jacksonville's beaches."

Although oceanfront properties here can be worth millions, a few blocks from the beach, things become more affordable. That means kids here grow up and go to school together, and then stick around to live in and govern the towns together. Instead of pouring money into attractions designed to rake in tourism dollars, locals are likely to concentrate on stodgy subjects like good schools and parks. Because of this some visitors might find area beaches here to be a little calmer and quieter than they expected.

But there's a real sense of community here—that and a laid-back pace. You might want to embrace it all. In fact, many vacationers like the easy pace so much that they decide to make the area their permanent home.

## EXPLORING

**Adventure Landing and Shipwreck Island Water Park.** With go-karts, two miniature-golf courses, laser tag, batting cages, kiddie rides, and an arcade, Adventure Landing is more like an old-time boardwalk than a high-tech amusement park. But when the closest theme park is more than two hours away, you make do. The largest family-entertainment center in northeast Florida also encompasses Shipwreck Island Water Park, which features a lazy river for tubing, a 500,000-gallon wave pool, and three extreme slides—the Rage, HydroHalfpipe, and Eye of the Storm. ⊠ *1944 Beach Blvd., Jacksonville Beach* ☎ *904/246–4386* ⊕ *www.adventurelanding.com* ⌨ *Adventure Landing free (fees for rides and games), Shipwreck Island $27.99* ☉ *Adventure Landing: Mon.– Thurs. and Sun. 10 am–10 pm, Fri. and Sat. 10 am–midnight; Shipwreck Island: call, hrs vary; Shipwreck Island closed late Sept.–late Mar.*

**Beaches Historical Museum.** This museum has exhibits about the history of the beaches communities, the St. Johns River, the fishing and shrimping industry, the area's settlers, and more. Its gift shop is a good place to find Florida souvenirs of every variety, from tasteful to pure kitsch. Admission here includes a guided tour of the adjacent Pablo Historical Park with its 1911 steam locomotive, railroad foreman's house, and the Mayport Depot. ⊠ *380 Pablo Ave., Jacksonville Beach* ☎ *904/241–5657* ⊕ *www.beachesareahistoricalsociety.com* ⌨ *$5* ☉ *Tues.–Sat. 10–4:30.*

**J. Johnson Gallery.** Built by photographer and art collector Jennifer Johnson, this stunning Mediterranean building just a block from the ocean in Jacksonville Beach hosts contemporary art exhibits you'd expect to find only in the nation's largest and most sophisticated cities. Exhibits like "Miami: Visions of Now" and "Contemporary China" include work by emerging artists as well as established names. The gallery also presents experimental and project work. ⊠ *177 4th Ave. N, Jacksonville Beach* ☎ *904/435–3200* ⊕ *www.jjohnsongallery.com* ⌨ *Free* ☉ *Tues.– Fri. 10–5, Sat. noon–5.*

## SPORTS AND THE OUTDOORS
### BIKING
**Champion Cycling.** Here you can rent beach cruisers by the hour and by the day. ⊠ *1303 N. 3rd St., Jacksonville Beach* ☎ *904/241–0900.*

Beaches make great places to drop a line and see if the fish are biting.

**Ponte Vedra Bicycles.** This outfitter includes free bike maps with your rental. ✉ *250 Solana Rd., Ponte Vedra Beach* ☎ *904/273-0199.*

## GOLF

Every May millions of golf fans are riveted to the TV, watching golf's most elite competitors vie for the prestige of winning THE PLAYERS Championship. The event—considered by many to be the sport's "unofficial fifth major"—takes place each year at the Tournament Players Club (TPC) Sawgrass in Ponte Vedra Beach, 20 mi southeast of Jacksonville. Designed and built for major tournament golf, its elevated seating area gives more than 40,000 fans a great view of the action. There's also a fine second course designed by Pete Dye.

**Tournament Players Club Sawgrass.** In conjunction with the Sawgrass Resort & Spa at Marriott, TPC offers packages like the Ultimate Tour: not only does it give you access to the player area of the TPC, but you get your own caddie, who proudly wears your name on the back of his golf shirt just like he does when caddying for the pros—how cool is that? If you just want to play a round of golf and aren't staying at the Marriott, check out the Resort Day Passes. And while you're in the area, be sure to visit the World Golf Hall of Fame a few miles down the road in St. Augustine. ✉ *1000 PGA Tour Blvd., Ponte Vedra Beach* ☎ *904/273-3235 or 800/457-GOLF* ⊕ *www.tpc.com/tpc-sawgrass.*

## SHOPPING

**The Book Mark.** It may be small in size but this book shop is big in prestige. Thanks to its knowledgeable owners, many famous authors love this place and always include it on their publicity tours. Once you've bought books here a time or two, the staff will be able to recommend books you'll like with an amazing accuracy. ⊠ *220 1st St., Atlantic Beach* ☎ *904/241–9026* ⊘ *Mon.–Wed. 10–7, Thurs.–Sat. 10–8, Sun. 11–5.*

## NIGHTLIFE

### JACKSONVILLE BEACH

**The Atlantic.** During the week, it's a groovy, low-key lounge. On weekends, it's jam-packed with twentysomethings. ⊠ *333 N. 1st St., Jacksonville Beach* ☎ *904/249–3338.*

**Fionn MacCool's.** This is, first and foremost, an Irish pub, but its menu is nothing to shake a shillelagh at. ⊠ *333 N. 1st St., Suite 150, Jacksonville Beach* ☎ *904/242–9499.*

**Free Bird Live.** This medium-size (it holds 700) concert venue owned by Judy Van Zant, (widow of Lynyrd Skynyrd's Ronnie Van Zant) draws some complaints about its standing-room-only tickets and slow bar service. But it also gets raves for the chance to see great blues, rock, funk, rockabilly and jam bands in an intimate setting. ⊠ *200 1st St. N, Jacksonville Beach* ☎ *904/246–2473* ⊕ *www.freebirdlive.com* ✍ *Admission varies by show* ⊘ *8 pm–2 am show days only.*

**Lynch's Irish Pub.** Hoist a pint o' Guinness and sing along with Emerald Isle troubadours. ⊠ *514 N. 1st St., Jacksonville Beach* ☎ *904/249–5181.*

**Ocean Club.** The beautiful people come here for dancing, flirting, and drinking—not necessarily in that order. ⊠ *401 N. 1st St., Jacksonville Beach* ☎ *904/242–8884.*

**Penthouse Lounge.** If you'd rather gawk at sports stars in person than on the tube, head to this oceanfront spot, where local NFL and PGA stars have been known to congregate. ⊠ *Casa Marina Hotel, 691 N. 1st St., Jacksonville Beach* ☎ *904/270–0025.*

**Sneakers Sports Grille.** With nearly 80 TVs and an impressive menu (by sports-bar standards anyway), this is the go-to sports bar at the beach. ⊠ *111 Beach Blvd., Jacksonville Beach* ☎ *904/482–1000.*

### NEPTUNE BEACH

**Pete's Bar.** The oldest bar in the Jacksonville area is also notable for the cheapest drinks, cheapest pool tables, and the most colorful clientele. ⊠ *117 1st St., Neptune Beach* ☎ *904/249–9158.*

**Sun Dog Steak & Seafood.** Entertainment here often includes acoustic guitarists. ⊠ *207 Atlantic Blvd.* ☎ *904/241–8221.*

## WHERE TO EAT

### ATLANTIC BEACH

$
SEAFOOD
✕ **The Fish Company Restaurant and Seafood Market.** If you want fresh fish, this is the place. Owners Bill and Ann Pinner have lots of street cred: among other area culinary achievements, they helped establish the Ragtime Tavern as an institution. Options include perfectly blended crab cakes, oh-so-lightly fried Mayport shrimp (never a heavy batter that might cover up the flavor), seafood salads, and delicious sides. And there are offerings for meat lovers in the family, too. There's also a raw bar, outdoor seating, and a full drinks bar with happy-hour prices 2–7 Monday through Saturday and all day on Sunday. ⊠ *Atlantic Blvd., Atlantic Beach* ☎ *904/246-0123* ⊕ *www.thefishcojax.com* ✍ *Reservations not accepted* ⊘ *Mon.–Thurs. 11–9, Fri. and Sat. 11–10, Sun. 11–9.*

**$$$**
ECLECTIC
Fodor's Choice
★

✕ **Ocean 60**. Despite being a block from the Atlantic Ocean, this lively restaurant–wine bar–martini room has gone largely undiscovered by visitors, who might think fine dining and flip-flops don't mix. Those who do stumble upon it, however, are pleasantly surprised to find that a casual aura befits Ocean 60's eclectic seasonal menu, with signature items like walnut-grilled salmon and Mayport prawns, Kona-coffee-grilled rack of lamb, and Buddha's Delight (vegetables sautéed with cellophane noodles and Thai coconut and Kaffir lime broth). Things are anything but laid-back on Friday and Saturday nights, however, thanks to live music and potent cocktails. ⊠ *60 Ocean Blvd., Atlantic Beach* ☎ *904/247–0060* ⊕ *www.ocean60.com* ⊗ *Closed Sun.*

**$$**
AMERICAN
★

✕ **Ragtime Tavern & Seafood Grill**. A New Orleans theme prevails at this loud place that attracts a lively crowd ranging in age from 21 to midlife crisis. Bayou bouillabaisse (lobster, shrimp, scallops, fish, crab, clams, and crawfish in a creole-court bouillon) and Ragtime shrimp (deep-fried fresh shrimp rolled in coconut) are specialties (as are microbrews made on the premises), or try a po'boy sandwich or fish sizzled on the grill. ⊠ *207 Atlantic Blvd., Atlantic Beach* ☎ *904/241–7877* ⊕ *www. ragtimetavern.com* ⌲ *Reservations not accepted.*

**$**
SOUTHERN

✕ **Sticky Fingers**. Like its counterpart across the ditch (beach-speak for the Intracoastal Waterway), the Atlantic Beach location of this über-popular barbecue joint is known for its inviting atmosphere, perky staff, and spectacular service. Oh, yeah, and some people really seem to like the ribs, too. Slow cooked over aged hickory, the ribs come in five versions, including Memphis-style dry, Tennessee whiskey, and Carolina sweet. The hickory-smoked chicken wings are arguably the best wings in town. ⊠ *363 Atlantic Blvd. #1, Atlantic Beach* ☎ *904/241–7427* ⊕ *www.stickyfingers.com* r*Reservations not accepted.*

## JACKSONVILLE BEACH

**¢**
AMERICAN
☺

✕ **Ellen's Kitchen**. Once upon a time, Ellen's Kitchen was a breakfast and lunch place inside Silver's Drug Store at First and Atlantic, a landmark from time immemorial. Silver's is no more, and Ellen's long ago relocated to a shopping strip, but it's still an institution, and probably will be for generations. It's also a great place to bring the kids, thanks to the kid-friendly menu, very reasonable prices, and relaxed atmosphere. Sure, you can get your eggs over easy and your bacon crisp, but if you want to be mistaken for a local, ask for a Hippie or a Surfer, two poached-egg-on-English-muffin creations that are far better than anybody's eggs Benedict. If it's hollandaise sauce you're craving, though, the crab cake Benedict is brunch perfection. Breakfast is served until the doors close at 2 pm, but the lunch menu is also fairly extensive. Don't expect too much chat from your server at "rush hour" on weekend mornings—everyone's usually working at warp speed. Regardless, though, the staffers do their best to please, no matter how crowded. ⊠ *1824 3rd St. S, Jacksonville Beach* ☎ *904/246–1572* ⌲ *Reservations not accepted* ⊗ *Mon.–Sun. 7 am–2 pm. No dinner.*

**¢**
AMERICAN

✕ **European Street Café**. After more than 25 years of dominance in Jacksonville, this colorful, quirky, family-owned eatery has finally landed a location at the beach. The menu has an ambitious list of sandwiches, salads, and soups; an overflowing gourmet-food section;

a mind-boggling beer list; and cookies big enough to knock someone unconscious. Thirsty locals belly up to the impressive, hand-carved bar for monthly beer tastings and daily happy hour (2–7 pm). The more mature crowds prefer to sip their zinfandel in the bustling dining room. ⊠ *992 Beach Blvd.* ☎ *904/249–3001* ⌲ *Reservations not accepted.*

$    ✕ **Mambo's Cuban Bistro.** So you think you can't dance? Don't let that
CUBAN    stop you from checking out the Salsa Sundays at Mambo's Cuban Bis-
☺    tro. In addition to authentic Cuban cuisine seven days a week, Mambo's offers live music and free dance lessons some evenings. Mambo's draws raves from a mix of the young and the restless, who love the live music and dancing, and families, who insist that even Miami doesn't offer better Cuban cuisine. The mojitos from the full bar are lauded, too. But the highest praise goes to the desserts from *tres leches* cake (cake soaked in evaporated milk, condensed milk, and heavy cream) to guava flan. ⊠ *311 3rd St. N, Beaches, Jacksonville Beach* ☎ *904/853–6360* ⊕ *www. mamboscubanbistro.com* ⌲ *Reservations not accepted.*

$    ✕ **Mojo's Kitchen BBQ Pit & Blues Bar.** True barbecue aficionados know
BARBECUE    that the country's really divided into four territories: North Carolina, Memphis, Kansas City, and Texas, each renowned for its own barbecue style. Owner Todd Lineberry did some serious research into each region before deciding his restaurants would honor all four traditions—along with some original flavor. In addition to great barbecue, you'll find Deep South sides like cheese grits and fried green tomatoes as well as some truly delicious sweet tea and banana pudding. The beach location means you'll find both young and old, blue collar and no-collar (plus puka-shells), all ready to chow down to generous portions, with a backdrop of bright, bold-color walls and edgy portraits of blues royalty. Mojo's appreciation for the blues doesn't end with the interior design. You'll find good recorded blues at all times, and on occasion, some great live blues as well. ⊠ *1500 Beach Blvd., Beaches, Jacksonville Beach* ☎ *904/247–6636* ⊕ *www.mojobbq.com* ⌲ *Reservations not accepted.*

### PONTE VEDRA BEACH

$$$    ✕ **The Augustine Grill.** The atmosphere at this Sawgrass Marriott restau-
NEW AMERICAN    rant is polished but informal, the service is attentive but not intrusive,
Fodor's Choice    and the menu is exquisite Executive chef David Scalise and chef de cui-
★    sine Brett Smith subscribe to the farm-to-table philosophy that focuses on sourcing food from regional farms and dairies. You can order an old favorite (for many, that means steak, both wet-aged and dry-aged on-site) or experiment with small-plate tasting combinations. Options include Mayport shrimp with grit cakes and greens; pork belly with red peas; andouille sausage; quail; gourmet mac and cheese; and tuna tartare. If you're feeling truly adventurous, put yourself into the chef's hands with their five-course tasting menu to which you can also add wine pairings. ⊠ *1000 PGA Tour Blvd., Ponte Vedra Beach* ☎ *800/416–7067* ⌲ *Reservations essential* ⊘ *No lunch. Closed Sun.*

**WHERE TO STAY**

*For expanded hotel reviews, visit Fodors.com.*

### ATLANTIC BEACH

**$$$** 🏨 **One Ocean.** Atlantic Beach's only high-rise oceanfront hotel captures
RESORT the serenity of the ocean through a color palette of sea-foam green, sand, and sky blue, and reflective materials like glass and marble. **Pros:** exceptional service; walking distance to restaurants and shops; all rooms have ocean view; 24-hour room service. **Cons:** tiny bathroom; no self-parking on property; resort fee. ☒ *1 Ocean Blvd.* ☎ *904/249–7402* ⊕ *www.oneoceanresort.com* ⮑ *190 rooms, 3 suites* ⚷ *In-room: Wi-Fi. In-hotel: restaurants, bar, pool, gym, spa, beach, children's programs, parking, some pets allowed.*

### JACKSONVILLE BEACH

**$$$** 🏨 **Casa Marina Hotel.** Compared with nearby oceanfront inns, it's small,
B&B/INN but Casa Marina's creature comforts and rich history—including hosting Franklin Delano Roosevelt and Al Capone in its early days—make it a hit with those looking for a peaceful, characterful retreat. **Pros:** oceanfront location; comfortable beds; continental breakfast, good alternative to chain hotels. **Cons:** no pool; inconsistent restaurant hours; room service only on weekends. ☒ *691 1st St. N* ☎ *904/270–0025* ⊕ *www. casamarinahotel.com* ⮑ *7 rooms, 16 suites* ⚷ *In-hotel: restaurants, bars, beach, parking* ❑ *Breakfast.*

### NEPTUNE BEACH

**$$** 🏨 **Sea Horse Oceanfront Inn.** This bright-pink-and-aqua '50s throwback
HOTEL caters to budget-minded guests seeking an ultracasual, laid-back vibe. **Pros:** beach access with private walk-over; popular bar on-site; walking distance to restaurants and shops; free breakfast baskets available at front desk. **Cons:** no-frills; no room service. ☒ *120 Atlantic Blvd.* ☎ *904/246–2175 or 800/881–2330* ⊕ *www.seahorseoceanfrontinn.com* ⮑ *39 rooms, 1 suite* ⚷ *In-room: kitchen, Wi-Fi. In-hotel: bar, pool, beach, parking.*

### PONTE VEDRA BEACH

**$$$$** 🏨 **The Lodge & Club.** This Mediterranean-revival oceanfront resort—with
RESORT its white-stucco exterior and Spanish roof tiles—is luxury lodging at its
Fodor'sChoice best. **Pros:** high-end accommodations; excellent service; private beach.
★ **Cons:** nonvalet parking—can be a hike to and from car; most recreation facilities are a few blocks away at Ponte Vedra Inn & Club; $18 gratuity charge automatically added to bill nightly. ☒ *607 Ponte Vedra Blvd.* ☎ *904/273–9500 or 800/243–4304* ⊕ *www.pvresorts.com* ⮑ *42 rooms, 24 suites* ⚷ *In-room: kitchen (some). In-hotel: restaurants, bars, pools, gym, beach, water sports, children's programs, parking.*

**$$$$** 🏨 **Ponte Vedra Inn & Club.** Considered northeast Florida's premier resort
RESORT for decades, this 1928 landmark continues to wow guests with its stel-
Fodor'sChoice lar service and large guest rooms housed in white-brick, Spanish-style
★ buildings lining the beach. **Pros:** accommodating, friendly staff; private beach; adults-only pool. **Cons:** charge for umbrellas and chaises on the beach; crowded pool; $18 gratuity charge automatically added to bill nightly. ☒ *200 Ponte Vedra Blvd.* ☎ *904/285–1111 or 800/234–7842* ⊕ *www.pvresorts.com* ⮑ *205 rooms, 45 suites* ⚷ *In-room: kitchen*

*(some), Wi-Fi. In-hotel: restaurants, bars, golf courses, tennis courts, pool, gym, spa, beach, children's programs, parking.*

**$$$**    ⛳ **Sawgrass Golf Resort & Spa, a Marriott Resort.** Here you can laze about
**RESORT** in the highly regarded spa or by one of four swimming pools, get active out on a golf course, or fish in a freshwater lake or pond. **Pros:** championship golf courses; beautiful surroundings; readily available shuttle; efficient staff. **Cons:** beach not within walking distance; no free parking; fee for in-room Wi-Fi. ⊠ *1000 PGA Tour Blvd.* ☎ *904/285–7777 or 800/457–4653* ⊕ *www.sawgrassmarriott.com* ⤴ *508 rooms, 24 suites, 80 villas* ⌂ *In-room: kitchen (some), Wi-Fi. In-hotel: restaurants, bars, golf course, tennis court, pool, gym, spa, children's programs, laundry facilities, parking, some pets allowed.*

## MAYPORT

*20 mi northeast of downtown Jacksonville, on Rte. A1A/105.*

Dating back more than 300 years, this is one of the oldest fishing communities in the United States. It has several excellent and very casual seafood restaurants and a commercial shrimp-boat fleet. It's also home to one of the largest naval facilities in the country, Naval Station Mayport.

### GETTING HERE AND AROUND

**St. Johns River Ferry.** The arrival of the *Jean Ribault* ferry in 1948 made everyday life here more convenient—and fun. The 153-vessel continues to delight passengers young and old as they embark on the 10-minute cruise across the river between Mayport and Fort George Island. The cost is $3 per motorcycle, $5 per car ($1 additional per axle). Pedestrians enjoy the ride for just $1 each way. Call for departure times. ☎ *904/241–9969* ⊕ *www.stjohnsriverferry.com.*

### EXPLORING

**Fodor's** Choice   **Kathryn Abbey Hanna Park.** This 450-acre oceanfront property just north
★ of Atlantic Beach is filled with spectacular beaches, biking and hiking trails, wooded campsites, and a 60-acre freshwater lake, perfect for swimming, kayaking, and canoeing. The lake area also includes picnic tables, grills, and a quarter-acre water park with fountains and squirting hoses. Throughout the park there are restrooms, showers, and snack bars, open April through Labor Day, as well as lifeguards supervising all water activities during summer. Surfers in the know head to "the poles" for the best wave action in town. The park includes nearly 300 campsites and cabins with fees ranging from $20 to $34 per day. ⊠ *500 Wonderwood Dr.* ☎ *904/249–4700* ⤴ *$3 per vehicle* ☉ *Apr.–Oct., daily 8–8; Nov.–Mar., daily 8–6.*

## FORT GEORGE ISLAND

*25 mi northeast of Jacksonville, on Rte. A1A/105.*

One of the oldest inhabited areas of Florida, Fort George Island is lush with foliage, natural vegetation, and wildlife. A 4-mi nature and bike trail meanders across the island, revealing shell mounds dating as far back as 5,000 years.

**EXPLORING**

**Kingsley Plantation.** Built in 1792 by Zephaniah Kingsley, an eccentric slave trader, this is the oldest remaining cotton plantation in the state. The ruins of 23 tabby (a concretelike mixture of sand and crushed shells) slave houses, a barn, and the modest Kingsley home are open to the public via self-guided tours and reachable by ferry or bridge. ✉ *Rte. A1A–Heckscher Dr., north of St. Johns River Ferry* ☎ *904/251–3537* ⊕ *www.nps.gov/timu/historyculture.kp.htm* ⊠ *Free* ☉ *Daily 9–5; ranger talks daily at 2.*

**Talbot Island State Parks.** The Talbot Island State Parks, including Big and Little Talbot islands, have 17 mi of gorgeous beaches, sand dunes, and golden marshes that hum with birds and native waterfowl. Come to picnic, fish, swim, snorkel, or camp. Little Talbot Island, one of the few undeveloped barrier islands in Florida, has river otters, marsh rabbits, raccoons, alligators, and gopher tortoises. Canoe and kayak rentals are available, and the north area is considered the best surfing spot in northeast Florida. A 4-mi nature trail winds across Little Talbot, and there are several smaller trails on Big Talbot. ✉ *12157 Heckscher Dr.* ☎ *904/251–2320* ⊕ *www.floridastateparks.org/littletalbotisland* ⊠ *$5 per vehicle, up to 8 people; $4 per motorcycle, $2 for pedestrians and bicyclists* ☉ *Daily 8–sundown.*

## AMELIA ISLAND AND FERNANDINA BEACH

*35 mi northeast of Jacksonville.*

At the northeastern-most reach of Florida, Amelia Island has beautiful beaches with enormous sand dunes along its eastern flank, a state park with a Civil War fort, sophisticated restaurants, interesting shops, and accommodations that range from B&Bs to luxury resorts. The town of Fernandina Beach is on the island's northern end; a century ago casinos and brothels thrived here, but those are gone. Today there's little reminder of the town's wild days, though one event comes close: the Isle of Eight Flags Shrimp Festival, held during the first weekend of May in Fernandina.

**ESSENTIALS**

**Visitor Information Amelia Island Tourist Development Council** (✉ *102 Centre St., Fernandina Beach* ☎ *904/277-0717* ⊕ *www.ameliaisland.com*).

**TAKE A TOUR**

**Amelia River Cruises and Charters.** The Cumberland Sound Ferry connects Fernandina Beach to the docks at St. Marys, Georgia. Narrated tours offered by this company glide near the area's marshes, rivers and wilderness beaches. ☎ *904/261–9972 or 877/264-9972* ⊕ *www.ameliarivercruises.com.*

**EXPLORING**

★ **Amelia Island Historic District.** In Fernandina Beach, this district has more than 50 blocks of buildings listed on the National Register of Historic Places; 450 ornate structures built before 1927 offer some of the nation's finest examples of Queen Anne, Victorian, and Italianate homes. Many date from the haven's mid-19th-century glory days. Pick up a self-guided-tour map at the chamber of commerce, in the old train depot—once a stopping point on the first cross-state railroad—and take your time exploring the quaint shops, restaurants, and boutiques that populate the district, especially along Centre Street.

★ **Fort Clinch State Park.** One of the country's best-preserved and most complete 19th-century brick forts, Fort Clinch was built to discourage further British intrusion after the War of 1812 and was occupied in 1863 by the Confederacy; a year later it was retaken by the North. During the Spanish-American War it was reactivated for a brief time, but no battles were ever fought on its grounds (which explains why it's so well preserved). Wander through restored buildings, including furnished barracks, a kitchen, and a repair shop. Living-history reenactments of Civil War garrison life are scheduled throughout the year. The 1,086-acre park surrounding the fort has camping, nature trails, carriage rides, a swimming beach, and surf and pier fishing. Nature buffs will enjoy the variety of flora and fauna, especially since Fort Clinch is the only state park in northeast Florida designated by the Florida Fish and Wildlife Conservation Commission as a viewing destination for the eastern brown pelican, green sea turtle, and loggerhead sea turtle. ✉ *2601 Atlantic Ave.* ☎ *904/277–7274* ⊕ *www.floridastateparks.org/ fortclinch* 🖾 *$6 per vehicle, up to 8 people, $2 pedestrians, bicyclists* ☉ *Daily 8–sundown.*

## BEACH

**Main Beach.** Amelia Island's eastern shore includes this 13-mi stretch of white-sand beach edged with dunes, some 40 feet high. It's one of the few beaches in Florida where horseback riding is allowed.

## SPORTS AND THE OUTDOORS

### HORSEBACK RIDING

**Kelly Seahorse Ranch.** At this ranch within the Amelia Island State Park, you can arrange horseback rides on the beach. ✉ *7500 1st Coast Hwy., Amelia Island* ☎ *904/491–5166* ⊕ *www.kellyranchinc.com.*

### KAYAKING

**Kayak Amelia** (✉ *13030 Heckscher Dr., Amelia Island* ☎ *904/251–0016* ⊕ *www.kayakamelia.com*) takes adventurous types on guided tours of salt marshes and Fort George River and also rents equipment for those looking to create their own adventures. Reservations required.

### NIGHTLIFE

**Falcon's Nest.** The 7,000-square-foot, aviation-themed club in Amelia Island Plantation has a dance floor and outdoor deck. ✉ *6800 1st Coast Hwy.* ☎ *904/261–6161* ⊕ *www.aipfl.com/falconsnest.*

**O'Kane's Irish Pub.** It's St. Patrick's Day every day at O'Kane's. ✉ *318 Centre St.* ☎ *904/261–1000.*

**Palace Saloon.** Florida's oldest continuously operating bar entertained the Rockefellers and Carnegies at the turn of the 20th century but now caters to common folk. It also operates a package store, the only one in downtown Fernandina. ✉ *117 Centre St.* ☎ *904/491–3332.*

**The Surf Restaurant and Bar.** Locals like to congregate on the outdoor deck here for drinks and good old-fashioned bar food (pizza, burgers, wings). ✉ *3199 S. Fletcher Ave.* ☎ *904/261–5711* ⊕ *www.thesurfonline.com.*

## WHERE TO EAT

**$$–$$$**
SEAFOOD
Fodor'sChoice
★

✕ **Beech Street Grill.** Housed in an 1889 sea-captain's house, this highly regarded Fernandina Beach restaurant caters to locals who crave its comfort-food-inspired dishes like tenderloin meat loaf with spinach, ham, and provolone cheese with shiitake-mushroom gravy and chive whipped potatoes, as well as visiting foodies who have heard the quiet buzz about this cozy, coastal, two-story Victorian from afar. Hardwood floors and marble fireplaces aside, one of Beech Street's most treasured fixtures is pianist John "If-you-can-hum-it-I-can-play-it" Springer, who has been entertaining diners for decades. Delicious nightly fish specials and outstanding wine list. ✉ *801 Beech St.* ☎ *904/2773662* ⊕ *www. beechstreetgrill.com* ⌂ *Reservations essential.*

**$$$$**
ECLECTIC
Fodor'sChoice
★

✕ **Salt.** The Ritz-Carlton restaurant's inventive cuisine highlights seasonal ingredients that might include peekytoe crab salad with watermelon and peanuts or Kurobuta pork chop and truffled potato gratin. The wine list has more than 500 bottles (20 by the glass), service is nothing short of impeccable, and there's a view of the Atlantic from every table. For a unique dining experience, reserve A Seat in the Kitchen, a private dining room within the kitchen, where you'll watch the chefs at work and enjoy a personalized five-course meal. To learn the secrets of Salt's cuisine, consider getting into the kitchen with the chefs by taking one of the two-day Salt cooking school sessions—they've proven so popular, the Ritz-Carlton has expanded the offerings to six a year. Collared shirts are recommended (for dining, we mean; cooking students get their own Ritz-Carlton aprons). ✉ *The Ritz-Carlton, 4750 Amelia Island Pkwy.* ☎ *904/277–1028* ⊕ *www.ritzcarlton.com* ⌂ *Reservations essential* ⊘ *Closed Mon. No lunch.*

**$$$**
SEAFOOD

✕ **Verandah Restaurant.** Although it's at the Amelia Island Plantation, this family-friendly restaurant is open to nonresort guests, many of whom drive in from Jacksonville. The dining room has a casual vibe, with floral prints and roomy booths, but the menu is all business. Seafood dishes are a highlight, including red snapper with pecan, crab meunière, pasta paella, and surf-and-turf, as is the "famous" Verandah salad, a meal in itself. And if you luck out and find she-crab soup on the menu (it's seasonal and not always available), order yourself the biggest bowl or bucket they have. ✉ *6800 1st Coast Hwy.* ☎ *904/321–5050* ⊕ *www. aipfl.com/Restaurants/Verandah_Menu.htm* ⊘ *No lunch.*

## WHERE TO STAY

*For expanded hotel reviews, visit Fodors.com.*

**$$$**
HOTEL
♻

🏨 **Amelia Hotel at the Beach.** Across the street from the beach, this midsize inn is not only convenient but an economical and family-friendly alternative to the area's luxury resorts and romantic and kid-unfriendly B&Bs. **Pros:** complimentary breakfast; free Wi-Fi; comfy beds. **Cons:** small pool; not all rooms have balconies; no on-site restaurant. ✉ *1997 S. Fletcher Ave.* ☎ *904/206–5200 or 877/263–5428* ⊕ *www.ameliahotel.com* ⇆ *86*

*rooms* ♿ *In-room: kitchen (some), Wi-Fi. In-hotel: pool, gym, parking* ⫪⦿⫪ *Breakfast.*

**$$$$**
**B&B/INN**
★
⫪⦿⫪ **Elizabeth Pointe Lodge.** Guests at this oceanfront inn, built to resemble an 1890s sea-captain's house, can't say enough about the impeccable personal service, legendary breakfasts, and enjoyable evening social hour. **Pros:** beachfront location; hospitable staff; 24-hour desk attendant; convenient to various recreation possibilities. **Cons:** pricey for a B&B; not all rooms are oceanfront. ✉ *98 S. Fletcher Ave.* ☎ *904/277–4851 or 800/772–3359* ⊕ *www.elizabethpointelodge.com* ⛵ *24 rooms, 1 2-bedroom cottage* ♿ *In-room: kitchen (some), Wi-Fi. In-hotel: beach, laundry facilities, parking* ⫪⦿⫪ *Breakfast.*

**$$$**
**B&B/INN**
⫪⦿⫪ **Florida House Inn.** The rambling two-story clapboard main building, more than 150 years old, is definitely of another era, and is full of character. **Pros:** proximity to Centre Street; free use of scooters; free Wi-Fi. **Cons:** bar can be noisy; loud air-conditioning. ✉ *22 S. 3rd St.* ☎ *904/451–3722 or 800/258–3301* ⊕ *www.floridahouseinn.com* ⛵ *22 rooms, 1 suite, 1 carriage house* ♿ *In-room: Wi-Fi. In-hotel: restaurant, bar, parking, some pets allowed.*

**$$$**
**RESORT**
☯
Fodor'sChoice
★
⫪⦿⫪ **Omni Amelia Island Plantation Resort and the Villas of Amelia Island Plantation.** The emphasis here is family-oriented resort accommodations and activities, including first-rate golf, tennis, and spa facilities. **Pros:** family-friendly; variety of outdoor activities; shuttle service throughout property. **Cons:** far removed from facilities (golf course, shops, tennis courts); quality of villas inconsistent; a hike to some hotel rooms. ✉ *6800 1st Coast Hwy.* ☎ *904/261–6161 or 800/843–6664* ⊕ *www.aipfl.com* ⛵ *249 rooms, 361 1-, 2-, and 3-bedroom villas* ♿ *In-room: kitchen (some). In-hotel: restaurants, bars, golf courses, tennis courts, pools, gym, spa, beach, water sports, children's programs, laundry facilities, some pets allowed.*

**$$$$**
**RESORT**
☯
Fodor'sChoice
★
⫪⦿⫪ **The Ritz-Carlton, Amelia Island.** Guests know what to expect from the Ritz—elegance, superb comfort, excellent service—and the Amelia Island location is no exception. **Pros:** fine-dining restaurant; world-class spa; private beach access; accommodating staff; great programs, activities, and amenities for kids, teens, and families. **Cons:** fee for Wi-Fi; no self-parking ($17 per day valet); lack of nightlife; a drive to sites and other restaurants. ✉ *4750 Amelia Island Pkwy.* ☎ *904/277–1100* ⊕ *www.ritzcarlton.com/ameliaisland* ⛵ *444 rooms, 44 suites* ♿ *In-room: safe, Wi-Fi. In-hotel: restaurants, bars, golf course, tennis courts, pools, gym, spa, beach, children's programs.*

---

**A BANNER BEACH**

Fernandina Beach is also known as the "Isle of Eight Flags," a moniker derived from the fact that it is the only American site to have been under eight different flags (French, Spanish, British, Patriots, Green Cross of Florida, Mexican Revolutionary Flag, National Flag of the Confederacy, and United States). Every May the Isle of Eight Flags Shrimp Festival also celebrates another of Fernandina's claims to fame: birthplace of the modern shrimping industry.

3

# ST. AUGUSTINE

*35 mi south of Jacksonville, on U.S. 1.*

Founded in 1565 by Spanish explorers, St. Augustine is the nation's oldest city. In addition to having many historic sites on the mainland, the city has 43 mi of beaches on two barrier islands to the east, both reachable by causeways. Several times a year St. Augustine holds historic reenactments, such as December's Grand Christmas Illumination, which commemorates the town's British occupation.

The core of any visit is a tour of the historic district, a showcase for more than 60 historic sites and attractions, plus 144 blocks of houses listed on the National Register of Historic Places. You could probably spend several weeks exploring these treasures, but don't neglect other, generally newer, attractions found elsewhere in town.

### ESSENTIALS

Centrally located between the south and north ends of St. Augustine's historic district, the St. John's County Visitor Information Center is a smart place to start your day. You can park in the multistoried garage here ($1.25 per hour, $7.50 per day), as well as pick up maps; get information on and advice about attractions and restaurants, and hop aboard the sightseeing trolley. Be sure to notice the large coquina ball outside. Built in 1929, it was placed here to note the 0 mile marker for the 3,000-mi Old Spanish Trail that was established by missionaries and stretched all the way to San Diego.

**Visitor Information St. Augustine, Ponte Vedra, & the Beaches Visitors and Convention Bureau** (✉ *500 San Sebastian View* ☎ *904/829–1711 or 800/653–2489* ⊕ *www.getaway4florida.com*) is open daily 8:30–5:30. **St. Johns County Visitor Information Center** (✉ *10 W. Castillo Dr.* ☎ *904/825–1000* ☽ *Daily 8:30–5:30*).

**TAKE A TOUR**

**Old Town Trolley Tour.** The Old Town Trolley's fully narrated tours ($23 adults/$10 children) cover more than 100 points of interest and are, perhaps, the best way to take in the historic district. Your pass is good for three days and, with parking at a premium and meters closely watched, park at one of their main stations for free and enjoy the ability to reboard at any of 16 stops throughout town—they even have shuttles to the beach. In the evening a macabre slant is added on the Ghosts and Graveyards Tour ($26 adults/$14 children), which includes visits to the Old Jail and Lighthouse. ☎ *904/829–3800* ⊕ *www.historictours.com/staugustine.*

**St. Augustine Transfer Company.** The nation's oldest continually operated carriage company (since 1877) knows quite a few things about the city's history. Guides fill you in on horse-drawn carriage tours ($25 adult/$18 children) that are as calming as they are informative. For a different slant, consider the Ghostly Gatherings evening carriage excursion. ☎ *904/829–2391* ⊕ *www.staugustinetransfer.com.*

Built to protect Spain's St. Augustine, the Castillo de San Marcos still stands along the shore.

## EXPLORING

### TOP ATTRACTIONS

Fodor'sChoice **Castillo de San Marcos National Monument.** The focal point of St. Augus-
★    tine, this massive and commanding structure was completed by the
Spaniards in 1695 (English pirates were handy with a torch back then),
and it looks every day of its three centuries. The fort was constructed of
coquina, a soft limestone made of broken shells and coral that, unex-
pectedly, could absorb the impact of British cannonballs. (Unlike solid
stone, the softer coquina wouldn't shatter when hit by large muni-
tions.) The fort was also used as a prison during the Revolutionary
and Civil wars.

Park rangers provide an introductory narration, after which you're
on your own to explore the moat, turrets, and 16-foot-thick walls.
Garrison rooms depict the life of the era, and special cannon-firing
demonstrations are held several times a day Fridays through Sunday
year-round. Children under 15 are admitted free and must be accompanied by an adult. Save the receipt, since admission is valid for seven
days. If you're over 62, spring for the $10 NPS America the Beautiful
pass which grants you free admission to this and other national parks
for a year. ⊠ 1 S. Castillo Dr. ☎ 904/829–6506 ⊕ www.nps.gov/casa
⊡ $6 ⊙ Daily 8:45–5:15, last ticket sold at 4:45.

**Cathedral Basilica of St. Augustine.** This cathedral has the country's oldest written parish records, dating from 1594. The circa-1797 structure
underwent changes after a fire in 1887 as well as restoration work in the
mid 1960s. If you're around for the holidays, stop in for Christmas Eve's
gorgeous midnight mass conducted amid banks of flickering candles

that reflect off gilded walls. Regular Sunday masses are held through-out the year at 7, 9, 11, and 5. ⊠ *38 Cathedral Pl.* ☎ *904/824–2806* ⊕ *www.thefirstparish.org* ✉ *Donation welcome* ⊘ *Weekdays 9–4:30.*

☺ **Colonial Spanish Quarter Museum.** To get a sense of how Spanish soldiers and their families lived in 1740s St. Augustine, stroll through this living-history museum housed in nine small buildings reconstructed on origi-nal foundations. In historic vignettes along the way you'll likely see a blacksmith, carpenter, leatherworker, and calligrapher/scribe at work. Even younger kids enjoy the costumes and recountings of history. The museum's grounds are also the meeting place for a tour (included in the admission) of the de Mesa-Sanchez House (aka the Pink House) and the chance to see life in the 1780s, when the city was, briefly, under British rule. ⊠ *29 St. George St.* ☎ *904/825–6830* ⊕ *www.historicstaugustine. com* ✉ *$7, $4 children 6–17* ⊘ *Daily 9–5:30, last ticket sold at 4:45.*

**NEED A BREAK?**

**St. George Tavern.** Although they serve food here (sandwiches, mostly), the appeal of this joint is that, in a city of historic recreations, this is the real deal: A noisy, packed, active bar where smokers smoke, drinkers drink, locals gather, and strangers blend right in. ⊠ *116 St. George St.* ☎ *904/824–4204.*

**Flagler College.** Originally one of two posh hotels Henry Flagler built in 1887, this building—now a small liberal-arts college—is a rivet-ing Spanish Renaissance revival structure with towers, turrets, and arcades decorated by Louis Comfort Tiffany. The former Hotel Ponce de León is a National Historic Landmark, having hosted U.S. presi-dents Grover Cleveland, Theodore Roosevelt, and Warren Harding. Tours are offered daily through Flagler's Legacy Tours. ⊠ *74 King St.* ☎ *904/829–6481, 904/823–3378 tour information* ⊕ *www.flagler.edu* ✉ *Tours $7* ⊘ *Daily 10 and 2 when school's in session, on the hr 10–3 when school's out.*

★ **Lightner Museum.** In his quest to turn Florida into an American Riviera, Henry Flagler built two fancy hotels in 1888: the Ponce de León, which became Flagler College, and the Alcazar, which closed during the Great Depression, was purchased by publisher Otto Lightner in 1946, and was donated to the city in 1948. It's now a museum with three floors of fur-nishings, costumes, and Victorian art glass, and not-to-be-missed ornate antique music boxes (demonstrations daily at 11 and 2). The Lightner Antiques Mall is on three levels of what was once the hotel's indoor pool. On other floors you'll find city staff since, apparently, the guest rooms of a former grand hotel also make nice municipal-government offices. ⊠ *75 King St.* ☎ *904/824–2874* ⊕ *www.lightnermuseum.org* ✉ *$10* ⊘ *Museum daily 9–5, last admission at 4.*

**Old Jail Museum.** At this 19th century prison, felons were detained and released or detained and hanged from the gallows in back. After learn-ing the history of local crime and punishment and seeing displays of weapons and other artifacts, you can browse the surfeit of souvenirs in Cracker Bob's Trading Post and the adjacent Old Store Museum. Note that the museum is at the starting point for the Old Town Trolley Tours. ⊠ *167 San Marco Ave.* ☎ *904/829–3800* ✉ *$9* ⊘ *Daily 8:30–4:30.*

🕐 **Pirate and Treasure Museum.** Inside this small museum established by entrepreneur and motivational speaker Pat Croce is a collection of more than 800 pirate artifacts, including one of only two Jolly Rogers (skull-and-crossbone flags) to have actually flown above a ship. Exhibits include a mock-up of a tavern, a captain's quarters, and a ship's deck. You'll learn about the lives of everyday and famous pirates, their navigation techniques, their weaponry, and the concoctions they drank (including something called Kill Devil, which is rum mixed with gunpowder). You'll get to touch an actual treasure chest; see piles of gold, jade, emeralds, and pearls; and leave knowing full well that there were pirates before Captain Jack Sparrow. ✉ *12 Castillo Dr.* ☎ *877/467–5863* ⊕ *www.thepiratemuseum.com* ▧ *$12* ☉ *Daily 9–8.*

🕐 **St. Augustine Alligator Farm Zoological Park.** Founded in 1893, the Alliga-
★ tor Farm is one of Florida's oldest (and, at times, smelliest) zoological attractions and is credited with popularizing the alligator in the national consciousness and helping to fashion an image for the state. In addition to oddities like Maximo, a 15-foot, 1,250-pound saltwater crocodile, and a collection of rare albino alligators, the park is also home to Land of Crocodiles, the only place in the world to see all 23 species of living crocodilians. Traversing the treetops in Crocodile Crossing is an inventive, ambitious, and expensive ($65) zipline/rope course with more than 50 challenges and seven zips. It's the only attraction of its kind through a zoological park. In many places, a thin cable is all that keeps you from becoming croc cuisine. Reptiles are the main attraction, but there's also a wading-bird rookery, an exotic-birds and mammals exhibit, and nature trails. Educational presentations are held throughout the day, and kids will love the wild-animal shows, alligator wrestling and all. ✉ *999 Anastasia Blvd.* ☎ *904/824–3337* ⊕ *www. alligatorfarm.us* ▧ *$21.95* ☉ *Daily 9–5.*

**St. Augustine Lighthouse & Museum.** It's unusual to find a lighthouse tucked into a residential neighborhood, but that's what you'll see here. This 1874 version replaced an earlier one built when the city was founded in 1565. Although its beacon no longer guides ships, it does draw thousands of visitors each year. The visitor center has a museum with exhibits on the U.S. Coast Guard, historic boat building, maritime archaeology, and the life of a lighthouse keeper—whose work involved far more than light housekeeping. You have to climb 219 steps to reach the peak, but the wonderful view and fresh ocean breeze are well worth it. Children must be at least 44" tall to make the ascent. ✉ *81 Lighthouse Ave.* ☎ *904/829–0745* ⊕ *www.staugustinelighthouse. com* ▧ *$9.50* ☉ *Daily 9–6.*

**WORTH NOTING**

**Anastasia State Park.** Anastasia Island park draws families that like to hike, bike, swim, and play on the beach to its 1,700 protected acres of bird sanctuary and 4 mi of secluded beachfront. There's an area for tent camping and RVs, as well as a camp store and snack bar for supplies and provisions. If you can forsake the grand hotels and inns of the historic district, this isn't a bad place to spend the night. ✉ *1340 Rte. A1A S* ☎ *904/461–2033* ⊕ *www.floridastateparks.org/anastasia* ▧ *$8 per vehicle, $2 for pedestrians or bicyclists* ☉ *Daily 8–sundown.*

**St. Augustine**

Genoply St.

Milton St.

San Marco Ave.

Douglas Ave.

Nelmar

May St.

Dufferin Ave.

Williams

Ballard Ave.

Ocean Ave.

Sebastian (Avenida Menendez)

Old Mission

San Sebastian River

Ponce de Leon Blvd.

Vista Cove Rd.

Hospital River

Pine St.

Locust St.

Rhode Ave.

Mulberry St.

Castillo Dr.

St. John's Cty. Visitors Center

Orange St.

Saragossa St.

Cuna St.

Carrera St.

Valencia St.

Ribería St.

Cordova St.

St. George St.

King St.

Bridge of Lions

Bridge St.

St. Francis St.

Weedon St.

Dehaven St.

Washington St.

Central Ave.

Marine St.

Lovel St.

Ribería St.

South St.

Duero St.

Cerro St.

San Sebastian River

Matanzas Bay

TO
ST. AUGUSTINE BEACH

St. Augustine Blvd.

Arpieka

Oglethorpe Blvd.

Anastasia Blvd.

Dolphin Dr.

TO
FT. MATANZAS
NAT'L PARK

0     1/2 mile

0     1/2 km

**City Gate.** At the northernmost end of the colorful shops and sites of St. George Street, the gate is a relic from the days when the Castillo's moat ran westward to the river, and the Cubo Defense Line (defensive wall) protected against approaches from the north. The old coquina gates set the tone for St. George Street, the historic lane filled with old-world balconies and quaint little shops. ⊠ *St. George and Orange Sts.*

**Flagler Memorial Presbyterian Church.** To look at a marvelous Venetian Renaissance–style structure, head to this church, built by Flagler in 1889 as a memorial to his daughter Jenny, who died during childbirth. In addition to Jenny, this is also the final resting place for Flagler himself, his first wife Mary, and their granddaughter Marjorie. A stunning sanctuary, the dome towers more than 100 feet and is topped by a 20-foot Greek cross. ⊠ *32 Sevilla St.* ☎ *904/829–6451* ⊕ *www.memorialpcusa.org* ⊙ *Weekdays 8:30–4:30.*

**Fountain of Youth National Archaeological Park.** Here's the thing about "North America's first historical site": you either love it, or you hate it. Fans of the grade-A tourist trap appreciate the kitsch factor. They laugh at the cheesy costumes and educational displays. They chuckle at the tired planetarium show. They wonder if the "national archaeological park" really means anything (it doesn't) or if it's affiliated with the National Park Service (it isn't). Eventually they sip from the legendary Fountain of Youth, if only to mock Ponce de León and his followers for believing such foul-tasting water could hold magical powers. If you don't appreciate kitsch, you'll be disappointed in the dated exhibits and disinterested employees and wish you had spent your money on a roast-beef sandwich. ⊠ *11 Magnolia Ave.* ☎ *904/829–3168 or 800/356–8222* ⊕ *www.fountainofyouthflorida.com* ⊠ *$10* ⊙ *Daily 9–5.*

OFF THE BEATEN PATH

**Ft. Matanzas National Monument.** As you drive south on Anastasia Island, you head toward what was, in the 1700s, St. Augustine's farthest reaches. With Castillo de San Marcos guarding the town, in 1740 the Spanish created the relatively small Ft. Matanzas to defend their southern flank. A short ferry ride across the Matanzas River takes you to the Ft. Matanzas National Monument. Although it's only 15 mi from town, the fort feels eerily remote, and it takes little imagination to picture the demanding lives of the soldiers sent here to protect the young colony. Ferry shuttles are free and run several times a day. ⊠ *8635 A1A S* ☎ *904/471–0116* ⊕ *www.nps.gov/foma* ⊠ *Free* ⊙ *Daily 9–5:30.*

**Government House Museum.** At different points in its history this has been a hospital, a courthouse, a customs house, a post office, and, during the American Revolution, the home of the British governors. And it was from here, in 1821, that the Spanish governor ceded control of East Florida to the United States to conclude 256 years of colonial control. Today, a collection of more than 300 artifacts from archaeological digs and Spanish shipwrecks off the coast are showcased in the museum, reflecting an amazing five centuries of history. ⊠ *48 King St.* ☎ *904/825–5079* ⊕ *www.staugustinegovernment.com/visitors/gov-house.cfm* ⊠ *$4* ⊙ *Daily 10–4.*

## CLOSE UP

# Newport of the South

Henry Morrison Flagler, who, with John D. Rockefeller, founded the Standard Oil Company, first visited the tiny town of St. Augustine in 1885 while honeymooning with his second wife. His choice proved to be very fortunate for the city. During the trip Flagler decided to make St. Augustine "the Newport of the South": a winter resort for wealthy northern industrialists. And to get his select clientele to Florida, he built the luxurious Florida East Coast Railway, which eventually stretched from New York all the way to the Florida Keys, with St. Augustine conveniently located just 24 hours from New York by rail.

To incorporate the city's Spanish heritage, Flagler chose Spanish Renaissance revival as his architectural theme. He created the St. Augustine

Golf Club and the St. Augustine Yacht Club, so there would be leisure activities to enjoy in the warm climate, and he built the city's hospital, churches, city hall, and winter residences.

The most visible manifestations of Flagler's dream, however, were the spectacular hotels with castlelike towers, turrets, and red-tile roofs. His most opulent hotel resort, the Ponce de León, is now the four-year liberal-arts college that bears his name. Another flagship resort, the Alcazar, has been turned into the Lightner Museum; the Casa Monica Hotel is again functioning as a luxury resort, more than a century after Flagler purchased it from its original owner. Despite the wrath of multiple hurricanes, many of the hotels and railroad routes Flagler built and developed are still in use today.

**OFF THE BEATEN PATH**

**Marineland's Dolphin Conservation Center.** The world's first oceanarium was constructed in 1938, 18 mi south of St. Augustine. This National Register of Historic Places designee has come a long way from marine film studio to theme park to its current iteration as dolphin research, education, and entertainment center. The formal dolphin shows are history, but you can have a far more memorable experience with interactive programs that allow you to swim with and feed the animals, become a dolphin trainer for a day, or create dolphin art. Programs start at $26 a day (for the simple "touch-and-feed" option) and go as high as $550 (for "trainer for a day"). Those who prefer not to get so up close and personal can watch the action in the dolphin habitats through 6-by-10-foot acrylic windows. The 1.3-million-gallon facility is home to a dozen dolphins, including Nellie who was born here on February 27, 1953, making her the oldest dolphin in captivity. Reservations are required. ⊠ 9600 Ocean Shore Blvd. ☎ 904/471–1111 or 888/279–9194 ⊕ www. marineland.net ☞ General admission $8.50; call for program prices ☉ Daily 8:30–4:30.

**Mission of Nombre de Dios.** The site, north of the historic district, commemorates where America's first mass was celebrated. A 208-foot-tall stainless-steel cross (purportedly the world's tallest) allegedly marks the spot where the mission's first cross was planted in 1565. Also on the property is the Shrine of Our Lady of La Leche, the first shrine devoted to Mary in the United States. The landscape is exquisitely maintained and the mission is crisscrossed with paths. ⊠ 27 Ocean

Get a bird's-eye view of St. Augustine from atop the historic city's 1874 lighthouse.

*Ave.* ☎ *904/824–2809 or 800/342–6529* ⊕ *www.missionandshrine.org* ✉ *Donation requested* ☉ *Weekdays 9–5, weekends 10–5.*

**Oldest House.** Known as the Gonzalez-Alvarez House, Florida's oldest surviving Spanish-colonial dwelling is a National Historic Landmark. The current site dates from the early 1700s, but there's been a structure here since the early 1600s. Much of the city's history is seen in the building's modifications and additions, from the coquina blocks—which came into use to replace wood soon after the town burned in 1702—to the house's enlargement during the British occupation. The complex also encompasses Tovar House, a circa 1750s home of a Spanish soldier; the Manucy Museum; the Page L. Edwards Gallery and its rotating exhibits; a gift shop; and an ornamental garden. ✉ *14 St. Francis St.* ☎ *904/824–2872* ⊕ *www.oldesthouse.com* ✉ *$8* ☉ *Daily 9–5, tours every ½ hr.*

**Oldest Wooden Schoolhouse.** This tiny 18th-century building of cypress and cedar served not only as a schoolhouse but also as a tearoom, a farmhouse, and a guardhouse and sentry shelter during the Seminole Wars. In 1939, members of the Class of '64 (1864, that is) dressed out the school as they remembered it, and today automated mannequins instruct you on the education of 150 years ago. Apparently teachers had more leeway then because miscreants were given "time out" in a cubby beneath the stairs. And the heavy chain wrapped around the building? It held the structure down during hurricanes. ✉ *14 St. George St.* ☎ *888/653–7245* ⊕ *www.oldestwoodenschoolhouse.com* ✉ *$4.50* ☉ *Sun.–Thurs. 9–5, Fri. 9–6, Sat. 9–7.*

**Plaza de la Constitución.** At the foot of the Bridge of Lions, this central area of the original settlement was laid out in 1598 by decree of Spain's King Philip II. At its core is a monument to the Spanish constitution of 1812, and at its east end is a portico dating from early American days. This is where products and, regrettably, people were sold, earning the area the twin names of "public market" and "slave market." Today, it's the gathering spot for holiday events, art shows, and evening concerts. Toward the bridge, look for the life-size statue of Ponce de León. The man who

> ## HOPE SPRINGS ETERNAL
>
> Whether St. Augustine's world-renowned Fountain of Youth has curative powers is debatable—as is the legend of Ponce himself. Many scholars believe he came ashore closer to Melbourne, 150 mi south, in 1513. Still, those caught in the trap of folklore are still tempted to drink the foul-smelling water, which packs a dose of 42 minerals, including iron and—not surprising—sulfur.

"discovered" Florida in 1513 was, apparently, all of 4' 11". ⊠ *St. George St. and Cathedral Pl.*

**Ripley's Believe It or Not! Museum.** The nation's first Ripley's museum is, appropriately enough, in a historic structure—Castle Warden, an 1887 Moorish Revival-style mansion. Like its younger siblings, this odditorium is packed with plenty of unusual items including Robert Ripley's personal collections; a mummified cat; a death mask of Abraham Lincoln; a scale model of the original Ferris Wheel created from an Erector set; and life-size models of Robert Wadlow, the world's tallest man, and Robert Hughes, the world's fattest man. ⊠ *19 San Marco Ave.* ☎ *904/824–1606* ⊕ *staugustine.ripleys.com* ☜ *$15* ☉ *Sun.–Thurs. 9–7, Fri. and Sat. 9–8.*

**World Golf Hall of Fame.** This stunning tribute to the game of golf is the centerpiece of World Golf Village, an extraordinary complex that includes 36 holes of golf, a golf academy, several accommodations options, a convention center, spa, and a variety of restaurants, including Murray Bros. Caddyshack. The Hall of Fame features an adjacent IMAX theater and houses a variety of exhibits combining historical artifacts and personal memorabilia with the latest in interactive technology. Stand up to the pressures of the TV camera and crowd noise as you try to sink a final putt, take a swing on the museum's simulator, or snap a photo as you walk across a replica of St. Andrews's Swilcan Burn Bridge. Once you're sufficiently inspired, see how you fare on the 18-hole natural-grass putting course. Note that admission includes a chance to score a hole-in-one on a 132-yard hole. If you do, you'll win a prize such as admission to THE PLAYERS Championship. ⊠ *1 World Golf Pl.* ☎ *904/940–4123* ⊕ *www.wgv.com* ☜ *$19.50 (includes all-day admission to museum, one round on 18-hole putting course, and a shot at hole-in-one challenge). IMAX price $13 for full-length features, $8.50 for documentaries* ☉ *Mon.–Sat. 10–6, Sun. noon–6.*

**Ximenez-Fatio House Museum.** Built as a merchant's house and store in 1798, the place became a boardinghouse in the 1800s and has been restored to look like it did during its inn days—romantic yet severe, with balconies that hearken back to Old Spain and sparely appointed rooms. Docents will lead you around the property; be sure to look at the fascinating St. Augustine street scenes, painted in 1854 by an itinerant artist. Amazingly, much of what you see in the paintings is extant. ⊠ *20 Aviles St.* ☏ *904/829–3575* ⊕ *www.ximenezfatiohouse.org* ▭ *$5* ⊙ *Tues.–Sat. 11–4.*

## BEACHES

**St. Augustine Beach.** The closest beach to downtown is very popular. It's on the northern end of Anastasia Island, directly east of the city. ⊠ *1200 Rte. A1A S* ▭ *Free.*

**Vilano Beach.** Two miles north of St. Augustine, Vilano Beach is slowly blossoming into a bustling community with a town center, cozy restaurants, outdoor cafés, condos, and hotels. The area is popular with fishermen, skimboarders, and bird-watchers (125 species of birds call it home). This isn't a good place to take little ones swimming, though, as the beaches aren't developed and currents can be fierce. ⊠ *Coastal Hwy. at Vilano Beach Causeway* ▭ *Free.*

## SPORTS AND THE OUTDOORS

### BOAT TOURS

**EcoTours.** Amidst America's most enduring human history, EcoTours investigates St. Augustine's natural history. Scenic cruises, kayak tours, and catamaran excursions on Matanzas Bay offer a chance to see bottlenose dolphins, bird habitats, lakes, creeks, and saltwater marshes. Along the way are incredible photo ops of the city and the Castillo from on the waterfront. Call for rates. ⊠ *111 Ave. Menendez* ☏ *907/377–7245* ⊕ *www.staugustineecotours.com.*

**Schooner** *Freedom.* Cutting a sharp profile, this 72-foot replica of a 19th-century blockade-runner sails from the marina for excursions across Matanzas Bay. You can relax and savor the breeze, nibbling on free snacks and drinks, or you can help the crew prepare to set sail. There are two-hour day ($35 per person) and sunset ($45) sails as well as one-hour nighttime ghost-story ($35) sails. Precise times vary by season. Reservations are advised. ⊠ *111 Ave. Menendez* ☏ *904/810–1010* ⊕ *www.schoonerfreedome.com.*

### BIKING

**Solano Cycle.** Here you can rent bicycles, scooters, and "scoot coups," which look like the offspring of a scooter and a bumper car and are $49 for the first hour (one-hour minimum) and $69 for two. ⊠ *32 San Marco Ave.* ☏ *904/825–6766* ⊕ *www.solanocycle.com.*

### FISHING

**Tailin' Spots Charters.** Tailin' Spots offers full- and half-day charters in addition to overnight and extended-stay trips. You won't need a license; the captain's license covers you. ⊠ *U.S. 1 and Rte. 207* ☏ *904/669–2775* ⊕ *www.tailinspots.com.*

**St. Augustine Deep Sea Fishing.** Tackle and bait are included on this outfit's half- or full-day fishing trips. ⊠ *Cat's Paw Marina, 220 Nix Boat Yard Rd.* ☎ *904/829–8040* ⊕ *www.sealovefishing.com.*

### GOLF

**Pine Course at the Grand Club.** Greens fees at this Arnold Palmer–designed course 30 minutes south of downtown are $45–$65. After 2 pm, you can play 9 holes for $21. ⊠ *400 Pine Lakes Pkwy., Palm Coast* ☎ *386/ 446–6330.*

**World Golf Village.** The World Golf Hall of Fame complex has two 18-hole layouts named for and partially designed by golf legends Sam Snead, Gene Sarazen, Arnold Palmer, and Jack Nicklaus. Greens fees at the Slammer & Squire are $109–$139; at the King & Bear, they're $139–$169. ⊠ *21 World Golf Pl.* ☎ *904/940–4000, 904/940–6088 Slammer & Squire, 904/940–6200 King & Bear.*

### WATER SPORTS

**Smile High Parasail.** Beneath huge canopies you can sit three abreast and soak in a commanding view of the city and the sea. Call in advance for weather conditions, and know that the higher the altitude, the higher the cost. ⊠ *111 Ave. Menendez* ☎ *904/819–0980* ⊕ *www. smilehighparasail.com.*

**Surf Station.** Here you can rent surfboards, skimboards, and bodyboards. ⊠ *1020 Anastasia Blvd.* ☎ *904/471–9463* ⊕ *www.surf-station.com.*

## SHOPPING

One of the most pleasing pastimes in St. Augustine is a stroll along St. George Street, a pedestrian mall with shoulder-to-shoulder art galleries and one-of-a-kind shops selling candles, home accents, handmade jewelry, aromatherapy products, pottery, books, clothing. There are also restaurants, clubs, and a veritable orchestra of street musicians.

Several blocks north of the Castillo and the popular St. George Street, a string of shops—galleries, antiques, a bookstore—line both sides of San Marco Avenue. Although this strip isn't as eclectic as it used to be, you'll still find some unique independent stores.

### MALLS

**Prime Outlets.** Several miles outside of the city, Prime Outlets has more than 60 name-brand stores including Gucci, Saks 5th Avenue's OFF 5TH, and Michael Kors. ⊠ *500 Belz Outlet Blvd.* ☎ *904/826–1311.*

**St. Augustine Premium Outlets.** Just north of St. Augustine, off Interstate 95, is this collection of 85 designer and brand-name outlet stores. ⊠ *2700 Rte. 16* ☎ *904/825–1555* ⊕ *www.premiumoutlets.com.*

## NIGHTLIFE

**A1A Aleworks.** The Aleworks always seems to be filled with students and visitors taste-driving the microbrews and other selections from the full bar. Seats on the 2nd-story balcony provide a great view of the marina and bay across the street. It's a little like being on Bourbon Street—but clean. ⊠ *1 King St.* ☎ *904/829–2977* ⊕ *www.A1Aaleworks.com.*

**Café Eleven.** This live music haven sets the stage for local groups, and tries to book national acts at least once a month. ✉ *501 Rte. A1A Beach Blvd.* ☎ *904/460–9311* ⊕ *www.cafeeleven.com.*

**Mill Top Tavern** The rustic Mill Top is famous for its live, local music. ✉ *19½ St. George St.* ☎ *904/829–2329.*

**Oasis Deck and Restaurant.** If you're staying on Anastasia Island, this is your best nightlife bet. It has 24-ounce draft beers, beach access, and what many locals consider the best burgers in town. ✉ *4000 Rte. A1A S, at Ocean Trace Rd.* ☎ *904/471–3424.*

**3**

**Scarlett O'Hara's.** It's a popular and convenient spot to stop for lunch or dinner (preferably enjoyed on the front porch); later in the evening it turns up the volume with blues, jazz, disco, Top 40, or karaoke. Whatever's playing, it's always packed. ✉ *70 Hypolita St.* ☎ *904/824–6535.*

**The Tini Martini Bar.** The veranda overlooking Matanzas Bay at this Casablanca Inn bar is the perfect place to enjoy a cocktail, people-watch, and listen to live music. ✉ *Casablanca Inn, 24 Ave. Menendez* ☎ *904/829–0928.*

**Tradewinds.** It's been showcasing bands—from country and western to rock and roll— since 1964. Thanks to the music and the beer and margaritas, you might feel as if you're in Key West. ✉ *124 Charlotte St.* ☎ *904/829–9336* ⊕ *www.tradewindslounge.com.*

## WHERE TO EAT

**$$$**  
ECLECTIC  
Fodor'sChoice  
★

✕ **95 Cordova.** On the first floor of the Casa Monica Hotel, this restaurant serves classic cuisine with an international flair. Sup in one of three dining rooms, including the main room with intricate Moroccan-style chandeliers, wrought-iron chairs, and heavy wood columns, or the Sultan's Room, a gold-dipped space accented with potted palms and a silk-draped ceiling. Innovative dishes with New World, Middle Eastern, and Asian flavors change seasonally and highlight local seafood and produce. Among the dinner items are several types of steak, roast duckling, corn-crusted mahimahi, crab and shrimp ravioli, and ahi tuna with a Thai peanut sauce. The tasting menu offers six international courses paired with outstanding wines. ✉ *95 Cordova St.* ☎ *904/810–6810* ⊕ *www.casamonica.com.*

**¢**  
CAFE

✕ **The Bunnery.** Hidden among the art galleries and trinket shops of St. George Street is this cozy little restaurant, which is very popular at breakfast and nearly as popular during lunch. There's nothing fancy—just high-back booths and a menu of pancakes, bacon, eggs, cinnamon buns, salads, and sandwiches. It's the perfect spot when you want something familiar in a new place. ✉ *121 St. George St.* ☎ *904/829–6166* ⊙ *No dinner.*

**$$$**  
SEAFOOD

✕ **Collage.** Foodies seeking a new dining experience in the Oldest City head to Collage for "artful global cuisine" in a warm and intimate setting. Tucked away on Hypolita Street in the historic district, the 48-seat restaurant highlights local seafood which, depending on the success of the fishermen, will include several fish entrées each day. The ever-changing menu also often has steak, lamb, or veal selections. For dessert, the bougainvillea, an original dessert inspired by the colorful flowering plants that frame the building, is made of strawberries, ice cream, and cabernet-vanilla sauce served in a leaf-shape phyllo cup. ⊠ *60 Hypolita St.* ☎ *904/829–0055* ⊕ *www.collagestaug.com* ☾ *No lunch.*

$$$ × **Columbia.** Arroz con pollo, fillet *salteado* (with a spicy sauce), and
SPANISH a fragrant seafood paella (allow 30 minutes for preparation) are the
★ time-honored Cuban and Spanish dishes served at this branch of the original Columbia, which was founded in Tampa in 1905. Befitting its cuisine, the restaurant is more like an airy Spanish villa, with many archival family photos; a white-stucco exterior; and an atrium dining room full of palm trees, hand-painted tiles, and decorative arches. Table not ready? Linger in the courtyard, listen to the fountains, and enjoy a glass of homemade sangria or a refreshing mojito. ⊠ *98 St. George St.* ☎ *904/824–3341* ⊕ *www.columbiarestaurant.com.*

$$ × **O.C. White's Seafood & Spirits.** Dining outside is a treat at this bustling
SEAFOOD little spot across from the marina. Set in the circa-1791 General Worth house, it has a homelike feel with a balanced clientele of locals, students, and visitors. Favorites include coconut shrimp, blue-crab cakes, and Caribbean jerk chicken. Beef lovers may want to try the 20-ounce porterhouse or the 12-ounce New York strip. From upstairs, you have a great marina view; in the courtyard you might enjoy the perfume of blooming jasmine. Note that reservations aren't accepted on weekends. ⊠ *118 Ave. Menendez* ☎ *904/824–0808* ⊕ *www.ocwhites.com.*

$ × **O'Steen's.** Across the Bridge of Lions from downtown, this hole-in-
SEAFOOD the-wall restaurant is recognizable for the line of customers who wait patiently for fried shrimp (the specialty), oysters, scallops, hush puppies, fried chicken, coleslaw, biscuits and cornbread with gravy, and banana cream pie. Needless to say it's been a popular local eatery for generations. ⊠ *205 Anastasia Blvd.* ☎ *904/829–6974* ☾ *No lunch weekdays.*

$ × **Salt Water Cowboy's.** Rustic handmade twig furniture and 100-year-old
SOUTHERN hardwood floors are reminders that this spot, hidden in the salt marshes
Fodor's Choice flanking the Intracoastal Waterway midway down Anastasia Island,
★ began as a secluded fish camp. Critically acclaimed Minorcan clam chowder, oyster stew, blackened or broiled fish, barbecued ribs, steaks, and crispy fried chicken are standard fare. For more adventuresome palates, the menu also includes frogs' legs, alligator, and cooter (fried soft-shell turtle rolled in seasoned bread crumbs). ⊠ *299 Dondanville Rd.* ☎ *904/471–2332* ⊕ *www.saltwatercowboys.com* ⌳ *Reservations not accepted* ☾ *No lunch.*

## WHERE TO STAY

*For expanded hotel reviews, visit Fodors.com.*

$$ ⌑ **Casablanca Inn Bed & Breakfast on the Bay.** Breakfast comes with sce-
B&B/INN nic views of the Matanzas Bay at this restored 1914 Mediterranean-
Fodor's Choice revival stucco-and-stone house, just north of the Bridge of Lions in
★ the historic district. **Pros:** comfy beds; friendly staff; free early evening snacks and beverages. **Cons:** some rooms have no view; street noise in some rooms. ⊠ *24 Ave. Menendez* ☎ *904/829–0928 or 800/826–2626* ⊕ *www.casablancainn.com* ⌐ *23 rooms, 2 suites* ⌳ *In-room: kitchen*

*(some), Internet. In-hotel: bar, parking, some pets allowed, some age restrictions* ¶©¶ *Breakfast.*

**$$**

B&B/INN

★

🏠 **Casa de Solana.** There's a reason you feel like you're stepping back in time when you enter this 1820s-era inn made of coquina and hand-made bricks: It's on the oldest street in the oldest European-settled city in the country. **Pros:** excellent service; delicious breakfast; location, free parking. **Cons:** some small rooms; the free parking's three blocks away; "forced" socialization. ⊠ *21 Aviles St.* ☎ *877/824–3555* ⊕ *www. casadesolana.com* 🔗 *10 rooms* ⚬ *In-room: Wi-Fi. In-hotel: parking, some pets allowed.*

**$$$**

HOTEL

Fodor's Choice

★

🏠 **Casa Monica Hotel.** Hand-stenciled Moorish columns and arches, handcrafted chandeliers, and gilded iron tables decorate the lobby of this late-1800s Flagler-era masterpiece. **Pros:** location; architecture and decor; service; Gilded Age heritage. **Cons:** busy lobby; expensive ($22) parking; small rooms. ⊠ *95 Cordova St.* ☎ *904/827–1888 or 800/648–1888* ⊕ *www.casamonica.com* 🔗 *138 rooms, 14 suites* ⚬ *In-room: kitchen (some), Wi-Fi. In-hotel: restaurant, bar, pool, gym, parking.*

**$$$**

HOTEL

🏠 **Hilton St. Augustine Historic Bayfront.** In the heart of historic St. Augus-tine, this Spanish-colonial-inspired hotel overlooking Matanzas Bay has 19 separate buildings in a village setting. ons: 4 pm check-in; expensive ($21) parking; noise from the road. ⊠ *32 Ave. Menendez* ☎ *904/829–2277 or 800/445–8667* ⊕ *www.hiltonhistoricstaugustine.com* 🔗 *72 rooms* ⚬ *In-room: Wi-Fi. In-hotel: restaurant, bar, pool, gym, laundry facilities, parking.*

**$$$**

B&B/INN

🏠 **Inn on Charlotte Bed & Breakfast.** Innkeeper Ronald Holeman says guests comment that staying at his inn reminds them of visiting a friend or family member's home, assuming that person offers an elegant two-course breakfast and cozy rooms with whirlpool tubs. It's on a quaint brick street just a block from the bay. **Pros:** location; excellent ser-vice; free parking. **Cons:** tight parking, compact lot, weekend street noise. ⊠ *52 Charlotte St.* ☎ *904/829–3819 or 800/355–5508* ⊕ *www. inoncharlotte.com* 🔗 *8 rooms* ⚬ *In-room: Wi-Fi. In-hotel: parking, some age restrictions.*

**$**

HOTEL

**Monterey Inn.** The basic offerings at this two-story motor-court-style hotel are offset by reasonable rates and a great location a few blocks from the Castillo. **Pros:** location; convenience; affordability; free park-ing; pets welcome. **Cons:** not as upscale as neighboring properties; packed parking lot; active street frontage. ⊠ *16 Ave. Menendez* ☎ *904/824–4482* ⊕ *www.themontereyinn.com* 🔗 *59 rooms In-room: Wi-Fi. In-hotel: parking, pool.*

**$**

B&B/INN

🏠 **Old City House Inn & Restaurant.** Touches of Paris, Venice, and India are just a few of the surprises within this small two-story inn's coquina walls, where innkeepers Ilse and James Philcox have decorated the rooms to reflect international cities or themes. **Pros:** location; roman-tic; on-site restaurant. **Cons:** thin walls; may have to share room with a ghost! ⊠ *115 Cordova St.* ☎ *904/826–0113* ⊕ *www.oldcityhouse.com* 🔗 *7 rooms, 2 suites* ⚬ *In-hotel: restaurant, parking, some age restric-tions* ¶©¶ *Breakfast.*

$$$
RESORT
★

⬚ **Renaissance Resort at World Golf Village.** If you want to be within walking distance of all World Golf Village has to offer, this full-service resort is an excellent choice. **Pros:** breakfast buffet; friendly staff; large bathrooms. **Cons:** small pool; no pets. ✉ *500 S. Legacy Trail* ☎ *904/940–8000 or 888/740–7020* ⊕ *www.worldgolfrenaissance.com* ⤵ *271 rooms, 30 suites* ⬚ *In-room: Wi-Fi. In-hotel: restaurant, bar, golf course, tennis court, pool, gym, laundry facilities, parking.*

$$$
B&B/INN

⬚ **St. Francis Inn Bed & Breakfast.** If the walls of this late-18th-century house in the historic district—and the oldest inn in the Oldest City—could talk, they would tell of slave uprisings, buried doubloons, and Confederate spies. **Pros:** warm hospitality; family-friendly cottage; Southern breakfast buffet; short walk to historic district. **Cons:** small rooms; small pool; dated decor. ✉ *279 St. George St.* ☎ *904/824–6068 or 800/824–6062* ⊕ *www.stfrancisinn.com* ⤵ *12 rooms, 4 suites, 1 2-bedroom cottage* ⬚ *In-room: kitchen (some), Wi-Fi. In-hotel: pool, parking, some pets allowed, some age restrictions* ⦿ *Breakfast.*

# DAYTONA BEACH AND INLAND TOWNS

The section of the coast around Daytona Beach offers considerable variety, from the unassuming bedroom community of Ormond Beach to the spring break and auto-racing capital of Daytona Beach—go just 75 mi to the south and you've got speeding rockets instead of speeding cars. (Down that way is the Canaveral National Seashore, nestled between New Smyrna Beach and Cocoa Beach.)

Inland, peaceful little towns are separated by miles of two-lane roads, running through dense forest and flat pastureland and skirting one lake after another. There's not much to see but cattle and the state's few hills. Gentle and rolling, they're hardly worth noting to people from true hill country, but they're significant enough in Florida for much of this area to be called the "hill and lake region."

## DAYTONA BEACH

*65 mi south of St. Augustine.*

Best known for the Daytona 500, Daytona has been the center of automobile racing since cars were first raced along the beach here in 1902. February is the biggest month for race enthusiasts, and there are weekly events at the International Speedway. During race weeks, bike weeks, spring break periods, and summer holidays, expect extremely heavy traffic. On the mainland, near the inland waterway, several blocks of Beach Street have been "streetscaped," and shops and restaurants open onto an inviting, broad brick sidewalk.

### GETTING HERE AND AROUND

Several airlines have regular service to Daytona Beach International Airport, which is next to Daytona International Speedway on International Speedway Boulevard, an east–west artery that stretches from I–95 to the beaches. The average drive time from the airport to beachside hotels is 20 minutes; Yellow Cab–Daytona Beach makes the trip for $12–$40.

DOTS Transit Service has scheduled service ($35 one-way, $65 round-trip) connecting Daytona Beach, DeLand, Deltona, and the Orlando International Airport, which serves more airlines and has more direct flights but is about a 70-mi commute via Interstate 4 and SR 417. (Allow at least 90 minutes.) Note that DOTS doesn't serve the Daytona airport. Indeed, outside of a few hotel shuttles, there's no shuttle service between the Daytona airport and town.

Daytona Beach has an excellent bus network, Votran, which serves the beach area, airport, shopping malls, and major arteries, including service to DeLand and NewSmyrna Beach and the Express Link to Orlando. Exact fare is required for Votran ($1.25) if using cash.

> ## HURRY UP AND WAIT
>
> To snowbirds, a trip to Daytona Beach in mid-February might sound like a great idea. Just don't plan it for the weekend of the Daytona 500. Assuming you can even find a hotel room, it will probably cost you double the usual rate. If you plan on leaving your hotel room, you'll most likely get stuck in bumper-to-bumper traffic. And when you get to your destination, it might not be open.

### ESSENTIALS

Transportation Contacts **Daytona Beach International Airport** (*DAB* ☎ *386/248–8069* ⊕ *www.flydaytonafirst.com*). **DOTS Transit Service** (☎ *386/257–5411 or 800/231–1965* ⊕ *www.dots-daytonabeach.com*). **Votran** (☎ *386/756–7496* ⊕ *www.votran.com*). **Yellow Cab–Daytona Beach** (☎ *386/255–5555*).

Visitor Information **Daytona Beach Area Convention and Visitors Bureau** (✉ *126 E. Orange Ave., Daytona Beach* ☎ *800/854–1234* ⊕ *www. daytonabeach.com*).

### EXPLORING

**Casements.** Built in 1912 for Reverend Harwood Huntington and named for its hand-crafted casement windows, it was purchased by John D. Rockefeller Sr. in 1918 as a winter retreat. Once considered the richest man in the world, Rockefeller entertained famous friends such as Henry Ford, Will Rogers, and Henry Flagler at the home while remaining an active member of the Ormond Beach community. After Rockefeller's death in 1937, the property was bought and sold numerous times and is now a cultural center and museum. The waterfront estate and its formal gardens host daily tours and an annual lineup of events and exhibits; there's also a permanent exhibit of Hungarian folk art. ✉ *25 Riverside Dr., Ormond Beach* ☎ *386/676–3216* ⊕ *www.ormondbeach. org* ✉ *Donations accepted* ☉ *Call for hrs and tour times.*

**Halifax Historical Museum.** Memorabilia from the early days of beach automobile racing are on display here, as are historic photographs, American Indian and Civil War artifacts, a postcard exhibit, and a video that details city history. There's a shop for gifts and antiques, too, and kids get free admission on Saturday. ✉ *252 S. Beach St.* ☎ *386/255–6976* ⊕ *www.halifaxhistorical.org* ✉ *$5* ☉ *Tues.–Sat. 10–4.*

🕲 **Museum of Arts & Sciences.** This behemoth museum has a humanities section with displays of Chinese art, and glass, silver, gold, and porcelain examples of decorative arts. The museum also has the largest collection of Cuban art outside of Cuba, Florida American Indian items, pre-Columbian art, Indian and Persian miniature paintings, and an eye-popping complete skeleton of a giant sloth that is 13 feet long and 130,000 years old. Kids will love the Charles and Linda Williams Children's Museum, which is filled with interactive science experiments; a 2½-acre outdoor contemporary-sculpture garden; and a planetarium with laser-light shows. ⊠ *352 S. Nova Rd.* ☎ *386/255–0285* ⊕ *www. moas.org* ✉ *$12.95* ⊗ *Tues.–Sat. 9–5, Sun. 11–5.*

**OFF THE BEATEN PATH**

**Ponce de León Inlet Light Station.** At the southern tip of the barrier island that includes Daytona Beach is the sleepy town of Ponce Inlet, with a small marina, a few bars, and casual seafood restaurants. Boardwalks traverse delicate dunes and provide easy access to the beach, although storms have caused serious erosion. Marking this prime spot is the bright-red, century-old Ponce de León Inlet Light Station, a National Historic Monument and museum, the tallest lighthouse in the state and the third-tallest in the country. Climb to the top of the 175-foot-tall lighthouse tower for a bird's-eye view of Ponce Inlet. ⊠ *4931 S. Peninsula Dr., Ponce Inlet* ☎ *386/761–1821* ⊕ *www.ponceinlet.org* ✉ *$5* ⊗ *Memorial Day–Labor Day, daily 10–9; after Labor Day, daily 10–6; last admission 1 hr prior to closing.*

**BEACH**

★ **Daytona Beach.** At the World's Most Famous Beach you can drive right onto the sand (at least from one hour after sunrise to one hour before sunset), spread out a blanket, and have all your belongings at hand (with the exception of alcohol, which is prohibited). All that said, heavy traffic during summer and holidays makes it dangerous for children, and families should be extra careful or stay in the designated car-free zones. The speed limit is 10 mph, and there's a $5 fee, collected at the beach ramps, for driving on the sands every month but December and January.

The wide, 23-mi-long beach can get crowded in the "strip" area (between International Speedway Boulevard and Seabreeze Boulevard) with its food vendors, beachfront bars, volleyball matches, and motorized water sports enthusiasts. Those seeking a quieter experience can head north or south in either direction toward car-free zones in more residential areas. The hard-packed sand that makes the beach suitable for driving is also perfect for running and cycling. There's also excellent surf fishing directly from the beach. **Best for:** Swimming, accessibility, sunrises, sunbathing, biking, families. **Amenities:** Lifeguards, food concessions, off- and on-beach parking, beachfront parks with playground, picnic and restroom facilities. ■TIP→ Signs on Route A1A indicate car access via beach ramps. Sand traps aren't limited to the golf course, though—cars can get stuck.

If the action on Daytona Beach is too much for you, soar above it by parasailing.

## SPORTS AND THE OUTDOORS

### BIRD-WATCHING

**Tomoka State Park.** With more than 160 species to see, this scenic park is perfect for bird-watching. It also has wooded campsites, bicycle and walking paths, and kayak and canoe rentals on the Tomoka and Halifax rivers. It's on the site of a Timucuan Indian settlement discovered in 1605 by Spanish explorer Alvaro Mexia. ☒ *2099 N. Beach St, 3 mi north of Ormond Beach* ☎ *386/676–4050, 800/326–3521 (Reserve America) for camping reservations* ⊕ *www.floridastateparks. org/tomoka* ☒ *$5 per vehicle, up to 8 people, $2 pedestrians, camping $27 per night* ☉ *Daily 8–sundown.*

### BOATING

**Cracker Creek.** At this eco-adventure park you can rent kayaks, canoes, and pontoon boats or take ecotours or a Pirate Cruise on scenic Spruce Creek. There are also on-site picnic facilities. ☒ *1795 Taylor Rd., Port Orange* ☎ *386/304–0778* ⊕ *www.oldfloridapioneer.com* ☉ *Fri.–Sun. 8–5; canoeing and kayaking by reservation only.*

### FISHING

**Finest Kind II Sport Fishing Charters.** This company offers everything you could need and (hopefully) more with half-day, full-day, and night fishing excursions, as well as burial at sea! ☒ *Inlet Harbor Marina, 133 Inlet Harbor Rd., Ponce Inlet* ☎ *386/527–0732* ⊕ *www.finestkind2fishing. com.*

**Sea Spirit Fishing.** Four- to 10-hour private and group charters are options with this operator. ☒ *Inlet Harbor Marina, 133 Inlet Harbor Rd., Ponce Inlet* ☎ *386/763–4388* ⊕ *www.seaspiritfishing.com.*

## GOLF

**Indigo Lakes Golf Club.** Greens fees to play the 18 holes here are $20–$40. ✉ *312 Indigo Dr.* ☎ *386/254–3607* ⊕ *www.indigolakesgolf.com.*

**LPGA International Legends Course.** The public courses here have 36 holes. Greens fees are $59–$64. ✉ *1000 Champions Dr., Daytona Beach* ☎ *386/523–2001* ⊕ *www.lpgainternational.com.*

**Pelican Bay South Country Club.** In addition to playing on one of two 18-hole courses, you can rent clubs, visit the pro shop, and a grab a bite in the restaurant. Greens fees are $35–$45. ✉ *350 Pelican Bay Dr.* ☎ *386/756–0034* ⊕ *www.pelicanbaycc.com.*

**Spruce Creek Golf & Country Club.** There's an 18-hole course at Spruce Creek, along with practice and driving ranges, rental clubs, a pro shop, and a restaurant. Greens fees are $39–$49. ✉ *1900 Country Club Dr., Port Orange* ☎ *386/756–6114* ⊕ *www.sprucecreekgolf.com.*

## MANATEE SPOTTING

**Blue Spring State Park.** January and February are the top months for sighting sea cows at this designated manatee refuge, but they begin to head here in November, as soon as the water gets cold enough (below 68°F). Your best bet for spotting a manatee is to walk along the boardwalk. The park, which is 30 mi southwest of Daytona Beach on Interstate 4, was once a river port where paddle wheelers stopped to take on cargoes of oranges. Home to the largest spring on the St. Johns River, the park offers hiking, camping, and picnicking facilities. It also contains a historic homestead that's open to the public. ✉ *2100 W. French Ave., Orange City* ☎ *386/775–3663* ⊕ *www.floridastateparks.org/bluespring* ▱ *$6 per vehicle, up to 8 people, $2 for pedestrians and bicyclists* ⊙ *Daily 8–sundown.*

☺ **Manatee Scenic Boat Tours.** This Ponce Inlet operator takes you on narrated cruises of the Intracoastal Waterway. Kids will love looking for the creatures also known as "sea cows," and your guide might tell you how (sun-delirious?) sailors may have mistaken them for mermaids. ✉ *133 Inlet Harbor Rd., Ponce Inlet* ☎ *386/761–2027 or 800/881–2628* ⊕ *www.manateecruise.com.*

## WATER SPORTS

**Daytona Beach Parasail.** Catch air with this Ponce Inlet outfitter. ✉ *4936 S. Peninsula, Ponce Inlet* ☎ *386/547–6067* ⊕ *www.daytonaparasailing.com.*

**Maui Nix.** Maui Nix is one of several outfitters that rent surf or boogie boards. ✉ *635 N. Atlantic Ave.* ☎ *386/253–1234* ⊕ *www.mauinix.com/store.*

**Salty Dog Surf Shop.** You can rent surfboards or boogie boards at Salty Dog Surf Shop ✉ *700 E. International Speedway Blvd.* ☎ *386/258–0457* ⊕ *www.saltydogsurfshop.com.*

## SHOPPING

**Daytona Flea and Farmers' Market.** One of the largest flea markets in the South draws residents from all over the state as well as visitors to the state. ✉ *2987 Bellevue Ave.* ☎ *386/253–3330.*

**Destination Daytona.** This 100-acre biker enclave is complete with an expansive Harley Davidson dealership; retail shops; a restaurant; bars; a tattoo parlor; a hotel; and a pavilion used for concerts, conventions—even biker-inspired weddings. ⊠ *1635 N. U.S. Hwy. 1, Ormond Beach* ⊕ *www.destinationdaytona.com.*

**The Pavilion at Port Orange.** Just off Interstate-95 (Port Orange Exit) is this outdoor shopping complex. It houses a 14-screen Hollywood Theaters; numerous restaurants; and retailers like the Southern department store, Belk, and ULTA beauty and cosmetics shop. ⊠ *5501 S. Williamson Blvd., Port Orange* ⊕ *www.thepavilionatportorange.com.*

**Volusia Mall.** This mall has more than 125 stores, including anchors like JCPenney, Macy's, and Dillard's. ⊠ *1700 W. International Speedway Blvd.* ☎ *386/253–6783.*

### NIGHTLIFE

**NIGHTLIFE**

**Boot Hill Saloon.** Despite its reputation as a biker bar, this place welcomes nonbikers and even nonbiker tourists! ⊠ *310 Main St.* ☎ *386/ 258–9506).*

**Ocean Walk Village.** Lively and always hopping, Ocean Walk is a cluster of shops, restaurants, and bars (the Mai Tai Bar is a good bet) stretching along Atlantic Avenue and the ocean.

**Ocean Deck.** It's the only oceanfront nightclub with live reggae music. ⊠ *127 S. Ocean Ave.* ☎ *386/253–5224.*

**The Oyster Pub.** Spring breakers congregate by the thousands here. ⊠ *555 Seabreeze Blvd.* ☎ *386/255–6348.*

**Razzle's Nightclub.** DJs play high-energy dance music from 8 pm–3 am. ⊠ *611 Seabreeze Blvd.* ☎ *386/257–6236.*

### WHERE TO EAT

$ ╳ **Aunt Catfish's on the River.** Don't be surprised if your server introduces herself as your cousin, though you've never seen her before in your life. You see, everybody is "cousin" at Aunt Catfish's (as in, "Can I get you another mason jar of sweet tea, Cousin?"). The silly Southern hospitality is only one of the draws at this wildly popular seafood restaurant just south of Daytona. The main lure, of course, is the food: fried chicken, fried shrimp, fried catfish, and crab cakes. Hot cinnamon rolls and hush puppies come with every entrée and can be a meal in themselves. Bring your appetite and your patience—a wait is practically guaranteed. Sunday brunch lures empty stomachs with made-to-order eggs and French toast, and a chocolate fountain. ⊠ *4009 Halifax Dr., Port Orange* ☎ *386/767–4768* ⊕ *auntcatfishontheriver.com* ⌧ *Reservations not accepted.*

SEAFOOD

$ ╳ **Daytona Brickyard.** It's not just the locals who swear that the Brickyard's charboiled sirloin burgers are the best they've ever tasted—devotees have been known to drive from Georgia just for lunch. Given its name and location in the heart of NASCAR country, the popular bar and grill is covered in racing memorabilia. Dang, even the floor and the tablecloths are black-and-white checkered. But don't mistake the racing theme to mean the place merely serves greasy bar food to Joe Sixpacks.

AMERICAN

*Continued on page 148*

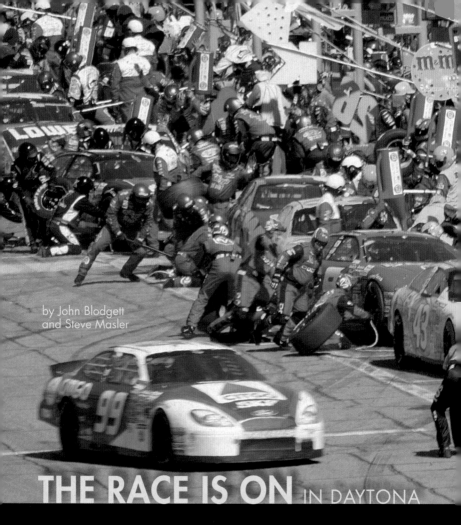

by John Blodgett
and Steve Masler

# THE RACE IS ON IN DAYTONA

It's morning on race day. Check the weather—rain or shine? The race won't run if it's raining, but bring a poncho just in case, and pack some sunscreen, too (maybe even throw in a beach umbrella). Oh, and don't forget your binoculars and ear plugs. Fill your cooler with snacks and drinks—yes, it's allowed. Got your waterproof padded seat? Good. If you have a radio scanner, bring it to listen in on the pit crews; if you don't, you can rent one at the track for $50 ($30 for Sprint customers). This handheld device, in addition to its scanning capabilities, provides live video feeds, driver statistics, and auto replay.

You're here! Welcome to Daytona International Speedway—the storied race track that is home to one of America's most famous races, the Daytona 500. Hope you like crowds, because you'll be jostling with upward of 200,000 fellow race fanatics. The gate generally opens at 8 AM, with the race starting at 1 PM. The hours in between are one of the best times to seek autographs from your favorite racers in their garages near the Sprint FANZONE (drivers also can be approached throughout race weekend as they hang out at their respective souvenir haulers).

Watching the race is a sensory experience: 43 cars powered by 800 or more horsepower make

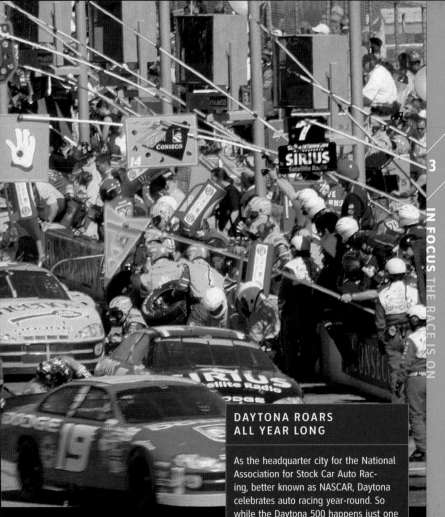

for a constant roar; there's the smell of hot rubber, fuel, and exhaust; and, if you happen to be down low by the track itself, you might be pelted by flecks of tire as the pack blasts by at speeds approaching 190 mph. Every so often, let your binoculars wander—you might just see a past champion or other celebrity.

A few hours later the adrenaline-packed race is finished and your ears will be ringing (unless you remembered plugs). Now it's time to cheer the victor and wait in line to go find your car. This is when you grab another beverage from your cooler and relive the race with the fans next to you.

## DAYTONA ROARS ALL YEAR LONG

As the headquarter city for the National Association for Stock Car Auto Racing, better known as NASCAR, Daytona celebrates auto racing year-round. So while the Daytona 500 happens just one day out of 365, there's plenty for you to see and do every day at the speedway's 480-acre complex. You can go to other races, go on a tour, or, as part of the Richard Petty Driving Experience, maybe even jump into a stock car yourself. Major races are held during nine weekends, and an assortment of other races take place throughout the year. On non-race days the Speedway is host to R&D of racing vehicles, car shows, and other events. For motorcycles, there's the Daytona 200 and the Daytona Supercross by Honda.

# THE LAPS ALONG THE WAY

For more than 50 years, the world's top NASCAR drivers have competed in the Daytona 500, considered by many to be the sport's premier race.

The first official Daytona 500 was held on February 22, 1959, with 59 cars in front of 41,000 fans. It has been held each year in late February ever since. In the half century that followed, cash awards have grown from $68,000 to $18 million, with fewer drivers—43—but triple the fans—200,000. Every year the 500-mi (200-lap) race marks the beginning of NASCAR's premier Sprint Cup series and generally offers the greatest monetary reward. Winning the Daytona 500 has been equated with a Super Bowl victory, and much as in that sport, the final moments can be the most memorable and most important.

## GETTING TICKETS

For tickets to the Daytona 500 or any other races held at the speedway, contact the Daytona Speedway ticket office (✉ 1801 W. International Speedway Blvd., Daytona Beach ☎ 800/PIT-SHOP [748–7467] ⊕ www.daytonainternationalspeedway.com). Single ticket prices to the Daytona 500 range from $55 to $185, primo seats go quickly, so the sooner you order the better. Grandstand seats typically sell out days or weeks in advance.

## NASCAR'S FINEST

**David Pearson**
"The Silver Fox"
105 NASCAR wins
retired in 1986.

**Dale Earnhardt**
"The Intimidator"
"Ironhead"
Killed during the
2001 Daytona 500.

**Richard Petty**
"King Richard,"
Most NASCAR wins
(200) and Daytona
victories (7).

**Jimmie Johnson**
Won his fifth
consecutive Sprint
Cup championship
in 2010.

Getting out and inspecting the track first hand is just one part of a Daytona Speedway tour.

**You don't have to wait** until race days to explore the World Center of Racing. Some of the best exploring can be done when the engines are silent. Narrated tours give you a look at the hallowed grounds where Fireball Roberts, Bobby Allison, Richard Petty, and Dale Earnhardt turned a regional sport into an international phenomenon.

The 60-minute All Access Tour ($22; hourly 10–3) brings you into the ritzy Daytona 500 Club and the Houston Lawing Press Box in the Sprint Tower, which features views not only of the 2.5-mile tri-oval, but also of the Atlantic Ocean nearby. You'll also visit the drivers' meeting room, the NASCAR Sprint Cup garages, Gatorade Victory Lane, and the Sprint FANZONE. There are three dramatic photo opportunities on the tour: Victory Lane, the start/finish line, and the daunting 31-degree banking in Turns 3 and 4.

Other options include the 30-minute Speedway Tour ($15; 11:30, 1:30, and 3:30) and the three-hour VIP Tour ($50; by reservation on select days). ✉ 1801 W. International Speedway Blvd. ☎ 800/748–7467 ⊕ www.daytonainternationalspeedway.com.

If you're not satisfied with merely viewing the historic speedway, driving opportunities

Driving Experience. You can ride shotgun—or, for more dough, drive yourself—in a stock car on Daytona International Speedway. You suit up, helmet and all, and slide into the car through the window, just like you're Jimmie Johnson. Be sure to get a photo afterward so your friends believe you when you tell them how you zoomed around at speeds in excess of 150 mph! Ride-alongs cost $135; call for driving prices and to reserve a ride. ☎ 800-BE PETTY (800/237–3389).

## LADIES WELCOME

Stock-car racing has long been a male-dominated sport, but icons such as Dale Earnhardt Jr. and Jeff Gordon have been, on occasion, overshadowed by women. Danica Patrick, the pint-sized, telegenic driver of Indy Car fame made her NASCAR debut at Daytona in a 2010 Nationwide Series race. Patrick, who is planning a transition into NASCAR, is among a growing number of women entering motorsports but one of only a few to break into NASCAR. Most people expect Patrick to be the first woman to race in the highest series, the Sprint Cup.

It also feeds T-bone and New York strip steaks to doctors. ✉ *747 International Speedway Blvd.* ☎ *386/253–2270* ⊕ *www.daytonabrickyard. com* ⚠ *Reservations not accepted.*

**$$$**
STEAK
★

✕ **Gene's Steak House.** Quiet and intimate, this family-operated restaurant and race-car-driver hangout has long upheld its reputation as the best place for steaks in the area (since 1948, to be exact) despite its nondescript exterior and somewhat out-of-the-way location west of town. Gene's has a decidedly old-school, supper-club vibe, with classics like escargot baked in puff pastry, French onion soup, and Gene's special-recipe Roquefort dressing. Signature entrées include cooked-to-order filet mignons, sirloins, and porterhouses. Seafood is also on the menu, and the wine list is one of the state's largest, with bottles ranging from $19 to $1,200. ✉ *3674 W. International Speedway Blvd.* ☎ *386/255–2059* ⊕ *www.genessteakhouse.com* ⊙ *Closed Mon. No lunch.*

**$$$$**
STEAK

✕ **Hyde Park Prime Steakhouse.** This chophouse provides an upscale alternative to Daytona's more prevalent shorts-and-flip-flop joints. The lively dining room—done in dark wood with soft lighting and splashes of colorful artwork—is complemented by dramatic ocean views. Attentive servers carry chalkboards detailing specials such as lobster or mac and cheese. But steaks, especially the cuts named after race-car drivers, and mouthwatering sides (don't miss the potatoes Gruyère gratin) are the main attractions. The 22-ounce bone rib eye named after beefy Tony Stewart is, appropriately the thickest, showing that these guys know their NASCAR. The popular Steak Earnhardt is a filet mignon over bordelaise crowned with lobster, béarnaise (yes, it has two sauces), asparagus, and mushroom caps. An expansive wine list includes over 40 options by the glass. And don't let this restaurant chain's Ohio roots fool you—the key lime pie is absolutely Florida-worthy. *Hilton Resort* ✉ *100 N. Atlantic Ave.* ☎ *386/226–9844* ⊕ *www.hydeparkrestaurants.com.*

**$$$**
SEAFOOD
Fodor's Choice
★

✕ **Martini's Chophouse.** Local beautiful people seem to flock to this trendy South Daytona Beach eatery and lounge as much for the scene as they do for the food. The bar area, done in gray with splashes of lime green, is a modern meeting place for the after-work crowd, and the outdoor deck and bar attract a livelier bunch. Those who do deign to dine will appreciate the chef's use of homegrown herbs and creative sauces in dishes such as marinated skirt steak with *chimichurri* (a sauce of parsely, garlic, olive oil, vinegar, and red pepper) and barbecue-grilled Chilean salmon with cucumber and melon relish, which can be enjoyed in the sleek dining room or in the garden, complete with a 20-foot lighted waterfall and fire pit. ✉ *1815 S. Ridgewood Ave., South Daytona* ☎ *386/763–1090* ⊙ *Closed Sun. and Mon.*

## WHERE TO STAY

*For expanded hotel reviews, visit Fodors.com.*

**$$$**
RESORT
★

▦ **Hilton Daytona Beach Oceanfront Resort.** Perched on the only traffic-free strip of beach in Daytona, this high-rise is as popular with families as it is with couples. **Pros:** spacious rooms; beach access. **Cons:** small pool; extra charges ✉ *100 N. Atlantic Ave.* ☎ *386/254–8200 or 866/536–8477* ⊕ *www.daytonahilton.com* 🛏 *744 rooms, 52 suites* ⚙ *In-room: Wi-Fi. In-hotel: restaurants, bars, pools, gym, beach, laundry facilities.*

The Florida Trail goes through Ocala National Forest, taking hikers past hardwoods, pines, and prairies.

**$$$**
RESORT
☼
**Perry's Ocean Edge Resort.** Perhaps more than any other property in Daytona, Perry's has a die-hard fan base, many of whom started coming to the oceanfront resort as children, then returned with their children and their children's children. **Pros:** spacious rooms; helpful staff; nice pools; family-friendly. **Cons:** small bathrooms; slow elevators; limited TV channels. ⊠ *2209 S. Atlantic Ave.* ☎ *386/255–0581 or 800/447–0002* ⊕ *www.perrysoceanedge.com* ↘ *200 rooms* ☼ *In-room: kitchen, Wi-Fi. In-hotel: restaurant, bar, pools, gym, beach, children's programs, laundry facilities, parking* ❑I *Breakfast.*

**$$$**
RESORT
Fodor's Choice
★
**The Shores Resort & Spa.** Rustic furniture and beds swathed in mosquito netting are a nod to Old Florida at this 11-story beachfront resort, but there's nothing rustic about the amenities, including a luxury four-poster bed and a 42-inch plasma TV in every room. **Pros:** beachfront; spa; friendly staff; 24-hour room service. **Cons:** expensive restaurant; crowded pool; not all rooms have balconies. ⊠ *2637 S. Atlantic Ave., Daytona Beach Shores* ☎ *386/767–7350 or 866/934–7467* ⊕ *www. shoresresort.com* ↘ *212 rooms, 1 suite* ☼ *In-room: Wi-Fi. In-hotel: restaurant, bars, pool, gym, spa, beach, parking, some pets allowed.*

**$$–$$$$**
RESORT
☼
Fodor's Choice
★
**Wyndham Ocean Walk Resort.** Kids definitely won't be bored at this all-suites high-rise beachfront resort with four swimming pools, a water-slide, lazy river, game room, indoor miniature-golf course, activities center, and the only traffic-free beach in Daytona Beach. **Pros:** family-friendly; beachfront; great facilities; in-room washers and dryers; spacious accommodations. **Cons:** no room service; very slow elevators. ⊠ *300 N. Atlantic Ave.* ☎ *386/323–4800 or 800/347–9092* ⊕ *www. oceanwalk.com* ↘ *200 1-, 2-, and 3-bedroom suites* ☼ *In-room:*

*kitchen. In-hotel: restaurants, bars, golf course, pools, gym, beach, water sports, children's programs.*

## OCALA NATIONAL FOREST

*Eastern entrance 40 mi west of Daytona Beach, northern entrance 52 mi south of Jacksonville.*

**Ocala National Forest.** This breathtaking 383,000-acre national forest off State Road 40 has lakes, springs, rivers, hiking trails, campgrounds, and historic sites. It also has the largest off-highway vehicle trail system in the Southeast and three major recreational areas: Alexander Springs, Salt Springs, and Juniper Springs. About 30 campsites are sprinkled throughout the park and range from bare sites to sites with electric hook-ups, showers, and bathrooms (credit cards are not accepted at them.) ⊠ *Visitor center, 17147 Rte. 40 E, Salt Springs* ☎ *352/625–2520* ⊕ *www.fs.fed.us/r8/florida.*

**Alexander Springs.** In this recreation area you'll find a stream and a campground. ⊠ *Off Rte. 40 via Rte. 445 S* ☎ *$4.*

**Salt Springs.** The draw here is a natural saltwater spring where Atlantic blue crabs come to spawn each summer. The area received a sidewalk and landscaping update in the latter half of 2009. ⊠ *Visitor center, 14100 State Rd. 19* ☎ *$4.*

**Juniper Springs.** Here you'll find a stone waterwheel house, a campground, a natural-spring swimming pool, and hiking trails. The 7-mi Juniper Springs run is a narrow, twisting, and winding canoe ride, which, although exhilarating, isn't for the novice. ⊠ *14100 Rte. 40 N* ☎ *$4.*

### SPORTS AND THE OUTDOORS

#### CANOEING

**Juniper Springs Canoe Rentals.** Canoe rentals and guided tours are available through this operator inside Ocala National Forest. ☎ *352/625–2808.*

#### FISHING

**Captain Tom's Custom Charters.** Charter fishing trips offered by this company range from three hours to a full day. You can arrange sightseeing cruises as well. Trips are by reservation only. ☎ *352/236–0872.*

#### HORSEBACK RIDING

**Adopt a Horse Club.** Located within the Ocala National Forest, this outfitter offers nature trail riding lessons (walk, gait, and canter) for ages 6 and older. ⊠ *22651 S.E. Hwy. 42* ☎ *352/821–4756 or 800/731–4756* ⊕ *www.adoptahorseclub.com.*

## OCALA

*78 mi west of Daytona Beach*

This is horse country: here at the forest's western edge are dozens of horse farms with grassy paddocks and white-wooden fences. Hills and sweeping fields of bluegrass make the area feel more like Kentucky than Florida, which is entirely appropriate. The peaceful town is considered a center for thoroughbred breeding and training, and Kentucky Derby winners have been raised in the region's training centers. Sometimes the farms are open to the public.

**Appleton Museum of Art.** Part of a three-building cultural complex, the Appleton is a marble-and-granite tour de force with a serene esplanade and reflecting pool. The collection lives up to its surroundings, thanks to a stellar collection of European, American and contemporary art plus more than 6,000 pre-Columbian, Asian, and African antiquities and artifacts. ⊠ *4333 E. Silver Springs Blvd.* ☎ *352/291–4455* ⊕ *www. appletonmuseum.org* ☞ *$6* ☉ *Tues.–Sat. 10–5, Sun. noon–5.*

**Don Garlits Museum of Drag Racing.** Retired drag racer Don Garlit pays tribute to the drag racing's cars and the drivers at this museum. Among his extensive collection are a 1963 Pontiac Firebird Jet, the only car to run more than 290 mph in the ¼ mi; a rare 1904 Orient Buckboard, a consumer automobile built predominantly out of wood; and a 1956 Chrysler sedan once owned by President Eisenhower. ⊠ *13700 S.W. 16th Ave.* ☎ *877/271–3278* ⊕ *www.garlits.com* ☞ *$15* ☉ *Daily 9–5.*

**Silver Springs.** The 350-acre natural theme park at the western edge of the Ocala National Forest has the world's largest collection of artesian springs. The state's first tourist attraction, it was established in 1890. Today the park presents wild-animal displays, glass-bottom-boat tours on the Silver River, a Jeep safari through 35 acres of wilderness, and walks through natural habitats. Exhibits include the Panther Prowl, which enables visitors to watch and photograph the endangered Florida panther, and the Big Gator Lagoon, a 1-acre cypress swamp with more than 30 alligators. Other attractions include the Fort King River Cruise and the Lighthouse Ride, a combination carousel/gondola ride giving guests a bird's-eye view of the park. ⊠ *Rte. 40, Exit 352 east off I–75 or Exit 268 west off I–95, 5656 E. Silver Springs Blvd., Silver Springs* ☎ *352/236–2121* ⊕ *www.silversprings.com* ☞ *$29.99; Silver Pass (with access to Wild Waters water park, concerts, and special events) $45.99* ☉ *Call for hrs.*

**Silver Springs Wild Waters.** This is a great place to cool off, thanks to a 450,000-gallon wave pool, a 220-foot-long speed flume, a three-story high wild-water flume, and a multilevel kids area. The water park is open April through September. Call for hours. ☎ *352/236–2121* ⊕ *www.wildwaterspark.com* ☞ *$23.99; Silver Pass (with access to Silver Springs Park, concerts, and special events) $45.99.*

## GAINESVILLE

*40 mi northwest of Ocala, 98 mi northwest of Daytona Beach.*

The University of Florida (UF) anchors this sprawling town. Visitors are mostly Gator football fans and parents of students, so the styles and costs of accommodations are aimed at budget-minded travelers rather than luxury-seeking vacationers. The surrounding area encompasses several state parks and interesting gardens and geological sites.

**GETTING HERE AND AROUND**

Gainesville Regional Airport is served by Delta and US Airways. From the airport, taxi fare to the center of Gainesville is about $20; some hotels provide free airport pickup.

**ESSENTIALS**

Transportation Contact Gainesville Regional Airport (*GNV* ☎ *352/373–0249* ⊕ *www.gra-gnv.com*).

Visitor Information Gainesville/Alachua County Visitors and Convention Bureau (✉ *30 E. University Ave., Gainesville* ☎ *352/374–5260 or 866/778–5002* ⊕ *www.visitgainesville.com*).

> **LATER, GATORS**
>
> Depending on what time of year you visit, Gainesville's population could be plus or minus 50,000. Home to one of the largest colleges in the country, the University of Florida, Gainesville takes on a different personality during the summer when most students return home. During the fall and spring terms, the downtown streets are teeming with students on bikes, scooters, and foot, but in summer it's much more laid-back.

**EXPLORING**

**Devil's Millhopper Geological State Park.** Scientists surmise that thousands of years ago an underground cavern collapsed and created this geological wonder that is designated as a National Natural Landmark. See the botanical wonderland of exotic subtropical ferns and trees growing in the 500-foot-wide, 120-foot-deep sinkhole. You pass a dozen small waterfalls as you head down 236 steps to the bottom. Pack your lunch and enjoy it in one of the park's picnic areas. And bring Spot, too; just keep him on a leash while he's at the park. Guided walks with the park ranger are offered Saturday mornings at 10. ✉ *4732 Millhopper Rd., off U.S. 441* ☎ *352/955–2008* ⊕ *www.floridastateparks.org/devilsmillhopper* 💲 *$4 per vehicle, up to 8 people, $2 for pedestrians and bicyclists* ⊙ *Wed.–Sun. 9–5.*

☺ **Florida Museum of Natural History.** On the campus of the University of Florida, the state's official museum of natural history and the largest natural-history museum in the Southeast has holdings of more than 30 million objects and specimens. In addition to active collections in anthropology, archaeology, botany, mammalogy, and ornithology, the museum features several interesting replicas, including nearly complete fossil skeletons of a mastodon and mammoth from the last Ice Age as well as a full-size model of a Florida cave and mangrove forest. The Butterfly Rainforest houses 60 to 80 species in a 6,400-square-foot, screened, free-flight vivarium. Butterfly releases take place Saturday and Sunday at 2, 3, and 4, weather permitting. ✉ *University of Florida Cultural Plaza, S.W. 34th St. at Hull Rd.* ☎ *352/846–2000* ⊕ *www.flmnh.ufl.edu* 💲 *Butterfly Rainforest $10.50* ⊙ *Mon.–Sat. 10–5, Sun. 1–5.*

**Samuel P. Harn Museum of Art.** The large (86,800 square feet) Harn Museum has five main collections: Asian, with works dating back to the Neolithic era; African, encompassing costumes, domestic wares, and personal adornments; Modern, featuring the works of Georgia O'Keeffe, William Morris Hunt, and George Bellows; Contemporary, with original pieces by Willem de Kooning and Andy Warhol; and Photography, including the work of Jerry N. Uelsmann, a retired University of Florida professor. ⊠ *University of Florida Cultural Plaza, S.W. 34th St. and Hull Rd.* ☎ *352/392–9826* ⊕ *www.harn.ufl.edu* ☒ *Free* ⊙ *Tues.–Fri. 11–5, Sat. 10–5, Sun. 1–5.*

## SPORTS AND THE OUTDOORS

### AUTO RACING

**Gainesville Raceway.** The site of professional and amateur auto and motor-cycle races, including Gatornationals in March, is also home to Frank Hawley's Drag Racing School (☎ *866/480–7223* ⊕ *www.frankhawley. com*). ⊠ *11211 N. County Rd. 225* ☎ *352/377–0046, 626/914–4761 for National Hot Rod Association* ⊕ *www.gainesvilleraceway.com.*

### FOOTBALL

**Ben Hill Griffin Stadium.** The University of Florida Gators play their home games in the largest stadium in the state, which is also referred to as "The Swamp." ⊠ *Lemerand Dr. and Stadium Rd.* ☎ *352/375–4683.*

## NIGHTLIFE

**1982 Bar.** There's music five nights a week and drinking games every night. ⊠ *919 W. University Ave.* ☎ *352/371–9836* ⊕ *www.1982bar.com.*

**Calico Jack's Oyster Bar.** Locals come here for seafood, beer, and, on Friday, live music. ⊠ *3501 S.W. 2nd Ave.* ☎ *352/375–2337* ⊕ *www. calicojacks.net.*

**Common Grounds.** You can get your caffeine and live-music fix here. The grounds have something in common, but the bands are an eclectic mix. ⊠ *210 S.W. 2nd Ave.* ☎ *352/372–7320* ⊕ *www.commongroundslive.com.*

**Lillian's Music Store.** Gainesville's oldest bar has rock and Top 40 music, bands, and karaoke. ⊠ *112 S.E. 1st St.* ☎ *352/372–1010.*

**The Swamp Restaurant.** This place attracts college students by the pitcher, especially on game day. ⊠ *1642 W. University Ave.* ☎ *352/377–9267* ⊕ *swamprestaurant.com.*

## WHERE TO EAT

$ ╳ **Bistro 1245.** Get high-quality meals at bargain-basement prices at
AMERICAN this trendy yet surprisingly down-to-earth restaurant that shares a roof with Leonardo's by the Slice. Some call the small dining room cramped, while others find the close quarters to be romantic. However you look at it, the menu is full of comfort foods with a twist, such as maple-roasted chicken breast, spicy shrimp pasta, seared-tuna club sandwich, and bison sirloin. In keeping with the bistro's lack of pretention, you're invited to pick your own wine from the restaurant's wine rack. For a lighter meal and a lighter price, order from the lunch menu in the evening. ⊠ *1245 W. University Ave.* ☎ *352/376–0000* ⊕ *www. leonardosgainesville.com.*

$$ ╳ **Emiliano's Café.** Linen tablecloths and art deco–style artwork create
LATIN AMERICAN a casual, elegant feel at this Gainesville institution serving Pan-Latin cuisine for more than 20 years. Dine indoors or beneath the stars on the sidewalk café. Start with the Gallician stew (a family recipe) or the black-bean soup, and then move on to one of the chef's signature dishes—Spanish saffron rice with shrimp, clams, mussels, fresh fish, chicken, artichoke hearts, peas, asparagus, and pimientos. Emiliano's also offers an extensive tapas menu with nearly 40 items to mix and

match, and tempting desserts like the original chipotle brownie cake. Live jazz fills the air Monday and Wednesday nights. ⊠ *7 SE 1st Ave.* ☎ *352/375–7381* ⊕ *www.emilianoscafe.com.*

¢    ✕ **Leonardo's by the Slice.** It's ironic that the kitschy pizza joint with a
ITALIAN   '50s flair is surrounded by a white-picket fence, since most of its patrons and employees are far from conventional. College students, especially the pierced and tatted kind, flock to the Gainesville landmark not only because it's cheap but because it has the best pizza in town. Available in thick or thin varieties, by the pie and, of course, by the slice, Leonardo's pizza comes in a handful of varieties (like veggie, pepperoni, Greek, and spinach tomato). It also offers calzones, salads, and pasta such as baked ziti and spinach lasagna, with no entrée over $8. ⊠ *1245 W. University Ave.* ☎ *352/378–2001* ⊕ *www.leonardosgainesville.com* ⌂ *Reservations not accepted.*

$$–$$$    ✕ **Paramount Grill.** This tiny, fine-dining restaurant may have single-
CONTINENTAL   handedly changed the perception of Gainesville from a college town
Fodor's Choice   fueled by pizza, chicken wings, and pitchers of beer to an up-and-
★   coming culinary destination with imaginative menus driven by fresh Florida produce. What Paramount lacks in size and glitz it makes up for with its menu. Try one of the five house salads and such entrées as grilled duck breast over wild-mushroom ravioli or blackened salmon with black-bean crepes. If you miss lunch here, try the Sunday brunch. ⊠ *12 S.W. 1st Ave.* ☎ *352/378–3398* ⊕ *www.paramountgrill.com* ☉ *No lunch Sat.*

## WHERE TO STAY

*For expanded hotel reviews, visit Fodors.com.*

$$$    ⊞ **Herlong Mansion.** Spanish moss clings to the stately oak trees sur-
B&B/INN   rounding this restored 1880s mansion in the town of Micanopy, 11 mi north of Gainesville. **Pros:** large private bathrooms; gourmet breakfast; evening wine-and-cookies reception. **Cons:** no phones in rooms; no TVs in some rooms; some small and windowless rooms; 14-day cancellation policy. ⊠ *402 N.E. Cholokka Blvd., Micanopy* ☎ *352/466–3322 or 800/437–5664* ⊕ *www.herlong.com* ⤳ *12 rooms, 2 cottages* ⌂ *In-room: no TV (some), Wi-Fi. In-hotel: parking, some age restrictions* ⑩ *Breakfast.*

$$$    ⊞ **Hilton University of Florida Conference Center Gainesville.** With 25,000
HOTEL   square feet of meeting space, the University of Florida's flagship hotel caters most obviously to business travelers, but its location on the southwest corner of the campus also makes it a good choice for UF visitors. **Pros:** proximity to college; free Internet; spacious rooms. **Cons:** 4 pm check-in; spotty service; overrated restaurant. ⊠ *1714 S.W. 34th St.* ☎ *352/371–3600* ⊕ *www.hilton.com* ⤳ *245 rooms, 3 suites* ⌂ *In-room: kitchen (some), Internet. In-hotel: restaurants, bar, pool, gym, parking, some pets allowed.*

$$$    ⊞ **Laurel Oak Inn.** Guests at this 1885 Queen Anne–style dwelling say
B&B/INN   they're so comfortable and at ease they feel like they're in a home, not an inn. **Pros:** three-course breakfast; location; hospitable staff. **Cons:** processing fee for cancelations; not family-friendly; no pool. ⊠ *221 S.E. 7th St.* ☎ *352/373–4535* ⊕ *www.laureloakinn.com* ⤳ *5 rooms* ⌂ *In-room: Wi-Fi. In-hotel: parking, some age restrictions* ⑩ *Breakfast.*

**$$$**
**B&B/INN**
**Fodor's Choice**
**★**

**The Magnolia Plantation Bed and Breakfast Inn.** You'll be within minutes of historic downtown and the University of Florida, and owners Joe and Cindy Montalto will welcome you like old friends, whether you stay in the main house, built in 1885, or in one of six adorable cottages. **Pros:** friendly service; breakfast; nightly social hour. **Cons:** small rooms; seven-day cancellation policy; some uncomfortable beds. ⊠ *309 S.E. 7th St.* ☎ *352/375–6653 or 800/201–2379* ⊕ *www.magnoliabnb.com* ⊅ *5 rooms, 5 cottages* ᐸ *In-room: kitchen (some). In-hotel: laundry facilities, parking, some pets allowed* †⊙ǀ *Breakfast.*

**$$$**
**B&B/INN**

**Sweetwater Branch Inn Bed & Breakfast.** You'll find such modern conveniences as hair dryers, Internet, and business services mixed with Southern charm and hospitality, all wrapped up in two grand Victorian homes surrounded by lush tropical gardens. **Pros:** Southern-style breakfast; Jacuzzi suites. **Cons:** spotty service; frequent on-site weddings. ⊠ *625 E. University Ave.* ☎ *352/373–6760 or 800/595–7760* ⊕ *www.sweetwaterinn.com* ⊅ *12 rooms, 5 cottages, carriage house* ᐸ *In-room: kitchen (some), Wi-Fi. In-hotel: parking* †⊙ǀ *Breakfast.*

# THE SPACE COAST

South of the Daytona Beach area along the coast is the Canaveral National Seashore, adjacent to the beach community of New Smyrna; Merritt Island National Wildlife Refuge; and the John F. Kennedy Space Center. This area is also home to the laid-back town of Cocoa Beach, which attracts visitors on weekends year-round because it's the closest beach to Orlando, 50 mi to the east.

**ESSENTIALS**

**Visitor Information Space Coast Office of Tourism** (⊠ *430 Brevard Ave., Suite 150, Cocoa Village* ☎ *877/572—3224 [877/57-BEACH] or 321/433-4470* ⊕ *www.space-coast.com*).

## NEW SMYRNA BEACH

*19 mi south of Daytona Beach, 56 mi northeast of Orlando*

The long, dune-lined beach of this small town abuts the Canaveral National Seashore. Behind the dunes sit beach houses, small motels, and an occasional high-rise (except at the extreme northern tip, where none is higher than seven stories). Canal Street, on the mainland, and Flagler Avenue, with many beachside shops and restaurants, have both been "streetscaped" with wide brick sidewalks and stately palm trees. The town is also known for its internationally recognized artists' workshop.

### EXPLORING

**Arts on Douglas.** In a warehouse that has been converted into a stunning 5,000-square-foot, high-ceiling art gallery, Arts on Douglas has a new exhibit of works by a Florida artist every month. Representing more than 50 Florida artists, the gallery has hosted exhibits on the handmade jewelry of Mary Schimpff Webb and landscape and still-life oils by Barbara Tiffany. ⊠ *123 Douglas St.* ☎ *386/428–1133*

⊕ *www.artsondouglas.net* ⊠ *Free* ⊙ *Tues.–Fri. 11–6, Sat. 11–3, and by appointment.*

**Atlantic Center for the Arts.** Changing exhibits every two months, the Atlantic Center for the Arts has works of internationally known artists. Mediums include sculpture, mixed materials, video, drawings, prints, and paintings. ⊠ *1414 Art Center Ave.* ☎ *386/427–6975* ⊕ *www.atlanticcenterforthearts.org* ⊠ *Free* ⊙ *Mon.–Sat. 10–4.*

★ **Canaveral National Seashore.** Miles of grassy windswept dunes and a virtually empty beach await you at this remarkable 57,000-acre park on a barrier island with 24 mi of undeveloped coastline spanning from New Smyrna to Titusville. The unspoiled area of hilly sand dunes, grassy marshes, and seashell-sprinkled beaches is a large part of NASA's buffer zone and is home to more than 1,000 species of plants and 300 species of birds and other animals. Surf and lagoon fishing are available, and a hiking trail leads to the top of an American Indian shell midden at Turtle Mound. For an additional charge, visitors can take a pontoon-boat tour ($20) or participate in the turtle-watch interpretive program ($14). Reservations required. A visitor center is on Route A1A at Apollo Beach. Weekends are busy, and parts of the park are closed before, during, and after launches, so call ahead. ⊠ *Visitor Information: 7611 S. Atlantic Ave., New Smyrna Beach* ☎ *386/428–3384* ⊕ *www.nps.gov/cana* ⊠ *$3* ⊙ *Nov.–Mar., daily 6–6; Apr.–Oct., daily 6 am–8 pm.*

**Smyrna Dunes Park.** In this park, on a barrier island at the northernmost tip of New Smyrna Beach peninsula, 1½ mi of boardwalks crisscross sand dunes and delicate dune vegetation to lead to beaches and a fishing jetty. Botanical signs identify the flora, and there are picnic tables and an information center. It's also one of the few county parks where pets are allowed (on leashes, that is). ⊠ *N. Peninsula Dr.* ☎ *386/424–2935* ⊕ *volusia.org/parks/smyrnadunes.htm* ⊠ *$5 per vehicle, up to 8 people* ⊙ *Daily sunrise–sundown.*

## BEACHES

**Apollo Beach.** In addition to typical beach activities, visitors to this beach on the northern end of Canaveral National Seashore can also ride horses here (with a permit), hike self-guided trails, and tour the historic Eldora Statehouse. **Best for:** Swimming, sunrises, sunbathing, families. **Amenities:** Seasonal lifeguards (May 30–Sept. 1), park visitor center, off-beach parking. ⊠ *Rte. A1A to southern end of New Smyrna Beach* ☎ *386/428–3384* ⊠ *$3 per person (admission to National Seashore)* ⊙ *Nov.–Mar., daily 6–6; Apr.–Oct., daily 6 am–8 pm; call for statehouse hrs.*

**New Smyrna Beach.** This public beach extends 7 mi from the northernmost part of New Smyrna's barrier island south to the Canaveral National Seashore. It's mostly hard-packed white sand, and at low tide can be stunningly wide. The beach is lined with heaps of sandy dunes, but because they're endangered, it's against the law to walk on or play in them or to pick the sea grass, which helps to stabilize the dunes. From sunrise to sunset cars are allowed on certain sections of the beach (speed limit: 10 mph). In season there's a nominal beach-access fee for cars. **Best for:** Swimming, surfing, accessibility, sunrises, sunbathing,

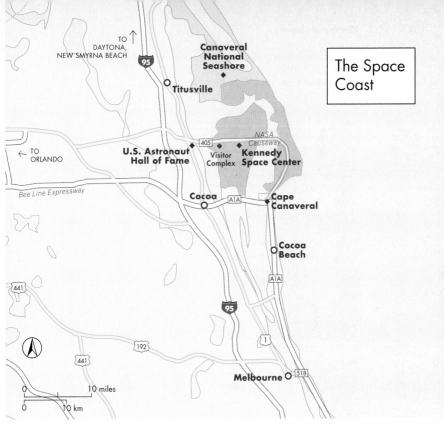

families. **Amenities:** Seasonal lifeguards, parking, restroom facilities, beach concessions.

**Playalinda Beach.** The southern access for the Canaveral National Seashore, remote Playalinda Beach has pristine sands and is the longest stretch of undeveloped coast on Florida's Atlantic seaboard. Hundreds of giant sea turtles come ashore here from May through August to lay their eggs. Fourteen parking lots anchor the beach at 1-mi intervals. To get here, take Exit 220 east off Interstate 95 and follow the signs. Take bug repellent in case of horseflies. **Best for:** Swimming, sunbathing, families. **Amenities:** Seasonal lifeguards, off-beach parking. ⊠ *Rte. 402/Beach Rd.* ☎ *321/867–4077* ⊕ *www.nps.gov/cana* ✉ *$3 per person (admission to the National Seashore)* ☉ *Nov.–Mar., daily 6–6; Apr.– Oct., daily 6 am–8 pm.*

### WHERE TO EAT

**$–$$** ✕ **Chase's on the Beach.** Eat on the deck beneath the stars—gazing at either the ocean or the pool—or dine indoors (the latter is recommended for folks who don't want to lose their lunch, literally, watching not-so-hard bodies covered in oil and splayed out on lounge chairs). Barefoot beachgoers wander up for beverages, hamburgers, and salads during the day (shoes required inside), whereas the evening crowd comes for fried shrimp, grouper sandwiches, and weekend entertainment. ⊠ *3401 S.*

Atlantic Ave. ☎ 386/423–8787 ⊕ www.chaseonthebeach.com ⌂ Reservations not accepted.

**$–$$** ╳ **J.B.'s Fish Camp and Restaurant.** Better known simply as J.B.'s, this
SEAFOOD local landmark is on the eastern shore of the Indian River (i.e., the middle of nowhere). Eat at picnic-style tables covered with brown paper inside and out, or belly up to the bar to dine on mounds of spicy seafood, Cajun alligator, J.B.'s famous crab cakes, and blue crabs by the dozen. It's a great place to catch the sunset, and there's live music weekend afternoons. Five bucks says at least one person at your table says their hush puppies are the best he's ever eaten. ✉ 859 Pompano Ave. ☎ 386/427–5747 ⊕ www.jbsfishcamp.com ⌂ Reservations not accepted.

**$–$$$** ╳ **New Smyrna Steakhouse.** You could find a fancier place to get your
STEAK steak on, but why bother? Superb steaks and ribs bring locals and visitors to this dark busy spot. Booths are lighted by individual, low-hanging lamps that provide intimacy but enough light to read the menu. Try the 12-ounce New York strip or sirloin, the 22-ounce porterhouse, the 8-ounce filet mignon, or a rack of tender ribs. Other popular menu items are the Cajun pizza, shrimp Caesar salad, mesquite chicken, and chocolate volcano for dessert. ✉ 723 3rd Ave. ☎ 386/424–9696 ⊕ www.mynewsmyrnasteakhouse.com ⌂ Reservations not accepted.

**$–$$$** ╳ **Norwood's Seafood Restaurant.** Fresh local fish and shrimp are the spe-
SEAFOOD cialties at this bustling New Smyrna Beach landmark, open since 1946. Built as a gas station, the building later served as a general store and piggy-bank factory, but the remodeled interior belies this backstory; the place is replete with wood, from the chairs and booths to the walls and rafters. Order steak, blackened-chicken breast, or pasta. Prices are reasonable, and more than 3,000 bottles of wine are on hand. Don't be fooled by the fancy wine list and linen tablecloths; you can still wear shorts (business casual, however, is the norm). ✉ 400 2nd Ave. ☎ 386/428–4621 ⊕ www.norwoods.com ⌂ Reservations not accepted.

**$–$$$** ╳ **Spanish River Grill.** Michele and Henry Salgado own this modern
CARIBBEAN Cuban and Spanish eatery, which many locals consider the best restaurant in New Smyrna Beach. Though many consider the cuisine to represent fine dining, overall the restaurant is casual and unpretentious. Henry combines his Cuban grandmother's recipes with local ingredients for knockout results. Start with fried-green plantains or clams tossed with garlic and avocado. For the main course, try the incredible paella, or a tender rib eye steak stuffed with chorizo. Be sure to save room for one of Michele's desserts. Sunday sees a brunch from 11 to 3. ✉ 737 E. 3rd Ave. ☎ 386/424–6991 ⊕ www.thespanishrivergrill.com ⌂ Reservations not accepted ⊘ Closed Mon. No lunch.

## WHERE TO STAY
For expanded hotel reviews, visit Fodors.com.

**$$–$$$** ⌂ **Riverview Hotel and Spa.** A landmark since 1885, this former bridge
B&B/INN tender's home is set back from the Intracoastal Waterway at the edge of the north causeway, which still has an operating drawbridge. **Pros:** on-site spa; hospitable staff; homey feel. **Cons:** small rooms in main

house; strict cancellation policy; blocks from the beach. ✉ *103 Flagler Ave.* ☎ *386/428–5858 or 800/945–7416* ⊕ *www.riverviewhotel.com* ⇆ *17 rooms, 1 suite* ⚴ *In-room: Wi-Fi. In-hotel: restaurant, pool, spa, parking* ⎰⫶⎱*Breakfast.*

## TITUSVILLE

*34 mi south of New Smyrna Beach, 67 mi east of Orlando.*

It's unusual that such a small, easily overlooked community of Titusville could accommodate what it does, namely the magnificent Merritt Island National Wildlife Refuge and the entrance to the Kennedy Space Center, the nerve center of the U.S. space program *(⇨ see In-Focus feature, "Soaring High at Kennedy Space Center").*

### EXPLORING

**American Police Hall of Fame & Museum.** You know police officers deserve your respect, and you'll be reminded why at this intriguing attraction. In addition to memorabilia like the Robocop costume and Blade Runner car from the films, informative displays offer insight into the dangers officers face every day: drugs, homicides, and criminals who can create knives from dental putty and guns from a bicycle spoke (really). Other historical exhibits include invitations to hangings, police patches, how you collect evidence at a crime scene, and a rotunda where more than 8,000 names are etched in marble to honor police officers who have died in the line of duty. The 24-lane shooting range provides rental guns (Tuesday to Friday noon–8, weekends noon–6). ✉ *6350 Horizon Dr.* ☎ *321/264–0911* ⊕ *www.aphf.org* 🎟 *$12* ⊙ *Daily 10–6.*

**Valiant Air Command Warbird Museum & Tico Airshow.** Although its exterior looks sort of squirrelly, what's inside here is certainly impressive. Aviation buffs won't want to miss memorabilia from World Wars I and II, Korea, and Vietnam, as well as extensive displays of vintage military flying gear and uniforms. There are posters that were used to identify Japanese planes, plus there's a Huey helicopter and the cockpit of an F-106 that you can sit in. In the north hangar it looks like activity day at the senior center as a volunteer team of retirees busily restores old planes. It's an inspiring sight, and a good place to hear some war stories. The lobby gift shop sells real flight suits, old flight magazines, bomber jackets, books, models, and T-shirts. ✉ *6600 Tico Rd.* ☎ *321/268–1941* ⊕ *www.vacwarbirds.org* 🎟 *$18* ⊙ *Daily 9–5.*

### SPORTS AND THE OUTDOORS

Fodor'sChoice
★

**Merritt Island National Wildlife Refuge.** Owned by the National Aeronautics and Space Administration (NASA), this 140,000-acre refuge, which adjoins the Canaveral National Seashore, acts as a buffer around Kennedy Space Center while protecting 1,000 species of plants and 500 species of wildlife, including 15 considered federally threatened or endangered. It's an immense area dotted by brackish estuaries and marshes and patches of land consisting of coastal dunes, scrub oaks, pine forests and flatwoods, and palm and oak hammocks. You can borrow field guides and binoculars at the visitor center (5 mi east of U.S. 1 in Titusville on State Road 402) to track down falcons, ospreys, eagles, turkeys, doves, cuckoos, owls, and woodpeckers, as well as loggerhead turtles, alligators, and otters. A 20-minute video about refuge wildlife and accessibility—only 10,000 acres are developed—can help orient you.

You might take a self-guided tour along the 7-mi Black Point Wildlife Drive. The dirt road takes you where there are no traces of encroaching malls or mankind and it's easy to visualize the tribes who made this their home 7,000 years ago. On the Oak Hammock Foot Trail you can see wintering migratory waterfowl and learn about the plants of a hammock community.

If you exit the north end of the refuge, look for the Manatee Observation Area just north of the Haulover Canal (maps are at the visitor center). They usually show up in spring and fall. There are also fishing camps, fishing boat ramps, and six hiking trails scattered throughout the area. Most of the refuge is closed 24 hours prior to a shuttle launch. ✉ *Rte. 402, across Titusville Causeway* ☎ *321/861–0667, 321/861–0669 visitor center* ⊕ *www.fws.gov/merrittisland* ✍ *Free* ☉ *Daily sunrise–sundown; visitor center weekdays 8–4:30, Sat. 9–5 and Sun. 9–5 (Nov.–Mar.).*

**WHERE TO EAT AND STAY**
*For expanded hotel reviews, visit Fodors.com.*

$
SEAFOOD
★
✕ **Dixie Crossroads.** This sprawling restaurant is always crowded and festive, but it's not just the rustic setting that draws the throngs—it's the seafood. The specialty is the difficult-to-cook rock shrimp, which are served fried, broiled, or steamed. Diners with a hearty appetite can opt for the all-you-can-eat rock shrimp, small shrimp, tilapia, or catfish. You might have to wait (up to 90 minutes) for a table, but if you don't have time to wait, you can order takeout or eat in the bar area. And a word to the wise: as tempting as those corn fritters dusted with powdered sugar are, don't fill up on them. ✉ *1475 Garden St., 2 mi east of I–95 Exit 220* ☎ *321/268–5000* ⊕ *www.dixiecrossroads.com* ✍ *Reservations not accepted.*

$$
HOTEL
☶ **Hampton Inn Titusville.** Proximity to the Kennedy Space Center and reasonable rates make this four-story hotel a top pick for seeing a launch. **Pros:** free Internet; extra-comfy beds; convenient to I–95. **Cons:** thin walls; no restaurant on-site; no room service. ✉ *4760 Helen Hauser Blvd.* ☎ *321/383–9191* ⊕ *www.hamptoninn.com* ✍ *86 rooms, 4 suites* ☶ *In-room: Internet. In-hotel: pool, gym, laundry facilities, parking* ☵ *Breakfast.*

# COCOA

*17 mi south of Titusville.*

Not to be confused with the seaside community of Cocoa Beach, the small town of Cocoa sits smack-dab on mainland Florida and faces the Intracoastal Waterway, known locally as the Indian River. There's a planetarium and a museum, as well as a rustic fish camp along the St. Johns River, a few miles inland.

Folks in a rush to get to the beach tend to overlook Cocoa's Victorian-style village, but it's worth a stop and is perhaps Cocoa's most interesting feature. Within the cluster of restored turn-of-the-20th-century buildings and cobblestone walkways you can enjoy several restaurants, indoor and outdoor cafés, snack and ice-cream shops, and more than 50 specialty shops and art galleries. The area hosts music performances in the gazebo, arts-and-crafts shows, and other family-friendly events throughout the year. To get to Cocoa Village, head east on Route 520—named King Street in Cocoa—and when the streets get narrow and the road curves, make a right onto Brevard Avenue; follow the signs for the free municipal parking lot.

## EXPLORING

**Brevard Museum of History & Natural Science.** This is the place to come to see what the lay of the local land looked like in other eras. Hands-on activities draw children, who especially migrate toward the Imagination Center, where they can act out history or reenact a space shuttle flight. Not to be missed is the Windover Archaeological Exhibit of 7,000-year-old artifacts indigenous to the region. In 1984, a shallow pond revealed the burial ground of more than 200 American Indians who lived in the area about 7,000 years ago. Preserved in the muck were bones, and, to the archaeologists' surprise, the brains of these ancient people. There's also a butterfly garden and a nature center with 22 acres of trails encompassing three distinct ecosystems—sand pine hills, lake lands, and marshlands. ✉ *2201 Michigan Ave.* ☎ *321/632–1830* ⊕ *www.brevardmuseum.org* 🎫 *$6* ☉ *Thurs.–Sat. 10–3.*

## SPORTS AND THE OUTDOORS

### BOATING

**Twister Airboat Rides.** If you haven't seen the swampy, alligator-ridden waters of Florida, then you haven't really seen Florida. Here you go on a unique and thrilling wildlife tour where eagles and wading birds coexist with water moccasins and gators. The Coast Guard–certified deluxe airboats hit speeds of up to 45 mph and offer unparalleled opportunities to photograph native species. The basic tour lasts 30 minutes, but 60- and 90-minute ecotours are also available at an additional cost by reservation only. Twister Airboat Rides is inside the Lone Cabbage Fish Camp, about 9 mi west of Cocoa's city limits, 4 mi west of Interstate 95. ✉ *8199 Rte. 520 at St. Johns River* ☎ *321/632–4199* ⊕ *www.twisterairboatrides.com* 🎫 *$22* ☉ *Daily 10–5:30.*

## SHOPPING

**Cocoa Flea Market.** With more than 1,000 booths, this is, essentially, the largest outdoor shopping center in Brevard County. The market is open Wednesday, Friday, and weekends from 8 to 4. ⊠ *5605 N. U.S. 1* ☎ *321/631–0241.*

**Cocoa Village.** You could spend hours browsing in the more than 50 boutiques here, along Brevard Avenue and Harrison Street (the latter has the densest concentration of shops). Although most stores are of the gift and clothing variety, the village is also home to 11 antiques shops, 13 art galleries, restaurants, a tattoo parlor, and a spa. ⊠ *Rte. 520 and Brevard Ave.* ☎ *321/631–9075*

**Super Flea & Farmers' Market.** You're sure to find a bargain at one of the 900 booths at this market, which is held every Friday, Saturday, and Sunday from 9 to 4. ⊠ *4835 W. Eau Gallie Blvd.* ☎ *321/242–9124* ⊕ *www.superfleamarket.com.*

## WHERE TO EAT

**\$\$\$**
CAFÉ
Fodor'sChoice
★

✕ **Café Margaux.** Eclectic, creative, and international is the perfect way to describe the cuisine and the decor at this charming Cocoa Village spot. The menu blends French, Italian, and Asian influences with dishes like tenderloin of beef brochette, sesame-seared ahi with green tea and bamboo risotto, and braised veal scaloppine, and also features more exotic fare such as duck and ostrich. The themed dining rooms are elaborately decorated with dramatic but not necessarily coordinating window treatments, wallpaper, and artwork. ⊠ *220 Brevard Ave.* ☎ *321/639–8343* ⊕ *www.margaux.com* ☾ *Closed Sun.*

**\$**
ECLECTIC

✕ **Lone Cabbage Fish Camp.** The word "rustic" doesn't even begin to describe this down-home, no-nonsense restaurant (translation: you eat off paper plates with plastic forks) housed in a weathered, old, clapboard shack along with a bait shop and airboat-tour company. Set your calorie counter for plates of catfish, frogs' legs, turtle, and alligator (as well as burgers and hot dogs). Dine inside or on the outdoor deck overlooking the St. Johns River with live music every Sunday. Who knows, you might even see your dinner swimming by. ⊠ *8199 Rte. 520 at St. Johns River* ☎ *321/632–4199* ⚑ *Reservations not accepted.*

# CAPE CANAVERAL

*5 mi east of Cocoa via Rte. A1A.*

The once-bustling commercial fishing area of Cape Canaveral is still home to a small shrimping fleet, charter boats, and party fishing boats, but its main business these days is as a cruise-ship port. Cocoa Beach itself isn't the spiffiest place around, but what is becoming quite clean and neat is the north end of the port where the Carnival, Disney, and Royal Caribbean cruise lines set sail. Port Canaveral is now Florida's second-busiest cruise port for multiday cruises, which makes this a great place to catch a glimpse of these giant ships.

## SPORTS AND THE OUTDOORS

**Jetty Park.** Come for a wonderful taste of the real Florida. The 4½-acre beach and oceanfront campground has more than 150 campsites for tents and RVs, picnic pavilions, bike paths, and a 1,200-foot-long fishing pier that doubles as a perfect vantage point from which to watch a liftoff from Cape Canaveral. Lifeguards are on duty all year, and beach wheelchairs are available for rent. A jetty constructed of giant boulders adds to the landscape, and a walkway that crosses it provides access to a less populated stretch of beach. Real and rustic, this is Florida without the theme-park varnish. ⊠ *400 E. Jetty Rd., Port Canaveral* ☎ *321/783–7111* ⊕ *www.jettypark.org* ⊠ *$5–$10 per car, $7–$15 for RVs for fishing or beach; camping $25–$35 for basic, $28–$42 with water and electric, $31–$47 full hook-up* ☉ *Daily 7 am–9 pm.*

## SHOPPING

**The Cove at Port Canaveral.** Whether you're at Port Canaveral for a cruise or are just passing through, this retail marketplace on the south side of the harbor has enough shops, restaurants, and entertainment venues to keep you occupied. Since most of the bars and eateries are located on the public waterfront area, you'll have a unique view of the cruise ships—and their colorful passengers. ⊠ *Glen Cheek Dr. and Scallop Dr., Port Canaveral* ⊠ *Free* ☉ *Hrs vary by business.*

## WHERE TO STAY

*For expanded hotel reviews, visit Fodors.com.*

**$$$**
RESORT

**Radisson Resort at the Port.** For cruise-ship passengers who can't wait to get under way, this splashy resort, done up in pink and turquoise, already feels like the Caribbean. **Pros:** cruise-ship convenience; pool area; free shuttle. **Cons:** rooms around the pool can be noisy; loud air-conditioning in some rooms; no complimentary breakfast. ⊠ *8701 Astronaut Blvd.* ☎ *321/784–0000 or 888/201–1718* ⊕ *www.radisson. com/capecanaveralfl* ⊠ *284 rooms, 72 suites* ⚐ *In-room: kitchen (some), Wi-Fi. In-hotel: restaurant, bar, tennis court, pool, gym, laundry facilities* ❧ *No meals.*

**$$$**
HOTEL

**Residence Inn Cape Canaveral/Cocoa Beach.** Billing itself as the closest all-suites hotel to the Kennedy Space Center, this four-story Residence Inn, painted cheery yellow, is also convenient to other area attractions such as Port Canaveral, the Cocoa Beach Pier, the Brevard Zoo, and Cocoa Village, and is only an hour from the Magic Kingdom. **Pros:** helpful staff; free breakfast buffet; pet-friendly. **Cons:** less than picturesque views; street noise in some rooms. ⊠ *8959 Astronaut Blvd.* ☎ *321/323–1100 or 800/331–3131* ⊕ *www.marriott.com* ⊠ *150 suites* ⚐ *In-room: kitchen, Wi-Fi. In-hotel: pool, gym, laundry facilities, parking, some pets allowed* ❧ *Breakfast.*

# COCOA BEACH

*5 mi south of Cape Canaveral, 58 mi southeast of Orlando.*

After crossing a long and high bridge just east of Cocoa Village, you'll drop down upon a barrier island. A few miles farther and you'll reach the Atlantic Ocean and picture-perfect Cocoa Beach at Route A1A.

*Continued on page 174*

The astronauts prepare for the launch
of Endeavour STS–118 on Pad 39–A.

# SOARING HIGH

by John Blodgett
and Steve Master

## AT THE KENNEDY SPACE CENTER

Ever since the National Aeronautics and Space Administration (NASA) was founded, in 1958, the United States has been working on missions that launch us heavenward. When these dreams are about to become reality, and it's time for blastoff, Kennedy Space Center in Cape Canaveral, Florida, is where the action is.

# NASA FROM COAST TO COAST

The Vehicle Assembly Building houses the space shuttle before a launch.

You've heard the words: "Houston, the *Eagle* has landed." And *Apollo 13*'s "Houston, we have a problem." But have you wondered, "Why are they talking to Houston if they left from Florida?"

NASA actually has operations at centers scattered across the United States. Its major centers are in Florida, Texas, and California. NASA's Launch Operations Center, known as the Kennedy Space Center, in Cape Canaveral, Florida, is where the famous countdowns are heard as a mission prepares for launch. You could say this is like NASA's big airport for outbound flights.

Once a mission (with a crew inside) is airborne, Houston takes over. In addition to operating all manned space flights, the Lyndon B. Johnson Space Center in Houston, Texas, is home base for American astronauts. They train here in laboratories that simulate weightlessness and other space-related concepts.

Not to be left out, the West Coast also gets a piece of the space-action pie. At Moffet Field, in California's Silicon Valley, the Ames Research Center is research and development central for NASA technology. If a mission can't happen because the technology isn't there yet, it's the job of the Ames Research Center to figure it out. Also in California is the Dryden Flight Research Center, at Edwards Air Force Base in Southern California. The center is where a lot of smart people who know a lot of about aerodynamics get to test out their ideas; it's also where space shuttle orbiters land.

So, in a nutshell, you could say California is the brains of NASA's operations, Texas is its heart, and Florida is its wings.

## NASA TIMELINE

**OCT. 1958:** NASA begins operating with 8,000 employees and $100 million. Ten days later, *Pioneer* I takes off.

**MAY 1961:** Alan B. Shepard, Jr., becomes the first person in space.

**FEB. 1962:** John Glenn is the first American to orbit the Earth.

**JUNE 1965:** Edward H. White II is the first American to walk in space.

**DEC. 1968:** Three astronauts orbit the moon aboard *Apollo 8*.

**JULY 1969:** *Apollo 11* brings man to the moon.

**JULY 1976:** *Viking 1* lands on Mars.

**APRIL 1981:** First space shuttle orbiter launches two astronauts into space.

**JAN. 1986:** Space shuttle *Challenger* explodes 73 seconds after launch; seven onboard astronauts die.

**APRIL 1990:** Hubble telescope launches.

**JULY 1997:** Mars Pathfinder lands on the red planet.

**JULY 1999:** Eileen Collins is the first woman to command a space shuttle mission.

**FEB. 2002:** Mars Odyssey begins mapping the red planet.

**FEB. 1, 2003:** Space shuttle *Columbia* explodes over Texas 15 minutes before scheduled landing; seven astronauts on board die.

**JULY 2004:** Cassini–Huygens spacecraft begins orbiting Saturn.

**MAY 2010:** Shuttle *Atlantis* delivers new Russian module and critical spare parts to International Space Station.

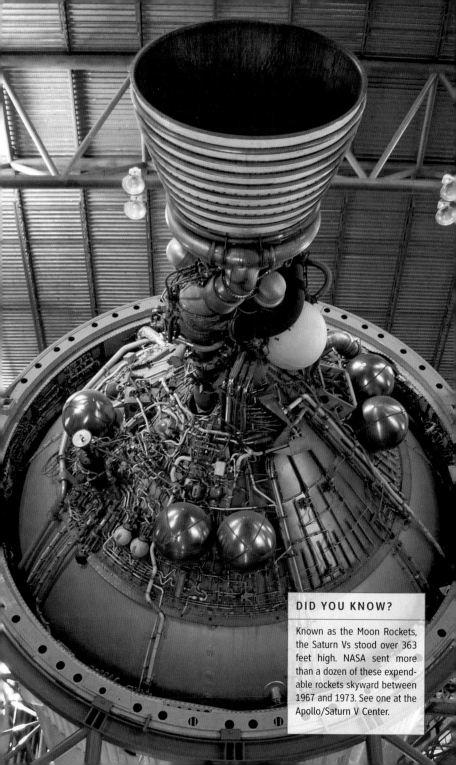

# THE KENNEDY SPACE CENTER

The 140,000-acre Kennedy Space Center is one of central Florida's most popular sights. The must-see attraction gives you a hands-on opportunity to learn about the past, present, and future of America's space program. View old rockets and other artifacts from space flight operations, talk with astronauts during Q&As, experience a simulated launch, and become part of the awed crowd on launch days as you watch the blastoff from a viewing site on the grounds or nearby.

**VISITOR COMPLEX**

Space Education

Children's Pla
Dome

Rocket Garden

Dr. Kurl H. Debus
Conference
Facility

Early Space
Exploration

PARKIN

## VISITOR COMPLEX

The Kennedy Space Center Visitor Complex is the starting place for your visit. It's home to several attractions and is also where you can board the bus for tours of the center beyond the visitor complex.

### EXHIBITS

The **Early Space Exploration** display highlights the rudimentary yet influential Mercury and Gemini space programs; **Robot Scouts** is a walk-through exhibit of unmanned planetary probes; and the **Exploration Space: Explorers Wanted** exhibit immerses visitors in exploration beyond Earth. Don't miss the outdoor **Rocket Garden,** with walkways winding beside rockets, from early Atlas spacecraft to a Saturn IB. The most moving exhibit is the **Astronaut Memorial.** The 70,400-pound black-granite tribute to astronauts who lost their lives in the name of space exploration stands 42½ feet high by 50 feet wide.

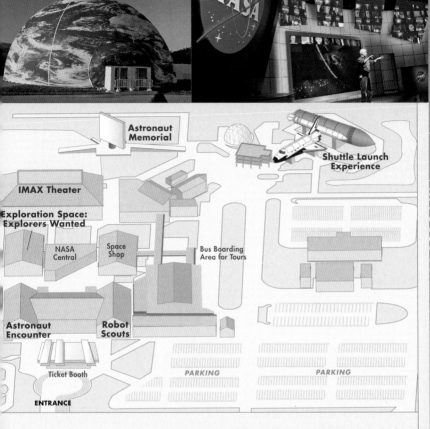

### Map Labels

- Astronaut Memorial
- Shuttle Launch Experience
- IMAX Theater
- Exploration Space: Explorers Wanted
- NASA Central
- Space Shop
- Bus Boarding Area for Tours
- Astronaut Encounter
- Robot Scouts
- Ticket Booth
- PARKING
- PARKING
- ENTRANCE

## INTERACTIVE SHOWS AND RIDES

**Astronaut Encounter Theater** has two daily programs where NASA astronauts share their adventures in space travel and show a short film. More befitting Walt Disney World or Universal Studios (complete with the health warnings), the **Shuttle Launch Experience** is the center's spectacular attraction. Designed by a team of astronauts, NASA experts, and renowned attraction engineers, the 44,000-square-foot structure uses a sophisticated motion-based platform, special-effects seats, and high-fidelity visual and audio components to simulate the sensations experienced in an actual space-shuttle launch, including MaxQ, Solid Rocker Booster separation, main engine cutoff, and External Tank separation. The journey culminates with a breathtaking view of Earth from space. For those under 48 inches, **Children's Play Dome** enables kids to play among the next generation of spacecraft, climb a moon-rock wall, and crawl through rocket tunnels.

## MOVIES

At the world's only back-to-back twin **IMAX Theater** the dream of space flight comes to life on a movie screen five stories tall with dramatic footage shot by NASA astronauts during missions. Realistic 3-D special effects will make you feel like you're in space with them. Films alternate throughout the year.

## BEYOND THE VISITOR COMPLEX

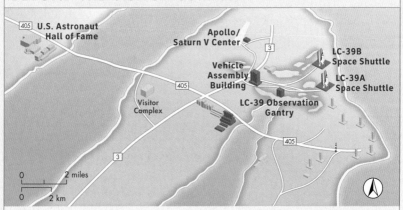

U.S. Astronaut
Hall of Fame

Apollo/
Saturn V Center

Vehicle
Assembly
Building

LC-39B
Space Shuttle

LC-39A
Space Shuttle

Visitor
Complex

LC-39 Observation
Gantry

0       2 miles

0    2 km

### SPACE CENTER TOURS

To explore the remainder of the space center, you will need to take a tour by bus. Buses depart every 15 minutes from the Visitor Complex; the tour duration is two hours, but you can get off and back on again at will at various sites. Bus stops include the **Launch Complex 39 Observation Gantry,** which has an unparalleled view of the launchpads and the **Apollo/Saturn V Center,** with a don't-miss presentation at the Firing Room Theatre, where the launch of America's first lunar mission, 1968's *Apollo VIII,* is re-created with a ground-shaking, window-rattling liftoff. The **Saturn V Center** features one of the three remaining Saturn V moon rockets. This bus tour is included with admission; two others are available for additional fees (*see Add-Ons*).

### U.S. ASTRONAUT HALL OF FAME

The original Mercury 7 team and the later Gemini, Apollo, Skylab, and shuttle astronauts contributed to make the United States Astronaut Hall of Fame the world's premium archive of astronauts' personal stories. Authentic memorabilia and equipment from their collections tell the story of human space exploration. This stand-alone attraction is across the

river from the Kennedy Space Center; admission to it is included with your Kennedy Space Center ticket.

You can see one-of-a-kind items like Wally Schirra's relatively archaic Sigma 7 Mercury space capsule, Gus Grissom's spacesuit (colored silver only because NASA thought silver looked more "spacey"), and a flag that made it to the moon. The exhibit First of the Moon focuses on crew selection for Apollo 11 and the Soviet Union's role in the space race. One of the more challenging activities at the hall of fame is a space-shuttle simulator that lets you try your hand at landing the craft—and afterward replays a side view of your rolling and pitching descent. Don't miss Simulation Station, an area with interactive exhibits about space travel. There are also videos of historic moments.

The life of an astronaut can mean a tight squeeze! See for yourself at the U.S. Astronaut Hall of Fame.

## ADD-ONS

The following tours and programs are available for extra cost beyond admission and should be reserved in advance.

■ **Discover KSC: Today and Tomorrow** ($21) brings visitors to sites seldom accessible to the public, such as the Vehicle Assembly Building, the shuttle landing strip, and the 6-million-pound crawler that transports the launch vehicles to the launch pads.

■ See how far the space program has come on the **Cape Canaveral: Then and Now Tour** ($21). It puts you up close to the original launch pads, brings you to the Air Force Space and Missile Museum, and lets you watch the active unmanned rocket program.

■ During **Lunch with an Astronaut** ($23), astronauts talk about their experiences and engage in Q&A (kids often ask "How do you eat/sleep/relieve yourself in space?").

■ If you want to live the life of an astronaut, you can enroll in the **Astronaut Training Experience** (ATX) at the U.S. Astronaut Hall of Fame. The half-day program combines hands-on training and preparation for the rigors of space flight. NASA astronauts helped design the program, and you'll hear first-hand from them as you progress through an exciting day at the busiest launch facility on Earth. The $145 cost includes flight training simulators, a full-scale space shuttle mission simulation, a meet-and-greet with a NASA astronaut, and ATX Gear. Age restrictions apply. Reserve your spot well in advance.

Cape Canaveral Then and Now Tour.

## PLANNING YOUR TRIP

### GETTING HERE

The Kennedy Space Center and the U.S. Astronaut Hall of Fame are near Titusville on Cape Canaveral, about a 45- to 60-minute drive from Orlando. From Orlando International Airport, take the north exit to 528 East (the Beeline Expressway) and drive east to the exit marked "407, Titusville, Kennedy Space Center." Take 407 until you reach Rte. 405 (Columbia Boulevard/NASA Parkway) and then turn right. After approximately 1 mi you will see the U.S. Astronaut Hall of Fame on your right. Continue another 5 mi until you reach the visitor complex, your starting point for all tours.

### BUDGETING YOUR TIME

Plan to spend a full day at the center and hall of fame, or at the very least, several hours.

### ADMISSION

Your $41 admission ticket grants you access for two days (within the span of one week) to Kennedy Space Center Visitor Complex and related tours as well as the U.S. Astronaut Hall of Fame, which is just across the causeway.

### CONTACT INFORMATION

✉ Off Rte. 405

☎ 877/313–2610

🌐 www.kennedyspacecenter.com

🎟 $41

🕘 Daily 9 AM; closing times vary. (Call ahead for restrictions if you're visiting on a launch day.)

# SHUTTLE COMPONENTS

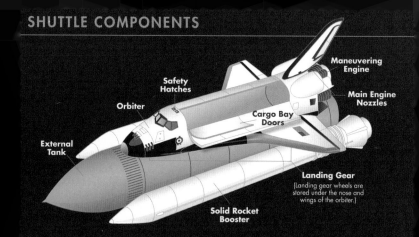

Maneuvering Engine

Main Engine Nozzles

Safety Hatches

Orbiter

Cargo Bay Doors

External Tank

Landing Gear
(Landing gear wheels are stored under the nose and wings of the orbiter.)

Solid Rocket Booster

## ROCKET VS. SHUTTLE

When the space shuttle orbiter *Columbia* blasted off on April 12, 1981, NASA launched its Space Transportation System—a planned fleet of manned, reusable spacecraft that can transport crew, cargo, and experiments into space and return to Earth to land like an aircraft. The system is a radical departure from the days when manned lunar modules were thrust into space at the tip of a disposable rocket, to return to the planet by parachute and then be plucked from the ocean. (Shuttles are launched piggyback on a huge, single-use fuel tank; its two solid rocket boosters return via parachute.) Modern traditional rockets are used only to deploy instruments like unmanned probes into space.

**EXTERNAL TANK**—provides a platform for the shuttle and fuel for the two booster rockets that transport the shuttle into space. It separates from the shuttle within the first 10 minutes of the flight and falls into the ocean.

**SOLID ROCKET BOOSTER**—one of two rockets used to launch the shuttle into space. Each returns to Earth via parachute to be restored for use on a future mission.

**ORBITER**—another name for the space shuttle, which rides piggyback on the fuel tank until it can launch into space under its own rocket power. The crew is inside.

**CARGO BAY DOORS**—the two long doors on the back of the orbiter that open to allow payload to be deployed into space by means of a manipulating arm.

**LANDING GEAR**—the retractable wheels under the nose and wings of the orbiter, which allow it to land like a typical aircraft.

**ENTRY HATCH**—this door allows astronauts to enter the shuttle, and doubles as an escape hatch.

**MANEUVERING ENGINES**—a number of smaller orbiter engines, on the nose and in the tail section, which allow the craft to make fine positioning adjustments while in space.

**MAIN ENGINE NOZZLES**—the three engines at the rear of the orbiter that propel the craft to space.

# BLASTOFF!

From Kennedy Space Center's launch pads most unmanned space flights and all manned space missions have found their origin, with many of them being momentous events—the first satellite launched into space, the first man in space, that giant leap onto the moon's surface. Over the years many flights have become rather routine, happening fairly frequently, but hundreds of spectators still line the cape's nearby roads to watch the countdown, the great explosions of rocket power, and the always-exciting liftoff—proving that NASA routine is never boring.

With the retirement of the Shuttle fleet, a new era at NASA brims with possibilities such as space tourism, commercial space transportation, and expanded frontiers in space. The future of manned space flight remains unclear, but unmanned vehicles such as Atlas and Delta rockets remain a spectacle to behold at Cape Canaveral. Tickets are available for viewing a launch from within the Kennedy Space Center at the visitor complex ($31–$41); prices include admission to the center. Popular off-site vantage points include:

■ Along the Indian River on Hwy. 1, especially in Titusville

■ Beach Line Expressway (Rte. 528), especially where it crosses over the Indian or Banana Rivers

■ Rte. A1A in Cocoa Beach

■ Jetty Park at Port Canaveral, just south of the Cape Canaveral Air Force Station border (park admission is $5)

In the early 1960s, Cocoa Beach was a sleepy, little-known town. But in 1965 the sitcom *I Dream of Jeannie* premiered. The endearing show centered around an astronaut, played by Larry Hagman, and his "Jeannie" in a bottle, Barbara Eden, and was set in Cocoa Beach. Though the series was never shot in Florida, creator Sidney Sheldon paid homage to the town with local references to Cape Kennedy (now known as the Kennedy Space Center) and Bernard's Surf. Today, the town and its lovely beach are mecca to Florida's surfing community.

## ESSENTIALS

**Visitor Information** Cocoa Beach Convention and Visitors Bureau (✉ *8501 Astronaut Blvd., Suite 4, Cape Canaveral* ☎ *321/454–2022 or 877/321–8474* ⊕ *www.visitcocoabeach.com*).

## EXPLORING

**Cocoa Beach Pier.** By day, it's a good place to stroll—if you don't mind weather-worn wood and sandy, watery paths. Although most of the pier is free to walk on, there's a $1 charge to enter the fishing area at the end of the 800-foot-long boardwalk, and a $5 fishing fee. You can rent rods and reels here for an additional $10. By night, visitors and locals—beach bums and surfers among them—head here to party. Come on Friday night for the Boardwalk Bash, with live acoustic and rock-and-roll music; Wednesday and Saturday also see live music. ■ TIP→ The pier is a great place to watch launches from Kennedy Space Center. ✉ *401 Meade Ave.* ☎ *321/783–7549* ⊕ *www.cocoabeachpier.com*.

## BEACHES

**Cocoa Beach.** Famous for its surfing, this is also one of the Space Coast's nicest beaches, with many wide stretches that are excellent for biking, jogging, power walking, or strolling In some places there are dressing rooms, showers, playgrounds, picnic areas with grills, snack shops, and surf-side parking lots. Beach vendors offer necessities, and guards are on duty in summer. ✉ *Rte. A1A.*

**Alan Shepard Park.** Named for the former astronaut, this 5-acre oceanfront park, aptly enough, provides excellent views of launches from Kennedy Space Center. Facilities include 10 picnic pavilions, shower and restroom facilities, and more than 300 parking spaces. Those spaces are in high demand on launch days, but the park's a nice break any other day, too. Beach vendors carry necessities for sunning and swimming. Parking is $7 per day, $10 per day on weekends and holidays from early March through Labor Day. Shops and restaurants are within walking distance. ✉ *East end of SR 520* ☎ *321/868–3258.*

**Sidney Fischer Park.** The 10-acre oceanfront has showers, playgrounds, changing areas, picnic areas with grills, snack shops, and plenty of well-maintained, inexpensive surf-side parking lots. The parking fee is $5 for cars and RVs under 26 feet. ✉ *2100 block of Rte. A1A* ☎ *321/868–3258.*

## SPORTS AND THE OUTDOORS

### KAYAKING

**Adventure Kayak of Cocoa Beach.** Specializing in manatee encounters, this outfitter organizes one- and two-person kayak tours of mangroves, channels, and islands. Rates run about $25 per person. ☎ 321/480–8632 ⊕ www.kayakcocoabeach.com.

### SURFING

**Cocoa Beach Surf Company.** The world's largest surf complex has three floors of boards, apparel, sunglasses, and anything else a surfer, wannabe-surfer, or souvenir-seeker could need. Also on-site are a 5,600-gallon fish and shark tank, the Shark Pit Bar & Grill, and the East Coast Surfing Hall of Fame and Museum. Here you can also rent surfboards, bodyboards, and wet suits, as well as umbrellas, chairs, and bikes. And staffers teach grommets (dudes) and gidgets (chicks)—from kids to seniors—how to surf. There are group, semi-private, and private lessons available in one-, two- and three-hour sessions. Prices range from $40 (for a one-hour group lesson) to $120 (three-hour private). All gear is provided. ✉ 4001 N. Atlantic Ave. ☎ 321/799–9930.

Fodor'sChoice **Ron Jon Surf Shop.** It's impossible to miss Ron Jon: it takes up nearly
★ two blocks along Route A1A and has a giant surfboard and an art deco facade painted orange, blue, yellow, and turquoise. What started in 1963 as a small T-shirt and bathing-suit shop has evolved into a 52,000-square-foot superstore that's open every day 'round the clock. The shop rents water-sports gear as well as chairs and umbrellas, and it sells every kind of beachwear, surf wax, plus the requisite T-shirts and flip-flops. ■TIP→ For up-to-the-minute surfing conditions, call the store and press 2 and then 7 for the Ron Jon Surf and Weather Report. ✉ 4151 N. Atlantic Ave., Rte. A1A ☎ 321/799–8888 ⊕ www.ronjonsurfshop.com.

**Ron Jon Surf School.** If you can't tell a tri-skeg stick from a hodaddy shredding the lip on a gnarly tube, then you may want to avail yourself of the Ron Jon Surf School. Private lessons and clinics are offered for surfers of all levels. The most popular sessions last two hours ($65 clinics, $95 private). Boards are provided, but you should bring your own towels and sunscreen. ✉ 150 E. Columbia La. ☎ 321/868–1980.

### SHOPPING

**Merritt Square Mall.** The area's only major shopping mall is about a 20-minute ride from the beach. Stores include Macy's, Dillard's, JCPenney, Sears, Foot Locker, Island Surf and Skate, and roughly 100 others. There's a 16-screen multiplex, along with a food court and several restaurant chains. ✉ 777 E. Merritt Island Causeway, Merritt Island ☎ 321/452–3270.

### NIGHTLIFE

The Cocoa Beach Pier has several nightspots as well as live-music sessions a couple nights a week.

**Heidi's Jazz Club.** Local and nationally known jazz musicians (Boots Randolph and Mose Allison have taken the stage) play Tuesday through Sunday, with showcase acts appearing on weekends. ✉ 7 Orlando Ave. N ☎ 321/783–4559.

Popular with families, Cocoa Beach is an easy day trip for Orlando or Kennedy Space Center visitors.

## WHERE TO EAT

**$$$**
**GERMAN**

✕ **Heidelberg.** The cuisine here is definitely German, from the sauerbraten served with potato dumplings and red cabbage to the beef Stroganoff and spaetzle to the classically prepared Wiener schnitzel. All the soups and desserts are homemade; try the Viennese-style apple strudel and the rum-zapped almond-cream tortes. Elegant interior touches include crisp linens and fresh flowers. There's live music Friday and Saturday evenings. You can also dine inside the jazz club, Heidi's, next door. ⊠ *7 N. Orlando Ave., opposite City Hall* ☎ *321/783–6806* ⊕ *www.heidisjazzclub.com* ⊗ *Closed Mon. No lunch Sun.*

**$**
**SEAFOOD**

✕ **Oh Shucks Seafood Bar.** At the only open-air seafood bar on the beach, at the entrance of the Cocoa Beach Pier, the main item is oysters, served on the half shell. You can also grab a burger here, crab legs by the pound, or Oh Shucks's most popular item, coconut beer shrimp. Some diners complain that the prices don't jibe with the ultracasual atmosphere (e.g., plastic chairs), but they're also paying for the "ex-Pierience." There's live entertainment on Wednesday, Friday, Saturday, and Sunday. ⊠ *401 Meade Ave., Cocoa Beach Pier* ☎ *321/783–7549.*

## WHERE TO STAY

*For expanded hotel reviews, visit Fodors.com.*

**$$**
**HOTEL**

⊞ **Best Western Ocean Beach Hotel & Suites.** Families love this Best Western for its affordable suites; everyone loves it for its location—just a half block from the Cocoa Beach Pier—and great views of launches from Kennedy Space Center. **Pros:** free Internet; complimentary breakfast. **Cons:** not all rooms have an ocean view; small bathrooms; noise from the pier. ⊠ *5600 N. Atlantic Ave.* ☎ *321/784–4343 or 800/367–1223*

⊕ *www.bestwesterncocoabeach.com* ⇆ *50 suites* & *In-room: Internet. In-hotel: restaurants, pools, laundry facilities* ⏃⃝ *Breakfast.*

**$$**    ⊟ **Doubletree Hotel Cocoa Beach Oceanfront.** Proximity to the beach and
HOTEL   comforts like microwaves and refrigerators—and Doubletree's famous
chocolate-chip cookies—make this six-story hotel a favorite of vacationing families, particularly Orlandoans on weekend getaways. **Pros:**
private beach access; refrigerator and microwave in every room; comfy
beds. **Cons:** extra charge for beach-chair rental; loud air-conditioning in
some rooms; slow elevators; no breakfast with standard room. ⊠ *2080
N. Atlantic Ave.* ☎ *321/783–9222* ⊕ *www.cocoabeachdoubletree.com*
⇆ *148 rooms, 12 suites* & *In-room: Wi-Fi. In-hotel: restaurant, bar,
pool, gym, beach, laundry facilities, parking.*

**$$$**    ⊟ **Hilton Cocoa Beach Oceanfront.** You can't get any closer to the beach
HOTEL   than this seven-story oceanfront hotel. **Pros:** beachfront; friendly staff;
★   clean. **Cons:** small pool and bathrooms; no balconies; room windows
don't open; breakfast not included with standard rate. ⊠ *1550 N.
Atlantic Ave.* ☎ *321/799–0003* ⊕ *www.hiltoncocoabeach.com* ⇆ *285
rooms, 11 suites* & *In-room: Wi-Fi. In-hotel: restaurants, bar, pools,
gym, beach, laundry facilities, parking.*

**$$$**    ⊟ **Inn at Cocoa Beach.** This charming oceanfront inn has spacious, indi-
B&B/INN   vidually decorated rooms with four-poster beds, upholstered chairs, and
★   balconies or patios; most have ocean views. **Pros:** quiet; romantic; honor
bar. **Cons:** no on-site restaurant; "forced" socializing. ⊠ *4300 Ocean
Beach Blvd.* ☎ *321/799–3460, 800/343–5307 outside Florida* ⊕ *www.
theinnatcocoabeach.com* ⇆ *50 rooms* & *In-room: safe. In-hotel: pool,
gym, beach parking* ⏃⃝ *Breakfast.*

**$$$**    ⊟ **The Resort on Cocoa Beach.** Even if the beach weren't in its back-
RESORT   yard, this family-friendly, oceanfront property offers enough activi-
☺   ties and amenities—from tennis and basketball courts to a game
Fodor's Choice   room and 50-seat movie theater—to keep everyone entertained. **Pros:**
★   full kitchens; in-room washers and dryers; large balconies. **Cons:**
check-in not until 4 and checkout at 10; not all rooms are oceanfront;
slow elevators. ⊠ *1600 N. Atlantic Ave.* ☎ *321/783–4000* ⊕ *www.
theresortoncocoabeach.com* ⇆ *124 suites* & *In-room: kitchen, Internet.
In-hotel: restaurant, bars, tennis court, pools, gym, children's programs,
laundry facilities, parking.*

**$–$$**    ⊟ **Wakulla Suites Resort.** This kitschy two-story motel in a converted
HOTEL   1970s apartment building is clean and comfortable, surrounded by
tropical gardens, and just off the beach. **Pros:** kitchen; barbecue grills.
**Cons:** lots of kid noise; a hike to the beach; seven-day cancelation
policy. ⊠ *3550 N. Atlantic Ave.* ☎ *321/783–2230 or 800/992–5852*
⊕ *www.wakullasuites.com* ⇆ *117 suites* & *In-room: kitchen, Wi-Fi.
In-hotel: pool, laundry facilities, parking.*

## MELBOURNE

*20 mi south of Cocoa Beach.*

Despite its dependence on the high-tech space industry, this town is
decidedly laid-back. Most of the city is on the mainland, but a small

portion trickles onto a barrier island, separated by the Indian River Lagoon and accessible by several inlets, including the Sebastian.

## EXPLORING

Ⓒ    **Brevard Zoo**. On a stroll along the shaded boardwalks you get a close-up
Fodor's Choice    look at rhinos, giraffes, cheetahs, alligators, crocodiles, giant anteaters,
★    marmosets, jaguars, eagles, river otters, kangaroos, exotic birds, and kookaburras. Alligator, crocodile, and river-otter feedings are held on alternate afternoons—although the alligators do not dine on the otters. Stop by Paws-On, an interactive learning playground with a petting zone, wildlife detective training academy, and the Indian River Play Lagoon. Hand-feed a giraffe in Expedition Africa or a lorikeet in the Australian Free Flight Aviary, and step up to the Wetlands Outpost, an elevated pavilion that's a gateway to 22 acres of wetlands through which you can paddle kayaks and keep an eye open for the 4,000 species of wildlife that live in these waters and woods. ⊠ *8225 N. Wickham Rd.* ☎ *321/254–9453* ⊕ *www.brevardzoo.org* ☑ *$13.75 for general admission; $18.75 for admission, a train ride, and food for lorikeets* ☉ *Daily 9:30–5, last admission at 4:15*.

## BEACHES

**Paradise Beach**. Small and scenic, this 1,600-foot stretch of sand is part of a 10-acre park north of Indialantic, about 20 mi south of Cocoa Beach on Route A1A. It has showers, restrooms, picnic tables, a refreshment stand, and lifeguards in summer. **Best for:** Swimming, accessibility, sunrises, sunbathing, families. **Amenities:** Seasonal lifeguards, parking, volleyball courts, beachfront park with pavilions, grills, picnic and restroom facilities, outside showers.

**Satellite Beach**. The beaches of this sleepy little community just south of Patrick Air Force Base, about 15 mi south of Cocoa Beach on Route A1A, are cradled between the balmy Atlantic Ocean and biologically diverse Indian River Lagoon. It's a popular spot for family vacations because of its slow pace and lack of crowds. **Best for:** Swimming, accessibility, sunrises, sunbathing, families. **Amenities:** Seasonal lifeguards, parking, beachfront park with playground, five pavilions, picnic and restroom facilities.

## SPORTS AND THE OUTDOORS

### BASEBALL

**Space Coast Stadium**. Even though they play in our nation's capital during the regular season, the Washington Nationals, formerly the Montreal Expos, use this stadium for their spring training site. For the rest of the season, the facility is home to the Brevard County Manatees (☎ *321/633–9200*), one of the Milwaukee Brewers's minor-league teams. ⊠ *5800 Stadium Pkwy., Viera* ☎ *321/633–4487* ⊕ *www.nationals.com*.

### GOLF

**Baytree National Golf Links**. Greens fees are $25–$75 at this 18-hole course. ⊠ *8207 National Dr.* ☎ *321/259–9060* ⊕ *www.baytreenational.com*.

**Viera East Golf Club**. This is a public, 18-hole course. Greens fees are $26–$50. ⊠ *2300 Clubhouse Dr., Viera* ✛ *5 mi from Melbourne* ☎ *321/639–6500* ⊕ *www.vieragolf.com*.

# Orlando and Environs

PLAN FOR THE PARKS, PICK YOUR
HOTEL, EXPLORE ORLANDO

**WORD OF MOUTH**

"Get the Park Hopper Pass . . . to visit all the parks. Check out
dining with Disney characters. My daughter loved the princess
breakfast. Now that she's 13, she prefers Universal Studios. If you
have time, spend a day there, too. One of the most memorable
experiences was [swimming with the dolphins] at Discovery Cove."
—KendraM

# WELCOME TO ORLANDO AND ENVIRONS

## TOP REASONS TO GO

★ **Magic and Fantasy:** Unleash your inner child, in the glow of Cinderella Castle, at WDW's Magic Kingdom. Fireworks transform the night skies—and you—at this park and at Epcot. And, over at Universal's Islands of Adventure we have just, two words: Harry Potter.

★ **The Planet and Beyond:** Visit Epcot's 11 countries, complete with perfect replicas of foreign monuments, unique crafts, and traditional cuisine. Then venture beyond the Earth with a trip to the Kennedy Space Center.

★ **Amazing Animals:** Safari through Africa in Disney's Animal Kingdom, get splashed by Shamu at SeaWorld, kiss a dolphin at Discovery Cove, and watch gators wrestle at Gatorland.

★ **Shopping Opps:** Hit the national chains at Orlando's upscale malls, or browse Winter Park's unique Park Avenue boutiques. Don't forget the mouse ears: Main Street U.S.A. and Downtown Disney are filled with the best classic souvenirs and some quirkier items as well.

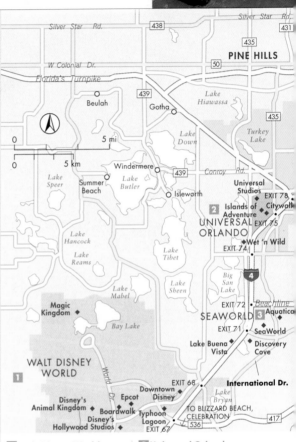

**1 Walt Disney World.**
Walt Disney's original decree that his parks be ever-changing, along with some healthy competition from Universal Studios and SeaWorld, has kept the Disney Imagineers dreaming up new entertainment and installing higher-tech thrills and attractions.

**2 Universal Orlando.**
While Disney creates a fantasy world for those who love fairy tales, Universal Orlando is geared to older kids, adults, and anyone who enjoys pop culture. Movie and TV fans love this place. Two other parks—Islands of Adventure (IOA) and Wet 'n Wild—add to the fun.

TO
LEESBURG
423

TO
DAYTONA

WINTER
PARK

Lake
Baldwin

W. Colonial Dr.

E. Colonial Dr.

50

TO
CHRISTMAS

Lake
Eola

Toll

408

**ORLANDO**

4

EXIT 82

Anderson St.

552

Katey St.

EXIT 80

527

Conway Rd.

Semoran

Rd.

Vineland Rd.

423

Edgewood

Hoffner Ave.

Oak Ridge Rd.

Lake
Conway

436

Pine
Castle

Judge Rd.

Sky Lake

Sand Lake Rd.

428

528

Expwy.

Taft

527

Orlando
International
Airport

Florida's Turnpike

John Young Pkwy.

Shingle

River

528

423

Flamingo

Mud
Lake

TO
KISSIMMEE

441

Central Florida Expwy.

417

436

# GETTING ORIENTED

Central Florida runs from Tampa/St. Petersburg in the west through Orlando and to the Space Coast attractions of Daytona Beach and Cape Canaveral on the east coast. Orlando is more or less equidistant, about 90 minutes by car to the Gulf of Mexico. Walt Disney World is not, contrary to advertising, in Orlando, but lies about 25 mi southwest of the city.

**4**

**3** SeaWorld and Discovery Cove. Less glitzy than Walt Disney World or Universal, SeaWorld and Discovery Cove are worth a visit for a low-key, relaxing, ocean-themed experience. If you want to get more keyed up, pay a call on SeaWorld's Aquatica water park.

**4** Orlando and Environs. Once you've exhausted the theme parks, or have been exhausted by them, turn your attention to a wealth of offerings, including museums, parks, and gardens, in Winter Park, Kissimmee, and elsewhere. The city sits about two hours east of Tampa.

# ORLANDO TRANSPORTATION

## Getting Here

All the major and most discount airlines fly into **Orlando International Airport** (*MCO* ☎ *407/825–2001*  ⊕ *www. orlandoairports.net*).

The **Beachline Expressway** (aka Beeline Expressway or Route 528), a toll road, gets you from the airport to area attractions. Depending on the location of your hotel, follow it west, and either exit at Sea-World for the International Drive (I-Drive) area or stay on it to Interstate 4, and head west for Disney and U.S. 192–Kissimmee or east for Universal and downtown Orlando.

The **Central Florida Greenway (SR 417)** is a faster way from the airport to Disney than the Beachline, but tolls are heftier.

## Magical Express

If you're staying at a Disney hotel, this free service will deliver your luggage from your home airport to your hotel (and back again) *and* shuttle you to and from your resort. ■ TIP→ You **must book before departure** (866/599–0951; www. disneysmagicalexpress.com); have your flight information handy.

## Getting Around

If you'll only be on Disney property, you can use its buses, trams, boats, and monorails. If you're staying outside Disney—or want to visit a non-Disney attraction—options are cabs, shuttles (your hotel may have a free one), and/or rental cars. Some hotels have shuttles to and from Universal and SeaWorld, which don't have transit systems.

### CABS, SHUTTLES, AND PUBLIC TRANSPORTATION

Many non-Disney hotels offer free airport shuttles. If yours doesn't, cab fare from the airport to the Disney area runs $55–$75. Try **Star Taxi** (☎ *407/857–9999*) or **Yellow Cab Co.** (☎ *407/422–2222*). **Town & Country Transportation** (☎ *407/828–3035*) charges $75 one-way for a town car. The **Mears Transportation Group** (☎ *407/423–5566* ⊕ *www.mearstransportation.com*) offers shuttle and charter services throughout the Orlando area. The **I-Ride Trolley** (☎ *407/248–9590* ⊕ *www.iridetrolley.com*)serves most attractions in the I-Drive area (including SeaWorld). It won't get you to Disney, but it does have a stop about a half mile from Universal. The **LYNX** (☎ *407/841–5969* ⊕ *www. golynx.com*)bus system provides service throughout Orlando.

### CAR RENTAL

Rates vary seasonally and can begin as low as $30 a day/$149 a week for an economy car (excluding 6.5% rental car tax). If you're staying on Disney property but want to rent car for a day, you might get a better daily rate if you reserve for two or more days, then return the car early. (Just be sure there aren't any penalties for this.)

### ROAD CONDITIONS AND SERVICE

Rush hours are weekdays 6–10 am and 4–7 pm. Dial *511 for traffic advisories (www.fl511.com). Dial *347 (*FHP) for the Florida Highway Patrol. Most Florida highways are also patrolled by Road Rangers, a free roadside service. The **AAA Car Care Center** (☎ *407/824–0976*) near the Magic Kingdom provides emergency services, including free towing even for non-AAA members on Disney property. Its office hours are weekdays 7–7, Saturday 7–4, but the trucks run the entire time the parks are open.

## Transit Times and Costs

| AIRPORT TO: | BY SHUTTLE | BY TAXI/CAR |
|---|---|---|
| Magic Kingdom | 30–45 min.; $34 round-trip (RT); $21 one way (OW) | 35 min.; approx. $62 (taxi fare) |
| Downtown Disney | 30–45 min.; $34 RT; $21 OW | 25–30 min.; approx. $45 |
| Animal Kingdom/ Hollywood Studios | 30–45 min.; $34 RT; $21 OW | 35 min.; approx. $61 |
| Universal | 30–40 min.; $30 RT; $19 OW | 20 min.; approx. $40 |
| Kissimmee | 30–45 min.; $46 RT; $27 OW | 30 min.; approx. $50 |
| I-Drive (midway/ Holiday Inn Resort Orlando—The Castle) | 30–40 min.; $30 RT; $19 OW | 20 min.; approx. $35 |
| Downtown Orlando | 30 min.; $29 RT; $18 OW | 20 min.; approx. $30 |
| **MAGIC KINGDOM TO:** | **BY SHUTTLE** | **BY TAXI/CAR** |
| Downtown Disney | N/A (use Disney transportation) | 10–15 min.; approx. $25 |
| Animal Kingdom/ Hollywood Studios | N/A (use Disney transportation) | 15 min.; approx. $23 |
| Universal | N/A | 25 min.; approx. $44 |
| Kissimmee | 30 min.; $16 RT | 25–30 min.; approx. $47 |
| I-Drive (midway/ Holiday Inn Resort Orlando—The Castle) | 35 min.; $19 RT | 30 min.; approx. $42 |
| Downtown Orlando | N/A | 40 min.; approx. $60 |
| **UNIVERSAL TO:** | **BY SHUTTLE** | **BY TAXI/CAR** |
| Magic Kingdom | N/A | 25 min.; approx. $41 |
| Downtown Disney | N/A | 20 min.; approx. $25 |
| Animal Kingdom/ Hollywood Studios | N/A | 30 min.; approx. $40 |
| Kissimmee | 30 min.; $19 RT | 25 min.; approx. $45 |
| I-Drive (midway/ Holiday Inn Resort Orlando—The Castle) | 25 min.; $16 RT | 5–10 min.; approx. $10 |
| Downtown Orlando | N/A | 10 min.; approx. $25 |

## Orlando Routes

**Beachline Expressway:** Toll road from the airport to International Drive (I-Drive) and Disney (roughly $2). Also good for Universal, SeaWorld, and Space Coast.

**Interstate 4:** Main east–west highway between Tampa and Daytona; it follows a north–south track through Orlando. ■ TIP→ Think north when I-4 signs say east (toward Daytona, say), and south when they say west (toward Tampa). Key exits are:

■ Exit 64B: Magic Kingdom/ U.S. 192; *heavy* peak-season traffic near this exit

■ Exit 65: Animal Kingdom, ESPN Wide World of Sports

■ Exit 67: Epcot/Downtown Disney, Typhoon Lagoon, Universal; less-congested exit

■ Exit 68: Downtown Disney, Typhoon Lagoon

■ Exits 71 and 72: SeaWorld

■ Exits 72, 74A, and 75A: I-Drive

■ Exits 74B and 75A: Universal Orlando Resort

**Semoran Blvd:** Main road to Winter Park. Heavily traveled but moves well; plenty of amenities.

**Spacecoast Parkway or Irlo Bronson Memorial Highway (U.S. 192):** Runs east–west to Kissimmee or Universal and downtown Orlando. Continues east to Space Coast. Crosses I-4 at Exits 64A and 64B.

# ORLANDO THEME PARKS

## Area Contacts

**Florida Tourist Board:** ☎ 850/488–5607 ⊕ www. visitflorida.com

**Kennedy Space Center:** ☎ 877/313–2610 ⊕ www. kennedyspacecenter.com

**Kissimmee Visitors Bureau:** ☎ 407/742–8200 ⊕ www. visitkissimmee.com

**Orlando Visitors Bureau:** ☎ 407/363–5872 or 800/972–3304 ⊕ www. visitorlando.com

**Space Coast Office of Tourism:** ☎ 877/572–3224 (877/57-BEACH) or 321/433–4470 ⊕ www.space-coast.com

**Tampa Bay & Company:** ☎ 800/448–2672 (800/44-TAMPA) or 813/223–1111 ⊕ www.visittampabay.com

**Winter Park Welcome Center:** ☎ 407/599–3399 ⊕ www. cityofwinterpark.org

## Disney Packages

**Cruises:** Disney Cruise Line ships have activities and amenities to thrill family members of all ages. From Florida's Port Canaveral you can sail to the Bahamas, Caribbean, or Panama Canal.

**Fairy Tale Weddings & Honeymoons.** Some 1,500 couples tie the knot at Disney World every year. At the Fairy Tale Wedding Pavilion and many other locations, the bride can ride in a Cinderella coach, have rings borne to the altar in a glass slipper, and spend time with Mickey and Minnie at the reception. Check out the interactive Web site, disney-weddings.disney.go.com.

**Magic Your Way Vacations.** These packages bundle hotel, parks admission, and an array of add-on options—dining plans, airfare, Park Hopper passes, spa treatments—that make it easy to customize your trip. They can also offer good value for money. Just do your homework so you'll know that, if you *aren't* interested in seeing Cirque du Soleil, it's best not to splurge on the Platinum Plan, which includes tickets to this show. You'll also be sure to determine how many park meals and snacks you'll truly need before investing in a dining plan.

**Grand Gatherings.** If you're planning a group trip, you must look into this service. It allows groups of eight or more to tailor entertainment and meals to their needs. Contact central reservations for information.

## Universal Packages

**Vacation Package.** Universal offers its own plans and ever-changing roster of deals to help you maximize valueBasic packages include hotel and park admission, but can be expanded to include airfare; dining; rental cars; show tickets; spa treatments; admission to SeaWorld, Wet 'n Wild, Aquatica, Busch Gardens, and Discovery Cove; and a VIP treatment that lets you skip many theme-park lines. Note, though, that this last perk is free to guests at on-site hotels at Universal Resorts.

# Parks Tickets

Per-day, per-person, at-the-gate admissions range from roughly $50 at Aquatica or Wet 'n Wild to about $80 at Universal, Disney, and SeaWorld. Discovery Cove runs from $189 without a dolphin swim to $299 with it, though prices vary seasonally. Combo ticket plans can save money, but be sure to weigh what they offer against your needs.

## DISNEY

**Magic Your Way:** With this plan, the more days you stay, the greater your per-day savings. For instance, a one-day ticket costs $82 for anyone age 10 and up, whereas a five-day ticket costs $237 (or just under $48 per day). There are also add-ons:

**Park Hopper:** This lets you move from park to park within a single day and adds $54 to the overall price of a ticket, no matter how many days your ticket covers. The flexibility is fantastic—you can spend the day at Animal Kingdom, for example, then hit Magic Kingdom for fireworks.

**Water Parks Fun and More:** With this $54-per-ticket add-on, you get admission to Typhoon Lagoon, Blizzard Beach, and other Disney attractions.

**No Expiration:** This add-on (prices vary) lets you use your ticket for more than one trip to Disney (e.g., use five days of a seven-day Magic Your Way ticket on one visit and two days on another).

## UNIVERSAL, SEAWORLD, BUSCH GARDENS TAMPA

**Universal Parks:** A one-day Park to Park ticket is $112 (ages 10 and up); a seven-day version is nearly $175 (a better per-day value at just under $25 a day). Add the Express PLUS (prices vary) option to skirt ride lines; City-Walk Party Pass (roughly $12) for one-night venue access; CityWalk Party Pass and Movie ($15) for a free movie; and Length-of-Stay Wet 'n Wild pass (about $50).

**SeaWorld and Busch Gardens Parks:** There are various ticket plans for SeaWorld Orlando parks and Busch Gardens Tampa Bay, which are all run by one company.

**Orlando FlexTicket:** This gives you 14 consecutive days' unlimited entry to (but not parking at) Universal and Sea-World parks, Wet 'n Wild, Aquatica, and select CityWalk venues. It costs nearly $248 (ages 10 and up). The Flex Ticket Plus (nearly $284) includes admission to Busch Gardens and free shuttle service between it and various Orlando locations.

# Parks Planning Contacts

## DISNEY

**Central Reservations:** ☎ 407/934–7639 (407/W–DISNEY)

**Dining:** ☎ 407/939–3463 (407/WDW–DINE)

**Fairytale Weddings:** ☎ 321/939–4610 ⊕ disneyweddings.disney.go.com

**Golf:** ☎ 407/939–4653 (407/WDW–GOLF)

**Hotel:** ☎ 407/939–7429

**Vacation Packages:** ☎ 407/939–7675

**Tickets:** ☎ 407/939–1289

**Web Site:** ⊕ disneyworld.disney.go.com

## SEAWORLD

**Discovery Cove:** ☎ 877/557–7404 ⊕ www.discoverycove.com

**SeaWorld:** ☎ 888/800–5447 ⊕ www.seaworld.com/orlando

## UNIVERSAL

**Main Number:** ☎ 407/363–8000

**Dining:** ☎ 407/224–3613, 407/224–4012 for character meals

**Hotel:** ☎ 888/273–1311

**Vacation Packages:** ☎ 877/801–9720

**Web Site:** ⊕ www.universalorlando.com

4

# Disney *Magic Your Way* Price Chart

| TICKET OPTIONS | | | | | | | | |
|---|---|---|---|---|---|---|---|---|
| **TICKET** | **1-DAY** | **2-DAY** | **3-DAY** | **4-DAY** | **5-DAY** | **6-DAY** | **7-DAY** | **10-DAY** |
| BASE TICKET | | | | | | | | |
| Ages 10-up | $85 | $168 | $232 | $243 | $251 | $259 | $267 | $291 |
| Ages 3-9 | $79 | $155 | $214 | $224 | $232 | $240 | $248 | $272 |
| *Base Ticket* admits guest to one of the four major theme parks per day's use. Park choices are: Magic Kingdom, Epcot, Disney's Hollywood Studios, Disney's Animal Kingdom. 8- and 9-day tickets are also available. | | | | | | | | |
| ADD: Park Hopper | $55 | $55 | $55 | $55 | $55 | $55 | $55 | $55 |
| *Park Hopper* option entitles guest to visit more than one theme park per day's use. Park choices are any combination of Magic Kingdom, Epcot, Disney's Hollywood Studios, Disney's Animal Kingdom. | | | | | | | | |
| ADD: Water Parks Fun & More | $55 2 visits | $55 2 visits | $55 3 visits | $55 4 visits | $55 5 visits | $55 6 visits | $55 7 visits | $55 10 visits |
| *Water Parks Fun & More* option entitles guest to a specified number of visits to a choice of entertainment and recreation venues. Choices are Blizzard Beach, Typhoon Lagoon, DisneyQuest, Disney's Oak Trail golf course, and Wide World of Sports. | | | | | | | | |
| ADD: No Expiration | n/a | $25 | $35 | $75 | $115 | $130 | $160 | $225 |
| *No expiration* means that unused admissions on a ticket may be used any time in the future. Without this option, tickets expire 14 days after first use. | | | | | | | | |

| MINOR PARKS AND ATTRACTIONS | | |
|---|---|---|
| **TICKET** | **AGES 10-UP** | **AGES 3-9** |
| Typhoon Lagoon or Blizzard Beach 1-Day 1-Park | $49 | $41 |
| DisneyQuest 1-Day | $43 | $37 |
| Disney's ESPN Wide World of Sports | $13.55 | $9.34 |
| Cirque du Soleil's *La Nouba* | $71–$124 | $57–$99 |
| *All prices are subject to Florida sales tax | | |

Get wet on the 12-story Summit Plummet at Disney's Blizzard Beach.

## Universal Orlando Ticket Price Chart

| TICKET OPTIONS | | | | |
|---|---|---|---|---|
| **TICKET** | **1-DAY** | **2-DAY** | **3-DAY** | **4-DAY** |
| BASE TICKET | | | | |
| Ages 10-up | $82 | $115 | $130 | $140 |
| Ages 3-9 | $74 | $102 | $115 | $123 |
| *Base Ticket* admits guest to one park per day, either Universal Studios or Islands of Adventure. | | | | |
| PARK-TO-PARK | | | | |
| Ages 10-up | $112 | $135 | $145 | $150 |
| Ages 3-9 | $104 | $122 | $130 | $133 |
| Park-to-Park Ticket allows guest to go back and forth between Universal Studios and Islands of Adventure; 7-day ticket available. | | | | |
| ADD: Wet 'n Wild Length of Stay Ticket | $48 | $48 | $48 | $48 |
| Wet 'n Wild Length of Stay Ticket gives guest admission to the water park for 14 consecutive days, beginning with the first day of use. | | | | |
| ADD: CityWalk Party Pass | $12 | Free | Free | Free |
| CityWalk Party Pass and Movie | $15 | N/A | N/A | N/A |
| CityWalk Party Pass gives guest one-night access to CityWalk clubs and venues (some of which require you to be at least 21). CityWalk Party Pass and Movie adds to that a free movie at the AMC Universal Cineplex 20. | | | | |
| ADD: Universal Express Pass | Prices vary greatly by options and season; check website for details. | | | |
| Gives guest access to much shorter lines at Universal Studios and Islands of Adventure rides. (Note that this pass is included in the room rate at Universal Resort hotels.) | | | | |
| All prices are subject to Florida sales tax | | | | |

4

Universal Orlando.

By Elise Allen, Rona Ginden, Megan Peck, Jennifer Greenhill-Taylor

There's magic in Orlando, and we don't just mean the NBA team. The city and its environs teem with magical experiences, both natural and Imagineered. With endless joys and excitements for people of all ages, it's no wonder that more than 50 million people visit every year.

The most obvious source of Orlando's magic is Disney World. And with four theme parks, two water parks, 20 or so themed hotels, shopping districts, and countless dining options, you could spend a lengthy vacation entirely on Disney property and still not see it all.

Universal Studios and Islands of Adventure offer their own thrills, including the Wizarding World of Harry Potter. There are also SeaWorld, Discovery Cove—where you can have the truly magical experience of swimming with the dolphins—and Busch Gardens Tampa. To take a break from the theme parks, you can visit Winter Park's Charles Hosmer Morse Museum for what may well be the world's largest collection of Tiffany glass; go hiking, swimming, or canoeing in Wekiwa Springs State Park; or head to Space Coast.

You could also just take it easy. Even in the midst of a whirlwind theme-park tour, you can laze by the pool, indulge in a spa treatment, play a round of golf, or leisurely shop an afternoon away.

The key to an ideal Orlando vacation is planning. Figure out well in advance who's going, what everyone wants to do on this trip, and what you'll save for the next. If your stay will center around theme parks, decide which parks to visit on which days, buy your ticket and hotel package, and make meal reservations—all long before leaving home.

When you're actually in Orlando, though, try to be flexible. Your plans form the backbone of your trip and you want it to be strong, but things will come up—moods will change, plans will alter. That's OK. For the most part, it's not difficult to change segments of your itinerary once you're on the ground. Planning is key to enjoying Orlando and all it offers, but so is taking a deep breath, allowing for the occasional detour, and going with the flow of your vacation.

# EXPLORING

There's more to an Orlando experience than walking 10 mi a day in the theme parks. Travelers were flocking to central Florida's communities, lakes, streams, and golf courses decades before Disney arrived. In addition to myriad outdoor activities, Orlando and its environs offer plenty of noteworthy cultural sights.

*Use the coordinate (✛ 1:B2) at the end of each review to locate a site on the Where to Explore, Eat, and Stay in the Orlando Area map.*

## ORLANDO

*85 mi northeast of Tampa; 56 mi southwest of New Smyrna Beach; 15 mi northeast of Walt Disney World; off I–4, take Exit 82C or 83B eastbound.*

Downtown has high-rises; sports venues; interesting museums, restaurants, and nightspots; and numerous parks. A few steps away are delightful residential neighborhoods with brick-paved streets and live oaks dripping with Spanish moss.

### EXPLORING

#### CENTRAL ORLANDO

Fodor's Choice
★

**Harry P. Leu Gardens.** A few miles outside of downtown—on the former lakefront estate of a citrus entrepreneur—is this 50-acre garden. Among the highlights are a collection of historical blooms (many varieties of which were established before 1900), ancient oaks, a 50-foot floral clock, and one of the largest camellia collections in eastern North America (in bloom November–March). Mary Jane's Rose Garden is filled with more than 1,000 bushes. The simple 19th-century Leu House Museum, once the Leu family home, preserves the furnishings and appointments of a well-to-do, turn-of-the-20th-century Florida family. ⊠ *1920 N. Forest Ave., Lake Ivanhoe* ☎ *407/246–2620* ⊕ *www.leugardens.org* ✆ *$7; free 1st Mon. of every month* ⊘ *Garden daily 9–5; guided house tours daily on hr and ½ hr 10–3:30* ✛ *1:F1.*

**Mennello Museum of American Folk Art.** One of the few museums in the United States devoted to folk art has intimate galleries, some with lovely lakefront views. Look for the nation's most extensive permanent collection of Earl Cunningham paintings as well as works by many other self-taught artists. There's a wonderful video about Cunningham and his "curio shop" in St. Augustine. ⊠ *900 E. Princeton St., Lake Ivanhoe* ☎ *407/246–4278* ⊕ *www.mennellomuseum.com* ✆ *$4* ⊘ *Tues.–Sat. 10:30–4:30, Sun. noon–4:30* ✛ *1:F1.*

Fodor's Choice
★

☺ **Orlando Science Center.** With exhibits about the human body, mechanics, computers, math, nature, the solar system, and optics, there's something for every child's inner geek. The four-story internal atrium is home to live gators and turtles and a great spot for simply gazing at what Old Florida once looked like. The 300-seat Dr. Phillips CineDome, a movie theater with a giant eight-story screen, offers large-format iWERKS films and planetarium programs. The Crosby Observatory and Florida's largest publicly accessible refractor telescope are here.

✉ *777 E. Princeton St., Lake Ivanhoe* ☎ *407/514–2000 or 888/672–4386* ⊕ *www.osc.org* 🎟 *$17; parking $5; tickets include all permanent and special exhibits, films, live science presentations, and planetarium shows* ⊙ *Thurs.–Tues. 10–5* ✛ *1:F1.*

### INTERNATIONAL DRIVE

☾ **Fun Spot.** Four go-kart tracks offer a variety of driving experiences for children and adults. Though drivers must be at least 10 years old and meet height requirements, parents can drive smaller children in two-seater cars on several of the tracks, including the Conquest Track. A dozen or so rides range from the dizzying Paratrooper to an old-fashioned Revolver Ferris Wheel to the twirling toddler Teacups. Inside the arcade, test your coordination with Dance Dance Revolution. ✉ *5551 Del Verde Way, I–4 to Exit 75A, I-Drive area* ☎ *407/363–3867* ⊕ *www.funspot.tutengraphics.com* 🎟 *$14.95–$34.95 depending on go-kart and ride package (discount coupon online); arcade tokens 25¢ each or $25 for 120* ⊙ *Daily 10 am–midnight* ✛ *1:D3.*

**Ripley's Believe It or Not! Odditorium.** A 10-foot-square section of the Berlin Wall. A pain and torture chamber. A Rolls-Royce constructed entirely of matchsticks. A 26-foot-by-20-foot portrait of van Gogh made from 3,000 postcards. These and almost 200 other oddities (shrunken heads included) speak for themselves in this museum-cum-attraction in the heart of tourist territory on International Drive. ■ TIP➜ Buy tickets online ahead of time, and you get a $1 discount. ✉ *8201 International Dr., I-Drive area* ☎ *407/351–5803 or 800/998–4418 Ext. 3* ⊕ *www.ripleysorlando.com* 🎟 *$18.95; free parking* ⊙ *Daily 9:30 am–midnight; last admission at 11 pm* ✛ *1:D3.*

☾ **WonderWorks.** The building seems to be sinking into the ground. Not only that, but it seems to be sinking into the ground at a precarious angle and upside down. Many people stop to take pictures in front of the topsy-turvy facade, complete with upended palm trees and broken skyward-facing sidewalks. Inside, the upside-down theme continues only as far as the lobby. After that, it's a playground of 100 interactive experiences—some incorporating virtual reality, others educational (similar to those at a science museum), and still others pure entertainment. You can experience an earthquake or a hurricane, pilot a fighter jet using simulator controls, make giant bubbles in the Bubble Lab, play laser tag, and design and ride your own roller coaster. ✉ *9067 International Dr., I-Drive area* ☎ *407/351–8800* ⊕ *www.wonderworksonline.com* 🎟 *$19.95; higher-price combo packages include laser tag and comedy dinner show; parking $2–$6; look for online coupons* ⊙ *Daily 9 am–midnight* ✛ *1:D4.*

## SPORTS AND THE OUTDOORS

### BALLOONING

Fodor'sChoice
★ **Bob's Balloons.** Bob's offers one-hour rides over protected marshland and will even fly over Disney World if wind and weather conditions are right. You meet in Lake Buena Vista at dawn, where Bob and his assistant take you by van to the launch site. It takes about 15 minutes to get the balloon in the air, and then you're off on an adventure that definitely surpasses Peter Pan's Flight in the Magic Kingdom. There

are seats in the basket, but you'll probably be too thrilled to sit down. ☎ 407/466–6380 or 877/824–4606 ⊕ *www.bobsballoons.com* ✉ *$90–$175 per person.*

## GOLF

★ **ChampionsGate Golf Club**, with the on-site David Leadbetter Golf Academy, has two distinct courses designed by Greg Norman. The 7,406-yard International has the feel of the best British Isles courses, whereas the 7,048-yard National course is designed in the style of the better domestic courses, with a number of par-3 holes with unusual bunkers. The club is less than 10 mi from Walt Disney World at Exit 72 on I–4. ⊠ *1400 Masters Blvd., Champions Gate* ☎ *407/787–4653 Champions Gate, 407/787–3330 or 888/633–5323 Leadbetter Academy* ⊕ *www. championsgategolf.com* ✉ *Greens fees $65–$147* ✦ *1:B6.*

**Grand Cypress Golf Resort**, fashioned after a Scottish glen, is comprised of three 9s: the North, South, and East courses, and the 18-hole New Course. In addition, the Grand Cypress Academy of Golf, a 21-acre facility, has lessons and clinics. The North and South courses have fairways constructed on different levels, giving them added definition. The New Course, designed by Jack Nicklaus, was inspired by the Old Course at St. Andrews, and has deep bunkers, double greens, a snaking burn, and even an old stone bridge. ⊠ *1 N. Jacaranda, Orlando* ☎ *407/239–1909 or 800/835–7377* ⊕ *www.grandcypress. com* ✉ *Greens fees $75–$175* ✦ *1:C5.*

## MINIATURE GOLF

○ **Hawaiian Rumble Adventure Golf.** Who can resist golfing around an erupting volcano? Hawaiian Rumble combines a tropical setting with waterfalls, tunnels, tiki gods, and flame-belching mountains. There's also a location in the Lake Buena Vista area. ⊠ *8969 International Dr., I-Drive area* ☎ *407/351–7733* ⊕ *www .hawaiianrumbleorlando.com* ✉ *$9.95–$14.95* ○ *Sun.–Thurs. 9 am–11:30 pm, Fri. and Sat. 9 am–midnight* ✦ *1:D4.*

Fodor'sChoice
★

○ **Pirate's Cove Adventure Golf.** Two 18-hole courses wind around artificial mountains, through caves, and into lush foliage. The beginner's course is called Captain Kidd's Adventure; the more advanced course is Blackbeard's Challenge. There's also a branch in the Crossroads of Lake Buena Vista shopping plaza, near Disney. ⊠ *8501 International Dr., I-Drive area* ☎ *407/352–7378* ⊕ *www.piratescove.net* ✉ *$10.95–$16.50* ○ *Daily 9 am–11:30 pm* ✦ *1:D3.*

## SHOPPING

### FACTORY OUTLETS

★ **Orlando Premium Outlets International Drive.** The massive complex at the north tip of International Drive includes Saks 5th Avenue OFF 5TH, Neiman Marcus Last Call, Victoria's Secret Outlet, the only outlet store for Baccarat and Lalique crystal, and a Disney outlet. Searching for bargains works up an appetite, and there are plenty of places to eat here, either in the well-lit food court or in one of several sit-down restaurants. ⊠ *5401 W. Oak Ridge Rd., I-Drive area* ☎ *407/352–9600* ⊕ *www. primeoutlets.com* ○ *Mon.–Sat. 10 am–11 pm, Sun. 10–9* ✦ *1:D3.*

**4**

**Orlando Premium Outlets Vineland Avenue.** Smart shoppers have lunch on International Drive and take the I-Ride Trolley right to the front entrance (it runs every 15 minutes). You'll find the Kleins (Anne and Calvin), Gap, Nike, Adidas, Timberland, Polo Ralph Lauren, Giorgio Armani, Burberry, Tommy Hilfiger, Reebok, and about 100 other stores. ⊠ *8200 Vineland Ave., I-Drive area* ☎ *407/238–7787* ⊕ *www. premiumoutlets.com/orlando* ⊘ *Mon.–Sat. 10 am–11 pm, Sun. 10–9* ✛ *1:D5.*

## MALLS

Fodor'sChoice  **Mall at Millenia.** Its high-end shops, include Gucci, Burberry, Chanel,
★  Jimmy Choo, Hugo Boss, Cartier, Tiffany, and Ferragamo. You'll also find Neiman Marcus, Bloomingdale's, IKEA, and an Apple store. ⊠ *4200 S. Conroy Rd., South Orlando* ☎ *407/363–3555* ⊕ *www. mallatmillenia.com* ⊘ *Mon.–Sat. 10–9:30, Sun. 11–7* ✛ *1:E3.*

**Pointe Orlando.** This entertainment and shopping complex is within walking distance of five top hotels and the Orange County Convention Center. Its home to WonderWorks; an IMAX theater; and specialty shops such as Armani Exchange, Tommy Bahama, Chico's, and Victoria's Secret. Among the restaurants are the very high-end Capital Grille, the Oceanaire Seafood Room, Cuba Libre, Funky Monkey Wine Company, B.B. King's Blues Club, and Taverna Opa. ⊠ *9101 International Dr., I-Drive area* ☎ *407/248–2838* ⊕ *www.pointeorlando.com* ⊘ *Mon.–Sat. noon–10, Sun. noon–8; restaurant hrs vary* ✛ *1:D4.*

## NIGHTLIFE
### BARS AND NIGHTCLUBS

Fodor'sChoice  **Antigua.** The multi-block-long entertainment complex called Church
★  Street is a restaurant and bar hot spot, with Antigua being a contender for flashiest of them all. The music in the multilevel, four-bar lounge is loud; the lighting is dramatic; and the waterfall (yes, you read that correctly) cascades 20 feet. No wonder the pretty people pack the place. ⊠ *46 W. Church St., Downtown Orlando* ☎ *407/649–4270* ⊕ *www. churchstreetbars.com* 🖅 *$5–$10* ⊘ *Wed.–Sat. 10 pm–2:45 am* ✛ *1:F1.*

**ICEBAR.** Thanks to the miracle of refrigeration, this is Orlando's coolest bar—literally and figuratively. Fifty tons of pure ice is kept at a constant 27°F and has been cut and sculpted by world-class carvers into a cozy (or as cozy as ice can be) sanctuary of tables, sofas, chairs, and a bar. The staff loans you a thermal cape and gloves, and when you enter the frozen hall you receive a complimentary drink served in a glass made of crystal-clear ice. ⊠ *Pointe Orlando, 8967 International Dr., I-Drive area* ☎ *407/426–7555* ⊕ *www.icebarorlando.com* ⊘ *Fri. and Sat. 7 pm–2 am, Sun.–Thurs. 7 pm–midnight* ✛ *1:D4*

**Wally's.** Some would say that one of Orlando's oldest bars (circa 1953) is a dive, but that doesn't matter to the students, bikers, lawyers, and barflies who land here to drink surrounded by the go-go-dancer wallpaper and '60s-era interior. ⊠ *1001 N. Mills Ave., Downtown Orlando* ☎ *407/896–6975* ⊘ *Mon.–Sat. 7:30 am–2 am* ✛ *1:F1.*

## MUSIC CLUBS

★ **B.B. King's Blues Club.** The blues-musician-turned-entrepreneur has clubs in Memphis, Nashville, Las Vegas, and West Palm Beach as well as Orlando. Like the others, the root of the club is music. There's a dance floor and two stages for live performances. You can't really experience Delta blues without Delta dining, so there's a menu with fried dill pickles, catfish bites, po' boys, ribs, and other comfort foods. Oh, yeah, and there's a full bar. ⊠ *Pointe Orlando, 9101 International Dr., I-Drive area* ☎ *407/370–4550* ⊕ *www.bbkingclubs.com* ☾ *Daily 11 am–2 am* ✛ *1:D4.*

**Firestone Live.** Based in an old automotive repair shop, this multilevel, high-energy club draws international music acts. Something's always going on to make the crowd hop: DJ mixes, big band, jazz, hip-hop, rock. Often the dance floor is more like semicontrolled chaos than a place to just listen, so be prepared. ⊠ *578 N. Orange Ave., Downtown Orlando* ☎ *407/872–0066* ⊕ *www.firestonelive.net* ✛ *1:F1.*

Fodor'sChoice **The Social.** Beloved by locals, The Social is a great place to see touring
★ and area musicians. Up to seven nights a week you can sip trademark martinis while listening to anything from indie rock to rockabilly to undiluted jazz. Hours vary. ⊠ *54 N. Orange Ave., Downtown Orlando* ☎ *407/246–1419* ⊕ *www.thesocial.org* ⌑ *$7–$30, depending on entertainment* ✛ *1:F1.*

# KISSIMMEE

*18 mi south of Orlando, 10 mi southeast of Walt Disney World (WDW).*

Although Kissimmee is primarily known as the gateway to Disney (technically, the park is in both Osceola and Orange counties), its non-WDW attractions just might tickle your fancy. They range from throwbacks to old-time Florida or to dinner shows for you and 2,000 of your closest friends. With at least 100,000 acres of freshwater lakes, the Kissimmee area brings anglers and boaters to national fishing tournaments and speedboat races. A 50-mi-long series of lakes, the Kissimmee Waterway, connects Lake Tohopekaliga—a Native American name that means "Sleeping Tiger"; locals call it Lake Toho—with huge Lake Ocheechobee in south Florida, and, from there, to both the Atlantic Ocean and the Gulf of Mexico.

☾ **Gatorland.** This campy attraction near the Orlando–Kissimmee border on U.S. 441 has endured since 1949 without much change. The Gator Gulley Splash Park is complete with giant "egrets" spilling water from their beaks, dueling water guns mounted atop giant gators, and other water-park splash areas. There's also a small petting zoo and an aviary. A free train ride is a high point, taking you through an alligator breeding marsh and a natural swamp setting where you can spot gators, birds, and turtles. A three-story observation tower overlooks the breeding marsh, swamped with gator grunts, especially come sundown during mating season. For a glimpse of 37 giant rare and deadly crocodiles, check out the Jungle Crocs of the World exhibit. To see eager gators leaping out of the water to catch their food, come on cool days for the Gator Jumparoo Show (summer heat just puts them to sleep). There's

also a Gator Wrestlin' Show. This is a real Florida experience, and you leave knowing the difference between a gator and a croc. ✉ *14501 S. Orange Blossom Trail, between Orlando and Kissimmee* ☎ *407/855–5496 or 800/393–5297* ⊕ *www.gatorland.com* 🎫 *$22.99; discount coupons online* ☉ *Daily 9–5* ✛ *1:E5.*

## SPORTS AND THE OUTDOORS

### FISHING

**Lake Charters.** This outfitter conducts trips from November to May on Lake Toho (January through April is high season, so reserve accordingly), and has done so for more than 20 years. It's possible to catch a 14-pound bass here. Rods and reels are included in the costs, and transportation is available. Half-day freshwater trips are $250, six-hour trips are $300, and full-day trips are $350. Prices are for one to two people. You can also buy your licenses here. ✉ *1650 Justin Matthew Way, St. Cloud* ☎ *407/891–2275 or 877/326–3575* ⊕ *www.lakecharter.com.*

### SHOPPING

**Lake Buena Vista Factory Stores.** Although it has scant curb appeal, it does have a good collection of outlets for Aeropostale, Bass, Eddie Bauer, Fossil, Gap, Izod, Liz Claiborne, Nike, Tommy Hilfiger, and Old Navy. Check out the coupons on the Web site, too. ✉ *15657 S. Apopka Vineland Rd., Lake Buena Vista* ☎ *407/238–9301* ⊕ *www.lbvfs.com* ☉ *Mon.–Sat. 10–9, Sun. 10–7* ✛ *1:D5.*

**192 Flea Market Outlet.** Its 400 booths are open daily. The all-new merchandise includes tons of items: toys, luggage, sunglasses, jewelry, clothes, beach towels, sneakers, electronics, and the obligatory T-shirts. ✉ *4301 W. Vine St., Hwy. 192, Kissimmee* ☎ *407/396–4555* ⊕ *www.192fleamarketprices.com* ☉ *Daily 9–6* ✛ *1:D6.*

### NIGHTLIFE

Fodor'sChoice ★  **Arabian Nights.** This palatial arena has seating for more than 1,200. The 25-act dinner show is complete with about 60 horses, centers around the quest of an Arabian princess to find her true love, and includes a buffoonish genie, a chariot race, and an intricate dance on horseback. The kitchen serves such things as USDA Choice and certified Black Angus sirloin. ✉ *3081 Arabian Nights Blvd., Kissimmee* ☎ *407/239–9223 or 800/553–6116* ⊕ *www.arabian-nights.com* 🎫 *$63.99, including tax* ☉ *Shows nightly, times vary* ✛ *1:C6.*

**Capone's Dinner and Show.** This show brings you back to gangland Chicago of the 1930s. The evening begins in an old-fashioned ice-cream parlor, but say the secret password, and you're ushered inside Al Capone's private Underworld Cabaret and Speakeasy. Dinner is an all-you-can-eat American and Italian buffet that includes beer, alcoholic mixed drinks, and cocktails for kids. ✉ *4740 W. Irlo Bronson Memorial Hwy., Kissimmee* ☎ *407/397–2378* ⊕ *www.alcapones.com* 🎫 *$51.99* ☉ *Daily 7:30* ✛ *1:D6.*

☾ **Medieval Times.** In a huge, ersatz-medieval manor you'll see a tournament of sword fights, jousting matches, and other games on a good-versus-evil theme. No fewer than 30 charging horses and a cast of 75 knights, nobles, wizards, and maidens participate. That the show takes precedence over the meat-and-potatoes fare is obvious: everyone sits facing forward at long, narrow banquet tables. ✉ *4510 W. Irlo Bronson Memorial Hwy., Kissimmee* ☎ *407/396–1518 or 800/229–8300* ⊕ *www.medievaltimes.com* 🎫 *$59.95; $20 per person "royalty" upgrade includes first-row seating* ⊙ *Castle daily 9–4, village daily 4:30–8, performances usually daily at 8 but call ahead* ✥ *1:D6.*

OFF THE
BEATEN
PATH

**LEGOLAND.** About 50 miles southwest of Orlando is the quiet town of Winter Haven, home to numerous lakes and a waterskiing school. It was also home to the Sunshine State's first theme park, Cypress Gardens, a mainstay of Florida tourism from 1936 until 2009. In October 2011 it reopened as the world's largest LEGOLAND, set on 150 acres and built using more than 50 million LEGOs. In addition to adding the 1:20-scale miniature reproductions of international cities—as is done at the Danish, German, British, and Californian parks—and more than 50 rides, attractions, and shows throughout 10 different zones, the owners have kept the marvelous botanical gardens from the original park. Among other things, look for replicas of Las Vegas, New York City, and Washington, D.C., as well as such Florida landmarks as the Kennedy Space Center. Check out the full-size, raceable LEGO cars—a nod to Daytona Beach racing—the a pirate-themed area and water-stunt show; and rides like Coastersauras, a wooden roller coaster, and the Lost Kingdom Adventure that has you navigating a Egyptian ruins and firing lasers. ✉ *One LEGOLAND Way, Winter Haven* ☎ *877/350–LEGO (877/350–5346)* ⊕ *www.LEGOLAND.com* ⊙ *Daily 10–5* 🎫 *$75 adults (13–59), $65 kids and senior citizens* ✥ *1:B6.*

## BOK TOWER GARDENS

*57 mi southwest of Orlando, 42 mi southwest of WDW.*

Fodor'sChoice
★

**Bok Tower Gardens.** You'll see citrus groves as you ride south along U.S. 27 to the small town of Lake Wales and the Bok Tower Gardens. This appealing sanctuary of plants, flowers, trees, and wildlife has been something of a local secret for years. Shady paths meander through pine forests with silvery moats, mockingbirds and swans, blooming thickets, and hidden sundials. The majestic, 200-foot Bok Tower is constructed of coquina—from seashells—and pink, white, and gray marble. The tower houses a carillon with 57 bronze bells that ring out each day at 1 and 3 pm during 30-minute live recitals of early American folk songs, Appalachian tunes, Irish ballads, or Latin hymns. The landscape was designed in 1928 by Frederick Law Olmsted Jr., son of the planner of New York's Central Park. The grounds include the 20-room, Mediterranean-style Pinewood Estate, built in 1930 and open for self-guided touring. ✉ *1151 Tower Blvd., Lake Wales* ☎ *863/676–1408* ⊕ *www.boktower.org* 🎫 *$10; Pinewood Estate general tour $6. 50% off admission Sat. 8–9 am; holiday tour prices higher* ⊙ *Daily 8–6* ✥ *1:B6.*

## WEKIWA SPRINGS STATE PARK

*13 mi northwest of Orlando, 28 mi north of WDW.*

Fodor's Choice ★

The river, springs, and surrounding 6,400-acre **Wekiwa Springs State Park** are well suited to camping, hiking, picnicking, swimming, canoeing, and fishing. The area is also full of Florida wildlife: otters, raccoons, alligators, bobcats, deer, turtles, and birds. You can rent canoes ($16 for two hours and $3.20 per hour after that) in the town of Apopka, near the park's southern entrance. ✉ *1800 Wekiva Circle, Apopka* ☎ *407/884–2008, 800/326–3521 for campsite bookings* ⊕ *www.floridastateparks.org* 🖅 *$2 per pedestrian or bicycle; $6 per vehicle* ☉ *Daily 8–dusk* ✛ *1:E1.*

## WINTER PARK

4

*6 mi northeast of Orlando, 20 mi northeast of WDW.*

This peaceful, upscale community may be just outside the hustle and bustle of Orlando, but it feels like a different country. The lovely, 8-square-mi village has brick-paved streets, boutique-lined Park Avenue, historic buildings, and well-maintained lakes and parkland. Even the town's bucolic 9-hole golf course is on the National Register of Historic Places.

Fodor's Choice ★

**Charles Hosmer Morse Museum of American Art.** The world's most comprehensive collection of work by Louis Comfort Tiffany—including immense stained-glass windows, lamps, watercolors, and desk sets—is in this museum. Many of the works were rescued from Tiffany's Long Island estate, Laurelton Hall, after a 1957 fire destroyed much of the property. Among the draws is the 1,082-square-foot Tiffany Chapel, originally built for the 1893 world's fair in Chicago. The museum also contains American decorative art and paintings from the mid-19th to the early-20th centuries. Exhibits in the new Laurelton Hall wing include architectural and decorative elements that survived the fire from Laurelton's dining room, living room, and Fountain Court reception hall. There's also a re-creation of the estate's Daffodil Terrace, so named for the glass daffodils that serve as the capitals for the terrace's marble columns. ✉ *445 N. Park Ave., Winter Park* ☎ *407/645–5311* ⊕ *www. morsemuseum.org* 🖅 *$3; Nov.–Apr., Fri. free 4–8* ☉ *Tues.–Sat. 9:30–4, Sun. 1–4; Nov.–Apr., Fri. until 8* ✛ *1:F1.*

**Cornell Fine Arts Museum.** On the Rollins College campus, this museum houses Florida's oldest art collection (its first paintings acquired in 1896)—one with more than 6,000 works, from Italian Renaissance to 19th- and 20th-century American and European paintings. Special exhibitions feature everything from Native American artifacts to Soviet propaganda posters. Outside the museum, a small but charming garden overlooks Lake Virginia. ✉ *Rollins College, 1000 Holt Ave., Winter Park* ☎ *407/646–2526* ⊕ *www.rollins.edu/cfam* 🖅 *$5* ☉ *Tues.–Fri. 10–4, weekends noon–5* ✛ *1:F1.*

**Scenic Boat Tour.** Head north from Park Avenue, and at the end of Morse Avenue you'll find the launching point for this tour, a Winter Park tradition since 1938. The one-hour cruise takes in 12 mi of waterways, including three lakes and oak- and cypress-shaded canals built

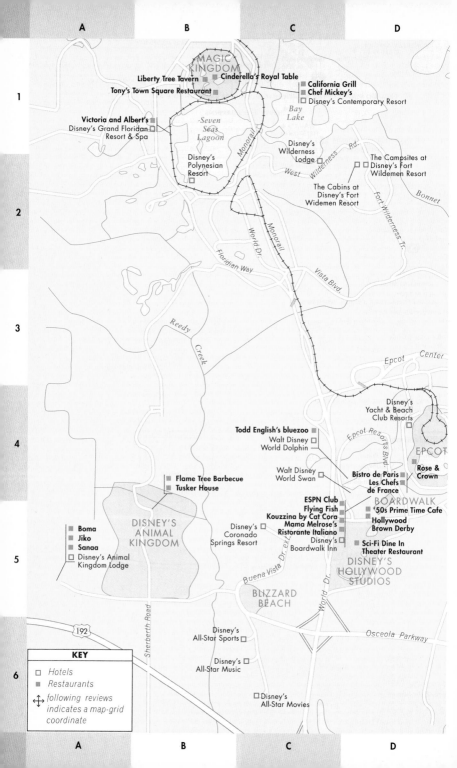

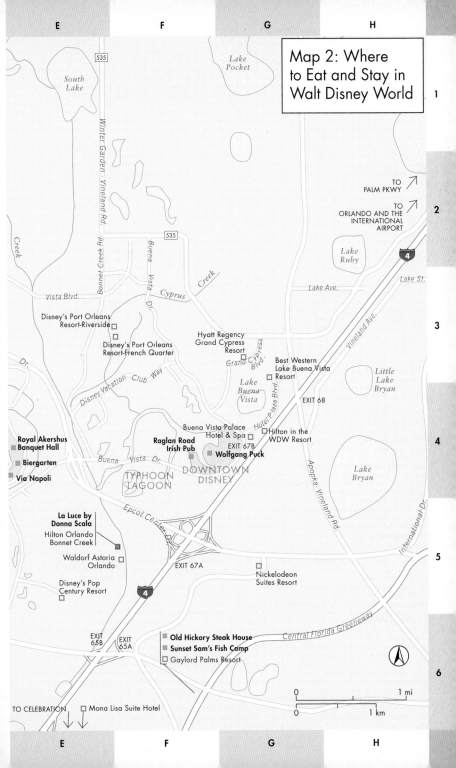

Map 2: Where to Eat and Stay in Walt Disney World

E    F    G    H

535

Lake Pocket

South Lake

1

TO PALM PKWY

TO ORLANDO AND THE INTERNATIONAL AIRPORT

2

Winter Garden - Vineland Rd.

535

Creek

Lake Ruby

Bonnet Creek Rd.

Buena Vista Dr.

Cyprus Creek

Lake Ave.

Lake St.

Vineland Ave.

Vista Blvd.

Disney's Port Orleans Resort-Riverside

Hyatt Regency Grand Cypress Resort

Grand Cypress Blvd.

Best Western Lake Buena Vista Resort

Little Lake Bryan

3

Disney's Port Orleans Resort-French Quarter

Lake Buena Vista

EXIT 68

Dr.

Disney Vacation Club Way

Hotel Plaza Blvd.

Royal Akershus Banquet Hall

Biergarten

Via Napoli

Buena    Vista Dr.

Buena Vista Palace Hotel & Spa

Raglan Road Irish Pub

EXIT 67B

Wolfgang Puck

Hilton in the WDW Resort

Apopka-Vineland Rd.

Lake Bryan

4

TYPHOON LAGOON

DOWNTOWN DISNEY

International Dr.

La Luce by Donna Scala

Epcot Center

Hilton Orlando Bonnet Creek

EXIT 67A

Nickelodeon Suites Resort

5

Waldorf Astoria Orlando

Disney's Pop Century Resort

EXIT 65B  EXIT 65A

Old Hickory Steak House

Sunset Sam's Fish Camp

Gaylord Palms Resort

Central Florida Greenway

6

0          1 mi

0          1 km

TO CELEBRATION

Mona Lisa Suite Hotel

E    F    G    H

# BEST BETS FOR
# ORLANDO AND THE PARKS DINING

If it can be fried and put under a heat lamp you can probably find it in Orlando, but the dining scene both within the parks and the city itself has long transcended fast food. Quality restaurants operate within the parks, Downtown Disney, and several Orlando neighborhoods. Here are our top recommendations, organized by price, cuisine, and experience. The restaurants we consider the very best are indicated in the listings with the Fodor's Choice logo.

## Fodor's Choice ★

50s Prime Time Café, p. 206
Bistro de Paris, p. 205
Boma—Flavors of Africa, p. 208
Emeril's, p. 211
Jiko, p. 209
Les Chefs de France, p. 205
Luma on Park, p. 216
Norman's, p. 213
Primo, p. 214
The Ravenous Pig, p. 216
Sanaa, p. 209
Seasons 52, p. 215
Todd English's bluezoo, p. 209
Victoria & Albert's, p. 210

## By Price

### ¢

Mel's Drive-In, p. 210

Pine 22, p. 215

### $

4Rivers Smokehouse, p. 216
Flame Tree Barbecue, p. 207
Mythos, p. 211

### $$

50s Prime Time Café, p. 206
Mama Melrose's Ristorante Italiano, p. 206
Sanaa, p. 209
Seasons 52, p. 215

### $$$

Les Chefs de France, p. 205
Luma on Park, p. 216
The Ravenous Pig, p. 216

### $$$$

Bistro de Paris, p. 205

Boma—Flavors of Africa, p. 208
Emeril's, p. 211
Jiko, p. 209
Norman's, p. 213
Primo, p. 214
Todd English's bluezoo, p. 209
Victoria & Albert's, p. 210

## By Cuisine

### AMERICAN

Chef Mickey's, p. 209
Cinderella's Royal Table, p. 199
The Ravenous Pig, p. 216
Seasons 52, p. 215

### ITALIAN

La Luce by Donna Scala, p. 214
Mama Melrose's Ristorante Italiano, p. 206
Primo, p. 214

### SEAFOOD

Flying Fish, p. 208
Sunset Sam's Fish Camp, p. 212

## By Experience

### BEST BUFFET

Boma—Flavors of Africa, p. 208
Tusker House, p. 207

### BEST DISNEY RESTAURANT

Bistro de Paris, p. 205
Boma—Flavors of Africa, p. 208
Jiko, p. 209
Victoria & Albert's, p. 210

### BEST OFF-SITE RESTAURANT

Luma on Park, p. 216
Norman's, p. 213
The Ravenous Pig, p. 216
Seasons 52, p. 215

### MOST ROMANTIC

Norman's, p. 213
Victoria & Albert's, p. 210

### BEST THEME RESTAURANTS

50s Prime Time Café, p. 206
Sci-Fi Dine-In Theater Restaurant, p. 206
Three Broomsticks, p. 211

on. Prices change seasonally. ✉ *Germany Pavilion* ☎ *407/939–3463* ⊹ *2:D4.*

**$$$$**
FRENCH
Fodor'sChoice
★

✕ **Bistro de Paris.** The great secret in the France pavilion—and, indeed, in all of Epcot—is the Bistro de Paris, upstairs from Les Chefs de France. The sophisticated menu changes regularly and reflects the cutting edge of French cooking; representative dishes include pan-seared scallops, venison medallions with caramelized apple and cranberries, and rack of lamb with thyme, ratatouille, and a thin onion tart. Come late, ask for a window seat, and plan to linger to watch the 9 pm Epcot light show. Moderately priced French wines are available by the bottle and the glass. If you want a value meal, the three-course, prix-fixe meal for $54 per person without wine, or $89 with wine parings, is a good way to go. ✉ *France Pavilion* ☎ *407/939–3463* ⊘ No lunch ⊹ *2:D4.*

**$$$**
FRENCH
Fodor'sChoice
★

✕ **Les Chefs de France.** What some consider the best restaurant at Disney was created by three of France's most famous chefs: Paul Bocuse, Gaston Lenôtre, and Roger Vergé. Classic escargots, a good starter, are prepared in a casserole with garlic butter; you might follow up with roasted breast of duck and leg confit, or grilled beef tenderloin with black pepper sauce. Make sure you finish with crepes *au chocolat*. The $40 three-course prix-fixe menu is a great value. The Boulangerie Pâtisserie, which is around the corner, offers tarts, croissants, éclairs, napoleons, and more, to go. ✉ *France Pavilion* ☎ *407/939–3463* ⊹ *2:D4.*

**$$**
BRITISH

✕ **Rose & Crown.** If you're an Anglophile and you love a beer so thick you could stand a spoon up in your mug, this is the place to soak up both the suds and British street culture. "Wenches" serve up traditional English fare—fish-and-chips, shepherd's pie (ground lamb with onions, carrots, and peas, topped with mashed potatoes and cheddar cheese), and the ever-popular bangers and mash (sausage over mashed potatoes). Potato-and-leek soup or Scotch egg make good appetizers. Vegetarians will even find a tasty vegetarian shepherd's pie. For dessert, try the sticky toffee pudding or lemon pie. The terrace has a splendid view of IllumiNations. ✉ *United Kingdom Pavilion* ☎ *407/939–3463* ⊹ *2:D4.*

**$$$$**
SCANDINAVIAN

✕ **Royal Akershus Banquet Hall.** This Norwegian restaurant has become the site of character buffets at all three meals, with an array of Disney princesses, including Ariel, Belle, Jasmine, Snow White, Mulan, Mary Poppins, and even an occasional cameo appearance by Cinderella. The ever-changing Norwegian menu is as extensive as you'll find on this side of the Atlantic. Appetizers are offered buffet style, and usually include herring, goat-milk cheese, peppered mackerel, and gravlax (cured salmon served with mustard sauce) or *fiskepudding* (a seafood mousse with herb dressing). For your main course, chosen à la carte, you might try traditional ground pork and beef *kjottkake* (dumplings), or mustard-glazed seared salmon. Aquavit, wine, and specialty drinks are offered. All meals are fixed price. ✉ *Norway Pavilion* ☎ *407/939–3463* ⌕ *Reservations essential* ⊹ *2:E4.*

**$$**
PIZZA

✕ **Via Napoli.** When the Patina Restaurant Group decided to open a second Italian eatery in Epcot (the first was Tutta Italia Ristorante), they decided to specialize in the authentic Neapolitan wood-fired pizza, importing the mozzarella from Italy and using only San Marzano tomatoes. The result is crusty, thin pies topped with your choice of pepperoni;

portobello and crimini mushrooms; or eggplant, artichokes, proscuitto, and mushrooms. The eggplant parmigiana is an outstanding alternative. ⊠ *Italy Pavilion, Epcot, Walt Disney World* ☎ *407/939–3463* ✛ *2:D4.*

## DISNEY'S HOLLYWOOD STUDIOS

**$$**
AMERICAN
Fodor's Choice
★

✕ **50's Prime Time Café.** Who says you can't go home again? If you grew up in middle America in the 1950s, just step inside. While *I Love Lucy* and *The Donna Reed Show* clips play on a television screen, you can feast on meat loaf, pot roast, or fried chicken, all served on a Formica tabletop. At $15, the meat loaf is one of the best inexpensive, filling dinners in any local theme park. Enjoy it with a malted-milk shake or root-beer float (or a bottle of wine). The place offers some fancier dishes, like the olive oil–poached salmon, which is a good choice for lighter eaters. If you're not feeling totally wholesome, go for Dad's Electric Lemonade (rum, vodka, blue curaçao, sweet-and-sour mix, and Sprite), which is worth every bit of the $10.50 price tag. Just like Mother, the menu admonishes, "Don't put your elbows on the table!" ⊠ *Hollywood Blvd.* ☎ *407/939–3463* ✛ *2:D5.*

**$$$$**
AMERICAN

✕ **Hollywood Brown Derby.** At this reproduction of the famous 1940s Hollywood restaurant, the walls are lined with movie-star caricatures, just as in Tinseltown. The specialty is the Cobb salad, which by legend was invented by Brown Derby founder Robert Cobb; the salad consists of finely chopped lettuce enlivened by loads of tomato, bacon, turkey, blue cheese, chopped egg, and avocado, all tossed table-side. Other menu choices include brown butter almond-crusted black grouper with lobster beurre blanc; and pork chops topped with smoked Gouda and apricot preserve with apple cider jus. Dining with an Imagineer is a special lunch option; you will have lunch with one of Disney's creative engineers while enjoying a set-price four-course meal including soup and choice of salad, entrée and dessert. If you request the Fantasmic! dinner package, make a reservation for no later than two hours before the start of the show. ⊠ *Hollywood Blvd.* ☎ *407/939–3463* ✛ *2:D5.*

**$$**
ITALIAN

✕ **Mama Melrose's Ristorante Italiano.** To replace the energy you've no doubt depleted by miles of theme-park walking, you can load up on carbs at this casual Italian restaurant that looks like an old warehouse. Good main courses include spaghetti with clams and pancetta, and grilled tuna with vegetable risotto and olive-caper butter. Wood-fired flatbreads are available as an entrée choice here (a great bargain at $12 and up) with toppings ranging from grilled chicken with sundried tomato pesto to a wonderful grilled shrimp and arugula combo. The sangria, available by the carafe, flows generously. Ask for the Fantasmic! dinner package if you want priority seating for the show. ⊠ *Backlot* ☎ *407/939–3463* ✛ *2:D4.*

**$$**
AMERICAN

✕ **Sci-Fi Dine-In Theater Restaurant.** If you don't mind zombies leering at you while you eat, then head to this enclosed faux drive-in, where you can sit in a fake candy-color '50s convertible and watch trailers from classics like *Attack of the Fifty-Foot Woman* and *Teenagers from Outer Space.* The menu includes choices like smoked St. Louis-style barbecue ribs, a beef-and-blue-cheese salad, sautéed shrimp with bow-tie pasta, and a huge Reuben sandwich with fries or cucumber salad. The hot-fudge sundaes are delicious. ⊠ *Backlot* ☎ *407/939–3463* ✛ *2:D5.*

## DISNEY'S ANIMAL KINGDOM

**$**
FAST FOOD

✗ **Flame Tree Barbecue.** This counter-service eatery is one of the relatively undiscovered gems of Disney's culinary offerings. There's nothing fancy here, but you can dig into ribs, barbecued chicken, and pulled pork and barbecued beef sandwiches with several sauce choices. For something with a lower calorie count, try the smoked turkey served in a multigrain bun, or a great barbecued chicken served with baked beans and corn on the cob. The outdoor tables, set beneath intricately carved wood pavilions, make great spots for a picnic, and they're not usually crowded. ⊠ *Discovery Island* ✛ *2:B5.*

**$$$**
AMERICAN

✗ **Tusker House.** This restaurant offers all-buffet dining three meals a day, starting with a character breakfast (Donald's Safari Breakfast), and lunch and dinner without Donald and his crew. Tusker House offers healthier fare like spice-rubbed rotisserie chicken, *peri-peri* (African hot pepper) marinated salmon, strip loin rubbed with *berbere* (an African spice mix), and saffron-infused root vegetables, along with the standard kids' fare. This restaurant has the largest vegetarian selection of any on Disney property. Prices rise during peak seasons. ⊠ *Africa* ☎ *407/939–3463* ⌕ *Reservations essential* ✛ *2:B5.*

## DOWNTOWN DISNEY

**$$$**
IRISH

✗ **Raglan Road Irish Pub.** An authentic Irish pub in Downtown Disney seems oxymoronic, particularly when that pub seats 600 people. But if Irish grub's your thing, Raglan's is the place to go. The shepherd's pie served here is of higher quality than the usual version, prepared with beef and lamb and jazzed up with house spices. And you don't have to settle for plain fish-and-chips (though you can for $19); there's also smoked salmon and maple glaze; shiitake risotto; and lamb shanks braised with rosemary jus. Three massive and ornate bars, all imported from Ireland and all more than a century old, help anchor the pub. The entertainment alone makes this place worth the visit. A house band, Creel, plays every evening except Sunday, and a trio of Irish dancers perform on Friday and Saturday evenings. ⊠ *Hyperion Wharf* ☎ *407/938–0300* ⊕ *www.raglanroadirishpub.com* ✛ *2:F4.*

**$$**
AMERICAN

✗ **Wolfgang Puck.** There are lots of choices here, from wood-oven pizza at the informal Puck Express to fine-dining meals in the upstairs formal Dining Room. There's also a sushi bar and an informal café; the café is quite literally a happy medium, and may be the best bet for families hoping for a bit of elegance without the pressure of a formal dinner. At Express try the roasted ruby beet, spinach, and goat cheese salad, or the spicy chicken pizza. At the café, midprice entrées like roasted organic chicken with lemon-rosemary sauce, and pumpkin ravioli with brown butter sauce, fried sage, and port wine glaze are winners, and you can always try the pizza pie that made Puck famous: smoked salmon with dill cream, red onion, chili oil, and chives. The Dining Room always offers inspired entrées like lobster risotto with lemon preserve. Three-and four-course menus are priced at $50 and $60, respectively. ⊠ *West Side* ☎ *407/938–9653* ⊕ *www.wolfgangpuckorlando.com* ✛ *2:F4.*

DISNEY'S BOARDWALK

$    ✕**ESPN Club.** Not only can you watch sports on a big-screen TV here
AMERICAN    (the restaurant has 108 monitors), but you can also periodically see
ESPN programs being taped in the club itself and be part of the audience of sports-radio talk shows. Food ranges from an outstanding half-
pound burger, made with Angus chuck, to an excellent Reuben with
plenty of corned beef, sauerkraut, and cheese. If you want an appetizer,
try the Macho Nachos, crispy corn tortilla chips piled high with spicy
chili, shredded cheddar cheese, sour cream, spicy salsa, and sliced jala-
peños. This place is open quite late by Disney standards—until 2 am on
Friday and Saturday. Beware, the place can be pretty loud during any
broadcast sports event, especially football games. ⊠ *Disney's Board-
Walk* ☎ *407/939–3463* ✛ *2:D4.*

$$$$    ✕**Flying Fish.** One of Disney's better restaurants, Flying Fish is whimsi-
SEAFOOD    cally decorated with murals along the upper portion of the walls paying
tribute to Atlantic seaboard spots of the early 1900s. This is a place
where you put on your "resort casual" duds to "dine," as opposed to
putting on your flip-flops and shorts to "chow down." The chefs take
the food so seriously that the entire culinary team takes day trips to
local farms to learn their foodstuffs' origins. Flying Fish's best dishes
include potato-wrapped red snapper, which is so popular it has been
on the menu for several years, and oak-grilled Bay of Fundy salmon.
Groups of up to six can sit at the counter that directly faces the exhibition kitchen for a six-course wine-tasting menu. ⊠ *Disney's BoardWalk*
☎ *407/939–2359* ✸ *No lunch* ✛ *2:D4.*

$$$    ✕**Kouzzina by Cat Cora.** Celebrity-chef Cat Cora and Disney joined forces
MEDITERRANEAN    in 2009 to open an upbeat family-oriented Greek restaurant along the
BoardWalk. From an exhibition *kouzzina* (Greek for kitchen), the culi-
nary team puts out hearty portions of Cora's family favorites, including
the familiar starter *spanakopita* (spinach pie) and an amazing side dish
of brussels sprouts sautéed with lemon and capers. Entrées range from a
sweet cinnamon-stewed chicken to a whole fish pan-roasted with braised
greens, olives, fennel, and smoked chili. Be sure to get a refreshing, sweet,
coffee frappé to go with your *loukoumades* (donuts with warm honey) or
baklava. ⊠ *Disney's BoardWalk* ☎ *407/939–3463* ✛ *2:D4.*

WDW RESORTS

$$$$    ✕**Boma–Flavors of Africa.** Boma takes Western-style ingredients and pre-
AFRICAN    pares them with an African twist—then invites guests to walk through
Fodor'sChoice    an African marketplace–style dining room to help themselves at the
★    extraordinary buffet. The dozen or so serving stations have entrées
such as roasted pork, chicken, beef, and fish served with tamarind and
other robust sauces; intriguing salads; and some of the best hummus
this side of the Atlantic. Don't pass up the soups, as the coconut-curry
seafood stew is excellent. The zebra dome dessert is chocolate mousse
covered with white chocolate and striped with dark chocolate. All meals
are prix fixe, and prices change seasonally. The South African wine list
is outstanding. ⊠ *Animal Kingdom Lodge, Animal Kingdom Resort
Area* ☎ *407/939–3463* ⌕ *Reservations essential* ✸ *No lunch* ✛ *2:A5.*

$$$$    ✕**California Grill.** The view of the surrounding Disney parks from this
AMERICAN    15th-floor restaurant—which just celebrated its 15th anniversary—is as

stunning as the food, especially at night when you can watch the nightly Magic Kingdom fireworks from the dining room. The menu changes regularly, but choices might include oak-fired filet of beef with smoked bacon-*Dauphinoise* potatoes (baked with cheese and cream), ginger-scented carrots, and teriyaki barbecue sauce; or pan-seared Florida snapper with roasted fig risotto, forest mushrooms, and a Pinot Noir reduction. Dozens of wines are available by both the glass and bottle. ✉ *Contemporary Resort, Magic Kingdom Resort Area* ☎ *407/939–3463* ⚓ *Reservations essential* ✣ *2:B2.*

**$$$$**
AMERICAN

✕ **Chef Mickey's.** This is the holy shrine for character meals, with Mickey, Minnie, or Goofy around for breakfast and dinner—it's not a quiet spot to read the *Orlando Sentinel.* Folks come here for entertainment and comfort food. The breakfast buffet includes omelets cooked to order, mountains of pancakes, and even a breakfast pizza. The dinner buffet doesn't disappoint with prime rib, roasted chicken, and changing specials like beef tips with mushrooms or tamarind-glazed salmon. Finish off your meal at the all-you-can-eat dessert bar of sundaes and chocolate cake. ✉ *Contemporary Resort, Magic Kingdom Resort Area* ☎ *407/939–3463* ✣ *2:B2.*

**$$$$**
AFRICAN
Fodor'sChoice
★

✕ **Jiko.** The name of this restaurant means "the cooking place" in Swahili, and it is certainly that. The dining area surrounds two big, wood-burning ovens and a grill area where you can watch cooks in North African-style caps working on your meal. The menu here is more African-inspired than purely African, but it does include authentic flavors in entrées like Swahili curry shrimp from an East African recipe and short ribs with a cabernet-tamarind sauce. Menu items often change, but entrées might include maize-crusted wreckfish with tomato-butter sauce, or chicken flavored with the spicy African *peri-peri* pepper and served with mango *sambal* (chili-based sauce) and onion jus. The restaurant offers more than 65 wines by the glass, including a large selection of South African vintages; vegetarian, vegan, and gluten-free menus are also available. ✉ *Animal Kingdom Lodge, Animal Kingdom Resort Area* ☎ *407/939–3463* ⚓ *Reservations essential* ☾ *No lunch* ✣ *2:A5.*

**$$**
INDIAN
Fodor'sChoice
★

✕ **Sanaa.** Most of the flavors are from India, yet Sanaa is really a celebration of the Spice Islands—locales off the coast of Africa that for centuries hosted traders from the world's corners. Exotic yet approachable lunches and dinners make Sanaa a true find on the outer edges of the Disney empire; views of zebras and giraffes right out the picture windows are another draw. Mustard seed–crusted scallops and pulled duck with red curry sauce are good starters. For the main course, be sure to try the shrimp in green curry sauce—only spicy upon request. ✉ *Disney's Animal Kingdom Villas, Animal Kingdom Resort Area* ☎ *407/989–3463* ✣ *2:A5*

**$$$$**
AMERICAN
Fodor'sChoice
★

✕ **Todd English's bluezoo.** Celebrity-chef Todd English oversees this cutting-edge seafood eatery, a sleek, modern restaurant that resembles an underwater dining hall, with blue walls and carpeting, aluminum fish suspended from the ceiling, and bubblelike lighting fixtures. The menu is creative and pricey, with entrées like the 2-pound Maine "Cantonese lobster," fried and tossed in a sticky soy glaze; and miso-glazed *mero* (Hawaiian sea bass) with shiitake-ginger rice and black garlic.

If you don't care for fish, alternatives include pork loin served with German potatoes and apple-mustard glaze. A five-course tasting menu ($79, plus $30 for wine pairings) is available to those who want to try a little bit of everything. ⊠ *Walt Disney World Dolphin, Epcot Resort Area* ☎ *407/934–1111* ⊕ *www.thebluezoo.com* ⊘ *No lunch* ✦ *2:D4.*

$$$$
CONTINENTAL
Fodor'sChoice
★

✕ **Victoria & Albert's.** At this ultraposh award-winning Disney restaurant, a well-polished service team will anticipate your every need during a gourmet extravaganza. This is one of the plushest, fine-dining experiences in Florida, with an ambience so sophisticated that children under 10 aren't on the guest list. The seven-course, prix-fixe menu changes daily, and you'd do well to supplement the $125 tab with a $60 wine pairing. Appetizer choices might include Maine Lobster with watermelon radish, *kohlrabi* (a type of cabbage), and vanilla aïoli; and entrées may feature duck three ways with *salsify* (a root vegetable with an oyster-like flavor) and squash puree followed by Japanese Wagyu strip loin with oxtail jus. For most of the year, there are two seatings, at 5:45 and 9 pm. In July and August, however, there's generally just one seating at 6:30 pm. For a more luxe experience, reserve a table in the intimate Queen Victoria Room, or at the Chef's Table, which will include more courses and numbers to your tab. ⊠ *Grand Floridian, Magic Kingdom Resort Area* ☎ *407/939–3862* ⊕ *www.victoria-alberts.com* ⚱ *Reservations essential; jacket required* ⊘ *No lunch* ✦ *2:B1.*

# UNIVERSAL ORLANDO AREA

## UNIVERSAL STUDIOS

$
IRISH

✕ **Finnegan's Bar & Grill.** In an Irish pub that would look just right in downtown New York during the Ellis Island era, Finnegan's offers classic Irish comfort food like shepherd's pie, Scotch eggs (eggs wrapped in sausage and bread crumbs and fried), corned beef and cabbage, bangers and mash (sausage and mashed potatoes), and fish-and-chips, plus Guinness, Harp, and Bass on tap. If shepherd's pie isn't your thing, opt instead for a steak, burger, entrée salad or sandwich. Irish folk music, sometimes live, completes the theme. ⊠ *New York* ☎ *407/224-3613* ✦ *1:D3.*

¢
AMERICAN

✕ **Mel's Drive-In.** At the corner of Hollywood Boulevard and Vine is a flashy '50s eatery with a pink-and-white 1956 Ford Crown Victoria parked out in front. For burgers and fries, this is one of the best choices in the park, and it comes complete with a roving doo-wop group during peak seasons. You're on vacation—go ahead and have that extra-thick shake or the decadent chili-cheese fries. Mel's is also a great place to meet up, in case you decide to go your separate ways in the park. ⊠ *Hollywood Blvd.* ☎ *407/363–8766* ⚱ *Reservations not accepted* ✦ *1:D3.*

## ISLANDS OF ADVENTURE

$
AMERICAN

✕ **Confisco Grille.** You could walk right past this full-service restaurant without noticing it, but if you want a good meal and sit-down service, don't pass by too quickly. This is one of the better eateries inside the theme parks. The menu changes often, but typical entrées include hickory-smoked barbecue ribs with fresh-roasted corn on the cob, grilled or blackened fresh fish of the day with mashed potatoes and sautéed spinach in a lemon-butter-cilantro sauce, and penne puttanesca—the vodka-cream tomato sauce is enhanced with sausage, kalamata olives, fried pepperocini, and roasted garlic. Wash it all down with refreshing sangria, available by glass, pitcher, and half pitcher. ⊠ *6000 Universal Blvd., Port of Entry* ☎ *407/224–4012* ⊘ *No lunch* ✢ *1:D3.*

$   ⨯ **Mythos.** The name is Greek, but the dishes are eclectic. The menu,
ECLECTIC   which changes seasonally, usually includes mainstays like blueberry-
and pistachio-crusted grilled pork with blue cheese and port wine sauce on smoky-cheddar mac-and-cheese, and cedar-plank salmon with citrus butter. The building itself is enough to grab your attention. It looks like a giant rock formation from the outside and a huge cave (albeit one with plush upholstered seating) from the inside. Mythos also has a waterfront view of the big lagoon in the center of the theme park. (When it's slow in the park, Mythos is only open for lunch.) ⊠ *6000 Universal Blvd., Lost Continent* ☎ *407/224–4012* ✢ *1:D3.*

$   ⨯ **Three Broomsticks.** For the first time ever, Harry Potter fans can taste
BRITISH   pumpkin juice (with hints of honey and vanilla) and butterbeer (sort
of like bubbly butterscotch cream soda; some say it tastes like short-bread cookies). They're on the menu along with British foodstuffs at Three Broomsticks, a Hogsmeade restaurant from the fantasy books' mileau. Rickety staircases and gaslit chandeliers set the tone for the counter-service restaurant, where families gobble down ample portions of shepherd's pie, fish-and-chips, chargrilled ribs, and smoked chicken. In the adjacent Hog's Head pub, a faux hog's head sneers now and then. ⊠ *6000 Universal Blvd., Wizarding World of Harry Potter* ☎ *407/224–4233* ⌓ *Reservations not accepted* ✢ *1:D3.*

## CITYWALK

$$$$   ⨯ **Emeril's.** The popular eatery is a culinary shrine to Emeril Lagasse, the
CREOLE   famous Food Network chef who occasionally makes an appearance.
**Fodor's** Choice   And while the modern interior of the restaurant with its 30-foot ceil-
★   ings, blond woods, second-story wine loft, and lots of galvanized steel
looks nothing like the Old French Quarter, the hardwood floors and linen tablecloths create an environment befitting the stellar nature of the cuisine. Entrées may include andouille-crusted pan-roasted redfish with Creole Meunière sauce; porcini-scented rib eye with garlic- and thyme-roasted potatoes and Emeril's Worcestershire sauce; lemongrass-smoked duck with ginger-stewed sushi rice and honey-soy butter sauce; and chipotle-barbecue-glazed salmon. Reservations are usually essential, but there's a chance of getting a walk-in seating if you show up for lunch (11:30 am) or early for dinner (5:30 pm). ⊠ *6000 Universal Blvd.* ☎ *407/224–2424* ⊕ *www.emerils.com* ⌓ *Reservations essential* ✢ *1:D3.*

$   ⨯ **NASCAR Sports Grille.** Filled with race-car simulator games, and arcade
AMERICAN   and racing memorabilia, this eatery might not look like the place to
grab a sublime meal, but that's not the case. This theme restaurant has a reputation as a good place for grub. Selections worth trying include the Southern-style pot roast, and the slow-roasted baby back rib plat-ter; the Talladega cheeseburger with a side of fries is a cut above the standard theme-park burger. ⊠ *6000 Universal Blvd.* ☎ *407/224–7223* ⊕ *www.nascarsportsgrille.com* ✢ *1:D3.*

### UNIVERSAL HOTELS

**$$$** ✕ **Mama Della's Ristorante.** Mama Della's is a playfully themed Italian res-
ITALIAN  taurant that happens to have excellent food. The premise is that you're
eating at a home-turned-restaurant owned by an Italian woman. That
woman, Mama Della, is played by an actress and her warmth enhances
the experience (as does the serenade by an accordianist and his and her
vocalists). The menu features Italian classics like chicken parmigiana,
and spaghetti with meatballs, but also offers more ambitious dishes
like the grilled veal chop with porcini mushrooms, polenta, and mar-
sala sauce; and risotto with butter-poached lobster, sea scallops, and
fava beans. Outdoor seating on the patio offers viewing of the hotel's
nightly *Musica Della Notte* (Music of the Night) opera show. ✉ *Loews
Portofino Bay Hotel, 5601 Universal Blvd.* ☎ *407/503–3463* ⊕ *www.
loewshotels.com* ☉ No lunch ✛ 1:D3.

**$$$** ✕ **Tchoup Chop.** The bold interior decor—with lots of bamboo, bright
HAWAIIAN  glazed tile, an exposition kitchen and a long zero-edge pool with porce-
lain lily pads running the length of the dining room—is just as ambitious
as the food at Emeril Lagasse's pacific-influenced restaurant. Following
the theme of the Royal Pacific Resort, Lagasse fuses his signature bold
flavors with Polynesian tastes. Entrées change regularly, but representative dishes include hot iron–seared yellowfin tuna steak with Thai
sticky rice and smoked bacon with wasabi-butter infusion; sake-braised
beef short ribs with carmelized onion mashed potatoes and hoisin-
honey-infused veal jus; and cilantro-cashew pesto-marinated tofu with
crispy rice cake and citrus soy. ✉ *Loews Royal Pacific Resort, 6300
Hollywood Way* ☎ *407/503–2467* ⊕ *www.emerils.com* ✍ Reservations
essential ✛ 1:D3.

## ORLANDO METRO AREA

### KISSIMMEE

**$$$$** ✕ **Old Hickory Steakhouse.** Old Hickory is an upscale steak house
STEAKHOUSE  designed to look like rustic cabins in the Everglades. Beyond the playful
facade is a polished restaurant with a classic steakhouse menu—bone-in
rib eye, Porterhouse, and filet mignon, supplemented by ostrich, buffalo, and the day's fish, all priced for the hotel's convention-goers. The
chef gets creative with appetizers like a warm pear gorgonzola tart and
wild boar ribs. Artisinal cheese plates are on the menu, and desserts are
ambitious, such as the white chocolate raspberry-bread pudding with
house-made sour cream ice cream. ✉ *Gaylord Palms Resort, 6000 W.
Osceola Pkwy., I–4 Exit 65* ☎ *407/586–1600* ⊕ *www.gaylordhotels.
com* ☉ No lunch ✛ 2:F6.

**$$$$** ✕ **Sunset Sam's Fish Camp.** Sunset Sam's looks gimmicky—its bar and
SEAFOOD  dining room encircle two 60-foot masts—yet the food is both excellent
and affordable, which is a nice surprise. Starters are big enough to be a
meal, and include conch fritters with scotch bonnet-pepper rémoulade
sauce, and mussels in curried coconut-lime broth. Share the three-tiered
tower for a taste of everything, including lobster skewers, blue crab
salad, and ahi tuna tartare. Entrées are pricey but not exorbitant, and
include sea scallops with corn risotto and citrus butter, and crispy whole
yellowtail snapper with citrus soy. For dessert, go for the traditional key

lime pie. ⊠ *Gaylord Palms Resort, 6000 W. Osceola Pkwy., I–4 Exit 65* ☎ *407/586–1101* ⊕ *www.gaylordhotels.com* ✛ *2:F6.*

## CELEBRATION

$$ × **Celebration Town Tavern.** This New England–cuisine eatery, operated by a family with Yankee roots, has a double personality. The interior is a brass, glass, and dark-wood-paneling kind of place, while the outside patio has table seating plus the Paddy O' Bar. The food ranges from landlubber treats like baby back ribs, prime rib (blackened or herb-crusted), and half-pound burgers to exquisite seafood including Ipswich clams, lobster rolls, Boston scrod, and 2-pound lobsters, plus, on occasion, a salute to the Sunshine State with its Florida stone crabs in season. While the place has a polished demeanor, there are plenty of menu choices right out of a working-class Boston bar—meatball hoagies, Philly cheesesteak sandwiches, and Buffalo-style chicken wings. For dessert there's great—what else?—Boston cream pie. ⊠ *721 Front St.* ☎ *407/566–2526* ⊕ *www.thecelebrationtowntavern.com* ✛ *1:B6.*

AMERICAN

$ × **Market Street Café.** The menu at this upscale diner ranges from the house-special baked-potato omelet and other breakfast classics served all day, like waffles and French toast, to comfort classics like beef Stroganoff and homemade chicken potpie. In addition to a hearty version of the quintessential American hamburger (best enjoyed with a creamy milk shake), there's also a salmon-and-veggie burger for the cholesterol wary. An outdoor seating section in front of the restaurant makes for a pleasant dining destination. ⊠ *701 Front St.* ☎ *407/566–1144* ⊕ *www.market-street-cafe.com* ⚅ *Reservations not accepted* ✛ *1:B6.*

AMERICAN

## INTERNATIONAL DRIVE

$$$ × **Café Tu Tu Tango.** The food here is served tapas-style—everything is appetizer-size but plentiful, and inexpensive. The eclectic menu is fitting for a restaurant on International Drive. If you want a compendium of cuisines at one go, try the black-bean soup with cilantro sour cream, the baby lamb chops with balsamic glaze, the pan-seared shrimp and chicken pot stickers, or the Cuban grilled steak skewers with poblanomashed potatoes and lime steak sauce. The wine list includes more than 50 wines from several countries, with more than half by the bottle and the glass. The restaurant is designed to resemble an artist's loft; artists paint at easels while diners take a culinary trip around the world. ⊠ *8625 International Dr., I-Drive area* ☎ *407/248–2222* ⊕ *www.cafetututango.com* ⚅ *Reservations not accepted* ✛ *1:D4.*

ECLECTIC

$$$$ × **Norman's.** Celebrity-chef Norman Van Aken brings impressive credentials to the restaurant that bears his name, as you might expect from the headline eatery in the Ritz-Carlton Orlando, Grande Lakes. Van Aken's culinary roots go back to the Florida Keys, where he's credited with creating "Floribbean" cuisine, a blend that is part Key West and part Caribbean—although he now weaves in flavors from all continents. The Orlando operation (there's another in Coral Gables, Florida) is a formal, sleek restaurant with marble floors, starched tablecloths, waiters in ties and vests, and a creative, if expensive, menu. The offerings change frequently, and are offered à la carte and in four-, five-, and seven-course tasting menus. In addition to exceptional ceviches and

AMERICAN
Fodor'sChoice
★

a signature appetizer called "Down Island" French toast made with Curacao-marinated foie gras, favorites include yucca-stuffed crispy shrimp with sour-orange sauce, pan-cooked yellowtail with citrus butter, and pork tenderloin "Havana Nueva" with smoky plantain crema and mole, a savory sauce made from chocolate and spices. ⊠ *Ritz-Carlton Grande Lakes, 4000 Central Florida Pkwy., I-Drive area* ☎ *407/393–4333* ⊕ *www.normans.com* ☽ *No lunch* ✛ *1:E4.*

**$$$$**
ITALIAN
**Fodor's Choice**
★

✕ **Primo.** James Beard Award winner Melissa Kelly cloned her Italian-organic Maine restaurant in an upscale Orlando hotel and brought her farm-to-table sensibilities with her. Here the daily dinner menu pays tribute to Sicily's lighter foods made with produce grown in the hotel garden. Homemade cavatelli is tossed Bolognese-style with wild boar, ricotta, and smoked *caciocavallo* cheese. Prime New York strip steak is enhanced with Oregon white truffles, chanterelles, cauliflower fritters, pumpkin lasagna, and roasted garlic sabayon. Desserts are just as special, with the likes of Meyer lemon–scented crème brûlée and a bowl of hot zeppole tossed in organic cinnamon and sugar. ⊠ *JW Marriott Orlando, Grande Lakes, 4040 Central Florida Pkwy., I-Drive area* ☎ *407/393–4444* ⊕ *www.primorestaurant.com* ⌖ *Reservations essential* ☽ *No lunch* ✛ *1:E4.*

**$$**
GREEK

✕ **Taverna Opa.** This high-energy Greek restaurant bills itself as offering "fun with a capital F," possibly because the ouzo flows like a mountain stream, the Greek music almost reaches the level of a rock concert, and the roaming belly dancers actively encourage diners to take part in the mass Zorba dancing (which often happens on the tops of dining tables). The only thing missing is the Greek restaurant tradition of throwing dinner plates, made up in part by the throwing of torn-up paper napkins, which sometimes reaches near-blizzard level. The food, by the way, is also excellent. Standouts include traditional staples like *spanakopita* (phyllo pastry with spinach and feta cheese), *saganaki* (the traditional flaming cheese appetizer), *avegolemono* (lemony chicken-rice soup), and perhaps the most famous Greek entrée, *moussaka* (layers of roasted eggplant, potatoes, and ground meat, topped with béchamel sauce). The best dessert is the *baklava* (phyllo filled with walnuts, cinnamon, cloves, and honey). ⊠ *Pointe Orlando, 9101 International Dr., I-Drive area* ☎ *407/879–2481* ⊕ *www.tavernaoparestaurant.com* ✛ *1:D4.*

## LAKE BUENA VISTA

**$$**
ITALIAN

✕ **La Luce by Donna Scala.** Donna Scala made a name for herself offering Italian food with that certain Napa Valley farm-fresh flair in California's Bistro Don Giovanni, and now she brings that same cuisine to the upscale Hilton located at the tip of Disney World. The art changes as the seasons do; a chalk mural is updated quarterly and is entirely different every time. Equal effort goes into the menu, where sausages are stuffed in house and pastas are made fresh. Try farfelle tossed with artichokes, mushrooms, and truffle pecorino; grilled sausage and duck confit with Tuscan bean ragout and aged balsamic; or a simpler sliced grass-fed ribeye with lemon and arugula. Don't be afraid to bring the kids; the "bambini" pizza comes with "no green stuff." ⊠ *Hilton Orlando Bonnett Creek, 14100 Bonnet Creek Resort La., Lake Buena Vista Area, Lake Buena Vista* ☎ *407/597–3600* ⊕ *www.laluceorlando.com* ✛ *2:E5.*

## SAND LAKE ROAD

$$$
HAWAIIAN

✕**Roy's.** Chef Roy Yamaguchi has more or less perfected his own cuisine type replete with tropical and Asian flavors melded together with lots of imagination. The menu changes seasonally, but typical dishes include Hawaiian-style butterfish with a sizzling peanut oil and tamari vinaigrette, or hibachi-style grilled Atlantic salmon with Japanese citrus ponzu sauce. If your tastes remain on the mainland, go for hearty fare like Hawaiian sea salt-smoked rib eye with a kimchee reduction, or the crab-stuffed pork chop. The crunchy golden lobster pot stickers are a Roy's classic. The three-course prix-fixe menu, at $36 per person, is a relative bargain, as you get your choice from three appetizers, four entrées, and two desserts. ✉ *7760 W. Sand Lake Rd., Plaza Venezia, I–4 Exit 74A* ☎ *407/352–4844* ⊕ *www.roysrestaurant.com* ☾ *No lunch* ✛ *1:D3.*

$$
AMERICAN
Fodor's Choice
★

✕**Seasons 52.** Parts of the menu change every week at this innovative restaurant that serves different foods at different times of year, depending on what's in season. Meals here tend to be healthful (butter is banned!) yet hearty and very flavorful. The buffalo chili starter is to die for. For an entrée, you might have wood-roasted pork tenderloin with polenta, cremini mushrooms, and a Dijon glaze, or roasted artichoke-stuffed shrimp in a light lemon sauce. An impressive wine list with dozens of selections by the glass complements the menu. For dessert, have "mini indulgence" classics like pecan pie, rocky road, carrot cake, and key lime pie served in petite portions. Although the cuisine is haute, the prices are modest—not bad for a snazzy, urbane bistro and wine bar. It has live music nightly to boot. ✉ *7700 Sand Lake Rd., I–4 Exit 75A* ☎ *407/354–5212* ⊕ *www.seasons52.com* ✛ *1:D3.*

$$$$
AMERICAN

✕**Vines Grill & Wine Bar.** Live jazz music fills the night at the bar section of this dramatically designed restaurant, but the food and drink in the snazzy main dining room are headliners in their own right. The kitchen bills itself as a steak house, but it really is far more than that. Entrées range from a dry-aged porterhouse to pan-seared Hawaiian big-eye tuna, from a one-pound Kobe burger with truffle fries to beef short rib osso bucco. Be sure to start with the grilled octopus, which is simply prepared with red onions, capers and roasted fennel. The wine list here is extensive, and the cocktails are serious business, too. The crowd tends to dress up, but suit jackets and ties are not required. ✉ *Plaza Venezia, 7533 W. Sand Lake Rd., I–4 Exit 74A* ☎ *407/351–1227* ⊕ *www.vinesgrille.com* ☾ *No lunch* ✛ *1:D3.*

## CENTRAL ORLANDO

¢
AMERICAN

✕**Pine 22.** Orlando farm-to-table pioneer Kathleen Blake is the chef-owner behind Pine 22, a chic downtown Orlando fast-casual burger joint where ingredients are "treated with love, admiration, and respect," according to their Web site. Here you can design your own sandwich; choose a burger of grass-fed Angus beef, holistically raised turkey, or black beans, and top it with your choice of house-made guacamole, farm-fresh eggs, chipotle aioli, or mango chutney. All told, there are 300-plus possible combinations. ✉ *22 E. Pine St., Downtown Orlando, Orlando* ☎ *407/574–2160* ⊕ *www.pine22.com* ✛ *1:F2.*

## WINTER PARK

**$**
BARBECUE

✕ **4Rivers Smokehouse.** Obsessed with Texas-style barbecue brisket, John Rivers decided to turn his passion into a business upon retiring from the corporate world. The result is the uber-popular 4Rivers, which brings this unique take on barbecue to Central Florida. Here, you'll find common items like pulled pork and cornbread, plus more unusual ones like the addicting bacon-wrapped smoked-jalapeno peppers, the "cochon de lait" pork-and-cabbage po' boy with Creole sauce, and a sausage-filled pastry called *kolache*. Old-time soft drinks such as Frostie Root Beer and Cheerwine are for sale, along with desserts like the kiddie favorite "chocolate awesomeness," an indulgent layering of chocolate cake, chocolate pudding, Heath Bar, whipped cream, and chocolate and caramel sauces. A second 4Rivers is located north of Disney in Winter Garden. ⊠ *2103 W. Fairbanks Ave.* ☎ *407/474–5641* ⊕ *www.4rbbq. com* ✛ *1:F1.*

**$$$**
AMERICAN
Fodor's Choice
★

✕ **Luma on Park.** Indisputably one of the Orlando area's best restaurants, Luma on Park is a popular spot for progressive American cuisine served in a fashionable setting. Every ingredient is carefully sourced from local producers when possible, and scratch-preparation—from pastas to sausages to pickled rhubarb—is the mantra among its dedicated clique of chefs. The menu changes daily. You might discover striped bass ceviche with local grapefruit or Maine lobster tortellini as starters, followed by tripletail with quinoa, aleppo pepper broth, and apple-tangerine chutney, or a free-range pork chop with Russian kale and bacon-braised cannelini beans. The wine cellar is a high point, holding 80 varieties, all available by the half glass, glass, and bottle. The restaurant offers a three-course, prix-fixe dinner Sunday through Tuesday for $35 per person, $45 with wine pairings. ⊠ *250 S. Park Ave.* ☎ *407/599–4111* ⊕ *www.lumaonpark.com* ⌖ *Reservations essential* ✛ *1:F1.*

**$$$**
AMERICAN
Fodor's Choice
★

✕ **The Ravenous Pig.** A trendy, vibrant gastropub in one of Orlando's most affluent enclaves, the Pig is arguably Orlando's most popular foodie destination. Run by husband-and-wife chefs James and Julie Petrakis, the restaurant dispenses delicacies such as Berkshire pork porterhouse with broccolini gratinée and pickled mustard butter, and olive oil-poached halibut with basil, beluga lentils, heirloom tomato, warm pistachio and cerignola olive vinaigrette. The menu changes daily and always includes less expensive pub fare like lobster tacos and homemade pretzels with a taleggio-porter fondue. All charcuterie is made in-house, from spiced orange salami to game bird terrine. A good dessert is the "Pig Tails," essentially a basket full of piping hot, pig tail–shape doughnuts with a chocolate-espresso dipping sauce. ⊠ *1234 N. Orange Ave.* ☎ *407/628–2333* ⊕ *www.theravenouspig.com* ⌖ *Reservations essential* ☾ *Closed Sun. and Mon.* ✛ *1:F1.*

# WHERE TO STAY

With tens of thousands of lodging choices available in the Orlando area, from tents to deluxe villas, there is no lack of variety in price or amenities. Narrowing down the possibilities can be part of the fun.

More upscale hotels are opening, as visitors demand more luxurious surroundings, such as luxe linens, tasteful and refined decor, organic toiletries and more. But no matter what your budget or desires, lodging comes in such a wide range of prices, themes, and guest-room amenities, that you will have no problem finding something that fits your needs.

*Use the coordinate (✛ 2:B1) at the end of each listing to locate a property on the Where to Explore, Eat, and Stay in the Orlando Area or Where to Eat and Stay in Walt Disney World maps.*

### RESERVATIONS

You can book many accommodations—Disney-owned hotels and some non-Disney-owned hotels—through the **WDW Central Reservations Office.** ☎ *407/934–7639* ⊕ *www.disneyworld.com.*

People with disabilities can call **WDW Special Request Reservations** ☎ *407/ 939–7807.* When booking by phone, expect to chat with a robot first, then a real person.

Packages can be arranged through the **Walt Disney Travel Co.** Avoid checkout headaches by asking about the resort fee. Many hotels and resorts charge this fee, and few tell you until checkout, so make sure to ask about it in advance. ☎ *407/934–7639* ⊕ *www.disneyworld.com.*

### PRICES

In the Orlando area, there's an inverse relationship between temperature and room rates. The hot and humid weather in late summer and fall brings low prices and possibly hurricanes. Conversely, the balmy days of late February, March, and April attract lots of visitors; hotel owners charge accordingly. Rates are often low from early January to mid-February, from late April to mid-June, and from mid-August to the third week in November.

| WHAT IT COSTS | | | | | |
|---|---|---|---|---|---|
| | ¢ | $ | $$ | $$$ | $$$$ |
| FOR TWO PEOPLE | under $100 | $100–$174 | $175–$249 | $250–$350 | over $350 |

Price categories reflect the range between the least and most expensive standard double rooms in nonholiday high season, based on the European Plan (with no meals) unless otherwise noted. County and resort taxes (10%–12%) are extra.

# HOTEL REVIEWS

*Listed alphabetically within theme park or neighborhood. The following reviews have been condensed for this book. Please go to Fodors. com for full reviews of each property.*

## WALT DISNEY WORLD

Disney-operated hotels are fantasies unto themselves. Each is designed according to a theme (quaint New England, the relaxed culture of the Polynesian Islands, an African safari village, etc.) and each offers the same perks: free transportation from the airport and to the parks, the option to

# BEST BETS FOR ORLANDO AND THE PARKS LODGING

With thousands of hotels to choose from, ask yourself first what your family truly wants to do in Orlando during your visit. This invariably leads to an on-property vs. off-property debate, and more questions. To assist you, here are our top recommendations by price (any property listed here has at least some rooms in the noted range) and experience. The very best properties—those that provide a particularly remarkable experience in their price range—are designated in the listings with the Fodor's Choice logo.

## Fodor's Choice ★

Best Western Lake Buena Vista Resort, p. 225

The Campsites at Disney's Fort Wilderness Resort, p. 220

Disney's All-Star Resorts, p. 223

Disney's Animal Kingdom Lodge, p. 223

Disney's Coronado Springs Resort, p. 223

Disney's Grand Floridian Resort & Spa, p. 220

Hyatt Regency Grand Cypress Resort, p. 229

Loews Portofino Bay Hotel at Universal Orlando, p. 226

Loews Royal Pacific Resort at Universal Orlando, p. 226

Mona Lisa Suite Hotel, p. 227

Nickelodeon Suites Resort, p. 229

Ritz-Carlton Orlando Grande Lakes, p. 229

Waldorf Astoria Orlando, p. 230

## By Price

### ¢

Best Western Lake Buena Vista Resort, p. 225

The Campsites at Disney's Fort Wilderness Resort, p. 220

### $

Disney's All-Star Resorts, p. 223

Disney's Pop Century Resort, p. 223

Mona Lisa Suite Hotel, p. 227

### $$

Disney's Coronado Springs Resort, p. 223

Hyatt Regency Grand Cypress Resort, p. 229

Nickelodeon Suites Resort, p. 229

### $$$

The Cabins at Disney's Fort Wilderness Resort, p. 220

Disney's Animal Kingdom Lodge, p. 223

Loews Portofino Bay Hotel at Universal Orlando, p. 226

Loews Royal Pacific Resort at Universal Orlando, p. 226

### $$$$

Disney's Grand Floridian Resort & Spa, p. 220

Disney's Polynesian Resort, p. 221

Ritz-Carlton Orlando Grande Lakes, p. 229

Waldorf Astoria Orlando, p. 230

## By Experience

### MOST KID-FRIENDLY

Disney's All-Star Resorts, p. 223

Disney's Pop Century Resort, p. 223

Nickelodeon Suites Resort, p. 229

### BEST POOLS

JW Marriott Orlando Grande Lakes, p. 227

Loews Portofino Bay Hotel at Universal Orlando, p. 226

Ritz-Carlton Orlando Grande Lakes, p. 229

### MOST ROMANTIC

Disney's Wilderness Lodge, p. 221

Hyatt Regency Grand Cypress Resort, p. 229

Loews Portofino Bay Hotel at Universal Orlando, p. 226

Park Plaza Hotel, p. 230

## WHERE SHOULD WE STAY?

| | VIBE | PROS | CONS |
|---|---|---|---|
| Disney | Thousands of rooms at every price; convenient to Disney parks; free transportation all over WDW complex. | Perks like early park entry, and Magical Express, which lets you circumvent airport bag checks. | Without a rental car, you likely won't leave Disney. On-site buses, while free, can take a big bite of time out of your entertainment day; convenience comes at a price. |
| Universal | On-site hotels offer luxury and convenience. There are less expensive options just outside the gates. | Central to Disney, Universal, SeaWorld, malls, and I–4; free water taxis to parks from on-site hotels. | On-site hotels are pricey; expect heavy rush-hour traffic during drives to and from other parks. |
| I-Drive | A hotel, convention center, and activities bonanza. A trolley runs from one end to the other. | Outlet malls provide bargains galore; diners enjoy world-class restaurants; it's central to parks; many hotels offer free shuttles. | Transportation can be pricey, in cash and in time, as traffic is often heavy. Crime is up, especially after dark, although area hotels and businesses have increased security. |
| Kissimmee | It offers mom 'n' pop motels and upscale choices, restaurants and places to buy saltwater taffy. | It's just outside Disney, very close to the Magic Kingdom. Lots of Old Florida charm and low prices. | Some of the older motels here are a little seedy. Petty crime in which tourists are victims is rare— but not unheard of. |
| Lake Buena Vista | Many hotel and restaurant chains here. Adjacent to WDW, which is where almost every guest in your hotel is headed. | Really close to WDW; plenty of dining and shopping options; easy access to I–4. | Heavy peak-hour traffic. As in all neighborhoods near Disney, a gallon of gas will cost 10%–15% more than elsewhere. |
| Central Orlando | Parts of town have the modern high-rises you'd expect. Other areas have oak-tree-lined brick streets winding among small, cypress-ringed lakes. | Lots of locally owned restaurants and some quaint B&Bs. City buses serve the parks. There's good access to I–4. | You'll need to rent a car. And you will be part of the traffic headed to WDW. Expect the 25-mi drive to take at least 45 minutes. |
| Orlando International Airport | Mostly business and flight-crew hotels and car-rental outlets. | Great if you have an early flight or just want to shop in a mall. There's even a Hyatt on-site. | Watching planes, buses, taxis, and cars arrive and depart is all the entertainment you'll get. |

charge all your purchases to your room, special guest-only park-visiting times, and much more. If you stay on-site, you'll have better access to the parks and you'll be more immersed in the Disney experience.

## MAGIC KINGDOM RESORT AREA

$$$ 🏕 **The Cabins at Disney's Fort Wilderness Resort.** The cabins in this 700-acre campground right across the lake from the Magic Kingdom don't exactly constitute roughing it, as they are small, air-conditioned log homes that accommodate four grown-ups and two youngsters. **Pros:** lots of traditional camping activities and a real campground community feel; you can save money by cooking, but you don't have to, as there is a three-meals-a-day restaurant and nightly barbecue; pricey for what is really just a mobile home encased in logs. **Cons:** shuttle to Disney theme parks is free, but slow; coin-op laundry is pricey. ✉ *Magic Kingdom Resort Area, 4510 N. Fort Wilderness Trail, Lake Buena Vista* ☎ *407/824–2900* 🛏 *421 cabins* ⚙ *In-room: kitchen, Internet. In-hotel: restaurant, golf course, pool, tennis court, beach, water sports, children's programs, laundry facilities, parking, some pets allowed, guest laundry, fire pit, grills, picnic table, food service, general store, play area, swimming* ✛ *2:D2.*

¢ 🏕 **The Campsites at Disney's Fort Wilderness Resort.** Bringing a tent or RV is
Fodor'sChoice one of the cheapest ways to stay on WDW property, especially consider-
★ ing that sites in this 700-acre campground can accommodate up to 10. **Pros:** Disney's most economical lodging; free bus or boat transportation around WDW; pets allowed. **Cons:** amount of walking within the camp (to reach the store, restaurants, etc.) can be a bit much for some; shuttle rides to Disney parks take a long time; the mosquitoes can be irritating especially around twilight, except in winter. ✉ *Magic Kingdom Resort Area, 4510 N. Fort Wilderness Trail, Lake Buena Vista* ☎ *407/939–6244 or 407/824–2742* 🛏 *799 campsites* ⚙ *In-hotel: restaurant, pool, tennis court, beach, water sports, children's programs, laundry facilities, some pets allowed, flush toilets, full hook-ups, drinking water, guest laundry, showers, grills, picnic table, food service, electricity, general store, play area, swimming* ✛ *2:D2.*

$$$$ 🏨 **Disney's Contemporary Resort.** You're paying for location at this sleek, modern resort in the heart of WDW, as the monorail runs right through the lobby, making park hopping a breeze, and offering quick respite for families in search of relief from the midday heat. **Pros:** easy access to parks via monorail; Chef Mickey's, the epicenter of the character-meal world, is here; launching point for romantic Bay Lake cruises. **Cons:** a mix of conventioneers and vacationers means it can be too frenzied for the former and too staid for the latter; if you don't like lots of kids around, look elsewhere; daily fee for high-speed Internet access. ✉ *Magic Kingdom Resort Area, 4600 N. World Dr., Lake Buena Vista* ☎ *407/824–1000* 🛏 *1,013 rooms, 25 suites* ⚙ *In-room: safe, Internet, Wi-Fi. In-hotel: restaurant, bar, golf course, pool, tennis court, gym, beach, water sports, children's programs, laundry facilities, business center, parking* ✛ *2:C1.*

$$$$ 🏨 **Disney's Grand Floridian Resort & Spa.** On the shores of the Seven Seas
Fodor'sChoice Lagoon, this red-roofed Victorian emulates the style of the great rail-
★ road resorts of a prior century with beautifully appointed guest rooms,

rambling verandas, delicate, white-painted gingerbread woodwork, and brick chimneys. **Pros:** old-Florida ambience; on the monorail route; Victoria & Albert's, one of Disney's best restaurants, offers an evening-long experience in dining; if you're a couple with no kids, this is definitely the most romantic on-property Disney hotel. **Cons:** pricey; convention clientele and vacationing singles may be more comfortable than families with young children. ✉ *Magic Kingdom Resort Area, 4401 Floridian Way, Lake Buena Vista* ☎ *407/824–3000* 🖥 *867 rooms, 90 suites* ♿ *In-room: safe, Internet. In-hotel: restaurant, bar, golf course, pool, tennis court, gym, spa, beach, water sports, children's programs, laundry facilities, business center, parking* ⊹ *2:B2.*

**$$$$** 🏨 **Disney's Polynesian Resort.** You may not think you're in Fiji, but families with kids can have fun pretending here, especially after hearing the drumming and chanting that occasionally fills the three-story atrium of the Great Ceremonial House—aka the lobby—or, in the case of the adults in the party, downing a few of the tropical drinks available at the bar. **Pros:** on the monorail; great atmosphere. **Cons:** pricey; not good for those bothered by lots of loud children. ✉ *Magic Kingdom Resort Area, 1600 Seven Seas Dr., Lake Buena Vista* ☎ *407/824–2000* 🖥 *847 rooms, 5 suites* ♿ *In-room: safe, Internet. In-hotel: restaurant, bar, golf course, pool, gym, beach, children's programs, laundry facilities, business center, parking* ⊹ *2:B2.*

**$$$** 🏨 **Disney's Wilderness Lodge.** The architects outdid themselves with this seven-story hotel modeled after majestic turn-of-the-20th-century lodges of the American Northwest. **Pros:** high wow-factor architecture; boarding point for romantic Bay Lake sunset cruises or free water taxi to Magic Kingdom; elegant dining options. **Cons:** no direct bus to Magic Kingdom; extra fee for high-speed Internet access. ✉ *Magic Kingdom Resort Area, 901 Timberline Dr., Lake Buena Vista* ☎ *407/824–3200* 🖥 *727 rooms, 31 suites* ♿ *In-room: safe, Internet. In-hotel: restaurant, bar, golf course, pool, gym, beach, children's programs, laundry facilities, business center, parking* ⊹ *2:C2.*

## EPCOT RESORT AREA

**$$$$** 🏨 **Disney's BoardWalk Inn.** Harking back to Atlantic City in its heyday, the striking red and white hotel has a lobby filled with atmospheric chintz-covered furniture, potted palms and wood floors, with porches looking out on a classic waterfront promenade, where ferries and water taxis tootle in and out of the bay, the smell of pretzels and popcorn hangs in the air, and hawkers entice you into arcade games. **Pros:** casual, upscale atmosphere; lots of activities just outside the door, including Epcot. **Cons:** pricey; long bus ride to Magic Kingdom; pool can get crowded; boat whistles can intrude if you have a waterfront room; additional fee for Internet. ✉ *Epcot Resort Area, 2101 Epcot Resorts Blvd., Lake Buena Vista* ☎ *407/939–5100* 🖥 *378* ♿ *In-room: safe, Internet. In-hotel: restaurant, bar, golf course, pool, gym, children's programs, laundry facilities, business center, parking* ⊹ *2:D4.*

**$$$$** 🏨 **Disney's Yacht and Beach Club Resorts.** These big Crescent Lake inns next door to Epcot seem straight out of a Cape Cod summer, with their nautical decor, waterfront locale, rockingchair porches and family-friendly water-based activities. **Pros:** location, location, location—it's easy to

# DISNEY AND UNIVERSAL RESORT PERKS

## DISNEY PERKS

**Extra Magic Hours.** You get special early and late-night admission to certain Disney parks on specified days. Call ahead for details so you can plan your early- and late-visit strategies.

**Free Parking.** Parking is free for Disney hotel guests at Disney hotel and theme-park lots.

**Magical Express.** If you're staying at a Disney hotel you don't need to rent a car or think about finding a shuttle or taxi or worry about baggage handling thanks to this free service.

At your hometown airport you'll check your bags in and won't see them again till you get to your Disney hotel. At Orlando International Airport you'll be met by a Disney rep who will lead you to a coach that takes you to your hotel. Your luggage will be delivered separately, and usually arrives in your room an hour or two after you do.

On departure, the process works in reverse (though only on some participating airlines, so check in advance). You get your boarding pass and check your bags at the hotel. At the airport you go directly to your gate, skipping check-in. You won't see your bags until you're in your hometown airport. Participating airlines include American, Continental, Delta, JetBlue, Southwest, United, and US Airways.

**Charging Privileges.** You can charge most meals and purchases throughout Disney to your hotel room.

**Package Delivery.** Anything you purchase at Disney—at a park, a hotel, or in Downtown Disney—can be delivered to the gift shop of your Disney hotel for free.

**Priority Reservations.** Disney hotel guests get priority reservations at Disney restaurants and choice tee times at Disney golf courses up to 30 days in advance.

**Guaranteed Entry.** Disney theme parks sometimes reach capacity, but on-site guests can enter even when others would be turned away.

## UNIVERSAL PERKS

**Head-of-the-Line Access.** Your hotel key lets you go directly to the head of the line for most Universal Orlando attractions. Unlike Disney's Fastpass program, you don't need to use this at a specific time; it's always good.

**Priority Seating.** Many of Universal's restaurants offer priority seating to those staying at on-site hotels.

**Charging Privileges.** You can charge most meals and purchases throughout Universal to your hotel room.

**Delivery Services.** If you buy something in the theme parks, you can have it sent directly to your room, so you don't have to carry it around.

**Free Loaners.** Some on-site hotels have a "Did You Forget?" closet that offers everything from kid's strollers to dog leashes to computer accessories. There's no fee for using this service.

walk or hop a ferry to Epcot, the BoardWalk, or Hollywood Studios. **Cons:** distances within the hotel—like, from your room to the front desk—can seem vast; high noise factor; extra fee for high-speed Internet. ⊠ *Epcot Resort Area, 1700 Epcot Resorts Blvd., Lake Buena Vista* 🕾 *407/934–8000 Beach Club, 407/934–7000 Yacht Club* 🖙 *1,213 rooms, 112 suites* ⚵ *In-room: safe, Internet, Wi-Fi. In-hotel: restaurant, bar, golf course, pool, tennis court, gym, beach, water sports, children's programs, laundry facilities, business center, parking* ✛ *2:D4.*

## ANIMAL KINGDOM RESORT AREA

$
☺
Fodor's Choice
★

🏨 **Disney's All-Star Sports, All-Star Music, and All-Star Movies Resorts.** Stay here if you want the quintessential Disney-with-your-kids experience, or if you're a couple that feels all that pitter-pattering of little feet is a reasonable tradeoff for a good deal on a room. (Hint: For a little peace, request a room away from pools and other common areas.) **Pros:** unbeatable price for a Disney property. **Cons:** no kids' clubs or programs, possibly because this is on the bottom tier of Disney hotels in terms of room rates; distances between rooms and on-site amenities can seem vast. ⊠ *Animal Kingdom Resort Area, 1701 W. Buena Vista Dr., Lake Buena Vista* 🕾 *407/939–5000 Sports, 407/939–6000 Music, 407/939–7000 Movies* 🖙 *1,700 rooms, 215 family suites at Music; 1,920 rooms at Movies and Sports* ⚵ *In-room: safe, Internet. In-hotel: bar, pool, laundry facilities, business center* ✛ *2:C6.*

$$$
Fodor's Choice
★

🏨 **Disney's Animal Kingdom Lodge.** Giraffes, zebras, and other wildlife roam three 11-acre savannas separated by the encircling arms of this grand hotel, designed to resemble a "kraal" or animal enclosure in Africa. **Pros:** extraordinary wildlife and cultural experiences; excellent on-site restaurants, Jiko, Boma and Sanaa. **Cons:** shuttle to parks other than Animal Kingdom can take more than an hour; guided savanna tours available only to guests on the concierge level, where the least expensive room is $100 a night higher than the least expensive rooms in other parts of the hotel. ⊠ *Animal Kingdom Resort Area, 2901 Osceola Pkwy., Lake Buena Vista* 🕾 *407/934–7639* 🖙 *972 rooms, 499 suites or villas* ⚵ *In-room: safe, Internet. In-hotel: restaurant, bar, golf course, pool, gym, spa, children's programs, laundry facilities, business center, parking* ✛ *2:A5.*

$$
Fodor's Choice
★

🏨 **Disney's Coronado Springs Resort.** Popular with convention-goers who love the huge meeting spaces, and with families who appreciate its casual Southwestern architecture, the lively, Mexican-style food court, and its elaborate swimming pool, colorful Coronado Springs Resort also offers a moderate price. **Pros:** great pool with a play-area arcade for kids and a bar for adults; lots of outdoor activities. **Cons:** some accommodations are a half-mile from the restaurants; standard rooms are on the small side; as in many Disney lakefront properties, the lake is for looking at and boating on, not for swimming in. ⊠ *Animal Kingdom Resort Area, 1000 W. Buena Vista Dr., Lake Buena Vista* 🕾 *407/939–1000* 🖙 *1,917 rooms* ⚵ *In-room: safe, Internet. In-hotel: restaurant, bar, golf course, pool, gym, spa, beach, children's programs, laundry facilities, business center, parking* ✛ *2:C5.*

$

🏨 **Disney's Pop Century Resort.** Giant jukeboxes, 65-foot-tall bowling pins, an oversize Big Wheel and Rubik's Cube, and other pop-culture

**4**

memorabilia are scattered throughout the grounds of this value resort. **Pros:** great room rates; hotel provides a trip down memory lane; proximity to ESPN Wide World of Sports and Disney's Hollywood Studios. **Cons:** big crowds at the front desk; big crowds (and noise) in the food court; small rooms; lots of small kids around. ⊠ *Animal Kingdom Resort Area, 1050 Century Dr., Lake Buena Vista* ☎ *407/938–4000 or 407/934–4639* ☍ *2,880 rooms* ⚹ *In-room: safe, Internet. In-hotel: restaurant, bar, golf course, pool, gym, laundry facilities, parking* ✛ *2:E5.*

## DOWNTOWN DISNEY RESORT AREA

$$    ⊡ **Disney's Port Orleans Resort–French Quarter.** Ornate Big Easy–style row houses with wrought-iron–clad balconies cluster around magnolia shaded squares in this relatively quiet resort, which appeals to couples more than families. **Pros:** authentic, or as authentic as you get at Disney; fun New Orleans–style atmosphere; moderate price; lots of water recreation options, including boat rentals. **Cons:** even though there are fewer kids here, public areas can still be quite noisy; shuttle service is slow; food court is the only on-site dining option. ⊠ *Downtown Disney Resort Area, 1251 Riverside Dr., Lake Buena Vista* ☎ *407/934–5000* ☍ *1,008 rooms* ⚹ *In-room: safe, Internet. In-hotel: restaurant, golf course, pool, water sports, laundry facilities, parking* ✛ *2:E3.*

$$    ⊡ **Disney's Port Orleans Resort–Riverside.** Buildings in this family-friendly, moderately priced resort look like Southern plantation-style mansions (in the Magnolia Bend section) and rustic bayou dwellings (in the Alligator Bayou section) and you can usually pick which section you want. **Pros:** carriage rides; river cruises; lots of recreation options for kids. **Cons:** shuttle can be slow; no shortage of extremely noisy youngsters, if that's a concern. ⊠ *Downtown Disney Resort Area, 1251 Riverside Dr., Lake Buena Vista* ☎ *407/934–6000* ☍ *2,048 rooms* ⚹ *In-room: safe, Internet. In-hotel: restaurant, bar, golf course, pool, gym, water sports, children's programs, laundry facilities, parking* ✛ *2:E3.*

# OTHER ON-SITE HOTELS

Although not operated by the Disney organization, the Swan and the Dolphin just outside Epcot, and the hotels along Hotel Plaza Boulevard near Downtown Disney call themselves "official" Walt Disney World hotels. While the Swan and Dolphin have the special privileges of on-site Disney hotels, such as free transportation to and from the parks and early park entry, the Downtown Disney resorts have their own systems to shuttle hotel guests to the parks.

## EPCOT RESORT AREA

$$$$    ⊡ **Walt Disney World Dolphin.** World-renowned architect Michael Graves designed the neighboring Dolphin and Swan hotels, which are dominated by giant sculptures of their namesakes, and are within easy ferry distance from Epcot; a pair of 56-foot-tall sea creatures bookend this 25-story glass pyramid. **Pros:** access to all facilities at the Walt Disney World Swan; easy walk or boat ride to BoardWalk and Epcot; good on-site restaurants. **Cons:** self-parking is $10 a day; a daily resort fee covers Wi-Fi and Internet access, use of health club, and local phone calls; room-charge privileges stop at the front door, and don't extend

to the Disney parks. ✉ *1500 Epcot Resorts Blvd., Lake Buena Vista* ☎ *407/934–4000 or 800/227–1500* 🌐 *www.swandolphin.com* ⇒ *1,509 rooms, 112 suites* ♁ *In-room: safe, Internet, Wi-Fi. In-hotel: restaurant, bar, golf course, pool, tennis court, gym, spa, beach, water sports, children's programs, laundry facilities, business center, parking* ⊕ *2:C4.*

$$$$ **Walt Disney World Swan.** The Grotto, a 3-acre water playground complete with waterslides and waterfalls, lies between and is shared by the Dolphin and Swan; Disney's BoardWalk and the Fantasia Gardens miniature-golf complex are nearby, giving guests lots to do between park hopping. **Pros:** charge privileges and access to all facilities at the Dolphin (but not inside Disney World); easy walk to BoardWalk; free boats take you to the BoardWalk and Epcot; good on-site restaurants. **Cons:** long bus ride to and from Magic Kingdom; daily resort fee. ✉ *1200 Epcot Resorts Blvd., Lake Buena Vista* ☎ *407/934–3000 or 800/248–7926* 🌐 *www.swandolphin.com* ⇒ *756 rooms, 55 suites* ♁ *In-room: safe, Internet, Wi-Fi. In-hotel: restaurant, bar, golf course, pool, tennis court, gym, spa, beach, water sports, children's programs, laundry facilities, business center, parking* ⊕ *2:C4.*

4

## DOWNTOWN DISNEY RESORT AREA

¢ **Best Western Lake Buena Vista Resort.** This Best Western resort is a few minutes walk from Downtown Disney and for a bargain price offers luxury linens, flat screen TVs, free Wi-Fi and parking, and in many of the rooms, a bird's-eye view of the nightly Disney World fireworks. **Pros:** free Wi-Fi and parking, not to mention the price, makes this one of the best bargains on Hotel Row; close to Downtown Disney. **Cons:** inconvenient to Universal and downtown Orlando. ✉ *2000 Hotel Plaza Blvd., Lake Buena Vista* ☎ *407/828–2424 or 800/348–3765* 🌐 *www.lakebuenavistaresorthotel.com* ⇒ *325 rooms* ♁ *In-room: safe, Wi-Fi. In-hotel: restaurant, pool, gym, laundry facilities, business center* ⊕ *2:G3.*

Fodor's Choice ★

$ **Buena Vista Palace Hotel & Spa.** This large and amenity-filled hotel gets kudos as much for its on-site charms as for its location, just yards from Downtown Disney. **Pros:** easy walk to Downtown Disney; good restaurants and bars on-site; spa is large and luxurious. **Cons:** inconvenient to Universal and downtown Orlando; daily resort fee for Wi-Fi and fitness center. ✉ *1900 Buena Vista Dr., Lake Buena Vista* ☎ *407/827–2727* 🌐 *www.buenavistapalace.com* ⇒ *1,014 rooms* ♁ *In-room: safe, Internet. In-hotel: restaurant, bar, pool, tennis court, gym, spa, children's programs, laundry facilities, business center* ⊕ *2:G3.*

$ **Hilton in the WDW Resort.** While this hotel offers full service to business travelers, families are not neglected, with scheduled Disney character breakfasts every Sunday. **Pros:** ergonomic work stations; 24-hour health club; character breakfasts; HDTV in rooms; free transporation to Disney parks. **Cons:** No children's programs; fee for Internet and parking; inconvenient to Universal and downtown Orlando. ✉ *1751 Hotel Plaza Blvd., Downtown Disney, Lake Buena Vista* ☎ *407/827–4000, 800/782–4414 reservations* 🌐 *www.hilton.com* ⇒ *814 rooms, 27 suites* ♁ *In-room: safe, Internet, Wi-Fi. In-hotel: restaurant, pool, gym, laundry facilities, business center* ⊕ *2:G4.*

## UNIVERSAL ORLANDO AREA

Universal Orlando's on-site hotels were built in a little luxury enclave that has everything you need, so you never have to leave Universal property. In minutes you can walk from any hotel to CityWalk, Universal's dining and entertainment district, or take a ferry that cruises the adjacent artificial river.

$ ⬚ **Doubletree Hotel at the Entrance to Universal Orlando.** The name is a mouthful, but it's an accurate description for this conveniently located hotel, which caters to business-trippers and pleasure-seekers alike thanks to a location right at the Universal Orlando entrance. **Pros:** four restaurants on-site; car rental onsite; within walking distance of Universal and area shops and restaurants; free shuttle to Universal. **Cons:** on a fast-lane tourist strip; need a rental car to reach Disney, I-Drive, or downtown Orlando. ⊠ *5780 Major Blvd., Universal Orlando, Orlando* ☎ *407/351–1000* ⊕ *www.doubltreeorlando.com* ↘ *742 rooms, 19 suites* ☐ *In-room: safe, Wi-Fi. In-hotel: restaurant, bar, pool, gym, laundry facilities, business center* ✛ *1:D3.*

$$$ ⬚ **Hard Rock Hotel.** Music rules in this California Mission–style building, where guests can pretend they are rock stars as their hotel key card lets them skip the lines at Universal and grants early admission to Islands of Adventure's Wizarding World of Harry Potter. **Pros:** shuttle, water taxi, or short walk to Universal and CityWalk; preferential treatment at Universal rides; charge privileges on your room extend to the two other on-property Universal hotels. **Cons:** rooms and meals are pricey; loud rock music in public areas; fee for gym and in-room Wi-Fi. ⊠ *5800 Universal Blvd., Universal Orlando, Orlando* ☎ *407/503–7625 or 800/232–7827* ⊕ *www.hardrockhotelorlando.com* ↘ *621 rooms, 29 suites* ☐ *In-room: safe, Internet, Wi-Fi. In-hotel: restaurant, bar, pool, gym, spa, children's programs, some pets allowed* ✛ *1:D3.*

$$$ ⬚ **Loews Portofino Bay Hotel at Universal Orlando.** The charm and romance
Fodor's Choice of Portofino, Italy, destination of the rich and famous in Europe, are
★ conjured up at this lovely luxury resort. **Pros:** Italian villa atmosphere; large spa; short walk or ferry ride to CityWalk, Universal Studios, and Islands of Adventure; preferential treatment at Universal rides; you can charge meals and services (and use the pools) at the Hard Rock and the Royal Pacific Resort. **Cons:** rooms and meals are pricey; daily fee for in-room high-speed Internet or Wi-Fi, as well as for access to the fitness center. ⊠ *5601 Universal Blvd., Universal Orlando, Orlando* ☎ *407/503–1000 or 800/232–7827* ⊕ *www.loewshotels.com/en/ Portofino-Bay-Hotel* ↘ *699 rooms, 51 suites* ☐ *In-room: safe, Internet, Wi-Fi. In-hotel: restaurant, bar, pool, gym, spa, children's programs, some pets allowed* ✛ *1:D3.*

$$$ ⬚ **Loews Royal Pacific Resort at Universal Orlando.** The entrance—a broad,
Fodor's Choice covered footbridge high above a tropical stream—sets the tone for
★ the Pacific Rim theme of this hotel, which lies amid 53 acres of lush shrubs, soaring bamboo, and palms. **Pros:** preferential treatment at Universal rides, early admission to Islands of Adventure (Wizarding World of Harry Potter); serene, Zen garden vibe. **Cons:** rooms can feel cramped; $10-a-day fee for in-room Internet access and fitness center unwarranted given rates. ⊠ *6300 Hollywood Way, Universal Orlando,*

*Orlando* ☎ *407/503–3000 or 800/232–7827* ⊕ *www.loewshotels.com/ en/Royal-Pacific-Resort* ⇩ *1,000 rooms, 113 suites* ♿ *In-room: safe, Wi-Fi. In-hotel: restaurant, bar, pool, gym, spa, children's programs, laundry facilities, some pets allowed* ✣ *1:D3.*

## ORLANDO METRO AREA

### KISSIMMEE

$$ ▧ **Gaylord Palms Resort.** Built in the style of a grand turn-of-the-20th-century Florida mansion, this resort is meant to inspire awe; inside its enormous atrium, covered by a 4-acre glass roof, are re-creations of Florida destination icons such as the Everglades, Key West, and old St. Augustine. **Pros:** you could have a great vacation without ever leaving the grounds; free shuttle to Disney. **Cons:** daily $20 resort fee; rooms are pricey; not much within walking distance (although the hotel is so big that you can take quite a hike inside the building); shuttles to Universal and SeaWorld are available for a fee. ⊠ *6000 W. Osceola Pkwy., I–4 Exit 65* ☎ *407/586–0000* ⊕ *www.gaylordpalms.com* ⇩ *1,406 rooms, 86 suites* ♿ *In-room: a/c, safe, Internet, Wi-Fi. In-hotel: restaurant, bar, golf course, pool, gym, spa, children's programs, laundry facilities, business center, parking* ✣ *2:F6.*

### CELEBRATION

$ ▧ **Mona Lisa Suite Hotel.** Much like a European boutique hotel in style,

Fodor's Choice the Mona Lisa is very human in scale, and crisply minimalist in decor.

★ **Pros:** free shuttle to downtown Celebration and all the theme parks; golf privileges at Celebration Golf; spa privileges at Celebration Day Spa; concierge service. **Cons:** busy U.S. 192 is close by; $12-a-day resort fee; if you want to go anywhere besides Celebration and the parks, you'll need a car. ⊠ *225 Celebration Pl., Celebration* ☎ *866/404–6662 or 407/964–7000* ⊕ *www.monalisasuitehotel.com* ⇩ *240 suites: 93 1-bedroom, 147 2-bedroom* ♿ *In-room: safe, kitchen, Wi-Fi. In-hotel: restaurant, bar, golf course, pool, gym, spa, laundry facilities, parking* ✣ *2:E6.*

### INTERNATIONAL DRIVE

$$$ ▧ **JW Marriott Orlando Grande Lakes.** With more than 70,000 square feet of meeting space, this hotel caters to a convention clientele, but it's also part of a lush resort with a European-style spa, a Greg Norman–designed golf course, and a huge, lazy-river style pool complex, giving it family and leisure appeal. **Pros:** pool is great for kids and adults; shares amenities with the Ritz, including a world-class, albeit pricey, health and beauty spa; golf course; free shuttle service to SeaWorld and Universal. **Cons:** things are spread out on the grounds; you need a rental car to reach Disney or shopping. ⊠ *4040 Central Florida Pkwy., I-Drive area* ☎ *407/206–2300 or 800/576–5750* ⊕ *www.grandelakes. com* ⇩ *1,000 rooms, 64 suites* ♿ *In-room: safe, Wi-Fi. In-hotel: restaurant, bar, golf course, pool, tennis court, gym, spa, children's programs, laundry facilities, business center, parking* ✣ *1:E4.*

$$ ▧ **Peabody Orlando.** This deluxe conference hotel underwent a $450-million expansion that transformed it into a full-service resort with richly appointed rooms, two pools with cabanas, a full-service spa and

Loews Royal Pacific Resort at Universal Orlando

All-Star Music Resort, Orlando

The Ritz-Carlton Orlando, Grande Lakes

Waldorf Astoria Orlando

Nickelodeon Suites Resort

Disney's Coronado Springs Resort

health center the size of your local Y, two restaurants and a 360-seat glass-walled lounge overlooking the pool. **Pros:** connected to Convention Center (business travelers take note); good spa; short walk to shops and restaurants. **Cons:** pricey; $15 daily resort fee includes Wi-Fi and other amenities. ⊠ *9801 International Dr., I-Drive area* ☎ *407/352–4000 or 800/732–2639* ⊕ *www.peabodyorlando.com* ➔ *1,641 rooms, 193 suites, 5 penthouse suites* ⌂ *In-room: safe, Internet, Wi-Fi. In-hotel: restaurant, bar, pool, tennis court, gym, spa* ✛ *1:D3.*

$$$$
Fodor's Choice
★
☷ **Ritz-Carlton Orlando Grande Lakes.** Orlando's first and only Ritz-Carlton is a particularly extravagant link in the luxury chain, with exemplary service that extends from the fully attended porte-cochere entrance to the 18-hole golf course and 40-room spa. **Pros:** truly luxurious; impeccable service; great spa; golf course; shares amenities with Marriott. **Cons:** pricey; need a rental car to reach theme parks, area shops, and restaurants. ⊠ *4012 Central Florida Pkwy., I-Drive area* ☎ *407/206–2400 or 800/576–5760* ⊕ *www.grandelakes.com* ➔ *582 rooms, 63 suites* ⌂ *In-room: Wi-Fi. In-hotel: restaurant, bar, golf course, pool, tennis court, gym, spa, water sports, children's programs, business center, parking* ✛ *1:E4.*

## LAKE BUENA VISTA AREA

$$
☷ **Hilton Orlando Bonnet Creek.** The Hilton is not quite as plush as its neighbor the Waldorf Astoria, but it has a load of amenities, and appeals to families, with its 2-acre lagoon pool, kids-eat-free program, free transportation to Disney World, and discounted tickets to Disney parks. **Pros:** wonderful setting for a hotel—Disney is just moments away, but the views southwest over the golf course and forest beyond give it a remote air; next door to the Waldorf, with its amenities easily at hand; free Disney shuttle; free Wi-fi. **Cons:** nothing within walking distance; you will need to rent a car; daily parking fee. ⊠ *14100 Bonnet Creek Resort La., Bonnet Creek, Orlando* ☎ *407/597–3600* ⊕ *www.hiltonbonnetcreek.com* ➔ *1,000 rooms, 36 suites* ⌂ *In-room: safe, Internet, Wi-Fi. In-hotel: restaurant, bar, golf course, pool, gym, spa, children's programs, business center, parking* ✛ *2:F5.*

$$
Fodor's Choice
★
☷ **Hyatt Regency Grand Cypress Resort.** Sitting amid 1,500 lushly landscaped acres just outside Disney's back gate, this luxury resort hotel has a private lake with watercraft, three golf courses, and miles of trails for strolling, bicycling, jogging, and horseback riding. **Pros:** great Sunday brunch at La Coquina restaurant; huge pool; lots of recreation options, including nearby equestrian center. **Cons:** pricey rooms, pricey resort fee; you'll need a car or taxi to get to downtown Orlando. ⊠ *1 Grand Cypress Blvd., Lake Buena Vista area, Orlando* ☎ *407/239–1234 or 800/233–1234* ⊕ *www.hyattgrandcypress.com* ➔ *815 rooms* ⌂ *In-room: safe, Internet, Wi-Fi. In-hotel: restaurant, bar, golf course, pool, tennis court, gym, spa, beach, water sports, children's programs, business center, parking, some pets allowed* ✛ *2:G3.*

$$
☼
Fodor's Choice
★
☷ **Nickelodeon Suites Resort.** This 24-acre Nickelodeon-themed resort is so kid friendly that you can barely take a step without bumping into images of SpongeBob, Dora the Explorer, Jimmy Neutron, or other Nick characters. **Pros:** extremely kid-friendly; Disney, Universal Orlando, and SeaWorld shuttles included in resort fee; discounts (up to

4

50% off standard rates) for active-duty military; mini-golf course. **Cons:** Daily resort fee of $25; not within walking distance of Disney or Downtown Disney; may be too frenetic for folks without kids. ✉ *14500 Continental Gateway, Lake Buena Vista area, Orlando* ☎ *407/387–5437 or 866/462–6425* ⊕ *www.nickhotels.com* ➲ *777 suites* ♿ *In-room: safe, kitchen, Internet. In-hotel: restaurant, bar, pool, gym, children's programs, laundry facilities, business center, parking* ✛ *2:G5.*

**$$$**
Fodor's Choice
★
**⊡ Waldorf Astoria Orlando.** While it doesn't duplicate the famed Waldorf Astoria Hotel in New York, the Waldorf Astoria Orlando echoes the original with imagination and flair, from the clock under the dome in the center of the circular lobby to tiny, black-and-white accent tiles on the floors of the guest rooms. **Pros:** a lavish and luxurious hotel, spa, and golf resort, next to Disney; free transportation to WDW parks; free Wi-Fi. **Cons:** if you can bear to leave the cabana you'll need a car to see anything else in the area. ✉ *14200 Bonnet Creek Resort La., Bonnet Creek, Orlando* ☎ *407/597–5500* ⊕ *www.waldorfastoriaorlando.com* ➲ *328 rooms, 169 suites* ♿ *In-room: safe, Internet. In-hotel: restaurant, bar, golf course, pool, gym, spa, children's programs, business center, parking* ✛ *2:F5.*

## CENTRAL ORLANDO

**$$**
**⊡ Grand Bohemian Hotel.** This European-style property is downtown Orlando's only Four-Diamond luxury hotel, and is part of the locally owned Kessler chain; decorated in a sophisticated and eclectic "Bohemian" style, the hotel showcases hundreds of pieces of art from the Kessler collection in a gallery and on the walls of the hotel. **Pros:** art gallery; quiet, adult-friendly atmosphere; great restaurant; sophisticated entertainment; short walk to Amway Center and downtown restaurants and clubs. **Cons:** kids may find it boring; meals are relatively expensive. ✉ *325 S. Orange Ave., Downtown Orlando* ☎ *407/313–9000 or 866/663–0024* ⊕ *www.grandbohemianhotel.com* ➲ *212 rooms, 35 suites* ♿ *In-room: safe, Wi-Fi. In-hotel: restaurant, bar, pool, gym, spa, business center, parking* ✛ *1:F2.*

## WINTER PARK

**$**
**⊡ Park Plaza Hotel.** Small and intimate, this 1922 establishment right on Park Avenue offers guests the charm of fern-bedecked wrought iron balconies, along with new furniture and free Wi-Fi. **Pros:** romantic; great balconies overlooking shops and restaurants; in-house restaurant is in a brick-walled courtyard. Amtrak station is about a block away. **Cons:** the railroad tracks are a lot closer than the station, and you can sometimes hear train noise at night; no small children allowed; small rooms. ✉ *307 Park Ave. S* ☎ *407/647–1072 or 800/228–7220* ⊕ *www.parkplazahotel.com* ➲ *27 rooms* ♿ *In-room: Wi-Fi. In-hotel: restaurant, parking, some age restrictions* ✛ *1:F1.*

# Walt Disney World

ENJOYING THE WHOLE WORLD

**WORD OF MOUTH**

"If I had one day only, I would spend it in the Magic Kingdom.
Epcot is nice but if you like rides and have never been to Disney,
it has to be MK. Nothing beats it."

—Nyetzy

# WELCOME TO WALT DISNEY WORLD

## TOP REASONS TO GO

★ **Nostalgia:** Face it— Mickey and company are old friends. And you probably have childhood pictures of yourself in front of Cinderella Castle. Even if you don't, nobody does yesteryear better: head to Main Street, U.S.A. or Hollywood Boulevard and see.

★ **Memories in the Making:** Who doesn't want to snap photos of Sis on the Dumbo ride or of Junior after his Splash Mountain experience? The urge to pass that Disney nostalgia on to the next generation is strong.

★ **The Thrills:** For some this means roller-coasting to an Aerosmith sound track or simulating space flight; for others it's about cascading down a waterslide or going on safari.

★ **The Chills:** If the Pirates of the Caribbean cave doesn't give you goose bumps, try the Haunted Mansion or Twilight Zone Tower of Terror.

★ **The Spectacle:** The list is long: fireworks, laserlight displays, arcade games, parades . . .

**1** Magic Kingdom. Disney's emblematic park is home to Space Mountain and Pirates of the Caribbean.

**2** Epcot. Future World's focus is science, technology, and hands-on experiences. In the World Showcase you can tour 11 countries without getting jet lagged.

**3** Disney's Hollywood Studios. Top attractions include Rock 'n' Roller Coaster starring Aerosmith and Twilight Zone Tower of Terror.

**4** Disney's Animal Kingdom. Amid a 403-acre wildlife preserve are an Asian-theme water ride, an African safari ride, and shows.

**5**–**6** Water Parks. Blizzard Beach's best (worst?) ride is the 55-mph dead-drop from Summit Plummet. Water babies love Typhoon Lagoon's Ketchakiddie Creek.

**7** Downtown Disney. It's a shopping, dining, and entertainment hub: the Marketplace, the West Side, and, someday, Hyperion Wharf.

**8** BoardWalk. At this lakeside district you can dine, shop, or cut a rug in an oldstyle dance hall.

**9** Celebration. Disney's utopian residential community recalls the Magic Kingdom's Main Street, U.S.A., but without the tourists.

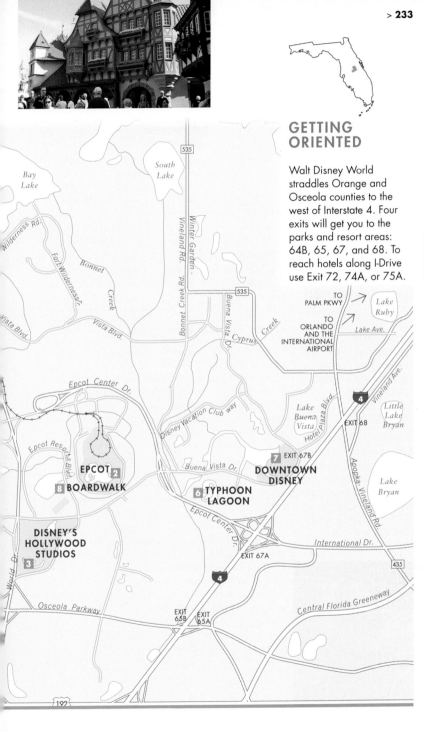

## GETTING ORIENTED

Walt Disney World straddles Orange and Osceola counties to the west of Interstate 4. Four exits will get you to the parks and resort areas: 64B, 65, 67, and 68. To reach hotels along I-Drive use Exit 72, 74A, or 75A.

5

Bay Lake

South Lake

535

Winter Garden - Vineland Rd.

Wilderness Rd.

Fort Wilderness Tr.

Bonnet Creek

Vista Blvd.

Bonnet Creek Rd.

Vista Blvd.

535

Buena Vista Dr.

Cyprus Creek

TO PALM PKWY

Lake Ruby

TO ORLANDO AND THE INTERNATIONAL AIRPORT

Lake Ave.

Epcot Center Dr.

I-4

Vineland Ave.

Disney Vacation Club Way

Lake Buena Vista

Hotel Plaza Blvd.

EXIT 68

Little Lake Bryan

Epcot Resorts Blvd.

EPCOT 2

8 BOARDWALK

Buena Vista Dr.

6 TYPHOON LAGOON

7 EXIT 67B

DOWNTOWN DISNEY

Apopka-Vineland Rd.

Lake Bryan

DISNEY'S HOLLYWOOD STUDIOS

3

Epcot Center Dr.

International Dr.

EXIT 67A

435

World Dr.

Osceola Parkway

I-4

EXIT 65B  EXIT 65A

Central Florida Greeneway

192

# WALT DISNEY WORLD PLANNER

## Operating Hours

Walt Disney World operates 365 days a year. Opening and closing times vary by park and by season, with the longest hours during prime summer months and year-end holidays. The parking lots open at least an hour before the parks do.

In general, openings hover around 9 am, though certain attractions might not start up till 10 or 11 am. Closings range between 5 and 8 pm in the off-season and between 8 and 10, 11, or even midnight in high season. Downtown Disney and BoardWalk shops stay open as late as 11 pm.

### EXTRA MAGIC HOURS

The Extra Magic Hours program gives Disney resort guests free early and late-night admission to certain parks on specified days—call ahead for information about each park's "magic hours" days to plan your early- and late-visit strategies.

## Getting In and Around

At the gate, the per-person per-day price is $82 adults (ages 10 and older) and $74 children (ages 3–9). You can buy tickets at the Ticket and Transportation Center (TTC) in the Magic Kingdom, from booths at other park entrances, in all on-site resorts if you're a guest, at the Disney store in the airport, and at various other sites around Orlando. You can also buy them in advance online—the best way to save time and money.

If you opt for a multiday ticket, you'll be issued a nontransferable pass that uses your fingerprint for ID. Slide your pass through the reader, just like people with single-day tickets, and also slip your finger into the V-shape reader.

### PARKING AND IN-PARK TRANSPORT

Parking at Disney parks is free to resort guests; all others pay $14 for cars and $15 for RVs and campers. Parking is free for everyone at Typhoon Lagoon, Blizzard Beach, Downtown Disney, and the BoardWalk. Trams take you between the theme-park lots (*note your parking location!*) and turnstiles. Disney's buses, boats, and monorails whisk you from resort to park and park to park. If you're staying on Disney property, you can use this system exclusively. Either take a Disney bus or drive to Typhoon Lagoon and Blizzard Beach. Once inside the water parks, your can walk, swim, slide, or chill out. Allow up to an hour for travel between parks and hotels on Disney transportation.

### FASTPASS

Fastpass helps you avoid lines, and it's included in regular park admission. Insert your theme-park ticket into the machines near several attractions. Out comes your Fastpass, printed with a one-hour window of time during which you can return to get into the fast line. *Don't forget to take your park ticket back, too.* You can't make a Fastpass for another attraction until you're within the window of time for your first appointment. It's best to make appointments only for the most popular attractions and to make new ones as soon as existing ones mature. Strategy is everything.

# Doing Disney Right

If you remember nothing else, keep in mind these essential strategies, tried and tested by generations of Disney fans.

■ **Buy tickets before leaving home**. It saves money and gives you time to look into all the ticket options. It also offers an opportunity for you to consider vacation packages and meal plans. Before you can sing "M-I-C-K-E-Y" you'll be organized and ready for a fun, successful Disney trip.

■ **Make dining reservations before leaving home.** If you don't, you might find yourself eating fast food (again) or leaving Disney for dinner. On-site restaurants, especially those featuring character appearances, book up fast.

■ **Arrive at least 30 minutes before the parks open.** We know, it's your vacation and you want to sleep in. But you probably want to make the most of your time and money, too. Plan to be up by 7:30 am each day to get the most out of your park visits. After transit time, it'll take you 15-20 minutes to park, get to the gates, and pick up your park guide maps and *Times Guide*.

■ **See top attractions in the morning.** And we mean *first thing*. Decide in advance on your can't-miss attractions, find their locations, and hotfoot it to them before 10 am.

■ **Use Fastpass.** Yes, use the Fastpass. It's worth saying twice. The system is free, easy, and it's your ticket to the top attractions with little or no waiting in line.

■ **Use Baby Swap.** Disney has a theme-park "rider switch" policy that works like this: one parent waits with the baby or toddler while the other parent rides the attraction. When the ride ends, they switch places with minimal wait.

■ **Build in rest time.** Who wants to become overly hot, tired, and grumpy? Start early and then leave the parks around 3 or 4 pm, thus avoiding the hottest and most crowded period. After a couple of hours' rest at your hotel, head back for a nighttime spectacle or to ride a big-deal ride or two (lines often are shorter around closing time).

■ **Create an itinerary, but leave room for spontaneity.** Decide which parks to see on each day, and know your priorities, but don't try to plot your trip hour by hour. If you're staying at a Disney resort, find out which parks have Extra Magic Hours on which days.

■ **Eat at off hours.** To avoid the mealtime rush hours have a quick, light breakfast at 7 or 8 am, lunch at 11 am, and dinner at 5 or 6 pm.

# Other Disney Services

If you can shell out $175–$315 an hour (with a six-hour minimum), you can take a customized **VIP Tour** with guides who help you park hop and get good seats at parades and shows. These tours don't help you skip lines, but they make navigating easy. Groups can have up to 10 people; book up to three months ahead.

At character meals—breakfasts, lunches, or dinners—Mickey, Belle, or other characters sign autographs and pose for photos. Book through Disney's dining reservations line up to 180 days out; these hugging-and-feeding frenzies are wildly popular. They're also a good way to spend the morning on check-out day.

# Disney Contacts

**Cruise Line:** ☎ *800/370–0097* ⊕ *www.disneycruise.com*

**Dining Reservations:** ☎ *407/939–3463*

**Fairytale Weddings:** ☎ *321/939–4610* ⊕ disneyweddings. disney.go.com

**Golf Reservations:** ☎ *407/939–4653*

**Guest Info:** ☎ *407/824–4321*

**VIP Tours:** ☎ *407/560–4033*

**WDW Travel Company:** ☎ *407/939–1289*

**Web:** ⊕ *disneyworld.disney. go.com*

5

By Jennie Hess    Mickey Mouse. Tinker Bell. Cinderella. What would childhood be like without the magic of Disney? When kids (and
let's be honest, adults, too) want to go to "the" theme park,
they're heading to Disney. Here you're walking amid people from around the world and meeting characters like
Snow White and Donald Duck while rides whirl nonstop
and the irrepressible "It's a Small World" tune and lyrics run
through your head. You can't help but believe dreams really
do come true here.

The secret to enjoying Disney is to have a good plan and the flexibility to
take detours when magical moments occur. You probably can persuade
your children to rush to the big-deal rides early in the morning when
timing matters most, but don't expect them to keep up that pace all day.

Cushion your itinerary with extra time so that kids can pause when
the spirit moves them. Let your motto be "quality over quantity." It's
better to tour the parks in a relaxed fashion. Why disappoint your little
ones by passing up the chance to hobnob with Princess Jasmine in your
hurry to get to Pirates of the Caribbean—only to find a 30-minute wait
at the ride entrance.

It's also important that your kids are involved in the vacation planning
and are aware of the need for a park strategy. Let each family member
choose one or two top rides or attractions for each park. Everything else
should be icing on the cake. Run through the plan before you enter the
park; if children know ahead of time that souvenirs are limited to one
per person and that ice-cream snacks come after lunch, they're likely
to be more patient than if they're clueless about your plans and dazzled
by every merchandise cart they encounter.

## DID YOU KNOW?

The quintessential Dis-
ney icon, the Cinderella
Castle, was inspired by the
palace built by the mad
Bavarian king Ludwig II at
Neuschwanstein. At 180
feet, it's 100 feet taller than
Disneyland's Sleeping Beauty
Castle.

# THE MAGIC KINGDOM
## ENTER A FAIRY TALE

The Magic Kingdom is the heart and soul of the Walt Disney World empire. It was the first Disney outpost in Florida when it opened in 1971, and it's the park that launched Disney's presence in France, Japan, and Hong Kong.

For a landmark that wields such worldwide influence, the 142-acre Magic Kingdom may seem small—indeed, Epcot is more than double the size of the Magic Kingdom, and Animal Kingdom is almost triple the size when including the park's expansive animal habitats. But looks can be deceiving. Packed into six different "lands" are nearly 50 major crowd pleasers and that's not counting all the ancillary attractions: shops, eateries, live entertainment, character meet-and-greet spots, fireworks shows, and parades. Many rides are geared to the young, but the Magic Kingdom is anything but a kiddie park. The degree of detail, the greater vision, the surprisingly witty spiel of the guides, and the tongue-in-cheek signs that crop up in the oddest places—"Prince" and "Princess" restrooms in Fantasyland, for instance—all contribute to a delightful sense of discovery.

## GETTING ORIENTED

The park is laid out on a north–south axis, with Cinderella Castle at the center and the various lands surrounding it in a broad circle.

As you pass underneath the railroad tracks, symbolically leaving behind the world of reality and entering a world of fantasy, you'll immediately notice the adorable buildings lining Town Square and Main Street, U.S.A., which runs due north and ends at the Hub (also called Central Plaza), in front of Cinderella Castle. If you're lost or have questions, cast members are available at almost every turn to help you.

## TOP ATTRACTIONS

### FOR AGES 7 AND UP

**Big Thunder Mountain Railroad.** An Old West–theme, classic coaster that's not too scary; it's just a really good, bumpy, swervy thrill.

**Buzz Lightyear's Space Ranger Spin.** A shoot-'em-up ride where space ranger wannabes compete for the highest score.

**Mickey's PhilharMagic.** The only 3-D film experience at Disney that features the main Disney characters and movie theme songs.

**Space Mountain.** The Magic Kingdom's scariest ride, recently renovated, zips you along the tracks in near-total darkness except for the stars.

**Splash Mountain.** A long, tame boat ride ends in a 52½-foot flume drop into a very wet briar patch.

**Haunted Mansion.** With its razzle-dazzle special effects, this classic is always a frightful hoot.

### FOR AGES 6 AND UNDER

**Dumbo the Flying Elephant.** The elephant ears get them every time—get in line very early or try later in the day.

**The Magic Carpets of Aladdin.** On this must-do for preschoolers you can make your carpet go up and down to avoid water spurts as mischievous camels spit at you.

**The Many Adventures of Winnie the Pooh.** Hang onto your honey pot as you get whisked along on a windy-day adventure with Pooh, Tigger, Eeyore, and friends.

**Pirates of the Caribbean.** Don't miss this family cruise through pirate territory, especially if you're a fan of the movies.

**Country Bear Jamboree.** Little ones may erupt in fits of giggles when these down-home bears break out their fiddles and "sing it" from the heart.

## VISITING TIPS

■ Try to come toward the end of the week, because most families hit the Magic Kingdom early in a visit.

■ Ride a star attraction during a parade; lines ease considerably. (But be careful not to get stuck on the wrong side of the parade route when it starts, or you may never get across.)

■ At City Hall, near the park's Town Square entrance, pick up a guide map and a *Times Guide*, which lists showtimes, character-greeting times, and hours for attractions and restaurants.

■ Book character meals early. Main Street, U.S.A.'s the Crystal Palace, A Buffet with Character has breakfast, lunch, and dinner with Winnie the Pooh, Tigger, and friends. All three meals at the Fairy Tale Dining experience in Cinderella Castle are extremely popular—so much so that you should reserve your spot six months out. At a Wonderland Tea Party weekday afternoons in the Grand Floridian Resort, kids can interact with Alice and help decorate (and eat) cupcakes.

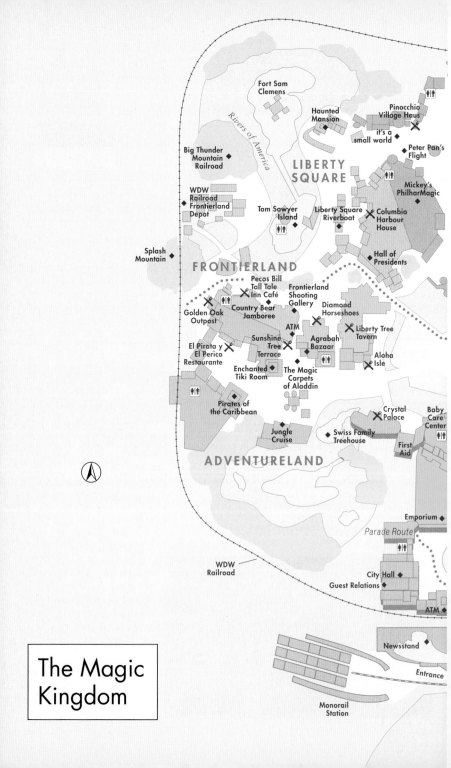

Fort Sam
Clemens

Haunted
Mansion

Pinocchio
Village Haus

it's a
small world

Peter Pan's
Flight

Big Thunder
Mountain
Railroad

**LIBERTY
SQUARE**

Mickey's
PhilharMagic

WDW
Railroad
Frontierland
Depot

Tom Sawyer
Island

Liberty Square
Riverboat

Columbia
Harbour
House

Splash
Mountain

**FRONTIERLAND**

Hall of
Presidents

Pecos Bill
Tall Tale
Inn Café

Frontierland
Shooting
Gallery

Golden Oak
Outpost

Country Bear
Jamboree

Diamond
Horseshoes

ATM

Liberty Tree
Tavern

El Pirata y
El Perico
Restaurante

Sunshine
Tree
Terrace

Agrabah
Bazaar

Enchanted
Tiki Room

The Magic
Carpets
of Aladdin

Aloha
Isle

Pirates of
the Caribbean

Jungle
Cruise

Swiss Family
Treehouse

Crystal
Palace

Baby
Care
Center

First
Aid

**ADVENTURELAND**

Emporium

*Parade Route*

WDW
Railroad

City Hall

Guest Relations

ATM

Newsstand

Entrance

# The Magic
Kingdom

Monorail
Station

*Rivers of America*

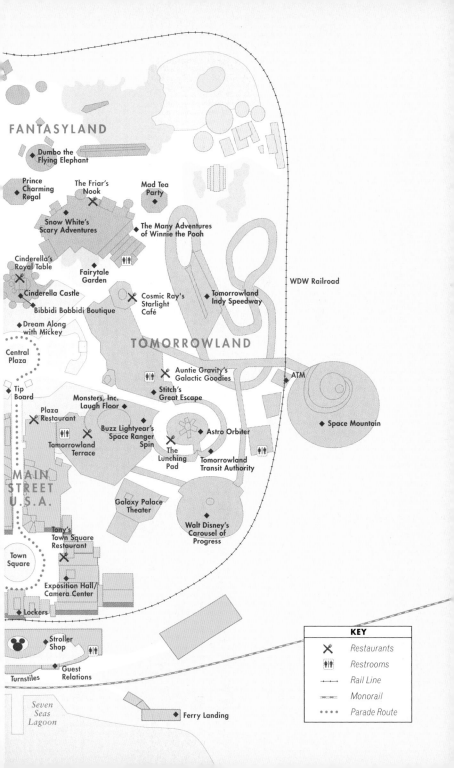

**FANTASYLAND**

◆ Dumbo the Flying Elephant

◆ Prince Charming Regal

The Friar's Nook ✖

Mad Tea Party ◆

Snow White's Scary Adventures

◆ The Many Adventures of Winnie the Pooh

🚻

Cinderella's Royal Table ✖

Fairytale Garden

◆ Cinderella Castle

✖ Cosmic Ray's Starlight Café

◆ Tomorrowland Indy Speedway

Bibbidi Bobbidi Boutique

**WDW Railroad**

◆ Dream Along with Mickey

Central Plaza

**TOMORROWLAND**

🚻 ✖ Auntie Gravity's Galactic Goodies

◆ ATM

◆ Tip Board

◆ Stitch's Great Escape

✖ Plaza Restaurant

Monsters, Inc. Laugh Floor ◆

🚻 ✖ Tomorrowland Terrace

◆ Buzz Lightyear's Space Ranger Spin

❋

◆ Astro Orbiter

◆ Space Mountain

The Lunching Pad

🚻

**MAIN STREET U.S.A.**

◆ Tomorrowland Transit Authority

Galaxy Palace Theater

◆ Tony's Town Square Restaurant ✖

Walt Disney's Carousel of Progress

Town Square

◆ Exposition Hall/Camera Center

◆ Lockers

◆ Stroller Shop 🚻

◆ Guest Relations

Turnstiles

*Seven Seas Lagoon*

◆ Ferry Landing

| KEY | |
|---|---|
| ✖ | *Restaurants* |
| 🚻 | *Restrooms* |
| —•— | *Rail Line* |
| ▬▬ | *Monorail* |
| •••• | *Parade Route* |

# MAGIC KINGDOM

| NAME | Height Req. | Type of Entertainment | Duration | Crowds | Audience | Tips |
|---|---|---|---|---|---|---|
| **Adventureland** | | | | | | |
| Enchanted Tiki Room | n/a | Show | 12 mins. | Light | All Ages | Come when you need a refresher in a/c. |
| Jungle Cruise | n/a | Cruise | 10 mins. | Heavy | All Ages | Use Fastpass or come during the parade. |
| The Magic Carpets of Aladdin | n/a | Thrill Ride for Kids | 3 mins. | Heavy | All Ages | Visit while waiting for Frontierland Fastpass appointment. |
| Pirates of the Caribbean | n/a | Cruise | 10 mins. | Moderate | All Ages | A good destination in the heat of the afternoon. |
| Swiss Family Treehouse | n/a | Walk-through | Up to you | Moderate | All Ages | Visit while waiting for Jungle Cruise Fastpass. |
| **Fantasyland** | | | | | | |
| Dumbo the Flying Elephant | n/a | Thrill Ride for Kids | 2 mins. | Moderate to Heavy | Small Kids | Come at rope drop. No shade in afternoon. |
| it's a small world | n/a | Cruise | 11 mins. | Moderate | All Ages | Tots may beg for a repeat ride; it's worth it. |
| Mad Tea Party | n/a | Thrill Ride for Kids | 2 mins. | Moderate | Small Kids | Come in the early morning. Skip it if wait is 30 mins. |
| ★ The Many Adventures of Winnie the Pooh | n/a | Thrill Ride for Kids | 3½ mins. | Heavy | All Ages | Use Fastpass. Come early, late in the afternoon, or after dark. |
| ★ Mickey's PhilharMagic | n/a | 3-D Film | 12 mins. | Heavy | All but Small Kids | Use Fastpass or arrive early or during a parade. |
| Peter Pan's Flight | n/a | Thrill Ride for Kids | 2½ mins. | Heavy | All Ages | Try evening or early morning. Use Fastpass first. |
| Prince Charming Regal Carrousel | n/a | Thrill Ride for Kids | 2 mins. | Moderate to Heavy | Families | Come while waiting for Peter Pan's Flight Fastpass, during afternoon parade, or after dark. |
| Snow White's Scary Adventures | n/a | Thrill Ride for Kids | 3 mins. | Moderate to Heavy | All Ages | Come very early, during the afternoon parade, or after dark. May scare toddlers and pre-schoolers. |
| **Frontierland** | | | | | | |
| ★ Big Thunder Mountain Railroad | At least 40" | Thrill Ride | 4 mins. | Absolutely! | All but Small Kids | Use Fastpass. Most exciting at night when you can't anticipate the curves. |
| Country Bear Jamboree | n/a | Show | 17 mins. | Heavy | All Ages | Visit before 11 am. Stand to the far left lining up for the front rows. |
| ★ Splash Mountain | At least 40" | Thrill Ride with Water | 11 mins. | Yes! | All but Small Kids | Use Fastpass. Get in line by 9:45 am, or ride during meal or parade time. You may get wet. |

| | n/a | Playground | Up to you | Light | Kids and Tweens | |
| --- | --- | --- | --- | --- | --- | --- |
| Tom Sawyer Island | n/a | Playground | Up to you | Light | Kids and Tweens | Afternoon refresher. It's hard to keep track of toddlers here. |
| **Liberty Square** | | | | | | |
| Hall of Presidents | n/a | Show/Film | 25 mins. | Moderate | All but Small Kids | Come in the morning or during the parade. |
| ★ Haunted Mansion | n/a | Thrill Ride | 8 mins. | Moderate | All Ages | Nighttime adds extra fear factor. |
| Liberty Square Riverboat | n/a | Cruise | 15 mins. | Light to Moderate | All Ages | Good for a break from the crowds. |
| **Main Street U.S.A.** | | | | | | |
| Walt Disney World Railroad | n/a | Railroad | 21 mins. | Moderate to Heavy | All Ages | Board with small children for an early start in Toontown or hop on midafternoon. |
| **Tomorrowland** | | | | | | |
| Astro-Orbiter | n/a | Thrill Ride for Kids | 2 mins. | Moderate to Heavy | All Ages | Skip unless there's a short line. |
| ★ Buzz Lightyear's Space Ranger Spin | n/a | Interactive Exp. | 5 mins. | Heavy | All Ages | Come in the early morning and use Fastpass. Kids will want more than one ride. |
| Monster's Inc. Laugh Floor | n/a | Film | 15 mins. | Moderate to Heavy | All Ages | Come when you're waiting for your Buzz Lightyear or Space Mountain Fastpass. |
| ★ Space Mountain | At least 44" | Thrill Ride | 2½ mins. | You Bet! | All but Small Kids | Use Fastpass, or come at the beginning or the end of day or during a parade. |
| Stitch's Great Escape | At least 40" | Simulator Exp. | 20 mins. | Moderate to Heavy | All but Small Kids | Use Fastpass. Visit early after Space Mountain, Splash Mountain, Big Thunder Mountain, or during a parade. |
| Tomorrowland Indy Speedway | 54" to drive | Thrill Ride for Kids | 5 mins. | Moderate | All but Small Kids | Come in the evening or during a parade; skip on a first-time visit; 32" height requirement to ride shotgun. |
| Tomorrowland Transit Authority PeopleMover | n/a | Railroad | 10 mins. | Light | All Ages | Come with young kids if you need a restful ride. |
| Walt Disney's Carousel of Progress | n/a | Show | 20 mins. | Light to Moderate | All Ages | Skip on a first-time visit unless you're heavily into nostalgia. |

★ FodorsChoice

# EPCOT
## TRAVEL THE GLOBE

Nowhere but at Epcot can you explore and experience the native food, entertainment, culture, and arts and crafts of countries in Europe, Asia, North Africa, and the Americas. What's more, employees at the World Showcase pavilions actually hail from the countries the pavilions represent.

Epcot, or "Experimental Prototype Community of Tomorrow," was the original inspiration for Walt Disney World. Walt envisioned a future in which nations coexisted in peace and harmony, reaping the miraculous harvest of technological achievement. The Epcot of today is both more and less than his original dream. Less, because the World Showcase presents views of its countries that are, as an Epcot guide once put it, "as Americans perceive them"—highly idealized. But this is a minor quibble in the face of the major achievement: Epcot is that rare paradox—a successful educational theme park that excels at entertainment, too.

## EPCOT BY BOAT

Epcot is a big place at 305 acres; a local joke suggests that the acronym actually stands for "Every Person Comes Out Tired." But still, the most efficient way to get around is to walk.

To vary things, you can cruise across the lagoon in an air-conditioned, 65-foot water taxi; they depart every 12 minutes from two World Showcase Plaza docks at the border of Future World.

The boat closer to Mexico zips to a dock by the Germany pavilion; the one closer to Canada heads to Morocco. You may have to stand in line to board, however.

## GETTING ORIENTED

Epcot is composed of two areas: Future World and the World Showcase. The inner core of Future World's pavilions has the Spaceship Earth geosphere and a plaza anchored by the computer-animated Fountain of Nations. Bracketing it are the crescent-shaped Innoventions East and West, with hands-on, high-tech exhibits, and immersion entertainment.

Six pavilions compose Future World's outer ring. Each of the three east pavilions has a ride and the occasional post-ride showcase; a visit rarely takes more than 30 minutes. The blockbuster exhibits on the west side contain rides and interactive displays; each exhibit can take up to 90 minutes for the complete experience.

World Showcase pavilions are on the promenade that circles the World Showcase Lagoon. Each houses shops, restaurants, and friendly foreign staffers; some have films or displays. Mexico and Norway offer tame rides. Live entertainment is scheduled at every pavilion except Norway.

## TOP ATTRACTIONS

**Soarin'.** Everyone's hands-down favorite: feel the sweet breeze as you "hang glide" over California landscapes.

**The American Adventure.** Many adults and older children love this patriotic look at American history; who can resist the Audio-Animatronics hosts, Ben Franklin and Mark Twain?

**IllumiNations.** This amazing musical laser-fountains-and-fireworks show is Disney nighttime entertainment at its best.

**Mission: SPACE.** Blast off on a simulated ride to Mars, if you can handle the turbulence.

**Test Track.** Your car revs up to 60 mph on a hairpin turn in this wild ride on a General Motors proving ground.

## MIND GAMES

Although several attractions provide high-octane kicks, Epcot's thrills are mostly for the mind. The park is best for school-age children and adults, but there's interactive entertainment for everyone at Innoventions. And most attractions provide some diversions for preschool children. At the 10 or so **Kidcot Fun Stops**, younger children can try their hands at crafts projects—like designing a mask and adding special touches at each pavilion along the way.

## VISITING TIPS

■ Epcot is so vast and varied you really need two days to explore. With just one day, you'll have to be highly selective.

■ Go early in the week, when others are at Magic Kingdom.

■ If you like a good festival, visit during the International Flower & Garden Festival (early to mid-March through May) or the International Food & Wine Festival (late September through mid-November).

# Epcot

## WORLD SHOWCASE

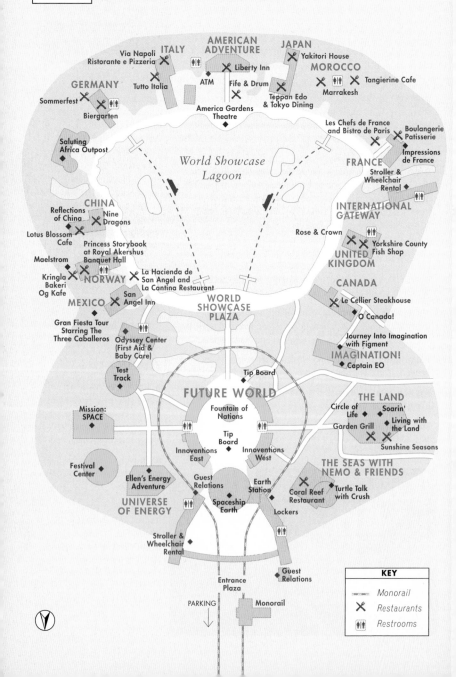

ITALY
Via Napoli
Ristorante e Pizzeria
Tutto Italia

AMERICAN ADVENTURE
ATM
Liberty Inn
Fife & Drum
America Gardens Theatre

JAPAN
Yakitori House
MOROCCO
Teppan Edo & Tokyo Dining
Marrakesh
Tangierine Cafe

GERMANY
Sommerfest
Biergarten

Saluting Africa Outpost

World Showcase Lagoon

FRANCE
Les Chefs de France and Bistro de Paris
Boulangerie Patisserie
Impressions de France
Stroller & Wheelchair Rental

CHINA
Reflections of China
Nine Dragons
Lotus Blossom Cafe
Princess Storybook at Royal Akershus Banquet Hall
Maelstrom
Kringla Bakeri Og Kafe
NORWAY
La Hacienda de San Angel and La Cantina Restaurant

INTERNATIONAL GATEWAY
Rose & Crown
Yorkshire County Fish Shop
UNITED KINGDOM

MEXICO
San Angel Inn
Gran Fiesta Tour Starring The Three Caballeros
Odyssey Center (First Aid & Baby Care)

CANADA
Le Cellier Steakhouse
O Canada!

WORLD SHOWCASE PLAZA

Journey Into Imagination with Figment
IMAGINATION!
Captain EO

Test Track

Tip Board

FUTURE WORLD
Fountain of Nations
Tip Board

THE LAND
Circle of Life
Soarin'
Garden Grill
Living with the Land
Sunshine Seasons

Mission: SPACE

Innoventions East
Innoventions West

THE SEAS WITH NEMO & FRIENDS
Coral Reef Restaurant
Turtle Talk with Crush

Festival Center

Ellen's Energy Adventure
Guest Relations
Earth Station

UNIVERSE OF ENERGY
Spaceship Earth
Lockers

Stroller & Wheelchair Rental

Guest Relations

Entrance Plaza
PARKING
Monorail

**DID YOU KNOW?**

Walt Disney's original conception for the Epcot Center—as a sort of futuristic master-planned community—didn't quite pan out in the park but instead took form in the town of Celebration, near Kissimmee.

## Future World

| NAME | Height Req. | Type of Entertainment | Duration | Crowds | Audience | Tips |
|---|---|---|---|---|---|---|
| Captain EO (Imagination!) | n/a | 3-D Film | 14 mins. | Moderate to Heavy | All Ages | Come in the early morning or just before closing. Take off the 3-D glasses if little kids get scared. |
| The Circle of Life (The Land) | n/a | Film | 20 mins. | Moderate to Heavy | All but Small Kids | Come early or for your toddler's afternoon nap. |
| Ellen's Energy Adventure (Universe of Energy) | n/a | Ride-Through | 45 mins. | Moderate | All Ages | Best seats are to the far left and front of the theater. |
| Innoventions | n/a | Walk-Through | Up to you | Moderate to Heavy | All Ages | Come before 11 am or after 2 pm. |
| Journey into Imagination with Figment (Imagination!) | n/a | Ride-Through | 8 mins. | Light | Small Kids | Ride while waiting for Captain EO Fastpass. Warn toddlers about darkness at the end of the ride. |
| Living with the Land (The Land) | n/a | Cruise | 14 mins. | Moderate | All but Small Kids | The line moves quickly, so come anytime. |
| ★ Mission: SPACE | At least 44" | Thrill Ride | 4 mins. | You Bet! | All but Small Kids | Come before 10 am or use Fastpass. Don't ride on a full stomach. |
| The Seas with Nemo & Friends | n/a | Ride- and Walk-Through | Up to you | Moderate to Heavy | Small Kids | Get Nemo fans here early in the morning. |

| Name | | Type | Duration | Crowds | Audience | Strategy |
|---|---|---|---|---|---|---|
| ★ Soarin' (The Land) | At least 40" | Simulator Ride | 5 mins. | Heavy | All but Small Kids | Use Fastpass, or come early, or just before closing. |
| Spaceship Earth | n/a | Ride-Through | 15 mins. | Moderate to Heavy | All Ages | Ride while waiting for Mission: SPACE Fastpass appointment or just before closing. |
| ★ Test Track | At least 40" | Thrill Ride | 5 mins. | Heavy | All but Small Kids | Come in morning with Fastpass. The ride can't function on wet tracks, so don't come after a downpour. |

## World Showcase

| Name | | Type | Duration | Crowds | Audience | Strategy |
|---|---|---|---|---|---|---|
| ★ The American Adventure Show | n/a | Show/Film | 20 mins. | Heavy | All Ages | Arrive 10 mins. before the Voices of Liberty or the Spirit of America Fife & Drum Corps are slated to perform. |
| America Gardens Theatre | n/a | Live Show | Varies | Varies | Varies | Arrive an hour or so ahead of time for holiday and celebrity performances. |
| Gran Fiesta Tour Starring the Three Caballeros | n/a | Cruise | 9 mins. | Moderate to Heavy | All Ages | Especially good if you have small children. |
| Impressions de France | n/a | Film | 20 mins. | Moderate | All but Small Kids | Come after dinner. |
| Maelstrom | n/a | Thrill Ride for Kids with Water | 10 mins. | Moderate to Heavy | All Ages | Use Fastpass for after lunch or dinner. |
| O Canada! | n/a | Film | 14 mins. | Moderate to Heavy | All Ages | Come when World Showcase opens or in the evening. No strollers permitted. |
| Reflections of China | n/a | Film | 14 mins. | Moderate | All Ages | Come anytime. No strollers permitted. |

★ Fodor's Choice

# HOLLYWOOD STUDIOS
## MAKE MOVIE MAGIC

Disney's Hollywood Studios were designed to be a trip back to Tinseltown's Golden Age, when Hedda Hopper, not tabloids, spread celebrity gossip and when the girl off the bus from Ohio could be the next Judy Garland.

The result is a theme park that blends movie-production capabilities and high-tech wonders with breathtaking rides and nostalgia. The park's old-time Hollywood ambience begins with a rosy-hue view of the movie-making business presented in a dreamy stage set from the 1930s and '40s, amid sleek Art Moderne buildings in pastel colors, funky diners, kitschy decorations, and sculptured gardens populated by roving actors playing, well, roving actors. There are also casting directors, gossip columnists, and other colorful characters.

Thanks to a rich library of film scores, the park is permeated with music, all familiar, all evoking the magic of the movies, and all constantly streaming from the camouflaged loudspeakers at a volume just right for humming along. The park icon, a 122-foot-high Sorcerer Mickey Hat that serves as a gift shop and Disney pin-trading station, towers over Hollywood Boulevard.

## WELCOME TO THE 'HOODS

The park is divided into sightseeing clusters. **Hollywood Boulevard** is the main artery to the heart of the park, and is where you find the glistening replica of Graumann's Chinese Theater.

Encircling it are **Sunset Boulevard**, the **Animation Courtyard, Mickey Avenue, Pixar Place, Commissary Lane**, the **Streets of America** area, and **Echo Lake**.

The entire park is 135 acres, and has just 20 major attractions (compared with Magic Kingdom's 40-plus). It's small enough to cover in a day and even repeat a favorite ride or two.

## TOP ATTRACTIONS

### FOR AGES 8 AND UP

**Twilight Zone Tower of Terror.** The TV classic theming of this free-fall "elevator" screamer is meticulous.

**Indiana Jones Epic Stunt Spectacular!** The show's Indy double and supporting cast reenact *Raiders of the Lost Ark* scenes with panache.

**Toy Story Midway Mania!** 3-D glasses? Check. Spring-action shooter? Check. Ride and shoot your way through with Buzz, Woody, and others.

**Star Tours.** Prepare for a high-speed chase on this updated simulator thrill ride through the *Star Wars* galaxy.

**Rock 'n' Roller Coaster Starring Aerosmith.** Blast off to rockin' tunes on a high-speed, hard-core coaster.

**The American Idol Experience.** If you don't get chosen to test your pipes, you can vote for your favorite Idol wannabe.

### FOR AGES 7 AND UNDER

**Beauty and the Beast—Live on Stage.** Memorable music, talented performers, dancing kitchen objects, and a fairy-tale ending make this a must-see show.

**Disney Junior—Live on Stage!** The preschool crowd can't get enough of the characters here from Disney Channel shows like *Jake and the Never Land Pirates, Mickey Mouse Clubhouse* and *Little Einsteins.*

**Honey I Shrunk the Kids Movie Set Adventure.** Youngsters love to romp among the giant blades of grass and bugs at this imaginative playground.

**MuppetVision 3-D.** Children (and most adults) shriek with laughter during this 3-D movie involving Kermit, Miss Piggy, and other lovable Muppets.

### VISITING TIPS

■ Visit early in the week, when most people are at Magic Kingdom and Animal Kingdom.

■ Check the Tip Board periodically for attractions with short wait times to visit between Fastpass appointments.

■ Be at the Fantasmic! amphitheater at least an hour before showtime if you didn't book the dinner package.

■ Need a burst of energy? On-the-run hunger pangs? Grab a slice at Pizza Planet Arcade at **Streets of America**. Alternatively, **Hollywood Scoops Ice Cream** on Sunset is the place to be on a hot day.

■ If you're planning on a fast-food lunch, eat before 11 am or after 2:30 pm. There are quick-bite spots are all over the park and several stands along Sunset. Get a burger (meat or veggie) or chicken strips at **Rosie's All-American Cafe**, a slice of pizza from **Catalina Eddie's**, or a hunk of smoked bird at **Toluca Legs Turkey Co.**

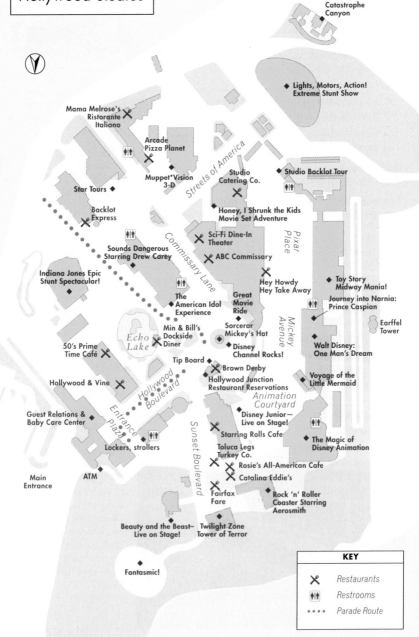

# Disney's Hollywood Studios

Catastrophe Canyon

Lights, Motors, Action! Extreme Stunt Show

Mama Melrose's Ristorante Italiano

Arcade Pizza Planet

Studio Catering Co.

Studio Backlot Tour

Muppet*Vision 3-D

Streets of America

Star Tours

Honey, I Shrunk the Kids Movie Set Adventure

Backlot Express

Pixar Place

Sci-Fi Dine-In Theater

Sounds Dangerous Starring Drew Carey

ABC Commissary

Indiana Jones Epic Stunt Spectacular!

Commissary Lane

Hey Howdy Hey Take Away

Toy Story Midway Mania!

Journey into Narnia: Prince Caspian

The American Idol Experience

Great Movie Ride

Earffel Tower

Sorceror Mickey's Hat

Walt Disney: One Man's Dream

Min & Bill's Dockside Diner

Mickey Avenue

Echo Lake

Disney Channel Rocks!

50's Prime Time Café

Tip Board

Voyage of the Little Mermaid

Brown Derby

Hollywood & Vine

Hollywood Junction Restaurant Reservations

Animation Courtyard

Hollywood Boulevard

Disney Junior— Live on Stage!

Guest Relations & Baby Care Center

Entrance Plaza

Starring Rolls Cafe

The Magic of Disney Animation

Lockers, strollers

Toluca Legs Turkey Co.

Sunset Boulevard

Rosie's All-American Cafe

Main Entrance

ATM

Catalina Eddie's

Fairfax Fare

Rock 'n' Roller Coaster Starring Aerosmith

Beauty and the Beast— Live on Stage!

Twilight Zone Tower of Terror

Fantasmic!

| KEY | |
|---|---|
| ✕ | *Restaurants* |
| 🚻 | *Restrooms* |
| •••• | *Parade Route* |

# DISNEY'S HOLLYWOOD STUDIOS

| NAME | Height Req. | Type of Entertainment | Duration | Crowds | Audience | Tips |
|------|-------------|----------------------|----------|--------|----------|------|
| **Animation Courtyard** | | | | | | |
| Disney Junior—Live on Stage! | n/a | Show | 22 mins. | Moderate to Heavy | Small Kids | Come first thing in the morning, when your child is most alert and lines are shorter. |
| The Magic of Disney Animation | n/a | Tour | 15+ mins. | Moderate | All Ages | Come in the morning or late afternoon. Toddlers may get bored. |
| Voyage of the Little Mermaid | n/a | Show | 17 mins. | Heavy | All Ages | Come first thing in the morning. Otherwise, wait until after 5. |
| **Echo Lake** | | | | | | |
| The American Idol Experience | n/a | Show | 25 mins./ 45 mins. | Yes! | All but Small Kids | Check *Times Guide*, for showtimes. Arrive at least 30 minutes early for seats inside the theater. |
| Indiana Jones Epic Stunt Spectacular! | n/a | Show | 30 mins. | Moderate to Heavy | All but Small Kids | Come at night, when the idol's eyes glow. Sit up front to feel the heat of a truck on fire. |
| Sounds Dangerous Starring Drew Carey | n/a | Show | 12 mins. | Moderate | All but Small Kids | Arrive 15 minutes before show. You sit in total darkness. |
| Star Tours 3-D | At least 40" | Simulator Exp. | 5 mins. | Heavy | All but Small Kids | Come before closing, early morning, or get a Fastpass. Keep to the left in line for the best seats. |
| **Hollywood Boulevard** | | | | | | |
| Great Movie Ride | n/a | Ride/Tour | 22 mins. | Moderate | All but Small Kids | Come while waiting for Fastpass appointment. Lines out the door mean 25-min. wait—or longer. |

## Mickey Avenue

| Name | Height | Type | Duration | Crowds | Audience | Comments |
|---|---|---|---|---|---|---|
| Journey Into Narnia: Prince Caspian | n/a | Walk-Through/Film | 15 mins. | Light | All but Small Kids | Come while waiting for Fastpass appointment. |
| Walt Disney: One Man's Dream | n/a | Walk-Through/Film | 20+ mins. | Light to Moderate | All but Small Kids | See this attraction while waiting for a Fastpass appointment. |

## Pixar Place

| Name | Height | Type | Duration | Crowds | Audience | Comments |
|---|---|---|---|---|---|---|
| Toy Story Midway Mania! | n/a | Interactive Ride | 7 mins. | Heavy | All Ages | Come early; use Fastpass. |

## Streets of America

| Name | Height | Type | Duration | Crowds | Audience | Comments |
|---|---|---|---|---|---|---|
| Honey, I Shrunk the Kids Movie Set Adventure | n/a | Playground | Up to you | Moderate | Small Kids | Come after you've done several shows and your kids need to cut loose. Keep an eye on toddlers who can quickly get lost in the caves and slides. |
| Lights, Motors, Action! Extreme Stunt Show | n/a | Show | 33 mins. | Heavy | All but Small Kids | For the best seats, line up for the show while others are lining up for the parade. |
| Muppet*Vision 3-D | n/a | 3-D Film | 25 mins. | Moderate to Heavy | All Ages | Arrive 10 mins. early. And don't worry—there are no bad seats. |
| Studio Backlot Tour | n/a | Tour | 35 mins. | Moderate | All but Small Kids | People sitting on the left can get wet. Come early; it closes at dusk. |

## Sunset Boulevard

| Name | Height | Type | Duration | Crowds | Audience | Comments |
|---|---|---|---|---|---|---|
| Beauty and the Beast— Live on Stage! | n/a | Show | 30 mins. | Moderate to Heavy | All Ages | Come 30 mins. before showtime for good seats. Performance days vary, so check ahead. |
| ★ Rock 'n' Roller Coaster Starring Aerosmith | At least 48" | Thrill Ride | 1 min., 22 secs. | Huge | All but Small Kids | Ride early, then use Fastpass for another go later. |
| ★ Twilight Zone Tower of Terror | At least 40" | Thrill Ride | 10 mins. | You Bet! | All but Small Kids | Use Fastpass. Come early or late evening. |

★ Fodor's Choice

# ANIMAL KINGDOM
## GO ON SAFARI

Disney's Animal Kingdom explores the stories of all animals—real, imaginary, and extinct. Enter through the Oasis, where you hear exotic background music and find yourself surrounded by gentle waterfalls and gardens alive with exotic birds, reptiles, and mammals.

At 403 acres and several times the size of the Magic Kingdom, Animal Kingdom is the largest in area of all Disney theme parks. Animal habitats take up much of that acreage. Creatures here thrive in careful re-creations of landscapes from Asia and Africa. Throughout the park, you'll also learn about conservation in a low-key way.

Amid all the nature are thrill rides, a 3-D show (housed in the "root system" of the iconic Tree of Life), two first-rate musicals, and character meet and greets. Cast members are as likely to hail from Kenya or South Africa as they are from Kentucky or South Carolina. It's all part of the charm.

### GETTING ORIENTED

Animal Kingdom's hub is the Tree of Life, in the middle of Discovery Island. The park's lands, each with a distinct personality, radiate from Discovery Island.

To the southwest is Camp Minnie-Mickey, a character-greeting location and live-show area. North of the hub is Africa, where Kilimanjaro Safaris travel across extensive savanna. In the northeast corner is Rafiki's Planet Watch with conservation activities.

Asia, with thrills like Expedition Everest and Kali River Rapids, is east of the hub, and DinoLand U.S.A. brings T. rex and other prehistoric creatures to life in the park's southeast corner.

## TOP ATTRACTIONS

### DISCOVERY ISLAND
**Tree of Life—It's Tough to Be a Bug!** This clever and very funny 3-D movie starring Flik from the Disney film *A Bug's Life* is full of surprises, including "shocking" special effects. Some kids under 7 are scared of the loud noises.

### AFRICA
**Kilimanjaro Safaris.** You're guaranteed to see dozens of wild animals, including giraffes, zebras, hippos, rhinos, and elephants, living in authentic, re-created African habitats. If you're lucky, the lions and cheetahs will be stirring, too.

### ASIA
**Expedition Everest.** This roller coaster is a spine-tingling trip into the snowy Himalayas to find the abominable snowman. It's best reserved for brave riders 7 and up.

### CAMP MINNIE-MICKEY
**Festival of the Lion King.** Singers and dancers dressed in fantastic costumes representing many wild animals perform uplifting dance and acrobatics numbers and interact with children in the audience.

### DINOLAND, U.S.A.
**DINOSAUR.** Extremely lifelike giant dinosaurs jump out as your vehicle swoops and dips. We recommend it for fearless kids 8 and up.

**Finding Nemo—The Musical.** Don't miss a performance of this outstanding musical starring the most charming, colorful characters ever to swim their way into your heart.

### TOUR
**TourWild Africa Trek.** The price tag is hefty, but this behind-the-scenes wild-animal adventure is a memory maker.

## VISITING TIPS

■ Try to visit during the week. Pedestrian areas are compact, and the park can feel uncomfortably packed on weekends.

■ Plan on a full day here. That way, while exploring Africa's Pangani Forest Exploration Trail, say, you can spend 10 minutes (rather than just two) watching vigilant meerkats stand sentry or tracking a mama gorilla as she cares for her infant.

■ Arrive a half hour before the park opens as much to see the wild animals at their friskiest (morning is a good time to do the safari ride) as to get a jump on the crowds.

■ For updates on line lengths, check the Tip Board, just after crossing the bridge into Discovery Island.

■ Good places to rendezvous include the outdoor seating area of Tusker House restaurant in Africa, in front of DinoLand U.S.A.'s Boneyard, and at the entrance to Festival of the Lion King at Camp Minnie-Mickey.

**5**

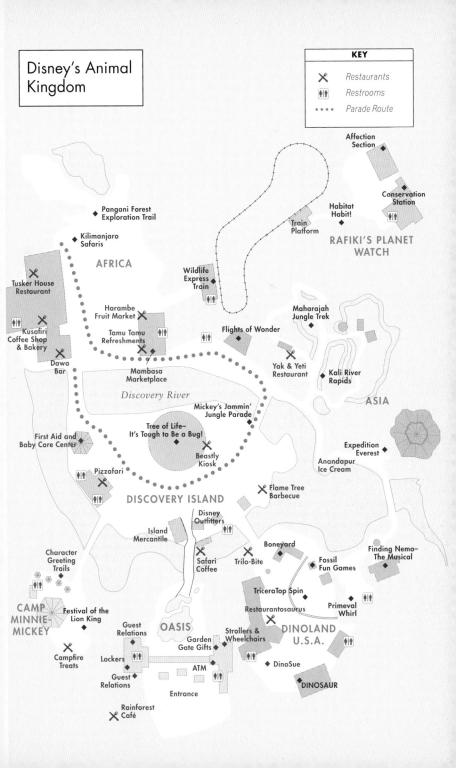

# Disney's Animal Kingdom

**KEY**

✗ Restaurants
🚹🚺 Restrooms
• • • • Parade Route

Affection Section

Conservation Station

Pangani Forest Exploration Trail

Habitat Habit!

Train Platform

**RAFIKI'S PLANET WATCH**

Kilimanjaro Safaris

**AFRICA**

Wildlife Express Train

Tusker House Restaurant

Maharajah Jungle Trek

Harambe Fruit Market

Flights of Wonder

Kusafiri Coffee Shop & Bakery

Tamu Tamu Refreshments

Yak & Yeti Restaurant

Kali River Rapids

Dawa Bar

Mombasa Marketplace

*Discovery River*

**ASIA**

Mickey's Jammin' Jungle Parade

First Aid and Baby Care Center

Tree of Life— It's Tough To Be a Bug!

Expedition Everest

Beastly Kiosk

Anandapur Ice Cream

Pizzafari

Flame Tree Barbecue

**DISCOVERY ISLAND**

Disney Outfitters

Island Mercantile

Boneyard

Finding Nemo— The Musical

Character Greeting Trails

Safari Coffee

Trilo-Bite

Fossil Fun Games

TriceraTop Spin

**CAMP MINNIE-MICKEY**

Festival of the Lion King

Restaurantosaurus

Primeval Whirl

Guest Relations

**OASIS**

Garden Gate Gifts

Strollers & Wheelchairs

**DINOLAND U.S.A.**

Campfire Treats

Lockers

Guest Relations

ATM

DinoSue

**DINOSAUR**

Entrance

Rainforest Café

# ANIMAL KINGDOM

| NAME | Height Req. | Type of Entertainment | Duration | Crowds | Audience | Tips |
|------|-------------|----------------------|----------|--------|----------|------|
| **Africa** | | | | | | |
| ★ Kilimanjaro Safaris | n/a | Tour | 20 mins. | Moderate to Heavy | All Ages | Do this first thing in the morning. If you arrive at the park late morning, save it for day's end, when it's not so hot. |
| Pangani Forest Exploration Trail | n/a | Zoo/Aviary | Up to you | Light to Moderate | All Ages | Come while waiting for your safari Fastpass; try to avoid coming at the hottest time of day, when the gorillas like to nap. |
| **Asia** | | | | | | |
| ★ Expedition Everest | At least 44" | Thrill Ride | 2½ mins. | Huge | All but Small Kids | Use Fastpass. This is the park's biggest thrill ride. |
| Flights of Wonder | n/a | Show | 30 mins. | Light | All Ages | Arrive 15 mins. before showtime, and find a shaded seat beneath one of the awnings—the sun can be brutal. |
| Kali River Rapids | At least 38" | Thrill Ride | 7 mins. | Heavy | All but Small Kids | Use your Fastpass or come during the parade. You'll get wet. |
| Maharajah Jungle Trek | n/a | Zoo/Aviary | Up to you | Light to Moderate | All Ages | Come anytime. |
| **Camp Minnie-Mickey** | | | | | | |
| ★ Festival of the Lion King | n/a | Show | 28 mins. | Light | All Ages | Arrive 40 mins. before showtime. Sit in one of the front rows to increase your kid's chance of being chosen. |
| **DinoLand U.S.A.** | | | | | | |
| Boneyard | n/a | Playground | Up to you | Moderate to Heavy | Small Kids | Play here while waiting for DINOSAUR Fastpass, or come late in the day. |

| | | | | | | |
|---|---|---|---|---|---|---|
| DINOSAUR | At least 40" | Thrill Ride | 4 mins. | Heavy | All but Small Kids | Come first thing in the morning or at the end of the day, or use Fastpass. |
| ★ Finding Nemo–The Musical | n/a | Show | 30 mins. | Heavy | All Ages | Arrive 40 mins. before showtime. Take little kids here while big kids wait for Expedition Everest. |
| Fossil Fun Games | n/a | Arcade/Fair | Up to you | Light | All but Small Kids | Bring a pocketful of change and a stash of ones. |
| Primeval Whirl | At least 48" | Thrill Ride | 2½ mins. | Heavy | All Ages | Kids may want to ride twice. Take your first spin early, then use Fastpass if the wait is more than 20 mins. |
| TriceraTop Spin | n/a | Thrill Ride for Kids | 2 mins. | Heavy | Small Kids | Ride early while everyone else heads for the safari or while waiting for your Fastpass appointment for DINOSAUR. |
| **Discovery Island** | | | | | | |
| ★ Tree of Life—It's Tough to Be a Bug! | n/a | 3-D film | 20 mins. | Moderate to Heavy | All but Small Kids | Do this after Kilimanjaro Safaris. Fastpass is available. Small children may be frightened. |
| **Rafiki's Planet Watch** | | | | | | |
| Affection Section | n/a | Petting Yard | Up to you | Light | Families | Pet exotic goats and other rare domesticated animals. |
| Conservation Station | n/a | Walk-Through | Up to you | Light to Moderate | All Ages | Wait for the critter encounter and learn how to protect endangered species. |
| Habitat Habit! | n/a | Trail Walk | Up to you | Light | All Ages | Watch cotton-top tamarins along this discovery trail. |
| Wildlife Express Train | n/a | Train Ride | 5 mins. | Moderate | All Ages | Head straight to Affection Section with little kids to come face-to-face with domesticated critters. |

★ **Fodor's**Choice

# DISNEY WATER PARKS
## RIDE THE WAVES

There's something about a water park that brings out the kid in us, and there's no denying that these are two of the world's best. What sets them apart? It's the same thing that differentiates all Disney parks—the detailed themes.

Whether you're cast away on a balmy island at Typhoon Lagoon or washed up on a ski resort–turned–seaside playground at Blizzard Beach, the landscaping and clever architecture will add to the fun of flume and raft rides, wave pools, and splash areas. Another plus: the vegetation has matured enough to create shade. The Disney water parks give you that lost-in-paradise feeling on top of all those high-speed wedgie-inducing waterslides. They're so popular that crowds often reach overflow capacity in summer.

Your children may like them so much that they'll clamor to visit more than once. If you're going to Disney for five days or more between April and October, add the Water Park Fun & More option to your Magic Your Way ticket. Of course, check the weather to make sure the temperatures are to your liking for running around in a swimsuit.

### SUPPLIES

**Typhoon Lagoon:** You can get inner tubes at Castaway Creek and inner tubes, rafts, or slide mats at the rides. Borrow snorkel gear at **Shark Reef** (your own isn't allowed) and life vests at **High 'N Dry.** Near the main entrance is **Singapore Sal's,** where you can pick up free life jackets, buy sundries, and rent (or buy) towels and lockers.

**Blizzard Beach:** Get free life vests or rent towels and lockers at **Snowless Joe's.** Inner tubes, rafts, and slide mats are provided at the rides. Buy beach gear or rent towels or lockers at **Beach Haus. Shade Shack** is the place for a new pair of sunglasses.

## WHAT TO EXPECT

Most people agree that kids under 7 and older adults prefer Typhoon Lagoon. Bigger kids and teens like Blizzard Beach better because it has more slides and big-deal rides. Indeed, devoted waterslide enthusiasts generally prefer Blizzard Beach to other water parks.

### TYPHOON LAGOON

You can speed down waterslides with names like Crush 'N' Gusher and Humunga Kowabunga or bump through rapids and falls at Mt. Mayday. You can also bob along in 5-foot waves in a surf pool the size of two football fields, or, for a mellow break, float in inner tubes along the 2,100-foot Castaway Creek. Go snorkeling in Shark Reef, rubberneck as fellow human cannonballs are ejected from the Storm Slides, or hunker down in a hammock or lounge chair and read a book. Ketchakiddie Creek for young children replicates adult rides on a smaller scale. It's Disney's version of a day at the beach—complete with friendly Disney lifeguards.

### BLIZZARD BEACH

Disney Imagineers have gone all out here to create the paradox of a ski resort in the midst of a tropical lagoon. Lots of verbal puns and sight gags play with the snow-in-Florida motif. The centerpiece is Mt. Gushmore, with its 120-foot-high Summit Plummet. Attractions have names like Teamboat Springs, a white-water raft ride. Themed speed slides include Toboggan Racer, Slush Gusher, and Snow Stormers. Between Mt. Gushmore's base and its summit, swim-skiers can also ride a chairlift converted from ski-resort to beach-resort use—with multihue umbrellas and snow skis on their undersides.

## VISITING TIPS

■ In summer, come first thing in the morning (early birds can ride several times before the lines get long), late in the afternoon when park hours run later, or when the weather clears after a thunder-shower (rainstorms drive away crowds). Afternoons are also good in cooler weather, as the water is a bit warmer. To make a whole day of it, avoid weekends, when locals and visitors pack in.

■ Women and girls should wear one-piece swimsuits unless they want to find their tops somewhere around their ears at the bottom of the waterslide.

■ Invest in sunscreen and water shoes. Plan to slather sunscreen on several times throughout the day. An inexpensive pair of water shoes will save tootsies from hot sand and walkways and from grimy restroom floors.

■ Arrive 30 minutes before opening so you can park, buy tickets, rent towels, and snag inner tubes before the crowds descend, and, trust us, it gets very crowded.

5

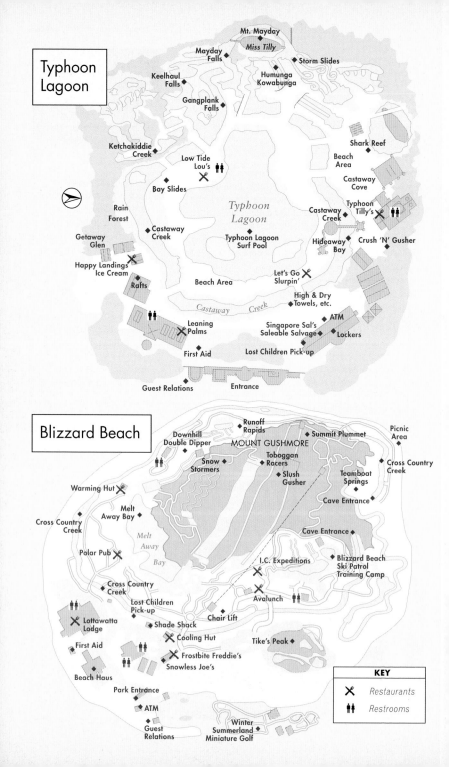

# Typhoon Lagoon

Mt. Mayday

Miss Tilly

Mayday Falls

Storm Slides

Keelhaul Falls

Humunga Kowabunga

Gangplank Falls

Ketchakiddie Creek

Shark Reef

Low Tide Lou's

Beach Area

Castaway Cove

Bay Slides

Typhoon Lagoon

Castaway Tilly's

Rain Forest

Castaway Creek

Typhoon Lagoon Surf Pool

Castaway Creek

Getaway Glen

Crush 'N' Gusher

Happy Landings Ice Cream

Hideaway Bay

Rafts

Let's Go Slurpin'

Beach Area

Castaway Creek

High & Dry Towels, etc.

Leaning Palms

ATM

Singapore Sal's Saleable Salvage

Lockers

First Aid

Lost Children Pick-up

Guest Relations

Entrance

# Blizzard Beach

Runoff Rapids

Summit Plummet

Picnic Area

Downhill Double Dipper

MOUNT GUSHMORE

Snow Stormers

Toboggan Racers

Cross Country Creek

Slush Gusher

Teamboat Springs

Warming Hut

Cave Entrance

Melt Away Bay

Cross Country Creek

Cave Entrance

Polar Pub

Melt Away Bay

I.C. Expeditions

Blizzard Beach Ski Patrol Training Camp

Cross Country Creek

Avalunch

Lost Children Pick-up

Chair Lift

Lottawatta Lodge

Shade Shack

First Aid

Cooling Hut

Tike's Peak

Frostbite Freddie's

Snowless Joe's

Beach Haus

Park Entrance

ATM

Guest Relations

Winter Summerland Miniature Golf

## KEY

| ✕ | Restaurants |
|---|---|
| 🚻 | Restrooms |

# DISNEY'S WATER PARKS

## Typhoon Lagoon

| NAME | Height Req. | Type of Entertainment | Duration | Crowds | Audience | Tips |
|---|---|---|---|---|---|---|
| Bay Slides | Under 60" | Waterslide for Kids | Up to You | Light to Moderate | Small Kids | Parents: be prepared for your kids to ride again and again. |
| Castaway Creek | n/a | River/Stream Ride | Up to 20 mins. | Vary by Season | All Ages | Spend 20 mins. on a full, leisurely circuit or zoom along with the current. |
| ★ Crush 'N' Gusher | At least 48" | Thrill Ride with Water | 1 min. | Moderate to Heavy | All but Small Kids | Ride first thing in the morning to avoid long lines. |
| Gangplank Falls | n/a | Waterslide | 1 min. | Vary by Season | All but Small Kids | It takes two people to carry the heavy inner tubes, and four or five to ride in them. |
| Humunga Kowabunga | At least 48" | Waterslide | 4 secs. | Heavy | All but Small Kids | You can race friends or family as there are three slides here. |
| Keelhaul Falls | n/a | Waterslide | 1 min. | Vary by Season | All but Small Kids | Ride before or after nearby Mayday Falls. |
| Ketchakiddee Creek | Under 48" | River/Stream Ride | Up to You | Light | Small Kids | Parents can take turns watching kiddies here and riding thrill slides elsewhere. |
| Mayday Falls | n/a | Waterslide | 1 min. | Vary by Season | All but Small Kids | While you're in the neighborhood, ride Keelhaul Falls too. |
| Shark Reef | n/a | Pool Area; Aquarium | Up to You | Heavy | All but Small Kids | It's popular: come early or late, especially if you want to linger. |
| Storm Slides | n/a | Waterslide | 15–20 secs. | Moderate to Heavy | All but Small Kids | Try each of the three slides for different twists. |
| ★ Typhoon Lagoon Surf Pool | n/a | Wave Pool; Beach Area | Up to You | Heavy | All Ages | Time your bodysurfing to the waves, which come every 90 seconds. |

**Blizzard Beach**

| Ride | Height | Type | Duration | Crowds | Age | Comments |
|---|---|---|---|---|---|---|
| Chair Lift | At least 48" alone; 32" w/ an adult | Thrill Ride | 2 mins. | Light to Moderate | All but Small Kids | Don't want to wait to get up Mt. Gushmore? Head for the single-rider line or just hike up. |
| Cross Country Creek | n/a | River/Stream Ride | 25 mins. | Vary by Season | All Ages | This is the best way to get around the park! |
| Downhill Double Dipper | At least 48" | Waterslide | Under 10 secs. | Heavy | All but Small Kids | Ride early or face the postlunch crowds. |
| Melt-Away Bay | n/a | Wave Pool; Beach Area | Up to You | Vary by Season | All Ages | Arrive early to snag an umbrella (for shade) and an inner tube (for deeper waters). |
| Runoff Rapids | n/a | Waterslide | 35 secs. | Light to Moderate | All but Small Kids | Be sure to try both slides. |
| Ski Patrol Training Camp | n/a | Waterslide; Thrill Ride with Water | Up to You | Light to Moderate | All but Small Kids | Hate lines? Come early or head to the zip-line drop or iceberg obstacle course. |
| ★ Slush Gusher | At least 48" | Waterslide | 15 secs. | You Bet! | All but Small Kids | Crowded days see 90-minute waits; come early. |
| Snow Stormers | n/a | Waterslide | 20 secs. | Moderate to Heavy | All Ages | Hold on tight! |
| ★ Summit Plummet | At least 48" | Waterslide | 10 crazy secs. | Absolutely | All but Small Kids | Make your first stop! Summer afternoon waits can be two hours. |
| Teamboat Springs | n/a | River/Stream Ride | 1½ mins. | Moderate | Families | There are no age or height requirements, tubes seat groups, and lines move fast. |
| ★ Tike's Peak | 48" and under | Pool Area | Up to You | Vary by Season | Small Kids | Adults must be accompanied by children no more than 48' tall! |
| Toboggan Racers | n/a | Waterslide/Game | 10 secs. | Moderate to Heavy | All but Small Kids | It's more fun if you race. |

# OTHER DISNEY ACTIVITIES

## EXPLORING THE REST OF THE WORLD

Try to budget in a few hours to explore Disney's "other" places. Several of them are no-admission-required charmers; one is a high-tech, high-cover-charge gaming wonderland.

### DISNEY'S BOARDWALK

In the good ol' days, Americans escaped their city routines for breezy seaside boardwalks. Disney's version is within walking distance of Epcot, across Crescent Lake from the Yacht and Beach Club Resorts, and fronting the Boardwalk Resort. You'll be drawn to some good restaurants, bars, shops, surreys, and performers. After sunset, the mood is festive.

### DOWNTOWN DISNEY

East of Epcot and close to Interstate 4 (I–4) along a large lake, this shopping, dining, and entertainment complex has three areas: the Marketplace, West Side, and the connecting district, Pleasure Island, which will become Hyperion Wharf. You can rent lockers, strollers, or wheelchairs, and there are two Guest Relations (aka Guest Services) centers.

**Hyperion Wharf.** The area once known as Pleasure Island had bars, comedy clubs, and dance spots. But the night spots have closed, and Disney is making it over into this family-oriented dining and entertainment district. That said, Raglan Road Irish Pub and Restaurant still offers live Irish music six nights a week, Paradiso 37 welcomes diners, and the upscale cigar bar, Fuego Cigars by Sosa, serves wine and spirits. Other restaurants and shops beckon as you stroll from the Marketplace to West Side.

**Marketplace.** In the easternmost Downtown Disney area, you can meander along winding sidewalks and explore hidden alcoves. Children love to splash in fountains that spring from the pavement and ride the miniature train and old-time carousel ($2). Toy stores also entice, and there are plenty of spots to grab a bite or sip a cappuccino along the lakefront.

**West Side.** The main attractions in the hip West Side are the House of Blues Music Hall, Cirque du Soleil, and DisneyQuest virtual indoor theme park and arcade. You can also ride the Characters in Flight ($18 ages 10 and up; $12 ages 3–9) helium balloon that's tethered here, shop in boutiques, or dine in such restaurants as the Wolfgang Puck Café and Planet Hollywood.

## SHOPPING

Though you can't turn a Disney corner without seeing a store or merchandise cart, certain areas offer the best shopping opportunities. And it really pays to know where these opportunities are: not only can you maximize your time, but you can also minimize your spending.

**Downtown Disney.** Why spend valuable touring time shopping in the theme parks when you can come here (for no entry fee) on your first or last day? Downtown Disney has dozens of stores, including the vast, hard-to-top World of Disney, the super-kid-friendly LEGO Imagination Center, and the über-hip Tren-D clothing and accessory shop.

**Epcot World Showcase.** Fine goods from the world over, some hand-crafted, are sold at the pavilions representing individual countries here. Check out the Japanese and Chinese kimonos, Moroccan fezzes, French wines, Norwegian sweaters, and Mexican wood carvings. A United Kingdom shop even helps you research your family coat of arms, which you can buy as a paper printout or dressed up with paint or embroidery.

**Main Street, U.S.A., Magic Kingdom.** The Main Street buildings, with forced-perspective architecture and elaborately decorated facades, beckon, but don't waste precious touring time shopping in the morning. Come back later for custom-made watches, hand-blown crystal, cookware, princess dresses, mouse ears, and, of course, fairy-tale-themed snow globes.

**Discovery Island, Animal Kingdom.** Although there are some great shops in Africa and Asia, many of the goods are concentrated in this hub. You'll find plush baby giraffes and Simba toys; several types of safari hats; and authentic, hand-decorated South African ostrich eggs produced by a Fair Trade Company.

**5**

**Hollywood Boulevard, Hollywood Studios.** If you're a size 0 or 2 fashionista like soap-opera diva Susan Lucci, you may want to take home the pink coat she wore on All My Children ($1,000 at Sid Cahuenga's One-of-a-Kind shop just inside the park). Or you can buy more affordable togs at the Boulevard's Keystone Clothiers (adults), L.A. Prop Cinema Storage (kids), and Mickey's of Hollywood (all in the family).

## OUTDOOR ACTIVITIES AND SPORTS

Tennis, anyone? A round of golf? Or maybe you'd rather surf, parasail, drive a racecar, or take yourself out to a ballgame at ESPN Wide World of Sports. For general Disney recreation information, call ☏ 407/939–7529; for golf and recreation reservations call ☏ 407/939–4653.

**Archery.** Make like Geronimo at Fort Wilderness Resort, where an archery guide oversees novice and expert marksmen (ages 6 and up).

**Biking.** You'll look sweet upon the seat of a bicycle built for two. You can even rent a covered surrey bike for four at the BoardWalk and other resort locations.

**Boating.** You can rent 12-foot sailboats, catamarans, motor-powered pontoon boats, pedal boats, kayaks, canoes, and tiny two-passenger Sea Racers for use on Bay Lake and the adjoining Seven Seas Lagoon, Crescent Lake at Epcot Resorts, Lake Buena Vista, or Buena Vista Lagoon.

**Fishing.** Depart from the Wilderness Lodge or Contemporary Resort on a Disney fishing charter to tranquil Bay Lake, where odds are good you'll discover a bass bonanza.

**Golf.** The Tom Fazio–designed Osprey Ridge course—one of several on Disney property—keeps players on their toes, and the scenery is lovely. Minigolf fans can putt-putt their way through the "winter chill" at the whimsical Winter Summerland next to the Blizzard Beach water park.

## TOP SOUVENIRS

If you're trying to figure out what could be the most memorable souvenir, you've got options—from classic to quirky.

**Make-Your-Own Mouse Ear Hat.** For $12 and up, you can customize your ears—from fuzzy pink to shiny silver—at The Chapeau in the Magic Kingdom.

**Indiana Jones Fedora.** This brown wool-felt fedora (about $37) is a Halloween favorite. Pick one up at Indiana Jones Adventure Outpost in Hollywood Studios.

**Hand-Decorated Ostrich Egg.** No ostriches are harmed to produce these beautiful pieces ($125–$185) available at Disney Outfitters in the Animal Kingdom. Each egg is sanded and painted by South African Fair Trade artists.

**Kimono.** Kids' and adults' poly-rayon or silk kimonos, at China or Japan shops in Epcot ($33–$170), never go out of style.

**Princess Dress.** Little girls treasure Cinderella, Aurora, Belle, or Ariel dresses ($60) from Tiana's Castle Couture, Magic Kingdom, or World of Disney, Downtown Disney Marketplace.

**Double Light Saber.** Let double the force be with you! At Tatooine Traders in Hollywood Studios, kids can customize a light saber ($19.95 single; $22.95 double) with crystals, hilts, and blades.

**Mickey Computer Mouse.** A wireless mouse styled after the Big Cheese's white-gloved hand is $30 at Mickey's of Hollywood in Hollywood Studios.

**Character Toy.** Dumbo, Goofy, Nemo—you name the character, and there's a plush toy—in many sizes and at just about any Disney park or Downtown Disney. Prices run $10 to $50.

**Horseback Riding.** Trail rides from Fort Wilderness Resort begin at 8:30 am and continue through the afternoon.

**Parasailing.** The sun is bright, and you've got the wind beneath your parasail as you soar hundreds of feet above sparkling Bay Lake.

**Race-Car Driving.** The Richard Petty Driving Experience lets you ride in or even drive a NASCAR-style stock car on the real racetrack. ☎ 800/237–3889 ⊕ www.1800bepetty.com.

**Surfing.** Surf's up in the early hours before Typhoon Lagoon water park officially opens—here's your chance to learn how to hang 10!

**Tennis.** Six Disney resorts have courts: the BoardWalk, Fort Wilderness, Old Key West, Saratoga Springs, Yacht Club, Grand Floridian.

# Universal Orlando

## THE STUDIOS, ISLANDS OF ADVENTURE, WET 'N WILD

**WORD OF MOUTH**

"You definitely should plan a day each for [Universal Studios and Islands of Adventure]. And it *is* worth it to get the front-of-line privileges . . . but [even with these] you still can spend a day at each park. If you finish one early, check out your hotel pool!"

—FL_Mom

# WELCOME TO UNIVERSAL ORLANDO

## TOP REASONS TO GO

★ **More Than You Bargain For:** Universal Orlando is more than just a single Hollywood-theme amusement park; it's also Islands of Adventure theme park, the CityWalk entertainment complex; and the Hard Rock Hotel, Portofino Bay, and Royal Pacific resorts. Wet 'n Wild water park is also affiliated with Universal.

★ **Theme-Park Powerhouse:** Neither SeaWorld nor any of Disney's four theme parks can match the energy at Universal Studios and Islands of Adventure. Wild rides, clever shows, and an edgy attitude all push the envelope here.

★ **A New Experience:** If your Orlando vacations have been based primarily at Disney, Universal will help you expand your range. In time, it may even become your first stop.

★ **Party Central:** Throughout the year, Universal hosts special events—Mardi Gras, Halloween Horror Nights, Grinchmas, the Rock the Universe Christian-music celebration.

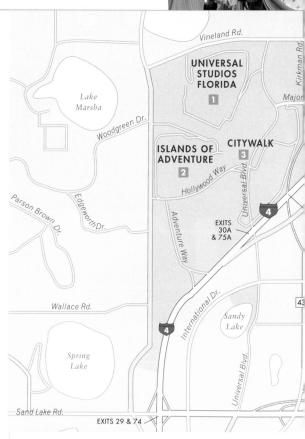

**1** **Universal Studios.** It's a creative and quirky tribute to Hollywood past, present, and future. Overall, the collection of wild rides, quiet retreats, live shows, street characters, and clever movies (both 3-D and 4-D) are as entertaining as the motion pictures they celebrate.

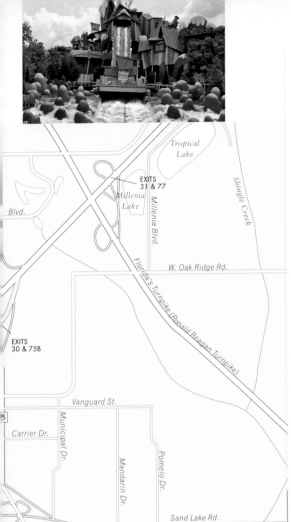

## GETTING ORIENTED

Universal Orlando is tucked into a corner created by the intersection of Interstate 4 and Kirkman Road (Highway 435), midway between downtown Orlando and the Walt Disney World Resort. Here you'll be about 15 minutes from each and 10 minutes from SeaWorld.

6

**2** Islands of Adventure. IOA has the ability to break new ground—as it did in 2010 with the premiere of an entire land dedicated to Harry Potter. Add a variety of attractions that bring you face-to-face with Spider-Man, the Hulk, velociraptors, and the Cat in the Hat, and there's every reason to head to the islands.

**3** CityWalk. Locals and visitors come to this sprawling entertainment and retail complex to watch movies; dine at theme restaurants; shop for everything from cigars to surf wear; and stay up late at nightclubs celebrating the French Quarter, Jamaica, and Latin America.

# UNIVERSAL ORLANDO PLANNER

## Operating Hours

Universal Studios and IOA are open 365 days a year, from 9 am to 7 pm, with hours as late as 10 pm in summer and at holidays. Wet 'n Wild is also open 365 days a year, weather permitting, but with widely varying hours. Usually it's open from 10 am to 5 pm, with summer hours from 9:30 am until 9 pm. Call for exact hours during holiday periods.

## Contacts

**Universal Dining Reservations:** ☎ *407/224–3613 general, 407/224–4012 IOA character meals*

**Universal Main Number:** ☎ *407/363–8000*

**Universal Room Reservations:** ☎ *888/273–1311*

**Universal Vacation Packages:** ☎ *877/801–9720*

**Universal Web:** ⊕ *www. universalorlando.com*

**Wet 'n Wild Main Number:** ☎ *407/351–1800 or 800/992–9453*

**Wet 'n Wild Web:** ⊕ *www. wetnwild.com*

## Getting Here and Around

East on Interstate 4 (from WDW and Tampa), exit at Universal Boulevard (75A); take a left into Universal Orlando, and follow the signs. West on Interstate 4 (from downtown or Daytona, even), exit at Universal Boulevard (74B), turn right, and follow Hollywood Way.

Both Universal Studios and IOA require a lot of walking—a whole lot of walking. Start off by using the parking area's moving walkways as much as possible. Arrive early, and you may be able to complete a single lap that will get you to each of the park's primary attractions.

## Parking

Universal's two garages total 3.4 million square feet, so *note your parking space*. The cost is a pain-inducing $15 for cars and motorcycles, $20 for RVs. Although moving walkways get you partway, you could walk up to a half mile to reach the gates. Valet parking ($15 for up to two hours $25 for over two hours) is much closer. From Universal hotels, it's either a short stroll or brief motor-launch trip to the entrance.

## Admission

The at-the-gate, per-person, per-day rate for either Universal Studios or IOA is $82 for adults (ages 10-plus) and $74 for children (ages 3–9). Wet 'n Wild costs $47.95 for ages 10 and up, $41.95 for ages 3 to 9.

## Express Passes

Formerly known as the Express PLUS Pass and ranging in price from about $20 off-season to $60 in peak season, this pass gets you to the front of most lines. It saves a tremendous amount of time, even if it seems like a tremendous outlay of cash. If crowds are thin and lines are moving fast, skip this pass. Also, if you're a guest at Universal hotel, this perk is free; your room key card serves as the pass.

## Universal and Wet 'n Wild Like a Pro

**Arrive early**—as early at 8 am if the parks open at 9. Seriously. Better to share Universal or Wet 'n Wild with hundreds of people rather than thousands.

**Visit on a weekday.** Crowds are lighter, especially fall through spring, when kids are in school.

**Don't forget anything in your car.** Universal's parking areas are at least a half-mile from park entrances and a round-trip hike will eat up valuable time. At Wet n' Wild parking's closer, but who wants to towel off, get dressed and walk across the street for a hairbrush?

**Know the rules.** A few things aren't allowed in the parks: alcohol and glass containers; hard-sided coolers; soft-sided coolers larger than 8½ inches wide by 6 inches high by 6 inches deep; coolers, suitcases, and other bags with wheels.

**Consider valet parking.** It costs almost twice as much as regular parking, but it puts you much closer to Universal's park entrances and just steps from CityWalk.

**Look into the Express Pass.** Jumping to the front of the line with this pass really is worth the extra cost—unless you stay at a resort hotel, in which case cutting in line is one of the perks.

**Ride solo.** At Universal some rides have a Single Rider line that moves faster than regular lines.

**Get expert advice.** The folks at Guest Services (aka Guest Relations) in both Universal and Wet 'n Wild have great insight. At Universal, reps will create a custom itinerary free of charge.

**Check out Child Swap.** At certain Universal attractions, one parent can enter the attraction, take a spin, and then return to take care of the baby while the other parent rides without having to wait in line again.

## Dining

All-you-can-eat, daylong **meal deals** are good at three sit-down restaurants in Universal (Mel's Drive-In, Louie's Italian, International Food and Film Festival) and three in IOA (Circus McGurkus Café Stoopendous, Comic Strip Café, the Burger Digs). The cost is $20 a day for adults, $10 daily for kids; an extra $9 a day buys all-you-can-drink soda. IOA's **character breakfasts** at Confisco's Grill feature Spider-Man, Scooby-Doo, Woody Woodpecker, Curious George, and Dr. Seuss characters. Reservations are a good idea. At CityWalk there's a Starbucks, a Cinnabon, a Burger King, and other affordable quick-bite eateries.

## For People with Disabilities

The *Studio Guide for Guests with Disabilities* (aka *Rider's Guide*) details attractions with special entrances and viewing areas, interpreters, Braille scripts, and assistance devices. In general, if you can transfer from your wheelchair unassisted or with the help of a friend, you can ride many attractions. Some rides have carts that accommodate manual wheelchairs, though not motorized wheelchairs or electric convenience vehicles (ECVs).

By Gary
McKechnie

For two decades or so Universal and Disney have been going head to head. While Disney creates a fantasy world for people—especially young children—who love fairy tales, Universal is geared to older kids, adults, and anyone who enjoys high-energy thrills, pop culture, and movies.

Where Disney may roll out a new land or retrofit an old ride once a decade, Universal knows that guests expect something different on each visit. And the park delivers. In recent years Univeral Studios alone has replaced Alfred Hitchcock with Shrek, Jimmy Neutron with Despicable Me, King Kong with The Mummy, Back to the Future with the virtual-reality Simpsons ride, and Earthquake with Disaster! They also launched Hollywood Rip Ride Rockit—an interactive roller coaster with a customized soundtrack.

Thanks to the opening of the Wizarding World of Harry Potter, things haven't been static at Islands of Adventure (IOA). And just when things seemed to be flagging at the CityWalk shopping/nightlife complex, a well-intentioned but less-than-successful jazz club became a karaoke stage, a Motown restaurant became the Red Coconut Lounge, and a series of stores were switched out. In addition, Universal created a wonderful theater specifically for the Blue Man Group.

A few miles away, on the tourist strip known as International Drive, is Wet 'n Wild—owned by Universal since 1998 and believed to be America's first water park. Wet 'n Wild does with aquatics what Universal does with theatrics: provide over-the-top entertainment, albeit in the form of super waterslides and fantastic plunges. (To wit: Bomb Bay, which drops you 76 nearly vertical feet down a slide and into the pool. Spooky, splashy fun.)

Despite the adrenaline-charging attractions at Wet n' Wild, it's not hard to chill out lazing about the park's beaches and pools. And, at Universal you can slow down with some leisurely shopping at CityWalk; a concert at Hard Rock Live; and a languorous, elegant dinner at Emeril's.

# UNIVERSAL STUDIOS
## STEP INTO THE MOVIES

Universal Studios appeals primarily to those who like loud, fast, high-energy attractions—generally teens and adults. Covering 444 acres, it's a rambling montage of sets, shops, and soundstages housing themed attractions, reproductions of New York and San Francisco, and some genuine moviemaking paraphernalia.

On a map, the park appears neatly divided into six areas positioned around a huge lagoon. There's Production Central, which covers the entire left side of the Plaza of the Stars; New York, with street performances at 70 Delancey; the bicoastal San Francisco/Amity; futuristic World Expo; Woody Woodpecker's KidZone; and Hollywood.

What's tricky is that—because it's designed like a series of movie sets—there's no straightforward way to tackle the park. You'll probably make some detours and do some backtracking. To save time and shoe leather, ask theme park hosts for itinerary suggestions and time-saving tips.

## TOURING TIPS

■ Upon entering, avoid the temptation to go left toward the towering soundstages, looping the park clockwise. Head right—bypassing shops, restaurants, and some crowds—to primary attractions like The Simpsons Ride and MEN IN BLACK.

■ Want to take a good picture? Universal Studios posts signs that indicate picture spots and show how best to frame your shot.

■ Good rendezvous points include the Lucy Tribute near the entrance, Mel's Drive-In, and Beetlejuice's Graveyard Revue.

## TOP ATTRACTIONS

### FOR AGES 7 AND UP

**Hollywood Rip Ride Rockit.** On this super-wild coaster, you select the sound track.

**MEN IN BLACK: Alien Attack.** The "world's first ride-through video game" gives you a chance to plug away at an endless swarm of aliens.

**Revenge of the Mummy.** It's a jarring, rocketing indoor coaster that takes you past scary mummies and billowing balls of fire (really).

**Shrek 4-D.** The 3-D film with sensory effects picks up where the original film left off—and adds some creepy extras in the process.

**The Simpsons Ride.** It puts you in the heart of Springfield on a wild-and-crazy virtual-reality experience.

**Terminator 2 3-D.** This explosive stage show features robots, 3-D effects, and sensations that all add extra punch to the classic film series.

**Twister . . . Ride It Out.** OK. It's just a special-effects show— but what special effects! You experience a tornado without having to head to the root cellar.

**Universal Horror Make-Up Show.** This sometimes gross, often raunchy, but always entertaining demonstration merges the best of stand-up comedy with creepy effects.

### FOR AGES 6 AND UNDER

**Animal Actors on Location!** It's a perfect family show starring a menagerie of animals whose unusually high IQs are surpassed only by their cuteness and cuddle-ability.

**A Day in the Park with Barney.** Small children love the big purple dinosaur and the chance to sing along.

**Curious George Goes to Town.** The celebrated simian visits the Man with the Yellow Hat in a small-scale water park.

## WHERE TO SNACK

The three restaurants on the Universal Meal Deal here are **Mel's Drive-In,** a Happy Days–era soda shop–burger joint; **Louie's Italian Restaurant** (pizza, spaghetti, salads); and the **International Food and Film Bazaar** (pizza, gyros, stir-fried beef, and other multicultural dishes). Full-service restaurants include **Finnegan's Bar and Grille** (Irish pub), and **Lombard's Seafood Grille** (seafood). Among the self-serve restaurants are **Classic Monsters Cafe** (seasonal, with pizzas, pasta, salads, rotisserie chicken); and **Richter's Burger Co.** (burgers, salads). Other choices include **Beverly Hills Boulangerie** for breakfast croissants and pastries; **Schwab's Pharmacy** for ice cream; and the **KidZone Pizza Company** for pizza, chicken tenders, and other kid-geared dishes.

**6**

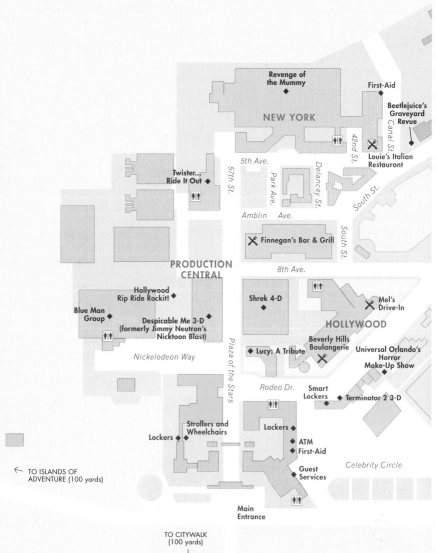

# Universal Studios

Revenge of
the Mummy

First-Aid

Beetlejuice's
Graveyard
Revue

**NEW YORK**

Canal St.

42nd St.

Louie's Italian
Restaurant

5th Ave.

Twister...
Ride It Out

57th St.

Park Ave.

Delancey St.

South St.

Amblin   Ave.

Finnegan's Bar & Grill

South St.

8th Ave.

**PRODUCTION
CENTRAL**

Hollywood
Rip Ride Rockit!

Shrek 4-D

Mel's
Drive-In

Blue Man
Group

Despicable Me 3-D
(formerly Jimmy Neutron's
Nicktoon Blast)

**HOLLYWOOD**

Beverly Hills
Boulangerie

Universal Orlando's
Horror
Make-Up Show

Nickelodeon Way

Lucy: A Tribute

Rodeo Dr.

Smart
Lockers

Terminator 2 3-D

Plaza of the Stars

Strollers and
Wheelchairs

Lockers

Lockers

ATM
First-Aid

Celebrity Circle

← TO ISLANDS OF
ADVENTURE (100 yards)

Guest
Services

Main
Entrance

TO CITYWALK
(100 yards)
↓

Midway Grill ✕

JAWS ◆

Disaster! ◆

**SAN FRANCISCO/AMITY**

Amity Ave.

The Embarcadero

🚻

San Francisco Pastry Co. ✕

Lombard's Landing ✕

✕ Richter's Burger Co.

*The Lagoon*

Exposition Blvd.

**MEN IN BLACK:** Alien Attack ◆

Smart Lockers ◆

**WORLD EXPO**

◆ The Simpsons Ride

Sunset Blvd.

🚻 International Food and Film Festival ✕

Animal Actors on Location! ◆

🚻

A Day in the Park with Barney ◆

**WOODY WOODPECKER'S KID ZONE**

E.T. Adventure ◆

Fievel's Playland ◆

Curious George Goes to Town ◆

Woody ◆ Woodpecker's Nuthouse Coaster

TO VINELAND RD. →

| **KEY** | |
|---|---|
| ✕ | *Restaurants* |
| 🚻 | *Restrooms* |

# UNIVERSAL STUDIOS

| NAME | Height Req. | Type of Entertainment | Duration | Crowds | Audience | Tips |
|---|---|---|---|---|---|---|
| **Hollywood** | | | | | | |
| Lucy: A Tribute | n/a | Walk-Through | 15 mins. | Light | Adults | Save this for a hot afternoon or for on your way out. |
| Terminator 2 3-D | n/a | 3-D Film / Simulator Exp. | 21 mins. | Heavy | All but Small Kids | Come first thing in the morning or use Express Pass. |
| ★ Universal Orlando's Horror Make-Up Show | n/a | Show | 25 mins. | Moderate | All but Small Kids | Come in the afternoon or evening. Young children may be frightened; older children eat up the blood-and-guts comedy. |
| **Production Central** | | | | | | |
| ★ Hollywood Rip Ride Rockit! | At least 51" | Thrill Ride | 2 mins. | You Bet! | All but Small Kids | Come early, late, or use a Express Pass. Be patient. |
| Shrek 4-D | n/a | 3-D Film | 12 mins. | Heavy | All Ages | Come early or late, or use Express Pass. |
| **New York** | | | | | | |
| Revenge of the Mummy | At least 48" | Thrill Ride | 3 mins. | Heavy | All but Small Kids | Use Express Pass, or come first thing in the morning. |
| Twister…Ride It Out | n/a | Show / Simulator Exp. | 3 mins. | Heavy | All but Small Kids | Come first thing in morning or at closing. This "ride" involves standing and watching the action unfold. |
| **San Francisco/Amity** | | | | | | |
| Beetlejuice's Graveyard Revue | n/a | Show | 25 mins. | Light to Moderate | All but Small Kids | You can use Express Pass here, but there's really no need as there's little chance of a wait. |
| Disaster! | n/a | Thrill Ride | 20 mins. | Heavy | All but Small Kids | Come early, before closing, or use Universal Express Pass. This is loud. |
| JAWS | n/a | Thrill Ride with Water | 7 mins. | Moderate | All but Small Kids | Come after dark for a more terrifying ride. Use Express Pass if needed. |

## Woody Woodpecker's KidZone

| | | | | | | |
|---|---|---|---|---|---|---|
| A Day in the Park with Barney | n/a | Show | 20 mins. | Light | Small Kids | Arrive 10–15 mins. early on crowded days for a good seat—up close and in the center. Can use Express Pass. |
| Animal Actors on Location! | n/a | Show | 20 mins. | Moderate to Heavy | All Ages | Stadium seating, but come early for a good seat. Express Pass accepted. |
| Curious George Goes to Town | n/a | Playground with Water | Up to you | Moderate | Small Kids | Come in late afternoon or early evening. Bring a towel. |
| E.T. Adventure | At least 34" | Thrill Ride for Kids | 5 mins. | Moderate to Heavy | All Ages | Come early morning or use Express Pass. |
| Fievel's Playland | n/a | Playground with Water | Up to you | Light to Moderate | Small Kids | Generally light crowds, but there are waits for the waterslide. On hot days come late. |
| Woody Woodpecker's Nuthouse Coaster | At least 36" | Thrill Ride for Kids | 1½ mins. | Moderate to Heavy | Small Kids | Come at park closing, when most little ones have gone home. Try Express Pass. |

## World Expo

| | | | | | | |
|---|---|---|---|---|---|---|
| MEN IN BLACK: Alien Attack | At least 42" | Thrill Ride | 4½ mins. | Heavy | All but Small Kids | Solo riders can take a faster line, so split up. This ride spins. Use Express Pass. |
| ★ The Simpsons Ride | 40" | Thrill Ride/ Simulator Exp. | 6 mins. | Heavy | All but Small Kids | Use Express Pass. |

★ Fodor's Choice

# ISLANDS OF ADVENTURE

## EXPLORE NEW LANDS

When Islands of Adventure (IOA) first opened in 1999 it took attractions to a new level. Most—from Marvel Super Hero Island and Toon Lagoon to Seuss Landing and the Lost Continent—are impressive; some even out-Disney Disney. And, in 2010, IOA received well-deserved worldwide attention when it opened the 20-acre Wizarding World of Harry Potter.

You pass through the turnstiles and into the Port of Entry plaza, a bazaar that brings together bits and pieces of architecture, landscaping, music, and wares from many lands—Dutch windmills, Indonesian pedicabs, African masks, restrooms marked Loo's Landing, and Egyptian figurines that adorn a massive archway inscribed with the notice the adventure begins. From here, theme islands—arranged around a large lagoon—are connected by walkways that make navigation easy. When you've done the full circuit, you'll recall the fantastic range of sights, sounds, and experiences and realize there can be truth in advertising. This park really *is* an adventure.

## TOURING TIPS

■ Ask hosts about their favorite experiences—and their suggestions for saving time.

■ Want to take a good picture? Islands of Adventure posts signs that indicate picture spots and show how best to frame your shot.

■ If the park's open late, split the day in half. See part of it in the morning, head off-site to a restaurant for lunch (your parking ticket is good all day), then head to your hotel for a swim or a nap (or both). Return in the cooler, less crowded evening.

■ Explore little-used sidewalks and quiet alcoves top counter IOA's manic energy.

## TOP ATTRACTIONS

### FOR AGES 7 AND UP

**Amazing Adventures of Spider-Man.** Get ready to fight bad guys and marvel at the engineering and technological wizardry on this dazzling attraction.

**Dudley Do-Right's Ripsaw Falls.** Even if its namesake is a mystery to anyone born after the 1960s, everyone loves the super splashdown at the end of this log-flume ride dedicated to the exploits of the animated Canadian Mountie.

**Eighth Voyage of Sindbad.** Jumping, diving, punching—is it another Tom Cruise action film? No, it's a cool, live stunt show with a love story to boot.

**Harry Potter and the Forbidden Journey.** This ride brings J.K. Rowling's books to life on a wild, virtual-reality adventure through Hogwarts and beyond with Harry, Hermione, and Ron.

**Incredible Hulk Coaster.** This super-scary coaster blasts you skyward before sending you on no less than seven inversions. It will be hard to walk straight after this one.

### FOR AGES 6 AND UNDER

**The Cat in the Hat.** It's like entering a Dr. Seuss book: all you have to do is sit on a moving couch and see what it's like when the Cat in the Hat drops by to babysit.

**Flight of the Hippogriff.** Some of the younger Hogwarts "students" will enjoy this low-key coaster in Harry Potter's world.

**Popeye and Bluto's Bilge-Rat Barges.** This tumultuous (but safe) raft ride lets younger kids experience a big-deal ride that's not too scary—just wild and wet.

### WHERE TO SNACK

The park's three Meal Deal (all-you-can-eat) options are **Circus McGurkus Café Stoo-pendous** (chicken, pasta, pizza, burgers, salads) in Seuss Landing; the **Burger Digs** (hamburgers, chicken sandwiches, chicken fingers, milk shakes) in Jurassic Park; and the **Comic Strip Café** (Asian, Italian, American, and fish) in Toon Lagoon. Also in Toon Lagoon is **Blondie's Deli** (jumbo sandwiches).
**Pizza Predattoria** and the seasonal **Thunder Falls Terrace** (rotisserie chicken and ribs) are in Jurassic Park, and, near the Port of Entry, is **Confisco's Grill**, with its steaks, salads, sandwiches, soups, and pasta. This is also where character breakfasts are held, and there's also a neat little pub.
The ultimate dining experience is the Lost Continent's **Mythos Restaurant**. Although its continental dishes change seasonally, the warm, gooey, chocolate-banana cake is a constant.

6

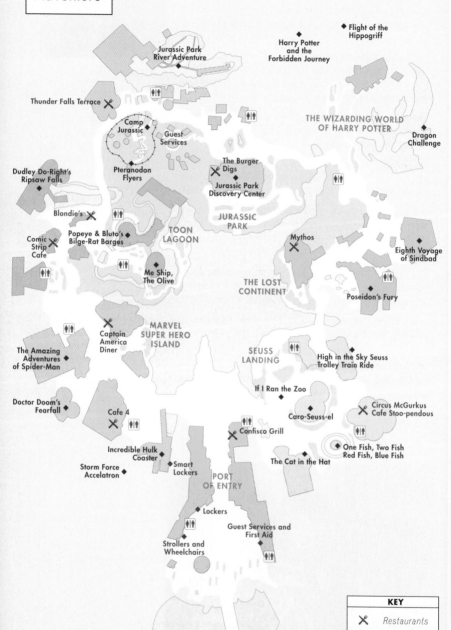

# Islands of Adventure

Jurassic Park River Adventure

Harry Potter and the Forbidden Journey

Flight of the Hippogriff

Thunder Falls Terrace

THE WIZARDING WORLD OF HARRY POTTER

Camp Jurassic

Guest Services

Dragon Challenge

Pteranodon Flyers

The Burger Digs

Dudley Do-Right's Ripsaw Falls

Jurassic Park Discovery Center

Blondie's

JURASSIC PARK

Comic Strip Cafe

Popeye & Bluto's Bilge-Rat Barges

TOON LAGOON

Mythos

Eighth Voyage of Sindbad

Me Ship, The Olive

THE LOST CONTINENT

Poseidon's Fury

The Amazing Adventures of Spider-Man

Captain America Diner

MARVEL SUPER HERO ISLAND

SEUSS LANDING

High in the Sky Seuss Trolley Train Ride

Doctor Doom's Fearfall

Cafe 4

If I Ran the Zoo

Circus McGurkus Cafe Stoo-pendous

Caro-Seuss-el

Incredible Hulk Coaster

Confisco Grill

One Fish, Two Fish Red Fish, Blue Fish

Storm Force Accelatron

Smart Lockers

PORT OF ENTRY

The Cat in the Hat

Lockers

Guest Services and First Aid

Strollers and Wheelchairs

| KEY | |
|---|---|
| ✕ | Restaurants |
| 🚻 | Rest rooms |

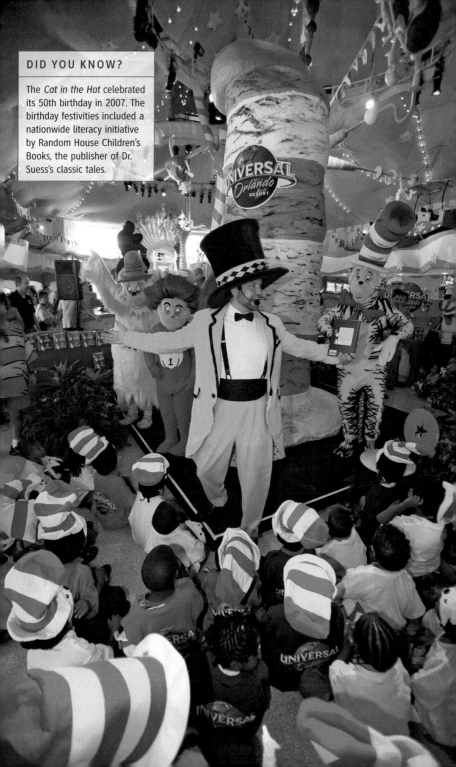

# ISLANDS OF ADVENTURE

| NAME | Height Req. | Type of Entertainment | Duration | Crowds | Audience | Tips |
|------|-------------|----------------------|----------|--------|----------|------|
| **Jurassic Park** | | | | | | |
| Camp Jurassic | n/a | Playground | Up to you | Light to Moderate | All Ages | Come anytime. |
| Jurassic Park Discovery Center | n/a | Walk-Through | Up to you | Light | Small Kids to Teens | Come anytime. |
| Jurassic Park River Adventure | At least 42" | Thrill Ride with Water | 6 mins. | Heavy | All but Small Kids | Use Express Pass. Come early or late. |
| Pteranodon Flyers | 36" to 56" | Thrill Ride for Kids | 2 mins. | Heavy | All Ages | Skip this on your first visit. 36" to 48" can ride but must do so with an adult. |
| **Lost Continent** | | | | | | |
| Eighth Voyage of Sindbad | n/a | Show | 25 mins. | Heavy | All but Small Kids | Stadium seating for everyone, but arrive at least 15 mins. early. Don't sit too far up front. Use Express Pass. |
| Poseidon's Fury | n/a | Walk-through Simulator Exp. | 20 mins. | Heavy | All but Small Kids | Come at the end of the day. Stay to the left for best spot. Get in first row each time. Express Pass accepted. |
| **Marvel Super Hero Island** | | | | | | |
| ★ The Amazing Adventures of Spider-Man | At least 40" | Simulator Exp. | 4½ mins. | Absolutely | All but Small Kids | Use Express Pass, or come early or late in day. Don't miss the bad guys in the wanted posters. Try it twice if you can. |
| Doctor Doom's Fearfall | At least 52" | Thrill Ride | 1 min. | Light to Moderate | All but Small Kids | Use Express Pass, or come later in the day. Regardless, come with an empty stomach. |
| Incredible Hulk Coaster | At least 54" | Thrill Ride | 2¼ mins. | Yes! | All but Small Kids | Come here first. Effects are best in the morning. The front row is best. |

| Name | Height | Type | Duration | Crowds | Ages | Comments |
|---|---|---|---|---|---|---|
| Storm Force Accelatron | n/a | Thrill Ride | 2 mins. | Light | All but Small Kids | Come whenever—except right after eating. |
| **Seuss Landing** | | | | | | |
| Caro-Seuss-el | n/a | Thrill Ride for Kids | 2 mins. | Moderate | All Ages | Use Express Pass, or end your day here. |
| The Cat in the Hat | n/a | Thrill Ride for Kids | 4½ mins. | Heavy | All Ages | Use Express Pass here, or come early or at the end of the day. |
| High in the Sky Seuss Trolley Train Ride! | At least 34" | Railroad | 3 mins. | Heavy | All Ages | Kids love trains, so plan to get in line! 34" to 48" can ride but must do so with an adult. Express Pass accepted. |
| If I Ran the Zoo | n/a | Playground with Water | Up to you | Heavy | Small Kids | Come toward the end of your visit. |
| One Fish, Two Fish, Red Fish, Blue Fish | n/a | Thrill Ride for Kids | 2+ mins. | Heavy | Small Kids | Use Express Pass, or come early or late in day. Skip it on your first visit. |
| **Toon Lagoon** | | | | | | |
| Dudley Do-Right's Ripsaw Falls | At least 44" | Thrill Ride with Water | 5½ mins. | Heavy | All but Small Kids | Ride the flume in late afternoon to cool down, or at day's end. There's no seat where you can stay dry. Express Pass accepted. |
| Me Ship, The Olive | n/a | Playground | Up to you | Heavy | Small Kids | Come in the morning or at dinnertime. |
| Popeye and Bluto's Bilge-Rat Barges | At least 42" | Thrill Ride with Water | 5 mins. | Heavy | All but Small Kids | Come early in the morning or before closing. You will get wet. Express Pass accepted. |
| **The Wizarding World of Harry Potter** | | | | | | |
| Dragon Challenge | At least 54" | Thrill Ride | 3 mins. | Heavy | All but Small Kids | Use Express Pass. Avoid if you're prone to motion sickness. |
| Flight of the Hippogriff | At least 36" | Thrill Ride for Kids | 1 min. | Moderate | Small Kids | Keep an eye on the line, and come when there's an opening. Express Pass accepted. |
| Harry Potter and the Forbidden Journey | At least 48" | Walk-Through/ Ride-Through/ Thrill Ride | 50 mins. | Yes! | All but Small Kids | Come early and use Express Pass. Steer clear if you have a queasy stomach. |

# WET 'N WILD
## THE WATERY WILD SIDE

Since 1977 Wet 'n Wild has been a place to cool off and take a break from the theme parks. Even though the Atlantic Ocean is a mere 50 mi east of Orlando and the Gulf of Mexico is just 90 mi to the west, neither has the massive slides, tube rides, knee-ski lines, and gentle rapids.

Thanks to Disney's Blizzard Beach and Typhoon Lagoon–theme water parks and SeaWorld's flashy, splashy Aquatica, Wet 'n Wild has plenty of competition. But Wet 'n Wild still has the advantage of its location: it's right on the International Drive tourist corridor and a short drive from Universal Orlando.

For decades the park has also earned credit of giving swimmers and aquatic thrill-seekers what they're looking for—incredible plunges, dives, spins, and swirls.

### WHERE TO EAT

A day here involves non-stop action, so eat a high-protein meal and plenty of snacks to keep your energy up. There isn't one large restaurant, but there are plenty of snack stands throughout the park.

One standout is the **Wild Tiki Lounge**, a Polynesian restaurant-bar overlooking the lake. It has a full menu, table service, and flat-screen TVs. There's also **Manny's Pizza** (pizza, spaghetti, and subs) and the **Surf Grill**, which serves burgers, hot dogs, BBQ sandwiches, and healthier choices like veggie burgers, baked potatoes, and salads. Smaller kiosks sell cotton candy, ice cream, funnel cakes, and other carnival-style snacks.

## TOURING TIPS

■ Want to save a bundle? Depending on closing time, admission drops to half price sometime around mid-afternoon. Call ahead for the magic hour.

■ To claim a prime beach spot, arrive 30 minutes before the park opens, or visit on a cloudy day. If it looks like rain all day, though, head elsewhere.

■ Men should wear a true bathing suit, and women should opt for a one-piece rather than a bikini. Cutoff shorts and garments with rivets, metal buttons, or zippers aren't allowed.

■ Wading slippers are a good idea (put them in a locker or plan to carry them when taking a plunge, though). The rough, hot sidewalks and sandpaper-like pool bottoms can do a number on your feet.

■ Stash money, keys, prescription glasses, and other valuables in a locker.

■ Be patient with the lines here. Just when you think you've arrived, you discover there's another level or two to go.

■ To bypass lines at the popular rides, get an Express Pass. Prices change based on park attendance, so call 407/351–1800 for details. Among the rides that accept the pass are The Black Hole: The Next Generation, Disco H2O, Surge, Mach V, Flyer, Brain Wash, Storm, and Bubba Tub. There are a limited number of passes sold each day; all the more reason to get here early.

■ OK. So you arrived armed with a swimsuit and a towel. But what about sunscreen? You can buy it and other necessities or souvenirs at the Breakers Beach Shop near the park entrance. And if you did forget your towel, renting one here costs $2 with a $2 deposit. Rent a three-pack, though, and you'll save $2.

## TOP WET 'N WILD ATTRACTIONS

**Bomb Bay.** You drop through the floor of a cylinder and plummet down a nearly vertical slide—as they say, the first step is a doozie.

**Storm.** Nestled in an inner tube, you slip into a surreal spin around a massive basin that slowly but surely washes you . . . down the drain.

**Disco H2O.** Why spin through a watery disco to a 1970s soundtrack? For the aquatic dance-hall sensation that makes this ride so popular.

**Brain Wash.** Lighting effects and surreal sounds accompany your five-story drop and spin around a 65-foot domed funnel.

**Lazy River.** This calming stream is a good antidote to all the adrenaline.

**Surf Lagoon.** If the beach is out of reach, take advantage of the sand and surf here.

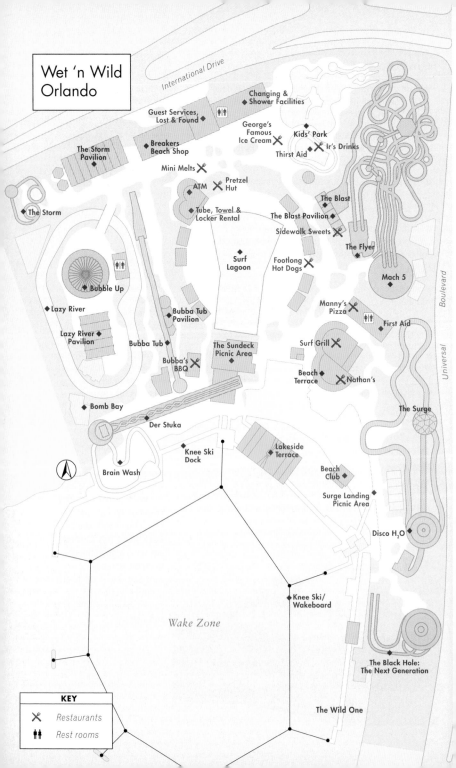

# WET 'N WILD WATER PARKS

| NAME | Height req. | Type of Entertainment | Duration | Crowds | Audience | Tips |
|---|---|---|---|---|---|---|
| Black Hole: The Next Generation | 36" with an adult, 48" without | Waterslide | 1 min. | Heavy | All but Small Kids | Try it very early (or very late) or invest in an Express Pass. |
| The Blast | 36" with an adult, 48" without | Waterslide | Under 1 min. | Heavy | Families | Keep an eye on the line and come when it looks short. |
| ★ Bomb Bay | At least 48" | Waterslide | Under 1 min. | Heavy | All but Small Kids | Watch the line. |
| ★ Brain Wash | At least 48" | Waterslide | 1 min. | Heavy | Families | Try it very early (or very late) or invest in an Express Pass. |
| Bubba Tub | 36" with an adult, 48" without | Waterslide | Under 1 min. | Moderate | Families | Early, late, or EXPRESS Pass. |
| Bubble Up | 42"–64" only | Pool Area | Up to You | Light | Small Kids | Come when your kids are ready. |
| Der Stuka | At least 48" | Waterslide | 1 min. | Moderate | All but Small Kids | Come early, late, or use an Express Pass. |
| ★ Disco H20 | 36" with an adult, 48" without | Waterslide | 1 min. | Heavy | Families | Come early, late, or use an Express Pass. |
| The Flyer | 36" with an adult, 48" without | Waterslide | 1 min. | Heavy | Families | Keep an eye on the line and head over when it's short. |
| Kids' Park | Under 48" to ride the rides | Pool Area | Up to You | Moderate to Heavy | Small Kids | Come when you need a break but the kids still have energy. |
| Knee Ski/Wakeboard | At least 56" | Thrill Ride with Water | Over 1 min. | Vary by Season | Tweens and Teens | It sosts extra, but the pass is good all day. |
| Lazy River | n/a | Pool Area | Up to You | Moderate | All Ages | Come whenever you wish. |
| Mach 5 | n/a | Waterslide | 1 min. | Moderate | All but Small Kids | Come early, late, or when the line looks short. |
| The Storm | At least 48" | Waterslide | 1 min. | Moderate | All but Small Kids | Come early or late. |
| Surf Lagoon | Those under 48" must wear flotation devices | Beach Area | Up to You | Moderate to Heavy | All Ages | Come anytime. |

# OTHER UNIVERSAL ACTIVITIES

## SHOPPING

If you just pass through the parks focused on the main rides, you may not notice that you're essentially walking through an outdoor mall. That said, there are a few key shopping areas.

### TOP AREAS

**Universal.** The largest collection of stores is near the park gates around Production Central and Hollywood. Here the inventory ranges from silver-screen collectibles to the usual souvenirs and kitsch. The Universal Studios Store offers one-stop shopping.

**Islands of Adventure.** The largest concentration of stores is near the gates at the Port of Entry. And a central emporium—the Trading Company—carries nearly every coveted collectible from nearly every park shop. Hogsmeade Village in the Wizarding World of Harry Potter is the place for Potter-related memorabilia and wizard supplies.

**CityWalk.** This 30-acre entertainment and retail complex is at the hub of promenades that lead to Universal Studios and Islands of Adventure. Shops here sell fine jewelry, cool beachwear, fashionable clothing, and stylish accessories.

**Wet 'n Wild.** You may not need a lot when you're hanging out wearing a bathing suit, but even Wet 'n Wild knows that you probably will need (or just want) something. One store—the Breakers Beach Shop—carries beachwear and other assorted gear.

## NIGHTLIFE

With an attitude that's distinctly non-Disney, Universal has created nightlife for adults who want to party. The epicenter is CityWalk, which has, among other things, an over-the-top discotheque, a theater for the popular Blue Man Group, and a huge hall where karaoke's king.

Clubs have individual cover charges, but it's far more economical to pay for the whole kit and much of the caboodle. Choose a Party Pass (a one-price-all-clubs admission) for $11.99; a Party Pass-and-a-Movie for $21 (plus tax); a Movie-and-a-Meal for $21.95; or a Party Pass-and-a-Meal for $21.

With 20 screens, there's certain to be a movie you'll like at AMC Universal cineplex. Meals (tax and gratuity included) are served at Jimmy Buffett's Margaritaville, the Hard Rock Cafe, NASCAR Sports Grille, and others. And as if these deals weren't sweet enough, after 6 pm the $15 parking fee drops to $3. However, it's a long haul from the garage to CityWalk—if you prefer, simply call a cab. They run at all hours.

### CITYWALK

**BARS AND CLUBS**

**Jimmy Buffett's Margaritaville.** Buffett tunes fill the air at the restaurant here and at Volcano, Land Shark, and 12 Volt bars. There's a Pan Am Clipper suspended from the ceiling, music videos projected onto sails,

## TOP SOUVENIRS

Each park has an item or two that tells folks where you've been (and that you're a savvy shopper).

**Shop like Homer.** At Apu Nahasapeemapetilon's Kwik-E-Mart, near the Simpsons Ride at Universal Studios, Marge wigs and Homer T-shirts or boxer shorts are natural choices.

**Shop like an Egyptian.** Several stores sell super-hero and film-themed souvenirs—from Spider-Man gear and Incredible Hulk fists to Egyptian hats and clothing from *The Mummy*.

**Pair Up.** At Seuss Landing in IOA, Thing 1 and Thing 2 T-shirts are always a hit with couples and siblings. Or how about a couple of red-and-white-striped Cat in the Hat mugs?

**Make Some Magic.** Visit IOA's Wizarding World of Harry Potter and you may head home with a wand, omni-oculars, quaffle ball, Hogwarts robe, or a Nimbus 2000 broomstick.

**Dry Off.** Check out Wet n' Wild's collection of beach towels—one of the few souvenirs you may actually use after you go home.

limbo and hula-hoop contests, a huge margarita blender that erupts "when the volcano blows," live music nightly—everything that Parrotheads need to roost. ☎ *407/224–2692* ⊕ *www.margaritaville.com* ✉ *$7 after 10 pm* ☾ *Daily 11:30 am–2 am.*

**Bob Marley—A Tribute to Freedom.** This club, modeled after the so-called King of Reggae's home in Kingston, Jamaica, is like a museum, with more than 100 photographs and paintings showing pivotal moments in Marley's life. Off the cozy bar is a patio where you can be jammin' to a (loud) live band that plays from 8 pm to 1:30 am nightly. ☎ *407/224–2692* ✉ *$7 after 9 pm* ☾ *Weekdays 4 pm–2 am, weekends 2 pm–2 am.*

**the groove.** Prepare for an under-thirty crowd, lots of fog, swirling lights, and sweaty bodies. The '70s-style Green Room is filled with the kind of stuff you threw out when Duran Duran hit the charts. The Blue Room is sci-fi Jetson-y, and the Red Room is hot and romantic in a bordello sort of way. ☎ *407/224–2692* ✉ *$7* ☾ *Daily 9 pm–2 am.*

**Latin Quarter.** A tribute to Latin music and dance, this place is spicy hot—salsa hot, even. Although there is a restaurant, most people come for the nightclub. It's a 21st-century version of Ricky Ricardo's Tropicana, with a design based on Aztec, Inca, and Maya architecture. There's even an Andes Mountain range, complete with waterfalls, around the dance floor. ☎ *407/224–2692* ✉ *$7; price may vary for certain performances* ☾ *Mon.–Thurs. 5 pm–2 am, Fri. and Sat. noon–2 am.*

**Pat O'Brien's.** It's an exact reproduction of the legendary New Orleans bar, complete with flaming fountain and dueling pianists. The draw here is the Patio Bar, where a wealth of tables and chairs allow you to do nothing but enjoy your potent, rum-based Hurricanes. ☎ *407/224–2692* ⊕ *www.patobriens.com* ✉ *$7 after 9 pm* ☾ *Patio Bar daily 4 pm–2 am; piano bar daily 6 pm–2 am.*

**Red Coconut Club.** The interior is part Vegas lounge, part Cuban club, and part Polynesian tiki bar—all circa the 1950s. There's a full bar, signature martinis, an extensive wine list, and VIP bottle service. Hang out in the Rat Pack–style lounge, on the balcony, or with the happening bar crowd. A DJ or live music pushes the energy with tunes ranging from Sinatra to rock. ☎ 407/224–2692 ➔ $7; price may vary for certain performances ⊙ Mon.–Thurs. 5 pm–2 am, Fri. and Sat. noon–2 am.

**Rising Star.** Here you and other hopeful (and hopeless) singers can let loose. Instead of singing to recorded music, you're accompanied by a band complete with backup singers—and all before an audience. Although the band's not here on Sunday and Monday, the backup singers are on hand every night. ☎ 407/224–2692 ➔ $7 ⊙ Nightly 8 pm–2 am, 21 and up; 18 and up on Thurs.

### SHOWS

**Blue Man Group.** The Sharp-Aquos Theatre is home to one act: the Blue Man Group, who present 90 minutes of surreal and silly routines—greatly appreciated by anyone who enjoys juvenile humor, which, as it turns out, happens to be most people. How many marshmallows can one Blue Man catch in his mouth? Many. Is it really art when a Blue Man spits paint onto a spinning canvas? Can someone really create music out of a spaghetti twist of PVC tubing? ☎ 407/BLUE–MAN (258–3626) ➔ Advance purchase from $64 (add $10 when buying at the box office) ⊙ Daily showtimes vary, call for schedule.

**Hard Rock Cafe.** The Hard Rock here is the largest on earth. This means more memorabilia than ever, including Beatles rarities such as cutouts from the *Sgt. Pepper* cover, John Lennon's famous "New York City" T-shirt, Paul's original lyrics for "Let It Be," and the doors from London's Abbey Road studios. At the Hard Rock Live concert hall, seats are hard and two-thirds don't face the stage, but there's a performance just about every night. Warning: you can't bring large purses or bags inside, and there are no lockers at CityWalk. ☎ 407/224–2692 ⊕ www.hardrocklive.com ➔ Cover prices vary ⊙ Daily from 11 am, with varying closing times, generally around midnight.

### RESORT BARS

There are several lounges within Universal's resort hotels, each themed and each a sanctuary where you can relax with a soothing libation.

**Hard Rock Hotel.** The **Beach Club** is a pool–beach bar and grill where you can sip a tropical drink or cold beer. The evening's certainly more upscale at the **Velvet Lounge**, a hip retreat that's home to the monthly Velvet Sessions rock-and-roll cocktail party.

**Portofino Bay.** At the dockside **Thirsty Fish** bar, sunsets are accompanied by wine and live jazz. **Bar American** specializes in martinis and other cocktails, and grappa.

**Royal Pacific Resort.** **Jake's American Bar** has a South Pacific look (it's themed as the retreat of an island-hopping airline pilot), English and Asian entrées, cocktails, a full liquor bar, and live background music. The **Orchid Court Lounge and Sushi Bar** is resplendent with orchids, hand-carved Balinese furniture, and South Seas martinis and drinks.

# SeaWorld Orlando

## SEAWORLD, DISCOVERY COVE, AQUATICA

**WORD OF MOUTH**

"SeaWorld has fewer rides but fewer lines. It also has animal shows. . . . the Shamu show is amazing, but Pets Ahoy is terrific."
—321go

"SeaWorld . . . is very manageable on a 100+ heat index day, with all the "splash" potential and air-conditioned areas. . . ."
—rattravelers

# WELCOME TO SEAWORLD ORLANDO

## TOP REASONS TO GO

★ **Animal Magnetism:** If you love animals—slick, shiny, feathery, or furry—SeaWorld, Discovery Cove, and Aquatica are where you want to be. No robotic wildlife here; just well-cared-for and talented dolphins, whales, seals, otters, penguins, cats, dogs. . . .

★ **A Slower Pace:** The shows and natural settings of SeaWorld and Discovery Cove let you enjoy a theme park vacation without racing from one attraction to the next. Living in the moment is the lesson here.

★ **Getting Smarter:** No one leaves these parks without learning a little something about nature through shows, backstage tours, instructional signage, and well-versed educators and naturalists who are always ready to answer questions.

★ **Memories in the Making:** Chances are SeaWorld and Discovery Cove will afford you the chance to pet a penguin, feed a dolphin, or watch a 5-ton whale leap out of the water. You can't forget things like that.

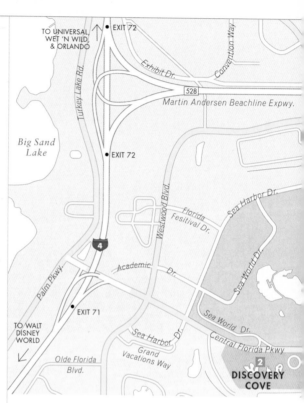

**1 SeaWorld.** With the exception of a handful of thrill rides, the original park (which opened in 1973 to siphon off visitors heading to the then recently opened Walt Disney World) maintains a slow and easy pace. Here it's all about clever shows, shaded sidewalks, and plenty of opportunities to enjoy the natural grace and intriguing personalities of marine life and other animals.

TO WET 'N WILD &
UNIVERSAL STUDIOS

Universal Blvd.

EXIT 3A

EXIT
3B

528

EXIT 2

AQUATICA **3**

Gateway Ave.

Orangewood Blvd.

International Dr.

**1**

SEAWORLD

423

0       1/4 mi

0       1/4 km

## GETTING ORIENTED

SeaWorld is just off the intersection of Interstate 4 and the Beachline Expressway, equidistant from Universal Orlando and the Walt Disney World Resort, which are about five minutes away. SeaWorld is also a mere 10 minutes from downtown Orlando and 15 minutes from the airport. Discovery Cove is its own oasis across the street from SeaWorld. Aquatica, a little ways down the road from both, is the first of the three that you'll see after exiting the expressway.

7

**2 Discovery Cove.** In 2000 SeaWorld spun off this park to give you the chance to enjoy a lot more time (and to spend a little more cash) with the animals. A trip to this park is a daylong, all-inclusive experience that includes breakfast and lunch, drinks, a private beach, snorkeling equipment, and—for an extra $100—the chance to swim with dolphins. Paradise

**3 Aquatica.** Opened in 2008, SeaWorld's water park offers the chance to slip and slide at adrenaline-rush speeds, relax in the current of two wave pools, laze on a wide beach, and take the wee ones to pint-size play areas of their very own. All in all, there's something for everyone showcased in a tropical, tiki-theme setting.

# SEAWORLD ORLANDO PLANNER

## Operating Hours

SeaWorld opens daily at 9 am and usually closes at 7 pm, with extended hours during the summer and holidays. Hours at Discovery Cove also vary seasonally, although it's generally open daily from 9 to 5:30, with check-in beginning at 8. Aquatica is open at 9 am, with closing times varying between 5 and 10 pm depending on the season. Allow a full day to see each attraction.

## Contacts

**Aquatica:** ☎ 888/800–5447 ⊕ www.aquaticabyseaworld. com

**Busch Gardens Tampa:** ☎ 888/800–5447 ⊕ www. buschgardens.com/bgt

**Discovery Cove:** ☎ 877/557– 7404 ⊕ www.discoverycove. com

**SeaWorld:** ☎ 888/800–5447 ⊕ www.seaworld.com

## Getting Here and Around

Heading west on Interstate 4 (toward Disney) take Exit 72; heading east, take Exit 71. After that you'll be going east on the Beachline Expressway (aka Route 528) and the first right-hand exit leads you to International Drive. Turn left, and you'll soon see the entrance to Aquatica on your left. Sea Harbor Drive—leading to SeaWorld's entrance—will be on your right. To reach Discovery Cove, follow International Drive past Aquatica ½-mi to the Central Florida Parkway and turn right. The park's entrance will be on your left.

### PARKING

Parking is $14 for a car or motorcycle, $15 for an RV or camper. For $20 you can pull into one of the six rows closest to the front gate. Parking is free at Discovery Cove.

## Admission

SeaWorld, Discovery Cove, Aquatica, and Busch Gardens Tampa Bay fall under the SeaWorld Parks & Entertainment umbrella, and you can save by buying combo tickets. Regular one-day tickets to **SeaWorld** cost $79.99 (adults) and $69.99 (children ages 3–9), excluding tax. **Aquatica** admission is $47.99 (adults) and $41.99 (children 3–9). Order online and save around $5 per ticket.

Reserve **Discovery Cove** visits well in advance—attendance is limited to about 1,000 a day. Tickets (with a dolphin swim) start at $199 (off-season) but are generally around $289. Forego the dolphin swim and save $100. Either fee includes access to all beach and snorkeling areas and the free-flight aviary; meals and snacks; use of a mask, snorkel, swim vest, towel, locker, and sunscreen; parking; and a pass for 14 days of unlimited admission to SeaWorld Orlando, Aquatica, or Busch Gardens Tampa.

### QUICK QUEUE PASSES

SeaWorld's one-time and unlimited Quick Queue passes ($15–$35 per person depending on the season), get you to the front of the line at major attractions and shows. Neither Discovery Cove nor Aquatica has such a pass.

## Smart SeaWorld

**Avoid weekend and school-holiday visits.** These are the busiest times, so plan around them if you can.

**Wear sneakers or water shoes**—no heels or slip-on sandals.

**Pack dry clothes.** You can get wet just by being toward the front at the One Ocean show or riding Journey to Atlantis. Alternatively, carry a rain poncho.

**Budget for food for the animals.** Participating in animal feedings is a major part of the SeaWorld experience. A small carton of fish costs $5.

**Pick up a map/show schedule inside the entrance.** Spend a few minutes planning so you can casually stroll from show to show and have time for learning, testing out thrill rides, *and* enjoying a leisurely meal.

**Be open to learning.** SeaWorld's trainers and educators are always at the ready to share information about the park's wildlife.

## Discovery Done Right

**Make reservations well in advance.** Prized June dates, for instance, can sell out in March. If there aren't openings when you call, though, don't despair. Call back often to inquire about cancellations.

**Think about your eyewear.** Park masks don't accommodate glasses, but there are a limited number of near- and far-sighted prescription masks (first-come, first-served) available. Consider wearing contacts as an alternative.

**Don't bring your own wet suit or fins.** Every guest must wear a Discovery Cove–issued wet suit or vest—not a bad idea, as the water can be cold.

**Leave belongings in your locker.** The plastic passes you're given are all you need to pick up your meals, soft drinks, and—if you're over 21—alcoholic drinks.

**Be flexible when it comes to weather.** If weather is really bad (e.g., a daylong thunderstorm) on your reserved day, attempts will be made to reschedule for while you're in town. If that's not possible, you'll have to settle for a refund.

**Have a dolphin relay a message.** The Special Occasion Package enlists the help of a bottlenose dolphin to deliver love notes, wedding proposals, birthday or anniversary greetings, and the like.

## Aquatica Advice

■ **Buy tickets in advance.** Tickets bought ahead of time online or at another park allow early entry to Aquatica, which, in turn, increases your chances of hitting all the big-deal flume and tube rides—possibly more than once.

■ **Be open to animal encounters.** The Commerson's dolphins of Dolphin Plunge have scheduled feeding times, and you can see macaws perched on tree limbs and small mammals on display in Conservation Cabanas—usually attended to by knowledgeable educators.

■ **Pack beach supplies.** You'll save a few bucks by having your own towels, lotion, water shoes, and snacks.

■ **Take care of yourself.** Fight fatigue by eating a good breakfast, drinking plenty of water, and nibbling on high-energy snacks. Avoid sunburn by reapplying sunscreen often—even the waterproof stuff washes off.

■ **Save your soles.** Water shoes protect your feet from hot sand and sidewalks and the rough surfaces in some pools.

7

By Gary
McKechnie

SeaWorld and Discovery Cove offer a relatively low-key, ocean-theme experience and are designed for animal lovers and those who prefer the natural to the man-made. Aquatica, on the other hand, suits those who are looking for the action of waterslides, wave lagoons, and beaches.

At SeaWorld you can catch high-energy shows involving dolphins, whales, sea lions, a huge walrus, and even cats and dogs. Plus, you can ride three thrilling coasters: Kraken, considered one of Florida's scariest rides; Journey to Atlantis, a splashy flume; and the park's newest coaster, Manta, which is designed to make you feel like you're sailing along with a giant manta ray.

Discovery Cove is more of a laid-back oasis. In your wet suit or swim vest (provided) you can spend a magical day snorkeling among tropical fish; getting up close to tropical birds in an aviary; relaxing on the beach; and, for a short period and extra charge, interacting with dolphins. You'll pay roughly three times as much as for a ticket to Sea-World, but your ticket includes 14 days of unlimited access to either SeaWorld or Aquatica or Tampa's Busch Gardens either before or after your visit to Discovery Cove. Or visit all three for an additional $50.

There's no denying that SeaWorld's water park, Aquatica, was designed to compete with Disney's Blizzard Beach and Typhoon Lagoon and Universal's Wet 'n Wild. There's also no denying that it does so—admirably. It's aesthetically pleasing, with tropical, tiki-theme, and eye-popping color schemes. It's also universally appealing, with 36 waterslides of varying thrill levels, six rivers and lagoons, and plenty of calm sandy stretches.

Are you a family with teens looking for adrenaline-rush rides? Do you have toddlers who need pint-size attractions? Are you honeymooners who simply want to sunbathe? All of you can find attractions here, whether lazing on the sands, bobbing in the wave pool, or screaming your heads off in a winding pitch-black tube en route to a super splashdown.

# SeaWorld Orlando

TO AQUATICA →

← TO DISCOVERY COVE

**KEY WEST**

Lagoon

- Manatees Rescue
- Dolphin Cove
- Stingray Lagoon
- First Aid
- Blue Horizons
- Journey to Atlantis
- Turtle Point
- Captain Pete's Island Eats
- Key West at SeaWorld
- Kraken
- Penguin Encounter
- Seaport Pizza
- Pacific Point Preserve
- Clyde and Seamore Take Pirate Island (Sea Lion & Otter Stadium)
- Antarctic Market
- Voyager's Smokehouse
- Shark's Underwater Grill
- Shark Encounter
- A'Lure the Call of the Ocean (Nautilus Theater)
- Spice Mill Cafe
- Paddle boats
- Sky Tower
- The Waterfront
- Pearl Dive
- Pets Ahoy (Seaport Theater)
- Manta
- Dolphin Nursery
- Makahiki Luau
- Seafire Inn
- Lockers
- Pet Care Center
- Cypress Bakery
- Guest Services; Information; Reservations and Show Schedules
- Main Entrance/Exit
- The Terrace
- One Ocean (Shamu Stadium)
- Dine with Shamu
- Atlantis Bayside Stadium
- Mango Joe's Café
- Coconut Cove Snacks
- Shamu's Happy Harbor
- First Aid
- Wild Arctic

**KEY**

✗ Restaurants

🚻 Rest rooms

# SEAWORLD ORLANDO
## SWIM WITH THE FISHIES

There's a whole lot more to SeaWorld and Discovery Cove than being splashed by Shamu. You can see manatees face-to-snout, learn to love an eel, swim with dolphins, and be spat at by a walrus. These two parks celebrate all the mammals, birds, fish, and reptiles that live in and near the ocean.

SeaWorld's performance venues, attractions, and activities surround a 17-acre lagoon, and the artful landscaping, curving paths, and concealing greenery sometimes lead to wrong turns. But armed with a map that lists showtimes, it's easy to plan an approach that lets you move fluidly from one show and attraction to the next and still have time for rest stops and meal breaks.

Thanks to Discovery Cove's daily cap on crowds, it may seem as if you have the park to yourself. Navigating the grounds is simple; signs point to swimming areas, cabanas, or the free-flight aviary—aflutter with exotic birds and accessible via a walkway or (even better) by swimming to it beneath a waterfall.

### TOURING TIPS

■ Before investing in front-of-the-line Quick Queue passes ($20–$35), remember that there are only a handful of big-deal rides, and space is seldom a problem at shows.

■ If you bring your own food, remove all straws and lids before you arrive—they can harm fish and birds.

■ Arrive at least 30 minutes early for the Shamu show, which generally fills to capacity. Prepare to get wet in the "splash zone" down front.

■ In Discovery Cove make the aviary one of your first stops, since the 250-plus birds within will be more active in the morning. Check-in starts at 8 am.

## TOP SEAWORLD ATTRACTIONS

**Clyde and Seamore Take Pirate Island.** Head for Sea Lion & Otter Stadium to watch this slapstick comedy routine starring an adorable team of water mammals and their trainers.

**Journey to Atlantis.** Although it seems a little dated, the Splash Mountain–esque ride still provides thrills—especially on its last, steep, wet drop.

**Kraken.** It takes you on a high-speed chase with a dragon. But who's chasing who? Fast and furious.

**Manta.** SeaWorld likes to claim that this is two attractions in one: while waiting in line, you walk past 10 supercool aquariums filled with rays and fish. But the big thrill is the amazingly fast coaster at the front of the line.

**One Ocean.** This show awes you with its audiovisual effects and killer-whale antics while inspiring you to care for the planet and its creatures.

**Pets Ahoy.** Anyone who has ever loved a pet (or simply wanted one) has to see the talented cats, dogs, birds, and pig in this cute and clever show.

## TOP DISCOVERY COVE ATTRACTIONS

**Private Cabanas.** Granted, admission to Discovery Cove isn't cheap, but if you can pony up a little more (about $175) you'll enjoy personalized service, complete privacy, a table, chairs, chaise lounges, rolled towels, and a well-stocked mini-refrigerator in these tropical waterfront sanctuaries.

**Snorkeling Pools.** The snorkeling pools may well be Discovery Cove's must under-hyped attractions. It's a real thrill to float lazily and silently amid tropical fish, to swim beneath a waterfall into an elaborate aviary, and to dive down a few feet to peer at sharks and barracuda through the porthole of a wrecked ship. There's also on-site snorkeling instruction.

### HOW IT BEGAN

Hard to believe that four frat brothers intent on creating a restaurant would inadvertently build the foundation for one of the world's most popular theme parks. In the early 1960s UCLA grads Milton Shedd, David DeMott, George Millay, and Ken Norris were ready to parlay their talent and ambition into an underwater restaurant, but as plans changed they ended up building San Diego's SeaWorld, which opened in early 1964.

Within the first year the park welcomed more than 400,000 visitors. It took several more years before the second SeaWorld, in Ohio, opened. This was followed in 1973 by Orlando's SeaWorld, and, in 1988—under the then-new ownership of publishing firm Harcourt Brace Jovanovich—a fourth park in San Antonio.

**7**

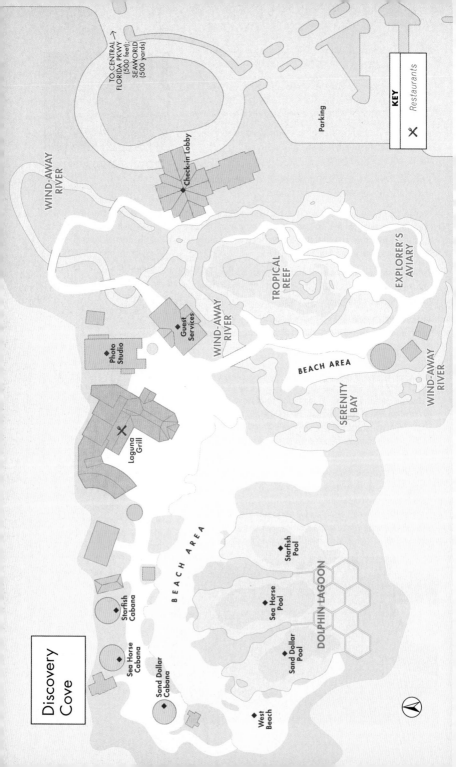

# Discovery Cove

KEY

✕ Restaurants

TO CENTRAL
FLORIDA PKWY →
(500 feet);
SEAWORLD
(500 yards)

WIND-AWAY RIVER

Check-in Lobby

Parking

TROPICAL REEF

EXPLORER'S AVIARY

Guest Services

WIND-AWAY RIVER

Photo Studio

BEACH AREA

SERENITY BAY

WIND-AWAY RIVER

✕ Laguna Grill

BEACH AREA

Starfish Cabana

Sea Horse Cabana

Sand Dollar Cabana

Starfish Pool

Sea Horse Pool

Sand Dollar Pool

DOLPHIN LAGOON

West Beach

**DID YOU KNOW?**

Commerson's dolphins (*Cephalorhynchus commersonii*) were named after Philibert Commerçon, an 18th-century scientist who saw them swimming in the Strait of Magellan in South America.

# SEAWORLD ORLANDO AND DISCOVERY COVE

| NAME | Height Req. | Type of Entertainment | Duration | Crowds | Audience | Tips |
|---|---|---|---|---|---|---|
| **SeaWorld** | | | | | | |
| A'Lure, the Call of the Ocean | n/a | Show | 20 mins. | Heavy | All Ages | Plenty of seats, but arrive 15 mins. early for a wide selection. |
| Blue Horizons | n/a | Show | 20 mins. | Heavy | All Ages | Arrive 20 mins. before showtime. |
| Dolphin Nursery | n/a | Aquarium | Up to you | Light | All Ages | Come during a Shamu show so the kids can be up front. |
| Journey to Atlantis | At least 42" | Thrill Ride with Water | 6 mins. | Heavy | All but Small Kids | You can make a beeline here first thing or come about an hour before closing. But the best time for this is at night. |
| Key West at SeaWorld | n/a | Walk-Through/ Aquarium | Up to you | Light to Moderate | All Ages | If too crowded, wander until crowds disperse. |
| ★ Kraken | At least 54" | Thrill Ride | 6 mins. | Heavy | All but Small Kids | Get to the park when it opens and head straight to Kraken; otherwise, hit it near closing time or during a Blue Horizons show. |
| Manatees Rescue | n/a | Aquarium | Up to you | Light to Moderate | All Ages | Come during a Shamu show but *not* right after a dolphin show. |
| ★ Manta | At least 54" | Thrill Ride with Water | 6 mins. | You Bet! | All but Small Kids | Come first thing or late in the day, or purchase a Quick Queue pass for front-of-ride access. |
| Pacific Point Preserve | n/a | Aquarium | Up to you | Light | All Ages | Come anytime. |
| Penguin Encounter | n/a | Aquarium | Up to you | Moderate to Heavy | All Ages | Come during dolphin and sea lion shows, and before you've gotten soaked at Journey to Atlantis, or you'll freeze. |
| Pets Ahoy | n/a | Show | 15–20 mins. | Moderate to Heavy | All Ages | Gauge the crowds, and come here early if necessary. |

| | | | | | | |
|---|---|---|---|---|---|---|
| ★ Sea Lion & Otter Stadium | n/a | Show | 40 mins. | Heavy | All Ages | Sit toward the center for the best view, and don't miss the pre-show mime. Plenty of seats. |
| Shamu's Happy Harbor | n/a | Playground with Water | Up to you | Heavy | Small Kids | Don't come first thing in morning, or you'll never drag your child away. Bring a towel to dry them off. |
| ★ Shamu Stadium (One Ocean) | n/a | Show | 25 mins. | Moderate to Heavy | All Ages | Show itself lasts 25 minutes, but there's a 30-minute pre-show; plan accordingly. |
| Shark Encounter | n/a | Aquarium | Up to you | Light to Moderate | All Ages | Come during the sea lion show. |
| Sky Tower | 48" | Tour/Thrill Ride | 6 mins. | Light | All Ages | Come whenever there's no line. Note the extra $4 charge, though. |
| Stingray Lagoon | n/a | Aquarium | Up to you | Moderate to Heavy | All Ages | Walk by if it's crowded, but return before dusk. |
| Turtle Point | n/a | Zoo | Up to you | Light | All Ages | Come anytime. |
| Wild Arctic | At least 42" | Simulator Exp./Aquarium | 5+ mins. | Moderate to Heavy | All Ages | Come during a Shamu show. You can skip the ride if you just want to see the mammals. |
| **Discovery Cove** | | | | | | |
| Beaches | n/a | Beach Area | Up to you | Light | All Ages | Arrive early and head to the far side for a private spot. |
| ★ Dolphin Lagoon | n/a | Pool | 45–60 mins. | n/a | All but Small Kids | Be mindful of your appointment time. |
| Explorer's Aviary | n/a | Aviary | Up to you | Light to Moderate | All Ages | Come early, when the birds are most active. |
| Tropical Reef | n/a | Aquarium/Pool Area | Up to you | Light to Moderate | All Ages | Monitor crowds and come when they're lightest. Popular with teens. |
| Wind-Away River | n/a | Aquarium | Up to you | Light to Moderate | All Ages | When it gets hot, slip into the water. Popular with teens. |

★ Fodor's Choice

# AQUATICA
## SPLASH IN TROPICAL SEAS

Aquatica takes cues from SeaWorld and Discovery Cove in design and mood—marine-life motifs are everywhere. It also gives competitor water parks a run for their money with thrilling slides, broad beaches, calming rivers, and an area for small kids.

The park also takes its cues from the tropics. Right after you clear the parking lot, you'll see a tropical pastiche of buildings. Yup. That's definitely an island vibe you're detecting. Upon entering, you feel as if you've left central Florida for the Caribbean or Polynesia, even.

Go with it. Get into a groove, and relax and enjoy yourself. You might be drawn to the series of super-fast waterslides (some of which conclude by sending you into serene streams). Or you might feel the pull of the white-sand beaches beside the twin wave pools, where you can laze in the sun, venturing out every so often to try a ride or climb into an inner tube and float down a river.

Hey, it's your vacation, and you're at Aquatica. Do whatever you like.

## TOURING TIPS

■ **Buy tickets in advance.** Prepurchased tickets get you early entrance, and this head start will enable you to hit the major flume and tube rides more than once.

■ **Commune with nature.** You can catch Commerson's dolphins at feeding times; spot macaws on tree limbs; or see small mammals in the Conservation Cabanas, where docents answer questions.

■ **Take care of yourself.** Avoid sunburn by reapplying sunscreen often— even waterproof sunblock washes off. Wear sandals or water shoes (or even socks) to protect your feet from hot sand, sidewalks, and rough pool surfaces.

## FOOD FOR THOUGHT

Even though the waters are exhilarating, you'll be amazed at how much energy it takes to cover all the rides and attractions at Aquatica. You need to stay hydrated and well-nourished, which can be a costly proposition.

The park allows guests to bring in a small cooler of "serving-size" snacks, bottled water, and baby food in plastic containers. It's not so keen on "family-size" servings (think sandwiches, pizza, and 2-liter bottles of soft drinks).

## TOP AQUATICA ATTRACTIONS

**Dolphin Plunge.** Aquatica's commercials love to showcase this attraction, where you slip through a winding string of pitch-black tubes and then a stretch of clear tubes through the Commerson's dolphins' habitat.

**Wave Pools.** The lagoons here aren't too deep and are perfect for cooling off. About every 10 minutes, a series of small waves move across them, enabling you to bob around like a cork.

**Tassie's Twisters.** After hopping into an inner tube and sloshing at a high speed through an enclosed tube, you're flung into a huge circular basin and spiraled into a drain and down a slide.

**Taumata Racer.** Eight colorful tubes are lined up and waiting for you. Following a countdown, you launch yourself into your chute, and, following a twisting and turning ride, end up on a long and slippery slide into the splash-down pool.

### WATER, WATER, EVERYWHERE

Since the days of the Roman baths, people have been on the lookout for new ways to enjoy water. For Americans, the big breakthrough came after World War II when a growing middle class with a little more money and a well-deserved desire to relax helped inspire the concept of a water park. Early parks included a few standard aquatic thrills: waterslides, tube slides, wave pools, and flowing rivers. Today there are well over 200 water parks in the United States (with Wisconsin claiming about 10% of the total). They range from a simple collection of slides and streams to incredible, over-the-top, exquisitely themed experiences like—Aquatica. For more information on water parks and where they are, check out www.waterparks.com.

7

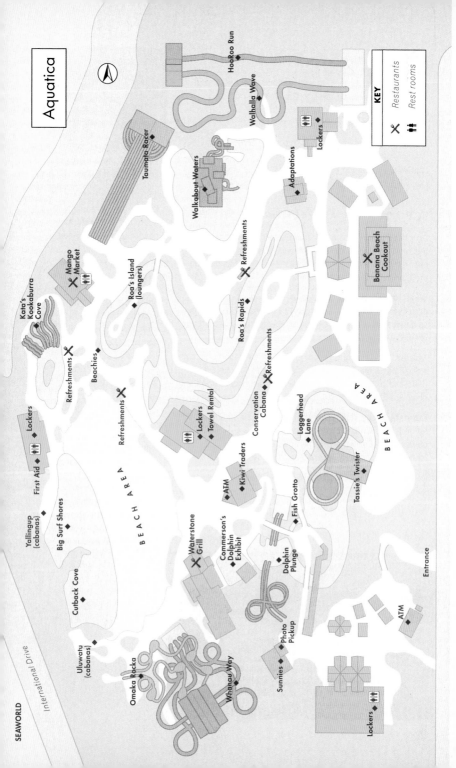

# AQUATICA WATER PARK

| NAME | Height Req. | Type of Entertainment | Duration | Crowds | Audience | Tips |
|---|---|---|---|---|---|---|
| ★ Big Surf Shores and Cutback Cove | n/a | Wave Pool | Up to you | Vary by Season | Tweens and Up | Arrive early to stake your claim on the beach. |
| Dolphin Plunge | At least 48" | Waterslide | 1 min. | Absolutely | Tweens and Up | Keep an eye on the line, and step up when it's light. |
| HooRoo Run/Walhalla Wave | At least 42" | Waterslide | 30 secs. | Heavy | All but Small Kids | Arrive early or later—or be patient. |
| Kata's Kookaburra Cove | Under 48" | Playground with Water | Up to you | Moderate to Heavy | Small Kids | Adults must be accompanied by a child no more than 48 inches tall. |
| Loggerhead Lane | At least 48" | River/Stream Ride | Up to you | Light | Tweens and Up | Try it during lunchtime. |
| Roa's Rapids | Under 51" must wear life vest | River/Stream Ride | Up to you | Light | All Ages | Visit during lunchtime. |
| Tassie's Twister | Under 48" must wear life vest | Waterslide | 1 min. | Heavy | Tweens and Up | Watch the line. |
| Taumata Racer | At least 42" | Waterslide | 30 secs. | Light to Moderate | All but Small Kids | Watch the line. |
| Walkabout Waters | 36"–42" (main pool); over 42" (large) slides. Under 48" wear life vest on larger slides. | Playground with Water | Up to you | Heavy | All but Small Kids | Save it for when you need a break. |
| Whanau Way | Under 48" must wear life vest | Waterslide | 1 min. | Heavy | All but Small Kids | Come during lunch or end of day. |

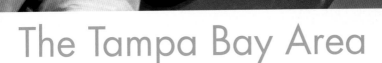

# The Tampa Bay Area

### WORD OF MOUTH

"Tampa has a great aquarium, Ybor City and Busch Gardens, of course, but the Gulf beaches are beautiful and full of fun things to do. No matter where you stay, you should include a trip to the Sponge docks in Tarpon Springs and a visit to Fort De Soto Park."
—stpetereb

# WELCOME TO
# THE TAMPA BAY AREA

## TOP REASONS
## TO GO

★ **Art Gone Wild:**
Whether you take the
guided tour or chart your
own course, experience
the one-of-a-kind col-
lection at the Salvador
Dalí Museum, which
relocated to a gorgeous
waterfront building in
Downtown St. Petersburg.

★ **Cuban Roots:** You'll
find great food and
vibrant nightlife in his-
toric Ybor City, just east
of downtown Tampa.

★ **Beachcomber Bonanza:**
Caladesi Island State Park
has some of the best shelling on the Gulf Coast, and
its five-star sunsets are a
great way to end the day.

★ **Culture Fix:** If you
love the arts, there's no
finer offering in the Bay
Area than at the Florida
State University Ringling
Center for the Cultural
Arts in Sarasota.

**1** Tampa/St. Petersburg
Area. State-of-the-art zoos
and museums in the com-
munities in the northwest
reaches of Tampa Bay
promise to broaden your
imagination, and some of
Florida's best beaches tempt
you with sparkling waters.
The area includes Clearwater, Dunedin, and Tarpon
Springs.

**2** South of Tampa Bay:
Sarasota County. Barrier
islands lure travelers to
another battery of white-
sand beaches, but Sarasota's
cultural treasures are the
true draw for many of its
visitors.

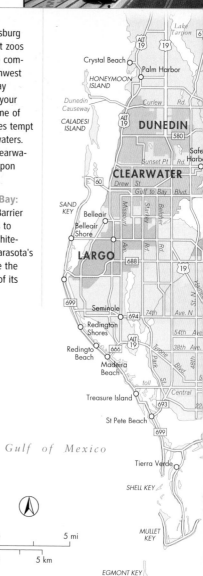

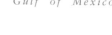

# GETTING ORIENTED

On the east side of the bay, Tampa is a sprawling cosmopolitan city offering attractions like Busch Gardens and Ybor City. To the west, St. Petersburg and Clearwater boast lovely barrier island beaches. Moving to the south, Sarasota's arts scene is among the finest in Florida.

**8**

Cosme

598

41 275 75

Fletcher Ave.

597 Gunn Hwy.

Fowler Ave.

Carrollwood

41 Temple Terrace

Busch Blvd.

586 Waters Sheldon Rd.

Oldsmar

580

Hillsborough Ave.

583

92

574

**Tampa International Airport**

Dale Mabry Hwy.

Nebraska Ave.

275

Ybor City

Courtney Campbell Causeway

60

Adamo St.

Rocky Point

*Old Tampa Bay*

Kennedy Blvd.

92

St Petersburg-Clearwater International Airport

275

Howard Frankland Bridge

**TAMPA**

BUS 41

BIG ISLAND

Gandy Bridge

South Crosstown Expwy.

West Shore Blvd.

*Hillsborough Bay*

41

East Tampa

92

1

Gibsonton

WEEDON I.

ROSS I.

62nd Ave. N

92

MacDill Air Force Base

Gadsden Point

Adamsville

38th St. N

9th St. N

19

Ave. M

**ST. PETERSBURG**

Apollo Beach

*T a m p a   B a y*

Boyd Hill Nature Park

Mangrove Point

Tamiami

54th Ave. S

COQUINA KEY

Pinellas Point

Gulf City

Ruskin

*Little*

75

Sun City

*Manatee River*

Valroy

41

Piney Point

301

Sunshine Skyway (to I)

2 TO SARASOTA ↓

Gillette

275

Parrish

19

75

# TAMPA BAY BEACHES

Tampa Bay gets rave reviews for having some of the state's best beaches. The allure includes warm water from spring through fall, gentle waves (when there are any at all), good shelling, and usually smaller crowds than ocean-front beaches. These are great places to go for romantic walks, or enjoy spectacular sunsets.

## WHEN TO GO

Tampa Bay area beaches are very popular and can get crowded in the summer, when families flock here, as well as in the winter, when snowbirds land to escape the cold in their home states. Early fall and late spring have fewer people and milder temperatures. But do check on red tide, an occasionally appearing algae that can cause breathing difficulty and itchy eyes; it is most common September to November (⊕ *research. myfwc.com*).

Tampa Bay–area beaches include Madeira Beach (called Mad Beach by locals), where you can see dolphins at play, and North Redington Beach, once a vacation spot for Marilyn Monroe and Joe DiMaggio. In Sarasota County, beaches range from artsy Siesta Key to the mansion-fronted Casey Key. **Tampa Bay Beaches Chamber of Commerce** (⊠ *6990 Gulf Blvd., St. Pete Beach* ☎ *800/ 944–1847* ⊕ *www.tampabaybeaches.com*) will give you the lowdown on the Pinellas County beaches. **Sarasota Convention & Visitors Bureau** (⊠ *701 N. Tamiami Trail, U.S. 41, Sarasota* ☎ *800/800–3906* ⊕ *www.sarasotafl.org*) has the skinny on South Tampa Bay.

## TAMPA BAY'S BEST BEACHES

### BEACH AT SOUTH LIDO PARK

At the southern tip of Sarasota's island, at 2201 Ben Franklin Drive in Lido Key, South Lido Park has one of the best beaches in the region, but note that there are no lifeguards. The sugar-sand beach offers little for shell collectors, but try your luck at fishing, take a dip in the gulf, or picnic as the sun sets through the Australian pines into the water. Facilities include nature trails, canoe and kayak trails, restrooms, and picnic grounds.

### CALADESI ISLAND STATE PARK

The beach at Caladesi, accessible by ferry from Honeymoon Island State Recreation Area, offers three reasons to visit: pure white beaches, beautiful sunsets, and, by Florida standards, relative seclusion. Oh, we left out the fact that this is an excellent spot for bird-watching.

### CLEARWATER BEACH

You will find crowds on weekends and during spring break, which are a turn-off for some, but this sun-worshippers' shrine off State Road 60 is the west coast's best muscle beach. Expect to see tanned bods draped with minimal bikinis and Speedos, plenty of hot cars, and sunsets nearly as grand as at Caladesi.

### PASS-A-GRILLE BEACH

Located where Tampa Bay meets the Gulf of Mexico in southern Pinellas County, this long-popular beach is wide and still dotted with small dunes and sea oats, two throwbacks that are rapidly vanishing in Florida. Pass-a-Grille (also called St. Pete Beach) tends to be crowded on weekends and during summer and spring break.

### SIESTA BEACH

This 40-acre park at 948 Beach Road in Siesta Key, Sarasota, has nature trails, a concession stand, fields for soccer and softball, picnic facilities, a playground, restrooms, a fitness trail, and tennis and volleyball courts. This beach has fine, powdery, quartz sand that squeaks under your feet, very much like the sand along the state's northwestern coast. It has been ranked as one of the country's top beaches.

### TURTLE BEACH

Only 14 acres, this beach-park at 8918 Midnight Pass Road in Siesta Key, Sarasota, is popular with families and is more secluded than most gulf beaches. It doesn't have the soft sand of Siesta Beach, but it does have boat ramps, a canoe and kayak launch, bay and gulf fishing, picnic facilities, restrooms, and a volleyball court.

**8**

Updated
by Kate
Bradshaw
and Connie
Sharpe

If you seek a destination that's no one-trick pony, the Tampa Bay region is a spot you can't miss. Encompassing an area from Tarpon Springs, to Tampa proper, and all the way south to Sarasota, it's one of those unsung places that's as dynamic as it is appealing—and word has definitely started to spread about its charms. With its long list of attractions—from pristine beaches to world-class museums—it's easy to see why.

First and foremost, Tampa Bay's beaches are some of the best in the country. Whether you want course or fine sand, and whether you seek a mellow day of shelling or a raucous romp on a crowded stretch of waterfront, this place has it all. Of course, you can choose from a range of water activities including charter fishing, parasailing, sunset cruises, kayaking, and more.

The region has its share of boutique districts spotted with shops and sidewalk cafés. Tampa's Hyde Park Village and Downtown St. Petersburg's Beach Drive are among the top picks if you're looking to check out some upscale shops and dine alfresco while getting the most of the area's pleasant climate. Vibrant nightlife tops off Tampa Bay's list of assets. Ybor City attracts the club set while barrier islands like St. Pete Beach offer loads of live music and barefoot dancing into the wee hours.

Tampa Bay has loads of family-friendly attractions, too. You can check out Busch Gardens, Adventure Island, and the Clearwater Marine Aquarium, to name a few. And art fanatics will find an astonishing array of attractions, including Sarasota's Ringling Museum of Art, St. Petersburg's enrapturing Salvador Dalí and Dale Chihuly collections (both permanent and housed in exquisite new digs), and Tampa's Museum of Art. Come prepared to explore and see for yourself what a compelling, unforgettable place the Tampa Bay area really is.

# TAMPA BAY AREA PLANNER

## WHEN TO GO

Winter and spring are high season, and the level of activity is double that in the off-season. Beaches do stay pretty packed throughout the sweltering summer, which is known for massive, almost daily afternoon thunderstorms. Summer daytime temperatures hover around or above 90°F. Luckily the mercury drops to the mid-70s at night, and the beaches have a consistent onshore breeze that starts just before sundown, which enabled civilization to survive here before air-conditioning arrived.

## GETTING HERE

### AIR TRAVEL

Tampa International Airport, the area's largest and busiest airport, with 19 million passengers per year, is served by most major carriers and offers ground transportation to surrounding cities. Many of the large U.S. carriers also fly into and out of Sarasota–Bradenton International Airport. St. Petersburg–Clearwater International Airport, 9 mi west of downtown St. Petersburg, is much smaller than Tampa International and has limited service.

SuperShuttle is one of the easiest ways to get to and from the airport if you forego a rental car. All you need to do is call or visit the SuperShuttle Web site to book travel—they'll pick you up and/or drop you off wherever you're staying at any hour. Basic service costs around $28.

Blue One Transportation provides service to and from Tampa International Airport for areas including Hillsborough (Tampa, Plant City), Pinellas (St. Petersburg, St. Pete Beach, Clearwater), and Polk (Lakeland) counties. Rates vary by pickup location/destination and fuel costs.

Airport Information **Sarasota–Bradenton International Airport** (☎ *941/359-2777* ⊕ *www.srq-airport.com*). **St. Petersburg–Clearwater International Airport** (☎ *727/453-7800* ⊕ *www.fly2pie.com*). **Tampa International Airport** (☎ *813/870-8700* ⊕ *www.tampaairport.com*).

Airport Transfers **Blue One Transportation** (☎ *813/282-7351* ⊕ *www.blueonetransportation.com*). **SuperShuttle** (☎ *727/572-1111 or 800/282-6817* ⊕ *www.supershuttle.com*).

### CAR TRAVEL

Interstates 75 and 275 span the Bay Area from north to south. Coming from Orlando, you're likely to drive west into Tampa on Interstate 4. Along with Interstate 75, U.S. 41 (the Tamiami Trail) stretches the length of the region and links the business districts of many communities; avoid this route during rush hours (7–9 am and 4–6 pm).

### TRAIN TRAVEL

Amtrak trains run from the Northeast, the Midwest, and much of the South into Tampa; the station is at 601 N. Nebraska Avenue.

Train Information **Amtrak** (☎ *800/872-7245* ⊕ *www.amtrak.com*).

8

## GETTING AROUND

Hillsborough Area Regional Transit and TECO Line Street Cars replicate Tampa's first electric streetcars, transporting cruise-ship passengers to Ybor City and, most recently, Downtown Tampa. Pinellas Suncoast Transit Authority offers bus service throughout Pinellas County, from the county's inland parts out to the beaches. PSTA also runs the Suncoast Beach Trolley, which takes passengers up and down the beaches—from Pass-A-Grille all the way up to Clearwater Beach and Downtown Clearwater—for $2 each way.

St. Petersburg Trolley will get you to key destinations throughout Downtown St. Pete, and even offers free service between the Chamber of Commerce Visitor's Bureau and certain destinations.

**Transportation Contacts Hillsborough Area Regional Transit** (☎ 813/254–4278 ⊕ www.hartline.org). **Pinellas Suncoast Transit Authority** (☎ 727/540–1900 ⊕ www.psta.net). **St. Petersburg Trolley** (☎ 727/821–5166 ⊕ www.loopertrolley.com). **TECO Line Street Cars** (☎ 813/254–4278 ⊕ www.tecolinestreetcar.org).

## ABOUT THE RESTAURANTS

Fresh gulf seafood is plentiful—raw bars serving oysters, clams, and mussels are everywhere. Tampa's many Cuban and Spanish restaurants serve paella with seafood and chicken, *boliche criollo* (sausage-stuffed eye-round roast) with black beans and rice, *ropa vieja* (shredded flank steak in tomato sauce), and other treats. Tarpon Springs adds classic Greek specialties. In Sarasota the emphasis is on ritzier dining, though many restaurants offer extra-cheap early-bird menus.

## ABOUT THE HOTELS

Many convention hotels in the Tampa Bay Area double as family-friendly resorts—taking advantage of nearby beaches, marinas, spas, tennis courts, and golf links. However, unlike Orlando and some other parts of Florida, the area has been bustling for more than a century, and its accommodations often reflect a sense of its history.

You'll find a turn-of-the-20th-century beachfront resort where Zelda and F. Scott Fitzgerald stayed, a massive all-wood building from the 1920s, plenty of art deco, and Spanish-style villas. But one thing they all have in common is a certain Gulf Coast charm.

| WHAT IT COSTS | | | | | |
|---|---|---|---|---|---|
| | ¢ | $ | $$ | $$$ | $$$$ |
| Restaurants | under $10 | $10–$15 | $15–$20 | $20–$30 | over $30 |
| Hotels | under $80 | $80–$100 | $100–$140 | $140–$220 | over $220 |

Restaurant prices are per person for a main course at dinner. Hotel prices are for a standard double room, excluding 6% sales tax (more in some counties) and 1%–4% tourist tax.

## BOAT TOURS

Dolphin Landings Charter Boat Center has daily four-hour cruises to unspoiled Egmont Key at the mouth of Tampa Bay. Aboard the glass-bottom boats of St. Nicholas Boat Line, you take a sightseeing cruise of Tarpon Springs' historic sponge docks and see a diver at work.

On Captain Memo's Pirate Cruise, crew members dressed as pirates take you on sightseeing and sunset cruises in a replica of a 19th-century sailing ship. The *Starlite Majesty*, a sleek, yacht-style vessel, and Starlite Princess, an old-fashioned paddle wheeler that sails out of St. Pete Beach, make lunch, sightseeing, and dinner cruises.

**Tour Operators Captain Memo's Pirate Cruise** (✉ *Clearwater Beach Marina, Clearwater Beach* ☎ *727/446-2587* ⊕ *www.captainmemo.com*). **Dolphin Landings Charter Boat Center** (✉ *4737 Gulf Blvd., St. Pete Beach* ☎ *727/360-7411* ⊕ *www.dolphinlandings.com*). **St. Nicholas Boat Line** (✉ *693 Dodecanese Blvd., Tarpon Springs* ☎ *727/942-6425*). The *Starlite Majesty* (✉ *Clearwater Beach Marina, at end of Rte. 60, Clearwater Beach* ☎ *727/462-2628* ⊕ *www.starlitecruises.com*).

# TAMPA/ST. PETERSBURG AREA

The core of the northern bay comprises the cities of Tampa, St. Petersburg, and Clearwater. A semitropical climate and access to the gulf make Tampa an ideal port for the cruise and freight industries. The waters around Clearwater and St. Petersburg are often filled with pleasure and commercial craft, including boats with day and night trips featuring gambling in international waters.

It's fitting that an area with a thriving international port should also show influence from a wide range of cultures. The center of the Cuban community is the east Tampa enclave of Ybor City, whereas north of Clearwater, in Dunedin, the heritage is Scottish. North of Dunedin, Tarpon Springs has been home to a large Greek population for decades and is the largest producer of natural sponges in the world. Inland, to the east and north of Tampa, it's all suburban sprawl, freeways, shopping malls, and—the main draw—Busch Gardens.

## TAMPA

*84 mi southwest of Orlando via I–4.*

Tampa, the west coast's business-and-commercial hub, has a sprinkling of high-rises and heavy traffic. A concentration of restaurants, nightlife, stores, and cultural events is amid the bustle.

### GETTING AROUND

Downtown Tampa's Riverwalk, on Ashley Drive at the Hillsborough River, connects waterside entities such as the Florida Aquarium, the Channelside shopping-and-entertainment complex, and Marriott Waterside. The landscaped park is 6 acres and extends along the Garrison cruise-ship channel and along the Hillsborough River downtown. The walkway is being expanded as waterside development continues.

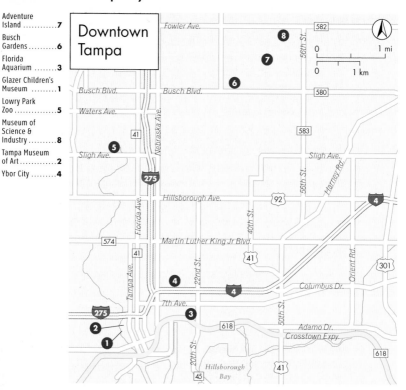

## ESSENTIALS

**Visitor Information Tampa Bay & Company** (✉ *401 E. Jackson St., Suite 2100, Tampa* ☎ *800/448-2672 or 813/223-1111* ⊕ *www.visittampabay.com*). **Ybor City Chamber Visitor Bureau** (✉ *1600 E. 8th Ave., Suite B104, Tampa* ☎ *813/241-8838* ⊕ *www.ybor.org*).

## EXPLORING

### TOP ATTRACTIONS

**Busch Gardens.** *See the highlighted listing in this chapter.*

**Florida Aquarium.** Although eels, sharks, and stingrays are the headliners, the Florida Aquarium is much more than a giant fishbowl. This architectural landmark features an 83-foot-high, multitier, glass dome, 250,000 square feet of air-conditioned exhibit space, and more than 20,000 aquatic plants, and animals representing species native to Florida and the rest of the world—from black-tip sharks to leafy sea dragons.

Floor-to-ceiling interactive displays, behind-the-scenes tours, and in-water adventures allow kids to really get hands-on—and even get their feet wet. Adventurous types (certified divers age 15 and up) can dive with mild-mannered sharks and sea turtles, participate in shark-feeding programs (age 12 and up), or shallow-water swim with reef fish such as eels and grouper (age six and up).

However, you don't have to get wet to have an interactive experience: the Ocean Commotion exhibit offers virtual dolphins and whales, multimedia displays and presentations, and even allows kids to upload video to become a part of the exhibit. The Coral Reef Gallery is a 500,000-gallon tank with viewing windows, an awesome 43-foot-wide panoramic opening, and a walk-through tunnel that gives the illusion of venturing into underwater depths. There you see a thicket of elkhorn coral teeming with tropical fish and a dark cave reveals sea life you would normally see only on night dives.

If you have two hours, try the Wild Dolphin Ecotour, which takes up to 130 passengers onto Tampa's bay in a 72-foot catamaran for an up-close look at bottlenose dolphins and other wildlife. The outdoor Explore a Shore exhibit, which gives younger kids a chance to release some energy, is an aquatic playground with a waterslide, water-jet sprays, and a climbable replica pirate ship. Last but not least, two black-footed African penguins make twice-daily appearances in the Coral Reef Gallery. ⊠ *701 Channelside Dr., Downtown, Tampa* ☎ *813/273–4000* ⊕ *www.flaquarium.org* ☜ *Aquarium $19.95, Ecotour $21.95; Aquarium/Ecotour combo $35.95; parking $6* ☉ *Daily 9:30–5.*

☼ **Glazer Children's Museum.** It's all about play here, and with 53,000-square-feet, 12 theme areas, and 175 "interactives" there's plenty of opportunity for it. Areas designed to nurture imagination and strengthen confidence allow children and families to experience everything from flying an airplane to shopping for groceries. Kids can also create art, navigate a mini–shipping channel, and "drive" a miniature (stationary) fire truck through Tampa. A Water's Journey Tree lets kids climb the tree to the second floor and mimics the water cycle. ⊠ *110 W. Gasparilla Plaza, Downtown* ☎ *813/443–3861* ⊕ *www.glazermuseum.org* ☜ *$15 adult, $9.50 children* ☉ *Weekdays 10–5, Sat. 10–6, Sun. 1–6.*

☼ **Lowry Park Zoo.** Natural-habitat exhibits featuring clouded leopards in ★ Asia Gardens make the 56-acre Lowry Park Zoo one of the best mid-size zoos in the country. Safari Africa is the home of a herd of African elephants, including Tamani, an elephant born in 2005, and residents of the nearby Ituri Forest include cheetahs and lovably plump pygmy hippos. The stars at Primate World range from cat-size lemurs to a family of heavyweight Bornean orangutans that love to ham for the camera.

For hands-on experiences, Lowry has more options than most large parks, including chances to ride a camel, feed a giraffe, or touch a slippery stingray. Majestic red-tailed hawks and other raptors put on a show at the Birds of Prey Center. You can come face-to-face with Florida manatees at the Manatee Aquatic Center, the only nonprofit manatee rehab center on the planet, Dwindling native species like Florida panthers, black bears, and red wolves may be tough to find in the wild, but you can easily find them at the Florida Wildlife Center. Kookaburras, koala, and wallabies populate the Wallaroo Station children's zoo. There are also water-play areas, rides (all of which are included with zoo admission), shows, and restaurants. ⊠ *1101 W. Sligh Ave., Central Tampa* ☎ *813/935–8552* ⊕ *www.lowryparkzoo.com* ☜ *$23.95; children $18.95* ☉ *Daily 9:30–5.*

8

# BUSCH GARDENS

Busch Gardens opened in Tampa on March 31, 1959 by the Anheuser-Busch company. It was originally designed as an admission-free animal attraction to accompany the plant, but it eventually was turned into a theme park, adding more exotic animals, tropical landscaping, and rides to entertain its guests.

Today the 335-acre park has nine distinct territories packed with roller coasters, rides, eateries, shops, and live entertainment. The park is best known for its incredible roller coasters and water rides, which draw thrill-seekers from around the globe. These rides tend to cater to those over the age of 10. With this in mind, Busch Gardens created the **Sesame Street Safari of Fun,** which is designed solely with children under 5 in mind. There's a lot packed into this area: junior thrill rides, play areas (some with water), and shows—all of which make it exciting for the kids.

### GETTING ORIENTED

The park is set up on a north–south axis with Nairobi being the center of the surrounding areas.

Your first encounter at the park is the Moroccan market (grab a map here). There are several small eateries and souvenir shops in this area. If you head west from Morocco you'll get to the Bird Gardens, Sesame Street Safari of Fun, Stanleyville, and Jungala. Heading north you'll find Nairobi, Timbuktu, and the Congo. Heading east takes you to Egypt and the Serengeti Plain. If you get lost, there are team members available almost everywhere to help you.

## TOP ATTRACTIONS

### FOR AGES 7 AND UP

**SheiKra.** This coaster is 200 feet tall and has a 200-foot vertical descent, and isn't for the faint of heart.

**Montu.** This 150-foot tall inverted coaster reaches speeds of 60 mph, and has a zero-G roll and seven inversions.

**Gwazi.** The largest, fastest wooden dueling roller coaster in the world, boasting crossing speeds of 100 mph.

**Kumba.** Riders on this coaster experience weightlessness, cobra rolls, corkscrews, and inverted rolls.

**Rhino Rally.** A Land Rover takes you on an off-road safari with up-close animal encounters and a raging river adventure.

**Cheetah Chase.** It's a pint-size roller coaster with twists and turns throughout.

**Cheetah Hunt.** Riders zoom over 4,000 feet of Serengeti-like landscape and down through a rocky cave.

### FOR AGES 6 AND UNDER

**Air Grover.** Take a ride on Grover's plane and soar through the Sahara on this junior coaster.

**Rosita's Djembe Fly-Away.** Rosita takes you on a swing ride that sends you above the African canopy.

**Oscar's Swamp Stomp.** Get wet stomping and splashing your way through this cool water area.

**Bert and Ernie's Watering Hole.** It's a water adventure filled with bubblers, geysers, jets, dumping buckets, and more.

**Zoe-Petra & the Hippos of the Nile.** A kid-size flume ride with Zoe's hippo friends that gives children a river glimpse of Africa.

**Walkabout Way.** You don't have to be a kid to enjoy this Australian-themed attraction, which allows you and the little ones to hand-feed a bunch of cuddly kangaroos.

## VISITING TIPS

■ The park is least crowded during the week, with weekends bringing in a lot of locals. Summer and the holidays also are crowded.

■ Ride the thrill rides as early as possible. Think about purchasing a Quick Queue pass for $14.95, which grants you no-wait access. It's only good once per ride but ensures you will hit all the big rides quickly.

■ Bring extra quarters for all the locker rentals at each of the coasters.

■ You can pick up a map at the entrance, which lists show times, meet-the-keeper times and special hours for attractions and restaurants.

■ Vegetarians will enjoy **Zagora Café** veggie burgers or the **Colony House's** delicious vegetable platter. Your best food bet's the All Day Dining Deal, $29.95 per adult and $13.95 per child. It's accepted at most dining venues. If eating at the Colony House, you'll want to make your reservations immediately upon entering the park.

8

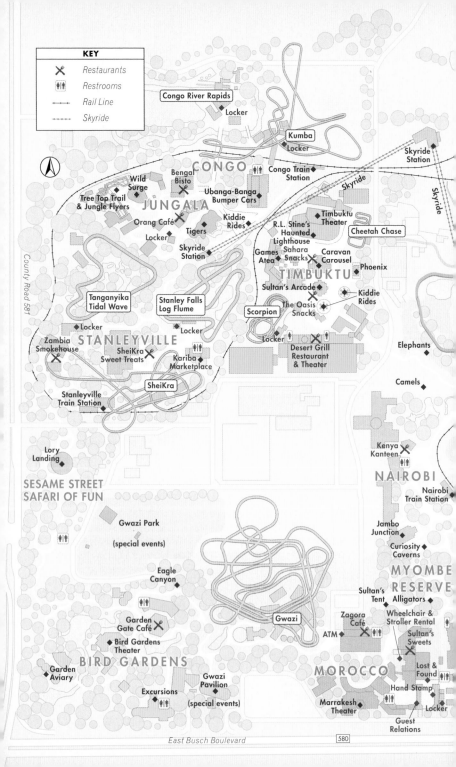

# Busch Gardens
# Tampa Bay

McKinley Drive

Rhino Rally

SERENGETI
PLAIN

Skyride

EDGE OF
AFRICA

Skyride
Station

Mandari Terrace
(special events)

Crown Colony
House

Crown
Colony
Pizza

Tut's
Tomb

Montu

Sand
Dig

Locker

EGYPT

Games
Area

Moroccan Palace
Theater

Katonga

Nairobi
Gate

ATM

PARK
ENTRANCE
& EXIT

PARKING

East Busch Boulevard    580

# BUSCH GARDENS

| NAME | Min. Height | Type of Entertainment | Duration | Suits | Crowds | Strategy |
|---|---|---|---|---|---|---|
| **EGYPT** | | | | | | |
| Montu | 54" | Thrill ride | 3 min. | 14 & up | Yes! | Go here first |
| Skyride | n/a | Ride | 5 min. | All | Yes | Can get busy |
| Tut's Tomb | n/a | Walk-Through | 10 min. | All | OK | Go after Montu |
| Edge of Africa | n/a | Walk-Through | up to you | All | OK | Go after lunch |
| **MOROCCO** | | | | | | |
| GWAZI | 48" | Thrill ride | 2.5 min. | 10 & up | Yes! | Expect to wait |
| Myombe Reserve | n/a | Walk-Through | Up to You | All | OK | Before noon photo op |
| Rock-A-Doo-Wop | n/a | Show | 20 min. | All | Yes | Arrive 15 min. early |
| **BIRD GARDENS** | | | | | | |
| Critter Castaway | n/a | Show | 25 min. | All | Yes | Do after Gwazi |
| Lory Landing | n/a | Walk-Through | Up to You | All | OK | Bring money to feed |
| Garden Aviary | n/a | Walk-Through | Up to You | All | OK | Go after lunch |
| Backyard Wildlife Habitat | n/a | Walk-Through | Up to You | All | Yes | Good anytime |
| **SESAME STREET SAFARI OF FUN** | | | | | | |
| Air Grover | n/a | Junior thrill ride | 2 min. | Under 6 | Yes! | Expect a wait |
| Zoe-Petra & the Hippos of the Nile | n/a | Junior thrill ride | 3 min. | Under 6 | Yes | Good cool-off spot |
| Elmo's Treehouse Trek | n/a | Play area | Up to You | Under 6 | OK | May be hard to keep track of toddlers. |
| Rosita's Djembe Fly-Away | n/a | Junior thrill ride | 2 min. | Under 6 | Yes | Older toddlers may enjoy this more. |
| The Count's Zambezi Rally | n/a | Ride | Up to You | Under 6 | Yes | Go early in the day. |
| Elmo's Safari Go-Round | n/a | Ride | 3 min. | Under 6 | Yes | Good anytime |
| Oscar's Swamp Stomp | n/a | Play area | Up to You | All | OK | Bring a towel |
| Bert and Ernie's Watering Hole | n/a | Play area | Up to You | All | OK | Bring a bathing suit |
| Slimey's Sawara Sand | n/a | Play area | Up to You | All | OK | Chance for parents to relax |
| Big Bird's Whirly Birdy | n/a | Ride | 3 min. | Under 6 | OK | Excellent for toddlers |
| Cookie Monster's Canopy Crawl | n/a | Play area | Up to You | Under 6 | OK | Good for energetic children |
| Telly's Jungle Jam | n/a | Play area | Up to You | All | OK | Slow- paced area |
| Big Bird's 123-Smile With Me | n/a | Walk-Through | Up to You | All | Yes | Photo/autograph op |

| Name | Height | Type | Duration | Age | | Notes |
|---|---|---|---|---|---|---|
| SheiKra | 54" | Thrill ride | 2.5 min. | 14 & up | Yes! | Use the lockers |
| Stanley Falls Flume | 46" | Thrill ride | 3 min. | 10 & up | Yes | Lengthy lines |
| Tanganyika Tidal Wave | 48" | Thrill ride | 2 min. | 10 & up | Yes | Bring a change of clothes or poncho |
| **JUNGALA** | | | | | | |
| Jungle Flyers | 48" | Junior thrill ride | 3 min. | 6 to 13 | Yes | Skip for other rides |
| Wild Surge | 38" | Thrill ride | 2 min. | 5 & up | Yes! | |
| Tree Top Trails | n/a | Walk-Through | Up to You | All | Yes | Gets crowded |
| Tiger Lodge | n/a | Walk-Through | Up to You | All | Yes | Close-up views |
| Orangutan Overlook | n/a | Walk-Through | Up to You | All | Yes | Morning photo op |
| Jungala Stiltwalkers | n/a | Show | 15 min. | All | ok | Very entertaining |
| **CONGO** | | | | | | |
| Congo River Rapids | 42" | Thrill ride | 6 min. | 10 & up | Yes! | Bring extra clothes or poncho |
| Kumba | 54" | Thrill ride | 3 min. | 14 & up | Yes! | Go early or before closing |
| Ubanga-Banga Bumper Cars | 42" | Ride | 2 min. | 8 & up | yes | Long wait times |
| **TIMBUKTU** | | | | | | |
| Carousel Caravan | n/a | Ride | 3 min. | All | ok | Slow- paced ride |
| Cheetah Chase | 46" | Junior thrill ride | 2 min. | All | yes | Very popular |
| Cheetah Hunt | n/a | Thrill ride | 3½ min. | 12 & up | Yes! | Newer ride, expect lines |
| Pirate 4-D Movie | n/a | Show | 15 min. | All | ok | Arrive 15 min. early |
| Phoenix | 48" | Thrill ride | 2 min. | 12 & up | yes | Go after Scorpion |
| Scorpion | 42" | Thrill ride | 2 min. | 14 & up | yes | Go during Dance to the Music show |
| Dance to the Music | n/a | Seasonal show | 20 min. | All | yes | Arrive 15 min. before show |
| Lights, Camera, Action! | n/a | Show | | All | | Good break from the sun |
| **NAIROBI** | | | | | | |
| Rhino Rally | 39" | Vehicle ride | 10 min. | 10 & up | yes | This ride is bumpy – hold onto your valuables |
| Serengeti Express | n/a | Vehicle ride | 12–35 min. | All | no | Great way to relax and see the park |
| Curiosity Caverns | n/a | Walk-Through | Up to You | All | no | Good to get out of the sun. |
| Elephant Habitat | n/a | Walk-Through | Up to You | All | ok | Go during Meet the Keeper |
| Rhino Habitat | n/a | Walk-Through | Up to You | All | yes | Earlier the better |
| Edge of Africa | n/a | Walk-Through | Up to You | All | ok | Great break from the crowds |

### DID YOU KNOW?

One of six roller coasters at Busch Gardens, the steel, 60-foot-tall Scorpion twists and turns at speeds near 50 mph and then throws you into a 360-degree vertical loop. During the 1½-minute ride you'll experience a 3.5 G-force.

**Fodor's Choice** **Ybor City.** Tampa's lively Latin quarter is one of only a few National
★ Historic Landmark districts in Florida. It has antique-brick streets and
wrought-iron balconies. Cubans brought their cigar-making industry
to Ybor (pronounced *ee*-bore) City in 1886, and the smell of cigars—
hand-rolled by Cuban immigrants—still wafts through the heart of this
east Tampa area, along with the strong aroma of roasting coffee. These
days the neighborhood is one of Tampa's hot spots, if at times a rowdy
one, as empty cigar factories and historic social clubs have been transformed into trendy boutiques, art galleries, restaurants, and nightclubs.

**Centennial Park.** You can step back into the past at Centennial Park,
which re-creates a period streetscape and hosts the Fresh Market every
Saturday. ⊠ *8th Ave. and 19th St.*

**Ybor City Museum State Park.** This park provides a look at the history of the cigar industry. Admission includes a tour of La Casita, one of
the shotgun houses occupied by cigar workers and their families in the
late 1890s. ⊠ *1818 E. 9th Ave., between Nuccio Pkwy. and 22nd St.,
from 7th to 9th Ave., Tampa* ☎ *813/247–6323* ⊕ *www.ybormuseum.
org* ⊒ *$4, walking tours $6* ⊙ *Daily 9–5; walking tours Sat. 10:30.*

**WORTH NOTING**

**ⓒ** **Adventure Island.** From spring until fall, rides named Splash Attack, Gulf
Scream, and Key West Rapids promise heat relief at this Busch Gardens–owned water park. Tampa's most popular "wet" park features
waterslides and artificial wave pools in a 30-acre package. One of the
attraction's headliners, Riptide, challenges you to race three other riders
on a sliding mat through twisting tubes and hairpin turns. Planners of
this park also took the younger kids into account, with offerings such as
Fabian's Funport, which has a scaled-down pool and interactive water
gym. Along with a volleyball complex and a rambling river, there are
cafés, snack bars, picnic and sunbathing areas, changing rooms, and,
the newest addition, private cabanas. ⊠ *4500 Bougainvillea Ave., less
than 1 mi north of Busch Gardens, Central Tampa* ☎ *813/987–5660
or 888/800–5447* ⊕ *www.adventureisland.com* ⊒ *$44.95; parking $12*
⊙ *Mid-Mar.–late Oct., daily 10–5.*

**Tampa Museum of Art.** The 35,000-square-foot Tampa Museum of Art
has an impressive permanent collection of Greek and Roman antiquities and 20th- to 21st-century sculpture, along with five galleries that
host traveling exhibits, which range from contemporary to classical.
⊠ *120 W. Gasparilla Plaza, Downtown* ☎ *813/274–8130* ⊕ *www.
tampamuseum.org* ⊒ *$10* ⊙ *Mon.–Wed. and Fri. 11–7, Thurs. 11–9,
Sun. 11–5.*

## SPORTS AND THE OUTDOORS

### BASEBALL

**Steinbrenner Field.** Locals and tourists flock each March to see the New
York Yankees play about 17 spring training games at this 11,000-seat
facility. (Call for tickets.) From April through September, the stadium
belongs to a Yankee farm team, the Tampa Yankees, who play 70
games against the likes of the Daytona Cubs and the Sarasota Red Sox.
⊠ *George M. Steinbrenner Field, 3802 Dr. Martin Luther King Jr. Blvd.,*

**8**

*near corner of Dale Mabry Hwy., off I–275 Exit 41B, Central Tampa* ☎ *813/879–2244 or 813/875–7753* ⊕ *www.steinbrennerfield.com.*

### FOOTBALL

**Tampa Bay Buccaneers.** Seeing the National Football Leagues play isn't easy without connections, since the entire stadium is booked by season-ticket holders years in advance. But tickets can be found in the classifieds of newspapers such as the *Tampa Tribune* and *St. Petersburg Times.* ⊠ *Raymond James Stadium, 4201 N. Dale Mabry Hwy., Central Tampa* ☎ *813/879–2827* ⊕ *www.buccaneers.com.*

### GOLF

**Babe Zaharias Golf Course.** The greens fees are $23–$39 at this challenging par-70, 18-hole public course with water hazards on eight holes. A pro is on hand to give lessons. ⊠ *11412 Forest Hills Dr., Northeast Tampa* ☎ *813/631–4374* ⊕ *www.babezahariasgc.com.*

**Bloomingdale Golfers Club.** In addition to an 18-hole, par-72 course, this club has a two-tiered driving range, a 1-acre putting green, and a restaurant. Greens fees are $30–$80. ⊠ *4113 Great Golfers Pl., Southeast Tampa* ☎ *813/685–4105* ⊕ *www.bloomingdalegolf.com.*

**The Claw at USF.** Named for its many doglegged fairways, the 18-hole, par-71 course is on a preserve with moss-draped oaks and towering pines. Greens fees are $20–$45. ⊠ *13801 N. 46th St., North Tampa* ☎ *813/632–6893* ⊕ *www.theclawatusf.com.*

**Tournament Players Club of Tampa Bay.** This public 18-hole 71-par course 15 mi north of Tampa was designed by Bobby Weed and Chi Chi Rodriguez; greens fee $99/$109. ⊠ *5300 W. Lutz Lake Fern Rd., Lutz* ☎ *813/949–0090* ⊕ *www.tpctampabay.com.*

### WALKING

**Bayshore Boulevard Trail.** This 8.6-mi trail is a good spot for just standing still and taking it all in, with its spectacular views of downtown Tampa and the Hillsborough Bay area. Of course, you can also walk, talk, jog, bike, and inline skate with locals. The trail is open from dawn to dusk daily. ⊠ *Bayshore Blvd.* ☎ *727/549–6099.*

## SHOPPING

### MALLS

**Centro Ybor.** Ybor City's destination within a destination is this dining-and-entertainment palace. It has shops, trendy bars and restaurants, and a 20-screen movie theater. ⊠ *1600 E. 8th Ave., Ybor City.*

**Channelside.** Downtown's Channelside has movie theaters, shops, restaurants, and clubs. ⊠ *615 Channelside Dr., Downtown.*

**International Plaza.** If you want to grab something at Neiman Marcus or Nordstrom this is the place. You'll also find Betsey Johnson, J.Crew, L'Occitane, Louis Vuitton, Tiffany & Co., and many other upscale shops. ⊠ *2223 N. West Shore Blvd., Airport Area.*

**Old Hyde Park Village.** It's a typical upscale shopping district in a quiet, shaded neighborhood near the water. Williams-Sonoma and Brooks Brothers are mixed in with bistros and sidewalk cafés. ⊠ *Swann Ave. near Bayshore Blvd., Hyde Park.*

## SPECIALTY SHOPS.

**King Corona Cigar Factory.** If you are shopping for hand-rolled cigars, head to Ybor City, where a few hand-rollers practice their craft in small shops. This is one of the more popular places. ⊠ *1523 E. 7th Ave., Ybor City* ☎ *888/248–3812.*

**Squaresville.** From the mildly unusual to the downright bizarre this store has it all—from the mid-20th century that is. Among the finds are Cuban clothing, Elvis posters, and Bettie Page clocks. ⊠ *508 S. Howard Ave., Hyde Park* ☎ *813/259–9944.*

## NIGHTLIFE

Although there are more boarded storefronts than in the past, the biggest concentration of nightclubs, as well as the widest variety, is found along 7th Avenue in Ybor City. It becomes a little like Bourbon Street in New Orleans on weekend evenings.

## BARS

**Blue Martini Lounge.** This spot in International Plaza has live entertainment nightly, except Monday, and a menu of killer martinis. ⊠ *2323 N. West Shore Blvd., West Tampa* ☎ *813/873–2583.*

**Centro Cantina.** There are lots of draws here: a balcony overlooking the crowds on 7th Avenue, live music Thursday through Sunday nights, a large selection of margaritas, and more than 30 brands of tequila. Food is served until 2 am. ⊠ *1600 E. 8th Ave., Ybor City* ☎ *813/241–8588.*

**Hub.** Considered something of a dive—but a lovable one—by a loyal and young local following that ranges from esteemed jurists to nose-ring-wearing night owls, the Hub is known for strong drinks and a jukebox that goes well beyond the usual. ⊠ *719 N. Franklin St., Downtown* ☎ *813/229–1553.*

## CASINO

**Seminole Hard Rock Hotel & Casino.** In addition to playing one of the hundreds of Vegas-style slot machines, gamers can also get their kicks at the casino's poker tables and video-gaming machines. The lounge serves drinks 24 hours a day. Floyd's restaurant has dinner and nightlife. There is a heavy smell of cigarette smoke here, as with most casinos. ⊠ *5223 N. Orient Rd., off I–4 at N. Orient Rd. Exit* ☎ *813/627–7625 or 866/502–7529* ⊕ *www.seminolehardrock.com* 🎫 *Free* 🕐 *Daily 24 hrs.*

## COMEDY CLUBS

**Side Splitters.** You can catch comedians Thursday through Sunday nights (and other nights, sporadically, throughout the week). ⊠ *12938 N. Dale Mabry Hwy., Central Tampa* ☎ *813/960–1197* ⊕ *www.sidesplitterscomedy.com.*

**Tampa Improv.** Top comedians perform here Wednesday through Sunday. ⊠ *Centro Ybor, 1600 E. 8th Ave., Ybor City* ☎ *813/864–4000* ⊕ *www.improvtampa.com.*

## MUSIC CLUB

**Skippers Smokehouse.** A junkyard-style restaurant and oyster bar, Skippers has live reggae on Wednesday, Uncle John's Band (a long-running Grateful Dead cover act) on Thursday, and great smoked fish every night. Check their calendar for exceptional musical lineups on the weekends. ✉ *910 Skipper Rd., Northeast Tampa* ☎ *813/971–0666* ⊕ *www.skipperssmokehouse.com.*

## THE ARTS

**Straz Center.** With 345,000 square feet, this is the largest arts complex south of the Kennedy Center in Washington, D.C. Among the facilities are the 2,500-seat Carol Morsani Hall, a 1,047-seat playhouse, the 200-seat TECO Theater, a 300-seat cabaret theater, and a 120-seat black-box theater. Opera, concerts, drama, and ballet performances are presented here. ✉ *1010 W. C. MacInnes Pl., Downtown* ☎ *813/229–7827* ⊕ *www.strazcenter.org.*

**Tampa Theatre.** This restored 1926 movie palace hosts films, concerts, and special events. ✉ *711 N. Franklin St., Downtown* ☎ *813/274–8982* ⊕ *www.tampatheatre.org.*

## WHERE TO EAT

**$$$$**
STEAK
Fodor'sChoice
★

✕**Bern's Steak House.** With the air of an exclusive club, this is one of Florida's finest steak houses. Rich mahogany paneling and ornate chandeliers define the legendary Bern's, where the chef ages his own beef, grows his own organic vegetables, and roasts his own coffee. There's also a Cave Du Fromage, housing a discriminating selection of artisanal cheeses from around the world. Cuts of topmost beef are sold by weight and thickness. There's a 60-ounce strip steak that's big enough to feed your pride (of lions), but for most appetites the veal loin chop or 8-ounce chateaubriand is more than enough. The wine list includes approximately 7,000 selections (with 1,000 dessert wines). After dinner, tour the kitchen and wine cellar before having dessert upstairs in a cozy booth. The dessert room is a hit. For a real jolt, try the Turkish coffee with an order of Mississippi mud pie. Casual business attire is recommended. ✉ *1208 S. Howard Ave., Hyde Park* ☎ *813/251–2421* ⊕ *www.bernssteakhouse.com* ⌕ *Reservations essential.*

**$$$**
VIETNAMESE

✕**BT.** Local restaurateur B.T. Nguyen has earned quite a following since opening her first two eateries more than two decades ago. In late 2010, Restaurant BT moved from its white tablecloth digs in Old Hyde Park Village and dropped the first part of its moniker. The new locale is supermodern, and the cuisine features fresh herbs grown on-site and a drink list that includes organic sake martinis. With a motto like "eat local, think global," the menu is inevitably sophisticated yet simple, with creative offerings like Deconstructed Beef Stroganoff James, which consists of grass-fed filet mignon, chanterelle mushrooms, and a Burgundy reduction served over fresh pasta. Vegetarians and vegans can rest easy here—entrée options include tofu-and-edamame Lauren (with cubed tofu, ginger, cilantro, diced ginger, edamame, and steamed jasmine rice). ✉ *2507 S. MacDill Ave., Suite B, Tampa* ☎ *813/258–1916* ⊕ *www.restaurantbt.com.*

**$$**
ECLECTIC

✕**Café Dufrain.** Dogs can tag along if you dine on the patio at pet-friendly Café Dufrain, a riverside eatery with an upscale crowd. Creative menu items include fried chicken and waffles (a Southern classic) and ceviche with vanilla bean and roast pumpkin. In mild weather, opt for the waterfront view of Downtown Tampa. ✉ *707 Harbour Post Dr., Downtown* ☎ *813/275–9701* ⊕ *www.cafedufrain.com.*

$$ ✕**Columbia**. Make a date for some of the best Latin cuisine in Tampa.
SPANISH A fixture since 1905, this magnificent structure with an old-world air
Fodor'sChoice and spacious dining rooms takes up an entire city block and seems to
★ feed the entire city—locals as well as visitors—throughout the week, but
especially on weekends. The paella, bursting with seafood, chicken, and
pork, arguably is the best in Florida, and the 1905 salad—with ham,
olives, cheese, and garlic—is legendary. The menu has Cuban classics
such as *boliche criollo* (tender eye of round stuffed with chorizo sau-
sage), *ropa vieja* (shredded beef with onions, peppers, and tomatoes),
and *arroz con pollo* (chicken with yellow rice). Don't miss the flamenco
dancing show every night but Sunday. This place is also known for its
sangria. If you can, walk around the building and check out the elabo-
rate, antique decor along every inch of the interior. ✉ *2117 E. 7th Ave.,
Ybor City* ☎ *813/248–4961* ⊕ *www.columbiarestaurant.com.*

$ ✕**Estela's**. On the quaint Davis Islands near Downtown Tampa, Estela's
MEXICAN is a favorite among those who enjoy authentic Central American cuisine
★ and Mexico's best beers. Expect the usual entrées (enchiladas, fajitas,
and chiles rellenos) mixed with delightful starters (chicken soup with
avocado slices) and a palate-pleasing rib-eye steak with rice, beans, and
guacamole. The place gets very crowded for weekday lunches. ✉ *209 E.
Davis Blvd., Downtown* ☎ *813/251–0558* ⊕ *www.estelas.com.*

$ ✕**Kojak's House of Ribs**. Few barbecue joints can boast the staying power
SOUTHERN of this family-owned and -operated pit stop. Located along a shaded
stretch in South Tampa, it debuted in 1978, and has since earned a fol-
lowing of sticky-fingered regulars who have turned it into one of the
most popular barbecue stops in central Florida. It's in a 1927 house
complete with veranda, pillars supporting the overhanging roof, and
brick steps. Day and night, three indoor dining rooms and an outdoor
dining porch have a steady stream of hungry patrons digging into ten-
der pork spareribs that are dry-rubbed and tanned overnight before
visiting the smoker for a couple of hours. Then they're bathed in the
sauce of your choice. Kojak's also has a nice selection of sandwiches,
including sloppy chicken and country-style sausage. This is definitely
not the kind of place you'd want to bring a vegan. ✉ *2808 Gandy Blvd.,
South Tampa* ☎ *813/837–3774* ⊕ *www.kojaksbbq.com* ⊘ *Closed Mon.*

¢ ✕**Mel's Hot Dogs**. This is a must after a long day of riding roller coasters
AMERICAN and scoping out zebras at Busch Gardens. Visitors as well as passersby
usually are greeted by a red wiener-mobile parked on the north side of
the highway near Busch Gardens. Venture inside to find walls dotted
with photos from fans and a hot-diggity menu that's heaven for tube-
steak fans. You can order a traditional dog, but try something with a
little more pizzazz, such as a bacon-cheddar Reuben-style bowwow on a
poppy-seed bun, or the Mighty Mel, a quarter-pounder decked out with
relish, mustard, and pickles. To avoid lunch crowds, arrive before 11:30
or after 1:30. ✉ *4136 E. Busch Blvd., Central Tampa* ☎ *813/985–8000*
⊕ *www.melshotdogs.com* ⊟ *No credit cards* ⊘ *Closed Sun.*

$$$ ✕**Roy's**. Chef Roy Yamaguchi's Pan-Asian restaurant has fresh ingre-
ASIAN dients flown in every day from around the Pacific. Regular dishes
include roasted macadamia-nut-crusted mahimahi with lobster sauce
and blackened ahi tuna with spicy soy-mustard sauce. Can't decide? Try

8

the prix-fixe menu, usually around $35 for three courses. For dessert, choices include chocolate soufflé and fruit cobbler. ⊠ *4342 Boy Scout Blvd., Airport Area* ☎ *813/873–7697* ⊕ *www.roysrestaurant.com.*

$$

SOUTHERN

✕ **Stumps Supper Club.** The menu is as lively as the entertainment at this popular restaurant-nightclub. Southern vittles are the house specialty—they're reminiscent of Sunday dinner at an aunt's house. The Brunswick stew (chicken mingling with butter beans and veggies in tomato broth) is close to perfection. The pulled-pork BBQ plate is a slow-cooked Southern essential, and the obligatory country-fried steak does not disappoint. Sides include corn bread, cheese grits, black-eyed peas, and collard greens. Decorated in flea-market chic, Stumps takes food quite seriously. Friday and Saturday nights after 9 you'll find a range of acts playing soul and rock, including Jimmy James & the Velvet Explosion, a six-piece band that relives Elvis, ABBA, Motown, and KC & the Sunshine Band. ⊠ *615 Channelside Dr., Downtown* ☎ *813/226–2261* ⊕ *www.stumpssupperclub.com* ☉ *No lunch weekdays.*

## WHERE TO STAY

*For expanded hotel reviews, visit Fodors.com.*

$$$

B&B/INN

★

**Don Vicente de Ybor Historic Inn.** Built as a home in 1895 by town founder Don Vicente de Ybor, this inn shows that the working-class cigar city had an elegant side, too. **Pros:** elegant rooms; rich in history; walking distance to nightlife. **Cons:** rowdy neighborhood on weekend nights. ⊠ *1915 Republica de Cuba, Ybor City* ☎ *813/241–4545 or 866/206–4545* ⊕ *donvicenteinn.com* ⤵ *13 rooms, 3 suites* ⌂ *In-room: Wi-Fi. In-hotel: restaurant, bar* ⏺❘ *BP.*

$$–$$$

HOTEL

★

**Hilton Garden Inn Tampa Ybor Historic District.** Although its modern architecture makes it seem out of place in this historic district, this chain hotel's location across from Centro Ybor is a plus. **Pros:** good location for business travelers; reasonable rates. **Cons:** chain-hotel feel; far from downtown. ⊠ *1700 E. 9th Ave., Ybor City* ☎ *813/769–9267* ⊕ *www.hiltongardeninn.com* ⤵ *84 rooms, 11 suites* ⌂ *In-room: Wi-Fi. In-hotel: restaurant, pool, laundry facilities.*

$$$–$$$$

RESORT

★

**Saddlebrook Resort Tampa.** If you can't get enough golf and tennis, here's your fix. **Pros:** away from urban sprawl; great choice for the fitness minded. **Cons:** a bit isolated. ⊠ *5700 Saddlebrook Way, Wesley Chapel* ☎ *813/973–1111 or 800/729–8383* ⊕ *www.saddlebrookresort. com* ⤵ *540 rooms, 407 suites* ⌂ *In-room: kitchen (some), Wi-Fi. In-hotel: restaurants, bars, golf courses, tennis courts, pools, gym, spa, children's programs.*

$$$–$$$$

HOTEL

**Tampa Marriott Waterside Hotel & Marina.** Across from the Tampa Convention Center, this downtown hotel was built for conventioneers but is also convenient to tourist spots such as the Florida Aquarium and the Channelside and Hyde Park shopping districts. **Pros:** great downtown location; near shopping. **Cons:** gridlock during rush hour; streets tough to maneuver; area sketchy after dark. ⊠ *700 S. Florida Ave., Downtown* ☎ *888/268–1616* ⊕ *www.marriott.com* ⤵ *683 rooms, 36 suites* ⌂ *In-room: Wi-Fi. In-hotel: restaurants, bars, pool, gym, spa, laundry facilities, parking.*

$$$–$$$$

HOTEL

**Westin Tampa Harbour Island.** Few folks think of the islands when visiting Tampa, but this 12-story hotel on a 177-acre man-made islet is a short drive from downtown Tampa. **Pros:** close to downtown; nice views; on the TECO streetcar line. **Cons:** a bit far from the action; chain-hotel feel. ⊠ *725 S. Harbour Island Blvd., Harbour Island* ☎ *813/229–5000* ⊕ *www.starwoodhotels.com/westin* ⤶ *299 rooms, 19 suites* ⚬ *In-room: Wi-Fi. In-hotel: restaurant, bar, pool, parking, some pets allowed.*

## ST. PETERSBURG

*21 mi west of Tampa.*

St. Petersburg and the Pinellas coast form the thumb of the hand that juts out of Florida's west coast and grasps Tampa Bay. Two distinct parts of St. Petersburg hold most of the appeal: the arty, sometimes upscale, sometimes rowdy downtown and cultural area on the bay front, and the mellow but pricey Pinellas beaches, a string of barrier island towns facing the gulf and including St. Pete Beach and Treasure Island. Causeways link beach communities to the mainland peninsula.

### GETTING HERE AND AROUND

Interstate 275 heads west from Tampa across Tampa Bay to St. Petersburg, swings south, and crosses the bay again on its way to Terra Ceia, near Bradenton. U.S. 19 is St. Petersburg's major north–south artery; traffic can be heavy, and there are many lights, so try to avoid it. Alternatives include 66th and 4th streets. One key thing to remember about St. Pete is that the roads form an easy-to-navigate grid: streets run north to south; avenues run east to west. Central Avenue connects Downtown to the beaches.

Around St. Petersburg, Pinellas Suncoast Transit Authority serves Pinellas County. Look for buses that cover the beaches and Downtown exclusively.

**TAKE A TOUR**

**All About Fun Tours.** What sets this tour apart from others is you are not going by bus or boat—your self-guided chariot is a motorized Segway. Each tour starts with an easy 15- to 20-minute training session. Tours are 60 or 90 minutes and are offered up to three times daily. It's a carefree way to see downtown St. Petersburg, the park system, and the waterfront while learning about local history. Reservations are required. ⊠ *335 N.E. 2nd Ave.* ☎ *727/896-3640* ⊕ *www.gyroglides.com* ⤶ *Tours $35–$50* ⊙ *Tues.–Sat. 10:30 and 2, Sun. 12:30 and 2:30, Mon. call for availability.*

### ESSENTIALS

Transportation Contacts **Pinellas Suncoast Transit Authority** (☎ *727/540–1900* ⊕ *www.psta.net*).

Visitor Information **St. Petersburg Area Chamber of Commerce** (⊠ *100 2nd Ave. N, St. Petersburg* ☎ *727/821–4069* ⊕ *www.stpete.com*). **St. Petersburg/Clearwater Area Convention and Visitors Bureau** (⊠ *13805 58th St. N, Suite 2-200, Clearwater* ☎ *727/464–7200 or 877/352–3224* ⊕ *www.floridasbeach.com*).

8

## CLEARWATER

*12 mi north of St. Petersburg via U.S. 19.*

Residential areas are a buffer between the commercial areas that center on U.S. 19 and the beach, which is moderately quiet during winter but buzzing with life during spring break and summer. There's a quaint downtown area on the mainland, just east of the beach.

### ESSENTIALS

**Visitor Information Clearwater Regional Chamber of Commerce** (⊠ *401 Cleveland St., Clearwater* ☎ *727/461–0011* ⊕ *www.clearwaterflorida.org*).

### EXPLORING

**Clearwater Marine Aquarium.** This aquarium gives you the opportunity to participate in the work of saving and caring for endangered marine species. Many of the sea turtles, dolphins, and other animals living at the aquarium were brought here to be rehabilitated from an injury or saved from danger. The dolphin exhibit has an open-air arena giving the dolphins plenty of room to jump during their shows (this aquarium is also home to Winter, a dolphin fitted with a prosthetic tail that's now the subject of a Hollywood flick). The aquarium conducts tours of the bays and islands around Clearwater, including a daily cruise on a pontoon boat (you might just see a wild dolphin or two), and kayak tours of Clearwater Harbor and St. Joseph Sound. ⊠ *249 Windward Passage* ☎ *727/441–1790* ⊕ *www.cmaquarium.org* 🖘 *$15* ☾ *Mon.–Thurs. 9–5, Fri. and Sat. 9–7, Sun. 10–5.*

**Suncoast Seabird Sanctuary.** When pelicans and other birds become entangled in fishing lines, locals sometimes carry them to this non-profit sanctuary, founded by Ralph Heath and dedicated to the rescue, repair, recuperation, and release of sick and injured birds. The sanctuary played a big role after the Gulf oil disaster in 2010. At times there are hundreds of land and sea birds in residence, including egrets, herons, gulls, terns, sandhill cranes, hawks, owls, and cormorants. ⊠ *18328 Gulf Blvd., Indian Shores* ☎ *727/391–6211* ⊕ *www.seabirdsanctuary. com* 🖘 *Donation suggested* ☾ *Tours Wed. and Sun. at 2.*

### BEACHES

Fodor's Choice ★ **Clearwater Beach.** On a narrow island between Clearwater Harbor and the gulf is a stretch of sand with a widespread reputation for beach volleyball. It's also the site of a nightly sunset celebration, complete with musicians and artisans. It's one of the area's nicest and busiest beaches, especially on weekends and during spring break, but it's also one of the costliest in terms of parking fees, which can reach $2 per hour. **Best for:** jetsking, parasailing, singles scene, people-watching, sunsets. **Amenities:** volleyball nets, showers, concessions, restrooms. ⊠ *Western end of Rte. 60, 2 mi west of downtown Clearwater.*

**Sand Key Park.** This is a mellow counterpart to often-crowded Clearwater Beach to the north. It has a lovely beach, plenty of green space, a playground, and a picnic area in an otherwise congested area. **Best for:** sunbathing, solitude, sunsets. **Amenities:** playground, dog zone, picnic area, concessions, showers. ⊠ *1060 Gulf Blvd.* ☎ *727/588–4852.*

# St. Petersburg and Environs

Waccasassa Bay

Cedar Key

Lake Rousseau

98

Crystal River

Crystal Bay

44

Homosassa Springs

Homosassa Bay

19

Chassahowitzka Bay

10 mi

10 km

Inverness

44

41

Withlacoochee State Forest

75

301

98

589

Brooksville

700

Ital

Weeki Wachee

41

Spring Hill

Dade City

19

Hudson

52

Pasco

52

700

Bayonet Point

589

41

New Port Richey

54

301

Gulf of Mexico

**22 - 24**

**Tarpon Springs**

St. John Sound

Caladesi Island

**Dunedin**

Oldsmar

39

See Downtown Tampa map

**TAMPA**

**1 - 8**

19

580

4

**21**

**20**

Gulf-to-Bay Blvd.

66th St.

Hillsborough Ave.

**Clearwater**

ALT 19

60

275

**19**

Starkey Rd.

Old Tampa Bay

60

**Largo**

74th St.

Ulmerton

92

41

**18**

699

19

Gandy Bridge

Gibsonton

**Seminole**

92

**9**

Madeira Beach

5th Ave.

**ST. PETERSBURG**

Gulf Blvd.

Central Ave.

**10** **11**

Apollo Beach

39

**St. Pete Beach**

**16**

**12**

**13**

Tampa Bay

Ruskin

679

Bayside Tours

**15**

Sun City

674

**14**

41

301

75

**Mullet Key**

**275**

62

**17**

A St. Petersburg pelican stares down passersby on the wharf; photo by Seymour Levy, Fodors.com member.

## EXPLORING

### TOP ATTRACTIONS

**Chihuly Collection.** For the uninitiated, those passing this collection's polished exterior may think it's a gallery like any other. Yet what's contained inside is an experience akin to *Alice in Wonderland*. This, the only permanent collection of renowned glass sculptor Dale Chihuly's work, has such impossibly vibrant, larger-than-life pieces as "Float Boat" and "Fire and Ice." You can tour the museum independently or with one of its volunteer docents (no added cost; tours given hourly on an as-needed basis). Each display is lit just so, which adds to the drama of Chihuly's designs. After passing under a hallway with a semi-transparent ceiling through which a brilliant array of smaller glass pieces shine, you'll wind up at the breathtaking finale, "Mille Fiore" ("Million Flowers"), a spectacular glass montage mimicking a wildflower patch, critters and all. Check out the gift shop at the end if you'd like to take some of the magic home with you. A combination ticket gets you a glimpse into the glass-blowing studio. ⊠ *400 Beach Dr., Downtown* ☎ *727/896–4527* ⊕ *www.chihulycollection.com* ✉ *$15* ⊗ *Mon.–Wed., Fri. and Sat. 10–6, Thurs. 10–8, Sun. noon–6.*

**Egmont Key.** In the middle of the mouth of Tampa Bay lies the small (350 acres), largely unspoiled but critically eroding island Egmont Key, now a state park, national wildlife refuge, national historic site, and bird sanctuary. On the island are the ruins of Fort De Soto's sister fortification, Fort Dade, built during the Spanish-American War to protect Tampa Bay. The primary inhabitants of the less-than-2-mi-long island are the threatened gopher tortoise and box turtles. The only way to get here is by boat—you can catch a ferry from Fort Se Soto. Nature lovers will find the trip well worth it—the beach here is excellent for shelling, secluded beach bathing, wildlife viewing, and snorkeling. (See ⊕ *www. egmontkeyferry.com* for more details.)

**Dolphin Landings Tours.** This operation runs a four-hour shelling trip, a two-hour dolphin-sighting excursion, back-bay or party-boat fishing, and other outings. ☎ *727/360–7411* ⊕ *www.dolphinlandings. com.*

Fodor's Choice
★

**The Dalí Museum.** Inside and out, the waterfront Dalí Museum, which opened on 1/11/11 (Dalí is said to have been into numerology), is almost as remarkable as the Spanish surrealist's work. The state-of-the-art building has a surreal geodesiclike glass structure called the Dalí Enigma as well as an outdoor labyrinth and a DNA-inspired spiral staircase leading up to the collection. All this, before you've even seen the collection, which is one of the most comprehensive of its kind—courtesy of Ohio magnate A. Reynolds Morse, a friend of Dalí's.

Here, you can scope out his early impressionistic works and see how the painter evolved into the visionary he's now seen to be. The mind-expanding paintings in this downtown headliner include *Eggs on a Plate Without a Plate, The Hallucinogenic Toreador,* and more than 90 other oils. You'll also discover more than 2,000 additional works including watercolors, drawings, sculptures, photographs, and objets d'art. Free hour-long tours are led by well-informed docents. ⊠ *1 Dali Blvd.* ☎ *727/823–3767 or 800/442–3254* ⊕ *www.thedali.org* ☜ *$21* ⊙ *Mon.–Wed., Fri. and Sat. 10–5:30, Thurs. 10–8, Sun. noon–5:30.*

**Sunken Gardens.** A cool oasis amid St. Pete's urban clutter, this lush 4-acre plot was created from a lake that was drained in 1903. Explore the cascading waterfalls and koi ponds, and walk through the butterfly house and exotic gardens where more than 50,000 tropical plants and flowers from across the globe thrive amid groves of some of the area's most spectacular palm trees. The on-site restaurant and hands-on kids' museum make this place a family favorite. ⊠ *1825 4th St. N* ☎ *727/551–3102* ⊕ *www.sunkengardens.org* ☜ *$8* ⊙ *Mon.–Sat. 10–4:30, Sun. noon–4:30.*

**WORTH NOTING**

**Florida Holocaust Museum.** The downtown Florida Holocaust Museum is one of the largest of its kind in the United States. It has the permanent History, Heritage, and Hope exhibit, an original boxcar, and an extensive collection of photographs, art, and artifacts. One compelling display includes portraits and biographies of Holocaust survivors. The museum, which also has a series of rotating exhibits, was conceived as a learning center for children, so many of the exhibits avoid overly graphic content; signs are posted outside galleries if the subject matter might be too intense for kids. ⊠ *55 5th St. S* ☎ *727/820–0100* ⊕ *www. flholocaustmuseum.org* ☜ *$14* ⊙ *Daily 10–5.*

**Fort De Soto Park.** Spread over five small islands, 1,136-acre Fort De Soto Park lies at the mouth of Tampa Bay. It has 7 mi of beaches, two fishing piers, a 4-mi hiking–skating trail, picnic-and-camping grounds, and a historic fort that kids of any age can explore. The fort for which

8

it's named was built on the southern end of Mullet Key to protect sea-lanes in the gulf during the Spanish-American War. Roam the fort or wander the beaches of any of the islands within the park. ⊠ *3500 Pinellas Bayway St., Tierra Verde* ☎ *727/582–2267* ⧉ *Free* ⊙ *Beaches, daily sunrise–sunset; fishing and boat ramp, 24 hrs.*

☾ **Great Explorations.** "Don't touch" are words never spoken here. The museum is hands-on through and through, with a Robot Lab, Climb Wall, Lie Detector, Fire House, Vet's Office, and other interactive play areas, including the new Tree House. Smart exhibits like the Tennis Ball Launcher, which uses compressed air to propel a ball through a series of tubes, and Sound Waves, where Styrofoam pellets in a clear tube show differences in sound frequencies, employ low-tech to teach high-tech principles. ⊠ *1925 4th St. N* ☎ *727/821–8992* ⊕ *www.greatexplorations.org* ⧉ *$10* ⊙ *Mon.–Sat. 10–4:30, Sun. noon–4:30.*

**Museum of Fine Arts.** One of the city's cornerstones, this museum is a gorgeous Mediterranean-revival structure that houses outstanding collections of European, American, pre-Columbian, and Asian art. Major works here by American artists range from Hassam to O'Keeffe to Bellows and Lichtenstein, but the museum is known for its collection of French artists, including Fragonard, Cézanne, Monet, Rodin, Gauguin, and Renoir. There are also photography exhibits that draw from a permanent collection of more than 14,000 works. The recent Hazel Hough Wing more than doubled the museum's exhibit space. A new café offers visitors a lunch respite and a beautiful view of the bay. Docents give narrated gallery tours. ⊠ *255 Beach Dr. NE* ☎ *727/896–2667* ⊕ *www.fine-arts.org* ⧉ *$17* ⊙ *Mon.–Sat. 10–5, Sun. noon–5.*

## BEACHES

**Pass-A-Grille Beach.** At the southern tip of St. Pete Beach (past the Don), is the epitome of Old Florida. One of the most popular beaches in the area, it skirts the west end of charming, historic Pass-A-Grille, a neighborhood that draws tourists and locals alike with its stylish yet low-key mom-and-pop motels and restaurants. **Best for:** families, kite-boarding, sunsets. **Amenities:** snack bar, showers, restrooms, parking meters. ⊠ *Off Gulf Blvd. (Rte. 699), St. Pete Beach.*

**Treasure Island.** Large wide swathes of sand that are sans crowd abound, but you can also find some good crowds, especially on weekends. The Sunday-evening drum circle, which happens around sunset just southwest of the Bilmar, makes for some interesting people-watching. It's also the only beach that allows alcohol, as long as it's not contained in glass. Plus, getting here is supereasy—just head west on St. Petersburg's Central Avenue, which dead-ends smack-dab in the middle of T.I. (that's what the locals call it). **Best for:** shelling, solitude, families, sunsets, accessibility. **Amenities:** bathrooms, cabanas, chairs and beach umbrellas for rent, parking (the lots are all metered now, but you can find free parking across Gulf Boulevard). ⊠ *11260 Gulf Blvd..*

**Sunset Beach.** Technically part of Treasure Island, this 2-mi-long outcrop is one of Tampa Bay's best-kept secrets. The northern end has a mixed crowd—from bikers to spring breakers—the middle portion is good for families (there's a pavilion and playground at around 78th and

West Gulf Boulevard), and the southern tip attracts the LGBT crowd. Surfers hit up Sunset Beach on the rare occasion that the gulf has some swells to offer. **Best for:** shelling, solitude, sunsets, singles scene, sunbathing, surfing/boogie boarding (when there are waves). **Amenities:** bathrooms, parking (free if you don't mind parking a block or two away; metered otherwise).

## SPORTS AND THE OUTDOORS

### BASEBALL

**Tampa Bay Rays.** Major League Baseball's Tampa Bay Rays completed an improbable worst-to-first turnaround when they topped the American League Eastern Division in 2008, and again in 2010. Tickets are available at the box office for most games, but you may have to rely on the classifieds sections of the *Tampa Tribune* and *St. Petersburg Times* for popular games. Get here early; parking is often at a premium (pregaming at Ferg's is always a safe bet). ⊠ *Tropicana Field, 1 Tropicana Dr., off I–175* ☎ *727/825–3137* ⊕ *tampabay.rays.mlb.com.*

## SHOPPING

**Florida Craftsmen Galleries.** Downtown St. Pete's bursting art revival is epitomized at Florida Craftsmen Galleries, which gives 125 local craftsmen a chance to exhibit glassware, jewelry, furniture, and more. While you're here, take a stroll along Central Avenue's 600 block for a real glimpse into Downtown St. Pete's burgeoning art scene. ⊠ *501 Central Ave.* ☎ *727/821–7391* ⊕ *www.floridacraftsmen.net.*

**Haslam's.** One of the state's most notable bookstores is a family-owned emporium that's been doing business just west of downtown St. Petersburg for more than 70 years. Rumored to be haunted by the ghost of On the Road author Jack Kerouac (indeed the renowned Beat Generation author used to frequent Haslam's before he died in St. Pete in 1969), the store carries some 300,000 volumes, from cutting-edge best sellers to ancient tomes. If you value a good book or simply like to browse, you could easily spend an afternoon here. ⊠ *2025 Central Ave.* ☎ *727/822–8616* ⊕ *www.haslams.com*).

**John's Pass Village and Boardwalk.** This collection of shops and restaurants is in an old-style fishing village, where you can watch pelicans cavorting and dive-bombing for food, taste kiwi wine and blood orange–flavored olive oil, or check out some mellow island music. ⊠ *12901 Gulf Blvd., Madeira Beach* ⊕ *www.johnspass.com.*

## NIGHTLIFE

**The Garden.** This multifaceted drinkery is a good place to start if you plan on barhopping in Downtown St. Pete, which gets packed on weekends—especially for the monthly first Friday festivities. ⊠ *217 Central Ave.* ☎ *727/896–3800* ⊕ *thegardendtsp.com.*

**Jimmy B's.** The default beach bar for tourists and locals alike overlooks the vast dunes leading down to the beach. There's live music virtually every night. ⊠ *Behind Beachcomber Resort on St. Pete Beach, 6200 Gulf Blvd.* ☎ *727/367–1902.*

**Marchand's.** Sophisticated locals and well-informed out-of-towners gather at the bar here for after-dinner cocktails and dancing to top-notch jazz bands Friday and Saturday. It's the most genteel place in town for a nightcap. ⊠ *Vinoy Hotel, 501 5th Ave. NE* ☎ *727/894–1000* ⊕ *www.marchandsbarandgrill.com.*

## WHERE TO EAT

**$$$$**
TAPAS

✕ **Ceviche.** A choice romantic destination as well as an excellent launch-pad for a night out, this tapas bar offers an astonishing spate of pleasant sensations for those with savvy taste buds. You can't go wrong with a huge order of seafood or chicken paella. The ceviche, Solomillo à la Parilla (prime filet with wild mushrooms and brandy cream sauce), and supergarlicky spinach (sautéed with figs) are good bets for tapas. In the catacomblike bar downstairs, there's jazz, salsa, and flamenco every night but Monday. While you're here, the sangria is a must. ⊠ *10 Beach Dr., Downtown, St. Pete* ☎ *727/209–2302* ⊕ *www.ceviche.com.*

**$**
SEAFOOD

✕ **Crabby Bill's.** Nothin' fancy about the crab-man's place—just some of the area's tastiest seafood served family style (picture long picnic-style tables) in a friendly atmosphere. The fried-grouper sandwich is tasty, but you can also order it grilled, broiled, or blackened. Crustaceans are the house specialty, meaning your choice of blue or soft-shell, and, from October to May, delicious—though costly—stone crabs, among others. There's also a good selection of other treats, including scallops and farm-raised oysters. Diners usually dress in the official uniform of Florida beaches: shorts, T-shirts, and flip-flops. ⊠ *5100 Gulf Blvd.* ☎ *727/360–8858* ⊕ *www.crabbybills.com.*

**$**
SEAFOOD

✕ **Hurricane Seafood Restaurant.** Sunsets and gulf views are the bait that hooks regulars as well as travelers who find their way to this somewhat hidden pit stop in Historic Pass-A-Grille. Dating to 1977, it's mainly heralded as a watering hole where you can hoist a cold one while munching on one of the area's better grouper sandwiches. (Speaking of this sweet white fish, it's the real deal here, which—be warned—isn't always a guarantee in some restaurants.) There's also a range of seafood and steak entrées, and the crab cakes are legendary. The aforementioned sunsets are best seen from the rooftop sundeck. ⊠ *807 Gulf Way, St. Pete Beach* ☎ *727/360–9558* ⊕ *www.thehurricane.com.*

**$$$$**
ECLECTIC
★

✕ **Marchand's Bar & Grill.** Opened in 1925, this wonderful eatery in the posh Renaissance Vinoy Resort has frescoed ceilings and a spectacular view of Tampa Bay. Upscale and special-occasion diners are drawn to Marchand's by an imaginative menu. A visit might offer crayfish mac-n-cheese or free-range chicken stuffed with bacon and goat cheese. The menu changes quite a bit, but mainstays include the crab cake and calamari. The wine list is extensive, including a number of by-the-glass selections. There's live jazz Friday and Saturday nights. ⊠ *Renaissance Vinoy Resort, 501 5th Ave. NE* ☎ *727/824–8072* ⊕ *www.marchandsbarandgrill.com.*

**$$$**
SEAFOOD

✕ **Salt Rock Grill.** This hot spot is where tourists and locals converge to enjoy a fun and lively beachside atmosphere. The rock-solid (if slightly less than imaginative) menu is the best reason to come. Don't believe the Caribbean lobster is a "monster"—at 1¼ pounds it's on the small side, but it's twice cooked—including a finish on the grill—and quite tasty. The showstopper is the cioppino (shrimp, king crab, lobster, mussels, fish, and clams with a sourdough crust). In fair weather, dine on

*Continued on page 352*

# SPRING TRAINING, FLORIDA-STYLE

8

by Jim Tunstall and Connie Sharpe

Sunshine, railroads, and land bargains were Florida's first tourist magnets, but baseball had a hand in things, too. The Chicago Cubs led the charge when they opened spring training in Tampa in 1913 — the same year the Cleveland Indians set up camp in Pensacola.

Over the next couple of decades, World War I and the Great Depression interrupted normal lives, but the Sunshine State became a great fit for the national pastime. Soon, big-league teams were flocking south to work off the winter rust.

At one point, the Florida "Grapefruit League" held a monopoly on spring training, but in 1947 Arizona's "Cactus League" started cutting into the action.

Today, roughly half of Major League Baseball's 30 teams arrive in Florida in February for six weeks of calisthenics, tryouts, and practice games. The clubs range from the Detroit Tigers, who have been in the same city (Lakeland) longer than any other team (since 1934), to the Tampa Bay Rays, who moved to a new spring home (Port Charlotte) in 2009.

The Los Angeles Dodgers play the Washington Nationals in Viera during a spring training game.

# HERE COME THE FANS

Cardinals fans take advantage of spring training's easier access to players.

Florida's spring training teams play 25 or 30 home and away games, to the delight of 1.68 million annual ticker buyers. Die-hards land as soon as the first troops—pitchers and catchers—come to practice around the third week of February. Inter-squad games start in the fourth week, while the real training schedule begins by the end of February or first of March and lasts until the end of the month or early April. These games don't count in the regular season, but they give managers and fans a good idea of which players will be on the opening-day rosters, and who will be traded, sent to the teams' minor leagues, or told it's time to find a regular day job.

Spring training games provide a great excuse for local baseball fans to cut out of work early, while visitors from the North can leave ice, snow, and sleet behind. And who doesn't want a few chili dogs, brats, burgers, and brews on a March day?

Spring training's draw is more than just a change of venue with an early sample of concession-stand staples. There is also the ample choice of game sites. Teams are scattered around most of the major tourist areas of central and southern Florida, so those coming to watch the games can try a different destination each spring—or even make a road trip to several. Baseball fans also like that it's a melting pot—teams from more than a dozen cities are represented here.

Finally, you can't beat the price—tickets are usually cheaper than during the regular season—nor the access you have to baseball celebrities. In fact, the relaxed atmosphere of spring training makes most players more willing to sign your ball, glove, or whatever. You can get autographs during pregame workouts (practice sessions), which are free, as well as after the game.

World champion Jimmy Rollins.

## 4 TIPS

■ **Have a game plan.** Don't just show up. Most teams only have about 15 home games, and those involving popular teams often sell out weeks in advance. Consider buying tickets ahead of time, and if needed, make hotel room reservations at the same time.

■ **Beat the crowds.** The best chance to do this is to go to a weekday game. You'll still encounter lots of fans, but weekday games generally aren't as well attended as weekenders. Also, each team only has a few night games.

■ **Pack a picnic.** Some stadiums let you bring coolers through the turnstiles. Many game attendees also gather for a tailgate party, grilling burgers and sipping a lemonade or beer while jawing with fellow fans (have a chair in tow).

■ West coast games get a lot of sun. Seats in the shade are premium.

(above) Hammond Stadium in Ft. Myers is where the Minnesota Twins practice.
(right) St. Louis Cardinals Chris Duncan is tagged out at Tradition Field in Port St. Lucie.

| | |
|---|---|
| Atlanta Braves ............... **2** | New York Yankees ........... **4** |
| Baltimore Orioles .......... **7** | Philadelphia Phillies ....... **1** |
| Boston Red Sox ............**14** | Pittsburgh Pirates .........**10** |
| Detroit Tigers ............... **9** | St. Louis Cardinals/ |
| Houston Astros .............**11** | Florida Marlins .............**12** |
| Minnesota Twins ........... **8** | Tampa Bay Rays ............. **3** |
| New York Mets .............. **6** | Toronto Blue Jays .......... **5** |
| | Washington Nationals ....**13** |

## PLAY BALL!

Spring training schedules are determined around Thanksgiving. Ticket prices change each year; 2010 prices are shown here. For all of these teams, you also can order spring training tickets through Ticketmaster (☎ 866/448–7849 ⊕ www.ticketmaster.com) or through the respective team's box office or team Web site. For more information about any of the teams, visit ⊕ www.floridagrapefruitleague.com.

**SPRING TRAINING GUIDE**
Order a free Guide to *Florida Spring Training* from the **Florida Sports Foundation** (✉ 2930 Kerry Forest Parkway, Tallahassee, FL ☎ 850/488–8347 ⊕ www.flasports. com). Published in February each year, it's packed with information about teams, sites, tickets, and more.

New York Mets catcher Ramon Castro.

### ATLANTA BRAVES
**Home Field:** Champion Stadium, Walt Disney World Wide World of Sports, 700 S. Victory Way, Lake Buena Vista. **Tickets:** $10–$42 ☎ 407/939–4263 ⊕ www.braves.mlb.com

### BALTIMORE ORIOLES
**Home Field:** Ed Smith Stadium, 2700 12th St., Sarasota. **Tickets:** $8–$29
☎ 941/954–4101 ⊕ www.orioles.mlb.com

### BOSTON RED SOX
**Home Field:** City of Palms Park, 2201 Edison Ave., Fort Myers. **Tickets:** $10–$46
☎ 239/334–4700, 877/733–7699 ⊕ www.redsox.mlb.com

### DETROIT TIGERS
**Home Field:** Joker Marchant Stadium, 2301 Lakeland Hills Blvd., Lakeland. **Tickets:** $9–$25
☎ 866/668–4437 ⊕ www.tigers.mlb.com

### FLORIDA MARLINS
**Home Field:** Roger Dean Stadium (shared with St. Louis Cardinals), 4751 Main St., Jupiter. **Tickets:** $15–$35
☎ 561/775–1818 ⊕ www.marlins.mlb.com

### HOUSTON ASTROS
**Home Field:** Osceola County Stadium, 631 Heritage Parkway, Kissimmee. **Tickets:** $10–$27
☎ 321/697–3200 ⊕ www.astros.mlb.com

### MINNESOTA TWINS
**Home Field:** Hammond Stadium, 14100 Six Mile Cypress Parkway, Fort Myers. **Tickets:** $13–$39
☎ 239/768-4270 ⊕ www.twins.mlb.com

### NEW YORK METS
**Home Field:** Tradition Field, 525 NW Peacock Blvd., Port St. Lucie. **Tickets:** $6–$20
☎ 772/871-2115 ⊕ www.mets.mlb.com

### NEW YORK YANKEES
**Home Field:** Steinbrenner Field, 1 Steinbrenner Dr., Tampa **Tickets:** $17–$33
☎ 813/879-2244 ⊕ www.yankees.mlb.com

### PHILADELPHIA PHILLIES
**Home Field:** Bright House Networks Field, 601 N. Old Coachman Rd., Clearwater. **Tickets:** $7–$34
☎ 727/467-4457 ⊕ www.phillies.mlb.com

### PITTSBURGH PIRATES
**Home Field:** McKechnie Field, 1611 9th St. W, Bradenton. **Tickets:** $12–$20
☎ 941/748-4610 ⊕ www.pirates.mlb.com

### ST. LOUIS CARDINALS
**Home Field:** Roger Dean Stadium (shared with Florida Marlins), 4751 Main St., Jupiter. **Tickets:** $15–$35
☎ 561/775-1818 ⊕ www.cardinals.mlb.com

### TAMPA BAY RAYS
**Home Field:** Charlotte County Sports Park, 2300 El Jobean Rd., Port Charlotte. **Tickets:** $8–$22
☎ 941/206-4487 ⊕ www.rays.mlb.com

### TORONTO BLUE JAYS
**Home Field:** Florida Auto Exchange Park, 373 Douglas Ave., Dunedin. **Tickets:** $15–$27
☎ 727/733-0429 ⊕ www.bluejays.mlb.com

### WASHINGTON NATIONALS
**Home Field:** Space Coast Stadium, 5800 Stadium Parkway, Viera. **Tickets:** $9–$26
☎ 321/633-4487 ⊕ www.nationals.mlb.com

the dock; otherwise ask for a table with a view of the water. ⊠ *19325 Gulf Blvd.* ☎ *727/593–7625* ⊕ *www.saltrockgrill.com.*

**$**
SEAFOOD
Fodor's Choice
★

✕ **Ted Peters Famous Smoked Fish.** Picture this: flip-flop-wearing anglers and beach-towel-clad bathers lolling on picnic benches, sipping a beer, and devouring oak-smoked salmon, mullet, mahimahi, and mackerel. Dinner comes to the table with heaped helpings of potato salad or coleslaw. If you're industrious enough to have hooked your own fish, the crew will smoke it for about $1.50 per pound. If not, there's always what many consider to be the best burger in the region. The popular smoked fish spread and Manhattan clam chowder are available to go. There's also indoor seating at Ted's, which has been a south-side fixture for more than six decades. Closing time is 7:30 pm. ⊠ *1350 Pasadena Ave. S, South Pasadena* ☎ *727/381–7931* ⟨ *Reservations not accepted* ⊟ *No credit cards* ⊘ *Closed Tues.*

## WHERE TO STAY

*For expanded hotel reviews, visit Fodors.com.*

**$$$–$$$$**
RESORT
Fodor's Choice
★

▦ **Don CeSar Beach Resort.** Today the "Pink Palace," as it's called thanks to its paint job, is a gulf-coast landmark with remarkable architecture, with exterior and public areas oozing turn-of-the-last-century elegance. **Pros:** romantic destination; great beach; tasty dining options. **Cons:** can be quite pricey. ⊠ *3400 Gulf Blvd., St. Pete Beach* ☎ *727/367–6952 or 800/282–1116* ⊕ *www.doncesar.com* ⤳ *277 rooms, 40 suites, 70 condos* ⟨ *In-room: Wi-Fi. In-hotel: restaurants, bars, pools, gym, spa, beach, children's programs, parking, some pets allowed.*

**$$$**
HOTEL
Fodor's Choice
★

▦ **Postcard Inn.** Take a Waikiki surf shack from back in Duke's day, shake it up with a little Miami chic (circa 1955), and give it a clean modern twist—that's this ultrahip beachfront hotel to a T. **Pros:** lively fresh feel; on the beach; walking distance to restaurants and nightlife; friendly staff. **Cons:** not for squares. ⊠ *6300 Gulf Blvd., St. Pete Beach* ☎ *727/367–2611 or 800/237–8918* ⊕ *www.postcardinn.com* ⤳ *196 rooms* ⟨ *In-room: Wi-Fi. In-hotel: restaurants, bars, pool, gym, beach, laundry facilities, parking* ▮◌▮CP.

**$$$–$$$$**
RESORT
Fodor's Choice
★

▦ **Renaissance Vinoy Resort & Golf Club.** Built in 1925, (making it the same vintage as the Don CeSar), the Vinoy is a luxury resort in St. Petersburg's gorgeous Old Northeast. **Pros:** charming property; friendly service; close to downtown museums. **Cons:** pricey; not on the beach. ⊠ *501 5th Ave. NE* ☎ *727/894–1000* ⊕ *www.vinoyrenaissanceresort. com* ⤳ *345 rooms, 15 suites* ⟨ *In-room: Internet. In-hotel: restaurants, bars, golf course, tennis courts, pools, gym, spa, laundry facilities.*

**$$$–$$$$**
RESORT

▦ **TradeWinds Islands Resort.** The only resort on the beach to put on its own fireworks display, the TradeWinds is very popular with foreign travelers and the go-to place for beach weddings. **Pros:** great beachfront location; close to restaurants. **Cons:** lots of conventions. ⊠ *5500 Gulf Blvd., St. Pete Beach* ☎ *727/363–2212* ⊕ *www.justletgo.com* ⤳ *584 rooms, 103 suites* ⟨ *In-room: kitchen, Wi-Fi. In-hotel: restaurants, bars, tennis courts, pools, gym, spa, beach, children's programs, laundry facilities, parking.*

## SPORTS AND THE OUTDOORS

### BASEBALL

**Philadelphia Phillies.** The Phillies get ready for the season with spring training here (late February to early April). The stadium also hosts the Phillies' farm team. ✉ *Bright House Networks Field, 601 N. Old Coachman Rd.* ☎ *727/441–8638.*

### BIKING

**Pinellas Trail.** This 35-mi paved route pans Pinellas County. Once a railway, the trail runs adjacent to major thoroughfares, no more than 10 feet from the roadway, so you can access it from almost any point. The trail, also popular with in-line skaters, has spawned trailside businesses such as repair shops and health-food cafés. There are also many lovely rural areas to bike through and plenty of places to rent bikes.

Be wary of traffic in downtown Clearwater and on the congested areas of the Pinellas Trail, which still needs more bridges for crossing over busy streets, and avoid the trail at night. To start riding from the route's south end, park at Trailhead Park (37th Street South at 8th Avenue South) in St. Petersburg. To ride south from the north end, park your car in downtown Tarpon Springs (East Tarpon Avenue at North Stafford Avenue). ☎ *727/464–8201.*

## WHERE TO EAT

**$$$** ✕ **Bob Heilman's Beachcomber.** The Heilman family has fed hungry din-
AMERICAN ers since 1920. Although it's very popular with tourists, you'll also rub shoulders with devoted locals. Despite the frequent crowds, the service is fast and friendly. The sautéed chicken is an American classic—arriving with mashed spuds, gravy, veggie du jour, and fresh baked bread. Or try the New Bedford sea scallops, broiled with lemon, capers, or pan-seared with roasted peppers. ✉ *447 Mandalay Ave., Clearwater Beach* ☎ *727/442–4144* ⊕ *www.bobheilmans.com.*

**$** ✕ **Frenchy's Rockaway Grill.** Quebec native Mike "Frenchy" Preston runs
SEAFOOD four eateries in the area, including the fabulous Rockaway Grill. Visitors and locals alike keep coming back for the grouper sandwiches that are moist and not battered into submission. (It's also real grouper, something that's not a given these days.) Frenchy also gets a big thumbs-up for the she-crab soup, and, on the march-to-a-different-drummer front, the cheddar-stuffed shrimp. In mild weather, eat on the deck, though the screaming yellow awning can be nearly as blinding as the sun. ✉ *7 Rockaway St.* ☎ *727/446–4844* ⊕ *www.frenchysonline.com.*

## WHERE TO STAY

*For expanded hotel reviews, visit Fodors.com.*

**$$$–$$$$** ▦ **Safety Harbor Resort & Spa.** Those who enjoy old-school pampering
RESORT love this hotel's 50,000-square-foot spa, which has the latest in therapies and treatments. **Pros:** charm to spare; good choice for pampering. **Cons:** far from beach; not ideal for families with children. ✉ *105 N. Bayshore Dr., Safety Harbor* ☎ *727/726–1161 or 888/237–8772* ⊕ *www.safetyharborspa.com* ⇌ *175 rooms, 16 suites* ⚒ *In-room: a/c, Wi-Fi. In-hotel: restaurant, tennis courts, pools, gym, spa, laundry facilities.*

8

Clearwater's Bait House lures in those heading to the pier to fish; photo by watland, Fodors.com member.

**$$$–$$$$**
**RESORT**
★
🏨 **Sheraton Sand Key Resort.** Expect something special—a modern property and one of the few uncluttered beaches in the area. **Pros:** private beach; great views; flat-screen TVs in rooms. **Cons:** near crowded Clearwater Beach; views come with a high price tag. ✉ *1160 Gulf Blvd., Clearwater Beach* ☎ *727/595–1611* ⊕ *www.sheratonsandkey. com* ↗ *375 rooms, 15 suites* ⚲ *In-room: Wi-Fi. In-hotel: restaurants, bars, tennis courts, pool, gym, beach, water sports, children's programs.*

**$$–$$$**
**B&B/INN**
🏨 **Wingate Inn—Clearwater/St. Pete.** This pleasant motel is close to the attractions of northern Pinellas County. **Pros:** friendly staff; waffle station at breakfast. **Cons:** a bit far from the sites. ✉ *5000 Lake Blvd., Clearwater* ☎ *727/299–9800* ⊕ *www.wingateinnclearwater.com* ↗ *84 rooms* ⚲ *In-room: Wi-Fi. In-hotel: pool, gym, laundry facilities* ⦿ *BP.*

## DUNEDIN

*3 mi north of Clearwater.*

If the sound of bagpipes and the sight of men in kilts appeals to you, you might catch an earful or a glimpse if your timing is right. Founded and named by two Scots in the 1880s, this town hosts the Highland Games in March and the Celtic Festival in November, both of which pay tribute to the town's heritage. Dunedin also has a nicely restored historic downtown—only about five blocks long—that has become a one-stop shopping area for antiques hunters and is also lined with gift shops and good nonchain eateries.

## GETTING HERE AND AROUND

From Clearwater, take U.S. 19 to Route 580, then go west about 8 to 10 mi.

## ESSENTIALS

Visitor Information **Greater Dunedin Chamber of Commerce** (✉ *301 Main St., Dunedin* ☎ *727/733–3197* ⊕ *www.dunedin-fl.com*).

## BEACH

**Caladesi Island State Park.** Quiet, secluded, and still wild, this 3½-mi-long barrier island is one of the best shelling beaches on the Gulf Coast, second only to Sanibel. The park also has plenty of sights for birders—from common sandpipers to majestic blue herons to rare black skimmers—and miles of trails through scrub oaks, saw palmettos, and cacti (with tenants such as armadillos, rabbits, and raccoons). The landscape also features mangroves and dunes, and the gradual slope of the sea bottom makes this a good spot for novice swimmers and kids. You have to get to Caladesi Island by private boat (there's a 108-slip marina) or through its sister park, Honeymoon Island State Recreation Area, where you take the hourly ferry ride across to Caladesi. Ferry rides cost $9 per person. Best for: shelling, solitude, kayaking, boating, fishing. Amenities: showers, playground, hiking trail, restrooms, concessions. ✉ *Dunedin Causeway* ☎ 727/469–5942 ☜ *$5 per car* ☉ *Daily 8–sunset.*

## SPORTS AND THE OUTDOORS

### BASEBALL

**Toronto Blue Jays.** The Jays play about 18 spring-training games here in March. ✉ *Knology Park, 373 Douglas Ave., north of Hwy. 580* ☎ 727/733–9302.

## WHERE TO EAT

$$$

CONTINENTAL

✕ **Bon Appétit.** Known for its creative fare, this waterfront restaurant has a menu that changes frequently, offering such entrées as broiled rack of lamb in herbed walnut crust and red snapper on a bed of lobster hash. The sautéed grouper gets well-deserved plaudits from many patrons. Bon Appétit has staying power, serving at the same location for more than three decades. It's a great place to catch a sunset over the Gulf of Mexico. There's a pianist Wednesday through Sunday evenings and a Sunday brunch. ✉ *148 Marina Plaza* ☎ 727/733–2151 ⊕ *www.bonappetitrestaurant.com.*

$$

MEXICAN

★

✕ **Casa Tina.** At this colorful Dunedin institution, vegetarians can veg out on roasted chiles rellenos (cheese-stuffed peppers), enchiladas with vegetables, and a cactus salad that won't prick your tongue but will tickle your taste buds with the tantalizing flavors of tender pieces of cactus, cilantro, tomatoes, onions, lime, and *queso fresco* (a mild white cheese). The stuffed sapote squash also makes the grade. Tamales, tacos, and tortillas are prepared in dozens of ways. The place is often crowded, and service can be slow as a result, but there's a reason everyone's eating here. ✉ *365 Main St.* ☎ 727/734–9226.

$$$

STEAK

✕ **Spoto's Italian Grille.** It's a simple formula: aged Angus beef expertly prepared and pasta cooked to perfection. This restaurant serves about every cut of beef you can imagine, from a huge porterhouse to a petit fillet to succulent prime rib. If red meat isn't what you're looking for, there's also a variety of fresh fish entrées. ✉ *1280 Main St.* ☎ *727/734–0008* ⊕ *www.spotossteakjoint2.com* ⊘ *No lunch*.

# TARPON SPRINGS

*10 mi north of Dunedin on Alternate U.S. 19.*

Tucked into a little harbor at the mouth of the Anclote River, this slowly growing town was settled by Greek immigrants at the end of the 19th century. They came to practice their generations-old craft of sponge diving. Although bacterial and market forces seriously hurt the industry in the 1940s, sponging has had a modest return, mostly as a focal point for tourism. The docks along Dodecanese Boulevard, the main waterfront street, are filled with sweet old buildings with shops and eateries. Tarpon Springs' other key street is Tarpon Avenue, about a mile south of Dodecanese. This old central business district has become a hub for antiques hunters.

The influence of Greek culture is omnipresent; the community's biggest celebration is the annual Greek Orthodox Epiphany celebration in January, in which teenage boys dive for a golden cross in Spring Bayou, a few blocks from Tarpon Avenue, during a ceremony followed by a street festival in the town's central business district.

### ESSENTIALS

Visitor Information **Tarpon Springs Chamber of Commerce** (✉ *11 E. Orange St.* ☎ *727/937–6109* ⊕ *www.tarponspringschamber.com*).

### EXPLORING

**Konger Tarpon Springs Aquarium.** Although it's not on par with larger tanks in Tampa and Clearwater, this is certainly an entertaining destination. There are some good exhibits, including a 120,000-gallon shark tank complete with a coral reef. (Divers feed the sharks several times daily.) Also look for tropical fish exhibits and a tank where you can touch baby sharks and stingrays. ✉ *850 Dodecanese Blvd., off U.S. 19* ☎ *727/938–5378* ⊕ *www.tarponspringsaquarium.com* 🔖 *$7.75* ⊘ *Mon.–Sat. 10–5, Sun. noon–5.*

**The Sponge Factory.** This shop, museum, and cultural center reveals more than you ever imagined about how a lowly sea creature created the industry that built this village. See a film about these much-sought-after creatures from the phylum *porifera* and how they helped the town prosper in the early 1900s. You'll come away converted to (and loaded up with) natural sponges. ✉ *15 Dodecanese Blvd., off U.S. 19* ☎ *727/938–5366* ⊕ *www.spongedocks.net* 🔖 *Free* ⊘ *Daily 10–9.*

### BEACHES

**Howard Park Beach.** It comes in two parts: a shady mainland picnic area and a white-sand beach island. The causeway is a popular hangout for windsurfers. The park has rest rooms, picnic tables, and grills. ✉ *Sunset Dr.*

**Sunset Beach.** This small public beach has rest rooms, picnic tables, grills, and a boat ramp. ✉ *Gulf Rd.*

**DID YOU KNOW?**

Sometimes called "sea cows," manatees are aquatic relatives of elephants. They can weigh more than 1,500 pounds and live 50-plus years. There are more than 3,000 in Florida's coastal waters.

crab-cake sandwich. Entrées from the land feature pork tenderloin and rack of lamb. Guests enjoy taking their cocktails on the extended veranda overlooking the river. On the way out, top off your meal with the purchase of a boat from the accompanying marina. ⊠ *102 Riviera Dunes Way, Palmetto* ☎ *941/723–2556* ⊘ *No lunch Mon.*

**$$–$$$** ✕ **Sandbar Seafood & Spirits**. If the grouper is not fresh, it is not on the
AMERICAN menu here. Ordered blackened, the grouper can hold its own against the Island Salad made with mangoes, Gorgonzola, passion fruit, and pralines. Other fresh fish options include crab cakes and crab-crusted sea scallops, a blend of the Chesapeake and the Gulf. The outside deck sits on the beach—the view is spectacular and a great place to watch the sunset. Sandbar has a formal indoor menu and a more casual outdoor menu. Options range from a spicy Szechuan tilapia sandwich to crab-crusted scallops. ⊠ *100 Spring Ave., Anna Maria Island* ☎ *941/778–0444* ⊕ *sandbar-restaurant-com.chewbacca.parcomweb.net.*

## WHERE TO STAY

*For expanded hotel reviews, visit Fodors.com.*

**$$$–$$$$** ⊟ **BridgeWalk**. This circa-1947 Caribbean colonial-style property is
RENTAL across from the beach and a community within itself. **Pros:** great loca-
★ tion; variety of lodging and dining experiences. **Cons:** can be pricey. ⊠ *100 Bridge St., Bradenton Beach* ☎ *941/779–2545 or 866/779–2545* ⊟ *941/779–0828* ⊕ *www.silverresorts.com* ⊐ *28 apartments* ⌂ *In-room: a/c, kitchen (some), Internet. In-hotel: restaurant, bar, pool, laundry facilities.*

**$$–$$$$** ⊟ **Silver Surf Gulf Beach Resort**. A sister to BridgeWalk, the Silver Surf
HOTEL has the air of a well-maintained 1960s motel with its studios and apartments. ⊠ *1301 Gulf Dr. N, Anna Maria Island, Bradenton Beach* ☎ *941/778–6626 or 800/441–7873* ⊕ *www.silverresorts.com* ⊐ *4 rooms, 46 suites* ⌂ *In-room: kitchen (some), Internet. In-hotel: pool, beach, laundry facilities.*

# SARASOTA

*30 mi south of Tampa and St. Petersburg.*

Sarasota is a year-round destination and in some cases permanent home to some of Florida's most affluent residents. Circus magnate John Ringling and his wife, Mable, started the city on the road to becoming one of the state's hotbeds for the arts. Today, sporting cultural events can be enjoyed year-round, and there is a higher concentration of upscale shops, restaurants, and hotels than in much of the Tampa Bay Area. Across the water from Sarasota lie the barrier islands of Siesta Key, Longboat Key, and Lido Key, with myriad beaches, shops, hotels, condominiums, and houses.

## GETTING HERE AND AROUND

Sarasota is accessible from Interstate 75 and Interstate 275, and U.S. 41. The town's public transit company is Sarasota County Area Transit (SCAT). Fares for local bus service range from 75¢ to $3 (for an all-day pass); exact change is required. A $60 monthly "R-Card" is available for unlimited rides on all SCAT and Manatee County Area Transit (MCAT) routes.

**ESSENTIALS**

Transportation Contact **Sarasota County Area Transit (SCAT)** (☎ *941/316–1234*).

Visitor Information **Sarasota Convention and Visitors Bureau** (✉ *701 N. Tamiami Trail, Sarasota* ☎ *941/957–1877 or 800/522–9799* ⊕ *www.sarasotafl.org*).

## EXPLORING
### TOP ATTRACTIONS

☺ **Florida State University Ringling Center for the Cultural Arts**. Along Sarasota
Fodor'sChoice  Bay, Ringling built a grand home that was patterned after Doges Palace
★  in Venice. This exquisite mansion of 32 rooms, 15 bathrooms, and a
61-foot Belvedere Tower was completed in 1925, and today is the site
of the Florida State University Ringling Center for the Cultural Arts.
Its 8,000-square-foot terrace overlooks the dock where Ringling's wife,
Mable, moored her gondola.

Within the center are the John and Mable Ringling Museum of Art—a
state-of-the-art museum with 500 years of art represented, including a
world-renowned collection of Rubens's paintings and tapestries—and
the Ringling Circus Museum, which displays circus memorabilia from
its ancient roots to modern day.

The Tibbals Learning Center focuses on the American circus and the
collection of Howard Tibbals, master model builder, who spent 40 years
building the world's largest miniature circus. This impressive to-scale
replica of the circa 1920s and '30s Ringling Bros. and Barnum & Bailey
Circus is authentic from the number of pancakes the circus cooks are
flipping, to the exact likenesses and costumes of the performers, to the
correct names of the animals marked on the miniature mess buckets.
Tibbals's passion to re-create every exact detail continues in his on-site
workshop, where kids can ask him questions and watch him carving
animals and intricate wagons.

If you're looking for clown noses, ringmaster hats, and circus-theme
T-shirts, don't leave before checking out the Ringling Museum of Art
Store. ✉ *U.S. 41, ½ mi west of Sarasota-Bradenton Airport* ☎ *941/359–
5700* ⊕ *www.ringling.org* 🎟 *$25* ⊙ *Fri.–Wed. 10–5, Thurs. 10–8.*

**Marie Selby Botanical Gardens**. Orchids make up nearly a third of the
20,000 species of flowers and plants here. You can stroll through the
Tropical Display House, home of orchids and colorful bromeliads gath-
ered from rain forests, and wander the garden pathway past plantings of
bamboo, ancient banyans, and mangrove forests along Little Sarasota
Bay. Although spring sees the best blooms, the greenhouses make this
an attraction for all seasons. The added bonus is a spectacular view of
downtown. There are rotating exhibits of botanical art and photography in a 1934 restored Southern Colonial mansion. Enjoy lunch at
the Selby Café. ✉ *811 S. Palm Ave.* ☎ *941/366–5731* ⊕ *www.selby.org*
🎟 *$17* ⊙ *Daily 10–5.*

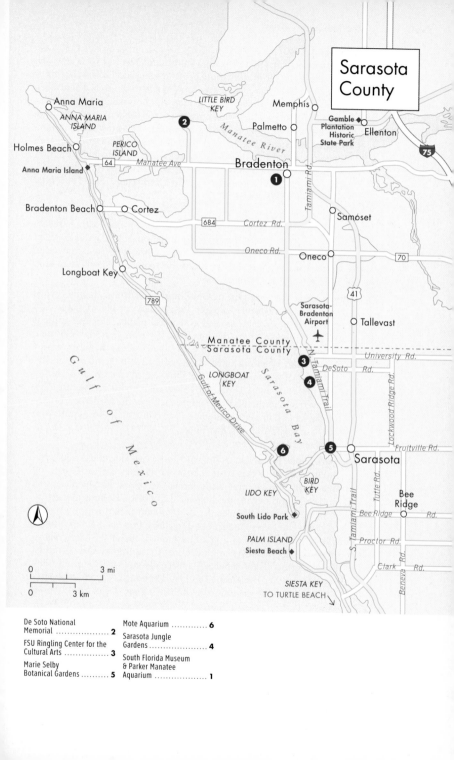

# Sarasota County

Anna Maria
*ANNA MARIA ISLAND*

*LITTLE BIRD KEY*

Memphis

Palmetto

*Manatee River*

Gamble Plantation Historic State Park ◆

Ellenton

I-75

Holmes Beach

*PERICO ISLAND*

64  *Manatee Ave*

**Bradenton**

Anna Maria Island ◆

❷

❶

Bradenton Beach    Cortez

684  *Cortez Rd.*

Samóset

*Tamiami Rd.*

*Oneco Rd.*

Oneco

70

Longboat Key

789

41

US 41

Sarasota-Bradenton Airport

Tallevast

✈

**Manatee County**
**Sarasota County**

❸  *Tamiami Trail*

*University Rd.*

*DeSoto   Rd.*

❹

*LONGBOAT KEY*

*Gulf of Mexico Drive*

*Sarasota Bay*

*Lockwood Ridge Rd.*

G  u  l  f

o  f

M  e  x  i  c  o

❻

❺  *Fruitville Rd.*

**Sarasota**

*Tuttle Rd.*

*BIRD KEY*

*LIDO KEY*

Bee Ridge

South Lido Park ◆

*Bee Ridge    Rd.*

*PALM ISLAND*
Siesta Beach ◆

*S. Tamiami Trail*

*Proctor Rd.*

*Clark    Rd.*

*SIESTA KEY*
TO TURTLE BEACH

*Beneva Rd.*

0 ___ 3 mi
0 ___ 3 km

De Soto National Memorial ................... **2**

FSU Ringling Center for the Cultural Arts ............... **3**

Marie Selby Botanical Gardens .......... **5**

Mote Aquarium ............ **6**

Sarasota Jungle Gardens ..................... **4**

South Florida Museum & Parker Manatee Aquarium ................... **1**

### WORTH NOTING

**Mote Aquarium.** The 135,000-gallon shark tank here lets you view various types of sharks from above and below the surface. Other tanks show off eels, rays, and other marine creatures native to the area. There's also a touch tank where you can get friendly with horseshoe crabs, conchs, and other creatures. Hugh and Buffett are the resident manatees and, though not as venerable as Snooty at the Parker Manatee Aquarium, they have lived here since 1996 as part of a research program. There's also a permanent sea-turtle exhibit. ✉ *1600 Ken Thompson Pkwy., City Island, Sarasota* ☎ *941/388–4441* ⊕ *www.mote.org* ✍ *Aquarium $17, boat excursion $26, combined ticket $36* ⊙ *Aquarium daily 10–5; boat tours daily 11, 1:30, and 4.*

**Sarasota Bay Explorers.** Many visitors to the Mote Aquarium take the 105-minute boat trip onto Sarasota Bay, conducted by Sarasota Bay Explorers. The crew brings marine life on board, explains what it is, and throws it back to swim away. You are almost guaranteed to see bottlenose dolphins. Reservations are required. ☎ *941/388–4200* ⊕ *www.sarasotabayexplorers.com.*

**Sarasota Jungle Gardens.** One of Old Florida's charming, family-owned and -operated attractions, Sarasota Jungle Gardens fills 10 acres with native and exotic animals as well as tropical plants. The lush gardens date to 1939, and still have the small-world feel of yesterday's Florida. You'll find red-tailed hawks and great horned owls in the birds of prey show, American alligators and a variety of snakes in the reptile encounter, and bugs of many varieties in a show called Critters and Things. You can talk to trainers and get to know such plants as the rare Australian nut tree and the Peruvian apple cactus in the gardens. Also onsite are flocks of flamingos that guests can hand-feed, plus reptiles and a butterfly garden. ✉ *3701 Bay Shore Rd.* ☎ *941/355–5305* ⊕ *www.sarasotajunglegardens.com* ✍ *$15* ⊙ *Daily 10–5.*

**OFF THE BEATEN PATH**

**Solomon's Castle.** For a visit to the wild and weird side, particularly fun for children, head to this castle about 45 minutes east of Bradenton through orange groves and cattle farms. Artist and Renaissance man Howard Solomon began building the 12,000-square-foot always-in-progress work out of thousands of aluminum offset printing plates. Inside, you'll find tons of intrigues—everything from a knight assembled with Volkswagen parts to a chair fashioned out of 86 beer cans to an elephant made from seven oil drums. A restaurant serves sit-down lunches in a full-scale model of a Spanish galleon. It is also open Friday and Saturday nights in season. ✉ *4533 Solomon Rd., Ona* ☎ *863/494–6037* ⊕ *www.solomonscastle.org* ✍ *$10* ⊙ *Tues.–Sun. 11–4; closed July–Sept.*

### SPORTS AND THE OUTDOORS

#### FISHING

**Flying Fish Fleet.** Several boats can be chartered for deep-sea fishing, and there are daily group trips on a "party" fishing boat. ✉ *U.S. 41, on bay front at Marina Jack* ☎ *941/366–3373* ⊕ *www.flyingfishfleet.com.*

"When my granddaughter saw the beach for the first time at Longboat Key the sand was so white that she thought it was snow and wanted to make angels." —photo by Elizabeth Shevloff, Fodors.com member.

### GOLF

**Bobby Jones Golf Course.** There are 45 holes and a driving range; greens fees are $17–$37. ✉ *1000 Circus Blvd.* ☎ *941/955–8097.*

### KAYAKING

**Siesta Sports Rentals.** Up for rent here are kayaks, bikes, beach chairs, scooters, and beach wheelchairs and strollers. Guided kayaking trips are also available. ✉ *6551 Midnight Pass Rd., Siesta Key* ☎ *941/346–1797* ⊕ *www.siestasportsrentals.com.*

## SHOPPING

St. Armands Circle has a cluster of oh-so-exclusive shops and laid-back restaurants. It's just east of Lido Beach.

**Elysian Fields Bookstore.** This unique bookstore carries a diverse selection of books and periodicals and hosts various events and art fairs. ✉ *1273 Tamiami Trail S* ☎ *941/361–3006.*

**Lotus.** The specialties here include denim, women's fashion, perfumes, and lingerie. ✉ *1451 Main St., Downtown* ☎ *941/906–7080* ⊕ *www.lotussarasota.com.*

**L. Boutique.** Find the trendiest fashions and most stylish handbags and shoes from top designers. ✉ *556 S. Pineapple Ave., Downtown* ☎ *941/906–1350* ⊕ *www.lboutiques.com.*

## NIGHTLIFE AND THE ARTS

### NIGHTLIFE

**Gator Club.** A famous nightclub located in a beautifully restored, brick historic cornerstone building downtown, the Gator Club has live music and dancing 365 days a year. ✉ *1490 Main St.* ☎ *941/366–5969.*

## THE ARTS

**Asolo Repertory Theatre.** One of the best theaters in Sarasota stages productions November to June. ⊠ *5555 N. Tamiami Trail* ☎ *941/351–8000* ⊕ *www.asolo.org.*

**The Players Theatre.** A long-established community theater, having launched such actors as Montgomery Clift and Paul Reubens, this troupe performs comedies, special events, live concerts, and musicals. ⊠ *838 N. Tamiami Trail U.S. 41 and 9th St.* ☎ *941/365–2494.*

**Sarasota Opera.** Performing from February through March in a historic 1,033-seat downtown theater, the Sarasota Opera features internationally known artists singing the principal roles, supported by a professional chorus of young apprentices. ⊠ *The Edwards Theater, 61 N. Pineapple Ave.* ☎ *941/366–8450.*

## WHERE TO EAT

**$$$**
CAFÉ
Fodor's Choice
★

✕ **Bijou Café.** Once a 50-seat 1920 gas station–turned-restaurant, the Bijou is now a 140-seat restaurant with the type of enchanting decor you might expect in a quaint, modern European café—think French windows and doors, sparkling glassware, bouquets of freshly picked flowers, and the soft glow of candlelight. Lunches begin with an inspired soup, salads, or sandwiches such as the Waldorf Chicken Salad Croissant. Dinners emphasize fresh local produce and sustainable seafood. Opera season—typically February and March—is the only time Sunday dinner is served. ⊠ *1287 1st St.* ☎ *941/366–8111* ⊕ *www.bijoucafe.net* ⊗ *Closed Sun. Apr.–Jan. No lunch weekends.*

**$$**
ITALIAN

✕ **Café Baci.** Specializing in Tuscan and Roman cuisine, Café Baci appeals to loyal locals and savvy travelers alike. Its menu highlights original family recipes; specialties range from fresh, succulent seafood dishes and homemade pastas to traditional veal recipes such as *piccata de vitella* simmered with white wine, lemon, and capers or grilled salmon served on spinach pesto risotto. From the moment you walk through the door, you'll enjoy the peaceful, elegant, Italian-inspired atmosphere. ⊠ *4001 S. Tamiami Trail* ☎ *941/921–4848* ⊕ *www.cafebaci.net.*

**$$$$**
CAFÉ

✕ **Café L'Europe.** Located in St. Armand's Circle, this sidewalk and indoor café has a spectacular menu featuring tableside specialties such as chateaubriand for two. Other popular entrées range from potato-crusted grouper and brandied duckling to rack of lamb and a horseradish salmon. There's also a nice choice of wines by the glass. Veranda tables are a great place to watch shoppers and strollers. ⊠ *431 St. Armands Circle, Lido Key* ☎ *941/388–4415* ⊕ *www.cafeleurope.net* ⊗ *Closed Sun.*

**$$**
SPANISH

✕ **Columbia.** On trendy St. Armand's Circle, patron perch for a good meal and amazing people-watching. The 1905 salad—with ham, olives, cheese, and garlic—deserves its cult status. October through May sees stone crabs fresh from the Gulf of Mexico. Order them chilled, steamed, with butter, with mustard sauce and lemon, or broiled "Carioca" style with Latin spices. The crusty bread and Spanish bean soup enhance the flavors. ⊠ *411 St. Armand's Circle, Lido Key* ☎ *941/388–3987* ⊕ *www.columbiarestaurant.com.*

**$$$$** ✕ **Euphemia Haye.** A lush tropical setting on the barrier island of Long-
STEAK/SEAFOOD boat Key, this is one of the most romantic restaurants around. The
Fodor'sChoice staff is friendly and gracious, the food delightful, and the atmosphere
★ contagious. Its popular dessert display is a sweet ending to the pricey
menu items that feature signature dishes such as crisp roast duckling
with bread and flambéed prime peppered steak. The upstairs Haye Loft,
once the home of the original owner's grandson, has been converted
into a bistro and lounge. ⊠ *5540 Gulf of Mexico Dr., Longboat Key*
☎ *941/383–3633* ⊕ *www.euphemiahaye.com.*

**$$$** ✕ **Michael's on East.** Not only do the lounge and piano bar, with their
AMERICAN extensive wines and vintage cocktails, lure the after-theater set, but
inspired cuisine and superior service also entice. Inside its Midtown
Plaza shopping center location, you'll find a decor similar to New York's
better bistros of the '30s and '40s, but there is plenty of veranda seat-
ing for enjoying Sarasota's balmy weather. The fare ranges from bow-
tie pasta with sun-dried tomatoes to porcini-rubbed rack of lamb to
roasted swordfish with red potatoes. The pecan-graham-crusted key
lime tart served under a cloud of baked meringue is only one of the
creative combinations for concluding your cuisine adventure. ⊠ *1212
East Ave. S* ☎ *941/366–0007* ⊕ *www.michaelsoneast.com* ☼ *Closed
Sun. No lunch Sat.*

**$** ✕ **The Old Salty Dog.** A menu of steamer and raw-bar options has been
AMERICAN added to the much-enjoyed old favorites, including quarter-pound
hot dogs, fish-and-chips, wings, and burgers. With views of New Pass
between Longboat and Lido Keys, this is a popular stop for locals and
visitors en route to Mote Aquarium and the adjoining bay-front park.
Open-air dining area is comfortable even in summer, thanks to a pleas-
ant breeze. Its bar is shaped from the hull of an old boat. ⊠ *1601 Ken
Thompson Pkwy., City Island* ☎ *941/388–4311* ⊕ *www.theoldsaltydog.
com* ⌕ *Reservations not accepted.*

**$$$$** ✕ **Ophelia's on the Bay.** Florida the way it should be: you can watch as
AMERICAN dolphins swim past while blue herons lounge on the dock. Enjoy the
flowering gardens while dining alfresco on the outdoor patio on its
dock at Market #48 or in one of two casually elegant dining rooms.
An ever-evolving menu highlights the Florida surroundings with selec-
tions such as red snapper with key lime–poblano relish and jumbo-lump
blue-crab guacamole. The tuna (bigeye, yellowfin, and more) is flown
in from Hawaii thanks to owner Jane Ferro, who is also the grandniece
of the restaurant's namesake. ⊠ *9105 Midnight Pass Rd., Siesta Key*
☎ *941/349–2212* ⊕ *www.opheliasonthebay.net* ☼ *No lunch.*

**$** ✕ **Yoder's.** Lines for meals stretch well beyond the hostess podium here.
AMERICAN Pies—key lime, egg custard, banana cream, peanut butter, strawberry
rhubarb, and others—are the main event at this family restaurant in the
heart of Sarasota's Amish community. Daily specials typically include
zesty goulash, chicken and dumplings, and pulled smoked pork. For
breakfast, choose from French toast stuffed with cream cheese or per-
haps a hearty stack of pancakes. Sandwiches include Manhattans (roast
beef, turkey, or meat loaf on homemade bread with mashed potatoes
and gravy). The entire village is always crowded, but there's plenty
of waitstaff who keep tables clean and cleared, so the flow is steady.

8

The decor retains its Old Florida efficiency appearance. ⊠ *3434 Bahia Vista* ☎ *941/955–7771* ⊕ *www.yodersrestaurant.com* ⌂ *Reservations not accepted* ⊘ *Closed Sun.*

## WHERE TO STAY

**$$–$$$**    ⊡ **Gulf Beach Resort.** Lido Key's first motel has been designated a historic
RESORT    property. **Pros:** near shopping; well maintained; lots of beach. **Cons:** basic rooms; motel feel. ⊠ *930 Ben Franklin Dr., Lido Key* ☎ *941/388–2127 or 800/232–2489* ⊕ *www.gulfbeachsarasota.com* ⇥ *8 rooms, 41 suites* ⌂ *In-room: a/c, Internet. In-hotel: pool, beach, laundry facilities.*

**$$$$**    ⊡ **Hyatt Regency Sarasota.** Popular among business travelers, the Hyatt
HOTEL    Regency is contemporary in design and sits in the heart of the city across from the Van Wezel Performing Arts Hall. **Pros:** great location; stellar views. **Cons:** chain-hotel feel. ⊠ *1000 Blvd. of the Arts* ☎ *941/953–1234 or 800/233–1234* ⊕ *www.sarasota.hyatt.com* ⇥ *294 rooms, 12 suites* ⌂ *In-room: Wi-Fi. In-hotel: restaurants, bars, pool, gym, laundry facilities, some pets allowed.*

**$$$–$$$$**    ⊡ **Lido Beach Resort.** Superb gulf views can be found at this stylish beach-
RESORT    front resort. **Pros:** beachfront location. **Cons:** bland furnishings; small parking area. ⊠ *700 Ben Franklin Dr.* ☎ *941/388–2161 or 800/441–2113* ⊕ *www.lidobeachresort.com* ⇥ *158 rooms, 64 suites* ⌂ *In-room: a/c, kitchen (some), Wi-Fi. In-hotel: restaurants, bars, pools, beach, children's programs, laundry facilities.*

**$$$$**    ⊡ **Longboat Key Club & Resort.** The debate is whether the 45 holes of chal-
RESORT    lenging golf attract guests to this property or whether it's the 291-slip marina. **Pros:** upscale vibe; lovely grounds; most rooms have private balcony. **Cons:** service can feel snooty. ⊠ *220 Sands Point Rd., Longboat Key* ☎ *941/383–8821, 800/237–8821, or 888/237–5545* ⊕ *www.longboatkeyclub.com* ⇥ *218 rooms and suites* ⌂ *In-room: a/c, kitchen (some), Wi-Fi. In-hotel: restaurants, bars, golf course, tennis courts, pool, gym, spa, beach, water sports, children's programs, laundry facilities, business center.*

**$$$$**    ⊡ **Ritz-Carlton, Sarasota.** With a style that developers like to say is circus
HOTEL    magnate John Ringling's realized dream, The Ritz is appointed with fine
★    artwork and fresh-cut flowers. **Pros:** Ritz-style glitz; lots of amenities; attentive staff. **Cons:** long distance to golf course; not on the beach. ⊠ *1111 Ritz-Carlton Dr.* ☎ *941/309–2000 or 800/241–3333* ⊕ *www.ritzcarlton.com/resorts/Sarasota* ⇥ *266 rooms, 30 suites* ⌂ *In-room: Wi-Fi. In-hotel: restaurants, bars, golf course, tennis courts, pool, gym, spa, children's programs, some pets allowed.*

**$$$–$$$$**    ⊡ **Turtle Beach Resort.** Reminiscent of a quieter time, many of the cottages
HOTEL    at this friendly, affordable, family- and pet-friendly resort date to the 1940s, a romantic plus for yesteryear lovers. **Pros:** nice location; romantic setting. **Cons:** far from the area's cultural attractions. ⊠ *9049 Midnight Pass Rd., Siesta Key* ☎ *941/349–4554* ⊕ *www.turtlebeachresort.com* ⇥ *16 apartments, 4 cottages* ⌂ *In-room: kitchen, Wi-Fi. In-hotel: pools, laundry facilities, parking.*

# The Lower Gulf Coast

## WITH FORT MYERS, NAPLES, AND THE COASTAL ISLANDS

### WORD OF MOUTH

"I would highly recommend Sanibel and Captiva for the beach, the biking, and peace and quiet."

—natinwpb

# WELCOME TO
# THE LOWER GULF COAST

## TOP REASONS TO GO

★ **Heavenly Beaches:** Whether you go to the beach to sun, swim, gather shells, or watch the sunset, the region's Gulf of Mexico beaches rank among the best.

★ **Edison and Ford Winter Estates:** A rare complex of two famous inventors' winter homes comes complete with botanical-research gardens, Edison's lab, and a museum.

★ **Island Hopping:** Rent a boat or jump aboard a charter for lunch, picnicking, beaching, or shelling on a subtropical island adrift from the mainland.

★ **Naples Shopping:** Flex your buying power in downtown Naples's charming downtown shopping districts or in lush outdoor centers around town.

★ **Watch for Wildlife:** On the edge of Everglades National Park, the region protects vast tracts of fragile land and water where you can see alligators, manatees, dolphins, roseate spoonbills, and hundreds of other birds.

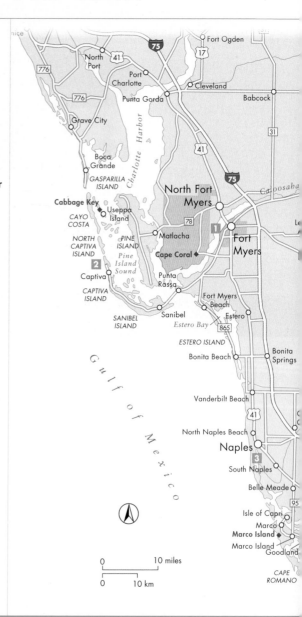

**1** **Fort Myers Area.** Don't miss the Edison and Ford Winter Estates along royal-palm-lined McGregor Boulevard. For museums, theater, and art, the up-and-coming downtown River District rules.

**2** **The Coastal Islands.** Shells and wildlife refuges bring nature-lovers to Sanibel and Captiva islands. Fort Myers Beach is known for its lively clubs and shrimp fleet. For true seclusion, head to the area's unbridged island beaches.

**3** **Naples Area.** Some of the region's best shopping and dining take up residence in historic buildings trimmed with blossoms and street sculptures in Old Naples. Hit Marco Island for the boating lifestyle and funky-fish-village character.

## GETTING ORIENTED

The Lower Gulf Coast of Florida, as its name suggests, occupies a stretch of coastline along southernmost west Florida, bordered by the Gulf of Mexico. It lies south of Tampa and Sarasota, directly on the other side of the state from West Palm Beach and Fort Lauderdale. In between the two coasts stretch heartland agricultural areas and Everglades wilderness. The region encompasses the major resort towns of Fort Myers, Fort Myers Beach, Sanibel Island, Naples, and Marco Island, along with a medley of suburban communities and smaller islands.

**9**

River
Alva
29
Falda
Corkscrew
Immokalee
29
Sunniland
*Everglades Parkway* (toll) 75
(Alligator Alley) Miles City
*Big Cypress National Preserve*
Royal Palm Hammock 29
Copeland
41
THOUSAND ISLANDS Everglades City
*Everglades National Park* Chokoloskee

# LOWER GULF COAST BEACHES

Gorgeous, long, white-sand beaches fringe the Lower Gulf Coast and barrier islands. Known ultimately for their great shelling and kid-friendly waves, the beaches here range from the natural, undeveloped sands of Sanibel Island to the manicured parks of Naples.

Sanibel Island holds the highest reputation for seashells on the seashore in these parts due to the east–west torque at its south end. Shelling is best at low tide and after a storm has washed shells ashore. Remember, collecting live shells (ones with flesh inside) is illegal on Sanibel Island and in all state and national parks, so look only for uninhabited specimens. Local laws outside of Sanibel and the parks limit the taking of live shells to two per person per species per day.

All of the beaches charge for parking; some are resident-only designated and require a car sticker. (Many of the latter you can walk or ride a bike to if you're looking for quiet and seclusion. If you're really looking to escape, rent a boat and hit the bridgeless islands of Don Pedro, Cayo Costa, North Captiva, and Keewaydin.)

## WORD OF MOUTH

"No franchise restaurants [on Sanibel] other than a Subway, a Dairy Queen and a 7/11 but there are lots of good restaurants that are sophisticated if that's your style or kid-friendly if that's a better fit. We began going there years ago when our family really needed some downtime, a chance to talk to each other and rest. We're now on the next generation and the kids love to rent bikes, play volleyball on the beach and pick up shells. It is a real vacation." —lukehead

## THE LOWER GULF COAST'S BEST BEACHES

### BAREFOOT BEACH PRESERVE

Although it's not easy to reach—the drive from Bonita Beach Road along Lely Barefoot Boulevard to this Collier County treasure takes you through a speed-bump-mined development—it's worth the inconvenience if you're looking for a natural encounter along with your beach play. Past the speed bumps, gopher tortoises crossing the road will slow you down. Beachgoers come for shells, canoeing, and to explore nature in gardens and exhibits off the beach.

### BOWMAN'S BEACH

Long, wide Bowman's Beach, on Sanibel's northwest end, is the island's most secluded strand. Walk the length of the beach and leave humanity behind, finding some of the area's greatest concentrations of shells along the way. In fact, while most beaches in Sanibel and Captiva are worthy hunting grounds for shell devotees, Bowman's tops them all. This is because Bowman's is the hardest to reach, most spread-out, and least populated of the island's many beaches. You might even score one of the island's most coveted shells, the Junonia. The sunsets at the north end are spectacular.

### DELNOR-WIGGINS PASS STATE PARK

Its placement across the pass from Barefoot Beach, along with a preserved bay

backdrop, make Delnor-Wiggins in North Naples popular with both fishermen and nature lovers. Rangers conduct birding and sea turtle programs at different times of year. Beach buffs adore its stretch of sand immune from the high-rise rash to the south. Picnic facilities and an observation tower attract families.

### LOVERS KEY STATE PARK

Among Florida's most visited parks, this barrier island south of Fort Myers Beach, on Route 865, is a natural haven. Birds flock to its estuary, kayakers paddle through, and a gazebo on the beach hosts many a wedding. Lovers Key got its name because, for years, it was accessible only by boat, and only lovers ventured here for a little remote romance.

### LOWDERMILK PARK

Looking for pure fun with your beach day, hold the nature lessons? That's what prettily landscaped Lowdermilk in Naples is all about. Families appreciate the grassy lawn, playground, volleyball nets, picnic facilities, shallow waters, duck pond, and food concession at this beach on Gulf Shore Boulevard at Banyan Boulevard.

### TURNER BEACH

This patch of undulating sand on the southern tip of Captiva is a good spot for catching the setting sun. Due to the strong currents here it's much better for surfing than swimming.

**9**

Updated by
Chelle Koster
Walton

With its subtropical climate and beckoning family-friendly beaches, the Lower Gulf Coast, also referred to as the state's southwestern region, is a favorite vacation spot of Florida residents as well as visitors. Vacationers tend to spend most of their time outdoors—swimming, sunning, shelling, fishing, boating, and playing tennis or golf.

The region has several distinct travel destinations. Small and historic downtown Fort Myers rises inland along the Caloosahatchee River, and the rest of the town sprawls in all directions. It got its nickname, the City of Palms, from the hundreds of towering royal palms that inventor Thomas Edison planted between 1900 and 1917 along McGregor Boulevard, a historic residential street and site of his winter estate. Edison's idea caught on, and more than 2,000 royal palms now line 14-mi-long McGregor Boulevard. Museums and educational attractions are the draw here. Across the river, Cape Coral has evolved from a mostly residential community to a resort destination for water-sports enthusiasts.

Off the coast west of Fort Myers are more than 100 coastal islands in all shapes and sizes. Connected to the mainland by a 3-mi causeway, Sanibel is known for its superb shelling, fine fishing, beachfront resorts, and wildlife refuge. Here and on Captiva, to which it is connected by a short bridge, multimillion-dollar homes line both waterfronts. Just southwest of Fort Myers is Estero Island, home of busy Fort Myers Beach, and farther south, Lovers Key State Park and Bonita Beach.

Farther down the coast lies Naples, once a small fishing village and now a thriving and sophisticated town. It's a smaller, more understated version of Palm Beach, with fine restaurants, chichi shopping areas, and—locals will tell you—more golf holes per capita than anywhere else in the world. A half-hour south basks Marco Island, best known for its beaches and fishing. See a maze of pristine miniature mangrove islands when you take a boat tour from the island's marinas into Ten Thousand Islands National Wildlife Refuge. Although high-rises line much of Marco's waterfront, the tiny fishing village of Goodland, an outpost of Old Florida, tries valiantly to stave off new development.

# LOWER GULF COAST PLANNER

## WHEN TO GO

In winter this is one of the warmest areas of the United States, although occasionally temperatures drop below freezing in December or January. From February through April you may find it next to impossible to find a hotel room.

Numbers drop the rest of the year, but visitors within driving range, European tourists, and convention clientele still keep things busy. Temperatures and humidity spike, but discounted room rates make summer attractive. Summer, however, is rainy season, but most storms occur in the afternoon. Hurricane season runs from June through November.

## GETTING HERE

**Southwest Florida International Airport (RSW)** (☎ *239/590–4800* ⊕ *www. flylcpa.com*) is the major airport for the region, with many airlines flying into and out of it.

Gulf Coast Airways to Key West and a couple of private charters service **Naples Municipal Airport** (☎ *239/643–0733* ⊕ *www.flynaples.com*).

Private pilots land at both RSW and Page Field in Fort Myers. North Captiva Island has a private airstrip.

Ground transportation companies include **Aaron Airport Transportation** (☎ *239/768–1898 or 800/998–1898*) and **Sanibel Island Taxi** (☎ *239/ 472–4160*).

## GETTING AROUND

If driving, U.S. 41 (the Tamiami Trail) runs the length of the region. Sanibel Island is accessible from the mainland via the Sanibel Causeway (toll $6 round-trip). Captiva Island lies across a small pass from Sanibel's north end, accessible by bridge.

Be aware that the destination's popularity, especially during winter, means traffic congestion at peak times of day. Avoid driving when the locals are getting to and from work and visitors to and from the beach.

## ABOUT THE RESTAURANTS

In this part of Florida fresh seafood reigns supreme. Succulent native stone-crab claws, a particularly tasty treat, in season from mid-October through mid-May, are usually served hot with drawn butter or chilled with tangy mustard sauce. Supplies are typically steady, since claws regenerate in time for the next season. Other seafood specialties include fried-grouper sandwiches and Sanibel pink shrimp. In Naples's highly hailed restaurants and sidewalk cafés, mingle with locals, winter visitors, and other travelers, and catch up on the latest culinary trends.

**9**

## ABOUT THE HOTELS

Lodging in Fort Myers, the islands, and Naples can be pricey, but there are affordable options even during the busy winter season. If these destinations are too rich for your pocket, consider visiting in the off-season, when rates drop drastically. Beachfront properties tend to be more expensive; to spend less, look for properties away from the water. In high season—Christmas time and President's Day through Easter—always reserve ahead for the top properties. Fall is the slowest season: rates are low and availability is high, but this is also the prime time for hurricanes.

| WHAT IT COSTS | | | | | |
|---|---|---|---|---|---|
| | ¢ | $ | $$ | $$$ | $$$$ |
| Restaurants | under $10 | $10–$15 | $15–$20 | $20–$30 | over $30 |
| Hotels | under $80 | $80–$100 | $100–$140 | $140–$220 | over $220 |

Restaurant prices are per person for a main course at dinner. Hotel prices are for a standard double room, excluding 6% sales tax (more in some counties) and 1%–4% tourist tax.

## SPECIAL TOURS

**Captiva Cruises.** Shelling, nature, luncheon, beach, sunset, and history cruises run to and around the out islands of Cabbage Key, Useppa Island, Cayo Costa, and Gasparilla Island. Night sky cruises and excursions also go to the Edison and Ford Winter Estates. Excursions cost $25 to $70 each. ⊠ *McCarthy's Marina, Captiva* ☎ *239/472–5300* ⊕ *www.captivacruises.com.*

**Manatee Sightseeing Adventure.** Tours to sight these gentle creatures run near Marco Island. ⊠ *525 Newport Dr., Naples* ☎ *239/642–8818* ⊕ *www.see-manatees.com.*

**Tarpon Bay Explorers.** One of the best ways to see the J.N. "Ding" Darling National Wildlife Refuge is by taking one of these kayak or nature boat tours. The knowledgeable naturalist guides can help you see so much more of what's there among the mangroves and under the water's surface. ⊠ *900 Tarpon Bay Rd., Sanibel* ☎ *239/472–8900* ⊕ *www. tarponbayexplorers.com.*

# FORT MYERS AREA

In parts of Fort Myers, old Southern mansions and their modern-day counterparts peek out from behind stately palms and blossomy foliage. Views over the broad Caloosahatchee River, which borders the city's small but businesslike cluster of office buildings downtown, soften the look of the area. These days, it's showing the effects of age and urban sprawl, but planners work at reviving what has been termed the River District. North of Fort Myers are small fishing communities and new retirement towns, including Boca Grande on Gasparilla Island;

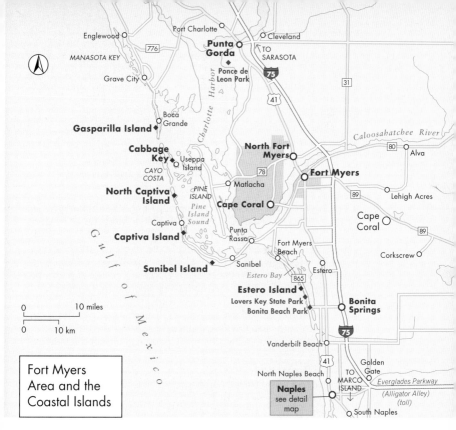

Englewood Beach on Manasota Key; Port Charlotte, north of the Peace River; and Punta Gorda, at the convergence of the Peace River and Charlotte Harbor.

## FORT MYERS

*90 mi southeast of Sarasota, 140 mi west of Palm Beach.*

The city core lies inland along the banks of the Caloosahatchee River, a half hour from the nearest beach. The town is best known as the winter home of inventors Thomas A. Edison and Henry Ford.

### GETTING HERE AND AROUND

The closest airport to Fort Myers is Southwest Florida International Airport (RSW), about 12 mi southwest of town. An on-demand taxi for up to three passengers costs about $20–$30. Extra people are charged at $10 each. LeeTran bus service serves most of the Fort Myers area. If you're driving here from Florida's East Coast, consider Alligator Alley, a toll section of Interstate 75 that runs from Fort Lauderdale to Naples. I–75 then runs north–south the length of the region. U.S. 41 (the Tamiami Trail) runs parallel to the interstate to the west and goes through downtown Naples and Fort Myers. McGregor Boulevard (Route 867) and Summerlin Road (Route 869), Fort Myers's main north–south city streets, head toward Sanibel and Captiva islands. San-Carlos Boulevard runs southwest from Summerlin Road to Fort Myers Beach, and Pine Island–Bayshore Road (Route 78) leads from North Fort Myers through northern Cape Coral onto Pine Island.

### ESSENTIALS

**Transportation Contact LeeTran** (☎ 239/275–8726 or 239/533–8726 ⊕ www.rideleetran.com).

**Visitor Information Lee County Visitor and Convention Bureau** (☎ 239/338–3500 or 800/237–6444 ⊕ www.fortmyers-sanibel.com).

## TOP ATTRACTIONS

★ **Art of the Olympians.** Opened in January 2010, this institution was the vision of the late four-time gold medalist and Fort Myers Beach resident Al Oerter. Upstairs, a gallery overlooks the river and displays artwork created by Olympian athletes including Oerter, Florence Griffith-Joyner, Peggy Fleming, Liston Bochette, and Bob Beamon. Based on the original Greek standard of well-rounded achievement in athletics and art, the Al Oerter Center for Excellence on the first floor inspires children and other visitors toward high achievement with interactive displays, Olympic videos, traveling exhibits, and guest Olympic programs. This is the only facility other than Olympic training centers that the U.S. Olympic Committee allows to use the Olympian name and display the five-ring logo. ⊠ *1300 Hendry St.* ☎ *239/322–5055* ⊕ *www.artoftheolympians. org* ⊡*$5* ⊙ *Tues.–Sat. 10–4.*

Fodor'sChoice **Edison and Ford Winter Estates.** Fort Myers's premier attraction pays hom-
★ age to two of America's most ingenious inventors: Thomas A. Edison, who gave the world the stock ticker, the incandescent lamp, and the phonograph, among other inventions; and his friend and neighbor, auto-maker Henry Ford. Donated to the city by Edison's widow, his once 12-acre estate has been expanded into a remarkable 26 acres, with two homes, two caretaker cottages, a laboratory, botanical gardens, and a museum. The laboratory contains the same gadgets and gizmos as when Edison last stepped foot into it. Visitors can see many of his inventions, along with historic photographs and memorabilia, in the museum. Edison traveled south from New Jersey and devoted much of his time here to inventing things (there are 1,093 patents to his name), experimenting with rubber for friend and frequent visitor Harvey Firestone, and planting hundreds of plant species collected around the world. Next door to Edison's two identical homes is Ford's "Mangoes," the more modest seasonal home of Edison's fellow inventor. It's said that the V-8 engine was, in essence, designed on the back porch. The property's oldest building, the Caretaker's House, dates to 1860. Research garden renovations are ongoing. Tours are guided or audio self-guided. One admission covers both homes; museum and laboratory-only tickets and botanical-garden tour tickets are also available. ⊠ *2350 McGregor Blvd.* ☎ *239/334–3614* ⊕ *www.efwefla.org* ⊡ *Complete Estate Tour $20, check Web site for other tour prices* ⊙ *Daily 9–5:30; hourly tours 10–4.*

Ⓒ **Imaginarium Hands-On Museum.** Kids can't wait to get their hands on the
★ wonderful interactive exhibits at this lively museum–aquarium combo that explores the environment, physics, anatomy, weather, and other

View 200 phonographs, an invention Thomas Edison patented in 1878, at his Fort Myers winter estate.

science and lifestyle topics. Check out the marine life in the aquariums, touch tanks, the living-reef tank, and the outdoor lagoon; visit a tarantula, python, hissing cockroach, juvenile alligator, and other live critters in the Animal Lab; dig for dinosaur bones; slap a hockey puck; watch a 3-D movie in the theater or a hands-on demonstration; then prepare to get blown away in the Hurricane Experience. Improvements made in 2010 upgraded Tiny Town and Animal Lab and brought the return of popular exhibits such as Busy Beehives, Puppet Theater, and Science of Motion. ⊠ *2000 Cranford Ave.* ☎ *239/321–7420* ⊕ *www. imaginariumfortmyers.com* ⊠ *$12* ⊙ *Mon.–Sat. 10–5, Sun. noon–5.*

9

☾ **Manatee Park.** You may glimpse Florida's most famous marine mammal.
★ When gulf waters are cold—usually from November to March—the gentle sea cows congregate in these waters, which are warmed by the outflow of a nearby power plant. Pause at any of the three observation decks (the first nearest the outflow and last at the lagoon usually yield the most sightings) and watch for bubbles. Hydrophones on the last deck allow you to eavesdrop on their songs. Periodically (more frequently on cold days) one of the mammoth creatures—mature adults weigh hundreds of pounds—will surface. The park rents kayaks in winter and on summer weekends and offers kayaking clinics (⊕ *www. calusablueweayoutfitters.com*) and free guided walks among the butterfly garden and other native vegetation. ⊠ *1¼ mi east of I–75 Exit 141 at 10901 Rte. 80* ☎ *239/690–5030* ⊕ *www.leeparks.org* ⊠ *Parking $1 per hr, $5 daily* ⊙ *Daily 8–sunset. Gates locked promptly at closing time. Visitor center daily 9–4.*

## WORTH NOTING

🔆 **Calusa Nature Center & Planetarium.** Get a look at Florida's native animals and habitats. Boardwalks lead through subtropical wetlands, a birds-of-prey aviary, and a butterfly house. There are snake, alligator, butterfly, and other live-animal demonstrations several times daily. Exhibits include exotic species, Mangrove/Living River display, and the Insectarium. The domed, state-of-the-art, 90-seat planetarium hosts astronomy shows daily and special laser shows. ⊠ *3450 Ortiz Ave.* ☎ *239/275–3435* ⊕ *www.calusanature.org* 🖅 *$9* ⊙ *Mon.–Sat. 9–5, Sun. 11–5.*

**Southwest Florida Museum of History.** A restored railroad depot serves as a showcase for the area's history dating to 800 BC. Displays include prehistoric animals and Calusa artifacts, a reconstructed *chickee* hut, a dugout canoe, clothing and photos from Seminole settlements, historical vignettes, changing exhibits, and a replicated Florida Cracker house. A favorite attraction is the *Esperanza,* a private, restored railcar from the 1930s. ⊠ *2031 Jackson St.* ☎ *239/321–7430* ⊕ *www.swflmuseumofhistory.com* 🖅 *$9.50* ⊙ *Tues.–Sat. 10–5.*

## SPORTS AND THE OUTDOORS

### BASEBALL

The region has become a popular outpost for spring training teams, with two in Fort Myers.

**Boston Red Sox.** As of January 2012, the Sox will move from their former downtown digs to a new $77 million, 10,357-capacity training facility in Fort Myers. ⊠ *11581 Daniels Pkwy.* ☎ *239/334–4700* ⊕ *boston. redsox.mlb.com.*

**Minnesota Twins.** The team plays exhibition games in town during March and early April. From April through August, the Miracle (☎ *239/768–4210* ⊕ *www.miraclebaseball.com*), a Twins single-A affiliate, plays home games at the Complex. ⊠ *Lee County Sports Complex, 14100 6 Mile Cypress Pkwy.* ☎ *800/338–9467* ⊕ *minnesota.twins.mlb.com.*

### BIKING

The longest bike path in Fort Myers is along Summerlin Road. It passes commercial areas and close to Sanibel through dwindling wide-open spaces. Linear Park, which runs parallel to Six Mile Cypress Parkway, offers more natural, less congested views. The new Trailhead Park links it to Ten Mile Linear Park to the east for 30 mi of pathway.

**Bike Route.** Come here for a good selection of rentals. ⊠ *8595 College Pkwy., Suite 200* ☎ *239/481–3376* ⊕ *thebikeroute.com.*

### FISHING

Anglers head for the gulf, its bays, and estuaries for saltwater fishing—snapper, sheepshead, mackerel, grouper, and other species. The Caloosahatchee River, Orange River, canals, and small lakes offer freshwater alternatives.

### GOLF

★ **Eastwood Golf Club.** The driving range and 18-hole course are affordable, especially if you don't mind playing at unfavorable times (midday in summer, for example). Many golfers enjoy the lack of development around the course, which poses challenges with its water hazards and doglegs. Fees include cart and tax; fees without cart are available at certain times; greens fee are $60/$20. ⊠ *4600 Bruce Herd La.* ☎ *239/321–7485* ⊕ *www.cityftmyers.com/eastwood.*

**Fort Myers Country Club.** Eighteen holes challenge golfers with its small greens. It's the town's oldest course. Lessons are available. Its clubhouse holds a lively restaurant and bar; greens fee $40/$15 without cart, $60/$25 with cart. ⊠ *3591 McGregor Blvd.* ☎ *239/321–7489* ⊕ *www. cityftmyers.com/countryclub.*

**Shell Point Golf Club.** Head here for an 18-hole course and a driving range; greens fee $99/$49 (including cart). ⊠ *17401 On Par Blvd.* ☎ *239/433–9790* ⊕ *www.shellpointgolf.com.*

### SAILING

★ **Southwest Florida Yachts.** Charter a sailboat or take lessons. ⊠ *3444 Marinatown La. NW* ☎ *239/656–1339 or 800/262–7939* ⊕ *www.swfyachts. com.*

## SHOPPING

★ **Bell Tower Shops.** This open-air shopping center has about 40 stylish boutiques and specialty shops, a Saks 5th Avenue, some of Fort Myers's best restaurants, and 20 movie screens. ⊠ *Cleveland Ave. and Daniels Pkwy.* ☎ *239/489–1221* ⊕ *www.thebelltowershops.com.*

**Edison Mall.** The largest air-conditioned indoor mall in Fort Myers houses several major department stores and some 160 specialty shops. ⊠ *Colonial Blvd. at Cleveland Ave.* ⊕ *www.edison-mall-fl.com.*

**Fleamasters Fleamarket.** Just east of Fort Myers, more than 900 vendors sell new and used goods Friday through Sunday 8–4. Its music hall hosts live entertainment. ⊠ *1.7 mi west of I–75 Exit 138 on Rte. 82* ☎ *239/334–7001* ⊕ *www.fleamall.com.*

**Sanibel Tanger Factory Outlets.** Its boardwalks are lined with outlets for Van Heusen, Maidenform, Coach, Coldwater Creek, Bath & Body Works, and Samsonite, among others. ⊠ *McGregor Blvd. and Summerlin Rd.* ☎ *888/471–3939* ⊕ *www.tangeroutlet.com.*

## NIGHTLIFE AND THE ARTS

### THE ARTS

**Barbara B. Mann Performing Arts Hall.** Catch Broadway plays, concerts, musicals, and comedy shows. ⊠ *Edison State College, 8099 College Pkwy.* ☎ *239/481–4849 or 800/440–7469* ⊕ *www.bbmannpah.com.*

★ **Broadway Palm Dinner Theatre.** Buffet dinners come along with some of Broadway's best comedies and musicals. There's also a 90-seat blackbox theater that hosts smaller-scale productions. ⊠ *1380 Colonial Blvd.* ☎ *239/278–4422* ⊕ *www.broadwaypalm.com.*

★ **Florida Rep.** In the restored circa-1920 Arcade Theatre downtown, this company stages professional entertainment from Neil Simon shows to musical revues mostly geared to a mature crowd. ⊠ *2267 1st St.* ☎ *239/332–4488 or 877/787–8053* ⊕ *www.floridarep.org.*

9

## NIGHTLIFE

**The Happy Buddha.** The casual dancing crowd grooves to popular music and squints in the smoky bar. ✉ *12701 McGregor Blvd., Fort Myers* ☎ *239/482–8838.*

**Laugh In Comedy Café.** South of downtown comedians perform Friday and Saturday. ✉ *College Plaza, 8595 College Pkwy.* ☎ *239/479–5233* ⊕ *www.laughincomedycafe.com.*

**Stevie Tomato's Sports Page.** Watch the big-screen TVs while feasting on good munchies. ✉ *11491 S. Cleveland Ave.* ☎ *239/939–7211* ⊕ *stevie-tomatossportspage.com.*

## WHERE TO EAT

**$$$**
SEAFOOD

✕ **Biddle's Piano Bar & Restaurant.** Besides moving its location across town in 2010, Biddle's moved "Piano Bar" to a new place of importance in its name—before "Restaurant." That doesn't mean, though, the food takes a back seat to the nightly entertainment and dancing. It's still diverse. It's still exciting. And it's still delicious. All of the old favorites have made the trip, along with the handsome jungle-motif décor. From the tower-of-tuna appetizer and outstanding lunchtime duck salad to dinner's seafood Wellington and the stunning chocolate piano dessert—it's all perfectly in tune. With Sunday brunch, enjoy bottomless mimosas for $5. ✉ *12984 S. Cleveland Ave.* ☎ *239/433–4449* ⊕ *www.biddlesrestaurant.com.*

**$$$**
AMERICAN
★

✕ **Bistro 41.** Shoppers and businesspeople meet here for some of the town's most dependable and inventive cuisine. Amid brightly painted, textured walls and a display kitchen, the menus roam from salmon BLT croissant and rotisserie chicken to pork chop mojo with roasted-corn–tomato salsa and seared salmon with orange-balsamic rosemary glaze. To experience the kitchen at its imaginative best, check the night's specials, which often include daringly done seafood (crabmeat-crusted tripletail fish with caramelized plantains and passion-fruit beurre blanc, for instance) and usually cost more than regular menu items (around $25). When weather permits, ask for a table on the patio. ✉ *13499 S. Cleveland Ave.* ☎ *239/466–4141* ⊕ *www.bistro41.com* ⌂ *Reservations essential.*

**$**
MEXICAN

✕ **Chile Ranchero.** Latinos and gringos alike converge on this authentic little corner of Mexicana along busy Tamiami Trail. You can't beat the prices or the portions. The staff speaks Spanish and so does the menu, with English subtitles. Dishes appeal to American and Latin palates, with a range from tongue tacos and steak ranchero to seafood soup and excellent nachos con ceviche. ✉ *11751 S. Cleveland Ave., No. 18* ☎ *239/275–0505* ⌂ *Reservations not accepted.*

**$$$**
ITALIAN

✕ **Cibo.** Its flavor-bursting Italian food and its propensity for fresh, quality ingredients keep it at the head of the class for local Italian restaurants. In contrast to the sophisticated black-and-white setting, the menu comes in colors from classic Caesar salad with shaved Grana Padano and spaghetti and meatballs to salmon piccata and veal porterhouse with porcini risotto. The lasagna Napoletana is typical of the standards set here—a generous square of pasta layered with fluffy ricotta, meat ragu, mozzarella, and the totally fresh-tasting, garlicky pomodoro sauce. ✉ *12901 McGregor Blvd.* ☎ *239/454–3700* ⊕ *www. cibofortmyers.com* ⟀ *Reservations essential* ⊙ *No lunch.*

$     ✗ **Il Pomodoro Cucina Italiana.** We say tomato or tomahtoe, but in Italy,
ITALIAN    they say pomodoro. But there's much more than the use of fresh tomatoes to recommend this place to the locals who find their way off the beaten culinary path. It starts with hot, crusty, garlic-glazed rolls, and Caesar salad with a flavorful Parmesan dressing. From there you have your pick from combinations of classic Italian subs, pastas and sauces, pizzas, and proteins. The same menu applies lunch and dinner, but with different pricing. It ranges from standard veal parmigiana and lasagna to gnocchi pomodoro (smothered in fresh tomatoes and basil) and chicken Sinatra (battered and layered with prosciutto, eggplant, roasted peppers, and fresh mozzarella in lemon wine sauce). ✉ *9681 Gladiolus Dr.* ☎ *239/985–0080* ⊕ *www.ilpomodororestaurant.com* ⊙ *Closed Sun. No lunch Sat.*

¢     ✗ **Philly Junction.** From the bread (Amorosa rolls) to the corned beef,
AMERICAN   almost everything here comes from Philadelphia. Not only are the Philly
★      cheesesteaks delicious and authentic, but the burgers and other sandwiches are excellent—and the prices are among the lowest around. Stay for an old-fashioned sundae, or join the Philly natives for pork roll and scrapple at breakfast. The strip-mall café occupies two rooms sided with natural wood board-and-bead paneling. Signs at every table humorously reveal "25 Ways to Tell You're from Philly." ✉ *4600 Summerlin Rd.* ☎ *239/936–6622* ⊙ *No dinner Sun.*

$$$    ✗ **Saigon Paris Bistro.** Irish omelet, Belgian waffles, crepes, table-side
VIETNAMESE steak au poivre, Vietnamese sea bass, Waldorf chicken salad: this eatery's extensive menu clearly travels farther abroad than its name implies. And it does so with utmost taste and flavor, as its faithful local clientele will attest. The best deals are the lunchtime Vietnamese entrées, chicken egg-drop soup, and the gigantic bowls of *pho* (traditional soup). It also offers three-course Vietnamese or Parisian dinners for $30. Leave room for crepes à la Grand Marnier table-side or something from the bakery, and a cup of fresh-roasted coffee. The interior provides a soothing surprise in this busy part of town, with a fireplace and classic columns. ✉ *12995 S. Cleveland. Ave., No. 118* ☎ *239/936–2233* ⊕ *www. saigonparisbistro.com.*

$     ✗ **Shrimp Shack.** Seafood lovers, families, and retired snowbirds flock
SEAFOOD   to this venue with its vivacious staff, bustle, and colorful, cartoon-
⟳      ish wall murals. There's a wait for lunch in winter season and a brisk take-out business with drive-through. Southern-style deep frying prevails—whole-belly clams, grouper, shrimp, onion rings, hush puppies, and fried pork loins—though you can get certain selections broiled or blackened, and there's some New England flavor with seafood rolls. Create your own combo by selecting two or three fried, broiled, or blackened choices. This is your place if you like your seafood simple. ✉ *13361 Metro Pkwy.* ☎ *239/561–6817* ⊕ *www.shrimpshackusa.com.*

$$$$   ✗ **The Veranda.** Restaurants come and go quickly as downtown reinvents
SOUTHERN itself, but this one has endured since 1979. A favorite of business and
★      government bigwigs at lunch (the fried green tomato salad is signature), it serves imaginative Continental fare with a trace of a Southern accent

9

for dinner. Notable are tournedos with smoky sour-mash-whiskey sauce, rack of lamb with rosemary-merlot sauce, herb-crusted honey-grilled salmon, and a grilled seafood sampler with prosciutto-cream fettuccine, all served with homemade honey-drizzled bread and muffins with pepper jelly. The restaurant is a combination of two turn-of-the-20th-century homes, with a two-sided central brick fireplace, and sconces and antique oil paintings on its pale-yellow walls. Ask for an outdoor courtyard table when weather permits. ⊠ *2122 2nd St.* ☎ *239/332–2065* ⊕ *www.verandarestaurant.com* ☉ *Closed Sun. No lunch Sat.*

## WHERE TO STAY

*For expanded hotel reviews, visit Fodors.com.*

**$$$**
HOTEL
🖼 **Hilton Garden Inn.** This compact, prettily landscaped low-rise is near Fort Myers's cultural and commercial areas, and a business clientele favors it for its convenience. **Pros:** near performing-arts center; enjoyable restaurant; large rooms. **Cons:** chain feel; small pool; at busy intersection. ⊠ *12600 University Dr.* ☎ *239/790–3500* ⊕ *www.fortmyers. gardeninn.com* ⇥ *126 rooms, 17 suites* ⛅ *In-room: a/c, no safe, Internet, Wi-Fi. In-hotel: restaurant, bar, pool, laundry facilities, business center* ⭘ *No meals.*

**$$$$**
RESORT
☾
Fodor's Choice
★
🖼 **Sanibel Harbour Marriott Resort & Spa.** Vacationing families and businesspeople who want luxury pick this high-rise resort complex. **Pros:** luxury accommodations; full amenities; great views. **Cons:** daily-amenities fee added to rate; unspectacular beach. ⊠ *17260 Harbour Pointe Dr., Fort Myers* ☎ *239/466–4000 or 800/767–7777* ⊕ *www.sanibel-resort. com* ⇥ *283 rooms, 64 suites, 37 condominiums* ⛅ *In-room: a/c, Internet, Wi-Fi. In-hotel: restaurants, bars, pools, tennis courts, gym, spa, beach, children's programs, business center* ⭘ *No meals.*

# CAPE CORAL, PINE ISLAND, AND NORTH FORT MYERS

*13 mi from downtown Fort Myers.*

## GETTING HERE AND AROUND

Four bridges cross from Fort Myers to Cape Coral and North Fort Myers. Pine Island–Bayshore Road (Route 78) leads from North Fort Myers through northern Cape Coral onto off-the-beaten path Pine Island, known for its art galleries and exotic fruit farms.

## EXPLORING

**Calusa Heritage Trail.** Affiliated with the University of Florida's natural history museum in Gainesville, this 3,700-foot interpretive walkway explores the site of an ancient Amerindian village—more than 1,500 years old—with excellent signage, an intact shell mound you can climb, the remains of a complex canal system, and ongoing archaeological research. ⊠ *Randell Research Center, 13810 Waterfront Dr.,* ☎ *239/282—2062* ⊕ *www.flmnh.ufl.edu/rrc* 🎟 *$7* ☉ *Daily 10–4.*

☾ **Shell Factory & Nature Park.** This entertainment complex, once a shopping attraction and a survivor from Florida's roadside-attraction era, contains restaurants, bumper boats, miniature golf, a money museum, and a mining sluice where kids can pan for shells, fossils, and gem stones.

Admission to the Shell Factory is free but it is $5 for golf and bumper boats; shops and amusements are open from 10 to 6. The Nature Park (✉ $12 ☉ 10–5) contains a petting zoo with camels, llamas, and goats; a walk-through aviary; an EcoLab with reptiles and small animals; a prairie-dog habitat; and a gator slough. Shell Factory also hosts annual events such as the Gumbo Fest in January. ✉ *2787 N. Tamiami Trail, North Fort Myers* ☎ *239/995–2141* ⊕ *www.shellfactory.com* ✉ *$5–$12 per attraction* ☉ *Closed Mon. and Tues. in summer.*

Ċ

Fodor'sChoice

★

**Sun Splash Family Waterpark.** Head here to cool off when summer swelters. A dozen wet and dry attractions include seven thrill waterslides; the Lilypad Walk, where you step from one floating "lily pad" to another; an arcade; a family pool and Tot Spot; and a river-tube ride. Rates go down after 2 pm, plus the park offers Family Fun Night specials. ✉ *400 Santa Barbara Blvd.* ☎ *239/574–0558* ⊕ *www.sunsplashwaterpark.com* ✉ *$17* ☉ *Mid-Mar.–Sept., call or visit the Web site for hrs.*

## SPORTS AND THE OUTDOORS
### GOLF
**Coral Oaks Golf Course.** There is an 18-hole layout and a practice range here. Arthur Hill designed the championship par-72 course, which has lots of lakes, ponds, wildlife, and mammoth live oaks. After 2 pm you can save money by walking the course; greens fee $45/$70 (including cart). ✉ *1800 N.W. 28th Ave.* ☎ *239/573–3100* ⊕ *www.coraloaksgolf.com.*

## WHERE TO EAT
Cape Coral determinedly moves from its pigeonhole as a residential community to attract tourism with its downtown reconfiguration, new Resort at MarinaVillage, and destination restaurants at the Cape Harbour residential marina development.

¢

AMERICAN

✕**Bert's Bar & Grill.** Looking to hang out with the locals on Pine Island? Here you'll find cheap eats, live entertainment, a pool table, and a water view to boot. Speaking of boots, you're likely to see some of the clientele wearing white rubber fishing boots, known here as Pine Island Reeboks. Order fried oysters, a burger, pizza, or a grouper Reuben melt from the no-nonsense menu, and enjoy live music most days. ✉ *4271 Pine Island Rd., Matlacha* ☎ *239/282–3232* ⊕ *www.bertsbar.com.*

$$

AMERICAN

★

✕**Rumrunners.** Cape Coral's best casual cuisine is surprisingly affordable, considering the luxury condo development that rises around it and the size of the yachts that pull up to the docks. Caribbean in spirit, with lots of indoor and outdoor views of a mangrove-fringed waterway, it serves bistro specialties such as conch fritters, seafood potpie, bronzed salmon, and a warm chocolate bread pudding that is addictive. Bar staff is affable and welcoming. ✉ *5848 Cape Harbour Dr., at Marina at Cape Harbour, off Chiquita Blvd.* ☎ *239/542–0200* ⊕ *www. capeharbourdining.com.*

$

THAI

✕**Siam Hut.** Lunch and dinner menus at this Cape Coral fixture let you design your own stir-fry, noodle, or fried-rice dish. Dinner specialties include fried crispy frogs' legs with garlic and black pepper, a sizzling shrimp platter, fried whole tilapia with curry sauce, salads, and pad thai (rice noodles, egg, ground peanuts, vegetables, and choice of protein). Get your food fiery hot or extra mild. Two traditional Thai tables

9

allow you to sit on floor pillows (conveniently with backs), or you can opt for a more conventional table or booth. ⊠ *4521 Del Prado Blvd.* ☎ *239/945–4247* ⊕ *siamhutcapecoral.com* ☉ *Closed Sun. No lunch Sat.*

## WHERE TO STAY

*For expanded hotel reviews, visit Fodors.com.*

**$$$**
RESORT

🛏 **Resort at MarinaVillage.** Cape Coral's only luxury resort, this 19-story high-rise sits alongside a marina fringed with mangroves. **Pros:** full-service marina; designer appointments; great kayaking. **Cons:** no beach; high-rise. ⊠ *5951 Silver King Blvd.* ☎ *239/541–5000 or 888/372–9256* ⊕ *www.marinavillageresort.com* ⤴ *82 studios, 82 1-bedroom condos, 83 2-bedroom condos, 15 3-bedroom condos* ⟁ *In-room: a/c, kitchen (some), Wi-Fi. In-hotel: restaurants, bars, pools, gym, spa, water sports, children's programs, laundry facilities, business center, some pets allowed* ⍓*No meals.*

**$$**
HOTEL

🛏 **Tarpon Lodge.** A no-frills escape, this lodge, named for a local game fish, was built in 1926 on a sweep of green lawn with magnificent views out to sea. **Pros:** waterfront view; historic property; great restaurant, near Calusa Heritage Trail. **Cons:** some rooms are basic; far from other restaurants; far from beach. ⊠ *13771 Waterfront Dr., Pineland* ☎ *239/283–3999* ⊕ *www.tarponlodge.com* ⤴ *21 rooms, 2 cottages* ⟁ *In-room: a/c, no safe. In-hotel: restaurant, bar, pool* ⍓*Breakfast.*

OFF THE BEATEN PATH

**Babcock Wilderness Adventures.** To see what Florida looked like centuries ago, visit Babcock Crescent B Ranch, northeast of Fort Myers. During the 90-minute swamp-buggy excursion you ride in a converted school bus through several ecosystems, including the unusual and fascinating Telegraph Cypress Swamp. Along the way an informative and typically amusing guide describes the area's social and natural history while you keep an eye peeled for alligators, wild pigs, all sorts of birds, and other denizens of the wild. The tour also takes in the ranch's resident cattle and Florida panthers in captivity. Reservations are needed for tours. An on-site restaurant servers "Cracker" chow. ⊠ *8000 Rte. 31* ☎ *941/637–4611 or 800/500–5583* ⊕ *www.babcockwilderness.com* ⍐ *Bus tour $19.95* ☉ *Tours by reservation only; call for tour times* ⍌ *Reservations essential.*

# THE COASTAL ISLANDS

A maze of islands in various stages of habitation fronts Fort Myers mainland, separated by the Intracoastal Waterway. Some are accessible via a causeway; to reach others, you need a boat. If you cut through bay waters, you have a good chance of being escorted by bottlenose dolphins. Mostly birds and other wild creatures inhabit some islands, which are given over to state parks. Traveler-pampering hotels on Sanibel, Captiva, and Fort Myers Beach give way to rustic cottages, old inns, and cabins on quiet Cabbage Key and Pine Island, which have no beaches because they lie between the barrier islands and mainland. Others are devoted to resorts. When exploring island beaches, keep one eye on the sand: shelling is a major pursuit in these parts.

## PUNTA GORDA DAY TRIP

A half hour (23 mi) north of Fort Myers, the small, old town of Punta Gorda merits a day trip for its restaurants and historic sites. If you're driving to Boca Grande via Highway 41, it also makes a nice stop along the way. On the mouth of the Peace River, where it empties into Charlotte Harbor, a new riverfront park, water views, and murals enliven the compact downtown historic district. Away from the downtown area, a classic car museum, wildlife rehabilitation center, and waterfront shopping complex built into an old fish-packing plant fills out a day of sightseeing. Fishing and nature-watching tours also depart from the Fishermen's Village complex.

## GASPARILLA ISLAND (BOCA GRANDE)

*43 mi northwest of Fort Meyers.*

Before roads to the Lower Gulf Coast were even talked about, wealthy Northerners came by train to spend the winter at the **Gasparilla Inn,** completed in 1913 in Boca Grande on Gasparilla Island, named, legend has it, for a Spanish pirate who set up headquarters in these waters. Although condominiums and modern sprawl creep up on the rest of Gasparilla, much of the town of Boca Grande evokes another era. The mood is set by the Old Florida homes and tree-framed roadways. The island's calm is disrupted in the spring when anglers descend with a vengeance on Boca Grande Pass, considered among the best tarpon-fishing spots in the world.

### GETTING HERE AND AROUND

Boca Grande is more than an hour's drive northwest of Fort Myers. Day-trippers can catch a charter boat or rent a boat, dock at a marina, and rent a bike or golf cart for a day of exploring and lunching. North of it stretches a long island, home to Don Pedro Island State Park and Palm Island Resort, both accessible only by boat, and the off-the-beaten-path but car-accessible island of Manasota Key and its fishing resort community of Englewood Beach.

### EXPLORING

**Gasparilla Island State Park and Port Boca Grande Lighthouse Museum.** The island's beaches are its greatest prize and lie within the state park at the south end. The long, narrow beach ends at Boca Grande Pass, famous for its deep waters and tarpon fishing. The pretty, two-story, circa-1890 lighthouse once marked the pass for mariners. In recent years it has been restored as a museum that explores the island's fishing and railroad heritage. ⊠ *Box 1150, Boca Grande* ☎ *941/964–0060* ⊕ *www. floridastateparks.org/gasparillaisland* ⊠ *$3 per vehicle; $2 suggested donation to lighthouse* ⊗ *Park daily 8–sunset; lighthouse Nov.–May, Mon.–Sat. 10–4, Sun. noon–4; June, July, Sept., and Oct., Wed.–Sat. 10–4, Sun. noon–4.*

## SPORTS AND THE OUTDOORS

### CANOEING AND KAYAKING

**Grande Tours.** Kayaking excursions travel along the creeks and open waters around Charlotte Harbor. The cost is $50 for two hours. Also available are kayaking lessons, fishing excursions, stand-up paddle-boarding, and rentals. ✉ *12575 Placida Rd., Placida* ☎ *941/697–8825* ⊕ *www.grandetours.com.*

### WHERE TO EAT AND STAY

*For expanded hotel reviews, visit Fodors.com.*

$$ \
AMERICAN

✕ **The Loose Caboose.** Revered by many—including Katherine Hepburn in her time—for its homemade ice cream, this is also a good spot for solid, affordable fare, from burgers and a Thanksgiving wrap (turkey and cranberry sauce) to chicken potpie and crispy duck with orange-teriyaki sauce. Housed in the town's historic depot, it offers indoor and patio seating in an all-American setting. ✉ *433 W. 4th St.* ☎ *941/964–0440* ⊕ *www.loosecaboose.biz* ⊗ *No dinner Wed. or Apr.–Dec.*

$$$$ \
HOTEL \
★

**Gasparilla Inn & Club.** Social-register members such as the Vanderbilts and DuPonts still winter at the gracious pale-yellow wooden hotel built by shipping industrialists in the early 1900s. Lodge rooms are not lavishly decorated by today's standards, but they match the inn's feminine Victorian air. **Pros:** historic property; nicely renovated. **Cons:** expensive rates; the quirks of a very old building. ✉ *500 Palm Ave., Boca Grande* ☎ *941/964–2201 or 800/996–1913* ⊕ *www.gasparillainn.com* ⇆ *139 rooms, 18 cottages and villas* ⌂ *In-room: a/c, Wi-Fi (some). In-hotel: restaurants, golf course, pools, tennis courts, gym, spa, beach, business center* †⊙† *No meals.*

# CABBAGE KEY

*5 mi south of Boca Grande.*

Cabbage Key is the ultimate in island-hopping escape in these parts. Some say Jimmy Buffett was inspired to write *Cheeseburger in Paradise* after a visit to its popular restaurant.

### GETTING HERE AND AROUND

You'll need to take a boat—from Bokeelia or Pineland, on Pine Island, or from Captiva Island—to get to this island, which sits at Mile Marker 60 on the Intracoastal Waterway. Local operators offer day trips and luncheon cruises.

### WHERE TO STAY

*For expanded hotel reviews, visit Fodors.com.*

$$ \
B&B/INN

**Cabbage Key Inn.** Atop an ancient Calusa Indian shell mound and accessible only by boat, the friendly, somewhat quirky inn built by novelist and playwright Mary Roberts Rinehart in 1938 welcomes guests seeking quiet and isolation. **Pros:** plenty of solitude; Old Florida character. **Cons:** two-night minimum stay; accessible only by boat; limited amenities, some rooms have no TV. ✉ *Box 200, Pineland 33945* ☎ *239/283–2278* ⊕ *www.cabbagekey.com* ⇆ *6 rooms, 7 cottages* ⌂ *In-room: a/c, no safe, kitchen (some), no TV (some), Wi-Fi (some). In-hotel: restaurant, bar* †⊙† *No meals.*

9

# SANIBEL AND CAPTIVA ISLANDS

*23 mi southwest of downtown Fort Myers.*

Sanibel Island is famous as one of the world's best shelling grounds, a function of the unusual east–west orientation of the island's south end. Just as the tide is going out and after storms, the pickings can be superb, and shell seekers performing the telltale "Sanibel stoop" patrol every beach carrying bags of conchs, whelks, cockles, and other bivalves and gastropods. (Remember, it's unlawful to pick up live shells.) Away from the beach, flowery vegetation decorates small shopping complexes, pleasant resorts and condo complexes, mom-and-pop motels, and casual restaurants. But much of the narrow road down the spine of the island is bordered by nature reserves that have made Sanibel as well known among bird-watchers as it is among seashell collectors.

Captiva Island, connected to the northern end of Sanibel by a bridge, is quirky and engaging. At the end of a twisty road lined with million-dollar mansions lies a delightful village of shops, eateries, and beaches.

## GETTING HERE AND AROUND

Sanibel Island is approximately 23 mi southwest of downtown Fort Myers, and Captiva lies north of 12-mi-long Sanibel. If you're flying into Southwest Florida International Airport, an on-demand taxi for up to three passengers to Sanibel or Captiva costs about $56–$75; additional passengers are charged $10 each. Sanibel Island is accessible from the mainland via the Sanibel Causeway (toll $6 round-trip). Captiva Island lies across a small pass from Sanibel's north end, accessible by bridge.

## ESSENTIALS

**Visitor Information Sanibel and Captiva Islands Chamber of Commerce** (⊠ *1159 Causeway Rd., Sanibel* ☎ *239/472–1080* ⊕ *www.sanibel-captiva.org*).

## EXPLORING

**Bailey-Matthews Shell Museum.** To help you choose your Sanibel Island beach, visit the shell-finder display, which identifies specimens from local waters in sizes ranging from tiny to huge. Thirty-five vignettes and exhibits explore shells in the environment, art, and history, including a life-size display of native Calusa and how they used shells for tools and vessels and exhibits on edible and record-sized mollusks. Handle shell specimens and play games in the colorful kids' lab. A 6-foot globe at the center of the museum rotunda highlights shells from around the world. ⊠ *3075 Sanibel–Captiva Rd., Sanibel* ☎ *239/395–2233 or 888/679–6450* ⊕ *www.shellmuseum.org* ⊠ *$7* ⊗ *Daily 10–5.*

Fodor's Choice ★

**Clinic for the Rehabilitation of Wildlife (C.R.O.W).** In existence for more than 40 years, the clinic currently cares for nearly 5,000 wildlife patients each year. The center offers a look inside the world of wildlife medicine through exhibits, videos, interactive displays, touch screens, and critter cams that feed live footage from four different animal spaces. ⊠ *3883 Sanibel–Captiva Rd., Sanibel* ☎ *239/472–3644* ⊕ *www.crowclinic.org* ⊠ *$5* ⊗ *May–Dec., Tues.–Sat. 10–4; Jan.–Apr., Tues.–Sun. 10–4.*

**J.N. "Ding" Darling National Wildlife Refuge.** More than half of Sanibel is occupied by the subtly beautiful 6,300 acres of wetlands and jungly

Fodor's Choice ★

9

mangrove forests named after a conservation-minded Pulitzer prize-winning political cartoonist. The masses of roseate spoonbills and ibis and the winter flock of white pelicans here make for a good show even if you're not a die-hard bird-watcher. Birders have counted some 230 species, including herons, ospreys, and the timid mangrove cuckoo. Raccoons, otters, alligators, and a lone American crocodile also can be spotted. The 4-mi Wildlife Drive is the main way to explore the preserve; drive, walk, or bicycle along it, or ride a specially designed open-air tram with an on-board naturalist. There are also a couple of short walking trails, including one to a Calusa shell mound. Or explore from the water via canoe or kayak (guided tours are available). The best time for bird-watching is in the early morning about an hour before or after low tide, and the observation tower along the road offers prime viewing. Interactive exhibits in the free visitor center, at the entrance to the refuge, demonstrate the refuge's various ecosystems and explain its status as a rest stop along a major bird-migration route. Because Wildlife Drive is closed to vehicular traffic on Friday, try to time your visit for another day. ⊠ *1 Wildlife Dr., off Sanibel–Captiva Rd. at MM 2, Sanibel* ☎ *239/472–1100 for refuge, 239/472–8900 for tram tours* ⊕ *www.fws.gov/dingdarling* ⊡ *$5 per car, $1 for pedestrians and bicyclists, tram $13* ⊘ *Education Center Jan.–Apr., daily 9–5; May–Dec., daily 9–4; Wildlife Drive Sat.–Thurs. 7:30–½ hr before sunset.*

Ü ★ **Sanibel–Captiva Conservation Foundation.** For a good look at snowy egrets, great blue herons, alligators, and other inhabitants of Florida's wetlands, follow the 4½ mi of walking trails on 1,800 acres of wetlands. See island research projects and nature displays, visit a butterfly house, and touch sea creatures. Guided walks are available on and off property; the beach walk is especially enjoyable and pleasantly educational. ⊠ *3333 Sanibel–Captiva Rd., Sanibel* ☎ *239/472–2329* ⊕ *www.sccf.org* ⊡ *$5* ⊘ *Oct., Nov., and May, weekdays 8:30–4; Dec.–Apr., weekdays 8:30–4, Sat. 10–3; June–Sept., weekdays 8:30–3.*

★ **Sanibel Historical Museum & Village.** Charming buildings from the island's past include a general store, a one-room schoolhouse, a 1927 post office, a garage housing a Model T Ford, a 1925 winter-vacation cottage, and the 1913 Rutland House Museum, containing old documents and photographs, artifacts, and period furnishings. ⊠ *950 Dunlop Rd., Sanibel* ☎ *239/472–4648* ⊕ *www.sanibelmuseum.org* ⊡ *$5* ⊘ *Nov.–Apr., Wed.–Sat. 10–4; May–mid-Aug., Wed.–Sat. 10–1; closed mid-Aug.-Oct.*

## BEACHES

Red tide, an occasional natural beach occurrence that kills fish, also has negative effects on the human respiratory system. It causes scratchy throats, runny eyes and noses, and coughing. Although the effects are not long-term, it's a good idea to avoid the beach when red tide is in the vicinity (look for posted signs).

**Alison Hagerup Beach Park.** The former Captiva Beach is acclaimed as one of the nation's most romantic beaches for its fabulous sunsets—the best view on Sanibel and Captiva. The parking lot is small, so arrive early. Facilities are limited to portable restrooms and a volleyball net,

*Continued on page 396*

# SHELL-BENT ON SANIBEL ISLAND

by Chelle Koster Walton

Sanibel Island beachgoers are an unusual breed: they pray for storms; they muck around tidal pools rather than play in the waves; and instead of lifting their faces to the sun, they have their heads in the sand—almost literally—as they engage in the so-called "Sanibel Stoop."

Odd? Not when you consider that this is Florida's prime shelling location, thanks to the island's east-west bend (rather than the usual north-south orientation of most beaches along the coastline). The lay of the land means a treasure trove of shells—more than 400 species—wash up from the Caribbean.

These gifts from the sea draw collectors of all levels. Come winter, when the cold and storms kill the shellfish and push them ashore, a parade of stoopers forms on Sanibel's shores.

The reasons people shell are as varied as the shellers themselves. The hardcore compete and sell, whereas others collect simply for the fun of discovery, for displaying, for use in gardens, or for crafts. The typical Sanibel tourist who comes seeking shells is usually looking for souvenirs and gifts to take home.

## WHERE TO SHELL

Shelling is good anywhere along Sanibel's gulf-front. Remote **Bowman's Beach** (*off Sanibel-Captiva Road at Bowman's Beach Rd.*) offers the least competition. Other public accesses include **Lighthouse Beach** (Periwinkle Way), **Tarpon Bay Beach** (Tarpon Bay Rd.), and **Turner Beach** (Sanibel-Captiva Rd.). If you want to ditch your car (and crowds), walk or bike using **resident access beaches** (along the Gulf drives). If you want to search with others and get a little guidance, you can join shelling cruises from Sanibel and Captiva islands to the un-bridged island of Cayo Costa. For information contact, **Captiva Cruises** (☎ 239/472-5300, ⊕ www.captivacruises.com) or **Adventures in Paradise** (☎ 239/472–8443, ⊕ www.adventureinparadiseinc.com).

Captiva
Island

○ **Captiva**

Turner
Beach

Bowman's
Beach

SANIBEL ISLAND

○ **Sanibel**

Lighthouse
Beach

Tarpon Bay
Beach

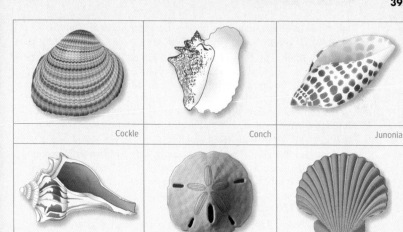

| | | |
|---|---|---|
| Cockle | Conch | Junonia |
| Lightning Whelk | Sand Dollar | Scallop |

## TYPES OF SHELLS

**Cockles:** The common Sanibel bivalve (hinged two-shelled mollusk), the heart cockle (named for its Valentine shape) is larger and more bowl-like than the scallop, which makes it a popular, colorful find for soap dishes, ashtrays, and catch-alls.

**Conchs:** Of the large family of conchs, fighting conchs are most commonly found on Sanibel. Contrary to its macho name, the fighting conch is one of the few vegetarian gastropods. While alive, the shell flames brilliant orange; it fades under tropical sunshine.

**Junonias:** These olive-shaped, spotted gastropods (single-shell mollusks) are Sanibel's signature, though somewhat rare, finds. People who hit upon one get their picture in the local paper. Resorts have been accused of planting them on their beaches for publicity.

**Lightning Whelks:** The lightning variety of whelk is "left-handed"—opening on the opposite side from most gastropods. Early islanders used them for tools. The animals lay their miniature shell eggs in papery egg-case chains on the beach.

**Sand Dollars:** Classified as an echinoderm not a mollusk, the thin sand dollar is brown and fuzzy while alive, studded with tiny tubes for breathing and moving. Unoccupied shells bleach to a beautiful white textured pattern, ideal for hanging on Christmas trees.

**Scallops:** No surprise that these pretty little bivalves have "scalloped" edges. They invented the word. Plentiful on Sanibel beaches, they come in a variety of colors and sizes.

## SHELLING LIKE A PRO

Veteran shell-seekers go out before the sun rises so they can be the first on the beach after a storm or night of high tides. (Storms and cold fronts bring in the best catches.)

Most shellers use a bag to collect their finds. But once you're ready to pack shells for transit, wash them thoroughly to remove sand and debris. Then wrap fragile species such as sand dollars and sea urchins in tissue paper or cotton, then newspaper. Last, place your shells in a cardboard or plastic box. To display them, restore the shell's luster by brushing it with baby oil.

Sanibel shops sell books and supplies for identifying your finds and turning them into craft projects.

but stores and restaurants are nearby. **Best for:** sunset. ⊠ *Captiva Dr., Captiva* 🕭 *Parking $2 per hr, $10 for 8 hrs.*

Ⅽ **Bowman's Beach.** This long, wide beach on Sanibel's northwest end is the island's most secluded strand and was once known for its nudists (no longer legal). Today it is famed for its shell collecting and spectacular sunsets at the north end—try to spot the green flash said to occur just as the sun sinks below the horizon. Facilities include a playground, a fitness trail, and a canoe launch. **Best for:** an all-day outing to the beach. ⊠ *Bowman Beach Rd., Sanibel* 🕭 *239/472–3700* 🕭 *Parking $2 per hr.*

Ⅽ **Gulfside Park Preserve.** The beach is quiet, safe from strong currents, and good for solitude, bird-watching, and shell-finding. There are restrooms, picnic tables, and long stretches to stroll, plus a loop trail to hike. **Best for:** swimming. ⊠ *Algiers La. off Casa Ybel Rd., Sanibel* 🕭 *239/472–3700* 🕭 *Parking $2 per hr.*

**Lighthouse Beach.** At Sanibel's southern tip, the beach is guarded by the frequently photographed **Sanibel Lighthouse,** built in 1884, before the island was settled. The lighthouse is not currently open to the public, but there's talk of refurbishing the tower so visitors can climb to the top. The 32-acre area around it was part of the "Ding" Darling wildlife refuge from 1950 until 2010, when it was sold to the city for $1 an acre. A fishing pier, nature trail, interpretive kiosk, and restrooms are available. **Best for:** birding. ⊠ *Periwinkle Way, Sanibel* 🕭 *239/472–3700* 🕭 *Parking $2 per hr.*

**Tarpon Bay Beach.** This centrally located beach is safer for swimming than beaches at the passes, where waters move swiftly. It is, however, one of the more populated beaches, lined with low-rise condos and resorts set back behind vegetation. The parking lot is a five-minute walk from the beach, so drop off your gang and gear before you park. At the beach, you can walk for miles in either direction. **Best for:** walking. ⊠ *Tarpon Bay Rd., off Sanibel–Captiva Rd., Sanibel* 🕭 *239/472–3700* 🕭 *Parking $2 per hr.*

**Turner Beach.** Looking for some romance? This is *the* sunset-watching spot on the southern tip of Captiva. Strong currents through the pass make swimming tricky, and parking is limited. Surfers head here when winds whip up the waves. **Best for:** fishing and surfing. ⊠ *Captiva Dr., Captiva* 🕭 *Parking $2 per hr.*

## SPORTS AND THE OUTDOORS

### BIKING

Everyone bikes around flat-as-a-pancake Sanibel and Captiva—on bikeways that edge the main highway in places, on the road through the wildlife refuge, and along side streets. Free maps are available at bicycle liveries.

**Billy's Bikes.** Rent by the hour or the day from this Sanibel outfitter, which also rents motorized scooters and leads Segway tours. ⊠ *1470 Periwinkle Way, Sanibel* 🕭 *239/472–5248* ⊕ *www.billysrentals.com.*

**Jim's Rentals.** Bikes are available at this Captiva operator. ⊠ *11534 Andy Rosse La., Captiva* 🕭 *239/472–1296* ⊕ *www.yolo-jims.com.*

### CANOEING AND KAYAKING

★ **Tarpon Bay Explorers.** One of the best ways to scout out the wildlife refuge is by paddle. Rent a canoe or kayak from the refuge's official concessionaire. Guided tours are also available and worthwhile for visitors unfamiliar with the ecosystem. ⊠ *900 Tarpon Bay Rd., Sanibel* ☎ *239/472–8900* ⊕ *www.tarponbayexplorers.com.*

### FISHING

Local anglers head out to catch mackerel, pompano, grouper, snook, snapper, tarpon, and shark.

**Sanibel Marina.** To find a charter captain on Sanibel, ask around the marina. ⊠ *634 N. Yachtsman Dr., Sanibel* ☎ *239/472–2723.*

**'Tween Waters Marina.** On Captiva, this is the place to look for guides. ⊠ *15951 Captiva Dr., Captiva* ☎ *239/472–5161* ⊕ *www.tween-waters. com/marina.*

### GOLF

**Dunes Golf & Tennis Club.** Rent clubs and take lessons as well as test your skills against the water hazards on the 18-hole course; greens fee $70/$110 (including cart). ⊠ *949 Sandcastle Rd., Sanibel* ☎ *239/472–2535* ⊕ *www.dunesgolfsanibel.com.*

### TENNIS

**Dunes Golf & Tennis Club.** There are 13 Har-Tru courts and a full-service pro shop. ⊠ *949 Sandcastle Rd., Sanibel* ☎ *239/472–3522.*

### SHOPPING

Sanibel is known for its art galleries, shell shops, and one-of-a-kind boutiques; the several small open-air shopping complexes are inviting, with their tropical flowers and shady ficus trees.

Fodor'sChoice **Jungle Drums.** Expect the unexpected in wildlife art, where fish, sea
★ turtles, and other wildlife are depicted with utmost creativity and touches of whimsy. If you're looking for souvenirs above and beyond the usual, this is the place to find them. ⊠ *11532 Andy Rosse La., Captiva* ☎ *239/395–2266* ⊕ *www.jungledrumsgallery.com.*

**Periwinkle Place.** The largest cluster of Sanibel shopping complexes has about 25 shops. ⊠ *2075 Periwinkle Way, Sanibel* ☎ *239/769–2289* ⊕ *www.periwinkleplace.com.*

**Sanibel Seashell Industries.** Among the island's cache of shell shops, this one is favored by serious collectors and crafters because of its reasonable prices and the knowledgeable family that runs it. For shell gifts, the family operates another little shop right behind the warehouse-sized one. ⊠ *905 Fitzhugh St., Sanibel* ☎ *239/472–1603* ⊕ *www.seashells. com.*

### WHERE TO EAT

$$$ ✕ **Bubble Room.** This lively, kitschy visitors' favorite is fun for families
AMERICAN and nostalgic types with fat wallets. Servers wear scout uniforms and
☺ funny headgear. Electric trains circle overhead, glossies of Hollywood stars past and present line the walls, and glass tabletops showcase old-time toys. There's so much going on that you might not notice your food is not quite as happening, and somehow that's okay. After grazing your basket of cheesy bubble bread and sweet, yeasty sticky buns,

go for slow-cooked prime rib or shrimp sautéed in spicy tequila garlic butter. The homemade triple-layer cakes, delivered in hefty wedges, are outstanding, and the gooey orange crunch cake is a signature favorite. Be prepared to wait for a table in season. ⊠ *15001 Captiva Dr., Captiva* ☎ *239/472–5558* ⊕ *www.bubbleroomrestaurant.com* ⚞ *Reservations not accepted.*

$$$
SEAFOOD

✕ **Green Flash.** Good food and sweeping views of quiet waters and a mangrove island keep boaters and others coming back to this casual indoor-outdoor restaurant. Seafood dominates, but there's a bit of everything on the menu, from barbecued shrimp and bacon to grilled swordfish to pork tenderloin wrapped in prosciutto and puff pastry. For lunch, try the Green Flash sandwich (smoked turkey and prosciutto or vegetables, both with cheese on grilled focaccia). On cool, sunny days, grab a table out back dockside. ⊠ *15183 Captiva Dr., Captiva* ☎ *239/472–3337* ⊕ *www.greenflashcaptiva.com.*

¢
AMERICAN
☺

✕ **Lazy Flamingo.** At two Sanibel locations, this is the friendly neighborhood hangout enjoyed by locals and visitors alike. The original in Santiva (near the beach between Sanibel and Captiva) has counter service only; the other is larger (but there's still often a wait) and provides table service. Both have a funky nautical look à la Key West and a popular following for their "Dead Parrot Wings" (Buffalo wings coated with tongue-scorching hot sauce), grouper sandwiches, burgers, and steamer pots. ⊠ *6520C Pine Ave., Sanibel* ☎ *239/472–5353* ⊠ *1036 Periwinkle Way, Sanibel* ☎ *239/472–6939* ⊕ *www.lazyflamingo.com* ⚞ *Reservations not accepted.*

$$$
SEAFOOD

✕ **The Mucky Duck.** A longtime fixture on Captiva's beach, it parodies British pubs with its name and sense of humor. (Beware of pranks and pratfalls.) Through its 35 years existence, it has consistently drawn crowds that occupy themselves with walking the beach and watching sunset while waiting for their name to be called. A little Brit, a lot Florida, the menu has kept some favored specialties such as barbecued shrimp wrapped in bacon, crab cakes, fish-and-chips, meat loaf, and frozen key lime pie. ⊠ *11546 Andy Rosse La., Captiva* ☎ *239/472–3434* ⊕ *www.muckyduck.com* ⚞ *Reservations not accepted* ⊗ *Closed Sun.*

$$
AMERICAN

✕ **Over Easy Café.** Locals head to this chicken-theme eatery mainly for breakfast and lunch, although it also serves dinner in season. Kick-start the day with the egg Reuben sandwich, veggie Benedict, or a custom omelet made with whole eggs, whites only, or egg substitute. Breakfast is available until 2:30. The lunch and dinner menu includes a vast variety of salads, omelets, and seafood. Indoor dining is cheerful; outdoors, pet-friendly. ⊠ *630-1 Tarpon Bay Rd., Sanibel* ☎ *239/472–2625* ⊕ *www.overeasycafesanibel.com* ⚞ *Reservations not accepted* ⊗ *No dinner Sun. and Mon. and May–mid-Nov.*

$$
SEAFOOD

✕ **Timbers Restaurant & Fish Market.** One of Sanibel's longest running restaurants successfully satisfies visitors and residents with consistent quality and a full net of nightly catches and specials. The fish market inside the door is a sure sign of freshness, and most of the dishes showcase seafood simply and flavorfully. The oysters Romanoff with caviar, shallots, and sour cream are a nice twist on oyster "sliders." Corn flakes grant the crunchy grouper and shrimp rights to their names. Choose to have your fresh catch blackened, fried, or broiled, or go for a sirloin or beef filet. House salad or soup du jour comes with each entrée, or you can upgrade to the crab bisque, which is tasty but a bit on the salty side. For lighter fare and a sports bar vibe, Sanibel Grill shares the same space. ⊠ *703 Tarpon Bay Rd., Sanibel* ☎ *239/472–3128* ⊕ *www. prawnbroker.com* ⚏ *Reservations not accepted.*

**$$$** ✕ **Traders Store & Café**. In the midst of a warehouse-size store, this bistro,
AMERICAN accented with artifacts from exotic places, is a favorite of locals. The
★ marvelous sesame-seared tuna lunch salad with Asian slaw and wasabi vinaigrette exemplifies the creative fare. For dinner, try the barbecued baby back ribs, macadamia-crusted grouper, or any of the day's finely crafted specials. A local band entertains two nights a week. The bar serves light nibbles and happy-hour twofers. ⊠ *1551 Periwinkle Way, Sanibel* ☎ *239/472–7242* ⚏ *Reservations not accepted.*

## WHERE TO STAY

*For expanded hotel reviews, visit Fodors.com.*

**$$$$** ⊞ **Casa Ybel Resort**. At this time-share resort, palm trees, quiet ponds,
RESORT and gazebos set the mood on 23 acres of gulf-facing grounds. **Pros:** on
☺ the beach; good restaurants; lots of recreational opportunities. **Cons:** spa treatments in-room only; minimum stay requirement in some units. ⊠ *2255 W. Gulf Dr., Sanibel* ☎ *239/472–3145 or 800/276–4753* ⊕ *www.casaybelresort.com* ↪ *40 1-bedroom units, 74 2-bedroom units* ⚒ *In-room: a/c, kitchen, Internet, Wi-Fi. In-hotel: restaurants, bars, pool, tennis courts, beach, children's programs* ❣ *No meals.*

**$$$** ⊞ **Sanibel's Seaside Inn**. Tucked among the tropical greenery, this beach-
RESORT front inn is a pleasant alternative to the area's larger resorts. **Pros:** intimate feel; lots of character; beautiful beachfront. **Cons:** no restaurant; cramped parking lot. ⊠ *541 E. Gulf Dr., Sanibel* ☎ *239/472–1400 or 888/295–4560* ⊕ *www.seasideinn.com* ↪ *32 rooms, 6 cottages, 4 suites* ⚒ *In-room: a/c, no safe, kitchen (some), Wi-Fi. In-hotel: pool, beach, laundry facilities* ❣ *Breakfast.*

**$$$$** ⊞ **South Seas Island Resort**. This 330-acre resort feels as lush as its name
RESORT suggests and is full-service with 19 swimming pools (one with two tubu-
☺ lar slides), private restaurants and shops, a nature center stocked with
Fodor's Choice small live animals, a family interactive center, and a 9-hole golf course
★ with attractive water features. **Pros:** full range of amenities; exclusive feel; car-free transportation. **Cons:** high rates; a bit isolated; spread out. ⊠ *5400 Plantation Rd., Captiva* ☎ *239/472–5111 or 888/222–7848* ⊕ *www.southseas.com* ↪ *106 rooms, 365 suites* ⚒ *In-room: a/c, no safe (some), kitchen (some), Wi-Fi. In-hotel: restaurants, bars, golf course, pools, tennis courts, gym, spa, beach, water sports, children's programs* ❣ *No meals.*

**$$$$** ⊞ **Sundial Beach & Golf Resort**. Sanibel's largest resort encompasses 400
RESORT privately owned one-, two-, and three-bedroom condos, about half of
☺ which are in its rental program. **Pros:** plenty of amenities; great beach.
★ **Cons:** conference crowds; packed pool area. ⊠ *1451 Middle Gulf Dr., Sanibel* ☎ *239/472–4151 or 866/565–5093* ⊕ *www.sundialresort.com* ↪ *200 1-, 2, and 3-bedroom units (varies according to rental program participants)* ⚒ *In-room: a/c, kitchen, Internet, Wi-Fi. In-hotel: restau-*

9

rants, bars, pools, tennis courts, gym, beach, water sports, children's programs, business center †◯┤ No meals.

**$$$**  ◻ **'Tween Waters Inn.** Besides its great beach-to-bay location, this inn has
**B&B/INN** historic value. In the 1930s, Pulitzer Prize–winning cartoonist and conservationist "Ding" Darling, namesake of Sanibel's refuge, stayed in its historic cottages, which are the most charming of the property's accommodations. **Pros:** great views; lots of water-sports options; free Internet. **Cons:** beach is across the road; rooms are bland. ✉ *Captiva Dr., Captiva* ☎ *239/472–5161 or 800/223–5865* ⊕ *www.tween-waters.com* ⤶ *32 rooms, 24 efficiencies, 40 suites, 4 2-bedroom suites, 2 3-bedroom suites, 19 cottages* ✦ *In-room: a/c, no safe, kitchen (some), Wi-Fi. In-hotel: restaurant, bar, pool, tennis courts, gym, spa, beach, laundry facilities, business center* †◯┤ *Breakfast.*

**$$$$**  ◻ **Waterside Inn.** Palm trees, sea-grape trees, pastel cottages, and white
**B&B/INN** sand set the scene at this quiet beachside vacation spot. **Pros:** beach-front location; intimate feel; small pets allowed in most cottages. **Cons:** no restaurants within walking distance; office closes at night. ✉ *3033 W. Gulf Dr., Sanibel* ☎ *239/472–1345 or 800/741–6166* ⊕ *www. watersideinn.net* ⤶ *4 rooms, 10 efficiencies, 13 cottages* ✦ *In-room: a/c, no safe, kitchen (some), Wi-Fi. In-hotel: pool, beach, laundry facilities, business center, some pets allowed* †◯┤ *No meals.*

## ESTERO ISLAND (FORT MYERS BEACH)

*18 mi southwest of Fort Meyers.*

Crammed with motels, hotels, and restaurants, this island is one of Fort Myers's more frenetic gulf playgrounds. Dolphins frequently frolic in Estero Bay, part of the Intracoastal Waterway, and marinas provide a starting point for boating adventures, including sunset cruises, sightseeing cruises, and deep-sea fishing. At the southern tip, a bridge leads to Lovers Key State Park.

### GETTING HERE AND AROUND

San Carlos Boulevard in Fort Myers leads to Fort Myers Beach's high bridge, Times Square, and Estero Boulevard, the island's main drag. Estero Island is 18 mi southwest of Fort Myers.

### BEACHES

⟳ **Lynn Hall Memorial Park.** At the 17-acre park in the commercial northern part of Estero Island, the shore slopes gradually into the usually tranquil and warm gulf waters, providing safe swimming for children. And since houses, restaurants, condominiums, and hotels line most of the beach, you're never far from civilization. There are picnic pavilions, barbecue grills, playground equipment, restrooms, and a free fishing pier. The park is part of a pedestrian mall with a number of beach shops and restaurants steps away. Parking is $2 per hour; the lot fills early on sunny days. **Best for:** families. ✉ *Estero Blvd.* ☎ *239/463–1116* ⊕ *www. leeparks.org* ⊙ *Daily 7 am–11 pm.*

OFF THE
BEATEN
PATH

**Lovers Key State Park.** Once a little-known secret, this out-of-the-way park encompassing 1,616 acres on four barrier islands and several uninhabited islets is gaining popularity among beachgoers and birders. Bike, hike, or walk the park's trails; go shelling on its 2½ mi of white-sand beach; take a boat tour; or rent a canoe, kayak, or bike. Trams run regularly from 9 to 5 to deliver you and your gear to South Beach. The ride is short but often dusty. North Beach is a five-minute walk from the concession area and parking lot. Watch for osprey, bald eagles, herons, ibis, pelicans, and roseate spoonbills, or sign up for a free excursion to learn fishing and cast-netting. There are also restrooms, picnic tables, a snack bar, and showers. On the bay side, playgrounds and another picnic area cater to families, plus there are boat ramps, kayak rentals, and a bait shop. ⊠ *8700 Estero Blvd.* ☎ *239/463–4588* ⊕ *www. floridastateparks.org/loverskey* ⊒ *$4–$8 per vehicle, $2 for pedestrians and bicyclists* ☉ *Daily 8–sunset.*

## SPORTS AND THE OUTDOORS

### BIKING

Fort Myers Beach has no designated trails, so most cyclists ride along the road or beach.

**Fun Rentals.** Bike-rental rates from anywhere between two hours and a week are available. ⊠ *1901 Estero Blvd.* ☎ *239/463–8844* ⊕ *www. funrentals.org.*

**Nature Recreation Management.** Rent bikes in Lovers Key State Park. Fees for adult bikes are $18 for a half day, $25 for a full day. ⊠ *8700 Estero Blvd., Fort Myers Beach* ☎ *239/765–7788* ⊕ *www.naturerecreationmanagement.com.*

### CANOEING

**Nature Recreation Management.** Lovers Key State Park offers both kayak rentals and guided kayaking tours of its bird-filled estuary. Guided tours cost $45 (call for dates and times). Rentals begin at $32 for a half day, $42 for a full day for a single kayak. ⊠ *8700 Estero Blvd., Fort Myers Beach* ☎ *239/765–7788* ⊕ *www.naturerecreationmanagement.com.*

### FISHING

**Getaway Deep Sea Fishing.** Arrange anything from half-day party-boat charters to full-day excursions, fishing equipment included. Rates start at $59 for a half-day trip. ⊠ *18400 San Carlos Blvd.* ☎ *800/641–3088 or 239/466–3600* ⊕ *www.getawaymarina.com.*

### GOLF

**Fort Myers Beach Golf Course.** Eighteen holes and a practice range sit in the midst of a condo community filled with birds; greens fee $56/$17. ⊠ *4200 Bay Beach La., off Estero Blvd.* ☎ *239/463–2064* ⊕ *www. fmbgc.com.*

## WHERE TO EAT

$$
SEAFOOD

✕ **Matanzas Inn.** Watch boats coming and going whether you sit inside or out at this rustic Old Florida–style restaurant right on the docks alongside the Intracoastal Waterway. When the weather cooperates, enjoy the view from the shaded outdoor tables. Inside, a rustic shack gives way to a more formal dining area in the back; there's a bar upstairs with sweeping views and live music nightly. You can't miss with shrimp from the local fleets—delicately cornmeal-breaded, stuffed, or done Alfredo with scallops. The Matanzas Steamer (market price), a house specialty, heaps on the fish and shellfish. This is true Fort Myers Beach style, meaning service can be a bit gruff—and slow. ✉ *416 Crescent St.* ☎ *239/463–3838* ⊕ *www.matanzasrestaurant.com* ⌕ *Reservations not accepted.*

**$$**
SEAFOOD

✕ **Parrot Key Caribbean Grill.** For something more contemporary than Fort Myers Beach's traditional shrimp and seafood houses, head to San Carlos Island on the east side of the high bridge where the shrimp boats dock. Parrot Key sits marina-side near the shrimp docks and exudes merriment with its Floribbean cuisine and island music. The all-day menu takes tropical cues with dishes such as habanero-pepper wings; corned beef, turkey, or grouper Reuben; fillet topped with blue cheese; and crab cakes with ancho pepper beurre blanc. There's live entertainment most nights. ✉ *2500 Main St.* ☎ *239/463–3257* ⊕ *www.myparrotkey.com* ⌕ *Reservations not accepted.*

**$**
GREEK

✕ **The Plaka.** A casual longtimer and a favorite for a quick breakfast, lunch breaks, and sunset dinners, Plaka—Greek for "fun"—has typical Greek fare such as moussaka, pastitsio, gyros, and roast lamb, as well as burgers, sandwiches, fried seafood, and strip steak. It lies along a row of casual sidewalk restaurants in a pedestrian mall near the beach. There's indoor dining, but grab a seat on the porch or under an umbrella on the patio for the best people-watching and sunset view. ✉ *1001 Estero Blvd.* ☎ *239/463–4707* ⌕ *Reservations not accepted.*

**$$$**
AMERICAN

✕ **The Sandy Butler.** Visitors to Fort Myers Beach can find fine dining—if they're willing to drive a few miles off the island. This huge complex is part market and part restaurant (it seats 150 diners next door), and a favorite haunt for Sanibel and Fort Myers foodies. Luncheon sandwiches dare beyond the norm: Caprese on a baguette and triple-decker vegetarian clubs, for instance. At dinner, there's everything from duck breast with port-berry demi-glaze to seared sesame ahi tuna and 12-ounce prime rib. The trio of crèmes brûlées is a true treat when it's on the changing dessert menu—especially the cayenne-chocolate selection. ✉ *17650 San Carlos Blvd.* ☎ *239/482–6765* ⊕ *www.sandybutler.com.*

## WHERE TO STAY

*For expanded hotel reviews, visit Fodors.com.*

**$$$$**
RESORT
☼

⌂ **DiamondHead.** This 12-story resort sits on the beach, and many of the suites, especially those on higher floors, have stunning views. **Pros:** on the beach; nice views; kitchen facilities. **Cons:** heavy foot and car traffic; tiny fitness center; not the best value on the beach. ✉ *2000 Estero Blvd.* ☎ *239/765–7654 or 888/765–5002* ⊕ *www.diamondheadfl.com* 🛏 *121 suites* ⌕ *In-room: a/c, no safe, kitchen, Internet, Wi-Fi. In-hotel: restaurants, bar, pool, gym, spa, beach, children's programs, laundry facilities, business center* ⏐◯⏐ *No meals.*

**$$$**
HOTEL

⌂ **Harbour House.** Opened in 2010, this condo-hotel adds a degree of beach luxury with brightly painted and sea-motif studios and one- and two-bedroom condos, all privately owned. **Pros:** close to lots of restaurants; roomy units; all have private balconies or lanais; free covered parking. **Cons:** a walk to the beach; not great views from most rooms. ✉ *450 Old San Carlos Blvd.* ☎ *239/463–0700 or 866/998–9250* ⊕ *www.harbourhouseattheinn.com* 🛏 *34 studios and 1- and 2-bedroom condos* ⌕ *In-room: a/c, no safe, kitchen, Internet, Wi-Fi. In-hotel: restaurant, pool, laundry facilities, parking* ⏐◯⏐ *No meals.*

**$$$$** 　🛏 **Lovers Key Resort.** Views can be stupendous from upper floors in this
RESORT 　14-story tower just north of Lovers Key State Park. **Pros:** excellent
★ 　views; off the beaten path; spacious accommodations. **Cons:** not a true
beach; far from shopping and restaurants; limited amenities. ⊠ *8771
Estero Blvd.* ☎ *239/765–1040 or 877/798–4879* ⊕ *www.loverskey.com*
⟿ *100 condominiums* ⚴ *In-room: a/c, no safe, kitchen, Internet, Wi-Fi.
In-hotel: restaurant, pool, gym, beach, laundry facilities, business center*
†⊚ *No meals.*

**$$$** 　🛏 **Outrigger Beach Resort.** On a wide gulf beach, this casual resort has
RESORT 　rooms and efficiencies with configurations to suit different guests' needs.
🕲 　**Pros:** beautiful beach; water-sports rentals; family-friendly vibe. **Cons:**
can be noisy; crowded pool area; old-school feel. ⊠ *6200 Estero Blvd.*
☎ *239/463–3131 or 800/657–5659* ⊕ *www.outriggerfmb.com* ⟿ *76
rooms, 68 efficiencies* ⚴ *In-room: a/c, kitchen (some), Wi-Fi. In-hotel:
restaurants, bar, pool, beach, business center* †⊚ *No meals.*

# NAPLES AREA

As you head south from Fort Myers on U.S. 41, you soon come to
Estero and Bonita Springs, followed by the Naples and Marco Island
areas, which are sandwiched between Big Cypress Swamp and the Gulf
of Mexico. East of Naples the land is largely undeveloped and mostly
wetlands, all the way to Fort Lauderdale. Naples itself is a major vaca-
tion destination that has sprouted pricey high-rise condominiums and
golfing developments, plus a spate of restaurants and shops to match.
A similar but not as thorough evolution has occurred on Marco Island,
the largest of the Ten Thousand Islands.

## ESTERO/BONITA SPRINGS

*10 mi south of Fort Meyers via U.S. 41.*

Towns below Fort Myers have started to flow seamlessly into one
another since the opening of Florida Gulf Coast University in San Car-
los Park and as a result of the growth of Estero and Bonita Springs,
agricultural communities until the 1990s. In recent years the area has
become a shopping mecca of mega-outdoor malls mixing big-box
stores, smaller chains, and restaurants. Bonita Beach, the closest beach
to Interstate 75, has evolved from a fishing community into a strip of
upscale homes and beach clubs built to provide access for residents of
inland golf developments.

### GETTING HERE AND AROUND
U.S. 41 (Tamiami Trail) runs right through the heart of these two adja-
cent communities. You can also reach them by exits 123 and 116 off
Interstate 75.

### EXPLORING
🕲 **Everglades Wonder Gardens.** Opened in 1936 and one of the first attrac-
tions of its kind in the state, this garden captures the beauty of untamed
Florida. The old-fashioned, rather cramped zoological gardens have
Florida panthers, black bears, crocodiles and alligators, tame Florida

**9**

deer, flamingos, otters, and birds. There's also a funky natural history museum. Tours, which include otter and alligator feedings, run continuously, the last starting at 4:15. The swinging bridge over the alligator pit is a real thrill. ⊠ *27180 Old U.S. 41* ☎ *239/992–2591* 🖰 *$15* ⊙ *Daily 9–5.*

★ **Koreshan State Historic Site.** Tour one of Florida's quirkier chapters from the past. Named for a religious cult that was active at the turn of the 20th century, Koreshan preserves a dozen structures where the group practiced arts, worshipped a male-female divinity, and created its own branch of science called cosmogony. The cult floundered when leader Cyrus Reed Teed died in 1908, and in 1961 the four remaining members deeded the property to the state. Rangers and volunteers lead tours and demonstrations, and the grounds are lovely for picnicking and camping. Canoeists paddle the Estero River, fringed by a forest of exotic vegetation the Koreshans planted. ⊠ *3800 Corkscrew Rd., at U.S. 41 (Tamiami Trail), Estero* ☎ *239/992–0311* ⊕ *www.floridastateparks.org/koreshan* 🖰 *$5 per vehicle with up to 8 passengers; $4 for single motorist; $2 per bicyclist, pedestrian, or extra passenger* ⊙ *Daily 8 am–sunset.*

**OFF THE BEATEN PATH**

**Corkscrew Swamp Sanctuary.** To get a feel for what this part of Florida was like before civil engineers began draining the swamps, drive 17 mi east of North Naples to these 11,000 acres of pine flatwood and cypress, grass-and-sedge "wet prairie," saw-grass marshland, and lakes and sloughs filled with water lettuce. Managed by the National Audubon Society, the sanctuary protects North America's largest remaining stand of ancient bald cypress, 600-year-old trees as tall as 130 feet, as well as endangered birds, such as wood storks, which often nest here. This is a favorite destination for serious birders and is the gateway to the Great Florida Birding South Trail. If you spend a couple of hours to take the 2¼-mi self-guided tour along the boardwalk, you'll spot ferns, orchids, and air plants, as well as wading birds and possibly alligators and river otters. A nature center educates you about this precious, unusual habitat with a dramatic re-creation of the preserve and its creatures in the Swamp Theater. ⊠ *375 Sanctuary Rd. W, 17 mi east of I–75 on Rte. 846* ☎ *239/348–9151* ⊕ *www.audubon.org* 🖰 *$10* ⊙ *Oct.–Apr. 10, daily 7–5:30; Apr. 11–Sept., daily 7 am–7:30 pm.*

**BEACHES**

★ **Barefoot Beach Preserve.** The 342-acre plot is a quiet, out-of-the-way place, accessible via a private neighborhood road around the corner from the buzzing public beach. It has picnic tables, a nature trail and learning center, an aquatic butterfly garden, a canoe trail, refreshment stands, and a beach rentals concession. Gopher tortoises often cross the road right in front of your car, so drive slowly. Park rangers lead nature walks and other interpretive programs. **Best for:** communing with nature. ⊠ *Barefoot Beach Rd. off Bonita Beach Rd.* ☎ *239/591–8596* ⊕ *www.colliergov.net/parks* 🖰 *$8.*

**Bonita Beach Park.** At the south end of Bonita Beach are picnic tables, beach concessions, volleyball, and a restaurant. As far as local beaches go, it's the easiest to access and the most popular south of Fort Myers Beach. It's also great for shelling fans. **Best for:** active beaching and partying. ⊠ *Hickory Blvd. at Bonita Beach Rd.* ☎ *239/707–1845* ⊕ *www.leeparks.org* 🅿 *Parking $2 per hr.*

## SPORTS AND THE OUTDOORS

### BIRDING

The last leg of the Great Florida Birding Trail has more than 20 stops in the Lower Gulf Coast. Go to ⊕ *floridabirdingtrail.com/index.php/ trip/trails/south/* for a complete listing.

### CANOEING

The meandering Estero River is pleasant for canoeing as it passes through Koreshan State Historic Site to the bay.

**Estero River Outfitters.** Rent canoes, kayaks, and equipment. ⊠ *20991 Tamiami Trail S, Estero* ☎ *239/992–4050* ⊕ *www.esteroriveroutfitters. com.*

### ICE HOCKEY

Fort Myers's minor-league hockey team, the **Florida Everblades** (⊠ *Germain Arena, 11000 Everblades Pkwy., Estero* ☎ *239/948–7825* ⊕ *www. floridaeverblades.com*), battle their opponents from October to April.

### ICE SKATING

Skaters can head to the **Germain Arena** (⊠ *11000 Everblades Pkwy., Estero* ☎ *239/948–7825* ⊕ *www.germainarena.com*) for ice skating, plus hockey and clinics.

## ⓒ SHOPPING

★ **Coconut Point.** A 500-acre planned community tops the Gulf Coast with even more upscale and big-box stores and restaurants. There's a boardwalk for a breather between impulse purchases, and a castle-theme kids' play area. ⊠ *23106 Fashion Dr., Estero* ☎ *239/992–9966* ⊕ *www. simon.com/mall/?id=1202.*

**Gulf Coast Town Center.** This a megamall of stores and chain restaurants includes a 123,000-square-foot Bass Pro Shops, Ron Jon Surf Shop, Best Buy, Costco, and movie theaters. ⊠ *9903 Gulf Coast Main St.* ⊕ *www. gulfcoasttowncenter.com.*

**9**

**Miromar Outlets.** The complex includes Adidas, Nike, Nautica, and more than 140 other stores and eateries, plus a free Playland for kids. ⊠ *Corkscrew Rd. at I–75 Exit 123 in Estero, near Germain Arena* ☎ *239/948–3766* ⊕ *www.miromaroutlets.com.*

## WHERE TO EAT

**$$$** ✕ **Blue Water Bistro.** For the convenience of shoppers at Coconut Point,
SEAFOOD several excellent restaurants cluster in the midst of the shopping center. Most are hooked to a chain. This one, although part of a Naples–Bonita Springs dining dynasty, has a personality all its own with a suave indoor–outdoor bar scene and seafood that's anything but timid. Its specialty is grilled fish from around the globe that you can mix and match with a choice of sauces and sides. For instance, try swordfish with a sweet-and-sour mango sauce and onion rings with chipotle barbecue sauce. Other specialties include a classic burger, chipotle baby back ribs, and excellent shrimp vodka penne. ⊠ *23151 Village Shops Way, Coconut Point, Estero* ☎ *239/949–2583* ⊕ *www.bluewaterbistro. net* ☉ *No lunch.*

¢  ✕ **Doc's Beach House.** Right next door to the public beach access, Doc's AMERICAN has fed hungry beachgoers for decades. Come barefoot and grab a quick 🕲 libation or meal downstairs, outside on the beach, or in the courtyard. When the thermometer reaches "searing" take refuge on the air-conditioned second floor, with its great view of beach action. Basic fare on the breakfast and all-day menu includes a popular Angus burger, Chicago-style pizza, and seafood plates. The conch chowder is some of the best in these parts, with just the right amount of fire. ✉ *27908 Hickory Blvd., Bonita Springs* 🕾 *239/992–6444* ⊕ *www.docsbeachhouse.com* ⌨ *Reservations not accepted* ═ *No credit cards.*

¢  ✕ **Old 41 Restaurant.** Locals vote this "best breakfast" and "best Philly AMERICAN cheesesteak," and mostly locals populate its cheery dining room with its Philadelphia allegiance. For breakfast, don't miss the incredible Texas French toast with homemade caramel and pecans, Carbon's malted Belgian waffles, or eggs and homemade hash with Boar's Head meat. Besides cheesesteak, lunch specialties include Boar's Head hoagies, burgers, open-faced beef or turkey sandwiches, and other comfort food it serves until 3 pm. ✉ *25091 Bernwood Dr., Bonita Springs* 🕾 *239/948–4123* ⌨ *Reservations not accepted* ☾ *No dinner.*

## WHERE TO STAY

*For expanded hotel reviews, visit Fodors.com.*

$$$$  ▦ **Hyatt Coconut Point Resort & Spa.** This secluded luxury resort, with RESORT its marble-and-mahogany lobby, makes a lovely sanctuary for fami-🕲 lies. **Pros:** top-notch amenities; pampering spa; great ceviche bar. **Cons:** Fodor'sChoice need shuttle to reach the beach; expensive restaurants. ✉ *5001 Coco-* ★ *nut Rd., Bonita Springs* 🕾 *239/444–1234 or 800/554–9288* ⊕ *www. coconutpoint.hyatt.com* ⟿ *426 rooms, 30 suites* ⚿ *In-room: a/c, safe, Internet, Wi-Fi. In-hotel: restaurants, bars, golf course, pools, tennis courts, gym, spa, beach, water sports, children's programs, business center* ⫪◎⫪ *No meals.*

$$$  ▦ **Trianon Bonita Bay.** Convenient to Bonita Springs' best shopping HOTEL and dining, this branch of a downtown Naples favorite has a peaceful, sophisticated feel and a poolside–lakeside alfresco bar and grill. **Pros:** shops and restaurants within walking distance; intimate atmosphere; refined amenities. **Cons:** sometimes less-than-friendly staff; far from beach; slightly stuffy. ✉ *3401 Bay Commons Dr., Bonita Springs* 🕾 *239/948–4400 or 800/859–3939* ⊕ *www.trianon.com* ⟿ *100 rooms* ⚿ *In-room: a/c, Internet, Wi-Fi. In-hotel: restaurant, bar, pool, business center* ⫪◎⫪ *Breakfast.*

# NAPLES

*21 mi south of Bonita Springs, on U.S. 41.*

Poised between the Gulf of Mexico and the Everglades, Naples belies its wild setting and Indian past with the trappings of wealth—neo-Mediterranean-style mansions, neatly manicured golfing developments, revitalized downtown streets lined with galleries and one-of-a-kind shops, and a reputation for lively and eclectic dining. Visitors come for its luxury hotels—including two Ritz-Carltons—its fabulous white-sand beaches, fishing, shopping, theater and arts, and a lofty reputation for golf. Yet with all the highfalutin living, Naples still appeals to families, especially with its water park and the new Golisano Children's Museum of Naples slated to open here in fall 2011.

### GETTING HERE AND AROUND

The Naples Municipal Airport is a small facility east of downtown principally serving private planes, commuter flights, and charters. An on-demand taxi for up to three passengers is about $60–$90 from Southwest Florida International Airport in Fort Myers to Naples. Extra people are charged $10 each. Once you have arrived, call Naples Taxi. Other transportation options include Aaron Airport Transportation and Naples Airport Shuttle. Greyhound Lines has service to Naples. In Naples and Marco Island, Collier Area Transit runs regular routes.

If you want someone to be your guide as you go about town, Naples Trolley Tours offers eight narrated tours daily, covering more than 100 points of interest in town. You can board at two places around town. The tour ($25) lasts about two hours, but you can get off and on at no extra cost.

Naples is 21 mi south of Bonita Springs, on U.S. 41. If you're driving here from Florida's East Coast, consider Alligator Alley, a toll section of Interstate 75 that runs from Fort Lauderdale to Naples. In Naples, east–west trunks exiting off Interstate 75 include, from north to south, Immokalee Road (Route 846) at the north edge of town, Pine Ridge Road (Route 896), and Route 951, which takes you also to Marco Island.

### ESSENTIALS

Transportation Contacts **Aaron Airport Limo & Taxi** (☎ *239/768–1898 or 800/998–1898* ⊕ *www.aarontaxi.com*).

**Collier Area Transit** (☎ *239/435–0000* ⊕ *www.colliergov.net*). **Greyhound Lines** (✉ *2669 Davis Blvd., Naples* ☎ *239/774–5660 or 800/231–2222* ⊕ *www.greyhound.com*). **Naples Airport Shuttle** (☎ *239/430–4747 or 888/569–2227* ⊕ *www.naplesairportshuttle.com*). **Naples Taxi** (☎ *239/435–0000 or 800/472–1371* ⊕ *naplestaxiflorida.com*). **Naples Trolley Tours** (☎ *239/262–7300 or 800/592–0848* ⊕ *www.naplestrolleytours.com*).

Visitor Information **Naples, Marco Island, Everglades Convention and Visitors Bureau** (✉ *2800 Horseshoe Dr., Naples* ☎ *239/252–2384 or 800/688–3600* ⊕ *www.paradisecoast.com*).

### EXPLORING

#### TOP ATTRACTIONS

**Collier County Museum.** To get a feel for local history, stroll the nicely presented indoor vignettes and traveling exhibits and outdoor park-like displays at this museum. A Seminole chickee village, native plant garden, swamp buggy, reconstructed 19th-century fort, steam logging locomotive, and more capture important Naples-area developments from prehistoric times to the World War II era. ✉ *3301 Tamiami Trail E* ☎ *239/252–8476* ⊕ *www.colliermuseums.com* 🎫 *Free* ⊙ *Weekdays 9–5, Sat. 9–4.*

**Naples Botanical Garden.** A two-year, $33 million renovation of the gardens, finished in November 2010, has elevated this attraction to one of Naples's most culturally and botanically exciting. Its "gardens with latitude" flourish with plants and architectural and decorative elements from Florida and other subtropical locales including Asia, Brazil, and the Caribbean. Highlights of the 170 acres include a Children's Garden with a Butterfly House, treehouse, waterfall, cave, Cracker house, and hidden garden; infinity water lily pool; an aromatic Enabling Garden; and a dramatic waterfall feature. ⊠ *4820 Bayshore Dr.* ☎ *239/643–7275* ⊕ *www.naplesgarden.org* 🏷 *$9.95* ⊙ *Daily 9–5.*

⟳ **Naples Nature Center.** On 14 acres bordering a tidal lagoon teeming with wildlife, the Naples Nature Center is undergoing a massive makeover with elements opening in stages. The new Dalton Discovery Center is expected to open the end of 2012 with interactive ecosystem exhibits, a sea turtle tank, and other live wildlife exhibits and programs. The opening of a new wildlife rehabilitation center in summer 2011 more than tripled the space of the old one and a theater opened to show orientation and other videos. Short trails are marked with interpretive signs, and there are guided walks and boat tours (ages 2 and older) on the mangrove-bordered Gordon River several times daily. Kayaks are available for rent. There may be closures at the Nature Center in late 2011, so call ahead before visiting. ⊠ *1450 Merrihue Dr.* ☎ *239/262–0304* ⊕ *www.conservancy.org* 🏷 *$9* ⊙ *May–Oct., Mon.–Sat. 9–4:30; Nov.–Apr., Mon.–Sat. 9–4:30, Sun. noon–4 (hrs subject to change; check the Web site for up-to-date information).*

⟳ **Naples Zoo.** The lush and entertaining 48-acre zoo, established in 1919, draws visitors curious to see lions, tigers, lemurs, antelope, panthers, leopards, and monkeys. Popular exhibits include the pair of endangered Madagascar fossas, ferocious carnivores related to the mongoose; the Florida black bears; and the new giraffes. Live shows like "Planet Predator" and "Serpents: Fangs & Fiction" star the animals at their wildest. The Primate Expedition Cruise takes you past islands populated with monkeys and lemurs. Youngsters can amuse themselves in three separate play areas, and there are meet-the-keeper times and alligator feedings. ⊠ *1590 Goodlette Rd.* ☎ *239/262–5409* ⊕ *www.napleszoo.org* 🏷 *$19.95* ⊙ *Daily 9–5; gates close at 4.*

**Fodor's**Choice
★ **Patty & Jay Baker Naples Museum of Art.** This cool, contemporary museum in the Naples Philharmonic Center for the Arts displays provocative, innovative pieces, including American miniatures, antique walking sticks, modern American and Mexican masters, and traveling exhibits. Dazzling installations by glass artist Dale Chihuly include a fiery cascade of a chandelier and an illuminated ceiling layered with many-hued glass bubbles, glass corkscrews, and other shapes that suggest the sea; alone, this warrants a visit. In 2010, the multimillion-dollar donation of a massive 12-piece Louise Nevelson sculpture greatly boosted the museum's importance. ⊠ *5833 Pelican Bay Blvd.* ☎ *239/597–1900 or 800/597–1900* ⊕ *www.thephil.org* 🏷 *$8* ⊙ *Oct.–June, Tues.–Sat. 10–4, Sun. noon–4.*

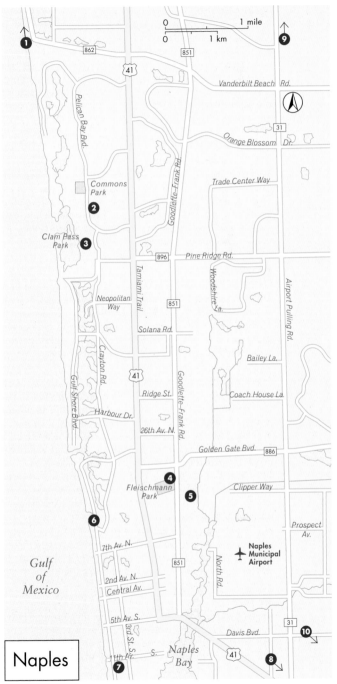

**WORTH NOTING**

**Palm Cottage.** Houses in 19th-century South Florida were often built of a concretelike material made of sand and seashells. For a fine example of such tabby construction, stop by Palm Cottage, built in 1895 and one of the Lower Gulf Coast's few surviving tabby homes. The historically accurate interior contains simple furnishings typical of the period. Next door to the cottage, Norris Gardens was designed to reflect turn-of-the-last-century garden trends. Docents give guided tours of the home or gardens and, for $15, a two-hour walking tour of the historic area. ✉ *137 12th Ave. S* ☎ *239/261–8164* ⊕ *www.napleshistoricalsociety.org* 🔁 *$10* ⊘ *Guided tours Nov.–Apr., Tues.–Sat. 1–4; May–Oct., Wed. and Sat. 1–4.*

Ⓒ **Sun-N-Fun Lagoon.** This is a splashy water park located in a county park east of town. Interactive water features such as water dumping buckets, water pistols, and a Tadpole pool are designed for children age seven and under. The whole family will go for the diving pool, lazy river, and slides. ✉ *15000 Livingston Rd., at North Collier Regional Park* ☎ *239/252–4021* ⊕ *www.colliergov.net* 🔁 *$12* ⊘ *10–5 daily; call to check for fall and winter closures.*

**BEACHES**

**Clam Pass Beach Park.** Besides soaking up sun on the beach here, you can kayak through the mangroves or into the surf. Next to the Naples Grande Beach Resort, a ¾-mi boardwalk winds through the mangrove area to the beach. Convenient for north-end Naples hotel guests, it provides tram service down the boardwalk and offers food and beach rentals. ✉ *Seagate Dr.* ☎ *239/252–4000* ⊕ *www.colliergov.net/parks* 🔁 *Parking $8* ⊘ *Daily 8–sunset.*

Fodor's Choice ★ **Delnor-Wiggins Pass State Park.** These well-maintained 166 acres comprise one of Naples's best beaches—all-natural with unobstructed views—plus barbecue grills, picnic tables, a boat ramp, an observation tower, restrooms with wheelchair access, bathhouses, showers, and lots of parking. Fishing is best in Wiggins Pass, at the north end of the park. Rangers conduct sea turtle programs in summer, and birding and other programs year-round. **Best for:** nature and fishing. ✉ *11100 Gulf Shore Dr. N, at Rte. 846* ☎ *239/597–6196* ⊕ *www.floridastateparks.org/delnorwiggins* 🔁 *$6 per vehicle with up to 8 people, $4 for single drivers, $2 for pedestrians and bicyclists* ⊘ *Daily 8–sunset.*

Ⓒ **Lowdermilk Park.** This stretch along Gulf Shore Boulevard is great for families. It has more than 1,000 feet of beach as well as volleyball courts, a playground, restrooms, showers, a snack bar, and picnic tables. **Best for:** families. ✉ *Gulf Shore Blvd. at Banyan Blvd.* ☎ *239/213–3029* 🔁 *Parking 25¢ per 10 min* ⊘ *Daily 7–sunset.*

**SPORTS AND THE OUTDOORS**

**BIKING**

**Naples Cyclery.** For daily rentals, rates range from $6 to $45 for two hours and selections include two- and four-passenger surreys, tandems, and more. ✉ *813 Vanderbilt Beach Rd. at Pavilion Shopping Center* ☎ *239/566–0600* ⊕ *www.naplescyclery.com.*

### BOATING

**Naples Watersports at Port-O-Call Marina.** Nineteen-foot pontoon boats and 21-foot deck boats starting at $130 for two hours. ✉ *550 Port-O-Call Way* ☎ *239/774–047* ⊕ *www.naples-boatrentals.com.*

### FISHING

**Lady Brett.** Half-day fishing trips run twice daily at $69 each. ✉ *Tin City, 1200 5th Ave. S* ☎ *239/263–4949* ⊕ *www.tincityboats.com.*

**Mangrove Outfitters.** Take a guided boat and learn to cast and tie flies. ✉ *4111 E. Tamiami Trail* ☎ *239/793–3370 or 888/319–9848* ⊕ *www. mangrove-outfitters.com.*

### GOLF

**Lely Flamingo Island Club.** There are three 18-hole courses—the Classics, Flamingo Island, and the Mustang—plus a golf school. Mustang is the easiest and most wide open; greens fee $165/$39. ✉ *8004 Lely Resort Blvd.* ☎ *239/793–2600* ⊕ *www.lely-resort.net.*

**Naples Beach Hotel & Golf Club.** This club has 18 holes, a golf school, and a putting green. The region's oldest course, a par 72, it was built in 1929 and last renovated in 1998; greens fee (includes cart) $85 (balls included)/$50. ✉ *851 Gulf Shore Blvd. N* ☎ *239/435–2475* ⊕ *www. naplesbeachhotel.com.*

**Riviera Golf Club.** This affordable 18-hole course has a greens fee of $37/$35 (includes cart). ✉ *48 Marseille Dr.* ☎ *239/774–2011* ⊕ *www. rivieragolf.com.*

★ **Tiburón Golf Club.** There are two 18-hole Greg Norman–designed courses, the Black and the Gold, and a golf academy. Challenging and environmentally pristine, the links include narrow fairways, stacked sod wall bunkers, coquina sand, and no roughs; greens fee $190/$95. ✉ *Ritz-Carlton Golf Resort, 2600 Tiburón Dr.* ☎ *239/593–2000.*

## SHOPPING

Old Naples encompasses two distinct shopping areas marked by historic buildings and flowery landscaping: 5th Avenue South and 3rd Street South. Both are known for their abundance of fine-art galleries and monthly musical entertainment.

★ **Gattle's.** This downtown shop stocks pricey-but-pretty linens. ✉ *1250 3rd St. S* ☎ *239/262–4791 or 800/344–4552* ⊕ *gattlesofnaples.com/*

**Marissa Collections.** Sample the designer women's wear here. ✉ *1167 3rd St. S* ☎ *239/263–4333* ⊕ *www.marissacollections.com*

★ **New to You.** The most upscale clothes sometimes go to this consignment shop. ✉ *933 Creech Rd.* ☎ *239/262–6869.*

**Options.** Naples's ladies who lunch often donate their year-old Armani castoffs and fine collectibles to this terrific thrift shop. ✉ *968 2nd Ave. N* ☎ *239/434–7115.*

**Regatta.** Among 5th Avenue South's upscale selection, this shop sells personal and home accessories with a sense of humor and style. ✉ *750 5th Ave. S* ☎ *239/262–3929.*

**Tin City.** Near 5th Avenue South, a collection of tin-roof former boat docks along Naples Bay has more than 30 boutiques, eateries, and

## DID YOU KNOW?

Beaches are for so much more than sunning and sandcastle building. Many are used for fishing, weddings, and horseback riding. And come July 4, some, like Naples Beach (shown here), draw people at night for viewing fireworks over the water.

souvenir shops, with everything from jewelry to T-shirts and seafood. ✉ *1200 5th Ave. S* ⊕ *www.tin-city.com.*

**Village on Venetian Bay.** Stroll along the classy shops and restaurants, nearly 60 in all, that line the water's edge. ✉ *4200 Gulf Shore Blvd.* ⊕ *www.venetianvillage.com.*

**Waterside Shops.** Only in South Florida can you find four dozen stores plus eateries wrapped around a series of waterfalls, waterways, and shaded open-air promenades. Saks 5th Avenue and Nordstrom are two of the anchors. ✉ *Seagate Dr. and U.S. 41* ⊕ *www.watersideshops.com.*

## NIGHTLIFE AND THE ARTS

### THE ARTS

Naples is the cultural capital of this stretch of coast.

★ **Naples Philharmonic Center for the Arts.** This 1,473-seat performance center hosts plays, concerts, and exhibits year-round. It's home to the 85-piece Naples Philharmonic, which presents both classical and pop concerts. The Miami Ballet Company performs here during its winter season. (✉ *5833 Pelican Bay Blvd.* ☎ *239/597–1900 or 800/597–1900* ⊕ *www.thephil.org*).

**Naples Players.** Musicals and dramas are performed year-round; winter shows often sell out well in advance. ✉ *Sugden Community Theatre, 701 5th Ave. S* ☎ *239/263–7990* ⊕ *www.naplesplayers.org.*

### NIGHTLIFE

Downtown's 5th Avenue South is the scene of lively nightclubs and sidewalk cafés.

**McCabe's Irish Pub.** Irish and other style bands perform most weekends and some weeknights. Audiences often join in on the lusty lyrics. ✉ *699 5th Ave. S* ☎ *239/403–7170* ⊕ *mccabesirishpub.com.*

**Ultra Naples.** DJ music and dancing keep the party going Thursday through Saturday, and there are occasional teen nights on Sunday. ✉ *15495 U.S. 41 N* ☎ *239/514–3790.*

## WHERE TO EAT

¢ ✕**Aurelio's Is Pizza.** Transplanted from Chicago, the pizza here is steeped
PIZZA in tradition and flavor. The selections are typical, with a few show-offs
☺ such as chicken Alfredo, BLT, and the low-cholesterol spinach Calabrese. There's also pasta with homemade sauces and chicken Parmesan or Alfredo. Black-and-white checkered tablecloths and old Illinois license plates accent this neighborhood-style strip mall café. ✉ *590 N. Tamiami Trail* ☎ *239/403–8882* ⊕ *www.aureliosofnaples.com* ⊗ *No lunch weekends.*

$$$$ ✕**Baleen.** The mood cast in this well-appointed dining room and the
SEAFOOD romantic gulf-view patio that spills out from it onto the sand feels like the perfect Florida restaurant experience. There's only one small problem: lighting is so low at dinner you can't read the menu, even with its built-in flashlight. Too bad, that means you also miss the effect of the beautifully presented dishes: Asian pear and arugula salad, black grouper with peppercorn sauce and red wine risotto, grilled scallops paired with a lemongrass lobster sauce, Grand Marnier crème brûlée, and the likes. (Thankfully, most entrées are available in half portions.)

At breakfast, the house-made corned beef hash is divine. For lunch, the lobster Cobb salad is a popular choice. ✉ *9891 Gulf Shore Dr.* ☎ *239/597–3123 or 800/237–6883* ⊕ *www.laplayaresort.com* ⚑ *Reservations essential.*

**$$$**
MIDDLE EASTERN
★

✕ **Bha! Bha!** Classic and fusion Middle Eastern cooking—some of Naples's finest ethnic food—fill the menu with wonderful, adventurous taste treats. Specialties include plum lamb with tomato-pomegranate sauce, garlic-eggplant chicken, mango-ginger shrimp, and spicy beef in saffron sauce with cucumber yogurt. Ocher walls, a stone fountain, and exotic tapestries confirm the "Persian Bistro" on the restaurant's sign. The service lags at times, but intrepid palates still declare it worth heading to the strip mall location. A belly dancer entertains Thursday (in season) or Saturday (out of season) nights. ✉ *847 Vanderbilt Rd.* ☎ *239/594–5557* ⊕ *www. bhabhapersianbistro.com* ☾ *Closed Mon. May–Dec.*

**$$$**
ECLECTIC
Fodor'sChoice
★

✕ **Chops City Grill.** Count on high-quality cuisine that fuses, as its name suggests, chopstick cuisine and fine cuts of meat. Sophisticated yet resort-wear casual, it draws everyone from young businesspeople to local retirees. Sushi and Pacific Rim inspirations such as beef spring rolls and mango chili-glazed yellowfin tuna represent its Asian persuasion; dry-aged rib eye, fillets, and prime rib, its meaty side. Grilled seafood comes with side options such as wild mushrooms and four-cheese mac. For dessert, sip a frothy Chocolate Kiss martini. Dine alfresco or inside with a view of the kitchen. ✉ *837 5th Ave. S, Naples* ☎ *239/262–4677* ✉ *U.S. 41 at Brooks Grand Plaza, Bonita Springs* ☎ *239/992–4677* ⊕ *www.chopsbonita.com* ⚑ *Reservations essential* ☾ *No lunch.*

**$**
MEXICAN

✕ **Cilantro Tamales.** The warm, crispy, and authentic-tasting salsa and chips alone are worth a visit to this bright and lively little spot, with slabs of clay tile for placemats. The signature dish, smoked Gouda–stuffed tamales, reveals freshness, authenticity, and flair. Imaginative touches are also added to other Tex-Mex standards, including enchiladas, fajitas, chiles rellenos, and a Mexican rice bowl. ✉ *10823 N. Tamiami Trail* ☎ *239/597–5855* ⊕ *www.cilantrotamales.com* ⚑ *Reservations not accepted* ☾ *Closed Sept. and Mon. May–Nov.*

**$$**
BRITISH

✕ **Jolly Cricket Gastropub.** As pub fare continues to grow in popularity, young and old crowd this new restaurant to relish Brit favorites along with fine steaks. Casual fare ranges from a ham, brie, and apple baguette at lunch to chicken pot pie, bangers and mash, and meatloaf for dinner. Or splurge on the New Zealand rack of lamb or grilled organic Scottish salmon with ginger-soy glaze. ✉ *720 5th Ave. S* ☎ *239/304–9460* ⊕ *thejollycricket.com.*

**¢**
ECLECTIC

✕ **Old Naples Pub.** Local blue- and white-collar workers gather with shoppers for affordable sandwiches and seafood in the courtyard of this 20-year-old traditional pub, tucked away from shopping traffic at 3rd Street Plaza. It strikes one as an everybody-knows-your-name kind of place, with jars of pickles on the tables and friendly bartenders. Taste any of 28 kinds of beer and order fried "ungrouper sandwiches" (made with "mild flaky white filet" as grouper becomes rarer), burgers, crispy chicken salad, and nachos, as well as such not-so-traditional pub snacks as grilled fresh catch-of-the-day and fried gator tail. There's musical entertainment Wednesday through Sunday between Thanksgiving and Easter. ⊠ *255 13th Ave. S* ☎ *239/649–8200* ⊕ *www.naplespubs.com* ⚑ *Reservations not accepted.*

$$$$

MEDITERRANEAN

Fodor'sChoice

★

✕ **Sea Salt.** Naples's hottest new restaurant draws a crowd of connoisseurs to its modern coral-rock dining room that spills out onto the sidewalk. Venetian-born Chef Fabrizio Aielli puts a New World spin on traditional Italian on his nightly changing menu. Start with the free sea-salt sampler and a charcuterie plate. The finest quality meats and seafood go into Wagyu cuts of beef and Kurobuta pork dishes, grilled black grouper, and local octopus. At lunch, dabble in European cheese before choosing between pasta and creative sandwiches. ⊠ *1186 3rd St. S* ☎ *239/434–7258* ⊕ *www.seasaltnaples.com* ⚑ *Reservations essential.*

$$$

CARIBBEAN

✕ **Tommy Bahama's Tropical Café.** Here Naples takes a youthful curve. Island music sounds on the umbrella-shaded courtyard at this eatery, the prototype for the chain. It has that trademark rattan look that identifies the Tommy Bahama label in clothing and furniture stores across the nation. Indoors and out, everybody's munching sandwiches, salads, and grilled seafood and meats with a tropical flair, like shrimp and scallops in curry-coconut sauce and blackberry-brandy barbecued ribs. Make sure to sample Tommy's Bungalow Brew beer. ⊠ *1220 3rd St. S* ☎ *239/643–6889* ⊕ *www.tommybahama.com.*

**WHERE TO STAY**
*For expanded hotel reviews, visit Fodors.com.*

$$$$

RENTAL

★

🏨 **Bellasera.** This place is just far enough "off 5th" to be away from the shopping-and-dining foot traffic and noise but close enough for convenience. Right off a Tuscany postcard, it feels quite villalike with its red-tile roofs and burnt-ochre stucco. **Pros:** near shops and restaurants; spacious rooms; screened patio or balcony. **Cons:** must take shuttle to beach; on a busy highway; average restaurant. ⊠ *221 9th St. S* ☎ *239/649–7333 or 888/612–1115* ⊕ *www.bellaseranaples.com* ⤵ *10 studios, 30 1-bedroom suites, 48 2-bedroom suites, 12 3-bedroom suites* ⚭ *In-room: a/c, kitchen (some), Internet, Wi-Fi. In-hotel: restaurant, bar, pool, gym, spa, business center* ⋈ *No meals.*

$$$$

RESORT

★

🏨 **Edgewater Beach Hotel.** This waterfront resort anchors the north end of fashionable Gulf Shore Boulevard. **Pros:** beautiful beach; spacious accommodations; fabulous restaurant. **Cons:** far from shopping; surrounded closely by high-rises; no tubs in some rooms. ⊠ *1901 Gulf Shore Blvd. N* ☎ *239/403–2000 or 800/821–0196* ⊕ *www.edgewaternaples.com* ⤵ *97 1-bedroom suites, 28 2-bedroom suites* ⚭ *In-room: a/c, kitchen, Wi-Fi. In-hotel: restaurants, bars, pool, gym, beach, water sports, laundry facilities, business center* ⋈ *No meals.*

$$$$

B&B/INN

🏨 **Inn on Fifth.** You can't beat this luxe property if you want to plant yourself in the heart of Naples nightlife and shopping. **Pros:** near shopping and restaurants; metro vibe; very comfortable rooms. **Cons:** among 5th Avenue's bustle; pool is eye-level with power lines; not on the beach. ⊠ *699 5th Ave. S* ☎ *239/403–8777 or 888/403–8778* ⊕ *www.innonfifth.com* ⤵ *76 rooms, 11 suites* ⚭ *In-room: a/c, safe, Internet, Wi-Fi. In-hotel: restaurant, bar, pool, gym, spa, business center* ⋈ *No meals.*

9

**$$$$**   LaPlaya Beach & Golf Resort. LaPlaya bespeaks posh and panache down
RESORT   to the smallest detail—note the custom-designed duvet covers, marble
Fodor'sChoice   bathrooms, and a stuffed sea turtle toy to cuddle during your stay. **Pros:**
★   right on the beach; high-end amenities; beautiful rooms. **Cons:** golf
course is off property; no locker rooms in spa. ⌂ *9891 Gulf Shore Dr.*
☏ *239/597–3123 or 800/237–6883* ⊕ *www.laplayaresort.com* ↰ *180
rooms, 9 suites* ♿ *In-room: a/c, no safe, Internet, Wi-Fi. In-hotel: restaurant, bars, golf course, pools, gym, spa, beach, water sports, business
center* ♚ *No meals.*

**$$$$**   Naples Bay Resort. This place boasts all the class and polish it takes to
RESORT   steal the hearts of those who thought the Ritz and Naples Grande were
★   the only top-of-the-line options. **Pros:** full range of amenities; walking
distance to downtown; $5 water shuttle to key stops. **Cons:** no beach;
some highway noise. ⌂ *1500 5th Ave. S* ☏ *239/530–1199 or 866/605–
1199* ⊕ *www.naplesbayresort.com* ↰ *20 rooms, 29 1-bedroom suites,
36 2-bedroom suites, 108 cottages (minimum 6-night stay in cottages)*
♿ *In-room: a/c, kitchen (some), Wi-Fi (some). In-hotel: restaurants,
bars, pools, tennis courts, gym, spa, water sports, laundry facilities,
business center* ♚ *Breakfast.*

**$$$$**   Naples Beach Hotel & Golf Club. Family-owned and -managed for more
RESORT   than 50 years, this beach resort is a piece of Naples history. **Pros:** ter-
☺   rific beach; good recreational amenities; complimentary kids' program.
**Cons:** expensive nightly rates; showing its age; have to cross street to
reach spa and golf facilities. ⌂ *851 Gulf Shore Blvd. N* ☏ *239/261–
2222 or 800/237–7600* ⊕ *www.naplesbeachhotel.com* ↰ *267 rooms,
42 suites, 10 efficiencies* ♿ *In-room: a/c, kitchen (some), Wi-Fi. In-
hotel: restaurants, bars, golf course, pool, tennis courts, gym, spa,
beach, children's programs, business center* ♚ *No meals.*

**$$$$**   Naples Grande Beach Resort. Beach access, golf nearby, and top-shelf
RESORT   luxury are all yours at the Naples Grande. **Pros:** great tennis and golf;
☺   attentive service; top-notch dining. **Cons:** not directly on the beach; high
Fodor'sChoice   room rates; golf course is 6 mi away from property. ⌂ *475 Seagate Dr.*
★   ☏ *239/597–3232 or 888/722–1269* ⊕ *www.naplesgrande.com* ↰ *395
rooms, 79 suites* ♿ *In-room: a/c, no safe, Internet, Wi-Fi. In-hotel: restaurants, bars, golf course, pools, tennis courts, gym, spa, beach, water
sports, children's programs, business center* ♚ *No meals.*

**$$$$**   Ritz-Carlton Golf Resort. Ardent golfers with a yen for luxury will find
RESORT   their dream vacation at Naples's most elegant golf resort. **Pros:** great
★   golfing; fine dining; very elegant. **Cons:** must take shuttle bus to beach;
expensive rates; valets not as careful with cars as they should be. ⌂ *2600
Tiburón Dr.* ☏ *239/593–2000 or 800/241–3333* ⊕ *www.ritzcarlton.
com* ↰ *295 rooms, 40 suites* ♿ *In-room: a/c, Wi-Fi. In-hotel: restaurants, bars, golf course, pool, tennis courts, children's programs, business center, parking, some pets allowed* ♚ *No meals.*

**$$$$**   Ritz-Carlton, Naples. This is a classic Ritz-Carlton, with marble
RESORT   statues, antique furnishings, and 19th-century European oil paint-
Fodor'sChoice   ings. **Pros:** free Wi-Fi in public areas; flawless service; great beach.
★   **Cons:** valet parking only; short walk to the beach. ⌂ *280 Vanderbilt
Beach Rd.* ☏ *239/598–3300 or 800/241–3333* ⊕ *www.ritzcarlton.com*
↰ *450 rooms, 30 suites* ♿ *In-room: a/c, Wi-Fi. In-hotel: restaurants,*

*bars, pools, tennis courts, gym, spa, beach, children's programs, business center, parking* ❑ *No meals.*

$$$$  ☎ **Trianon Old Naples.** Oh-so-European in feel, this boutique hotel is
HOTEL  just enough removed from 5th Avenue's traffic to feel private, but close
enough to be convenient. **Pros:** close to shops and restaurants; elegant
setting; spacious rooms. **Cons:** limited facilities; must drive to beach.
✉ *955 7th Ave. S* ☎ *239/435–9600 or 877/482–5228* ⊕ *www.trianon.
com* ➟ *55 rooms, 3 suites* ⚒ *In-room: a/c, Internet, Wi-Fi. In-hotel:
bar, pool, business center* ❑ *Breakfast.*

## MARCO ISLAND

*20 mi south of Naples via Rte. 951.*

High-rises line part of the shore of Marco Island, which is connected
to the mainland by two bridges. Yet it retains an isolated feeling much
appreciated by those who love this corner of the world. Some natural
areas have been preserved, and the down-home fishing village of Goodland resists change. Fishing, boating, sunning, swimming, and tennis
are the primary activities.

### GETTING HERE AND AROUND
From Naples, Route 951 takes you to Marco Island, about 20 mi to
the south. Collier Area Transit runs regular buses through the area.
Key West Express operates a ferry from Marco Island (from Christmas
through Easter) and Fort Myers Beach (year-round) to Key West. The
cost for the round-trip (four hours each way) from Fort Myers Beach
is $145, from Marco Island $119.

### ESSENTIALS
Transportation Contacts **Collier Area Transit** (☎ *239/596–7777* ⊕ *www.
colliergov.net*). **Key West Express** (☎ *239/394–9700 or 888/539–2628* ⊕ *www.
keywestshuttle.com*).

Visitor Information **Marco Island Area Chamber of Commerce** (✉ *1102
N. Collier Blvd., Marco Island* ☎ *239/394–7549 or 800/788–6272* ⊕ *www.
marcoislandchamber.org*). **Naples, Marco Island, Everglades Convention and
Visitors Bureau** (✉ *2800 Horseshoe Dr., No. 218, Naples* ☎ *239/403–2384*
⊕ *www.paradisecoast.com*).

### EXPLORING
**Marco Island Historical Museum.** Marco Island was once part of the ancient
Calusa kingdom. The Marco Cat, a statue found in 1896 excavations,
has become symbolic of the island's prehistoric significance. The original is part of the Smithsonian Institution's collection, but a replica of
the Marco Cat is among displays illuminating the ancient past at this
museum, which opened its new facility in January 2011 (with more
developments to come). Three rooms examine the island's history with
dioramas, artifacts, and signage: the Calusa Room, Pioneer Room, and
Modern Marco Room. A fourth will host changing exhibits. Outside,
the yard was built to look like a Calusa village atop a shell mound
with a water feature and chickee structure. ✉ *180 S. Heathwood Dr.*
☎ *239/389–6447* ⊕ *www.themihs.org* 🎟 *Free* ⊙ *Tues.–Sat. 9–4.*

9

☺
★ **Rookery Bay Environmental Learning Center.** In the midst of 110,000-acre Rookery Bay National Estuarine Reserve, the center dramatically interprets the Everglades environment and local history with interactive models, aquariums, original art, a film, tours, and classes. It's on the edge of the estuary, about five minutes east of Marco's north bridge on Collier Boulevard. In 2009 the center debuted a $1 million, 250-foot pedestrian bridge that spans the reserve's creek from the center's second floor, and connects with a half-mile nature trail that can be followed by guided or self-guided tour. Kayak tours are also available. Other new exhibits include an interactive research boat with bird sounds and glass-bottom-boat video, and exhibits about the Gulf of Mexico and global climate change. ✉ *300 Tower Rd.* ☎ *239/417–6310* ⊕ *www.rookerybay.org* ✆ *$5* ☉ *Nov.–Apr., Mon.–Sat. 9–4; May–Oct. weekdays 9–4.*

### BEACHES

☺ **Tigertail Beach.** On the southwest side of the island is 2,500 feet of both developed and undeveloped areas. Once gulf front, in recent years a sand spit known as Sanddollar Island has formed, which means the beach, especially at the north end, has become mud flats—great for birding. There's still plenty of sand on the south end and across the lagoon on the sand spit. Facilities include playgrounds, volleyball, a butterfly garden, free use of a beach wheelchair, a concession stand, restrooms, and showers. Kayak rentals are available, and rangers conduct nature programs. ■TIP→ The Conservancy of Southwest Florida conducts free educational beach walks at Tigertail Beach every weekday from 8:30 to 9:30 am January to mid-April. ✉ *490 Hernando Ct.* ☎ *239/353–0404, 239/353–0404 for ranger programs* ✆ *Parking $8* ☉ *Daily 8–sunset.*

### SPORTS AND THE OUTDOORS

#### FISHING

**Sunshine Tours.** Try a deep-sea ($99 per person for half day) or backcountry ($60 per person for three hours) fishing charter with this outfitter. ✉ *Rose Marco River Marina, 951 Bald Eagle Dr.* ☎ *239/642–5415* ⊕ *www.sunshinetoursmarcoisland.com.*

### WHERE TO EAT

**$$**
ITALIAN
Fodor'sChoice
★
✕ **Arturo's.** This place is huge, with expansive Romanesque dining rooms and more seating on the patio. Still, it fills up year-round with a strong well-dressed following that appreciates a fun attitude and serious Italian cuisine done comprehensively and traditionally. Start with the plump mussels marinara, then choose from three pages of classic Italian entrées, including homemade pasta. The stuffed pork chop, a nightly special, is a winner, as is the New York–style cheesecake. ✉ *844 Bald Eagle Dr.* ☎ *239/642–0550* ⊕ *www.arturosmarcoisland.com* ✆ *Reservations essential.*

$ ✕**Crazy Flamingo**. Burgers, conch fritters, and chicken wings draw
AMERICAN mostly locals to this neighborhood bar, where there's counter service
only and seating indoors and outdoors on the sidewalk. Try the peel-
and-eat shrimp, sushi, mussels marinara, chicken bistro salad, or fried
grouper basket. ✉ *Marco Island Town Center, 1035 N. Collier Blvd.*
☎ *239/642–9600* ⊕ *www.thecrazyflamingo.com.*

$$ ✕**Old Marco Lodge**. Built in 1869, this waterfront restaurant is Good-
SEAFOOD land's oldest landmark. Boaters often cruise in and tie up dockside to
sit on the veranda and dine on local seafood and pasta entrées. The
crab-cake sandwich is a popular lunch option. For dinner, start with
a wholesome bowl of vegetable crab soup and then a trip to the salad
bar (included in the price of entrées). The menu includes all manner of
seafood dishes, such as crab-stuffed grouper, coconut shrimp, and jerk
seafood pasta. There's also steak and chicken dishes for landlubbers.
Save room for the authentic key lime pie. ✉ *401 Papaya St., Goodland*
☎ *239/642–7227* ⊕ *www.oldmarcolodge.com* ☉ *Closed July–Sept.*

$$$ ✕**Sale e Pepe**. Marco's best dining view comes also with some of its fin-
ITALIAN est cuisine. The name means "salt and pepper," an indication that this
★ palatial restaurant with terrace seating overlooking the beach adheres
to the basics of home-style Italian cuisine. Pastas, sausages, and ice
cream are made right here in the kitchen. Simple dishes—veal ravioli, mushroom risotto, yellow-pepper-and-shrimp soup, baked salmon
with lobster sauce, roasted red snapper with saffron sauce, and grilled
marinated strip steak—explode with home-cooked, long-simmered flavors. With the exception of a handful of pizzas, lunch is more traditional, less Italian. ✉ *Marco Beach Ocean Resort, 480 S. Collier Blvd.*
☎ *239/393–1600* ⊕ *www.sale-e-pepe.com.*

$$ ✕**Snook Inn**. On the water with live entertainment in the tiki bar and a
SEAFOOD loaded salad bar: no wonder this place has been a casual favorite for
locals and visitors for decades. Signature items include the spicy conch
chowder, battered grouper sandwich, Caribbean BBQ baby back ribs,
and grouper in a bag with mushroom crab sauce. ✉ *1215 Bald Eagle*
*Dr., Old MarcoMarco Island* ☎ ⊕ *www.snookinn.com* ⌂ *Reservations*
*not accepted.*

$$$ ✕**Verdi's**. There's a Zen feel to this American bistro built on creative
ECLECTIC American-Italian-Asian fusion cuisine. You might start with steamed
littleneck clams in garlic butter or duck potstickers, then move on to
entrées such as grilled swordfish with pumpkin seeds, crispy duck, pasta
pomodoro, or the New Zealand rack of lamb. Cuban coffee crème
brûlée and deep-dish apple strudel are among the tempting desserts.
✉ *Sand Dollar Plaza, 241 N. Collier Blvd.* ☎ *239/394–5533* ⊕ *www.*
*verdisbistro.com* ☉ *No lunch. Closed Aug. and Sept.*

## WHERE TO STAY

*For expanded hotel reviews, visit Fodors.com.*

$$ ▦ **Boat House Motel**. For a great location at a good price, check into
HOTEL this two-story motel. **Pros:** away from busy beach traffic; affordable;
boating docks and access. **Cons:** no beach; hard to find; tight parking
area. ✉ *1180 Edington Pl.* ☎ *239/642–2400 or 800/528–6345* ⊕ *www.*
*theboathousemotel.com* ⤺ *20 rooms, 3 condominiums, 1 2-bedroom*

9

*house* ⟡ *In-room: a/c, no safe, kitchen (some), Wi-Fi. In-hotel: pool, some pets allowed* ⦿ *No meals.*

**$$$$**  🛏 **Hilton Marco Island Beach Resort.** This 11-story beachfront hotel is
RESORT  smaller and more conservative than the Marriott, but it seems less busy
and crowded. **Pros:** gorgeous wide beach; complete business services;
exclusive feel. **Cons:** a little stuffy; charge for Wi-Fi and self-parking;
business focus. ✉ *560 S. Collier Blvd.* ☎ *239/394–5000 or 800/394–
5000* ⊕ *www.hiltonmarcoisland.com* ↪ *271 rooms, 22 suites, 4 penthouses* ⟡ *In-room: a/c, Wi-Fi. In-hotel: restaurants, bar, pool, tennis
courts, gym, spa, beach, water sports, children's programs, business
center, parking* ⦿ *No meals.*

**$$$$**  🛏 **Marco Beach Ocean Resort.** One of the island's first condo hotels, this
RESORT  12-story class act has one- and two-bedroom suites decorated in tasteful
Fodor's Choice  neutral tones. **Pros:** top-rate dining; beach location; boutique hotel feel.
★  **Cons:** high prices; a rather squeezed feel because of neighboring condo
buildings; near busy resort. ✉ *480 S. Collier Blvd.* ☎ *239/393–1400
or 800/260–5089* ⊕ *www.marcoresort.com* ↪ *83 1-bedroom and 15
2-bedroom suites* ⟡ *In-room: a/c, kitchen, Wi-Fi. In-hotel: restaurants,
bars, pool, tennis courts, gym, spa, beach, business center* ⦿ *No meals.*

**$$$$**  🛏 **Marco Island Marriott Resort, Golf Club & Spa.** A circular drive and mani-
RESORT  cured grounds front this hilltop, beachfront resort made up of twin
☾  11-story towers and villas. **Pros:** terrific beach; top-notch amenities;
★  great spa. **Cons:** huge size; lots of convention business; paid parking
across the street in uncovered lot. ✉ *400 S. Collier Blvd.* ☎ *239/394–
2511 or 800/438–4373* ⊕ *www.marcoislandmarriott.com* ↪ *664
rooms, 63 suites* ⟡ *In-room: a/c, safe, Internet, Wi-Fi. In-hotel: restaurants, bars, golf course, pools, tennis courts, gym, spa, beach, water
sports, children's programs, business center, parking* ⦿ *No meals.*

**$$$$**  🛏 **Olde Marco Island Inn & Suites.** This Victorian with tin roofs and royal-
B&B/INN  blue shutters and awnings used to be the only place to stay on the island.
**Pros:** quiet part of the island; modern and upscale facilities; fine restaurants. **Cons:** not on the beach; part of a shopping center, office closes
at night. ✉ *100 Palm St.* ☎ *239/394–3131 or 877/475–3466* ⊕ *www.
oldemarcoinn.com* ↪ *51 suites, 2 penthouses* ⟡ *In-room: a/c, kitchen
(some). In-hotel: restaurants, bar, pool, business center* ⦿ *No meals.*

# Palm Beach and the Treasure Coast

## WORD OF MOUTH

"If you really want to be close to restaurants and shops in the Palm Beach area, check out the Marriott in Delray Beach or even the adjacent Residence Inn by Marriott . . . about 30 minutes south of Palm Beach."

—rattravlers

# WELCOME TO PALM BEACH AND THE TREASURE COAST

## TOP REASONS TO GO

★ **Beautiful Beaches:** From Jupiter's sandy shoreline, where leashed dogs are welcome, to the broad stretches of sand in Delray Beach and Boca Raton, swimmers, sunbathers, and surfers—and sea turtles looking for a place to hatch their eggs—all find happiness.

★ **Exquisite Resorts:** The Ritz-Carlton and the Four Seasons continue to sparkle with service fit for royalty. Two historic gems—the Breakers in Palm Beach and the Boca Raton Resort—perpetually draw the rich, the famous, and anyone else who can afford the luxury.

★ **Horse Around:** Wellington, with its jumping events and its popular polo season, is often called the winter equestrian capital of the world.

★ **Have a Reel Good Time:** From Lake Okeechobee, a great place to catch bass and perch, to the Atlantic Ocean, teeming with kingfish, sailfish, dolphinfish, and wahoos, anglers will find the waters here a treasure chest.

**1** Palm Beach. With Gatsby-era architecture, stone-and-stucco estates, extravagant landscaping, and highbrow shops, Palm Beach is a must-see for travelers to the area. Plan to spend some time on Worth Avenue, also called the Mink Mile, a collection of more than 200 chic shops, and Whitehall, once the winter retreat for Henry Flagler, Palm Beach's founder.

**2** West Palm Beach. Bustling with its own affluent identity, West Palm Beach has much to offer. Palm Beach–style homes line lovely Flagler Drive, and golf courses are abundant. Culture fans have plenty to cheer about, from the Kravis Center for the Performing Arts, to the Norton Museum of Art and the Armory Arts Center. Kids will love the Palm Beach Zoo.

**3** South to Boca Raton. The territory from Palm Beach south to Boca Raton defines old-world glamour and new age sophistication. Delray Beach boasts a lively downtown, with galleries, shops, and restaurants. To the west are the Morikami Japanese Gardens and the headquarters of the American Orchid Society. Boca Raton's Mizner Park has tony boutiques, restaurants, and the Boca Raton Museum of Art.

**4** Treasure Coast. Much of the shoreline north of Palm Beach remains blissfully undeveloped. Along the coast, the broad tidal lagoon separates barrier islands from the mainland.

## GETTING ORIENTED

This South Florida region extends 120 mi from Sebastian to Boca Raton. The golden stretch of the Atlantic from Palm Beach southward defines old-world glamour and new age sophistication. North of Palm Beach, you'll uncover the comparatively undeveloped Treasure Coast, where towns and wide-open spaces along the road await your discovery. Altogether, there's a delightful disparity, from Palm Beach, pulsing fast with old-money wealth, to low-key Hutchinson Island and Manalapan. The burgeoning equestrian community of Wellington lies 10 mi west of Palm Beach. It is the site of much of the county's new development.

**10**

### Map labels

ATLANTIC OCEAN

Jupiter Island
Hobe Sound
Tequesta
Jupiter
1A
Juno Beach
Singer Island
Palm Beach Gardens
Palm Beach Shores
Riviera Beach
1
West Palm Beach **1**
**2** Palm Beach
1A
Lake Worth
9
South Palm Beach
inland Manalapan
Boynton Beach
95 **3**
Gulf Stream
Delray Beach
Highland Beach
1A
Boca Raton
1

# PALM BEACH AND TREASURE COAST BEACHES

While not as white and fine as the shores on Florida's west coast, the beaches here provide good stomping grounds for hikers, well-guarded waters for swimmers, decent waves for surfers, and plenty of opportunities for sand-castle building and shell collecting.

Miles of sandy shoreline can be found here beside gorgeous blue-green waters you won't find farther north. The average year-round water temperature is 74°F, much warmer than Southern California beaches that average a comparatively chilly 62°F.

Humans aren't alone in finding the shores inviting. Migratory birds flock to the beaches, too, as do sea turtles, who come between May and August to lay their eggs in the sand. Locally organized watches take small groups out at night to observe mother turtles as they waddle onto shore, dig holes with their flippers and deposit their golf-ball-size eggs into the sand. Hatchlings emerge about 45 days later.

## WHEN TO GO

Palm Beach and Treasure Coast beaches are warm, clear, and sparkling all year long, but the best time to get in the water is between December and March. The shorelines are often more crowded then, but you don't have to worry about jellyfish or sea lice when you take a dip. Sea lice can cause welts, blisters, and rashes. The crowds thin out during summer and fall months, which is inviting, but jellyfish and sea lice can be a problem then.

# BEST PALM BEACH AND TREASURE COAST BEACHES

## DELRAY

If you're looking for a place to see and be seen, head for Delray's wide expanse of sand, which stretches 2 mi, half of it supervised by lifeguards. Reefs off the coast are popular with divers, as is a sunken Spanish galleon less than ½ mi offshore from the Seagate Club on the south end of the beach. **Pros:** good for swimmers and sunbathers; bars and restaurants across the street; cabanas and catamarans available for rent. **Cons:** often a long walk to the public restrooms. Best for families.

## JOHN D. MACARTHUR STATE PARK

If getting far from the madding crowd is your goal, John D. MacArthur State Park on the north end of Singer Island is a good choice. You will find a great place for snorkeling, kayaking, bird-watching, and fishing. Part of the beach was once dedicated to topless bathers, but that is no longer the case. **Pros:** guides to local flora and fauna are available; a good place to spot sea turtles. **Cons:** beach is a long walk from the parking lot. Best for sand-castle builders and nature lovers.

## JUNO BEACH

Juno Beach sports a 990-foot pier and a bait shop for those who like to spend their morning fishing. But the shoreline

itself is a favorite for families with kids who drag along sand toys, build castles, and hunt for shells. **Pros:** concession stand and a bait shop. **Cons:** beach isn't as wide as others. Best for anglers.

## RED REEF PARK

Looking for a great place to snorkel? This Boca Raton beach is just the ticket, and it doesn't matter if you're a beginner or a pro. The reef is only about 50 feet offshore. Expect to see tropical fish and maybe even a manatee or two. **Pros:** the park's showers and bathrooms are kept clean and there's a playground for kids. **Cons:** if you go at low tide, you're not going to see as many tropical fish. Best for snorkelers.

## STUART BEACH

When the waves robustly roll in at Stuart Beach, the surfers are rolling in, too. Beginning surfers are especially keen on Stuart Beach because of its ever-vigilant lifeguards, while pros to the sport like the challenges the choppy waters here bring. Beachgoers with kids like the snack bar known for its chicken fingers, and for those who like a side of museum musing with their day in the sun, there's an impressive collection of antique cars at a museum just steps from the beach. **Pros:** parking is easy to find, and there are three boardwalks for easy access to the beach. **Cons:** sand and surf can be rocky. Best for surfers.

10

Updated
by Mary
Thurwachter

This golden stretch of Atlantic coast resists categorization, and for good reason. The territory from Palm Beach south to Boca Raton defines old-world glamour and new age sophistication.

North of Palm Beach you'll uncover the comparatively undeveloped Treasure Coast—liberally sprinkled with coastal gems—where towns and wide-open spaces along the road await your discovery. Altogether, there's a delightful disparity, from Palm Beach, pulsing fast with plenty of old-money wealth, to low-key Hutchinson Island and Manalapan. Seductive as the beach scene interspersed with eclectic dining options can be, you should also take advantage of flourishing commitments to historic preservation and the arts, as town after town yields intriguing museums, galleries, theaters, and gardens.

Palm Beach, with Gatsby-era architecture, stone-and-stucco estates, extravagant landscaping, and highbrow shops, can reign as the focal point for your sojourn any time of year. From Palm Beach, head off in any of three directions: south via the Gold Coast toward Boca Raton along an especially scenic route known as A1A, back to the mainland and north to the barrier-island treasures of the Treasure Coast, or west for more rustic inland activities such as bass fishing and biking on the dikes around Lake Okeechobee.

# WEST PALM BEACH PLANNER

## WHEN TO GO

The weather is optimal from November through May, but the trade-off is that roadways and facilities are more crowded and prices higher. In summer it helps to have a tolerance for heat, humidity, and afternoon downpours. Hurricane season runs from June through November, not necessarily a bad time for a trip here as there's always plenty of warning before the big storms. For the best lodging rates consider summer months or the early weeks of December. Make sure to bring insect repellent for outdoor activities.

## SPECIALTY TOURS

☪ **DivaDuck Tours.** Amphibious tours, running 75 minutes, go in and out of the water around West Palm Beach/Palm Beach. Cruises run two or three times a day for $25. ✉ *Rosemary Ave. and Hibiscus St.* ☎ *561/ 844–4186* ⊕ *www.divaduck.com.*

**Old Northwood Historic District Tours.** Two-hour walking tours include visits to historic home interiors in this West Palm Beach neighborhood. In season tours start Sunday at 2; a $5 donation is suggested. Tours for groups of six or more can be scheduled almost any day. (☎ *No phone* ⊕ *www.oldnorthwood.org*).

## GETTING HERE

The best place to fly into is **Palm Beach International Airport** (*PBI* ☎ *561/ 471–7420*).

For a cab, call **Palm Beach Transportation** (☎ *561/689–4222*), the hotline for the Yellow cab company.

**Tri-Rail Commuter Bus Service** (☎ *800/874–7245*), the commuter rail system, provides taxi and limousine service. For either, the lowest fares are $2.50 per mile, with the meter starting at $2.50. Tri-Rail has 18 stops altogether between West Palm Beach and Miami, where tickets can be purchased. The one-way fare is $5.50.

The city's bus service, **Palm Tran** (☎ *561/841–4200*), runs routes 44 and 40 from the airport to Tri-Rail's nearby Palm Beach airport station daily.

**Amtrak** (☎ *800/872–7245* ⊕ *www.amtrak.com*) connects West Palm Beach with cities along Florida's east coast and the northeast daily.

## GETTING AROUND

Interstate 95 runs north–south, linking West Palm Beach with Fort Lauderdale and Miami to the south and with Daytona, Jacksonville, and the rest of the Atlantic Coast to the north. Florida's turnpike runs from Miami north through West Palm Beach before angling northwest to reach Orlando. U.S. 1 threads north–south along the coast, connecting most coastal communities, whereas the more scenic Route A1A ventures out onto the barrier islands. Interstate 95 runs parallel to U.S. 1 but a few miles inland.

**10**

## ABOUT THE RESTAURANTS

Numerous elegant establishments offer upscale Continental and contemporary fare, but the area also teems with casual waterfront spots serving affordable burgers and fresh seafood feasts. Grouper, fried or blackened, is especially popular here, along with the ubiquitous shrimp. An hour's drive west of the coast, around Lake Okeechobee, dine on catfish panfried to perfection and so fresh it seems barely out of the water. Early-bird menus, a Florida hallmark, typically entice the budget-minded with several dinner entrées at reduced prices offered during certain hours, usually before 5 or 6.

## ABOUT THE HOTELS

Palm Beach has a number of smaller hotels in addition to the famous Breakers. Lower-priced hotels and motels can be found in West Palm Beach and Lake Worth. To the south, the coastal town of Manalapan has the Ritz-Carlton, Palm Beach; and the posh Boca Raton Resort & Club is near the beach in Boca Raton. To the north in suburban Palm Beach Gardens is the PGA National Resort & Spa. To the west, small towns near Lake Okeechobee offer country-inn accommodations.

| WHAT IT COSTS | | | | | |
|---|---|---|---|---|---|
| | ¢ | $ | $$ | $$$ | $$$$ |
| Restaurants | under $10 | $10–$15 | $15–$20 | $20–$30 | over $30 |
| Hotels | under $80 | $80–$100 | $100–$140 | $140–$220 | over $220 |

Restaurant prices are per person for a main course at dinner. Hotel prices are for a standard double room, excluding 6½% sales tax (more in some counties) and 1%–4% tourist tax.

## INLAND SIGHTS

Want to get away from the water? Head 40 mi west of West Palm Beach on to Lake Okeechobee for some wildlife viewing, bird-watching, and fishing.

You are likely to see alligators in the tall grass along the shore, as well as birds, including herons, ibises, and bald eagles, which have made a comeback in the area. A 110-mi trail encircles Lake Okeechobee atop the 34-foot Herbert Hoover Dike. On the lake you'll spot happy anglers hooked on some of the best bass fishing in North America. There are 40 species of fish in "Lake O," including largemouth bass, bluegill, Okeechobee catfish, and speckled perch.

**Okee-Tantie Recreation Area.** Direct lake access makes this a popular fishing outpost, with two public boat ramps, fish-cleaning stations, and a bait shop that stocks groceries. There are also picnic areas and a restaurant. ⊠ *10430 Rte. 78 W, Okeechobee* ☎ *863/763–2622.*

**Getting Here:** The best way to drive here from West Palm is to go west on Southern Boulevard from Interstate 95 past the cutoff road to Lion Country Safari. From there, the boulevard is designated U.S. 98/441.

# PALM BEACH

*78 mi north of Miami, off I–95.*

Long reigning as the place where the crème de la crème go to shake off winter's chill, Palm Beach continues to be a seasonal hotbed of platinum-grade consumption. Other towns like Jupiter Island may rank higher on the per-capita-wealth meter, but there's no competing with the historic social supremacy of Palm Beach. It has been the winter address for heirs of the iconic Rockefeller, Vanderbilt, Colgate, Post, Kellogg, and Kennedy families. Even newer power brokers, with names like Kravis, Peltz, and Trump, are made to understand that strict laws govern everything from building to landscaping, and not so much as a pool awning gets added without a town council nod. If Palm Beach were to fly a flag, it's been observed, there might be three interlocking Cs, standing not only for Cartier, Chanel, and Christian Dior but also for clean, civil, and capricious. Only three bridges allow access to the island, and huge tour buses are a no-no.

To learn who's who in Palm Beach, it helps to pick up a copy of the *Palm Beach Daily News*—locals call it the Shiny Sheet because its high-quality paper avoids smudging society hands or Pratesi linens—for, as it is said, to be mentioned in the Shiny Sheet is to be Palm Beach. All this fabled ambience started with Henry Morrison Flagler, Florida's premier developer, and cofounder, along with John D. Rockefeller, of Standard Oil. No sooner did Flagler bring the railroad to Florida in the 1890s than he erected the famed Royal Poinciana and Breakers hotels. Rail access sent real estate prices soaring, and ever since, princely sums have been forked over for personal stationery engraved with 33480, the zip code of Palm Beach. To provide Palm Beach with servants and other workers, Flagler also developed an off-island community a mile or so west. West Palm Beach now bustles with its own affluent identity.

Setting the tone in this town of unparalleled Florida opulence is the ornate architectural work of Addison Mizner, who began designing homes and public buildings here in the 1920s and whose Moorish-Gothic style has influenced virtually all community landmarks. Thanks to Mizner and his lasting influence, Palm Beach remains a playground of the rich, famous, and discerning.

### GETTING HERE AND AROUND

Palm Beach is 78 mi north of Miami. To access Palm Beach off Interstate 95, exit east at Southern Boulevard, Belvedere Road, or Okeechobee Boulevard. The city's Palm Tran buses run between Worth Avenue and Royal Palm Way in Palm Beach and major areas of West Palm Beach and require exact change. Regular fares are $1.50.

For a taste of what it's like to jockey for position in this status-conscious town, stake out a parking place on Worth Avenue or parallel residential streets, and squeeze in among the Mercedeses, Rolls-Royces, and Bentleys. Between admiring your excellent parking skills and feeling car-struck at the surrounding fine specimens of automobile, be sure to note the "Parking By Permit Only" and "Two-hour" parking signs, as a $25 parking ticket might take the shine off your spot. ■ TIP➔ The best course for a half-day visit is to valet-park at the parking deck next to Saks 5th Avenue. Away from downtown, along County Road and Ocean Boulevard (the shore road, also designated as Route A1A), are Palm Beach's other defining landmarks: Mediterranean-style residences, some built of coral rock, that are nothing short of palatial, topped by barrel-tile roofs and often fronted by 10-foot ficus and sea-grape hedges. The low wall that separates the dune-top shore road from the sea hides shoreline that varies in many places from expansive

## A GOOD TOUR: PALM BEACH

Start at the **Henry Morrison Flagler Museum**—a 55-room villa Flagler built for his third wife—to get your first look at the eye-popping opulence of the Gilded Age, which defined Palm Beach. From here, turn left on Cocoanut Row, and right onto Royal Poinciana Way—outdoor cafés on the left and the Breakers golf course to your right—then right onto North County Road. Head south and look for the long stately driveway on the left that leads to the **Breakers**, built by Flagler in the style of an Italian Renaissance palace. Parking costs $20, and there are many valets under the porte cochere. Have your parking ticket validated while lunching at the Breakers and the parking fee is waived.

Continue south on South County Road to **Bethesda-by-the-Sea**, a Spanish Gothic Episcopal church. Keep driving south on South County Road until you reach Royal Palm Way; turn right, and drive a few blocks until you see the **Society of the Four Arts**. Turn left back onto Royal Palm Way and drive until it ends at the ocean, and turn right onto Ocean Boulevard until you reach famed **Worth Avenue** on the right, which is a one-way street running east to west. Park, stroll, and ogle designer goods. Then drive south back on Ocean Boulevard to peek at magnificent estates, including **El Solano**, designed by Addison Mizner, and the fabled **Mar-a-Lago**, a Mediterranean-revival palace with a distinctive 75-foot tower, now owned by Donald Trump and operating as a private club. At this point, if you want some sun and fresh air, continue south on South County Road until you reach **Phipps Ocean Park** and its stretch of beach, or head back toward town along South Ocean Boulevard to the popular Mid-Town Beach at the east end of Worth Avenue.

### TIMING
You'll need half a day, minimum, for these sights. A few shops and attractions are closed Sunday and May through October. From November through April, often-heavy traffic gets worse as the day wears on, so plan to explore in the morning.

to eroded. Here and there, where the strand deepens, homes are built directly on the beach.

### ESSENTIALS
Transportation Contact **Palm Tran** (☎ 561/841–4287).

Visitor Information **Town of Palm Beach Chamber of Commerce** (✉ *400 Royal Palm Way, Suite 106, Palm Beach* ☎ *561/655–3282*).

## EXPLORING

### TOP ATTRACTIONS
**Bethesda-by-the-Sea.** Donald Trump and his wife Melania were married here in 2005, but this Spanish Gothic Episcopal church had a claim to fame upon its creation in 1925: it was built by the first Protestant congregation in southeast Florida. Guided tours follow 11 am services on the second and fourth Sunday of the month. Adjacent are

Draped in European elegance, the Breakers in Palm Beach sits on 140 acres along the oceanfront.

the formal, ornamental **Cluett Memorial Gardens**. ✉ *141 S. County Rd.* ☎ *561/655–4554* ⊕ *www.bbts.org* ✆ *Free* ☉ *Church and gardens daily 8–5.*

**Fodor's Choice** **The Breakers**. Built by Henry Flagler in 1896 and rebuilt by his descendants
★ after a 1925 fire, this magnificent Italian Renaissance–style resort helped launch Florida tourism with its Gilded Age opulence, attracting influential wealthy Northerners to the state. The hotel, still owned by Flagler's heirs, is a must-see even if you aren't staying here. Walk through the 200-foot-long lobby, which has soaring arched ceilings painted by 72 Italian artisans and hung with crystal chandeliers, and the ornate Florentine Dining Room is decorated with 15th-century Flemish tapestries. ✉ *1 S. County Rd.* ☎ *561/655–6611* ⊕ *www.thebreakers.com.*

**Fodor's Choice** **Henry Morrison Flagler Museum**. The opulence of Florida's Gilded Age
★ lives on at Whitehall, the palatial 55-room "marble palace" Henry Flagler commissioned in 1901 for his third wife, Mary Lily Kenan. Architects John Carrère and Thomas Hastings were instructed to create the finest home imaginable—and they outdid themselves. Whitehall rivals the grandeur of European palaces and has an entrance hall with a baroque ceiling similar to Louis XIV's Versailles. Here you'll see original furnishings; a hidden staircase Flagler used to sneak from his bedroom to the billiards room; an art collection; a 1,200-pipe organ; and Florida East Coast Railway exhibits, along with Flagler's personal railcar, the *Rambler,* showcased in an 8,000-square-foot beaux arts–style pavilion behind the mansion. Tours take about an hour and are offered at frequent intervals. The café, open after Thanksgiving through mid-April, offers snacks and afternoon tea. ✉ *1 Whitehall*

**10**

Palm Beach and
West Palm Beach

*Way* ☎ *561/655–2833* ⊕ *www.flagler.org* 🖾 *$18* ⊙ *Tues.–Sat. 10–5, Sun. noon–5.*

★ **Worth Avenue.** Called the Avenue by Palm Beachers, this ¼-mi-long street is synonymous with exclusive shopping. Nostalgia lovers recall an era when faces or names served as charge cards, purchases were delivered home before customers returned from lunch, and bills were sent directly to private accountants. Times have changed, but a stroll amid the Moorish architecture of its shops offers a tantalizing taste of the island's ongoing commitment to elegant consumerism. Explore the labyrinth of eight pedestrian vias, on both sides of Worth Avenue, that wind past boutiques, tiny plazas, bubbling fountains, and the bougainvillea-festooned wrought-iron balconies of second-floor apartments. The avenue underwent a $15 million makeover in 2010. Two hundred mature coconut palm trees were planted along the road, and a magnificent $600,000 clock tower was built on the beach to mark the entrance from A1A. ⊠ *Between Cocoanut Row and S. Ocean Blvd.*

## WORTH NOTING

**El Solano.** No Palm Beach mansion better represents the town's luminous legacy than the Spanish-style home built by Addison Mizner as his own residence in 1925. Mizner later sold El Solano to Harold Vanderbilt, and the property was long a favorite among socialites for parties and photo shoots. Vanderbilt held many a gala fund-raiser here. Beatle John Lennon and his wife, Yoko Ono, bought it less than a year before Lennon's death. It's still privately owned and not open to the public. ⊠ *721 S. County Rd.*

**Mar-a-Lago.** Breakfast-food heiress Marjorie Merriweather Post commissioned a Hollywood set designer to create Ocean Boulevard's famed Mar-a-Lago, a 118-room, 110,000-square-foot Mediterranean-revival palace. Its 75-foot Italianate tower is visible from most areas of Palm Beach and from across the Intracoastal Waterway in West Palm Beach. Owner Donald Trump has turned it into a private membership club. ⊠ *1100 S. Ocean Blvd.* ☎ *561/832–2600* ⊕ *www.maralagoclub.com.*

**Phipps Ocean Park.** In addition to the shoreline, tennis courts, picnic tables, and grills, this park has a Palm Beach County landmark in the **Little Red Schoolhouse.** Dating from 1886, it served as the first schoolhouse in what was then Dade County. No alcoholic beverages are permitted in the park. ⊠ *2185 S. Ocean Blvd.* ☎ *561/838–5400* 🖾 *Free* ⊙ *Daily dawn–dusk.*

**Society of the Four Arts.** Despite widespread misconceptions of members-only exclusivity, this privately endowed institution—founded in 1936 to encourage appreciation of art, music, drama, and literature—is funded for public enjoyment. A gallery building—designed by Addison Mizner, of course—artfully melds an exhibition hall, library, and the Philip Hulitar Sculpture Garden, which underwent a major renovation in 2006. Open from about Thanksgiving to Easter, the museum's programs are extensive, and there's ample free parking. In addition to showcasing traveling art exhibitions, the museum offers films, lectures, workshops, and concerts. ⊠ *2 Four Arts Plaza* ☎ *561/655–7226*

10

*⊕ www.fourarts.org ✉ Program admission varies ☉ Galleries Dec.–mid-Apr., Mon.–Sat. 10–5, Sun. 2–5; library, weekdays 10–5, Sat. 10–1; gardens 10–5 daily.*

## SPORTS AND THE OUTDOORS

### BIKING

Bicycling is a great way to get a closer look at Palm Beach. Only 14 mi long, ½ mi wide, flat as the top of a billiard table, and just as green, it's a perfect biking place.

**Lake Trail.** This palm-fringed trail skirts the backyards of many palatial mansions and the edge of Lake Worth. ✉ *Parallel to Lake Way.*

**Palm Beach Bicycle Trail Shop.** The Palm Beach Bicycle Trail starts at the Society of the Four Arts, heading north 8 mi to the end and back—just follow the signs. You can rent bikes by the hour or day at this shop, a block from the bike trail. It's open daily. ✉ *223 Sunrise Ave.* ☎ *561/659–4583* ⊕ *www.palmbeachbicycle.com.*

### GOLF

**The Breakers Palm Beach.** The historic Ocean Course, as well as its contemporary counterpart the Breakers Rees Jones Course and the John Webster Golf Academy by the Breakers, is open to members and hotel guests only. A $190 greens fee includes range balls, cart, and bag storage at The Breakers Rees Jones Course or at the Ocean Course. ✉ *1 S. County Rd.* ☎ *561/655–6611.*

**Town of Palm Beach Golf Club.** The 18 holes include six on the Atlantic and three on the inland waterway; greens fee $45 riding, $32 to walk. The course was redesigned by Raymond Floyd and is a gem of a short-game course. ✉ *2345 S. Ocean Blvd.* ☎ *561/547–0598.*

## SHOPPING

★ **Worth Avenue.** One of the world's premier showcases for high-quality shopping runs ¼ mi east–west across Palm Beach, from the beach to Lake Worth. The street has more than 250 shops (more than 40 of them sell jewelry), and many upscale chain stores (Gucci, Hermès, Pucci, Saks Fifth Avenue, Neiman Marcus, Louis Vuitton, Emanuel Ungaro, Chanel, Dior, Cartier, Tiffany & Co., and Tourneau) are represented—their merchandise appealing to the discerning tastes of the Palm Beach clientele. ✉ *Between Cocoanut Row and S. Ocean Blvd.*

**South County Road.** The six blocks of South Country Road north of Worth Avenue have interesting, and somewhat less expensive, stores.

**Royal Poinciana Way.** For specialty items like out-of-town newspapers, health foods, and books, try the shops along the north side of Royal Poinciana Way. Most stores are closed on Sunday, and many go on hiatus in summer.

**Church Mouse.** Many high-end resale boutique owners grab their merchandise at this thrift store. ✉ *374 S. County Rd.* ☎ *561/659–2154.*

**Déjà Vu.** There are so many gently used, top-quality pieces from Chanel that this could be a resale house for the brand. There's no digging

Worth Avenue is the place in Palm Beach for high-end shopping, from international boutiques to art galleries.

through piles here; clothes are in impeccable condition and are well organized. ⊠ *Via Testa, 219 Royal Poinciana Way* ☎ *561/833–6624.*

**Giorgio's.** Over-the-top indulgence comes in the form of 50 colors of silk and cashmere sweaters and 22 colors of ostrich and alligator adorning everything from bags to bicycles. ⊠ *230 Worth Ave.* ☎ *561/655–2446.*

**Greenleaf & Crosby.** Jewelry is very important in Palm Beach, and for more than 100 years the divers selection here has included investment pieces. ⊠ *236 Worth Ave.* ☎ *561/655–5850.*

**Spring Flowers.** Beautiful children's clothing starts with a newborn gown set by Kissy Kissy or Petit Bateau and grows into fashions by Cacharel and Lili Gaufrette. ⊠ *337 Worth Ave.* ☎ *561/832–0131.*

**Van Cleef & Arpels.** Holding court for more than 60 years this shop is where legendary members of Palm Beach society shop for tiaras and formal jewels. ⊠ *202 Worth Ave.* ☎ *561/655–6767.*

## NIGHTLIFE AND THE ARTS

### NIGHTLIFE

Palm Beach is teeming with restaurants that turn into late-night hot spots, plus hotel lobby bars perfect for tête-à-têtes.

**Brazilian Court.** Thursday night happy hours spiked by creatively named cocktails and live jazz draw a local crowd to the lobby lounge and outdoor patio. ⊠ *301 Australian Ave.* ☎ *561/655–7740.*

**Cucina Dell'Arte.** Though popular for lunch and dinner, the younger trendier set comes late. ⊠ *257 Royal Poinciana Way* ☎ *561/655–0770.*

**Leopard Lounge.** The old guard gathers for live music during cocktail hour and later to dance until the wee hours every night of the year. ⊠ *Chesterfield Hotel, 363 Cocoanut Row* ☎ *561/659–5800.*

**THE ARTS**

**Society of the Four Arts.** This venue hosts concerts, lectures, and films from November through March. ⊠ *2 Four Arts Plaza* ☎ *561/655–7226.*

# WHERE TO EAT

$$$

ITALIAN

✕ **Amici.** The town's premier celebrity-magnet bistro is still a crowd pleaser. When it moved across the street and down the block from its original location, the Palm Beach crowd followed. The northern Italian menu highlights house specialties such as rigatoni with spicy tomato sauce and roasted eggplant, potato gnocchi, grilled veal chops, risottos, and pizzas from a wood-burning oven. There are nightly pasta and fresh fish specials as well. To avoid the crowds, stop by for a late lunch or early dinner. ⊠ *375 S. County Rd.* ☎ *561/832–0201* ⊕ *www. amicipalmbeach.com* ⟡ *Reservations essential.*

$$$$

FRENCH

Fodor's Choice

★

✕ **Café Boulud.** Celebrated chef Daniel Boulud opened his outpost of New York's Café Boulud in the Brazilian Court hotel. The warm and welcoming French-American venue is casual yet elegant, with a palette of honey, gold, and citron. Plenty of natural light spills through arched glass doors opening to a lush courtyard. Lunch and dinner entrées on Boulud's signature four-muse menu include classic French, seasonal, vegetarian, and a rotating selection of international dishes. The lounge, with its illuminated amber glass bar, is the perfect perch to take in the jet-set crowd that comes for a hint of the south of France in South Florida. A DJ plays on Saturday nights. ⊠ *Brazilian Court, 301 Australian Ave.* ☎ *561/655–6060* ⊕ *www.cafeboulud.com* ⟡ *Reservations essential.*

$$$$

ECLECTIC

✕ **Café L'Europe.** Even after 25 years, the favorite lunch spot of society's movers and shakers remains a regular stop on foodie itineraries. The management pays close attention to service and consistency, a big reason for its longevity. Best sellers include rack of lamb, Dover sole, and Wiener schnitzel, along with such inspired creations as crispy sweetbreads with poached pears and mustard sauce. Depending on your mood, the champagne-caviar bar can serve up appetizers or desserts. The place has an extensive wine list. A pianist plays nightly from 7 to 11 and a quartet plays dance music Friday and Saturday nights until 1 am. ⊠ *331 S. County Rd.* ☎ *561/655–4020* ⊕ *www.cafeleurope.com* ☻ *Lunch Wed.–Fri. Closed Mon. May–Dec.*

$$$$

FRENCH

Fodor's Choice

★

✕ **Chez Jean-Pierre.** With walls adorned with Dalí- and Picasso-like art, this is where the Palm Beach old guard likes to let down its guard, all the while partaking of sumptuous French cuisine and an impressive wine list. Forget calorie or cholesterol concerns and indulge in scrambled eggs with caviar or homemade duck foie gras, along with desserts like hazelnut soufflé or profiteroles au chocolat. Waiters are friendly and very attentive. Jackets are not required, although many men wear them. ⊠ *132 N. County Rd.* ☎ *561/833–1171* ⟡ *Reservations essential* ☻ *Closed Sun. No lunch.*

$  ✕ **Hamburger Heaven.** A favorite with locals since 1945, this quintessen-
AMERICAN  tial diner with horseshoe-shape counter as well as booths and tables is
loud and casual and has some of the best burgers on the island. Fresh
salads, homemade pastries, and daily soup and hot-plate specials featuring comfort foods like meat loaf and chicken potpie are also available. During the week, it's a popular lunch stop for working stiffs. The
staff is friendly and efficient. ✉ *314 S. County Rd.* ☎ *561/655–5277*
🕑 *Closed Sun.*

$$  ✕ **Pizza Al Fresco.** The secret-garden setting is the secret to the success
PIZZA  of this popular European-style pizzeria, where you can dine under
a canopy of century-old banyans in a charming courtyard. Special-
ties are 12-inch hand-tossed brick-oven pizzas with such interesting
toppings as prosciutto, arugula, and caviar. There's even a dessert
pizza topped with Nutella. Piping-hot calzones, salads, and sand-
wiches round out the selection. Look for the grave markers of Addi-
son Mizner's beloved pet monkey, Johnnie Brown, and Rose Sachs's
dog Laddie (she and husband Morton bought Mizner's villa and lived
there 47 years) next to the patio. Delivery is available. This bistro
is dog-friendly. ✉ *14 Via Mizner, at Worth Ave.* ☎ *561/832–0032*
🌐 *www.pizzaalfresco.com.*

$$$  ✕ **Ta-boó.** This 60-year-old landmark with peach stucco walls and green
AMERICAN  shutters attracts Worth Avenue shoppers looking for a two-hour lunch
★  and a dinner crowd ranging from tuxed-and-sequined theatergoers to
polo-shirted vacationers. Entrées include Black Angus dry-aged beef or
roast duck. Don't miss Coconut Lust, a signature dessert. Drop in late
night during the winter season when the nightly music is playing and
you'll probably spot a celebrity or two. ✉ *221 Worth Ave.* ☎ *561/835–
3500* 🌐 *www.taboorestaurant.com.*

# WHERE TO STAY

*For expanded hotel reviews, visit Fodors.com.*

$$$$  ▦ **Brazilian Court.** A short stroll from Worth Avenue, the yellow-stucco
HOTEL  Spanish-style facade and red-tile roof, and lobby with cypress ceilings
★  and stone floors, underscore this boutique hotel's Roaring '20s origins.
**Pros:** one of the best restaurants in town; attracts a hip crowd; gorgeous
courtyard; close to shopping and not far from the beach; free shuttle to
the hotel's sister property on the beach, the Omphoy. **Cons:** fitness center is tiny; small pool. ✉ *301 Australian Ave.* ☎ *561/655–7740* 🌐 *www.
thebraziliancourt.com* 🛏 *80 rooms* ⏷ *In-room: a/c, Internet, Wi-Fi.
In-hotel: restaurant, bar, pool, gym, spa, laundry facilities, some pets
allowed* ⍐ *No meals.*

$$$$  ▦ **The Breakers.** More than an opulent hotel, the Breakers is a modern
HOTEL  resort, built in an Italian Renaissance style, packed with amenities, from
Fodor'sChoice  a 20,000-square-foot luxury spa and Medditerranean-style beach club
★  to clubhouses for the 10 tennis courts and two 18-hole golf courses.
**Pros:** fine attention to detail throughout; beautiful room views; top-
rate golf and tennis facilities. **Cons:** big price tag. ✉ *1 S. County Rd.*
☎ *561/655–6611 or 888/273–2537* 🌐 *www.thebreakers.com* 🛏 *540
rooms, 68 suites* ⏷ *In-room: a/c, Internet, Wi-Fi. In-hotel: restaurants,*

**10**

*bars, golf courses, tennis courts, pools, gym, spa, beach, water sports, children's programs, business center, parking* ⁝◎⊦*No meals.*

**$$$$** ⊞ **The Chesterfield.** Two blocks north of Worth Avenue, the distinctive
HOTEL white-stucco hotel with coral-color stucco walls and red-and-white-striped awnings offers 54 inviting rooms ranging from small to spacious. **Pros:** turndown service; complimentary beverages in king rooms and suites; elegant rooms; you can open guest-room windows, which is a treat for those who hate air-conditioning **Cons:** small elevator; narrow steps leading to presidential suite. ✉ *363 Cocoanut Row* ☎ *561/659–5800 or 800/243–7871* ⊕ *www.chesterfieldpb.com* ⤴ *44 rooms, 11 suites* ⚒ *In-room: a/c, Internet. In-hotel: restaurant, bar, pool, business center, parking, some pets allowed* ⁝◎⊦*No meals.*

**$$$$** ⊞ **The Colony.** What distinguishes this legendary British colonial–style
HOTEL hotel is that it's only one block from Worth Avenue and one block from a beautiful beach on the Atlantic Ocean. **Pros:** close to shopping; rich history; lots of luxury. **Cons:** elevators are small; price tag is high. ✉ *155 Hammon Ave.* ☎ *561/655–5430 or 800/521–5525* ⊕ *www. thecolonypalmbeach.com* ⤴ *64 rooms, 16 suites, 3 penthouse suites, 7 2-bedroom villas with Jacuzzis* ⚒ *In-room: a/c, Wi-Fi. In-hotel: restaurant, bar, pools, spa, business center, parking, some pets allowed* ⁝◎⊦ *No meals.*

**$$$$** ⊞ **Four Seasons Resort Palm Beach.** Relaxed elegance is the watchword
RESORT at this four-story resort, which sits on 6 acres with a delightful beach
★ at the south end of town. **Pros:** outstanding restaurants; all rooms have balconies and ocean views; kids eat free; top-notch spa. **Cons:** far from nightlife; pricey. ✉ *2800 S. Ocean Blvd.* ☎ *561/582–2800 or 800/432–2335* ⊕ *www.fourseasons.com* ⤴ *210 rooms, 13 suites* ⚒ *In-room: a/c, Internet. In-hotel: restaurants, bars, tennis courts, pool, gym, spa, beach, children's programs, parking, some pets allowed* ⁝◎⊦*No meals.*

**$$$$** ⊞ **The Omphoy Ocean Resort.** From exotic ebony pillars in the lobby to
RESORT bronze-infused porcelain tile floors and a lounge area with a row of gongs guests are welcome to bang on, this Zen-like boutique hotel has a sexy sophisticated look. **Pros:** Michelle Bernstein restaurant; rooms have ocean views and most have balconies. **Cons:** the infinity pool is surrounded by a parking lot and you have to walk through or around the hotel to get to the beach from it. ✉ *2842 S. Ocean Blvd.* ☎ *561/540–6440 or 888/344–4321* ⊕ *www.omphoy.com* ⤴ *134 rooms, 10 suites* ⚒ *In-room: a/c, Wi-Fi. In-hotel: restaurants, bars, pool, gym, spa, beach, business center, parking, some pets allowed* ⁝◎⊦*No meals.*

# WEST PALM BEACH

*Across the Intracoastal Waterway from Palm Beach.*

Long considered Palm Beach's less-privileged stepsister, sprawling West Palm has evolved into an economically vibrant destination of its own, ranking as the cultural, entertainment, and business center of the entire county and territory to the north. High-rise buildings like the mammoth Palm Beach County Judicial Center and Courthouse and the State Administrative Building underscore the breadth of the city's governmental and corporate activity. The glittering Kravis Center for the Performing Arts is Palm Beach County's principal entertainment venue.

### GETTING HERE AND AROUND

West Palm Beach is across the Intracoastal Waterway from Palm Beach. The city's Palm Tran buses run between Worth Avenue and Royal Palm Way in Palm Beach and major areas of West Palm Beach and require exact change. Regular fares are $1.50. Alternatively, share space with local lawyers and shoppers on the free and frequent Molly's Trolleys, which makes continuous loops down Clematis Street, the city's main street, and through CityPlace, a shopping-restaurant-theater district. Hop on and off at any of the seven stops. The trolleys run Sunday to Wednesday 11–9 and Thursday to Saturday 11–11.

### ESSENTIALS

Transportation Contacts **Molly's Trolleys** (☎ *561/838–9511*). **Palm Tran** (☎ *561/841–4200*).

Visitor Information **Chamber of Commerce of the Palm Beaches** (✉ *401 N. Flagler Dr.* ☎ *561/833–3711*). **Palm Beach County Convention & Visitors Bureau** (✉ *1555 Palm Beach Lakes Blvd., Suite 800* ☎ *561/233–3000*).

## EXPLORING

With the $154 million City Center municipal and library complex and a $30 million waterfront complex with piers, a pavilion and a beach, downtown West Palm has an attractive, easy-to-walk downtown area. Along five blocks of beautifully landscaped Clematis Street, which ends at the Intracoastal Waterway and the new waterfront complex, are boutiques and outdoor cafés, plus the 400-seat Cuillo Centre for the Arts, which features shows and concerts; and Palm Beach Dramaworks, an intimate theater that often shows new plays. An exuberant nightlife has taken hold of the area. In fact, downtown rocks every Thursday from 6 pm on with Clematis by Night, a celebration of music, dance, art, and food at Centennial Square. Even on downtown's fringes there are sights of cultural interest.

West Palm Beach's outskirts, flat stretches lined with fast-food outlets and car dealerships, may not inspire, but are worth driving through to reach attractions scattered around the city's southern and western reaches. Several sites are especially rewarding for children and other animal and nature lovers.

### DOWNTOWN

**Ann Norton Sculpture Gardens.** This monument to the late American sculptor Ann Weaver Norton, second wife of Norton Museum founder Ralph H. Norton, includes a complex of art galleries in the main house and studio, plus 2½ acres of gardens, where you'll find 300 varieties of palm trees, seven granite figures, and six brick megaliths. The plantings were designed to attract native birds. Call ahead—hours sometimes vary. ✉ *253 Barcelona Rd.* ☎ *561/832–5328* ⊕ *www.ansg.org* ▭ *$5* ⊙ *Wed.–Sun. 10–4.*

The Armory Art Center in West Palm Beach helps students of all ages create works or art in various media.

**Armory Art Center.** Built by the WPA in 1939, the facility is now a non-profit art school hosting rotating exhibitions and art classes throughout the year. ✉ *1700 Parker Ave.* ☎ *561/832–1776* ⊕ *www.armoryart.org* ✉ *Free* ☼ *Weekdays 10–4, weekends 10–2.*

**Currie Park.** Frequent weekend festivals, including an annual celebration of seafood, take place at the scenic city park next to the Intracoastal Waterway. Sit on one of the piers and watch the yachts and fishing boats pass by. Put on your jogging shoes—the park is at the north end of a 6.3-mi biking-jogging-skating path. ✉ *N. Flagler Dr. at 23rd St.*

Fodor'sChoice
★
**Norton Museum of Art.** Constructed in 1941 by steel magnate Ralph H. and Elizabeth Norton, the museum has an extensive collection of 19th- and 20th-century American and European paintings—including works by Picasso, Monet, Matisse, Pollock, and O'Keeffe—and Chinese, contemporary, and photographic art. There are a sublime outdoor covered loggia, Chinese bronze and jade sculptures, and a library. Galleries, including the Great Hall, also showcase traveling exhibits. There's a good museum store, and lectures, programs, and concerts for children and adults. ■TIP→ One of the city's best-kept secrets is this museum's Café 1451, with its artfully presented dishes that taste as good as they look. ✉ *1451 S. Olive Ave.* ☎ *561/832–5196* ⊕ *www.norton.org* ✉ *$12* ☼ *Tues.–Sat. 10–5, Sun. 1–5.*

**Palm Beach Photographic Centre.** Fatima NeJame, who started the center in Delray Beach in 1977, achieved her dream of a larger exhibition center by moving it to the City Hall complex in West Palm Beach in 2009. The bright spacious gallery is devoted to photography. The second

## A GOOD TOUR: WEST PALM BEACH

Head south from downtown and turn right on Southern Boulevard, left onto Parker Avenue, and right onto Summit Boulevard to reach the **Palm Beach**. In the same area (turn right onto Dreher Trail) and also appealing to kids, the **South Florida Science Museum**, with its Aldrin Planetarium and McGinty Aquarium, is full of hands-on exhibits. If a quick game of croquet intrigues you, head to the **National Croquet Center**, less than 2 mi from the museum, by turning onto Summit Boulevard from Dreher Trail north and proceeding to Florida Mango Road, where you will turn left. Backtrack to Summit Boulevard and go west to the 150-acre **Pine Jog Environmental Education Center**. For more natural adventures, head farther west on Summit until you reach Forest Hill Boulevard, where you turn right to reach the **Okeeheelee Nature Center** and its miles of wooded trails. Now retrace your route to Summit Boulevard, drive east until you reach Military Trail, and take a left. Drive north to Southern Boulevard and turn west to reach **Lion Country Safari**, a 500-acre cageless zoo. For the last stop on this tour, backtrack to Military Trail and travel north to the **Mounts Botanical Gardens**.

### TIMING

Tailor your time based on specific interests, because you could easily spend most of a day at any of these attractions. Prepare yourself for heavy rush-hour traffic, and remember that sightseeing in the morning (not *too* early, to avoid rush hour) will be less congested.

floor is reserved for classes and has a large photo studio, but, with the digital age in mind, no darkroom. ⊠ *415 Clematis St.* ☎ *561/253–2600* ⊕ *www.workshop.org* ⊠ *Free* ☉ *Mon.–Thurs. 10–7, Fri. and Sat. 10–5, Sun. 1–5.*

### AWAY FROM DOWNTOWN

#### TOP ATTRACTIONS

**Lion Country Safari.** Drive your own vehicle along 8 mi of paved roads through a 500-acre cageless zoo with a thousand free-roaming animals. Lions, elephants, white rhinos, giraffes, zebras, antelopes, chimpanzees, and ostriches are among the wild things in residence. Lions are fenced away from roads, but there's a good chance you'll have a giraffe or two nudging at your window. Exhibits include the Kalahari, designed after a South African bush plateau and containing water buffalo and nilgai (the largest type of Asian antelope), and the Gir Forest, modeled after a game forest in India and showcasing a pride of lions. (For obvious reasons, no convertibles or pets are allowed.) A walk-through area has bird feeding and a petting zoo. You can also take a pontoon-boat tour, go paddleboating, play miniature golf, or send the kids off to the play area with rides and sports fields. There's also a restaurant and a snack shop. ⊠ *2003 Lion Country Safari Rd., at Southern Blvd. W, Loxahatchee* ☎ *561/793–1084* ⊕ *www. lioncountrysafari.com* ⊠ *$26.50; $5 parking fee* ☉ *Daily 9:30–5:30; last entrance 4:30.*

**10**

★ **Mounts Botanical Gardens.** Take advantage of balmy weather by walking among the tropical and subtropical plants here. Join a free tour or explore the 14 acres of exotic trees, rain-forest area, and butterfly and water gardens on your own. Many plants were significantly damaged during the 2004 and 2005 hurricanes, and new plantings will take years to reach maturity. There are lots of free brochures about tropical trees, flowers, and fruits in the main building. If you're feeling inspired, be sure to check out the gift shop's wide range of gardening books. ⊠ *531 N. Military Trail* ☎ *561/233–1757* ⊕ *www.mounts.org* ⊠ *Gardens: $5 suggested donation; tours $5* ☉ *Mon.–Sat. 8:30–4, Sun. noon–4.*

★ **National Croquet Center.** The world's largest croquet complex, the 10-acre center is also the headquarters for the U.S. Croquet Association. Vast expanses of manicured lawn are the stage for fierce competitions—in no way resembling the casual backyard games where kids play with wide wire wickets. There's also a clubhouse with a pro shop and Café Croquet, with verandas for dining and viewing, and a museum hall. You have to be a member, or a guest of a member, to reserve a lawn every day but Saturday, when lessons are free and lawns are open to all. ⊠ *700 Florida Mango Rd., at Summit Blvd.* ☎ *561/478–2300* ⊕ *www. croquetnational.com* ⊠ *Free admission; full day of play $25* ☉ *June– Sept., Tues.–Sat. 9–5; Oct.–May, daily 9–5.*

☾ **Palm Beach Zoo.** At this 23-acre wild kingdom there are more than 125 species of animals, from Florida panthers to the giant Aldabra tortoise. Here you'll find the country's first outdoor exhibit of Goeldi's monkeys. The Tropics of America exhibit has 6 acres of rain forest plus an aviary, Maya ruins, and an Amazon River village. Also notable are a nature trail, the otter exhibit, a children's petting zoo, merry-go-round, interactive fountain and a restaurant overlooking the river. ⊠ *1301 Summit Blvd.* ☎ *561/533–0887* ⊕ *www.palmbeachzoo.org* ⊠ *$16.95* ☉ *Daily 9–5.*

### WORTH NOTING

☾ **Okeeheelee Nature Center.** Explore 5 mi of trails through 90 acres of western Palm Beach County's native pine flatwoods and wetlands. A visitor center gift shop has hands-on exhibits and offers guided walks by the center's volunteers. ⊠ *7715 Forest Hill Blvd.* ☎ *561/233–1400* ⊠ *Free* ☉ *Visitor center Tues.–Fri. 10–4:35, Sat. 8:15–4:30, Sun 10-4:30; trails daily dawn–dusk.*

☾ **Pine Jog Environmental Education Center.** The draw here is 135 acres of mostly undisturbed Florida pine flatwoods with 2½-mi of self-guided trails. Demonstration landscaping and interpretive signs around the Gold L.E.E.D. certified buildings teach kids about sustainable living. School groups use the trails during the week; special events include camping and campfires. The gift shop is closed on Saturday. Call for an event schedule. ⊠ *6301 Summit Blvd.* ☎ *561/686–6600* ⊕ *www. pinejog.fau.edu* ⊠ *Free* ☉ *Weekdays 9–4, Sat. 9–2 (trails only).*

☾ **South Florida Science Museum.** Here at the museum, which includes the Aldrin Planetarium and McGinty Aquarium, there are hands-on exhibits with touch tanks and laser shows with music by the likes of

Dave Matthews. Galaxy Golf is a 9-hole science challenge. Weather permitting you can observe the heavens on Friday night through the most powerful telescope in South Florida. ⊠ *4801 Dreher Trail N* ☎ *561/832–1988* ⊕ *www.sfsm.org* ⌂ *$11.95, planetarium $4, laser show $10, galaxy golf $2* ⊙ *Weekdays 10–5, Sat. 10–6, Sun. noon–6.*

**OFF THE
BEATEN
PATH**

Forty miles west of West Palm Beach, rimming the western edges of Palm Beach and Martin counties, **Lake Okeechobee,** the second-largest freshwater lake completely within the United States, is girdled by 120 mi of road yet remains shielded from sight for almost its entire circumference. Lake Okeechobee—the Seminole's Big Water and the gateway of the great Everglades watershed—measures 730 square mi, roughly 33 mi north–south, and 30 mi east–west, with an average natural depth of only 10 feet (flood control brings the figure up to 12 feet and deeper). Six major lock systems and 32 separate water-control structures manage the water. Encircling the lake is a 34-foot-high grassy levee—locals call it "the wall"—and the Lake Okeechobee Scenic Trail, a segment of the Florida National Scenic Trail, an easy flat ride for bikers. ∎TIP➔ There's no shade, so wear a hat, sunscreen, and bug repellent. Be sure to bring lots of bottled water, too, because restaurants and stores are few and far between.

## SPORTS AND THE OUTDOORS

### GOLF

**Palm Beach National Golf & Country Club.** This classic course has 18 holes and a Joe Lee championship layout; greens fees $49/$75. The Joanne Carner Golf Academy is based here. ⊠ *7500 St. Andrews Rd., Lake Worth* ☎ *561/965–3381* ⊕ *www.palmbeachnational.com.*

## SHOPPING

The free downtown trolley runs a continuous loop linking Clematis Street and CityPlace, so you won't miss a shop.

★ **Antique Row.** West Palm's "South Dixie Highway" is the destination for those who are interested in interesting home decor. From thrift shops to the most exclusive stores, it is all here—furniture, lighting, art, junk, fabric, frames, tile, and rugs. So if you're looking for an art deco, French-provincial, or Mizner pièce de résistance, big or small, schedule a few hours for an Antique Row stroll. You'll find bargains during the off-season (May to November). Antique Row runs north–south from Belvedere Road to Forest Hill Boulevard, although most stores are bunched between Belvedere Road and Southern Boulevard.

**Clematis Street.** If you're looking for a mix of food, art, performance, landscaping, and retailing, then head to renewed downtown West Palm around Clematis Street, which runs west-east from Dixie Highway to Flagler Drive and the new waterfront complex. Water-view parks with attractive gardens—and fountains where kids can cool off—add to the pleasure of browsing, window-shopping, and resting at an outdoor café. Hip national retailers such as Design Within Reach and the Jean Bar blend in with restaurants, pubs, and nightclubs.

**10**

**CityPlace.** The 55-acre, four-block-by-four-block commercial and residential complex centered on Rosemary Avenue attracts people of all ages to with restaurants, cafés, outdoor bars, a 20-screen Muvico, the Harriet Himmel Theater, and a 36,000-gallon dance, water, and light show. The dining, shopping, and entertainment are all family-friendly. Among CityPlace's stores are popular national retailers Macy's, Armani Exchange, Pottery Barn, Lucky Brand Jeans, Nine West, Sephora, BCBG Maxazria, Gap, Banana Republic, Anthropologie, and Restoration Hardware. There are also shops unique to Florida. Behind the punchy, brightly colored clothing in the front window of C. Orrico (☎ *561/832–9203*) are family fashions and accessories by Lily Pulitzer. ⊠ *700 S. Rosemary Ave.* ☎ *561/366–1000* ⊕ *www.cityplace.com.*

## NIGHTLIFE AND THE ARTS

### NIGHTLIFE

**Blue Martini.** CityPlace comes alive at this bar, where eclectic music attracts a diverse crowd. ⊠ *550 S. Rosemary Ave.* ☎ *561/835–8601.*

**Dr. Feelgood's Rock Bar & Grill.** There are guitars hanging above the bar and a DJ booth made from a 1957 Chevy. Vince Neil, Mötley Crüe's lead singer, is the owner. ⊠ *219 Clematis St.* ☎ *561/833–6500.*

**ER Bradley's Saloon.** People of all ages congregate to hang out and socialize at this open-air restaurant and bar to gaze at the Intracoastal Waterway. ⊠ *104 Clematis St.* ☎ *561/833–3520.*

### THE ARTS

**Palm Beach Opera.** Five productions, including the Vocal Competition Grand Finals, are staged from December to April at the Kravis Center with English translations projected above the stage. The family opera series includes matinee performances such as *Hansel & Gretel*; tickets are $20 to $165. ⊠ *415 S. Olive Ave.* ☎ *561/833–7888* ⊕ *www.pbopera.org.*

★ **Raymond F. Kravis Center for the Performing Arts.** This center stars amid the treasury of local arts attractions and the crown jewel is the 2,193-seat Dreyfoos Hall, a glass, copper, and marble showcase just steps from the restaurants and shops of CityPlace. The center also boasts the 300-seat Rinker Playhouse and the Gosman Amphitheatre, which holds 1,400 in seats and on the lawn. A packed year-round schedule unfolds here with drama, dance, and music. Kravis on Broadway features a blockbuster lineup of Broadway's biggest touring productions; Miami City Ballet, the Palm Beach Pops, and Florida Stage, a theater company that presents new and emerging plays, also perform here. ⊠ *701 Okeechobee Blvd.* ☎ *561/832–7469* ⊕ *www.kravis.org.*

## WHERE TO EAT

$ ✕ **Havana.** Decorated with vintage travel posters of its namesake city,
CUBAN this two-level restaurant serves such authentic Cuban specialties as roast-pork sandwiches and chicken slowly cooked in Spanish sauce. Lunch and dinner dishes are enhanced by the requisite black beans and rice. Open until 1 am Friday and Saturday, this friendly place

attracts a late-night crowd. The popular walk-up window serves strong Cuban coffee, sugary fried churros, and fruit juices in exotic flavors like mamey, mango, papaya, guava, and *guanabana.* ✉ *6801 S. Dixie Hwy.* ☎ *561/547–9799* ⊕ *www.havanacubanfood.com.*

$ ✕**Howley's.** Since 1950 this diner's eat-in counter and "cooked in
AMERICAN sight, it must be right" motto has made a congenial setting for meeting old friends and making new ones. Forgo the counter for the 1950s-style tables or sit out on the patio. The café attracts a loyal clientele for breakfast, lunch, and dinner with such specialties as turkey and dressing, burgers, and chicken salad. ✉ *4700 S. Dixie Hwy.* ☎ *561/833–5691.*

$$ ✕**Il Bellagio.** In the center of CityPlace, this European-style bistro offers
ITALIAN Italian specialties and a wide variety of fine wines. The menu includes classics like chicken parmigiana, risotto, and fettuccine Alfredo. Pizzas from the wood-burning oven are especially tasty. Service is friendly and efficient, but the overall noise level tends to be high. Sit at the outdoor tables next to the main plaza's dancing fountains. ✉ *CityPlace, 600 S. Rosemary Ave.* ☎ *561/659–6160* ⊕ *www.ilbellagiocityplace.com.*

¢ ✕**Middle East Bakery.** This hole-in-the-wall Middle Eastern bakery, deli,
MEDITERRANEAN and market is packed at lunchtime with regulars who are on a first-name basis with the gang behind the counter. From the nondescript parking lot the place doesn't look like much, but inside, delicious hot and cold Mediterranean treats await. Choose from traditional gyro sandwiches and lamb salads with sides of grape leaves, tabbouleh, and couscous. ✉ *327 5th St., at Olive Ave.* ☎ *561/659–7322* ⊗ *Closed Sun.*

## WHERE TO STAY

*For expanded hotel reviews, visit Fodors.com.*

$$$ ⊞ **Grandview Gardens Bed & Breakfast.** This 1923 Spanish-style bed-and-
B&B/INN breakfast, housed in a cheery yellow building, is conveniently located
★ next to Howard Park, across from the Armory Art Center, and a short walk from the Convention Center, CityPlace, and the Kravis Center. **Pros:** private entrances; pool; multilingual owners. **Cons:** not close to the beach; steps to climb. ✉ *1608 Lake Ave.* ☎ *561/833–9023* ⊕ *www. grandview-gardens.net* ⚓ *5 rooms, 1 cottage* ⚓ *In-room: a/c, Internet. In-hotel: pool, parking* ⊙| *Breakfast.*

$$$$ ⊞ **Hampton Inn & Suites in Wellington.** The four-story hotel, about 10 mi
HOTEL west of downtown West Palm Beach, has the feeling of a ritzy clubhouse, with rich wood paneling, hunt prints, and elegant chandeliers. **Pros:** complimentary hot breakfast; free high-speed Internet access; near shopping. **Cons:** no restaurant. ✉ *2155 Wellington Green Dr.* ☎ *561/472–9696* ⊕ *www.hamptoninn.com* ⚓ *122 rooms, 32 suites* ⚓ *In-room: a/c, Wi-Fi. In-hotel: pool, gym* ⊙| *Breakfast.*

$$$ ⊞ **Hotel Biba.** In the El Cid historic district, this 1940s-era motel has got-
HOTEL ten a fun stylish revamp from designer Barbara Hulanicki: each room has a vibrant mélange of colors, along with handcrafted mirrors, mosaic bathroom floors, and custom mahogany furnishings. **Pros:** cool design; popular wine bar. **Cons:** water pressure is weak; bathrooms are tiny;

10

noisy when the bar is open late. ⊠ *320 Belvedere Rd.* ☎ *561/832–0094* ⊕ *www.hotelbiba.com* ⇆ *43 rooms* ⅛ *In-room: a/c, Wi-Fi. In-hotel: bar, pool* ⊺⊙⊺ *No meals.*

# SOUTH TO BOCA RATON

Strung together by Route A1A, the towns between Palm Beach and Boca Raton are notable for their variety, from high-rise condominiums to small-town public beaches. In one town you'll find a cluster of art galleries and fancy dining, and the very next town will yield mostly hamburger joints and mom-and-pop stores.

## LAKE WORTH

*2 mi south of West Palm Beach, off I–95 or Federal Hwy.*

For years, tourists looked here mainly for inexpensive lodging and easy access to Palm Beach, since a bridge leads from the mainland to a barrier island with Lake Worth's beach. Now Lake Worth has several blocks of restaurants, nightclubs, shops, and art galleries, making this a worthy destination on its own.

### GETTING HERE AND AROUND

To drive to Lake Worth from West Palm Beach, drive 2 mi south on Interstate 95 or Federal Highway.

### ESSENTIALS

**Visitor Information Lake Worth Chamber of Commerce** (⊠ *501 Lake Ave.* ☎ *561/582–4401*).

### EXPLORING

**Museum of Polo & Hall of Fame.** Start here for an introduction to polo. See polo memorabilia, art, and a film on the history of the sport. ⊠ *9011 Lake Worth Rd.* ☎ *561/969–3210* ⊕ *www.polomuseum.com* ⊠ *Free* ⊙ *May–Dec., weekdays 10–4; Jan.–Apr., weekdays 10–4, Sat. 10–2.*

### WHERE TO EAT

¢  ✕ **Benny's on the Beach.** Perched on the Lake Worth Pier, Benny's has

AMERICAN  diner-style food that's cheap and filling, but the spectacular view of the sun glistening on the water and the waves crashing directly below is what dining here is all about. Get here early—it doesn't serve dinner. ⊠ *10 Ocean Ave.* ☎ *561/582–9001* ⊕ *www.bennysonthebeach.com* ⊙ *No dinner.*

$  ✕ **Bizaare Avenue Café.** Decorated with a mix of artwork and antiques,

ECLECTIC  this cozy bistro, inspired by TV's *Friends,* fits right into downtown Lake Worth's groovy, eclectic scene. Artwork and furnishings can be purchased. Daily specials are available on both the lunch and dinner menus, where crepes, pizzas, pastas, and salads are the staples. ⊠ *921 Lake Ave.* ☎ *561/588–4488* ⊕ *www.bizaareavecafe.com.*

$$$  ✕ **Paradiso.** Arguably downtown Lake Worth's finest Italian restaurant,

ITALIAN  this is the place to go for a romantic evening. Veal chops, seafood, cheese ravioli, and risotto are all good choices. Don't miss the chocolate Grand Marnier soufflé for dessert. As the name implies, the food is heavenly. ⊠ *625 Lucerne Ave.* ☎ *561/547–2500* ⊕ *www.paradisolakeworth.com.*

The posh Palm Beach area has its share of luxury villas on the water; many are Mediterranean in style.

## WHERE TO STAY

*For expanded hotel reviews, visit Fodors.com.*

$$$–$$$$ B&B/INN ★ **Mango Inn.** It's only a 15-minute walk to the beach from this B&B dating from 1915. **Pros:** close to shops and restaurants; breakfasts served poolside; some suites have whirlpool tubs. **Cons:** some rooms are quite small. ✉ *128 N. Lakeside Dr.* ☎ *561/533–6900 or 888/626–4619* *www.mangoinn.com* *7 rooms, 3 suites, 1 cottage* *In-room: a/c, kitchen, Internet. In-hotel: pool, some age restrictions* *Breakfast.*

$$$ B&B/INN ★ **Sabal Palm House.** Built in 1936, this two-story B&B is a short walk from the Intracoastal Waterway, and each room is inspired by a different artist—including Renoir, Dalí, Norman Rockwell, and Chagall. **Pros:** fresh flowers in guest rooms; extra pillows; close to shops and restaurants. **Cons:** no pool. ✉ *109 N. Golfview Rd.* ☎ *561/582–1090 or 888/722–2572* *www.sabalpalmhouse.com* *5 rooms, 2 suites* *In-hotel: some pets allowed* *Breakfast.*

10

# LANTANA

*2 mi south of Lake Worth, off I–95 or Federal Hwy.*

Lantana—just a bit farther south from Palm Beach than Lake Worth—has inexpensive lodging and a bridge connecting the town to its own beach on a barrier island. Tucked between Lantana and Boynton Beach is **Manalapan,** a tiny but posh residential community.

### ESSENTIALS

Visitor Information **Lantana Chamber of Commerce** (✉ *212 Iris Ave.* ☎ *561/585–8664*).

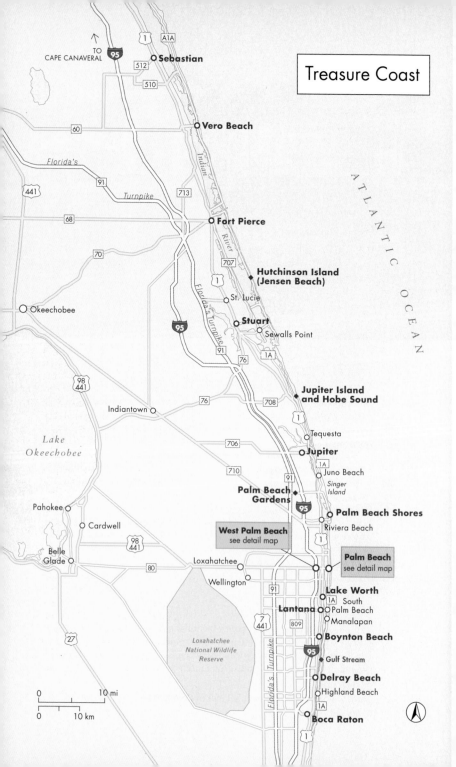

# Treasure Coast

TO CAPE CANAVERAL

95

1

A1A

512

510

Sebastian

60

Vero Beach

Florida's

91

441

Turnpike

713

68

70

Indian

River

Fort Pierce

707

Hutchinson Island
(Jensen Beach)

1

95

St. Lucie

Florida's Turnpike

Okeechobee

Stuart

Sewalls Point

76

91

76

1A

98
441

Jupiter Island
and Hobe Sound

708

1

Indiantown

706

Tequesta

Lake
Okeechobee

710

Jupiter

1A

91

Juno Beach

Singer
Island

Palm Beach
Gardens

95

Pahokee

Cardwell

Palm Beach Shores

Riviera Beach

West Palm Beach
see detail map

1

Belle
Glade

98
441

Palm Beach
see detail map

80

Loxahatchee

Wellington

91

Lake Worth

1A    South
Palm Beach

27

Lantana

Manalapan

7
441

809

Boynton Beach

Loxahatchee
National Wildlife
Reserve

95

Gulf Stream

Delray Beach

Highland Beach

1A

0        10 mi

Florida's Turnpike

Boca Raton

0     10 km

1

ATLANTIC OCEAN

## BEACHES

**Lantana Public Beach.** Ideal for sprawling, beachcombing, or power-walking, Lantana is also worthy for its proximity to one of the most popular food concessions in town, the **Dune Deck Café.** Here the choices are standard, but the food is particularly fresh and the portions are hearty. Try an omelet with a side of fries and melon wedges, Greek salad, homemade yogurt with seasonal fruit topped with honey, or a side of banana-nut bread. There are daily breakfast and lunch specials; dining is outdoors under yellow canopies perched over the beach. ⊠ *100 N. Ocean Ave.* ☎ *561/582–0472* 🅿 *Parking $1.50 for 1 hr* ☉ *Daily 9–4:45.*

## SPORTS AND THE OUTDOORS

### FISHING

**B-Love Fleet.** Three deep-sea fishing excursions depart daily: 8–noon, 1–5, and 6:30–10:30. No reservations are needed; just show up 30 minutes before the boat is scheduled to leave. The cost is $37 per person and includes fishing license, bait, and tackle. ⊠ *314 E. Ocean Ave.* ☎ *561/588–7612.*

## WHERE TO EAT AND STAY

*For expanded hotel reviews, visit Fodors.com.*

$$$
SEAFOOD
✗ **Old Key Lime House.** Overlooking the Intracoastal Waterway, the 1889 Lyman family house has grown in spurts over the years and its latest addition is the Manatee Observation Deck. This is an informal seafood house covered by a chickee hut built by the Seminole Indians. It's the largest viewing home for Gator Football. The panoramic water views are the main appeal here for adults—kids love to feed the fish and rock in the glider seats on the dock. Don't miss key lime pie—the house specialty was featured in *Bon Appétit* magazine. ⊠ *300 E. Ocean Ave.* ☎ *561/533–5220* ⊕ *www.oldkeylimehouse.com.*

$$$
SEAFOOD
✗ **Station House.** The best Maine lobster in South Florida might well reside at this delicious dive, where all the seafood is cooked to perfection. Sticky seats and tablecloths are an accepted part of the scene, so don't wear your best duds. Although it's casual and family-friendly, reservations are recommended since it's a local favorite. Station Grill, across the street, is less seafood oriented but every "bite" as good. ⊠ *233 Lantana Rd.* ☎ *561/547–9487* ⊕ *www.stationhouserestaurants. com* ☉ *No lunch.*

$$$$
RESORT
★
🏨 **Ritz-Carlton, Palm Beach.** A huge double-sided marble fireplace dominates the elegant lobby of this hotel (which is actually in Manalapan) and foreshadows the luxury of the guest rooms, which have richly upholstered furnishings and marble tubs. **Pros:** gorgeous rooms; magnificent ocean views; shops across the street. **Cons:** not close to golf course; 15-minute drive to Palm Beach. ⊠ *100 S. Ocean Blvd., Manalapan* ☎ *561/533–6000 or 800/241–3333* ⊕ *www.ritz-carlton.com* 🛏 *310 rooms* ⅃ *In-room: a/c, Internet, Wi-Fi. In-hotel: restaurants, bars, tennis courts, pools, spa, beach, water sports, children's programs, business center, parking* ⦿ *No meals.*

**10**

# BOYNTON BEACH

*3 mi south of Lantana, off I–95 or Federal Hwy.*

In 1884, when fewer than 50 settlers lived in the area, Nathan Boynton, a Civil War veteran from Michigan, paid $25 for 500 acres with a mile-long stretch of beachfront thrown in. How things have changed, with today's population at about 118,000 and property values still on an upswing. Far enough from Palm Beach to remain low-key, Boynton Beach has two parts, the mainland and the barrier island—the town of Ocean Ridge—connected by two bridges.

### GETTING HERE AND AROUND

From Lantana, drive south 3 mi on Interstate 95 or south on Federal Highway (U.S. 1) to reach Boynton Beach.

### ESSENTIALS

Visitor Information **Boynton Beach Chamber of Commerce** (⊠ *1880 N. Congress Ave., Suite 106* ☎ *561/732–9501).*

## EXPLORING

**Arthur R. Marshall–Loxahatchee National Wildlife Refuge.** The most robust part of the Everglades, this 221-square-mi refuge is one of three huge water-retention areas accounting for much of the Everglades outside the national park. These areas are managed less to protect natural resources, however, than to prevent flooding to the south. Start from the visitor center, where there is a marsh trail to a 20-foot-high observation tower overlooking a pond. The boardwalk takes you through a dense cypress swamp. There's also a 5½-mi canoe trail, best for experienced canoeists since it's overgrown. Wildlife viewing is good year-round, and you can fish for bass and panfish. ⊠ *10216 Lee Rd., off U.S. 441 between Rte. 804 and Rte. 806* ☎ *561/734–8303* 🖼 *$5 per vehicle, pedestrians $1* ⊙ *Daily sunrise–sunset; visitor center, weekdays 9–4, weekends 9–4:30.*

**Schoolhouse Children's Museum.** Boynton Beach's history is highlighted through interactive exhibits that make the museum a kid-and-parent pleaser. In this 1913 schoolhouse children can milk a mock cow or pick and wash plastic vegetables at the Pepper Patch Farm. Kids can buy tickets and dress up for a "time travel" train ride that immerses them in Boynton's history. A great outdoor playground castle is adjacent to the museum. ⊠ *129 E. Ocean Ave.* ☎ *561/742–6780* ⊕ *www. schoolhousemuseum.org* 🖼 *$5* ⊙ *Tues.–Sat. 10–5.*

## BEACH

**Boynton Beach Oceanfront Park.** An inviting beach, boardwalk, concessions, grills, and playground await. ⊠ *6415 Ocean Blvd.* ☎ *No phone* 🖼 *Parking $10 per day* ⊙ *Daily 7:30 am–11 pm.*

## SPORTS AND THE OUTDOORS

### FISHING

**Arthur R. Marshall–Loxahatchee National Wildlife Refuge.** West of Boynton Beach, fish the canal. There's a boat ramp, and the waters are decently productive, but bring your own equipment. ⊠ *10119 Lee Rd., off U.S. 441 between Rte. 804 and Rte. 806* ☎ *561/734–8303.*

**Boynton Beach Inlet Pier.** Here you can catch fish swimming between the Atlantic and Intracoastal Waterway. ✉ *6990 N. Ocean Blvd.* ☎ *No phone.*

### GOLF

**Links at Boynton Beach.** Find both an 18-hole course and 9-hole executive course; greens fees $27–$39 champion course, $39–$49 family course (rates vary with time of day; it's busier and costs more in the morning). ✉ *8020 Jog Rd.* ☎ *561/742–6500.*

### WHERE TO EAT

$

AMERICAN

✕ **Banana Boat.** A mainstay for local boaters who cruise up and down the Intracoastal Waterway, Banana Boat is easily recognizable by the lighthouse on its roof. On weekends, casual crowds clad in tank tops, flip-flops, and bikinis dance to live island music while downing frozen drinks. The kitchen serves fish-and-chips, burgers, and ribs. ✉ *739 E. Ocean Ave.* ☎ *561/732–9400* ⊕ *www.bananaboatboynton.com.*

## DELRAY BEACH

*2 mi south of Gulf Stream via I–95 or Federal Hwy.*

A onetime artists' retreat with a small settlement of Japanese farmers, Delray has grown into a sophisticated beach town. Atlantic Avenue, the once dilapidated main drag, has evolved into a more-than-a-mile-long stretch of palm-dotted sidewalks, lined with stores, art galleries, and dining establishments. Running east–west and ending at the beach, it's a pleasant place for a stroll, day or night. Another active pedestrian way begins at the eastern edge of Atlantic Avenue and runs along the big, broad swimming beach that extends north to George Bush Boulevard and south to Casuarina Road.

### GETTING HERE AND AROUND

To get to Delray Beach from Boynton Beach, drive 2 mi south on Interstate 95 or Federal Highway (U.S. 1).

### ESSENTIALS

**Visitor Information Delray Beach Chamber of Commerce** (✉ *64-A S.E. 5th Ave.* ☎ *561/278–0424*).

10

### EXPLORING

**Colony Hotel.** The chief landmark along Atlantic Avenue since 1926 is this Mediterranean revival–style hotel, which is a member of the National Trust for Historic Preservation. Walk through the lobby to the parking lot of the hotel where original stable "garages" still stand—relics of the days when hotel guests would arrive via horse and carriage. ✉ *525 E. Atlantic Ave.* ☎ *561/276–4123.*

Fodor's Choice

★

**Morikami Museum and Japanese Gardens.** Out in the boonies west of Delray Beach seems an odd place to encounter the East, but this is exactly where you can find a cultural and recreational facility heralding the Yamato Colony of Japanese farmers. The on-site Cornell Café serves light Asian fare. If you don't get your fill of orchids, the American Orchid Society's 20,000-square-foot headquarters is across the street. ✉ *4000 Morikami Park Rd.* ☎ *561/495–0233* ⊕ *www.morikami.org* ✉ *$12* ☉ *Tues.–Sun. 10–5.*

Morikami Museum and Japanese Gardens gives a taste of the Orient through its exhibits and tea ceremonies.

**Old School Square Cultural Arts Center.** Just off Atlantic Avenue is this cluster of several museums set in restored school buildings dating from 1913 and 1926. The **Cornell Museum of Art & History** offers ever-changing art exhibits. During its season, the **Crest Theatre** showcases performances by local and touring troupes in the restored 1925 Delray High School building. ⊠ *51 N. Swinton Ave.* ☎ *561/243–7922* ⊕ *www. oldschool.org* ☞ *$6* ⊙ *Tues.–Sat. 10:30–4:30, Sun. 1–4:30.*

### BEACHES

**Delray Beach Municipal Beach.** A scenic walking path follows the main stretch of this public beach, which stretches 2 mi, half of it supervised by lifeguards. Reefs off the coast are popular with divers. ⊠ *Atlantic Ave. at Rte. A1A*

★ **Seagate Beach.** Enjoy many types of water-sports rentals—sailing, kayaking, windsurfing, Boogie boarding, surfing, snorkeling—or scuba diving at a sunken Spanish galleon less than ½ mi offshore. ⊠ *½ mi south of Atlantic Ave. at Rte. A1A.*

### SPORTS AND THE OUTDOORS

#### BIKING

There's a bicycle path in Barwick Park and a special oceanfront lane along Route A1A.

**Richwagen's Bike & Sport.** Rent bikes by the hour or day and they'll come along with locks, baskets, helmets, and maps. ⊠ *298 N.E. 6th Ave.* ☎ *561/276–4234.*

**WATERSKIING**

**Lake Ida Park.** You can water-ski whether you're a beginner or a veteran. The park has a boat ramp, a slalom course, and a trick ski course. ⊠ *2929 Lake Ida Rd.*

## SHOPPING

**Atlantic Avenue.** This charming area, from Swinton Avenue east to the ocean, has maintained much of its small-town integrity. It showcases art galleries, shops, and restaurants.

**Escentials Apothecaries.** In the historic Colony Hotel, this shop is packed with all things good smelling for your bath, body, and home. ⊠ *533 Atlantic Ave.* ☎ *561/276–7070.*

**Snappy Turtle.** Mackenzie-Childs and Lilly Pulitzer mingle with other fun fashions for the home and family. ⊠ *1100 Atlantic Ave.* ☎ *561/ 276–8088.*

## NIGHTLIFE

**Boston's on the Beach.** Groove to reggae on Monday night and live music from jazz to country to rock most other nights. ⊠ *40 S. Ocean Blvd.* ☎ *561/278–3364.*

**Dada.** Bands play in the living room of a historic house. It's a place where those who don't drink will also feel comfortable. ⊠ *52 N. Swinton Ave.* ☎ *561/330–3232.*

**Delux.** A young hip crowd dances all night long. ⊠ *16 E. Atlantic Ave.* ☎ *561/279–4792.*

## WHERE TO EAT

$$$

AMERICAN

★

✕ **32 East.** Although restaurants come and go on a trendy street like Atlantic Avenue, 32 East remains one of the best restaurants in Delray Beach. A daily menu of wood-oven pizzas, salads, soups, seafood, and meat is all based on what is fresh and plentiful. Dark-wood accents and dim lighting make this large restaurant seem cozy. There's a packed bar in front and an open kitchen in back. ⊠ *32 E. Atlantic Ave.* ☎ *561/276– 7868* ⊕ *www.32east.com* ⊙ No lunch.

$$

BRITISH

✕ **Blue Anchor.** Yes, this pub was actually shipped from England, where it stood for 150 years in London's historic Chancery Lane. There it was a watering hole for famed Englishmen, including Winston Churchill. The Delray Beach incarnation has stuck to authentic British pub fare. Chow down on a ploughman's lunch (a chunk of Stilton cheese, a hunk of bread, and pickled onions), shepherd's pie, fish-and-chips, and bangers and mash (sausages with mashed potatoes). Don't be surprised to find a rugby game on TV. English beers and ales are on tap and by the bottle. It's a late-night place open until at least 2. Classic rock and swing music are featured on Thursday nights. ⊠ *804 E. Atlantic Ave.* ☎ *561/272–7272* ⊕ *www.theblueanchor.com.*

¢

AMERICAN

★

✕ **Old School Bakery.** This place concentrates on sandwich making at its best. Particularly worthy is the cherry chicken salad sandwich with Brie on multigrain. Apart from sandwiches and soups served for lunch every day, order from a diverse baked-goods menu with artisan breads, pastries, several kinds of cookies, and even biscotti. The bakery is pri-

**10**

marily takeout, but there are a few small tables in an adjacent open-air courtyard. ⊠ *814 E. Atlantic Ave.* ☎ *561/243–8059.*

### WHERE TO STAY

*For expanded hotel reviews, visit Fodors.com.*

**$$$**
HOTEL
⚏ **Colony Hotel & Cabana Club.** In the heart of downtown Delray, this charming building dates back to 1926. **Pros:** great location; close to restaurants; shuttle to the beach. **Cons:** pool is a car or tram ride away at the beach club; breakfast buffet servings are repetitious. ⊠ *525 E. Atlantic Ave.* ☎ *561/276–4123 or 800/552–2363* ⊕ *www.thecolonyhotel. com* ⤳ *69 rooms* ⌂ *In-room: a/c, Internet, Wi-Fi. In-hotel: bar, pool, beach, parking* ⦿| *Breakfast.*

**$$$$**
HOTEL
⚏ **Delray Beach Marriott.** By far the largest property in Delray Beach, this five-story hotel has a stellar location at the east end of Atlantic Avenue. **Pros:** great location; near nightlife; luxurious spa. **Cons:** sprawling resort; chain-hotel feel; service can be impersonal. ⊠ *10 N. Ocean Blvd.* ☎ *561/274–3200* ⊕ *www.delraybeachmarriott.com* ⤳ *269 rooms, 84 suites* ⌂ *In-room: a/c, Wi-Fi. In-hotel: restaurants, bars, pool, gym, spa, beach, laundry facilities, parking* ⦿| *No meals.*

**$$$**
B&B/INN
★
⚏ **Sundy House.** Just about everything in this bungalow-style B&B is executed to perfection. **Pros:** beautiful property; excellent restaurant; quiet area. **Cons:** not on the beach. ⊠ *106 Swinton Ave.* ☎ *561/272–5678 or 877/434–9601* ⊕ *www.sundyhouse.com* ⤳ *11 rooms* ⌂ *In-room: Wi-Fi. In-hotel: restaurant, bar, pool* ⦿| *Breakfast.*

# BOCA RATON

*6 mi south of Delray Beach, off I–95.*

Less than an hour south of Palm Beach and anchoring the county's south end, upscale Boca Raton has much in common with its fabled cousin. Both reflect the unmistakable architectural influence of Addison Mizner, their principal developer in the mid-1920s. The meaning of the name Boca Raton (pronounced boca rah-*tone*) often arouses curiosity, with many folks mistakenly assuming it means "rat's mouth." Historians say the probable origin is Boca Ratones, an ancient Spanish geographical term for an inlet filled with jagged rocks or coral. Miami's Biscayne Bay had such an inlet, and in 1823 a mapmaker copying Miami terrain confused the more northern inlet, thus mistakenly labeling this area Boca Ratones. No matter what, you'll know you've arrived in the heart of downtown when you spot the town hall's gold dome on the main street, Federal Highway.

### GETTING HERE AND AROUND

To get to Boca Raton from Delray Beach, drive south 6 mi on Interstate 95 or Federal Highway (U.S. 1).

TOURS **Boca Raton Historical Society.** Trolley tour city sites on Thursday. The tours are seasonal; call for information. ⊠ *71 N. Federal Hwy.* ☎ *561/395–6766* ⊕ *www.bocahistory.org.*

### ESSENTIALS

**Visitor Information Boca Raton Chamber of Commerce** (⊠ *1800 N. Dixie Hwy.* ☎ *561/395–4433*).

## EXPLORING

**2 East El Camino Real**. Built in 1925 as the headquarters of the Mizner Development Corporation, this is an example of Mizner's characteristic Spanish-revival architectural style, with its wrought-iron grilles and handmade tiles. As for Mizner's grandiose vision of El Camino Real, the architect-promoter once prepared brochures promising a sweeping wide boulevard with Venetian canals and arching bridges. Camino Real is attractive, heading east to the Boca Raton Resort & Club, but don't count on feeling like you're in Venice. ⊠ *2 E. Camino Real*.

**Boca Raton Museum of Art**. An interactive children's gallery and changing exhibition galleries showcase internationally known artists at this museum in a spectacular building in the Mizner Park shopping center. The permanent collection upstairs includes works by Picasso, Degas, Matisse, Klee, and Modigliani, as well as notable pre-Columbian art. ⊠ *501 Plaza Real* ☎ *561/392–2500* ⊕ *www.bocamuseum.org* ☐ *$8* ⊙ *Tues. 10–5, Wed. 10–9, Thurs. and Fri. 10–7, Sat. noon–7, Sun. noon–5.*

**Children's Science Explorium**. This hands-on science center offers interactive exhibits, programs, and camps designed to enhance 5- to 12-year-old explorers' understanding of everyday physical sciences. The Explorium is in Sugar Sand Community Center. ⊠ *300 S. Military Trail* ☎ *561/347–3912* ⊕ *www.scienceexplorium.org* ☐ *Suggested donaton: $5* ⊙ *Weekdays 9–6, weekends 10–5.*

**Gumbo Limbo Nature Center**. A big draw for kids, this nifty nature center has four huge saltwater tanks brimming with sea life—from coral to stingrays—and a boardwalk through dense forest with a 40-foot tower you can climb to overlook the tree canopy. In spring and early summer, staffers lead nocturnal turtle walks: you can watch nesting females come ashore and lay eggs. (Purchase tickets in advance; see Web site for details.) A great hiking spot, the park has a sturdy boardwalk and a 40-foot observation tower. Spend a little time there and you're likely to see brown pelicans and osprey. Kids love the aquariums, insect tanks, and the butterfly garden. ⊠ *1801 N. Ocean Blvd.* ☎ *561/338–1473* ⊕ *www.gumbolimbo.org* ☐ *Free but $3 donation suggested; turtle walks $5* ⊙ *Mon.–Sat. 9–4, Sun. noon–4; turtle walks May–July, Mon.–Thurs. 9 pm–midnight.*

**Old Floresta**. This residential area was developed by Addison Mizner starting in 1925 and landscaped with palms and cycads. It includes houses that are mainly Mediterranean in style, many with balconies supported by exposed wood columns. Home tours are held twice a year. ⊠ *Behind Boca Raton Art School on Palmetto Park Rd.*

## BEACHES

**Red Reef Park**. The beach comes with a playground, picnic tables, and grills. The reef is close to shore, so this is a good snorkeling spot. ⊠ *1400 N. Rte. A1A.*

**South Beach Park**. This pretty stretch of sand is popular with sunbathers. ⊠ *400 N. Rte. A1A.*

**Spanish River Park**. In addition to its beach, the park has picnic tables, grills, and a large playground. ⊠ *3001 N. Rte. A1A.*

10

## SPORTS AND THE OUTDOORS

### BOATING

**Palm Breeze Charters.** For the thrill of blasting across the water at up to 80 mph, choose a trip from the variety of weekly cruises and boat charters. ⊠ *107 E. Palmetto Park Rd., Suite 330* ☎ *561/368–3566.*

### GOLF

**Boca Raton Resort & Club.** Visit two championship courses and the Dave Pelz Golf School at this country club. Greens fees are $214, including a cart with GPS. ⊠ *501 E. Camino Real* ☎ *561/447–3078.*

## SHOPPING

★ **Mizner Park.** This distinctive 30-acre shopping center intersperses apartments and town houses among its gardenlike retail and restaurant spaces. Some three dozen stores, including national and local retailers, mingle with fine restaurants, sidewalk cafés, galleries, a movie theater, a museum, and an amphitheater. ⊠ *Federal Hwy., 1 block north of Palmetto Park Rd.*

## NIGHTLIFE

**Rustic Cellar.** Warm and intimate, this is perhaps the best wine bar in Palm Beach County. More than 300 hand-selected vintages from across the globe are served. ⊠ *409 S.E. Mizner Blvd., Royal Palm Place, Boca Raton* ☎ *561/392–5237* ⊕ *www.rusticcellar.com.*

## WHERE TO EAT

**$$$$** ✕ **Racks Downtown Eatery & Tavern.** Whimsical indoor–oudoor decor
AMERICAN and comfort food with a twist help define this popular eatery in tony Mizner Park. Instead of dinner rolls, pretzel bread and mustard get things started. Share plates like house-smoked salmon bits and sea bass lettuce cups to promote convivial social dining. Happy hour is 4–7 and offers half-price drinks and appetizers. ⊠ *402 Plaza Real, Mizner Park Boca Raton* ☎ *561/395–1662* ⊕ *www.grrestaurant.com.*

**$$$** ✕ **Tiramisu.** The food is an extravaganza of taste treats; veal chops, tuna,
ITALIAN and anything with mushrooms draw raves, but count on hearty fare rather than a light touch. Start with the portobello mushroom with garlic or the Corsican baby sardines in olive oil. For a main course, try ricotta ravioli; scaloppine of veal stuffed with crabmeat, lobster, and Gorgonzola; or Tuscan fish stew. Enjoy it all in an intimate setting as Andrea Bocelli music plays in the background. ⊠ *170 W. Camino Real* ☎ *561/338–9692* ☾ *No lunch.*

**$$$$** ✕ **Truluck's.** This popular chain is so serious about seafood that it boasts
SEAFOOD its own fleet of 16 boats. Stone crabs are the signature dish, and you can have all you can eat on Monday night from December to May. Other recommended dishes include jalapeño salmon topped with blue crabmeat, hot-and-crunchy trout, crab cakes, and bacon-wrapped shrimp. Portions are huge, so you might want to make a meal of appetizers. The place comes alive each night with its popular piano bar. ⊠ *Mizner Park, 351 Plaza Real* ☎ *561/391–0755* ⊕ *www.trulucks.com.*

**$$$** ✕ **Uncle Tai's.** The draw at this upscale eatery is some of the best Sze-
CHINESE chuan food on Florida's east coast. Specialties include sliced duck with snow peas and water chestnuts in a tangy plum sauce, and orange beef delight—flank steak stir-fried until crispy and then sautéed with

pepper sauce, garlic, and orange peel. They'll go easy on the heat on request. The service is quietly efficient. ⊠ *5250 Town Center Circle* ☎ *561/368–8806* ⊕ *www.uncle-tais.com* ⊗ *No lunch Sun.*

### WHERE TO STAY
*For expanded hotel reviews, visit Fodors.com.*

**$$$$** ▪ **Boca Raton Resort & Club.** Addison Mizner built this Mediterranean-
RESORT  style hotel in 1926, and additions over time have created a sparkling,
★       sprawling resort with many lodging options. **Pros:** historical property; loaded with luxury; plenty of activities. **Cons:** all this luxury is costly; conventions crowd common areas. ⊠ *501 E. Camino Real* ☎ *561/447–3000 or 800/327–0101* ⊕ *www.bocaresort.com* ⊿ *1,047 rooms, 134 suites, 60 2-bedroom bungalows* ⌂ *In-room: a/c, kitchen (some), Wi-Fi. In-hotel: restaurants, bars, golf course, tennis courts, pools, gym, water sports, children's programs, parking* ¶◎¶ *No meals.*

**$$$$** ▪ **Boca Raton Waterfront Bridge Hotel.** This boutique hotel on the Intra-
HOTEL  coastal Waterway has views of Lake Boca and the ocean that can't be beat, especially from Carmine's, the top-floor restaurant. **Pros:** great location; affordable rates, pet-friendly. **Cons:** can be noisy if you're near the bridge. ⊠ *999 E. Camino Real* ☎ *561/368–9500 or 800/333–3333* ⊕ *www.bocaratonbridgehotel.com* ⊿ *121 rooms, 25 suites* ⌂ *In-room: a/c, Internet. In-hotel: restaurants, bars, pool, gym, beach, laundry facilities, parking* ¶◎¶ *No meals.*

**$** ▪ **Ocean Breeze Inn.** If golf is your game, this smaller resort is an excel-
HOTEL  lent choice because guests can play the outstanding course at the adjoining Ocean Breeze Golf & Country Club, otherwise available only to club members. **Pros:** great spot for golfers; bargain rates. **Cons:** rooms are dated. ⊠ *5800 N.W. 2nd Ave.* ☎ *561/994–0400 or 800/344–6995* ⊕ *www.oceanbreezegolf.com* ⊿ *46 rooms* ⌂ *In-room: a/c. In-hotel: restaurant, golf course, tennis courts, pool, laundry facilities, parking* ¶◎¶ *No meals.*

# THE TREASURE COAST

**10**

In contrast to the Gold Coast—as the Palm Beach/West Palm Beach area is known—is the more rural Treasure Coast, covering northernmost Palm Beach County, plus Martin, St. Lucie, and Indian River counties. Along the coast are barrier islands all the way to Sebastian and beyond. Inland there's cattle ranching in tracts of pine and palmetto scrub, along with sugar and citrus production. Shrimp farming uses techniques for acclimatizing shrimp from saltwater—land near seawater is costly—to freshwater, all the better to serve demand from restaurants popping up all over the region. Despite a growing number of malls and beachfront condominiums, much of the Treasure Coast remains largely blissfully undeveloped.

## PALM BEACH SHORES

*7 mi north of Palm Beach, on Singer Island.*

Rimmed by mom-and-pop motels, this residential town is at the southern tip of Singer Island, across Lake Worth Inlet from Palm Beach. To travel between the two, however, you must cross over to the mainland before returning to the beach.

#### GETTING HERE AND AROUND

The best way to drive to Palm Beach Shores from West Palm Beach is to head 7 mi north on Interstate 95. Head east on Blue Heron Boulevard/Route 708 across the Intracoastal Waterway to Atlantic Avenue. Head south and you'll be in Palm Beach Shores.

#### ESSENTIALS

Visitor Information **Northern Palm Beach County Chamber of Commerce** (*✉ 800 N. U.S. 1, Jupiter ☎ 561/746–7111 🌐 www.npbchamber.com*).

### SPORTS AND THE OUTDOORS

**Peanut Island.** In the Intracoastal Waterway between Palm Beach Shores and Riviera Beach, this 79-acre island was opened in 1999 as a recreational park. There's a 20-foot-wide walking path surrounding the island, a 19-slip boat dock, a 170-foot T-shape fishing pier, six picnic pavilions, a visitor center, and 20 overnight campsites. The small **Palm Beach Maritime Museum** (*☎ 561/832–7428*) is open daily except Friday and showcases the "Kennedy Bunker," a bomb shelter prepared for President John F. Kennedy. Call for tour hours. To get to the island, you can take a water taxi. *☎ 561/339–2504 🌐 www.pbmm.org 🎟 $2 donation ⏲ Daily dawn–dusk for noncampers.*

#### FISHING

**Sailfish Marina and Resort.** Book a full or half day of deep-sea fishing for up to six people with the seasoned captains and large fleet of 28- to 60-foot boats. *✉ 98 Lake Dr. ☎ 561/844–1724 🌐 www.sailfishmarina.com.*

### WHERE TO EAT AND STAY

*For expanded hotel reviews, visit Fodors.com.*

$$ SEAFOOD ✕ **Sailfish Marina Restaurant.** This waterfront restaurant overlooking Peanut Island is a great place to chill out after a long day of mansion gawking, boating, or beach-bumming. Choose a table in the dining room or under an umbrella on the terrace and enjoy mainstays like conch chowder or grilled swordfish. More upscale entrées—this, after all, is still Palm Beach County—include lobster tail and baby sea scallops sautéed in garlic-and-lemon butter. Breakfast is a winner here, too. Sportfishing charters are available at Sailfish's store. *✉ 98 Lake Dr. ☎ 561/842–8449 🌐 www.sailfishmarina.com.*

$$ HOTEL **Sailfish Marina Resort.** This waterfront lodging has a marina with deep-water slips and accommodations that include motel-style rooms, efficiencies, and even a three-bedroom house. **Pros:** inexpensive rates; on the Intracoastal Waterway; water taxi stops here. **Cons:** can be noisy; area attracts a party crowd; dated rooms. *✉ 98 Lake Dr. ☎ 561/844–1724 or 800/446–4577 🌐 www.sailfishmarina.com ⇆ 30 units 👍 In-room: a/c, kitchen (some), Internet. In-hotel: restaurant, bar, pool, parking 🍽 No meals.*

**DID YOU KNOW?**

According to the United
States Department of Agriculture, 75% of all of the citrus
fruits (including oranges,
grapefruit, tangerines, lem-
ons, and limes) grown in the
United States are grown in
Florida.

# Florida's Sea Turtles: The Nesting Season

From May to October it's turtle-nesting season all along the Florida coast. Female loggerhead, Kemp's ridley, and other species living in the Atlantic Ocean or Gulf of Mexico swim up to 2,000 mi to the Florida shore. By night they drag their 100- to 400-pound bodies onto the beach to the dune line. Then each digs a hole with her flippers, drops in 100 or so eggs, covers them up, and returns to sea.

The babies hatch about 60 days later. Once they burst out of the sand, the hatchlings must get to sea rapidly or risk becoming dehydrated from the sun or being caught by crabs, birds, or other predators.

Instinctively, baby turtles head toward bright light, probably because for millions of years starlight or moonlight reflected on the waves was the brightest light around, serving to guide hatchlings to water. But now light from beach development can lead the babies in the wrong direction, toward the street rather than the water. To help, many coastal towns enforce light restrictions during nesting months. Florida home owners are requested to dim their lights on behalf of baby sea turtles.

At night, volunteers walk the beaches, searching for signs of turtle nests. Upon finding telltale scratches in the sand, they cordon off the sites, so beachgoers will leave the spots undisturbed. Volunteers also keep watch over nests when babies are about to hatch and assist if the hatchlings get disoriented.

It's a hazardous world for baby turtles. They can die after eating tar balls or plastic debris, or they can be gobbled by sharks or circling birds. Only about one in a thousand survives to adulthood. After reaching the water, the babies make their way to warm currents. East Coast hatchlings drift into the Gulf Stream, spending years floating around the Atlantic.

Males never return to land, but when females attain maturity, in 15–20 years, they return to shore to lay eggs. Remarkably, even after migrating hundreds and even thousands of miles out at sea, most return to the very beach where they were born to deposit their eggs. Each time they nest, they come back to the same stretch of beach. In fact, the more they nest, the more accurate they get, until eventually they return time and again to within a few feet of where they last laid their eggs. These incredible navigation skills remain for the most part a mystery despite intense scientific study. To learn more, check out the Sea Turtle Survival League's and Caribbean Conservation Corporation's website at ⊕ *www.cccturtle.org.*

—Pam Acheson

# PALM BEACH GARDENS

*5 mi north of West Palm Beach, off I–95.*

About 15 minutes northwest of Palm Beach is this relaxed, upscale residential community known for its high-profile golf complex, the PGA National Resort & Spa. Although not on the beach, the town is less than a 15-minute drive from the ocean.

### GETTING HERE AND AROUND

To reach Palm Beach Shores from West Palm Beach, head north for 5 mi on Interstate 95.

### ESSENTIALS

**Visitor Information Northern Palm Beach County Chamber of Commerce** (⌂ *800 N. U.S. 1, Jupiter* ☎ *561/746–7111* ⊕ *www.npbchamber.com*).

## SPORTS AND THE OUTDOORS

### GOLF

**PGA National Resort & Spa.** If you're the kind of traveler who takes along a set of clubs, this is the place for you. The resort has five championship courses that are challenging enough for the pros. Among them are the Champion Course, designed by Tom Fazio and Jack Nicklaus (greens fee $350); the General Course, designed by Arnold Palmer ($250); the Haig Course, the first course opened at the resort ($210); the Estate Course, with a practice range and putting green ($210); and the Tom Fazio–designed Squire Course ($210). Lessons are available at the Golf Digest Academy. ⌂ *1000 Ave. of the Champions* ☎ *561/627–1800.*

**EN ROUTE** **John D. MacArthur Beach State Park & Nature Center.** Almost 2 mi of beach, good fishing and shelling, and one of the finest examples of subtropical coastal habitat remaining in southeast Florida are among the treasures here. To learn about what you see, take an interpretive walk to a mangrove estuary along the upper reaches of Lake Worth. The nature center, open daily 9–5, has exhibits on the coastal environment. ⌂ *10900 Rte. A1A, North Palm Beach* ☎ *561/624–6950* ⊕ *www.macarthurbeach.org* ⎙ *$5 per vehicle, up to 8 people* ⊙ *Daily 8–sundown.*

**10**

## WHERE TO EAT

$$$
AMERICAN
★
✕ **Café Chardonnay.** At the end of a strip mall, Café Chardonnay is surprisingly elegant. Soft lighting, warm woods, and cozy banquettes set the scene for a quiet lunch or romantic dinner. The place consistently receives praise for its innovative menu and outstanding wine list. Starters include wild-mushroom strudel and truffle-stuffed diver sea scallops. Entrées might include Gorgonzola-crusted filet mignon or pan-seared veal scaloppine with rock shrimp. ⌂ *4533 PGA Blvd.* ☎ *561/627–2662* ⊕ *www.cafechardonnay.com* ⊙ *No lunch weekends.*

$$$
AMERICAN
✕ **Ironwood Grille.** Chef Kenny Gilbert of TV's *Top Chef* oversees the kitchen at this contemporary eatery, located at the PGA National Resort

> ### WORD OF MOUTH
>
> "Palm Beach Gardens is quiet and undiscovered. Lots of local golf. Very low key. It is convenient to Juno Beach—the most gorgeous Florida Beach with free beachside parking." —LindaBrinck

& Spa. The menu features beef and seafood dishes made with locally grown organic produce. Choices include she-crab soup with sherry and grilled filet mignon. The chic lobby restaurant and the adjoining bar share an extensive wine cellar and a room for private wine tastings. On Thursday nights, a DJ plays music from 6 until 9. ⊠ *400 Ave. of the Champions* ☎ *561/627–2000* ⊕ *www.ironwoodgrille.com.*

$$    ✕ **Spoto's.** If you like oysters, head to this place where black-and-white
SEAFOOD    photographs of oyster fisherman adorn the walls. The polished tables give the eatery a country club look. Spoto's serves up a delightful bowl of New England clam chowder and an impressive variety of oysters and clams. The prime-rib Caesar salad with crispy croutons never disappoints. Sit outside on the patio to take advantage of the area's perfect weather. ⊠ *4560 PGA Blvd.* ☎ *561/776–9448* ⊕ *www. spotosoysterbar.com.*

## WHERE TO STAY
*For expanded hotel reviews, visit Fodors.com.*

$$$$    🍽 **PGA National Resort & Spa.** Golf draws in about 40% of the guests
RESORT    here, but the rest come for amenities, such as the extensive sports facili-
★    ties, excellent dining, and 240-acre nature preserve. **Pros:** a golfer's paradise; short drive to shopping; large rooms. **Cons:** not on the beach. ⊠ *400 Ave. of the Champions* ☎ *561/627–2000 or 800/633–9150* ⊕ *www.pgaresort.com* ⟿ *280 rooms, 59 suites* ⌂ *In-room: a/c, kitchen (some), Wi-Fi. In-hotel: restaurants, bars, golf courses, tennis courts, pools, gym, spa, parking* ⍒*No meals.*

# JUPITER

*12 mi north of Palm Beach Shores via I–95 and Rte. 706.*

Jupiter is one of the few little towns in the region not fronted by an island. Beaches here are part of the mainland, and Route A1A runs for almost 4 mi along the beachfront dunes and beautiful estates.

## ESSENTIALS
Visitor Information **Northern Palm Beach County Chamber of Commerce** (⊠ *800 N. U.S. 1, Jupiter* ☎ *561/746–7111* ⊕ *www.npbchamber.com*).

## EXPLORING
★    **Jupiter Inlet Lighthouse.** Designed by Civil War hero General George Meade, this brick lighthouse has been operated by the Coast Guard since 1860. Tours of the 105-foot-tall landmark unfold every half hour. (Children must be at least 4 feet tall to go to the top.) There's a small museum that tells about efforts to restore this graceful spire to the way it looked from 1860 to 1918. ⊠ *500 Capt. Armour's Way, U.S. 1 and Beach Rd.* ☎ *561/747–8380* ⊕ *www.jupiterlighthouse.org* 🎫 *Tour $9* ☉ *Tues.–Sun. 10–5; last tour at 4.*

## BEACHES
**Carlin Park.** A beach is just one of the draws here. The park also has picnic pavilions, hiking trails, a baseball diamond, a playground, six tennis courts, and fishing sites. The Lazy Loggerhead Café, serving snacks

Away from developed shorelines, Blowing Rocks Preserve on Jupiter Island lets you wander the dunes.

and burgers, is open daily 9–5. ✉ *A1A at Juno Beach* ☎ *561/799–0185* ☉ *Daily dawn–dusk.*

**Juno Beach.** A 990-foot pier and a bait shop are the big draws here, but a section is available for surfing, and there's a snack bar, too. ✉ *14775 S. Rte. A1A* ☎ *561/624–0065* ☉ *Daily dawn–dusk.*

## SPORTS AND THE OUTDOORS

### BASEBALL

**Roger Dean Stadium.** Both the St. Louis Cardinals and the Florida Marlins train at the 7,000-seat stadium. ✉ *4751 Main St.* ☎ *561/775–1818.*

### CANOEING

**Canoe Outfitters of Florida.** See animals, from otters to eagles, along 8 miles of the Loxahatchee River. Canoe or kayak rental for two to three hours is $25, including drop-off and pickup. ✉ *9060 W. Indiantown Rd.* ☎ *561/746–7053.*

### GOLF

**Abacoa Golf Club.** This 18-hole course is a good alternative to nearby private courses; greens fee $60/$119. ✉ *105 Barbados Dr.* ☎ *561/ 622–0036.*

**Golf Club of Jupiter.** There are 18 holes of varying difficulty; greens fee $49/$69. ✉ *1800 Central Blvd.* ☎ *561/747–6262.*

**Jupiter Dunes Golf Club.** Head for the 18-hole golf course named Little Monster and a putting green near the Jupiter River estuary; greens fee $36/$65. ✉ *401 Rte. A1A* ☎ *561/746–6654.*

## WHERE TO EAT

**$$** ✕ **Food Shack.** This local favorite is a bit tricky to find, but worth the
SEAFOOD search. The fried-food standards you might expect at such a casual place
are not found on the menu; instead there are fried-tuna rolls with basil
and fried grouper cheeks with a fruity slaw. A variety of beers are fun
to pair with the creatively prepared seafood dishes that include wahoo,
mahimahi, and snapper. ⊠ *103 South U.S. 1* ☎ *561/741–3626* ⊕ *www.
littlemoirsfoodshack.com* ☾ *Closed Sun.*

**$$** ✕ **Guanabanas.** Expect a wait for dinner, which is not necessarily a bad
SEAFOOD thing at this island paradise of a waterfront restaurant and bar. Take
the wait time to explore the bridges and trails of this open-air oasis
and nibble on really good conch fritters. Try the lemon-butter hogfish
for dinner and stick around for the live music. The waterfront eatery
is next to the Jupiter Outdoor Center, where you can rent a kayak and
burn some calories after lunch or breakfast. ⊠ *960 N. A1A, Jupiter*
☎ *561/747–8878* ⊕ *www.guanabanas.com.*

**$$$** ✕ **Sinclair's Ocean Grill.** This popular spot in the Jupiter Beach Resort
SEAFOOD has sunlight streaming through the glass doors overlooking the pool.
The menu has a daily selection of fresh fish, such as cashew-encrusted
grouper, Cajun-spice tuna, and mahimahi with pistachio sauce. There
are also thick juicy steaks—filet mignon is the house specialty—and
chicken and veal dishes. The Sunday buffet is a big draw. ⊠ *5 N. Rte.
A1A* ☎ *561/745–7120* ⊕ *www.jupiterbeachresort.com.*

**$$** ✕ **Taste Casual Dining.** Located in the center of historic Hobe Sound, this
AMERICAN cozy dining spot with a pleasant, screened-in patio offers piano dinner
music on Fridays and an occasional band on Saturday nights. Locals like
to hang out at the old, English-style wine bar, but the food is the biggest
draw here. Try a lobster roll and some Gorgonzola salad for lunch, and
prime rib or any fish dish for dinner. ⊠ *11750 S.E. Dixie Hwy., Hobe
Sound* ☎ *772/546–1129* ⊕ *www.tastehobesound.com.*

## WHERE TO STAY

*For expanded hotel reviews, visit Fodors.com.*

**$$$$** ⊡ **Jupiter Beach Resort.** This time-share resort has a 7,500-square-foot
RESORT spa and a nine-story tower filled with Caribbean-style rooms containing
mahogany sleigh beds and armoires. **Pros:** fabulous views; good location; family-friendly. **Cons:** very high beds; pricey rates. ⊠ *5 N. Rte.
A1A* ☎ *561/746–2511 or 800/228–8810* ⊕ *www.jupiterbeachresort.
com* ⇗ *133 rooms, 44 suites* ⚹ *In-room: a/c, Wi-Fi. In-hotel: restaurants, bars, tennis court, pool, gym, spa, beach, water sports, laundry
facilities, parking* ℟⚙ *No meals.*

# JUPITER ISLAND AND HOBE SOUND

*5 mi north of Jupiter, off Rte. A1A.*

Northeast across the Jupiter Inlet from Jupiter is the southern tip of
Jupiter Island. Here expansive and expensive estates often retreat from
the road behind screens of vegetation, and at the north end of the island
turtles come to nest in a wildlife refuge. To the west, on the mainland,
is the little community of Hobe Sound.

**GETTING HERE AND AROUND**

The best way to get to Jupiter Island and Hobe Sound from Jupiter is to drive north 5 mi on Interstate 95 to Indiantown Road. From there, head east to Federal Highway (U.S. 1), then north on U.S. 1.

**EXPLORING**

**Blowing Rocks Preserve.** Protected within this 73-acre preserve are plants native to beachfront dune, coastal strand (the landward side of the dunes), mangrove forests, and tropical hardwood forests. The best time to visit is when high tides and strong offshore winds coincide, causing the sea to blow spectacularly through holes in the eroded outcropping. Park in the lot; police ticket cars parked along the road. ⊠ *574 S. Beach Rd., Rte. 707, Jupiter Island* ☎ *561/744–6668* 🗐 *$2* ⊗ *Daily 9–4:30.*

**Hobe Sound National Wildlife Refuge.** Two tracts make up this refuge: 232 acres of sand-pine and scrub-oak forest in Hobe Sound, and 735 acres of coastal sand dune and mangrove swamp on Jupiter Island. Trails are open to the public in both places. Turtle's nest and shells wash ashore on the 3½-mi-long beach, which has been severely eroded by high tides and strong winds. ⊠ *13640 S.E. Federal Hwy., Hobe Sound* ☎ *772/546–6141* 🗐 *$5 per vehicle* ⊗ *Daily dawn–dusk.*

☾ **Hobe Sound Nature Center.** It's located in the Hobe Sound National Wildlife Refuge, but this nature center is an independent organization. Its museum, which has baby alligators and crocodiles and a scary-looking tarantula, is a child's delight. A ½-mi trail winds through a forest of sand pine and scrub oak—one of Florida's most unusual and endangered plant communities. It lost its original building in 2004 due to hurricanes and moved into a new building in 2007. A new visitor center opened in 2009. ⊠ *13640 S.E. Federal Hwy., Hobe Sound* ☎ *772/546–2067* ⊕ *www.hobesoundnaturecenter.com* 🗐 *Donation suggested* ⊗ *Trail daily dawn–dusk; nature center weekdays 9–3.*

**Jonathan Dickinson State Park.** From Hobe Mountain, an ancient dune topped with a tower, you are treated to a panoramic view of this park's 10,285 acres of varied terrain and the Intracoastal Waterway. The Loxahatchee River, which cuts through the park, is home to manatees in winter and alligators all year. Two-hour boat tours of the river depart daily at 9, 11, 1, and 3 and cost $20 per person. Among amenities are a dozen cabins for rent, tent sites, bicycle and hiking trails, a campground, and a snack bar. ⊠ *16450 S.E. Federal Hwy., Hobe Sound* ☎ *772/546–2771* 🗐 *$6 per vehicle* ⊗ *Daily 8–dusk.*

**SPORTS AND THE OUTDOORS**

**OUTFITTER**

**Jonathan Dickinson's River Tours.** Boat tours of the Loxahatchee River are offered, as are canoe, kayak, and boat rentals from 9 to 5 daily. ⊠ *Jonathan Dickinson State Park, 16450 S.E. Federal Hwy., Hobe Sound* ☎ *561/746–1466.*

10

## STUART

*7 mi north of Hobe Sound.*

This compact little town on a peninsula that juts out into the St. Lucie River has a remarkable amount of shoreline for its size and also has a charming historic district. The ocean is about 5 mi east.

**GETTING HERE AND AROUND**

To get to Stuart from Jupiter and Hobe Sound, drive north on Federal Highway (U.S. 1).

**ESSENTIALS**

Visitor Information **Stuart Main Street** (✉ *201 S.W. Flagler Ave.* ☎ *772/286–2848*). **Stuart/Martin County Chamber of Commerce** (✉ *1650 S. Kanner Hwy.* ☎ *772/287–1088*).

### EXPLORING

Strict architectural and zoning standards guide civic-renewal projects. Stuart has antiques shops, restaurants, and more than 50 specialty shops within a two-block area. A self-guided walking-tour pamphlet is available at assorted locations downtown to clue you in on this once-small fishing village's early days.

★ **Maritime & Yachting Museum.** Linking the watery past with a permanent record of maritime and yachting events contributing to Treasure Coast lore, this museum near a marina has many old ships as well as historic exhibits to explore. Among those leading Saturday tours is a retired ship captain who has many interesting stories to share. ✉ *1707 N.E. Indian River Dr.* ☎ *772/692–1234* ⊕ *www.mcbmfl.org* ✏ *$5* ☉ *Mon.–Sat. 10–5, Sun. 1–5.*

### BEACHES

**Stuart Beach.** With its ever-vigilant lifeguards, this is a good spot for beginning surfers. More experienced wave riders enjoy the challenges of the choppy waters. Fishing and shelling are also draws. ✉ *801 N.E. Ocean Blvd.* ☎ *772/221–1418.*

### SPORTS AND THE OUTDOORS

**FISHING**

**Sailfish Marina.** Nab a deep-sea charter here. ✉ *3565 S.E. St. Lucie Blvd.* ☎ *772/221–9456.*

### SHOPPING

More than 60 restaurants and shops with antiques, art, and fashion have opened downtown along Osceola Street.

**B&A Flea Market.** Operating for more than two decades the oldest and largest such enterprise on the Treasure Coast has a street-bazaar feel, with shoppers happily scouting for the practical and unusual. ✉ *2885 S.E. Federal Hwy.* ☎ *772/288–4915* ✏ *Free* ☉ *Weekends 8–3.*

### THE ARTS

**Lyric Theatre.** On the National Register of Historic Places, this theater has been revived for live performances. A gazebo has free music performances. ✉ *59 S.W. Flagler Ave.* ☎ *772/286–7827* ⊕ *www.lyrictheatre.com.*

## WHERE TO EAT AND STAY

*For expanded hotel reviews, visit Fodors.com.*

$$  
FRENCH
✕ **Courtine's.** A husband-and-wife team oversees this quiet and hospitable restaurant under the Roosevelt Bridge. French and American influences are clear in the Swiss chef's dishes, from rack of lamb with Dijon mustard to grilled filet mignon stuffed with Roquefort and fresh spinach. The formal dining room has subtly elegant touches, such as fresh flowers on each table. A more casual menu is available at the bar. ☒ *514 N. Dixie Hwy.* ☎ *772/692–3662* ⊕ *www.courtines.com* ☽ *Closed Sun. and Mon. No lunch.*

$$  
SEAFOOD
✕ **Finz Waterfront Grille.** Located on the southern end of the Manatee Pocket in Port Salerno, the popular island-style restaurant is surrounded by boatyards and a lively gallery scene. Sit on the covered dock and take in the breeze while eating the tastiest crab cakes south of Chesapeake Bay. The kitchen also serves up savory teriyaki-marinated steak tips, Maryland crab soup, peel-and-eat shrimp, and maple-glazed salmon. There's live island music on Sunday afternoons 2–5 and entertainment every weekend night. ☒ *4290 S.E. Salerno Rd.* ☎ *772/283–1929* ⊕ *www.finzwaterfrontgrille.com.*

$$$  
RESORT
⌂ **Pirate's Cove Resort & Marina.** On the banks of the St. Lucie River, this cozy enclave is the perfect place to recoup after a day at sea. The resort is relaxing and casual but packed with plenty of recreational activities. **Pros:** pretty location; great for boaters. **Cons:** lounge gets noisy at night. ☒ *4307 S.E. Bayview St., Port Salerno* ☎ *772/287–2500 or 800/332–1414* ⊕ *www.piratescoveresort.net* ⇌ *48 rooms, 2 suites* ⌂ *In-room: a/c, Wi-Fi. In-hotel: restaurant, bar, pool, parking* ⍾ *Breakfast.*

# HUTCHINSON ISLAND (JENSEN BEACH)

*5 mi northeast of Stuart.*

The down-to-earth town of Jensen Beach, occupying the core of the island, stretches across both sides of the Indian River. Between late April and August more than 600 turtles come here to nest along the town's Atlantic beach. Area residents have taken pains to curb the runaway development that has created the commercial crowding found to the north and south, although some high-rises have popped up along the shore.

**10**

### GETTING HERE AND AROUND

The best way to reach Jensen Beach from Stuart is to drive north on Federal Highway (U.S. 1) to Northwest Jensen Boulevard, then east on Jensen Beach Boulevard.

### ESSENTIALS

Visitor Information **Jensen Beach Chamber of Commerce** (☒ *1900 N.E. Ricou Terr., Jensen Beach* ☎ *772/334–3444*).

## EXPLORING

**Elliott Museum.** This pastel-pink museum was erected in 1961 in honor of Sterling Elliott, inventor of an early automated-addressing machine and a four-wheel cycle. The museum, with its antique cars, dolls, toys, and vintage baseball cards, is a nice stop for anyone fond of nostalgic goods. There are also antique fixtures from an early general store, blacksmith shop, and apothecary shop. ⊠ *825 N.E. Ocean Blvd., Jensen Beach* 🕾 *772/225–1961* ⊕ *www.elliottmuseumfl.org* 🖅 *$8* ⊙ *Mon.–Sat. 10–4, Sun. 1–4.*

★   **Florida Oceanographic Coastal Center.** Explore a ½-mi interpretive boardwalk through coastal hardwood and mangrove forest. Guided nature walks through trails and stingray feedings are offered at various times during the day. Dolphins, manatees, and turtles are often seen on the boat tour, for which reservations are required. ⊠ *890 N.E. Ocean Blvd., Jensen Beach* 🕾 *772/225–0505* ⊕ *www.floridaoceanographic.org* 🖅 *$8* ⊙ *Mon.–Sat. 10–5, Sun. noon–4; guided nature walks Mon.–Sat. 11 and 3, Sun. at 2.*

**Gilbert's House of Refuge Museum.** Built in 1875 on Hutchinson Island, the museum is the only remaining building of nine such structures built by the U.S. Life-Saving Service (a predecessor of the Coast Guard) to aid stranded sailors. Exhibits include antique lifesaving equipment, maps, artifacts from nearby wrecks, and boatbuilding tools. ⊠ *301 S.E. MacArthur Blvd., Jensen Beach* 🕾 *772/225–1875* 🖅 *$6* ⊙ *Mon.–Sat. 10–4, Sun. 1–4.*

## BEACHES

**Bathtub Reef Park.** At the north end of the Indian River Plantation, is this ideal swimming spot for children because the waters are shallow and usually calm. At low tide you can walk to the reef. Facilities include restrooms and showers. ⊠ *MacArthur Blvd., off Rte. A1A, Jensen Beach.*

## SPORTS AND THE OUTDOORS

### BASEBALL

**Tradition Field.** The **New York Mets** train here, and it's also the home of the St. Lucie Mets Minor League Team. ⊠ *525 N.W. Peacock Blvd., Port St. Lucie* 🕾 *772/871–2115.*

### GOLF

**Hutchinson Island Marriott Golf Club.** There are 18 holes for members and hotel guests; greens fee $60 for 18 holes. ⊠ *555 N.E. Ocean Blvd., Jensen Beach* 🕾 *772/225–6819.*

**PGA Golf Club at the PGA Villages.** The PGA–operated public facility designed by Pete Dye and Tom Fazio has three separate courses; greens fee $62/$111. ⊠ *1916 Perfect Dr., Port St. Lucie* 🕾 *772/467–1300 or 800/800–4653.*

## WHERE TO EAT AND STAY

*For expanded hotel reviews, visit Fodors.com.*

$$$ ✕ **11 Maple Street.** This cozy spot is as good as it gets on the Treasure

CONTINENTAL Coast. Soft music and a friendly staff set the mood in the antiques-

★ filled dining room, which holds only 20 tables. Appetizers run from panfried conch to crispy calamari, and entrées include seared rainbow trout, wood-grilled venison with onion-potato hash, and beef tenderloin with white-truffle-and-chive butter. Desserts like white-chocolate custard with blackberry sauce are seductive, too. ⊠ *3224 Maple Ave.,*

*Jensen Beach* ☎ 772/334–7714 ⊕ *www.11maplestreet.net* ⬥ *Reservations essential* ⊘ *Closed Mon. and Tues. No lunch.*

$ ╳**Conchy Joe's.** Like a hermit crab sliding into a new shell, Conchy Joe's
SEAFOOD moved up from West Palm Beach in 1983. Built in the 1920s, this rustic stilt house is full of antique fish mounts, gator hides, and snakeskins. It's a popular tourist spot, but the waterfront location, casual vibe, and delicious seafood attract locals, too. Staples include grouper marsala, broiled sea scallops, and fried cracked conch. There's live reggae Thursday through Sunday. ⊠ *3945 N.E. Indian River Dr., Jensen Beach* ☎ 772/334–1130 ⊕ *www.conchyjoes.com.*

$$$–$$$$ ⌂**Hutchinson Island Marriott Beach Resort & Marina.** With a 77-slip marina,
RESORT a full water-sports program, a golf course, tennis courts, and a wide range of restaurants, this self-contained resort is excellent for families. **Pros:** attentive staff; challenging golf course. **Cons:** no children's program. ⊠ *555 N.E. Ocean Blvd., Hutchinson Island* ☎ 772/225–3700 *or* 800/775–5936 ⊕ *www.marriott.com* ⇆ *213 rooms, 70 suites* ♿ *In-room: a/c, kitchen (some), Internet. In-hotel: restaurants, bars, golf course, tennis courts, pools, gym, spa, beach, laundry facilities, parking, some pets allowed* ¶⊘ *No meals.*

# FORT PIERCE

*11 mi north of Stuart, off Federal Hwy. (U.S. 1).*

About an hour north of Palm Beach, this community has a distinctive rural feel, focusing on ranching and citrus farming. There are several worthwhile stops, including those easily seen while following Route 707.

### GETTING HERE AND AROUND
You can reach Fort Pierce from Stuart by driving 11 mi north on Federal Highway (U.S. 1).

### ESSENTIALS
**Visitor Information St. Lucie County Tourist Development Council** (⊠ *2300 Virginia Ave.* ☎ *800/344–8443*).

### EXPLORING
**Heathcote Botanical Gardens.** Take a self-guided tour of this 3½-acre park, which includes a palm walk, a Japanese garden, and an orchid house. There is also a gift shop with whimsical and botanical knickknacks. Guided tours are available Tuesday through Saturday by appointment. ⊠ *210 Savannah Rd.* ☎ 772/464–4672 ⊕ *www.heathcotebotanicalgardens.org* ☑ *$6* ⊘ *May–Oct., Tues.–Sat. 9–5; Nov.–Apr., Tues.–Sat. 9–5, Sun. 1–5.*

★ **Navy SEAL Museum.** Commemorating more than 3,000 troops who trained here during World War II, the museum has weapons and equipment on view and exhibits depicting the history of the Underwater Demolition Teams. Patrol boats and vehicles are displayed outdoors. ⊠ *3300 N. Rte. A1A* ☎ 772/595–5845 ⊕ *www.navysealmuseum.com* ☑ *$6* ⊘ *Tues.–Sat. 10–4, Sun. noon–4.*

☾ **Savannas Recreation Area.** Once a reservoir, the 550 acres have been returned to a natural state. Today the wilderness area has campsites, boat ramps, and trails. ⊠ *1400 E. Midway Rd.* ☎ *772/464–7855* ⊙ *Daily 8–6.*

🔄 **Smithsonian Marine Ecosystems Exhibit.** Run by the Smithsonian Institute and housed in the St. Lucie County Marine Center, this is where scientists come to study local ecosystems. A highlight is the 3,000-gallon coral-reef tank, originally shown in the Smithsonian's National Museum of Natural History in Washington, D.C. The parklike setting, where children love to play, makes it an ideal picnic destination. ⊠ *420 Seaway Dr.* ☎ *772/462–3474* 🎫 *$3, free 1st Tues. of month* ⊙ *Tues.–Sat. 10–4.*

### BEACHES

**Fort Pierce Inlet State Recreation Area.** Sand dunes and coastal forests cover this 340-acre reserve. The park has swimming, surfing, picnic facilities, and a self-guided nature trail. ⊠ *905 Shorewinds Dr.* ☎ *772/468–3985* 🎫 *$6 per vehicle* ⊙ *Daily 8–dusk.*

**Fort Pierce State Park.** Accessible only by footbridge, the reserve has 4 mi of trails around Jack Island. The 1½-mi Marsh Rabbit Trail across the island traverses a mangrove swamp to a 30-foot-tall observation tower overlooking the Indian River. ⊠ *Rte. A1A* ☎ *772/468–3985* 🎫 *$4 for one, $6 for a vehicle* ⊙ *Daily 8–5:30.*

### SPORTS AND THE OUTDOORS

#### FISHING

**Dockside Harborlight Resort.** For charter boats and fishing guides, contact the dockmaster. ⊠ *1160 Seaway Dr.* ☎ *772/461–4824.*

#### SCUBA DIVING

**Urca de Lima Underwater Archaeological Preserve.** On North Hutchinson Island, 200 yards from shore and under 10–15 feet of water, this preserve contains remains of a flat-bottom, round-bellied store ship. Once part of a treasure fleet bound for Spain, it was destroyed by a hurricane. ⊠ *3375 N. A1A.*

### THE ARTS

**A.E. "Bean" Backus Museum & Gallery.** Works of one of Florida's foremost landscape artists are on display at this museum, which is also home to the Treasure Coast Art Association. It also mounts changing exhibits and offers exceptional buys on work by local artists. ⊠ *500 N. Indian River Dr.* ☎ *772/465–0630* ⊕ *www.backusgallery.com* 🎫 *Free but $2 donation suggested* ⊙ *Wed.–Sun. 10–4.*

### WHERE TO EAT AND STAY

*For expanded hotel reviews, visit Fodors.com.*

$$$ ✕ **Mangrove Mattie's.** This upscale spot on Fort Pierce Inlet provides daz-
SEAFOOD zling waterfront views and delicious seafood. Dine on the terrace or in the dining room, and don't forget to try the coconut-fried shrimp or the chicken and scampi. Happy hour (weekdays 4–7) features roast beef or ham sandwiches, or oysters, clams and shrimp. Many locals come by for the Champagne Sunday brunch. ⊠ *1640 Seaway Dr.* ☎ *772/466–1044* ⊕ *www.mangrovematties.com.*

$ 🛏 **Dockside Harborlight Resort Inn.** Formerly two adjacent motels, this
RESORT resort is the best of the lodgings lining the Fort Pierce Inlet along Seaway

Drive. **Pros:** good value; good spot for anglers; reasonable rates at marina. **Cons:** basic decor; some steps to climb. ⊠ *1160 Seaway Dr.* ☎ *772/468–3555 or 800/286–1745* ⊕ *www.docksideinn.com* ⇆ *72 rooms, 4 apartments* ♿ *In-room: a/c, kitchen (some). In-hotel: restaurant, pools, laundry facilities, parking* ⊙ *Breakfast.*

# VERO BEACH

*12 mi north of Fort Pierce.*

Tranquil and charming, this Indian River County town has a strong commitment to the environment and the arts. There are plenty of outdoor activities here, even though many visitors to the area opt to do little at all. In the town's exclusive Riomar Bay area, roads are shaded by massive live oaks, and a popular cluster of restaurants and shops is just off the beach.

## GETTING HERE AND AROUND

To get here, you have two options—Route A1A, along the coast, or Route 605 (also called Old Dixie Highway), on the mainland. As you approach Vero on the latter, you pass through an ungussied landscape of small farms and residential areas. On the beach route, part of the drive is through an unusually undeveloped section of the Florida coast.

## ESSENTIALS

**Visitor Information Indian River Chamber of Commerce** (⊠ *1216 21st St.* ☎ *772/567–3491*).

## EXPLORING

**Environmental Learning Center.** In addition to aquariums filled with Indian River creatures, the 51 acres here have a 600-foot boardwalk through the mangrove shoreline and a 1-mi canoe trail. The center is on the northern edge of Vero Beach, and the pretty drive is worth the trip. ⊠ *255 Live Oak Dr.* ☎ *772/589–5050* ⊕ *www.elcweb.org* 💲 *$5* ⊙ *Tues.–Fri. 10–4, Sat. 9–4, Sun. 1–4.*

**Heritage Center and Indian River Citrus Museum.** You'll learn that more grapefruit is shipped from the Indian River area than anywhere else in the world at this museum. The memorabilia harks back to when families washed and wrapped the luscious fruit to sell at roadside stands, and oxen hauled citrus-filled crates with distinctive Indian River labels to the rail station. ⊠ *2140 14th Ave.* ⊕ *www.veroheritage.org* ☎ *772/770–2263* 💲 *Free* ⊙ *Tues.–Fri. 10–4.*

Fodor'sChoice
★ **McKee Botanical Garden.** On the National Register of Historic Places, the 18 acres here are both a tropical garden and a horticulture museum. The historic Hall of Giants, a rustic structure built from cedar and hearts of pine, features a beautiful stained glass, bronze bells, and the world's largest single-plank mahogany table. There's a 529-square-foot bamboo pavilion, a gift shop, and the Garden Café, which serves tasty snacks and sandwiches and locally grown tea. This is the place to see spectacular water lilies. ⊠ *350 U.S. 1* ☎ *772/794–0601* ⊕ *www.mckeegarden. org* 💲 *$9* ⊙ *Tues.–Sat. 10–5, Sun. noon–5.*

**Vero Beach Museum of Art.** Part of a 26-acre campus dedicated to the arts, the museum is where a full schedule of exhibitions, art movies,

**10**

lectures, workshops, and classes are hosted. The museum's five galleries and sculpture garden make it the largest art facility in the Treasure Coast. ⊠ *3001 Riverside Park Dr.* 🕾 *772/231–0707* ⊕ *www. verobeachmuseum.org* 🖃 *Free* ⊘ *Mon.–Sat. 10–4:30, Sun. 1–4:30.*

### BEACHES

**Treasure Shores Park.** There are picnic tables, restrooms, and a nice playground for kids. ⊠ *11300 A1A, 3 mi north of County Rd. 510* 🕾 *772/581–4997.*

**Wabasso Beach Park.** Lifeguards, restrooms, a boardwalk, and showers make this a pleasant beach to visit. ⊠ *County Rd. 510, east of A1A* 🕾 *772/581–4998.*

### SPORTS AND THE OUTDOORS
#### GOLF

**Sandridge Golf Club.** These two public 18-hole courses were designed by Ron Garl; greens fee $42. ⊠ *5300 73rd St.* 🕾 *772/770–5000.*

### SHOPPING

Along Ocean Drive near Beachland Boulevard, a shopping area includes art galleries, antiques shops, and upscale clothing stores. The eight-block area of Oceanside has an interesting mix of boutiques, specialty shops, and eateries.

**Outlets at Vero Beach.** Just west of Interstate 95 is a discount shopping destination with 70 brand-name stores, including Ann Taylor, Ralph Lauren Polo, and Jones New York. ⊠ *1824 94th Dr.* 🕾 *772/770–6097.*

### THE ARTS

ℭ **Riverside Children's Theatre.** A series of professional touring and local productions are staged here. ⊠ *Agnes Wahlstrom Youth Playhouse, 3280 Riverside Park Dr.* 🕾 *772/234–8052* ⊕ *www.riversidetheatre.com.*

**Riverside Theatre.** Five productions go up each season at the 650-seat Mainstage and three at its 200-seat Second Stage. ⊠ *3250 Riverside Park Dr.* 🕾 *772/231–6990* ⊕ *www.riversidetheatre.com.*

### WHERE TO EAT AND STAY

*For expanded hotel reviews, visit Fodors.com.*

$$$   ✕ **Ocean Grill.** Opened as a hamburger shack in 1938, the Ocean Grill
SEAFOOD   combines its ocean view with Tiffany-style lamps, wrought-iron chandeliers, and paintings of pirates. Count on at least three kinds of seafood any day on the menu, along with steaks, pork chops, soups, and salads. The house drink is "Pusser's Painkiller"—a curious blend first mixed by British sailors in the Virgin Islands and rationed in a tin cup. It commemorates the 1894 wreck of the *Breconshire*, which occurred offshore and from which 34 British sailors escaped. ⊠ *Sexton Plaza, 1050 Ocean Dr.* 🕾 *772/231–5409* ⊕ *www.ocean-grill.com* ⊘ *Closed 2 wks after Labor Day. No lunch weekends.*

$$   ⛶ **Aquarius Oceanfront Resort.** Right on beautiful South Beach, this small
RESORT   unpretentious resort has loyal guests who book a year in advance. **Pros:** relaxed vibe; great location; faces the beach. **Cons:** steps to climb; nothing too fancy. ⊠ *1526 Ocean Dr.* 🕾 *772/231–5218 or 877/767–1526* ⊕ *www.aquariusverobeach.com* ⏎ *28 rooms* ⛰ *In-*

*room: a/c, kitchen (some). In-hotel: pool, beach, laundry facilities, parking* ⦿ *No meals.*

**$$$** 🏨 **Costa d'Este.** Many people know this hotel because of its famous
HOTEL owners, singer Gloria Estefan and producer Emilio Estefan, who brought in a new design and a lively ambience. **Pros:** great location; huge showers; faces the beach. **Cons:** marble floors can be cold. ✉ *3244 Ocean Dr.* ☎ *772/562–9919* ⊕ *www.costadeste.com* ↳ *90 rooms, 4 suites* ⚐ *In-room: a/c, Wi-Fi. In-hotel: restaurant, pool, gym, spa, parking* ⦿ *No meals.*

**$$$$** 🏨 **Disney's Vero Beach Resort.** This oceanfront, family-oriented retreat
RESORT operates as a hotel and a Disney Vacation Club. **Pros:** fun for fami-
☺ lies; lots to do for kids. **Cons:** not the best place if you don't have children; a bit kitschy. ✉ *9250 Island Grove Terr.* ☎ *772/234–2000 or 800/359–8000* ⊕ *www.disneybeachresorts.com* ↳ *161 rooms, 14 suites, 6 cottages* ⚐ *In-room: a/c, kitchen (some), Internet. In-hotel: restaurants, bar, tennis courts, pool, gym, beach, children's programs, laundry facilities, parking* ⦿ *No meals.*

**$$$** 🏨 **Driftwood Resort.** On the National Register of Historic Places, this
RESORT 1935 inn was built entirely from ocean-washed timbers and decorated with such artifacts as ship bells, Spanish tiles, and a cannon from a 16th-century Spanish galleon. **Pros:** great seaside location; near restaurants and shops. **Cons:** older property; rooms can be musty. ✉ *3150 Ocean Dr.* ☎ *772/231–0550* ⊕ *www.thedriftwood.com* ↳ *96 1- and 2-bedroom suites, 4 hotel rooms* ⚐ *In-room: a/c, kitchen. In-hotel: restaurant, bar, pools, beach, parking* ⦿ *No meals.*

**$$$$** 🏨 **The Vero Beach Hotel & Spa.** This comfortable five-story hotel is right
RESORT on the beach and near restaurants and boutiques. **Pros:** great ocean views; fabulous pool. **Cons:** spa under construction until fall 2010. ✉ *3500 Ocean Dr.* ☎ *772/231–5666* ⊕ *www.verobeachhotelandspa. com* ↳ *32 rooms, 32 studios, 15 1-bedroom suites and 23 2-bedroom suites* ⚐ *In-room: a/c, Wi-Fi. In-hotel: restaurant, bar, pool, beach, parking* ⦿ *No meals.*

## SEBASTIAN

*14 mi north of Vero Beach, off Federal Hwy. (U.S. 1).*

One of the few sparsely populated areas on Florida's east coast, this fishing village has as remote a feeling as you're likely to find between Jacksonville and Miami Beach. That adds to the appeal of the recreation area around Sebastian Inlet, where you can walk for miles along quiet beaches and catch some of Florida's best waves for surfing.

### ESSENTIALS

**Visitor Information Sebastian Chamber of Commerce** (✉ *700 Main St.* ☎ *772/589–5969*).

### EXPLORING

**McLarty Treasure Museum.** A National Historic Landmark, this museum underscores this credo: "Wherever gold glitters or silver beckons, man will move mountains." It has displays of coins, weapons, and tools salvaged from a fleet of Spanish treasure ships that sank in the 1715 storm, leaving some 1,500 survivors struggling to shore between Sebastian and

Fort Pierce. The museum's last video showing begins at 3:15. ⊠ *13180 N. Rte. A1A* ☎ *772/589–2147* 🖃 *$2* ⊙ *Daily 10–4.*

**Mel Fisher's Treasures.** You'll really come upon hidden loot when you enter this museum operated by the late Mel Fisher's family. See some of what was recovered in 1985 from the Spanish treasure ship *Atocha* and its sister ships of the 1715 fleet. The museum certainly piques one's curiosity about what is still buried at sea: treasures continue to be discovered each year. ⊠ *1322 U.S. 1* ☎ *772/589–9875* ⊕ *www.melfisher. com* 🖃 *$6.50* ⊙ *Mon.–Sat. 10–5, Sun. noon–5.*

**Pelican Island National Wildlife Refuge.** Within the Indian River Lagoon and on the barrier island across from Sebastian, Pelican Island was founded in 1903 by President Theodore Roosevelt as the nation's first national wildlife refuge. The island is a closed wilderness area. The historic Pelican Island rockery is viewable from a distance by commercial boat and kayak tours and from a public observation tower on the adjacent barrier island. The Refuge has more than 6 mi of foot trails through the barrier island habitats. A boardwalk and observation tower enable visitors to see birds, endangered species, and habitats. ⊠ *1339 20th St.* ☎ *772/562–3909 Ext. 275* 🖃 *Free* ⊙ *Daily 7:30–sunset.*

**Sebastian Inlet State Recreation Area.** Because of the highly productive fishing waters of Sebastian Inlet, this 578-acre property at the north end of Orchid Island is one of the Florida park system's biggest draws. Both sides of the high bridge spanning the inlet—views are spectacular—attract anglers as well as those eager to enjoy the fine sandy shores, known for having some of the best waves in the state. A concession stand on the inlet's north side sells short-order food, rents various craft, and has a small apparel and surf shop. There's a boat ramp, and not far away is a dune area that's part of the **Archie Carr National Wildlife Refuge.** ⊠ *9700 S. Rte. A1A, Melbourne Beach* ☎ *321/984–4852* ⊕ *www. floridastateparks.org* 🖃 *$5 per vehicle* ⊙ *Daily 7–sunset.*

## SPORTS AND THE OUTDOORS
### FISHING
**Big Easy Fishing Charters.** For sportfishing, try this outfitter. ⊠ *Capt. Hiram's Restaurant, 1606 N. Indian River Dr.* ☎ *772/664–4068.*

**Incentive Charter Fishing.** This outfit will set you up for bottom-fishing. ⊠ *Capt. Hiram's Restaurant, 1606 N. Indian River Dr.* ☎ *321/676–1948.*

# Fort Lauderdale and Broward County

**WORD OF MOUTH**

"I think you'll enjoy Fort Lauderdale. The Riverwalk/Las Olas area has lots of good restaurants—you can take a water taxi there from just about anywhere on the Intracoastal waterway."

—321go

# WELCOME TO FORT LAUDERDALE AND BROWARD COUNTY

## TOP REASONS TO GO

★ **Blue Waves:** Sparkling Lauderdale beaches spanning Broward County's entire coast were Florida's first to capture Blue Wave Beach status from the Clean Beaches Council.

★ **Inland Waterways:** More than 300 mi of inland waterways, including downtown Fort Lauderdale's historic New River, create what's known as the Venice of America.

★ **Everglades Access:** Just minutes from luxury hotels and golf courses, the rugged Everglades tantalize with alligators, colorful birds, and other wildlife.

★ **Vegas-Style Gaming:** Since Vegas-style slots and blackjack tables hit Hollywood's glittering Seminole Hard Rock Hotel & Casino in 2008, smaller competitors seem to be following this lucrative trend on every square inch of Indian territory.

★ **Cruise Gateway:** Port Everglades—homeport for *Allure* and *Oasis of the Seas,* the world's largest cruise vessels—hosts cruise ships from major lines

**1 Fort Lauderdale.** Anchored by the fast-flowing New River and its attractive Riverwalk, Fort Lauderdale embraces high-rise condos along with single-family homes, museums, parks, and attractions. Las Olas Boulevard, lined with boutiques, sidewalk cafés, and restaurants, links downtown and the beaches.

**2 North on Scenic A1A.** Stretching north on Route A1A, seaside attractions range from high-rise Galt Ocean Mile to low-rise resort communities—and a glimpse of a lighthouse, inspiration for the community of Lighthouse Point.

**3 South Broward.** From Hollywood's beachside Broadwalk and historic Young Circle (the latter transformed into an Arts Park) to Seminole gaming, South Broward provides grit, glitter, and diversity in attractions.

Deerfield
Beach

Hillsboro
Beach

**Hillsboro
Lighthouse**

Pompano
Beach

Lauderdale-
by-the-Sea

Fort
Lauderdale

Port Everglades

Fort Lauderdale-Hollywood
International Airport

Dania Beach
Blvd.

Dania
Beach

Hollywood

Hallandale

0        3 mi

0        3 km

## GETTING
## ORIENTED

Along the southeast's Gold
Coast, Fort Lauderdale and
Broward County anchor
a delightfully chic middle
ground between the posh
and elite Palm and West
Palm beaches and the
international hubbub of
Miami. From downtown
Fort Lauderdale, it's about
a four-hour drive to either
Orlando or Key West,
but there's plenty to keep
you in Broward. All told,
Broward boasts 31 com-
munities from Deerfield
Beach to Hallandale
Beach along the coast,
and from Coral Springs to
Southwest Ranches closer
to the Everglades. Big—in
fact, huge—shopping
options await in Sunrise,
home of Sawgrass Mills,
the upscale Colonnade
Outlets at Sawgrass,
and IKEA Sunrise.

# FORT LAUDERDALE AND BROWARD COUNTY BEACHES

A wave-capped, 20-mi shoreline with wide ribbons of golden sand for beachcombing and sunbathing remains the anchor draw for Fort Lauderdale and Broward County.

Fort Lauderdale isn't just for spring breakers. In fact, ever since investors started pouring money into the waterfront scene, beginning in the '90s, the beach has lured a more upscale clientele. That said, it still has great people-watching and opportunities for partying.

Beyond the city, Broward County's beachfront extends for miles without interruption, although character of communities along the shoreline varies. To the south in Hallandale, the beach is backed by towering condominiums, while tee times and nightlife beckon in Hollywood. Deerfield Beach and Lauderdale-by-the-Sea to the north are magnets for active families, and nearby Pompano Beach attracts anglers. Many places along Broward shorelines—blessedly, for purists—are uncluttered with nothing but sand and turquoise waters.

## SAFETY TIPS

⚠ **Avoid unguarded waters, and be aware of color codes.** In Fort Lauderdale, double red flags mean water is closed to the public, often because of lightning or sharks; a lone red flag signals strong currents; purple indicates the presence of marine pests like men-of-war, jellyfish, or sea lice; green means calm conditions. In Hollywood, orange signals rip currents with easterly onshore winds; blue warns of marine life like jellyfish; red means hazardous; green signals good conditions.

# FORT LAUDERDALE'S BEST BEACHES

### FORT LAUDERDALE BEACH

Alone among Florida's major beachfront communities, Fort Lauderdale's beach remains gloriously open and uncluttered. A wave theme unifies the Fort Lauderdale Beachfront setting—from the low, white, wave-shape wall between the beach and beachfront promenade to the widened and bricked inner promenade in front of shops, restaurants, and hotels. Walkways line both sides of the beach roadway, and traffic has been trimmed to two gently curving northbound lanes, where in-line skaters skim past slow-moving cars. On the beach side, a low masonry wall doubles as an extended bench, separating sand from the promenade. At night the wall is accented with pretty ribbons of fiberoptic color, often on the blink despite an ongoing search for a permanent fix. The beach is most crowded between Las Olas and Sunrise boulevards.

### HOLLYWOOD'S BROADWALK

The name might be Hollywood, but there's nothing hip or chic about Hollywood North Beach Park, which sits at the north end of Hollywood (Route A1A and Sheridan Street). And that's a good thing. It's just a laid-back, old-fashioned place to enjoy the sun, sand, and sea. No high-rises overpower the scene here. Parking is $5. The main part of the Broadwalk is quite a bit more fashionable. Thanks to a $14 million makeover, this popular beach has spiffy new features like a pedestrian walkway, a concrete bike path, a crushed-shell jogging path, an 18-inch decorative wall separating the Broadwalk from the sand, and places to shower off after a dip. Fido fans take note: the film *Marley & Me*, starring Jennifer Aniston and Owen Wilson and filmed in Greater Fort Lauderdale, spurred a comeback for dog beaches in South Florida, including the year-round Dog Beach of Hollywood.

### LAUDERDALE-BY-THE-SEA

For a small village with a pier, Lauderdale-by-the-Sea packs a big punch for beach pleasure. Especially popular with divers and snorkelers, this laid-back stretch of sand provides great access to lovely coral reefs. When you're not down in the waters, look up and you'll likely see a pelican flying by. Gentle trade winds make this an utterly relaxing retreat from the hubbub of the Fort Lauderdale party scene. Things do liven up with nightly entertainment at a couple of local watering holes, but L-B-T-S, as it's known, still provides a small-town, easygoing, family-friendly feel.

Updated by
Paul Rubio

Collegians of the 1960s returning to Fort Lauderdale would be hard-pressed to recognize the onetime "Sun and Suds Spring Break Capital of the Universe." Back then, Fort Lauderdale's beachfront was lined with T-shirt shops, and downtown consisted of a lone office tower and dilapidated buildings waiting to be razed.

The beach and downtown have since exploded with upscale shops, restaurants, and luxury resort hotels equipped with enough high-octane amenities to light up skies all the way to western Broward's Alligator Alley. At risk of losing small-town 45-rpm magic in iPod times—when hotel parking fees alone eclipse room rates of old—Greater Fort Lauderdale somehow seems to meld disparate eras into nouveau nirvana, seasoned with a little Gold Coast sand.

The city was named for Major William Lauderdale, who built a fort at the river's mouth in 1838 during the Seminole Indian wars. It wasn't until 1911 that the city was incorporated, with only 175 residents, but it grew quickly during the Florida boom of the 1920s. Today's population hovers around 150,000, and suburbs keep growing—1.6 million live in Broward County's 31 municipalities and unincorporated areas. As elsewhere, many speculators busily flipping property here got caught when the sun-drenched real-estate bubble burst, leaving Broward's foreclosure rate to skyrocket.

Despite economic downturns, gaming options have expanded. South Florida's Indian tribes have long offered bingo, poker, and machines resembling slots. In 2005, Broward became Florida's first county to offer gambling with true slot machines at four wagering facilities referred to as racinos: Gulfstream Park Racing & Casino, the Mardi Gras Racetrack & Gaming, Dania Jai Alai Casino, and the Isle Casino & Racing of Pompano Park. In 2008, Hollywood's Seminole Hard Rock Hotel & Casino, which ranks as the most glittering example of Vegas-style gaming with a tropical twist, cut a deal with the state to replace bingo-style machines with genuine Vegas-style slots.

# FORT LAUDERDALE PLANNER

## WHEN TO GO

Peak season runs Thanksgiving through April, when concert, art, and entertainment seasons go full throttle. Expect rain, heat, and humidity in summer. Hurricane winds come most notably in August and September. Golfing tee-time waits are longer on weekends year-round. Fort Lauderdale sunshine can burn even in cloudy weather.

## TOP FESTIVALS

**Fort Lauderdale International Boat Show.** In late October Fort Lauderdale hosts the world's largest boat show, the end-all, be-all of marine envy, with more than $2 billion worth of boats, yachts, superyachts, electronics, engines, and thousands of accessories from every major marine manufacturer and builder worldwide. ☎ *954/764–7642* ⊕ *www. showmanagement.com.*

**Seminole Hard Rock Winterfest Boat Parade.** Weeks of pre-events culminate in the largest one-day spectator event in Florida each December, drawing a crowd of 1 million onlookers as a stampede of 1,500 jaw-dropping yachts cruise 10 mi of Fort Lauderdale's waterways, complete with original themes and decorations. Over the years, celebrity grand marshals have included Joan Rivers, Brooke Burke, and Kim Kardashian. ☎ *954/767–0686* ⊕ *www.winterfestparade.com.*

## GETTING HERE AND AROUND

### AIR TRAVEL

Serving more than 21 million travelers a year, **Fort Lauderdale–Hollywood International Airport** is 3 mi south of downtown Fort Lauderdale, just off U.S. 1 between Fort Lauderdale and Hollywood, and near Port Everglades and Fort Lauderdale Beach. Other options include **Miami International Airport**, about 32 mi to the southwest, and the far less chaotic **Palm Beach International Airport**, about 50 mi to the north. All three airports link to **Tri-Rail**, a commuter train operating seven days through Palm Beach, Broward, and Miami-Dade counties.

### BUS TRAVEL

**Broward County Transit** operates bus route No. 1 between the airport and its main terminal at Broward Boulevard and Northwest 1st Avenue, near downtown Fort Lauderdale. Service from the airport is every 20 minutes and begins at 5:22 am on weekdays, 5:37 am Saturday, and 8:41 am Sunday; the last bus leaves the airport at 11:38 pm Monday–Saturday and 9:41 pm Sunday. The fare is $1.75. ⚠ **The Northwest 1st Avenue stop is in a crime-prone part of town. Exercise special caution there, day or night. Better yet, take a taxi to and from the airport.** Broward County Transit (BCT) also covers the county on 303 fixed routes. The fare is $1.75. Service starts around 5 am and continues to 11:30 pm, except on Sunday.

## CAR TRAVEL

Renting a car to get around Fort Lauderdale is highly recommended. Taxis are scarce and costly. Traditional public transportation is rarely used, but a water taxi makes transport between waterfront destinations quite easy (albeit slow).

## TRAIN TRAVEL

**Amtrak** provides daily service to Fort Lauderdale and stops at Deerfield Beach and Hollywood.

By car, access to Broward County from north or south is via Florida's Turnpike, Interstate 95, U.S. 1, or U.S. 441. Interstate 75 (Alligator Alley, requiring a toll despite being part of the nation's interstate-highway system) connects Broward with Florida's west coast and runs parallel to State Road 84 within the county. East–west Interstate 595 runs from westernmost Broward County and links Interstate 75 with Interstate 95 and U.S. 1, providing handy access to the airport and seaport. Route A1A, designated a Florida Scenic Highway by the state's Department of Transportation, parallels the beach.

## ESSENTIALS

**Airport information Fort Lauderdale–Hollywood International Airport** (*FLL* ☎ *866/435–9355* ⊕ *www.broward.org/airport).* **Miami International Airport** (*MIA* ☎ *305/876–7000* ⊕ *www.miami-airport.com).* **Palm Beach International Airport** (*PBI* ☎ *561/471–7420* ⊕ *www.pbia.org).* **Tri-Rail** (☎ *800/874–7245* ⊕ *www.tri-rail.com).*

**Bus information Broward County Transit** (☎ *954/357–8400* ⊕ *www.broward. org/BCT).*

# ABOUT THE RESTAURANTS

References to "Fort Liquordale" from spring-break days of old have given way to au courant allusions for the decidedly cuisine-oriented "Fork Lauderdale." Greater Fort Lauderdale offers some of the finest, most varied dining of any U.S. city its size, spawned in part by the advent of new luxury hotels and upgrades all around. From among more than 4,000 wining-and-dining establishments in Broward, choose from basic Americana or cuisines of Asia, Europe, or Central and South America, and enjoy more than just food in an atmosphere with subtropical twists.

# ABOUT THE HOTELS

Not as posh as Palm Beach or as deco-trendy as Miami Beach, Fort Lauderdale has a growing roster of more-than-respectable lodging choices, from beachfront luxury suites to intimate bed-and-breakfasts to chain hotels along the Intracoastal Waterway. Relatively new on the luxury beachfront are the Atlantic, the Hilton Fort Lauderdale Beach Resort, the Ritz-Carlton, Fort Lauderdale, and W resort, and more upscale places to hang your hat are on the horizon while smaller family-run lodging spots disappear. If you want to be *on* the beach, be sure to ask specifically when booking your room, since many hotels advertise "waterfront" accommodations that are along inland waterways or overlooking the beach from across Route A1A.

| WHAT IT COSTS | | | | | |
|---|---|---|---|---|---|
| | ¢ | $ | $$ | $$$ | $$$$ |
| Restaurants | under $10 | $10–$15 | $15–$20 | $20–$30 | over $30 |
| Hotels | under $80 | $80–$100 | $100–$140 | $140–$220 | over $220 |

Restaurant prices are per person for a main course at dinner. Hotel prices are for a standard double room, excluding 6% sales tax (more in some counties) and 1%–5% tourist tax.

## BOAT TOURS

For a similar experience to these tours but with a local flair, explore Fort Lauderdale's waterways on the public water taxis. ⇨ *See Exploring the Venice of America, below, for more information.*

**Carrie B.** Board a 300-passenger day cruiser for a 90-minute tour on the New River and Intracoastal Waterway. Cruises depart at 11, 1, and 3 daily November through May and Thursday–Monday between June and October. The cost is $19.95. ⊠ *440 N. New River Dr. E, Fort Lauderdale* ☎ *954/768–9920* ⊕ *www.carriebcruises.com.*

**Fort Lauderdale Duck Tours.** This outfitter provides 90 minutes of land/water family fun on a 45-passenger amphibious Hydra-Terra, cruising Venice of America neighborhoods, historic areas, and the Intracoastal Waterway. Several tours depart daily (schedule varies) and cost $30. ⊠ *17 S. Fort Lauderdale Beach Blvd., at Beach Pl., Fort Lauderdale* ☎ *954/761–4002* ⊕ *www.fortlauderdaleducktours.com.*

**Jungle Queen.** The *Jungle Queen III* and *Jungle Queen IV* tour boats seat more than 550 for cruises up New River through the heart of Fort Lauderdale. Sightseeing cruises at 9:30 and 1:30 cost $17.50, and the 6 pm all-you-can-eat BBQ dinner cruise costs $39.95. ⊠ *Bahia Mar Beach Resort, 801 Seabreeze Blvd., Fort Lauderdale* ☎ *954/462–5596* ⊕ *www.junglequeen.com.*

**Sea Experience.** Glass-bottom-boat and snorkeling combination trips on the *Sea Experience I* explore Fort Lauderdale's offshore reefs. Daily two-hour trips at 10:15 am and 2:15 pm cost $28 for the ride or $35 to snorkel, equipment provided. ⊠ *Bahia Mar Beach Resort, 801 Seabreeze Blvd., Fort Lauderdale* ☎ *954/770–3483* ⊕ *www.seaxp.com.*

# FORT LAUDERDALE

Like many southeast Florida neighbors, Fort Lauderdale has long been revitalizing. In a state where gaudy tourist zones often stand aloof from workaday downtowns, Fort Lauderdale exhibits consistency at both ends of the 2-mi Las Olas corridor. The sparkling look results from upgrades both downtown and on the beachfront. Matching the downtown's innovative arts district, cafés, and boutiques is an equally inventive beach area, with hotels, cafés, and shops facing

## GREAT ITINERARIES

Many Broward County attractions are close, so you can pack a lot into a day—if you have wheels. Catch the history, museums, and shops and bistros in Fort Lauderdale's downtown and along Las Olas Boulevard. Then if you feel like hitting the beach, head east to the intersection of Las Olas and Route A1A and you're there. Neighboring communities like Lauderdale-by-the-Sea and Pompano Beach (to the north) or Dania Beach and Hollywood (to the south) have attractions of their own, and you may not realize when you've crossed municipal lines. As a result, you'll be able to cover most high points in three days.

**3 DAYS**

With a bigger concentration of hotels, restaurants, and attractions

than its suburbs, Fort Lauderdale makes a logical base for any visit. On your first day, see downtown, especially **Las Olas Boulveard** between Southeast 3rd and Southeast 15th avenues. After lunch at a sidewalk café, head for the nearby Arts and Science District and the downtown **Riverwalk**, which you can enjoy at a leisurely pace in half a day or less. On your second day, spend time at the **Fort Lauderdale Beachfront**, sunbathing or having a cooling libation at an oceanfront lounge. Tour the waterways on the third day, either on a rented boat from one of the marinas along Route A1A, or via the Water Taxi.

an undeveloped shoreline, and new resort-style hotels replacing faded icons of yesteryear. Despite wariness of pretentious overdevelopment, city leaders have allowed a striking number of glittering high-rises. Nostalgic locals and frequent visitors fret over the diminishing vision of sailboats bobbing in waters near downtown, now that a boxy high-rise has erased one of the area's oldest marinas. Sharp demographic changes are also altering the faces of Greater Fort Lauderdale communities, increasingly cosmopolitan with more minorities, including Hispanics and people of Caribbean descent, as well as gays and lesbians. In Fort Lauderdale, especially, a younger populace is growing, whereas longtime residents are heading north, to a point where one former city commissioner likens the change to that of historic New River—moving with the tide and sometimes appearing at a standstill. "The river of our population is at still point, old and new in equipoise, one pushing against the other."

### GETTING HERE AND AROUND

The Fort Lauderdale metro area is laid out in a grid system, and only myriad canals and waterways interrupt the mostly straight-line path of streets and roads. Nomenclature is important here. Streets, roads, courts, and drives run east–west. Avenues, terraces, and ways run north–south. Boulevards can (and do) run any which way. For visitors, trendy Las Olas Boulevard is one of the most important east–west thoroughfares from the beach to downtown, whereas Route A1A—referred to as Atlantic Boulevard, Ocean Boulevard, and Fort Lauderdale Beach along some stretches—runs along the north–south oceanfront. These names can confuse visitors, since there are separate streets called Atlantic and Ocean in Hollywood and Pompano Beach. Boulevards, composed of either pavement or water, give Fort Lauderdale its distinct "Venice of America" character.

The city's transportation system, though less congested than elsewhere in South Florida, suffers from traffic overload. Interstate 595 connects the city and suburbs and provides a direct route to the Fort Lauderdale–Hollywood International Airport and Port Everglades, but lanes slow to a crawl during rush hours. The Intracoastal Waterway, paralleling Route A1A, is the nautical equivalent of an interstate highway. It runs north–south between downtown Fort Lauderdale and the beach and provides easy boating access to neighboring beach communities.

The major taxi company serving the area is Yellow Cab, with vehicles equipped for major credit cards.

TOURS Honeycombed with some 300 mi of navigable waterways, Fort Lauderdale is home port for about 44,000 privately owned vessels, but you don't need to be a boat owner to ply the waters. For a scenic way to really see this canal-laced city, simply hop on a Water Taxi, sometimes called a Water Bus, part of Fort Lauderdale's water-transportation system, made up of a fleet of vessels carrying up to 70 passengers each. Providing transport and quick, narrated tours, a water taxi is a good way to bar-hop or access many waterfront hotels and restaurants. Larger, multiple-deck touring vessels and motorboat rentals for self-guided adventure are other sightseeing options.

Boats won't get you everywhere; you may need to call for taxi service when getting to and from the airport, seaport, or major hotels. Meters run at rates of $4.50 for the first mile and $2.40 for each additional mile; waiting time is 40¢ per minute. There's a $10-fare minimum from seaport or airport, and an additional $2 service charge when you are collected from the airport.

Catch an orange-bottomed, yellow-topped Sun Trolley, running every 15 minutes, free on Friday and for 50¢ each way, on any route. Sun Trolley's *Convention Connection*, 50¢ per person, runs round-trip from Cordova Road's Harbor Shops near Port Everglades (where you can park free) to past the Convention Center, over the 17th Street Causeway, and north along Route A1A to Beach Place. Wave at trolley drivers— yes, they will stop—for pickups anywhere along the route.

### ESSENTIALS

Transportation Contacts **Sun Trolley** (☎ *954/761–3543* ⊕ *www.suntrolley. com*). **Water Taxi** (☎ *954/467–0008* ⊕ *www.watertaxi.com*). **Yellow Cab** (☎ *954/565–5400*).

Visitor Information **Greater Fort Lauderdale Convention and Visitors Bureau** (☎ *954/765–4466* ⊕ *www.sunny.org*).

This couple tours Fort Lauderdale via a three-wheeled scooter; photo by rockindom, Fodors.com member.

## EXPLORING

### DOWNTOWN AND LAS OLAS

The jewel of downtown along New River is the Arts and Entertainment District, with Broadway shows, ballet, and theater at the riverfront Broward Center for the Performing Arts. Clustered within a five-minute walk are the Museum of Discovery & Science, the expanding Fort Lauderdale Historical Museum, and the Museum of Art, home to stellar touring exhibits. Restaurants, sidewalk cafés, bars, and blues, folk, jazz, reggae, and rock clubs flourish along Las Olas and its downtown extension. Tying these areas together is the Riverwalk, extending 2 mi along the New River's north and south banks. Tropical gardens with benches and interpretive displays fringe the walk on the north, boat landings on the south.

### TOP ATTRACTIONS

**Fort Lauderdale History Center.** Surveying city history from the Seminole era to more recent times, the Fort Lauderdale Historical Society's museum has expanded into several adjacent buildings, including the historic King-Cromartie House (typical early 20th-century style Fort Lauderdale home), the 1905 New River Inn (Broward's oldest remaining hotel building), and the Hoch Heritage Center, a public research facility archiving original manuscripts, maps, and more than 250,000 photos. Daily docent-led tours run on the hour 1 pm–3 pm. ⊠ *231 S.W. 2nd Ave.* ☎ *954/463–4431* ⊕ *www.oldfortlauderdale.org* ✉ *$10* ⊗ *Tues.–Sun. noon–4.*

★ **Las Olas Boulevard.** What Lincoln Road is to South Beach, Las Olas Boulevard is to Fort Lauderdale. The terrestrial heart and soul of Broward

County, Las Olas is the premiere street for restaurants, art galleries, shopping, and people-watching. From west to east the landscape of Las Olas transforms from modern downtown high-rises to original boutiques and ethnic eateries. Beautiful mansions and traditional Floridian homes line the Intracoastal and define Fort Lauderdale. The streets of Las Olas connect to the pedestrian friendly Riverwalk, which continues to the edge of the New River on Avenue of the Arts. ⊕ *www.lasolasboulevard.com*.

**Museum of Art Fort Lauderdale.** Currently in an Edward Larrabee Barnes–designed building that's considered an architectural masterpiece, activists started this museum in a nearby storefront about 50 years ago. MOAFL now coordinates with Nova Southeastern University to host world-class touring exhibits and has an impressive permanent collection of 20th-century European and American art, including works by Picasso, Calder, Dalí, Mapplethorpe, Warhol, and Stella, as well as works by celebrated Ashcan School artist William Glackens. ⊠ *1 E. Las Olas Blvd.* ☎ *954/763–6464* ⊕ *www.moafl.org* ☜ *$10* ⊘ *Tues.–Wed., Fri., and Sat. 11–5, Thurs.11–8, Sun. noon–5.*.

Ⓒ **Museum of Discovery & Science/AutoNation IMAX Theater.** With more than
★ 200 interactive exhibits, the aim here is to entertain children—*and* adults—with wonders of science. Exhibits include Kidscience, encouraging youngsters to explore the world; and Gizmo City, a look at how gadgets work. Florida Ecoscapes has a living coral reef, plus sharks, rays, and eels. *Runways to Rockets* offers stimulating trips to Mars and the moon while nine different cockpit stimulators let you try out your pilot skills. The AutoNation IMAX theater, part of the complex, shows films, some in 3-D, on an 80-foot by 60-foot screen with 15,000 watts of digital surround sound broadcast from 42 speakers. ⊠ *401 S.W. 2nd St.* ☎ *954/467–6637 museum, 954/463–4629 IMAX* ⊕ *www.mods.org* ☜ *Museum $11, $16 with one IMAX show (not including full-length feature films)* ⊘ *Mon.–Sat. 10–5, Sun. noon–6*.

★ **Riverwalk.** Lovely views prevail on this paved promenade on the New River's north bank. On the first Sunday of every month a free jazz festival attracts visitors as does an organic, urban farmers' market each Saturday from 9 to 1. From west to east, the Riverwalk begins at the residential New River Sound, passes through the Arts and Science District, then the historic center of Fort Lauderdale, and wraps around the New River until it meets with Las Olas Boulevard's shopping district.

**Stranahan House.** The city's oldest residence, on the National Register of Historic Places, and increasingly dwarfed by high-rise development, was once home for businessman Frank Stranahan, who arrived in 1892. With his wife, Ivy, the city's first schoolteacher, he befriended and traded with Seminole Indians, and taught them "new ways." In 1901 he built a store that would later become his home after serving as a post office, a general store, and a restaurant. Frank and Ivy's former residence is now a museum, with many period furnishings, and tours. The historic home remains Fort Lauderdale's principal link to its brief 110-year history. Note that self-guided tours are not allowed. ⊠ *335 S.E.*

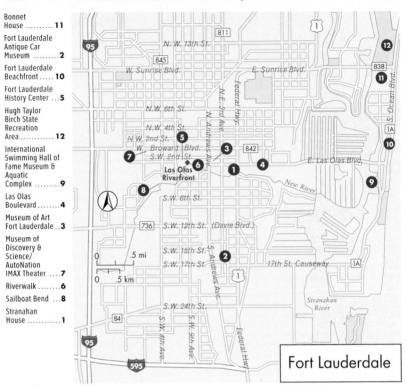

Fort Lauderdale

*6th Ave., at Las Olas Blvd.* ☎ *954/524–4736* ⊕ *www.stranahanhouse.
org* ☞ *$12* ⊘ *Tours daily at 1, 2, and 3 pm; closed Sept.*

**QUICK
BITES**

**Kilwin's of Las Olas.** The sweet smell of waffle cones lures pedestrians
to an old-fashioned confectionery that also sells hand-paddled fudge and
scoops of homemade ice cream. ⊠ *809 E. Las Olas Blvd.* ☎ *954/523–8338.*

### WORTH NOTING

**Fort Lauderdale Antique Car Museum.** Retired floral company owner
Arthur O. Stone set up a foundation to preserve these eyepoppers. Nostalgia includes around two dozen Packards (all in running condition)
from 1900 to the 1940s, along with a gallery saluting Franklin Delano
Roosevelt. This sparkling museum sports everything from grease caps,
spark plugs, and gearshift knobs to Texaco Oil signage, plus a newer
wing and an enlarged library. ⊠ *1527 S.W. 11th Ave. (Packard Ave.)*
☎ *954/779–7300* ⊕ *www.antiquecarmuseum.net* ☞ *$8* ⊘ *Weekdays
10–4, Sat. 10–3.*

**Sailboat Bend.** Between Las Olas and the river lies a neighborhood with
a character reminiscent of Key West's Old Town and Miami's Coconut
Grove. Although without shops or much in the way of services, it's still
worth a visit to be reminded of bygone days. The circa-1927 Fire Station
No. 3, designed by local architect Francis Abreu and now housing the

## THE GHOSTS OF STRANAHAN HOUSE

These days the historic Stranahan House is equally famous for its nighttime ghost tours as it is for its daytime history tour. Originally built as a trading post in 1901 and later expanded into a town hall, a post office, a bank, and the personal residence of Frank Stranahan and wife, Ivy Cromartie, the historic Stranahan House was more than plagued by a number of tragic events and violent deaths, including Frank's tragic suicide. After financial turmoil, Stranahan tied himself to a concrete sewer grate and jumped into New River, leaving his widow to carry on. Sunday nights at 7:30, house staff reveal the multiple tragic tales from the Stranahan crypt during the River House Ghost Tour ($25) and help visitors communicate with "the other side." Using special tools and snapping photos to search for orbs, guests are encouraged to field energy from the supposed five ghosts in the house. Given the high success rate of reaching out to the paranormal, the Stranahan House has become a favorite campground for global ghost hunters and television shows. Advance reservations are required.

Fort Lauderdale Fire Museum, is at the corner of West Las Olas Boulevard and Southwest 11th Avenue. Across the river lies the tree-lined Tarpon River neighborhood, alluding to the canal-like river looping off New River from the southeast quadrant and running to the southwest section, returning to New River near Sailboat Bend.

### ALONG THE BEACH

★ **Bonnet House.** A 35-acre oasis in the heart of the beach area, this subtropical estate on the National Register of Historic Places stands as a tribute to the history of Old South Florida. This charming home, built in the roaring '20s, was the winter residence of the late Frederic and Evelyn Bartlett, artists whose personal touches and small surprises are evident throughout. For architecture, artwork, or the natural environment, this place is special. After admiring the fabulous gardens, be on the lookout for playful monkeys swinging from trees. Hours can vary, so call first. ⌂ *900 N. Birch Rd.* ☎ *954/563–5393* ⊕ *www.bonnethouse. org* ⌖ *$20 for house tours, $10 for grounds only* ☉ *Tues.–Sat. 10–4, Sun. 11–4. Closed Sept.*

Fodor's Choice
★

**Fort Lauderdale Beachfront.** Fort Lauderdale's increasingly stylish beachfront offers easy access not only to a wide band of downy sands but also to restaurants and shops. Heading north for 2 mi, beginning at the Bahia Mar yacht basin along Route A1A, you'll have clear ocean views (typically across rows of colorful beach umbrellas) to ships passing in and out of nearby Port Everglades. If you're on the beach, gaze back on an exceptionally graceful promenade.

**Hugh Taylor Birch State Recreation Area.** Amid the tropical greenery of this 180-acre park, stroll along a nature trail, visit the Birch House Museum, picnic, play volleyball, or paddle a rented canoe. Since parking is limited on Route A1A, park here and take a walkway underpass to the beach (which can be accessed 9–5, daily). ⌂ *3109 E. Sunrise Blvd.*

☎ *954/564–4521* ⊕ *www.floridastateparks.org* ✉*$6 per vehicle, $2 per pedestrian* ☉ *Daily 8–sunset.*

**International Swimming Hall of Fame Museum.** This monument to underwater accomplishments has photos, medals, and other souvenirs from major swim events, and the Huizenga Theater provides an automated video experience where you can select vintage-Olympic coverage or old films such as Esther Williams' *Million Dollar Mermaid.* Connected to the museum, the **Fort Lauderdale Aquatic Complex**(⊕ *www.ci.ftlaud. fl.us/flac*) has two 50-meter pools plus a dive pool open daily to the public (except mid-December to mid-January). ✉ *501 Sea Breeze Blvd., 1 block south of Las Olas at Rte. A1A* ☎ *954/462–6536 or 954/828–4580* ⊕ *www.ishof.org* ✉ *Museum $8, pool $4* ☉ *Museum daily 9–5; pool 8–4 daily, plus 6 pm–8 pm weekday evening.*

**NEED A BREAK?**

**Casablanca Café.** For respite from the sun, duck in for a nice glass of chardonnay. ✉ **3049 Alhambra St.** ☎ **954/764–3500.**

**Steak 954.** Recover from a long day in the sun with a much-deserved, refreshing cocktail. ✉ **401 N. Fort Lauderdale Beach Blvd.** ☎ **954/414–8333.**

Starbucks addicts can get their iced coffee fix at the beachfront outpost at the Westin Hotel, smack-dab in the center of Fort Lauderdale beach.

## WESTERN SUBURBS AND BEYOND

West of Fort Lauderdale is ever-growing suburbia, with most of Broward's golf courses, landlocked attractions, and shopping. As you head farther west, the terrain takes on more characteristics of the Everglades, and you'll occasionally see alligators sunning on canal banks. Eventually, you reach the Everglades themselves after hitting the airboat outfitters on the park's periphery. Tourists flock to these airboats, but the best way of seeing the Everglades is to visit the National Park itself.

♻ **Big Cypress Seminole Reservation.** On the way to the Everglades from Fort Lauderdale is this reservation's two very different attractions.

At the **Billie Swamp Safari,** experience the majesty of the Everglades firsthand. Daily tours of wildlife-filled wetlands and hammocks yield sightings of deer, water buffalo, raccoons, wild hogs, hawks, eagles, and alligators. Sighting of the rare Florida panther are limited to the two captive felines on-site. Animal and reptile shows entertain audiences. Ecotours are conducted aboard motorized swamp buggies, and airboat rides are available, too. The on-site Swamp Water Café serves gator nuggets, frogs' legs, catfish, and Indian fry bread with honey. ✉ *Big Cypress Seminole Indian Reservation, 30000 Gator Tail Trail, Clewiston* ☎ *863/983–6101 or 800/949–6101* ⊕ *www.swampsafari. com* ✉*Swamp Safari Day Package (ecotour, shows, exhibits, and airboat ride) $49.95* ☉ *Daily 10–5.*

A couple of miles from Billie Swamp Safari is **Ah-Tah-Thi-Ki Museum,** whose name means "a place to learn, a place to remember." This museum documents the traditions and culture of the Seminole Tribe

# FORT LAUDERDALE SPAS

Most of Fort Lauderdale's upscale spas are located within elegant beachfront hotels but remain open to the public. During low season (September and October), top spas offer $99 treatments during the "Spa Chic" promotion (⊕ *www.sunny.org/spachic*).

**Bliss Spa, W Fort Lauderdale.** The menu at this quiet respite matches that of other Bliss spas and features Bliss products. A local favorite is the "carrot and sesame body buff" —a carrot mulch and hot oil rubdown, warm milk and honey drizzle, skin-softening wrap, sesame seed and sea salt scrub, and Vichy shower.

**Body Treatments:** Massage: Swedish, aromatherapy, stone, couples massage, Ashiatsu, deep tissue, mother-to-be massage, hydromassage, reflexology, exfoliation.

**Beauty Treatments:** Anti-aging treatments, anti-cellulite, facials, manicure, pedicure, waxing.

**Prices:** Body Treatments, $70–$235. Facials, $80–$280. Manicure/Pedicure, $25–$90. Waxing, $15–$220.

✉ *W Fort Lauderdale, 401 N. Fort Lauderdale Beach Blvd., Along the beach, Fort Lauderdale* ☎ *954/414-8200* ⊕ *www.blissworld.com.*

**The Spa at the Ritz-Carlton, Fort Lauderdale.** The expansive 8,500-foot hideaway exudes tranquillity and relaxation, from the seashell color palate to the magical hands of Fort Lauderdale's top therapists.

**Body Treatments:** Massage options run the gamut, including Swedish, aromatherapy, stone, couples massage, deep tissue, hydrotherapy, reflexology, Thai massage, mother-to-be, and Sea Spray.

**Beauty Treatments:** Dermatologist-developed skincare treatments, anti-cellulite treatments, anti-aging treatments, facials, manicure, pedicure, and waxing.

**Prices:** Body Treatments, $130–$230. Facials, $75–$195. Manicure/Pedicure, $45–$110. Waxing, $30–$90.

✉ *The Ritz-Carlton, Fort Lauderdale, 1 N. Fort Lauderdale Beach Blvd., Along the beach, Fort Lauderdale* ☎ *954/465-2300* ⊕ *www.RitzCarlton.com/FortLauderdale.*

**Spa Atlantic.** The 10,000-foot Spa Atlantic boasts a relaxed glamour and offers a menu of perfected core spa services. Many treatments are rooted in India, Arabia, the Orient, and the Mediterranean but alongside are modern approaches, like the health-boosting beer scrubs and beer hair treatments.

**Body Treatments:** Swedish, aromatherapy, stone, couples massage, deep tissue, hydrotherapy, reflexology, mother-to-be, Thai, and chair massage. Baths, body wraps, body glows (exfoliation).

**Beauty Treatments:** Skincare enhancements, anti-aging treatments, facials, manicure, pedicure, waxing, hair, makeup.

**Prices:** Body Treatments, $75–$330. Facials, $75–$175. Manicure/Pedicure, $26–$70. Waxing, $20–$90.

✉ *The Atlantic Hotel, 601 N. Fort Lauderdale Beach Blvd., Along the beach, Fort Lauderdale* ☎ *954/567-8085* ⊕ *www.atlantichotelfl.com.*

of Florida through artifacts, exhibits, and reenactments of rituals and ceremonies. The 60-acre site includes a living-history Seminole village, nature trails, and a wheelchair-accessible boardwalk through a cypress swamp. ⊠ *34725 W. Boundary Rd., Clewiston* ☎ *863/902–1113* ⊕ *www.ahtahthiki.com* ⌑ *$9* ☉ *Tues.–Sun. 9–5.*

**Sawgrass Mills.** Twenty-six million visitors a year flock to this mall, 10 mi west of downtown Fort Lauderdale, making it Florida's second-biggest tourist attraction (after the one with the mouse). The ever-growing complex has a basic alligator shape, and walking it all amounts to about a 2-mi jaunt. Count on 11,000 self-parking spaces (note your location, or you'll be working those soles), valet parking, and two information centers. More than 400 shops—many manufacturer's outlets, retail outlets, and name-brand discounters—include Chico's Outlet, Super Target, and Ron Jon Surf Shop. Chain restaurants such as P.F. Chang's, the Cheesecake Factory, Grand Lux Cafe, and Rainforest Café are on-site. Wannado City, an "interactive-empowerment environment" is geared toward ages four and up. The adjacent Shops at Colonnade cater to well-heeled patrons with a David Yurman jewelry outlet and other shops including Valentino, Prada, Burberry, Kate Spade New York, and Barneys New York. ⊠ *12801 W. Sunrise Blvd., at Flamingo Rd., Sunrise.*

**Sawgrass Recreation Park.** For Everglades thrills, take a half-hour airboat ride here. You'll see all manner of plants and wildlife, from birds and alligators to turtles, snakes, and fish. Besides the ride, your entrance fee covers admission to an Everglades nature exhibit; a native Seminole village; and exhibits on alligators, other reptiles, and birds of prey. ⊠ *1006 N. U.S. Hwy. 27, Weston* ☎ *888/424–7262* ⊕ *www.evergladestours. com* ⌑ *$19.50* ☉ *Airboat rides daily 9–5.*

## SPORTS AND THE OUTDOORS

### BIKING

Among the most popular routes are Route A1A and Bayview Drive, especially in early morning before traffic builds, and a 7-mi bike path that parallels State Road 84 and New River and leads to Markham Park, which has mountain bike trails. ■ TIP→ Alligator alert: Do not dangle your legs from seawalls.

### BIRD-WATCHING

**Evergreen Historic Cemetery.** North of Fort Lauderdale's 17th Street Causeway, amid a Gothic setting, lies an avid bird-watchers' haven. The circa 1879 graveyard, shaded by gumbo limbo and strangler figs, doubles as a place of fleeting repose for Bahama mockingbirds and other species winging through urban Broward. Warblers are big here, and there are occasional sightings of red-eyed vireos, northern waterthrushes, and scarlet tanagers. ⊠ *1300 S.E. 10th Ave.* ☎ *954/745–2140* ⊕ *www.browardcemeteries.com.*

## EXPLORING THE VENICE OF AMERICA

While a number of tour outfitters offer an opportunity to journey the aqua back lots of Fort Lauderdale, the best way to experience the multimillion-dollar homes, hotels, and seafood restaurants along Fort Lauderdale's waterways is via the public **Water Taxi.** An unlimited day pass serves as both a tour and a means of transportation between Fort Lauderdale's most notable sights.

For sightseeing, the Water Taxi can pick you up at any of several docks along the Intracoastal Waterway or New River, and you can stop off at attractions like the Performing Arts Center, Beach Place, and the Stranahan House. For lunch or dinner, sail away to restaurants on Las Olas Boulevard, Las Olas Riverfront, or Fort Lauderdale beach. Water taxis are also a superb way to barhop, letting your pilot play the sober role of designated driver. Even just cruising on the water taxi for an afternoon is a fun way to take in the waterfront sights. Captains and helpers tend to be real characters, indulging guests in fun factoids about Fort Lauderdale, white lies about the city's history, and bizarre tales about the celebrity homes along the Intracoastal.

The Water Taxi has a direct pickup point at Hyatt Regency 66 and two stops a few minutes walk from the Ritz-Carlton, the Atlantic, and the W Fort Lauderdale. Since the service runs hourly, check the schedule before setting off to begin your tour.

The water-transport venture was started by Bob Bekoff, a longtime Broward resident and outspoken tourism promoter, who decided to combine the need for transportation with one of the area's most captivating features: waterways that make Fort Lauderdale the Venice of America.

Ride all you want with a day pass, purchased onboard or at a kiosk at the Gallery at Beach Place, 10:30 am–12:30 am, for $20. Family all-day passes for two adults and up to three youths are $55, and after 7 pm, passes are $7. The taxis have fourteen scheduled stops.

In addition to regular service throughout Fort Lauderdale, the winter season brings the much-welcomed South Beach Express Water Taxi service. This express service first travels south 45 minutes to Hollywood, then continues another hour to the Art Deco District of Miami Beach ($38). From mid-December through February, the service leaves Fort Lauderdale at 10:15 am, returning by 6:30 pm. From early March through April, the service leaves Fort Lauderdale at 10:45 am, returning at 7 pm. To get around town by boat, contact **Water Taxi** (☎ 954/467–6677 ⊕ www.watertaxi.com).

### FISHING

**Bahia Mar Beach Resort.** If you're interested in a saltwater charter, check out the offerings at this resort. Sportfishing and drift-fishing bookings can be arranged. ✉ *801 Seabreeze Blvd.* ☎ *954/627–6357.*

Sand can sometimes be forgiving if you fall, and bicyclists also appreciate the ocean views.

### SCUBA DIVING AND SNORKELING

**Lauderdale Diver.** This PADI–affiliated outfit arranges dive charters up and down Broward's shoreline. Dive trips typically last four hours. Nonpackage reef trips are open to divers for around $50; scuba gear is extra. ⊠ *1334 S.E. 17th St. Causeway* ☎ *954/467–2822.*

**Pro Dive.** The area's oldest diving operation has downsized and joined forces with another company, Sea Experience. Snorkelers can go out for $35 on a two-hour snorkeling trip, including equipment, with Sea Experience. Pro Dive offers daily trips for scuba divers to Broward's natural coral reefs or over two-dozen shipwrecks including the famous "Mercedes I." Expect to pay $55 if using your own gear or $115 with full scuba gear included. Pro Dive: ⊠ *801 Seabreeze Blvd.* ☎ *954/776–3483* ⊕ *www.prodiveusa.com.* Sea Experience: ⊠ *Bahia Mar Beach Resort, 801 Seabreeze Blvd., Fort Lauderdale* ☎ *954/770– 3483* ⊕ *www.seaxp.com.*

## SHOPPING

### MALLS

**Galleria Mall.** Just west of the Intracoastal Waterway, the split-level emporium entices with Neiman Marcus, Dillard's, and Macy's, plus 150 specialty shops for anything from cookware to exquisite jewelry. Recent upgrades include marble floors and fine dining options. Chow down at Capital Grille, Truluck's, Blue Martini, P.F. Chang's or Seasons 52, or head for the food court, which will defy expectations with its international food-market feel. Galleria is open 10–9 Monday through

Saturday, noon–5:30 Sunday. ⊠ *2414 E. Sunrise Blvd.* ☎ *954/564–1015* ⊕ *www.galleriamall-fl.com.*

**Sawgrass Mills.** This alligator-shape megamall draws 26 million dollars a year to its collection of 400 outlet stores and name-brand discounters. Themed restaurants keep the whole family fed and entertained. If the kids (or even the adults) would rather not shop til they drop, they can have their own kind of fun at Wannado City, an "interactive-empowerment environment" (four and up) while the shopaholics do their thing. ⊠ *12801 W. Sunrise Blvd., at Flamingo Rd., Sunrise.*

**Swap Shop.** The South's largest flea market, with 2,000 vendors, is open daily. While exploring this indoor–outdoor entertainment-and-shopping complex, hop on the carousel or stick around for movies at the 14-screen Swap Shop drive-in. ⊠ *3291 W. Sunrise Blvd.*

### SHOPPING DISTRICTS

**Las Olas Boulevard.** The city's best boutiques plus top restaurants and art galleries line a beautifully landscaped street. Window shopping allowed. ⊠ *1 block off New River east of Andrews Ave.* ⊕ *www.lasolasboulevard.com.*

## NIGHTLIFE AND THE ARTS

For the most complete weekly listing of events, check "Showtime!" the *South Florida Sun-Sentinel*'s tabloid-sized entertainment section and events calendar published on Friday. "Weekend," in the Friday Broward edition of the *Herald,* also lists area happenings. The weekly *City Link* is principally an entertainment and dining paper with an "underground" look. *New Times* is a free alternative weekly circulating a Broward–Palm Beach County edition.

### THE ARTS

**Broward Center for the Performing Arts.** More than 500 events unfold annually at the 2,700-seat architectural gem, including Broadway-style musicals, plays, dance, symphony, opera, rock, film, lectures, comedy, and children's theater. An enclosed elevated walkway links the centerpiece of Fort Lauderdale's arts district to a parking garage across the street. ⊠ *201 S.W. 5th Ave.* ☎ *954/462–0222* ⊕ *www.browardcenter.org.*

★ **Chef Jean-Pierre Cooking School.** Catering to locals, seasonal snowbirds, and folks winging in for even shorter stays, Jean-Pierre Brehier (former owner of the much-missed Left Bank Restaurant on Las Olas) teaches the basics, from boiling water onward. The enthusiastic Gallic transplant has appeared on NBC's *Today* and CNN's *Larry King Live.* For souvenir hunters, this fun cooking facility also sells nifty pots, pastas, oils, and other great items. ⊠ *1436 N. Federal Hwy.* ☎ *954/563–2700* ⊕ *www.chefjp.com* ⊠ *$65 per demonstration class, $125 hands-on class* ⊙ *Store Mon.–Sat. 10–7, class schedules vary.*

**Cinema Paradiso.** This art-house movie theater operates out of a former church, south of New River near the county courthouse. The space doubles as headquarters for FLIFF, the Fort Lauderdale International Film Festival. ⊠ *503 S.E. 6th St.* ☎ *954/525–3456.*

**11**

## NIGHTLIFE
### BARS AND LOUNGES
The majority of Fort Lauderdale nightlife takes place near downtown though some of the high-end bars and clubs along Fort Lauderdale beach's luxury row have become popular. Nightlife options begin in the heart of downtown on Himmarshee Street (2nd Street), continuing on to the Riverfront and then to Las Olas Bouleveard. Fort Lauderdale's gay nightlife is concentrated in the Wilton Manors area.

The Downtown Riverfront tends to draw a younger demographic somewhere between underage teens and late twenties. On Himmarshee Street, a half dozen rowdy bars entice a wide range of partygoers, ranging from the seedy to the sophisticated.

**Coyote Ugly.** Pick up where the film left off with wild girls and wild nights. ⊠ *214 S.W. 2nd St.* ☎ *954/764–8459* ⊕ *www.coyoteuglysaloon.com.*

**Living Room.** This dance palladium, near the Riverfront, is Fort Lauderdale's hottest Saturday club experience. Friday nights are alternative/ gay night. The club is also open on Thursday for ladies night, where ladies drink free and get in free. ⊠ *300 S.W. 1st Ave, Suite 200, 2nd fl.* ☎ *888/992–7555* ⊕ *www.livingroomclub.com.*

**O Lounge.** This lounge and two adjacent establishments, **Yolo** and **Vibe,** on Las Olas and under the same ownership, cater to Fort Lauderdale's sexy yuppies, business men, desperate housewives, and hungry cougars letting loose during happy hour and on the weekends. Crowds alternate between Yolo's outdoor fire pit, O Lounge's chilled atmosphere and lounge music, and Vibe's more intense beats. Expect flashy cars in the driveway. ⊠ *333 E. Las Olas Blvd.* ☎ *954/523–1000* ⊕ *www. yolorestaurant.com.*

**Tarpon Bend.** Expect casual fun along with a few beers and some great bar food at this consistently busy joint. ⊠ *200 S.W. 2nd St.* ☎ *954/523– 3233* ⊕ *www.tarponbend.com.*

**Voodoo Lounge.** The party gets going late at night. The lounge plays the latest club music and packs the house for ladies night on Wednesday and the gay-straight mixer, "Life's a Drag" on Sunday. ⊠ *111 S.W. 2nd Ave.* ☎ *954/522–0733* ⊕ *www. voodooloungeflorida.com.*

## WHERE TO EAT

### ALONG THE BEACH

**$$$**
ECLECTIC
✕ **Casablanca Cafe.** You'll get a fabulous ocean view and a good meal to boot at this historic two-story Moroccan-style villa, built in the 1920s by local architect Francis Abreu. This piano bar's menu is a potpourri with both tropical and Asian influence (try the Korean-style roasted duck) along with North African specialties like lamb shank and couscous. There's a deck for outside dining. It's a lively spot with friendly service. ⊠ *3049 Alhambra St.* ☎ *954/764–3500* ⊕ *www. casablancacafeonline.com.*

**$$$**
ITALIAN
✕ **Da Campo Osteria.** Todd English makes his Fort Lauderdale debut with this upscale Tuscan-inspired restaurant. On the ground floor of the sleek Il Lugano hotel, the stylish restaurant impresses with its tableside

mozzarella showcase and exceptional array of antipasti, primi, and secondi. The mozzarella barista makes the cheese fresh at your table from raw ingredients and then provides a choice of six toppings, including heirloom tomatoes and sweet basil or green and olive tapenade. Five pastas are handcrafted in house daily, usually two special ones and the three staples—spaghetti, tagliatelle, and *angnolotti.* ⊠ *3333 N.E. 32nd Ave., Along the beach, Fort Lauderdale* ☎ *954/225–5002* ⊕ *www. dacampoosteria.com* ♦ *Reservations essential.*

$$$
MEXICAN
Fodor's Choice
★

✕ **Dos Caminos.** After taking over the Manhattan Mexican dining scene, Dos Caminos has settled into its Florida home, bringing the robust flavors of Mexico and the hospitality culture of NYC to Fort Lauderdale. Rounds of traditional and nontraditional margaritas (like the Pineapple Brown Sugar Margarita) begin an evening of new flavors and foodie fantasia. Chips are served with a trio of authentic salsas, usually followed by chunky guacamole, made to order. The ceviches vary from classic Mexican preparations, like the "Snapper Ceviche Veracruz" and the more modern, Asian-influenced "Tuna Ceviche Chino-Latino" and the "Shrimp Ceviche Yucateco," marinated in citrus and coconut foam. The house specialties, tacos, quesadillas, and enchiladas impress with a commingling of truly traditional Mexican dishes and neo-Mexican cuisine reinvented with an American flair. For example, the "Grilled Shrimp Quesadilla" is a creative tour de force—an open-faced crispy flour tortilla topped with chile-marinated shrimp, Mexican cheeses, wild mushrooms, and oven-dried tomatoes. Basically, heaven on a plate! ⊠ *Sheraton Fort Lauderdale Beach Resort,1140 Seabreeze Blvd., Along the beach, Fort Lauderdale* ☎ *954/727–7090* ⊕ *www.doscaminos.com.*

$$$$
STEAKHOUSE
Fodor's Choice
★

✕ **Steak 954.** Steak 954 has quickly become an institution for Fort Lauderdale's foodies and visitors alike. It's not just the steaks that impress here. The lobster and crab-coconut ceviche and the red snapper tiradito are divine; the butter-poached Maine lobster is perfection; and the raw bar showcases only the best and freshest seafood on the market. Located on the 1st floor of the swanky W Fort Lauderdale, Steak 954 offers spectacular views of the ocean for those choosing outdoor seating; or a sexy, sophisticated ambience for those choosing to dine in the main dining room, with bright tropical colors balanced with dark woods and an enormous jellyfish tank spanning the width of the restaurant. Sunday brunch is very popular, so arrive early for the best views. ⊠ *401 N. Fort Lauderdale Beach Blvd., Along the beach, Fort Lauderdale* ☎ *954/414–8333* ⊕ *www.steak954.com.*

## DOWNTOWN AND LAS OLAS

$$$
ECLECTIC

✕ **Big City Tavern.** A Las Olas landmark, Big City Tavern is the boulevard's most consistent spot for good food, good spirits, and good times. The diverse menu commingles Asian entrées like pad thai, Italian options like homemade meatballs and cheese ravioli, and American dishes like the grilled skirt steak Cobb salad. The Asian Calamari with peanuts, apricots, and sweet-and-sour sauce and the Pistachio Brown Butter Bundt Cake with honey-roasted spiced peaches and pistachio gelato are two of the tavern's best creations. Big City is open late night for drinks, desserts, and even offers a late-night menu. ⊠ *609 E. Las*

*Olas Blvd., Downtown and Las Olas, Fort Lauderdale* ☎ *954/727–0307* ⊕ *www.bigtimerestaurants.com.*

**$$$$**
BRAZILIAN

✕ **Chima.** Fort Lauderdale's snazzy Brazilian steak house is located at the far eastern end of Las Olas, in a lushly landscaped enclave. Similar to other restaurants of its type, Chima has an entourage of meat carvers parading around the restaurant with different cuts as well as a massive salad bar with seafood options, fancy greens, and grilled vegetables to accompany the never-ending plates of protein. ✉ *2400 E. Las Olas Blvd., Downtown and Las Olas, Fort Lauderdale* ☎ *954/712–0580* ⊕ *www.chima.cc* ⊗ *No lunch.*

**$$**
AMERICAN

✕ **Floridian.** This classic diner is plastered with photos of Monroe, Nixon, and local notables past and present in a succession of brightly painted rooms with funky chandeliers. The kitchen dishes up typical grease-pit breakfast favorites (no matter the hour), with oversize omelets that come with biscuits, toast, or English muffins, plus a choice of grits or tomato. The restaurant also has good hangover eats but don't expect anything exceptional (besides the location). It's open 24 hours—even during hurricanes, as long as the power holds out. ✉ *1410 E. Las Olas Blvd.* ☎ *954/463–4041* ▭ *No credit cards.*

**$**
ITALIAN

✕ **Grand Forno Cafe.** The gamble of importing an entire Italian bakery direct from Brescia, Italy definitely paid off. Most days, the sandwiches, fresh baked breads, and pastries sell out even before lunchtime. All products are made fresh daily, beginning at 4 am, by a team of bakers who can be seen hard at work through the café's glass windows. Customers line up at the door early in the morning to get their piping-hot artisanal breads, later returning for the scrumptious paninis and decadent desserts. A second branch, five blocks east on Las Olas, called Grand Forno Pronto, serves a more limited menu. ✉ *1235 E. Las Olas Blvd., Downtown and Las Olas, Fort Lauderdale* ☎ *954/467–2244* ⊕ *www.granforno.com* ⊗ *Tues.–Sun. 7:30–7; closed Mon.*

**$$$**
AMERICAN
Fodor's Choice
★

✕ **Himmarshee Bar and Grill.** There's a reason that Himmarshee Bar and Grill has survived all of downtown Fort Lauderdale's ups and downs--the food is utterly fantastic. While the restaurant is constantly evolving based on customer feedback and the chef's ingenuity, it has perfected a number of dishes in its 15 years while pushing the envelope of flavorful American cuisine with its ever-changing menu. Some items, like the butternut squash purses and the buttermilk blue cheese stuffed dates, have been the talk of the town since the 1990s and remain a fixture with each seasonal menu. Thankfully, so does the amazing herb-seared rare tuna served over a ragout of white bean, wild mushroom, broccolini, shallot, oil poached tomato, and balsamic jus. However, by virtue of using fresh, seasonal products, some good things (or entrees) must come to an end; but on the flip side, it's a great reason to return with each passing season to discover a new favorite dish. ✉ *210 S.W. 2nd St., Downtown and Las Olas, Fort Lauderdale* ☎ *954/524–1818* ⊕ *www.himmarshee.com.*

**$**
AMERICAN
★

✕ **ROK: BRG.** It took a while, but Fort Lauderdale finally welcomed its first personality-driven gastro pub in early 2011, giving the grown-ups something to enjoy in teenage-infested Downtown. The long and narrow venue, adorned with exposed brick walls and flat-screen TVs, serves up the city's best burgers from Angus beef monsters to the more en vogue sushi-grade ahi tuna burger. The hand-cut original fries and sweet potato fries are served in their own mini fryers, accompanied by a series of sauces made from scratch every day (try the Bourbon BBQ sauce). Scrumptious starters include hand-battered onion rings with jalapeño-cheddar sauce and "Lobster Corn Dogs." With several beers on tap, a huge cocktail menu, and a great vibe, ROK: BRGR is the perfect place for amazing cheap eats and good times, any night of the week. ☒ *208 S.W. 2nd St., Downtown and Las Olas, Fort Lauderdale* ☎ *954/525–7656* ⊕ *www.rokbrgr.com.*

**$$$**     ✕ **YOLO.** YOLO stands for "You Only Live Once," but you will defi-
AMERICAN    nitely want to eat here more than once. For Fort Lauderdale's bour-
geoisie, this is the place to see and be seen and to show off your hottest wheels in the driveway. For others, it's an upscale restaurant with affordable prices and a great ambience. The restaurant serves the full gamut of new American favorites like tuna sashimi, fried calamari, garden burgers, and short ribs with a sophisticated spin. For example, the Szechuan Calamari is flash fried, and then covered in garlic-chili sauce, chopped peanuts, and sesame seeds; the garden burger is made from bulgur wheat, cremini mushrooms, and cashews and served with thin-cut fries. ☒ *333 E. Las Olas Blvd., Downtown, Fort Lauderdale* ☎ *954/523–1000* ⊕ *www.yolorestaurant.com.*

## INTRACOASTAL AND INLAND

**$$$$**        ✕ **Canyon Southwest Cafe.** Southwestern fusion fare helps you escape
SOUTHWESTERN    the ordinary at this small magical enclave. It's been run for the past
Fodor'sChoice   dozen years by owner and executive chef Chris Wilber. Order, for exam-
★         ple, bison medallions with scotch bonnets, a tequila-jalapeño smoked salmon tostada, coriander-crusted tuna, or blue-corn fried oysters. Chipotle, wasabi, mango, and red chilies accent fresh seafood and wild game. Start off with a signature prickly pear margarita or choose from a well-rounded wine list or beer selection. Save room for the divine chocolate bread pudding. ☒ *1818 E. Sunrise Blvd.* ☎ *954/765–1950* ⊕ *www.canyonfl.com* ☽ *No lunch.*

**$$$**     ✕ **Casa D'Angelo.** Owner-chef Angelo Elia has created a gem of a Tuscan-
ITALIAN     style white-tablecloth restaurant, tucked in the Sunrise Square shopping center. Casa D'Angelo's oak oven turns out marvelous seafood and beef dishes. The pappardelle with porcini mushrooms takes pasta to pleasant heights. Another favorite is the calamari and scungilli salad with garlic and lemon. Ask about the oven-roasted fish of the day or the snapper *oreganta* at market price. ☒ *1201 N. Federal Hwy.* ☎ *954/564–1234* ⊕ *www.casa-d-angelo.com* ☽ *No lunch.*

**$$$$**    ✕ **China Grill.** China Grill takes the best of Asian cuisine and adds an
ASIAN       American flair to create a pan-Asian eating extravaganza. This concept of global Asian fusion draws inspiration from Marco Polo and his descriptions of the Far East and its riches. While Marco Polo's travels are imprinted on the restaurant floor, the flavors of his destinations are all over the menu. Try the crackling calamari salad—a taste explosion of zest with crispy lettuce, calamari, and citrus in lime-miso dressing—or the Shanghai Lobster —a 2.5-pound female lobster, unbelievably soft

and tender, drenched in ginger and curry and accompanied by crispy spinach. ⊠ *1881 S.E. 17th St., Intracoastal and Inland, Fort Lauderdale* ☎ *954/759–9950* ⊕ *www.chinagrillmgt.com.*

**$$**
PIZZA
Fodor'sChoice
★
× **Giorgio's Brick Oven Pizza.** The delicious brick oven pizza lures customers to this tiny restaurant, but it's really the salads and sandwiches that provide the wow factor. The blackened chicken Caesar salad and the monstrous grilled chicken sandwiches (with grilled peppers and fresh mozzarella on freshly baked bread) are both memorable. Nevertheless, the homemade seafood salad is still Giorgio's best seller, a healthy mix of baby squid, shrimp, calamari, and scallops in a light vinaigrette. All meals are served with piping hot rolls and homemade hummus. ⊠ *1499 S.E. 17th St., Intracoastal and Inland, Fort Lauderdale* ☎ *954/767–8300.*

**$$**
GERMAN
× **Old Heidelberg Restaurant & Deli.** Likened to a Bavarian mirage plucked from the Alps and plopped along State Road 84 near the airport and seaport, the Old Heidelberg's beer stein–cowbell–cuckoo-clock decor accents the Bavarian lamb shanks, various schnitzels, sauerkraut, and other specialties, from apple strudel to Black Forest cake. The restaurant boats a great selection of German beers on tap. Old Heidelberg Deli next door (open Tuesday through Saturday 9–6) stocks kielbasa, liver dumplings, Bitburger beer, breads, and nearly a dozen mustards. ⊠ *900 State Rd. 84* ☎ *954/463–6747* ⊕ *www.oldheidelbergdeli.com* ⊗ *Closed Mon. No lunch Sat.*

**$**
SEAFOOD
× **Southport Raw Bar.** You can't go wrong at this unpretentious spot where the motto, on bumper stickers for miles around, proclaims, "eat fish, live longer, eat oysters, love longer, eat clams, last longer." Raw or steamed clams, raw oysters, and peel-and-eat shrimp are market priced. Sides range from Bimini bread to key lime pie, with conch fritters, beer-battered onion rings, and corn on the cob in between. Order wine by the bottle or glass, and beer by the pitcher, bottle, or can. Eat outside overlooking a canal, or inside at booths, tables, or in the front or back bars. Limited parking is free, and a grocery-store parking lot is across the street. ⊠ *1536 Cordova Rd.* ☎ *954/525–2526* ⊕ *www. southportrawbar.com.*

**$$$**
VEGETARIAN
× **Sublime.** Pamela Anderson and her celebrity pals are not the only vegetarians that love this vegan powerhouse. The vegan sushi, the portobello stack, and innovative pizzas and pastas surprisingly satisfy carnivore cravings. All dishes are organic and void of any animal by-products, showing the world how vegan eating does not compromise flavor or taste. Even items like the key lime cheesecake, and chicken scaloppini use alternative ingredients and headline an evening of health-conscious eating. ⊠ *1431 N. Federal Hwy., Intracoastal and Inland, Fort Lauderdale* ☎ *954/539–9000* ⊕ *www.sublimerestaurant. com* ⊗ *Closed Mon.*

**¢**
MEXICAN
Fodor'sChoice
★
× **Zona Fresca.** A local favorite, Zona Fresca leads the healthy, Mexican fast-food revolution with the best chips, salsas, and burritos in town. Everything is made fresh on premises, including the authentic salsas, presented in a grand salsa bar. Known locally for its fantastic value and great products, Zona is busy seven days a week for both lunch and dinner and offers both indoor and outdoor seating. ⊠ *1635 N.*

*Federal Hwy., Intracoastal and Inland, Fort Lauderdale* ☎ *954/566–1777* ⊕ *www.zonafresca.com.*

## WESTERN SUBURBS

**$$** ✕**Alligator Alley.** At this taproom and music hall big on nightly music
AMERICAN from rockabilly to funk rock, chefs ladle up memorable gumbo, and
alligator ribs so good they once were featured on the Food Network.
Wash down your beer with Gator Bites or Buffalo Fingers, or for
delicacy, go for an appetizer of scallopini of gator with Szechuan
sauce. Vegetarians can bulk up on cheese fries, or keep trim with a
garden salad. ✉ *1321 E. Commercial Blvd.* ☎ *954/771–2220* ⊕ *www.
alligatoralleyflorida.com.*

**$$$$** ✕**Ireland Steakhouse.** Don't let the name fool you. Ireland Steakhouse is
IRISH not particularly Irish nor is it just a steak house. In fact, this restaurant
is most popular for its sustainable seafood menu. Promoting a holis-
tic philosophy of green eating, the restaurant meticulously chooses its
ingredients and the purveyors that supply them, while staying true to
the international "Seafood Watch" guide. The restaurant is a warm and
woodsy enclave in the back corner of the Hyatt Bonaventure. In keeping
with trends of other steak houses, hearty mains (like the Orange Glaze
Wild Canadian Arctic Char and the Cherry Balsamic Yellowfin Tuna)
are paired with loads of decadent sides made for sharing (like Lobster
Mac n' Cheese and Lobster Fries). ✉ *250 Racquet Club Rd., Weston*
☎ *954/349–5656* ⊕ *www.bonaventure.hyatt.com* ☽ *Dinner Tues.–Sat.
5:30–10:30 pm; closed Sun. and Mon.*

## WILTON MANORS AND OAKLAND PARK

**$** ✕**Diner 24.** It's still a mystery why Fort Lauderdale's newest diner added
AMERICAN the magic 2-4 to its name when it's open 24 hours on just Friday and
Saturday, until 11 pm other nights. Regardless, the awesome diner
favorites are served at rock-bottom prices, at nearly the same price as
neighboring McDonald's. With promotions nightly, a kitsch fish shack
decor, and a superwelcoming environment, Diner 24 merits a large fol-
lowing for the hours it is actually open. ✉ *301 W. Oakland Park Blvd.,
Oakland Park, Fort Lauderdale* ☎ *954/765–6349.*

**$$$** ✕**Galanga.** Serving both Thai and Japanese cuisine under one roof,
ASIAN Galanga manages to deliver authenticity and extreme satisfaction to
patrons who often find it hard to choose between the fabulous sushi
and the succulent coconut curries and Thai specialties. Located on the
main strip in Wilton Manors, the restaurant offers a sophisticated and
intimate ambience. ✉ *2389 Wilton Dr., Wilton Manors, Fort Lauderdale* ☎ *954/202–0000* ⊕ *www.galangarestaurant.com.*

**$$** ✕**Rosie's Bar and Grill.** Rosie's is consistently lively, pumping out tons of
AMERICAN pop tunes and volumes of joyous laughter to surrounding streets. The
former Hamburger Mary's has become an institution in South Florida,
as the go-to gay-friendly place for cheap drinks, decent bar food, and
great times. Most of the fun at Rosie's is meeting new friends and engag-
ing in conversation with the person seated next to you. Drink specials
change daily. Sunday brunch with alternating DJ's is wildly popular.
✉ *2449 Wilton Dr., Wilton Manors, Fort Lauderdale* ☎ *954/567–1320*
⊕ *www.rosiesbarandgrill.com.*

$ **✕ Stork's Café**. At the edge of Wilton
CAFÉ Manors, Stork's Café stands out
as a gay-friendly, straight-friendly,
and just plain friendly place to plot
sightseeing strategies (or catch up
on local papers). Sit indoors or outside under tables with red umbrellas. Custom Barbie cakes (real
dolls, edible ball gowns) are Stork's
signature as is the pistachio cheesecake. Divine baked goods range
from croissants, tortes, cakes, and pies to "Monster Cookies," including
gingersnap and snicker doodle. Pilgrim (turkey) or Hello Kitty (tuna)
sandwiches go with salads or made-from-scratch soups like Vegan Split
Pea. ☒ *2505 N.E. 15th Ave., Wilton Manors* ☎ *954/567–3220* ⊕ *www.
storkscafe.com.*

> **WORD OF MOUTH**
>
> "Loved Lago Mar. The rooms are
> spacious and clean, nice pools
> and nice beach. Restaurant is very
> good. You would need a car to
> get to other places in Fort Lau-
> derdale but I think it is worth it."
> —lindafromNJ

# WHERE TO STAY

*For expanded hotel reviews, visit Fodors.com.*

### ALONG THE BEACH

$$$$ **⊡ The Atlantic Hotel**. Functional but elegant, this luxury condo hotel
HOTEL overlooks the Atlantic Ocean. **Pros:** sophisticated lodging option; rooms
★ have high-tech touches. **Cons:** no complimentary water bottles in room;
expensive parking. ☒ *601 N. Fort Lauderdale Beach Blvd.* ☎ *954/567–
8020 or 877/567–8020* ⊕ *www.atlantichotelfl.com* ⟿ *61 rooms, 58
suites, 4 penthouses* ⚇ *In-room: a/c, kitchen, Internet, Wi-Fi. In-hotel:
restaurants, bar, pool, gym, spa, parking* ⎥⊙⎢ *No meals.*

$$ **⊡ Lago Mar Resort and Club**. The sprawling Lago Mar, owned by the
RESORT Banks family since the early 1950s, has retained its sparkle thanks
☺ to frequent renovations. **Pros:** secluded setting; plenty of activities;
★ on the beach. **Cons:** not the easiest to find; far from restaurants and
beach action. ☒ *1700 S. Ocean La.* ☎ *954/523–6511 or 800/524–
6627* ⊕ *www.lagomar.com* ⟿ *52 rooms, 160 suites* ⚇ *In-room: a/c,
kitchen, Wi-Fi. In-hotel: restaurants, tennis court, pool* ⎥⊙⎢ *No meals.*

$$$–$$$$ **⊡ Pelican Grand Beach Resort**. Smack on the beach, this already lovely
RESORT property has been transformed with a new tower, restaurant and lounge,
☺ an old-fashioned ice-cream parlor, and a circulating lazy-river pool that
★ allows guests to float 'round and 'round. **Pros:** you can't get any closer
to the beach in Fort Lauderdale. **Cons:** you'll need wheels to access Las
Olas's beach-area action. ☒ *2000 N. Atlantic Blvd.* ☎ *954/568–9431 or
800/525–6232* ⊕ *www.pelicanbeach.com* ⟿ *121 rooms (remainder of
155 total are condominiums)* ⚇ *In-room: a/c, Internet, Wi-Fi. In-hotel:
restaurant, bar, pool* ⎥⊙⎢ *No meals.*

$$$ **⊡ The Pillars Hotel**. A "small secret" kept by locals in the know, this
B&B/INN gem is one block from the beach and on the Intracoastal Waterway.
**Pros:** attentive staff; lovely decor; idyllic pool area. **Cons:** small
rooms; not for families with young kids given proximity to dock and
water with no lifeguard on duty. ☒ *111 N. Birch Rd.* ☎ *954/467–
9639* ⊕ *www.pillarshotel.com* ⟿ *13 rooms, 5 suites* ⚇ *In-room: a/c,*

Internet, Wi-Fi. In-hotel: restaurant, pool, some age restrictions ⦿ No meals.

$$$–$$$$
HOTEL
Fodor'sChoice
★
**Ritz-Carlton, Fort Lauderdale.** It's an eyepopper, with 24 dramatically tiered, glass-walled stories rising behind a tropical sundeck and a pool looking out toward the ocean. **Pros:** golfers have privileges at the private Grande Oaks Golf Course, where *Caddyshack* was filmed. **Cons:** golf facilities off-site; no complimentary Wi-Fi in public spaces. ⊠ 1 N. Fort Lauderdale Beach Blvd. ☎ 954/465–2300 ⊕ www.ritzcarlton.com ⧄ 138 rooms, 54 suites ⧉ In-room: a/c, Wi-Fi. In-hotel: restaurants, bar, pool, gym, spa, parking ⦿ No meals.

$$$–$$$$
HOTEL
Fodor'sChoice
★
**W Fort Lauderdale.** Fort Lauderdale's trendiest hotel, this pair of 23-story towers of the W Hotel rise over the Atlantic blues like a massive luxury boat at full sail. **Pros:** newest of the beach luxury leaders; tony scene; great spa. **Cons:** across highway from beach. ⊠ 435 N. Fort Lauderdale Beach Blvd. ☎ 954/462–1633 ⊕ www.starwood.com ⧄ 346 hotel rooms, 171 hotel condominiums ⧉ In-room: a/c, Internet, Wi-Fi. In-hotel: restaurants, bars, pools, gym, spa, parking, some pets allowed ⦿ No meals.

$$–$$$
HOTEL
**The Worthington and the Alcazar.** Side by side and sharing common amenities, the Worthington and the Alcazar are two of Fort Lauderdale beach's 27 clothing-optional resorts for gay men. **Pros:** fresh-squeezed orange juice in the morning; nice pool area. **Cons:** not on the beach; no view. ⊠ 543–555 N. Birch Rd. ☎ 954/563–6819 or 954/567–2525 ⊕ www.worthington.com, www.alcazarresort.com ⧄ 17 rooms; 20 rooms and suites ⧉ In-room: a/c, kitchen (some). In-hotel: pool ⦿ Breakfast.

## DOWNTOWN AND LAS OLAS

$$$
B&B/INN
**Pineapple Point.** Tucked a few blocks behind Las Olas Boulevard in the residential neighborhood of Victoria Park, Pineapple Point is a spectacular maze of tropical cottages and dense foliage catering to the gay community. **Pros:** superior service; tropical setting. **Cons:** away from the beach; need a vehicle. ⊠ 315 N.E. 16th Terrace, Victoria Park ☎ 954/527–0094 ⊕ www.pineapplepoint.com ⧄ 25 rooms ⧉ In-room: a/c, kitchen (some), Wi-Fi. In-hotel: gym, spa, parking, some age restrictions ⦿ Breakfast.

$$$
HOTEL
**Riverside Hotel.** On Las Olas Boulevard, just steps from boutiques, restaurants, and art galleries, Fort Lauderdale's oldest hotel debuted in 1936, but frequent renovations have kept it looking great in true

---

## ULTIMATE WINE TASTING

The seductive Wine Room and sensual Wine Vault at the Ritz-Carlton, Fort Lauderdale impress with 5,000 global bottles, classic elegance, and the haute design minutia that has given the Ritz-Carlton its flawless reputation. The surprisingly affordable "Take Flight in the Wine Vault" experience entails the hotel sommelier creating a private wine tasting for guests inside the signature wine vault. Experience a journey across France, Australia, Argentina, or California through six glasses of red or white wine while enjoying informative and fascinating lessons between sips! Reservations required, $50.

Lago Mar Resort & Club in Fort Lauderdale has its own private beach on the Atlantic Ocean.

Tommy Bahamas style. **Pros:** historic appeal; in the thick of Las Olas action; nice views. **Cons:** no quick access to beach. ⊠ *620 E. Las Olas Blvd.* ☎ *954/467–0671 or 800/325–3280* ⊕ *www.riversidehotel.com* ⊸ *203 rooms, 10 suites* ⌂ *In-room: a/c, Internet. In-hotel: restaurants, bars, pool* ⊺⊙⊺ *No meals.*

### INTRACOASTAL AND INLAND

**\$\$\$–\$\$\$\$**
RESORT

🛏 **Hyatt Regency Pier Sixty-Six Resort & Spa.** The iconic 17-story tower dominates a lovely 22-acre spread that includes the full-service Spa 66. **Pros:** great views; plenty of activities; free shuttle to beach; easy water taxi access. **Cons:** not on the beach; '70s exterior. ⊠ *2301 S.E. 17th St. Causeway* ☎ *954/525–6666* ⊕ *www.pier66.com* ⊸ *384 rooms and suites* ⌂ *In-room: a/c, Wi-Fi. In-hotel: restaurants, bars, tennis courts, pools, gym, spa, water sports* ⊺⊙⊺ *No meals.*

### WESTERN SUBURBS

**\$\$–\$\$\$\$**
RESORT

🛏 **Hyatt Regency Bonaventure Conference Center & Spa.** This upscale venue targets conventioneers and business executives as well as vacationers who value golf, Everglades, and shopping over beach proximity. **Pros:** lush landscaping; pampering spa. **Cons:** in the suburbs; poor views from some rooms. ⊠ *250 Racquet Club Rd., Westin* ☎ *954/616–1234* ⊕ *www.bonaventure.hyatt.com* ⊸ *501 rooms* ⌂ *In-room: a/c, Wi-Fi. In-hotel: restaurants, bars, golf courses, tennis courts, pools, gym, spa, some pets allowed* ⊺⊙⊺ *No meals.*

# NORTH ON SCENIC A1A

North of Fort Lauderdale's Birch Recreation Area, Route A1A edges away from the beach through a stretch known as Galt Ocean Mile, and a succession of ocean-side communities line up against the sea. Traffic can line up, too, as it passes through a changing pattern of beach-blocking high-rises and modest family vacation towns and back again. As far as tourism goes, these communities tend to cater to a different demographic than Fort Lauderdale. Europeans and cost-conscious families head to Lauderdale-by-the-Sea, Pompano, and Deerfield for fewer frills and longer stays.

*Towns are shown on the Broward County map.*

## LAUDERDALE-BY-THE-SEA

*5 mi north of Fort Lauderdale.*

Just north of Fort Lauderdale's northern boundary, this low-rise family resort town traditionally digs in its heels at mere mention of high-rises. The result is choice shoreline access that's rapidly disappearing in nearby communities. Without a doubt, Lauderdale-by-the-Sea takes delight in embracing its small beach-town feel and welcoming guests to a different world of years gone by.

### GETTING HERE AND AROUND

Lauderdale-by-the-Sea is just north of Fort Lauderdale. If you're driving from Interstate 95, exit east onto Commercial Boulevard and head over the Intracoastal Waterway. From U.S. 1 (aka Federal Highway), turn east on Commercial Boulevard. If coming from A1A, just continue north from Fort Lauderdale Beach.

### ESSENTIALS

Visitor Information Lauderdale-by-the-Sea Chamber of Commerce (✉ 4201 N. Ocean Dr., Lauderdale-by-the-Sea ☎ 954/776–1000 ⊕ www.lbts. com).

### SPORTS AND THE OUTDOORS

★ **Anglin's Fishing Pier.** This longtime favorite for 24-hour fishing has a fresh, renovated appearance after shaking off repeated storm damage that closed the pier at intervals during the past decade. ☎ 954/491–9403.

### WHERE TO EAT

$$ ✕ **Aruba Beach Café.** This massive, beachfront eatery is always crowded
CAFÉ and always fun. One of Lauderdale-by-the-Sea's most famous restaurants, Aruba Beach serves a wide range of American and Caribbean cuisine, including Caribbean conch chowder and conch fritters. There are also fresh tropical salads, sandwiches, and seafood. The café is famous for its divine fresh-baked Bimini Bread with Aruba Glaze (think challah with donut glaze). A band performs day and night, so head for the back corner with eye-popping views of the beach if you want conversation while you eat and drink. Sunday breakfast buffet starts at 9 am. ✉ 1 Commercial Blvd. ☎ 954/776–0001 ⊕ www.arubabeachcafe.com.

$$$$ ✕ **Blue Moon Fish Company.** Most tables have stellar views of the Intra-
SEAFOOD coastal Waterway, but Blue Moon East's true magic comes from the
**Fodor's** Choice
★

kitchen, where the chefs create moon-and-stars-worthy seafood dishes. It's also the best deal in town with a two-for-one word-of-mouth lunch special Monday through Saturday. Start with whole roasted garlic and bread and continue on to the mussels, the langostino salad (with pecan-crusted goat cheese, spinach, and carmelized onions) or pan-seared fresh-shucked oysters. For Sunday champagne brunches book early, even in the off-season. ⊠ *4405 W. Tradewinds Ave.* ☎ *954/267–9888* ⊕ *www.bluemoonfishco.com.*

$   ✕**LaSpada's Original Hoagies.** The crew at this seaside hole-in-the-wall
AMERICAN   puts on quite a show of ingredient-tossing flair while assembling takeout hoagies, subs, and deli sandwiches. Locals rave that they are the best around. Fill up on the foot-long Monster (ham, cheese, roast beef, and turkey, $10.95), Hot Meatballs Marinara ($8.50), or an assortment of salads. ⊠ *4346 Seagrape Dr.* ☎ *954/776–7893* ⊕ *www.laspadashoagies. com.*

## WHERE TO STAY
*For expanded hotel reviews, visit Fodors.com.*

$$–$$$   ▦ **Blue Seas Courtyard.** Innkeeper Cristie Furth, with her husband, Marc,
B&B/INN   runs this small motel in a quiet resort area across from the beach. **Pros:** south-of-the-border vibe; friendly owners; vintage stoves from 1971; memory foam mattress toppers. **Cons:** rooms lack ocean views; old bath tubs in some rooms. ⊠ *4525 El Mar Dr.* ☎ *954/772–3336* ⊕ *www. blueseascourtyard.com* ⤷ *12 rooms* ⌂ *In-room: a/c, kitchen, Wi-Fi. In-hotel: pool, laundry facilities* ¶❍¶ *Breakfast.*

$$–$$$   ▦ **High Noon Beach Resort.** Family-run since 1961, this resort sits on
HOTEL   300 feet of beautiful beach, where you'll find a comfortable place to relax morning, noon, or night. **Pros:** smack on the beach; friendly vibe. **Cons:** early booking required. ⊠ *4424 El Mar Dr.* ☎ *954/776–1121 or 800/382–1265* ⊕ *www.highnoonresort.com* ⤷ *40 rooms* ⌂ *In-room: a/c, kitchen (some), Wi-Fi. In-hotel: pool, beach* ¶❍¶ *Breakfast.*

$$–$$$   ▦ **Sea Lord Hotel & Suites.** This attractive ocean-side hotel has undergone
HOTEL   a major transformation in recent years, adding a pool deck, restaurant, lobby, sundeck, a new entranceway, a small fitness center, and room upgrades. **Pros:** terrific beach location; void of the moldy smell in other hotels. **Cons:** shaky elevators; limited parking. ⊠ *4140 El Mar Dr.* ☎ *954/776–1505 or 800/344–4451* ⊕ *www.sealordhotel.com* ⤷ *47 rooms* ⌂ *In-room: a/c, kitchen (some), Wi-Fi. In-hotel: pool, laundry facilities, beach* ¶❍¶ *Breakfast.*

$$–$$$   ▦ **Tropic Seas Resort Motel.** This two-story property has an unbeatable
HOTEL   location—directly on the beach, flanking 150 feet of pristine sands and sparkling blues. **Pros:** family-owned friendliness; great lawn furniture. **Cons:** must reserve far ahead; older style bathrooms ⊠ *4616 El Mar Dr.* ☎ *954/772–2555 or 800/952–9581* ⊕ *www.tropicseasresort. com* ⤷ *16 rooms* ⌂ *In-room: a/c, kitchen (some), Wi-Fi. In-hotel: pool, beach* ¶❍¶ *Breakfast.*

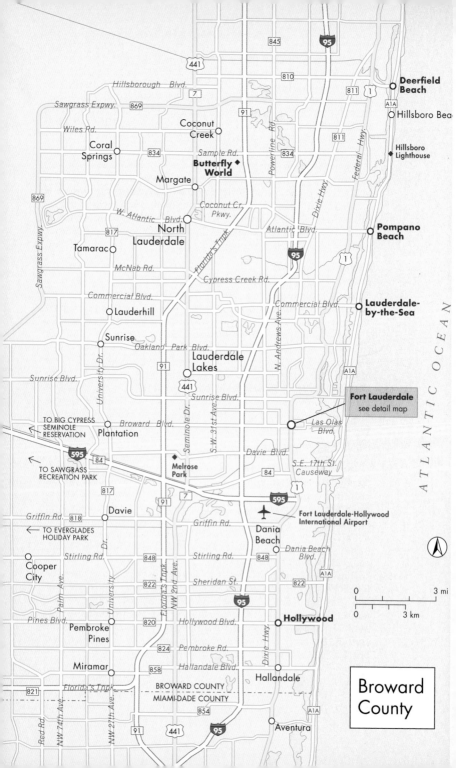

Broward
County

## POMPANO BEACH

*Pompano Beach is 3 mi north of Lauderdale-by-the-Sea.*

As Route A1A enters this town directly north of Lauderdale-by-the-Sea the high-rise scene resumes. Sportfishing is big in Pompano Beach, as its name implies, but there's more to beachside attractions than the popular Fisherman's Wharf. Behind a low coral-rock wall, Alsdorf Park (also called the 14th Street boat ramp) extends north and south of the wharf along the road and beach.

### GETTING HERE AND AROUND

From Interstate 95, Pompano Beach exits include Sample Road, Copans Road, or Atlantic Boulevard.

### ESSENTIALS

**Visitor Information Greater Pompano Beach Chamber of Commerce** (☎ 954/941-2940 ⊕ www.pompanobeachchamber.com).

### EXPLORING

**Butterfly World.** As many as 80 butterfly species from South and Central America, the Philippines, Malaysia, Taiwan, and other Asian nations are typically found within the serene 3-acre site inside Tradewinds Park, at the western edge of Pompano Beach, several miles inland. A screened aviary called North American Butterflies is reserved for native species. The Tropical Rain Forest Aviary is a 30-foot-high construction, with observation decks, waterfalls, ponds, and tunnels filled with thousands of colorful butterflies. Kids bug out at the bug zoo with Asian cockroaches as big as your hand. ☒ *3600 W. Sample Rd., Coconut Creek* ☎ *954/977-4400* ⊕ *www.butterflyworld.com* ☒ *$24.95* ☽ *Mon.–Sat. 9–5, Sun. 11–5.*

### SPORTS AND THE OUTDOORS

#### FISHING

**Pompano Pier.** The 24-hour pier extends more than 1,000 feet into the Atlantic. The pier tackle shop sells beer and snacks. Admission is $4 to fish, $1 to sightsee; rod-and-reel rental is $16.50 (including admission, plus a $20 deposit) for the day. Anglers brag about catching barracuda, jack, and snapper here in the same sitting, along with bluefish, cobia, and, yes, even pompano. ☎ *954/226–6411.*

OUTFITTERS **Fish City Pride.** Morning, afternoon, and evening drift-fishing trips cost $37 and include fishing gear and bait. ☒ *Fish City Marina, 2621 N. Riverside Dr., Pompano Beach* ☎ *954/781–1211.*

**Hillsboro Inlet Marina.** The eight-boat fleet offers saltwater half-day charters for $550, six hours for $750, or a full day for $950, including gear for up to six anglers. ☒ *2705 N. Riverside Dr., Pompano Beach* ☎ *954/943–8222.*

#### SCUBA DIVING

**SS *Copenhagen* State Underwater Archaeological Preserve.** The wreck of the SS *Copenhagen* lies in 15- to 30-foot depths just outside the second reef on the Pompano Ledge, 3.6 mi south of Hillsboro Inlet. The 325-foot-long steamer's final voyage, from Philadelphia bound for Havana, began May 20, 1900, ending six days later when the captain—attempting to avoid gulf currents—crashed onto a reef off what's now Pompano Beach. In 2000, the missing bow section was identified a half mile to the south. The wreck, a haven for colorful fish and corals and a magnet for skin and scuba divers, became Florida's fifth Underwater Archaeological Preserve in 1994, listed on the National Register of Historic Places in 2001.

## SHOPPING

**Sugar Chest Antique Mall.** Bargain hunters and antique junkies browse the 200 vendors' collectibles and antiques. ⊠ *906 N. Federal Hwy., Pompano Beach* ☎ *954/942–8601* ⊕ *www.thesugarchestantiquemall.com.*

## WHERE TO EAT

**$$$$**
ECLECTIC
★
✕ **Cafe Maxx.** New-wave epicurean dining had its South Florida start here in the early 1980s, and Cafe Maxx remains fresh. The menu changes nightly but showcases tropical appeal with jerk-spiced sea scallops or jumbo stone crab claws with honey-lime mustard sauce and black-bean-and-banana-pepper chili with Florida avocado. Appetizers include caviar pie and crispy sweetbreads. Desserts such as Trio of Sorbet (or ice cream) with a flurry of fruit sauces, including mango, stay the tropical course. Select from 300 wines by the bottle, and many by the glass. ⊠ *2601 E. Atlantic Blvd., Pompano Beach* ☎ *954/782–0606* ⊕ *www.cafemaxx.com* ⊙ *No lunch.*

**$$$**
SEAFOOD
✕ **Cap's Place.** On an island once a bootlegger's haunt, Lighthouse Point's ramshackle seafood spot reached by launch has served the famous as well as the infamous, including the likes of Winston Churchill, FDR, JFK, and Al Capone. Cap was Captain Theodore Knight, born in 1871, who, with partner-in-crime Al Hasis, floated a derelict barge to the area in the 1920s. Broward's oldest restaurant, built on the barge, is run by Hasis's descendants. Sesame-crusted mahimahi is served with soy-ginger sauce, flaky rolls are baked fresh, and tangy lime pie is a great finale. Clams and oysters are shucked to order. Cap's is no cheapie; even a plate of linguine and clams will cost you $24. ⊠ *Cap's Dock, 2765 N.E. 28th Ct.* ☎ *954/941–0418* ⊕ *www.capsplace.com* ⊙ *No lunch. Closed Mon. May–Dec.*

## WHERE TO STAY

*For expanded hotel reviews, visit Fodors.com.*

**$$–$$$**
HOTEL
**Beachcomber Resort & Villas.** This property's beachfront location is close to most local attractions and a mile from the Pompano Pier. **Pros:** Old Florida feel; on the water. **Cons:** worn around the edges; moldy smell in some rooms. ⊠ *1200 S. Ocean Blvd.* ☎ *954/941–7830 or 800/231–2423* ⊕ *www.beachcomberresort.com* ⋈ *143 rooms, 9 villas, 4 suites* ⚒ *In-room: a/c, Internet, Wi-Fi. In-hotel: restaurant, bar, pools, beach* ⍟*No meals.*

**EN ROUTE**
**Hillsboro Lighthouse.** About 2 mi north of Pompano Beach you are afforded a beautiful view across Hillsboro Inlet to this lighthouse, often called the brightest lighthouse in the Southeast and used by mariners as a landmark for decades. When at sea you can see its light from almost halfway to the Bahamas. Although the octagonal-pyramid, iron-skeletal tower lighthouse is on private property inaccessible to the public, it's well worth a peek, even from afar. The Hillsboro Lighthouse

Preservation Society offers tours about four times a year; call for schedule and tips on viewing vantage points. ☎ *954/942–2102* ⊕ *www. hillsborolighthouse.org.*

EN
ROUTE

**Hillsboro Mile.** To the north, Route A1A traverses the so-called Hillsboro Mile (actually more than 2 mi), a millionaire's row of some of Broward's most beautiful and expensive homes. The road runs along a narrow strip of land between the Intracoastal Waterway and the ocean, with bougainvillea and oleander edging the way and yachts docked along both banks. Traffic often moves at a snail's pace, especially in winter, as vacationers (and sometimes even envious locals) gawk.

## DEERFIELD BEACH

*Deerfield Beach is 2 mi north of Pompano Beach.*

As posh Hillsboro Mile comes to an end, Route A1A spills out onto Deerfield Beach, Broward's northernmost ocean-side community.

**GETTING HERE AND AROUND**
From Interstate 95, take the Hillsboro Boulevard exit east. From A1A, continue north past Pompano Beach and Hillsboro Beach.

**ESSENTIALS**
Visitor Information **Greater Deerfield Beach Chamber of Commerce**
(☎ *954/427–1050* ⊕ *www.deerfieldchamber.com*).

### EXPLORING

☺ **Quiet Waters Park.** Its name belies what's in store for kids here. Splash Adventure is a high-tech water-play system with slides and tunnels, among other activities. A Rent-A-Tent program ($35 per night for up to four campers) provides already set-up tents or teepees. There's also cable water-skiing and boat rental on this county park's lake, and a skate park. Note that this space functions mostly as a public park for locals than as a tourist attraction and is located near a highway. ⊠ *401 S. Powerline Rd., Deerfield Beach* ☎ *954/360–1315* ⊕ *www.broward. org/parks* ☜ *Park $1 weekends, free weekdays* ☉ *Apr.–Sept., daily 8–6; Oct.–Mar., daily 8–5:30.*

OFF THE
BEATEN
PATH

**Deerfield Island Park.** Reached only by boat (and with a new dock in the works for vessels longer than 25 feet), this officially designated Urban Wilderness Area showcases coastal hammock island and contains a mangrove swamp that provides a critical habitat for gopher tortoises, gray foxes, raccoons, and armadillos. County-operated boat shuttles run 10–3 on weekends (on the hour only). Amenities include a boardwalk, walking trails, and an observation tower. ⊠ *1720 Deerfield Island Park* ☎ *954/360–1320* ⊕ *www.broward.org/parks/ DeerfieldIslandPark* ☜ *Free.*

### SPORTS AND THE OUTDOORS

**FISHING**
**Deerfield Pier.** This picturesque pier teems with fishermen and tourists. Admission is $4 to fish, $1 to sightsee. Common catches include king mackerel, snapper, blue fish, and barracuda. ☎ *954/426–9206.*

OUTFITTERS **Cove Marina.** The deep-sea charter fleet does excellent runs of sailfish, kingfish, dolphin, and tuna in winter. A half-day charter for six costs about $600, or $1,000 for a full day. ⊠ *Hillsboro Blvd. and Intracoastal Waterway, Deerfield Beach* ☎ 954/427–9747.

## SCUBA DIVING

**Dixie Divers.** Among the area's most popular dive operators, this outfit has morning and afternoon dives aboard the 48-foot *Lady-Go-Diver,* plus evening dives on weekends. Snorkelers and certified divers can explore the marine life of nearby reefs and shipwrecks. The cost is $60; ride-alongs are welcome for $35. ⊠ *Cove Marina, Hillsboro Blvd. and Intracoastal Waterway, Deerfield Beach* ☎ 954/420–0009 ⊕ *www.dixiedivers.com.*

## WHERE TO EAT

$$$
FRENCH
★
✕ **Brooks.** This is one of Broward's more elegant dining spots, thanks to French perfectionist Bernard Perron. Brooks is now run by Perron's son-in-law John Howe. Updated Continental fare is served in a series of rooms filled with old-master replicas, cut glass, antiques, and floral wallpaper. Fresh ingredients go into distinctly Floridian dishes, including sautéed Key Largo yellowtail snapper. Roast rack of lamb is also popular. Put your order in early for the chocolate or Grand Marnier soufflé. ⊠ *500 S. Federal Hwy., Deerfield Beach* ☎ 954/427–9302 ⊕ *www.brooks-restaurant.com.*

$
SEAFOOD
★
✕ **Olympia Flame Diner.** The family-owned Flame burned white-hot in 2009 when finance guru Suze Orman did a star turn as a waitress here for an *Oprah* TV segment. Orman has a condo nearby, and her fitness trainer—who dines here regularly—suggested the blue-awning diner as an illuminated best bet for a hot, home-style meal accompanied by megawatt chatter. Greek specialties from spinach pie to baklava dominate the menu, but you can order seafood, deli-style sandwiches, and burgers along with beer or wine. And no, Oprah and Orman mega-exposure hasn't changed the homey mood here at all. ⊠ *80 S. Federal Hwy., Deerfield Beach* ☎ 954/480–8402 ⊕ *www.olympiaflamediner.com.*

$$
SEAFOOD
★
✕ **Whale's Rib.** For a casual, almost funky, nautical experience near the beach, look no farther. If you want to blend in, order a fish special with whale fries—thinly sliced potatoes that look like hot potato chips. People come from near and far for the famous whale fries. Those with smaller appetites can choose from salads and fish sandwiches, or raw-bar favorites like Ipswich clams. ⊠ *2031 N.E. 2nd St., Deerfield Beach* ☎ 954/421–8880.

## WHERE TO STAY

*For expanded hotel reviews, visit Fodors.com.*

$
HOTEL
 **Carriage House Resort Motel.** This tidy motel, accredited as an SSL (Superior Small Lodging), is less than a block from the ocean, and the two-story, colonial-style building with black shutters has two sections connected by a second-story sundeck. **Pros:** friendly staff; bargain rates. **Cons:** nothing fancy. ⊠ *250 S. Ocean Blvd.* ☎ 954/427–7670 ⊕ *www.carriagehouseresort.com* ⌁ 6 rooms, 14 efficiencies, 10

*apartments* ⛄ *In-room: a/c, Internet, Wi-Fi. In-hotel: pool, laundry facilities.* ⧄ *No meals.*

# SOUTH BROWARD

South Broward's roots are in early Florida settlements. Thus far it has avoided some of the glitz and glamour of neighbors to the north and south, and folks here like it that way. Still, there's plenty to see and do—excellent restaurants in every price range, world-class pari-mutuels, and a new focus on the arts.

## HOLLYWOOD

*Hollywood is 8 mi south of Fort Lauderdale.*

Hollywood has had a face-lift, with more nips and tucks to come. Young Circle, once down-at-heel, has become Broward's first Arts Park. On Hollywood's western outskirts, the flamboyant Seminole Hard Rock Hotel & Casino has permanently etched the previously downtrodden section of State Road 7/U.S. 441 corridor on the map of trendy excitement, drawing local weekenders, architecture buffs, and gamblers. But Hollywood's redevelopment effort doesn't end there: new shops, restaurants, and art galleries open at a persistent clip, and the city has spiffed up its Broadwalk (not Boardwalk)—a wide pedestrian walkway along the beach—where Rollerbladers are as commonplace as snowbirds from the north.

### GETTING HERE AND AROUND
From Interstate 95, exit east on Sheridan Street or Hollywood Boulevard.

### ESSENTIALS
Visitor Information **Hollywood Chamber of Commerce** (✉ *330 N. Federal Hwy., Hollywood* ☎ *954/923–4000* ⊕ *www.hollywoodchamber.org*).

### EXPLORING

**Art and Culture Center of Hollywood**. This is a visual- and performing-arts facility with an art reference library, outdoor sculpture garden, and arts school. It's southeast of Young Circle, melding urban open space with a fountain, a 2,000-plus-seat amphitheater, and an indoor theater. Nearby, on trendy Harrison Street and Hollywood Boulevard, are chic lunch places, bluesy entertainment spots, and shops. ✉ *1650 Harrison St.* ☎ *954/921–3274* ⊕ *artandculturecenter.org* 🗐 *$7* ☉ *Tues.–Fri. 10–5, weekends noon–4. Closed Mon.*

### BEACHES

**Broadwalk.** With the Intracoastal Waterway to the west and the beach and ocean immediately east, this spiffed-up 2-mi paved promenade has lured pedestrians and cyclists since 1924. With a recent $14 million makeover, this stretch has taken on added luster for the buff, the laid-back, and the retired. Kids also thrive here: there are play areas, rental bikes, trikes, and other pedal-powered gizmos. Expect to hear French spoken here, since Hollywood Beach has long been a favorite getaway for Quebecois. Conversations in Spanish and Portuguese are

Fodor's Choice
★

also frequently overheard on this path. ⊠ *Rte. A1A and Sheridan St.* 🚗 *Parking in public lots is $1.50 per hr.*

**John U. Lloyd Beach State Recreation Area.** The once pine-dotted natural area was restored to its natural state, thanks to government-driven efforts to pull out all but indigenous plants. Now native sea grape, gumbo-limbo, and other native plants offer shaded ambience. Nature trails and a marina remain are large draws as is canoeing on Whiskey Creek. ⊠ *6503 N. Ocean Dr.* 🕾 *954/923–2833* 🚗 *$6 per vehicle for 2 to 8 passengers, $4 for lone driver* ⊘ *Daily 8–sunset.*

## SPORTS AND THE OUTDOORS

⟳ **West Lake Park.** Rent a canoe, kayak, or take the 40-minute boat tour at this park bordering the Intracoastal Waterway. At 1,500 acres, it is one of Florida's largest urban nature facilities. Extensive boardwalks traverse mangrove forests that shelter endangered and threatened species. A 65-foot observation tower showcases the entire park. At the free **Anne Kolb Nature Center,** named after Broward's late environmental advocate, there's a 3,500-gallon aquarium. The center's exhibit hall has 27 interactive displays. ⊠ *751 Sheridan St.* 🕾 *954/926–2480* 🚗 *Weekends $1.50, weekdays free* ⊘ *Daily 9–5.*

### FISHING

**Sea Leg's III.** Drift-fishing trips run during the day and bottom-fishing trips at night. Trips cost $35–$38, including rod rental. ⊠ *5398 N. Ocean Dr.* 🕾 *954/923–2109*

### GOLF

**Diplomat Country Club & Spa.** There are 18 holes and a spa; greens fee $69/$209. ⊠ *501 Diplomat Pkwy., Hallandale* 🕾 *954/883–4000.*

**Emerald Hills.** The course has 18 holes; greens fee $55/$190. ⊠ *4100 N. Hills Dr.* 🕾 *954/961–4000.*

## NIGHTLIFE AND THE ARTS

### THE ARTS

**Harrison Street Art and Design District.** In downtown Hollywood, this collection of galleries features original artwork (eclectic paintings, sculpture, photography, and mixed media). Friday night the artists' studios, galleries, and shops stay open later while crowds meander along Hollywood Boulevard and Harrison Street.

### NIGHTLIFE

Although Hollywood has a small-town feel, it has an assortment of coffee shops, sports bars, martini lounges, and dance clubs.

**Sushi Blues.** Since 1989, this Japanese-American-theme establishment has served up revolving entertainment, especially on weekends. ⊠ *2009 Harrison St.* 🕾 *954/929–9560* ⊕ *www.sushiblues.com.*

**Whisky Tango.** The comfy couches are available nightly. ⊠ *1903 Hollywood Blvd.* 🕾 *954/925–2555* ⊕ *www.whiskeytangofl.com.*

## WHERE TO EAT

$$$ ✕ **Azia.** Located on the Intracoastal across from the Westin Hollywood
ASIAN FUSION Diplomat, Azia remains somewhat a well-kept secret in greater Fort
Fodor's Choice Lauderdale. Before the restaurant transforms into a chic and seductive
★ Asian-inspired nightclub on the weekends, a phenomenal team presents

an Asian fusion extravaganza seven nights a week. While classics are indeed on the menu, the chef puts a welcomed and successful twist on most dishes. For example, Azia's pad thai is infused with Tamarind sauce while the summer rolls are made with mango instead of shrimp. The shrimp tempura roll also has fried green tomatoes inside and the Lava Seafood appetizer mixes curried seafood with cream cheese to create mouth-watering heaven! The presentation is nothing less than spectacular. Even if you're not staying in Hollywood, Azia is worth the drive from Fort Lauderdale proper. ⊠ *3660 S Ocean Dr., Hollywood* ☎ *954/602–8347* ⊕ *www.aiziahollywood.com.*

**$$$** ✕ **Café Martorano.** Located within Hard Rock Hollywood's massive
ITALIAN  entertainment and restaurant zone, this Italian-American institution pays homage to anything and everything that has to do with the "Godfather" and impresses with massive family-style portions. Dishes run the full Italian-American gamut, from the classic parmigianas to the lobster and snapper francaise. The homemade mozzarella and fried calamari are excellent choices for starters. It's easy to gorge here since each dish is so succulent and savory. The ever-present "Godfather" motif is taken to the extreme—dinner is interrupted hourly with clips from the movie played on the surrounding flat screens. ⊠ *5751 Seminole Way, Hollywood* ☎ *954/584–4450* ⊕ *www.cafemartorano.com.*

**$$$** ✕ **Giorgio's Grill.** Good food and service are hallmarks of this expan-
SEAFOOD  sive 400-seat restaurant overlooking the Intracoastal Waterway. Seafood is a specialty, but you'll also find pasta and meat dishes, and a solid Sunday brunch for around $20. A great watery view—especially around sunset—and friendly staff add to the experience, and there's a surprisingly extensive, reasonably priced wine list. ⊠ *606 N. Ocean Dr.* ☎ *954/929–7030* ⊕ *www.giorgiosgrill.com.*

**$$$** ✕ **Las Brisas.** Next to the beach, this cozy bistro offers seating inside
ARGENTINE  or out, and the food is Argentine with Italian flair. A small pot, filled with *chimichurri*—a paste of oregano, parsley, olive oil, salt, garlic, and crushed pepper—for spreading on steaks, sits on each table. Grilled fish is a favorite, as are pork chops, chicken, and pasta entrées. Desserts include a flan like *mamacita* used to make. ⊠ *600 N. Surf Rd.* ☎ *954/923–1500* ☾ *No lunch.*

**$$** ✕ **LeTub.** Formerly a Sunoco gas station, this quirky waterside saloon
AMERICAN  has an enduring affection for claw-foot bathtubs. Hand-painted porcelain is everywhere—under ficus, sea grape, and palm trees. If a potty doesn't appeal, there's a secluded swing facing the water north of the main dining area. Despite molasses-slow service and an abundance of flies at sundown, this eatery is favored by locals, and management seemed genuinely appalled when hordes of trend-seeking city slickers started jamming bar stools and tables after Oprah declared its thick, juicy Angus burgers the best around. A plain burger and small fries will run you around $15. ⊠ *1100 N. Ocean Dr.* ☎ *954/921–9425* ⊕ *www. theletub.com* ▭ *No credit cards.*

**$$** ✕ **Sushi Blues Café.** Run by husband-and-wife-team Kenny Millions and
JAPANESE  Junko Maslak, this place proves that sushi has gone global. Japanese
Fodor's Choice  chefs prepare conventional and macrobiotic-influenced dishes, includ-
★  ing lobster teriyaki and steamed snapper with miso sauce. Poached

pears steamed in Cabernet sauce and cappuccino custard are popular desserts. Music is a big part of the appeal of this place, especially when the Sushi Blues Band performs on weekends. ⊠ *2009 Harrison St.* ☎ *954/929–9560* ⊕ *www.sushiblues.com.*

## WHERE TO STAY

*For expanded hotel reviews, visit Fodors.com.*

**$$–$$$**  ⊡ **Manta Ray Inn.** Canadians Donna and Dwayne Boucher run this immac-
HOTEL  ulate, affordable, two-story inn on the beach. **Pros:** on the beach; low-key
★  atmosphere. **Cons:** no restaurant. ⊠ *1715 S. Surf Rd.* ☎ *954/921–9666 or 800/255–0595* ⊕ *www.mantarayinn.com* ⇨ *12 units* ⬙ *In-room: a/c, kitchen, Wi-Fi. In-hotel: beach, parking* ◎ *No meals.*

**$$–$$$**  ⊡ **Sea Downs.** Facing the Broadwalk and ocean, this three-story lodging
HOTEL  is a good choice for families, as one-bedroom units can be joined to create two-bedroom apartments. **Pros:** facing ocean; reasonable rates. **Cons:** minimum stay often required. ⊠ *2900 N. Surf Rd.* ☎ *954/923–4968* ⊕ *www.seadowns.com* ⇨ *4 efficiencies, 8 1-bedroom apartments* ⬙ *In-room: a/c, Internet. In-hotel: pool, laundry facilities, parking* ⊟ *No credit cards* ◎ *No meals.*

**$$$–$$$$**  ⊡ **Seminole Hard Rock Hotel & Casino.** On the flatlands of western Hol-
HOTEL  lywood, the Seminole Hard Rock Hotel & Casino serves as a magnet for pulsating Vegas-style entertainment. Poker unfolds at 40 tables, to the delight of spectators, near a phalanx of slot machines. **Pros:** non-stop entertainment; plenty of activities. **Cons:** not on the beach; endless entertainment can be exhausting. ⊠ *1 Seminole Way* ☎ *866/502–7529 or 800/937–0010* ⊕ *www.hardrock.com* ⇨ *395 rooms, 86 suites* ⬙ *In-room: a/c, Internet, Wi-Fi. In-hotel: restaurants, bars, pool, gym, spa* ◎ *No meals.*

**$$$–$$$$**  ⊡ **The Westin Diplomat Resort & Spa.** This 39-story property has been
RESORT  instrumental in bringing new life and new style to Hollywood Beach
★  with its massive, 60-foot high ceilinged atrium. **Pros:** heavenly beds for adults and kids now, too; in-room workouts and great spa; eye-popping architecture. **Cons:** beach is eroding. ⊠ *1995 E. Hallandale Beach Blvd.* ☎ *954/602–6000 or 800/327–1212* ⊕ *www.starwoodhotels.com* ⇨ *900 rooms, 100 suites* ⬙ *In-room: a/c, Internet, Wi-Fi. In-hotel: restaurants, bars, golf course, tennis courts, pools, gym, spa* ◎ *No meals.*

# Miami and
# Miami Beach

**WORD OF MOUTH**

"South beach is perfect . . . plenty of shopping, beautiful beach . . .
 great restaurants, lots of fun."

—flep

# WELCOME TO MIAMI AND MIAMI BEACH

## TOP REASONS TO GO

★ **The Beach:** Miami Beach has been rated as one of the 10 best in the world. White sand, warm water, and bronzed bodies everywhere provide just the right mix of relaxation and people-watching.

★ **Dining Delights:** Miami's eclectic residents have transformed the city into a museum of epicurean wonders, ranging from Cuban and Argentine fare to fusion haute cuisine.

★ **Wee-Hour Parties:** A 24-hour liquor license means clubs stay open until 5 am, and after-parties go until noon the following day.

★ **Picture-Perfect People:** Miami is a watering hole for the vain and beautiful of South America, Europe, and the Northeast. Watch them—or join them—as they strut their stuff and flaunt their tans on the white beds of renowned art deco hotels.

★ **Art Deco District:** Iconic pastels and neon lights accessorize the architecture that first put South Beach on the map in the 1930s.

**1 Downtown Miami.** Weave through the glass-and-steel labyrinth of new condo construction to catch a Miami Heat game at the American Airlines Arena or a ballet at the spaceshiplike Adrienne Arsht Center for the Performing Arts. To the north is artsy and edgy Wynwood and the Design District.

**2 South Beach.** People-watch from sidewalk cafés along Ocean Drive, lounge poolside at posh Collins Avenue hotels, and party 'til dawn at the nation's hottest clubs.

**3 Coral Gables.** Dine and shop on family-friendly Miracle Mile, and take a driving tour of the Mediterranean-style mansions in the surrounding neighborhoods.

**4 Mid-Beach.** Home to the latest and greatest hotel trends and a booming restaurant scene, Mid-Beach is now rivaling South Beach as a trendy hotspot.

**5 Coconut Grove.** Catch dinner and a movie and listen to live music at Coco-Walk, or cruise the bohemian shops and locals' bars in this hip neighborhood.

**6 Key Biscayne.** Pristine parks and tranquillity make this upscale enclave a total antithesis to the South Beach party.

**12**

## GETTING ORIENTED

Long considered the gateway to Latin America, Miami is as close to Cuba and the Caribbean as you can get within the United States. The 36-square-mi city is located at the southern tip of the Florida peninsula, bordered on the east by Biscayne Bay. Over the bay lies a series of barrier islands, the largest being a thin 18-square-mi strip called Miami Beach. To the east of Miami Beach is the Atlantic Ocean. To the south are the Florida Keys.

# MIAMI BEACHES

Almost every side street in Miami Beach dead-ends at the ocean. Sandy shores also stretch along the southern side of the Rickenbacker Causeway to Key Biscayne, where you'll find more popular beaches.

Beaches tend to have golden, light brown, or gray-tinted sand with coarser grains than the fine white stuff on Florida's Gulf Coast beaches. Although pure white-sand beaches are many peoples' idea of picture-perfect, darker beach sand is much easier on the eyes on a sunny day and—bonus!—your holiday photos (and the people in them) will have a subtle warm glow rather than harsh highlights.

Expect gentle waves, which can occasionally turn rough, complete with riptides, depending on what weather systems are lurking out in the ocean—always check and abide by the warnings posted on the lifeguard's station. One thing that isn't perfect here is shelling, but for casual shell collectors Bal Harbour Beach is the best bet; enter at 96th Street and Collins Avenue.

## SOUTH BEACH PARKING TIPS

Several things are plentiful in South Beach. Besides the plethora of cell phones and surgically enhanced bodies, there are a lot of cars for a small area, and plenty of seriously attentive meter maids. On-street parking is scarce, tickets are given freely, and towing charges are high. Check your meter to see when you must pay to park; times vary. It's $1 per hour for meters north of 23rd Street (8 am–6 pm) and $1.50 per hour for meters south of 23rd Street (9 am–3 am). There are also public parking lots that accept cash and credit cards. Or, buy a Parking Meter Card at Miami Beach Visitors Center and Publix supermarkets for $25.

## MIAMI'S BEST BEACHES

### BILL BAGGS CAPE FLORIDA STATE PARK

At the end of Key Biscayne, at 1200 S. Crandon Boulevard, is a wide peachy-brown beach with usually gentle waves. The beach has been named several times in Dr. Beach's coveted America's Top Ten Beaches list. The picnic area is popular with local families on the weekends, but the beach itself never feels crowded. The park also includes miles of nature trails; bike, boat, beach chair, and umbrella rentals; and casual dining at the Lighthouse Café. You can fish off the piers by the marina, too. Come here for an escape from city madness.

### CRANDON PARK BEACH

The 3-mi sliver of beach paradise is dotted with palm trees to provide a respite from the steamy sun, until it's time to take a dip in the clear-blue waters. On weekends, be prepared for a long hike from your car to the beach. There are bathrooms, outdoor showers, plenty of picnic tables, and concession stands. The family-friendly park offers abundant options for kids who find it challenging to simply sit and build sand castles. There are marine-theme play sculptures, a dolphin-shape spray fountain, an old-fashioned outdoor roller rink, and a restored carousel.

### HAULOVER BEACH

Want to bare it all? Just north of Bal Harbour, at 10800 Collins Avenue in Sunny Isles, sits the only legal clothing-optional beach in the area. Haulover has more claims to fame than its casual attitude toward swimwear—it's also the best beach in the area for bodyboarding and surfing as it gets what passes for impressive swells in these parts. Plus the sand here is fine-grain white, unusual for the Atlantic coast. There's a section for families, singles, and a gay beach at Haulover.

### MATHESON HAMMOCK PARK BEACH

Kids will love the gentle waves and warm water of the beach at 4000 Crandon Boulevard in Key Biscayne. The golden sands of this 3-mi beach are only part of the attraction: the park includes a playground, picnic areas, even a golf course. The man-made lagoon is perfect for inexperienced swimmers, and it's the best place in Miami for a picnic. But the water can be a bit murky, and with the emphasis on families, it's not the best place for singles.

### SOUTH BEACH (LUMMUS PARK BEACH)

Want glitz and glamour? On South Beach's Ocean Drive from 6th to 14th streets, this beach is crowded with beautiful people working hard on their tans, muscle tone, and social lives. It's also the place for golden sands, blue water, and gentle waves.

Updated by
Paul Rubio

Even an ailing real estate market and plummeting property values have failed to dethrone Miami from its status as one of the world's trendiest and flashiest hotspots. In 2012, it almost feels as if the recession never happened. Downtown Miami's megamakeover, which began in 2006, and came to a screeching halt in 2008, was later resumed in 2010. No longer are high-end restaurants luring customers with three-course $30 specials nor are five-star hotels offering bargain basement $149/night rooms. Miami is back and with this revival of glam and economy return higher price tags and longer guest lists!

Luckily for visitors, South Beach is no longer the only place to stand and pose in Miami. The growing Design District is home to Miami's hipster and fashionista scene while South Beach continues to extend both north and west, with the addition of new venues north of 20th Street and along the bay on West Avenue. Following the reopening of the mammoth Fontainebleau and its enclave of nightclubs and restaurants along Mid-Beach, other globally renowned resorts have moved into the neighborhood, like the Soho Beach House and Canyon Ranch.

Visit Miami today and it's hard to believe that 100 years ago, it was a mosquito-infested swampland, with an Indian trading post on the Miami River. Then hotel builder Henry Flagler brought his railroad to the outpost known as Fort Dallas. Other visionaries—Carl Fisher, Julia Tuttle, William Brickell, and John Sewell, among others—set out to tame the unruly wilderness. Hotels were erected, bridges were built, the port was dredged, and electricity arrived. The narrow strip of mangrove coast was transformed into Miami Beach—and the tourists started to come. They haven't stopped since!

Greater Miami is many destinations in one. At its best it offers an unparalleled multicultural experience: melodic Latin and Caribbean tongues, international cuisines and cultural events, and an unmistakable joie de vivre—all against a beautiful beach backdrop. In Little Havana the air is tantalizing with the perfume of strong Cuban coffee. In Coconut Grove, Caribbean steel drums ring out during the Miami/Bahamas Goombay Festival. Anytime in colorful Miami Beach restless crowds wait for entry to the hottest new clubs.

Many visitors don't know that Miami and Miami Beach are really separate cities. Miami, on the mainland, is South Florida's commercial hub. Miami Beach, on 17 islands in Biscayne Bay, is sometimes considered America's Riviera, luring refugees from winter with its warm sunshine; sandy beaches; graceful, shady palms; and tireless nightlife. The natives know well that there's more to Greater Miami than the bustle of South Beach and its Art Deco District. In addition to well-known places such as Ocean Drive and Lincoln Road, the less reported spots—like the burgeoning Design District in Miami, the historic buildings of Coral Gables, and the secluded beaches of Key Biscayne—are great insider destinations.

# MIAMI PLANNER

## WHEN TO GO

Miami and Miami Beach are year-round destinations. Most visitors come November through April, when the weather is close to perfect; hotels, restaurants, and attractions are busiest; and each weekend holds a festival or event. "Season" kicks off in December with Art Basel Miami Beach, and hotel rates don't come down until after the college kids have left from spring break in late March.

It's hot and steamy from May through September, but nighttime temperatures are usually pleasant. Also, summer is a good time for the budget traveler. Many hotels lower their rates considerably, and many restaurants offer discounts—especially during **Miami Spice** in August, when slews of top restaurants offer special tasting menus at a steep discount (sometimes Spice runs for two months, check ⊕ *www.iLoveMiamiSpice. com* for details).

## TOP EVENTS

**Art Basel.** The most prestigious art show in the United States is held every December. ⊕ *www.artbaselmiamibeach.com.*

**South Beach Food and Wine Festival.** The Food Network's star-studded weekend every February showcases the flavors and ingenuity of the country's top chefs. ⊕ *www.sobewineandfoodfest.com.*

**Winter Music Conference.** The largest DJ showcase in the world rocks Miami every March. ⊕ *www.wintermusicconference.com.*

## GETTING HERE

**Air Travel:** Miami is serviced by Miami International Airport (MIA) 8 mi northwest of downtown and Fort Lauderdale-Hollywood International Airport (FLL) 26 mi northeast. Many discount carriers, like Spirit Airlines, Southwest Airlines, and AirTran fly into FLL, making it a smart bargain if you are renting a car. Otherwise, look for flights to MIA on American Airlines, Delta, and Continental. MIA recently underwent an extensive face-lift improving facilities, common spaces, and the overall aesthetic of the airport.

**Car Travel:** Interstate 95 is the major expressway connecting South Florida with points north; State Road 836 is the major east–west expressway and connects to Florida's Turnpike, State Road 826, and Interstate 95. Seven causeways link Miami and Miami Beach, Interstate 195 and Interstate 395 offering the most convenient routes; the Rickenbacker Causeway extends to Key Biscayne from Interstate 95 and U.S. 1. The high-speed lanes on the left hand side of I–95 require a prepaid toll gadget called a "Sunpass," available in most drug and grocery stores.

Remember U.S. 1 (aka Biscayne Boulevard)—you'll hear it often in directions. It starts in Key West, hugs South Florida's coastline, and heads north straight through to Maine.

**Train Travel:** Amtrak provides service from 500 destinations to the Greater Miami area. The trains make several stops along the way; north–south service stops in the major Florida cities of Jacksonville, Orlando, Tampa, West Palm Beach, and Fort Lauderdale. Note that these stops are often in less than ideal locations for immediate city access. For extended trips, or if you want to visit other areas in Florida, you can come via Auto Train (where you bring your car along) from Lorton, Virginia, just outside Washington, D.C., to Sanford, Florida, just outside Orlando. From there it's less than a four-hour drive to Miami. Fares vary, but expect to pay between $269 and $346 for a basic sleeper seat and car passage each way. ■ TIP→ You must be traveling with an automobile to purchase a ticket on the Auto Train.

## GETTING AROUND

Greater Miami resembles Los Angeles in its urban sprawl and traffic. You'll need a car to visit many attractions and points of interest. If possible, avoid driving during the rush hours of 7–9 am and 5–7 pm—the hour just after and right before the peak times also can be slow going. During rainy weather, be especially cautious of flooding in South Beach and Key Biscayne. Miami's main north and south thoroughfare, I–95, now offers an express lane to get more quickly between Miami and Fort Lauderdale. A prepaid Sunpass is required to use this lane.

Some sights are accessible via the public transportation system, run by the **Metro-Dade Transit Agency**, which maintains 740 Metrobuses on 90 routes; the 23-mi Metrorail elevated rapid-transit system; and the Metromover, an elevated light-rail system. Those planning on using public transportation should get an EASY Card or EASY Ticket available at any Metrorail station and most supermarkets. Fares are discounted and transfer fees are nominal. The bus stops for the **Metrobus** are marked with blue-and-green signs with a bus logo and route information. The fare is $2 (exact change only if paying cash). Cash-paying customers must pay for another ride if transferring. Some express routes carry a surcharge of 35¢. Elevated **Metrorail** trains run from downtown Miami north to Hialeah and south along U.S. 1 to Dadeland. The system operates daily 5 am–midnight. The fare is $2; 50¢ transfers to Metrobus are available only for EASY Card and EASY ticket holders. **Metromover** resembles an airport shuttle and runs on two loops around downtown Miami, linking major hotels, office buildings, and shopping areas. The system spans 4 mi, including the 1-mi Omni Loop and the 1-mi Brickell Loop. There is no fee to ride; transfers to Metrorail are $2.

**Tri-Rail,** South Florida's commuter-train system, stops at 18 stations north of MIA along a 71-mi route. There is a Metrorail transfer station 2 stops north of MIA. Prices range from $2.50 to $6.90 for a one-way ticket.

Transportation Information **Metro-Dade Transit Agency** (☎ 305/891–3131 ⊕ www.miamidade.gov/transit). **Tri-Rail** (☎ 800/874–7245 ⊕ www.tri-rail.com).

## CAB IT

Except in South Beach, it's difficult to hail a cab on the street; in most cases you'll need to call a cab company or have a hotel doorman hail one for you. Fares run $4.50 for the first mile and $2.40 every mile thereafter; flat-rate fares are also available from the airport to a variety of zones. Many cabs now accept credit cards; inquire before you get in the car.

Taxi Companies **Central Cabs** (☎ 305/532–5555). **Diamond Cab Company** (☎ 305/545–5555). **Flamingo Taxi** (☎ 305/599–9999). **Metro Taxi** (☎ 305/888–8888). **Society Cab Company** (☎ 305/757–5523). **Super Yellow Cab Company** (☎ 305/888–7777). **Tropical Taxi** (☎ 305/945–1025). **Yellow Cab Company** (☎ 305/633–0503).

## VISITOR INFORMATION

For additional information about Miami and Miami Beach, contact the city's visitor bureaus. You can also pick up a Free Miami Beach INcard at the Miami Beach Visitors Center 10 am–4 pm seven days a week, entitling you to discounts and offers at restaurants, shops, galleries, and more.

Visitor Information **Coconut Grove Chamber of Commerce** (✉ 2820 McFarlane Rd., Coconut Grove, Miami ☎ 305/444–7270 ⊕ www.coconutgrovechamber.com)). **Coral Gables Chamber of Commerce** (✉ 224 Catalonia Ave., Coral Gables ☎ 305/446–1657 ⊕ www.gableschamber.org). **Greater Miami Convention & Visitors Bureau** (✉ 701 Brickell Ave., Suite 2700, Miami ☎ 305/539–3000, 800/933–8448 in U.S. ⊕ www.miamiandbeaches.com). **Key Biscayne Chamber of Commerce and Visitors Center** (✉ 88 W. McIntyre St., Suite 100, Key Biscayne ☎ 305/361–5207 ⊕ www.keybiscaynechamber.org). **Miami Beach**

**Visitors Center** (✉ *1920 Meridian Ave., 1st fl., Miami Beach* ☎ *305/674–1300* ⊕ *www.miamibeachguestservices.com*).

# EXPLORING MIAMI AND MIAMI BEACH

If you had arrived here 50 years ago with a guidebook in hand, chances are you'd be thumbing through listings looking for alligator wrestlers and you-pick strawberry fields or citrus groves. Things have changed. While Disney sidetracked families in Orlando, Miami was developing a unique culture and attitude that's equal parts beach town/big business, Latino/Caribbean meets European/American—all of which fuels a great art and food scene, as well as exuberant nightlife and myriad festivals.

To find your way around Greater Miami, learn how the numbering system works (or better yet, use a GPS). Miami is laid out on a grid with four quadrants—northeast, northwest, southeast, and southwest—which meet at Miami Avenue and Flagler Street. Miami Avenue separates east from west and Flagler Street separates north from south. Avenues and courts run north–south; streets, terraces, and ways run east–west. Roads run diagonally, northwest–southeast. But other districts—Miami Beach, Coral Gables, and Hialeah—may or may not follow this system, and along the curve of Biscayne Bay the symmetrical grid shifts diagonally. It's best to buy a detailed map, stick to the major roads, and ask directions early and often. However, make sure you're in a safe neighborhood or public place when you seek guidance; cabdrivers and cops are good resources.

## DOWNTOWN MIAMI

Downtown Miami dazzles from a distance. The skyline is fluid, thanks to the sheer number of sparkling glass high-rises between Biscayne Boulevard and the Miami River. Business is the key to downtown Miami's daytime bustle. Traffic congestion from the high-rise offices and expensive parking tend to keep the locals away by day; however, downtown has become a nighttime hotspot in recent years.

The free, 23-mi, elevated commuter system known as the Metromover runs inner and outer loops through downtown and to nearby neighborhoods south and north. Many attractions are conveniently located within about a few blocks of a station.

Note that you can combine a visit to this neighborhood with one to Little Havana, which is just southwest of downtown. ⇨ *See our "Caribbean Infusion" spotlight for a map of Little Havana as well as one of Little Haiti in north Miami.*

### TOP ATTRACTIONS

**Adrienne Arsht Center for the Performing Arts.** Lovers of culture and other artsy types are drawn to this stunning home of the Florida Grand Opera, Miami City Ballet, New World Symphony, Concert Association of Florida, and other local and touring groups, which have included Broadway hits like *Wicked* and *Jersey Boys*. Think of it as a sliver of savoir faire to temper Miami's often-over-the-top vibe. Designed

## DOWNTOWN MIAMI ENCLAVES

The influx of massive, modern, and affordable condos has lured a young and trendy demographic to downtown, leading to the establishment of restaurant-centric enclaves and headlining eateries and nightclubs in hotels like the Viceroy and the Tempo.

**Bayfront Park.** Monuments dot this park, and both it and the streets that face it really pull in shoppers—particularly those from South America and especially those from Brazil. In the park's southwest corner is the white *Challenger* Memorial, commemorating the space shuttle that exploded in 1986. A little north is Plaza Bolivar, a tribute by Cuban immigrants to

their adopted country; the JFK Torch of Friendship, a plaza with plaques representing all the South and Central American countries except Cuba; and the Bayside Marketplace entertainment, dining, and retail complex. *To get here:* Metromover to Bayfront Park, 1st Street, College/Basyide, or Freedom Tower stations.

**Mary Brickell Village.** This burgeoning neighborhood of low-rise condos and shops clustered around South Miami Avenue also has some rather popular restaurants, so you might want to plan a visit for some late-afternoon shopping followed by dinner. *To get here:* Metromover to 5th or 8th Street stops.

by architect César Pelli, the massive development contains a 2,400-seat opera house, 2,200-seat concert hall, a black-box theater, and an outdoor Plaza for the Arts. Restaurateur Barton G. opened up his pre-theater dining restaurant, **Prelude by Barton G.** (☎ *305/357–7900* ⊕ *www.preludebybartong.com*) in early 2010 to rave reviews. ⊠ *1300 Biscayne Blvd., at N.E. 13th St., Downtown* ☎ *305/949–6722* ⊕ *www. arshtcenter.org.*

**Freedom Tower.** In the 1960s this ornate Spanish-baroque structure was the Cuban Refugee Center, processing more than 500,000 Cubans who entered the United States after fleeing Fidel Castro's regime. Built in 1925 for the *Miami Daily News,* it was inspired by the Giralda, an 800-year-old bell tower in Seville, Spain. Preservationists were pleased to see the tower's exterior restored in 1988. Today, it is owned by Miami-Dade College, and continues to maintain the tower as a cultural and educational center, which includes a museum depicting Cuban history, the experiences of refugees, and the achievements of Cuban-Americans. ⊠ *600 Biscayne Blvd., at N.E. 6th St., Downtown* ☎ *305/237–7700* ۞ *Tues.–Fri. noon–5.*

**Miami-Dade Cultural Center.** Containing three cultural resources, this fortresslike 3-acre complex is a downtown focal point. ⊠ *101 W. Flagler St., between N.W. 1st and 2nd Aves., Downtown.*

The **Miami Art Museum** (☎ *305/375–3000* ⊕ *www.miamiartmuseum. org* ⬚ *$8 [free for families every 2nd Sat.]* ۞ *Tues.–Fri. 10–5, weekends noon–5*) is waiting to move into its new 120,000-square-foot home in Museum Park, which is to be completed in mid-2013. Meanwhile, the museum presents major touring exhibitions of work by international artists, with an emphasis on art since 1945. Every second Saturday, entrance is free for families.

Discover a treasure trove of colorful stories about the region's history at **HistoryMiami** (☎ *305/375–1492* ⊕ *www.historymiami.org* ✉ *$8 museum, $10 combo ticket art and history museums* ⊙ *Tues.–Fri. 10–5, weekends noon–5*), formerly known as the Historical Museum of Southern Florida. Exhibits celebrate Miami's multicultural heritage, including an old Miami streetcar, and unique items chronicling the migration of Cubans to Miami.

★  **Wynwood Art District.** Just north of downtown Miami, the funky, urban, and edgy Wynwood Art District is peppered with galleries, art studios, and private collections accessible to the public. Visit during Wynwood's monthly gallery walk on the second Saturday evening of each month when studios and galleries are all open at the same time.

Make sure a visit includes a stop at the **Margulies Collection at the Warehouse** (⊠ *591 N.W. 27th St., between N.W. 5th and 6th Aves., Downtown* ☎ *305/576–1051* ⊕ *www.margulieswarehouse.com*). Martin Margulies's collection of vintage and contemporary photography, videos, and installation art in a 45,000-square-foot space makes for eye-popping viewing. Entrance fee is a $10 donation, which goes to a local homeless shelter for women and children. It's open November to April only, Wednesday to Saturday 11–4.

Fans of edgy art will appreciate the **Rubell Family Collection** (⊠ *95 N.W. 29th St., between N. Miami and N.W. 1st Aves., Downtown* ☎ *305/573–6090* ⊕ *www.rfc.museum*). Mera and Don Rubell have accumulated work by artists from the 1970s to the present, including Jeff Koons, Cindy Sherman, Damien Hirst, and Keith Haring. Admission is $10, and the gallery is open December to August, Wednesday to Saturday 10–6.

## WORTH NOTING

🄫  **Jungle Island.** Originally located deep in south Miami and known as Parrot Jungle, South Florida's original tourist attraction opened in 1936 and moved closer to Miami Beach in 2003. Located on Watson Island, a small stretch of land off of I-395 between Downtown Miami and South Beach, Jungle Island is far more than a park where cockatoos ride tricycles; this interactive zoological park is home to just about every unusual and endangered species you would want to see, including a rare albino alligator, a liger (lion and tiger mix), a 28-foot-long "crocosaur," and a myriad of exotic birds. The most intriguing offerings are the VIP animal tours, including the Lemur Experience ($45 for 45 minutes), in which the highly social primates make themselves at home on your lap or shoulders, and the Penguin Encounter ($30 for 30 minutes), where you can pet and feed warm-weather South African penguins. ⊠ *1111 Parrot Jungle Trail, off MacArthur Causeway (I–395)* ☎ *305/400–7000* ⊕ *www.jungleisland.com* ✉ *$32.95, plus $8 parking* ⊙ *Weekdays 10–5, weekends 10–6.*

🄫  **Miami Children's Museum.** This Arquitectonica-designed museum, both imaginative and geometric in appearance, is directly across the MacArthur Causeway from Jungle Island. Twelve galleries house hundreds of

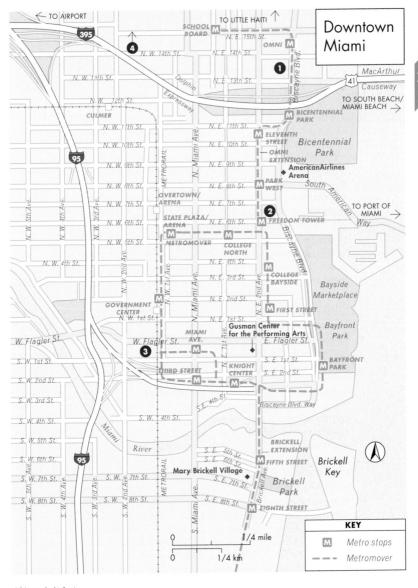

Downtown Miami

12

KEY

Ⓜ Metro stops
--- --- Metromover

interactive, bilingual exhibits. Children can scan plastic groceries in the supermarket, scramble through a giant sand castle, climb a rock wall, learn about the Everglades, and combine rhythms in the world-music studio. ✉ *980 MacArthur Causeway* ☎ *305/373–5437* ⊕ *www. miamichildrensmuseum.org* ✎ *$15, parking $1/hr* ⊙ *Daily 10–6.*

## MIAMI BEACH

The hub of Miami Beach is South Beach (better known as SoBe), with its energetic Ocean Drive, Collins Avenue, and Washington Avenue. Here, life unfolds 24 hours a day. Beautiful people pose in hotel lounges and sidewalk cafés, bronzed cyclists zoom past palm trees, and visitors flock to see the action. On Lincoln Road, café crowds spill onto the sidewalks, weekend markets draw all kinds of visitors and their dogs, and thanks to a few late-night lounges the scene is just as alive at night. A Mid-Beach renaissance is unfolding on Collins Avenue, with haute new hotels and restaurants popping up between 40th and 60th streets.

Quieter areas to the north on Collins Avenue are Surfside (from 88th to 96th streets), fashionable Bal Harbour (beginning at 96th Street), and Sunny Isles (between 157th and 197th streets). If you're interested in these areas and you're flying in, the Fort Lauderdale airport might be a better choice than Miami International.

### SOUTH BEACH
#### TOP ATTRACTIONS

★ **Española Way.** There's a bohemian feel to this street lined with Mediter-ranean-revival buildings constructed in 1925. Al Capone's gambling syn-dicate ran its operations upstairs at what is now the Clay Hotel, a youth hostel. At a nightclub here in the 1930s, future bandleader Desi Arnaz strapped on a conga drum and started beating out a rumba rhythm. Visit this quaint avenue on a weekend afternoon, when merchants and crafts-people set up shop to sell everything from handcrafted bongo drums to fresh flowers. Between Washington and Drexel avenues the road has been narrowed to a single lane and Miami Beach's trademark pink sidewalks have been widened to accommodate sidewalk café's and shops selling imaginative clothing, jewelry, and art. ✉ *Española Way, between 14th and 15th Sts. from Washington to Jefferson Aves.*

★ **Holocaust Memorial.** A bronze sculpture depicts refugees clinging to a giant bronze arm that reaches out of the ground and 42 feet into the air. Enter the surrounding courtyard to see a memorial wall and hear the music that seems to give voice to the 6 million Jews who died at the hands of the Nazis. It's easy to understand why Kenneth Treister's dra-matic memorial is in Miami Beach: the city's community of Holocaust survivors was once the second-largest in the country. ✉ *1933–1945 Meridian Ave., at Dade Blvd.* ☎ *305/538–1663* ⊕ *www.holocaustmmb. org* ✎ *Free (donations welcome)* ⊙ *Daily 9–9.*

Ⓒ
Fodor's Choice
★

**Lincoln Road Mall.** A playful 1990s redesign spruced up this open-air pedestrian mall, adding a grove of 20 towering date palms, five linear pools, and colorful broken-tile mosaics to the once-futuristic 1950s vision of Fontainebleau designer Morris Lapidus. Some of the shops are owner-operated boutiques with a delightful variety of clothing, furnishings, jewelry, and decorative design. Others are the typical chain stores of American malls. Remnants of tired old Lincoln Road—beauty supply and discount electronics stores on the Collins end of the strip—somehow fit nicely into the mix. The new Lincoln Road is fun, lively, and friendly for people old, young, gay, and straight—and their dogs. Folks skate, scoot, bike, or jog here. The best times to hit the road are during Sunday morning farmers' markets and on weekend evenings, when cafés bustle, art galleries open shows, street performers make the sidewalk their stage, and stores stay open late.

12

Two of the landmarks worth checking out at the eastern end of Lincoln Road are the massive 1940s keystone building at 420 Lincoln Road, which has a 1945 Leo Birchanky mural in the lobby, and the 1921 mission-style Miami Beach Community Church, at Drexel Avenue. The Lincoln Theatre (No. 541–545), at Pennsylvania Avenue, is a classical four-story art deco gem with friezes. The New World Symphony, a national advanced-training orchestra led by Michael Tilson Thomas, rehearses and performs here, and concerts are often broadcast via loud-speakers, to the delight of visitors. Just west, facing Pennsylvania, a fabulous Cadillac dealership sign was discovered underneath the facade of the Lincoln Road Millennium Building, on the south side of the mall. At Euclid Avenue there's a monument to Lapidus, who in his 90s watched the renaissance of his whimsical creation. At Lenox Avenue, a black-and-white art deco movie house with a Mediterranean barrel-tile roof is now the Colony Theater (No. 1040), where live theater and experimental films are presented. ⊠ *Lincoln Rd., between Collins Ave. and Alton Rd.* ⊕ *www.lincolnroad.org.*

**QUICK BITES**

Lincoln Road is a great place to cool down with an icy treat while touring South Beach. If you visit on a Sunday, stop at one of the many juice vendors, who will whip up made-to-order smoothies from mangoes, oranges, and other fresh local fruits.

**Frieze Ice Cream Factory.** Delight in homemade ice cream and sorbets—including Indian mango, key lime pie, cashew toffee crunch, and chocolate decadence. ⊠ *1626 Michigan Ave., south of Lincoln Rd.* ☎ *305/538–2028* ⊕ *www.thefrieze.com.*

**Gelateria Parmalat.** Authentic Italian gelato (or the Spanish-inspired delicious *dulce de leche* gelato) is scooped up at this sleek glass-and-stainless-steel sweet spot. ⊠ *670 Lincoln Rd., between Euclid and Pennsylvania Aves.* ☎ *786/276–9475.*

*Continued on page 543*

# CARIBBEAN INFUSION

by Michelle Delio

Miami has sun, sand, and sea, but unlike some of Florida's other prime beach destinations, it also has a wave of cultural traditions that spice up the city.

It's with good reason that people in Miami fondly say that the city is an easy way for Americans to visit another country without ever leaving the United States. According to the U.S. Census Bureau, approximately half of Miami's population is foreign born and more than 70% speak a language other than English at home (in comparison, only 35.7% of New York City residents were born in another country). The city's Latin/Caribbean immigrants and exiles make up the largest segments of the population.

Locals merrily merge cultural traditions, speaking "Spanglish" (a mix of Spanish and English), sipping Cuban coffee with Sicilian pastries, eating Nuevo Latino fusion food, and dancing to the beat of other countries' music. That said, people here are just as interested in keeping to their own distinct ways—think of the city as a colorful mosaic composed of separate elements rather than a melting pot.

Miami's diverse population creates a city that feels alive in a way that few other American cities do. And no visit to the city would be complete without a stop at one of the two neighborhoods famed for their celebrations of cultural traditions—Little Haiti and Little Havana—places that have a wonderful foreign feel even amid cosmopolitan Miami.

⚠ Safety can be an issue in Little Haiti. Exercise special caution and do not visit at night.

Playing dominoes is a favorite pastime at Maximo Gomez Park in Little Havana (left).

# LA PETITE HAÏTI—LITTLE HAITI

Little Haiti is a study in contrasts. At first glance you see the small buildings painted in bright oranges, pinks, reds, yellows, and turquoises, with signs, some handwritten, touting immigration services, lunch specials with *tassot* (fried cubed goat), and voodoo supplies.

But as you adjust to this dazzle of color, you become aware of the curious juxtapositions of poverty and wealth in this evolving neighborhood. Streets dip with potholes in front of trendy art galleries, and dilapidated houses struggle to survive near newly renovated soccer fields and arts centers.

Miami's Little Haiti is the largest Haitian community outside of Haiti itself, and while people of different ethnic backgrounds have begun to move to the neighborhood, people here tend to expect to primarily see other Haitians on these streets. Obvious outsiders may be greeted with a few frozen stares on the streets, but owners of shops and restaurants tend to be welcoming. Creole is commonly spoken, although some people—especially younger folks—also speak English.

## WHEN TO GO

The neighborhood is best visited during the daytime, combined with a visit to the nearby Miami Design District, an 18-block section of art galleries, interior design showrooms, and restaurants between N.E. 41st Street and N.E. 36th Street, Miami Avenue, and Biscayne Boulevard.

## CREOLE EXPRESSIONS

Creole, one of Haiti's two languages (the other is French), is infused with French, African, Arabic, Spanish, and Portuguese words.

*Komon ou ye?* How are you? *(also spelled Kouman)
*N'ap boule!* Great!
*Kisa ou ta vla?* What would you like?
*Mesi.* Thanks.
*Souple.* Please.

## MANGÉ KRÉYOL (HAITIAN FOOD)

Traditional Caribbean cuisines tend to combine European and African culinary techniques. Haitian can be a bit spicier—though never mouth-scorching hot—than many other island cuisines. Rice and beans are the staple food, enlivened with a little of whatever people might have: fish, goat, chicken, pork, usually stewed or deep-fried, along with peppers, plantains, and tomatoes.

**Chez Le Bebe** (⊠ *114 N.E. 54th St.* ☎ *305/751–7639* ⊕ *www.chezlebebe.com*) offers Haitian home cooking—if you want to try stewed goat, this is the place to do it. Chicken, fish, oxtail, and fried pork are also on the menu; each plate comes with rice, beans, plantains, and salad for less than $12.

**Tap Tap restaurant** (⊠ *819 Fifth St.* ☎ *305/672–2898*) is outside of Little Haiti, but this Miami institution will immerse you in the island's culture with an extensive collection of Haitian folk art displayed everywhere in the restaurant. On the menu is pumpkin soup, *spageti kreyol* (pasta, shrimp, and a Creole tomato sauce), goat stewed in Creole sauce (a mildly spicy tomato-based sauce), conch, and "grilled goat dinner." You can eat well here for $15 or less.

## GETTING ORIENTED

Little Haiti, once a small farming community outside of Miami proper, is slowly becoming one of the city's most vibrant neighborhoods. Its northern and southern boundaries are 85th Street and 36th Street, respectively, with Interstate–95 to the west and Biscayne Boulevard to the east. The best section to visit is along North Miami Avenue from 54th to 59th streets. Driving is the best way to get here; parking is easy to find on North Miami Avenue. Public transit (☎ *305/891–3131*) is limited.

## SHOPPING

The cluster of botanicas at N.E. 54th Street and N.E. 2nd Avenue offer items intended to sway the fates, from candles to plastic and plaster statues of Catholic saints that, in the voodoo tradition, represent African deities. While exploring, don't miss **Sweat Records** (⊠ *5505 N.E. 2nd Ave.* ☎ *786/693–9309* ⊕ *www.sweatrecordsmiami. com*). Sweat sells a wide range of music—rock, pop, punk, electronic, hip-hop, and Latino. Check out the vegan-friendly organic coffee bar at the store, which is open from noon to 10 PM every day but Sunday.

# LITTLE HAVANA

First settled en masse by Cubans in the early 1960s, after Cuba's Communist revolution, Little Havana is a predominantly working-class area and the core of Miami's Hispanic community. Spanish is the main language, but don't be surprised if the cadence is less Cuban than Salvadoran or Nicaraguan: the neighborhood is now home to people from all Latin American countries.

If you come to Little Havana expecting the Latino version of New Orleans's French Quarter, you're apt to be disappointed—it's not yet that picturesque. But if great, inexpensive food (not just Cuban; there's Vietnamese, Mexican, and Argentinean here as well), distinctive, affordable art, cigars, and coffee interest you, you'll enjoy your time in Little Havana. It's not a prefab tourist destination, so don't expect Disneyland with a little Latino flair—this is real life in Miami.

## WHEN TO GO

The absolute best time to visit Calle Ocho is the last Friday evening of every month, between 6:30 and 11 PM on 8th Street from 14th to 17th avenues. Known as **Viernes Culturales** (🌐 *www.viernes-culturales.org*), it's a big block party that everyone is welcome to attend. Art galleries, restaurants, and stores stay open late, and music, mojitos, and avant-garde street performances bring a young, hip crowd to the neighborhood where they mingle with locals.

If you come in mid-March, your visit may coincide with the annual **Calle Ocho festival** (🌐 *www.carnavalmiami.com*), which draws more than a million visitors in search of Latin music, food, and shopping.

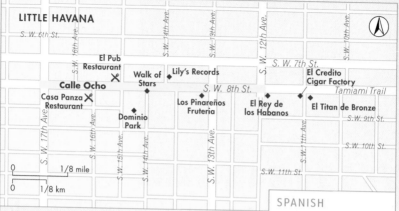

**LITTLE HAVANA**

S. W. 6th St.

S.W. 16th Ave.

S.W. 14th Ave.

S.W. 13th Ave.

S.W. 12th Ave.

S.W. 10th Ave.

S. W. 7th St.

El Pub Restaurant ✕

Walk of Stars

Lily's Records

El Credito Cigar Factory

Tamiami Trail

**Calle Ocho**

S. W. 8th St.

Casa Panza ✕ Restaurant

S.W. 17th Ave.

S.W. 16th Ave.

Dominio Park

Los Pinareños Frutería

El Rey de los Habanos

S.W. 15th Ave.

S.W. 14th Ave.

El Titan de Bronze

S.W. 9th St.

S.W. 13th Ave.

S.W. 11th Ave.

S.W. 10th St.

0    1/8 mile

0    1/8 km

S.W. 11th St.

## GETTING ORIENTED

Little Havana's semi-official boundaries are 27th Avenue to 4th Avenue on the west, Miami River to the north, and S.W. 11th Street to the south. Much of the neighborhood is residential, but its heart and tourist hub is Calle Ocho (8th Street), between 14th and 18th avenues.

The best way to get here is by car. Park on the side streets off **Calle Ocho** (some spots have meters; most don't). Other options include the free **Metromover** (☎ 305/891–3131) and a cab ride. From Miami Beach the 15-minute ride should cost just under $30 each way.

## THE SIGHTS

Stroll down Calle Oche from 12th to 17th avenues and look around you: cafés are selling guava pastries and rose petal flan, a botanica brims with candles and herbs to heal whatever ails you. Small galleries showcasing modern art jostle up next to mom-and-pop food shops and high-end Cuban clothes and crafts. At Domino Park (officially Maximo Gomez Park), guayabera-clad seniors bask in the sun and play dominoes, while at corner bodegas and coffee shops (particularly Versailles) regulars share neighborhood gossip and political opinions. A few steps away is the "Paseo de las Estrellas" (Walk of Stars), honoring the likes of Julio Iglesias and Gloria Estefan.

At SW 13th Street, the Cuban Memorial Boulevard fills 2 blocks with monuments to Cuba's freedom fighters. At family-owned El Credito Cigar Factory, watch workers assemble cigars fit for presidents and celebs.

### SPANISH EXPRESSIONS

*Algo más?* Anything else?

*Muchas gracias!* Thank you very much!

*No hay de qué. / De nada.* You're welcome.

*No entiendo.* I don't understand.

*Oye!* All-purpose word used to get attention or express interest, admiration, and appreciation.

Calle Ocho Carnaval

Rolling cigars by hand in a Little Havana factory.

## THE SOUNDS

Salsa and merengue pour out of storefronts and restaurants, while other businesses cater to the snap and shuffles of flamenco performances and Sevillańa *tablaos* (dances performed on a wood-plank stage, using castanets). If you want to join in the merriment along Calle Ocho, dance with locals on the patio of **El Pub Restaurant** (near 15th Avenue), or snack on tapas at **Casa Panza Restaurant** (near 16th), where the background music is the restaurant owner's enthusiastic singing. Any time of day, you can hear the constant backbeat of people speaking Spanish and the occasional crowing of a stray, time-confused rooster. To take these sounds home with you, wander over to **Lily's Records** (✉ *1419 S.W. 8th St, near 14th* ☎ *305/856–0536*), for its huge selection of Latin music.

## THE SCENTS

Bottled, the essence of Little Havana would be tobacco, café cubano, and a whiff of tropical fruit. To indulge your senses in two of these things, head to **Los Pinareños Fruteria** on Calle Ocho just west of 13th Avenue. Here you can sip a sweet, hot *cortadito* (coffee with milk), a *cafecito* (no milk), or a cool *coco frio* (coconut water). For more subsistence, dig into a Cuban-style tamale. There are stools out front of the shop, or take your drink to go and wander over to S.W. 13th Avenue, which has monuments to Cuban heroes, and sit under the ceiba trees. For cigars, head to Calle Ocho near 11th Avenue and visit any of these three stores: **El Credito Cigar Factory**, **El Rey de los Habanos**, and **El Titan de Bronze**. At these family-owned businesses employees deftly hand-roll millions of stogies a year.

## TOURS

If a quick multicultural experience is your goal, set aside an hour or two to do your own self-guided walking tour of the neighborhood. For real ethnic immersion, allow more time; eating is a must, as well as a peek at the area's residential streets lined with distinctive homes.

Especially illuminating are **History Miami, Little Havana City Tours** (✉ *101 W. Flagler St.* ☎ *305/375–1621* ⊕ *www.hmsf.org/programs=adult.htm*). Those led by Dr. Paul George, a history professor at Miami Dade College and historian for History Miami, covers architecture and community history. These take place only a few times a year.

Private three-hour tours are available for groups of up to 20 people for $400 ($20 per person above 20 people).

A PDF on the Web site has up-to-date information on tour dates and times.

For customized offerings, try **Miami Cultural Tours** (✉ *305/416-6868* ⊕ *www.miamiculturaltours.com*), interactive tours that introduce people to Little Havana and Little Haiti. Group and private tours are available, with prices ranging from $39 to $79 a person.

# GREAT ITINERARIES

**12**

## 3 DAYS

Grab your lotion and head to the ocean, more specifically **Ocean Drive** on **South Beach**, and catch some rays while relaxing on the warm sands. Afterward, take a guided or self-guided tour of the **Art Deco District** to see what all the fuss is about, drop in at the News Café for breakfast anytime (or a snack), great coffee, and an outstanding selection of international magazines. Keep the evening free to socialize at Ocean Drive cafés or have a special dinner at one of the many Latin-European–fusion restaurants. The following day drive through **Little Havana** to witness the heartbeat of Miami's Cuban culture (stop for a high-octane Cuban coffee at Versaille's outside-counter window) on your way south to Coconut Grove's Vizcaya. Wrap up the evening a few blocks away in downtown **Coconut Grove**, enjoying its laid-back party mood and many nightspots. On the last day

head over to **Coral Gables** to take in the eye-popping display of 1920s Mediterranean-revival architecture in the neighborhoods surrounding the city center and the majestic **Biltmore Hotel**; then take a dip in the fantastic thematic **Venetian Pool**. Early evening, stroll and shop Coral Gable's Miracle Mile—contrary to its name it's just a half mile, but every bit is packed with upscale shops, art galleries, and interesting restaurants.

## 5 DAYS

Follow the suggested three-day itinerary, and on Day 4 visit the beaches of **Virginia Key** and **Key Biscayne**. Take a diving trip or fishing excursion, learn to windsurf, or just watch the water. On Day 5, tour the 18-block Design District and browse its 130-plus art galleries, home-decor shops, and interesting restaurants, or explore the Fairchild Tropical Botanic Garden. Then return to **South Beach** for an evening of shopping, drinking, and outdoor dining at **Lincoln Road Mall**.

### WORTH NOTING

**Art Deco District Welcome Center.** Run by the Miami Design Preservation League, the center provides information about the buildings in the district. An improved gift shop sells 1930s–50s art deco memorabilia, posters, and books on Miami's history. Several tours—covering Lincoln Road, Española Way, North Beach, and the entire Art Deco District, among others—start here. You can choose from a self-guided iPod audio tour or join one of the regular morning walking tours at 10:30 am, every day except Thursday when the tour takes place at 6:30 pm. Arrive at the center 15 minutes beforehand. All of the options provide detailed histories of the art deco hotels as well as an introduction to the art deco, Mediterranean revival, and Miami Modern (MiMo) styles found within the Miami Beach Architectural Historic District. Don't miss the special boat tours during Art Deco Weekend, in early January. (⇨ *For a map of the Art Deco District and info on some of the sites there, see the "A Stroll Down Deco Lane" in-focus feature.*) ✉ *1001 Ocean Dr., at Barbara Capitman Way (10th St.)* ☎ *305/763-8026* ⊕ *www.mdpl.org* 🎫 *Tours $20* ☾ *Daily 9:30–7.*

**Bass Museum of Art.** The Bass, in historic Collins Park, is part of the Miami Beach Cultural Park, which includes the Miami City Ballet's Arquitectonica-designed facility and the Miami Beach Regional Library. The original building, constructed of keystone, has unique Maya-inspired carvings. The expansion designed by Japanese architect Arata Isozaki houses another wing and an outdoor sculpture garden. Special exhibitions join a diverse collection of European art. Works on permanent display include *The Holy Family,* a painting by Peter Paul Rubens; *The Tournament,* one of several 16th-century Flemish tapestries; and works by Albrecht Dürer and Henri de Toulouse-Lautrec. Special exhibits often cost a little extra. Docent tours are by appointment. ⊠ *2100 Collins Ave.* ☎ *305/673–7530* ⊕ *www.bassmuseum.org* ◰ *$8* ⊙ *Wed.–Sun. noon–5.*

> ### THE OCEAN DRIVE HUSTLE
>
> As you stroll by the sidewalk restaurants lining Ocean Drive, don't be surprised if you are solicited by a pretty hostess, who will literally shove a menu in your face to entice you to her café—which is exactly like every other eatery on the strip. Be warned that reputable restaurants refrain from these aggressive tactics. If you are indeed enticed by the fishbowl drinks, use the chance to bargain. A request for free drinks with dinner may very well be accommodated!

**Sanford L. Ziff Jewish Museum of Florida.** Listed on the National Register of Historic Places, this former synagogue, built in 1936, contains art deco chandeliers, 80 impressive stained-glass windows, and a permanent exhibit, MOSAIC: Jewish Life in Florida, which depicts more than 235 years of the Florida Jewish experience. The museum, which includes a store filled with books, jewelry, and other souvenirs, also hosts traveling exhibits and special events. ⊠ *301 Washington Ave., at 3rd St.* ☎ *305/672–5044* ⊕ *www.jewishmuseum.com* ◰ *$6, free on Sat.* ⊙ *Tues.–Sun. 10–5. Museum store closed Sat.*

★ **Wolfsonian–Florida International University.** An elegantly renovated 1926 storage facility is now a research center and museum showcasing a 120,000-item collection of modern design and "propaganda arts" amassed by Miami native Mitchell ("Micky") Wolfson Jr., a world traveler and connoisseur. Broad themes of the 19th and 20th centuries—nationalism, political persuasion, industrialization—are addressed in permanent and traveling shows. Included in the museum's eclectic holdings, which represent art deco, art moderne, art nouveau, Arts and Crafts, and other aesthetic movements, are 8,000 matchbooks collected by Egypt's King Farouk. ⊠ *1001 Washington Ave., at 10th St.* ☎ *305/531–1001* ⊕ *www.wolfsonian.org* ◰ *$7, free after 6 pm Fri.* ⊙ *Mon., Tues., Thur., and weekends noon–6, Fri. noon–9. Closed Wed.*

**World Erotic Art Museum (WEAM).** The sexy collection of more than 4,000 erotic items, all owned by millionaire Naomi Wilzig, unfolds with unique art of varying quality—fertility statues from around the globe and historic Chinese *shunga* books (erotic art offered as gifts to new brides on the wedding night) share the space with some kitschy knickknacks. If this is your thing, an original phallic prop from Stanley

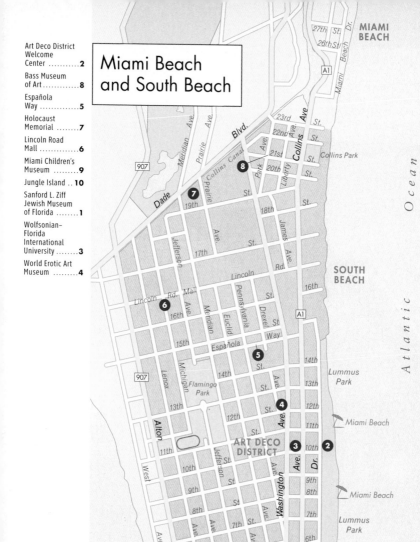

# Miami Beach and South Beach

MIAMI BEACH

A1

Miami Beach Dr.

27th St.

26th St.

23rd St.

Collins Ave.

Blvd.

Meridian Ave.

Prairie Ave.

Collins Canal

Dade

22nd Ave.

Park Ave.

21st Ave.

Liberty Ave.

Collins Park

8

20th St.

Collins

7

19th St.

18th St.

James Ave.

17th Ave.

Jefferson

Lincoln Rd.

SOUTH BEACH

16th

Ocean

Atlantic Ocean

Lincoln Rd. Mall

6

16th

Meridian Ave.

Pennsylvania

Euclid

Drexel

Española St.

Way

5

15th

14th St.

14th

13th

Michigan

Flamingo Park

Lenox

13th

12th St.

Lummus Park

4

12th

11th

Miami Beach

Alton

11th

10th

Ave.

Washington

ART DECO DISTRICT

Ave.

Dr.

3

2

10th

Miami Beach

9th

West

10th St

9th St

8th St

Jefferson

7th St

Ave.

Ave.

Ave.

8th

7th

6th

5th

8th

Miami Beach

Lummus Park

Rd.

6th

5th St.

Collins

Ocean

907

907

41

A1

A1

4th St.

3rd St.

2nd St.

1st St.

Biscayne St.

Harley St.

1

SOUTH POINTE

Ocean Front Park

Ocean Beach

Pier Park

Miami Beach Pier

MacArthur Causeway

9 10

Inlet Blvd.

South Pointe Park

SOUTH POINTE

0        400 yrds

0        400 meters

Kubrick's *A Clockwork Orange* and an over-the-top Kama Sutra bed is worth the price of admission, but the real standout is "Miss Naomi," who is usually on hand to answer questions and provide behind-the-scenes anecdotes. Kids 17 and under are not admitted. ⊠ *1205 Washington Ave., at 12th St.* ☎ *305/532–9336* ⊕ *www.weam.com* 🖃 *$15* ⊙ *Mon.–Thurs. 11 am–10 pm, Fri.–Sun. 11 am–midnight.*

**12**

## CORAL GABLES

You can easily spot Coral Gables from the window of a Miami-bound jetliner—just look for the massive orange tower of the Biltmore Hotel rising from a lush green carpet of trees concealing the city's gracious homes. The canopy is as much a part of this planned city as its distinctive architecture, all attributed to the vision of George E. Merrick nearly 100 years ago.

The story of this city began in 1911, when Merrick inherited 1,600 acres of citrus and avocado groves from his father. Through judicious investment he nearly doubled the tract to 3,000 acres by 1921. Merrick dreamed of building an American Venice here, complete with canals and homes. Working from this vision, he began designing a city based on centuries-old prototypes from Mediterranean countries. Unfortunately for Merrick, the devastating no-name hurricane of 1926, followed by the Great Depression, prevented him from fulfilling many of his plans. He died at 54, an employee of the post office. Today Coral Gables has a population of about 45,000. In its bustling downtown, more than 150 multinational companies maintain headquarters or regional offices, and the University of Miami campus in the southern part of the Gables brings a youthful vibrancy to the area. A southern branch of the city extends down the shore of Biscayne Bay through neighborhoods threaded with canals.

### EXPLORING
#### TOP ATTRACTIONS

★ **Biltmore Hotel.** Bouncing back stunningly from its dark days as an Army hospital, this hotel has become the jewel of Coral Gables—a dazzling architectural gem with a colorful past. First opened in 1926, it was a hot spot for the rich and glamorous of the Jazz Age until it was converted to an Army–Air Force regional hospital in 1942. Until 1968, the Veterans Administration continued to operate the hospital after World War II. The Biltmore then lay vacant for nearly 20 years before it underwent extensive renovations and reopened as a luxury hotel in 1987. Its 16-story tower, like the Freedom Tower in downtown Miami, is a replica of Seville's Giralda Tower. The magnificent pool, reportedly the largest hotel pool in the continental United States, is steeped in history—Johnny Weissmuller of Tarzan fame was a lifeguard here, and in the 1930s grand aquatic

**WORD OF MOUTH**

"The best people-watching spots are News Cafe on Ocean Drive and Van Dyke Cafe or Segafredo on Lincoln Road. Go in the evening when it's cooler and the beautiful people are out."
—SoBchBud1

galas featuring alligator wrestling, synchronized swimming, and bathing beauties drew thousands. More recently it was President Clinton's preferred place to stay and golf. To the west is the Biltmore Country Club, a richly ornamented beaux arts–style structure with a superb colonnade and courtyard; it was reincorporated into the hotel in 1989. Sunday champagne brunch is a local legend; try to get a table in the courtyard. ⊠ *1200 Anastasia Ave., near De Soto Blvd., Coral Gables* ☎ *305/445–1926* ⊕ *www.biltmorehotel.com.*

♻ **Fairchild Tropical Botanic Garden.** With 83 acres of lakes, sunken gardens,
Fodor's Choice  a 560-foot vine pergola, orchids, bellflowers, coral trees, bougainvil-
★  lea, rare palms, and flowering trees, Fairchild is the largest tropical botanical garden in the continental United States. The tram tour highlights the best of South Florida's flora; then you can set off exploring on your own. A 2-acre rain-forest exhibit showcases tropical plants from around the world complete with a waterfall and stream. The conservatory, Windows to the Tropics, is home to rare tropical plants, including the Titan Arum (*Amorphophallus titanum*), a fast-growing variety that attracted thousands of visitors when it bloomed in 1998. (It was only the sixth documented bloom in this country in the 20th century.) The Keys Coastal Habitat, created in a marsh and mangrove area in 1995 with assistance from the Tropical Audubon Society, provides food and shelter to resident and migratory birds. Check out the Montgomery Botanical Center, a research facility devoted to palms and cycads. Spicing up Fairchild's calendar are plant sales, afternoon teas, and genuinely special events year-round, such as the International Mango Festival the second weekend in July. The excellent bookstore–gift shop carries books on gardening and horticulture, and the Garden Café serves sandwiches and, seasonally, smoothies made from the garden's own crop of tropical fruits. ⊠ *10901 Old Cutler Rd., Coral Gables* ☎ *305/667–1651* ⊕ *www.fairchildgarden.org* ⊒ *$25* ⊙ *Daily 9:30–4:30.*

Fodor's Choice  **Venetian Pool.** Sculpted from a rock quarry in 1923 and fed by artesian
★  wells, this 820,000-gallon municipal pool had a major face-lift in 2010. It remains quite popular because of its themed architecture—a fantasy version of a waterfront Italian village—created by Denman Fink. The pool has earned a place on the National Register of Historic Places and showcases a nice collection of vintage photos depicting 1920s beauty pageants and swank soirees held long ago. Paul Whiteman played here, Johnny Weissmuller and Esther Williams swam here, and you should, too (but no kids under 3). A snack bar, lockers, and showers make this must-see user-friendly as well. ⊠ *2701 De Soto Blvd., at Toledo St., Coral Gables* ☎ *305/460–5306* ⊕ *www.gablesrecreation.com* ⊒ *$11; free parking across De Soto Blvd.* ⊙ *Times vary month to month. Call ahead.*

**WORTH NOTING**
**Coral Gables Congregational Church.** With George Merrick as a charter member (he donated the land on which it stands) this parish was organized in 1923. Rumor has it that Merrick built Coral Gables's first church, in honor of his father, a congregational minister. It's only natural then that this was the first church in the state of Florida to

**12**

be listed on the National Register of Historic Places. Nowadays, this functioning church is welcoming, regardless of age, sexual orientation, or faith. The original interior is still in magnificent condition. The church is located directly across from the Biltmore Hotel. ⊠ *3010 De Soto Blvd., at Anastasia Ave., Coral Gables* ☎ *305/448–7421* ⊕ *www. coralgablescongregational.org* ⊙ *Weekdays 8:30–5, Sun. services at 9 at Chapel and 11 at the Sanctuary.*

**Coral Gables Merrick House and Gardens.** In 1976 the city of Coral Gables acquired Merrick's boyhood home. Restored to its 1920s appearance, it contains Merrick family furnishings and artwork. The breezy veranda and coral-rock construction are details you'll see repeated on many of the grand homes along Coral Way. Note that the telephone is disconnected except during open hours. ⊠ *907 Coral Way, at Toledo St., Coral Gables* ☎ *305/460–5361* ☜ *$5* ⊙ *45-min house tours Wed. and most Sun. at 1, 2, and 3.*

**Miracle Mile.** Even with competition from some impressive malls, this half-mile stretch of retail stores continues to thrive because of its intriguing mixture of unique boutiques, bridal shops, art galleries, charming restaurants, and upscale nightlife venues. ⊠ *Coral Way between S.W. 37th and S.W. 42nd Aves., Coral Gables* ⊕ *www.shopcoralgables.com.*

OFF THE
BEATEN
PATH

**Zoo Miami.** Don't miss a visit to this top-notch zoo, 14 mi southwest of Coral Gables. The only subtropical zoo in the continental United States, it has 320 plus acres that are home to more than 2,000 animals, including 40 endangered species, which roam on islands surrounded by moats. Take the monorail ($3 for an all-day pass) for a cool overview, then walk around for a closer look, including the latest attraction Amazon & Beyond, which encompasses 27 acres of simulated tropical rain forests showcasing 600 animals indigenous to the region, such as giant river otters, harpy eagles, anacondas, and jaguars. Other exhibits include Tiger Temple, where white tigers roam, and the African Plains exhibit, where giraffes, ostriches, and zebras graze in a simulated natural habitat. You can even feed veggies to the giraffes at Samburu Station. The Wings of Asia aviary has about 300 exotic birds representing 70 species flying free within the jungle-like enclosure. There's also a petting zoo with a meerkat exhibit and interactive opportunities, such as those at Dr. Wilde's World and the Ecology Theater, where kids can touch Florida animals like alligators and opossums. An educational and entertaining wildlife show is given three times daily. ⊠ *12400 S.W. 152nd St., Richmond Heights, Miami* ☎ *305/251–0400* ⊕ *www.miamimetrozoo.com* ☜ *$15.95, $11.95 children ages 3 to 12; 45-min tram tour $4.95* ⊙ *Daily 9:30–5:30, last admission 4.*

## COCONUT GROVE

Eclectic and intriguing, Miami's Coconut Grove can be considered a loose tropical equivalent of New York's Greenwich Village. A haven for writers and artists, the neighborhood has never quite outgrown its image as a small village. During the day it's business as usual in Coconut Grove, much as in any other Miami neighborhood. But in the evening, especially on weekends, it seems as if someone flips a switch and the streets come alive. Locals and tourists jam into small boutiques, sidewalk cafés, and stores lodged in two massive retail-entertainment complexes. For blocks in every direction, students, families, and prosperous retirees flow in and out of a mix of galleries, restaurants, bars, bookstores, comedy clubs, and theaters. With this weekly influx of traffic, parking can pose a problem. There's a well-lighted city garage at 3315 Rice Street (behind the Mayfair and Cocowalk), or look for police to direct you to parking lots where you'll pay $10 and up for an evening's slot. If you're staying in the Grove, leave the car behind, and your night will get off to an easier start.

Nighttime is the right time to see Coconut Grove, but in the day you can take a casual drive around the neighborhood to see its diverse architecture. Posh estates mingle with rustic cottages, modest frame homes, and stark modern dwellings, often on the same block. If you're into horticulture, you'll be impressed by the Garden of Eden–like foliage that seems to grow everywhere without care. In truth, residents are determined to keep up the Grove's village-in-a-jungle look, so they lavish attention on exotic plantings even as they battle to protect any remaining native vegetation.

### EXPLORING

**Barnacle Historic State Park.** A pristine bay-front manse sandwiched between cramped luxury developments, Barnacle is Miami's oldest house still standing on its original foundation. To get here, you'll hike along an old buggy trail through a tropical hardwood hammock and landscaped lawn leading to Biscayne Bay. Built in 1891 by Florida's first snowbird—New Yorker Commodore Ralph Munroe—the large home, built of timber that Munroe salvaged from wrecked ships, has many original furnishings, a broad sloping roof, and deeply recessed verandas that channel sea breezes into the house. If your timing is right, you may catch one of the monthly Moonlight Concerts, and the old-fashioned picnic on July 4 is popular. ⊠ *3485 Main Hwy.* 🕾 *305/442–6866* ⊕ *www.floridastateparks.org/thebarnacle* 🖃 *$2 park entry, tours $3, concerts $7* ⊙ *Fri.–Mon. 9–5; tours at 10, 11:30, 1, and 2:30; groups Wed. and Thurs.; closed Tues.; concerts Sept.–May on evenings near the full moon 6–9, call or check the Web site for date.*

☺ **Miami Museum of Science and Planetarium.** This small fun museum is chock-full of hands-on sound, gravity, and electricity displays for children and adults alike. For animal lovers, its wildlife center houses native Florida snakes, turtles, tortoises, and birds of prey. Check the museum's schedule for traveling exhibits that appear throughout the year. If you're here the first Friday of the month—called Fabulous First Fridays—stick around for the free star show at 7:30 pm and then gaze at the planets through two powerful Meade telescopes at the Weintraub Observatory. Also enjoy a laser-light rock-and-roll show at either 9, 10, or 11 pm to the tunes of the Doors, the Beatles, or Pink Floyd to name a few. ⊠ *3280 S. Miami Ave.* 🕾 *305/646–4200* ⊕ *www.miamisci.org* 🖃 *Museum exhibits, planetarium shows, and wildlife center $14.95, laser show $7* ⊙ *Museum daily 10–6.*

Fodor's Choice
★ **Vizcaya Museum and Gardens.** Of the 10,000 people living in Miami between 1912 and 1916, about 1,000 of them were gainfully employed by Chicago industrialist James Deering to build this European-inspired residence. Once comprising 180 acres, this national historic landmark now occupies a 30-acre tract that includes a native hammock and more than 10 acres of formal gardens with fountains overlooking Biscayne Bay. The house, open to the public, contains 70 rooms, 34 of which are filled with paintings, sculpture, antique furniture, and other fine and decorative arts. The collection spans 2,000 years and represents the Renaissance, baroque, rococo, and neoclassical periods. The 90-minute self-guided Discover Vizcaya Audio Tour is available in both English and Spanish for an additional $5. Guided tours are also available. Moonlight tours, offered on evenings that are nearest the full moon, provide a magical look at the gardens; call for reservations. ⊠ *3251 S. Miami Ave.* ☎ *305/250–9133* ⊕ *www.vizcayamuseum.org* ⊠ *$15* ☾ *Wed.–Mon. 9:30–4:30.*

## KEY BISCAYNE

Once upon a time, these barrier islands were an outpost for fishermen and sailors, pirates and salvagers, soldiers and settlers. The 95-foot Cape Florida Lighthouse stood tall during Seminole Indian battles and hurricanes. Coconut plantations covered two-thirds of Key Biscayne, and there were plans as far back as the 1800s to develop the picturesque island as a resort for the wealthy. Fortunately, the state and county governments set much of the land aside for parks, and both keys are now home to top-ranked beaches and golf, tennis, softball, and picnicking facilities. The long and winding bike paths that run through the islands are favorites for in-line skaters and cyclists. Incorporated in 1991, the village of Key Biscayne is a hospitable community of about 10,500; Virginia Key remains undeveloped at the moment, making these two playground islands especially family-friendly.

### EXPLORING

🐚 **Miami Seaquarium.** This classic family attraction stages shows with sea lions, dolphins, and Lolita the killer whale. The Crocodile Flats exhibit has 26 Nile crocodiles. Discovery Bay, an endangered mangrove habitat, is home to sea turtles, alligators, herons, egrets, and ibis. You can also visit a shark pool, a tropical reef aquarium, and West Indian and Florida manatees. A popular interactive attraction is the Stingray Touch Tank, where you can touch and feed cow-nose rays and southern stingrays. Another big draw is the Swim with Our Dolphins program. For $199, a two-hour session

### SAIL AWAY

If you can sail in Miami, do. Blue skies, calm seas, and a view of the city skyline make for a pleasurable outing—especially at twilight, when the fabled "moon over Miami" casts a soft glow on the water. Key Biscayne's calm waves and strong breezes are perfect for sailing and windsurfing, and although Dinner Key and the Coconut Grove waterfront remain the center of sailing in Greater Miami, sailboat moorings and rentals sit along other parts of the bay and up the Miami River.

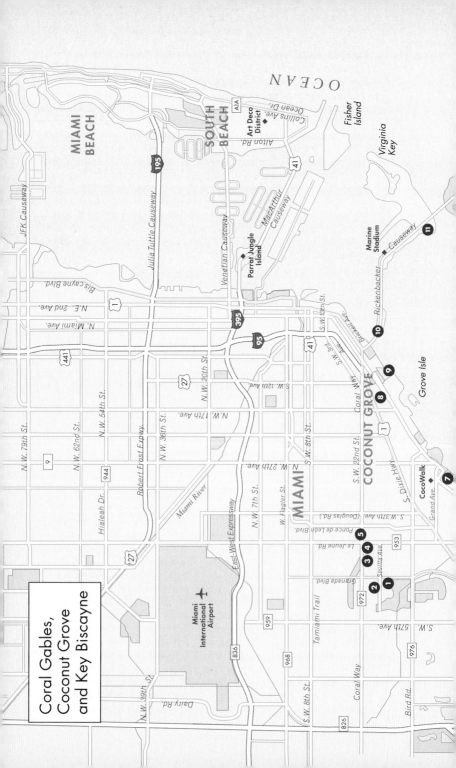

Coral Gables, Coconut Grove and Key Biscayne

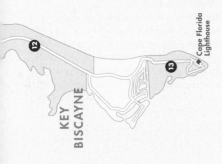

ATLANTIC

*Biscayne Bay*

KEY
BISCAYNE

Cape Florida
Lighthouse

**12**

**13**

Coral Gables

Maynada St.

Sunset Dr.

Ponce de León Rd.

Red Rd.

Old Cutler Rd.

Waterway

Cartagena
Plaza

CORAL
GABLES

S. W. 72nd St.

Ponce de León Blvd.

986

SOUTH
MIAMI

**6**

**14**

0   3 km
0   3 miles

allows you to touch, kiss, and swim with the gentle marine mammals on the Dolphin Odyssey, $139 ($99 for kids) to participate in the shallow water Dolphin Encounter. It may seem pricey but it does include park admission, towel, and a wet suit. Reservations required. ⊠ *4400 Rickenbacker Causeway, Virginia Key* ☎ *305/361–5705* ⊕ *www. miamiseaquarium.com* ▦ *$37.95, children 3–9 $27.95, parking $8* ⊙ *Daily 9–6, last admission 4:30; dolphin swim daily at 9:30, 10, 11:30, 1, and 2:30; dolphin encounter daily at 12:15 and 3:15.*

**Old Rickenbacker Causeway Bridge.** Here you can watch boat traffic pass through the channel, pelicans and other seabirds soar and dive, and dolphins cavort in the bay. Park at the bridge entrance, about a mile from the tollgate, and walk past anglers tending their lines to the gap where the center draw span across the Intracoastal Waterway was removed. On the right, on cool, clear winter evenings, the water sparkles with dots of light from hundreds of shrimp boats. ⊠ *Rickenbacker Causeway south of Powell Bridge, east of Coconut Grove.*

# BEACHES

## MIAMI BEACH

### NORTH BEACH AND AVENTURA

**Haulover Beach Park.** This popular clothing-optional beach is embraced by naturists of all ages, shapes, and sizes. Once you park in the North Lot, you'll walk through a short tunnel covered with trees and natural habitat until you emerge on the unpretentious beach, where nudity is rarely met by gawkers. There are volleyball nets, and plenty of beach chair and umbrella rentals to protect your birthday suit from too much exposure—to the sun, that is. The sections of beach requiring swimwear are popular, too, given the park's ample parking and relaxed atmosphere. Lifeguards stand watch. More active types might want to check out the kite rentals, charter-fishing excursions, and a par-3, 9-hole golf course. ⊠ *10800 Collins Ave., north of Bal Harbour in Sunny Isles* ☎ *305/947–3525* ⊕ *www.hauloverbeach.org* ▦ *$6 per vehicle if park in lot* ⊙ *Daily sunrise–sunset.*

☾ ★ **Oleta River State Park.** Tucked away in North Miami Beach is a ready-made family getaway. Nature lovers will find it easy to embrace the 1,128 acres of subtropical beauty along Biscayne Bay. Swim in the calm bay waters and bicycle, canoe, kayak, and bask among egrets, manatees, bald eagles, and fiddler crabs. Dozens of picnic tables, along with 10 covered pavilions, dot the stunning natural habitat, which has recently been restored with red mangroves to revitalize the ecosystem and draw endangered birds, like the roseate spoonbill. There's a playground for tots, a mangrove island accessible only by boat, 15 mi of mountain-bike trails, a half-mile exercise track, concessions,

> **WORD OF MOUTH**
>
> "Stay in South Beach and take a drive out to Key Biscayne—you'll love it!! Nice place to ride bikes."
> —JerseySue

Not all the fun is for grown-ups. With sandy shores great for kite flying, Miami beaches appeal to kids, too.

and outdoor showers. If you want to continue the nature adventure into the evening, reserve an overnight stay in minimalist (but still air-conditioned) cabins, which run $55 per night. ⊠ *3400 N.E. 163rd St., North Miami Beach* ☎ *305/919–1844* ⊕ *www.floridastateparks. org/oletariver* ⊡ *$6 per vehicle; $2 per person on foot or bike; free entrance if renting a cabin* ☉ *Daily 8–sunset.*

### SOUTH BEACH

Fodor'sChoice
★

**South Beach.** A 10-block stretch of white sandy beach hugging the turquoise waters along Ocean Drive—from 5th to 15th streets—is one of the most popular in America, known for drawing unabashedly modelesque sunbathers and posers. With the influx of new luxe hotels and hotspots from 16th to 25th streets, the South Beach stand-and-pose scene is now bigger than ever. The beaches crowd quickly on the weekends with a blend of European tourists, young hipsters, and sun-drenched locals offering Latin flavor. Separating the sand from the traffic of Ocean Drive is palm-fringed Lummus Park, with its volleyball nets and chickee huts (huts made of palmetto thatch over a cypress frame) for shade. The beach at 12th Street is popular with gays, in a section often marked with rainbow flags. Locals hang out on 3rd Street beach, in an area called SoFi (South of Fifth) where they watch fit Brazilians play foot volley, a variation of volleyball that uses everything but the hands. Because much of South Beach leans toward skimpy sunning—women are often in G-strings and casually topless—many families prefer the tamer sections of Mid- and North Beach. Metered parking spots next to the ocean are a rare find. Instead, opt for a public garage a few blocks away and enjoy the people-watching as you walk to find your perfect spot on the sand. ⊠ *Ocean Dr. from 5th to 15th Sts., then Collins Ave. to 25th St., Miami Beach* ☎ *305/673–7714.*

## KEY BISCAYNE

FodorsChoice   **Bill Baggs Cape Florida State Park.** Thanks to inviting beaches, sunsets,
★    and a tranquil lighthouse, this park at Key Biscayne's southern tip is worth the drive. In fact, the 1-mi stretch of pure beachfront has been ranked among Florida's best on several occasions. It has 19 picnic shelters, and two cafés that serve light lunches. A stroll or ride along walking and bicycle paths provides wonderful views of Miami's dramatic skyline. From the southern end of the park you can see a handful of houses rising over the bay on wooden stilts, the remnants of Stiltsville, built in the 1940s and now protected by the Stiltsville Trust. The nonprofit group was established in 2003 to preserve the structures as they showcase the park's rich history. Bill Baggs has bicycle rentals, a playground, fishing piers, and guided tours of the **Cape Florida Lighthouse,** South Florida's oldest structure. The lighthouse was erected in 1845 to replace an earlier one damaged in an 1836 Seminole attack, in which the keeper's helper was killed. The restored cottage and lighthouse offer free tours at 10 am and 1 pm Thursday to Monday. Be there a half hour beforehand. ⊠ *1200 S. Crandon Blvd., Key Biscayne* ☎ *305/361–5811* ⊕ *www.floridastateparks.org/ capeflorida* ⊟ *$8 per vehicle; $2 per person on bicycle, bus, motorcycle, or foot* ⊘ *Daily 8–dusk.*

Ↄ    **Crandon Park Beach.** This relaxing oasis in northern Key Biscayne is
★    popular with families. The sand is soft, there are no riptides, there's a great view of the Atlantic, and parking is both inexpensive and plentiful. The park is dotted with picnic tables and grills and cabanas are available for rent on a first-come, first-served basis.

**Crandon Gardens** at Crandon Park was once the site of a zoo. There are swans, waterfowl, and dozens of huge iguanas running loose. Nearby are a restored carousel (it's open weekends and major holidays 10–5, until 6 in summer, and you get three rides for $1), outdoor roller rink, and playground.

At the north end of the beach is the free **Marjory Stoneman Douglas Biscayne Nature Center** (☎ *305/361–6767* ⊘ *Daily 10–4*), where you can explore sea-grass beds on a tour with a naturalist; see red, black, and white mangroves; and hike along the beach and hammock in the Bear Cut Preserve. The park also sponsors hikes and tours. ⊠ *6747 Crandon Blvd., Key Biscayne* ☎ *305/361–5421* ⊕ *www. biscaynenaturecenter.org* ⊟ *$5 per vehicle* ⊘ *Daily 8–sunset.*

## MIAMI TOURS

### BOAT TOURS

**Duck Tours Miami.** Amphibious vehicles make daily 90-minute tours of Miami that combine land and sea views. Comedy and music are part of the mix. Tickets are $18 for children 4–12. ⊠ *1661 James Ave., Miami Beach* ☎ *305/673–2217* ⊕ *www.ducktourssouthbeach.com* ☞ *$32.*

**Island Queen, Island Lady, and Miami Lady.** Double-decker, 140-passenger tour boats docked at Bayside Marketplace set sail daily for 90-minute narrated tours of the Port of Miami and Millionaires' Row. ⊠ *401 Biscayne Blvd., Miami* ☎ *305/379–5119* ⊕ *www.islandqueencruises.com* ☞ *$26.*

**RA Charters.** For something a little more private and luxe, sail out of the Dinner Key Marina in Coconut Grove. Full- and half-day charters include sailing lessons, with occasional extended trips to the Florida Keys.

For a romantic night, have Captain Masoud pack some gourmet fare and sail sunset to moonlight while you enjoy Biscayne Bay's spectacular skyline view of Miami. ☎ *305/666–7979* or *305/989–3959* ⊕ *www.racharters.com* ☞ *Call for prices.*

### WALKING TOURS

**Art Deco District Tour.** Operated by the Miami Design Preservation League, this is a 90-minute guided walking tour that departs from the league's welcome center at Ocean Drive and 10th Street. It starts at 10:30 am Friday through Wednesday, and at 6:30 pm Thursday. Alternatively, you can go at your own pace with the league's self-guided iPod audio tour, which takes roughly an hour and a half. ⊠ *1001 Ocean Dr., South Beach, Miami Beach* ☎ *305/763–8026* ⊕ *www.mdpl.org* ☞ *$20 guided tour, $15 audio tour.*

# SPORTS AND THE OUTDOORS

Sun, sand, and crystal-clear water mixed with an almost nonexistent winter and a cosmopolitan clientele make Miami and Miami Beach ideal for year-round sunbathing and outdoor activities. Whether the priority is showing off a toned body, jumping on a Jet Ski, or relaxing in a tranquil natural environment, there's a beach tailor-made to please. But tanning and water sports are only part of this sun-drenched picture. Greater Miami has championship golf courses and tennis courts, miles of bike trails along placid canals and through subtropical forests, and skater-friendly concrete paths amidst the urban jungle. For those who like their sports of the spectator variety, the city offers up a bonanza of pro teams for every season. The Miami Dolphins remain the only NFL team to have ever played a perfect season (back in 1972), the scrappy Florida Marlins took the World Series title in 2003, and the Miami Heat were the 2006 NBA champions (hopes for more have risen with the dream three of Chris Bosch, Dwayne Wade, and LeBron James on the court). There's even a crazy ball-flinging game called jai alai that's billed as the fastest sport on earth.

In addition to contacting venues directly, get tickets to major events from **Ticketmaster** (☎ *800/745–3000* ⊕ *www.ticketmaster.com*).

## BASEBALL

**Miami Marlins.** Miami's baseball team, formerly known as the Florida Marlins, is settling into its new home, Miami Ballpark—a 37,000-seat retractable-roof baseball stadium on the grounds of Miami's famous Orange Bowl. Go see the team that came out of nowhere to beat the New York Yankees and win the 2003 World Series. Home games are April through early October. ⊠ *Miami Ballpark, 1501 N.W. 3rd St., 2 mi west of Downtown. Miami* ☎ *305/626–7378 or 877/627–5467* ⊕ *www.marlins.com* ☜ *$10–$315, parking $10.*

## BASKETBALL

**Miami Heat.** The 2006 NBA champs play at the 19,600-seat, waterfront AmericanAirlines Arena. The state-of-the-art venue features restaurants, a wide patio overlooking Biscayne Bay, and a silver sun-shape special-effects scoreboard with rays holding wide-screen TVs. During Heat games, when the 1,100 underground parking spaces are reserved for season-ticket holders, you can park across the street at Miami's Bayside Marketplace ($20), at metered spaces along Biscayne Boulevard, or in lots on side streets, where prices range from $5 to $25, depending on the distance from the arena (a limited number of spaces for people with disabilities are available on-site for non-season-ticket holders). Better yet, take the Metromover to the Park West or Freedom Tower station. Home games are held November through April. ⊠ *AmericanAirlines Arena, 601 Biscayne Blvd., Downtown* ☎ *800/462–2849 ticket hotline* ⊕ *www.nba.com/heat* ☜ *$10–$500.*

## BICYCLING

Perfect weather and flat terrain make Miami-Dade County a popular place for cyclists; however, biking here can also be quite dangerous. Be very vigilant when biking on Miami Beach, or better yet, steer clear and bike the beautiful paths of Key Biscayne.

**Key Cycling.** Rent bikes for $15 for two hours, $24 for the day, and $80 for the week. ⊠ *328 Crandon Blvd., Key Biscayne* ☎ *305/361–0061* ⊕ *www.keycycling.com.*

## BOATING AND SAILING

Boating, whether on sailboats, powerboats, luxury yachts, WaveRunners, or windsurfers, is a passion in greater Miami. The Intracoastal Waterway, wide and sheltered Biscayne Bay, and the Atlantic Ocean provide ample opportunities for fun aboard all types of watercraft.

The best windsurfing spots are on the north side of the Rickenbacker Causeway at Virginia Key Beach or to the south at, go figure, Windsurfer Beach. Kite surfing adds another level to the water-sports craze.

### MARINAS

**Bayshore Landing Marina.** This bustling marina is home to a lively seafood restaurant that's good for viewing the nautical eye candy. ⊠ *2560 S. Bayshore Dr., Coconut Grove* ☎ *305/854–7997.*

**Haulover Marine Center.** It may be low on glamour, but this marina, with a bait-and-tackle shop and a 24-hour marine gas station, is high on service. ⊠ *15000 Collins Ave., north of Bal Harbour, Miami Beach* ☎ *305/945–3934* ⊕ *www.haulovermarinecenter.net.*

**12**

**Miami Beach Marina.** Near the Art Deco District there is plenty to entice sailors and landlubbers alike: restaurants, charters, boat rentals, a complete marine-hardware store, a dive shop, excursion vendors, a large grocery store, a fuel dock, concierge services, and 400 slips accommodating vessels of up to 250 feet. There's also a U.S. Customs clearing station and a charter service, Florida Yacht Charters. Picnic tables along the docks make this marina especially visitor-friendly. ⊠ *MacArthur Causeway, 300 Alton Rd., Miami Beach* ☎ *305/673–6000* ⊕ *www. miamibeachmarina.com.*

### OUTFITTERS AND EXPEDITIONS

**Club Nautico.** You can rent 18- to 34-foot powerboats and 52- to 54-foot yachts through this national boat rental company with two Miami locations. Half- to full-day rentals range from $399 to $3,600. ⊠ *Miami Beach Marina, 300 Alton Rd., #112, Miami Beach* ☎ *305/673–2502* ⊕ *www.club-nautico.com* ⊠ *Crandon Park Marina, 4000 Crandon Blvd., Key Biscayne.*

**Playtime Watersports.** A number of high-end hotels get their water-sports equipment, including WaveRunners and wind-driven devices, here. ☎ *786/234–0184 or 305/216-6967* ⊕ *www.playtimewatersport.com.*

**Sailboards Miami.** In addition to renting equipment, these friendly folks say they teach more windsurfers each year than anyone in the United States and promise to teach you to windsurf within two hours—for $79. Rentals average $30 for the first hour and $25 for each additional hour. ⊠ *.7 mi after toll plaza on Rickenbacker Causeway, Key Biscayne* ☎ *305/361–7245* ⊕ *www.sailboardsmiami.com.*

## FOOTBALL

Fodor'sChoice
★

**Miami Dolphins.** The Dolphins have one of the largest average attendance figures in the league. September through January, on home-game days the Metro Miami-Dade Transit Agency runs buses to the stadium. ⊠ *Sun Life Stadium, 2269 Dan Marino Blvd., 16 mi northwest of Downtown, between I–95 and Florida's Tpke.* ☎ *305/623–6100* ⊕ *www.miamidolphins.com.*

## GOLF

Greater Miami has more than 30 private and public courses. Costs at most courses are higher on weekends and in season, but you can save by playing on weekdays and after 1 or 3 pm, depending on the course—call ahead to find out when afternoon-twilight rates go into effect. For information on most courses in Miami and throughout Florida, you can visit ⊕ *www.floridagolferguide.com.*

**Biltmore Golf Course.** The 18-hole, par-71 championship course, known for its scenic layout, has been restored to its original Donald Ross design, circa 1925. Greens fees in season range from $145 to $165 for nonresidents. The optional cart is $27. ⊠ *1210 Anastasia Ave., Coral Gables* ☎ *305/460–5364* ⊕ *www.biltmorehotel.com.*

**Crandon Golf.** Overlooking the bay, this top-rated 18-hole, par-72 public course comes with a beautiful tropical setting. Nonresidents should expect to pay $180 for a round in season (December 15– April) and roughly half that off-season. Twilight rates apply after 3 pm. ⊠ *6700 Crandon Blvd., Key Biscayne* ☎ *305/361–9129* ⊕ *www. crandongolfclub.com.*

**Don Shula's Hotel & Golf Club.** In northern Miami, this hotel has one of the longest championship courses in the area (7,055 yards, par 72), a lighted par-3 course, and a golf school. Greens fees are $134–$175, depending on the season. Hotel guests get discounted rates. You'll pay in the lower range on weekdays, more on weekends, and $45 after 3 pm. Golf carts are included. The par-3 course is $12 weekdays, $15 weekends. The club hosts more than 75 tournaments a year. ⊠ *7601 Miami Lakes Dr., 154th St. Exit off Rte. 826, Miami Lakes* ☎ *305/820–8106* ⊕ *www.donshulahotel.com.*

Fodor'sChoice **Doral Golf Resort and Spa.** Of its five courses and many annual tour-
★ naments this resort, just west of Miami proper, is best known for the par-72 Blue Monster course and the PGA's annual World Golf Championship. (The week of festivities planned around this tournament, which offers $8 million in prize money, brings hordes of pro-golf aficionados in late March.) Greens fees range from $65 to $325. Carts are not required. ⊠ *4400 N.W. 87th Ave., 36th St. Exit off Rte. 826, Doral, Miami* ☎ *305/592–2000 or 800/713–6725* ⊕ *www. doralresort.com.*

**Miami Beach Golf Club.** Hit the links in the heart of South Beach at a lovely 18-hole, par-72 course. Greens fees are $100 in summer, $200 in winter, including mandatory cart. ⊠ *2301 Alton Rd., Miami Beach* ☎ *305/532–3350* ⊕ *www.miamibeachgolfclub.com.*

## SCUBA DIVING AND SNORKELING

Diving and snorkeling on the offshore coral wrecks and reefs on a calm day can be very rewarding. Chances are excellent you'll come face-to-face with a flood of tropical fish. One option is to find Fowey, Triumph, Long, and Emerald reefs in 10- to 15-foot dives that are perfect for snorkelers and beginning divers. On the edge of the continental shelf a little more than 3 mi out, these reefs are just ¼ mi away from depths greater than 100 feet. Another option is to paddle around the tangled prop roots of the mangrove trees that line the coast, peering at the fish, crabs, and other creatures hiding there. ⇨ *For the best snorkeling in Miami-Dade, head to Biscayne National Park. See the Everglades chapter for more information.*

**Artificial Reefs.** Perhaps the area's most unusual diving options are its artificial reefs. Since 1981, Miami-Dade County's Department of Environmental Resources Management has sunk tons of limestone boulders and a water tower, army tanks, and almost 200 boats of all descriptions to create a "wreckreational" habitat where divers can swim with yellow

*Continued on page 566*

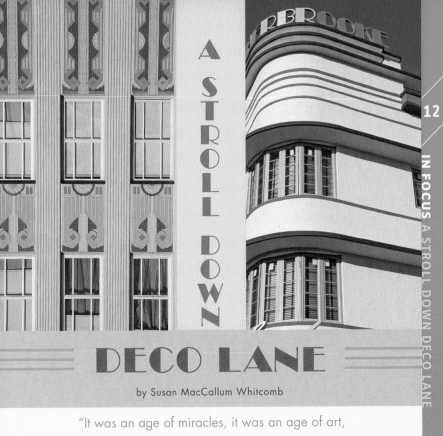

# A STROLL DOWN

# DECO LANE

by Susan MacCallum Whitcomb

"It was an age of miracles, it was an age of art,

it was an age of excess, and it was an age of satire."

—F. Scott Fitzgerald, *Echoes of the Jazz Age*

The 1920s and '30s brought us flappers and gangsters, plunging stock prices and soaring skyscrapers, and plenty of headline-worthy news from the arts scene, from talking pictures and the jazz craze to fashions where pearls piled on and sequins dazzled. These decades between the two world wars also gave us an art style reflective of the changing times: art deco.

Distinguished by geometrical shapes and the use of industrial motifs that fused the decorative arts with modern technology, art deco became the architectural style of choice for train stations and big buildings across the country (think New york's Radio City Music Hall and Empire State Building).

Using a steel-and-concrete box as the foundation, architects dipped into art deco's grab bag of accessories, initially decorating facades with spheres, cylinders, and cubes. They later borrowed increasingly from industrial design, stripping elements used in ocean liners and automobiles to their streamlined essentials.

The style was also used in jewelry, furniture, textiles, and advertising. The fact that it employed inexpensive materials, such as stucco or terrazzo, helped art deco thrive during the Great Depression.

# MIAMI BEACH'S ART DECO DISTRICT

With its warm beaches and tropical surroundings, Miami Beach in the early 20th century was establishing itself as America's winter playground. During the roaring '20s luxurious hostelries resembling Venetian palaces, Spanish villages, and French châteaux sprouted up. In the 1930s, middle-class tourists started coming, and more hotels had to be built. Designers like Henry Hohauser chose art deco for its affordable yet distinctive design.

An antidote to the gloom of the Great Depression, the look was cheerful and tidy. And with the whimsical additions of portholes, colorful racing bands, and images of rolling ocean waves painted or etched on the walls, these South Beach properties created an oceanfront fantasy world for travelers.

Many of the candy-colored hotels have survived and been restored. They are among the more than 800 buildings of historical significance in South Beach's art deco district. Composing much of South Beach, the 1-square-mi district is bounded by Dade Boulevard on the north, the Atlantic Ocean on the east, 6th Street on the south, and Alton Road on the west.

Because the district as a whole was developed so rapidly and designed by like-minded architects—**Henry Hohauser, L. Murray Dixon, Albert Anis,** and their colleagues—it has amazing stylistic unity. Nevertheless, on this single street you can trace the evolution of period form from angular, vertically emphatic early deco to aerodynamically rounded Streamline Moderne. The relatively severe Cavalier and more curvaceous Cardozo are fine examples of the former and latter, respectively.

To explore the district, begin by loading up on literature in the **Art Deco Welcome Center** (⌂ *1001 Ocean Dr.* ☎ *305/763–8026* ⊕ *www.mdpl.org*). If you want to view these historic properties on your own, just start walking. A four-block stroll north on Ocean Drive gets you up close to camera-ready classics: the **Clevelander** (1020), the **Tides** (1220), the **Leslie** (1244), the **Carlyle** (1250), the **Cardozo** (1300), the **Cavalier** (1320), and the **Winterhaven** (1400).

# ART DECO TOURS

See the bold looks of classic Art Deco architecture along Ocean Drive.

## SELF-GUIDED AUDIO TOURS

Expert insight on the architecture and the area's history is yours on the Miami Design Preservation League's (MDPL) 90-minute self-guided walks that use an iPod or cell phone and include a companion map. You can pick up the iPod version and companion map at the Art Deco Welcome Center from 9:30 AM to 5 PM daily; the cost is $15. The cellphone option ($10) is available anytime by calling 786/312–1229 and charging the amount to your credit card; your payment allows you access to audio commentary for up to 24 hours after purchase.

## WALKING TOURS

The MDPL's 90-minute "Ocean Drive and Beyond" group walking tour gives you a guided look at area icons, inside and out. (A number of interiors are on the itinerary, so it's a good chance to peek inside spots that might otherwise seem off-limits.) Morning tours depart at 10:30 AM from the Art Deco Welcome Center Gift Shop on Tuesday, Wednesday, Friday, Saturday, and Sunday. An evening tour departs at 6:30 PM on Thursdays. Reservations can't be made in advance, so arrive 15–20 minutes early to buy tickets ($20).

## BIKE TOURS

Rather ride than walk? Half-day cycling tours of the city's art deco history are organized daily for groups (5 or more) by **South Beach Bike Tours** (☎ 305/673–2002 ⊕ www.southbeach-biketours.com). The $59 cost includes equipment, snacks, and water.

## ART DECO WEEKEND

Tours, lectures, film screenings, and dozens of other '30s-themed events are on tap in mid-January, during the annual **Art Deco Weekend** (☎ 305/672–2014, ⊕ www.ArtDecoWeekend.com). Festivities—many of them free—kick off with a Saturday morning parade and culminate in a street fair. More than a quarter of a million people join in the action, which centers on Ocean Drive between 5th and 15th streets.

Celebrate the 1930s during Art Deco Weekend.

# ARCHITECTURAL HIGHLIGHTS

Cavalier Hotel

### FRIEZE DETAIL, CAVALIER HOTEL

The decorative stucco friezes outside the Cavalier Hotel at 1320 Ocean Drive are significant for more than aesthetic reasons. Roy France used them to add symmetry (adhering to the "Rule of Three") and accentuate the hotel's verticality by drawing the eye upward. The pattern he chose also reflected a fascination with ancient civilizations engendered by the recent rediscovery of King Tut's tomb and the Chichén Itzá temples.

Park Central Hotel

### LOBBY FLOOR, PARK CENTRAL HOTEL

Terrazzo—a compound of cement and stone chips that could be poured, then polished—is a hallmark of deco design. Terrazzo floors typically had a geometric pattern, like this one in the Park Central Hotel, a 1937 building by Henry Hohauser at 640 Ocean Drive.

Essex House Hotel

### CORNER FACADE, ESSEX HOUSE HOTEL

Essex House Hotel, a 1938 gem that appears permanently anchored at 1001 Collins Avenue, is a stunning example of Maritime deco (also known as Nautical Moderne). Designed by Henry Hohauser to evoke an ocean liner, the hotel is rife with marine elements, from the rows of porthole-style windows and natty racing stripes to the towering smokestack-like sign. With a prow angled proudly into the street corner, it seems ready to steam out to sea.

The Hotel

### NEON SPIRE, THE HOTEL

The name spelled vertically in eye-popping neon on the venue's iconic aluminum spire—Tiffany—bears evidence of the hotel's earlier incarnation. When the L. Murray Dixon–designed Tiffany Hotel was erected at 801 Collins Avenue in 1939, neon was still a novelty. Its use, coupled with the spire's rocket-like shape, combined to create a futuristic look influenced by the sci-fi themes then pervasive in popular culture.

Jerry's Famous Deli

### ENTRANCE, JERRY'S FAMOUS DELI

Inspired by everything from car fenders to airplane noses, proponents of art deco's Streamline Moderne look began to soften buildings' hitherto boxy edges. But when Henry Hohauser designed Hoffman's Cafeteria in 1940 he took moderne to the max. The landmark at 1450 Collins Avenue (now Jerry's Famous Deli) has a sleek, splendidly curved facade. The restored interior echoes it through semicircular booths and rounded chair backs.

## ARCHITECTURAL TERMS

**The Rule of Three:** Early deco designers often used architectural elements in multiples of three, creating tripartite facades with triple sets of windows, eyebrows, or banding.

**Eyebrows:** Small shelf-like ledges that protruded over exterior windows were used to simultaneously provide much-needed shade and serve as a counterpoint to a building's strong vertical lines.

**Tropical Motifs:** In keeping with the setting, premises were plastered, painted, or etched with seaside images. Palm trees, sunbursts, waves, flamingoes, and the like were particularly common.

**Banding:** Enhancing the illusion that these immobile structures were rapidly speeding objects, colorful horizontal bands (also called "racing stripes") were painted on exteriors or applied with tile.

**Stripped Classic:** The most austere version of art deco (sometimes dubbed Depression Moderne) was used for buildings commissioned by the Public Works Administration.

(top) Hotel Marlin; (left) Sherbrooke Hotel; (right) U.S. Post Office in Miami Beach.

For locals, the beach scene is often incorporated into daily life, from getting exercise to walking the dog.

tang, barracudas, nurse sharks, snapper, eels, and grouper. Most dive shops sell a book listing the locations of these wrecks. Information on wreck diving can be obtained from the Miami Beach Chamber of Commerce. ⊠ *1920 Meridian Ave., Miami Beach* ☎ *305/672–1270.*

**Divers Paradise of Key Biscayne.** This complete dive shop and diving-charter service next to the Crandon Park Marina, includes equipment rental and scuba instruction with PADI and NAUI affiliation. Dive trips are offered Tuesday through Friday at 10 and 1, weekends 8:30 and 1:30. The trip is $60. ⊠ *4000 Crandon Blvd., Key Biscayne* ☎ *305/361–3483* ⊕ *www.keydivers.com.*

**South Beach Dive and Surf Center.** The Discover Scuba course trains diving newcomers on Tuesday, Thursday, and Saturday at 8 am at a PADI-affiliated dive shop. Advance classes follow at 9:45 am. Night dives take place each Wednesday at 4:30, and wreck and reef dives on Sundays at 7:30 am and noon. The center also runs dives in Key Largo's Spiegel Grove, the second-largest wreck ever to be sunk for the intention of recreational diving, and in the Neptune Memorial Reef, inspired by the city of Atlantis and created in part using the ashes of cremated bodies. Boats depart from marinas in Miami Beach and Key Largo, in the Florida Keys. ⊠ *850 Washington Ave., Miami Beach* ☎ *305/531–6110* ⊕ *www.southbeachdivers.com.*

# SHOPPING

Miami teems with sophisticated shopping malls and the bustling avenues of commercial neighborhoods. But this is also a city of tiny boutiques tucked away on side streets—such as South Miami's Red, Bird, and Sunset roads intersection—and outdoor markets touting unusual and delicious wares. Stroll through Spanish-speaking neighborhoods where shops sell clothing, cigars, and other goods from all over Latin America. At an open-air flea-market stall, score an antique glass shaped like a palm tree and fill it with some fresh Jamaican ginger beer from the table next door. Or stop by your hotel gift shop and snap up an alligator magnet for your refrigerator, an ashtray made of seashells, or a bag of gum balls shaped like Florida oranges. Who can resist?

People fly to Miami from all over the world just to shop, and the malls are high on their list of spending spots. Stop off at one or two of these climate-controlled temples to consumerism, many of which double as mega-entertainment centers, and you'll understand what makes Miami such a vibrant shopping destination.

If you're over the climate-controlled slickness of shopping malls and can't face one more food-court "meal," you've got choices in Miami. Head out into the sunshine and shop the city streets, where you'll find big-name retailers and local boutiques alike. Take a break at a sidewalk café to power up on some Cuban coffee or fresh-squeezed OJ and enjoy the tropical breezes.

Beyond the shopping malls and the big-name retailers, Greater Miami has all manner of merchandise to tempt even the casual browser. For consumers on a mission to find certain items—art deco antiques or cigars, for instance—the city streets burst with a rewarding collection of specialty shops.

Pass the mangoes! Greater Miami's farmers' markets and flea markets take advantage of the region's balmy weather and tropical delights to lure shoppers to open-air stalls filled with produce and collectibles.

## COCONUT GROVE

### MALLS

**CocoWalk.** This popular three-story indoor-outdoor mall has three floors of nearly 40 shops that stay open almost as late as its popular restaurants and clubs. Chain stores like Victoria's Secret and Gap blend with specialty shops like Koko & Palenki and Edward Beiner; the space blends the bustle of a mall with the breathability of an open-air venue. Kiosks with cigars, beads, incense, herbs, and other small items are scattered around the ground level, and restaurants and nightlife (Cheesecake Factory, Fat Tuesday, and a 16-screen AMC theater, to name a few) line the upstairs perimeter. Hanging out and people-watching is something of a pastime here. ✉ *3015 Grand Ave., Coconut Grove, Miami* ☎ *305/444–0777* ⊕ *www.cocowalk.net.*

## SPECIALTY STORES
### ANTIQUES
★ **Architectural Antiques.** Find an enormous selection of antique lighting, as well as large and eclectic items—railroad crossing signs, statues, English roadsters. There's also antique furniture, paintings, and silverware, all in a cluttered setting that makes shopping an adventure. ⊠ *2520 S.W. 28th La., Coconut Grove* ☎ *305/285–1330* ⊕ *www.miamiantique.com.*

### OUTDOOR MARKETS
★ **Coconut Grove Farmers' Market.** The most organic of Miami's outdoor markets specializes in a mouthwatering array of local produce as well as such ready-to-eat goodies as cashew butter, homemade salad dressings, and fruit pies (some of the offerings can taste stodgy to the nonorganic eater). If you are looking for a downright granola crowd and experience, pack your Birkenstocks because this is it. It's open Saturdays only, from 10 to 7, rain or shine. ⊠ *3300 Grand Ave., Coconut Grove* ☎ *305/238–7747* ⊕ *www.glaserorganicfarms.com.*

## WORD OF MOUTH

"South Beach is filled with cutting-edge, hip clothing shops for young women, and in addition has great nightlife and a lively street scene."
—montereybob

# CORAL GABLES

## MALLS
Fodor'sChoice **Village of Merrick Park.** At this Mediterranean-style shopping-and-dining
★ venue, Neiman Marcus and Nordstrom anchor 115 specialty shops. Designers such as Etro, Tiffany & Co., Burberry, CH Carolina Herrera, and Gucci fulfill most high-fashion needs, and Brazilian contemporary-furniture designer Artefacto provides a taste of the haute-decor shopping options. International food venues like C'est Bon and a day spa, Elemis, offer further indulgences. ⊠ *358 San Lorenzo Ave., Coral Gables* ☎ *305/529–0200* ⊕ *www.villageofmerrickpark.com.*

## SHOPPING DISTRICTS
**Miracle Mile.** The centerpiece of the downtown Coral Gables shopping district, lined with trees and busy with strolling shoppers, is home to men's and women's boutiques, jewelry and home-furnishings stores, and a host of exclusive couturiers and bridal shops. Running from Douglas Road to LeJeune Road and Aragon Avenue to Andalusia Avenue, more than 30 first-rate restaurants offer everything from French to Indian cuisine, and art galleries and the Actors' Playhouse give the area a cultural flair. ⊠ *Douglas Rd. to LeJeune Rd. and Aragon Ave. to Andalusia Ave., Coral Gables* ⊕ *www.shopcoralgables.com.*

## SPECIALTY SHOPS
### ANTIQUES
**Valerio Antiques.** This shop carries fine French art deco furniture, bronze sculptures, shagreen boxes, and original art glass by Gallé and Loetz, among others. ⊠ *250 Valencia Ave., Coral Gables* ☎ *305/448–6779* ⊕ *www.valerioartdeco.com.*

**12**

## BOOKS

Fodor's Choice ★ **Books & Books, Inc.** Greater Miami's only independent English-language bookshops specialize in contemporary and classical literature as well as in books on the arts, architecture, Florida, and Cuba. At any of its three locations you can lounge at a café or, at the Coral Gables store, browse the photography gallery. All stores host regular poetry and other readings. ✉ *265 Aragon Ave., Coral Gables* ☎ *305/442–4408* ✉ *927 Lincoln Rd., South Beach, Miami Beach* ☎ *305/532–3222* ✉ *9700 Collins Ave., Bal Harbour* ☎ *305/864–4241* ⊕ *www.booksandbooks.com.*

## CIGARS

**Sabor Havana Cigars.** Spanish wine helps patrons relax while browsing the selection of rare cigars. ✉ *2309 Ponce de León Blvd., Coral Gables* ☎ *305/444–1764* ⊕ *www.saborhavana.com.*

## CLOTHING

★ **Silvia Tcherassi.** The Colombian designer's signature boutique in the Village of Merrick Park features feminine and frilly dresses and separates accented with chiffon, tulle, and sequins. ✉ *350 San Lorenzo Ave., Coral Gables* ☎ *305/461–0009* ⊕ *www.silviatcherassi.com.*

## JEWELRY

**Jose Roca Fine Jewelry Designs.** Jose Roca designs fine jewelry from precious metals and stones. If you have a particular piece that you would like to create, this is the place to have it meticulously executed. ✉ *297 Miracle Mile, Coral Gables* ☎ *305/448–2808.*

## OUTDOOR MARKETS

**Coral Gables Farmers' Market.** Some 25 local produce growers and plant vendors sell herbs, fruits, fresh-squeezed juices, chutneys, cakes, and muffins at this market between Coral Gables's City Hall and Merrick Park. Artists also join in. Regular events include gardening workshops, children's activities, and cooking demonstrations offered by Coral Gables's master chefs. The market opens on Saturday, mid-January through late March only. ✉ *405 Biltmore Way, Coral Gables* ☎ *305/460–5311.*

# DOWNTOWN MIAMI

## MIAMI DESIGN DISTRICT

★ **Miami Design District.** Miami is synonymous with good design, and this visitor-friendly shopping district is an unprecedented melding of public space and the exclusive world of design. There are more than 200 showrooms and galleries, including Kartell, Ann Sacks, Poliform, and Luminaire. Restaurants like Michael's Genuine Food & Drink, Joey's, and Sra. Martinez also make this trendy neighborhood a hip place to dine. Unlike most showrooms, which are typically the beat of decorators alone, the Miami Design District's showrooms are open to the public and occupy windowed, street-level spaces. Bring your quarters, as all of the parking is on the street and metered. The neighborhood even has its own high school (of art and design, of course) and hosts street parties and gallery walks. Although in many cases you'll need a decorator to secure your purchases, browsers are encouraged to consider for themselves the array of rather exclusive furnishings, decorative objects, antiques, and art. ⊠ *N.E. 2nd Ave. and N.E. 40th St., Miami Design DistrictMiami* ⊕ *www.miamidesigndistrict.net.*

### SPECIALTY SHOPS

ANTIQUES **Artisan Antiques Art Deco.** These purveyors of china, crystal, mirrors, and armoires from the French–art deco period also draw customers in with an assortment of 1930s radiator covers, which can double as funky sideboards. The shop is open weekdays. ⊠ *110 N.E. 40th St., Miami Design District, Miami* ☎ *305/573–5619* ⊕ *www. artisanartdeco.com.*

### LITTLE HAVANA

### SPECIALTY SHOPS

ONLY IN MIAMI **La Casa de las Guayaberas.** Like the name says, this shop sells custom-made guayaberas, the natty four-pocket dress shirts favored by Latin men. Hundreds are also available off the rack. ⊠ *5840 S.W. 8th St., Little Havana* ☎ *305/266–9683.*

CIGARS **Sosa Family Cigars.** There is a wide selection of premium and house cigars in a humidified shop, once known as Macabi. There's a selection of wines for purchase. Humidors and other accessories are also available. ⊠ *3475 S.W. 8th St., Little Havana* ☎ *305/446–2606.*

# MIAMI BEACH

## NORTH BEACH AND AVENTURA

Fodor's Choice **Aventura Mall.** This three-story mall offers the ultimate in South Flor-
★ ida retail therapy. Aventura houses many global top performers such
MALLS as the most lucrative Abercrombie & Fitch in the United States, a massive Crate & Barrel, the latest, greatest Nordstrom and Bloomingdale's, and 250 other shops, which together create the fifth-largest mall in the United States. This is the one-stop, shop-'til-you-drop retail palladium for locals, out-of-towners, and, frequently, celebrities. ⊠ *19501 Biscayne Blvd., Aventura* ☎ *305/935–1110* ⊕ *www. aventuramall.com.*

Fodor's Choice **Bal Harbour Shops.** Local and international shoppers flock to this swank
★ collection of 100 high-end shops, boutiques, and department stores,
MALLS which include such names as Christian Dior, Gucci, Hermès, Salvatore Ferragamo, Tiffany & Co., and Valentino. Many European designers open their first North American signature store at this outdoor, pedestrian-friendly mall, and many American designers open their first boutique outside of New York here. Restaurants and cafés, in tropical garden settings, overflow with style-conscious diners. People-watching at outdoor café Carpaccio is the best in town. ⊠ *9700 Collins Ave., Bal Harbour* ☎ *305/866–0311* ⊕ *www.balharbourshops.com.*

## SOUTH BEACH

### SHOPPING DISTRICTS

★ **Collins Avenue.** Give your plastic a workout in South Beach shopping at the many high-profile tenants on this densely packed two-block stretch like Club Monaco, M.A.C., Kenneth Cole, Barney's Co-Op, and A/X

Armani Exchange. Sprinkled among the upscale vendors are hair salons, spas, cafés, and such familiar stores as the Gap, Urban Outfitters, and Banana Republic. Be sure to head over one street east and west to catch the shopping on Ocean Drive and Washington Avenue. ⊠ *Collins Ave. between 5th and 10th Sts., South Beach* *Miami Beach.*

**Fodor's** Choice ★  **Lincoln Road Mall.** The eight-block-long pedestrian mall is the trendiest place on Miami Beach. Home to more than 150 shops, 20-plus art galleries and nightclubs, about 50 restaurants and cafés, and the renovated Colony Theatre, Lincoln Road, between Alton Road and Washington Avenue, is like the larger, more sophisticated cousin of Ocean Drive. The see-and-be-seen theme is furthered by outdoor seating at every restaurant, where well-heeled patrons lounge and discuss the people (and pet) parade passing by. An 18-screen movie theater anchors the west end of the street, which is where most of the worthwhile shops are; the far east end is mostly discount and electronics shops. Sure, there's a Pottery Barn, a Gap, and a Williams-Sonoma, but the emphasis is on emporiums with unique personalities, like En Avance, Chroma, Base, and Jonathan Adler. ⊠ *Lincoln Rd., between Alton Rd. and Washington Ave., South Beach, Miami Beach* ⊕ *www. lincolnroad.org.*

### SPECIALTY SHOPS

★  CLOTHING  **Base.** Constantly evolving, this shop features an intriguing magazine section, an international CD station with DJ, and groovy home accessories. Stop here for men's and women's eclectic clothing, shoes, and accessories that mix Japanese design with Caribbean-inspired materials. The often-present house-label designer may help select your wardrobe's newest addition. ⊠ *939 Lincoln Rd., South Beach, Miami Beach* ☎ *305/531–4982* ⊕ *www.baseworld.com.*

**Fodor's** Choice ★ BEAUTY  **Brownes & Co.** An entire store dedicated to beauty, body, and soul, Brownes & Co. is a one-stop shop for pampering and high-end vanity. Cosmetics include Molton Brown, Nars, Le Clerc, and others. It also sells herbal remedies and upscale hair and body products from Bumble and bumble. Just try to resist something from the collection of French, Portuguese, and Italian soaps in various scents and sizes. There's also a fabulous spa and salon on-site. ⊠ *841 Lincoln Rd., South Beach, Miami Beach* ☎ *305/532–8703* ⊠ *87 N.E. 40 St., Design District* ☎ *305/538– 7544* ⊕ *www.brownesbeauty.com.*

★ ONLY IN MIAMI  **Dog Bar.** Just north of Lincoln Road's main drag, this over-the-top pet boutique caters to enthusiastic animal owners with a variety of unique items for the pampered pet, including a luxurious pet sofa imported from Italy and offered in cowhide, leather, or vinyl fitted into a chrome frame. ⊠ *1684 Jefferson Ave., South Beach, Miami Beach* ☎ *305/532– 5654* ⊠ *3301 N.E. 1st Ave., Midtown 4, Wynwood* ☎ *786/837–0904* ⊕ *www.dogbar.com.*

CLOTHING  **Intermix.** This modern New York–based boutique has the variety of a department store. You'll find fancy dresses, stylish shoes, slinky accessories, and trendy looks by sassy and somewhat pricey designers like Chloé, Stella McCartney, Marc Jacobs, Moschino, and Diane von Furstenberg. ⊠ *634 Collins Ave., South Beach, Miami Beach* ☎ *305/531–5950* ⊕ *www.intermixonline.com.*

★    **MIA Jewels.** On Alton Road, this jewelry and accessories boutique is
JEWELRY   known for its colorful, gem- and bead-laden, gold and silver earrings,
necklaces, bracelets, and brooches by lines such as Cousin Claudine,
Amrita, and Alexis Bittar. This is a shoo-in store for everyone: you'll
find things for trend lovers (gold-studded chunky Lucite bangles),
classicists (long, colorful, wraparound beaded necklaces), and ice
lovers (long Swarovski crystal cabin necklaces) alike. ⊠ *1439 Alton
Rd., South Beach, Miami Beach* ☎ *305/532–6064* ⊠ *19575 Biscayne
Blvd., Aventura* ☎ *305/931–2000* ⊕ *www.miajewels.com.*

★    **Morgan Miller Shoes.** Design your own couture stiletto or stylish sandal
CLOTHING   in just a half hour (cobblers are fast at work while you wait). The
selection of materials is seemingly endless: wood, resin, or cork heels
or sandals; leather, alligator, snake, or ostrich straps in a myriad of
vibrant colors; and more than 100 crystals and jewels to choose from.
Prices range from a basic sandal with a denim strap for about $70 to
an over-the-top pair of strappy lime-green, snakeskin stilettos laced
with Swarovski crystals, colored tacks, and hanging jewels, topping
$500. This is a great store for footwear fashionistas, but you don't
have to be a shoe addict to enjoy finding the right fit here. ⊠ *618
Lincoln Rd., South Beach, Miami Beach* ☎ *305/672–8700* ⊕ *www.
morganmillershoes.com.*

CLOTHING   **South Beach Dive and Surf Center.** The one-stop shop for beach gear—from
clothing and swimwear for guys and gals to wake-, surf-, and skate-
boards—also offers multilingual surfing, scuba, snorkeling, and dive
lessons and trips. ⊠ *850 Washington Ave., South Beach, Miami Beach*
☎ *305/531–6110* ⊕ *www.southbeachdivers.com.*

**OUTDOOR MARKETS**

★    **Lincoln Road Outdoor Antique and Collectibles Market.** Interested in picking up samples of Miami's ever-present modern and moderne furniture and accessories? This outdoor show takes place every other
Sunday and offers eclectic goods that should satisfy postimpression-
ists, deco-holics, Edwardians, Bauhausers, Goths, and '50s junkies. ⊠ *Lincoln and Alton Rds., South Beach, Miami Beach* ⊕ *www.
antiquecollectiblemarket.com.*

**Lincoln Road Farmers' Market.** With all the familiar trappings of a farmers'
market (except for farmers—most of the people selling veggies appear
to be resellers), this is a weekly South Beach Sunday (9–6:30) ritual. It
brings local produce and bakery vendors to Lincoln Road and often
features plant workshops, art sales, and children's activities. This is a
good place to pick up live orchids, too. ⊠ *Lincoln Rd. between Meridian and Washington Aves., South Beach, Miami Beach* ☎ *305/531–0038*
⊕ *www.themarketcompany.org/mkts.html.*

From salsa and merengue to disco and hip-hop, Miami's dance clubs cater to diverse styles of music.

# NIGHTLIFE

One of Greater Miami's most popular pursuits is barhopping. Bars range from intimate enclaves to showy see-and-be-seen lounges to loud, raucous frat parties. There's a New York–style flair to some of the newer lounges, which are increasingly catering to the Manhattan party crowd who escape to South Beach for long weekends. No doubt, Miami's pulse pounds with nonstop nightlife that reflects the area's potent cultural mix. On sultry, humid nights with the huge full moon rising out of the ocean and fragrant night-blooming jasmine intoxicating the senses, who can resist Cuban salsa, Jamaican reggae, and Dominican merengue, with some disco and hip-hop thrown in for good measure? When this place throws a party, hips shake, fingers snap, bodies touch. It's no wonder many clubs are still rocking at 5 am. If you're looking for a relatively nonfrenetic evening, your best bet is one of the chic hotel bars on Collins Avenue.

The *Miami Herald* (⊕ *www.miamiherald.com*) is a good source for information on what to do in town. The Weekend section of the newspaper, included in the Friday edition, has an annotated guide to everything from plays and galleries to concerts and nightclubs. The "Ticket" column of this section details the week's entertainment highlights. Or, you can pick up the *Miami New Times* (⊕ *www. miaminewtimes.com*), the city's largest free alternative newspaper, published each Thursday. It lists nightclubs, concerts, and special events; reviews plays and movies; and provides in-depth coverage of the local music scene. "Night & Day" is a rundown of the week's cultural highlights. *Ocean Drive* (⊕ *www.oceandrive.com*),

## THE VELVET ROPES

How to get past the velvet ropes at the hottest South Beach nightspots? First, if you're staying at a hotel, use the concierge. Decide which clubs you want to check out (consult *Ocean Drive* magazine celebrity pages if you want to be among the glitterati), and the concierge will email, fax, or call in your names to the clubs so you'll be on the guest list when you arrive. This means much easier access and usually no cover charge (which can be upward of $20) if you arrive before midnight. Guest list or no guest list, follow these pointers: make sure there are more women than men in your group. Dress up—casual chic is the dress code. For men this means no sneakers, no shorts, no sleeveless vests, and no shirts unbuttoned past the top button. For women, provocative and seductive is fine; overly revealing is not. Black is always right. At the door: don't name-drop—no one takes it seriously. Don't be pushy while trying to get the doorman's attention. Wait until you make eye contact, then be cool and easygoing. If you decide to tip him (which most bouncers don't expect), be discreet and pleasant, not big-bucks obnoxious—a $10 or $20 bill quietly passed will be appreciated, however. With the right dress and the right attitude, you'll be on the dance floor rubbing shoulders with South Beach's finest clubbers in no time.

Miami Beach's model-strewn, upscale fashion and lifestyle magazine, squeezes club, bar, restaurant, and events listings in with fashion spreads, reviews, and personality profiles. Paparazzi photos of local party people and celebrities give you a taste of Greater Miami nightlife before you even dress up to paint the town.

The Spanish-language *El Nuevo Herald* (⊕ *www.elnuevoherald.com*), published by the *Miami Herald,* has extensive information on Spanish-language arts and entertainment, including dining reviews, concert previews, and nightclub highlights.

## COCONUT GROVE

### BARS AND LOUNGES

**Monty's in the Grove.** The outdoor bar here has Caribbean flair, thanks especially to live calypso and island music. It's very kid-friendly on weekends, when Mom and Dad can kick back and enjoy a beer and the raw bar while the youngsters dance to live music. Evenings bring a DJ and reggae music. ✉ *2550 S. Bayshore Dr., at Aviation Ave.* ☎ *305/856–3992.*

## CORAL GABLES

### BARS AND LOUNGES

**Bar at Ponce and Giralda.** One of the oldest bars in South Florida, the old Hofbrau has been reincarnated and now serves vibrant, live reggae music on Saturday nights and a nontouristy vibe. ✉ *172 Giralda Ave., at Ponce de León Blvd., Coral Gables* ☎ *305/442–2730.*

**Globe.** The centerpiece of Coral Gables's emphasis on nightlife draws crowds of twentysomethings who spill into the street for live jazz on Saturday evenings and a bistro-style menu nightly. Free appetizers and drink specials every weekday attract a strong happy-hour following. Outdoor tables and an art-heavy, upscale interior are comfortable, if you can find space to squeeze in. ⊠ *377 Alhambra Circle, at Le Jeune Rd.* ☎ *305/445–3555* ⊕ *www.theglobecafe.com.*

**John Martin's Restaurant and Irish Pub.** The cozy upscale Irish pub hosts an Irish cabaret on Saturday night with live contemporary and traditional music—sometimes by an Irish band—storytelling, and dancers. ⊠ *253 Miracle Mile, at Ponce de León Blvd.* ☎ *305/445–3777* ⊕ *www. johnmartins.com.*

## DOWNTOWN MIAMI

### BARS AND LOUNGES

Fodor'sChoice ★ **Tobacco Road.** Opened in 1912, this classic holds Miami's oldest liquor license: No. 0001! Upstairs, in a space that was occupied by a speakeasy during Prohibition, local and national blues bands perform nightly. There is excellent bar food, a dinner menu, and a selection of single-malt scotches, bourbons, and cigars. This is the hangout of grizzled journalists, bohemians en route to or from nowhere, and club kids seeking a way station before the real parties begin. Live blues, R&B, and jazz bands are on tap, along with food and drink, seven days a week. ⊠ *626 S. Miami Ave., Downtown Miami* ☎ *305/374–1198* ⊕ *www. tobacco-road.com.*

### DANCE CLUBS

Fodor'sChoice ★ **Space Miami.** Want 24-hour partying? Here's the place. Space revolutionized the Miami party scene 10 years ago and still gets accolades as one of the country's best dance clubs. Created from four downtown warehouses, it has two levels (one blasts house music; the other reverberates with hip-hop), an outdoor patio, a New York–style industrial look, and a 24-hour liquor license. It's open on weekends only, and you'll need to look good to be allowed past the velvet ropes. ⊠ *34 N.E. 11th St.* ☎ *305/375–0001* ⊕ *www.clubspace.com.*

## SOUTH BEACH

### BARS AND LOUNGES

**B.E.D.** Innocently standing for "beverages, entertainment, and dining," B.E.D. also offers king-pillow-strewn beds in place of tables. Not only were the sheets washed in 2010 but B.E.D. got an entire makeover, too, including new beds. ⊠ *929 Washington Ave., Miami Beach* ☎ *305/532– 9070* ⊕ *www.bedmiami.com.*

★ **Buck 15.** This hidden lounge above popular Lincoln Road eatery Miss Yip Café is one of Miami's best-kept secrets. The tiny club manages to play amazing music—a rock-heavy mix of songs you loved but haven't heard in ages—and maintain a low-key, unpretentious attitude. It's a bit of a kitschy frat party for grown-ups. The drinks are reasonably priced, and the well-worn couches are great to dance on. The club attracts local hipsters. ✉ *707 Lincoln Rd., Miami Beach* ☎ *305/538–3815* ⊕ *www. buck15.net.*

**Club Deuce.** Although it's completely unglam, this pool hall attracts a colorful crowd of clubbers, locals, celebs—and just about anyone else. Locals consider it the best spot for a cheap drink and one of the best dive bars. ✉ *222 14th St., at Collins Ave., Miami Beach* ☎ *305/531–6200.*

**Lost Weekend.** Players at this pool hall are serious about their pastime, so it's hard to get a table on weekends. The full bar, which has 150 kinds of beer, draws an eclectic crowd, from yuppies to drag queens to slumming celebs like Lenny Kravitz. ✉ *218 Española Way, at Collins Ave., Miami Beach* ☎ *305/672–1707.*

> ### CULTURAL FRIDAYS
>
> On the last Friday of every month Little Havana takes its culture to the streets for *Viernes Culturales* (Cultural Friday ⊕ *www. viernesculturales.org*), held between 7 and 11 pm on 8th Street from 14th to 17th avenues. Art galleries and stores stay open late, and music, mojitos, and avant-garde street performances bring a young hip crowd to the neighborhood where they mingle with locals. The annual Calle Ocho festival, held in March, draws more than a million visitors in search of Latin music, food, and shopping.

**Mynt Ultra Lounge.** The name of this upscale nightclub, which opens its doors at midnight, is meant to be taken literally—not only are the walls bathed in soft green shades, but an aromatherapy system pumps out different fresh scents, including mint. Celebs like Enrique Iglesias, Angie Everhart, and Queen Latifah have cooled down here. ✉ *1921 Collins Ave., Miami Beach* ☎ *305/532-0727* ⊕ *www.myntlounge.com.*

★ **The National.** Don't miss a drink at the hotel's nifty wooden bar, one of many elements original to the 1939 building, which give it such a sense of its era that you'd expect to see Ginger Rogers and Fred Astaire hoofing it along the polished lobby floor. The adjoining Martini Room has a great collection of cigar and old airline stickers and vintage Bacardi ads on the walls. Don't forget to take a peek at the long, sexy pool. ✉ *1677 Collins Ave., Miami Beach* ☎ *305/532–2311* ⊕ *www. nationalhotel.com.*

FodorsChoice **Rose Bar at the Delano.** The airy lobby lounge at South Beach's trendiest
★ hotel manages to look dramatic but not cold, with long, snow-white, gauzy curtains and huge white pillars separating conversation nooks (this is where Ricky Martin shot the video for "La Vida Loca"). A pool table brings the austerity down to earth. There's also an expansive poolside bar, dotted with intimate poolside beds (bottle service required) and private cabanas to reserve for the evening—for a not-so-nominal fee, of course. ✉ *1685 Collins Ave., South Beach, Miami* ☎ *305/672–2000* ⊕ *www.delano-hotel.com.*

FodorsChoice **SkyBar at the Shore Club.** Splendor-in-the-garden is the theme at this
★ haute spot by the sea, where multiple lounging areas are joined together. Daybeds, glowing Moroccan lanterns, and maximum atmosphere make a visit to this chic outdoor lounge worthwhile. Groove to dance music in the Red Room, or enjoy an aperitif and Japanese bar

bites at Nobu Lounge. The Red Room, Nobu Restaurant and Lounge, Italian restaurant Ago, and SkyBar all connect around the Shore Club's pool area. ⊠ *1901 Collins Ave., Miami Beach* ☎ *305/695–3100* ⊕ *www.shoreclub.com.*

### DANCE CLUBS

**Fodor's Choice**
★

**Cameo.** One of Miami's ultimate dance clubs, Cameo, formerly known as Crobar, has emerged after a welcomed face-lift. Gone is the industrial feel, but all-star DJs and plentiful dance space remain, and plush VIP lounges have been added. If you can brave the velvet rope, Saturday-night parties are the best. ⊠ *1445 Washington Ave.* ☎ *305/531–5535* ⊕ *www.cameomiami.com.*

**Nikki Beach Club.** Smack-dab on the beach, the full-service Nikki Beach Club was once a favorite of SoBe's pretty people and celebrities. Nowadays, it's filled with more suburbanites than the "in" crowd. Tepees and hammocks on the sand, dance floors both under the stars and inside, and beach parties make this a true South Beach experience circa 2003. ⊠ *1 Ocean Dr.* ☎ *305/538–1111* ⊕ *www.nikkibeach. com/miami.*

**Score.** This popular bar is the see-and-be-seen central of Miami's gay community. DJs spin every night of the week except Sunday, a popular karaoke night where everything goes. Latin Tuesdays are popular as is the upstairs party at Crème Lounge on Thursday and the weekend dance offs. ⊠ *727 Lincoln Rd.* ☎ *305/535–1111* ⊕ *www. scorebar.net.*

**Twist.** This longtime hot spot with the local gay clientele has two levels, an outdoor patio, and a game room that's crowded from 8 pm on, especially on Monday, Thursday (two-for-one), and Friday nights. ⊠ *1057 Washington Ave., Miami Beach* ☎ *305/538–9478* ⊕ *www. twistsobe.com.*

### LIVE MUSIC

★ **Jazid.** If you're looking for an unpretentious alternative to the velvet-rope nightclubs, this unassuming, live-music hot spot is a standout on the strip. Eight-piece bands play danceable Latin rhythms, as well as reggae, hip-hop, and fusion sounds. Get ready for a late night though, as bands are just getting started at midnight. They play every night of the week. Call ahead to reserve a table. ⊠ *1342 Washington Ave.* ☎ *305/673–9372* ⊕ *www.jazid.net.*

# WHERE TO EAT

Miami's restaurant scene has exploded in the last few years, with dozens of great new restaurants springing up left and right. The melting pot of residents and visitors has brought an array of sophisticated, tasty cuisine. Little Havana is still king for Cuban fare, while Miami Beach is swept up in a trend of fusion cuisine, which combines Asian, French, American, and Latin cuisine with sumptuous—and pricy—results. Downtown Miami and the Design District especially are home to some of the city's best spots, and they're all new. Since Miami dining is a part of the trendy nightlife scene, most dinners don't start until 8 or 9 pm, and may go well into the night. To avoid a long wait amongst the late night partiers at hot spots come before 7 or make reservations. Attire is usually casual-chic, but patrons like to dress to impress. Don't be surprised to see large tables of women in skimpy dresses—this is common in Miami. Prices tend to stay high in hot spots like Lincoln Road; but if you venture off the beaten path, you can find delicious food for reasonable prices. When you get your bill, check whether a gratuity is already included; most restaurants add between 15% and 18% (ostensibly for the convenience of, and protection from, the many Latin American and European tourists who are used to this practice in their homelands), but supplement it depending on your opinion of the service.

*Use the coordinate (✛ C2) at the end of each review to locate a property on the Where to Eat in the Miami Area map.*

| WHAT IT COSTS | | | | | |
|---|---|---|---|---|---|
| | ¢ | $ | $$ | $$$ | $$$$ |
| AT DINNER | under $10 | $10–$15 | $15–$20 | $20–$30 | over $30 |

Price per person for a median main course or equivalent combination of smaller dishes.

## COCONUT GROVE, CORAL GABLES, AND KEY BISCAYNE

### COCONUT GROVE

**$$$**
PERUVIAN
Fodor's Choice
★
✕ **Jaguar Ceviche Spoon Bar & Grill.** A fabulous fusion of Peruvian and Mexican flavors, Jaguar is a gastronomic tour of Latin America in a single restaurant. As the name implies, there is a heavy emphasis on ceviches. The best option for experiencing this delicacy is the sampler, which includes six distinct Peruvian and Mexican ceviches served in oversized spoons. Meals come with blue corn tortilla and pita chips served with authentic Mexican salsa. Dishes, such the Mexican Tortilla Lasagna (chicken, poblano peppers, corn, tomato sauce, and cream, topped with melted cheese), are colorful, flavorful, and innovative. ✉ *3067 Grand Ave., Coconut Grove* ☎ *305/444–0216* ⊕ *www.jaguarspot.com.*

**$$$**
FRENCH
✕ **Le Bouchon du Grove.** This French bistro with a supercharged atmosphere is a great spot in the heart of the Grove. Waiters tend to lean on chairs while taking orders, and managers and owners freely mix with the clientele, making Le Bouchon perhaps the last remaining vestige of the Grove's bohemian days. The result is one big happy family, all enjoying traditional French pâtés, gratins, quiches, chicken fricassee, mussels, duck-leg confit, and steak frites. The lively mood inside is matched by the throngs that parade outside the French doors. Breakfast is served daily. ✉ *3430 Main Hwy.* ☎ *305/448–6060* ⊕ *www.lebouchondugrove. com* ✛ *5C.*

# BEST BETS FOR MIAMI DINING

**12**

Fodor's writers and editors have selected their favorite restaurants by price, cuisine, and experience in the Best Bets lists below. In the first column, Fodor's Choice designations represent the "best of the best" in every price category. Find specific details about a restaurant in the full reviews, listed alphabetically by neighborhood.

## Fodor'sChoice★

**Blue Door Fish,** South Beach, p. 588

**Cecconi's,** Mid-Beach, p. 585

**Cioppino,** Key Biscayne, p. 581

**The Forge,** Mid-Beach, p. 585

**Joe's Stone Crab Restaurant,** South Beach, p. 589

**Joey's,** Wynwood, p. 582

**Michael's Genuine Food & Drink,** Design District, p. 582

**Michy's,** Mid-Beach, p. 586

**Palacio de los Jugos,** Coral Gables, p. 580

**Pascal's on Ponce,** Coral Gables, p. 581

**Perricone's Marketplace and Café,** Downtown, p. 584

**Sra. Martinez,** Design District, p. 583

**The Villa by Barton G – The Restaurant,** South Beach, p. 596

## By Price

### ¢

**Palacio de los Jugos,** Coral Gables, p. 580

### $

**Las Culebrinas,** Coral Gables, p. 580

**Tutto Pasta,** Little Havana, p. 584

**Versailles,** Little Havana, p. 585

### $$

**Hy-Vong Vietnamese Cuisine,** Little Havana, p. 585

**Joey's,** Wynwood, p. 582

**Sra. Martinez,** Design District, p. 583

### $$$

**Michael's Genuine Food & Drink,** Downtown Miami, p. 582

### $$$$

**Cioppino,** Key Biscayne, p. 581

**The Forge,** Mid-Beach, p. 585

**Pascal's on Ponce,** Coral Gables, p. 581

## By Cuisine

### AMERICAN

**Big Pink,** South Beach, p. 588

**Joe Allen,** South Beach, p. 589

**Michael's Genuine Food & Drink,** Downtown Miami, p. 582

### ASIAN

**Hakkasan,** Mid-Beach, p. 586

**SushiSamba Dromo,** South Beach, p. 596

### CUBAN

**Havana Harry's,** Coral Gables, p. 580

**Versailles,** Little Havana, p. 585

### ITALIAN

**Cecconi's,** Mid-Beach, p. 585

**Cioppino,** Key Biscayne, p. 581

### SEAFOOD

**Chef Allen's,** North Miami and Aventura, p. 587

**Joe's Stone Crab Restaurant,** South Beach, p. 589

### STEAKHOUSE

**Bourbon Steak,** North Miami and Aventura, p. 587

**The Forge,** Mid-Beach, p. 585

**Prime One Twelve,** South Beach, p. 595

**Red, the Steakhouse,** South Beach, p. 595

## By Experience

### CHILD-FRIENDLY

**Tutto Pasta,** Little Havana, p. 584

**Versailles,** Little Havana, p. 585

### HOT SPOTS

**Blue Door Fish,** South Beach, p. 588

**Meat Market,** South Beach, p. 594

**Michael's Genuine Food & Drink,** Downtown Miami, p. 582

## CORAL GABLES

**$**   ✕ **Havana Harry's.** When Cuban families want a home-cooked meal
CUBAN   but don't want to cook it themselves or go supercheap at the Cuban
fast-food joint, Pollo Tropical, they come to this big, unassuming restaurant. In fact, you're likely to see whole families here, from babes
in arms to grandmothers. The fare is traditional Cuban: the long thin
steaks known as *bistec palomilla* (a panfried steak), roast chicken with
citrus marinade, and fried pork chunks; contemporary flourishes—
mango sauce and guava-painted pork roast—are kept to a minimum.
Most dishes come with white rice, black beans, and a choice of ripe
or green plantains. The sweet ripe ones offer a good contrast to the
savory dishes. Start with the $5.95 *mariquitas* (plantain chips) with
guacamole. ⊠ *4612 Le Jeune Rd.* ☎ *305/661–2622* ⊕ *www.hharrys.
com* ✣ *5C.*

**$**   ✕ **Las Culebrinas.** Each of Las Culebrinas's five locations in Miami tends
SPANISH   to draw throngs of adoring diners for Spanish tapas and Cuban steaks.
Tapas here are not small; some are entrée size like the Frisbee-size
Spanish *tortilla* (omelet). Our suggestion: indulge in a tender fillet of
crocodile, fresh fish, or the grilled fish stuffed with mashed bananas,
followed by a dessert of *crema Catalana*, caramelized at your table with
a blowtorch—this is a good time to remind your kids not to touch.
⊠ *4700 W. Flagler St., at N.W. 47th Ave.* ☎ *305/445–2337* ⊠ *2890
S.W. 27 Ave., Coconut Grove* ☎ *305/448–4090* ⊕ *www.culebrinas.
com* ✣ *4C.*

**$$$$**   ✕ **Ortanique on the Mile.** Cascading *ortaniques*, a Jamaican hybrid
CARIBBEAN   orange, are hand-painted on columns in this warm, welcoming yellow dining room. Food is vibrant in taste and color, as delicious as it
is beautiful. Though there is no denying that the strong, full flavors
are imbued with island breezes, chef-partner Cindy Hutson's personal
cuisine goes beyond Caribbean refinements. The menu centers on fish,
since Hutson has a special way with it, and the Caribbean bouillabaisse
is not to be missed. On Sunday there is live jazz. ⊠ *278 Miracle Mile*
☎ *305/446–7710* ⊕ *www.cindyhutsoncuisine.com* ☾ *No lunch weekends* ✣ *5C.*

**¢**   ✕ **Palacio de los Jugos.** Nearby and to the west of Coral Gables, this
CUBAN   joint is one of the easiest and truest ways to see Miami's local Latin life
Fodor's Choice   in action. It's also one of the best fruit-shake shacks you'll ever come
★   across (ask for a juice of—"*jugo de*"—mamey, melón, or guanabana,
a sweet-tart equatorial fruit, and you can't go wrong). Besides the
rows and rows of fresh tropical fruits and vegetables, and the shakes
you can make with any of them, this boisterous indoor-outdoor market has numerous food counters where you can get just about any
Cuban food—tamales, rice and beans, a *pan con lechón* (roast pork
on Cuban bread), fried pork rinds, or a coconut split before you and
served with a straw. Order your food at a counter and eat it along with
local families at rows of outdoor picnic-style tables next to the parking lot. It's disorganized, chaotic, and not for those cutting calories,
but it's delicious and undeniably the real thing. ⊠ *5721 W. Flagler St.*
☎ *305/264–4557* ⊕ *www.elpalaciodelosjugosonline.com* ⊟ *No credit
cards* ✣ *4B.*

**12**

$$$$ ✕ **Pascal's on Ponce.** This French

FRENCH gem amid the Coral Gables restau-

Fodor'sChoice rant district is always full, thanks

★ to chef-proprietor Pascal Oudin's assured and consistent cuisine. Oudin forgoes the glitz and fussiness often associated with French cuisine, and instead opts for a simple, small, refined dining room that won't overwhelm patrons. The equally sensible menu includes a superb gnocchi appetizer (ask for mushrooms on top). The main course is a tough choice between oven-roasted duck with poached pears, milk-fed veal loin, and diver sea scallops with beef short rib. It opened in 2000. Ask your expert waiter to pair dishes with a selection from Pascal's impressive wine list, and, for dessert, order the bittersweet chocolate soufflé. ✉ *2611 Ponce de León Blvd.* ☎ *305/444–2024* ⊕ *www.pascalmiami.com* ☾ *Closed Sun. No lunch Sat.* ✢ *5C.*

> **FULL-MOON DINNERS**
>
> The Moonrise Dinner Series at Cioppino is fun, romantic, geeky, and one of Miami's most memorable experiences. Held from October to May on the exact night of the full moon, the dinner is a four-course Italian gastronomic extravaganza under the magical path of the rising full moon. Tabletop telescopes serve as centerpieces. The restaurant's Constellation Connoisseur visits each table to point out key stars and constellations, and then invites guests to look at the moon through the mega telescope. Meanwhile the highly attentive staff serve the divine creations of Chef de Cuisine Ezio Gamba.

### KEY BISCAYNE

$$ ✕ **Cantina Beach.** Leave it to the Ritz-Carlton Key Biscayne to bring a

MEXICAN small sumptuous piece of coastal Mexico to Florida's fabulous beaches. The pool- and ocean-side Cantina Beach showcases authentic and divine Mexican cuisine, including fresh guacamole at your table. The restaurant also boasts the country's only *tequilier*, mixing and matching 85 high-end tequilas. It's no surprise then that Cantina Beach has phenomenal margaritas. And the best part is that you can enjoy them with your feet in the sand, gazing at the ocean. ✉ *Ritz-Carlton, 455 Grand Bay Dr.* ☎ *305/365–4622* ⊕ *www.RitzCarlton.com/KeyBiscayne* ✢ *6E.*

$$$$ ✕ **Cioppino.** Few visitors think to venture out to the far end of Key Bis-

ITALIAN cayne for dinner, but making the journey to the soothing grounds of

Fodor'sChoice this quiet Ritz-Carlton property on the beach is well worth it. Choose

★ your view: the ornate dining room near the exhibition kitchen or the alfresco area with views of landscaped gardens or breeze-brushed beaches. Choosing your dishes may be more difficult, given the many rich, luscious Italian options, including imported cheeses, olive oils, risottos and fresh fish flown in daily. Items range from the creamy *burrata* mozzarella and authentic pasta dishes to tantalizing risotto with organic spinach and roasted quail, all expertly matched with fine, vintage, rare, and boutique wines. An after-dinner drink and live music at the old-Havana-style RUMBAR inside the hotel is another treat. ✉ *Ritz-Carlton, 455 Grand Bay Dr.* ☎ *305/365–4156* ⊕ *www.RitzCarlton.com/KeyBiscayne* ✢ *6E.*

Daniel Boulud brings his celebrated take on French cuisine to Miami at db Bistro.

# MIAMI

### DESIGN DISTRICT

$$  
ITALIAN  
Fodor's Choice  
★

✕ **Joey's.** This joyfully good and merrily buzzing new place is literally the only restaurant in Wynwood, an emerging neighborhood to the south of the Design District. But this new restaurant already has that rarest of blessings—the sizzling vibe of a thriving neighborhood restaurant that everyone seems to adore. Its contagious charm begins with the service: informal but focused, very professional, and attentive. Then comes the food: Veneto native chef Ivo Mazzon does homage to fresh ingredients prepared simply and perfectly. A full line of flatbread pizzas contend for tops in Miami. The *dolce e piccante* has figs, Gorgonzola, honey, and hot pepper; it's unexpectedly sweet at first bite, and at bite 10 you'll be swearing it's the best you've ever had. The wine list is small but the product of much discernment. Because it's little and in a weird spot, Joey's makes you feel that you're the first to discover it, and that you've made a new friend in Miami—one you'll need to visit again very soon. ✉ *2506 N.W. 2 Ave., Design District* ☎ *305/438–0488* ⊕ *www. joeyswynwood.com* ✛ *4D.*

$$$  
AMERICAN  
Fodor's Choice  
★

✕ **Michael's Genuine Food & Drink.** Michael's is often cited as Miami's top restaurant. This indoor-outdoor bistro in Miami's Design District relies on fresh ingredients and a hip but unpretentious vibe to lure diners. Beautifully arranged combinations like crispy beef cheek with whipped celeriac, and sweet-and-spicy pork belly with kimchi explode with unlikely but satisfying flavor. Owner and chef Michael Schwartz aims for sophisticated American cuisine with an emphasis on local and organic ingredients. He gets it right. Portions are divided into small, medium, and large plates, and the smaller plates are more inventive, so you can order several and explore. Reserve two weeks in advance for weekend tables; also, consider brunch. ⊠ *130 N.E. 40th St., Design District* ☎ *305/573–5550* ⊕ *www.michaelsgenuine.com* ⚠ *Reservations essential* ☽ *No lunch Sat.* ✛ *3D.*

$$ ✕ **Sra. Martinez**. For a good time with food, dial up Sra. Martinez.
SPANISH Michelle Bernstein's second restaurant (her, first, Michy's, is a must-
Fodor's Choice visit for Miami foodies); the name is a sly take on her name—her
★ husband is David Martinez—which is good, because something as artful as this new restaurant deserves a signature. Bernstein anchors her menu at Sra. Martinez in traditional Spanish cuisine, a brilliant jumping-off point for her wildly successful experiments in flavor, texture, and plate composition. Order several dishes from the Cold & Crisp ($5–$18) and Warm & Lush ($8–$23) sections, which feature small plates of takes on traditional tapas. The cuisine is modern, colorful and, above all, fun. Cocktail lovers will be delighted by the inventive, high-quality selections like the Jalisco Mule, a spicy take on the traditional Moscow Mule, made with tequila and ginger beer, and laced with chili syrup. It's no wonder this restaurant has already become one of the best and most exciting in the city. ⊠ *4000 N.E. 2 Ave., Design District* ☎ *305/573–5474* ⊕ *www.chefmichellebernstein. com* ☽ *Closed Sun. No Lunch Sat.* ✛ *3D.*

## DOWNTOWN MIAMI

$$$$ ✕ **db Bistro Moderne Miami**. At long last, one of America's most celebrated
FRENCH French chefs, Daniel Boulud, brings his renowned cooking to the Miami scene. The menu of Boulud's latest outpost pays homage to the different cuisines and specialties of his homeland and surrounding regions, beginning with a fabulous raw bar alongside regional tasting plates such as the "Assiette Provencale" with mackerel escabeche, black olive tapenade, goat cheese with pear, and Swiss chard *barbajuan*. Moving on to the second course, chose from a dozen hot and cold small plates, like the signature "Daniel Boulud's Smoked Salmon," "Escargots Persillade" with wild burgundy snails simmered in parsley, garlic, salted butter with yellow tomatoes and wild mushrooms, and the "Tomato Tarte Tatin." For the main course, the authentic "Coq Au Vin" and the "Moules Piquante" are guaranteed crowd pleasers, channeling images and/or memories of France through the tastes and smells of the restaurant's flagship dishes. ⊠ *255 Biscayne Boulevard Way, Downtown, Miami* ☎ *305/421–8800* ⊕ *www.danielnyc.com* ✛ *4D.*

$$ ✕ **Eos**. This restaurant at the snazzy Viceroy Hotel on Brickell is
MEDITERRANEAN definitely worth a visit if you're downtown. Chef Michael Psilakis and restaurateur Donatella Arpaia are culinary superstars whose involvement gives this restaurant a lot of attention. The sophisticated, bold design is by Kelly Wearstler. The large menu of inexpensive light dishes is divided by ingredients—cheese and crostini; vegetable and potato; pasta; fish; and meats, poultry, and game. The influences are vast, with Greek, Italian, French, and Spanish flavors all evident. There's also a sushi and sashimi selection. ⊠ *485 Brickell Ave., Downtown Miami* ☎ *305/503–4400 or 866/781–9923* ⊕ *www. viceroymiami.com* ✛ *4D.*

12

$$    ✕ **Novecento.** This Argentine eatery is the Financial District's answer
ARGENTINE   to Ocean Drive: the people are still beautiful, but now they're wear-
ing suits. Known for its empanadas (tender chicken or spinach and
cheese), simple grilled meats (luscious grilled skirt steak with *chimi-
churri* sauce), and the innovative Ensalada Novecento (grilled skirt
steak, french fries, and baby mixed greens), it's no wonder Novecento
is Brickell Avenue's best power-lunch and happy-hour spot. Come for
Sunday brunch and enjoy the signature *parillada*, a small grill with
an assortment of steaks, sausages, and sweetbreads (not sweet bread,
but rather the sweet pancreas of a lamb or calf). ⊠ *1414 Brickell Ave.,
Downtown Miami* ☎ *305/403–0900* ⊕ *www.novecento.com* ✦ *5D.*

$$    ✕ **Perricone's Marketplace and Café.** Brickell Avenue south of the Miami
ITALIAN   River is burgeoning with Italian restaurants, and this lunch place for
Fodor's Choice   local bigwigs is the biggest and most popular among them. It's housed
★   partially outdoors and partially indoors in a 125-year-old Vermont
barn. Recipes were handed down from generation to generation,
and the cooking is simple and good. Buy your wine from the on-
premises deli, and enjoy it (for a small corking fee) with homemade
minestrone; a generous antipasto; linguine with a sauté of jumbo
shrimp, scallops, and calamari; or gnocchi with four cheeses. The
homemade tiramisu and cannoli are top-notch. ⊠ *Mary Brickell Village, 15 S.E. 10th St., Downtown Miami* ☎ *305/374–9449* ⊕ *www.
perricones.com* ✦ *5D.*

$    ✕ **Tobacco Road.** If you like your food (or your drink) the way you
AMERICAN   like your blues—gritty, honest, and unassuming—then this almost-
100-year-old joint will earn your respect. This is Miami's oldest bar
and restaurant, and it manages to stay up the latest, too: 5 am. A
live band plays daily, making this hangout one of Miami's low-key
gems. The road burger is a popular choice, as are appetizers like
nachos and chicken wings; the chili may induce a call for a fire hose.
Fine single-malt scotches are stocked behind the bar. ⊠ *626 S. Miami
Ave., Downtown Miami* ☎ *305/374–1198* ⊕ *www.tobacco-road.com*
✦ *4D.*

$    ✕ **Tutto Pasta.** Tourists might pay $30 for linguine elsewhere, but locals
ITALIAN   are more likely to frequent Tutto Pasta, where they feast on the deli-
☺   cious homemade pasta for less than $15. Start with fresh-baked goat-
cheese focaccia with truffle oil. Then try the famous lobster ravioli
garnished with plantain chips, or the tilapia sautéed with shrimp,
calamari, scallops, and tomato sauce. Hop over to Tutto Pizza next
door to enjoy innovative Brazilian-inspired thin pizzas like the Portu-
guesa, topped with ham, mozzarella, black olives, eggs, and onions.
Finish with Tutto chocolate cake or creamy Brazilian Pave. ⊠ *1751
S.W. 3rd Ave. at S.W. 18th Rd., Downtown Miami* ☎ *305/857–0709*
⊕ *www.tuttopasta.com* ✦ *5D.*

## LITTLE HAVANA

$$$$    ✕ **Casa Juancho.** This meeting place for the movers and shakers of
SPANISH   the Cuban *exilio* community is also a haven for lovers of fine Spanish regional cuisine. Strolling balladeers serenade amid brown brick,
rough-hewn dark timbers, hanging smoked meats, ceramic plates,
and oil still lifes: a bit of old España dropped on Calle Ocho. Try the

**12**

hake prepared in a fish stock with garlic, onions, and Spanish white wine or the *carabineros a la plancha* (jumbo red shrimp with head and shell on, split and grilled). For dessert, *crema Catalana* is a rich pastry custard with a delectable crust of burnt caramel. The house features one of the largest lists of reserve Spanish wines in the United States. Jackets are recommended for men at dinner. ✉ *2436 S.W. 8th St., Little Havana* ☎ *305/642–2452* ⊕ *www.casajuancho.com* ✛ *5C.*

$$ ╳ **Hy-Vong Vietnamese Cuisine.** Spring springs forth in spring rolls of
VIETNAMESE ground pork, cellophane noodles, and black mushrooms wrapped in homemade rice paper. People are willing to wait on the sidewalk for hours—come before 7 pm to avoid a wait—to sample the fish panfried with mango or with *nuoc man* (a garlic-lime fish sauce), not to mention the thinly sliced pork barbecued with sesame seeds, almonds, and peanuts. Beer-savvy proprietor Kathy Manning serves a half-dozen top brews (Double Grimbergen, Peroni, and Spaten, among them) to further inoculate the experience from the ordinary—well, as ordinary as a Vietnamese restaurant on Calle Ocho can be. ✉ *3458 S.W. 8th St., Little Havana* ☎ *305/446–3674* ⊕ *www.hyvong.com* ☾ *Closed Mon. No lunch* ✛ *5C.*

$ ╳ **Versailles.** *¡Bienvenido a Miami!* To the area's Cuban population,
CUBAN Miami without Versailles is like rice without black beans. The sto-
★ ried eatery, where old émigrés opine daily about all things Cuban, is a stop on every political candidate's campaign trail, and it should be a stop for you as well. Order a heaping platter of *lechon asado* (roasted pork loin), *ropa vieja* (shredded beef), or *picadillo* (spicy ground beef), all served with rice, beans, and fried plantains. Battle the oncoming food coma with a cup of the city's strongest *cafecito*, which comes in the tiniest of cups but packs a lot of punch. Versailles oper-ates a bakery next door as well—take some *pastelitos* home. ✉ *3555 S.W. 8th St., between S.W. 35th and S.W. 36th Aves., Little Havana* ☎ *305/444–0240* ✛ *5C.*

## MIAMI BEACH

### MID-BEACH

$$$$ ╳ **Cecconi's.** After the New York restaurant scene invaded Miami Beach,
ITALIAN it was only a matter of time until L.A. made its way down southeast,
**Fodor's**Choice too. With the unveiling of the new Soho House in Miami came the
★ company's iconic Italian restaurant, Cecconi's. The wait for a table at this outpost is just as long as its West Hollywood counterpart, and the dining experience just as fabulous. Eating here is a real scene of who's who and who's eating what. Without a doubt, the truffle pizza, which servers shave huge hunks of black or white truffle onto table-side, is the restaurant's most talked about dish. The fish carpaccios are light and succulent while the classically hearty pastas and risottos provide authentic Italian fare. ✉ *4385 Collins Ave., Mid-Beach, Miami Beach* ☎ *786/507–7900* ⊕ *www.cecconismiamibeach.com* ⌲ *Reservations essential* ✛ *4F.*

$$$–$$$$ ╳ **The Forge.** Legendary for its opulence, this restaurant has been wow-
STEAKHOUSE ing patrons since 1968. After a renovation, The Forge reemerged in
**Fodor's**Choice 2010 more decadent than ever! It is a steak house, but a steak house
★

the likes of which you haven't seen before. Antiques, gilt-framed paintings, a chandelier from the Paris Opera House, and Tiffany stained-glass windows from New York's Trinity Church are the fitting background for some of Miami's best steaks. The tried-and-true menu also includes prime rib, bone-in fillet, lobster *thermidor*, chocolate soufflé, and sinful side dishes like creamed spinach and roasted-garlic mashed potatoes. The focaccia bread is to die for. For its walk-in humidor alone, the over-the-top Forge is worth visiting. The automated wine machine spans the perimeter of the restaurant and allows you to pick your own pour and sample several wines throughout your meal. ⊠ *432 Arthur Godfrey Rd., Mid-Beach, Miami Beach* ☎ *305/538–8533* ⊕ *www.theforge.com* ⌂ *Reservations essential* ⊗ *No lunch.* ✛ *4F.*

**$$$$**
CANTONESE

✕ **Hakkasan.** This stateside sibling of the Michelin-starred London restaurant is one of the best-looking restaurants on Miami Beach. Intricately carved, lacquered-black-wood Chinois panels divide seating sections, creating a deceptively cozy dining experience. The music is clubby, the waitresses' matching outfits are slinky, and the shadowy lighting is thoughtfully designed to make everyone look about as good as they can. Chef Alan Yau, a pioneer of the haute-Chinese-food movement, has collected mostly simple and authentic Cantonese recipes, many featuring fresh seafood. Don't overlook the tofu dishes in lieu of other proteins: this isn't supermarket soy. The braised tofu and aubergine claypot in black bean pairs glorious little pillows of silken tofu with expertly cooked eggplant in a perfectly seasoned, thick, funky sauce. ⊠ *4441 Collins Ave., Mid-Beach, Miami Beach* ☎ *305/538–2000* ⊕ *www.hakkasan.com* ⌂ *Reservations essential* ⊗ *No lunch* ✛ *2F.*

**$$$$**
ARGENTINIAN

✕ **Las Vacas Gordas.** For more than 15 years, this Argentinean steak house has welcomed the who's who of Latin high society, fulfilling their wildest carnivore cravings. Recently expanded and reinvented as a glamorous enclave where the Pampas meets contemporary Miami, Vacas's grill sizzles day and nights to the troves of patrons who patiently wait to feast on mounds of fresh meat from the Argentinean lowlands. The reasonably priced house Malbecs complemented the high-end selections showcased in the floor-to-ceiling, glass-enclosed wine cellar. Those less enthused about massive meat slabs can opt for the Berecava (eggplant with tomato sauce and cheese), homemade pastas, grilled peppers, fish and shrimp, or fill up on homemade rolls with spicy chimmichurri. ⊠ *933 Normandy Dr., Mid-Beach, Miami Beach* ☎ *305/867–1717* ⊕ *www.lasvacasgordas.com* ✛ *3F.*

**$$$**
MEDITERRANEAN
Fodor's Choice
★

✕ **Michy's.** Miami's homegrown star chef Michelle Bernstein made a huge splash with the shabby-chic decor and self-named restaurant on the north end of Miami's Design District. Bernstein serves exquisite French- and Mediterranean-influenced seafood dishes at over-the-causeway (read: non-tourist-trap) prices. Plates come in half portions and full portions, which makes the restaurant even more of a deal. Can't-miss entrées include the blue cheese and *jamón serrano* (serrano ham) *croquetas*, the beef short rib, and the steak frites au poivre. ⊠ *6927 Biscayne Blvd., Mid-Beach* ☎ *305/759–2001* ⊕ *www.chefmichellebernstein.com* ⊗ *Closed Mon. No lunch* ✛ *3E.*

**12**

$    ✕ **Roasters 'N Toasters.** This small Jewish delicatessen chain took over
DELICATESSEN    from Arnie and Richie's, a longtime family establishment, in 2008.
🕐    Gone are the baskets of plastic silverware. The prices are slightly higher,
but the faithful still come for the onion rolls, smoked whitefish salad,
as well as the new "Corky's Famous Zaftig Sandwich," a deliciously
juicy skirt steak served on twin challah rolls with a side of apple sauce.
Service can be brusque, but it sure is quick. ✉ *525 Arthur Goddrey Rd.,
Mid-Beach, Miami Beach* ☎ *305/531–7691* ⊕ *www.roastersntoasters.
com* ✛ *3F.*

## NORTH BEACH AND AVENTURA

$$$$    ✕ **Bourbon Steak.** Michael Mina's sole restaurant in the southeastern
STEAKHOUSE    United States is arguably his best. The restaurant design is seductive,
Fodor'sChoice    the clientele sophisticated, the wine list outstanding, the service phe-
★    nomenal, and the food exceptional. Dinner begins with a skillet of fresh
potato focaccia and chive butter. Mina then presents a bonus starter—
his trio of famous fries (fried in duck fat) with three robust sauces.
Appetizers are mainly seafood. The raw bar impresses and classic appetizers like the ahi tuna tartare are delightful and super fresh. Entrees like
the Maine lobster pot pie and any of the dozen varieties of wood-grilled
steaks (from natural, organic, hormone-free beef) are cooked to perfection. ✉ *19999 W. Country Club Dr., Aventura, Miami* ☎ *786/279–6600*
⊕ *www.michaelmina.net* ⟡ *Reservations essential* ✛ *1F.*

$$$    ✕ **Café Prima Pasta.** If Tony Soprano lived in Miami, this is where
ITALIAN    you'd find him. This famous, bustling Italian eatery is infused with
the energy of the Argentine Cea family, whose clan cooks, serves, and
operates this place, while somehow finding the time to pose for photos
with the hundreds of celebrities who have eaten here over the years
(see them in the photos on the walls). It's on a busy street, yet the low
light, soothing music, and intimate seating on this restaurant's outdoor
veranda can make Café Prima Pasta a romantic spot. Everything is
made in-house—from the fragrant rosemary butter to the pasta, which
tastes best as crab-stuffed ravioli or as linguine dyed in squid ink and
served with seafood in a lobster sauce. ✉ *414 71st St., North Beach,
Miami* ☎ *305/867–0106* ⊕ *www.primapasta.com* ☾ *No lunch* ✛ *3F.*

$$$    ✕ **Chef Allen's.** Chef Allen Susser has long been a figure of Miami's culi-
SEAFOOD    nary scene, a member of the original, self-designated "Mango Gang,"
who created contemporary American masterpieces from a global menu.
Over the past couple of years, though, his namesake restaurant has
been renovated with a new look and jolt of fresh energy as a "modern
seafood bistro," focusing on sustainable fish. The restaurant is still the
best in northern Miami. After trying the famous Devil's on a Horseback
(manchego- and mango-stuffed dates wrapped in bacon), order a salad
of baby greens and warm wild mushrooms or a rock-shrimp hash with
roasted corn. Allen serves only locally caught seafood, so you may
want to consider the swordfish with conch-citrus couscous, macadamia
nuts, and lemon. It's hard to resist the dessert soufflé; order it when you
order your appetizer to eliminate a mouthwatering wait at the end of
your meal. ✉ *19088 N.E. 29th Ave., Aventura, Miami* ☎ *305/935–2900*
⊕ *www.chefallens.com* ✛ *1F.*

**$$$$**
JAPANESE
Fodor's Choice
★

✕**NAOE.** Once in a rare while, you discover a restaurant so authentic, so special, yet still undiscovered by the masses. By virtue of its petite size (16 person max) and strict seating times (twice per night at 6:30 and 9:30), the Japanese gem, NAOE, will forever remain intimate and original. The menu changes daily, based on the day's best and freshest seafood. Beginning with a Bento Box and continuing on to rounds of Nigirizushi, every visit ushers in a new exploration of the senses. Chef Kevin Corey prepares the gastronomic adventure a few feet from his patrons, using only the best ingredients and showcasing family treasures, like the renowned products of his centuries' old family shoyu (soy sauce) brewery and sake brewery. From start to finish, you'll be transported to Japan through the stellar service, the tastes of bizarre sea creatures, the planching of live scallops, and the smoothness of spectacular sakes. ⊠ *175 Sunny Isles Blvd., Sunny Isles Beach* ☎ *305/947–6263* ⊕ *www.naoemiami.com* ♨ *Reservations essential* ✣ *1F.*

**$$$**
ITALIAN
★

✕**Timó.** Located in a glorified strip mall 5 mi north of South Beach, Timó (Italian for "thyme") is worth the trip from anywhere in South Florida. It's a kind of locals' secret that it's the best food in South Florida. The handsome bistro, co-owned by chef Tim Andriola and Rodrigo Martinez (former general manager and wine director at Norman's), has dark-wood walls, Chicago brick, and a stone-encased wood-burning stove. Andriola has an affinity for robust Mediterranean flavors: sweetbreads with bacon, honey, and aged balsamic vinegar; inexpensive, artisanal pizzas; and homemade pastas. Wood-roasted meats and Parmesan dumplings in a truffle broth are not to be missed. Every bite of every dish attests to the care given, and the service is terrific. ⊠ *17624 Collins Ave., Sunny Isles* ☎ *305/936–1008* ⊕ *www.timorestaurant.com* ☾ *No lunch weekends* ✣ *1F.*

## SOUTH BEACH

**$**
AMERICAN

✕**Big Pink.** The decor in this innovative, superpopular diner may remind you of a roller-skating rink—everything is pink Lucite, stainless steel, and campy (think sports lockers as decorative touches)—and the menu is 3 feet tall, complete with a table of contents. Food is solidly all-American, with dozens of tasty sandwiches, pizzas, turkey or beef burgers, and side dishes, each and every one composed with gourmet flair. Big Pink also makes a great spot for brunch. ⊠ *157 Collins Ave., South Beach* ☎ *305/532–4700* ⊕ *www.mylesrestaurantgroup.com* ✣ *5H.*

**$$$$**
STEAKHOUSE

✕**BLT Steak.** Miami suddenly has a plethora of good steak houses. This Ocean Drive favorite is in the light-filled, open lobby of the snazzy Betsy Hotel at the very northern end of South Beach and has the distinction of being open for breakfast daily—get the sensational steak and eggs. The clever name stands for Bistro Laurent Tourondel, Mr. T being the highly regarded chef who created the chain of BLTs. You can count on the highest quality cuts of USDA prime, certified Black Angus, and American Wagyu beef, in addition to blackboard specials and raw-bar selections. The grilled Kobe beef–skirt salad is juicy and delicious. The popovers are even better. ⊠ *1440 Ocean Dr., South Beach* ☎ *305/673–0044* ⊕ *www.bltrestaurants.com* ✣ *2H.*

**$$$$**
SEAFOOD
Fodor's Choice
★

✕**Blue Door Fish.** In a hotel where style reigns supreme, this high-profile restaurant at the Delano Hotel provides both glamour and solid cuisine.

Thankfully, Master Chef Claude Troisgros kept a dozen of the most popular dishes from the restaurant's predecessor, Blue Door at the Delano, including the famous Crabavocat, Big Ravioli, Homard Banana and Boeuf Gorgonzola. He, also thankfully, added 50 inventive seafoodcentric items like Shrimp over Risotto with a saffron bouillabaisse-style sauce and Scallops a la Plancha with brown butter sauce, garlic, lemon, parsley and pine nuts. The restaurant also serves sushi from its Philippe Starck countertop sushi bar across the hall, Blue Sea: remarkable creations include the Wild Coho Salmon Tartare (with olive and soy tapenade and fried ginger), the rice-less Smokey Roll (with four types of smoked fish and caviar), the Yakuza Roll (BBQ eel, avocado, and Boursin cheese with spicy *masago* and eel sauce), and California rolls with real blue or king crab. ⊠ *1685 Collins Ave., South Beach* ☎ *305/674–6400* ⊲ *Reservations essential* ✛ *2H.*

**$$** ╳ **Emeril's.** "It's getting happy in here" is one of Emeril Lagasse's stock
SOUTHERN phrases, and now he has brought his brand of happy to Miami Beach. You can expect a different gumbo each day and other New Orleans specialties at Lagasse's chain, which appears to have the winning formula down. The seafood naturally shines in these parts (an andouille-crusted redfish signals the imported Lagasse touch), and the chef has his own take on mango pie and banana-cream pie. As a bonus, the restaurant delivers without even a hint of South Beach attitude—though a view of the pool at its Loews hotel location is a perk. ⊠ *1601 Collins Ave., at Loews Miami Beach Hotel, South Beach* ☎ *305/695–4550* ⊕ *www. emerils.com* ✛ *2H.*

**$$$** ╳ **Joe Allen.** Crave a good martini along with a terrific burger? Locals
AMERICAN head to this hidden hangout in an exploding neighborhood of condos, town houses, and stores. The eclectic crowd includes kids and grandparents, and the menu has everything from pizzas to calves' liver to steaks. Start with an innovative salad, such as arugula with pear, prosciutto, and a Gorgonzola dressing, or roast-duck salad with blue cheese and pears. Home-style desserts include banana-cream pie and ice-cream-and-cookie sandwiches. Comfortable and homey, this is the perfect place to go when you don't feel like going to a restaurant. ⊠ *1787 Purdy Ave., South Beach* ☎ *305/531–7007* ⊕ *www.joeallenrestaurant. com* ✛ *4E.*

**$$$$** ╳ **Joe's Stone Crab Restaurant**. In South Beach's decidedly new-money
SEAFOOD scene, the stately Joe's Stone Crab is an old-school testament to good
Fodor'sChoice food and good service. South Beach's most storied restaurant started
★ as a turn-of-the-century eating house when Joseph Weiss discovered succulent stone crabs off the Florida coast. Almost a century later, the restaurant stretches a city block and serves 2,000 dinners a day to local politicians and moneyed patriarchs. Stone crabs, served with legendary mustard sauce, crispy hash browns, and creamed spinach, remain the staple. Though stone crab season runs from October 15 to May 15, Joe's remains open year-round serving other phenomenal seafood dishes. Finish your meal with tart key lime pie, baked fresh daily. ■TIP➡ Joe's famously refuses reservations, and weekend waits can be three hours long—yes, you read that correctly—so come early or order from Joe's Take Away next door. ⊠ *11 Washington Ave., South*

# CUBAN FOOD

If the tropical vibe has you hankering for Cuban food, you've come to the right place. Miami is the top spot in the country to enjoy authentic Cuban cooking.

The flavors and preparations of Cuban cuisine are influenced by the island nation's natural bounty (yucca, sugarcane, guava), as well as its rich immigrant history, from near (Caribbean countries) and far (Spanish and African traditions). Chefs in Miami tend to stick with the classic versions of beloved dishes, though you'll find some variation from restaurant to restaurant as recipes have often been passed down through generations of home cooks. Try the popular **Versailles** (⊠ *3555 S.W. 8th St.* ☎ *305/444–0240*) in Little Havana or Coral Gables's **Havana Harry's** (⊠ *4612 Le Jeune Rd.* ☎ *305/661–2622*), appealing to families seeking a home-cooked, Cuban-style meal. The South Beach late-night institution **David's Café** (⊠ *1058 Collins Ave.* ☎ *305/534–8736* ⊠ *1654 Meridian Ave.* ☎ *305/672–8707*) is a hole-in-the-wall with excellent eats.

## THE CUBAN SANDWICH

A great *cubano* (Cuban sandwich) requires pillowy Cuban bread layered with ham, garlic-citrus-marinated slow-roasted pork, Swiss cheese, and pickles (plus salami, in Tampa; lettuce and tomatoes in Key West), butter and/or mustard. The sandwich is grilled in a sandwich press until the cheese melts and all the elements are fused together. Try one at **Enriqueta's Sandwich Shop** (⊠ *186 N.E. 29th St.* ☎ *305/573–4681* ⊘ *Weekdays 6 am–4 pm, Sat. 6 am–2 pm*) in the Design District, or **Exquisito Restaurant** (⊠ *1510 S.W. 8th St.* ☎ *305/643-0227* ⊘ *Open daily 7 am–midnight*) in Little Havana.

## KEY CUBAN DISHES

**12**

### ARROZ CON POLLO
This chicken-and-rice dish is Cuban comfort food. Found throughout Latin America, the Cuban version is typically seasoned with garlic, paprika, and onions, then colored golden or reddish with saffron or achiote (a seed paste), and enlivened with a sizable splash of beer near the end of cooking. Green peas and sliced, roasted red peppers are a standard topping.

### BISTEC DE PALOMILLA
This thinly sliced sirloin steak is marinated with lime juice and garlic, and fried with onions. The steak is often served with chimichurri sauce, an olive oil, garlic, and cilantro sauce that is sometimes served with bread as a dip (slather bread with butter and dab on the chimichurri). Also try *ropa vieja*, a slow-cooked, shredded flank steak in a garlic-tomato sauce.

### DESSERTS
Treat yourself to a slice of *tres leches* cake. The "three milks" come from the sweetened condensed milk, evaporated milk, and heavy cream that are poured over the cake until it's an utterly irresistible gooey mess. Also, don't miss the *pastelitos*, Cuban fruit-filled turnovers. Traditional flavors include plain guava, guava with cream cheese, and cream cheese with coconut. Yum!

### DRINKS
Sip *guarapo* (gwa-RA-poh), a fresh sugarcane juice that isn't really as sweet as you might think, or grab a straw and enjoy a frothy *batido* (bah-TEE-doe), a Cuban-style milk shake made with tropical fruits like mango, *piña* (pineapple), or *mamey* (mah-MAY, a tropical fruit with a melon-cherry taste). For a real twist, try the *batido de trigo*—a wheat shake that will remind you of sugarglazed breakfast cereal.

### FRITAS
If you're in the mood for an inexpensive, casual Cuban meal, have a *frita*—a hamburger with distinctive Cuban flair. It's made with ground beef that's mixed with ground or finely chopped chorizo, spiced with pepper, paprika, and salt, topped with sautéed onions and shoestring potato fries, and then served on a bun slathered with a special tomatobased ketchuplike sauce.

### LECHON ASADO
Fresh ham or an entire suckling pig marinated in *mojo criollo* (parsley, garlic, sour orange, and olive oil) are roasted until fork tender and served with white rice, black beans, and *tostones* (fried plantains) or yucca (pronounced YUkah), a starchy tuber with a mild nut taste that's often sliced into fat sticks and deep-fried like fries.

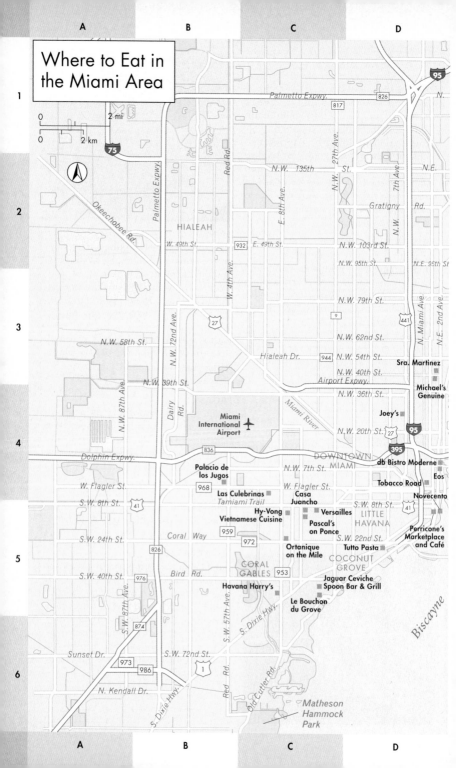

# Where to Eat in the Miami Area

0 ——— 2 mi
0 ——— 2 km

A

B

C

D

1

Palmetto Expwy.

826

817

N.

2

HIALEAH

N.W. 135th St.

Gratigny Rd.

N.E.

Red Rd.

E. 8th Ave.

N.W. 27th Ave.

7th Ave.

Okeechobee Rd.

Palmetto Expwy.

N.W.

W. 49th St.

932

E. 49th St.

N.W. 103rd St.

N.W. 95th St.

N.E. 95th St.

W. 4th Ave.

3

N.W. 58th St.

N.W. 72nd Ave.

27

N.W. 79th St.

9

441

N.W. 62nd St.

N. Miami Ave.

N.E. 2nd Ave.

Hialeah Dr.

944

N.W. 54th St.

**Sra. Martinez**

N.W. 39th St.

N.W. 40th St.

Dairy Rd.

Airport Expwy.

**Michael's Genuine**

N.W. 36th St.

N.W. 87th Ave.

Miami River

**Joey's**

4

Miami International Airport

N.W. 20th St.

27

95

836

395

DOWNTOWN MIAMI

**db Bistro Moderne**

Dolphin Expwy.

**Palacio de los Jugos**

N.W. 7th St.

**Eos**

W. Flagler St.

968

W. Flagler St.

**Tobacco Road**

**Novecento**

S.W. 8th St.

41

**Las Culebrinas**

Tamiami Trail

**Casa Juancho**

S.W. 8th St.

41

**Hy-Vong Vietnamese Cuisine**

**Versailles**

LITTLE HAVANA

**Perricone's Marketplace and Café**

959

**Pascal's on Ponce**

972

S.W. 24th St.

Coral Way

S.W. 22nd St.

826

**Ortanique on the Mile**

5

CORAL GABLES

953

COCONUT GROVE

S.W. 40th St.

976

Bird Rd.

**Jaguar Ceviche Spoon Bar & Grill**

S.W. 87th Ave.

**Havana Harry's**

S.W. 57th Ave.

S. Dixie Hwy.

**Le Bouchon du Grove**

Biscayne

874

Sunset Dr.

973

986

S.W. 72nd St.

6

N. Kendall Dr.

1

Red Rd.

S. Dixie Hwy.

Old Cutler Rd.

Matheson Hammock Park

A

B

C

D

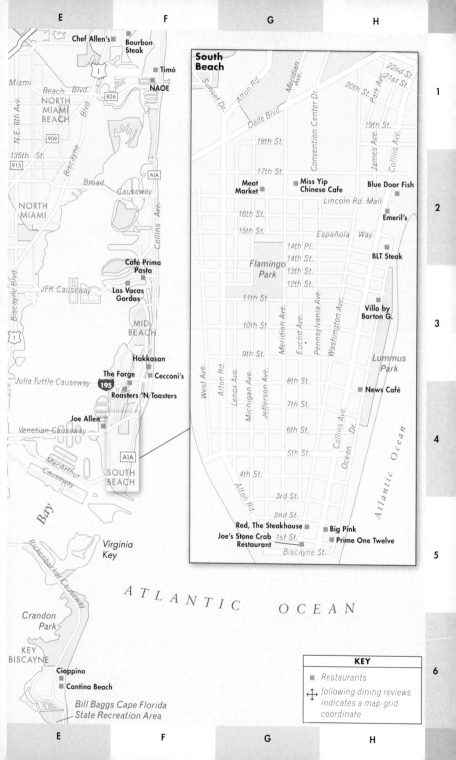

Pink as cotton candy and bubble gum, the Big Pink diner fits right in with its art deco surroundings.

*Beach* ☎ *305/673–0365, 305/673–4611 for takeout, 800/780–2722 for overnight shipping* ⊕ *www.joesstonecrab.com* 🚢 *Reservations not accepted* ⊘ *No lunch Wed.–Sun. Closed Mon. and Tues. May 15–Oct. 15* ✚ *5G.*

**$$$** ✕ **Meat Market**. Yes, it's a great name for a steak-inspired restaurant,
STEAKHOUSE and a name seemingly destined for a place like this on Lincoln Road,
★ where sexy people amble by in skimpy clothes year-round. But here's
the great news: this is a sophisticated place with a large non-steak-
house menu. Appetizers such as cedar-scented *hamachi* (yellowtail
sashimi) topped with mango caviar, white truffle, fresh lime, and
rice-paper tuna tacos with *guajillo* chili, cabbage, grilled watermelon,
micro watercress, and roasted garlic are just the beginning of the
incredible variety. The seafood selection, like the seared Florida grou-
per in browned goat butter and bacon-chipotle conch broth, is also
excellent. Naturally, there are the steaks, which range from simple
à la carte cuts to thoughtful creations like the braised prime bris-
ket with coconut, mango, Cuban sweet potatoes, and wild mush-
rooms. ✉ *915 Lincoln Rd., South Beach* ☎ *305/532–0088* ⊕ *www.
meatmarketmiami.com* ⊘ *No lunch* ✚ *2G.*

**$$** ✕ **Miss Yip Chinese Cafe**. At the most popular of only a handful of
CHINESE Chinese restaurants on South Beach, the hip Miss Jennie Yip serves
authentic dim sum and steaming fresh Cantonese dishes just off Lincoln Road. Try the Peking duck and the "Princess Jade" sea bass,
made of cubes of tender battered fish with Chinese mayo sauce. Wash
it down with one of Miss Yip's many specialty cocktails: a few favorites include the lychee mojito and the ginger martini. A small market
sells dozens of sauce and spice mixes. The crowds here are lively,

## CHEAP EATS ON SOUTH BEACH

Miami Beach is notorious for over-priced eateries, but locals know better. **Half Moon Empanadas** (✉ *1616 Washington Ave., at Lincoln Rd.*) has the colorful and polished look of a national franchise but is a genuine local start-up serving 17 delicious flavors of baked (or fried) empanadas for $1.99 each. **Pizza Rustica** (✉ *8th St. and Washington Ave., 14th St. and Washington Ave., and at 667 Lincoln Rd.*) serves up humongous slices overflowing with mozzarella, steak, olives, and barbecue chicken until 4 am. **La Sandwicherie** (✉ *14th St. between Collins and Washington Aves.*) is a South Beach classic since 1988, serving gourmet French sandwiches, a delicious pro-sciutto salad, and healthy smooth-ies from a walk-up bar. **Lime Fresh Mexican Grill** (✉ *1439 Alton Rd. at 14th St.*) serves fresh and tangy fish tacos and homemade guacamole.

the design vividly colorful and contemporary, and the food flavor-ful. ✉ *1661 Meridian Ave., South Beach* ☎ *305/534–5488* ⊕ *www. missyipchinesecafe.com* ✛ *2G*.

$    ✕ **News Café.** No trip to Miami is complete without a stop at this Ocean
AMERICAN    Drive landmark. The 24-hour café attracts a crowd with snacks, light meals, drinks, periodicals, and the people-parade on the sidewalk out front. Most prefer sitting outside, where they can feel the salt breeze and gawk at the human scenery. Sea-grape trees shade a patio where you can watch from a quiet distance. Offering a little of this and a little of that—bagels, pâtés, chocolate fondue, sandwiches, and a ter-rific wine list—this joint has something for everyone. Although service can be indifferent to the point of laissez-faire and the food is mediocre at best, News Café is just one of those places visitors just can't miss! ✉ *800 Ocean Dr., South Beach* ☎ *305/538–6397* ⊕ *www.newscafe.com* ⌨ *Reservations not accepted* ✛ *4H*.

$$$$    ✕ **Prime One Twelve.** This wildly busy steak house is particularly
STEAKHOUSE    renowned for its highly marbleized prime beef (try the 30-ounce bone-in rib eye for two, $68), creamed corn, truffle macaroni and cheese, and buzzing scene: while you stand at the bar awaiting your table (every-one has to wait—at least a little bit), you'll clamor for a drink with all facets of Miami's high society, from the city's top real estate devel-opers and philanthropists to striking models and celebrities (Lenny Kravitz, Jay-Z, and Matt Damon are among a big list of celebrity regulars). ✉ *112 Ocean Dr., South Beach* ☎ *305/532–8112* ⊕ *www. mylesrestaurantgroup.com* ✛ *5H*.

$$$$    ✕ **Red, the Steakhouse.** Just when it seemed that South Beach had become
STEAKHOUSE    all too saturated with steak houses, Red arrived and raises the bar on SoBe's steak house experience. The carnivore glamour den seduces with its red and black dominatrix color scheme and overloads the senses with the divine smells and tastes of the extensive menu. Red boasts an equal number of seafood and traditional carnivorous offerings, each delicately prepared, meticulously presented, and gleefully consumed. Start with the tuna tartare, the mussels *diavolo*, or crisp chili calamari and then continue with fresh lobster or the many variations of Angus Beef Prime. And don't forget about the dozen or so sides, often the most

exciting part of any steak house experience. ⊠ *119 Washington Ave., South Beach* ☎ *305/534–3688* ⊕ *www.redthesteakhouse.com* ⌂ *Reservations essential* ✛ *4G.*

**$$$**   ✕ **SushiSamba Dromo.** This sibling to the New York City SushiSamba
JAPANESE   makes an eclectic pairing of Japanese, Peruvian, and Brazilian cuisines. The results are fabulous if a bit mystifying: miso-marinated sea bass, hamachi *taquitos* (basically a yellowtail tartare), *mocqueca mista* (Brazilian seafood stew), and caramel–passion fruit sponge cake. Loaded with customers in the heart of pedestrian Lincoln Road, colorful Sushi-Samba has a vibe that hurts the ears but warms the trendy heart. ⊠ *600 Lincoln Rd., South Beach* ☎ *305/673–5337* ⊕ *www.sushisamba.com* ⌂ *Reservations essential* ✛ *2G.*

**$$$$**   ✕ **The Villa by Barton G. – the Restaurant.** Set within the glitz, the glamour,
ECLECTIC   and the ostentation of Gianni Versace's former mansion, the Villa by
**Fodor's**Choice   Barton G. is an international destination. Famous for the area where
★   Versace spent his last moments, the mansion provides a more intimate experience inside. Eating here or enjoying afternoon tea allows you to roam the front terrace, the inner courtyard, and the magical black pool garden of this historic Mediterranean fantasy home. Dinner is usually served in courses with suggested wine pairings. The avant-garde dishes served in the intimate 30-seat dining room are a gastronome's delight—Caesar salad with grilled artichokes and frozen Caesar dressing, vodka-cured salmon, and out-of-this-world clementine carrot veloute. Traditional afternoon tea, with a full spread of pastries and sandwiches, is served from 2:30 to 4 Thursday through Sunday in the Mosaic Garden ($55). ⊠ *1116 Ocean Dr., South Beach* ☎ *305/576–8003* ⊕ *www.thevillabybartong.com* ⌂ *Reservations essential* ✛ *3H.*

# WHERE TO STAY

*For expanded hotel reviews, visit Fodors.com.*

Room rates in Miami tend to swing wildly. In high season, which is January through May, expect to pay at least $150 per night, even at budget hotels. In summer, however, prices can be as much as 50% lower than the dizzying winter rates. You can also find great values between Easter and Memorial Day, which is actually a delightful time in Miami. Business travelers tend to stay in downtown Miami, while most vacationers stay on Miami Beach, as close as possible to the water. If money is no object, stay in one of the glamorous hotels lining Collins Avenue between 15th and 23rd streets. Otherwise, stay on the quiet beaches farther north, or in one of the small boutique hotels on Ocean Drive, Collins, or Washington avenues between 10th and 15th streets. Two important considerations that affect price are balcony and view. If you're willing to have a room without an ocean view, you can sometimes get a much lower price than the standard rate. Mid-Beach and Downtown have taken the hotel scene by storm in the past few years, unveiling some of Miami's most avant-garde and luxurious properties to date.

*Use the coordinate (✛ C2) at the end of each review to locate a property on the Where to Stay in the Miami Area map.*

| WHAT IT COSTS | | | | | |
|---|---|---|---|---|---|
| | ¢ | $ | $$ | $$$ | $$$$ |
| FOR TWO PEOPLE | under $150 | $150–$200 | $200–$300 | $300–$400 | over $400 |

Prices for hotels are for two people in a standard double room in high season, excluding 12.5% city and resort taxes.

**12**

## COCONUT GROVE, CORAL GABLES, AND KEY BISCAYNE

### COCONUT GROVE

Coconut Grove is blessed with a number of excellent luxury properties. All are within walking distance of its principal entertainment center, Coco Walk, as well as its marinas. Although this area certainly can't replace the draw of Miami Beach or the business convenience of downtown, about 20 minutes away, it's an exciting bohemian-chic neighborhood with a gorgeous waterfront.

$$$
HOTEL

**Ritz-Carlton, Coconut Grove.** Overlooking Biscayne Bay, the hotel has rooms that are appointed with marble baths, a choice of down or nonallergenic foam pillows, and private balconies. **Pros:** best service in Coconut Grove; high-quality spa. **Cons:** of the three Miami Ritz-Carltons this one has the least interesting location and the fewest amenities. ⊠ 3300 S.W. 27th Ave. ☎ 305/644–4680 or 800/241–3333 ⊕ www.ritzcarlton. com ➷ 88 rooms, 27 suites ♿ In-room: a/c, Internet, Wi-Fi. In-hotel: restaurants, bar, pool, gym, spa, business center, parking, some pets allowed ⊖| No meals ✥ 5D.

### CORAL GABLES

The beautiful Coral Gables is set around its beacon, the national landmark Biltmore Hotel. It also has a couple of big business hotels and one smaller boutique property. The University of Miami is nearby.

$$$
HOTEL
Fodor's Choice
★

**Biltmore Hotel.** Built in 1926, this landmark hotel has had several incarnations over the years—including a stint as a hospital during World War II—but through it all, this grande dame remains an opulent reminder of yesteryear, with its palatial lobby and grounds, enormous pool, and distinctive 315-foot tower, which rises above the canopy of trees shading Coral Gables. **Pros:** historic property; possibly best pool in the Miami area; great tennis and golf. **Cons:** far from Miami Beach. ⊠ 1200 Anastasia Ave. ☎ 305/445–1926 or 800/727–1926 ⊕ www. biltmorehotel.com ➷ 241 rooms, 39 suites ♿ In-room: a/c, Wi-Fi. In-hotel: restaurants, bars, golf course, tennis courts, pool, gym, spa, business center, parking ⊖| No meals ✥ 5C.

### KEY BISCAYNE

There is probably no other place in Miami where slowness is lifted to a fine art. On Key Biscayne there are no pressures, there's no nightlife outside of the Ritz-Carlton's great live Latin music weekends, and the dining choices are essentially limited to the hotel (which has four dining options, including the languorous, Havana-style RUMBAR).

# BEST BETS FOR MIAMI LODGING

Fodor's offers a selective listing of quality lodging experiences in every price range, from the city's best budget beds to its most sophisticated luxury hotels. Here, we've compiled our top recommendations by price and experience. The very best properties are designated in the listings with the Fodor's Choice logo. Find specific details about a hotel in the full reviews, listed alphabetically by neighborhood.

## Fodor's Choice ★

**Acqualina Resort & Spa on the Beach,** p. 604

**Biltmore Hotel,** p. 597

**Circa 39 Hotel,** p. 603

**Fisher Island Hotel & Resort,** p. 602

**Four Seasons Hotel Miami,** p. 599

**Mandarin Oriental Miami,** p. 599

**National Hotel,** p. 608

**Ritz-Carlton Key Biscayne,** p. 599

**Ritz-Carlton South Beach,** p. 608

**W South Beach,** p. 610

## By Price

### ¢

**Circa 39 Hotel,** p. 603

**Villa Paradiso,** p. 609

### $$

**Catalina Hotel & Beach Club,** p. 605

**National Hotel,** p. 608

**Townhouse,** p. 609

### $$$

**Biltmore Hotel,** p. 597

**Fontainebleau,** p. 603

### $$$$

**Acqualina Resort,** p. 604

**Fisher Island Hotel,** p. 602

**Four Seasons Hotel Miami,** p. 599

**Mandarin Oriental Miami,** p. 599

**Ritz-Carlton Key Biscayne,** p. 599

**Setai,** p. 609

**W South Beach,** p. 610

## By Experience

### BEST POOL

**Biltmore Hotel,** p. 597

**National Hotel,** p. 608

**Ritz-Carlton South Beach,** p. 608

**The Standard,** p. 602

**The Viceroy,** p. 602

### BEST HOTEL BAR

**National Hotel,** p. 608

**The Standard,** p. 602

**The Viceroy (rooftop bar),** p. 602

**W South Beach,** p. 610

### BEST SERVICE

**Acqualina Resort,** p. 604

**Four Seasons Hotel Miami,** p. 599

**Ritz-Carlton Key Biscayne,** p. 599

### BEST VIEWS

**Mandarin Oriental Miami,** p. 599

**W South Beach,** p. 610

### HIPSTER HOTELS

**Catalina Hotel & Beach Club,** p. 605

**Hotel Victor,** p. 608

**Shore Club,** p. 609

**Soho Beach House Miami,** p. 604

### BEST LOCATION

**National Hotel,** p. 608

**Pelican,** p. 608

### BEST-KEPT SECRET

**Acqualina Resort,** p. 604

**Soho Beach House Miami,** Mid-Beach, p. 604

**$$$**
RESORT
Fodor'sChoice
★
**Ritz-Carlton, Key Biscayne.** In this ultra-laid-back Key Biscayne setting, it's natural to appreciate the Ritz brand of pampering with luxurious rooms, attentive service, and ample recreational activities for the whole family. **Pros:** private beach; quiet, luxurious family retreat. **Cons:** it will be too quiet if you're looking for a party—so you have to drive to Miami for nightlife. ✉ *455 Grand Bay Dr.* ☎ *305/365–4500 or 800/241–3333* ⊕ *www.ritzcarlton.com/keybiscayne* ⤢ *365 rooms, 37 suites* ⚇ *In-room: a/c, Internet, Wi-Fi. In-hotel: restaurants, bars, tennis courts, pools, gym, spa, beach, water sports, business center, parking, some pets allowed* ⦿ *No meals* ✛ *6E.*

12

# DOWNTOWN MIAMI

**$$**
HOTEL
**Doubletree Grand Hotel Biscayne Bay.** This elegant waterfront option is at the north end of downtown off a scenic marina, and near many of Miami's headline attractions: the Port of Miami, Bayside, the Arena, and the Carnival Center. **Pros:** great bay views; deli and market on-site. **Cons:** need a cab to get around. ✉ *1717 N. Bayshore Dr., Downtown Miami* ☎ *305/372–0313 or 800/222–8733* ⊕ *www.doubletree. com* ⤢ *152 suites* ⚇ *In-room: a/c, kitchen (some), Wi-Fi. In-hotel: restaurant, bar, pool, gym, spa, business center, parking* ⦿ *No meals* ✛ *4E.*

**$$$**
HOTEL
**Epic Hotel.** Located in the heart of downtown, alongside glittery high-rise condominiums, the Epic Hotel is a real gem. **Pros:** sprawling pool deck with a view of the water; complimentary wine in the lobby every day from 5 to 6 pm; complimentary in-room yoga mats and yoga television programming; tennis courts and golf courts available through partnerships with nearby tennis clubs and golf courses. **Cons:** not located directly near the beach; some rooms overlook tall condominiums and office buildings. ✉ *270 Biscayne Blvd., Downtown Miami* ☎ *305/424–5226* ⊕ *www.epichotel.com* ⤢ *411 rooms* ⚇ *In-room: a/c, Wi-Fi. In-hotel: restaurant, bar, pool, gym, spa, water sports, children's programs, business center, parking, some pets allowed* ⦿ *No meals* ✛ *5D.*

**$$$$**
HOTEL
Fodor'sChoice
★
**Four Seasons Hotel Miami.** Stepping off busy Brickell Avenue into this hotel, you see a soothing water wall trickling down from above, and the serenity continues in the yoga classes and poolside. **Pros:** sensational service; amazing gym and pool deck. **Cons:** no balconies. ✉ *1435 Brickell Ave., Downtown Miami* ☎ *305/358–3535 or 800/819–5053* ⊕ *www.fourseasons.com/miami* ⤢ *182 rooms, 39 suites* ⚇ *In-room: a/c. In-hotel: restaurant, bars, pools, gym, spa, business center, parking* ⦿ *No meals* ✛ *5D.*

**$$$$**
HOTEL
Fodor'sChoice
★
**Mandarin Oriental, Miami.** Clandestinely hidden at the tip of Brickell Key in Biscayne Bay, the Mandarin feels as exclusive as it does glamorous. **Pros:** only beach (man-made) in downtown; intimate feeling; top luxury hotel. **Cons:** small pool; few beach cabanas. ✉ *500 Brickell Key Dr., Downtown Miami* ☎ *305/913–8288 or 866/888–6780* ⊕ *www. mandarinoriental.com* ⤢ *326 rooms, 31 suites* ⚇ *In-room: a/c, Internet. In-hotel: restaurants, bars, pool, gym, spa, children's programs, business center, parking* ⦿ *No meals* ✛ *5E.*

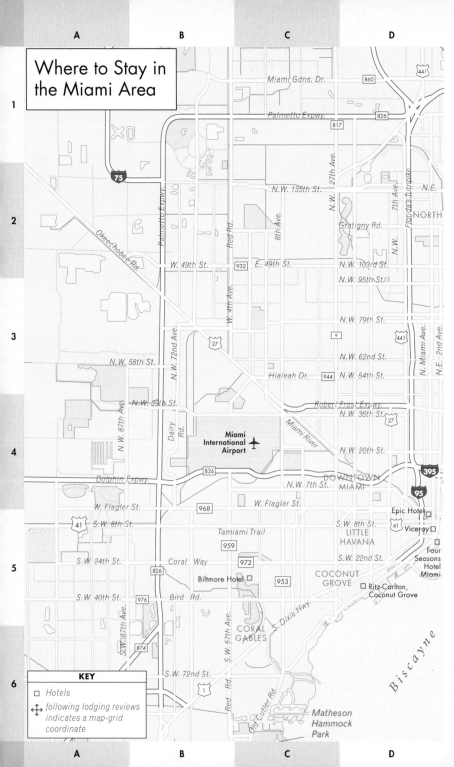

# Where to Stay in the Miami Area

**KEY**

☐ Hotels

⬌ following lodging reviews indicates a map-grid coordinate

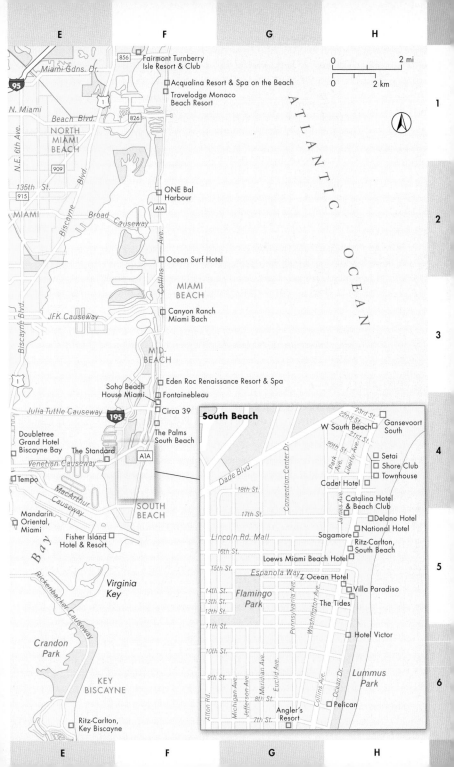

E    F    G    H

95

Miami Gdns. Dr.

856  Fairmont Turnberry Isle Resort & Club

□ Acqualina Resort & Spa on the Beach

□ Travelodge Monaco Beach Resort

N. Miami

Beach Blvd.
826

NORTH MIAMI BEACH

N.E. 6th Ave.

909

135th St.
915

MIAMI

Biscayne Blvd.

Broad Causeway

Collins Ave.

□ ONE Bal Harbour
A1A

□ Ocean Surf Hotel

MIAMI BEACH

JFK Causeway

Biscayne Blvd.

1

□ Canyon Ranch Miami Bach

MID-BEACH

□ Eden Roc Renaissance Resort & Spa

Soho Beach House Miami □ Fontainebleau

Julia Tuttle Causeway  195

□ Circa 39

The Palms South Beach

Doubletree Grand Hotel Biscayne Bay
□
The Standard □
A1A

Venetian Causeway

□ Tempo

MacArthur Causeway

Mandarin Oriental, Miami
□

SOUTH BEACH

Fisher Island □ Hotel & Resort

Bay

Rickenbacker Causeway

Virginia Key

Crandon Park

KEY BISCAYNE

□ Ritz-Carlton, Key Biscayne

ATLANTIC OCEAN

0   2 mi
0   2 km

1

2

3

4

5

6

**South Beach**

23rd St.
22nd St.
W South Beach □ □ Gansevoort South
21st St.
20th St.
Liberty Ave.
Park Ave.

Convention Center Dr.

Dade Blvd.

□ Setai
□ Shore Club
□ Townhouse

Cadet Hotel □

18th St.

James Ave.

Catalina Hotel & Beach Club

17th St.

□ Delano Hotel
□ National Hotel

Sagamore □

Lincoln Rd. Mall

Ritz-Carlton, South Beach

16th St.

Loews Miami Beach Hotel □

15th St.

Espanola Way   Z Ocean Hotel

14th St.
13th St.
12th St.

Flamingo Park

Pennsylvania Ave.

Washington Ave.

□ Villa Paradiso

The Tides □

11th St.

10th St.

□ Hotel Victor

9th St.

Alton Rd.

Michigan Ave.

Meridian Ave.

Jefferson Ave.

Euclid Ave.

Collins Ave.

Ocean Dr.

Lummus Park

8th St.

□ Pelican

7th St.

Angler's Resort

E    F    G    H

$$ **:: Tempo, A Rock Resort.** In the
HOTEL    Marquis high-rise in downtown,
Tempo, offers a splendid boutique
experience steps from major ven-
ues such as the Arsht Performing
Arts Center and the American Air
lines Arena. **Pros:** spacious rooms;
great restaurant; amazing bath-
rooms. **Cons:** some bathrooms
do not have doors. ✉ *1100 Bis-
cayne Blvd., Downtown* ☎ *786/
369–0300* ⊕ *www.tempomiami.*

*rockresorts.com* ⤳ *56 rooms* ♿ *In-room: a/c, Wi-Fi. In-hotel: restau-
rant, bar, pool, gym, spa, business center, parking* ⦿ *No meals* ✛ *4E.*

$$    **:: Viceroy.** This hotel has a brash, supersophisticated South Beach atti-
HOTEL    tude—something that distinguishes it wholly from every other Miami
nonbeach hotel. **Pros:** sensationally designed spa area; fantastic pool
deck; sleek rooms. **Cons:** downtown location rather than the beach;
tiny lobby. ✉ *485 Brickell Ave., Downtown Miami* ☎ *305/503–4400
or 866/781–9923* ⊕ *www.viceroymiami.com* ⤳ *150 rooms, 18 suites*
♿ *In-room: a/c, kitchen (some), Wi-Fi. In-hotel: restaurant, bars, pools,
gym, spa, business center, parking, some pets allowed* ⦿ *No meals*
✛ *5D.*

## FISHER AND BELLE ISLANDS

$$$$    **:: Fisher Island Hotel & Resort.** Assuming you don't have a private yacht,
RESORT    there are three ways to gain access to Fisher Island just off South Beach:
Fodor'sChoice    you can either become a club member (initiation fee alone: $25,000),
★    be one of the 750 equity members who have vacation places here (starting price: $8 million), or book a night at the club hotel (basic villa:
$900 a night). **Pros:** great private beaches; exclusive surroundings; var-
ied dining choices. **Cons:** expensive ferry rides take time. ✉ *1 Fisher
Island Dr., Fisher Island* ☎ *305/535–6000 or 800/537–3708* ⊕ *www.
fisherislandclub.com* ⤳ *5 junior suites, 50 condo units, 6 villas, 3 cottages* ♿ *In-room: a/c, Wi-Fi. In-hotel: restaurants, golf course, tennis
courts, pools, gym, spa, beach, water sports, business center, parking,
some pets allowed* ⦿ *No meals* ✛ *5E.*

$$    **:: The Standard.** An extension of André Balazs's trendy, budget hotel
RESORT    chain, the Standard is a Hollywood newcomer that set up shop a few
minutes from South Beach on an island just over the Venetian Cause-
way. **Pros:** interesting island location; free bike and kayak rentals;
swank pool scene; great spa; inexpensive. **Cons:** removed from South
Beach nightlife; small rooms with no views. ✉ *40 Island Ave., Belle
Isle* ☎ *305/673–1717* ⊕ *www.standardhotel.com* ⤳ *104 rooms, 1 suite*
♿ *In-room: a/c, Internet, Wi-Fi. In-hotel: restaurant, bars, pool, gym,
spa, water sports, business center, parking, some pets allowed, some
age restrictions* ⦿ *No meals* ✛ *4E.*

## MID-BEACH

Where does South Beach end and Mid-Beach begin? With the massive amount of money being spent on former 1950s pleasure palaces like the Fontainebleau and Eden Roc, it could be that Mid-Beach will soon just be considered part of South Beach. North of 24th Street, Collins Avenue curves its way to 44th Street, where it takes a sharp left turn after running into the Soho House Miami and then the Fontainebleau resort. The area between these two points—24th Street and 96th Street—is Mid-Beach. This stretch is undergoing a renaissance, as formerly run-down hotels are renovated and new hotels and condos are being built.

**$$$**
RESORT

🏨 **Canyon Ranch Miami Beach.** When you're not lounging around your well-appointed suite, with its 400-thread-count Mascioni linens and flat-panel HDTVs, or swimming in one of the hotel's four pools, take your meals at the Canyon Ranch Grill, where you can indulge in tasty cuisine with a healthy slant: each dish's nutritional information (including calories) is printed on the menu, and all wines served here are sustainable, organic, or biodynamic. *6801 Collins Ave., Mid-Beach* ☎ *305/514–7000* ⊕ *www.canyonranch.com* ⤶ *150 suites* △ *In-room: a/c, kitchen, Wi-Fi. In-hotel: restaurants, pools, gym, spa, beach, business center, parking* ⎮⊘⎮ *No meals* ⊹ *3F.*

**¢–$**
HOTEL
**Fodor's**Choice
★

🏨 **Circa 39 Hotel.** This stylish budget boutique hotel pays attention to every detail and gets them all right. **Pros:** affordable; chic; intimate; beach chairs provided; art deco fireplace. **Cons:** not on the beach side of Collins Avenue. ⊠ *3900 Collins Ave., Mid-Beach* ☎ *305/538–4900 or 877/824–7223* ⊕ *www.circa39.com* ⤶ *96 rooms* △ *In-room: a/c, kitchen, Internet. In-hotel: restaurant, bar, pool, gym, parking, some pets allowed* ⎮⊘⎮ *No meals* ⊹ *4F.*

**$$$–$$$$**
RESORT

🏨 **Eden Roc Renaissance Resort & Spa.** This grand 1950s hotel designed by Morris Lapidus retains its old glamour while renovations have updated and added sparkle to the rooms and grounds. *4525 Collins Ave., Mid-Beach* ☎ *305/531–0000 or 800/327–8337* ⊕ *www.edenrocresort.com* ⤶ *631 rooms* △ *In-room: a/c, kitchen (some), Wi-Fi. In-hotel: restaurants, bars, pools, gym, spa, beach, business center, parking* ⎮⊘⎮ *No meals* ⊹ *3F.*

**$$–$$$**
RESORT

🏨 **Fontainebleau.** This classic property is Miami's biggest hotel—twice the size of the Loews, with more than 1,500 rooms; 11 restaurants and lounges, a huge nightclub, sumptuous pool with cabana islands, a state-of-the-art fitness center, a 40,000-square-foot-spa, and more than 100,000 square feet of meeting and ballroom space come along with all those rooms. **Pros:** historic design mixed with all-new facilities; fabulous pools. **Cons:** away from the South Beach pedestrian scene; too big to be intimate. ⊠ *4441 Collins Ave., Mid-Beach* ☎ *305/538–2000 or 800/548–8886* ⊕ *www.fontainebleau.com* ⤶ *1,504 rooms* △ *In-room: a/c, kitchen (some), Wi-Fi. In-hotel: restaurants, bars, pools, gym, spa, water sports, business center, parking* ⎮⊘⎮ *No meals* ⊹ *4F.*

**¢–$**
HOTEL

🏨 **Ocean Surf Hotel.** Don't expect luxury in this colorful art deco lodge, but if you want a cheap stay away from everybody and ideal beach access, you can't beat the tiny Ocean Surf Hotel. **Pros:** adorable art deco hotel; cheap. **Cons:** basic rooms; no Internet; spotty service. ⊠ *7436*

*Ocean Terr., Mid-Beach* ☎ *305/866–1648 or 800/555–0411* ⊕ *www.
theoceansurfhotel.com* ⤳ *49 rooms* ⚇ *In-room: a/c. In-hotel: beach,
parking* ❑ *No meals* ✢ *2F.*

**$–$$**
HOTEL

📷 **The Palms South Beach**. Stay here if you're seeking an elegant, relaxed
property away from the noise but still near South Beach. **Pros:** tropical garden; relaxed and quiet. **Cons:** no balconies; away from South
Beach. ⊠ *3025 Collins Ave., Mid-Beach* ☎ *305/534–0505 or 800/550–
0505* ⊕ *www.thepalmshotel.com* ⤳ *220 rooms, 22 suites* ⚇ *In-room:
a/c, Wi-Fi. In-hotel: restaurant, bars, pool, beach, parking* ❑ *No
meals* ✢ *4F.*

**$$$$**
HOTEL
★

📷 **Soho Beach House Miami.** Though a stay usually requires membership
to the House, if you are lucky enough to land a room through a sales
promotion, then do so! **Pros:** trendy; two pools; fabulous restaurant
**Cons:** patchy Wi-Fi; members have priority for rooms. ⊠ *4385 Collins
Ave., Mid-Beach, Miami* ☎ *786/507–7900* ⊕ *www.sohobeachhouse.
com* ⤳ *55 rooms* ⚇ *In-room: a/c, Wi-Fi. In-hotel: restaurant, bar, pool,
gym, spa, beach, business center, parking* ❑ *No meals* ✢ *4F.*

---

## NORTH MIAMI BEACH AND AVENTURA

Nearing the 100th Street mark on Collins Avenue, Mid-Beach gives way
to North Beach. In particular, at 96th Street, the town of Bal Harbour
takes over Collins Avenue from Miami Beach. The town runs a mere
10 blocks to the north before the bridge to Sunny Isles. Bal Harbour is
famous for its outdoor upscale shops. If you take your shopping seriously, you'll probably want to stay in this area. At 106th Street, the
town of Sunny Isles is an appealing, calm, predominantly upscale choice
for families looking for a beautiful beach. There is no nightlife to speak
of in Sunny Isles, and yet the half-dozen megaluxurious skyscraper
hotels that have sprung up here since 2005 have created a niche-resort
town from the demolished ashes of much older, affordable hotels. Further west are the high-rises of Aventura.

**$$$$**
RESORT
Fodor's Choice
★

📷 **Acqualina Resort & Spa on the Beach**. When it opened in 2006, this
hotel raised the bar for luxury in Miami, and it stands as one of
the city's best hotels. **Pros:** in-room check-in; luxury amenities; huge
spa. **Cons:** no nightlife near hotel. ⊠ *17875 Collins Ave., Sunny Isles*
☎ *305/918–8000* ⊕ *www.acqualinaresort.com* ⤳ *54 rooms, 43 suites*
⚇ *In-room: a/c, Wi-Fi. In-hotel: restaurants, bars, pools, gym, spa,
beach, water sports, children's programs, business center, parking*
❑ *No meals* ✢ *1F.*

**$$$$**
RESORT

📷 **Fairmont Turnberry Isle Resort & Club**. Golfers and families will enjoy
this upscale resort with one of the best service staffs in the city. **Pros:**
great golf, pools, and restaurants; free shuttle to Aventura Mall. **Cons:**
far from the beach; no nightlife. ⊠ *19999 W. Country Club Dr., Aventura* ☎ *305/932–6200 or 800/327–7028* ⊕ *www.turnberryisle.com*
⤳ *392 rooms, 41 suites* ⚇ *In-room: a/c, kitchen (some), Wi-Fi. In-
hotel: restaurants, bars, golf courses, tennis courts, pools, gym, spa,
water sports, business center, parking, some pets allowed* ❑ *No meals*
✢ *1F.*

$$$$ RESORT **ONE Bal Harbour.** The tiny, tony town of Bal Harbour finally has a hotel worthy of its ultra-high-end mall. *10295 Collins Ave., Bal Harbour ☎ 305/455–5400 🌐 www.oneluxuryhotels.com 124 rooms, 63 suites In-room: a/c, kitchen, Wi-Fi. In-hotel: restaurant, bar, tennis courts, pools, gym, spa, beach, water sports, parking No meals ✢ 2F.*

¢ HOTEL **Travelodge Monaco Beach Resort.** The last of a dying breed, the Travelodge Monaco is a no-frills step up from a youth hostel. **Pros:** steps to great beach; bottom-dollar cost; free shuttle to South Beach and Aventura. **Cons:** older rooms; not service-oriented; no Wi-Fi in room, and public Wi-Fi in hotel has a fee. *✉ 17501 Collins Ave., Sunny Isles ☎ 305/932–2100 or 800/227–9006 🌐 www.monacomiamibeachresort.com 110 rooms In-room: a/c, kitchen (some). In-hotel: restaurant, bar, pool, beach, parking No meals ✢ 1F.*

## SOUTH BEACH

$$ HOTEL **Angler's Boutique Resort.** Angler's has the feel of a sophisticated private Mediterranean villa community. **Pros:** gardened private retreat. **Cons:** on busy Washington Ave. *✉ 660 Washington Ave., South Beach ☎ 305/534–9600 🌐 www.theanglersresort.com 24 rooms, 20 suites In-room: a/c, kitchen (some), Wi-Fi. In-hotel: restaurant, bar, pool, business center, parking, some pets allowed No meals ✢ G6.*

¢ HOTEL **Cadet Hotel.** You can trace the fact that this is one of the sweetest, quietest hotels in South Beach to the ways of its independent female owner, a local doctor named Vilma Biaggi. **Pros:** well run with friendly service; lovely garden; great value. **Cons:** no pool. *✉ 1701 James Ave., South Beach ☎ 305/672–6688 or 800/432–2338 🌐 www.cadethotel.com 32 rooms, 3 suites In-room: a/c, Wi-Fi. In-hotel: restaurant, bar Breakfast ✢ 4H.*

$–$$ HOTEL **Catalina Hotel & Beach Club.** The Catalina is the budget party spot in the heart of South Beach's hottest block. **Pros:** free drinks; free bikes; free airport shuttle; good people-watching. **Cons:** $15 wireless fee; service not a high priority; loud. *✉ 1732 Collins Ave., South Beach ☎ 305/674–1160 🌐 www.catalinahotel.com 200 rooms In-room: a/c, Wi-Fi. In-hotel: restaurant, bars, pool, parking, some pets allowed No meals ✢ 5H.*

$$$$ HOTEL **Delano Hotel.** The decor of this grand hotel is inspired by Lewis Carroll's *Alice in Wonderland*, and as you make your way from the sparse, busy, spacious lobby past cascading white curtains and through rooms dotted with strange, whimsical furniture pieces, you will feel like you are indeed falling down a rabbit hole. **Pros:** electrifying design; lounging among the beautiful and famous. **Cons:** crowded; scene-y; small rooms; expensive. *✉ 1685 Collins Ave., South Beach ☎ 305/672–2000 or 800/555–5001 🌐 www.delano-hotel.com 184 rooms, 24 suites In-room: a/c, Wi-Fi. In-hotel: restaurants, bars, pool, gym, spa, beach, business center, parking No meals ✢ 5H.*

$$$$ RESORT **Gansevoort South.** For the well-heeled, party-seeking, jet-setting crowd, there's a South Beach hotel to toy with: this southern cousin of New York's trendsetting Meatpacking District hotel is better than the original, starting with a fantastic beachfront setting. *2377 Collins Ave., South Beach ☎ 305/604–1000 🌐 www.gansevoortsouth.*

Acqualina Resort & Spa on the Beach

Circa 39 Hotel

Biltmore Hotel

Delano Hotel

Ritz-Carlton, Key Biscayne

Four Seasons Hotel Miami

The Tides South Beach

Mandarin Oriental

*com* ⤴ *334 rooms* ☐ *In-room: a/c, kitchen (some), Internet, Wi-Fi. In-hotel: restaurants, bar, pool, gym, spa, beach, water sports, business center, parking* ▯◯▮ *No meals* ⊹ *4H.*

$$$$    **Hotel Victor.** The sleek look of
HOTEL   the Hotel Victor was created by
the Parisian designer Jacques Garci
and unusually organized rooms
draw a sleek set of customers.
**Pros:** great design; views of Ocean
Drive from the pool deck; high hip
factor; good service. **Cons:** small
rooms; small pool. ☒ *1144 Ocean
Dr., South Beach* ☎ *305/428–
1234 or 800/327–7028* ⊕ *www.
hotelvictorsouthbeach.com* ⤴ *91 rooms* ☐ *In-room: a/c, kitchen
(some), Wi-Fi. In-hotel: restaurants, bar, pool, gym, spa, business
center, parking, some pets allowed* ▯◯▮ *No meals* ⊹ *5H.*

> ## WORD OF MOUTH
>
> "If you can get a hotel room at a good price than you should come to Miami during Art Basel week (first weekend in Dec.). It's a very, very cosmopolitan atmosphere. It will be busy but if you like being in a city then you'll enjoy the energy with all sorts of interesting people, art lovers, artists, celebrities, and art everywhere. It's the best week to feel alive in Miami."
> —SoBchBud1

$$$–$$$$   **Loews Miami Beach Hotel.** Loews Miami Beach is marvelous for fami-
HOTEL   lies, businesspeople, groups, and pet-lovers. **Pros:** top-notch amenities
include a beautiful oceanfront pool and immense spa; pets welcome.
**Cons:** intimacy is lost due to its large size. ☒ *1601 Collins Ave., South
Beach* ☎ *305/604–1601 or 800/235–6397* ⊕ *www.loewshotels.com/
miamibeach* ⤴ *733 rooms, 57 suites* ☐ *In-room: a/c, Internet, Wi-Fi.
In-hotel: restaurants, bars, pool, gym, spa, beach, business center,
parking, some pets allowed* ▯◯▮ *No meals* ⊹ *5H.*

$$    **National Hotel.** This luxurious, beautiful hotel serves as a bastion
HOTEL   of calm in the sea of white-on-white mod decor and raucous revel-
Fodor'sChoice   ing usually reserved for the beachfront masterpieces lining Collins
★   Avenue between 15th and 20th streets. **Pros:** stunning pool; perfect
location. **Cons:** tower rooms aren't impressive; neighboring hotels
can be noisy on the weekends. ☒ *1677 Collins Ave., South Beach*
☎ *305/532–2311 or 800/327–8370* ⊕ *www.nationalhotel.com* ⤴ *143
rooms, 9 suites* ☐ *In-room: a/c, Internet, Wi-Fi. In-hotel: restaurants,
bars, pools, gym, beach, business center, parking, some pets allowed*
▯◯▮ *No meals* ⊹ *5H.*

$$    **Pelican.** The spirit of Diesel clothing company, which owns this Ocean
HOTEL   Drive boutique, permeates the hotel: Each room is completely different,
fashioned from a mix of antique and garage-sale furnishings selected by
the designer of Diesel's clothing-display windows. **Pros:** unique, over-
the-top design; central Ocean Drive location. **Cons:** rooms are so tiny
that the quirky charm wears off quickly; no no-smoking rooms. ☒ *826
Ocean Dr., South Beach* ☎ *305/673–3373 or 800/773–5422* ⊕ *www.
pelicanhotel.com* ⤴ *28 rooms, 4 suites* ☐ *In-room: a/c, Wi-Fi. In-hotel:
restaurant, bar, beach, parking* ▯◯▮ *No meals* ⊹ *6H.*

$$$$    **Ritz-Carlton, South Beach.** A sumptuous affair, the Ritz-Carlton is the
HOTEL   only truly luxurious property on the beach that *feels* like it's on the
Fodor'sChoice   beach, because its long pool deck leads you right out to the water.
★   **Pros:** luxury rooms; great service; great location. **Cons:** too big to be

intimate. ✉ *1 Lincoln Rd., South Beach* ☎ *786/276–4000 or 800/241–3333* ⊕ *www.ritzcarlton.com* 🛏 *375 rooms* 🛇 *In-room: a/c, Wi-Fi. In-hotel: restaurants, bars, pools, gym, spa, beach, children's programs, business center, parking, some pets allowed* ⍥ *No meals* ✛ *5H.*

**$$** ⊞ **Sagamore.** This supersleek, all-white hotel in the middle of the action
HOTEL looks and feels more like a Chelsea art gallery, filled with brilliant contemporary art. **Pros:** sensational pool; great location; quiet on weekdays; good rate specials. **Cons:** basic rooms are not as stylish as public areas; service can be spotty. ✉ *1671 Collins Ave.* ☎ *305/535–8088* ⊕ *www.sagamorehotel.com* 🛏 *93 suites* 🛇 *In-room: a/c, kitchen, Wi-Fi. In-hotel: restaurant, bars, pool, spa, beach, business center, parking* ⍥ *No meals* ✛ *5H.*

**$$$$** ⊞ **Setai.** The place feels like an Asian museum, serene and beautiful,
HOTEL with heavy granite furniture lifted by orange accents, warm candlelight, and the soft bubble of seemingly endless pools and ponds. **Pros:** quiet and classy; beautiful grounds. **Cons:** somewhat cold aura; TVs are far from the beds. ✉ *101 20th St., South Beach* ☎ *305/520–6000 or 888/625–7500* ⊕ *www.setai.com* 🛏 *110 rooms* 🛇 *In-room: a/c, Wi-Fi. In-hotel: restaurant, bars, pools, gym, spa, beach, business center, parking, some pets allowed* ⍥ *No meals* ✛ *4H.*

**$$$$** ⊞ **Shore Club.** Shore Club is the perfect adult playground; in terms
HOTEL of lounging, people-watching, and poolside glitz, this is the best of South Beach. **Pros:** good restaurants and bars; nightlife in your backyard. **Cons:** uninviting rooms; snooty service. ✉ *1901 Collins Ave., South Beach* ☎ *305/695–3100 or 877/640–9500* ⊕ *www.shoreclub.com* 🛏 *309 rooms, 79 suites* 🛇 *In-room: a/c, Wi-Fi. In-hotel: restaurants, bars, pools, gym, spa, beach, business center, parking, some pets allowed* ⍥ *No meals* ✛ *4H.*

**$$$$** ⊞ **The Tides.** The Tides is arguably Miami's most exclusive Ocean Drive
HOTEL art deco hotel. **Pros:** superior service; great beach location; ocean views from all suites plus the terrace restaurant. **Cons:** tiny elevators; ubiquitous taxidermy. ✉ *1220 Ocean Dr., South Beach* ☎ *305/604–5070 or 866/438–4337* ⊕ *www.thetideshotel.com* 🛏 *45 suites* 🛇 *In-room: a/c, Internet, Wi-Fi. In-hotel: restaurant, pool, gym, beach, business center, parking* ⍥ *No meals* ✛ *5H.*

**$** ⊞ **Townhouse.** Though sandwiched between the Setai and the Shore
HOTEL Club—two of the coolest hotels on the planet—the Townhouse doesn't
★ try to act all dolled up: it's comfortable being the shabby-chic, lighthearted, relaxed, no-frills, fun hotel on South Beach. **Pros:** a great budget buy for the style-hungry; direct beach access; hot rooftop lounge. **Cons:** no pool; small rooms not designed for long stays. ✉ *150 20th St., east of Collins Ave., South Beach* ☎ *305/534–3800 or 877/534–3800* ⊕ *www.townhousehotel.com* 🛏 *69 rooms, 2 suites* 🛇 *In-room: a/c, Internet, Wi-Fi. In-hotel: restaurant, bar, laundry facilities, business center, parking* ⍥ *Breakfast* ✛ *4H.*

**¢** ⊞ **Villa Paradiso.** One of South Beach's best deals, Paradiso has huge
HOTEL rooms with kitchens and a charming tropical courtyard with benches for hanging out at all hours. **Pros:** great hangout spot in courtyard; good value; great location. **Cons:** no pool; no restaurant. ✉ *1415 Collins Ave., South Beach* ☎ *305/532–0616* ⊕ *www.villaparadisohotel.com*

↘ *17 studios* ⚭ *In-room: a/c, kitchen, Internet, Wi-Fi. In-hotel: some pets allowed* ⦿ *No meals* ✛ *5H.*

**$$$**

**HOTEL**

**Fodor's Choice**

★

⊡ **W South Beach.** Fun, fresh, and funky, this W is also the flagship for the brand's evolution towards young sophistication, which means less club music in the lobby, more lighting, and more attention to the $40 million art collection lining the lobby's expansive walls. **Pros:** pool scene; masterful design; ocean-view balconies in each room. **Cons:** not a classic art deco building. ⊠ *2201 Collins Ave., South BeachMiami Beach* ☎ *305/938–3000* ⊕ *www.WHotels.com/SouthBeach* ↘ *334 rooms* ⚭ *In-room: a/c, kitchen, Wi-Fi. In-hotel: restaurant, bars, pools, gym, spa, beach, business center, parking, some pets allowed* ⦿ *No meals* ✛ *4H.*

**$$**

**HOTEL**

⊡ **Z Ocean Hotel.** The lauded firm of Arquitectonica designed the rooms and suites at this glossy and bold hideaway that began as an über-exclusive Regent property, before changing hands a few times. **Pros:** incredible balconies; huge rooms. **Cons:** gym is just a small "cardio room;" no spa; not much privacy on private decks. ⊠ *1437 Collins Ave., South Beach* ☎ *305/672–4554* ⊕ *www.zoceanhotelsouthbeach. com* ↘ *79 suites* ⚭ *In-room: a/c, Wi-Fi. In-hotel: restaurant, bar, pool, gym, parking* ⦿ *No meals* ✛ *5H.*

# The Everglades

**WORD OF MOUTH**

"Sign up at the Ernest Coe Visitor Center or call the Flamingo Visitor Center for the free ranger-led canoe tour. . . . No experience necessary—maneuvering the long canoe through the twists and turns of the mangroves was a challenge, but very fun."

—JC98

# WELCOME TO THE EVERGLADES

## TOP REASONS TO GO

★ **Fun Fishing:** Cast for some of the world's fight-ingest game fish—600 species of fish in all—in the Everglades' backwaters.

★ **Abundant Birdlife:** Check hundreds of birds off your life list, includ-ing—if you're lucky—the rare Everglades snail kite.

★ **Cool Kayaking:** Do a half-day trip in Big Cypress National Preserve or reach for the ultimate—the 99-mi Wilderness Trail.

★ **Swamp Cuisine:** Hankering for alligator tail and frogs' legs? Or how about swamp cabbage, made from hearts of palm? Better yet, try stone crab claws fresh from the traps.

★ **Great Gator-Spotting:** This is ground zero for alligator viewing in the United States, and there's a good bet you'll leave having spotted your quota.

**1** **Everglades National Park.** Alligators, Florida panthers, black bears, mana-tees, dolphins, bald eagles, and roseate spoonbills call this vast habitat home.

**2** **Biscayne National Park.** Mostly underwater, here's where the string of coral reefs and islands that form the Florida Keys begin.

**13**

**3** Big Cypress National
Preserve. Neighbor to
Everglades National Park, it's
an outdoor-lover's paradise.

## GETTING ORIENTED

The southern third of
the Florida peninsula is
largely taken up by pro-
tected government land
that includes Everglades
National Park, Big Cypress
National Preserve, and
Biscayne National Park.
Miami lies to the northeast,
while Naples and Marco
Island are northwest.
Land access to Everglades
National Park is primarily
by two roads. The park's
main road traverses the
southern Everglades from
the gateway towns of
Homestead and Florida
City to the outpost of
Flamingo, on Florida Bay.
In the northern Everglades,
Tamiami Trail (U.S. 41) runs
from the Greater Miami
area on the east coast or
from Naples on the west
coast to the western park
entrance in Everglades
City at Route 29.

# THE FLORIDA
# EVERGLADES

by Lynne Helm

Alternately described as elixir of life or swampland muck, the Florida Everglades is one of a kind—a 50-mi-wide "river of grass" that spreads across hundreds of thousands of acres. It moves at varying speeds depending on rainfall and other variables, sloping south from the Kissimmee River and Lake Okeechobee to estuaries of Biscayne Bay, Florida Bay, and the Ten Thousand Islands.

Today, apart from sheltering some 70 species on America's endangered list, the Everglades also embraces more than 7 million residents, 50 million annual tourists, 400,000 acres of sugarcane, and the world's largest concentration of golf courses.

Demands on the land threaten the Everglades' finely balanced ecosystem. Irrigation canals for agriculture and roadways disrupt natural water flow. Drainage for development leaves wildlife scurrying for new territory. Water runoff, laced with fertilizers, promotes unnatural growth of swamp vegetation. What remains is a miracle of sorts, given decades of these destructive forces.

Creation of the Everglades required unique conditions. South Florida's geology, linked with its warm, wet subtropical climate, is the perfect mix for a marshland ecosystem. Layers of porous, permeable limestone create water-bearing rock,

soil, and aquifers, which in turn affects climate, weather, and hydrology.

This rock beneath the Everglades reflects Florida's geologic history—its crust was once part of the African region. Some scientists theorize that continental shifting merged North America with Africa, and then continental rifting later pulled North America away from the African continent but took part of northwest Africa with it—the part that is today's Florida. The Earth's tectonic plates continued to migrate, eventually placing Florida at its current location as a land mass jutting out into the ocean, with the Everglades at its tip.

# EXPERIENCING THE ECOSYSTEMS

Eight distinct habitats exist within Everglades National Park, Big Cypress National Preserve, and Biscayne National Park.

Carnestown ○   Ochopee ○
29   41
Gulf Coast   ○ Everglades City
Visitor Center ●
○ Chokoloskee
TEN THOUSAND ISLANDS

| ECOSYSTEMS | EASY WAY | MORE ACTIVE WAY |
|---|---|---|
| **COASTAL PRAIRIE:** An arid region of salt-tolerant vegetation lies between the tidal mud flats of Florida Bay and dry land. **Best place to see it: The Coastal Prairie Trail** | Take a guided boat tour of Florida Bay, leaving from Flamingo Marina. | Hike the Coastal Prairie Trail from Eco Pond to Clubhouse Beach. |
| **CYPRESS:** Capable of surviving in standing water, cypress trees often form dense clusters called "cypress domes" in natural water-filled depressions. **Best place to see it: Big Cypress National Preserve** | Drive U.S. 41 (also known as Tamiami Trail—pronounced Tammy-Amee), which cuts across Southern Florida, from Naples to Miami. | Hike (or drive) the scenic Loop Road, which begins off Tamiami Trail, running from the Loop Road Education Center to Monroe Station. |
| **FRESH WATER MARL PRAIRIE:** Bordering deeper sloughs are large prairies with marl (clay and calcium carbonate) sediments on limestone. Gators like to use their toothy snouts to dig holes in prairie mud. **Best place to see it: Pahayokee Overlook** | Drive there from the Ernest F. Coe Visitor Center. | Take a guided tour, either through the park service or from permitted, licensed guides. You also can set up camp at Long Pine Key. |
| **FRESH WATER SLOUGH AND HARDWOOD HAMMOCK:** Shark River Slough and Taylor Slough are the Everglades' two sloughs, or marshy rivers. Due to slight elevation amid sloughs, dense stands of hardwood trees appear as teardrop-shaped islands. **Best place to see it: The Observation Tower** | Take a two-hour guided tram tour from the Shark Valley Visitor Center to the tower and back. | Walk or bike (rentals available) the route to the tower via the tram road and (walkers only) Bobcat Boardwalk trail and Otter Cave Hammock Trail. |
| **MANGROVE:** Spread over South Florida's coastal channels and waterways, mangrove thrives where Everglades fresh water mixes with salt water. **Best place to see it: The Wilderness Waterway** | Picnic at the area near Long Pine Key, which is surrounded by mangrove, or take a water tour at Biscayne National Park. | Boat your way along the 99-mi Wilderness Waterway. It's six hours by motorized boat, seven days by canoe. |
| **MARINE AND ESTUARINE:** Corals, sponges, mollusks, seagrass, and algae thrive in the Florida Bay, where the fresh waters of the Everglades meet the salty seas. **Best place to see it: Florida Bay** | Take a boat tour from the Flamingo Visitor Center marina. | Canoe or kayak on White Water Bay along the Wilderness Waterway Canoe Trail. |
| **PINELAND:** A dominant plant in dry, rugged terrain, the Everglades' diverse pinelands consist of slash pine forest, saw palmettos, and more than 200 tropical plant varieties. **Best place to see it: Long Pine Key trails** | Drive to Long Pine Key, about 6 mi off the main road from Ernest F. Coe Visitor Center. | Hike or bike the 28 mi of Long Pine Key trails. |

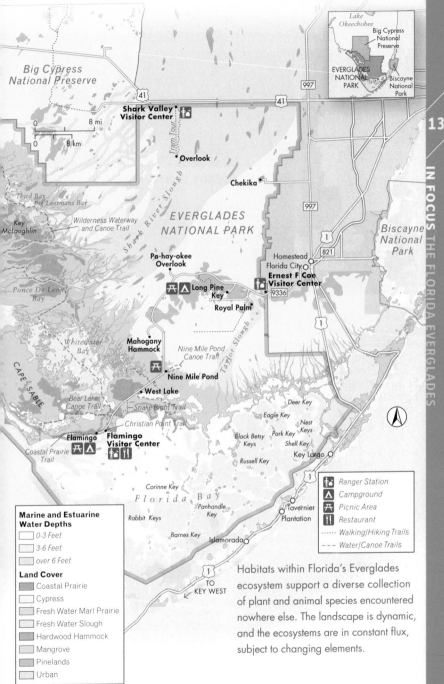

**Big Cypress National Preserve**

Lake Okeechobee
Big Cypress National Preserve
EVERGLADES NATIONAL PARK
Biscayne National Park

Shark Valley Visitor Center

Tram Tour

Overlook

Chekika

**EVERGLADES NATIONAL PARK**

Third Bay
Big Lostmans Bay

Key McLaughlin

Wilderness Waterway and Canoe Trail

Shark River Slough

Pa-hay-okee Overlook

Homestead
Florida City

Ernest F Coe Visitor Center

Ponce De Leon Bay

Long Pine Key

Royal Palm

Mahogany Hammock

Nine Mile Pond Canoe Trail

Taylor Slough

Whitewater Bay

Nine Mile Pond

West Lake

**Biscayne National Park**

Bear Lake Canoe Trail

Snake Bight Trail

Christian Point Trail

**CAPE SABLE**

Deer Key

Eagle Key

Nest Keys

Black Betsy Keys

Park Key

Shell Key

Key Largo

Flamingo
Flamingo Visitor Center

Coastal Prairie Trail

Russell Key

Corinne Key

*Florida Bay*

Panhandle Key

Tavernier
Plantation

Rabbit Keys

Barnes Key

Islamorada

TO KEY WEST

**Marine and Estuarine Water Depths**
- 0-3 Feet
- 3-6 Feet
- over 6 Feet

**Land Cover**
- Coastal Prairie
- Cypress
- Fresh Water Marl Prairie
- Fresh Water Slough
- Hardwood Hammock
- Mangrove
- Pinelands
- Urban

Ranger Station
Campground
Picnic Area
Restaurant
Walking/Hiking Trails
Water/Canoe Trails

0      8 mi
0      8 km

Habitats within Florida's Everglades ecosystem support a diverse collection of plant and animal species encountered nowhere else. The landscape is dynamic, and the ecosystems are in constant flux, subject to changing elements.

# FLORA

### ❶ Cabbage Palm
It's virtually impossible to visit the Everglades and not see a cabbage palm, Florida's official state tree. The cabbage palm (or sabal palm), graces assorted ecosystems and grows well in swamps. **Best place to see them:** At Loxahatchee National Wildlife Refuge (embracing the northern part of the Everglades, along Alligator Alley), throughout Everglades National Park, and at Big Cypress National Preserve.

### ❷ Sawgrass
With spiny, serrated leaf blades resembling saws, sawgrass inspired the term "river of grass" for the Everglades. **Best place to see them:** Both Shark Valley and Pahayokee Overlook provide terrific vantage points for gazing over sawgrass prairie; you also can get an eyeful of sawgrass when crossing Alligator Alley, even when doing so at top speeds.

### ❸ Mahogany
Hardwood hammocks of the Everglades live in areas that rarely flood because of the slight elevation of the sloughs, where they're typically found. **Best place to see them:** Everglades National Park's Mahogany Hammock Trail (which has a boardwalk leading to the nation's largest living mahogany tree).

### ❹ Mangrove
Mangrove forest ecosystems provide both food and protected nursery areas for fish, shellfish, and crustaceans. **Best place to see them:** Along Biscayne National Park shoreline, at Big Cypress National Preserve, and within Everglades National Park, especially around the Caple Sable area.

### ❺ Gumbo Limbo
Sometimes called "tourist trees" because of peeling reddish bark (not unlike sunburns). **Best place to see them:** Everglades National Park's Gumbo Limbo Trail and assorted spots throughout the expansive Everglades.

## FAUNA

**❶ American Alligator**
In all likelihood, on your visit to the Everglades you'll see at least a gator or two. These carnivorous creatures can be found throughout the Everglades swampy wetlands.
**Best place to see them:** Loxahatchee National Wildlife Refuge (also sheltering the endangered Everglades snail kite) and within Everglades National Park at Shark Valley or Anhinga Trail. Sometimes (logically enough) gators hang out along Alligator Alley, basking in early morning or late-afternoon sun along four-lane I–75.

**❷ American Crocodile**
Crocs gravitate to fresh or brackish water, subsisting on birds, fish, snails, frogs, and small mammals.
**Best place to see them:** Within Everglades National Park, Big Cypress National Preserve, and protected grounds in or around Billie Swamp Safari.

**❸ Eastern Coral Snake**
This venomous snake burrows in underbrush, preying on lizards, frogs, and smaller snakes.
**Best place to see them:** Snakes typically shy away from people, but try Snake Bight or Eco Pond near Flamingo, where birds are also prevalent.

**❹ Florida Panther**
Struggling for survival amid loss of habitat, these shy, tan-colored cats now number around 100, up from lows of near 30.
**Best place to see them:** Protected grounds of Billie Swamp Safari sometimes provide sightings during tours. Signage on roadway linking Tamiami Trail and Alligator Alley warns of panther crossings, but sightings are rare.

**❺ Green Tree Frog**
Typically bright green with white or yellow stripes, these nocturnal creatures thrive in swamps and brackish water.
**Best place to see them:** Within Everglades National Park, especially in or near water.

● =Extremely Common ● =Very Common ● =Somewhat Common ● =Rare

# BIRDS

### ❶ Anhinga

The lack of oil glands for waterproofing feathers helps this bird to dive as well as chase and spear fish with its pointed beak. The Anhinga is also often called a "water turkey" because of its long tail, or a "snake bird" because of its long neck.

**Best place to see them:** The Anhinga Trail, which also is known for attracting other wildlife to drink during especially dry winters.

### ❷ Blue-Winged Teal

Although it's predominantly brown and gray, this bird's powder-blue wing patch becomes visible in flight. Next to the mallard, the blue-winged teal is North America's second most abundant duck, and thrives particularly well in the Everglades.

**Best place to see them:** Near ponds and marshy areas of Everglades National Park or Big Cypress National Preserve.

### ❸ Great Blue Heron

This bird has a varied palate and enjoys feasting on everything from frogs, snakes, and mice to shrimp, aquatic insects, and sometimes even other birds! The all-white version, which at one time was considered a separate species, is quite common to the Everglades.

**Best place to see them:** Loxahatchee National Wildlife Refuge or Shark Valley in Everglades National Park.

### ❹ Great Egret

Once decimated by plume hunters, these monogamous, long-legged white birds with S-shaped necks feed in wetlands, nest in trees, and hang out in colonies that often include heron or other egret species.

**Best place to see them:** Throughout Everglades National Park, along Alligator Alley, and sometimes even on the fringes of Greater Fort Lauderdale.

### ❺ Greater Flamingo

Flocking together and using long legs and webbed feet to stir shallow waters and mud flats, color comes a couple of years after hatching from ingesting shrimplike crustaceans along with fish, fly larvae, and plankton.

**Best place to see them:** Try Snake Bight or Eco Pond, near Flamingo Marina.

### ❻ Osprey

Making a big comeback from chemical pollutant endangerment, ospreys (sometimes confused with bald eagles) are distinguished by black eyestripes down their faces. Gripping pads on feet with curved claws help them pluck fish from water.

**Best place to see them:** Look near water, where they're fishing for lunch in the shallow areas. Try the coasts, bays, and ponds of Everglades National Park. They also gravitate to trees You can usually spot them from the Gulf Coast Visitor Center, or you can observe them via boating in the Ten Thousand Islands.

### ❼ Roseate Spoonbill

These gregarious pink-and-white birds gravitate toward mangroves, feeding on fish, insects, amphibians, and some plants. They have long, spoon-like bills, and their feathers can have a touch of red and yellow. These birds appear in the Everglades year-round.

**Best place to see them:** Sandy Key, southwest of Flamingo, is a spoonbill nocturnal roosting spot, but at sunrise these colorful birds head out over Eco Pond to favored day hangouts throughout Everglades National Park.

### ❽ Wood Stork

Recognizable by featherless heads and prominent bills, these birds submerge in water to scoop up hapless fish. They are most common in the early spring and often easiest to spot in the morning.

**Best place to see them:** Amid the Ten Thousand Island areas, Nine Mile Pond, Mrazek Pond, and in the mangroves at Paurotis Pond.

●=*Extremely Common* ●=*Very Common* ●=*Somewhat Common* ●=*Rare*

# THE BEST EVERGLADES ACTIVITIES

## HIKING

**Top experiences:** At Big Cypress National Preserve, you can hike along designated trails or push through unmarked acreage. (Conditions vary seasonally, which means you could be tramping through waist-deep waters.) Trailheads for the Florida National Scenic Trail are at Loop Road off U.S. 41 and Alligator Alley at mile marker 63.

**What will I see?** Dwarf cypress, hardwood hammocks, prairies, birds, and other wildlife.

**For a short visit:** A 6.5-mi section from Loop Road to U.S. 41 crosses Robert's Lake Strand, providing a satisfying sense of being out in the middle nowhere.

**With more time:** A 28-mi stretch from U.S. 41 to I–75 (Alligator Alley) reveals assorted habitats, including hardwood hammocks, pinelands, prairie, and cypress.

**Want a tour?** Big Cypress ranger-led exploration starts from the Oasis Visitor Center, late November through mid-April.

## WALKING

**Top experiences:** Everglades National Park magnets: wheelchair accessible walkways at Anhinga Trail, Gumbo Limbo Trail, Pahayokee Overlook, Mahogany Hammock, and West Lake Trail.

**What will I see?** Birds and alligators at Anhinga; tropical hardwood hammock at Gumbo Limbo; an overlook of the River of Grass from Pahayokee's tower; a subtropical tree island with massive mahogany growth along Mahogany Hammock; and a forest of mangrove trees on West Lake Trail.

**For a short visit:** Flamingo's Eco Pond provides for waterside wildlife viewing.

**With more time:** Shark Valley lets you combine the quarter-mile Bobcat Boardwalk (looping through sawgrass prairie and a bayhead) with the 1-mi-long round-trip Otter Cave, allowing you to steep in subtropical hardwood hammock.

**Want a tour?** Pahayokee and Flamingo feature informative ranger-led walks.

*The Anhinga Trail near the Royal Palm Visitor Center at Everglades National Park*

## BOATING

**Top experiences:** Launch a boat from the Gulf Coast Visitors Center or Flamingo Marina. Bring your own watercraft or rent canoes or skiffs at either location.

**What will I see?** Birds from bald eagles to roseate spoonbills, plus plenty of mangrove and wildlife—and maybe even some baby alligators with yellow stripes.

**For a short visit:** Canoe adventurers often head for Hells Bay, a 3-mi stretch about 9 mi north of Flamingo. Or put in at the Turner River alongside the Tamiami Trail in the Big Cypress National Preserve and paddle all the way (about eight hours) to Chocoloskee Bay at Everglades City.

**With more time:** Head out amid the Ten Thousand Islands and lose yourself in territory once exclusively the domain of only the hardiest pioneers and American Indians. If you've got a week or more for paddling, the 99-mi Wilderness Waterway stretches from Flamingo to Everglades City.

**Want a tour?** Sign on for narrated boat tours at the Gulf Coast or Flamingo visitor center.

## BIRD WATCHING

**Top experiences:** Anhinga Trail, passing over Taylor Slough.

**What will I see?** Anhinga and heron sightings are a nearly sure thing, especially in early morning or late afternoon. Also, alligators can be seen from the boardwalk.

**For a short visit:** Even if you're traveling coast to coast at higher speeds via Alligator Alley, chances are you'll spot winged wonders like egrets, osprey, and heron.

**With more time:** Since bird-watching at Flamingo can be a special treat early in the morning or late in the afternoon, try camping overnight even if you're not one for roughing it. Reservations are recommended. (Flamingo Lodge remains under reconstruction from 2005 hurricane damage.)

**Want a tour?** Ranger-led walks at Pahayokee and from Everglades National Park visitor centers provide solid birding background for novices.

*(top left) Tourists cruise the Everglades by airboat; (bottom left) Green Heron; (right) Eastern Meadowlark*

# THE BEST EVERGLADES ACTIVITIES

## BIKING

**Top experiences:** Shark Valley (where bicycling is allowed on the tram road) is great for taking in the quiet beauty of the Everglades. Near Ernest F. Coe Visitor Center, Long Pine Key's 14-mi nature trail also can be a way to bike happily away from folks on foot.

**What will I see?** At Shark Valley, wading birds, turtles, and, probably alligators. At Long Pine Key, shady pinewood with subtropical plants and exposed limestone bedrock.

**For a short visit:** Bike on Shark Valley tram road but turn around to fit time schedule.

**With more time:** Go the entire 15-mi tram road route, which has no shortcuts. Or try the 22-mi route of Old Ingraham Highway near the Royal Palm Visitor Center, featuring mangrove, sawgrass, and birds (including hawks).

**Want a tour?** In Big Cypress National Preserve, Bear Island Bike Rides (8 mi round-trip over four to five hours) happen on certain Saturdays.

## SNORKELING

**Top experiences:** Biscayne National Park, where clear waters incorporate the northernmost islands of the Florida Keys.

**What will I see?** Dense mangrove swamp covering the park shoreline, and, in shallow waters, a living coral reef and tropical fish in assorted colors.

**For a short visit:** Pick a sunny day to optimize your snorkeling fun, and be sure to use sunscreen.

**With more time:** Advanced snorkel tours head out from the park on weekends to the bay, finger channels, and around shorelines of the barrier islands. Biscayne National Park also has canoe and kayak rentals, picnic facilities, walking trails, fishing, and camping.

**Want a tour?** You can swim and snorkel or stay dry and picnic aboard tour boats that depart from Biscayne National Park's visitor center.

*(top left) Biking near the Shark Valley Visitor Area. (top right) Snorkeling on the surface in the Atlantic Ocean.*

## DID YOU KNOW?

You can tell you're looking at a crocodile if you can see its lower teeth protruding when its jaws are shut, whereas an alligator shows no teeth when his mouth is closed. Gators are much darker in color—a gray-ish black—compared with the lighter tan color of crocodiles. Alligators' snouts are also much broader than their long, thin crocodilian counterparts.

# THE STORY OF THE EVERGLADES

Dreams of draining southern Florida took hold in the early 1800s, expanding in the early 1900s to convert large tracts from wetlands to agricultural acreage. By the 1920s, towns like Fort Lauderdale and Miami boomed, and the sugar industry—which came to be known as "Big Sugar"—established its first sugar mills. In 1947 Everglades National Park opened as a refuge for wildlife.

**KEY**

*Extent of the Everglades*

1900
1999

Meanwhile, the sugar industry grew. In its infancy, about 175,000 tons of raw sugar per year was produced from fields totaling about 50,000 acres. But once the U.S. embargo stopped sugar imports from Cuba in 1960 and laws restricting acreage were lifted, Big Sugar took off. Less than five years later, the industry produced 572,000 tons of sugar and occupied nearly a quarter of a million acres.

Fast-forward to 2008, to what was hailed as the biggest conservation deal in U.S. history since the creation of the national parks. A trailblazing restoration strategy hinged on creating a water flow-way between Lake Okeechobee and the Everglades by buying up and flooding 187,000 acres of land. The country's largest producers of cane sugar agreed to sell the necessary 187,000 acres to the state of Florida for $1.75 billion. Environmentalists cheered.

But within months, news broke of a scaled-back land acquisition plan: $1.34 billion to buy 180,000 acres. By spring 2009, the restoration plan had shrunk to $536,000 to buy 73,000 acres. With the purchase still in limbo, critics claim the state might overpay for acreage appraised at pre-recession values and proponents fear dwindling revenues may derail the plan altogether.

The Big Sugar land deal is part of a larger effort to preserve the Everglades. In 2010, two separate lawsuits charged the state, along with the United States Environmental Protection Agency, with stalling Everglades cleanup that was supposed to begin in 2006. "Glacial delay" is how one judge put it. The state must reduce phosphorus levels in water that flows to the Everglades or face fines and sanctions for violating the federal Clean Water Act. The fate of the Everglades remains in the balance.

13

# THE EVERGLADES PLANNER

## WHEN TO GO

Updated by
Lynne Helm

Winter is the best, and busiest time to visit the Everglades. Temperatures and mosquito activity are more tolerable, low water levels concentrate the resident wildlife, and migratory birds swell the avian population. In late spring the weather turns hot and rainy, and tours and facilities are less crowded. Migratory birds depart, and you must look harder to see wildlife. Summer brings intense sun and afternoon rainstorms. Water levels rise and mosquitoes descend, making outdoor activity virtually unbearable, unless you swath yourself in netting. Mosquito repellent is a necessity any time of year.

## FLYING IN

Miami International Airport (MIA) is 34 mi from Homestead and 47 mi from the eastern access to Everglades National Park. ⇨ *For MIA airline carrier information, refer to the Miami chapter.* Shuttles run between MIA and Homestead. Southwest Florida International Airport (RSW) in Fort Myers, a little over an hour's drive from Everglades City, is the closest major airport to the Everglades's western access. On-demand taxi transportation from the airport to Everglades City is available, and costs $150 for up to three passengers ($10 each for additional passengers).

## ABOUT THE RESTAURANTS

Dining in the Everglades area centers on mom-and-pop places that serve hearty home-style food, and small eateries that specialize in fresh local fare: alligator, fish, stone crab, frogs' legs, and Florida lobster from the Keys. American Indian restaurants serve local favorites as well as catfish, Indian fry bread (a flour-and-water flatbread), and pumpkin bread. A growing Hispanic population around Homestead means plenty of authentic, inexpensive Latin cuisine, with an emphasis on Cuban and Mexican dishes. Restaurants in Everglades City, especially those along the river, have fresh seafood, particularly succulent, sustainable stone crab. These places are mostly casual to the point of rustic, and are often closed in late summer or fall. For finer dining, go to Marco Island or Naples.

## ABOUT THE HOTELS

Accommodations near the parks range from inexpensive to moderate and offer off-season rates in summer, when rampant mosquito populations preclude spending much time outdoors, especially at dusk. If you're spending several days exploring the east coast Everglades, stay in one of the park's campgrounds; 11 mi away in Homestead–Florida City, where there are reasonably priced motels and RV parks; or in the Florida Keys or the Greater Miami–Fort Lauderdale area. Lodgings and campgrounds are also available on the Gulf Coast in Everglades City, Marco Island, and Naples, which has the most upscale accommodations in the area. Florida City's selection is mostly of the chain variety and geared toward business travelers.

| WHAT IT COSTS | | | | | |
|---|---|---|---|---|---|
| | ¢ | $ | $$ | $$$ | $$$$ |
| Restaurants | under $10 | $10–$15 | $15–$20 | $20–$30 | over $30 |
| Hotels | under $80 | $80–$100 | $100–$140 | $140–$220 | over $220 |

Restaurant prices are per person for a main course at dinner. Hotel prices are for a standard double room, excluding 6% sales tax (more in some counties) and 1%–5% tourist tax.

## EVERGLADES NATIONAL PARK

More than 1.5 million acres of South Florida's 4.3 million acres of subtropical, watery wilderness were given national-park status and protection in 1947 with the creation of Everglades National Park. It is one of the country's largest national parks and is recognized by the world community as a Wetland of International Importance, an International Biosphere Reserve, and a World Heritage Site. Come here if you want to spend the day biking, hiking, or boating in deep, raw wilderness with lots of wildlife.

## BISCAYNE NATIONAL PARK

To the east of Everglades National Park, Biscayne National Park brings forth a pristine, magical, subtropical Florida. It is the nation's largest marine park and the largest national park within the continental United States boasting living coral reefs. A small portion of the park's 172,000 acres consists of mainland coast and outlying islands, but 95% remains under water. Of particular interest are the mangroves and their tangled masses of stiltlike roots that thicken the shorelines. These "walking trees," as some locals call them, have curved prop roots, which arch down from the trunk, and aerial roots that drop from branches. The trees draw freshwater from saltwater and create a coastal nursery that sustains myriad types of marine life.

You can see Miami's high-rise buildings from many of Biscayne's 44 islands, but the park is virtually undeveloped and large enough for escaping everything that Miami and the Upper Keys have become. To truly escape, don scuba diving or snorkeling gear, and lose yourself in the wonders of the coral reefs.

## BIG CYPRESS NATIONAL PRESERVE

On the northern edge of Everglades National Park is Big Cypress National Preserve, one of South Florida's least-developed watersheds. Established by Congress in 1974 to protect the Everglades, it comprises extensive tracts of prairie, marsh, pinelands, forested swamps, and sloughs. Hunting is allowed, as is off-road-vehicle use. Come here if you like alligators. Stop at the Oasis Visitor Center to walk the boardwalk with alligators lounging underneath and then drive Loop Road for a backwoods experience. If time permits, kayak the Turner River. ■TIP➡ Many activities in the parks and preserve are based on water, so be prepared to get a bit damp on the marshy trails.

## NEARBY TOWNS

Surrounding the parks and preserve are several small communities: Everglades City, Florida City, and Homestead, home to many area outfitters.

⇨ *While outfitters are listed with the parks and preserve, see our What's Nearby section later in this chapter for information about each town.*

## CAMPING IN THE EVERGLADES

For an intense stay in the "real" Florida, consider one of some four-dozen backcountry campsites deep in Everglades National Park, many inland, some on the beach. You'll have to carry in your food, water, and supplies, and carry out all your trash. You'll also need a site-specific permit, available on a first-come, first-served basis from the Flamingo or Gulf Coast visitors centers. Permits cost $10, plus $2 per person per night for sites, with a 14-night limit, and are only issued up to 24 hours in advance. Front-country camping fees at park campgrounds are $16 per night.

# EVERGLADES NATIONAL PARK

*45 mi southwest of Miami International Airport.*

If you're heading across South Florida on U.S. 41 from Miami to Naples, you'll breeze right through the Everglades. Also known as Tamiami Trail, this mostly two-lane road along much of the route skirts the edge of Everglades National Park and cuts across the Big Cypress National Preserve. You'll also be near the park if you're en route from Miami to the Florida Keys on U.S. 1, which travels through Homestead and Florida City, two communities east of the main park entrance. Basically, if you're in South Florida you can't get away from at least fringes of the Everglades. With tourist strongholds like Miami, Naples, and the Florida Keys so close by, travelers from all over the world typically make day trips to the park.

Everglades National Park has three main entry points: the park headquarters at Ernest F. Coe Visitor Center, southwest of Homestead and Florida City; the Shark Valley area, in the northern reaches and accessed by Tamiami Trail (U.S. 41); and the Gulf Coast Visitor Center, just south of Everglades City to the west and closest to Naples.

You can explore on your own or participate in free ranger-led hikes, bicycle tours, bird-watching tours, and canoe trips; the number and variety of these excursions are greatest from mid-December through Easter, and some excursions (canoe trips, for instance) typically aren't offered in the sweltering summer. Among the more popular are the Anhinga Amble, a 50-minute walk around the Taylor Slough (departs from the Royal Palm Visitor Center), and the Early Bird Special, a 90-minute walk centered on birdlife (departs from Flamingo Visitor Center at 7:30 am). Ask at the visitor centers for details.

### PARK ESSENTIALS

**Admission Fees** $10 per vehicle, $5 per pedestrian, bicycle, or motorcycle. Admission, payable at gates, is good for seven consecutive days at all park entrances. Annual passes are $25.

**Admission Hours** The park is open daily, year-round, and both the main entrance near Florida City and Homestead, and the Gulf Coast entrance are open 24 hours. The Shark Valley entrance is open 8:30 am to 6 pm.

## COE VISITOR CENTER TO FLAMINGO

*About 30 mi from Miami.*

The most popular access to Everglades National Park is via the park headquarters entrance just southwest of Homestead and Florida City. If you're coming to the Everglades from Miami, the highway you'll take is Route 836 west to Route 826/874 south to the Homestead Extension of Florida's Turnpike, U.S. 1, and Krome Avenue (Route 997/old U.S. 27). To reach the Ernest F. Coe Visitor Center from Homestead, go right (west) from U.S. 1 or Krome Avenue onto Route 9336 (Florida's only four-digit route) in Florida City and follow signs to the park entrance.

### EXPLORING

To explore this section of the park, follow Route 9336 from the park entrance to Flamingo; there are many opportunities to stop along the way, and an assortment of activities to pursue in the Flamingo area. The following is arranged in geographic order.

**Ernest F. Coe Visitor Center.** Don't just grab your park map and go; this visitor center's numerous interactive exhibits and films are well worth your time. The 15-minute film *River of Life,* updated frequently, provides a succinct park overview with emphasis on the river of grass. There is also a movie on hurricanes and a 35-minute wildlife film for children available upon request. A bank of telephones offers differing viewpoints on the Great Water Debate, detailing how last century's gung ho draining of swampland for residential and agricultural development also cut off water-supply routes for precious wetlands in the Everglades ecosystem. Here you'll also find a schedule of daily ranger-led activities, mainly walks and talks, and information on canoe rentals and boat tours at Flamingo. The Everglades Discovery Shop stocks books and jewelry including bird-oriented earrings, and you can browse through cool nature, science, and kids' stuff or pick up extra insect repellent. Coe Visitor Center, which has restrooms, is outside park gates, so you can stop in without paying park admission. ⊠ *11 mi southwest of Homestead at 40001 State Rd. 9336* ☎ *305/242–7700* ◷ *Daily 8–4:30; hrs sometimes shortened in off-season.*

**Main road to Flamingo.** Route 9336 travels 38 mi from the Ernest F. Coe Visitor Center southwest to the Florida Bay at Flamingo. It crosses a section of the park's eight distinct ecosystems: hardwood hammock, freshwater prairie, pinelands, freshwater slough, cypress, coastal prairie, mangrove, and marine-estuarine. Route highlights include a dwarf cypress forest, the transition zone between saw grass and mangrove forest, and a wealth of wading birds at Mrazek and Coot Bay ponds—where in early morning or late afternoon you can observe the hundreds of birds feeding. Boardwalks, looped trails, several short spurs, and observation platforms help you stay dry. You also may want to stop along the way to walk several short trails (each takes about 30 minutes): the popular, wheelchair-accessible **Anhinga Trail**, which cuts through saw grass marsh and allows you to see lots of wildlife (be on the lookout for alligators and the trail's namesake, water birds known as anhingas); and junglelike—yet, also wheelchair-accessible—**Gumbo-Limbo Trail;** the **Pinelands Trail,** where you can see the limestone bedrock that underlies the park; the **Pahayokee Overlook Trail,** which ends at an observation tower; and the **Mahogany Hammock Trail** with its dense growth.

■TIP→ Before you head out on the trails, inquire about insect and weather conditions and plan accordingly, stocking up on bug repellent, sunscreen, and water as necessary. Also, even on seemingly nice days, it's probably smart to bring along rain gear.

★ **Royal Palm Visitor Center.** A must for anyone wanting to experience the real Everglades, and ideal for when there's limited time, this small center with a bookstore and vending machines permits access to the **Anhinga Trail boardwalk,** where in winter catching sight of alligators congregating in watering holes is almost guaranteed. Or follow the neighboring **Gumbo Limbo Trail** through a hardwood hammock. Both strolls are short (½ mi) and expose you to two Everglades ecosystems. Rangers conduct daily Anhinga Ambles in season (check for dates by calling ahead) starting at 10:30. At 1:30 the Glades Glimpse program takes place daily in season. Ask also about starlight walks and bike tours in season. ⊠ *4 mi west of Ernest F. Coe Visitor Center on Rte. 9336* ☎ *305/242–7700* ◷ *Daily 8–4:15.*

**NEED A BREAK?** Good spots to pull over for a picnic lunch are Paurotis Pond, about 10 mi north of Florida Bay, or Nine Mile Pond, less than 30 mi from the main visitor center. Another option is along Bear Lake, 2 mi north of the Flamingo Visitor Center.

**Flamingo.** At the far end of the main road to Flamingo lies this community along Florida Bay, where you'll find a marina, visitor center, and campground, with nearby hiking and nature trails. Before hurricanes Katrina and Wilma washed them away in 2005, a lodge, cabins, and restaurants in Flamingo provided Everglades National Park's only accommodations. At press time, the rebuilding of Flamingo Lodge was projected to materialize sometime after 2012 (and has been for quite some time), but for now, you can still pitch a tent or bring an RV to the campground, where improvements include solar-hot-water showers and electricity for RV sites. A popular houseboat rental concession returned in December 2010. The 35-foot floating homes sleep six and are equipped with a shower, a toilet, bedding, pots, flatware, a stereo, and depth finder. Houseboats (thankfully air-conditioned) with 60-horsepower outboards rent for $350 per night, plus fuel.

**Flamingo Visitor Center.** Check the schedule here for ranger-led activities, such as naturalist discussions, hikes along area trails, and evening programs in the 100-seat campground amphitheater, which replaced the old gathering spot destroyed by hurricanes in 2005. Also, find natural history exhibits and pamphlets on canoe, hiking, and biking trails in the small Florida Bay Flamingo Museum on the 2nd floor of the visitor center. ⊠ *1 Flamingo Lodge Hwy., Flamingo* ☎ *239/695–2945, 239/695–3101 marina* ⊙ *Exhibits are always open, staffed mid-Nov.–mid-Apr., daily 8–4:30.*

## SPORTS AND THE OUTDOORS

### BIRDING
Some of the park's best birding is in the Flamingo area.

### BOATING
The 99-mi inland **Wilderness Trail** between Flamingo and Everglades City is open to motorboats as well as canoes, although, depending on the water level, powerboats may have trouble navigating the route above Whitewater Bay. Flat-water canoeing and kayaking are best in winter, when temperatures are moderate, rainfall diminishes, and mosquitoes back off—a little, anyway. You don't need a permit for day trips, although there is a seven-day, $5 launch fee for all motorized boats brought into the park. The Flamingo area has well-marked canoe trails, but be sure to tell someone where you're going and when you expect to return. Getting lost is easy, and spending the night without proper gear can be unpleasant, if not dangerous.

OUTFITTER **Flamingo Lodge, Marina, and Everglades National Park Tours.** The official Everglades National Park concessionaire runs tours and operates a marina. The 1.75-hour backcountry *Pelican* cruise ($26.50) winds through the water under a heavy canopy of mangroves, revealing abundant wildlife—from alligators, crocodiles, and turtles to herons, hawks, and egrets. A second boat, *Sawgrass,* follows the same route in peak season (November–April). Flamingo Marina charters boats, and rents 17-foot power skiffs from 7 am for $195 per day (eight hours, if returned by 4 pm), $150 per half day, $80 for two hours. Canoes for up to three paddlers rent for $16 for two hours (minimum), $22 for four hours, and $40 overnight. Family canoes for up to four rent for $20 for two hours (minimum), $30 for four hours, $40 for eight hours, and $50 for 24 hours. Two-person charter fishing trips can be arranged for weekends ($350 for a half day or $450 a day; each additional person pays $25). Cost includes tackle, ice, and license. The concessionaire also rents bikes, binoculars, rods, reels, and other equipment by the half and full day. Feeling sticky after a day in the 'Glades? Hot showers are $3. The Flamingo Lodge, a victim of massive hurricane damage in 2005, remains closed pending funding for a fresh start. ⌂ *1 Flamingo Lodge Hwy., on Buttonwood Canal, Flamingo* ☎ *239/695–3101.*

## GOOD READS

■ *The Everglades: River of Grass.* This circa-1947 classic by pioneering conservationist Marjory Stoneman Douglas (1890–1998) is a must-read.

■ *Everglades Wildguide.* Jean Craighead George gives an informative account of the park's natural history in this official National Park Service handbook.

■ *Everglades: The Park Story.* Wildlife biologist William B. Robertson Jr. presents the park's flora, fauna, and history.

**13**

### WHERE TO CAMP

*For expanded campground reviews, visit Fodors.com.*

■ TIP→ In the dry winter season, be careful with campfires and matches; this is when the wildfire-prone saw grass prairies and pinelands are most vulnerable.

★ ⛺ **Flamingo.** This campground has 234 drive-in sites; 55 have a water view, and nine of 64 walk-in sites are along water. *Flush toilets, dump station, drinking water, showers, general store ↰ 234 drive-up sites, 64 walk-in sites* ☎ *877/444–6777 campsite reservations, 305/242–7700 park information, 239/695–0124 camping information* ⊕ *www.recreation.gov.*

¢ ⛺ **Long Pine Key.** About 6 mi west of the park's main entrance, Long Pine Key has drive-up sites for tents and RVs, several area hiking trails, and a pond for fishing (permit required). *Flush toilets, dump station, drinking water, picnic tables ↰ 108 drive-up sites* ☎ *305/242–7700* ⊕ *www.nps.gov/ever.*

## GULF COAST ENTRANCE

To reach the park's western gateway, take U.S. 41 west from Miami for 77 mi, turn left (south) onto Route 29, and travel another 3 mi through Everglades City to the Gulf Coast Ranger Station. From Naples on the Gulf Coast, take U.S. 41 east for 35 mi, then turn right onto Route 29.

**Gulf Coast Visitor Center.** The best place to bone up on Everglades National Park's watery western side is at this visitor center just south of Everglades City, where rangers are on hand to answer any of your questions. In winter, canoeists check in here for trips to the Ten Thousand Islands and 99-mi Wilderness Waterway Trail, nature lovers view

Much skill is required to navigate boats through the shallow, muddy waters of the Everglades.

interpretive exhibits on local flora and fauna while waiting for naturalist-led boat trip departures, and backcountry campers purchase permits. In season (Christmas through Easter), rangers lead bike tours and canoe trips. No direct roads run from here to other sections of the park, and admission is free only to this section of the park. ⊠ *Rte. 29, Everglades City* ☎ *239/695–3311* ☉ *Mid-Nov.–mid-Apr., daily 8–4:30; mid-Apr.–mid-Nov., daily 9–4:30.*

## OUTFITTERS

**Everglades National Park Boat Tours.** Operating in conjunction with boat tours at Flamingo, this company runs 1½-hour trips ($26.50) through the Ten Thousand Islands National Wildlife Refuge. Adventure-seekers often see dolphins, manatees, bald eagles, and roseate spoonbills. In peak season (November–April), 49-passenger boats run on the hour and half-hour daily. Mangrove wilderness tours are also conducted on smaller boats for up to six passengers. These one-hour, 45-minute trips ($35) are the best option to see alligators. The outfitter also rents canoes. ⊠ *Gulf Coast Visitor Center, Everglades City* ☎ *239/695–2591 or 866/628–7275* ⊕ *evergladesnationalparkboattoursflamingo.com/ index.php.*

Fodor's Choice  **Everglades Rentals & Eco Adventures.** Inside the Ivey House Inn there is
★  an established, year-round source for canoes, sea kayaks, and guided Everglades paddling tours. Canoe rentals cost $35 the first day, $27 for each day thereafter. Day-long kayak rentals are from $65. All half-day rentals are from 1 to 5 pm. Shuttles deliver you to major launching areas such as Turner River ($30 for up to two people) and Collier-Seminole State Park ($60). Tour highlights include bird and

gator sightings, mangrove forests, no-man's-land beaches, relics of hideouts for infamous and just-plain-reclusive characters, and spectacular sunsets. Longer adventures ($859 for two nights to $1,439 for six nights, per person with a two-person minimum) include canoe/kayak and equipment rental, all necessary camping equipment, a guide, and meals. ⊠ *Ivey House, 107 Camellia St., Everglades City* ☐ *Box 5038, Everglades City 34139* ☎ *877/567–0679 or 239/695–3299* ⊕ *www. evergladesadventures.com.*

13

## SHARK VALLEY

*23½ mi west of Florida's Turnpike, off Tamiami Trail. Approximately 45 minutes west of Miami.*

One thing you won't see at Shark Valley is sharks. The name comes from the Shark River, also called the River of Grass, which flows through the area. Several species of shark swim up this river from the coast (about 45 mi south of Shark Valley) to give birth. Young sharks (called pups), vulnerable to being eaten by adult sharks and other predators, gain strength in waters of the slough before heading out to sea to fend for themselves.

### EXPLORING

Though Shark Valley is the national park's north entrance, no roads here lead directly to other parts of the park. However, it's still worth stopping here to take a tram tour. Be sure to stop at the halfway point and ascend to the top of the observation tower via a ramp.

Prefer to do the trail on foot? It takes a bit of nerve to walk the paved 15-mi loop in Shark Valley because in the winter months alligators lie on and alongside the road, basking in the sun—most, however, do move quickly out of the way.

You also can ride a bicycle (the outfitter here rents one-speed, well-used bikes daily 8:30–4 for $7 per hour) or take a two-hour guided tram tour (reservations recommended in winter). Just behind the bike-rental area a short boardwalk trail meanders through the saw grass, and another one passes through a tropical hardwood hammock. An underwater live camera in the canal behind the center (viewed from the gift shop) lets visitors sporadically see the alligators and otters.

**Observation Tower.** At the Shark Valley trail's end (really, the halfway point of the 15-mi loop), you can pause to navigate this tower, first built in 1984, spiraling 50 feet upward. Once on top, the River of Grass gloriously spreads out as far as your eye can see. Observe water birds as well as alligators, and perhaps even river otters crossing the road. The tower has a wheelchair-accessible ramp to the top.

**Shark Valley Visitor Center.** The small center has rotating exhibits, a bookstore, and park rangers ready for your questions. ⊠ *23½ mi west of Florida's Turnpike, off Tamiami Trail* ☎ *305/221–8776* ⊙ *Late Mar.– late Dec., daily 9:15–5:15; late Dec.–late Mar., daily 8:45–5:15; gate daily 8:30–6.*

### TOURS

★ **Shark Valley Tram Tours.** Starting at the Shark Valley visitor center, two-hour, narrated tours ($18.25) follow a 15-mi loop road—especially good for viewing gators—into the interior, stopping at a 50-foot observation tower. Reservations are recommended December through April. ⊠ *Valley Visitor Center* ☎ *305/221–8455* ⊕ *www.sharkvalleytramtours.com* ⊠ *$16.25 per person* ⊙ *Tours Dec.–Apr., hourly 9–4; May–Nov., hourly 9–3.*

### SPORTS AND THE OUTDOORS

#### BOATING

Many Everglades-area tours operate only in season, roughly November through April.

**Buffalo Tiger's Airboat Tours.** A former chief of Florida's Miccosukee tribe operates this Shark Valley area company. Though at 90 (or so) years old he no longer skippers the boat, the chief still gets out to meet and greet customers when he can. Guides narrate the trip to an old Indian camp on the north side of Tamiami Trail from the American Indian perspective. Don't worry about airboat noise, since guides shut down the engines during informative talks. The 45-minute round-trip tours go 10–5 Saturday through Thursday and cost $30 per person for two, $20 per person for more than two, up to 12 people. Reservations are not required, but cash is—no credit cards accepted. ⊠ *29708 S.W. 8th St., Miami, 5 mi east of Shark Valley, 25 mi west of Florida's Turnpike* ☎ *305/559–5250* ⊕ *www.buffalotigersairboattours.com.*

# BIG CYPRESS NATIONAL PRESERVE

Through the 1950s and early 1960s the world's largest cypress-logging industry prospered in Big Cypress Swamp. As the industry died out, the government began buying parcels. Today, more than 729,000 acres, or nearly half of the swamp, form this national preserve. The word "big" refers not to the size of the trees but to the swamp, which juts into the north edge of Everglades National Park like a jigsaw-puzzle piece. Size and strategic location make Big Cypress an important link in the region's hydrological system, where rainwater first flows through the preserve, then south into the park, and eventually into Florida Bay. Its variegated pattern of wet prairies, ponds, marshes, sloughs, and strands provides a wildlife sanctuary, and thanks to a policy of balanced land use—"use without abuse"—the watery wilderness is devoted to recreation as well as research and preservation.

The preserve allows—in limited areas—hiking, hunting, and off-road-vehicle (airboat, swamp buggy, four-wheel-drive vehicles) use by permit.

Compared with Everglades National Park, the preserve is less developed and hosts fewer visitors. That makes it ideal for naturalists, birders, and hikers who prefer to see more wildlife than humans.

Several scenic drives link from Tamiami Trail; some require four-wheel-drive vehicles, especially in wet summer months. A few lead to camping areas, and roadside picnic areas.

### PARK ESSENTIALS

Admission Fees There is no admission fee to visit the preserve.

Admission Hours The park is open daily, year-round. Accessible only by boat, Adams Key is for day use only.

Contact Information **Big Cypress National Preserve** (✉ HCR 61, Box 11, Ochopee 34141 ☎ 239/695–1201 ⊕ www.nps.gov/bicy).

## EXPLORING

**Oasis Visitor Center.** The big attraction here is the observation deck where you can view huge gators as well as fish, birds, and other wildlife. There's also a small butterfly garden where native plants seasonally attract winged wonders. Inside the information center you'll find a small exhibit area, a bookshop, and a theater that shows a dated but informative 15-minute film on the Big Cypress Preserve swamplands. ✉ *24 mi east of Everglades City, 50 mi west of Miami, 20 mi west of Shark Valley* ☎ *239/695–1201* ▨ *Free* ☉ *Daily 9–4:30.*

**Ochopee Post Office.** This former irrigation pipe shed, on the south side of Tamiami Trail, is North America's smallest post office. Don't blink or you'll miss it. To help keep this picturesque outpost in business during times of governmental cutbacks and layoffs, buy a postcard of the one-room shack, and mail it to someone who would appreciate such a rustic spot. ✉ *4 mi east of Rte. 29, at 38000 E. Tamiami Trail, Ochopee* ☎ *239/695–2099* ☉ *Weekdays 10–noon and 1–4:30, Sat. 10–11:30.*

## RANGER PROGRAMS

From the Oasis Visitor Center you can get in on one of the seasonal ranger-led or self-guided activities, such as campfire and wildlife talks, hikes, slough slogs, and canoe excursions. The 8-mi Turner River Canoe Trail begins nearby and crosses through Everglades National Park before ending in Chokoloskee Bay, near Everglades City. Rangers lead four-hour canoe trips and two-hour swamp walks in season; call for days and times. Bring shoes and long pants for the swamp walks and be prepared to wade at least knee-deep in water. Ranger program reservations are accepted up to 14 days in advance.

## SPORTS AND THE OUTDOORS

There are three types of trails—walking (including part of the extensive Florida National Scenic Trail), canoeing, and bicycling. All three trail types are easily accessed from the Tamiami Trail near the preserve visitor center, and one boardwalk trail departs from the center. Canoe and bike equipment can be rented from outfitters in Everglades City, 24 mi west, and Naples, 40 mi west.

Hikers can tackle the Florida National Scenic Trail, which begins in the preserve and is divided into segments 6.5 to 28 mi each. Two 5-mi trails, Concho Billy and Fire Prairie, can be accessed off Turner River Road, a few miles east. Turner River Road and Birdon Road form a 17-mi gravel loop drive that's excellent for birding. Bear Island has about 32 mi of scenic, flat, looped trails that are ideal for bicycling. Most trails are hard-packed lime rock, but a few miles are gravel. Cyclists share the road with off-road vehicles, most plentiful from mid-November through December.

To see the best variety of wildlife from your car, follow 26-mi Loop Road, south of U.S. 41 and west of Shark Valley, where alligators, raccoons, and soft-shell turtles crawl around beside the gravel road, often swooped upon by swallowtail kites and brown-shouldered hawks. Stop at H. P. Williams Roadside Park, west of the Oasis, and walk along the boardwalk to spy gators, turtles, and garfish in the river waters.

## WHERE TO CAMP

*For expanded campground reviews, visit Fodors.com. For lodging options in the area, see the Where to Stay sections under each town in What's Nearby, later in this chapter.*

¢ ⚠ **Big Cypress National Preserve.** There are four no-fee primitive campgrounds within the preserve along Tamiami Trail and Loop Road, including Burns Lake, Bear Island, Pinecrest, and Mitchell's Landing. *Flush toilets, dump station, showers* ⤵ *40 sites at Burns Lake; 40 sites at Bear Island; 10 sites at Pinecrest; 15 sites at Mitchell's Landing; 10 tent, 26 RV sites at Monument Lake; 10 tent, 26 RV sites at Midway* ✉ *Tamiami Trail (Hwy. 41), between Miami and Naples* ✆ *HCR 61, Box 110, Ochopee 34141* ☏ *239/695–1201* ⬛ *No credit cards.*

¢ ⚠ **Trail Lakes Campground.** Close to Everglades City and Big Cypress National Preserve, Trail Lakes spreads out over 30 acres, is near a canoe launch, and has the added attraction of a nature park and wildlife exhibits. *Flush toilets, drinking water, electricity, public telephone, general store* ⤵ *80 RV sites, 25 tent sites* ✉ *40904 E. Tamiami Trail (Hwy. 41), Ochopee* ☏ *239/695–2275* ⊕ *www.skunkape.info.*

# BISCAYNE NATIONAL PARK

Occupying 172,000 acres along the southern portion of Biscayne Bay, south of Miami and north of the Florida Keys, this national park is 95% submerged, and its altitude ranges from 4 feet above sea level to 60 feet below. Contained within from shore to sea are four distinct zones: mangrove forest along the coast, Biscayne Bay, the undeveloped upper Florida Keys, and coral reefs. Mangroves line the mainland shore much as they do elsewhere along South Florida's protected bay waters. Biscayne Bay functions as a lobster sanctuary and a nursery for fish, sponges, and crabs. Manatees and sea turtles frequent its warm shallow waters.

### GETTING HERE

To reach Biscayne National Park from Homestead, take Krome Avenue to Route 9336 (Palm Drive) and turn east. Follow Palm Drive for about 8 mi until it becomes S.W. 344th Street and follow signs to park headquarters in Convoy Point. The entry is 9 mi east of Homestead and 9 mi south and east of Exit 6 (Speedway Boulevard/S.W. 137th Avenue) off Florida's Turnpike.

**13**

### PARK ESSENTIALS

**Admission Fees** There is no fee to enter Biscayne National Park, and you don't pay a fee to access the islands, but there is a $20 overnight camping fee that includes a $5 dock fee to berth vessels at some island docks. The park concessionaire charges for trips to the coral reefs and the islands *(⇨ see Outfitters and Expeditions)*.

**Admission Hours** The park is open daily, year-round.

**Contact Information Biscayne National Park** (✉ *Dante Fascell Visitor Center, 9700 S.W. 328th St., Homestead* ☎ *305/230–7275* ⊕ *www.nps.gov/bisc)*.

## EXPLORING

Biscayne is a great place if you want to dive, snorkel, canoe, camp, birdwatch, or learn about marine ecology. The best place to hike is Elliott Key *(⇨ see Islands, below)*.

### THE CORAL REEF

Biscayne's corals range from the soft, flagellant fans, plumes, and whips found chiefly in the shallower patch reefs to the hard brain corals, elkhorn, and staghorn forms that can withstand the depths and heavier wave action along the ocean's edge.

### THE ISLANDS

To the east, about 8 mi off the coast, lie 44 tiny keys, stretching 18 nautical mi north–south and accessible only by boat. There's no commercial transportation between the mainland and the islands, and only a handful can be visited: Elliott, Boca Chita, Adams, and Sands keys. The rest are wildlife refuges, are too small, or have rocky shores or waters too shallow for boats. It's best to explore the Keys between December and April, when the mosquito population is less aggressive. Repellent is a must.

**Adams Key**. A stone's throw from the western tip of Elliott Key and 9 mi southeast of Convoy Point, the onetime site of the Cocolobo Club, a yacht club famous for once hosting presidents Harding, Hoover, Johnson, Nixon and other luminaries, is open for day use. It has picnic areas, restrooms, dockage, and a short trail that runs along the shore and through a hardwood hammock. Rangers live on-island. Access is by private boat, and no pets or overnight docking are allowed.

★  **Boca Chita Key**. Ten miles northeast of Convoy Point, this key was once owned by the late Mark C. Honeywell, former president of Honeywell Company. A ½-mi hiking trail curves around the south side of

the island. Climb the 65-foot-high ornamental lighthouse (by ranger tour only) for a panoramic view of Miami or check out the cannon from the HMS *Fowey*. There's no freshwater, access is by private boat only, and no pets are allowed. Only portable toilets are on-site, and there are no sinks or showers. A $20 fee for overnight docking between 6 pm and 6 am covers a campsite; pay at the automated kiosk near the harbor. Boca Chita Key, about 12 mi south of the Cape Florida Lighthouse on Key Biscayne, is listed on the National Register of Historic Places for its 10 historic structures.

### BISCAYNE IN ONE DAY

Most visitors come to snorkel or dive. Divers should plan to spend the morning on the water and the afternoon exploring the Convoy Point Visitor Center. The opposite is true for snorkelers, as snorkel trips (and one-tank shallow-dive trips) depart in the afternoon. If you want to hike as well, turn to the trails at Elliott Key—just be sure to apply insect repellent (and sunscreen, too, no matter what time of year).

**Elliott Key.** The largest of the islands, 9 mi east of Convoy Point, has a mile-long loop trail on the bay side of the island at the north end of the campground. Boaters may dock at any of 36 slips, and a $20 fee for stays between 6 pm and 6 am covers a campsite. Take an informal, ranger-led nature walk or head out on your own to hike the 6-mi trail along so-called Spite Highway, a 225-foot-wide swath of green that developers mowed down in hopes of linking this key to the mainland. Luckily the federal government stepped in, and now it's a hiking trail through tropical hardwood hammock. Facilities include restrooms, picnic tables, fresh drinking water, cold (or, occasionally, lukewarm) water showers, grills, and a campground. Leashed pets are allowed in developed areas only, not on trails. A 30-foot-wide sandy shoreline about a mile north of the harbor on the west (bay) side of the key is the only one in the national park. Boaters like to anchor off it to swim. The beach, fun for families, is for day use only; it has picnic areas and a short trail that follows the shore and cuts through the hammock.

### VISITOR CENTER

**Dante Fascell Visitor Center.** Go outside on the wide veranda to take in views across mangroves and Biscayne Bay. Inside the museum, artistic vignettes and on-request videos including the 11-minute *Spectrum of Life* explore the park's four ecosystems, while the Touch Table gives both kids and adults a feel for bones, feathers, and coral. Facilities include the park's canoe and tour concessionaire, restrooms with showers, a ranger information area, gift shop with books, and vending machines. Various ranger programs take place daily during busy fall and winter seasons. On the second Sunday of each month from January through May, the Family Fun Fest program offers three hours of hands-on activities for kids and families. Rangers also give informal tours of Elliott and Boca Chita keys; arrange in advance. Outside are picnic tables and grills. A short trail and boardwalk lead to a jetty. This is the only area of the park accessible without a boat. ⊠ *9700 S.W.*

Native plants along the Turner River Canoe Trail hem paddlers in on both sides, and alligators lurk nearby.

*328th St., Homestead/Convoy Point* ☎ *305/230–7275* ⊕ *www.nps.gov/ bisc* ✉ *Free* ☉ *Daily 9–4:30.*

## SPORTS AND THE OUTDOORS

### BIRD-WATCHING

More than 170 species of birds have been identified around the park. Expect to see flocks of brown pelicans patrolling the bay—suddenly rising, then plunging beak first to capture prey in their baggy pouches. White ibis probe exposed mud flats for small fish and crustaceans. Although all the Keys are excellent for birding, Jones Lagoon (south of Adams Key, between Old Rhodes Key and Totten Key) is outstanding. It's approachable only by nonmotorized craft.

### DIVING AND SNORKELING

Diving is great year-around, but best in summer, when calmer winds and smaller seas result in clearer waters. Ocean waters, another 3 mi east of the Keys, showcase the park's main attraction—the northernmost section of Florida's living tropical coral reefs. Some are the size of an office desk, others as large as a football field. You can take a glass-bottom-boat ride to see this underwater wonderland, but you really should snorkel or scuba dive to fully appreciate it.

A diverse population of colorful fish—angelfish, gobies, grunts, parrot fish, pork fish, wrasses, and many more—flits through the reefs. Shipwrecks from the 18th century are evidence of the area's international maritime heritage, and a Maritime Heritage Trail is being developed to link six of the major shipwreck and underwater cultural sites. Thus far, three sites, including a 19th-century wooden sailing vessel, have been plotted with GPS coordinates and marked with mooring buoys. Plastic dive cards are being developed that will contain navigational and background information.

## WHERE TO CAMP

*For expanded campground reviews, visit Fodors.com. For lodging options in the area, see the Where to Stay sections under each town in What's Nearby, later in this chapter.*

13

⟨ ⚠ **Boca Chita Campground.** This small flat island has a grassy, waterside campground shaded by palms whispering in the breeze. *Flush toilets, picnic tables* ⟶ *39 sites⊠ Visitor center: 9700 S.W. 328th St., Homestead* ☎ *305/230–7275* ⊟ *No credit cards.*

⟨ ⚠ **Elliott Key Campground.** You'll need a private boat to get here, but grassy, beachfront tent sites with awesome views and populated with plenty of native hardwood trees make it worth the inconvenience. *Flush toilets, drinking water, showers, picnic tables, swimming (ocean)* ⟶ *40 sites⊠ Visitor center: 9700 S.W. 328th St., Homestead* ☎ *305/230–7275, 305/230–1100 transportation, 305/230–1144 Ext. 3074 for group campsite* ⊕ *www.nps.gov/bisc* ⊟ *No credit cards.*

# WHAT'S NEARBY

## EVERGLADES CITY

*35 mi southeast of Naples and 83 mi west of Miami.*

Aside from a chain gas station or two, Everglades City is perfect Old Florida. No high-rises (other than an observation tower) mar the landscape at this western gateway to Everglades National Park, just off the Tamiami Trail. It was developed in the late 19th century by Barron Collier, a wealthy advertising entrepreneur, who built it as a company town to house workers for his numerous projects including construction of the Tamiami Trail. It grew and prospered until the Depression and World War II. Today this ramshackle town draws adventure-seekers heading to the park for canoeing, fishing, and bird-watching excursions. Airboat tours, though popular, are banned within the preserve and park because of the environmental damage they cause to the mangroves. The Everglades Seafood Festival, going strong for nearly 40 years and held the first full weekend of February, draws crowds of up to 75,000 for delights from the sea, music, and craft displays. At quieter times, dining choices are limited to a handful of basic eateries. The town is small, fishing-oriented, and unhurried, making it excellent for boating, bicycling, or just strolling around. Pedal along the waterfront on a 2-mi ride along the strand out to Chokoloskee Island.

Visitor Information **Everglades Area Chamber of Commerce** (⊠ *Rte. 29 and Tamiami Trail* ☎ *239/695–3172* ⊕ *www.evergladeschamber.com*).

### EXPLORING

★ **Fakahatchee Strand Preserve State Park.** The ½-mi boardwalk through this linear swamp forest gives you an opportunity to see rare plants, bald cypress, nesting eagles, and North America's largest stand of native royal palms and largest concentration and variety of epiphytic orchids, including more than 30 varieties of threatened and endangered species blooming most extravagantly in hotter months. It's particularly famous for its ghost orchids (as featured in the novel *The Orchid Thief* by Susan Orlean), visible only on guided hikes. In your quest for ghost orchids, also keep a hopeful eye out for white-tailed deer, black bears, bobcats, and the Florida panther. For park nature on parade, take the 12-mi-long (one-way) W. J. Janes Memorial Scenic Drive, and, if you have the time, hike the spur trails leading off it. Rangers lead swamp walks and canoe trips November through April. ⊠ *Boardwalk on north side of Tamiami Trail, 7 mi west of Rte. 29; W. J. Janes Scenic Dr., ¾ mi north of Tamiami Trail on Rte. 29; ranger station on W. J. Janes Scenic Dr.* ☎ *239/695–4593* ⊕ *www.floridastateparks.org/fakahatcheestrand* ☜ *Free* ⊙ *Daily 8 am–sunset.*

OFF THE
BEATEN
PATH

**Collier-Seminole State Park.** Nature trails, biking, hiking, camping, and canoeing into Everglades territory make this park a prime introduction to this often forbidding land. Of historical interest, a Seminole War blockhouse has been re-created to hold the interpretive center, and one of the "walking dredges"—a towering black machine invented to carve the Tamiami Trail out of the muck—stands silent on the grounds amid tropical hardwood forest. Campsites ($22 per night) include electricity, water, and picnic table. Restrooms have hot water, and one has laundry. ⊠ *20200 E. Tamiami Trail, Naples* ☎ *239/394–3397* ⊕ *www.floridastateparks.org/collier-seminole* ☜ *$5 per car, $4 with lone driver* ⊙ *Daily 8–sunset.*

**Museum of the Everglades.** Through artifacts and photographs you can meet the American Indians, pioneers, entrepreneurs, and fishermen who played a role in the development of southwest Florida. Exhibits and a short film chronicle the tremendous feat of building the Tamiami Trail through the mosquito-ridden, gator-infested Everglades wetlands. In addition to the permanent displays, monthly exhibits rotate the work of local artists. ⊠ *105 W. Broadway* ☎ *239/695–0008* ☜ *Free* ⊙ *Tues.–Sat. 10–4.*

### SPORTS AND THE OUTDOORS
#### BOATING AND CANOEING

On the Gulf Coast explore the nooks, crannies, and mangrove islands of Chokoloskee Bay and Ten Thousand Islands National Wildlife Refuge, as well as the many rivers near Everglades City. The Turner River Canoe Trail, a pleasant day trip with a guarantee of bird and alligator sightings, passes through mangrove, dwarf cypress, coastal prairie, and freshwater slough ecosystems of Everglades National Park and Big Cypress National Preserve.

OUTFITTER **Glades Haven Marina.** Get on the water to explore the Ten Thousand Islands in 16-foot Carolina skiffs and 24-foot pontoon boats. Rates start at $150 a day, with half-day and hourly options. The outfitter also rents kayaks and canoes and has a 24-hour boat ramp and dockage for vessels up to 24 feet long. ⊠ *801 Copeland Ave. S, Everglades City* ☎ *239/695–2628* ⊕ *www.gladeshaven.com*

## WHERE TO EAT

**$$$**
SEAFOOD
✕ **City Seafood.** Owner Richard Wahrenberger serves up gems from the sea delivered fresh from his own boat. Even better, patrons can chow down on the delectable stone crabs—which come in sizes medium, large, jumbo, and colossal based on weight—with a clear conscience. The sustainable dishes are made only with the meaty claws, and the crabs are returned to the water where they grow new ones. Sure you can have lunch or dinner inside this rustic haven, but if you pick outdoor seating you can watch pelicans, gulls, tarpon, manatee, and the occasional gator play off the dock in the Barron River. Relax with a beer or wine by the glass. Appetizers run from deep-fried corn to fried conch and sandwiches from hot dogs to pulled pork. But it's the stone crabs and the plates and baskets of smoked mullet, grouper, shrimp, oysters, blue crab, gator, or frog legs that keep people coming back. Got a cooler? Florida lobster tail, scallops, clams, and gator can be wrapped for the road. City Seafood's market also ships nationwide, and a gift shop sells cutesy crabby-style tanks, boxers and tees. ⊠ *702 Begonia St., Everglades City* ☎ *239/695-4700* ⊕ *www.cityseafood1.com.*

**$$–$$$**
SEAFOOD
✕ **Everglades Seafood Depot.** Count on an affordable, scenic breakfast, lunch, or dinner at this storied 1928 Spanish-style stucco structure fronting Lake Placid. Beginning life as the original Everglades train depot, the building later was deeded to the University of Miami for marine research, and appeared in scenes from the film Winds across the Everglades, before becoming a haven for assorted restaurants through the years. Well-prepared seafood including shrimp, frogs' legs, and alligator—much from local boats—dominates the menu. For big appetites, there are generously portioned entrées of steak and fish specials and combination platters that include warm, fresh-baked biscuits. All-you-can-eat specials, such as fried chicken, a taco bar, or a seafood buffet are staged on selected nights. There's also an all-you-can-eat salad bar. Save room for the coconut guava cake. Ask for a table on the back porch or for a window seat overlooking the lake. Bargain hunters arrive early for the 99¢ breakfast menu specials, served Friday and Saturday 5:30 am–10:30 am. ⊠ *102 Collier Ave.* ☎ *239/695–0075* ⊕ *www. evergladesseafooddepot.com.*

**$**
CUBAN
✕ **Havana Cafe.** Cuban specialties are a tasty change from the shanty seafood houses of Everglades City; brightly painted walls and floral tablecloths make this little eatery with 10 indoor tables and four porch tables a cheerful spot. Service is order-at-the-counter for breakfast and lunch (8 am–3 pm; with dinner on Friday and Saturday nights in season). Jump-start your day with *café con leche* and a pressed-egg sandwich. For lunch, you'll find the ubiquitous Cuban sandwich, burgers, shrimp, grouper, steak, and pork plates with rice and beans and yucca. ⊠ *191 Smallwood Dr., Chocoloskee* ☎ *239/695-2214* ▭ *No credit cards* ☾ *No dinner Apr.–Oct. No dinner Sun.–Thurs. Nov.–Mar.*

13

$$ ✕**Oyster House Restaurant.** One of the town's oldest and most old-
SEAFOOD fashioned fish houses, Oyster serves all the local staples—shrimp,
🕒 gator tail, frogs' legs, oysters, stone crab, and grouper—in a lodgelike
setting where mounted wild game decorates walls and rafters. Shrimp
and grouper smothered in tomatoes are among the few exceptions
to fried preparation. Deep-frying remains an art in these parts, so if
you're going to indulge, do it here. Consider the stone crab soup, in
season, and try to dine at sunset for golden rays with your watery
view. Outside, a 75-foot observation tower affords a terrific view of
the Ten Thousand Islands. ✉ *Hwy. 29 S* ☎ *239/695–2073* ⊕ *www.
oysterhouserestaurant.com.*

$$$ ✕**Rod and Gun Club.** The striking, polished pecky-cypress woodwork
SEAFOOD in this historic building dates from the 1920s when wealthy hunters,
anglers, and yachting parties from around the world arrived for the
winter season. Presidents Hoover, Roosevelt, Truman, Eisenhower,
and Nixon have stopped by here, as have Ernest Hemingway, Burt
Reynolds, and Mick Jagger. The main dining room holds the overflow
from the popular, enormous screened porch overlooking the river.
Like life in general here, friendly servers move slowly and upkeep is
minimal. Fresh seafood dominates, from stone crab claws in season
(October 15–May 15) to a surf-and-turf combo of steak and grouper, a swamp-and-turf combo of frogs' legs and steak, and seafood
and pasta pairings. For $14.95 you can have your own catch fried,
broiled, or blackened, and served with salad, veggies, and potato.
Pie offerings include key lime and chocolate–peanut butter. Be aware
separate checks are discouraged and there's a $5 plate-sharing charge.
Yesteryear's main lobby is well worth a look—even if you plan to eat
elsewhere. Arrive by boat or land. Adjacent cottages with private
baths and air-conditioning run $95 to $140 depending on the season.
✉ *200 Riverside Dr.* ☎ *239/695–2101* ⊕ *www.evergladesrodandgun.
com* ▭ *No credit cards.*

$ ✕**Triad Seafood.** Along the Barron River, seafood houses, fishing boats,
SEAFOOD and crab traps populate one shoreline; mangroves the other. Some of
the seafood houses, selling fresh off the boat, added picnic tables and
eventually grew into restaurants. Family-owned Triad is one, with a
screened dining area seating 44, and additional outdoor seating under
a breezeway and on a deck overhanging the scenic river where you can
savor fresh seafood during stone crab season, October 15 to May 15.
Nothing fancy (although smoked salmon and blue crab salad have been
added to the lineup), but you'd be hard-pressed to find a better grouper sandwich. An all-you-can-eat fresh stone crab jumbo feast will set
you back around $85; or $59.95 for large; $42, medium, with prices
fluctuating. Hours for lunch and dinner vary but lunch starts at 10:30
am with fried shrimp, oyster, crab cake, and soft-shell blue crab baskets, plus Reubens, hamburgers, Philly cheesesteak sandwiches, and,
on Friday, smoked ribs. ✉ *401 School Dr.* ☎ *239/695–0722* ⊕ *www.
triadseafood.com* ◔ *Closed May 16–Oct. 15.*

## SHUTTLES FROM MIAMI

**Airporter.** Shuttle buses run three times daily and stop at the Ramada Inn in Florida City on the way between MIA and the Florida Keys. Shuttle service, which takes about an hour, runs 6:10 am–5:20 pm from Florida City, 7:30 am–6 pm from the airport. Reserve at least 48 hours in advance. Pickups can be arranged for all baggage-claim areas. The cost is $30 one-way. ☎ 800/830–3413

**Super Shuttle.** This 24-hour service runs 11-passenger air-conditioned vans between MIA and the Homestead-Florida City area; pickup is outside baggage claim and costs around $53 per person depending on your destination. For the return to MIA, reserve 24 hours in advance and know your pickup zip code for a price quote. Taxi fare from MIA to Everglades City runs about $115. ☎ 305/871–2000 ⊕ www.supershuttle.com.

**13**

### WHERE TO STAY

*For expanded hotel reviews, visit Fodors.com.*

$     ⊡ **Glades Haven Cozy Cabins.** Bob Miller wanted to build a Holiday Inn
HOTEL   next to his Oyster House Restaurant on marina-channel shores, but
when that didn't fly, he sent for cabin kits and set up mobile-home-size units around a pool on his property. **Pros:** good food options; convenient to ENP boating; free docking; marina. **Cons:** crowded trailer-park feel; no phones. ⊠ *801 Copeland Ave.* ☎ *239/695–2746 or 888/956–6251* ⊕ *www.gladeshaven.com* ↬ *24 cabins, 4 3-bedroom houses* ⌂ *In-room: a/c, kitchen (some). In-hotel: restaurants, pool, laundry facilities* ⦿ *No meals.*

$$$   ⊡ **Ivey House.** A remodeled 1928 boardinghouse originally for work-
B&B/INN   ers building the Tamiami Trail, Ivey House today fits many budgets.
Fodor's Choice   **Pros:** canoe and kayak rentals and tours; pleasant; affordable. **Cons:**
★   not on water; some small rooms. ⊠ *107 Camellia St.* ☎ *877/567–0679 or 239/695–3299* ⊕ *www.iveyhouse.com* ↬ *30 rooms, 18 with bath; 1 2-bedroom cottage* ⌂ *In-room: a/c, Internet, Wi-Fi (some). In-hotel: pool, laundry facilities* ⦿ *Breakfast.*

## FLORIDA CITY

*3 mi southwest of Homestead on U.S. 1.*

Florida's Turnpike ends in Florida City, the southernmost town on the peninsula, spilling thousands of vehicles onto U.S. 1 and eventually west to Everglades National Park, east to Biscayne National Park, or south to the Florida Keys. Florida City and Homestead run into each other, but the difference couldn't be more noticeable. As the last outpost before 18 mi of mangroves and water, this stretch of U.S. 1 is lined with fast-food eateries, service stations, hotels, bars, dive shops, and restaurants. Hotel rates increase significantly during NASCAR races at the nearby Homestead Miami Speedway. Like Homestead, Florida City is rooted in agriculture, with hundreds of acres of farmland west of Krome Avenue and a huge farmers' market that processes produce shipped nationwide.

## VISITOR INFORMATION

**Tropical Everglades Visitor Center** (✉ *160 U.S. 1* ☎ *305/245–9180 or 800/388–9669* ⊕ *www.tropicaleverglades.com*).

## SHOPPING

☾ **Robert Is Here.** This remarkable fruit stand sells vegetables, fresh-fruit
★ milk shakes (try the key lime shake), 10 flavors of honey, more than 100 types of jams and jellies, fresh juices, salad dressings, and some 30 kinds of tropical fruits, including (in season) carambola, lychee, egg fruit, monstera, sapodilla, dragonfruit, genipa, sugar apple, and tamarind. The stand started in 1960, when seven-year-old Robert sat at this spot selling his father's bumper crop of cucumbers. Today, Robert (still on the scene daily with his wife and kids), ships all over the United States and donates seconds to needy area families. An odd assortment of animals out back—from goats to emus—adds entertainment value for kids. Picnic tables, benches, and a waterfall with a koi pond add some serenity to the experience. The stand, on the way to Everglades National Park, opens at 8 am and stays open until at least 7. It shuts down between September and October. ✉ *19200 S.W. 344th St.* ☎ *305/246–1592*.

## WHERE TO EAT

$$ ✕ **Capri Restaurant.** Locals have come to this family-owned enterprise for
ITALIAN affordable Italian-American classics since 1958. Interior dining areas have redbrick accent walls with plenty of round tables; the sunny courtyard has umbrella-covered tables. Tasty options range from pizza with a light, crunchy crust and ample toppings to broiled steaks and seafood-pasta classics; spaghetti comes 16 ways. Old Time Capri Favorites, at $12.95, include chop steak with mushroom gravy or sausage and pepper, with either soup or salad. Daily early-bird entrées (4:30–6:30 for $12–$14) include soup or salad and potato or spaghetti. The Tuesday family night (after 4 pm, $6.95) comes with all-you-can-eat pasta and salad or soup. Specialty martinis and fruity cocktails supplement the international wine list. ✉ *935 N. Krome Ave.* ☎ *305/247–1542* ⊕ *www. dinecapri.com* ☯ *No lunch Sun.*

$$ ✕ **Captain's Restaurant and Seafood Market.** A comfortable place where
SEAFOOD the chef prepares seafood with flair, this is among the town's best bets. Locals and visitors alike gather in the cozy dining room or outdoors on the patio. Blackboards describe a varied menu of sandwiches, pasta, seafood, steak, and nightly specials running up to $28.95, plus stone crabs in season. Inventive offerings include a lobster Reuben sandwich, crawfish pasta, and pan-seared tuna topped with balsamic onions and shallots. ✉ *404 S.E. 1st Ave.* ☎ *305/247–9456.*

$ ✕ **Farmers' Market Restaurant.** Although it's in the farmers' market on the
AMERICAN edge of town and serves fresh vegetables, seafood figures prominently
★ on the menu. A family of fishermen runs the place, so fish and shellfish are only hours from the sea, and there's a fish fry on Friday nights. Catering to anglers and farmers, it opens at 5:30 am, serving pancakes, jumbo eggs, and fluffy omelets with home fries or grits in a pleasant dining room with checkered tablecloths. Lunch and dinner menus have fried shrimp, seafood pasta, country-fried steak, roast turkey, and fried

conch, as well as burgers, salads, and sandwiches. ⊠ *300 N. Krome Ave.* ☎ *305/242–0008.*

**$$$**
SEAFOOD
☺

✕ **Mutineer Restaurant.** Families and older couples flock to the quirky yet well-dressed setting of this roadside steak-and-seafood outpost with a fish-and-duck pond and a petting zoo for kids. It was built in 1980 to look like a ship, back when Florida City was barely on the map. Etched glass divides the bi-level dining rooms, with velvet-upholstered chairs, an aquarium, and nautical antiques. Topping the menu of about a dozen seafood entrées is the stuffed grouper, Florida lobster tails, and snapper Oscar, plus another half-dozen daily seafood specials, as well as poultry, ribs, and steaks. Burgers and seafood sandwiches are popular for lunch, as is a happy-hour buffet until 7 pm in the lounge for $2.25 and the purchase of a drink. You also can dine in the restaurant's Wharf Lounge. Most Friday and Saturday nights feature live entertainment and dancing. ⊠ *11 S.E. 1st Ave. (U.S. 1), at Palm Dr.* ☎ *305/245–3377* ⊕ *www.mutineer.biz.*

**¢**
MEXICAN
★

✕ **Rosita's Restaurante.** With its growing Mexican population this area can boast the authenticity that you just don't get in the Tex-Mex chains. Order à la carte specialties or dinners and combos with beans and rice, and salad. A large variety of breakfast, lunch, and dinner entrées are served all day and range from Mexican eggs, enchiladas, and taco salad to stewed beef, shrimp ranchero-style, and fried pork chop. Food is on the spicy side, and if you like more fire, each table is equipped with fresh-tasting salsa, pickled jalapeños, and bottled habanero sauce. Clean (with lingering whiffs of bleach to prove it) and pleasant, with an open kitchen, take-out counter, and Formica tables, it's a favorite with locals and budget-minded guests at the Everglades International Hostel across the street. ⊠ *199 W. Palm Dr.* ☎ *305/246–3114.*

### WHERE TO STAY
*For expanded hotel reviews, visit Fodors.com.*

**$$–$$$**
HOTEL

▥ **Best Western Gateway to the Keys.** If you want easy access to Everglades and Biscayne national parks as well as the Florida Keys, you'll be well-placed at this modern, two-story motel two blocks off Florida's Turnpike. **Pros:** convenient to national parks, outlet shopping, and Keys; business services; pretty pool area. **Cons:** traffic noise; generic rooms; fills up fast during high season. ⊠ *411 S. Krome Ave.* ☎ *305/246–5100 or 888/981–5100* ⊕ *www.bestwestern.com/gatewaytothekeys* ⏎ *114 rooms* ⟡ *In-room: a/c Internet. In-hotel: pool, laundry facilities* †⊚† *Breakfast.*

**$**
HOTEL

▥ **Econo Lodge.** Close to Florida's Turnpike and with access to the Keys, this is a good overnight pullover spot. **Pros:** convenient location; business services; microwaves and refrigerators in rooms. **Cons:** urban-ugly location; noisy. ⊠ *553 N.E. 1st Ave.* ☎ *305/248–9300 or 800/553–2666* ⊕ *www.econolodge.com* ⏎ *42 rooms* ⟡ *In-room: a/c, Internet, Wi-Fi. In-hotel: pool, laundry facilities, business center* †⊚† *Breakfast.*

**¢**
HOTEL

▥ **Everglades International Hostel.** Stay in clean and spacious private or dorm-style rooms (generally six to a room), relax in indoor or outdoor quiet areas, and watch videos or TV on a big screen. **Pros:** affordable; Everglades tours; free services. **Cons:** communal living; no elevator; old structure. ⊠ *20 S.W. 2nd Ave.* ☎ *305/248–1122 or 800/372–3874*

13

⊕ *www.evergladeshostel.com* ↪ *46 beds in dorm-style rooms with shared bath, 2 private rooms with shared bath, 2 suites, tent space* ⚘ *In-room: a/c, no TV. In-hotel: water sports, laundry facilities, business center, some pets allowed* ⦿ *No meals.*

**$**  🏨 **Fairway Inn.** Two stories high with a waterfall pool, this motel has
HOTEL  some of the area's lowest chain rates, and it's next to the Chamber of Commerce visitor center so you'll never be short of reading and planning material. **Pros:** affordable; convenient to restaurants, parks, and raceway. **Cons:** plain, small rooms; no-pet policy. ✉ *100 S.E. 1st Ave.* ☎ *305/248–4202 or 888/340–4734* ↪ *160 rooms* ⚘ *In-room: a/c, Internet, Wi-Fi. In-hotel: pool, laundry facilities* ⦿ *Breakfast.*

**$$**  🏨 **Ramada Inn.** If you're looking for an upgrade from the other chains,
HOTEL  this pet-friendly property offers more amenities and comfort, such as
★  32-inch flat-screen TVs, duvet-covered beds, closed closets, and stylish furnishings. **Pros:** extra room amenities; business clientele perks; convenient location. **Cons:** chain anonymity. ✉ *124 E. Palm Dr.* ☎ *305/247–8833* ⊕ *www.hotelfloridacity.com* ↪ *123 rooms* ⚘ *In-room: a/c, Internet, Wi-Fi. In-hotel: pool* ⦿ *Breakfast.*

**$–$$$**  🏨 **Travelodge.** This bargain motor lodge is close to Florida's Turnpike,
HOTEL  Everglades and Biscayne national parks, the Florida Keys, and the Homestead Miami Speedway. **Pros:** pet-friendly for a $10 per night fee; convenience to U.S. 1; complimentary breakfast. **Cons:** small rooms; busy location. ✉ *409 S.E. 1st Ave.* ☎ *305/248–9777 or 800/758–0618* ⊕ *www.tlflcity.com* ↪ *88 rooms* ⚘ *In-room: a/c, Internet, Wi-Fi. In-hotel: pool, laundry facilities, business center* ⦿ *Breakfast.*

## HOMESTEAD

*30 mi southwest of Miami.*

In recent years Homestead has redefined itself as a destination for tropical agro- and ecotourism. At the juncture between Miami and the Keys as well as Everglades National Park and Biscayne National Park, the area has the added dimension of shopping centers, residential development, hotel chains, and the Homestead-Miami Speedway—when car races are scheduled, hotels hike up their rates and require minimum stays. The historic downtown has become a preservation-driven Main Street. Krome Avenue, where it cuts through the city's heart, is lined with restaurants, an arts complex, antiques shops, and low-budget, sometimes undesirable accommodations. West of north–south Krome Avenue, miles of fields grow fresh fruits and vegetables. Some are harvested commercially, and others beckon with "U-pick" signs. Stands selling farm-fresh produce and nurseries that grow and sell orchids and tropical plants abound. In addition to its agricultural legacy, the town has an eclectic flavor, attributable to its population mix: descendants of pioneer Crackers, Hispanic growers and farm workers, professionals escaping Miami hubbub, and latter-day Northern retirees.

Are baby alligators more to your liking than their daddies? You can pet one at Everglades Gator Park.

## WHAT TO SEE

**Coral Castle.** Driven by unrequited love, 100-pound Latvian immigrant Ed Leedskalnin (1887–1951) built this castle in the early 1900s out of massive slabs of coral rock, a feat he likened to the building of the pyramids. Visitors can learn how he peopled his fantasy world with his imaginary wife and three children, studied astronomy, and created a simple home and elaborate courtyard with no engineering education and tools he mostly fashioned himself. Highlights of this National Register of Historic Places site include the Polaris telescope built to spot the North Star, a working sundial, a 5,000-pound heart-shape table featured in Ripley's *Believe It or Not,* a banquet table in the shape of Florida, and a playground Ed named "Grotto of the Three Bears." ⊠ *28655 S. Dixie Hwy.* ☎ *305/248–6345* ⊕ *www.coralcastle. com* ⊠ *$9.75* ☉ *Daily 8–6.*

## SPORTS AND THE OUTDOORS

### AUTO RACING

**Homestead-Miami Speedway.** Buzzing more than 280 days each year with racing, manufacturer testing, car-club events, driving schools and ride-along programs, this facility with 65,000 grandstand seats, has club seating eight stories above racing action, and two tracks—a 2.21-mi continuous road course and a 1.5-mi oval. A packed schedule includes GRAND-AM and NASCAR events. ⊠ *1 Speedway Blvd.* ☎ *866/409– 7223* ⊕ *www.homesteadmiamispeedway.com.*

## WATER SPORTS

**Homestead Bayfront Park.** Boaters, anglers, and beachgoers give high ratings to the facilities at this recreational area adjacent to Biscayne National Park. The 174-slip marina has a ramp, dock, bait-and-tackle shop, fuel station, ice, and dry storage. The facility can handle vessels up to 50 feet long. The park also has a tidal swimming area, a beach with lifeguards, a playground, ramps for people with disabilities (including a ramp that leads into the swimming area), and a picnic pavilion with grills, showers, and restrooms. ⊠ *9698 S.W. 328th St.* ☎ *305/230–3033* 🖅 *$6 per passenger vehicle; $12 per vehicle with boat Mon.–Thurs., $15 Fri.–Sun.; $15 per RV or bus* ☉ *Daily sunrise–sunset.*

## WHERE TO EAT

¢  ✕ **Bobbie Jo's Diner.** Head to Bobbie Jo's with the locals for good, old, Southern-style home cooking. Burgers, sandwiches, and dinners—including chicken livers, chicken and dumplings, and fried clams—come with fresh-baked corn bread and a daily selection of sides such as okra with tomatoes, turnip greens, pickled beets, or onion rings. The Bobbie Jo burger comes with fries for under five bucks. Don't miss out on the changing selection of homemade soups and desserts. All this goodness comes cheap, but at the expense of anything-but-glamorous dining environs and often slow service. ⊠ *1320 N. Krome Ave.* ☎ *305/246–2990* ☉ *No dinner Sun.*

SOUTHERN

¢  ✕ **NicaMex.** Among the local Latin population this 68-seat eatery is a low-budget favorite for Nicaraguan and Mexican flavors. It helps if you speak Spanish, but usually some staffers on hand speak English, and the menu is bilingual. Although they term it *comidas rapidas* (fast food), the cuisine is not Americanized. You can get authentic huevos rancheros or *chilaquiles* (corn tortillas cooked in red-pepper sauce) for breakfast, and specialties such as *chicharron en salsa verde* (fried pork skin in hot-green-tomato sauce) and shrimp in garlic all day. Hearty seafood and beef soups are best sellers. Choose a domestic or imported beer, pop a coin into the Wurlitzer jukebox, select a Latin tune, and escape south of the border. ⊠ *32 N.W. 1st St., across from Krome Ave. bandstand* ☎ *305/247–0727.*

MEXICAN

## WHERE TO STAY

*For expanded hotel reviews, visit Fodors.com.*

$  🏨 **Grove Inn Country Guesthouse.** Away from downtown but close to Homestead's agricultural attractions, Grove Inn offers notably personalized service and lushly landscaped environs. **Pros:** fresh fruit; privacy; delicious breakfast; rural location. **Cons:** far from downtown and national parks; no restaurants nearby; not suited to families. ⊠ *22540 S.W. Krome Ave., 6 mi north of downtown* ☎ *305/247–6572 or 877/247–6572* ⊕ *www.groveinn.com* 🛏 *13 rooms, 1 2-bedroom suite, 1 cottage* ♿ *In-room: a/c, kitchen (some), Wi-Fi. In-hotel: pool, laundry facilities, some pets allowed* ⊠⊙ *Breakfast.*

B&B/INN
★

$–$$  🏨 **Redland Hotel.** Of downtown Homestead's smattering of mom-and-pop lodging options, this historic inn is the most desirable with its Victorian-style rooms decorated in pastels and reproduction antique furniture. **Pros:** historic character; convenient to downtown; well

HOTEL
★

maintained; smoke free. **Cons:** traffic noise; some small rooms; ugly street location. ⊠ *5 S. Flagler Ave.* ☎ *305/246–1904 or 800/595–1904* ⊕ *www.redlandhotel.com* 🛏 *13 rooms* ⚖ *In-room: a/c, Internet, Wi-Fi. In-hotel: bar* ⦿ *No meals.*

## TAMIAMI TRAIL

An 80-mi stretch of U.S. 41 (known as the Tamiami Trail) traverses the Everglades, Big Cypress National Preserve, and Fakahatchee Strand Preserve State Park. The road was conceived in 1915 to link Miami to Fort Myers and Tampa. When it finally became a reality in 1928, it cut through the Everglades and altered the natural flow of water and lives of the Miccosukee Indians, who were trying to eke out a living fishing, hunting, farming, and frogging here. The landscape is surprisingly varied, changing from hardwood hammocks to pinelands, then abruptly to tall cypress trees dripping with Spanish moss and back to saw grass marsh. Slow down to take in the scenery and you'll likely be rewarded with glimpses of alligators sunning themselves along the banks of roadside canals or in the shallow waters, and hundreds of waterbirds, especially in the dry winter season. The man-made landscape has American Indian villages, chickee huts, and airboats parked at roadside enterprises. Between Miami and Naples the road goes by several names, including Tamiami Trail, U.S. 41, 9th Street in Naples, and, at the Miami end, S.W. 8th Street. ■TIP→ Businesses along the trail give their addresses either based on their distance from Krome Avenue, Florida's Turnpike, and Miami on the east coast or Naples on the west coast.

### WHAT TO SEE

🖙 **Everglades Gator Park.** Here you can get face-to-face with and even touch an alligator—albeit a baby one—during the park's exciting Wildlife Show. You also can squirm in a "reptilium" of venomous and nonpoisonous native snakes or learn about American Indians of the Everglades through a reproduction of a Miccosukee village. The park also has 35-minute airboat tours and RV campsites ($30 per night), as well as a gift shop and restaurant serving fare from burgers to gator tail. ⊠ *24050 Tamiami Trail, 12 mi west of Florida's Turnpike, Miami* ☎ *305/559–2255 or 800/559–2205* ⊕ *www.gatorpark.com* 🛥 *Tours, wildlife show, and park $22.95; show and park $10* ⊙ *Daily 9–5.*

**Everglades Safari Park.** A perennial favorite with tour-bus operators, the park has an arena, seating up to 300, for an alligator show and wrestling demonstration. Before and after the show, get a closer look

---

**CROCS OR GATORS?**

You can tell you're looking at a crocodile, not an alligator, if you can see its lower teeth protruding when its jaws are shut. Gators are much darker in color—a grayish black—compared with the lighter tan color of crocodiles. Alligator snouts—sort of U-shape—are also much broader than their long, thin A-shape crocodilian counterparts. South Florida is the world's only place where both coexist. Alligators are primarily found in freshwater habitats, while crocodiles (better at expelling salt from water) are typically in coastal estuaries.

**13**

at both alligators and crocodiles on Gator Island; walk through a small wildlife museum, follow the jungle trail, or climb aboard an airboat for a 40-minute ride on the River of Grass (included in admission). There's also a restaurant, gift shop, and an observation platform looking out over the Glades. Smaller, private airboats are available for an extra charge for tours lasting 40 minutes to 2 hours. ⊠ *26700 Tamiami Trail, 15 mi west of Florida's Turnpike, Miami* ☎ *305/226–6923 or 305/223–3804* ⊕ *www.evsafaripark.com* 🖙 *$23* ⊙ *Daily 9–5, last tour departs 3:30.*

ℭ **Miccosukee Indian Village and Gift Shop.** Showcasing the culture, skills,
★ and lifestyle of the Miccosukee Tribe of Florida, this cultural center offers crafts demonstrations and insight into the interactions between alligators and the American Indians. Narrated 30-minute airboat rides take you into the wilderness where these American Indians hid after the Seminole Wars and Indian Removal Act of the mid-1800s. In modern times many of the Miccosukee have relocated to this village along Tamiami Trail, but most still maintain their hammock farming and hunting camps. The village museum shows a film and displays chickee structures and artifacts. Guided tours run throughout the day, and a gift shop stocks dolls, apparel for adults and children, silver jewelry, beadwork, and other handcrafted items. The Miccosukee Everglades Music and Craft Festival falls on a July weekend, and the 10-day Miccosukee Indian Arts Festival is in late December. ⊠ *Just west of Shark Valley entrance on U.S. 41/Tamiami Trail, 25 mi west of Florida's Turnpike at MM 70, Miami* ☎ *305/552–8365* ⊕ *www.miccosukee.com* 🖙 *Village $8, airboat rides $10* ⊙ *Daily 9–5.*

## SPORTS AND THE OUTDOORS

### BOAT TOURS

Many Everglades-area tours operate only in season, roughly November through April.

**Coopertown Airboats.** Running since 1945, this is the oldest airboat operator in the Everglades. The 35- to 40-minute tour ($21) takes you 9 mi to hammocks and alligator holes. Private charters of up to two hours are also available. ⊠ *11 mi west of Florida's Turnpike, on Tamiami Trail* ☎ *305/226–6048* ⊕ *www.coopertownairboats.com.*

**Everglades Alligator Farm.** Southwest of Florida City near the entrance to Everglades National Park, this outfit runs a 4-mi, 30-minute airboat tour of the River of Grass with departures 20 minutes after the hour. The tour ($23) includes free hourly alligator, snake, and wildlife shows, or see the 2,000-strong gator farm and shows only ($15.50). ⊠ *40351 S.W. 192nd Ave.* ☎ *305/247–2628* ⊕ *www.everglades.com.*

**Everglades Safari Park.** Try a 40-minute eco-adventure airboat ride for $23 or smaller, private airboat tours for an extra charge, lasting from 40 minutes to 2 hours. The price includes the alligator show, natural-museum admission, and walking-trail access. ⊠ *26700 S.W. 8th St., 15 mi west of Florida's Turnpike, on Tamiami Trail* ☎ *305/226–6923 or 305/223–3804* ⊕ *www.evsafaripark.com.*

**Gator Park Airboat Tours.** Forty-five minute narrated airboat tours ($22.95) include a park tour and wildlife show. ⊠ *12 mi west of*

*Florida's Turnpike, on Tamiami Trail* ☎305/559–2255 *or* 800/559–2205 ⊕ *www.gatorpark.com.*

**Wooten's Everglades Airboat Tour.** A classic Florida roadside attraction runs airboat tours through the Everglades and swamp-buggy tours through the Big Cypress Swamp lasting approximately 30 minutes each (swamp buggies are giant tractorlike vehicles with oversize rubber wheels). More personalized airboat tours on smaller boats (seating six to eight) are also available for 45 minutes to one hour and start at $37.10. The on-site animal sanctuary offers the typical Everglades array of alligators, snakes, panthers, and other creatures. Discounts are available online. ⊠ *Wooten's Alligator Farm, 1½ mi east of Rte. 29 on Tamiami Trail, Ochopee* ☎239/695–2781 *or* 800/282–2781 ⊕ *www.wootensairboats.com* ⬚ *$25 for ½-hr tour, $8 for animal exhibits; $59.36 combo ticket for all attractions* ☉ *Daily 8:30–5; last ride departs at 4:30.*

## SHOPPING

**Miccosukee Indian Village.** Wares include American Indian crafts such as beadwork, moccasins, dolls, pottery, baskets, and patchwork fabric and clothing. ⊠ *Just west of Shark Valley entrance, 25 mi west of Florida's Turnpike at MM 70* ☎305/223–8380.

## WHERE TO EAT

$
ECLECTIC
✕**Coopertown Restaurant.** Make this a pit stop for local color and cuisine fished straight from the swamp. Starting a half century ago as a sandwich stand, this small casual eatery inside an airboat concession storefront has attracted the famous and the humbly hungry. House specialties are frogs' legs and alligator tail breaded in cornmeal and deep-fried, casually served on paper ware with a lemon wedge and Tabasco. More conventional options include catfish, shrimp, burgers, hot dogs, or grilled cheese sandwiches. ⊠ *22700 S.W. 8th St., 11 mi west of Florida's Turnpike, on Tamiami Trail, Miami* ☎305/226–6048 ⊕ *www.coopertownairboats.com.*

$
SOUTHWESTERN
★
✕**Miccosukee Restaurant.** For a taste of culture at breakfast or lunch (or dinner until 9 November–April), this roadside cafeteria a quarter mile from the Miccosukee Indian Village and overlooking the River of Grass, provides the best variety of food along Tamiami Trail in Everglades territory where you won't find all that much choice. Atmosphere comes from the River of Grass view, servers wearing traditional Miccosukee patchwork vests, and a mural depicting American Indian women cooking and men engaged in a powwow. Catfish and frogs' legs are breaded and deep-fried. Other favorites include Indian fry bread and pumpkin bread, but you'll also find burgers, salads, and dishes from south of the border. The Miccosukee Platter ($24.95) offers a sampling of local favorites, including gator bites. Gator Nuggets (slightly larger than gator bites) are $2.25 each. ⊠ *U.S. 41 (Tamiami Trail), 18 mi west of Miccosukee Resort and Gaming; 25 mi west of Florida's Turnpike* ☎305/894–2374.

$
SOUTHERN
✕**Pit Bar-B-Q.** At the edge of Miami, this old-fashioned roadside eatery along Tamiami Trail near Krome Avenue was launched in 1965 by the late Tommy Little, who wanted anyone heading into or out

13

of the Everglades to have access to cold drinks and rib-sticking fare. His vision remains a holdout from the Everglades' backwoods heritage and a popular, affordable option for families. Order at the counter, pick up your food, and eat at one of the picnic tables on the screened porch or outdoors. Specialties include barbecued chicken and ribs with a tangy sauce, fries, coleslaw, and a fried biscuit, plus burgers and fish sandwiches. The whopping double-decker beef or pork sandwich with slaw requires at least five napkins. Latin specialties include deep-fried pork and fried green plantains. Beer is by the bottle or pitcher. Locals flock here with kids on weekends for pony rides. ⊠ *16400 Tamiami Trail, 5 mi west of Florida's Turnpike, Miami* ☎ *305/226–2272* ⊕ *www.thepitbarbq.com.*

## WHERE TO STAY

*For expanded hotel reviews, visit Fodors.com.*

**$$$**
RESORT
⬚ **Miccosukee Resort & Gaming.** Like an oasis on the horizon of endless sawgrass, this nine-story resort at the southeastern edge of the Everglades can't help but attract your attention, even if you're not on the lookout for 24-hour gaming action. **Pros:** casino; most modern resort in these parts; golf. **Cons:** cigarette odor in lobby; parking lot fills with gamblers; feels incompatible with the Everglades. ⊠ *500 S. W. 177th Ave., 6 mi west of Florida's Turnpike, Miami* ☎ *305/925–2555 or 877/242–6464* ⊕ *www.miccosukee.com* ⬚ *256 rooms, 46 suites* ⬚ *Inroom: a/c, Wi-Fi. In-hotel: restaurants, bars, golf course, pool, gym, spa, children's programs, business center, parking* ⦿⦿ *No meals.*

# The Florida Keys

**WORD OF MOUTH**

"The Keys are definitely a get out on the water type place instead of a driving up and down U.S. 1 kind of place. Bars and restaurants open early and close early. Get out over the water. That is where the most amazing things in the keys are."

—GoTravel

# WELCOME TO THE FLORIDA KEYS

## TOP REASONS TO GO

★ **John Pennekamp Coral Reef State Park:** A perfect introduction to the Florida Keys, this nature reserve offers snorkeling, diving, camping, and kayaking. An underwater highlight is the massive Christ of the Deep statue.

★ **Under the Sea:** Whether you scuba, snorkel, or ride a glass-bottom boat, don't miss gazing at the coral reef and its colorful denizens.

★ **Sunset at Mallory Square:** Sure it's touristy, but just once while you're here you've got to witness the circus-like atmosphere of this nightly event.

★ **Duval Crawl:** Shop, eat, drink, repeat. Key West's Duval Street and the nearby streets make a good day's worth of window-shopping and people-watching.

★ **Get on the Water:** From angling for trophy-size fish to zipping out to the Dry Tortugas, a boat trip is in your future. It's really the whole point of the Keys.

**1 The Upper Keys.** As the doorstep to the islands' coral reefs and blithe spirit, the Upper Keys introduce all that is sporting and sea-oriented about the Keys. They stretch from Key Largo to the Long Key Channel (MM 106–65).

**2 The Middle Keys.** Centered around the town of Marathon, the Middle Keys hold most of the chain's historic and natural attractions outside of Key West. They go from Conch (pronounced *konk*) Key through Marathon to the south side of the Seven Mile Bridge, including Pigeon Key (MM 65–40).

**3 The Lower Keys.** Pressure drops another notch in this laid-back part of the region, where wildlife and the fishing lifestyle peak. The Lower Keys go from Little Duck Key south through Big Coppitt Key (MM 40–9).

```
0              10 mi
0              10 km
```

Gulf o

National Deer Ref

**3 THE LOWER KEYS**

Big Torch Key
Little Torch Key
No Name Key
Cudjoe Key
Mud Keys
Saddlebunch Keys
Sugarloaf Key
Summerland Key
Ramrod Key
Big Pine Key
Key West
Big Coppitt Key
Boca Chica Key
Stock Island

**Key West**
Key West International Airport

**4 Key West.** The ultimate in Florida Keys craziness, the party town Key West isn't the place for those seeking a quiet retreat. The Key West area encompasses MM 9–0.

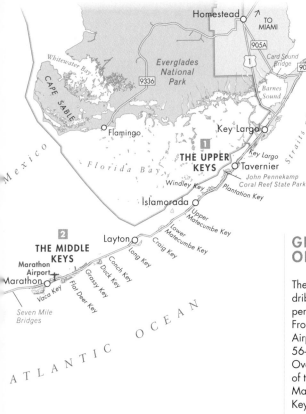

**14**

Homestead
TO MIAMI
905A
Card Sound Bridge
905
1
Everglades National Park
9336
Barnes Sound
Whitewater Bay
CAPE SABLE
Flamingo
Key Largo
Straits of Florida
Florida Bay
Key Largo
**THE UPPER KEYS**
Tavernier
John Pennekamp Coral Reef State Park
Windley Key
Plantation Key
Islamorada
Upper Matecumbe Key
Lower Matecumbe Key
2
Layton
Craig Key
**THE MIDDLE KEYS**
Long Key
Marathon Airport
Conch Key
Duck Key
Marathon
Grassy Key
Vaca Key
Flat Deer Key
Seven Mile Bridges
ATLANTIC OCEAN

## GETTING ORIENTED

The Florida Keys are the dribble of islands off the peninsula's southern tip. From Miami International Airport, Key Largo is a 56-mi drive along the Overseas Highway. The rest of the keys—Islamorada, Marathon, Bahia Honda Key, Big Pine Key—fall in succession for the 106 mi between Key Largo and Key West. At their north end, the Florida Keys front Florida Bay, part of Everglades National Park. The Middle and Lower Keys front the Gulf of Mexico; the Atlantic Ocean borders the length of the chain on its eastern shores.

# THE FLORIDA KEYS BEACHES

Because the Bahamas steal the Keys' offshore sand, the region has fewer natural beaches than one might expect. But the ones it does have are award-winning, specifically those at Bahia Honda State Park.

Also, just because a beach is not natural, doesn't mean it should be overlooked. Some of the Keys' public man-made beaches provide solid recreation and sunning options for visitors looking to work on their tan. Many resorts provide their own private beachfronts.

The Keys may not have a surplus of beaches, but a surplus of camping makes that one of many ways to enjoy nature while on the beach. Another is keeping an eye out for sea turtles. April through October female sea turtles lay their eggs into the sand for a nearly two-month period of nesting.

■ TIP→ Don't let pests ruin your day at the beach. To avoid the stings of sea lice, remove your swimsuit and shower thoroughly upon exiting the water. Sand fleas (aka no-see-ums) are tiny insects with big teeth that are most likely to attack in the morning and around sunset.

## BIRD-WATCHING ON THE BEACH

The Florida Keys beaches can be great places to look to the skies and waters for all varieties of birds. Permanent residents include shorebirds—plovers, ruddy turnstones, willets, and short-billed dowitchers; wading birds—roseate spoonbills, great blue herons, great white egrets, snowy egrets, tri-colored herons, and white ibis; brown pelicans; osprey; and turkey vultures. In the autumn, hawks migrate through the region, while in winter ducks and white pelicans make their debut. In the summer, white-crowned pigeons are commonly seen.

## FLORIDA KEYS' BEST BEACHES

### BAHIA HONDA STATE PARK

This state park at MM 37 holds three beaches, all of different character. Sandspur Beach is the most removed from crowds with long stretches of powdery sands and a campground. Loggerhead Beach is closer to the park's concession area, where you can rent snorkel equipment and kayaks. Like Sandspur, it faces the Atlantic Ocean, but waves are typically wimpy. Near Loggerhead, Calusa Beach on the gulf side near the marina is popular with families, offering a small and safe swimming venue and picnic facilities, as well as camping.

### HIGGS BEACH, KEY WEST

Situated on Atlantic Boulevard, this is as urban as beaches in the Keys get, with lots of amenities, activities, and distractions. Visitors can check out a historic site, eat at a popular beachfront Italian restaurant, rent a kayak, play volleyball, tennis, or at the playground—and all within walking distance of the long sweep of man-made beach and sparkling clear, shallow, and calm water.

### LONG KEY STATE PARK

The beach at Long Key State Park at MM 67.5 is typical of Middle Key's beaches, which are more like sand flats where low tide reveals the coral bedrock of the ecosystem. Here you can snorkel or fish (bonefishing is quite popular)

14

during the day and then be lulled to sleep by the sound of gentle sea waves if you spend the night camping. (The beach is accessible only to campers.)

### SOMBRERO BEACH

Something of a local hangout—especially on weekends, when it can get crowded—Sombrero Beach in Marathon is worth getting off the beaten Overseas Highway path for (exit at MM 50 onto Sombrero Beach Road). Families will find much to do on the man-made coved beach and its grassy green, manicured lawn, and in its playground area and clear calm waters. Separate sections also accommodate boaters and windsurfers.

### ZACHARY TAYLOR HISTORIC STATE PARK

This man-made beach is part of a Civil War–era fort complex at the end of Southard Street and is arguably the best beach in Key West with its typically small waves, swaying Australian pines, water-sports rentals, and shaded picnic grounds. It also hosts, from mid-January through mid-April, an alfresco collection of oversized art called Sculpture Key West, which changes annually and showcases artists from across the country.

Updated by
Chelle Koster
Walton

Being a Conch is a condition of the heart, and foreclosure on the soul. Many throughout the Florida Keys wear that label proudly, yet there's anything but a shared lifestyle here.

To the south, Key West has a Mardi Gras mood with Fantasy Festivals, Hemingway look-alike contests, and the occasional threat to secede from the Union. It's an island whose melting-pot character allows crusty natives to mingle (more or less peacefully) with eccentrics and escape artists who lovingly call this 4-mi sandbar "Paradise." Although life elsewhere in the island chain isn't quite as offbeat, it's nearly as diverse. Flowering jungles, shimmering seas, and mangrove-lined islands are also, conversely, overburdened. Key Largo, nearest the mainland, is becoming more congested as it evolves into a bedroom community and weekend hideaway for residents of Miami and Fort Lauderdale.

A river of tourist traffic gushes along Overseas Highway, the 110-mi artery linking the inhabited islands. Take pleasure, nonetheless, as you cruise down Overseas Highway along the islands. Gaze over the silvery blue-and-green Atlantic and its still-living reef, with Florida Bay, the Gulf of Mexico, and the backcountry on your right (the Keys extend southwest from the mainland). At a few points the ocean and gulf are as much as 10 mi apart; in most places, however, they are from 1 to 4 mi apart, and on the narrowest landfill islands they are separated only by the road. Try to get off the highway. Once you do, rent a boat, anchor, and then fish, swim, or marvel at the sun, sea, and sky. In the Atlantic, dive spectacular coral reefs or pursue grouper, blue marlin, dolphinfish, and other deepwater game fish. Along Florida Bay's coastline, kayak and canoe to secluded islands and bays or seek out the bonefish, snapper, snook, and tarpon that lurk in the grass flats and in the shallow, winding channels of the backcountry.

# THE FLORIDA KEYS PLANNER

## WHEN TO GO

High season in the Keys falls between Christmas and Easter. November to mid-December crowds are thinner, the weather is wonderful, and hotels and shops drastically reduce their prices. Summer, which is hot and humid, is becoming a second high season, especially among Floridians, families, and European travelers. If you plan to attend the wild Fantasy Fest in October, book your room at least six months in advance. Accommodations are also scarce during the last consecutive Wednesday and Thursday in July (lobster sport season) and starting the first weekend in August, when the commercial lobster season begins.

Winter is typically 10°F warmer than on the mainland; summer is usually a few degrees cooler. The Keys also get substantially less rain, around 40 inches annually, compared with an average 55–60 inches in Miami and the Everglades. Most rainfalls are quick downpours on summer afternoons, except in June through October, when tropical storms can dump rain for two or more days. Winter cold fronts occasionally stall over the Keys, dragging overnight temperatures down to the low 50s.

## GETTING HERE AND AROUND

About 450,000 passengers use the **Key West International Airport (EYW)** each year. In 2009, the airport completed its four-year renovation, which includes a beach where travelers can catch their last blast of rays after clearing security. Because flights are few, many prefer flying into Miami International Airport (MIA) and driving the 110-mi Overseas Highway (aka U.S. 1).

By car, from Miami International Airport, follow signs to Coral Gables and Key West, which puts you on LeJeune Road, then Route 836 west. Take the Homestead Extension of Florida's Turnpike south (toll road), which ends at Florida City and connects to the Overseas Highway (U.S. 1, currently under construction so expect delays). Tolls from the airport run approximately $3. Payment is collected via **SunPass**, a prepaid toll program, or with **Toll-By-Plate**, a system that photographs each vehicle's license plate and mails a monthly bill for tolls, plus a $2.50 administrative fee, to the vehicle's registered owner. Vacationers traveling in their own cars can obtain a mini-SunPass sticker via mail before their trips for $4.99 and receive the cost back in toll credits and discounts. The pass also is available at many major Florida retailers and turnpike service plazas. It works on all Florida toll roads and many bridges. For details on purchasing a mini-SunPass, call or visit the Web site. For visitors renting cars in Florida, most major rental companies have programs allowing customers to use the Toll-By-Plate system. Tolls, plus varying service fees, are automatically charged to the credit card used to rent the vehicle. For details, including pricing options at participating rental-car agencies, check the program Web site. Under no circumstances should motorists attempt to stop in high-speed electronic

14

tolling lanes. Travelers can contact Florida's Turnpike Enterprise for more information about the all-electronic tolling on Florida's Turnpike.

The alternative from Florida City is Card Sound Road (Route 905A), which has a bridge toll of $1. Continue to the only stop sign and turn right on Route 905, which rejoins Overseas Highway 31 mi south of Florida City. The best Keys road map, published by the Homestead–Florida City Chamber of Commerce, can be obtained for $5.50 from the **Tropical Everglades Visitor Center.**

Those unwilling to tackle the route's 42 bridges and peak-time traffic can take **Greyhound's** Keys Shuttle, which has multiple daily departures from Miami International Airport.

Boaters can travel to and along the Keys either along the Intracoastal Waterway through Card, Barnes, and Blackwater sounds and into Florida Bay or along the deeper Atlantic Ocean route through Hawk Channel. The Keys are full of marinas that welcome transient visitors, but there aren't enough slips for all the boats heading to these waters. Make reservations far in advance and ask about channel and dockage depth—many marinas are quite shallow.

### ESSENTIALS

**Airport Information Key West International Airport (EYW)** (☎ 305/296–5439 ⊕ www.keywestinternationalairport.com).

**Bus Information Greyhound** (☎ 800/231–2222 ⊕ www.greyhound.com).

**Car Information Florida's Turnpike Enterprise** (☎ 800/749–7453 ⊕ www. FloridasTurnpike.com/all-electronictolling). **SunPass** (☎ 888/865–5352 ⊕ www. sunpass.com). **TOLL-BY-PLATE** (⊕ www.sunpass.com/rentalcar).

**Visitor Information Tropical Everglades Visitor Center** (☎ 305/245–9180 or 800/388–9669 ⊕ www.tropicaleverglades.com).

## ABOUT THE RESTAURANTS

Seafood rules on the Keys, which is full of chef-owned restaurants with not-too-fancy food. Things get more exotic once you reach Key West. Restaurants serve cuisine that reflects the proximity of the Bahamas and Caribbean. Tropical fruits figure prominently—especially on the beverage side of the menu. Florida spiny lobster should be local and fresh from August to March, and stone crabs from mid-October to mid-May. And don't dare leave the islands without sampling conch, be it in a fritter or in ceviche. Keep an eye out for authentic key lime pie—yellow custard in a graham-cracker crust. If it's green, just say "no." Note: Particularly in Key West and particularly during spring break, the more affordable and casual restaurants can get loud and downright rowdy, with young visitors often more interested in drinking than eating. Live music contributes to the decibel levels. If you're more of the quiet, intimate dining type, avoid such overly exuberant scenes by eating early or choosing a restaurant where the bar is not the main focus.

## ABOUT THE HOTELS

Throughout the Keys, the types of accommodations are remarkably varied, from '50s-style motels to cozy inns to luxurious resorts. Most are on or near the ocean, so water sports are popular. Key West's lodging portfolio includes historic cottages, restored Conch houses, and large resorts. Some larger properties throughout the Keys charge a mandatory daily resort fee of $15 or more, which can cover equipment rental, fitness-center use, and other services, plus expect another 12.5% (or more) sales/resort tax. Some guesthouses and inns do not welcome children, and many do not permit smoking.

| WHAT IT COSTS | | | | | |
|---|---|---|---|---|---|
| | ¢ | $ | $$ | $$$ | $$$$ |
| Restaurants | under $10 | $10–$15 | $15–$20 | $20–$30 | over $30 |
| Hotels | under $80 | $80–$100 | $100–$140 | $140–$220 | over $220 |

Restaurant prices are per person for a main course at dinner. Hotel prices are for a standard double room, excluding 12.5% sales tax (or more) in sales and resort taxes.

**14**

## THE MILE MARKER SYSTEM

Getting lost in the Keys is almost impossible once you understand the unique address system. **Many addresses are simply given as a mile marker (MM) number.** The markers are small, green, rectangular signs along the side of the Overseas Highway (U.S. 1). They begin with MM 126, 1 mi south of Florida City, and end with MM 0, in Key West. **Keys residents use the abbreviation BS for the bay side of Overseas Highway and OS for the ocean side.** From Marathon to Key West, residents may refer to the bay side as the gulf side.

## THE UPPER KEYS

Diving and snorkeling rule in the Upper Keys, thanks to the tropical coral reef that runs a few miles off the seaward coast. Divers of all skill levels benefit from accessible dive sites and an established tourism infrastructure. Fishing is another huge draw, especially around Islamorada, known for its sportfishing in both deep offshore waters and in the backcountry. Offshore islands accessible only by boat are popular destinations for kayakers. In short, if you don't like the water you might get bored here.

Other nature lovers won't feel shortchanged. Within 1½ mi of the bay coast lie the mangrove trees and sandy shores of Everglades National Park, to where naturalists lead tours of one of the world's few saltwater forests. Here you'll see endangered manatees, curious dolphins, and other underwater creatures. Although the number of birds has dwindled since John James Audubon captured their beauty on canvas, the rare Everglade snail kite, bald eagles, ospreys, and a colorful array of egrets and herons delight bird-watchers. At sunset flocks take to the skies as

## GREAT ITINERARIES

### 3 DAYS

Spend your first morning diving or snorkeling at John Pennekamp Coral Reef State Park in Key Largo. If you aren't certified, sign up for a resort course and you'll be exploring the reefs by the afternoon. Dinner at a bay-side restaurant will give you your first look at a fabulous Keys sunset. On Day 2 get an early start to savor the breathtaking views on the two-hour drive to Key West. Along the way make a stop at the natural-history museum that's part of Crane Point Museum, Nature Center and Historic Site in Marathon. Another worthwhile detour is Bahia Honda Key State Park on Bahia Honda Key, where you can stretch your legs on a forest trail or snorkel on an offshore reef. Once you arrive in Key West, watch the sunset at one of the island's restaurants. The next day, take a trolley tour of Old Town, stroll Duval Street, visit a museum or two, and spend some beach time at Fort Zachary Taylor State Park.

### 7 DAYS

Spend your first three days as you would in the above itinerary, but spend both the second and third nights in Islamorada. In the morning catch a boat or rent a kayak to paddle to Lignumvitae Key Botanical State Park before making the one-hour drive to Marathon. Visit Crane Point Museum, Nature Center and Historic Site and walk out on the Old Seven Mile Bridge or take the ferry to Pigeon Key. The next stop is just 10 mi away at Bahia Honda State Park on Bahia Honda Key. Take a walk on a wilderness trail, go snorkeling around the offshore reef, or wriggle your toes in the beach's soft sand. Spend the night in a waterfront cabin, letting the waves lull you to sleep. Your sixth day starts with either a half day of fabulous snorkeling or diving at Looe Key Reef or a visit to the National Key Deer Refuge on Big Pine Key. Then continue on to Key West, and get in a little sightseeing before watching the sunset.

they gather to find their night's roost, adding a swirl of activity to an otherwise quiet time of day.

The Upper Keys are full of low-key eateries where the owner is also the chef and the food is tasty and never too fussy. The one exception is Islamorada, where you'll find the more upscale restaurants. Restaurants may close for a two- to four-week vacation during the slow season between mid-September and late October.

In the Upper Keys, the accommodations are as varied as they are plentiful. The majority of lodgings are in small waterfront complexes with efficiencies and one- or two-bedroom units. These places offer dockage and often arrange boating, diving, and fishing excursions. There are also larger resorts with every type of activity imaginable and smaller boutique hotels where the attraction is personalized service.

Depending on which way the wind blows and how close the property is to the highway, there may be some noise from Overseas Highway. If this is an annoyance for you, ask for a room as far from the traffic as possible. Some properties require two- or three-day minimum stays during holiday and high-season weekends. Conversely, discounts apply for midweek, weekly, and monthly stays.

### GETTING HERE AND AROUND

Airporter operates scheduled van and bus pick-up service from all Miami International Airport (MIA) baggage areas to wherever you want to go in Key Largo ($50) and Islamorada ($55). Groups of three or more passengers receive discounts. There are three departures daily; reservations are required 48 hours in advance. The SuperShuttle charges about $165 for two passengers for trips from Miami International Airport to the Upper Keys; reservations are required. For a trip to the airport, place your request 24 hours in advance.

### ESSENTIALS

**Transportation Contacts Airporter** (☎ *305/852–3413 or 800/830–3413*). **SuperShuttle** (☎ *305/871–2000 ⊕ www.supershuttle.com*).

14

## KEY LARGO

The first of the Upper Keys reachable by car, 30-mi-long Key Largo is also the largest island in the chain. Key Largo—named Cayo Largo ("Long Key") by the Spanish—makes a great introduction to the region.

The history of Largo is similar to that of the rest of the Keys, with its succession of native people, pirates, wreckers, and developers. The first settlement on Key Largo was named Planter, back in the days of pineapple and later key lime plantations. For a time it was a convenient shipping port, but when the railroad arrived Planter died on the vine. Today three communities—North Key Largo, Key Largo, and Tavernier—make up the whole of Key Largo.

If you've never tried diving, Key Largo is the perfect place to learn. Dozens of companies will be more than happy to show you the ropes. Nobody comes to Key Largo without visiting John Pennekamp Coral Reef State Park, one of the jewels of the state-park system. Also popular is the adjacent Key Largo National Marine Sanctuary, which encompasses about 190 square mi of coral reefs, sea-grass beds, and mangrove estuaries. Both are good for underwater exploration.

Fishing is the other big draw, and world records are broken regularly. There are plenty of charter operations to help you find the big ones and teach you how to hook the elusive bonefish, sometimes known as the ghost fish. On land, restaurants will cook your catch or dish up their own offerings with inimitable style.

Key Largo offers all the conveniences of a major resort town, with most businesses lined up along Overseas Highway (U.S. 1), the four-lane highway that runs down the middle of the island. Cars whiz past at all hours—something to remember when you're booking a room. Most lodgings are on the highway, so you'll want to be as far back as possible.

### GETTING HERE AND AROUND

Key Largo is 56 mi south of Miami International Airport, with the mile markers going from 106 to 91. The island runs northeast–southwest, with Overseas Highway running down the center. If the highway is your only glimpse of the island, you're likely to feel barraged by its tacky commercial side. Make a point of driving Route 905 in North Key Largo and down side streets to the marinas to get a better feel for it.

**ESSENTIALS**

Visitor Information **Key Largo Chamber of Commerce** (⊠ *MM 106 BS, Key Largo* ☎ *305/451–4747 or 800/822–1088* ⊕ *www.keylargochamber.org*).

## EXPLORING

**Dagny Johnson Key Largo Hammock Botanical State Park.** American crocodiles, mangrove cuckoos, white-crowned pigeons, Schaus swallowtail butterflies, mahogany mistletoe, wild cotton, and 100 other rare critters and plants inhabit these 2,400 acres, sandwiched between Crocodile Lake National Wildlife Refuge and Pennekamp Coral Reef State Park. The park is also a user-friendly place to explore the largest remaining stand of the vast West Indian tropical hardwood hammock and mangrove wetland that once covered most of the Keys' upland areas. Interpretive signs describe many of the tropical tree species along a wide 1-mi paved road (2-mi round-trip) that invites walking and biking. There are also more than 6 mi of nature trails accessible to bikes and wheelchairs. Pets are welcome if on a leash no longer than 6 feet. You'll also find restrooms, information kiosks, and picnic tables. ⊠ *0.5 mi north of Overseas Hwy. on Rte. 905 OS, North Key Largo* ☎ *305/451–1202* ⊕ *www.floridastateparks.org/keylargohammock* ☞ *$2.50* ☾ *Daily 8–sundown.*

**Dolphin Cove.** This educational program begins at the facility's lagoon with a get-acquainted session from a platform. After that, you slip into the water for some frolicking with your new dolphin pals. The cost is $135 to $185. Spend the day shadowing a dolphin trainer for $630. Admission for nonparticipants is $10 for adults. ⊠ *MM 101.9 BS, 101900 Overseas Hwy., Key Largo* ☎ *305/451–4060 or 877/365–2683* ⊕ *www.dolphinscove.com.*

**Dolphins Plus.** A sister property to Dolphin Cove, Dolphin Plus offers some of the same programs. Costing $135, the Natural Swim program begins with a one-hour briefing; then you enter the water to become totally immersed in the dolphins' world. In this visual orientation, participants snorkel but are not allowed to touch the dolphins. For tactile interaction (kissing, fin tows, etc.), sign up for the Structured Swim program ($185). The same concept with different critters, the sea lion swim costs $120. ⊠ *MM 99, 31 Corrine Pl., Key Largo* ☎ *305/451–1993 or 866/860–7946* ⊕ *www.dolphinsplus.com.*

⟳ **Jacobs Aquatic Center.** Take the plunge at one of three swimming pools: an 8-lane, 25-meter lap pool with a diving well; a 3- to 4-foot-deep pool accessible to people with mobility problems; and an interactive play pool with a waterslide, pirate ship, waterfall, and sloping zero entry instead of steps. ⊠ *MM 99.6 OS, 320 Laguana Ave.* ☎ *305/453–7946* ⊕ *www.jacobsaquaticcenter.org* ☞ *$8–$10* ☾ *Daily 10–6, 10–7 in summer).*

**Laura Quinn Wild Bird Center.** Have a nose-to-beak encounter with ospreys, hawks, herons, and other unreleasable birds at this bird rehabilitation center, recently renamed for its founder, who passed away in 2010 (formerly the Florida Keys Wild Bird Center). The birds live in spacious screened enclosures along a boardwalk running through some of the best waterfront real estate in the Keys. Rehabilitated birds are set free, whereas these have become permanent residents. Free birds—especially pelicans and egrets—come to visit. The center is popular among photographers, who arrive at 3:30 pm, when hundreds of wild waterbirds fly in and feed within arm's distance as the staff tries to draw in injured animals. A short nature trail runs into the mangrove forest (bring bug spray May to October). ⊠ *MM 93.6 BS, 93600 Overseas Hwy., Tavernier* ☎ *305/852–4486* ⊕ *www.fkwbc.org* ☐ *Free, donations accepted* ⊙ *Daily sunrise–sunset.*

### BEACHES

**John Pennekamp Coral Reef State Park.** This state park is on everyone's list for close access to the best diving and snorkeling sites in the Sunshine State. The underwater treasure encompasses 78 square mi of coral reefs, sea-grass beds, and mangrove swamps and lies adjacent to the Florida Keys National Marine Sanctuary, which contains 40 of the 52 species of coral in the Atlantic Reef System and nearly 600 varieties of fish, from the colorful stoplight parrot fish to the demure cocoa damselfish. The park's visitor center has a 30-gallon floor-to-ceiling fish tank surrounded by smaller ones, so you can get a closer look at many of the underwater creatures. When you want to head out to sea, a concessionaire rents kayaks and powerboats, as well as snorkeling and diving equipment. You can also sign up for snorkeling and diving trips ($30 and $60, respectively, equipment extra) and glass-bottom-boat rides to the reef ($24). One of the most popular excursions is the snorkeling trip to see *Christ of the Deep,* the 2-ton underwater statue of Jesus. The park also has short nature trails, two man-made beaches, picnic shelters, a snack bar, and a campground. ⊠ *MM 102.5 OS, 102601 Overseas Hwy.* ☎ *305/451–1202 for park, 305/451–6300 for excursions* ⊕ *www.pennekamppark. com, www.floridastateparks.org/pennekamp* ☐ *$4.50 for 1 person in vehicle, $8 for 2–8 people, $2 for pedestrians and cyclists or extra people* ⊙ *Daily 8–sunset.*

### SPORTS AND THE OUTDOORS

#### BOATING

**Everglades Eco-Tours.** Captain Sterling operates Everglades and Florida Bay ecology tours ($50 per person) and sunset cruises ($75 per person). ⊠ *MM 104 BS, Sundowners Restaurant, 103900 Overseas Hwy., Key Largo* ☎ *305/853–5161 or 888/224–6044* ⊕ *www.captainsterling.com.*

**M.V. Key Largo Princess.** Two-hour glass-bottom-boat trips and sunset cruises on a luxury 75-foot motor yacht with a 280-square-foot glass viewing area (each $30) depart from the Holiday Inn docks three times a day. ⊠ *MM 100 OS, 99701 Overseas Hwy., Key Largo* ☎ *305/451–4655 or 877/648–8129* ⊕ *www.keylargoprincess.com.*

#### CANOEING AND KAYAKING

Sea kayaking continues to gain popularity in the Keys. You can paddle for a few hours or the whole day, on your own or with a guide. Some outfitters even offer overnight trips. The **Florida Keys Overseas Paddling Trail,** part of a statewide system, runs from Key Largo to Key West. You can paddle the entire distance, 110 mi on the Atlantic side, which takes 9–10 days. The trail also runs the chain's length on the bay side, which is a longer route.

**Coral Reef Park Co.** At John Pennekamp Coral Reef State Park, this operator has a fleet of canoes and kayaks for gliding around the 2½-mi mangrove trail or along the coast. It also rents powerboats. ⊠ *MM 102.5 OS, 102601 Overseas Hwy.* ☎ *305/451–6300* ⊕ *www. pennekamppark.com.*

**Florida Bay Outfitters.** Rent canoes or sea kayaks from this company, which sets up self-guided trips on the Florida Keys Overseas Paddling Trail, helps with trip planning, and matches equipment to your skill level. It also runs myriad guided tours around Key Largo. Take a full-moon paddle or a one- to seven-day canoe or kayak tour to the Everglades, Lignumvitae Key, or Indian Key. Trips start at $60 for a half-day. ⊠ *MM 104 BS, 104050 Overseas Hwy.* ☎ *305/451–3018* ⊕ *www.kayakfloridakeys.com.*

### FISHING

Private charters and big head boats (so named because they charge "by the head") are great for anglers who don't have their own vessel.

**Sailors Choice.** Fishing excursions depart twice daily ($40 cash for half-day trips). The 65-foot boat leaves from the Holiday Inn docks. Rods, bait, and license are included. ⊠ *MM 100 OS, Holiday Inn Resort & Marina, 99701 Overseas Hwy.* ☎ *305/451–1802 or 305/451–0041* ⊕ *www.sailorschoicefishingboat.com.*

### SCUBA DIVING AND SNORKELING

Much of what makes the Upper Keys a singular dive destination is variety. Places like Molasses Reef, which begins 3 feet below the surface and descends to 55 feet, have something for everyone from novice snorkelers to experienced divers. The *Spiegel Grove,* a 510-foot vessel, lies in 130 feet of water, but its upper regions are only 60 feet below the surface. On rough days, Key Largo Undersea Park's Emerald Lagoon is a popular spot. Expect to pay about $80 for a two-tank, two-site-dive trip with tanks and weights, or $35–$40 for a two-site-snorkel outing. Get big discounts by booking multiple trips.

**Amy Slate's Amoray Dive Resort.** This outfit makes diving easy. Stroll down to the full-service dive shop (NAUI, PADI, TDI, and BSAC certified), then onto a 45-foot catamaran. The rate for a two-dive trip is $80. ⊠ *MM 104.2 BS, 104250 Overseas Hwy.* ☎ *305/451–3595 or 800/426–6729* ⊕ *www.amoray.com.*

★ **Conch Republic Divers.** Book diving instruction as well as scuba and snorkeling tours of all the wrecks and reefs of the Upper Keys. Two-location dives are $80 with tank and weights or $65 without the equipment. ⊠ *MM 90.8 BS, 90800 Overseas Hwy.* ☎ *305/852–1655 or 800/274–3483* ⊕ *www.conchrepublicdivers.com.*

**Coral Reef Park Co.** At John Pennekamp Coral Reef State Park, this company gives 3½-hour scuba ($60) and 2½-hour snorkeling ($30) tours of the park. In addition to the great location and the dependability it's also suited for water adventurers of all levels. ⊠ *MM 102.5 OS, 102601 Overseas Hwy.* ☎ *305/451–6300* ⊕ *www.pennekamppark.com.*

**Ocean Divers.** The PADI five-star Caribbean Drive facility offers day and night dives, a range of courses, and dive-lodging packages. The cost is $80 for a two-tank reef dive with tank and weight rental. Snorkel trips cost $45 without equipment, $50 including snorkel, mask, and fins provided. There are two shops in Key Largo. ⊠ *MM 100 OS, 522 Caribbean Dr.* ⊠ *MM 105.8 BS, 105800 Overseas Hwy.* ☎ *305/451–1113 (Caribbean Dr. location), 305/451–0037 (Overseas Hwy. location) or 800/451–1113* ⊕ *www.oceandivers.com.*

**Quiescence Diving Services.** This operator sets itself apart in two ways: it limits groups to six to ensure personal attention and offers day and night dives, as well as twilight dives when sea creatures are most active. Two-dive trips start at $66 without equipment. ⊠ *MM 103.5 BS, 103680 Overseas Hwy.* ☎ *305/451–2440* ⊕ *www.quiescence.com.*

## SHOPPING

For the most part, shopping is sporadic in Key Largo, with a couple of shopping centers and fewer galleries than you find on the other big islands. If you're looking to buy scuba or snorkel equipment, you'll have plenty of places from which to choose.

## NIGHTLIFE

The semiweekly *Keynoter* (Wednesday and Saturday), weekly *Reporter* (Thursday), and Friday through Sunday editions of the *Miami Herald* are the best sources of information on entertainment and nightlife. Daiquiri bars, tiki huts, and seaside shacks pretty well summarize Key Largo's bar scene.

**Breezers Tiki Bar & Grille.** Mingle with locals over cocktails and sunsets at Marriott's Key Largo Bay Beach Resort. ⊠ *MM 103.8 BS, 103800 Overseas Hwy.* ☎ *305/453–0000.*

★ **Caribbean Club.** Walls plastered with Bogart memorabilia remind customers that the classic 1948 Bogart–Bacall flick *Key Largo* has a connection with this club. It draws boaters, curious visitors, and local barfly types, all of whom happily mingle and shoot pool. Postcard-perfect sunsets and live music draw revelers on weekends. ⊠ *MM 104 BS* ☎ *305/451–4466.*

**Coconuts.** Live music fills both the indoor and outdoor areas of this Marina Del Mar Resort throughout most of the week. Outside around the resort pool it's a family scene, with food service and a bar. Inside is strictly a thirty- and fortysomething crowd, including a few seasoned townies, playing pool, watching sports TV, and enjoying the music. ⊠ *MM 100 OS, Marina Del Mar Resort, 528 Caribbean Dr.* ☎ *305/453–9794.*

## WHERE TO EAT

$ ✕ **Alabama Jack's.** Calories be damned—the conch fritters here are
SEAFOOD heaven on a plate. The crab cakes, made from local blue crabs, earn
★ hallelujahs, too. The conch salad is as good as any you'll find in the Bahamas and a third of the price in trendy Keys restaurants. This weathered, circa-1950 restaurant floats on two roadside barges in an old fishing community. Regulars include weekend cyclists, Miamians on the lam, and boaters, who come to admire tropical birds in the nearby

mangroves, the occasional crocodile in the canal, or the bands that play on weekend afternoons. ■TIP→ It's about a half-hour drive from Key Largo, so you may want to plan a visit for your drive in or out. Jack's closes by 7, when the mosquitoes start biting. ⊠ *58000 Card Sound Rd., Key Largo* ☎ *305/248–8741* ⊕ *www.alabamajacks.com* ⌂ *Reservations not accepted.*

**$$$** ✕ **The Fish House.** Restaurants not on the water have to produce the
SEAFOOD   highest quality food to survive in the Keys. That's how the Fish House
★   has succeeded since the 1980s—so much so that it built the Fish House Encore next door to accommodate fans. The pan-sautéed black grouper will make you moan with pleasure, but it's just one of many headliners in this nautical eatery. On the fin side, the choices include mahimahi, swordfish, tuna, and yellowtail snapper that can be broiled, blackened, baked, or fried. The Matecumbe Catch prepares the day's fresh fish so simply and flavorfully it should be patented—baked with tomatoes, capers, olive oil, and lemon juice. Prefer shellfish? Choose from shrimp, lobster, and (mid-October to mid-May) stone crab. For a sweet ending, try the homemade key lime pie. ⊠ *MM 102.4 OS, 102341 Overseas Hwy.* ☎ *305/451–4665* ⊕ *www.fishhouse.com* ⌂ *Reservations not accepted* ⊘ *Closed Sept.*

**¢** ✕ **Harriette's Restaurant.** If you're looking for comfort food—like melt-
AMERICAN   in-your-mouth buttermilk biscuits—try this refreshing throwback. The kitchen makes fresh muffins daily, in flavors like mango, chocolate, and key lime. Little has changed over the years in this yellow-and-turquoise eatery. Owner Harriette Mattson often personally greets guests who come for steak and eggs with hash browns or old-fashioned hotcakes with sausage or bacon. Stick to simple dishes; the eggs Benedict are a disappointment. At lunch- and dinnertime, Harriette's shines in the burger department, but there are also hot meals such as chicken-fried steak and steak-and-shrimp combo. ⊠ *MM 95.7 BS, 95710 Overseas Hwy.* ☎ *305/852–8689* ⌂ *Reservations not accepted* ⊘ *No dinner Fri.–Sun.*

**$** ✕ **Mrs. Mac's Kitchen.** Townies pack the counters and booths at this tiny
SEAFOOD   eatery, where license plates are stuck on the walls and made into chandeliers. Got a hankering for meat loaf or crab cakes? You'll find them here, along with specials like grilled yellowfin tuna. Bring your appetite for the all-you-can-eat fish specials on Tuesday and Thursday. There's also champagne breakfast, an assortment of tasty burgers and sandwiches, and its famous chili and key lime freeze (somewhere between a shake and a float). Ask about the hogfish special du jour. ⊠ *MM 99.4 BS, 99336 Overseas Hwy.* ☎ *305/451–3722* ⊕ *www.mrsmacskitchen. com* ⌂ *Reservations not accepted* ⊘ *Closed Sun.*

**$$$** ✕ **Rib Daddy's Chop House.** Two Key Largo sister operations combined
SEAFOOD   to create a comfort-food haven open for breakfast, lunch, and din-
☺   ner. Dieters, keep driving. Sunday's brunch buffet has everything the restaurant is famous for with a $14.95 price tag. You'll swoon after tasting the Memphis-style smoked prime rib, bison strip steak, and barbecue chicken flavored with specially formulated rubs and sauces. The menu includes seafood options, too, such as crab cakes and all-you-can-eat lobster and stone crab specials. Try the Hemingway (fried mahimahi, eggs, and grits) for breakfast or either the hand-pulled pork

14

sandwich or blackened chicken wrap for lunch. Save room for the key lime pie, creamy mango pie, or coconut cake. Kids love staring at the reef aquarium, the highlight of this rather plain, open dining room. ⊠ *MM 102.2 BS, 102570 Overseas Hwy.* ☎ *305/451–0900* ⊕ *www. ribdaddysrestaurant.com* ⌲ *Reservations not accepted.*

$$$
SEAFOOD
★

✕ **Snapper's.** "You hook 'em, we cook 'em" is the motto here. Alas, "cleanin' 'em" is not part of the bargain. If you bring in your ready-for-the-grill fish, dinner here is $12 for a single, $13.95 per person family style. Otherwise, they'll catch and prepare you a plank-roasted yellowtail snapper, a grilled tuna steak, fish of the day baked with 36 herbs and spices, or a little something from the raw bar. The ceviche of yellowtail, shrimp, and conch (merrily spiced) wins raves, too. Lunch's seafood burrito is a keeper. All this is served up in a lively, mangrove-ringed waterfront setting with live music, an aquarium bar, Sunday brunch (including a Finlandia Bloody Mary bar), killer rum drinks, and seating alongside the fishing dock. Three-course early-bird dinner specials are available 5–6 for $18.50. ⊠ *MM 94.5 OS, 139 Seaside Ave.* ☎ *305/852–5956* ⊕ *www. snapperskeylargo.com* ⌲ *Reservations not accepted.*

$$$
AMERICAN

✕ **Sundowners.** The name doesn't lie. If it's a clear night and you can snag a reservation, this restaurant will treat you to a sherbet-hue sunset over Florida Bay. If you're here in mild weather—anytime other than the dog days of summer or the rare winter cold snap—the best seats are on the patio. The food is excellent: try the key lime seafood, a happy combo of sautéed shrimp, lobster, and lump crabmeat swimming in a tangy sauce spiked with Tabasco served over penne or rice. Wednesday and Saturday are all about prime rib, and Friday draws the crowds with an all-you-can-eat fish fry ($16). Sunday brunch features Bloody Marys. ⊠ *MM 104 BS, 103900 Overseas Hwy.* ☎ *305/451–4502* ⊕ *sundownerskeylargo.com* ⌲ *Reservations essential.*

## WHERE TO STAY

*For expanded hotel reviews, visit Fodors.com.*

$$$
HOTEL
★

🛏 **Azul del Mar.** The dock points the way to many beautiful sunsets at this adults-only boutique hotel. **Pros:** great garden; good location; sophisticated design. **Cons:** small beach; close to highway; high-priced. ⊠ *MM 104.3 BS, 104300 Overseas Hwy.* ☎ *305/451–0337 or 888/253–2985* ⊕ *www.azulhotels.us* ⟿ *2 studios, 3 1-bedroom suites, 1 2-bedroom suite* ⌂ *In-room: a/c, kitchen, Wi-Fi. In-hotel: beach, water sports, some age restrictions* ❖ *No meals.*

$$
RESORT

🛏 **Coconut Bay Resort & Bay Harbor Lodge.** Some 200 feet of waterfront is the main attraction at this property, a combination of two lodging options. **Pros:** bay front; neatly kept gardens; walking distance to restaurants; complimentary kayak and paddleboat use. **Cons:** a bit dated; small sea-walled sand beach. ⊠ *MM 97.7 BS, 97702 Overseas Hwy.* ☎ *305/852–1625 or 800/385–0986* ⊕ *www.coconutbaykeylargo.com* ⟿ *7 rooms, 5 efficiencies, 2 suites, 1 2-bedroom villa, 6 1-bedroom cottages* ⌂ *In-room: a/c, kitchen (some), Wi-Fi (some). In-hotel: pool, beach, some pets allowed* ❖ *No meals.*

$$$$
B&B/INN

🛏 **Dove Creek Lodge.** Old-school anglers will likely be scandalized by this 2004 fishing camp's sherbet-hue paint and plantation-style furnishings. **Pros:** great for fishing enthusiasts; luxurious rooms; close to

Snapper's restaurant with charging privileges. **Cons:** loud music next door. ⊠ *MM 94.5 OS, 147 Seaside Ave.* ☎ *305/852–6200 or 800/401–0057* ⊕ *www.dovecreeklodge.com* ⇆ *4 room, 10 suites* ♺ *In-room: a/c, kitchen (some), Internet, Wi-Fi. In-hotel: pool* ⦿ *Breakfast.*

**$$$$**
**RESORT**
**Fodor'sChoice**
★
🏨 **Kona Kai Resort & Gallery.** Brilliantly colored bougainvilleas, coconut palms, guava trees, and a new botanical garden make this 2-acre hideaway one of the prettiest places to stay in the Keys. **Pros:** lush landscaping; free use of sports equipment; knowledgeable staff. **Cons:** expensive; some rooms are very close together. ⊠ *MM 97.8 BS, 97802 Overseas Hwy.* ☎ *305/852–7200 or 800/365–7829* ⊕ *www.konakairesort.com* ⇆ *8 suites, 3 rooms* ♺ *In-room: a/c, kitchen (some). In-hotel: tennis court, pool, beach, some age restrictions* ⦿ *No meals* ☾ *Closed Sept.*

**$$$**
**B&B/INN**
★
🏨 **Largo Lodge.** When you drive under the dense canopy of foliage at the entrance to Largo Lodge you'll feel like you've escaped Overseas Highway's bustle. **Pros:** lush grounds; great sunset views; affordable rates; boat docking. **Cons:** no pool; some traffic noise outdoors. ⊠ *MM 101.7 BS, 101740 Overseas Hwy.* ☎ *305/451–0424 or 800/468–4378* ⊕ *www.largolodge.com* ⇆ *2 rooms, 6 cottages* ♺ *In-room: a/c, kitchen (some), Wi-Fi. In-hotel: beach, some age restrictions* ⦿ *No meals.*

**$$$$**
**RESORT**
☺
★
🏨 **Marriott's Key Largo Bay Beach Resort.** Park the car and toss the keys in the bottom of your bag; there's no need to go anywhere else (except maybe John Pennekamp Coral Reef State Park, just a half mile north). **Pros:** lots of activities; free covered parking; dive shop on property; free Wi-Fi. **Cons:** rooms facing highway can be noisy; thin walls; unspectacular beach. ⊠ *MM 103.8 BS, 103800 Overseas Hwy.* ☎ *305/453–0000 or 866/849–3753* ⊕ *www.marriottkeylargo.com* ⇆ *132 rooms, 20 2-bedroom suites, 1 penthouse suite* ♺ *In-room: a/c, kitchen (some), Wi-Fi. In-hotel: restaurants, bars, pool, gym, spa, beach, water sports, children's programs, laundry facilities* ⦿ *No meals.*

**¢**
**HOTEL**
🏨 **The Pelican.** This 1950s throwback is reminiscent of the days when parents packed the kids into the station wagon and headed to no-frills seaside motels, complete with an old-timer fishing off the dock. **Pros:** free use of kayaks and paddleboats; well-maintained dock; reasonable rates. **Cons:** some small rooms; basic accommodations and amenities. ⊠ *MM 99.3, 99340 Overseas Hwy.* ☎ *305/451–3576 or 877/451–3576* ⊕ *www.thepelicankeylargo.com* ⇆ *13 rooms, 4 efficiencies, 4 suites* ♺ *In-room: a/c, kitchen (some), Wi-Fi. In-hotel: beach, water sports* ⦿ *No meals.*

**$**
**HOTEL**
🏨 **Seafarer Resort.** It's budget lodging, but the Seafarer Resort is not without its charms. **Pros:** sandy beach; complimentary kayak use. **Cons:** some rooms close to road noise; basic accommodations. ⊠ *MM 97.6 BS, 97684 Overseas Hwy.* ☎ *305/852–5349* ⊕ *www.seafarerresort.com* ⇆ *8 rooms, 3 studios, 3 1-bedroom cottages, 1 2-bedroom cottage, 2 apartments* ♺ *In-room: kitchen (some), Wi-Fi. In-hotel: beach, water sports, laundry facilities* ⦿ *No meals.*

### CAMPING

☺
★
⛰ **John Pennekamp Coral Reef State Park.** Divers and snorkelers won't find a better location in the Upper Keys. Pennekamp's campsites are carved out of hardwood hammock, providing shade and privacy away from the heavy day-use areas. Activities include boating, fishing, scuba

**14**

diving, snorkeling, and hiking. There's no restaurant, but there are vending machines for late-night snack attacks. ☝ *Flush toilets, partial hook-ups (electric and water), dump station, drinking water, showers, fire pits, picnic tables, electricity, public telephone, general store, ranger station, swimming (ocean)* ☞*47 partial hook-ups for RVs and tents*✉ *MM 102.5 OS, 102601 Overseas Hwy.* ☏ *305/451–1202 park, 800/326–3521 reservations* ⊕ *www.reserveamerica.com.*

## ISLAMORADA

*Islamorada is between mile markers 90.5 and 70.*

Early settlers named this key after their schooner, *Island Home*, but to make it sound more romantic they translated it into Spanish: *Isla Morada.* The chamber of commerce prefers to use its literal translation "Purple Island," which refers either to a purple-shelled snail that once inhabited these shores or to the brilliantly colored orchids and bougainvilleas.

Early maps show Islamorada as encompassing only Upper Matecumbe Key. But the incorporated "Village of Islands" is made up of a string of islands that the Overseas Highway crosses, including Plantation Key, Windley Key, Upper Matecumbe Key, Lower Matecumbe Key, Craig Key, and Fiesta Key. In addition, two state-park islands accessible only by boat—Indian Key and Lignumvitae Key—belong to the group.

Islamorada (locals pronounce it "*eye*-la-mor-*ah*-da") is one of the world's top fishing destinations. For nearly 100 years, seasoned anglers have fished these clear, warm waters teeming with trophy-worthy fish. There are numerous options for those in search of the big ones, including chartering a boat with its own crew or heading out on a vessel rented from one of the plethora of marinas along this 20-mi stretch of the Overseas Highway. Islamorada is one of the more affluent resort areas of the Keys. Sophisticated resorts and restaurants meet the needs of those in search of luxury, but there's also plenty for those looking for something more casual and affordable. Art galleries and boutiques make Islamorada's shopping scene the best in the Upper Keys, but if you're shopping for groceries, head to Marathon or Key Largo.

### ESSENTIALS

Visitor Information **Islamorada Chamber of Commerce & Visitors Center** (✉ *MM 83.2 BS, 83224 Overseas Hwy,. Upper Matecumbe Key, Islamorada* ☏ *305/664–4503 or 800/322–5397* ⊕ *www.islamoradachamber.com*).

Islamorada's warm waters attract large fish and the anglers, including charters, who want to catch them.

## EXPLORING

**History of Diving Museum.** Adding to the region's reputation for world-class diving, this museum plunges into the history of man's thirst for undersea exploration. Among its 13 galleries of interactive and other interesting displays are a submarine and helmet from the film *20,000 Leagues Under the Sea.* Historic equipment, sunken treasures, and photographs are part of the extensive collection donated by a local couple. ⊠ *MM 83 BS, 82990 Overseas Hwy., Upper Matecumbe Key* ☎ *305/664-9737* ⊕ *www.divingmuseum.org* ✉ *$12* ☉ *Daily 10–5.*

**Robbie's Marina.** Huge, prehistoric-looking denizens of the not-so-deep, silver-sided tarpon congregate around the docks at this marina on Lower Matecumbe Key. Children—and lots of adults—pay $4 to feed them sardines or $1 just to watch. Spend some time hanging out at this authentic Keys community, where you can grab a bite to eat, do a little shopping, or charter a boat. ⊠ *MM 77.5 BS, 77522 Overseas Hwy., Lower Matecumbe Key* ☎ *305/664-9814 or 877/664-8498* ⊕ *www. robbies.com* ✉ *Dock access $1* ☉ *Daily 8–5.*

**Theater of the Sea.** The second-oldest marine-mammal center in the world doesn't attempt to compete with more modern, more expensive parks. Even so, it's among the better attractions north of Key West, especially if you have kids in tow. Like the pricier parks, there are dolphin, sea lion, and stingray encounters ($55–$175, which includes general admission; reservations required) where you can get up close and personal with underwater creatures. These are popular, so reserve in advance. Ride a "bottomless" boat to see what's below the waves and take a guided tour of the marine-life exhibits. Entertaining educational shows highlight conservation issues. You can stop for lunch at the grill, shop in the boutique, or sunbathe at a lagoon-side beach. This easily could be an all-day attraction. ⊠ *MM 84.5 OS, 84721 Overseas Hwy., Windley Key* ☎ *305/664–2431* ⊕ *www.theaterofthesea.com* 🖃 *$26.95* ⊙ *Daily 9:30–5 (last ticket sold at 3:30).*

**Upper Matecumbe Key.** This was one of the first of the Upper Keys to be permanently settled. Early homesteaders were so successful at growing pineapples in the rocky soil that at one time the island yielded the country's largest annual crop. However, foreign competition and the hurricane of 1935 killed the industry. Today, life centers on fishing and tourism, and the island is filled with bait shops, marinas, and charter-fishing boats. ⊠ *MM 84–79.*

**OFF THE BEATEN PATH**

**Indian Key Historic State Park.** Mystery surrounds 10-acre Indian Key, on the ocean side of the Matecumbe islands. Before it became one of the first European settlements outside of Key West, it was inhabited by American Indians for several thousand years. The islet served as a base for 19th-century shipwreck salvagers until an Indian attack wiped out the settlement in 1840. Dr. Henry Perrine, a noted botanist, was killed in the raid. Today his plants grow in the town's ruins. Most people kayak or canoe here from Indian Key Fill to explore the nature trails and the town ruins or to snorkel. Florida Keys Kayak has an office at Robbie's Marina. There are no restrooms or picnic facilities on the island. ⌂ *Box 1052* ☎ *305/664–2540* ⊕ *www.floridastateparks.org/indiankey* 🖃 *Free* ⊙ *Daily sunrise–sunset.*

**OFF THE BEATEN PATH**

**Lignumvitae Key Botanical State Park.** On the National Register of Historic Places, this 280-acre bay-side island is the site of a virgin hardwood forest and the 1919 home of chemical magnate William Matheson. His caretaker's cottage serves as the park's visitor center. Access is by boat— your own, a rented vessel, or a ferry operated by Robbie's Marina (reservations required). Paddling here from Indian Key Fill, at MM 78.5, is a popular pastime. The only way to do the trails is by a guided ranger walk, offered at 10 am and 2 pm Friday to Sunday. Wear long sleeves and pants, and bring mosquito repellent. On the first weekend in December is the Lignumvitae Christmas Celebration. ⌂ *Box 1052* ☎ *305/664–2540* park, *305/664–9814* ferry ⊕ *www.floridastateparks. org/lignumvitaekey* 🖃 *$1 for tours; ferry prices fluctuate according to season* ⊙ *Park (Matheson yard/picnic grounds) open daily 9–5; house tours Fri.–Sun 10 and 2.*

**Windley Key Fossil Reef Geological State Park.** The fossilized-coral reef, dating back about 125,000 years, demonstrates that the Florida Keys were once beneath the ocean. Excavation of Windley Key's limestone bed by the Florida East Coast Railway exposed the petrified reef, full of beautifully fossilized brain coral and sea ferns. Visitors can see the fossils along a 300-foot quarry wall when hiking the park's three trails. There are guided (Friday, Saturday, and Sunday only) and self-guided tours along the trails, which lead to the railway's old quarrying equipment and cutting pits, where you can make rubbings of the quarry walls. The **Alison Fahrer Environmental Education Center** holds historic, biological, and geological displays about the area, including videos. The first Saturday in March is Windley Key Day, when the park sells native plants and hosts environmental exhibits. ⊠ *MM 84.9 BS, Windley Key* ☎ *305/664–2540* ⊕ *www. floridastateparks.org/windleykey* ◪ *Education center free, $2.50 for park self-tours, $1 for ranger-guided tours* ☉ *Education center Fri.– Sun. 9–5 (tours at 10 and 2).*

### BEACHES

**Anne's Beach Park.** On Lower Matecumbe Key is a popular village park, named for a local environmental activist. Its "beach" (really a typical Keys-style sand flat) is best enjoyed at low tide. The nicest feature here is a ½-mi, elevated, wooden boardwalk that meanders through a natural wetland hammock. Covered picnic areas along the way give you places to linger and enjoy the view. Restrooms are at the north end. Weekends are packed with Miami day-trippers as it's the only public beach until you reach Marathon. ⊠ *MM 73.5 OS, Lower Matecumbe Key* ☎ *305/853–1685.*

### SPORTS AND THE OUTDOORS

#### BOATING

Marinas pop up every mile or so in the Islamorada area, so finding a rental or tour is no problem. Robbie's Marina is a prime example of a salty spot where you can find it all—from fishing charters and kayaking rentals to lunch and tarpon feeding.

**Bump & Jump.** This one-stop shop for windsurfing, sailboat and powerboat rentals, sales, and lessons delivers to your hotel or house, or drops equipment off right at the beach. ⊠ *MM 81.2 OS, 81197 Overseas Hwy., Upper Matecumbe Key* ☎ *305/664–9404 or 877/453–9463* ⊕ *www.keysboatrental.com.*

**Houseboat Vacations of the Florida Keys.** See the islands from the comfort of your own boat (captain's cap optional). The company maintains a fleet of 42- to 55-foot boats that accommodate up to 10 people and come outfitted with everything you need besides food. You may provision yourself at a nearby grocery store. The three-day minimum starts at $1,112; one week costs $1,950 and up. Kayaks, canoes, and skiffs suitable for the ocean are also available. ⊠ *MM 85.9 BS, 85944 Overseas Hwy. Plantation Key* ☎ *305/664–4009* ⊕ *www.floridakeys.com/houseboats.*

**Robbie's Boat Rentals & Charters.** This full-service company will even give you a crash course on how not to crash your boat. The rental fleet includes an 18-foot skiff with a 60-horsepower outboard for $150 for four hours and $200 for the day to a 23-foot deck boat with a 130-horsepower engine for $185 for a half day and $235 for eight hours. Robbie's also rents fishing and snorkeling gear (there's good snorkeling nearby) and sells bait, drinks and snacks, and gas. Want to hire a guide who knows the local waters and where the fish lurk? Robbie's offers offshore-fishing trips, patch-reef trips, and party-boat fishing. Backcountry flats trips are a specialty. ⊠ *MM 77.5 BS, 77522 Overseas Hwy., Lower Matecumbe Key* ☎ *305/664–9814 or 877/664–8498* ⊕ *www.robbies.com.*

**Treasure Harbor Marine.** Captains Pam and Pete Anderson provide everything you'll need for a sailing vacation at sea. They also give excellent

14

Renting wave runners is a fun way to catch some surf and sun in Florida Keys. Each fits one to three people.

advice on where to find the best anchorages, snorkeling spots, or lobstering sites. Vessels range from a 23.5-foot Hunter to a 41-foot Morgan Out Island. Rates start at $160 a day; $700 a week. Hire a captain for $175–$200 a day. Marina facilities are basic—water, electric, ice machine, laundry, picnic tables, and restrooms with showers. A store sells snacks, beverages, and sundries. ⊠ *MM 86.5 OS, 200 Treasure Harbor Dr., Plantation Key* ☎ *305/852–2458 or 800/352–2628* ⊕ *www.treasureharbor.com.*

### FISHING

Here in the self-proclaimed "Sportfishing Capital of the World," sailfish is the prime catch in the winter and dolphinfish in the summer. Buchanan Bank just south of Islamorada is a good spot to try for tarpon in the spring. Blackfin tuna and amberjack are generally plentiful in the area, too. ■TIP→ The Hump at Islamorada ranks highest among anglers' favorite fishing spots in Florida due to the incredible offshore marine life.

**Captain Ted Wilson.** Go into the backcountry for bonefish, tarpon, redfish, snook, and shark aboard a 17-foot boat that accommodates up to three anglers. For two people, half-day trips run $375, full-day trips $550, two-hour sunset bonefishing $225, and evening excursions $400. There's a $100 charge for an extra person. ⊠ *MM 79.9 OS, 79851 Overseas Hwy., Upper Matecumbe Key* ☎ *305/942–5224 or 305/664–9463* ⊕ *www.captaintedwilson.com.*

**Florida Keys Fly Fish.** Like other top fly-fishing and light-tackle guides, Captain Geoff Colmes helps his clients land trophy fish in the waters around the Keys ($500–$550). ⊠ *105 Palm La., Upper Matecumbe Key* ☎*305/853–0741* ⊕ *www.floridakeysflyfish.com.*

**Florida Keys Outfitters.** Long before fly-fishing became popular, Sandy Moret was fishing the Keys for bonefish, tarpon, and redfish. Now he attracts anglers from around the world on a quest for the big catch. Weekend fly-fishing classes, which include classroom instruction, equipment, and daily lunch, cost $985. Add $1,070 for two additional days of fishing. Guided fishing trips cost $395 for a half day, $535 for a full day. Packages combining fishing and accommodations at Islander Resort are available. ⊠ *Green Turtle, MM 81.2, 81219 Overseas Hwy., Upper Matecumbe Key* ☎*305/664–5423* ⊕ *www. floridakeysoutfitters.com.*

★ **Hubba Hubba Charters.** Captain Ken Knudsen quietly poles his flatboat through the shallow water, barely making a ripple. Then he points and his clients cast. Five seconds later there's a zing, and the excitement of bringing in a snook, redfish, trout, or tarpon begins. Knudsen has fished Keys waters for more than 40 years. Now a licensed backcountry guide, he's ranked among Florida's top 10 by national fishing magazines. He offers four-hour sunset trips for tarpon ($425) and two-hour sunset trips for bonefish ($200), as well as half- ($375) and full-day ($550) outings. Prices are for one or two anglers, and tackle and bait are included. ⊠ *MM 79.8 OS, Upper Matecumbe Key* ☎*305/664–9281.*

*Miss Islamorada.* The 65-foot party boat has full-day trips for $60. Bring your lunch or buy one from the dockside deli. ⊠ *Bud n' Mary's Marina, MM 79.8 OS, 79851 Overseas Hwy., Upper Matecumbe Key* ☎*305/664–2461 or 800/742–7945* ⊕ *www.budnmarys.com.*

## SCUBA DIVING AND SNORKELING

About 1¼ nautical mi south of Indian Key is the **San Pedro Underwater Archaeological Preserve State Park** (⊠ *MM 85.5 OS* ☎*305/664–2540* ⊕ *www.floridastateparks.org/sanpedro*), which includes the wreck of a Spanish treasure-fleet ship that sank in 1733. The state of Florida protects the site for divers; no spearfishing or souvenir collecting is allowed. Resting in only 18 feet of water, its ruins are visible to snorkelers as well as divers and attract a colorful array of fish.

**Florida Keys Dive Center.** Dive from John Pennekamp Coral Reef State Park to Alligator Light with this outfitter. The center has two 46-foot Coast Guard–approved dive boats, offers scuba training, and is one of the few Keys dive centers to offer Nitrox and Trimix (mixed gas) diving. Two-tank dives cost $60 with no equipment; two-location snorkeling is $38. ⊠ *MM 90.5 OS, 90451 Overseas Hwy. Plantation Key* ☎*305/852–4599 or 800/433–8946* ⊕ *www.floridakeysdivectr.com.*

**Holiday Isle Dive Shop.** With a resort, pool, restaurant, lessons, and twice-daily dive and snorkel trips this a one-stop dive shop. Rates start at $50 for a two-tank dive without equipment. ⊠ *MM 84 OS, 84001 Overseas Hwy., Windley Key* ☎*305/664–3483 or 800/327–7070* ⊕ *www. diveholidayisle.com.*

14

**WATER SPORTS**

**Florida Keys Kayak.** Rent kayaks for trips to Indian and Lignumvitae keys, two favorite destinations for paddlers. Kayak rental half-day rates (and you'll need plenty of time to explore those mangrove canopies) are $40 for a single kayak and $55 for a double. Pedal kayaks are available for $50 single and $65 double. The company also offers guided three-hour tours, including a snorkel trip to Indian Key ($45). It also rents stand-up paddleboards, at $50 for a half-day including lessons, and canoes. ⊠ *Robbie's Marina, MM 77.5 BS, 77522 Overseas Hwy., Lower Matecumbe Key* ☎ *305/664–4878* ⊕ *www. kayakthefloridakeys.com.*

**SHOPPING**

Art galleries, upscale gift shops, and the mammoth World Wide Sportsman (if you want to look the part of a local fisherman, you must wear a shirt from here) make up the variety and superior style of Islamorada shopping.

**Banyan Tree.** A sharp-eyed husband-and-wife team successfully combines antiques and contemporary gifts for the home and garden with plants, pots, and trellises in a stylishly sophisticated indoor–outdoor setting. ⊠ *MM 81.2 OS, 81197 Overseas Hwy., Upper Matecumbe Key* ☎ *305/664–3433 or 877/453–9463* ⊕ *www.banyantreegarden.com.*

**Gallery Morada.** The go-to destination for one-of-a-kind gifts beautifully displays blown-glass objects, original sculptures, paintings, lithographs, and jewelry by top South Florida artists. ⊠ *MM 81.6 OS, 81611 Old Hwy., Upper Matecumbe Key* ☎ *305/664–3650* ⊕ *www. gallerymorada.com.*

**Hooked on Books.** Among the best buys in town are the used best sellers at this bookstore, which also sells new titles, audiobooks, and CDs. ⊠ *MM 82.6 OS, 82681 Overseas Hwy., Upper Matecumbe Key* ☎ *305/517– 2602* ⊕ *www.hookedonbooksfloridakeys.com.*

**Island Silver & Spice.** The shop stocks tropical-style furnishings, rugs, and home accessories, as well as women's and men's resort wear and a large jewelry selection with high-end watches and marine-theme pieces. ⊠ *MM 82 OS, 81981 Overseas Hwy., Upper Matecumbe Key* ☎ *305/664–2714.*

**Rain Barrel.** This is a natural and unhurried shopping showplace. Set in a tropical garden of shady trees, native shrubs, and orchids, the crafts village has shops with works by local and national artists and resident artists in studios, including John Hawver, noted for Florida landscapes and seascapes. The Main Gallery up front showcases the craftsmanship of the resident artisans, who create marine-inspired artwork while you watch. ⊠ *MM 86.7 BS, 86700 Overseas Hwy. Plantation Key* ☎ *305/852–3084.*

**Redbone Gallery.** One of the largest sportfishing–art galleries in Florida stocks hand-stitched clothing and giftware, in addition to work by wood and bronze sculptors such as Kendall van Sant; watercolorists Chet Reneson, Jeanne Dobie, and Kathleen Denis; and painters C.D. Clarke and Tim Borski. Proceeds benefit cystic fibrosis research. ⊠ *MM*

*81.5 OS, 200 Industrial Dr., Upper Matecumbe Key* ☎ *305/664–2002*
⊕ *www.redbone.org.*

**World Wide Sportsman.** Former U.S. presidents, celebrities, and record
holders beam alongside their catches in black-and-white photos on the
walls of this two-level retail center that sells upscale fishing equipment,
resort clothing, sportfishing art, and other gifts. When you're tired of
shopping, relax at the Zane Grey Long Key Lounge just above World
Wide Sportsman. ✉ *MM 81.5 BS, 81576 Overseas Hwy., Upper Matecumbe Key* ☎ *305/664–4615 or 800/327–2880.*

### NIGHTLIFE

Islamorada is not known for its raging nightlife, but for local fun Lorelei's is legendary. Others cater to the town's sophisticated clientele and
fishing fervor.

★ **Lorelei Restaurant & Cabana Bar.** Behind a larger-than-life mermaid, this is
the kind of place you fantasize about during those long cold winters up
north. It's all about good drinks, tasty pub grub, and beautiful sunsets
set to live bands playing island tunes and light rock nightly. ✉ *MM 82
BS, 81924 Overseas Hwy., Upper Matecumbe Key* ☎ *305/664–2692*
⊕ *www.loreleicabanabar.com.*

### WHERE TO EAT

$$$ ╳ **Green Turtle Inn.** This circa-1928 landmark inn and its vintage neon
SEAFOOD sign is a slice of Florida Keys history. Period photographs decorate the
wood-paneled walls. Breakfast and lunch options include surprises like
coconut French toast made with Cuban bread and yellowfin tuna tartare.
Chef Dan Harris relies heavily on Cajun cuisine with Italian touches for
the dinner menu; think turtle chowder (don't gasp; it's made from farm-
raised freshwater turtles), barbecued shrimp, gumbo, and lobster lasagna.
Naturally, there's a Turtle Sundae on the dessert menu. ✉ *MM 81.2 OS,
81219 Overseas Hwy., Upper Matecumbe Key* ☎ *305/664–2006* ⊕ *www.
greenturtlekeys.com* ⚏ *Reservations essential* ◯ *Closed Mon.*

$$ ╳ **Island Grill.** Don't be fooled by appearances; this shack on the water-
SEAFOOD front takes island breakfast, lunch, and dinner cuisine up a notch. The
★ eclectic menu tempts you with such dishes as tuna nachos and lobster
rolls. Southern-style shrimp and andouille sausage with grits join island-
style specialties such as grilled ribs with guava barbecue sauce on the
list of entrées. There's an air-conditioned dining room and bar as well
as outdoor seating under the trees. The outdoor bar hosts live entertainment Wednesday to Sunday. ✉ *MM 85.5 OS, 85501 Overseas Hwy.,
Windley Key* ☎ *305/664–8400* ⊕ *www.keysislandgrill.com* ⚏ *Reservations not accepted.*

$$ ╳ **Kaiyó Grill & Sushi.** Kaiyó's decor—an inviting setting that includes
JAPANESE colorful abstract mosaics, polished wood floors, and upholstered ban-
quettes—almost steals the show here, but the food is equally interest-
ing. The menu, a fusion of East and West, offers sushi and sashimi
and rolls that combine local ingredients with traditional Japanese
tastes. A wood grill dimension is used to prepare such dishes as grilled
catch-of-the-day with a smoked Scotch bonnet pepper aioli crust and
hardwood grilled rack of lamb. ✉ *MM 81.5 OS, 81701 Overseas*

*Continued on page 693*

# UNDER THE SEA
## SNORKELING AND DIVING IN THE FLORIDA KEYS
by Lynne Helm

Up on the shore they work all day...

    While we devotin',

      Full time to floatin',

        Under the sea...

        –"Under the Sea,"
from Disney's *Little Mermaid*

All Floridians—even those long-accustomed to balmy breezes and swaying palms—turn ecstatic at the mere thought of tripping off to the Florida Keys. Add the prospect of underwater adventure, and hot diggity, it's unparalleled bliss.

Perennially laid back, the Keys annually attract nearly 800,000 snorkeling and scuba diving aficionados, and why not? There's arguably no better destination to learn these sports that put you up close to the wonders of life under the sea.

### THE BARRIER REEF
The continental United States' only living coral barrier reef stretches 5 mi offshore of the Keys and is a teeming backbone of marine life, ranging from brilliant corals to neon-colored fish from blue-striped grunts to green moray eels. This is the prime reason why the Keys are where you descend upon intricate natural coral formations and encrusted shipwrecks, some historic, others sunk by design to create artificial reefs that attract divers

and provide protection for marine life. Most diving sites have mooring buoys (nautical floats away from shore, sometimes marking specific sites); these let you tie up your boat so you don't need to drop anchor, which could damage the reef. Most of these sites also are near individual keys, where dozens of dive operators can cater to your needs.

Reef areas thrive in waters as shallow as 5 feet and as deep as 50 feet. Shallow reefs attract snorkelers, while deeper reefs suit divers of varying experience levels. The Keys' shallow diving offers two benefits: longer time safely spent on the bottom exploring, and more vibrant colors because of sunlight penetration. Most divers log maximum depths of 20 to 30 feet.

(left) Shallow-water coral reef, (top) Nine Foot Stake is a popular site for underwater photography.

# WHERE TO SNORKEL AND DIVE

## KEY WEST
### Mile Marker 0–4

You can soak up a mesmerizing overview of submerged watery wonders at the **Florida Keys Eco-Discovery Center**, opened in 2007 on Key West's Truman

Nine Foot Stake

Annex waterfront. Both admission and parking are free at the 6,000 square–foot center (⏱ *9–4 Tues.–Sat.* ☎ *305/809–4750*); interactive exhibits here focus on Keys marine life and habitats. Key West's offshore reefs are best accessed via professional charters, but it's easy to snorkel from shore at **Key West Marine Park**. Marked by a lighthouse, **Sand Key Reef** attracts snorkelers and scuba divers. **Joe's Tug**, at 65-foot depths, sets up encounters with Goliath grouper. **Ten-Fathom Ledge**, with coral caves and dramatic overhangs, shelters lobster. The **Cayman Salvor**, a buoy tender sunk as an artificial reef in 1985, shelters baitfish. Patch reef **Nine Foot Stake**, submerged 10 to 25 feet, has soft corals and juvenile marine life. **Kedge Ledge** features a pair of coral-encrusted anchors from 18th-century sailing vessels. 🚩 *Florida Keys main visitor line at* ☎ *800/FLA-KEYS (352-5397).*

## BIG PINE KEY/LOWER KEYS
### Mile Marker 4–47

Many devotees feel a Florida dive adventure would not be complete without heading 5 mi from Big Pine Key to **Looe Key National Marine Sanctuary**, an underwater preserve named for the HMS Looe running aground in 1744. If you time your visit for July, you might hit the one-day free underwater music festival for snorkelers

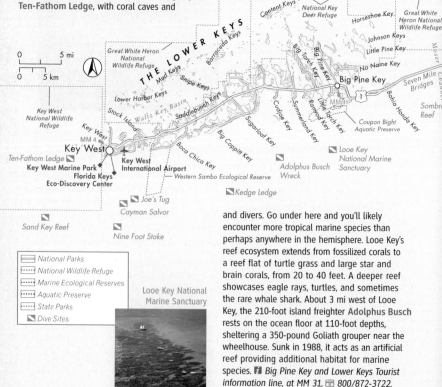

Legend:
- National Parks
- National Wildlife Refuge
- Marine Ecological Reserves
- Aquatic Preserve
- State Parks
- Dive Sites

Looe Key National Marine Sanctuary

and divers. Go under here and you'll likely encounter more tropical marine species than perhaps anywhere in the hemisphere. Looe Key's reef ecosystem extends from fossilized corals to a reef flat of turtle grass and large star and brain corals, from 20 to 40 feet. A deeper reef showcases eagle rays, turtles, and sometimes the rare whale shark. About 3 mi west of Looe Key, the 210-foot island freighter **Adolphus Busch** rests on the ocean floor at 110-foot depths, sheltering a 350-pound Goliath grouper near the wheelhouse. Sunk in 1988, it acts as an artificial reef providing additional habitat for marine species. 🚩 *Big Pine Key and Lower Keys Tourist information line, at MM 31,* ☎ *800/872-3722.*

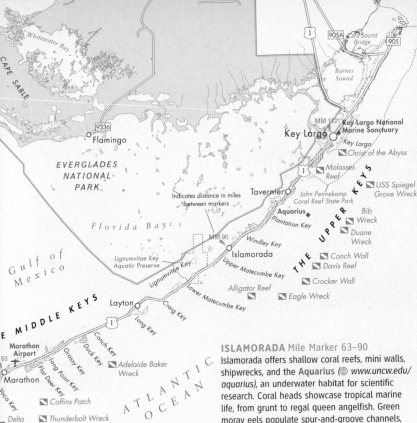

## MARATHON/MIDDLE KEYS

Mile Marker 47–63

The Middle Keys yield a marine wilderness of a spur-and-groove coral and patch reefs. The **Adelaide Baker** historic shipwreck has a pair of stacks in 25 feet of water.

Sombrero Reef

Popular **Sombrero Reef**, with coral canyons and archways, is marked by a 140-foot lighted tower. Six distinct patch reefs known as **Coffin's Patch** have shallow elkhorn forests. **Delta Shoals**, a network of coral canyons fanning seaward from a sandy shoal, attracts divers to its elkhorn, brain, and star coral heads. Marathon's **Thunderbolt**, a 188-foot ship sunk in 1986, sits upright at 115-foot depths, coated with sponge, coral, and hydroid, and attracting angelfish, jacks, and deep-water pelagic creatures. 🗊 *Greater Marathon Chamber and visitors center at MM 53.5,* ☎ *800/262-7284.*

## ISLAMORADA Mile Marker 63–90

Islamorada offers shallow coral reefs, mini walls, shipwrecks, and the **Aquarius** (⊕ www.uncw.edu/aquarius), an underwater habitat for scientific research. Coral heads showcase tropical marine life, from grunt to regal queen angelfish. Green moray eels populate spur-and-groove channels, and nurse sharks linger around overhangs. Submerged attractions include the **Eagle**, a 287-foot ship in 110 feet of water; **Davis Reef**, with gorgonian coral; **Alligator Reef**, where the *USS Alligator* sank while fighting pirates; the sloping **Conch Wall**, with barrel sponges and gorgonian; and **Crocker Wall**, featuring spur-and-groove and block corals. 🗊 *Islamorada Chamber and visitor center at MM 83.2,* ☎ *800/322–5397.*

## KEY LARGO Mile Marker 90–112

Key Largo marine conservation got a big leg up with creation of **John Pennekamp Coral Reef State Park** in 1960, the nation's first undersea preserve, followed by 1975's designation of the **Key Largo National Marine Sanctuary**. A popular underwater attraction is the bronze statue of **Christ of the Abyss** between coral formations. Explorers with a "lust for rust" can dive down to 60 to 90 feet and farther to see the murky cemetery for two twin 327-foot U.S. Coast Guard cutters, *Duane* and *Bibb*, used during World War II; *USS Spiegel Grove*, a 510-foot Navy transport ship sunk in 2002 to create an artificial reef; and **Molasses Reef**, showcasing coral heads. 🗊 *Key Largo Chamber at MM 106,* ☎ *800/822–1088.*

# SCUBA DIVING

A diver explores the coral reef in the Florida Keys National Marine Sanctuary off Key Largo.

Florida offers wonderful opportunities to spend your vacation in the sun and become a certified diver at the same time. In the Keys, count on setting aside three to five days for entry-level or so-called "Open Water" certification offered by many dive shops. Basic certification (covering depths to about 60 feet) involves classroom work and pool training, followed by one or more open-water dives at the reef. After passing a knowledge test and completing the required water training (often starting in a pool), you become a certified recreational scuba diver, eligible to rent dive gear and book dive trips with most operations worldwide. Learning through video or online computer programs can enable you to complete classroom work at home, so you can more efficiently schedule time in the Keys for completing water skills and getting out to the reef for exploration.

Many would-be divers opt to take the classroom instruction and pool training at home at a local dive shop and then spend only two days in the Keys completing four dives. It's not necessarily cheaper, but it can be far more relaxing to commit to only two days of diving.

**Questions you should ask:** Not all dive shops are created equal, and it may be worthwhile to spend extra money for a better diving experience. Some of the larger dive shops take out large catamarans that can carry as many as 24 to 40 people. Many people prefer the intimacy of a smaller boat.

**Good to know:** Divers can become certified through PADI *(www.padi.com)*, NAUI *(www.naui.org)*, or SSI *(www.divessi.com)*. The requirements for all three are similar, and if you do the classroom instruction and pool training with a dive shop associated with one organization, the referral for the open water dives will be honored by most dive shops. Note that you are not allowed to fly for at least 24 hours after a dive, because residual nitrogen in the body can pose health risks upon decompression. While there are no rigid rules on diving after flying, make sure you're well-hydrated before hitting the water.

**Cost:** The four-day cost can range from $300 to $475, but be sure to ask if equipment, instruction manuals, and log books are extra. Some dive shops have relationships with hotels, so check for dive/stay packages. Referral dives (a collaborative effort among training agencies) run from $285 to $300 and discover scuba runs around $175 to $200.

## SNUBA

Beyond snorkeling or the requirements of scuba, you also have the option of "Snuba." The word is a trademarked portmanteau or combo of snorkel and scuba. Marketed as easy-to-learn family fun, Snuba lets you breathe underwater via tubes from an air-supplied vessel above, with no prior diving or snorkel experience required.

## NOT CERTIFIED?

Not sure if you want to commit the time and money to become certified? Not a problem. Most dive shops and many resorts will offer a discover scuba day-long course. In the morning, the instructor will teach you the basics of scuba diving: how to clear your mask, how to come to the surface in the unlikely event you lose your air supply, etc. In the afternoon, instructors will take you out for a dive in relatively shallow water—less than 30 feet. Be sure to ask where the dive will take place. Jumping into the water off a shallow beach may not be as fun as actually going out to the coral. If you decide that diving is something you want to pursue, the open dive may count toward your certification.

■TIP→ You can often book the discover dives at the last minute. It may not be worth it to go out on a windy day when the currents are stronger. Also the underwater world looks a whole lot brighter on sunny days.

(top) Scuba divers; (bottom) Diver ascending line.

14

IN FOCUS UNDER THE SEA

# SNORKELING

Snorkling lets you see the wonders of the sea from a new perspective.

**The basics:** Sure, you can take a deep breath, hold your nose, squint your eyes, and stick your face in the water in an attempt to view submerged habitats . . . but why not protect your eyes, retain your ability to breathe, and keep your hands free to paddle about when exploring underwater? That's what snorkeling is all about.

**Equipment needed:** A mask, snorkel (the tube attached to the mask), and fins. In deeper waters (any depth over your head), life jackets are advised.

**Steps to success:** If you've never snorkeled before, it's natural to feel a bit awkward at first, so don't sweat it. Breathing through a mask and tube, and wearing a pair of fins take getting used to. Like any activity, you build confidence and comfort through practice.

If you're new to snorkeling, begin by submerging your face in shallow water or a swimming pool and breathing calmly through the snorkel while gazing through the mask.

Next you need to learn how to clear water out of your mask and snorkel, an essential skill since splashes can send water into tube openings and masks can leak. Some snorkels have built-in drainage valves, but if a tube clogs, you can force water up and out by exhaling through your mouth. Clearing a mask is similar: lift your head from water while pulling forward on mask to drain. Some masks have built-in purge valves, but those without can be cleared underwater by pressing the top to the forehead and blowing out your nose (charming, isn't it?), allowing air to bubble into the mask, pushing water out the bottom. If it sounds hard, it really isn't. Just try it a few times and you'll soon feel like a pro.

14

Now your goal is to get friendly with fins—you want them to be snug but not too tight—and learn how to propel yourself with them. Fins won't help you float, but they will give you a leg up, so to speak, on smoothly moving through the water or treading water (even when upright) with less effort.

Flutter stroking is the most efficient underwater kick, and the farther your foot bends forward the more leg power you'll be able to transfer to the water and the farther you'll travel with each stroke. Flutter kicking movements involve alternately separating the legs and then drawing them back together. When your legs separate, the leg surface encounters drag from the water, slowing you down. When your legs are drawn back together, they produce a force pushing you forward. If your kick creates more forward force than it causes drag, you'll move ahead.

Submerge your fins to avoid fatigue rather than having them flailing above the water when you kick, and keep your arms at your side to reduce drag. You are in the water—stretched out, face down, and snorkeling happily away—but that doesn't mean you can't hold your breath and go deeper in the water for a closer look at some fish or whatever catches your attention. Just remember that when you do this, your snorkel will be submerged, too, so you won't be breathing (you'll be holding your breath). You can dive head-first, but going feet-first is easier and less scary for most folks, taking less momentum. Before full immersion, take several long, deep breaths to clear carbon dioxide from your lungs.

If your legs tire, flip onto your back and tread water with inverted fin motions while resting. If your mask fogs, wash condensation from lens and clear water from mask.

## TIPS FOR SAFE SNORKELING

■ Snorkel with a buddy and stay together.

■ Plan your entry and exit points prior to getting in the water.

■ Swim into the current on entering and then ride the current back to your exit point.

■ Carry your flippers into the water and then put them on, as it's difficult to walk in them.

■ Make sure your mask fits properly and is not too loose.

■ Pop your head above the water periodically to ensure you aren't drifting too far out, or too close to rocks.

■ Think of the water as someone else's home—don't take anything that doesn't belong to you, or leave any trash behind.

■ Don't touch any sea creatures; they may sting.

■ Wear a T-shirt over your swimsuit to help protect you from being fried by the sun.

■ When in doubt, don't go without a snorkeling professional; try a guided tour.

Cayman Salvor

# TOP OUTFITTERS

| COMPANY | ADDRESS & PHONE | COST | DESCRIPTION |
|---------|-----------------|------|-------------|
| AMY SLATE'S AMORAY DIVE CENTER ⊕ www.amoray.com | ✉ 104250 Overseas Hwy. (MM 104.2), Key Largo ☎ 305/451–3595 | ☺ Daily ⛟ Scuba classes for kids ages 8 and up and adults $100-$200. | Sign up for dive/ snorkel trips, scuba instruction and kid programs. |
| DIVE KEY WEST ⊕ www.divekeywest.com | ✉ 3128 N. Roosevelt Blvd., Key West ☎ 305/296–3823 | ⛟ Snorkel from $49, dive from $69 | Operating nearly 40 years. Has charters, instruction, and gear. |
| ECO SCUBA KEY WEST ⊕ www.ecoscuba.com | ✉ 5930 Peninsular Ave. (MM 5), Key West ☎ 305/851–1899 | ☺ Daily ⛟ Snorkel from $35, scuba from $99. | Debuted in 2009. Offers eco-tours, lobstering, snorkeling, and scuba. |
| FLORIDA KEYS DIVE CENTER ⊕ www.floridakeys-divectr.com | ✉ 90451 Old Hwy. (MM 90.5), Tavernier ☎ 305/852–4599 | ☺ Daily ⛟ Classes from $175. | Charters for snorkelers and divers go to Pennekamp, Key Largo, and Islamorada. |
| HORIZON DIVERS ⊕ www.horizondivers.com | ✉ 100 Ocean Dr. #1, Key Largo ☎ 305/453–3535 | ☺ Daily ⛟ Snorkel from $50, scuba from $80. | Take customized dive/ snorkel trips on a 45-foot catamaran. |
| ISLAND VENTURES ⊕ www.islandventure.com | ✉ 103900 Overseas Hwy. (MM 103.9), Key Largo ☎ 305/451–4957 | ☺ Two trips daily ⛟ Snorkel $45, scuba from $80. | Go on snorkeling and scuba explorations to the Key Largo reef and shipwrecks. |
| KEYS DIVER SNORKEL TOURS ⊕ www.keysdiver.com | ✉ 99696 Overseas Hwy. (MM 99.6), Key Largo ☎ 305/451–1177 | ⛟ Three daily snorkel tours from $28. Includes gear. | Family-oriented snorkel-only tours head to coral reefs such as Pennekamp. |
| LOOE KEY REEF RE-SORT & DIVE CENTER ⊕ www.diveflakeys.com | ✉ 27340 Overseas Hwy. (MM 27.5), Ramrod Key ☎ 305/872–2215 | ☺ Daily ⛟ Snorkel from $44, scuba from $85. | Beginner and advanced scuba instruction, a photographer course, and snorkel gear rental. |
| RON JON SURF SHOP ⊕ www.ronjons.com | ✉ 503 Front St., Key West ☎ 305/293–8880 | ☺ Daily ⛟ Sells snorkel gear. | Several locations in Florida; its HQ is in Cocoa Beach. |
| SNUBA OF KEY WEST ⊕ www.snubakeywest.com | ✉ 600 Palm Ave., Key West ☎ 305/292–4616 | ☺ Daily ⛟ $99 per person, $44 for ride-alongs. | Swimmers ages 8 and up can try Snuba. |
| TILDENS SCUBA CENTER ⊕ www.tildensscuba-center.com | ✉ 4650 Overseas Hwy. (MM 49.5), Marathon ☎ 305/743–7255 | ☺ Daily ⛟ Snorkel from $35.99, scuba from $60.99. | Operating for 25 years. Has lessons, tours, snorkeling, scuba, snuba, gear, and a kids club. |

*Hwy., Upper Matecumbe Key* ☎*305/664–5556* ⊕*www.kaiyogrill. com* ⊙ *No lunch.*

**$$$**
SEAFOOD
★
✕**Marker 88.** A few yards from Florida Bay, this seafood restaurant has been popular for more than 40 years. Large picture windows offer great sunset views, but the bay is lovely no matter what time of day you visit. Chef Sal Barrios serves such irresistible entrées as onion-crusted mahimahi, crispy yellowtail snapper, and mangrove-honey-and-chipotle–glazed rib eye. In addition, there are a half-dozen burgers and sandwiches, and you can't miss the restaurant's famous key lime baked Alaska dessert. The extensive wine list is an oenophile's delight. ⊠ *MM 88 BS, 88000 Overseas Hwy., Plantation Key* ☎*305/852–9315* ⊕*www. marker88.info* ⌂ *Reservations essential.*

**$$$**
ECLECTIC
☾
★
✕**Morada Bay Beach Café.** This bay-front restaurant wins high marks for its surprisingly stellar cuisine, tables planted in the sand, and tiki torches that bathe the evening in romance. Entrées feature alluring combinations like banana curry lobster, and coconut-crusted yellowtail snapper. Seafood takes center stage, but you can always get grilled chicken pasta or a Wagyu burger. A tapas menu caters to smaller appetites or those who can't decide with offerings like grouper ceviche, conch fritters, and tuna rolls. Lunch adds interesting sandwiches to the mix. Sit in a dining room outfitted with surfboards, or outdoors on a beach, where the sunset puts on a mighty show and kids (and your feet) play in the sand. There's nightly live music and a monthly full-moon party. ⊠ *MM 81 BS, 81600 Overseas Hwy., Upper Matecumbe Key* ☎*305/664–0604* ⊕*www.moradabay-restaurant.com.*

**$$$**
FRENCH
Fodor's Choice
★
✕**Pierre's.** One of the Keys' most elegant restaurants, Pierre's marries colonial style with modern food trends. Full of interesting architectural artifacts, the place oozes style, especially the wicker chair–strewn veranda overlooking the bay. Save your best "tropical chic" duds for dinner here, so you don't stand out from your surroundings. The food, drawn from French and Floridian influences, is multilayered and beautifully presented. Among the appetizer choices, few can resist the lamb ravioli or shrimp bisque. A changing list of entrées might include hogfish meunière and steak au poivre. The downstairs bar is a perfect spot for catching sunsets, sipping martinis, and enjoying light eats. ⊠ *MM 81.5 BS, 81600 Overseas Hwy., Upper Matecumbe Key* ☎*305/664–3225* ⊕*www.pierres-restaurant.com* ⌂ *Reservations essential.*

**$$$**
ITALIAN
✕**Uncle's Restaurant.** Former fishing guide Joe LePree adds Italian flair to standard seafood dishes. Here you can have your seafood almandine, Milanese (breaded and fried), LePree (with artichokes, mushrooms, and lemon-butter wine sauce), or any of five other different preparations. For starters, feast on mussels or littleneck clams in a marinara or garlic sauce. Specials sometimes combine game (bison, caribou, or elk) with seafood. Portions are huge, so share dishes or take home a doggie bag. Alternatively arrive early (between 5 and 7) for the lighter menu, priced $12.95 to $17.95. Weather permitting, sit outdoors in the garden; poor acoustics make dining indoors unusually noisy. ⊠ *MM 81 OS, 80939 Overseas Hwy., Upper Matecumbe Key* ☎*305/664–4402* ⊕*www.unclesrestaurant.com* ⊙ *Closed Mon.*

**WHERE TO STAY**

*For expanded hotel reviews, visit Fodors.com.*

**$$$$**   ⊞ **Casa Morada.** This relic from the 1950s was rescued and restyled into
HOTEL   a suave, design-forward, all-suites property in 2000. **Pros:** cool design;
Fodor'sChoice   complimentary snacks and bottled water; complimentary use of bikes,
★   kayaks, and snorkel gear. **Cons:** trailer park across the street; beach is
small and inconsequential. ✉ *MM 82 BS, 136 Madeira Rd., Upper Matecumbe Key* ☎ *305/664–0044 or 888/881–3030* ⊕ *www.casamorada.
com* ⤳ *16 suites* ♿ *In-room: a/c, Wi-Fi. In-hotel: restaurant, room service, bar, pool, water sports, some age restrictions* ¶◎¶ *Breakfast.*

**$$$$**   ⊞ **Cheeca Lodge & Spa.** In the main lodge, West Indian–style rooms boast
RESORT   luxurious touches like elegant balcony tubs that fill from the ceiling.
★   **Pros:** beautifully landscaped grounds; new designer rooms; dive shop
on property. **Cons:** expensive rates; $39 resort fee for activities; busy.
✉ *MM 82 OS, Box 527, Upper Matecumbe Key* ☎ *305/664–4651 or
800/327–2888* ⊕ *www.cheeca.com* ⤳ *214 rooms, 44 1-bedroom suites,
4 2-bedroom suites* ♿ *In-room: a/c, kitchen (some) Wi-Fi. In-hotel: restaurants, bars, golf course, tennis courts, pools, gym, spa, beach, water
sports, children's programs, business center* ¶◎¶ *No meals.*

**$$**   ⊞ **Drop Anchor Resort and Marina.** It's easy to find your cottage here, as
RESORT   they are painted in an array of Crayola colors. **Pros:** bright and color-
★   ful; attention to detail; laid-back charm. **Cons:** noise from the highway;
beach is better for fishing than swimming. ✉ *MM 85 OS, 84959 Over-
seas Hwy., Windley Key* ☎ *305/664–4863 or 888/664–4863* ⊕ *www.
dropanchorresort.com* ⤳ *18 suites* ♿ *In-room: a/c, kitchen (some),
Wi-Fi. In-hotel: pool, beach, laundry facilities* ¶◎¶ *No meals.*

**$$$$**   ⊞ **The Islander Resort.** Although the vintage sign is straight out of a
RESORT   *Happy Days* rerun, this property has undergone a top-to-bottom
transformation while the general layout retained a 1950s feel. **Pros:**
spacious rooms; nice kitchens; eye-popping views. **Cons:** pricey for
what you get; beach has rough sand; no a/c in the screened gym.
✉ *MM 82.1 OS, 82200 Overseas Hwy., Upper Matecumbe Key*
☎ *305/664–2031 or 800/753–6002* ⊕ *www.islanderfloridakeys.com*
⤳ *114 rooms* ♿ *In-room: a/c, kitchen, Wi-Fi. In-hotel: restaurant,
bar, pools, gym, beach, water sports, laundry facilities, some pets
allowed* ¶◎¶ *Breakfast.*

**$$$$**   ⊞ **The Moorings Village.** This tropical retreat is everything you imagine
HOTEL   when you think of the Keys—from hammocks swaying between tow-
Fodor'sChoice   ering trees to sugar-white sand (arguably the Keys' best resort beach)
★   lapped by aqua-green waves. **Pros:** romantic setting; good dining
options with room-charging privileges; beautiful beach. **Cons:** no room
service; extra fee for housekeeping; daily resort fee for activities. ✉ *MM
81.6 OS, 123 Beach Rd., Upper Matecumbe Key* ☎ *305/664–4708*
⊕ *www.themooringsvillage.com* ⤳ *4 cottages, 14 houses* ♿ *In-room:
a/c, kitchen, Wi-Fi. In-hotel: tennis court, pool, gym, spa, beach, water
sports, laundry facilities* ¶◎¶ *No meals.*

**$**   ⊞ **Ragged Edge Resort.** Tucked away in a residential area at the ocean's
HOTEL   edge, this hotel is big on value but short on style. **Pros:** oceanfront
location; boat docks and ramp; cheap rates. **Cons:** dated decor; guests
can be noisy. ✉ *MM 86.5 OS, 243 Treasure Harbor Rd., Plantation*

*Key* ☎ *305/852–5389 or 800/436–2023* ⊕ *www.ragged-edge.com* ⇆ *6 studios, 1 efficiency, 3 2-bedroom suites* ♿ *In-room: a/c, kitchen (some), Wi-Fi. In-hotel: pool.* ⦿ *No meals.*

## LONG KEY

Long Key isn't a tourist hot spot, making it a favorite destination for those looking to avoid the masses and enjoy some ecological history in the process.

### GETTING HERE AND AROUND

Long Key runs from mile markers 70 to 65.5, with the tiny town of Layton at its heart. Many people get around by bike.

14

### EXPLORING

★ **Long Key State Park.** Come here for solitude, hiking, fishing, and camping. On the ocean side, the Golden Orb Trail leads to a boardwalk that cuts through the mangroves (may require some wading) and alongside a lagoon where waterfowl congregate (as do mosquitoes, so be prepared). A 1¼-mi canoe trail leads through a tidal lagoon, and a broad expanse of shallow grass flats is perfect for bonefishing. Bring a mask and snorkel to observe the marine life in the shallow water. The park is particularly popular with campers who long to stake their tent at the campground on a beach. In summer, no-see-ums (biting sand flies) also love the beach, so again—be prepared. The picnic area is on the water, too, but lacks a beach. Canoes rent for $10 per day, and kayak rentals start at $17 for a single for two hours, $21.50 for a double. Rangers lead tours every Thursday at 10 on birding, boating, or beachcombing. ⊠ *MM 67.5 OS, 67400 Overseas Hwy.* ☎ *305/664–4815* ⊕ *www.floridastateparks.org/longkey* 💲 *$4.50 for 1 person, $5.50 for 2 people, and 50¢ for each additional person in the group* ⊙ *Daily 8–sunset.*

### BEACHES

**Long Key State Park.** Camping, snorkeling, and bonefishing are the favored activities along this narrow strip of natural, rocky beach. It lines the park's campground, which is open only to registered campers. ⊠ *MM 67.5 OS, 67400 Overseas Hwy.* ☎ *305/664–4815* ⊕ *www.floridastateparks.org/longkey* 💲 *$4.50 for 1 person, $5.50 for 2 people, and 50¢ for each additional person in the group* ⊙ *Daily 8–sunset.*

### WHERE TO EAT AND STAY

*For expanded hotel reviews, visit Fodors.com.*

$$
RESORT

🏨 **Lime Tree Bay Resort.** Easy on the eye and the wallet, this 2½-acre resort on Florida Bay is far from the hustle and bustle of the larger islands. **Pros:** great views; friendly staff; close to Long Key State Park. **Cons:** only one restaurant nearby, shared balconies. ⊠ *MM 68.5 BS, 68500 Overseas Hwy., Layton* ☎ *305/664–4740 or 800/723–4519* ⊕ *www.limetreebayresort.com* ⇆ *10 rooms, 10 studios, 8 suites, 5 apartments, 4 efficiencies* ♿ *In-room: a/c, kitchen (some), Wi-Fi. In-hotel: tennis court, pool, beach, business center, some pets allowed* ⦿ *No meals.*

**Long Key Viaduct.** As you cross Long Key Channel, look beside you at the old viaduct. The second-longest bridge on the former rail line, this

EN
ROUTE

2-mi-long structure has 222 reinforced-concrete arches. The old bridge is popular with cyclists and anglers, who fish off the sides day and night.

# THE MIDDLE KEYS

Most of the activity in this part of the Florida Keys centers on the town of Marathon—the region's third-largest metropolitan area. On either end of it, smaller keys hold resorts, wildlife research and rehab facilities, a historic village, and a state park. The Middle Keys make a fitting transition from the Upper Keys to the Lower Keys not only geographically but mentally. Crossing Seven Mile Bridge prepares you for the slow pace and don't-give-a-damn attitude you'll find a little farther down the highway. Fishing is one of the main attractions—in fact, the region's commercial-fishing industry was founded here in the early 1800s. Diving is another popular pastime. There are many beaches and natural areas to enjoy in the Middle Keys, where mainland stress becomes an ever more distant memory.

If you get bridge fever—the heebie-jeebies when driving over long stretches of water—you may need a pair of blinders (or a couple of tranquilizers) before tackling the Middle Keys. Stretching from Conch Key to the far side of the Seven Mile Bridge, this zone is home to the region's two longest bridges: Long Key Viaduct and Seven Mile Bridge, both historic landmarks.

Overseas Highway takes you from one end of the region to the other in a direct line that takes in most of the sights, but you'll find some interesting resorts and restaurants off the main drag.

## DUCK AND GRASSY KEYS

*Grassy Key is between mile markers 60 and 57.*

Duck Key holds one of the region's nicest marina resorts, Hawks Cay. To its south, sleepy little Grassy Key, local lore has it, was named not for its vegetation—mostly native trees and shrubs—but for an early settler by the name of Grassy. There's no marked definition between it and Marathon, so it feels sort of like a suburb of its much larger neighbor to the south. Grassy Key's sights-to-see tend toward the natural, including a worthwhile dolphin attraction and a small state park.

### EXPLORING

**Dolphin Connection.** Hawk's Cay Resort's Dolphin Connection offers three programs, including Dockside Dolphins, a 30-minute encounter from the dry training docks ($60); Dolphin Discovery, an in-water program that lasts about 45 minutes and lets you kiss, touch, and feed the dolphins ($155); and Trainer for a Day, a three-hour session with the animal training team ($295). ⊠ *MM 61 OS, 61 Hawks Cay Blvd., Duck Key* ☎ *305/743–7000* ⊕ *www.dolphinconnection.com.*

**Dolphin Research Center.** The 1963 movie *Flipper* popularized the notion of humans interacting with dolphins, and Milton Santini, the film's creator, also opened this center, which is home to a colony of dolphins and sea lions. The nonprofit center has tours, narrated programs, and

### DID YOU KNOW?

Dolphins come in various forms, from the Atlantic bottlenose dolphin to the killer whale. These playful and smart creatures love to leap out of the water and synchronize their movements with others. By swimming next to ships, dolphins can conserve energy.

programs that allow you to greet the dolphins from dry land or play with them in their watery habitat. You can even paint a T-shirt with a dolphin—you pick the paint, the dolphin "designs" your shirt ($55). The center also offers five-day programs for children and adults with disabilities. ⊠ *MM 59 BS, 58901 Overseas Hwy.* ☎ *305/289–1121 or 305/289–0002* ⊕ *www.dolphins.org* ⊠ *$19.50* ⊙ *Daily 9–4:30.*

**OFF THE BEATEN PATH**

**Curry Hammock State Park.** Looking for a slice of the Keys that's far removed from tiki bars? On the ocean and bay sides of Overseas Highway are 260 acres of upland hammock, wetlands, and mangroves. On the bay side, there's a trail through thick hardwoods to a rocky shoreline. The ocean side is more developed, with a sandy beach, a clean bathhouse, picnic tables, a playground, grills, and a 28-site campground open November to May. Locals consider the paddling trails under canopies of arching mangroves one of the best kayaking spots in the Keys. Manatees frequent the area, and it's a great spot for bird-watching. Herons, egrets, ibis, plovers, and sanderlings are commonly spotted. Raptors are often seen in the park, especially during migration periods. ⊠ *MM 57 OS, 56200 Overseas Hwy., Little Crawl Key* ☎ *305/289–2690* ⊕ *www. floridastateparks.org/curryhammock* ⊠ *$4.50 for 1 person, $6 for 2, 50¢ per additional person* ⊙ *Daily 8–sunset.*

## WHERE TO EAT AND STAY

*For expanded hotel reviews, visit Fodors.com.*

**$$$**

**LATIN AMERICAN**

**★**

✕ **Alma.** A refreshing escape from the Middle Keys' same-old menus, Alma serves expertly prepared Florida and Latin-Caribbean dishes in an elegant setting. Nightly changing menus often include yellowtail snapper ceviche with Peruvian popcorn, the divine calabaza-squash-and-lobster risotto, roasted breadfruit gnocchi, curried goat stew with breadfruit tostones, and the grilled bone-in rib eye. Finish your meal with the silky, smooth, passion fruit crème brûlée, which has just the right amount of tartness to balance the delicate caramelized crust. ⊠ *Hawks Cay Resort, 61 Hawks Cay Blvd., Duck Cay* ☎ *305/743– 7000 or 888/432–2242* ⊕ *www.hawkscay.com* ⊙ *No lunch.*

**$$$**

**AMERICAN**

✕ **Hideaway Café.** The name says it all. Tucked between Grassy Key and Marathon, it's easy to miss if you're barnstorming through the middle islands. When you find it (upstairs at Rainbow Bend Resort), you'll discover a favorite of locals who appreciate a well-planned menu, lovely ocean view, and quiet evening away from the crowds. For starters, dig into escargots à la Edison (sautéed with vegetables, pepper, cognac, and cream). Then feast on several specialties, such as a rarely found chateaubriand for one, a whole roasted duck, or the seafood medley combining the catch of the day with scallops and shrimp in a savory sauce. ⊠ *MM 58 OS, Rainbow Bend Resort, 57570 Overseas Hwy., Grassy Key* ☎ *305/289–1554* ⊕ *www.hideawaycafe.com* ⊙ *No lunch.*

**$$**

**RESORT**

▯ **Bonefish Resort.** Set on a skinny lot bedecked with palm trees, banana trees, and hibiscus plantings, this motel-style hideaway is the best choice among the island's back-to-basics properties. **Pros:** decent price for the location; ocean-side setting. **Cons:** decks are small; simple decor. ⊠ *MM 58 OS, 58070 Overseas Hwy.* ☎ *305/743–7107 or 800/274–9949* ⊕ *www.bonefishresort.com* ⤳ *3 rooms, 11 efficiencies* ⌂ *In-room: a/c,* *kitchen (some), Wi-Fi. In-hotel: beach, pool, laundry facilities, some pets allowed* ⦿ *No meals.*

**$$$** ⬚ **Hawks Cay Resort.** An in-the-water program that lets you get up close

RESORT and personal with dolphins makes this sprawling resort a family favor-

☽ ite. **Pros:** huge rooms; restful spa; full-service marina and dive shop.

Fodor's Choice **Cons:** no real beach; far from Marathon's attractions. ⊠ *MM 61 OS,*

★ *61 Hawks Cay Blvd., Duck Key* ☎ *305/743–7000 or 888/432–2242*
⊕ *www.hawkscay.com* ⤶ *161 rooms, 16 suites, 225 2- to 4-bedroom villas* ☽ *In-room: a/c, kitchen (some), Wi-Fi. In-hotel: restaurants, bars, tennis courts, pools, gym, spa, water sports, children's programs, laundry facilities* ⦿ *No meals.*

# MARATHON

**14**

*Marathon runs from mile markers 53 to 47.5.*

*Most of what there is to see lies right off the Overseas Highway, with the exception of a couple of hidden restaurants.*

Marathon is a bustling town, at least compared to other communities in the Keys. As it leaves something to be desired in the charm department, Marathon will probably not be your first choice of places to stay. But there are a number of good dining options, so you'll definitely want to stop for a bite even if you're just passing through on the way to Key West.

Outside of Key West, Marathon has the most historic attractions, which merit a visit, along with its Sombrero Beach. Fishing, diving, and boating are the main events here. It throws tarpon tournaments in April and May, more fishing tournaments in June and September, a seafood festival in March, and lighted boat parades around the winter holidays.

### GETTING HERE AND AROUND

The SuperShuttle charges $102 per passenger for trips from Miami International Airport to the Upper Keys. To go farther into the Keys, you must book an entire 11-person van, which costs about $250 to Marathon. For a trip to the airport, place your request 24 hours in advance.

Miami Dade Transit provides daily bus service from MM 50 in Marathon to the Florida City Walmart Supercenter on the mainland. The bus stops at major shopping centers as well as on-demand anywhere along the route during daily round trips on the hour from 6 am to 10 pm. The cost is $2 one-way, exact change required. The Lower Keys Shuttle bus runs from Marathon to Key West ($3 one-way), with scheduled stops along the way.

### ESSENTIALS

**Transportation Contacts Lower Keys Shuttle** (☎ *305/809–3910* ⊕ *www. kwtransit.com*). **Miami Dade Transit** (*formerly the Dade–Monroe Express* ☎ *305/770–3131*). **SuperShuttle** (☎ *305/871–2000* ⊕ *www.supershuttle.com*).

**Visitor Information Greater Marathon Chamber of Commerce and Visitor Center** (⊠ *MM 53.5 BS, 12222 Overseas Hwy., Marathon* ☎ *305/743–5417 or 800/262–7284* ⊕ *www.floridakeysmarathon.com*).

### EXPLORING

☾ **Crane Point Museum, Nature Center, and Historic Site.** Tucked away from the
★ highway behind a stand of trees, Crane Point—part of a 63-acre tract
that contains the last-known undisturbed thatch-palm hammock—is
delightfully undeveloped. This multiuse facility includes the **Museum
of Natural History of the Florida Keys,** which has displays about
local wildlife, a seashell exhibit, and a marine-life display that makes
you feel you're at the bottom of the sea. Kids love the replica 17th-
century galleon and pirate dress-up room where they can play, and the
re-created **Cracker House** filled with insects, sea-turtle exhibits, and
children's activities. On the 1-mi indigenous loop trail, visit the **Laura
Quinn Wild Bird Center** and the remnants of a Bahamian village,
site of the restored **George Adderly House.** It is the oldest surviving
example of Bahamian tabby (a concretelike material created from sand
and seashells) construction outside of Key West. A boardwalk crosses
wetlands, rivers, and mangroves before ending at Adderly Village.
From November to Easter, docent-led tours are available; bring good
walking shoes and bug repellent during warm weather. ⊠ *MM 50.5
BS, 5550 Overseas Hwy.* ☎ *305/743–9100* ⊕ *www.cranepoint.net*
🖙 *$12.50* ⊙ *Mon.–Sat. 9–5, Sun. noon–5; call to arrange trail tours.*

**QUICK
BITES**

**Leigh Ann's (More Than Just A) Coffee House.** If you don't get a buzz
just from breathing in the robust aroma order an espresso shot, Cuban or
Italian, for a satisfying jolt. Pastries are baked fresh daily, but the biscuits
with sausage gravy and the breakfast burrito with homemade salsa are
among the big movers. Leigh Ann's also serves lunch—quiche, and hot
and cold sandwiches. It's open weekdays 7–5, Saturday 7–3, and Sunday 8–noon. ⊠ *MM 50 OS, 7537 Overseas Hwy.* ☎ *305/743–2001* ⊕ *www.
leighannscoffeehouse.com.*

**Seven Mile Bridge.** This is one of the most photographed images in the
Keys. Actually measuring slightly less than 7 mi, it connects the Middle
and Lower Keys and is believed to be the world's longest segmental
bridge. It has 39 expansion joints separating its various concrete sections. Each April runners gather in Marathon for the annual Seven Mile
Bridge Run. The expanse running parallel to Seven Mile Bridge is what
remains of the **Old Seven Mile Bridge,** an engineering and architectural
marvel in its day that's now on the National Register of Historic Places.
Once proclaimed the Eighth Wonder of the World, it rested on a record
546 concrete piers. No cars are allowed on the old bridge today, but a
2-mi segment is open for biking, walking, and fishing.

**OFF THE
BEATEN
PATH**

**Pigeon Key.** There's much to like about this 5-acre island under the
Old Seven Mile Bridge. You can reach it by walking across a 2-mi
section of the bridge or by ferry. Once there, tour the island on your
own or join a guided tour to explore the buildings that formed the
early-20th-century work camp for the Overseas Railroad that linked
the mainland to Key West. Later the island became a fish camp, a state
park, and then government-administration headquarters. Exhibits in
a small museum recall the history of the Keys, the railroad, and railroad baron Henry M. Flagler. Pick up the ferry outside the gift shop,

which occupies an old railroad car on Knight's Key (MM 47 OS), for a two-hour excursion. Visitors can self-tour and catch the ferry back in a half hour. ⊠ *MM 45 OS, 1 Knights Key Blvd., Pigeon Key* ☎ *305/289–0025 general information, 305/743–5999 reservations* ⊕ *www.pigeonkey.net* ⊠ *$11* ⊘ *Daily 9:30–4; ferryboat departures at 10, 11:30, 1, 2:30.*

**The Turtle Hospital.** More than 100 injured sea turtles check in here every year. The 90-minute guided tours take you into recovery and surgical areas at the world's only state-certified veterinary hospital for sea turtles. If you're lucky, you can visit hatchlings. In the "hospital bed" tanks, you can see recovering patients and others that are permanent residents due to their injuries. If you're lucky, you can visit hatchlings. Call ahead—tours are sometime cancelled due to medical emergencies. ⊠ *MM 48.5 BS, 2396 Overseas Hwy.* ☎ *305/743–2552* ⊕ *www.turtlehospital.org* ⊠ *$15* ⊘ *Daily 9–5; tours at 10, 1, and 4.*

## SPORTS AND THE OUTDOORS

### BEACH

**Sombrero Beach.** Here, pleasant, shaded picnic areas overlook a coconut palm–lined grassy stretch and the Atlantic Ocean. Separate areas allow swimmers, boaters, and windsurfers to share the narrow cove. Facilities include barbecue grills, showers, and restrooms, as well as a large playground, a pier, and a volleyball court. Sunday afternoons draw lots of local families toting coolers. The park is accessible for those with disabilities and allows leashed pets. Turn east at the traffic light in Marathon and follow signs to the end. Best for: families. ⊠ *MM 50 OS, Sombrero Beach Rd.* ☎ *305/743–0033 Ext. 6* ⊠ *Free* ⊘ *Daily 8–sunset.*

### BIKING

Tooling around on two wheels is a good way to see Marathon. There's easy cycling on a 1-mi off-road path that connects to the 2 mi of the Old Seven Mile Bridge leading to Pigeon Key.

**Bike Marathon Bike Rentals.** "Have bikes, will deliver" could be the motto of this company, which gets beach cruisers to your hotel door for $35 per week, including a helmet and basket. Note that there's no physical location, but services are available Monday through Saturday 9–4 and Sunday 9–2. ☎ *305/743–3204* ⊕ *www.bikemarathonbikerentals.com.*

**Bubba's.** Book a custom biking tour through the Keys along the heritage trail. A van accompanies tours to carry luggage and tired riders. Operated by former police officer Bubba Barron, Bubba's hosts an annual one-week ride down the length of the Keys every November. Riders can opt for tent camping ($595) or motel-room accommodations (prices vary). Meals are included on the annual ride and bike rentals are extra. ☎ *321/759–3433* ⊕ *www.bubbafestbiketours.com.*

**Overseas Outfitters.** Aluminum cruisers and hybrid bikes are available for rent for $10 to $15 per day. The company also rents tandem bikes. It's open weekdays 9–6, Saturday 9–3, and Sunday 10–2. ⊠ *MM 48 BS, 1700 Overseas Hwy.* ☎ *305/289–1670* ⊕ *www.overseasoutfitters.com.*

### BOATING

Sail, motor, or paddle—whatever your choice of modes, boating is what the Keys is all about. Brave the Atlantic waves and reefs or explore the backcountry islands on the gulf side. If you don't have a lot of boating and chart-reading experience, it's a good idea to tap into local knowledge on a charter.

**Captain Pip's.** This operator rents 19- to 24-foot outboards, $195–$330 per day, as well as tackle and snorkeling gear. You also can charter a small boat with a guide, $500–$550 for a half day and $750–$800 for a full day. ⊠ *MM 47.5 OS,1410 Overseas Hwy.* 🕾 *305/743–4403 or 800/707–1692* ⊕ *www.captainpips.com.*

**Fish 'n Fun.** Get out on the water on 19- to 26-foot powerboats starting at $140 for a half day, $190 for a full day. The company offers free delivery in the Middle Keys. You also can rent Jet Skis and kayaks. ⊠ *MM 49.5 OS, 4590 Overseas Hwy., at Banana Bay Resort & Marina* 🕾 *305/743–2275 or 800/471–3440* ⊕ *www.fishnfunrentals.com.*

### FISHING

For recreational anglers, the deepwater fishing is superb in both bay and ocean. Marathon West Hump, one good spot, has depths ranging from 500 to more than 1,000 feet. Locals fish from a half-dozen bridges, including Long Key Bridge, the Old Seven Mile Bridge, and both ends of Tom's Harbor. Barracuda, bonefish, dolphinfish, and tarpon all frequent local waters. Party boats and private charters are available.

★ *Marathon Lady.* Morning, afternoon, and night, fish for mahimahi, grouper, and other tasty catch aboard this 73-footer, which departs on half-day ($45) excursions from the Vaca Cut Bridge, north of Marathon. Join the crew for night fishing ($55) from 6:30 to midnight from Memorial Day to Labor Day; it's especially beautiful on a full-moon night. ⊠ *MM 53 OS, at 117th St.* 🕾 *305/743–5580* ⊕ *fishfloridakeys. com/marathonlady.*

**Sea Dog Charters.** Captain Jim Purcell, a deep-sea specialist for ESPN's *The American Outdoorsman,* provides one of the best values in Keys fishing. Next to the Seven Mile Grill, his company offers half- and full-day offshore, reef and wreck, and backcountry fishing trips, as well as fishing and snorkeling trips aboard 30- to 37-foot boats. The cost is $60 per person for a half day, regardless of whether your group fills the boat, and includes bait, light tackle, ice, coolers, and fishing licenses. If you prefer an all-day private charter on a 37-foot boat, he offers those, too, for $600 for up to six people. A fuel surcharge may apply. ⊠ *MM 47.5 BS, 1248 Overseas Hwy.* 🕾 *305/743–8255* ⊕ *www.seadogcharters.net.*

### SCUBA DIVING AND SNORKELING

Local dive operations take you to Sombrero Reef and Lighthouse, the most popular down-under destination in these parts. For a shallow dive and some lobster-nabbing, Coffins Patch, off Key Colony Beach, is a good choice. A number of wrecks such as *Thunderbolt* serve as artificial reefs. Many operations out of this area will also take you to Looe Key Reef.

**Hall's Diving Center & Career Institute.** The institute has been training divers for more than 40 years. Along with conventional twice-a-day snorkel and two-tank dive trips ($30–$55) to the reefs at Sombrero Lighthouse and wrecks like the *Thunderbolt*, the company has more unusual offerings like digital and video photography. ⊠ *MM 48.5 BS, 1994 Overseas Hwy.* ☎ *305/743–5929 or 800/331–4255* ⊕ *www. hallsdiving.com.*

**Spirit Snorkeling.** Snorkeling excursions to Sombrero Reef and Lighthouse Reef cost $30 a head. ⊠ *MM 47.5 BS, 1410 Overseas Hwy., Slip No. 1* ☎ *305/289–0614* ⊕ *www.spiritsnorkeling.net.*

## WHERE TO EAT

¢ ✕ **Fish Tales Market and Eatery.** This roadside eatery with its own seafood
SEAFOOD market serves signature dishes such as oysters on a roll and snapper on grilled rye with coleslaw and melted Muenster cheese. You also can slurp lobster bisque or red-conch chowder. There are burgers, chicken, and dogs for those who don't do seafood. Plan to dine early; it's only open until 6:30 pm. This is a no-frills kind of place with a loyal local following, a couple of picnic tables, and friendly service. ⊠ *MM 52.5 OS, 11711 Overseas Hwy.* ☎ *305/743–9196 or 888/662–4822* ⊕ *www.floridalobster.com* ⚏ *Reservations not accepted* ☽ *Closed Sun.*

$$ ✕ **Key Colony Inn.** The inviting aroma of an Italian kitchen pervades this
ITALIAN family-owned favorite with a supper-club atmosphere. As you'd expect, the service is friendly and attentive. For lunch there are fish and steak entrées served with fries, salad, and bread in addition to Italian specialties. At dinner you can't miss with traditional dishes like veal Oscar and New York strip, or such specialties as seafood *Italiano,* a dish of scallops and shrimp sautéed in garlic butter and served with marinara sauce over a bed of linguine. The place is renowned for its Sunday brunch, served from November to April. ⊠ *MM 54 OS, 700 W. Ocean Dr., Key Colony Beach* ☎ *305/743–0100* ⊕ *www.kcinn.com.*

$$ ✕ **Keys Fisheries Market & Marina.** From the parking lot, this commercial
SEAFOOD warehouse flanked by fishing boats and lobster traps barely hints at the
☺ restaurant inside. Order at the window outside, pick up your food, then
★ dine at one of the waterfront picnic tables outfitted with rolls of paper towels. The menu is comprised of fresh seafood and a token hamburger and chicken sandwich. A huge lobster Reuben ($15.95) served on thick slices of toasted bread is the signature dish. Other delights include the shrimp burger, very rich whiskey-peppercorn snapper, and the Keys Kombo (broiled or grilled lobster, shrimp, scallops, and mahimahi for $29). There are also sushi and a bar serving beer and wine. Kids like feeding the fish while they wait for their food. ⊠ *MM 49 BS, 3390 Gulfview Ave. (turn west on 35th St.), end of 35th St.* ☎ *305/743–4353 or 866/743–4353* ⊕ *www.keysfisheries.com* ⚏ *Reservations not accepted.*

$$$ ✕ **Lazy Days South.** Tucked into Marathon Marina a half-mile north of
SEAFOOD the Seven Mile Bridge, the restaurant offers views just as spectacular
★ as the highly lauded food. A spin-off of an Islamorada favorite, here you'll find a wide range of daily offerings from garlic-baked clams and a coconut-fried fish du jour sandwich to seafood pastas and beef tips over rice. Choose a table on the outdoor deck, or inside underneath paddle fans and surrounded by local art. ⊠ *MM 47.3 OS, 725 11th St.* ☎ *306/289–0839* ⊕ *www.keysdining.com/lazydays.*

¢  ✕ **The Stuffed Pig**. With only eight tables and a counter inside, this break-
AMERICAN  fast-and-lunch place is always hopping. When the weather's right, grab
a table out back. The kitchen whips up daily lunch specials like burgers, seafood platters, or pulled pork with hand-cut fries, but a quick
glance around the room reveals that the all-day breakfast is the main
draw. You can get the usual breakfast plates, but most newcomers opt
for oddities like the lobster omelet, alligator tail and eggs, or "grits and
grunts" (that's fish, to the rest of us). ✉ *MM 49 BS, 3520 Overseas
Hwy.* ☎ *305/743–4059* ⊕ *www.thestuffedpig.com* ⬧ *Reservations not
accepted* ⊟ *No credit cards* ◷ *No dinner.*

### WHERE TO STAY
*For expanded hotel reviews, visit Fodors.com.*

$$$$  ⛉ **Tranquility Bay**. Ralph Lauren could have designed the rooms at this
RESORT  luxurious beach resort. **Pros:** secluded setting; gorgeous design; lovely
☾  crescent beach. **Cons:** a bit sterile; no real Keys atmosphere; cramped
★  building layout. ✉ *MM 48.5 BS, 2600 Overseas Hwy.* ☎ *305/289–0888
or 866/643–5397* ⊕ *www.tranquilitybay.com* ⬐ *45 2-bedroom suites,
41 3-bedroom suites* ⚬ *In-room: a/c, kitchen, Wi-Fi. In-hotel: restaurants, bars, pools, gym, beach, water sports* ⓞ *No meals.*

# THE LOWER KEYS

Beginning at Bahia Honda Key, the islands of the Florida Keys become
smaller, more clustered, and more numerous—a result of ancient tidal
water flowing between the Florida Straits and the gulf. Here you're
likely to see more birds and mangroves than other tourists, and more
refuges, beaches, and campgrounds than museums, restaurants, and
hotels. The islands are made up of two types of limestone, both denser
than the highly permeable Key Largo limestone of the Upper Keys. As
a result, freshwater forms in pools rather than percolating through
the rock, creating watering holes that support alligators, snakes, deer,
rabbits, raccoons, and migratory ducks. Many of these animals can
be seen in the National Key Deer Refuge on Big Pine Key. Nature was
generous with her beauty in the Lower Keys, which have both Looe
Key Reef, arguably the Keys' most beautiful tract of coral, and Bahia
Honda State Park, considered one of the best beaches in the world for
its fine-sand dunes, clear warm waters, and panoramic vista of a historic bridge, hammocks, and azure sky and sea. Big Pine Key is fishing
headquarters for a laid-back community that swells with retirees in
the winter. South of it, the dribble of islands can flash by in a blink of
an eye if you don't take the time to stop at a roadside eatery or check
out tours and charters at the little marinas. In truth, the Lower Keys
include Key West, but since it is as different from the rest of the Lower
Keys as peanut butter is from jelly, it is covered in its own section.

### GETTING HERE AND AROUND
The Lower Keys in this section include the keys between MM 37 and
MM 9. The Seven Mile Bridge drops you into the lap of this homey,
quiet part of the Keys.

Heed speed limits in these parts. They may seem incredibly strict given the traffic is lightest of anywhere in the Keys, but the purpose is to protect the resident Key deer population, and officers of the law pay strict attention and will readily issue speeding tickets.

## BAHIA HONDA KEY

*Bahia Honda Key is between mile markers 38 and 36.*

All of Bahia Honda Key is devoted to its eponymous state park, which keeps it in a pristine state. Besides the park's outdoor activities, it offers an up-close look at the original railroad bridge.

### EXPLORING

**Bahia Honda State Park.** Most first-time visitors to the region are dismayed by the lack of beaches—but then they discover sun-soaked Bahia Honda Key. The 524-acre park here sprawls across both sides of the highway, giving it 2½ mi of fabulous sandy coastline. The snorkeling isn't bad, either; there's underwater life (soft coral, queen conchs, random little fish) just a few hundred feet offshore. Although swimming, kayaking, fishing, and boating are the main reasons to visit, you shouldn't miss biking along the 2½ mi of flat roads or hiking the Silver Palm Trail, with rare West Indian plants and several species found nowhere else in the nation. Along the way you'll be treated to a variety of butterflies. Seasonal ranger-led nature programs take place at or depart from the Sand and Sea Nature Center. There are rental cabins, a campground, snack bar, gift shop, 19-slip marina, nature center, and facilities for renting kayaks and arranging snorkeling tours. Get a panoramic view of the island from what's left of the railroad—the Bahia Honda Bridge. ⊠ *MM 37 OS, 36850 Overseas Hwy.* ☎ *305/872-2353* ⊕ *www.floridastateparks.org/bahiahonda* ☜ *$4.50 for 1 person, $9 for 2 people, 50¢ per additional person* ☽ *Daily 8–sunset.*

Fodor's Choice ★

14

### BEACHES

**Bahia Honda State Park.** The park contains three beaches in all—on both the Atlantic Ocean and the Gulf of Mexico. Sandspur Beach, the largest, is regularly declared the best beach in Florida, and you'll be hard-pressed to argue. The sand is baby-powder soft, and the aqua water is warm, clear, and shallow. With their mild currents, the beaches are great for swimming, even with small fry. **Best for:** snorkeling. ⊠ *MM 37 OS, 36850 Overseas Hwy.* ☎ *305/872-2353* ⊕ *www.floridastateparks.org/bahiahonda* ☜ *$4.50 for 1 person, $9 for 2 people, 50¢ per additional person* ☽ *Daily 8–sunset.*

### SPORTS AND THE OUTDOORS

#### SCUBA DIVING AND SNORKELING

**Bahia Honda Dive Shop.** The concessionaire at Bahia Honda State Park manages a 19-slip marina; rents wet suits, snorkel equipment, and corrective masks; and operates twice-a-day offshore-reef snorkel trips ($30 plus $9 for equipment). Park visitors looking for other fun can rent kayaks ($10 per hour for a single, $18 for a double) and beach chairs. ⊠ *MM 37 OS, 36850 Overseas Hwy.* ☎ *305/872-3210* ⊕ *www.bahiahondapark.com.*

## WHERE TO STAY

*For expanded hotel reviews, visit Fodors.com.*

**$$$**  ⛺ **Bahia Honda State Park**. Elsewhere you'd pay big bucks for the won-
HOTEL  derful water views available at these cabins on Florida Bay. **Pros:** great
★  bay-front views; beachfront camping; affordable rates. **Cons:** books
up fast; area can be buggy. ⊠ *MM 37 OS, 36850 Overseas Hwy.*
☎ *305/872–2353 or 800/326–3521* ⊕ *www.reserveamerica.com* ⤴ *80
partial hook-up campsites, 6 cabin units* ᗕ *In-room: a/c, kitchen, no
TV. In-hotel: beach, water sports* ❍*No meals.*

# BIG PINE KEY

*Big Pine Key runs from mile marker 32 to 30.*

Welcome to the Keys' most natural holdout, where wildlife refuges pro-
tect rare and endangered animals. Here you have left behind the com-
mercialism of the Upper Keys for an authentic backcountry atmosphere.

## ESSENTIALS

**Visitor Information Big Pine and the Lower Keys Chamber of Commerce**
⊠ *MM 31 OS, 31020 Overseas Hwy., Big Pine Key* ☎ *305/872–2411 or 800/872–
3722* ⊕ *www.lowerkeyschamber.com.*

## EXPLORING

★ **National Key Deer Refuge**. This 84,351-acre refuge was established in
1957 to protect the dwindling population of the Key deer, one of more
than 20 animals and plants classified as endangered or threatened in
the Florida Keys. The Key deer, which stands about 30 inches at the
shoulders and is a subspecies of the Virginia white-tailed deer, once
roamed throughout the Lower and Middle Keys, but hunting, destruc-
tion of their habitat, and a growing human population caused their
numbers to decline to 27 by 1957. The deer have made a comeback,
increasing their numbers to approximately 750. The best place to see
Key deer in the refuge is at the end of Key Deer Boulevard and on
No Name Key, a sparsely populated island just east of Big Pine Key.
Mornings and evenings are the best time to spot them. Deer may turn
up along the road at any time of day, so drive slowly. They wander
into nearby yards to nibble tender grass and bougainvillea blossom,
but locals do not appreciate tourists driving into their neighborhoods
after them. Feeding them is against the law and puts them in danger.
The refuge also has 21 other listed endangered and threatened spe-
cies of plants and animals, including five that are found nowhere else.

**Blue Hole**. A quarry left over from railroad days, the Blue Hole is the
largest body of freshwater in the Keys. From the observation platform
and nearby walking trail, you might see the resident alligator, turtles,
and other wildlife. There are two well-marked trails: the Jack Watson
Nature Trail (.6 mi), named after an environmentalist and the refuge's
first warden; and the Fred Mannillo Nature Trail, one of the most
wheelchair-accessible places to see an unspoiled pine-rockland forest
and wetlands. The visitor center has exhibits on Keys biology and ecol-
ogy. The refuge also provides information on the Key West National
Wildlife Refuge and the Great White Heron National Wildlife Refuge.

## DID YOU KNOW?

An old railroad bridge used
to connect Bahia Honda
Key with Key West until a
hurricane destroyed it in
1935. While it is no longer in
operation, the bridge is used
by visitors as a place for
viewing the island.

Accessible only by water, both are popular with kayak outfitters. ✉ *MM 30.5 BS, Visitor Center–Headquarters, Big Pine Shopping Center, 28950 Watson Blvd.* ☎ *305/872–2239* ⊕ *www.fws.gov/nationalkeydeer* 🖃 *Free* ☉ *Daily sunrise–sunset; headquarters weekdays 8–5.*

## SPORTS AND THE OUTDOORS

### BIKING

A good 10 mi of paved roads run from MM 30.3 BS, along Wilder Road, across the bridge to No Name Key, and along Key Deer Boulevard into the National Key Deer Refuge. Along the way you might see some Key deer. Stay off the trails that lead into wetlands, where fat tires can do damage to the environment.

**Big Pine Bicycle Center.** Owner Marty Baird is an avid cyclist and enjoys sharing his knowledge of great places to ride. He's also skilled at selecting the right bike for the journey, and he knows his repairs, too. His old-fashioned single-speed, fat-tire cruisers rent for $8 per half day and $10 for a full day. Helmets, baskets, and locks are included. Although the shop is officially closed on Sunday, Marty leads free off-road fun rides on Sunday mornings at 8 from December to Easter. ✉ *MM 30.9 BS, 31 County Rd.* ☎ *305/872–0130.*

### BOATING

**Strike Zone Charters.** Glass-bottom-boat excursions venture into the backcountry and Atlantic Ocean. The five-hour Island Excursion ($55 plus fuel surcharge) emphasizes nature and Keys history; besides close encounters with birds, sea life, and vegetation, there's a fish cookout on an island. Snorkel and fishing equipment, food, and drinks are included. This is one of the few nature outings in the Keys with wheelchair access. ✉ *MM 29.6 BS, 29675 Overseas Hwy., Big Pine Key* ☎ *305/872–9863 or 800/654–9560* ⊕ *www.strikezonecharter.com.*

### KAYAKING

★ **Big Pine Kayak Adventures.** There's no excuse to skip a water adventure with this convenient kayak rental service, which delivers them to your lodging or anywhere between Seven Mile Bridge and Stock Island. The company, headed by *The Florida Keys Paddling Guide* author Bill Keogh, will rent you a kayak and then ferry you—called taxi-yakking—to remote islands with clear instructions on how to paddle back on your own. Rentals are by the half day or full day. Group kayak tours ($50 each for three hours) explore the mangrove forests of Great White Heron and Key Deer National Wildlife Refuges. Custom tours ($125 and up, four hours) transport you to exquisite backcountry areas teeming with wildlife. Kayak fishing charters are also popular. ✉ *MM 30 BS, Old Wooden Bridge Fishing Camp, turn right at traffic light, continue on Wilder Rd. toward No Name Key* ☎ *305/872–7474* ⊕ *www.keyskayaktours.com.*

### SCUBA DIVING AND SNORKELING

**Strike Zone Charters.** Dive excursions head to the wreck of the 110-foot *Adolphus Busch* ($55), and scuba ($45) and snorkel ($35) trips to Looe Key Reef, prime scuba and snorkeling territory, aboard glass-bottom boats. Strike Zone also offers a five-hour island excursion that combines snorkeling, fishing, and an island cookout for $55 per person.

A large dive shop is on-site. ⊠ *MM 29.5 BS, 29675 Overseas Hwy.* ☎ *305/872–9863 or 800/654–9560* ⊕ *www.strikezonecharter.com.*

## WHERE TO EAT

¢ ✕ **Good Food Conspiracy.** Like good wine, this small natural-foods eatery
VEGETARIAN and market surrenders its pleasures a little at a time. Step inside to the aroma of brewing coffee, and then pick up the scent of fresh strawberries or carrots blending into a smoothie, the green aroma of wheatgrass juice, followed by the earthy odor of hummus. Order raw or cooked vegetarian and vegan dishes, organic soups and salads, and organic coffees and teas. Bountiful sandwiches (available halved) include the popular tuna melt or hummus and avocado. If you can't sit down for a bite, stock up on healthful snacks like dried fruits, raw nuts, and carob-covered almonds. Dine early: The shop closes at 7 pm Monday to Saturday, and at 5 pm on Sunday. ⊠ *MM 30.2 OS, 30150 Overseas Hwy.* ☎ *305/872–3945* ⊕ *www.goodfoodconspiracy.com* ⚅ *Reservations not accepted.*

$ ✕ **No Name Pub.** This no-frills honky-tonk has been around since 1936,
AMERICAN delighting inveterate locals and intrepid vacationers who come for the excellent pizza, cold beer, and *interesting* companionship. The decor, such as it is, amounts to the autographed dollar bills that cover every inch of the place. The full menu printed on place mats includes a tasty conch chowder, a half-pound fried-grouper sandwich, spaghetti and meatballs, and seafood baskets. The lighting is poor, the furnishings are rough, and the music is oldies. This former brothel and bait shop is just before the No Name Key Bridge. It's a bit hard to find, but worth the trouble if you want a singular Keys experience. ⊠ *MM 30 BS, turn west on Wilder Rd., left on South St., right on Ave. B, right on Watson Blvd.* ☎ *305/872–9115* ⊕ *www.nonamepub.com* ⚅ *Reservations not accepted.*

## WHERE TO STAY

*For expanded hotel reviews, visit Fodors.com.*

¢ ⛫ **Big Pine Key Fishing Lodge.** There's a congenial atmosphere at this lively
HOTEL family-owned lodge-campground-marina. **Pros:** local fishing crowd; nice pool; great price. **Cons:** RV park is too close to motel; deer will eat your food if you're camping. ⊠ *MM 33 OS, 33000 Overseas Hwy.* ☎ *305/872–2351* ⤴ *16 rooms; 158 campsites, 97 with full hook-ups, 61 without hook-ups* ⚅ *In-room: kitchen (some), refrigerator. In-hotel: pool, laundry facilities* ⦿ *No meals.*

$$$$ ⛫ **Deer Run Bed & Breakfast.** Key deer wander the grounds of this beach-
B&B/INN front bed-and-breakfast, set on a quiet street lined with buttonwoods
★ and mangroves. **Pros:** quiet location; healthy breakfasts; complimentary bike and kayak use. **Cons:** price is a bit high; hard to find. ⊠ *MM 33 OS, 1997 Long Beach Dr.* ☎ *305/872–2015* ⊕ *www.deerrunfloridabb. com* ⤴ *4 rooms* ⚅ *In-room: Wi-Fi. In-hotel: pool, beach, water sports, some age restrictions* ⦿ *Breakfast.*

## LITTLE TORCH KEY

*Little Torch Key is between mile markers 29 and 10.*

Little Torch Key and its neighbor islands, Ramrod Key and Summerland Key, are good jumping-off points for divers headed for Looe Key Reef.

The islands also serve as a refuge for those who want to make forays into Key West but not stay in the thick of things.

The undeveloped backcountry at your door makes Little Torch Key an ideal location for fishing and kayaking. Nearby **Ramrod Key,** which also caters to divers bound for Looe Key, derives its name from a ship that wrecked on nearby reefs in the early 1800s.

<table>
<tr>
<td>

**NEED A BREAK?**

</td>
<td>

**Baby's Coffee.** The aroma of rich roasting coffee beans arrests you at the door of "the Southernmost Coffee Roaster." Buy it by the pound or by the cup along with fresh baked goods. ⊠ *MM 15 OS, 3178 Overseas Hwy., Saddlebunch Keys* ☎ *305/744–9866 or 800/523–2326* ⊕ *www.babyscoffee.com.*

</td>
</tr>
</table>

## SPORTS AND THE OUTDOORS

### SCUBA DIVING AND SNORKELING

★ **Looe Key Reef.** In 1744 the HMS *Looe,* a British warship, ran aground and sank on one of the most beautiful coral reefs in the Keys. Today the key owes its name to the ill-fated ship. The 5.3-square-nautical-mi reef, part of the **Florida Keys National Marine Sanctuary,** has strands of elkhorn coral on its eastern margin, purple sea fans, and abundant sponges and sea urchins. On its seaward side, it drops almost vertically 50 to 90 feet. In its midst, **Shipwreck Trail** plots the location of nine historic wreck sites in 14 to 120 feet of water. Buoys mark the sites, and underwater signs tell the history of each site and what marine life to expect. Snorkelers and divers will find the sanctuary a quiet place to observe reef life—except in July, when the annual Underwater Music Festival pays homage to Looe Key's beauty and promotes reef awareness with six hours of music broadcast via underwater speakers. Dive shops, charters, and private boats transport about 500 divers and snorkelers to hear the spectacle, which includes classical, jazz, new age, and Caribbean music, as well as a little Jimmy Buffett. There are even underwater Elvis impersonators. ⊠ *MM 27.5 OS, 216 Ann St., Key West* ☎ *305/292–0311.*

**Looe Key Reef Resort & Dive Center.** Rather than the customary morning and afternoon two-tank, two-location trips offered by most dive shops, this center, the closest dive shop to Looe Key Reef, runs a single three-tank, three-location dive ($84 for divers, $44 for snorkelers). The maximum depth is 30 feet, so snorkelers and divers go on the same boat. On Wednesday it runs a trip that visits a wreck and reefs in the area for the same price for either snorkeling or diving. The dive boat, a 45-foot catamaran, is docked at the full-service Looe Key Reef Resort. ⊠ *Looe Key Reef Resort, MM 27.5 OS, 27340 Overseas Hwy., Ramrod Key* ☎ *305/872–221 or 877/816–3483* ⊕ *www.diveflakeys.com.*

### WATER SPORTS

**Sugarloaf Marina.** Rent a paddle-propelled vehicle for exploring local gulf waters. Rates for one-person kayaks start at $25 for one hour to $30 for a full day. Two-person kayaks are also available. Delivery is free for multiple-day rentals. ⊠ *MM 17 BS, 17015 Overseas Hwy., Sugarloaf Key* ☎ *305/745–3135.*

14

## WHERE TO EAT

**$$**
AMERICAN
✕ **Geiger Key Smokehouse Bar & Grill**. There's a strong hint of the Old Keys at this oceanside marina restaurant, which came under new management in 2010. "On the backside of paradise," as the sign says, its tiki structures overlook quiet mangroves at an RV park marina. Locals usually outnumber tourists; they come for the daily dinner specials: pot roast on Tuesday, Italian on Wednesday, prime rib on Friday, and so on. For lunch, try a fish sandwich or pulled pork. The all-day menu spans an ambitious array of sandwiches, tacos, seafood, and steaks. In season, local fishermen stop here for breakfast before heading out in search of the big one. ⊠ *MM 10, Geiger Key at 5 Geiger Key Rd., off Boca Chica Rd.* ☎ *305/296–3553 or 305/294–1230* ⊕ *www.geigerkeymarina.com.*

**$$$$**
ECLECTIC
★
✕ **Little Palm Island Restaurant**. The oceanfront setting calls to mind St. Barts and the other high-end destinations of the Caribbean. Keep that in mind as you reach for the bill, which can also make you swoon. The restaurant at the exclusive Little Palm Island Resort—its dining room and adjacent outdoor terrace lit by candles and warmed by live music—is one of the most romantic spots in the Keys. The seasonal menu is a melding of French and Caribbean flavors, with exotic little touches. Think shrimp and yellowtail ceviche or coconut lobster bisque as a starter, followed by mahimahi with cilantro and creamy polenta. The Saturday and Sunday brunch buffet, the full-moon dinners with live entertainment, and Chef's Table Dinner are very popular. The dining room is open to nonguests on a reservations-only basis. ⊠ *MM 28.5 OS, 28500 Overseas Hwy.* ☎ *305/872–2551* ⊕ *www.littlepalmisland.com* ⌂ *Reservations essential.*

## WHERE TO STAY

*For expanded hotel reviews, visit Fodors.com.*

**$$$$**
RESORT
Fodor's Choice
★
🏠 **Little Palm Island Resort & Spa**. *Haute tropicale* best describes this luxury retreat, and "second mortgage" might explain how some can afford the extravagant prices. **Pros:** secluded setting; heavenly spa; easy wildlife viewing. **Cons:** expensive; might be too quiet for some. ⊠ *MM 28.5 OS, 28500 Overseas Hwy.* ☎ *305/872–2524 or 800/343–8567* ⊕ *www.littlepalmisland.com* ⌨ *30 suites* ⌂ *In-room: a/c, no TV, Wi-Fi. In-hotel: restaurant, bars, pool, gym, spa, beach, water sports, parking, some age restrictions* ⊞*Some meals.*

**$**
HOTEL
🏠 **Looe Key Reef Resort & Center**. If your Keys vacation is all about diving, you'll be well served at this scuba-obsessed operation. **Pros:** guests get discounts on dive and snorkel trips; fun bar. **Cons:** small rooms; unheated pool; close to road. ⊠ *MM 27.5 OS, 27340 Overseas Hwy. Ramrod Key* ☎ *305/872–2215 Ext. 2 or 877/816–3483* ⊕ *www.diveflakeys.com* ⌨ *23 rooms, 1 suite* ⌂ *In-room: a/c, Wi-Fi. In-hotel: bar, pool* ⊞*No meals.*

**$$**
HOTEL
🏠 **Parmer's Resort**. Almost every room at this budget-friendly option has a view of South Pine Channel, with the lovely curl of Big Pine Key in the foreground. **Pros:** bright rooms; pretty setting; good value. **Cons:** a bit out of the way; housekeeping costs extra; little shade around the pool. ⊠ *MM 28.7 BS, 565 Barry Ave.* ☎ *305/872–2157* ⊕ *www.parmersresort.com* ⌨ *18 rooms, 12 efficiencies, 15 apartments, 1*

*penthouse, 1 2-bedroom cottage* 🏊 *In-room: a/c, kitchen (some). In-hotel: pool, laundry facilities* 🍴 *Breakfast.*

EN
ROUTE
The huge object that looks like a white whale floating over Cudjoe Key (MM 23–21) is not a figment of your imagination. It's Fat Albert, a radar balloon that monitors local air and water traffic.

# KEY WEST

Situated 150 mi from Miami, 90 mi from Havana, and an immeasurable distance from sanity, this end-of-the-line community has never been like anywhere else. Even after it was connected to the rest of the country—by the railroad in 1912 and by the highway in 1938—it maintained a strong sense of detachment.

Key West reflects a diverse population: Conchs (natives, many of whom trace their ancestry to the Bahamas), freshwater Conchs (longtime residents who migrated from somewhere else years ago), Hispanics (primarily descendants of Cuban immigrants), recent refugees from the urban sprawl of mainland Florida, military personnel, and an assortment of vagabonds, drifters, and dropouts in search of refuge. The island was once a gay vacation hot spot, and it remains a decidedly gay-friendly destination. Some of the most renowned gay guesthouses, however, no longer cater to an exclusively gay clientele. Key Westers pride themselves on their tolerance of all peoples, all sexual orientations, and even all animals. Most restaurants allow pets, and it's not surprising to see stray cats, dogs, and even chickens roaming freely through the dining rooms. The chicken issue is one that government officials periodically try to bring to an end, but the colorful iconic fowl continue to strut and crow, particularly in the vicinity of Old Town's Bahamian Village.

Although the rest of the Keys are known for outdoor activities, Key West has something of a city feel. Few open spaces remain, as promoters continue to churn out restaurants, galleries, shops, and museums to interpret the city's intriguing past. As a tourist destination, Key West has a lot to sell—an average temperature of 79°F, 19th-century architecture, and a laid-back lifestyle. Yet much has been lost to those eager for a buck. Duval Street looks like a miniature Las Vegas lined with garish signs for T-shirt shops and tour company offices. Cruise ships dwarf the town's skyline and fill the streets with day-trippers gawking at the hippies with dogs in their bike baskets, gay couples walking down the street holding hands, and the oddball lot of locals, some of whom bark louder than the dogs.

**GETTING HERE AND AROUND**

Between mile markers 4 and 0, Key West is the one place in the Keys where you could conceivably do without a car, especially if you plan on staying around Old Town. If you've driven the 106 mi down the chain, you're probably ready to abandon your car in the hotel parking lot anyway. Trolleys, buses, bikes, scooters, and feet are more suitable alternatives. To explore the beaches, New Town, and Stock Island, you'll probably need a car.

## KEY WEST'S COLORFUL HISTORY

The United States acquired Key West from Spain in 1821, along with the rest of Florida. The Spanish had named the island Cayo Hueso, or Bone Key, after the American Indians' skeletons they found on its shores. In 1823, President James Monroe sent Commodore David S. Porter to chase pirates away. For three decades the primary industry in Key West was wrecking—rescuing people and salvaging cargo from ships that foundered on the nearby reefs. According to some reports, when pickings were lean the wreckers hung out lights to lure ships aground. Their business declined after 1849 when the federal government began building lighthouses.

In 1845 the army began construction on Fort Taylor, which kept Key West on the Union side during the Civil War, even though most of Florida seceded. After the fighting ended, an influx of Cubans unhappy with Spain's rule brought the cigar industry here. Fishing, shrimping, and sponge-gathering became important industries, as did pineapple canning. Through much of the 19th century and into the 20th, Key West was

Florida's wealthiest city in per-capita terms. But in 1929 the local economy began to unravel. Cigar-making moved to Tampa, Hawaii dominated the pineapple industry, and the sponges succumbed to blight. Then the Depression hit, and within a few years half the population was on relief.

Tourism began to revive Key West, but that came to a halt when a hurricane knocked out the railroad bridge in 1935. To help the tourism industry recover from that crushing blow, the government offered incentives for islanders to turn their charming homes—many of them built by shipwrights—into guesthouses and inns. The wise foresight has left the town with more than 100 such lodgings, a hallmark of Key West vacationing today. In the 1950s the discovery of "pink gold" in the Dry Tortugas boosted the economy of the entire region. Harvesting Key West shrimp required a fleet of up to 500 boats and flooded local restaurants with sweet luscious shrimp. The town's artistic community found inspiration in the colorful fishing boats.

**14**

Greyhound Lines runs a special Keys shuttle two times a day (depending on the day of the week) from Miami International Airport (departing from Concourse E, lower level) and stops throughout the Keys. Fares run about $39 for Key West (3535 S. Roosevelt, Key West International Airport). Keys Shuttle runs scheduled service six times a day in 15-passenger vans between Miami Airport and Key West with stops throughout the Keys for $70 to $90 per person. Key West Express operates air-conditioned ferries between the Key West Terminal (Caroline and Grinnell streets) and Marco Island and Fort Myers Beach. The trip from Fort Myers Beach takes at least four hours each way and costs $85.50 one-way, $145 round-trip. Ferries depart from Fort Myers Beach at 8:30 am and from Key West at 6 pm. The Marco Island ferry costs $85.50 one-way and $119 round-trip, and departs at 8:30 am. A photo ID is required for each passenger. Advance reservations are recommended. The SuperShuttle charges $102 per passenger for trips from Miami International Airport to the Upper Keys. To go farther into the Keys, you must book an entire 11-person van, which costs about $350 to Key West. You need to place your request for transportation back to the airport 24 hours in advance.

The City of Key West Department of Transportation has six color-coded bus routes traversing the island from 6:30 am to 11:30 pm. Stops have signs with the international bus symbol. Schedules are available on buses and at hotels, visitor centers, and shops. The fare is $2 one-way. The Lower Keys Shuttle bus runs from Marathon to Key West ($3 one-way), with scheduled stops along the way.

Old Town Key West is the only place in the Keys where parking is a problem. There are public parking lots that charge by the hour or day (some hotels and B&Bs provide parking or discounts at municipal lots). If you arrive early, you can sometimes find a spot on side streets off Duval and Whitehead, where you can park for free—just be sure it's not marked for residential parking only. Your best bet is to bike or take the trolley around town if you don't want to walk. You can disembark and reboard the trolley at will.

### ESSENTIALS

**Transportation Contacts City of Key West Department of Transportation** (☎ 305/809-3910). **Greyhound Lines** (☎ 800/410-5397 or 800/231-2222). **Keys Shuttle** (☎ 305/289-9997 or 888/765-9997 ⊕ www.floridakeysshuttle.com). **Key West Express** (✉ 100 Grinnell St. ☎ 888/539-2628 ⊕ www.seakeywestexpress.com). **Lower Keys Shuttle** (☎ 305/809-3910 ⊕ www.monroecounty-fl.gov). **SuperShuttle** (☎ 305/871-2000 ⊕ www.supershuttle.com).

**Visitor Information Greater Key West Chamber of Commerce** (✉ 510 Greene St. ☎ 305/294-2587 or 800/527-8539 ⊕ www.keywestchamber.org).

# EXPLORING

## OLD TOWN

The heart of Key West, this historic Old Town area runs from White Street to the waterfront. Beginning in 1822, wharves, warehouses, chandleries, ship-repair facilities, and eventually in 1891 the U.S. Custom House sprang up around the deep harbor to accommodate the navy's large ships and other sailing vessels. Wreckers, merchants, and sea captains built lavish houses near the bustling waterfront. A remarkable number of these fine Victorian and pre-Victorian structures have been restored to their original grandeur and now serve as homes, guesthouses, shops, restaurants, and museums. These, along with the dwellings of famous writers, artists, and politicians who've come to Key West over the past 175 years, are among the area's approximately 3,000 historic structures. Old Town also has the city's finest restaurants and hotels, lively street life, and popular nightspots.

### TOP ATTRACTIONS

**Audubon House and Tropical Gardens.** If you've ever seen an engraving by ornithologist John James Audubon, you'll understand why his name is synonymous with birds. See his works in this three-story house, which was built in the 1840s for Captain John Geiger and filled with period furniture. It now commemorates Audubon's 1832 stop in Key West while he was traveling through Florida to study birds. Docents lead a guided tour ($7.50) that points out the rare indigenous plants and trees in the garden. An art gallery sells lithographs of the artist's famed portraits. ✉ *205 Whitehead St.* ☎ *305/294–2116 or 877/294–2470* ⊕ *www.audubonhouse.com* ✏ *$12; additional $7.50 for tours* ☉ *Daily 9:30–5, last tour starts at 4:30.*

★ **Ernest Hemingway Home and Museum.** Amusing anecdotes spice up the guided tours of Ernest Hemingway's home, built in 1801 by the town's most successful wrecker. While living here between 1931 and 1942, Hemingway wrote about 70% of his life's work, including classics like *For Whom the Bell Tolls.* Few of his belongings remain aside from some books, and there's little about his actual work, but photographs help you visualize his day-to-day life. The supposed six-toed descendants of Hemingway's cats—many named for actors, artists, authors, and even a hurricane—have free rein of the property. Tours begin every 10 minutes and take 30 minutes; then you're free to explore on your own. ✉ *907 Whitehead St.* ☎ *305/294–1136* ⊕ *www.hemingwayhome.com* ✏ *$12* ☉ *Daily 9–5.*

★ **Fort Zachary Taylor Historic State Park.** Construction of the fort began in 1845 but was halted during the Civil War. Even though Florida seceded from the Union, Yankee forces used the fort as a base to block Confederate shipping. More than 1,500 Confederate vessels were detained in Key West's harbor. The fort, finally completed in 1866, was also used in the Spanish-American War. Take a 30-minute guided walking tour of the redbrick fort, a National Historic Landmark, at noon and 2, or self-tour anytime between 8 and 5. In February a celebration called Civil War Heritage Days includes costumed reenactments and demonstrations. From mid-January to mid-April the park serves as an open-air gallery for pieces created for Sculpture Key West. One of its most popular features is its man-made beach, a rest stop for migrating birds in the spring and fall; there are also hiking and biking trails and a kayak launch. ✉ *Box 6565; end of Southard St., through Truman Annex* ☎ *305/292–6713* ⊕ *www.floridastateparks.org/forttaylor* ✏ *$4.50 for 1 person, $7 for 2 people, 50¢ per additional person* ☉ *Daily 8–sunset, tours noon and 2.*

**NEED A BREAK?**

**Key West Library.** Check out the pretty palm garden next to the Key West Library at 700 Fleming Street, just off Duval. This leafy, outdoor reading area, with shaded benches, is the perfect place to escape the frenzy and crowds of downtown Key West. There's free Internet access in the library, too. ✉ *700 Fleming St.*

**Harry S. Truman Little White House Museum.** Recent renovations to this circa-1890 landmark have restored the home and gardens to the Truman era, down to the wallpaper pattern. A free photographic review of visiting dignitaries and presidents—John F. Kennedy, Jimmy Carter, and Bill Clinton are among the chief executives who passed through here—is on display in the back of the gift shop. Engaging 45-minute tours begin every 15 minutes until 4:30. They start with an excellent 10-minute video on the history of the property and Truman's visits. On the grounds

**14**

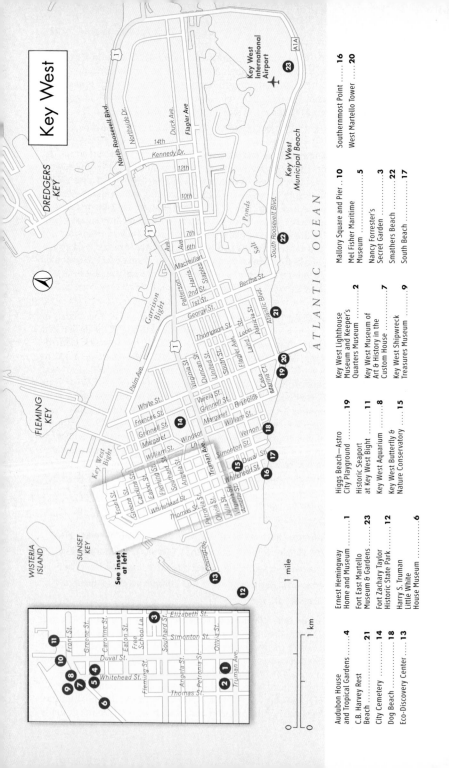

# Key West

DREDGERS KEY

WISTERIA ISLAND

SUNSET KEY

FLEMING KEY

See inset at left

Key West International Airport

A1A

Key West Municipal Beach

ATLANTIC OCEAN

GARRISON BIGHT

Key West Bight

**Inset streets:** Elizabeth St., Simonton St., Duval St., Whitehead St., Thomas St., Front St., Greene St., Caroline St., Eaton St., Southard St., Free School La., Fleming St., Angela St., Petronia St., Olivia St., Truman Ave.

**Map streets:** North Roosevelt Blvd., Northside Dr., Duck Ave., Flagler Ave., 14th, Kennedy Dr., 12th, 10th, 7th, 6th, Ave., Ave., Machllian, Palm Ave., White St., Frances St., Grinnell St., Margaret, William St., Windsor, Ln., Simonton St., Truman Ave., Duval St., Whitehead St., Front St., Greene St., Caroline St., Eaton St., Southard St., Angela St., Thomas St., Petronia St., Olivia St., Julia St., Amelia St., Virginia St., Varela St., Grinnell St., Margaret, Reynolds, Vernon, Patterson, Harris, 2nd St., Staples, 1st St., George St., Thompson St., Duncan St., United St., South St., Flagler Ave., Leon, Laird, Patricia St., Atlantic Blvd., Casa Ct., Marina Ct., Bertha St., South Roosevelt Blvd., Ponds, Salt, Thomas Shar., Eisenhower Dr.

0 ⊢ 1 km
0 ⊢ 1 mile

# KEY WEST: A GOOD TOUR

To cover many sights, take the **Old Town Trolley**, which lets you get off and reboard a later trolley, or the **Conch Train**, which is a set guided tour. Old Town is also manageable by foot, bicycle, moped, or electric car. The area is expansive, so you'll want either to pick and choose from the stops on this tour or break it into two or more days. Start on Whitehead Street at the **Ernest Hemingway Home and Museum**, and then cross the street and climb to the top of the **Key West Lighthouse Museum & Keeper's Quarters Museum** for a spectacular view. Return to Whitehead Street and follow it north to Angela Street, where you'll turn right. At Margaret Street, the **City Cemetery** is worth a look for its aboveground vaults and unusual headstone inscriptions. Head north on Margaret Street, turn left onto Southard Street, then right onto Simonton Street. Halfway up the block, **Nancy Forrester's Secret Garden** occupies Free School Lane. Follow Southard Street south through Truman Annex to **Fort Zachary Taylor Historic State Park**.

Walk west into Truman Annex to see the **Harry S. Truman Little White House Museum**, President Truman's vacation residence. Return east on Caroline and turn left on Whitehead to visit the **Audubon House and Tropical Gardens**, honoring the famed artist and naturalist. Follow Whitehead north to Greene Street and turn left to see the salvaged sea treasures of the **Mel Fisher Maritime Museum**. At Whitehead's northern end are the **Key West Aquarium** and the **Key West Museum of Art & History**, in the historic former U.S. Custom House. By late afternoon you should be ready to cool off with a dip or catch a few rays at the beach. From the aquarium, head east about a mile, where you'll find **South Beach**, located at Southernmost Hotel at the Beach and named for its location at the southern end of Duval Street. If you've brought your pet, stroll a few blocks east to **Dog Beach**, at the corner of Vernon and Waddell streets. A little farther east is **Higgs Beach–Astro City Playground**, on Atlantic Boulevard between White and Reynolds streets. As the sun starts to sink, return to the west side of Old Town and follow the crowds to Mallory Square, behind the aquarium, to watch Key West's nightly sunset spectacle. Those lucky enough may see a green flash—the brilliant splash of green or blue that sometimes appears as the sun sinks into the ocean on a clear night. For dinner, head east on Caroline Street to **Historic Seaport at Key West Bight**, a renovated area where there are numerous restaurants and bars.

### TIMING

Allow two full days to see all the Old Town museums and homes, especially with a little shopping thrown in. For a narrated trip on the Conch Train or trolley, budget 1½ hours to ride the loop without getting off, or an entire day if you plan to get off and on the trolley at sights and restaurants.

14

Sailboats big and small make their way into Key West Harbor; photo by John Franzis, Fodors.com member.

of **Truman Annex,** a 103-acre former military parade grounds and barracks, the home served as a winter White House for presidents Truman, Eisenhower, and Kennedy. Note: The tour does require climbing steps. Visitors can do a self-guided botanical tour of the grounds with a free brochure from the museum store. ⊠ *111 Front St.* ☎ *305/294–9911* ⊕ *www.trumanlittlewhitehouse.com* ✉ *$15* ⊘ *Daily 9–5, grounds 7–6; last tour at 4:30.*

**Historic Seaport at Key West Bight.** What used to be a funky—in some places even seedy—part of town is now an 8½-acre historic restoration of 100 businesses, including waterfront restaurants, open-air bars, museums, clothing stores, bait shops, dive shops, docks, a marina, and water-sports concessions. It's all linked by the 2-mi waterfront **Harborwalk,** which runs between Front and Grinnell streets, passing big ships, schooners, sunset cruises, fishing charters, and glass-bottom boats. ⊠ *100 Grinnell St.* ☎ *305/293–8309.*

| NEED A BREAK? | **Coffee Plantation.** Get your morning (or afternoon) buzz, and hook up to the Internet in the comfort of a homelike setting in a circa-1890 Conch house. Munch on sandwiches, wraps, and pastries, and sip a hot or cold espresso beverage. ⊠ *713 Caroline St.* ☎ *305/295–9808* ⊕ *www. coffeeplantationkeywest.com.* |

☺
★ **Key West Butterfly & Nature Conservatory.** This air-conditioned refuge for butterflies, birds, and the human spirit gladdens the soul with hundreds of colorful wings—more than 45 species of butterflies alone—in a lovely glass-encased bubble. Waterfalls, artistic benches, paved pathways, birds, and lush, flowering vegetation elevate this above most

butterfly attractions. The gift shop and gallery are worth a visit on their own. ✉ *1316 Duval St.* ☎ *305/296–2988 or 800/839–4647* ⊕ *www.keywestbutterfly.com* 💲 *$12* ⊙ *Daily 9–5 (last admission 4:30); gallery and shop open until 5:30.*

**Key West Lighthouse Museum & Keeper's Quarters Museum.** For the best view in town, climb the 88 steps to the top of this 1847 lighthouse. The 92-foot structure has a Fresnel lens, which was installed in the 1860s at a cost of $1 million. The keeper lived in the adjacent 1887 clapboard house, which now exhibits vintage photographs, ship models, nautical charts, and lighthouse artifacts from all along the Key reefs. A kids' room is stocked with books and toys. ✉ *938 Whitehead St.* ☎ *305/295–6616* ⊕ *www.kwahs.com* 💲 *$10* ⊙ *Daily 9:30–5; last admission at 4:30.*

Fodor's Choice ★ **Key West Museum of Art & History in the Custom House.** When Key West was designated a U.S. port of entry in the early 1820s, a customhouse was established. Salvaged cargoes from ships wrecked on the reefs were brought here, setting the stage for Key West to become--for a time--the richest city in Florida. The imposing redbrick-and-terra-cotta Richardsonian Romanesque–style building reopened as a museum and art gallery in 1999. Smaller galleries have long-term and changing exhibits about the history of Key West, including a Hemingway room and a fine collection of folk artist Mario Sanchez's wood paintings. In 2011, to commemorate the 100th anniversary of the railroad's arrival to Key West in 1912, a new permanent Flagler exhibit opened. ✉ *281 Front St.* ☎ *305/295–6616* ⊕ *www.kwahs.com* 💲 *$7* ⊙ *Daily 9:30–5.*

**Mallory Square and Pier.** For cruise-ship passengers, this is the disembarkation point for an attack on Key West. For practically every visitor, it's the requisite venue for a nightly sunset celebration that includes street performers—human statues, sword swallowers, tightrope walkers, musicians, and more—plus craft vendors, conch fritter fryers, and other regulars who defy classification. (Wanna picture with my pet iguana?) With all the activity, don't forget to watch the main show: a dazzling tropical sunset. ✉ *Mallory Sq.* ☎ *No phone.*

**The Southernmost Point.** Possibly the most photographed site in Key West (even though the actual geographic southernmost point in the continental United States lies across the bay on a naval base, where you see a satellite dish), this is a must-see. Who wouldn't want his picture taken next to the big striped buoy that marks the southernmost point in the continental United States? A plaque next to it honors Cubans who lost their lives trying to escape to America and other signs tell Key West history. ✉ *Whitehead and South Sts.* ☎ *No phone.*

## WORTH NOTING

**City Cemetery.** You can learn almost as much about a town's history through its cemetery as through its historic houses. Key West's celebrated 20-acre burial place may leave you wanting more, with headstone epitaphs such as "I told you I was sick," and, for a wayward husband, "Now I know where he's sleeping at night." Among the interesting plots are a memorial to the sailors killed in the sinking of the battleship USS *Maine,* carved angels and lambs marking graves of children, and grand aboveground crypts that put to shame many of the town's dwellings for

14

See the typewriter Hemingway used at his home office in Key West. He lived here from 1931 to 1942.

the living. There are separate plots for Catholics, Jews, and refugees from Cuba. You're free to walk around the cemetery on your own, but the best way to see it is on a 90-minute tour given by the staff and volunteers of the Historic Florida Keys Foundation. Tours leave from the main gate, and reservations are required. ⊠ *Margaret and Angela Sts.* ☎ *305/292–6718* 🖃 *Tours $15* ⊙ *Daily sunrise–6 pm, tours Tues. and Thurs. at 9:30 year-round; call for additional times.*

**Dog Beach.** Next to Louie's Backyard, this tiny beach—the only one in Key West where dogs are allowed unleashed—has a shore that's a mix of sand and rocks. **Best for:** dog owners. ⊠ *Vernon and Waddell Sts.* ☎ *No phone* 🖃 *Free* ⊙ *Daily sunrise–sunset.*

**Eco-Discovery Center.** While visiting Fort Zachary Taylor Historic State Park, stop in at this 6,400-square-foot interactive attraction, which encourages visitors to venture through a variety of Florida Keys habitats from pinelands, beach dunes, and mangroves to the deep sea. Walk through a model of NOAA's (National Oceanic and Atmospheric Administration) Aquarius, a unique underwater ocean laboratory 9 mi off Key Largo, to virtually discover what lurks beneath the sea. Touch-screen computer displays, a dramatic movie, a 2,450-gallon aquarium, and live underwater cameras show off North America's only contiguous barrier coral reef. ⊠ *35 E. Quay Rd., at end of Southard St. in Truman Annex* ☎ *305/809–4750* ⊕ *floridakeys.noaa.gov* 🖃 *Free, donations accepted* ⊙ *Tues.–Sat. 9–4.*

**Key West Aquarium.** Pet a nurse shark and explore the fascinating underwater realm of the Keys without getting wet at this historic aquarium. Hundreds of tropical fish and enormous sea creatures live here. A touch

## CLOSE UP
# Hemingway Was Here

In a town where Pulitzer Prize–winning writers are almost as common as coconuts, Ernest Hemingway stands out. Bars and restaurants around the island claim that he ate or drank there (except Bagatelle, where the sign reads "Hemingway never liked this place").

Hemingway came to Key West in 1928 at the urging of writer John dos Passos and rented a house with wife number two, Pauline Pfeiffer. They spent winters in the Keys and summers in Europe and Wyoming, occasionally taking African safaris. Along the way they had two sons, Patrick and Gregory. In 1931, Pauline's wealthy uncle Gus gave the couple the house at 907 Whitehead Street. Now known as the Ernest Hemingway Home & Museum, it's Key West's number-one tourist attraction. Renovations included the addition of a pool and a tropical garden.

In 1935, when the visitor bureau included the house in a tourist brochure, Hemingway promptly built the brick wall that surrounds it today. He wrote of the visitor bureau's offense in a 1935 essay for *Esquire,* saying, "The house at present occupied by your correspondent is listed as number eighteen in a compilation of the forty-eight things for a tourist to see in Key West. So there will be no difficulty in a tourist finding it or any other of the sights of the city, a map has been prepared by the local F.E.R.A. authorities to be presented to each arriving visitor. This is all very flattering to the easily bloated ego of your correspondent but very hard on production."

During his time in Key West, Hemingway penned some of his most important works, including *A Farewell to Arms, To Have and Have Not, Green Hills of Africa,* and *Death in the Afternoon.* His rigorous schedule consisted of writing almost every morning in his second-story studio above the pool, then promptly descending the stairs at midday. By afternoon and evening he was ready for drinking, fishing, swimming, boxing, and hanging around with the boys.

One close friend was Joe Russell, a craggy fisherman and owner of the rugged bar Sloppy Joe's, originally at 428 Greene Street but now at 201 Duval Street. Russell was the only one in town who would cash Hemingway's $1,000 royalty check. Russell and Charles Thompson introduced Hemingway to deep-sea fishing, which became fodder for his writing. Another of Hemingway's loves was boxing. He set up a ring in his yard and paid local fighters to box with him, and he refereed matches at Blue Heaven, then a saloon at 729 Thomas Street.

Hemingway honed his macho image, dressed in cutoffs and old shirts, and took on the name Papa. In turn, he gave his friends new names and used them as characters in his stories. Joe Russell became Freddy, captain of the *Queen Conch* charter boat in *To Have and Have Not.*

Hemingway stayed in Key West for 11 years before leaving Pauline for wife number three. Pauline and the boys stayed on in the house, which sold in 1951 for $80,000, 10 times its original cost.

—Jim and Cynthia Tunstall

14

tank enables you to handle starfish, sea cucumbers, horseshoe and hermit crabs, even horse and queen conchs—living totems of the Conch Republic. Built in 1934 by the Works Progress Administration as the world's first open-air aquarium, most of the building has been enclosed for all-weather viewing. Guided tours, included in the admission price, feature shark feedings. ⊠ *1 Whitehead St.* ☎ *305/296–2051* ⊕ *www. keywestaquarium.com* ⊠ *$12* ☉ *Daily 10–6; tours at 11, 1, 3, and 4:30.*

**Key West Shipwreck Treasures Museum.** Much of Key West's history, early prosperity, and interesting architecture come from ships that ran aground on its coral reef. Artifacts from the circa-1856 *Isaac Allerton,* which yielded $150,000 worth of wreckage, comprise the museum portion of this multifaceted attraction. Actors and films add a bit of Disneyesque drama. The final highlight is climbing to the top of the 65-foot lookout tower, a reproduction of the 20 or so towers used by Key West wreckers during the town's salvaging heydays. ⊠ *1 Whitehead St.* ☎ *305/292–8990* ⊕ *www.shipwreckhistoreum.com* ⊠ *$12* ☉ *Daily 9:40–5.*

**Mel Fisher Maritime Museum.** In 1622 two Spanish galleons laden with riches from South America foundered in a hurricane 40 mi west of the Keys. In 1985 diver Mel Fisher recovered the treasures from the lost ships, the *Nuestra Señora de Atocha* and the *Santa Margarita.* Fisher's incredible adventure tracking these fabled hoards and battling the state of Florida for rights is as amazing as the loot you'll see, touch, and learn about in this museum. Artifacts include a gold bar (that you can lift to get an idea of what $15,000 feels like) and a 77.76-carat natural emerald crystal worth almost $250,000. Exhibits on the second floor rotate and might cover slave ships, including the excavated 17th-century *Henrietta Marie,* or the evolution of Florida maritime history. ⊠ *200 Greene St.* ☎ *305/294–2633* ⊕ *www.melfisher.org* ⊠ *$12* ☉ *Weekdays 8:30–6, weekends 9:30–6 (last tickets sold at 5:15).*

**Nancy Forrester's Secret Garden.** It's hard to believe that this green escape still exists in the middle of Old Town Key West. Despite damage by hurricanes and pressures from developers, Nancy Forrester has maintained her naturalized garden for more than 40 years. Growing in harmony are rare palms and cycads, ferns, bromeliads, bright gingers and heliconias, gumbo-limbo trees strewn with orchids and vines, and a colorful crew of birds, reptiles, cats, and a few surprises. An art gallery has botanical prints and environmental art. One-hour private tours cost $35 per person, four-person minimum. ⊠ *1 Free School La. (off 500 block of Simonton)* ☎ *305/294–0015* ⊕ *www.nancyforrester.com* ⊠ *$10* ☉ *Daily 10–5.*

## NEW TOWN

The Overseas Highway splits as it enters Key West, the two forks rejoining to encircle New Town, the area east of White Street to Cow Key Channel. The southern fork runs along the shore as South Roosevelt Boulevard (Route A1A) skirting Key West International Airport. Along the north shore, North Roosevelt Boulevard (U.S. 1) leads to Old Town. Part of New Town was created with dredged fill. The island would have continued growing this way had the Army Corps of Engineers not determined in the early 1970s that it was detrimental to the nearby reef.

★   **Fort East Martello Museum & Gardens.** This redbrick Civil War fort never saw a lick of action during the war. Today it serves as a museum, with historical exhibits about the 19th and 20th centuries. Among the latter are relics of the USS *Maine,* cigar factory and shipwrecking exhibits, and the citadel tower you can climb to the top. The museum, operated by the Key West Art and Historical Society, also has a collection of Stanley Papio's "junk art" sculptures inside and out, and a gallery of Cuban folk artist Mario Sanchez's chiseled and painted wooden carvings of historic Key West street scenes. ⊠ *3501 S. Roosevelt Blvd.* ☎ *305/296–3913* ⊕ *www.kwahs.com* ✉ *$6* ⊗ *Daily 9:30–4:30.*

**14**

**West Martello Tower.** Among the arches and ruins of this redbrick Civil War–era fort, the Key West Garden Club maintains lovely gardens of native and tropical plants, fountains, and sculptures. It also holds art, orchid, and flower shows February through April and leads private garden tours one weekend in March. ⊠ *Atlantic Blvd. and White St.* ☎ *305/294–3210* ⊕ *www.keywestgardenclub.com* ✉ *Donation welcome* ⊗ *Tues.–Sat. 9:30–5.*

**OFF THE BEATEN PATH**

History buffs might remember long-deactivated Fort Jefferson as the prison that held Dr. Samuel Mudd for his role in the Lincoln assassination. But today's "guests" are much more captivated by this sanctuary's thousands of birds and marine life.

**Dry Tortugas National Park.** This park, 70 mi off the shores of Key West, consists of seven small islands. Tour the fort; then lay out your blanket on the sunny beach for a picnic before you head out to snorkel on the protected reef. Many people like to camp here ($3 per person per night, eight sites plus group site and overflow area; first come, first served), but note that there's no freshwater supply and you must carry off whatever you bring onto the island. ⌂ *Box 6208, Key West 33040* ☎ *305/242–7700* ⊕ *www.nps.gov/drto* ✉ *$5.*

**Dry Tortugas National Park Ferry.** The fast, sleek, 100-foot catamaran *Yankee Freedom II* cuts the travel time to the Dry Tortugas to 2¼ hours. The time passes quickly on the roomy vessel equipped with three restrooms, two freshwater showers, and two bars. Stretch out on two decks: one an air-conditioned salon with cushioned seating, the other an open sundeck with sunny and shaded seating. Continental breakfast and lunch are included. On arrival, a naturalist leads a 40-minute guided tour, which is followed by lunch and a free afternoon for swimming, snorkeling (gear included), and exploring. The vessel is ADA–certified for visitors using wheelchairs. ■ TIP➔ The Dry Tortugas lies in the central time zone.

⊠ *Lands End Marina, 240 Margaret St., Key West* ☎ *305/294–7009 or 800/634–0939* ⊕ *www.yankeefreedom.com* ✉ *$160, plus $5 park fee* ⊗ *Trips daily at 8 am; check in 7:15.*

**BEACHES**

**C. B. Harvey Rest Beach.** This beach and park were named after Cornelius Bradford Harvey, former Key West mayor and commissioner. It has half a dozen picnic areas, dunes, and a wheelchair and bike path. **Best for:**

quiet. ⊠ *Atlantic Blvd., east side of White St. Pier* ☎ *No phone* 🖅 *Free* ⊘ *Daily 7 am–11 pm.*

☏ ★ **Fort Zachary Taylor Historic State Park.** The park's beach is the best and safest place to swim in Key West. There's an adjoining picnic area with barbecue grills and shade trees, a snack bar, and rental equipment, including snorkeling gear. A café serves sandwiches and other munchies. **Best for:** history-lovers and families. ⊠ *Box 6565; end of Southard St., through Truman Annex* ☎ *305/292–6713* ⊕ *www.floridastateparks. org/forttaylor* 🖅 *$4.50 for 1 person, $7 for 2 people, 50¢ per additional person* ⊘ *Daily 8–sunset, tours noon and 2.*

☏ **Higgs Beach–Astro City Playground.** This Monroe County park with its groomed pebbly sand is a popular sunbathing spot. A nearby grove of Australian pines provides shade, and the West Martello Tower provides shelter should a storm suddenly sweep in. Kayak and beach-chair rentals are available, as is a volleyball net. The beach also has a marker and cultural exhibit commemorating the gravesite of 295 enslaved Africans who died after being rescued from three South America–bound slave ships in 1860. Across the street, **Astro City Playground** is popular with young children. **Best for:** families. ⊠ *Atlantic Blvd. between White and Reynolds Sts.* ☎ *No phone* 🖅 *Free* ⊘ *Daily 6 am–11 pm.*

**Smathers Beach.** This wide beach has nearly 2 mi of sand, plus restrooms, picnic areas, and volleyball courts, all of which make it popular with the spring-break crowd. Trucks along the road rent rafts, windsurfers, and other beach "toys." Metered parking is on the street. **Best for:** partying. ⊠ *S. Roosevelt Blvd.* ☎ *No phone* 🖅 *Free* ⊘ *Daily 7 am–11 pm.*

**South Beach.** On the Atlantic, this stretch of sand, also known as City Beach, is popular with travelers staying at nearby motels. It is now part of the new Southernmost Hotel on the Beach resort, but is open to the public with a fun beach bar and grill. There's no parking however, so visitors must walk or bike to the beach. ⊠ *Foot of Duval St.* ☎ *No phone* 🖅 *Free* ⊘ *Daily 7 am–11 pm.*

## SPORTS AND THE OUTDOORS

Unlike the rest of the region, Key West isn't known primarily for outdoor pursuits. But everyone should devote at least half a day to relaxing on a boat tour, heading out on a fishing expedition, or pursuing some other adventure at sea. The ultimate excursion is a boat trip to Dry Tortugas National Park for snorkeling and exploring Fort Jefferson. Other excursions cater to nature lovers, scuba divers and snorkelers, fishing anglers, and those who would just like to get out in the water and enjoy the scenery and sunset. For those who prefer their recreation land based, biking is the way to go. Hiking is limited, but walking the streets of Old Town provides plenty of exercise.

### BIKING

Key West was practically made for bicycles, but don't let that lull you into a false sense of security. Narrow and one-way streets along with car traffic result in several bike accidents a year. Some hotels rent or lend bikes to guests; others will refer you to a nearby shop and reserve

## KEY WEST TOURS

### BICYCLE TOURS

**Lloyd's Original Tropical Bike Tour.** Explore the natural, noncommercial side of Key West at a leisurely pace, stopping on backstreets and in backyards of private homes to sample native fruits and view indigenous plants and trees with a 30-year Key West veteran. The behind-the-scenes tours run two hours and cost $37, including bike rental. ⊠ *Truman Ave. and Simonton St., Key West* ☎ *305/304–4700 or 305/294–1882* ⊕ *www.lloydstropicalbiketour.com.*

### BOAT TOURS

**Dancing Dolphin Spirit Charters.** Victoria Impallomeni, a 34-year wilderness guide and marine scientist, invites up to six nature lovers—especially children—aboard the *Imp II*, a 25-foot Aquasport, for four-hour ($500) and seven-hour ($700) ecotours that frequently include encounters with wild dolphins. While island-hopping, you visit underwater gardens, natural shoreline, and mangrove habitats. For her Dolphin Day for Humans tour, Impallomeni pulls you through the water, equipped with mask and snorkel, on a specially designed "dolphin water massage board" that simulates dolphin swimming motions. Sometimes dolphins follow the boat and swim among participants. All equipment is supplied. ⊠ *MM 5 OS, Murray's Marina, 5710 Overseas Hwy., Key West* ☎ *305/304–7562 or 888/822–7366* ⊕ *www.captainvictoria.com.*

**White Knuckle Thrill Boat Ride.** For something with an adrenaline boost, book with this speedboat. It holds up to 10 people and does 360s, fishtails, and other water stunts in the gulf. Cost is $59 each, and includes pickup shuttle. ⊠ *Sunset Marina, 555 College Rd., Key West* ☎ *305/797–0459* ⊕ *www.whiteknucklethrillboatride.com.*

### KAYAK TOURS

**Lazy Dog Kayak Guides.** Take a four-hour guided sea kayak-snorkel tour around the mangrove islands just east of Key West. The $60 charge covers transportation, bottled water, a snack, and supplies, including snorkeling gear. A $35 two-hour guided kayak tour is also available. ⊠ *5114 Overseas Hwy., Key West* ☎ *305/295–9898* ⊕ *www.lazydog.com.*

### WALKING TOURS

**Historic Florida Keys Foundation.** In addition to publishing several good guides on Key West, the foundation conducts tours of the City Cemetery Tuesday and Thursday at 9:30. ⊠ *510 Greene St., Old City Hall, Key West* ☎ *305/292–6718.*

a bike for you. Rentals usually start at about $10 a day, but some places also rent by the half day. ■ TIP➔ Lock up! Bikes—and porch chairs!—are favorite targets for local thieves.

**A&M Rentals.** Rent beach cruisers with large baskets for $10 a day. Rates for scooters start at $30 for four hours. Look for the huge American flag on the roof. ⊠ *523 Truman Ave.* ☎ *305/294–0399* ⊕ *www.amscooterskeywest.com.*

**Eaton Bikes.** Tandem, three-wheel, and children's bikes are available in addition to the standard beach cruisers ($18 for first day) and seven-

## THE CONCH REPUBLIC

Beginning in the 1970s, pot smuggling became a source of income for islanders who knew how to dodge detection in the maze of waterways in the Keys. In 1982, the U.S. Border Patrol threw a roadblock across the Overseas Highway just south of Florida City to catch drug runners and undocumented aliens. Traffic backed up for miles as Border Patrol agents searched vehicles and demanded that the occupants prove U.S. citizenship. Officials in Key West, outraged at being treated like foreigners by the federal government, staged a protest and formed their own "nation," the so-called Conch Republic. They hoisted a flag and distributed mock border passes, visas, and Conch currency. The embarrassed Border Patrol dismantled its roadblock, and now an annual festival recalls the city's victory.

speed cruisers ($18). It delivers free to all Key West rentals. ⊠ *830 Eaton St.* ☎ *305/295–0057* ⊕ *www.eatonbikes.com.*

**Moped Hospital.** This outfit supplies balloon-tire bikes with yellow safety baskets for adults and kids ($12 for the first day, $8 for extra days), as well as scooters ($35) and double-seater scooters ($55). ⊠ *601 Truman Ave.* ☎ *305/296–3344 or 866/296–1625* ⊕ *www.mopedhospital.com.*

### FISHING

**Key West Bait & Tackle.** Prepare to catch a big one with the live bait, frozen bait, and fishing equipment provided here. It also has the Live Bait Lounge, where you can sip ice-cold beer while telling fish tales. ⊠ *241 Margaret St.* ☎ *305/292–1961* ⊕ *www.keywestbaitandtackle.com.*

**Key West Pro Guides.** Trips include flats and backcountry fishing ($400–$425 for a half day) and reef and offshore fishing (starting at $550 for a half day). ⊠ *G-31 Miriam St.* ☎ *866/259–4205* ⊕ *www.keywestproguides.com.*

### GOLF

**Key West Resort Golf Course.** Key West isn't a major golf destination, but there is one course on Stock Island. This 18-hole, par 70 course has $70–$95 greens fees. Book your tee time early in the season. ⊠ *6450 E. College Rd.* ☎ *305/294–5232* ⊕ *www.keywestgolf.com.*

### KAYAKING

**Key West Eco-Tours.** Key West is surrounded by marinas, so it's easy to find what you're looking for, whether it's sailing with dolphins or paddling in the mangroves. These sail-kayak-snorkel excursions take you into backcountry flats and mangrove forests. The 4½-hour trip costs $95 per person and includes lunch. Sunset sails ($295) and private charters ($495) are also available. ⊠ *Historic Seaport, 100 Grinnell St.* ☎ *305/294–7245* ⊕ *www.javacatcharters.com.*

### SCUBA DIVING AND SNORKELING

**Captain's Corner.** This PADI–certified dive shop has classes in several languages and twice-daily snorkel and dive trips ($40–$65) to reefs and wrecks aboard the 60-foot dive boat *Sea Eagle.* Use of weights, belts, masks, and fins is included. ⊠ *125 Ann St.* ☎ *305/296–8865* ⊕ *www. captainscorner.com.*

**Snuba of Key West.** Safely dive the coral reefs without getting a scuba certification. Ride out to the reef on a catamaran, then follow your guide underwater for a one-hour tour of the coral reefs. You wear a regulator with a breathing hose that is attached to a floating air tank on the surface. No prior diving or snorkeling experience is necessary, but you must know how to swim. The $99 price includes beverages. ⊠ *Garrison Bight Marina, Palm Ave. between Eaton St. and N. Roosevelt Blvd.* ☎ *305/292–4616* ⊕ *www.snubakeywest.com.*

## SHOPPING

On these streets you'll find colorful local art of widely varying quality, key limes made into everything imaginable, and the raunchiest T-shirts in the civilized world. Browsing the boutiques—with frequent pub stops along the way—makes for an entertaining stroll down Duval Street.

### MALLS AND SHOPPING CENTERS

**Bahama Village.** Where to start your shopping adventure? This cluster of spruced-up shops, restaurants, and vendors is responsible for the restoration of the colorful historic district where Bahamians settled in the 19th century. The village lies roughly between Whitehead and Fort streets and Angela and Catherine streets. Hemingway frequented the bars, restaurants, and boxing rings in this part of town.

### ARTS AND CRAFTS

Key West is filled with art galleries, and the variety is truly amazing. Much is locally produced by the town's large artist community, but many galleries carry international artists from as close as Haiti and as far away as France. Local artists do a great job of preserving the island's architecture and spirit.

**Alan S. Maltz Gallery.** The owner, declared the state's official wildlife photographer by the Wildlife Foundation of Florida, captures the state's nature and character in stunning portraits. Spend four figures for large-format images on canvas or save on small prints and closeouts. ⊠ *1210 Duval St.* ☎ *305/294–0005* ⊕ *www.alanmaltz.com.*

**Cuba, Cuba!** Check out the stock of paintings, sculptures, and photos by Cuban artists. ⊠ *814 Duval St.* ☎ *305/295–9442 or 800/621–3596* ⊕ *cubacubastore.com.*

**Gallery on Greene.** Showcasing politically incorrect art by Jeff MacNelly and three-dimensional paintings by Mario Sanchez, this is the largest gallery–exhibition space in Key West. ⊠ *606 Greene St.* ☎ *305/294– 1669* ⊕ *www.galleryongreene.com.*

**Gingerbread Square Gallery.** The oldest private art gallery in Key West represents local and internationally acclaimed artists on an annually changing basis, in mediums ranging from graphics to art glass. ⊠ *1207 Duval St.* ☎ *305/296–8900* ⊕ *www.gingerbreadsquaregallery.com.*

**Glass Reunions.** Find a collection of wild and impressive fine-art glass here. It's worth a stop in just to see the imaginative and over-the-top glass chandeliers, jewelry, dishes, and platters. ✉ *825 Duval St.* ☎ *305/294–1720* ⊕ *www.glassreunions.com.*

**KW Light Gallery.** Historian, photographer, and painter Sharon Wells opened this gallery to showcase her own fine-art photography and painted tiles and canvases, as well as the works of other national artists. You can find historic photos here as well. ✉ *1203 Duval St.* ☎ *305/294–0566* ⊕ *www.kwlightgallery.com.*

**Lucky Street Gallery.** High-end contemporary paintings are the focus. There are also a few pieces of jewelry by internationally recognized Key West–based artists. Changing exhibits, artist receptions, and special events make this a lively venue. ✉ *1130 Duval St.* ☎ *305/294–3973* ⊕ *luckystreetgallery.com.*

**Pelican Poop Shoppe.** Caribbean art sells in a historic building (with Hemingway connections, of course). For a $2 admission or a $10 purchase, you can stroll the tropical courtyard garden. The owners buy directly from the artisans every year, so the prices are very attractive. ✉ *314 Simonton St.* ☎ *305/292–9955* ⊕ *www.pelicanpoopshoppe.com.*

**Whitehead St. Pottery.** Potters Charles Pearson and Timothy display their porcelain stoneware and raku-fired vessels. The setting, around two koi ponds with a burbling fountain, is as sublime as the art. ✉ *322 Julia St.* ☎ *305/294–5067* ⊕ *www.whiteheadstreetpottery.com.*

## BOOKS

**Key West Island Bookstore.** This home away from home for the large Key West writers' community carries new, used, and rare titles. It specializes in Hemingway, Tennessee Williams, and South Florida mystery writers. ✉ *513 Fleming St.* ☎ *305/294–2904.*

## CLOTHING AND FABRICS

**Fairvilla Megastore.** Don't leave town without a browse through the legendary shop, where you'll find an astonishing array of fantasy wear, outlandish costumes (check out the pirate section), and other interesting souvenirs. ✉ *520 Front St.* ☎ *305/292–0448* ⊕ *www.fairvilla.com.*

**Seam Shoppe.** Take home a shopping bag full of scarlet hibiscus, fuchsia heliconias, blue parrot fish, and even pink flamingo fabric, selected from the city's widest selection of tropical-print fabrics. ✉ *1114 Truman Ave.* ☎ *305/296–9830* ⊕ *www.tropicalfabricsonline.com.*

## FOOD AND DRINK

**Fausto's Food Palace.** Since 1926 Fausto's has been the spot to catch up on the week's gossip and to chill out in summer—it has groceries, organic foods, marvelous wines, a sushi chef on duty 8 am–6 pm, and box lunches to go. ✉ *522 Fleming St.* ☎ *305/296–5663* ✉ *1105 White St.* ☎ *305/294–5221* ⊕ *www.faustos.com.*

★ **Kermit's Key West Lime Shoppe.** You'll see Kermit himself standing on the corner every time a trolley passes, pie in hand. Besides pie, his shop carries a multitude of key lime products from barbecue sauce to jellybeans. His prefrozen pies, dressed with a special long-lasting whipped cream instead of meringue, travels well. ✉ *200 Elizabeth St., Historic Seaport* ☎ *305/296–0806 or 800/376–0806* ⊕ *www.keylimeshop.com.*

Nightlife, shops, and some interesting street art can all be found on Key West's Duval Street.

**Key West Winery.** You'll be pleasantly surprised with the fruit wines sold here. Display crates hold bottles of wines made from blueberries, blackberries, pineapples, cherries, mangoes, watermelons, tomatoes, and, of course, key limes. Stop in for a free tasting. ⊠ *103 Simonton St.* ☎ *305/292–1717 or 866/880–1717* ⊕ *www.thekeywestwinery.com.*

**Peppers of Key West.** If you like it hot, you'll love this collection of hundreds of sauces, salsas, and sweets guaranteed to light your fire. ⊠ *602 Greene St.* ☎ *305/295–9333 or 800/597–2823* ⊕ *www. peppersofkeywest.com.*

## GIFTS AND SOUVENIRS

**Cayo Hueso y Habana.** Part museum, part shopping center, this circa-1879 warehouse includes a hand-rolled cigar shop, one-of-a-kind souvenirs, a Cuban restaurant, and exhibits that tell of the island's Cuban heritage. Outside, a memorial garden pays homage to the island's Cuban ancestors. ⊠ *410 Wall St., Mallory Sq.* ☎ *305/293–7260.*

★ **Fast Buck Freddie's.** Find a classy, hip selection of gifts, including every flamingo item imaginable here. It also has a whole department called "Tropical Trash," and carries such imaginative items as an electric fan in the shape of a rooster. ⊠ *500 Duval St.* ☎ *305/294–2007* ⊕ *www. fastbuckfreddies.com.*

★ **Montage.** For that unique (but slightly overpriced) souvenir of your trip to Key West head here, where you'll discover hundreds of hand-crafted signs of popular Key West guesthouses, inns, hotels, restaurants, bars, and streets. If you can't find what you're looking for, they'll make it for you. ⊠ *512 Duval St.* ☎ *305/395–9101 or 877/396–4278* ⊕ *montagekeywest.com.*

## NIGHTLIFE

Rest up: Much of what happens in Key West does so after dark. Open your mind and have a stroll. Scruffy street performers strum next to dogs in sunglasses. Brawls tumble out the doors of Sloppy Joe's. Drag queens strut across stages in Joan Rivers garb. Tattooed men lick whipped cream off of women's body parts. And margaritas flow like a Jimmy Buffett tune.

### BARS AND LOUNGES

**Capt. Tony's Saloon.** When it was the original Sloppy Joe's in the mid-1930s Hemingway was a regular. Later, a young Jimmy Buffett sang here and made this watering hole famous in his song "Last Mango in Paris." Bands play nightly. ⊠ *428 Greene St.* ☎ *305/294–1838* ⊕ *www. capttonyssaloon.com.*

**Durty Harry's.** The megasize entertainment complex has live music in a variety of indoor-outdoor bars including Rick's Dance Club Wine & Martini Bar and the tiny Red Garter strip club. ⊠ *208 Duval St.* ☎ *305/296–5513* ⊕ *www.ricksanddurtyharrys.com.*

**Green Parrot Bar.** Pause for a libation in the open-air. Built in 1890, the bar is said to be Key West's oldest. The sometimes-rowdy saloon has locals outnumbering out-of-towners, especially on weekends when bands play. ⊠ *601 Whitehead St., at Southard St.* ☎ *305/294–6133* ⊕ *www.greenparrot.com.*

**Hog's Breath Saloon.** Belly up to the bar for a cold mug of the signature Hog's Breath Lager at this infamous joint, a must-stop on the Key West bar crawl. Live bands play daily 1 pm–2 am. ⊠ *400 Front St.* ☎ *305/296–4222* ⊕ *www.hogsbreath.com.*

**Margaritaville Café.** A youngish, touristy crowd mixes with aging Parrot Heads. It's owned by former Key West resident and recording star Jimmy Buffett, who has been known to perform here. The drink of choice is, of course, a margarita, made with Jimmy's own brand of Margaritaville tequila. There's live music nightly, as well as lunch and dinner. ⊠ *500 Duval St.* ☎ *305/292–1435* ⊕ *www.margaritaville.com.*

**Pier House.** The party begins with a steel-drum band to celebrate the sunset on the beach (on select Thursdays and Fridays), then moves indoors to the Wine Galley piano bar for live jazz. ⊠ *1 Duval St.* ☎ *305/296–4600 or 800/327–8340* ⊕ *www.pierhouse.com.*

**Schooner Wharf Bar.** An open-air waterfront bar and grill in the historic seaport district retains its funky Key West charm and hosts live entertainment daily. Its margarita ranks among Key West's best. ⊠ *202 William St.* ☎ *305/292–3302* ⊕ *www.schoonerwharf.com.*

**Sloppy Joe's.** There's history and good times at the successor to a famous 1937 speakeasy named for its founder, Captain Joe Russell. Decorated with Hemingway memorabilia and marine flags, the bar is popular with travelers and is full and noisy all the time. A Sloppy Joe's T-shirt is a de rigueur Key West souvenir, and the gift shop sells them like crazy. ⊠ *201 Duval St.* ☎ *305/294–5717* ⊕ *www.sloppyjoes.com.*

14

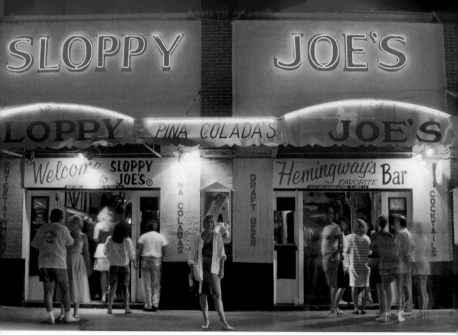

Sloppy Joe's is one must-stop on most Key West visitors' barhop stroll, also known as the Duval Crawl.

**The Top.** On the seventh floor of the La Concha Crowne Plaza, this is one of the best places in town to view the sunset and enjoy live entertainment. ✉ *430 Duval St.* ☎ *305/296–2991* ⊕ *www.laconchakeywest.com.*

**Virgilio's.** In the best traditions of a 1950s cocktail lounge, this bar serves chilled martinis to the soothing tempo of live jazz and blues nightly. ✉ *524 Duval St.* ☎ *305/296–8118* ⊕ *www.virgilioskeywest.com.*

## WHERE TO EAT

**$$–$$$**
JAPANESE

✕ **Ambrosia.** Ask any savvy local where to get the best sushi on the island and you'll undoubtedly be pointed to this tiny wood-and-tatami-paneled dining room with indoor waterfall tucked away into a resort near the beach. Grab a seat at the sushi bar and watch owner and head sushi chef Masa prepare an impressive array of superfresh sashimi delicacies. Sushi lovers can't go wrong with the Ambrosia special ($35), a sampler of five kinds of sashimi, seven pieces of sushi, and sushi rolls. There's an assortment of lightly fried tempura and teriyaki dishes and a killer bento box at lunch. Enjoy it all with a glass of premium sake or a cold glass of Sapporo beer. ✉ *Santa Maria Resort, 1401 Simonton St.* ☎ *305/293–0304* ⊕ *www.keywestambrosia.com* ☉ *No lunch weekends. Closed 2 weeks after Labor Day.*

**$$$**
CARIBBEAN
★

✕ **Blue Heaven.** The outdoor dining area here is often referred to as "the quintessential Keys experience," and it's hard to argue. There's much to like about this historic restaurant where Hemingway refereed boxing matches and customers cheered for cockfights. Although these events are no more, the free-roaming chickens and cats add that "what-a-hoot" factor. Nightly specials include black bean soup, Provençal sea scallops, jerk chicken, and sautéed yellowtail snapper in citrus beurre blanc sauce. Desserts and breads are baked on the premises; the banana bread and lobster Benedict with key lime hollandaise are hits during "breakfast with the roosters." Breakfast is the signature meal here. ⊠ *729 Thomas St.* ☎ *305/296–8666* ⊕ *www.blueheavenkw.com* ⌬ *Reservations not accepted* ⊘ *Closed after Labor Day for 6 weeks.*

¢    ✕ **B.O.'s Fish Wagon.** What started out as a fish house on wheels appears
SEAFOOD    to have broken down on the corner of Caroline and William streets and is today the cornerstone for one of Key West's junkyard-chic dining institutions. Step up to the wood-plank counter window and order the specialty: a grouper sandwich fried or grilled and topped with key lime sauce. Other choices include fish nuts (don't be scared, they're just fried nuggets), hot dogs, and shrimp or soft-shell-crab sandwich. Talk sass with your host and find a picnic table or take a seat at the plank. Grab some paper towels off one of the rolls hanging around and busy yourself reading graffiti, license plates, and irreverent signs. It's a must-do Key West experience. ⊠ *801 Caroline St.* ☎ *305/294–9272* ⊕ *www. bosfishwagon.com* ⌬ *Reservations not accepted* ⊟ *No credit cards.*

$    ✕ **The Café, A Mostly Vegetarian Place.** You don't have to be a vegetarian to
VEGETARIAN    love this new-age café decorated with bright artwork and a corrugated tin–fronted counter. Local favorites include homemade soup, veggie burgers (order them with a side of sweet potato fries), grilled portobello mushroom salad, seafood, vegan specialties, and grilled Gorgonzola pizza. For bigger appetites there are offerings like the Szechuan-style vegetable stir-fry. ⊠ *509 Southard St.* ☎ *305/296–5515* ⌬ *Reservations not accepted.*

$$$    ✕ **Café Marquesa.** Chef Susan Ferry presents seven or more inspired
CONTINENTAL    entrées on her changing menu each night; delicious dishes can include
**Fodor's**Choice    yellowtail snapper with pear, ricotta pasta purses with caponata, and
★    red pepper coulis; and Australian rack of lamb crusted with goat cheese and a port-fig sauce. End your meal on a sweet note with key lime napoleon with tropical fruits and berries. There's also a fine selection of wines and custom martinis such as the key limetini and the Irish martini. Adjoining the intimate Marquesa Hotel, the dining room is equally relaxed and elegant. ⊠ *600 Fleming St.* ☎ *305/292–1244* ⊕ *www.marquesa.com* ⌬ *Reservations essential* ⊘ *No lunch.*

$$$    ✕ **Café Solé.** Welcome to the "home of the hog snapper," a deliciously
FRENCH    roasted local fish seasoned with a red-pepper-custard sauce. This little piece of France is concealed behind a high wall and a gate in a residential neighborhood. Inside, chef John Correa marries his French training with local ingredients, creating delicious takes on classics, including portobello mushroom soup, snapper with mango salsa, and some of the best bouillabaisse that you'll find outside of Marseilles. From the land, there is filet mignon with a wild-mushroom demi-glaze. The restaurant serves lunch and Sunday brunch in the winter and spring. ⊠ *1029 Southard St.* ☎ *305/294–0230* ⊕ *www.cafesole.com* ⌬ *Reservations essential.*

$$    ✕ **El Meson de Pepe.** If you want to get a taste of the island's Cuban
CARIBBEAN    heritage, this is the place. Perfect for after watching a Mallory Square sunset, you can dine alfresco or in the dining room on refined versions of Cuban classics. Begin with a megasized mojito while you enjoy the

**14**

# EVERYTHING'S FISHY IN THE KEYS

Fish. It's what's for dinner in the Florida Keys. The Keys's runway between the Gulf of Mexico or Florida Bay and Atlantic warm waters means fish of many fin. Restaurants take full advantage by serving it fresh, whether you caught it or a local fisherman did.

Menus at a number of colorful waterfront shacks such as **Snapper's** (⊠ *139 Seaside Ave., Key Largo* ☎ *305/852–5956*) in Key Largo and **Half Shell Raw Bar** (⊠ *231 Margaret St., Key West* ☎ *305/294–7496*) range from basic raw, steamed, broiled, grilled, or blackened fish to some Bahamian and New Orleans–style interpretations. Other seafood houses dress up their fish in creative haute-cuisine styles, such as **Pierre's** (⊠ *MM 81.5 BS, Islamorada* ☎ *305/664–3225*) hogfish *meunière* or yellowtail snapper with pear, ricotta pasta purses with caponata, and red pepper coulis at **Café Marquesa** (⊠ *600 Fleming St., Key West* ☎ *305/292–1244* ⊕ *www.marquesa.com*). Try a Keys–style breakfast of "grits and grunts"—fried fish and grits—at the **Stuffed Pig** (⊠ *3520 Overseas Hwy., Marathon* ☎ *305/743–4059*).

## BUILT-IN FISH

You know it's fresh when you see a fish market as soon as you open the door to the restaurant where you're dining. It happens all the time in the Keys. You can even peruse the seafood showcases and pick the fish fillet or lobster tail you want.

Many of the Keys' best restaurants are found in marina complexes, where the commercial fishermen bring their catches straight from the sea. Those in **Stock Island** (one island north of Key West) and at **Keys Fisheries Market & Marina** (⊠ *MM 49 BS, end of 35th St., Marathon* ☎ *305/743–4353 or 866/743–4353*) take some finding.

## CONCH

One of the tastiest legacies of the Keys' Bahamian heritage, conch shows up on nearly every restaurant menu. It's so prevalent in local diets that natives refer to themselves as Conchs. Conch fritter is the most popular culinary manifestation, followed by cracked (pounded, breaded, and fried) conch, and conch salad, a ceviche-style refresher. Since the harvesting of queen conch is now illegal, most of the islands' conch comes from the Bahamas.

## FLORIDA LOBSTER

What happened to the claws? Stop looking for them: Florida spiny lobsters don't have 'em, never did. The sweet tail meat, however, makes up for the loss. Commercial and sports divers harvest these glorious crustaceans from late July through March. Check with local dive shops on restrictions, then get ready for a fresh feast. Restaurants serve them broiled with drawn butter or in creative dishes such as lobster Benedict, lobster sushi rolls, lobster Reuben, and lobster tacos.

## GROUPER

Once central to Florida's trademark seafood dish—fried grouper sandwich—its populations have been overfished in recent years, meaning that the state has exerted more control over bag regulations and occasionally closes grouper fishing on a temporary basis during the

winter season. Some restaurants have gone antigrouper to try to bring back the abundance, but most grab it when they can. Black grouper is the most highly prized of the several varieties.

## STONE CRAB

In season October 15 through May 15, it gets its name from its rock-hard shell. Fishermen take only the claws, which can regenerate in a sustainable manner. Connoisseurs prefer them chilled with tangy mustard sauce. Some restaurants give you a choice of hot claws and drawn butter, but this means the meat will be cooked twice, because it's usually boiled or steamed quickly after taken from its crab trap.

## YELLOWTAIL SNAPPER

The preferred species of snappers, it is more plentiful in the Keys than any other Florida waters. As pretty as it is tasty, it's a favorite of divers and snorkelers. Mild, sweet, and delicate, its meat lends itself to any number of preparations. It is available pretty much year-round, and many restaurants will give you a choice of broiled, baked, fried, or blackened. Chefs top it with everything from key lime beurre blanc to mango chutney. **Ballyhoo's** in Key Largo (⊠ *MM 97.8, in the median* ☎ *305/852–0822*) serves it 10 different ways.

basket of bread and savory sauces. The expansive menu offers *tostones rellenos* (green plantains with different traditional fillings), ceviche (raw fish "cooked" in lemon juice), and more. Choose from Cuban specialties such as roasted pork in a cumin mojo sauce and *ropa vieja* (shredded beef stew). At lunch, the local Cuban population and cruise-ship passengers enjoy Cuban sandwiches and smaller versions of dinner's most popular entrées. A salsa band performs outside at the bar during sunset celebration. ✉ *Mallory Sq., 410 Wall St.* ☎ *305/295–2620* ⊕ *www. elmesondepepe.com.*

**$**  ✕ **El Siboney.** Dining at this family-style restaurant is like going to Mom's
CARIBBEAN  for Sunday dinner—if your mother is Cuban. The dining room is noisy, and the food is traditional *cubano*. There are well-seasoned black beans, a memorable paella, traditional ropa vieja (shredded beef and roast pork), and local seafood served grilled, stuffed, and breaded. Dishes come with Cuban bread, salad or plantains, and rice or fries. To make a good thing even better, the prices are very reasonable. ✉ *900 Catherine St.* ☎ *305/296–4184* ⊕ *www.elsiboneyrestaurant.com* ⌂ *Reservations not accepted.*

**$**  ✕ **Finnegan's Wake Irish Pub and Eatery.** "Come for the beer. Stay for the
IRISH  food. Leave with the staff," is the slogan of this popular pub. The pictures of Beckett, Shaw, Yeats, and Wilde on the walls and the creaky wood floors underfoot exude Irish country warmth. The certified Angus beef is priciest; most of the other dishes are bargains. Traditional fare includes bangers and mash, chicken potpie, and colcannon—rich mashed potatoes with scallions, sauerkraut, and melted white cheddar cheese. Bread pudding soaked with a honey-whiskey sauce is a true treat. Live music on weekends and daily happy hours from 4 to 7 and midnight to 2 featuring nearly 30 beers on tap make it popular with the spring break and sometimes-noisy drinking crowd. ✉ *320 Grinnell St.* ☎ *305/293–0222* ⊕ *www.keywestirish.com.*

**$$**  ✕ **Half Shell Raw Bar.** Smack-dab on the docks, this legendary institution
SEAFOOD  gets its name from the oysters, clams, and peel-and-eat shrimp that are
☺  a departure point for its seafood-based diet. It's not clever recipes or fine dining (or even air-conditioning) that packs 'em in; it's fried fish, po'boy sandwiches, and seafood combos. For a break from the deep fryer, try the fresh and light conch ceviche "cooked" with lime juice. The potato salad is flavored with dill, and the "Pama Rita" is a new twist in Margaritaville. ✉ *Lands End Village at Historic Seaport, 231 Margaret St.* ☎ *305/294– 7496* ⊕ *www.halfshellrawbar.com* ⌂ *Reservations not accepted.*

**¢**  ✕ **Lobo's Mixed Grill.** Famous for its selection of wrap sandwiches, Lobo
AMERICAN  has a reputation among locals for its 8-ounce, charcoal-grilled ground
☺  chuck burger—thick and juicy and served with lettuce, tomato, and pickle on a toasted bun. Mix it up with toppings like Brie, blue cheese, or portobello mushroom. The menu of 30 wraps includes rib eye, oyster, grouper, Cuban, and chicken Caesar. The menu includes salads and quesadillas, as well as a fried-shrimp-and-oyster combo. Beer and wine are served. This courtyard food stand closes at 6, so eat early. Most of Lobo's business is takeout (it has a half-dozen outdoor picnic tables), and it offers free delivery within Old Town. ✉ *5 Key Lime Sq., east of intersection of Southard and Duval Sts.* ☎ *305/296–5303* ⊕ *www.*

*loboskeywest.com* ⌂ *Reservations not accepted* ▭ *No credit cards* ⊗ *Closed Sun. Apr.–early Dec.*

**$$$$**  ✕ **Louie's Backyard**. Feast your eyes
ECLECTIC  on a steal-your-breath-away view
★  and beautifully presented dishes
prepared by executive chef Doug
Shook. Once you get over sticker
shock on the seasonally changing menu (appetizers cost around
$9–$18; entrées can hover around

**WORD OF MOUTH**

"My favorite fine dining restaurant is Louie's Backyard, though we always go for lunch rather than dinner. The food is just as good, the view is wonderful during the day, and the prices are reason-able." —SusanCS

**14**

the $36 mark), settle in on the outside deck and enjoy dishes like grilled scallops with shrimp cream, sautéed veal sweetbreads with crabmeat, and greens-stuffed chicken breast. A more affordable option upstairs is the Upper Deck, which serves tapas such as flaming ouzo shrimp, roasted olives with onion and feta, and Gruyère and duck confit pizza. If you come for lunch, the menu is less expensive but the view is just as fantastic. For night owls, the tin-roofed Afterdeck Bar serves cocktails on the water until the wee hours. ✉ *700 Waddell Ave.* ☎ *305/294–1061* ⊕ *www.louiesbackyard.com* ⌂ *Reservations essential* ⊗ *Closed Labor Day to mid-Sept, Upper Deck closed Sun. and Mon.*

**$–$$**  ✕ **Mangia Mangia**. This longtime favorite serves large portions of home-
ITALIAN  made pastas that can be matched with any of the homemade sauces. Tables are arranged in a brick garden hung with twinkling lights and in a cozy, casual dining room in an old house. Everything out of the open kitchen is outstanding, including the *bollito misto di mare* (fresh seafood sautéed with garlic, shallots, white wine, and pasta) or the memorable spaghettini "schmappellini," homemade pasta with aspara-gus, tomatoes, pine nuts, and Parmesan. The wine list—with more than 350 offerings—includes old and rare vintages, and also has a good by-the-glass selection. ✉ *900 Southard St.* ☎ *305/294–2469* ⊕ *www.mangia-mangia.com* ⌂ *Reservations not accepted* ⊗ *No lunch*.

**$$$**  ✕ **Michaels Restaurant**. White tablecloths, subdued lighting, and romantic
AMERICAN  music give Michaels the feel of an urban eatery. Garden seating reminds you that you are in the Keys. Chef–owner Michael Wilson flies in prime rib, cowboy steaks, and rib eyes from Allen Brothers in Chicago, which has supplied top-ranked steak houses for more than a century. Also on the menu is a melt-in-your-mouth grouper stuffed with jumbo lump crab, Kobe and tenderloin meat loaf, veal saltimbocca, and a variety of made-to-order fondue dishes (try the pesto pot, spiked with hot pepper and basil). To lighten up, smaller portions of many of the favorites are available until 7:30 Sunday through Thursday. The Hemingway (mojito-style) and the Third Degree (raspberry vodka and white crème de cacao) top the cocktail menu. ✉ *532 Margaret St.* ☎ *305/295–1300* ⊕ *www.michaelskeywest.com* ⌂ *Reservations essential* ⊗ *No lunch*.

**$$$**  ✕ **Nine One Five**. Twinkling lights draped along the lower- and upper-
ECLECTIC  level outdoor porches of a 100-year-old Victorian mansion set an ele-gant—though unstuffy—stage at this very cool tapas-style eatery. If you like to sample and sip, you'll appreciate the variety of smaller plate selections and wines by the glass. Taster-portioned tapas include

olives, cheese, shrimp, and pâté, or try a combination with the tapas platter or the signature "tuna dome" with fresh crab, lemon-miso dressing, and an ahi tuna–sashimi wrapping. There are also larger plates if you're craving something like seafood soup or steak au poivre frites. Dine outdoors and people-watch along upper Duval, or sit at a table inside while listening to light jazz. ⊠ *915 Duval St.* ☎ *305/296–0669* ⊕ *www.915duval.com* ☾ *No lunch.*

**$$$$**
CONTINENTAL
★

✕**Pisces.** In a circa-1892 former store and home, chef William Arnel and staff create a contemporary setting with a stylish granite bar, Andy Warhol originals, and glass oil lamps. Favorites include "lobster tango mango," flambéed in cognac and served with saffron butter sauce and sliced mangoes; Pisces Aphrodite (seafood in puff pastry); veal tenderloin with wild mushrooms; and black grouper bouillabaise. ⊠ *1007 Simonton St.* ☎ *305/294–7100* ⊕ *www.pisceskeywest.com* ☝ *Reservations essential* ☾ *No lunch.*

**$$**
ITALIAN
★

✕**Salute Ristorante at the Beach.** This colorful restaurant sits on Higgs Beach, giving it one of the island's best lunch views—and a bit of sand and salt spray on a windy day. Owners of the popular Blue Heaven restaurant took it over and have designed an intriguing dinner menu that includes linguine with mussels, vegetable or three-meat lasagna, and white bean soup. At lunch the gazpacho refreshes with great flavor and texture, and the calamari marinara, antipasti sandwich, pasta primavera, and yellowtail sandwich do not disappoint. ⊠ *1000 Atlantic Blvd., Higgs Beach* ☎ *305/292–1117* ⊕ *saluteonthebeach.com* ☝ *Reservations not accepted.*

**$$**
SEAFOOD
★

✕**Seven Fish.** A local hot spot, this intimate, off-the-beaten-track eatery is good for an eclectic mix of dishes like tropical shrimp salsa, wild-mushroom quesadilla, seafood marinara, and old-fashioned meat loaf with real mashed potatoes. For dessert, the sweet potato pie provides an added measure of down-home comfort. Those in the know arrive for dinner early to snag one of the 12 or so tables clustered in the bare-bones dining room. ⊠ *632 Olivia St.* ☎ *305/296–2777* ⊕ *www.7fish. com* ☾ *Closed Tues. No lunch.*

**$$**
SEAFOOD
☾

✕**Turtle Kraals.** Named for the kraals, or corrals, where sea turtles were once kept until they went to the cannery, this place calls to mind the island's history. The lunch–dinner menu offers an assortment of marine cuisine that includes seafood enchiladas, mesquite-grilled fish of the day, and mango crab cakes. The slow-cook wood smoker results in wonderfully tender ribs, brisket, mesquite-grilled oysters with Parmesan and cilantro, and mesquite grilled chicken sandwich. Breakfast offers some interesting and quite tasty options like barbecued hash and eggs or huevos rancheros. The open restaurant overlooks the marina at the Historic Seaport. Turtle races entertain during happy hour on Monday and Friday at 6 pm. ⊠ *231 Margaret St.* ☎ *305/294–2640* ⊕ *www. turtlekraals.com* ☝ *Reservations not accepted.*

## WHERE TO STAY

Historic cottages, restored century-old Conch houses, and large resorts are among the offerings in Key West, the majority charging from $100 to $300 a night. In high season, December through March, you'll be hard-pressed to find a decent room for less than $200, and most places raise prices considerably during holidays. Many guesthouses and inns do not welcome children under 16, and most do not permit smoking indoors; rates often include an expanded continental breakfast and afternoon wine or snack.

*For expanded hotel reviews, visit Fodors.com.*

**$$$$**
**B&B/INN**
★
**Ambrosia Key West.** If you desire personal attention, a casual atmosphere, and a dollop of style, stay at these twin inns spread out on nearly 2 acres. **Pros:** spacious rooms; poolside breakfast; friendly staff. **Cons:** on-street parking can be tough to come by; a little too spread out. ⊠ *615, 618, 622 Fleming St.* ☎ *305/296–9838 or 800/535–9838* ⊕ *www.ambrosiakeywest.com* ⊐ *6 rooms, 3 town houses, 1 cottage, 10 suites* ⟳ *In-room: a/c, kitchen (some), Wi-Fi. In-hotel: pools, parking, some pets allowed* ⦿ *Breakfast.*

**$$**
**B&B/INN**
**Angelina Guest House.** The high rollers and ladies of the night were chased away long ago, but this charming guesthouse revels in its past as a gambling hall and bordello. **Pros:** good value; nice garden; friendly staff. **Cons:** thin walls; basic rooms; shared balcony. ⊠ *302 Angela St.* ☎ *305/294–4480 or 888/303–4480* ⊕ *www.angelinaguesthouse.com* ⊐ *13 rooms* ⟳ *In-room: a/c, no TV, Wi-Fi. In-hotel: pool, some age restrictions* ⦿ *Breakfast.*

**$$$**
**HOTEL**
**Azul Key West.** The ultramodern—nearly minimalistic—redo of this classic circa-1903 Queen Anne mansion is a break from the sensory overload of Key West's other abundant Victorian guesthouses. **Pros:** lovely building; marble-floored baths; luxurious linens. **Cons:** on a busy street. ⊠ *907 Truman Ave.* ☎ *305/296–5152 or 888/253–2985* ⊕ *www.azulhotels.us* ⊐ *10 rooms, 1 suite* ⟳ *In-room: Wi-Fi. In-hotel: pool, some age restrictions* ⦿ *Breakfast.*

**$$$$**
**RESORT**
☾
★
**Casa Marina Resort & Beach Club.** At any moment, you expect the landed gentry to walk across the oceanfront lawn, just as they did when this 13-acre resort was built back in the 1920s. **Pros:** nice beach; historic setting; away from the crowds. **Cons:** long walk to Old Town; $25 resort fee. ⊠ *1500 Reynolds St.* ☎ *305/296–3535 or 866/203–6392* ⊕ *www.casamarinaresort.com* ⊐ *241 rooms, 70 suites* ⟳ *In-room: a/c, Internet, Wi-Fi. In-hotel: restaurant, bars, tennis courts, pools, gym, spa, beach, water sports, business center, some pets allowed* ⦿ *No meals.*

**$$$**
**B&B/INN**
**Courtney's Place.** If you like kids, cats, and dogs, you'll feel right at home in this collection of accommodations ranging from cigar-maker cottages to shotgun houses. **Pros:** near Duval Street; fairly priced. **Cons:** small parking lot; small pool. ⊠ *720 Whitemarsh La., off Petronia St.* ☎ *305/294–3480 or 800/869–4639* ⊕ *www.courtneysplacekeywest.com* ⊐ *6 rooms, 2 suites, 2 efficiencies, 8 cottages* ⟳ *In-room: a/c, kitchen (some), Internet. In-hotel: pool, laundry facilities, parking, some pets allowed* ⦿ *Breakfast.*

**$$$$**
**HOTEL**
★
**Eden House.** From the vintage metal rockers on the street-side porch to the old neon hotel sign in the lobby, this 1920s rambling Key West mainstay hotel is high on character, low on gloss. **Pros:** sunny garden; hot tub is actually hot; daily happy hour around the pool. **Cons:** pricey. ⊠ *1015 Fleming St.* ☎ *305/296–6868 or 800/533–5397* ⊕ *www.*

14

*edenhouse.com* ⌂ *36 rooms, 8 suites* ⚭ *In-room: a/c, kitchen (some). In-hotel: restaurant, pool, parking* ⚑*No meals.*

**$$$$**
HOTEL
Fodor's Choice
★

⊞ **The Gardens Hotel.** Built in 1875, this gloriously shaded property covers a third of a city block in Old Town, among orchids, ponytail palms, black bamboo, walks, fountains, and earthen pots imported from Cuba. **Pros:** luxurious bathrooms; secluded garden seating; free phone calls. **Cons:** hard to get reservations; expensive. ⊠ *526 Angela St.* ☎ *305/294–2661 or 800/526–2664* ⊕ *www.gardenshotel.com* ⌂ *17 rooms* ⚭ *In-room: a/c, Wi-Fi. In-hotel: bar, pool, parking, some age restriction* ⚑*Breakfast.*

**$$$$**
RESORT
☉

⊞ **Hyatt Key West Resort and Spa.** With its own man-made beach, the Hyatt Key West is one of few resorts where you can dig your toes in the sand, then walk a short distance away to the streets of Old Town. **Pros:** a little bit away from the bustle of Old Town; plenty of activities. **Cons:** beach is small; cramped-feeling property; chain-hotel feel. ⊠ *601 Front St.* ☎ *305/809–1234* ⊕ *www.keywest.hyatt.com* ⌂ *118 rooms* ⚭ *In-room: a/c, Internet, Wi-Fi. In-hotel: restaurants, bars, pool, gym, spa, beach, water sports, business center, parking* ⚑*No meals.*

**$$$**
B&B/INN

⊞ **Key Lime Inn.** This 1854 Grand Bahama–style house on the National Register of Historic Places succeeds by offering amiable service, a great location, and simple rooms with natural-wood furnishings. **Pros:** free parking; some rooms have private outdoor spaces. **Cons:** standard rooms are pricey; pool faces a busy street; mulch-covered paths. ⊠ *725 Truman Ave.* ☎ *305/294–5229 or 800/549–4430* ⊕ *www.keylimeinn.com* ⌂ *37 rooms* ⚭ *In-room: a/c, Internet, Wi-Fi. In-hotel: pool, parking* ⚑*Breakfast.*

**$$**
B&B/INN
★

⊞ **Key West Bed and Breakfast/The Popular House.** Local art—large, splashy canvases and a Gauguinesque mural—decorates the walls, while handmade textiles (owner Jody Carlson is a talented weaver) drape chairs, couches, and beds at this historic home. **Pros:** lots of art; tiled outdoor shower; hot tub and sauna area is a welcome hangout. **Cons:** some rooms are small. ⊠ *415 William St.* ☎ *305/296–7274 or 800/438–6155* ⊕ *www.keywestbandb.com* ⌂ *8 rooms, 6 with bath* ⚭ *In-room: a/c, no TV, Wi-Fi (some). In-hotel: pool, some age restrictions* ⚑*Breakfast.*

**$$$$**
HOTEL

⊞ **Key West Marriott Beachside Hotel.** This new hotel vies for convention business with the biggest ballroom in Key West. **Pros:** private beach; poolside cabanas. **Cons:** small beach; can't walk to Old Town; cookie-cutter facade. ⊠ *3841 N. Roosevelt Blvd., New Town* ☎ *305/296–8100 or 800/546–0885* ⊕ *www.keywestmarriottbeachside.com* ⌂ *93 rooms, 93 1-bedroom suites, 10 2-bedroom suites, 26 3-bedroom suites* ⚭ *In-room: a/c, kitchen (some), Internet. In-hotel: restaurants, bars, pool, gym, business center, parking* ⚑*No meals.*

**$$$$**
HOTEL
Fodor's Choice
★

⊞ **Marquesa Hotel.** In a town that prides itself on its laid-back luxury, this complex of four restored 1884 houses stands out. **Pros:** elegant setting; romantic atmosphere; turndown service. **Cons:** street-facing rooms can be noisy; expensive rates. ⊠ *600 Fleming St.* ☎ *305/292–1919 or 800/869–4631* ⊕ *www.marquesa.com* ⌂ *27 rooms* ⚭ *In-room: a/c, Wi-Fi. In-hotel: restaurant, pools, business center, parking, some age restrictions* ⚑*No meals.*

$$$
B&B/INN
★
**Merlin Guesthouse**. Key West guesthouses don't usually welcome families, but this laid-back jumble of rooms and suites is an exception. **Pros:** good location near Duval Street; good rates. **Cons:** neighbor noise; common areas are dated; street parking. ⊠ *811 Simonton St.* ☎ *305/296–3336 or 800/642–4753* ⊕ *www.merlinguesthouse.com* ⇨ *10 rooms, 6 suites, 4 cottages* ◊ *In-room: a/c, kitchen (some), Wi-Fi. In-hotel: pool* ❘⊙❘ *Breakfast.*

$$$
B&B/INN
★
**Mermaid & the Alligator**. An enchanting combination of flora and fauna makes this 1904 Victorian house a welcoming retreat. **Pros:** hot plunge pool; massage pavilion; island-getaway feel. **Cons:** minimum stay required (length depends on season); dark public areas; plastic lawn chairs. ⊠ *729 Truman Ave.* ☎ *305/294–1894 or 800/773–1894* ⊕ *www.kwmermaid.com* ⇨ *9 rooms* ◊ *In-room: a/c, no TV, Wi-Fi. In-hotel: pool, some age restrictions* ❘⊙❘ *Breakfast.*

$$$$
RESORT
★
**Ocean Key Resort & Spa**. A pool and lively open-air bar and restaurant sit on Sunset Pier, a popular place to watch the sun sink into the horizon. **Pros:** well-trained staff; lively pool scene; best spa on the island. **Cons:** confusing layout; too bustling for some. ⊠ *Zero Duval St.* ☎ *305/296–7701 or 800/328–9815* ⊕ *www.oceankey.com* ⇨ *64 rooms, 36 suites* ◊ *In-room: a/c, kitchen (some), Wi-Fi In-hotel: restaurants, bars, pool, spa, water sports, laundry facilities, parking* ❘⊙❘ *No meals.*

$$$$
HOTEL
★
**Parrot Key Resort**. The same people who created Tranquility Bay in Marathon opened this high-end Key West resort in 2008. **Pros:** four pools; finely appointed units; access to marina and other facilities at three sister properties in Marathon. **Cons:** outside of walking distance to Old Town and no transportation provided; expensive; hefty resort fee. ⊠ *2801 N. Roosevelt Blvd., New Town* ☎ *305/809-2200* ⊕ *www.parrotkeyresort.com* ⇨ *44 2-bedroom town houses, 30 3-bedroom town houses* ◊ *In-room: a/c, kitchen, Wi-Fi. In-hotel: restaurant, bar, pools, beach* ❘⊙❘ *No meals.*

$$$$
RESORT
★
**Pier House Resort and Caribbean Spa**. The location—on a quiet stretch of beach at the foot of Duval—is ideal as a buffer from and gateway to the action. **Pros:** beautiful beach; good location; nice spa. **Cons:** lots of conventions; cookie-cutter feel; poolside rooms are small; minimum stays during busy times. ⊠ *1 Duval St.* ☎ *305/296–4600 or 800/327–8340* ⊕ *www.pierhouse.com* ⇨ *113 rooms, 29 suites* ◊ *In-room: a/c, Wi-Fi. In-hotel: restaurants, bars, pool, gym, spa, beach* ❘⊙❘ *No meals.*

$$$$
RESORT
★
**The Reach Resort**. Embracing Key West's only natural beach, this recently reinvented and reopened full-service resort has its roots in the 1980s when locals rallied against the loss of the topless beach it displaced. **Pros:** removed from Duval hubbub; great sunrise views; pullout sofas in most rooms. **Cons:** $20 per day per room resort fee; expensive. ⊠ *1435 Simonton St.* ☎ *305/296–5000 or 888/318–4316* ⊕ *www.reachresort.com* ⇨ *72 rooms, 78 suites* ◊ *In-room: a/c, Wi-Fi. In-hotel: restaurant, room service, bars, pools, gym, beach, water sports, business center, parking, some pets allowed* ❘⊙❘ *No meals.*

$$$$
B&B/INN
★
**Simonton Court**. A small world all of its own, this lodging makes you feel deliciously sequestered from Key West's crasser side, but close enough to get there on foot. **Pros:** lots of privacy; well-appointed accommodations; friendly staff. **Cons:** minimum stays required in

Sunset Key cottages are right on the water's edge, far away from the action of Old Town.

high season. ⊠ *320 Simonton St.* ☎ *305/294–6386 or 800/944–2687* ⊕ *www.simontoncourt.com* ⟿ *17 rooms, 6 suites, 6 cottages* ⚒ *In-room: a/c, kitchen (some), Wi-Fi. In-hotel: pools, some age restrictions* ⊠❶ *Breakfast.*

**$$$$**
HOTEL
❖ **Southernmost Hotel**. This hotel's location on the quiet end of Duval means you don't have to deal with the hustle and bustle of downtown unless you want to—it's within a 20-minute walk (but around sunset, this end of town gets its share of car and foot traffic). **Pros:** pool attracts a lively crowd; access to nearby properties; free parking. **Cons:** public beach is small; can get crowded around the pool and public areas. ⊠ *1319 Duval St.* ☎ *305/296–6577 or 800/354–4455* ⊕ *www. southernmostresorts.com* ⟿ *126 rooms* ⚒ *In-room: a/c, Wi-Fi. In-hotel: pool, laundry facilities* ⊠❶ *No meals.*

**$$$**
B&B/INN
❖ **Speakeasy Inn**. During Prohibition, Raul Vasquez made this place popular by smuggling in liquor from Cuba. **Pros:** good location; reasonable rates; kitchenettes. **Cons:** no pool; basic decor. ⊠ *1117 Duval St.* ☎ *305/296–2680* ⊕ *www.speakeasyinn.com* ⟿ *2 rooms* ⚒ *In-room: a/c, Wi-Fi. In-hotel: bar* ⊠❶ *Breakfast.*

**$$$$**
RESORT
Fodor'sChoice
★
❖ **Sunset Key**. This private island retreat feels completely cut off from the world, yet you're just minutes away from the action. **Pros:** peace and quiet; roomy verandas; free 24-hour shuttle. **Cons:** luxury doesn't come cheap. ⊠ *245 Front St.* ☎ *305/292–5300 or 888/477–7786* ⊕ *westinsunsetkeycottages.com* ⟿ *40 cottages* ⚒ *In-room: a/c, kitchen, Internet, Wi-Fi. In-hotel: restaurant, bars, tennis courts, pool, gym, spa, beach, parking* ⊠❶ *Breakfast.*

# Travel Smart
# Florida

## WORD OF MOUTH

". . . . The vast majority of U.S. colleges have spring break in [early to mid March]. There are a handful of schools that might be in late February or the first week of April but not many. . . ."

—cheryllj

". . . . The way to avoid spring breakers [isn't to avoid one area of the Florida coast or another but rather] to stay at very expensive resorts and properties . . . ."

—garyt22

# GETTING HERE AND AROUND

## ■ AIR TRAVEL

Average flying times to Florida's international airports are 3 hours from New York, 4 hours from Chicago, 2¾ hours from Dallas, 4½–5½ hours from Los Angeles, and 8–8½ hours from London.

### AIRPORTS

Florida's 21 commercial airports give you myriad choices. Most people begin and end their trip at Orlando International Airport (MCO). Destinations like St. Augustine and Kennedy Space Center, plus beaches on both the Atlantic and Gulf of Mexico are within a 100-mi radius. Just as busy is Miami International Airport (MIA), which welcomes the most international passengers to the United States after New York's John F. Kennedy (JFK). Tampa (TPA) is also an international hub.

Note, though, that flying to alternate airports can save you time and money. Take, for example, Fort Lauderdale-Hollywood International (FLL), which is close to Miami, and Sarasota Bradenton International (SRQ), which is close to Tampa. FLL is just a 30-minute drive from MIA (and as close to certain neighborhoods of Miami!). And what you might lose in driving time between Sarasota and downtown Tampa, you'll make up for in spades with shorter security lines and fewer in-terminal navigation woes at SRQ.

■TIP➔ Flying to secondary airports can save you money—sometimes even when there are additional ground transportation costs—so price things out before booking.

Airport Information **Daytona Beach International Airport (DAB)** (🕾 386/248–8069 ⊕ www.volusia.org/airport). **Fort Lauderdale–Hollywood International Airport (FLL)** (🕾 866/435–9355 ⊕ www.broward.org/airport). **Jacksonville International Airport (JAX)** (🕾 904/741–4902 ⊕ www.jaa.aero). **Key West International Airport (EYW)** (🕾 305/296–5439 ⊕ www.keywestinternational airport. com). **Miami International Airport (MIA)** (🕾 305/876–7000 ⊕ www.miami-airport.com). **Orlando International Airport (MCO)** (🕾 407/825–2001 ⊕ www.orlandoairports.net). **Palm Beach International Airport (PBI)** (🕾 561/471–7420 ⊕ www.pbia.org). **Northwest Florida Beaches International Airport (ECP)** (🕾 850/763–6751 ⊕ www.iflybeaches.com). **Sarasota Bradenton International Airport (SRQ)** (🕾 941/359–5200 ⊕ www.srq-airport.com). **Southwest Florida International Airport (RSW)** (🕾 239/590–4800 ⊕ www.flylcpa.com). **St. Petersburg–Clearwater International Airport (PIE)** (🕾 727/453–7800 ⊕ www.fly2pie.com). **Tampa International Airport TPA)** (🕾 813/870–8700 ⊕ www.tampaairport.com).

### GROUND TRANSPORTATION

There's SuperShuttle service from several Florida airports: Miami, Orlando, Sarasota, St. Petersburg/Clearwater, and Tampa. That said, most airports have some type of shuttle service or another.

Although buying a round-trip ticket and reserving for the return trip doesn't save you any money, it does make departure that much easier. Otherwise book a shuttle from your hotel to the airport at least 24 hours in advance. Expect to be picked up 2½ before your scheduled departure.

Cab fares from Florida's larger airports into town average $35. Note that in some cities airport fares are a single flat rate; in others, flat-rate fares vary by zone; in still others, the fare is determined by the meter. Private car service fares run between $50 and $150, depending on the locale and the type of vehicle.

Shuttle Service **SuperShuttle** (🕾 800/258–3826 ⊕ www.supershuttle.com).

# ▌CAR TRAVEL

Three major interstates lead to Florida. Interstate 95 begins in Maine, runs south through the Mid-Atlantic states, and enters Florida just north of Jacksonville. It continues south past Daytona Beach, the Space Coast, Vero Beach, Palm Beach, and Fort Lauderdale, ending in Miami.

Interstate 75 begins in Michigan at the Canadian border and runs south through Ohio, Kentucky, Tennessee, and Georgia, then moves south through the center of the state before veering west into Tampa. It follows the west coast south to Naples, then crosses the state through the northern section of the Everglades, and ends in Fort Lauderdale.

| SAMPLE FLORIDA DRIVING TIMES | | |
|---|---|---|
| FROM–TO | MILES | HOURS +/- |
| Pensacola–Panama City | 140 | 2:30 |
| Tallahassee–Jacksonville | 165 | 3 |
| Jacksonville–St. Augustine | 40 | 0:45 |
| Gainesville–Orlando | 115 | 2:15 |
| Cape/Port Canaveral–Orlando | 65 | 1 |
| Orlando–Tampa | 85 | 1:30 |
| Ft. Lauderdale–Miami | 30 | 0:30 |
| Miami–Naples | 125 | 2:15 |
| Miami–Key Largo | 65 | 1 |
| Key Largo–Key West | 100 | 2 |

California and most Southern and Southwestern states are connected to Florida by Interstate 10, which moves east from Los Angeles through Arizona, New Mexico, Texas, Louisiana, Mississippi, and Alabama; it enters Florida at Pensacola and runs straight across the northern part of the state ending in Jacksonville.

## RENTAL CARS

Unless you plan to plant yourself at a beach or theme-park resort, you really need a car to get around. In-season rental rates average $35 a day/$160 a week, plus tax ($2 per day). In Florida you must be 21 to rent a car, and rates are higher if you're under 25.

## ROAD CONDITIONS

Downtown areas of such major cities as Miami, Orlando, and Tampa can be extremely congested during rush hours, usually 7–9 am and 3:30–6:30 pm on weekdays. When you drive the interstate system in Florida, try to plan your trip so that you are not entering, leaving, or passing through a large city during rush hour when traffic can slow to 10 mph for 10 mi or more.

▌TIP➔ Florida has a website (⊕ www.fl511.com) with real-time traffic information—including details on congestion owing to construction or accidents.

## ROADSIDE EMERGENCIES

If you need emergency assistance while traveling on roads in Florida, dial 911 or the Florida Highway Patrol at *FHP (*347) from your cell phone.

## RULES OF THE ROAD

Speed limits are 60 mph on state highways, 30 mph within city limits and residential areas, and 70 mph on interstates and Florida's Turnpike. Be alert for signs announcing exceptions.

Children younger than four years old must be strapped in a separate carrier or child seat; children four through five can be secured in a separate carrier, integrated child seat, or by a seat belt. The driver will be held responsible for passengers under the age of 18 who are not wearing seat belts, and all front-seat passengers are required to wear seat belts.

Florida's Alcohol/Controlled Substance DUI Law is one of the toughest in the United States. A blood-alcohol level of .08

or higher can have serious repercussions even for a first-time offender.

### Local Agencies

| | | |
|---|---|---|
| Continental (Fort Lauderdale, Miami, Orlando) | 800/221–4085 or 954/332–1125 | www.continentalcar.com |
| Sunshine Rent A Car (Fort Lauderdale) | 888/786–7446 or 954/467–8100 | www.sunshinerentacar.com |

### Major Agencies

| | | |
|---|---|---|
| Alamo | 877/222–9075 | www.alamo.com |
| Avis | 800/230–4898 | www.avis.com |
| Budget | 800/527–0700 | www.budget.com |
| Hertz | 800/654–3131 | www.hertz.com |
| National Car Rental | 800/227–7368 | www.nationalcar.com |

# ❚ CRUISE TRAVEL

Many major cruise lines make Florida a point of embarkation for sails to the Caribbean and Mexico. Occasionally a cruise line actually offers an itinerary in which Florida is a port of call, but this is rare.

The port of Miami has the world's largest year-round fleet. It also handles more megaships—vessels capable of transporting more than 2,000 people at a time—than any other port in the world.

Port Everglades, 30 mi north of Miami in the greater Fort Lauderdale area, is also a cruise-ship mecca, and it's been vying to eclipse its neighbor. In 2010 it got a step closer to this goal when it welcomed the second of Royal Caribbean's 5,400-passenger ships with a sparkling new terminal to handle the increased traffic.

Port Canaveral, 65 mi west of Orlando, is the home port for Disney Cruise Line vessels—the *Magic*, the *Wonder*, and the two newest ships, the *Dream*, and the *Fantasy*. DCL offers five- and seven-day cruises to the Bahamas, the Caribbean, Mexico and, increasingly, elsewhere in the world.

Canaveral is also home for Carnival Cruise Lines's Sensation (three- and four-night Bahamian cruises) and Dream (yes, Carnival has a Dream, too; seven-night eastern and western Caribbean cruises) and Royal Caribbean International's Monarch of the Seas (three- and four-night Bahamian cruises) and Freedom of the Seas (seven-night eastern- and western-Caribbean itineraries).

# ESSENTIALS

## ▋ ACCOMMODATIONS

In the busy seasons, reserve ahead for the top properties. In general, the peak seasons are over Christmas and from late January through Easter in the southern half of the state, during the summer along the Panhandle and around Jacksonville and St. Augustine, in both time frames in Orlando and central Florida, and all over the state during holiday weekends at any point during the year but especially in summer.

Fall is the slowest season, with only a few exceptions (Key West is jam-packed for Fantasy Fest at Halloween). Rates are low and availability is high, but this is also the prime time for hurricanes.

Children are welcome generally everywhere in Florida. Pets are another matter, so inquire ahead of time if you're bringing an animal with you.

### APARTMENT AND HOUSE RENTALS

Contacts **American Realty** (☎ 800/547–0127 ⊕ www.captiva-island.com). **Florida Keys Rental Store/Marr Properties** (☎ 800/585–0584 or 305/451–3879 ⊕ www.floridakeysrentalstore.com). **Freewheeler Vacations** (☎ 866/664–2075 or 305/664–2075 ⊕ www.freewheeler-realty.com). **Interhome** (☎ 954/791–8282 or 800/882–6864 ⊕ www.interhomeusa.com). **ResortQuest** (☎ 800/336–4853 ⊕ www.resortquest.com). **Sand Key Realty** (☎ 800/257–7332 or 727/595–5441 ⊕ www.sandkey.com). **Suncoast Vacations Rentals** (☎ 800/341–2021 ⊕ www.uncommonflorida.com). **Villas International** (☎ 415/499–9490 or 800/221–2260 ⊕ www.villasintl.com). **Wyndham Vacation Resorts** (☎ 800/251–8736 ⊕ www.wyndhamvacationresorts.com).

### BED-AND-BREAKFASTS

Small inns and guesthouses in Florida range from modest cozy places with home-style breakfasts and owners who treat you like family, to elegantly furnished Victorian houses with four-course breakfasts and rates to match. The associations listed below offer descriptions and suggestions for B&Bs throughout the state.

Reservation Services **BedandBreakfast.com** (☎ 512/322–2710 or 800/462–2632 ⊕ www.bedandbreakfast.com). **Bed & Breakfast Inns Online** (☎ 800/215–7365 ⊕ www.bbonline.com). **BnBFinder.com** (☎ 888/547–8226 ⊕ www.bnbfinder.com). **Florida Bed & Breakfast Inns** (☎ 877/303–3224 ⊕ www.florida-inns.com).

### HOME EXCHANGES

With a direct home exchange you stay in someone else's home while they stay in yours. Some outfits also deal with vacation homes, so you're not actually staying in someone's full-time residence, just their weekend place.

Exchange Clubs **Home Exchange.com** (☎ 800/877–8723 ⊕ www.homeexchange.com); $119.40 for a 1-year membership. **HomeLink International** (☎ 800/638–3841 ⊕ www.homelink.org); $119 for a 1-year membership. **Intervac USA Home Exchange** (☎ 800/756–4663 ⊕ www.intervacus.com); $99.99 for 1-year membership.

### HOTELS

Wherever you look in Florida you'll find lots of plain inexpensive motels and luxurious resorts, independents alongside national chains, and an ever-growing number of modern properties as well as quite a few classics. In fact, since Florida has been a favored travel destination for some time, vintage hotels are everywhere: there are grand edifices like the Breakers in Palm Beach, Boca Raton Resort & Club in Boca Raton, the Biltmore in Coral Gables, and Casa Marina in Key West.

All hotels listed have private bath unless otherwise noted.

# ▌ EATING OUT

Smoking is banned statewide in most enclosed indoor workplaces, including restaurants. Exemptions are permitted for stand-alone bars where food takes a backseat to the libations.

One caution: raw oysters are a potential problem for people with chronic illness of the liver, stomach, or blood, or who have immune disorders. All Florida restaurants that serve raw oysters must post a notice in plain view warning of the risks associated with consuming them.

## FLORIBBEAN FOOD

A true marriage of downstate's Floridian, Caribbean, and Latin cultures yields home-grown Floribbean cuisine. (Think freshly caught fish with tropical fruit salsa.) A trip to the Tampa area or South Florida, however, is not complete without a taste of Cuban food. The cuisine is heavy, with pork dishes like *lechon asado*, served in garlic-based sauces. The two most typical dishes are *arroz con frijoles* (the staple side dish of rice and black beans) and *arroz con pollo* (chicken in sticky yellow rice).

Key West is famous for its key lime pie (the best is found here) and conch fritters. Stone-crab claws, a South Florida delicacy, can be savored from October through May.

## MEALS AND MEALTIMES

Unless otherwise noted, the restaurants listed in this guide are open daily for lunch and dinner.

## RESERVATIONS AND DRESS

We discuss reservations only when they're essential (there's no other way you'll ever get a table) or when they are not accepted. It's always smart to make reservations when you can, particularly if your party is large. It's critical to do so at popular restaurants (book as far ahead as possible, often 30 days, and reconfirm on arrival).

We mention dress only when men are required to wear a jacket or a jacket and

tie. Expect places with dress codes to truly adhere to them.

**Contacts OpenTable** (⊕ *www.opentable.com*). **DinnerBroker** (⊕ *www.dinnerbroker.com*).

# ▌ HEALTH

Sunburn and heat prostration are concerns, even in winter. So hit the beach or play tennis, golf, or another outdoor sport before 10 am or after 3 pm. If you must be out at midday, limit exercise, drink plenty of nonalchoholic liquids, and wear a hat. If you feel faint, get out of the sun and sip water slowly.

Even on overcast days, ultraviolet rays shine through the haze, so use a sunscreen with an SPF of at least 15, and have children wear a waterproof SPF 30 or higher.

While you're frolicking on the beach, steer clear of what look like blue bubbles on the sand. These are Portuguese men-of-war, and their tentacles can cause an allergic reaction. Also be careful of other large jellyfish, some of which can sting.

If you walk across a grassy area on the way to the beach, you'll probably encounter the tiny, light-brown, incredibly prickly sand spurs. If you get stuck with one, just pull it out.

# ▌ HOURS OF OPERATION

Many museums are closed Monday but have late hours on another weekday and are usually open on weekends. Some museums have a day when admission is free. Popular attractions are usually open every day but Thanksgiving and Christmas Day.

# ▌ MONEY

Prices throughout this guide are given for adults. Substantially reduced fees are almost always available for children, students, and senior citizens.

## CREDIT CARDS

We cite information about credits only if they aren't accepted at a restaurant or a hotel. Otherwise, assume that most major credit cards are acceptable.

It's good to inform your credit-card company before you travel to prevent it from putting a hold on your card owing to unusual activity—not a good thing halfway through your trip. Record all your credit-card numbers—as well as the phone numbers to call if your cards are lost or stolen—in a safe place, so you're prepared should something go wrong.

Both MasterCard and Visa have general numbers you can call if your card is lost, but you're better off calling the number of your issuing bank, since MasterCard and Visa usually just transfer you to your bank; your bank's number is usually printed on your card.

**Reporting Lost Cards American Express** (☎ 800/992–3404 ⊕ www.americanexpress. com). **Diners Club** (☎ 800/234–6377 ⊕ www. dinersclub.com). **Discover** (☎ 800/347–2683 ⊕ www.discovercard.com). **MasterCard** (☎ 800/622–7747 ⊕ www.mastercard.com). **Visa** (☎ 800/847–2911 ⊕ www.visa.com).

# ▌ PACKING

Northern Florida is much cooler in winter than southern Florida, so pack a heavy sweater. Even in summer, ocean breezes can be cool, so it's good to have a lightweight sweater or jacket.

Aside from an occasional winter cold spell (when the mercury drops to, say, 50), Miami and the Naples–Fort Myers areas are warm year-round and extremely humid in summer. Be prepared for sudden storms all over in summer, and note that plastic raincoats are uncomfortable in the high humidity. Often storms are quick and the sun comes back in no time.

Dress is casual throughout the state— sundresses, jeans, or walking shorts are appropriate during the days. A few restaurants request that men wear jackets and ties, but most do not. Where there are dress codes, they tend to be fully adhered to. Be prepared for air-conditioning working in overdrive.

You can generally swim year-round in peninsular Florida from about New Smyrna Beach south on the Atlantic coast and from Tarpon Springs south on the Gulf coast. Bring a sun hat and sunscreen.

# ▌ SAFETY

Stepped-up policing of thieves who prey on tourists in rental cars has helped address what was a serious issue in the early 1990s. Still, visitors should be especially wary when driving in strange neighborhoods and leaving the airport, especially in the Miami area. Don't assume that valuables are safe in your hotel room; use in-room safes or the hotel's safety-deposit boxes. Try to use ATMs only during the day or in brightly lighted, well-traveled locales. Don't leave valuables unattended while you walk the beach or go for a dip.

If you are visiting Florida during the June through November hurricane season and a hurricane is imminent, be sure to follow directions from local authorities.

# TAXES

Florida's sales tax is 6% or higher depending on the county, and local sales and tourist taxes can raise what you pay considerably. Miami Beach hoteliers, for example, collect 13% for city and resort taxes. It's best to ask about additional costs up front, to avoid a rude awakening.

# TIME

The western portion of the Panhandle is in the central time zone, while the rest of mainland Florida is in the Eastern time zone.

# TIPPING

Whether they carry bags, open doors, deliver food, or clean rooms, hospitality employees work to receive a portion of your travel budget. In deciding how much to give, base your tip on what the service is and how well it's performed.

| FLORIDA TIPPING GUIDELINES | |
|---|---|
| Airport Valet or Hotel Bellhop | $1–$3 per bag |
| Chambermaid | $1–$2 a night per guest |
| Hotel Room-Service Waiter | 15% (unless a service charge was added) |
| Helpful doorman or a parking valet | $1–$3 |
| Taxi Driver | 15%–20% |
| Waiter/Bartender | 15%–20% before tax |
| Golf Caddies | 15% of the greens fee |
| Spa Therapist | 15%–20% of the treatment before tax |

## FLORIDA'S SCENIC TRAILS

Florida has some 8,000 mi of land-based routes (plus another 4,000 mi for paddling!). About 1,400 mi of these connect to create the Florida Trail, one of only 11 National Scenic Trails in the United States. Info on top segments is available at ⊕ *www.floridatrail.org*, and you can find a searchable list of all trails at ⊕ *www.visitflorida.com/trails.*

# VISITOR INFORMATION

Florida has a terrific visitors website with information about the state as a whole as well as that for individual cities and regions. There are Florida welcome centers are on Interstate 10 (near Pensacola), Interstate 75 (near Jennings), Interstate 95 (near Yulee, north of Jacksonville), and U.S. 231 (near Campbellton), and in the lobby of the New Capitol in Tallahassee.

In addition, many cities, regions, and towns have their own visitor information offices and/or booths. What's more, some tourism offices are pumping out helpful (and smart) apps—Miami's just added one to instantly locate the hottest, latest dining spots, and Orlando has parkIN', which searches and compares rates at parking facilities closest to you.

Contacts **Visit Florida** (☎ *850/488–5607or 866/972–5280 toll-free* ⊕ *www.visitflorida.com*).

# INDEX

## PHOTO CREDITS

1, Visit Florida. 2-3, Tim Souter, Fodors.com member. 5, PhotoStockFile/Alamy. Chapter 1: Experience Florida: 8-9, Steven Widoff/Alamy. 10, Fritz Poelking/age fotostock. 11 (left), Stuart Pearce/World Pictures/age fotostock. 11 (right), J.D. Heaton/Picture Finders/age fotostock. 12, ACE STOCK LIMITED/Alamy. 13 (left), Richard Cummins/viestiphoto.com. 13 (right), Jeff Greenberg/age fotostock. 14 (left), Cogoli Franco/SIME/eStock Photo. 14 (right) and 15 (left), Visit Florida. 15 (top right), John Henshall/Alamy. 15 (bottom right), Jeremy Edwards/iStockphoto. 16 (left) Visit Florida. 16 (right), Rob Keaton/wikipedia.org. 17 (left), Martin Sasse/Laif/Aurora Photos. 17 (top right), RIEGER Bertrand/age fotostock. 17 (bottom right), Danita Delimont/Alamy. 18 (left), Jeff Greenberg/Alamy. 18 (top right), the SuperStar/Flickr. 18 (bottom right), Ken Canning/Shutterstock. 19 (left), Cogoli Franco/SIME/eStock Photo. 19 (right), Robert Harding Picture Library Ltd/Alamy. 20 and 21, Jeff Greenberg/age fotostock. 22, GlyndaK, Fodors.com member. 23, Jeff Greenberg/age fotostock. 24, Joe Viesti/viestiphoto.com. 25 (left), culliganphoto/Alamy. 25 (right), Orlando CVB. 26, J Loveland/Shutterstock. 29, Visit Florida. 30, Jeff Greenberg/Alamy. 31 (left), St. Petersburg/Clearwater Area CVB. 31 (right), Regina Stancel/iStockphoto. 32 (left), Kirk Peart Professional Imaging/Shutterstock. 32 (right), PhotoStockFile/Alamy. 33 (left), Stephen Frink Collection/Alamy. 33 (right), Dennis MacDonald/Alamy. Chapter 2: Panhandle: 35 and 36 (top and bottom), Cheryl Casey/Shutterstock. 37 (top), Todd Taulman/Shutterstock. 37 (bottom), Visit Florida. 38, Cheryl Casey/Shutterstock. 39 (top), Jeff Kinsey/Shutterstock. 39 (bottom), Cheryl Casey/Shutterstock. 40, divemasterking2000/Flickr. 48, Kathy Hicks/iStockphoto. 56, Brandon Cole Marine Photography/Alamy. 59, Visit Florida. 60 (top), Ernest Hemingway Photograph Collection, John F. Kennedy Presidential Library and Museum, Boston. 60 (bottom), Visit Florida. 61 (top), Linda Brinck, Fodors.com member. 61 (bottom), George Peters/iStockphoto. 62, Michael Zegers/imagebroker.net/photolibrary.com. 65, Andrew Woodley/Alamy. 68, geishaboy500/Flickr. 73, Gorilla/Shutterstock. 84-85, imagebroker/Alamy. 86, Dennis MacDonald/age fotostock. Chapter 3: Northeast Florida: 91, FRILET Patrick/age fotostock. 92 (top), The Freewheeling Daredevil/Flickr. 92 (bottom), Henryk Sadura/Shutterstock. 93 (top and bottom), Cogoli Franco/SIME/eStockPhoto. 94, Visit Florida. 95 (top), Tom Hirtreiter/Shutterstock. 95 (bottom), Deborah Wolfe/Shutterstock. 96, Visit Florida. 100, Karel Gallas/Shutterstock. 106, Jeff Greenberg/age fotostock. 113, Therese McKeon/iStockphoto. 122, funinthetub, Fodors.com member. 125, Roberto A Sanchez/iStockphoto. 131, Visit Florida. 141, Visit Florida. 144-45, Visit Florida. 146 (top) Visit Florida. 146 (bottom left), David Allio/Icon SMI. 146 (bottom 2nd from left), JACK BRADEN/wikipedia.org. 146 (bottom 3rd from left), Arni Katz/Alamy. 146 (bottom right), Motorsports Images and Archives/Datona International Speedway. 147, Daytona Frontstretch Grandstand by Nancy Nally www.flicker.com/photos/scrapnancy/3289448500/ Attribution-ShareAlike License. 149, greg pelt/iStockphoto. 164-65, jurvetson/Flickr. 166, thelastminute/Flickr. 167, yeowatzup/Flickr. 168 (top left), hyku/Flickr. 168 (top right and bottom) and 169 (left), thelastminute/Flickr. 169 (right), Kennedy Space Center Visitor Complex. 170, by jonworth/Flickr. 171, bnhsu/Flickr. 172-73, jurvetson/Flickr. 176, breezy421/Flickr. Chapter 4: Orlando & Environs: 179, Visit Florida. 180, SeaWorld Orlando. 181 (top), Nick Hotel. 181 (bottom), Universal Orlando. 186, © Disney. 187, @ LaRsNoW@Flicker. 188, Universal Orlando. 194, Gary Bogdon/Visit Florida. 228 (top left), Universal Orlando Resort. 228 (top right), erin MC hammer/Flickr. 228 (center left), The Ritz-Carlton. 228 (center right), Daniels & Roberts INC/The Waldorf Astoria Orlando. 228 (bottom left), Nick Hotel. 228 (bottom right), Greencolander/Flickr. Chapter 5: Walt Disney World: 231, © Disney. 232, d4rr3ll/Flickr. 233, vanguardist/Flickr. 234, Universal Orlando. 236 and 237, Orlando CVB. 238, © Disney. 239 (top), vanguardist/Flickr. 239 (bottom), FAN travelstock/Alamy. 244, Orlando CVB. 245 (top), Joe Shlabotnik/Flickr. 245 (bottom), Orlando CVB. 247, © Disney. 250, Universal Orlando. 251 (top), wikipedia.org. 251 (bottom), Universal Orlando Resort. 253, dawnzy58/Flickr. 256, Joe Shlabotnik/Flickr. 257 (top and bottom), Allie_Caulfield/Flickr. 258, dawnzy58/Flickr. 262-63 (all) and 265, © Disney. Chapter 6: Universal Orlando: 271 and 272 (both), Universal Orlando Resort. 273, bea&txm/Flickr. 276, divemasterking/Flickr. 277, Visit Florida. 278-87, Universal Orlando Resort. 290-91, Wet 'n Wild. Chapter 7: SeaWorld Orlando: 297-304 and 305 (top), SeaWorld Parks & Entertainment. 305 (bottom), Visit Florida. 307, Orlando CVB. 310-11, Jason Collier/SeaWorld Parks & Entertainment. 314, SeaWorld Parks & Entertainment. Chapter 8: The Tampa Bay Area: 315, Joe Stone/Shutterstock. 316 (top), gppilot, Fodors.com member. 316 (bottom), Visit Florida. 317 (top), Marje Cannon/iStockphoto. 317 (bottom), William Hamilton/SuperStock. 318, St. Petersburg/Clearwater Area CVB. 319 (top), Visit Florida. 319 (bottom), Graca Victoria/Shutterstock. 320, iStockphoto. 326-27, Busch Entertainment Corporation. 332, Martin Bennett/Alamy. 342, Seymour Levy, Fodors.com member. 347, Ed Wolfstein/Icon SMI. 348 (top), Palm Beach Post/ZUMA Press/Icon SMI. 348 (bottom), Cliff Welch/Icon SMI. 349 (top), Evan Meyer/Shutterstock. 349 (bottom) and 350 (top), GARY I ROTHSTEIN/Icon SMI. 350 (bottom background photo), Ed Wolfstein/Icon SMI. 351 (background photo), Ed Wolfstein/Icon SMI. 350-51 (logos), wikipedia.org. 354, watland, Fodors.com member. 357, Richard T. Nowitz/age fotostock. 360, TIPTON DONALD/age fotostock. 365, Elizabeth Shevloff, Fodors.com member. Chapter 9: The Lower Gulf Coast: 369, Dan Leffel/age fotostock. 371 (top), Cogoli Franco/SIME/eStock Photo. 371 (center), Visit Florida. 371 (bottom), Heeb Photos/eStock Photo. 372, Travelshots.com/Alamy. 373 (top), jeff gynane/iStockphoto. 373 (bottom), Visit Florida. 374, Alan Briere/SuperStock. 379 and 387, Visit Florida. 390, Walter Bibikow/age fotostock. 393, blewisphotography/Shutterstock. 394, Mitch Aunger/Shutterstock. 412, Dennis Guyitt/iStockphoto. Chapter 10: Palm Beach and the Treasure Coast: 421, RIEGER Bertrand/age fotostock. 423 (top), Perry Correll/Shutterstock. 423 (bottom), Bill Bachmann/Alamy. 424, Masa Ushioda/Alamy. 425 (top), Stephen Frink Collection/Alamy. 425 (bottom), Denny Medley/Random Photography/iStockphoto. 426, FloridaStock/Shutterstock. 431, Jon Arnold Images Ltd/Alamy. 435, Andre Jenny/Alamy. 440, mrk_photo/Flickr. 447, FloridaStock/Shutterstock. 452, wikipedia.org. 459, Paddy Eckersley/age fotostock. 460, Tap10/Shutterstock. 463 and 473, Visit Florida. Chapter 11: Fort Lauderdale and Broward County: 477, Visit Florida. 478, Rick Gomez/age fotostock. 479 (top), Dean Bergmann/iStockphoto. 479 (bottom), Jeff Greenberg/Alamy. 480, Nicholas Pitt/Alamy. 481 (top), Medioimages/Photodisc/Thinkstock. 481 (bottom), Claudette, Fodors.com member. 482, Qole Pejorian/Flickr. 488, rockindom, Fodors.com member. 493, Nicholas Pitt/Alamy. 497, Eric Gevaert/Shutterstock. 507, Lago Mar Resort & Club - Fort Lauderdale. 513, Pat Cahill/iStockphoto. Chapter 12: Miami and Miami Beach: 521, iStockphoto. 522, Stuart Westmorland/age fotostock. 523 (top), Jeff Greenberg/age fotostock. 523 (bottom), VISUM Foto GmbH/Alamy. 524, Jeff Greenberg/age fotostock. 525 (top), Picasa 2.7/Flickr. 525 (bottom), murray cohen/iStockphoto. 526, Ivan Cholakov/Shutterstock. 536, Chuck Mason/Alamy. 537 (top), Jeff Greenberg/Alamy. 537 (bottom), David R. Frazier Photolibrary, Inc./Alamy. 538 and 540, Jeff Greenberg/Alamy. 541, Jeff Greenberg/age fotostock. 542, Gregory Wrona/Alamy. 546, Robert Harding Picture Library Ltd/Alamy. 555, Visit Florida. 561 (left), dk/Alamy. 561 (right), Nicholas Pitt/Alamy. 563 (top), M. Timothy O'Keefe/Alamy. 563 (bottom), Miami Design Preservation League. 564 (top), Nicholas Pitt/Alamy. 564 (2nd from top), Park Central Hotel. 564 (3rd from top), Ian Patrick Alamy. 564 (4th from top), Laura Paresky. 564 (bottom), ICIMAGE/Alamy. 565 (top), INTERFOTO Pressebildagentur/Alamy. 565 (bottom left), Ian Patrick/Alamy. 565 (bottom right), culliganphoto/Alamy. 566, iStockphoto. 573, alexdecarvalho/Flickr. 582, Claudia Uribe. 590, Roxana Gonzalez/Shutterstock. 591 (top), JUPITERIMAGES/Brand X/Alamy. 591 (bottom), iStockphoto. 594, Jeff Greenberg/Alamy. 606 (top), Acqualina Resort & Spa on the Beach. 606 (bottom left), Nile Young. 606 (center right), Circa 39. 606 (bottom right), Morgans Hotel Group. 607 (top), Mark Wieland. 607 (center left), Kevin Syms/Four Seasons Hotels and Resorts. 607 (bottom left), Kor Hotel Group. 607 (bottom right), Mandarin Oriental Hotel Group. Chapter 13: The Everglades: 611, David Lyons/Alamy. 612 (top), Visit Florida. 612 (bottom), Jeff Greenberg/age fotostock. 613 (top), FloridaStock/Shutterstock. 613 (middle), Pamela McCreight/Flickr. 613 (bottom), Walter Bibikow/age fotostock. 614-15, tbkmedia.de/Alamy. 618 (left), inga spence/Alamy. 618 (top center), FloridaStock/Shutterstock. 618 (bottom center), Andrewtappert/wikipedia.org. 618 (top right), wikipedia.org. 618 (bottom right), David R. Frazier Photolibrary, Inc./Alamy. 619 (top left), Larsek/Shutterstock. 619 (bottom left), Caleb Foster/Shutterstock. 619 (bottom center), mlorenz/Shutterstock. 619 (top right), umar faruq/Shutterstock. 619 (bottom right), Peter Arnold, Inc./Alamy. 620 (left), John A. Anderson/Shutterstock. 620 (top right), FloridaStock/Shutterstock. 620 (bottom center), Norman Bateman/Shutterstock. 620 (bottom right), FloridaStock/Shutterstock. 621 (top left), David Drake & Deborah Jaffe. 621 (bottom left), Krzysztof Slusarczyk/Shutterstock. 621 (bottom center), Norman Bateman/Shutterstock. 621 (right), Jerry Zitterman/Shutterstock. 622, Patricia Schmidt/iStockphoto. 623 (top left), Brett Charlton/iStockphoto. 623 (bottom left, bottom center, and right), David Drake & Deborah Jaffe. 624 (left), Walter Bibikow/age fotostock. 624 (right), Stephen Frink Collection/Alamy. 625, Leatha J. Robinson/Shutterstock. 627, Larsek/Shutterstock. 634, Steven Widoff/Alamy. 640, Marc Muench/Alamy. 642, Sarah and Jason/Flickr. 651, Visit Florida. Chapter 14: The Florida Keys: 657, Stephen Frink/Aurora Photos. 658 (top), Pawel Lipiec/iStockphoto. 658 (bottom), David L Amsler/iStockphoto. 659 (top), Pacific Stock/SuperStock. 659 (bottom), Visit Florida. 660, Nick Greaves/Alamy. 661 (top), Ingolf Pompe 77/Alamy. 661 (bottom), Visit Florida. 662, iStockphoto. 671, Stephen Frink/ Florida Keys News Bureau. 677, flasporty/Flickr. 680, Visit Florida. 684, PBorowka/Shutterstock. 685 and 686 (top), Douglas Rudolph. 686 (bottom), ANDY NEWMAN/Visit Florida. 687, M. Timothy O'Keefe/Alamy. 688 (top), Bob Care/Florida Keys News Bureau. 688 (bottom), Julie de Leseleuc/iStockphoto. 689 (left), Visit Florida. 689 (right), Charles Stirling (Diving)/Alamy. 690 (top), Visit Florida. 690 (bottom), Gert Vrey/iStockphoto. 691, Scott Wilson, FKCC Student. 697, Melissa Schalke/iStockphoto. 707, Henryk Sadura/Alamy. 718, John P Franzis. 720, CedarBendDrive/Flickr. 725, John P Franzis. 730, Laure Neish/iStockphoto. 732, Harold Smith/Alamy. 734, Gregory Wrona/Alamy. 735 (top), Claudio Lovo/Shutterstock. 735 (bottom), Michael Ventura/Alamy. 742, Starwood Hotels & Resorts.

# ABOUT OUR WRITERS

Tampa Bay updater and beach lover Kate Bradshaw lives in the small Gulf Coast town of Treasure Island and is a news reporter for various outlets, namely WMNF 88.5 FM, an eclectic nonprofit community radio station. Born in the Chicago area, Kate has lived in Hawaii, New Zealand, and New Mexico, among other places. She is proud to now be a Florida resident, and with her coverage for Fodor's, hopes to convey to visitors all the beauty and wonder of her adopted home.

After being hired sight unseen by a South Florida newspaper, Fort Lauderdale–based freelance travel writer and editor Lynne Helm arrived from the Midwest anticipating a few years of palm-fringed fun. More than a quarter century later (after covering the state for several newspapers, consumer magazines, and trade publications), she's still enamored of Florida's sun-drenched charms. Lynne updated the Everglades chapters.

Dorothea Hunter Sönne, who updated Experience Florida and Travel Smart, is a freelance writer who has been enchanted by Florida since her youth—so much so that after dozens of vacations, she relocated to its sunny shores in 2010. Prior to that she was a magazine editor, spending nearly five years at O, The Oprah Magazine. She also co-edited the book, Words That Matter, and her work has appeared in publications including The Knot and Chicago.

From her home of more than 25 years on Sanibel Island, Chelle Koster Walton—author of the Keys and Lower Gulf Coast chapters—has written and contributed to a dozen guidebooks (among them Fodor's Bahamas), two of which have won Lowell Thomas Awards. She has penned thousands of articles about Florida and the Caribbean for Miami Herald, USA Today, Concierge.com, FoxNews.com, and other print and digital media.

Space Coast and Daytona updater Steve Master can hear the engines roar, literally, from his Port Orange, Florida, home, 10 mi south of famed Daytona International Speedway. Steve spent 20 years as a sports writer for the Daytona Beach News Journal, where he won many awards, including a 2007 national honor from the Associated Press Sports Editors. He has written commentary for NASCAR Illustrated and covered travel for Orbitz Worldwide. Currently, he's an assistant professor of communication at Embry-Riddle Aeronautical University in Daytona Beach.

Gary McKechnie, who reported on St. Augustine, Universal Studios, and SeaWorld, knows a lot about Florida, his native state. He's traveled its back roads and explored its small towns on weekend trips and has taken several "voyages of discovery" on a series of motorcycles. He's also explored the rest of the country for his award-winning guidebook Great American Motorcycle Tours. National Geographic published his latest book, USA 101, which highlights iconic American places, events, and festivals. He also speaks on America's cultural heritage aboard the Cunard Line ships Queen Mary 2 and Queen Victoria.

Paul Rubio's insatiable quest to discover and learn has taken him to the far corners of the world—81 countries and counting. A Harvard-trained economist with a double masters degree, he took on his passion for travel writing full-time in 2008 and hasn't looked back. Paul, who updated the Fort Lauderdale and Miami chapters, currently contributes to Ocean Home Magazine, Palm Beach Illustrated, and Weddings Illustrated as well as other Fodor's guides, jetsetter.com, and various outlets of Modern Luxury Media.

Baseball, beaches, and boats were among the things that lured Connie Sharpe back to Sarasota from Detroit, Michigan, nearly 30 years ago. Connie, who writes for newspapers in Michigan, Maryland, Nebraska, and Florida, updated the Spring Training and Sarasota County sections of Fodor's Florida. When she's not writing she's teaching writing, communications, and marketing at the University of Tampa; scouting out whacky, quirky, old-time Florida haunts; or playing tennis or sailing.

Palm Beach and the Treasure Coast writer Mary Thurwachter, a Florida resident since 1979, writes travel stories for *The Palm Beach Post, Miami Herald* and INNsideFlorida.com, a travel site she launched in 2008.

Jacksonville updater Sharon Weightman Hoffmann is a writer and researcher who has lived in the Jacksonville Beaches area for more than 20 years. (She is also a poet who has won an individual fellowship from Florida's Division of Cultural Affairs.) Her work has appeared in many magazines and other publications including *Alice Walker: Critical Perspectives* by Harvard University Press. Sharon was assisted by Jaimie Wilson, a Neptune Beach–based writer who has covered many aspects of the arts and pop culture from fine dining and the symphony to skateboarding and square-dancing. She is also the recipient of a fellowship to the Atlantic Center for the Arts in New Smyrna, Florida.

Panhandle updater Ashley Wright is a northwest Florida native and a master-of-all-trades in the publishing world, including (but certainly not limited to) writing, editing, graphic design, and photography. She contributes to a number of local and regional publications and loves sharing the hidden treasures of her native coast with travelers both near and far.

The Orlando and Walt Disney World chapters were updated by a very talented team of freelance writers, including Elise Allen (Orlando Planner), Rona Gindin (Where to Eat), Jennifer Greenhill-Taylor, (Where to Stay), Jennie Hess (all of Disney World), and Megan Peck (Orlando and environs sights and attractions).